*Access to Literature*

# Access to Literature

Understanding
Fiction, Drama, and Poetry

Edited by
Elliott L. Smith
and
Wanda V. Smith

**St. Martin's Press**
**New York**

cover design: Tom McKeveny

typography: Patricia Smythe

ISBN: 0–312–00213–0

ACKNOWLEDGMENTS

W. H. AUDEN: "As I Walked Out One Evening." Copyright 1940 and renewed 1968 by
W. H. Auden. "O What Is That Sound." Copyright 1937 and renewed 1965 by W.
H. Auden. Both reprinted from W. H. Auden: *Collected Poems* by W. H. Auden, edited
by Edward Mendelson, by permission of Random House, Inc. and Faber and Faber
Ltd.

AMIRI BARAKA: "Preface to a Twenty Volume Suicide Note." From *Preface to a Twenty
Volume Suicide Note*, Totem/Corinth, 1961. Copyright © 1961 by LeRoi Jones (Amiri
Baraka). Reprinted by permission of The Sterling Lord Agency.

DONALD BARTHELME: "Report." "Report" from *Unspeakable Practices, Unnatural Acts*
by Donald Barthelme. Copyright © 1967, 1968 by Donald Barthelme. Reprinted by
permission of Farrar, Straus and Giroux, Inc.

STEPHEN VINCENT BENÉT: "By the Waters of Babylon" by Stephen Vincent Benét.
From: *The Selected Works of Stephen Vincent Benét.* Copyright, 1942 by Stephen Vincent
Benét. Copyright renewed © 1966 by Thomas C. Benét, Stephanie B. Mahin & Rachel
Benét Lewis. Reprinted by permission of Brandt & Brandt Literary Agents, Inc.

GINA BERRIAULT: "The Stone Boy" by Gina Berriault. Published by *Mademoiselle.* Copyright 1957. By permission of Toni Strassman, Agent.

ROBERT BLY: "Waking from Sleep." Reprinted from *Silence in the Snowy Fields*, Wesleyan
University Press, 1962, copyright © 1962 by Robert Bly, reprinted with his permission.
"The Great Society" from *The Light Around the Body* by Robert Bly. Copyright © 1962
by Robert Bly. Reprinted by permission of Harper & Row, Publishers, Inc.

MAXWELL BODENHEIM: "Poet to His Love." Reprinted with permission from Liveright
Publishing Corporation.

ARNA BONTEMPS: "A Summer Tragedy." Reprinted by permission of Dodd, Mead &
Company, Inc. from *The Old South* by Arna Bontemps. Copyright 1933, 1961 by Arna
Bontemps. Copyright © 1973 by Alberta Bontemps, Executrix.

Acknowledgments and copyrights continue at the back of the book on pages 806–810,
which constitute an extension of the copyright page.

# Contents

## PART IV   *Poetry*

# Preface

Over the years we have become more and more convinced that a continuing interest in literature can grow only out of literary encounters that reward the beginning student's efforts with understanding and enjoyment. We have therefore chosen the stories, novellas, plays, and poems in *Access to Literature* not only because of their intrinsic excellence but also because they appeal strongly to today's college students. Our own students have shown us that they are perfectly capable of responding to literature with excitement and delight—but not to *all* literature. Some works that appeal to advanced readers and to teachers, including ourselves, can strike beginning readers as obscure, joyless, and peculiar. Nabokov, Pinter, and Pound, for instance, are evidently tastes that appeal mainly to the trained palate. Nevertheless, there are great numbers of stories, plays, and poems that both teachers and students can enjoy, and it is from such works that we have compiled *Access to Literature*.

Nearly all of our selections are quite short, even the novellas and most of the plays. Moreover, nearly all are understandable—at least on the surface—at first reading, requiring little or no special knowledge. Nearly all are artful in ways that most freshmen students can discern and appreciate. Not all are equally accessible, though; we like to have a few more challenging pieces in reserve whenever our students are ready for them. But even the "easiest" pieces reward attentive reading. From beginning to end, *Access to Literature* gives students the real thing.

The introductions to the four genres—short story, novella, drama, and poetry—teach elements of literature that are standard in the introductory course. Experience has shown us that beginning students enjoy learning about literary form, and that what they learn does in fact increase their appreciation of literature. We exclude a few topics, such as the relation between drama and poetry in verse plays like *Oedipus Rex* and *Othello*, because they have proved unprofitable with our students. "Completeness of coverage," whatever that may be, is frankly not one of our objectives. On the other hand, we cover such topics as poetic meter, stanza forms, and free verse in greater than usual detail, again because we find that our own students are genuinely interested in these matters, and gain a sense of growing mastery as they learn what the various forms and techniques are and what they are called.

Writing even short papers about literature can be a daunting exercise for students who are just beginning to read literature with pleasure. As a consequence, we have found it absolutely vital to offer explicit and detailed guidance in the matter of suitable topics and approaches. Our chapter on writing about literature is, therefore, rather long and full. We offer model paragraphs or short papers for several kinds of topics, and we often provide a series of thesis statements—each making an observation about a specific work or pair of works—which students can develop into papers or use as models for constructing thesis statements of their own. We also permit papers that stop short of relating the elements of a work to the whole. If a student offers a summary of a poem's chief formal devices, without going further to show how they coalesce into a satisfying structure or how they relate to meaning, such a paper still represents a significant step in the appreciation of poetry and we acknowledge it as such. Indeed, in our own course—at least early on—we admit papers of a more subjective kind, such as those relating the situation or theme of a literary work to a student's own experience. After all, such echoes between art and life are part of literature's appeal and power; and later on we find that our students are no less able, and perhaps more willing, to adopt a more purely literary approach if their direct, emotional responses have been legitimized from the start.

The texts used are normalized to contemporary American spelling, but are based on authoritative sources. Annotation is light, as we gloss no words or phrases that appear in standard college dictionaries, and annotate allusions only when the information is absolutely essential to an adequate understanding of the work's surface meaning or to an appreciation of its craftsmanship. We give birth and death dates for the authors in the index of authors, titles, and poetic first lines. There is also an index of literary terms that refers back to the definitions and examples provided in the introductions. In general, we have tried to keep the selections unencumbered by scholarly or teaching apparatus, so that they will be all the more inviting—or, at least, less intimidating.

*Access to Literature* is hardly the product of our efforts alone. We would like to thank our many students, who helped us choose selections through the enthusiasm, or puzzlement, or boredom with which they received each new story, play, or poem we tried on them. We also wish to acknowledge the patient assistance and professional guidance of John Francis, Nancy Perry, Charles Thurlow, and Lynne Williams of St. Martin's Press. For keeping us on track day by day, John Francis gets special thanks. Finally, among our colleagues at Ferris State College, we would like to acknowledge the generous help of Ada Lou Carson, Joseph Dugas, Andrew Hart, Mary Kilgallen, Daniel Mullet, and Lucy Wright.

*Elliott L. Smith*
*Wanda V. Smith*

# Access to Literature

# PART I *The Short Story*

# Introduction

As far back as we have been able to push our knowledge of human behavior, people have been telling stories. The traditions of primitive tribes and ancient cultures, and even pictures on the walls of prehistoric cave dwellings, show us again and again the seemingly innate human desire to tell tales and to hear them. Stories can explain or instruct; and of course they also entertain. Sometimes they even help people to build and sustain their courage.

Although written short fiction has flourished in almost every period of civilized history, the form we know as the literary short story did not evolve until the early nineteenth century. Then it came to life more or less at the same time in several countries: the United States, France, Germany, and Russia. The short story emerged because of the rise of popular education, resulting in greater numbers of people who could read; improved economic conditions, giving people more free time for reading; a steady rise in sophistication among these readers; and the growing interest among writers in the short narrative form, as well as the rapidly expanding number of popular magazines in the United States and Europe to publish their stories.

The new short story of the nineteenth century was a much more carefully structured work than many of the earlier types of short fiction, and if anything craftsmanship has continued to increase. So has variety, as contemporary writers seek new and individual ways to tell their stories, ways that may sometimes seem disjointed, incoherent, and even absurd. But most modern short stories have certain characteristics in common. First, of course, they are fictional, even though some stories contain elements taken from history or contemporary life, and may even read like eyewitness accounts. They are short, seldom longer than twenty-five printed pages (12,000 words) long and often much briefer. They are written in prose, although some stories employ brief passages of verse. Virtually all center on a single incident, make just one point or impression, and emphasize the personality of the central character or characters.

The modern short story is far too multifaceted a literary form to be summed up in a brief, tidy definition, and we will offer no such definition here. But there are certain elements which are typical of the form and which we will discuss. Knowing about these elements will help you to read and compare stories critically, and to write about them knowledgeably. They are plot; setting; character; tone, mood, and emotion; irony; imagery and symbolism; theme; and point of view.

## Plot

Plot is what happens in a story, the sequence of events comprising the narrative. Usually a short story treats a single major incident, and all the other occurrences in the story support that incident. You may be told step by step what is taking place, or you may have to sort out an implicit or internalized plot, one revealed through the details of memories, dreams, thoughts, and imaginings occurring in the minds of the major characters. An internalized plot is more difficult to follow, and more subtle, than the plot of a fast-moving action story whose events follow a chronological order.

The conventional short story plot includes several important elements. To begin with, there is the **protagonist,** the most important character. The protagonist does not have to be heroic, but he or she normally tries to accomplish something decisive during the course of the story. This goal may be obvious to the other characters, or it may be private—for example, trying to discover why a husband and wife, after years of marriage, still do not understand each other.

The character who opposes the protagonist is the **antagonist.** Although the antagonist may well be unpleasant or actually evil, this is by no means always the case. Many times—especially in contemporary fiction—the protagonist and the antagonist will be presented as equally good or bad individuals.

The struggle between the protagonist and the antagonist results in another important element of plot—**conflict.** It is a rare short story that does not contain at least some degree of conflict. But the conflict need not arise exclusively from the protagonist's struggle with another person. The protagonist may struggle against a force of nature—a tornado, a stormy sea, a disease—or against an entire society, or some large segment of society. The protagonist may experience an inner struggle between conflicting personal impulses. Or the struggle may be against what seems to be the inevitability of the universe, against fate or destiny or even God.

The more intense the conflict and uncertain the outcome, the more gripping the story is likely to be for the reader. Therefore, the protagonist and antagonist are often presented as possessing very nearly equal abilities for their struggle with each other. This **balancing of forces** gives the main characters at least the appearance of an even chance. In stories with a particularly forceful protagonist, the balancing of forces may be achieved through a **multiple struggle,** a struggle against multiple antagonists—one or more characters, nature, society, conflicting inner impulses, perhaps even fate. At its best, a multiple struggle blends external and internal antagonistic forces.

A story's conflict usually begins with a **precipitating incident,** some large or small happening early in the narrative that sets the plot in motion and makes all the subsequent events possible or even necessary. Often the precipitating incident **foreshadows** the major conflict—that is, it gives readers a hint of what is to come. For instance, a protagonist who is later to confront his wife's secret lover may overhear a remark suggesting that an affair may be taking place. Although foreshadowing mainly prepares readers for future plot developments, it may sometimes actually arise in other elements of the story, such as a suggestive description of the setting, a comment by the narrator, or simply the author's general tone and the story's resultant mood.

In a traditionally plotted story, the precipitating incident is followed by a period of increasing tension and conflict called **rising action.** Eventually the conflict reaches a level of intensity that the protagonist finally cannot tolerate: a situation called the **crisis** that requires decisive action or the making of an important decision. Sometimes the crisis situation will include a dilemma, in which every possible action or decision appears to promise equally undesirable consequences for the protagonist.

The **climax** is the high point of the story's plot. It is the point at which the protagonist makes an irrevocable decision or performs some act that can never be undone. Everything following the climax is part of the falling action, leading to the final unraveling of the plot, the **denouement** (pronounced *day*-new-MAHN). The denouement may consist of a solution or explanation, as in a detective story, or a final thematic statement by one of the characters, or a description that suggests the story's theme. Occasionally it will even reestablish some kind of relationship between the contending forces.

At any point in a story the author may introduce a flashback or a narrative projection. A **flashback** is a brief episode that actually occurred at a time earlier than its placement in the story; a **narrative projection** depicts a possible future. These devices allow the author to depart from strict chronology so as to give the events of the story in a more effective order. Information may be withheld until a strategic point—perhaps the crisis—then supplied in a flashback that takes the form of a memory or a dream, as in John's dream vision in "By the Waters of Babylon." Or the author may use one of these techniques to organize an entire story, as in Chekhov's "The Lottery Ticket," in which nearly everything between the precipitating incident and the denouement is a narrative projection, showing us what Ivan Dmitritch expects to happen if his wife wins the lottery.

These elements of the traditional short story—and of all fiction, and often of drama too, as you will see—are not present in every story you will read. Nor does the lack of one or several elements necessarily mean that a plot is defective. But with this discussion in mind as a guide, you can read and discuss the plotting of any short story with sharpness and confidence.

The first three stories in this book were chosen because they offer examples of the two main types of plots discussed here. These stories are Richard Connell's "The Most Dangerous Game," Stephen Vincent Benét's "By the Waters of Babylon," and Anton Chekhov's "The Lottery Ticket." (The Chekhov story features an implicit or internalized plot.) Other stories in the book that lend themselves especially well to plot analysis include W. W. Jacobs's "The Monkey's Paw," Gina Berriault's "The Stone Boy," D. H. Lawrence's "The Shades of Spring," Irwin Shaw's "The Dry Rock," and Harry Mark Petrakis's "The Wooing of Ariadne."

## Setting

Although setting is closely related to plot, as it is to all other elements of the short story, it is a distinct element in itself. A story is set in a specific place and time, has a plot of a specific duration, and reflects a particular psychological or spiritual state. We can say, then, that setting involves place, time, and frame of mind. Generally speaking, writers use setting to provide a scenic backdrop, to help establish mood and atmosphere, and to assist in dramatizing the inner thoughts and emotions of characters.

The physical environment of a story can tell the reader much about the characters. Similarly, the social atmosphere can reveal what kinds of people the story is dealing with—rich people or poor people, educated people or primitive people, aggressive and assertive people, or passive and insecure people. Stories set in the nostalgic past—the good old days—are likely to affect many readers quite differently from stories set in a computerized and mechanized future. Settings may be intentionally described in positive or negative terms, depending on what sort of mood an author wishes to create or what emotional response to draw from the reader. Settings may even be used as symbols to reinforce the workings of the other elements of the story. For example, the sea or a broad flowing river may symbolize time, fate, or aging; a mountain may symbolize strength of character or faith; a vast and arid desert may symbolize a kind of primitive purity unspoiled by the elaborate paraphernalia of civilization.

Whenever you read a story, you should take careful note of the degree to which setting is featured. Pay attention to the actual geographical location and the tone in which the author presents its characteristics. Note the occupations and life styles of the characters, the period within which the story occurs, and the religious, moral, social, emotional, and spiritual condition of the characters. On occasion a story will emphasize setting to the point of outweighing the other narrative elements. For example, in many pioneer or western stories the vast landscape of mountains, prairies, or forests reduces the importance of plot, character, and theme. Other stories on religious or political themes emphasize the social or spiritual aspects of setting to such a degree that the story line is trite and the characters seem little more than puppets. In other stories, however, the setting may be merely sketched in.

In both "The Most Dangerous Game" and "By the Waters of Babylon," the setting lies at the heart of the story, making the plot possible. Also consider the contributions of location, time, and spiritual condition or mental outlook to Katherine Brush's "Night Club" and Honoré de Balzac's "A Passion in the Desert." Other stories that lend themselves quite well to a look at the importance of setting are Eudora Welty's "Powerhouse," D. H. Lawrence's "The Shades of Spring," Stephen Crane's "The Bride Comes to Yellow Sky," James Joyce's "The Boarding House," and Shirley Jackson's "The Lottery."

## Character

Most readers get special pleasure from reading about fictional characters, just as they are interested in the real people in their lives. But understanding the characters in a short story is more complex than taking in its plot and setting. Whereas plot and setting are usually presented directly, character is usually dramatized—acted out—or presented through other elements in the story.

For example, setting can tell you much about the characters, because setting includes not only the places where the action occurs but also the characters' backgrounds, friends, and social position. How the characters look, dress, and move may tell you much about them. What the characters do and say—their actions and the dialogue—also reveal their personalities. Authors can invade the minds of their characters and reveal what thoughts are and are not there, and frequently use the opinions of other characters in the story to contribute to your understanding of a particular character. (Of course, those opinions may or may not be reliable, depending on the context.) You will rarely come across a story in which the author tells you straight out that an individual is mean, immoral, untruthful, vengeful, or the like. Modern readers prefer to be shown rather than told.

Well-dramatized fictional characters have three specific qualities: consistency, motivation, and plausibility. **Consistency** requires that once introduced and established as a certain type, a character must not change markedly unless the story provides convincing reasons for the change. For example, in "Night Club" Mrs. Brady, the aged dressing room attendant at the Club Français, is introduced to us as a woman who does not care much for her job and pays little attention to the remarkable things going on around her, and she remains unchanged until the end of the story.

**Motivation** is the "why" behind what the characters do. In a well-written story, characters do not act without observable reasons, and each action fits the reason for it. For example, Rainsford's actions at the end of "The Most Dangerous Game" have sufficient motivation by any standards, even if such actions would have been unthinkable to him at the beginning of the story.

**Plausibility** means believability: a plausible character is one who seems basically true to life. Of course, there is hardly room in the few pages of a short story to capture a complete personality, and so the author must create the illusion of lifelikeness by offering a blend of a few characteristic details that readers will accept as believable. For example, old Mrs. Brady in "Night Club," with her cheap magazines and her indifference to what is happening around her, is plausible because we have all known people like her. On the other hand, General Zaroff, in "The Most Dangerous Game," is rather too quirky and evil to be plausible.

When the exaggeration of a few character traits is taken to an extreme, the result is a **caricature.** A literary caricature is a sort of written cartoon sketch of a character, such as Ivan in "The Most Dangerous Game" and a couple of the minor gangsters in Irwin Shaw's "The Dry Rock." A **stock character,** although usually more thoroughly developed than a caricature, is no more plausible. A stock character is a stereotype that has appeared many times in popular writing and entertainment, and whose thoughts and actions are completely predictable: the bluff Irish cop, the domineering mother-in-law, the mad scientist, the prudish schoolteacher, the masked seeker of justice. Of course an author may make such a character come to life by supplying individual, plausible details; what makes a stock character implausible is the lack of such details, the reliance on the stereotype.

Alice Walker's "To Hell with Dying" explores the nuances of a single character—Mr. Sweet. Grace Paley's "The Loudest Voice," on the other hand, offers a constellation of interesting characters. Other stories that emphasize character include Carson McCullers's "The Sojourner," Eudora Welty's "Powerhouse," D. H. Lawrence's "The Shades of Spring," Irwin Shaw's "The Dry Rock," Harry Mark Petrakis's "The Wooing of Ariadne," James T. Farrell's "Studs," and James Joyce's "The Boarding House."

## Tone, Mood, and Emotion

Good fiction can make us feel as well as understand. Tone, mood, and emotion all contribute to our emotional response to a story. **Tone** reveals the author's attitude toward the story, including its subject and its readers. The tone may be matter-of-fact, grim, humorous, angry, ironic, nostalgic, or whatever the author chooses to make it. **Mood,** on the other hand, has to do with the story's predominating atmosphere. Mood arises only partly from the author's tone and may actually contrast with it. The narrative tone in "The Cask of Amontillado" is controlled and rational, but the story's mood is one of rising terror. It is to a story's overall atmosphere—its mood—that readers often experience an emotional response. That mood, created by Poe more through plot and setting than through tone, is what triggers our emotional response to the story.

"The Cask of Amontillado" is, among other things, a tale of **suspense.** We know from the beginning that the narrator has planned a terrible revenge against his enemy, but he withholds until the end what that revenge is to be and whether he achieves it. Keeping readers uncertain of the outcome, yet anxious to know what it is, produces one kind of suspense. Another type involves informing the readers of impending disaster while keeping the characters in the dark. Some degree of suspense is built into most stories, growing with the rising action and relieved by the climax and denouement. Suspense has much to do with the intensity of our emotional reponse to fiction.

Another source of our emotional response to a story is the **emotions** of the characters themselves. Their feelings can become our feelings; we can share, for example, in John's curiosity and fear in "By the Waters of Babylon," as the young priest searches for the truth about the Place of the Gods, and also feel a suspenseful anxiety for his safety. We know he is afraid because he says he is, but also because he describes his physical sensations—"My heart was cold as a frog and my knees like water"—and we can sense what that might feel like. Perhaps the description evokes memories of our own experiences, and of the emotions that went with them.

Memories can be of almost anything: early incidents such as learning to swim, watching a pet slowly give up life, experiencing a love affair, crashing the family car, getting caught in a grand lie, visiting a large city for the first time. Memories may also include brief sensory experiences, like the smell of finger-paint or hot cinnamon toast, the taste of heavily spiced chili or fresh corn on the cob, the feel of a warm bath or a cool autumn wind blowing in one's face, or the sound of a mosquito in a dark room or a dentist's drill. Scenes of all sorts can also become memories—a rolling meadow in the late summer, golden brown with tall grass gone to seed and swaying back and forth under an uncertain breeze; an entire hillside blighted by a sprawling junkyard; an antique car show in the city park; or a gym filled with deliriously anxious fans at the beginning of a big game.

Through dialogue, descriptions of setting, the presentation of incidents, and the delineation of images, authors can call up such memories in our minds. These memories heighten our receptiveness for the duration of the story; when we are reminded of our own sensations and past experiences, the chances of our responding emotionally are greatly increased. But such an appeal to readers' emotions must not be taken too far. Authors who try too hard and obviously to make us laugh or cry usually succeed only in turning us off. And so the better writers handle the element of emotion with restraint, stimulating our emotions while still respecting our minds.

Although tone, mood, and emotion are crucial to any short story, they are especially prominent in Edgar Allan Poe's "The Cask of Amontillado," W. W. Jacobs's "The Monkey's Paw," Donald Barthelme's "Report," Eudora Welty's "Powerhouse," and Arna Bontemps's "A Summer Tragedy." Other stories that emphasize these elements are John Collier's "De Mortuis," Gina Berriault's "The Stone Boy," Ivan Turgenev's "The Tryst," and Shirley Jackson's "The Lottery."

## Irony

Irony always involves some discrepancy or incongruity, some difference between appearance and fact. Three types of irony are particularly important to the short story: verbal irony, dramatic irony, and irony of plot.

**Verbal irony** occurs when a character knowingly says something whose meaning turns out to be very different from what the other characters believe. For example, Montresor in "The Cask of Amontillado" claims to be a mason, and it is not until the end of the story that Fortunato—and we—understand the point of his ironic joke. In **dramatic irony,** on the other hand, the reader or audience has important knowledge of which the characters are ignorant. In "By the Waters of Babylon" we know, as John never will, the meaning not only of such details as "UBTREAS" and "ASHING" but also of his dream about the Place of the Gods.

**Irony of plot,** perhaps the most important variety for the short story, involves a discrepancy between appearance and reality, or between what we expect to happen and what actually does happen. For example, the ending of Maupassant's "The Necklace" is crushingly ironic, as Mme. Loisel discovers that she has labored needlessly for ten years because she once mistook appearance for reality. And in "The Monkey's Paw," the fulfillment of Mr. White's first wish is horribly ironic because whatever he (and we) may have expected is far different from the ghastly way his wish was granted—and because it was his son Herbert who suggested the wish in the first place.

Occasionally, even symbols may be used ironically. An **ironic symbol** makes use of an image, object, situation, or action that normally symbolizes something quite different. In "The Most Dangerous Game" General Zaroff is surrounded by symbols of European civilization, which prove ironic because of the barbaric sport for which he lives. And the necklace in Maupassant's story is an ironic symbol for several reasons, for example because it symbolizes the brilliant life Mme. Loisel longs for, yet in reality reduces her and her husband to desperation and poverty.

Life is filled with ironies large and small, and so are short stories. The three stories we have specifically chosen to illustrate irony are Guy de Maupassant's "The Necklace," John Collier's "De Mortuis," and Gina Berriault's "The Stone Boy." Other stories that make important use of irony are W. W. Jacobs's "The Monkey's Paw," Harry Mark Petrakis's "The Wooing of Ariadne," Anton Chekhov's "The Lottery Ticket," and Katherine Brush's "Night Club."

## Imagery and Symbolism

Literary images are of two broad types: literal and figurative. A **literal image** consists of a literal and concrete delineation of an actual object, person, or brief "frozen" incident, without the suggestion of an abstract, extended, or hidden meaning. Figurative images, on the other hand, involve some "twist" on the literal meaning of the words used to describe whatever the image is comprised of. Figurative imagery involves the use of figures of speech such as similes, metaphors, and personifications, which do suggest special meanings, and which will not concern us until later on, when we look at the structure of poetry.

From childhood, we can all remember the impressions that certain early images made on our minds. A horizon of spindly trees evenly bent by the force of a steady winter wind, the rushing muddy waters of a river in flood after heavy rains, shimmering heat rising off hot pavement or sand, a mother's silhouette against a table lamp or night light, a grandfather's thick and gnarled fingers wrapped around some sort of tool, a roaring locomotive rushing through the valley, a dragon kite soaring against the blue heavens—all of these are literal images, and they become literal literary images when used by an author in a story.

When an image has also been given a meaning beyond itself—when meaning is added to it—it becomes a literary **symbol**. A line of large black starlings sitting along a telephone wire against a gray sky is only an image when we look out the window and see it, or when we remember it years later. When such an image appears in a story it is a literary image. And when this literary image is used to suggest how fate patiently waits to claim all of us, it has become a literary symbol.

Since an author may assign characters names that suggest something about their natures or their roles, the careful reader should be alert for name symbolism. For example, General Zaroff, in "The Most Dangerous Game," is in effect the czar of Ship-Trap Island, with absolute and unlimited power within his domain. Mr. Sweet, in "To Hell with Dying," is a diabetic, an alcoholic, a guitar player who likes to play "Sweet Georgia Brown," and a very sweet man to the children who love him, especially the narrator. His name is symbolic of his character.

Objects are generally more important as literary symbols than are names, however. For example, in Pär Lagerkvist's "Father and I" the two trains symbolize two different views of life, the father's and the boy's. When Hilda wraps herself in an animal skin in "The Shades of Spring," the skin symbolizes her primitive, animal side. An inattentive reader might well overlook these symbols, and miss an important point—in "Father and I," the whole point of the story.

How can one tell a literal image from a symbol? Some readers find symbols everywhere, with or without justification from the context, and others miss them entirely. The answer is that the story itself will provide clues that a particular image is being used as a symbol. The qualities of the symbol will be relevant to its symbolic meaning, as with the animal skin and Hilda's animal nature. The symbol will be important to the story, referred to repeatedly or even dominating the action, like the necklace in Maupassant's story. Finally, the specific meaning of the symbol will be suggested and supported within the story, not imposed on the story by a reader with conventional or personal ideas of what symbolic meaning a particular image is supposed to have. For example, a catacomb like that in "The Cask of Amontillado" might in a different context symbolize safety or sanctuary, but in this story, as a result of elaborate and suggestive description, it may be taken as symbolic of the narrator's crazed brain.

There are, however, certain symbols that have a conventional meaning. Many authors, for example, symbolize life as a voyage. In modern fiction a class of sexual symbols, also sometimes called Freudian symbols, has also taken on more or less universal meaning. Typically, long, pointed, rigid objects like guns or towers may be used as symbols of masculinity; dark enclosed places can be taken as reminiscent of the womb and used as feminine symbols. Physical actions or movements suggesting sexual activity—for example, riding a horse—are often intended by writers to symbolize sexual desire or suppression. D. H. Lawrence makes much use of sexual symbolism in his fiction, including "The Shades of Spring."

Such fixed or conventional symbols should not be assumed always to have the same meaning, however. Some readers assume that whenever a story contains a river it symbolizes time, that every tree is a masculine sexual symbol, that each character's name is a clue to his or her nature and destiny. Authors sometimes protest against being interpreted in this pat way. Shirley Jackson, for example, insists that the lottery in her well-known story was not meant to symbolize any particular social ritual, and she might have added that the black lottery box is not a symbolic stand-in for the womb.

Not recognizing a symbol is preferable to seeing symbols where none exist. If you read a story only on the literal level, you can still grasp an important part of its meaning; but if you start imposing your own symbolism on the story, even the literal meaning will be obscured. Nevertheless, keep in mind that it is through the use of symbolism that the author hopes to bring to the story a breadth and depth beyond the literal level.

Three good stories for demonstrating symbolism are Nathaniel Hawthorne's "The Minister's Black Veil," Pär Lagerkvist's "Father and I," and D. H. Lawrence's "The Shades of Spring." Other stories that emphasize symbolism are W. W. Jacobs's "The Monkey's Paw," Guy de Maupassant's "The Necklace," Arna Bontemps's "A Summer Tragedy," and Ivan Turgenev's "The Tryst."

## Theme

A story's **theme** is what the work is all about, its controlling idea or central insight into human nature or the human condition. In most good stories, all of the other elements—plot, setting, character, tone, mood, emotion, irony, symbolism, and point of view—work together to dramatize the theme. Theme, therefore, gives a story unity and reveals the author's artistic purpose in writing the piece.

A theme is not the same thing as a moral. The traditional "moral to the story" is much more limited in scope than a full thematic statement. For example, the moral to "By the Waters of Babylon" might go something like, "Sometimes it is okay not to obey your father." The story's theme, on the other hand, is much more comprehensive. It embodies the irrepressible drive of the human spirit to seek the truth; it contrasts the primitive life with modern urban civilization; and it prophesies that after even the worst imaginable disaster, the survivors will sooner or later begin the climb back toward civilization.

Since different stories may be stronger in one element than in another, you should not always weigh each element equally in trying to determine theme. Nathaniel Hawthorne's "The Minister's Black Veil" is built around a symbol, the veil, and so readers should naturally expect symbolism to make a major contribution to theme. Likewise, in Arna Bontemps's "A Summer Tragedy," a work that is essentially about its characters' feelings, you should expect emotion to make a substantial contribution to theme. Theme, then, may develop primarily out of the one or two elements that dominate the story.

As we have suggested, a thematic statement should contain some generalization about life, human character, or the human experience. However, the generalization should not be too broad. For example, if you try to say that the theme of Pär Lagerkvist's "Father and I" offers the observation that sooner or later all fathers come up short in the eyes of their sons, you have expressed a theme that reaches beyond the bounds of the story. A more suitable theme statement for "Father and I" might say that while a child may normally see life as ordered and friendly, and parents as all-knowing and powerful, he may sometimes gain a frightening and painful insight into the dark, unpredictable future beyond his or his parents' control.

Any thematic statement must be consistent with the story as the story is written. It must take into account all the major details of the story without contradicting or going beyond them. As with symbolism, you must beware of reading into the story a meaning that it does not have.

What we have said about theme does not mean that every story has only one theme, or that a theme may be stated in just one way. Many good stories are open to multiple interpretations. Arna Bontemps's "A Summer Tragedy" is such a story. Some readers might see the work as offering a thematic statement about the treatment of black Americans, while others might see it as being about the mistreatment and neglect of old people, whether black or white. Similarly, some readers might regard the theme of Crane's "The Bride Comes to Yellow Sky" as being about the triumph of persuasion over violence, while others might think it to be about the end of the old, wild west.

We have included two stories to be read for thematic emphasis. They are Stephen Crane's "The Bride Comes to Yellow Sky" and Irwin Shaw's "The Dry Rock." Other stories in the text that can be read for similar emphasis include Anton Chekhov's "The Lottery Ticket," Arna Bontemps's "A Summer Tragedy," Gina Berriault's "The Stone Boy," D. H. Lawrence's "The Shades of Spring," and Shirley Jackson's "The Lottery."

## Point of View

Nothing is more important to a full and informed reading of a short story than an understanding of its narrative **point of view**—the physical vantage point from which the events of the story are told. Said another way, point of view encompasses the position, location, person, or voice from which or through which the author tells the story.

All possible narrative points of view can be divided into two broad categories: first-person point of view and third-person point of view. Any story in which the narrator refers to himself or herself as "I" is told from the first-person point of view. Stories told from the third-person point of view do not include an "I" narrator. As a matter of fact, in most third-person stories you do not really know who the narrator is. You know who wrote the story, but you do not know by name who is telling the story; and you should not make the mistake of assuming that the author and the unknown narrative voice are one and the same. You may think of the third-person narrator as existing outside the story or as being submerged within it, depending on the specific circumstances of the story.

There are three important varieties of first-person narration: first-person central character, first-person secondary character, and first-person observer. In the first of these the "I" narrator is the major character—the protagonist—and the story is really all about some experience this "I" has had. Marko in "The Wooing of Ariadne" occupies such a narrative position, and so does John in "By the Waters of Babylon." The first-person narrator who is a secondary character in the story will often be a sidekick or acquaintance of the protagonist—a minor participant in the action whose primary function is to tell someone else's story. This is the case with the narrator in James T. Farrell's "Studs." Finally, the first-person narrator who occupies the position of observer does not actually participate in the action but rather stands on the sidelines telling you what he or she has seen or heard. The first-person narrator in Turgenev's "The Tryst" is essentially an observer.

Like any other character in the story, the first-person narrator has a distinct personality, and that personality affects how "well" he or she tells the story. For the narrator may be naive, or unobservant, or stupid, or biased, or a liar. When reading a story with a first-person narrator, you should test the probability of what the narrator tells you as much as you can within the limits of the story, to make sure whether he or she is to be trusted.

There are also three important varieties of third-person narration: third-person limited, third-person omniscient, and third-person dramatic. Stories told from the third-person limited point of view employ an unnamed narrative voice that concentrates on the thoughts, feelings, actions, and observations of a single character. We may say that such a narrator is submerged within this character, as in Carson McCullers's "The Sojourner." In stories told from the third-person omniscient point of view, the narrative voice is all-knowing; it can report what is going on anywhere, and can go into the minds of any or all of the characters and tell us what they think and feel. James Joyce's "The Boarding House" is an example of a story written from the omniscient point of view. Finally, in stories told from the third-person dramatic point of view, the narrative voice operates much like a roving movie camera, giving us the story's action, dialogue, and setting, but not directly revealing any character's thoughts and feelings. The narrator in stories told from the dramatic point of view is often said to be effaced. Shirley Jackson's "The Lottery" is narrated from the dramatic point of view, and so is Dorothy Parker's "You Were Perfectly Fine," which incidentally has so much dialogue and so little description that it much resembles a one-act play.

Generally speaking, all three types of first-person point of view and also the third-person limited point of view focus most clearly and sharply on the events of the story. This is true because readers are pretty well forced to experience the world of the story through the senses and mind of a single person—the central character, a secondary character, or an observer. The omniscient point of view has the advantage of revealing to us much more fully than would be possible in real life what is taking place in all the characters' minds. By contrast, the great advantage of dramatic narration is that the thoughts and feelings of all the characters can be withheld from the reader, creating suspenseful situations or making possible plausible surprise endings. In stories written from the dramatic point of view, almost everything is dramatized; little or nothing—beyond the most generalized thoughts of large numbers of people or sketchy historical background information—is directly told to the reader.

Each of our seven concluding stories—Harry Mark Petrakis's "The Wooing of Ariadne," James T. Farrell's "Studs," Ivan Turgenev's "The Tryst," Carson McCullers's "The Sojourner," James Joyce's "The Boarding House," Dorothy Parker's "You Were Perfectly Fine," and Shirley Jackson's "The Lottery"—demonstrates a different point of view.

# The Most Dangerous Game

RICHARD CONNELL

"Off there to the right—somewhere—is a large island," said Whitney.
"It's rather a mystery—"

"What island is it?" Rainsford asked.

"The old charts call it 'Ship-Trap Island,'" Whitney replied. "A
suggestive name, isn't it? Sailors have a curious dread of the place. I
don't know why. Some superstition—"

"Can't see it," remarked Rainsford, trying to peer through the dank
tropical night that was palpable as it pressed its thick warm blackness
in upon the yacht.

"You've good eyes," said Whitney, with a laugh, "and I've seen you
pick off a moose moving in the brown fall bush at four hundred yards,
but even you can't see four miles or so through a moonless Caribbean
night."

"Nor four yards," admitted Rainsford. "Ugh! It's like moist black
velvet."

"It will be light in Rio," promised Whitney. "We should make it in
a few days. I hope the jaguar guns have come from Purdey's. We should
have some good hunting up the Amazon. Great sport, hunting."

"The best sport in the world," agreed Rainsford.

"For the hunter," amended Whitney. "Not for the jaguar."

"Don't talk rot, Whitney," said Rainsford. "You're a big-game hunter,
not a philosopher. Who cares how a jaguar feels?"

"Perhaps the jaguar does," observed Whitney.

"Bah! They've no understanding."

"Even so, I rather think they understand one thing—fear. The fear
of pain and the fear of death."

"Nonsense," laughed Rainsford. "This hot weather is making you
soft, Whitney. Be a realist. The world is made up of two classes—the
hunters and the huntees. Luckily, you and I are the hunters. Do you
think we've passed that island yet?"

"I can't tell in the dark. I hope so."

"Why?" asked Rainsford.

"The place has a reputation—a bad one."

"Cannibals?" suggested Rainsford.

"Hardly. Even cannibals wouldn't live in such a God-forsaken place.
But it's gotten into sailor lore, somehow. Didn't you notice that the
crew's nerves seemed a bit jumpy to-day?"

"They were a bit strange, now you mention it. Even Captain Niel-
sen—"

"Yes, even that tough-minded old Swede, who'd go up to the devil
himself and ask him for a light. Those fishy blue eyes held a look I never
saw there before. All I could get out of him was: 'This place has an evil

name among sea-faring men, sir.' Then he said to me, very gravely:
'Don't you feel anything?'—as if the air about us was actually poisonous.
Now, you mustn't laugh when I tell you this—I did feel something like
a sudden chill.

"There was no breeze. The sea was as flat as a plate-glass window.
We were drawing near the island then. What I felt was a—a mental
chill; a sort of sudden dread."

"Pure imagination," said Rainsford. "One superstitious sailor can
taint the whole ship's company with his fear."

"Maybe. But sometimes I think sailors have an extra sense that tells
them when they are in danger. Sometimes I think evil is a tangible
thing—with wave lengths, just as sound and light have. An evil place
can, so to speak, broadcast vibrations of evil. Anyhow, I'm glad we're
getting out of this zone. Well, I think I'll turn in now, Rainsford."

"I'm not sleepy," said Rainsford. "I'm going to smoke another pipe
on the after deck."

"Good night, then, Rainsford. See you at breakfast."

"Right. Good night, Whitney."

There was no sound in the night as Rainsford sat there, but the
muffled throb of the engine that drove the yacht swiftly through the
darkness, and the swish and ripple of the wash of the propeller.

Rainsford, reclining in a steamer chair, indolently puffed on his
favorite brier. The sensuous drowsiness of the night was on him. "It's
so dark," he thought, "that I could sleep without closing my eyes; the
night would be my eyelids—"

An abrupt sound startled him. Off to the right he heard it, and his
ears, expert in such matters, could not be mistaken. Again he heard the
sound, and again. Somewhere, off in the blackness, some one had fired
a gun three times.

Rainsford sprang up and moved quickly to the rail, mystified. He
strained his eyes in the direction from which the reports had come, but
it was like trying to see through a blanket. He leaped upon the rail and
balanced himself there, to get greater elevation; his pipe, striking a rope,
was knocked from his mouth. He lunged for it; a short, hoarse cry came
from his lips as he realized he had reached too far and had lost his
balance. The cry was pinched off short as the blood-warm waters of the
Caribbean Sea closed over his head.

He struggled up to the surface and tried to cry out, but the wash
from the speeding yacht slapped him in the face and the salt water in
his open mouth made him gag and strangle. Desperately he struck out
with strong strokes after the receding lights of the yacht, but he stopped
before he had swum fifty feet. A certain cool-headedness had come to
him; it was not the first time he had been in a tight place. There was
a chance that his cries could be heard by some one aboard the yacht,
but that chance was slender, and grew more slender as the yacht raced
on. He wrestled himself out of his clothes, and shouted with all his

power. The lights of the yacht became faint and ever-vanishing fireflies; then they were blotted out entirely by the night.

Rainsford remembered the shots. They had come from the right, and doggedly he swam in that direction, swimming with slow, deliberate strokes, conserving his strength. For a seemingly endless time he fought the sea. He began to count his strokes; he could do possibly a hundred more and then—

Rainsford heard a sound. It came out of the darkness, a high screaming sound, the sound of an animal in an extremity of anguish and terror.

He did not recognize the animal that made the sound; he did not try to; with fresh vitality he swam toward the sound. He heard it again; then it was cut short by another noise, crisp, staccato.

"Pistol shot," muttered Rainsford, swimming on.

Ten minutes of determined effort brought another sound to his ears— the most welcome he had ever heard—the muttering and growling of the sea breaking on a rocky shore. He was almost on the rocks before he saw them; on a night less calm he would have been shattered against them. With his remaining strength he dragged himself from the swirling waters. Jagged crags appeared to jut into the opaqueness, he forced himself upward, hand over hand. Gasping, his hands raw, he reached a flat place at the top. Dense jungle came down to the very edge of the cliffs. What perils that tangle of trees and underbrush might hold for him did not concern Rainsford just then. All he knew was that he was safe from his enemy, the sea, and that utter weariness was on him. He flung himself down at the jungle edge and tumbled headlong into the deepest sleep of his life.

When he opened his eyes he knew from the position of the sun that it was late in the afternoon. Sleep had given him new vigor; a sharp hunger was picking at him. He looked about him, almost cheerfully.

"Where there are pistol shots, there are men. Where there are men, there is food," he thought. But what kind of men, he wondered, in so forbidding a place? An unbroken front of snarled and ragged jungle fringed the shore.

He saw no sign of a trail through the closely knit web of weeds and trees; it was easier to go along the shore, and Rainsford floundered along by the water. Not far from where he had landed, he stopped.

Some wounded thing, by the evidence a large animal, had thrashed about in the underbrush; the jungle weeds were crushed down and the moss was lacerated; one patch of weeds was stained crimson. A small, glittering object not far away caught Rainsford's eye and he picked it up. It was an empty cartridge.

"A twenty-two," he remarked. "That's odd. It must have been a fairly large animal too. The hunter had his nerve with him to tackle it with a light gun. It's clear that the brute put up a fight. I suppose the first three shots I heard was when the hunter flushed his quarry and wounded it. The last shot was when he trailed it here and finished it."

He examined the ground closely and found what he had hoped to find—the print of hunting boots. They pointed along the cliff in the direction he had been going. Eagerly he hurried along, now slipping on a rotten log or a loose stone, but making headway; night was beginning to settle down on the island.

Bleak darkness was blacking out the sea and jungle when Rainsford sighted the lights. He came upon them as he turned a crook in the coast line, and his first thought was that he had come upon a village, for there were many lights. But as he forged along he saw to his great astonishment that all the lights were in one enormous building—a lofty structure with pointed towers plunging upward into the gloom. His eyes made out the shadowy outlines of a palatial château; it was set on a high bluff, and on three sides of it cliffs dived down to where the sea licked greedy lips in the shadows.

"Mirage," thought Rainsford. But it was no mirage, he found, when he opened the tall spiked iron gate. The stone steps were real enough; the massive door with a leering gargoyle for a knocker was real enough; yet about it all hung an air of unreality.

He lifted the knocker, and it creaked up stiffly, as if it had never before been used. He let it fall, and it startled him with its booming loudness. He thought he heard steps within; the door remained closed. Again Rainsford lifted the heavy knocker, and let it fall. The door opened then, opened as suddenly as if it were on a spring, and Rainsford stood blinking in the river of glaring gold light that poured out. The first thing Rainsford's eyes discerned was the largest man Rainsford had ever seen—a gigantic creature, solidly made and black-bearded to the waist. In his hand the man held a long-barreled revolver, and he was pointing it straight at Rainsford's heart.

Out of the snarl of beard two small eyes regarded Rainsford.

"Don't be alarmed," said Rainsford, with a smile which he hoped was disarming. "I'm no robber. I fell off a yacht. My name is Sanger Rainsford of New York City."

The menacing look in the eyes did not change. The revolver pointed as rigidly as if the giant were a statue. He gave no sign that he understood Rainsford's words, or that he had even heard them. He was dressed in uniform, a black uniform trimmed with gray astrakhan.

"I'm Sanger Rainsford of New York," Rainsford began again. "I fell off a yacht. I am hungry."

The man's only answer was to raise with his thumb the hammer of his revolver. Then Rainsford saw the man's free hand go to his forehead in a military salute, and he saw him click his heels together and stand at attention. Another man was coming down the broad marble steps, an erect, slender man in evening clothes. He advanced to Rainsford and held out his hand.

In a cultivated voice marked by a slight accent that gave it added precision and deliberateness, he said: "It is a very great pleasure and honor to welcome Mr. Sanger Rainsford, the celebrated hunter, to my home."

Automatically Rainsford shook the man's hand.

"I've read your book about hunting snow leopards in Tibet, you see," explained the man. "I am General Zaroff."

Rainsford's first impression was that the man was singularly handsome; his second was that there was an original, almost bizarre quality about the general's face. He was a tall man past middle age, for his hair was a vivid white; but his thick eyebrows and pointed military mustache were as black as the night from which Rainsford had come. His eyes, too, were black and very bright. He had high cheek bones, a sharp-cut nose, a spare, dark face, the face of a man used to giving orders, the face of an aristocrat. Turning to the giant in uniform, the general made a sign. The giant put away his pistol, saluted, withdrew.

"Ivan is an incredibly strong fellow," remarked the general, "but he has the misfortune to be deaf and dumb. A simple fellow, but, I'm afraid, like all his race, a bit of a savage."

"Is he Russian?"

"He is a Cossack," said the general, and his smile showed red lips and pointed teeth. "So am I."

"Come," he said, "we shouldn't be chatting here. We can talk later. Now you want clothes, food, rest. You shall have them. This is a most restful spot."

Ivan had reappeared, and the general spoke to him with lips that moved but gave forth no sound.

"Follow Ivan, if you please, Mr. Rainsford," said the general. "I was about to have my dinner when you came. I'll wait for you. You'll find that my clothes will fit you, I think."

It was to a huge, beam-ceilinged bedroom with a canopied bed big enough for six men that Rainsford followed the silent giant. Ivan laid out an evening suit, and Rainsford, as he put it on, noticed that it came from a London tailor who ordinarily cut and sewed for none below the rank of duke.

The dining room to which Ivan conducted him was in many ways remarkable. There was a medieval magnificence about it; it suggested a baronial hall of feudal times with its oaken panels, its high ceiling, its vast refectory table where twoscore men could sit down to eat. About the hall were the mounted heads of many animals—lions, tigers, elephants, moose, bears; larger or more perfect specimens Rainsford had never seen. At the great table the general was sitting, alone.

"You'll have a cocktail, Mr. Rainsford," he suggested. The cocktail was surpassingly good; and, Rainsford noted, the table appointments were of the finest—the linen, the crystal, the silver, the china.

They were eating *borsch*, the rich, red soup with whipped cream so dear to Russian palates. Half apologetically General Zaroff said: "We do our best to preserve the amenities of civilization here. Please forgive any lapses. We are well off the beaten track, you know. Do you think the champagne has suffered from its long ocean trip?"

"Not in the least," declared Rainsford. He was finding the general a most thoughtful and affable host, a true cosmopolite. But there was one small trait of the general's that made Rainsford uncomfortable. Whenever he looked up from his plate he found the general studying him, appraising him narrowly.

"Perhaps," said General Zaroff, "you were surprised that I recognized your name. You see, I read all books on hunting published in English, French, and Russian. I have but one passion in my life, Mr. Rainsford, and it is the hunt."

"You have some wonderful heads here," said Rainsford as he ate a particularly well cooked filet mignon. "That Cape buffalo is the largest I ever saw."

"Oh, that fellow. Yes, he was a monster."

"Did he charge you?"

"Hurled me against a tree," said the general. "Fractured my skull. But I got the brute."

"I've always thought," said Rainsford, "that the Cape buffalo is the most dangerous of all big game."

For a moment the general did not reply; he was smiling his curious red-lipped smile. Then he said slowly: "No. You are wrong, sir. The Cape buffalo is not the most dangerous big game." He sipped his wine. "Here in my preserve on this island," he said in the same slow tone, "I hunt more dangerous game."

Rainsford expressed his surprise. "Is there big game on this island?"

The general nodded. "The biggest."

"Really?"

"Oh, it isn't here naturally, of course. I have to stock the island."

"What have you imported, general?" Rainsford asked. "Tigers?"

The general smiled. "No," he said. "Hunting tigers ceased to interest me some years ago. I exhausted their possibilities, you see. No thrill left in tigers, no real danger. I live for danger, Mr. Rainsford."

The general took from his pocket a gold cigaret case and offered his guest a long black cigaret with a silver tip; it was perfumed and gave off a smell like incense.

"We will have some capital hunting, you and I," said the general. "I shall be most glad to have your society."

"But what game—" began Rainsford.

"I'll tell you," said the general. "You will be amused, I know. I think I may say, in all modesty, that I have done a rare thing. I have invented a new sensation. May I pour you another glass of port, Mr. Rainsford?"

"Thank you, general."

The general filled both glasses, and said: "God makes some men poets. Some He makes kings, some beggars. Me He made a hunter. My hand was made for the trigger, my father said. He was a very rich man with a quarter of a million acres in the Crimea, and he was an ardent sportsman. When I was only five years old he gave me a little gun, specially made in Moscow for me, to shoot sparrows with. When I shot some of his prize turkeys with it, he did not punish me; he complimented me on my marksmanship. I killed my first bear in the Caucasus when I was ten. My whole life has been one prolonged hunt. I went into the army—it was expected of noblemen's sons—and for a time commanded a division of Cossack cavalry, but my real interest was always the hunt. I have hunted every kind of game in every land. It would be impossible for me to tell you how many animals I have killed."

The general puffed at his cigaret.

"After the debacle in Russia I left the country, for it was imprudent for an officer of the Czar to stay there. Many noble Russians lost everything. I, luckily, had invested heavily in American securities, so I shall never have to open a tea room in Monte Carlo or drive a taxi in Paris. Naturally, I continued to hunt—grizzlies in your Rockies, crocodiles in the Ganges, rhinoceroses in East Africa. It was in Africa that the Cape buffalo hit me and laid me up for six months. As soon as I recovered I started for the Amazon to hunt jaguars, for I had heard they were unusually cunning. They weren't." The Cossack sighed. "They were no match at all for a hunter with his wits about him, and a high-powered rifle. I was bitterly disappointed. I was lying in my tent with a splitting headache one night when a terrible thought pushed its way into my mind. Hunting was beginning to bore me! And hunting, remember, had been my life. I have heard that in America business men often go to pieces when they give up the business that has been their life."

"Yes, that's so," said Rainsford.

The general smiled. "I had no wish to go to pieces," he said. "I must do something. Now, mine is an analytical mind, Mr. Rainsford. Doubtless that is why I enjoy the problems of the chase."

"No doubt, General Zaroff."

"So," continued the general, "I asked myself why the hunt no longer fascinated me. You are much younger than I am, Mr. Rainsford, and have not hunted as much, but you perhaps can guess the answer."

"What was it?"

"Simply this: hunting had ceased to be what you call 'a sporting proposition.' It had become too easy. I always got my quarry. Always. There is no greater bore than perfection."

The general lit a fresh cigaret.

"No animal had a chance with me any more. That is no boast; it is a mathematical certainty. The animal had nothing but his legs and his instinct. Instinct is no match for reason. When I thought of this it was a tragic moment for me, I can tell you."

Rainsford leaned across the table, absorbed in what his host was saying.

"It came to me as an inspiration what I must do," the general went on.

"And that was?"

The general smiled the quiet smile of one who has faced an obstacle and surmounted it with success. "I had to invent a new animal to hunt," he said.

"A new animal? You're joking."

"Not at all," said the general. "I never joke about hunting. I needed a new animal. I found one. So I bought this island, built this house, and here I do my hunting. The island is perfect for my purposes—there are jungles with a maze of trails in them, hills, swamps—"

"But the animal, General Zaroff?"

"Oh," said the general, "it supplies me with the most exciting hunting in the world. No other hunting compares with it for an instant. Every day I hunt, and I never grow bored now, for I have a quarry with which I can match my wits."

Rainsford's bewilderment showed in his face.

"I wanted the ideal animal to hunt," explained the general. "So I said: 'What are the attributes of an ideal quarry?' And the answer was, of course: 'It must have courage, cunning, and above all, it must be able to reason.' "

"But no animal can reason," objected Rainsford.

"My dear fellow," said the general, "there is one that can."

"But you can't mean—" gasped Rainsford.

"And why not?"

"I can't believe you are serious, General Zaroff. This is a grisly joke."

"Why should I not be serious? I am speaking of hunting."

"Hunting? Good God, General Zaroff, what you speak of is murder."

The general laughed with entire good nature. He regarded Rainsford quizzically. "I refuse to believe that so modern and civilized a young man as you seem to be harbors romantic ideas about the value of human life. Surely your experiences in the war—"

"Did not make me condone cold-blooded murder," finished Rainsford stiffly.

Laughter shook the general. "How extraordinarily droll you are!" he said. "One does not expect nowadays to find a young man of the educated class, even in America, with such a naive, and, if I may say so, mid-Victorian point of view. It's like finding a snuff-box in a limousine. Ah, well, doubtless you had Puritan ancestors. So many Americans appear to have had. I'll wager you'll forget your notions when you go hunting with me. You've a genuine new thrill in store for you, Mr. Rainsford."

"Thank you, I'm a hunter, not a murderer."

"Dear me," said the general, quite unruffled, "again that unpleasant word. But I think I can show you that your scruples are quite ill founded."

"Yes?"

"Life is for the strong, to be lived by the strong, and, if need be, taken by the strong. The weak of the world were put here to give the strong pleasure. I am strong. Why should I not use my gift? If I wish to hunt, why should I not? I hunt the scum of the earth—sailors from tramp ships—lascars, blacks, Chinese, whites, mongrels—a thorobred horse or hound is worth more than a score of them."

"But they are men," said Rainsford hotly.

"Precisely," said the general. "That is why I use them. It gives me pleasure. They can reason, after a fashion. So they are dangerous."

"But where do you get them?"

The general's left eyelid fluttered down in a wink. "This island is called Ship-Trap," he answered. "Sometimes an angry god of the high seas sends them to me. Sometimes, when Providence is not so kind, I help Providence a bit. Come to the window with me."

Rainsford went to the window and looked out toward the sea.

"Watch! Out there!" exclaimed the general, pointing into the night. Rainsford's eyes saw only blackness, and then, as the general pressed a button, far out to sea Rainsford saw the flash of lights.

The general chuckled. "They indicate a channel," he said, "where there's none: giant rocks with razor edges crouch like a sea monster with wide-open jaws. They can crush a ship as easily as I crush this nut." He dropped a walnut on the hardwood floor and brought his heel grinding down on it. "Oh, yes," he said, casually, as if in answer to a question, "I have electricity. We try to be civilized here."

"Civilized? And you shoot down men?"

A trace of anger was in the general's black eyes, but it was there for but a second, and he said, in his most pleasant manner: "Dear me, what a righteous young man you are! I assure you I do not do the thing you suggest. That would be barbarous. I treat these visitors with every consideration. They get plenty of good food and exercise. They get into splendid physical condition. You shall see for yourself to-morrow."

"What do you mean?"

"We'll visit my training school," smiled the general. "It's in the cellar. I have about a dozen pupils down there now. They're from the Spanish bark San Lucar that had the bad luck to go on the rocks out there. A very inferior lot, I regret to say. Poor specimens and more accustomed to the deck than to the jungle."

He raised his hand, and Ivan, who served as waiter, brought thick Turkish coffee. Rainsford, with an effort, held his tongue in check.

"It's a game, you see," pursued the general blandly. "I suggest to one of them that we go hunting. I give him a supply of food and an excellent hunting knife. I give him three hours' start. I am to follow, armed only with a pistol of the smallest caliber and range. If my quarry eludes me for three whole days, he wins the game. If I find him"—the general smiled—"he loses."

"Suppose he refuses to be hunted?"

"Oh," said the general, "I give him his option, of course. He need not play that game if he doesn't wish to. If he does not wish to hunt, I turn him over to Ivan. Ivan once had the honor of serving as official knouter to the Great White Czar, and he has his own ideas of sport. Invariably, Mr. Rainsford, invariably they choose the hunt."

"And if they win?"

The smile on the general's face widened. "To date I have not lost," he said.

Then he added hastily: "I don't wish you to think me a braggart, Mr. Rainsford. Many of them afford only the most elementary sort of problem. Occasionally I strike a tartar. One almost did win. I eventually had to use the dogs."

"The dogs?"

"This way, please. I'll show you."

The general steered Rainsford to a window. The lights from the windows sent a flickering illumination that made grotesque patterns on the courtyard below, and Rainsford could see moving about there a dozen or so huge black shapes; as they turned toward him, their eyes glittered greenly.

"A rather good lot, I think," observed the general. "They are let out at seven every night. If anyone should try to get into my house—or out of it—something extremely regrettable would occur to him." He hummed a snatch of song from the Folies Bergère.[1]

"And now," said the general, "I want to show you my new collection of heads. Will you come with me to the library?"

"I hope," said Rainsford, "that you will excuse me to-night, General Zaroff. I'm really not feeling at all well."

"Ah, indeed?" the general inquired solicitously. "Well, I suppose that's only natural, after your long swim. You need a good, restful night's sleep. To-morrow you'll feel like a new man, I'll wager. Then we'll hunt, eh? I've one rather promising prospect—"

Rainsford was hurrying from the room.

"Sorry you can't go with me to-night," called the general. "I expect rather fair sport—a big, strong black. He looks resourceful—Well, good night, Mr. Rainsford; I hope you have a good night's rest."

The bed was good, and the pajamas of the softest silk, and he was tired in every fiber of his being, but nevertheless Rainsford could not quiet his brain with the opiate of sleep. He lay, eyes wide open. Once he thought he heard stealthy steps in the corridor outside his room. He sought to throw open the door; it would not open. He went to the window and looked out. His room was high up in one of the towers. The lights of the château were out now, and it was dark and silent, but there was a fragment of sallow moon, and by its wan light he could see, dimly, the courtyard; there, weaving in and out in the pattern of shadow, were black, noiseless forms; the hounds heard him at the window and looked up, expectantly, with their green eyes. Rainsford went back to the bed and lay down. By many methods he tried to put himself to sleep. He had achieved a doze when, just as

[1] A famous Parisian music hall.

morning began to come, he heard, far off in the jungle, the faint report of a pistol.

General Zaroff did not appear until luncheon. He was dressed fault-lessly in the tweeds of a country squire. He was solicitous about the state of Rainsford's health.

"As for me," sighed the general, "I do not feel so well. I am worried, Mr. Rainsford. Last night I detected traces of my old complaint."

To Rainsford's questioning glance the general said: "Ennui. Bore-dom."

Then, taking a second helping of Crêpes Suzette, the general ex-plained: "The hunting was not good last night. The fellow lost his head. He made a straight trail that offered no problems at all. That's the trouble with these sailors; they have dull brains to begin with, and they do not know how to get about in the woods. They excessively stupid and obvious things. It's most annoying. Will you have another glass of Chablis, Mr. Rainsford?"

"General," said Rainsford firmly, "I wish to leave this island at once."

The general raised his thickets of eyebrows; he seemed hurt. "But, my dear fellow," the general protested, "you've only just come. You've had no hunting—"

"I wish to go to-day," said Rainsford. He saw the dead black eyes of the general on him, studying him. General Zaroff's face suddenly brightened.

He filled Rainsford's glass with venerable Chablis from a dusty bottle.

"To-night," said the general, "we will hunt—you and I."

Rainsford shook his head, "No, general," he said. "I will not hunt."

The general shrugged his shoulders and delicately ate a hothouse grape. "As you wish, my friend," he said. "The choice rests entirely with you. But may I not venture to suggest that you will find my idea of sport more diverting than Ivan's?"

He nodded toward the corner to where the giant stood, scowling, his thick arms crossed on his hogshead of chest.

"You don't mean—" cried Rainsford.

"My dear fellow," said the general, "have I not told you I always mean what I say about hunting? This is really an inspiration. I drink to a foeman worthy of my steel—at last."

The general raised his glass, but Rainsford sat staring at him.

"You'll find this game worth playing," the general said enthusiasti-cally. "Your brain against mine. Your woodcraft against mine. Your strength and stamina against mine. Outdoor chess! And the stake is not without value, eh?"

"And if I win—" began Rainsford huskily.

"I'll cheerfully acknowledge myself defeated if I do not find you by midnight of the third day," said General Zaroff. "My sloop will place you on the mainland near a town."

The general read what Rainsford was thinking.

"Oh, you can trust me," said the Cossack. "I will give you my word as a gentleman and a sportsman. Of course you, in turn, must agree to say nothing of your visit here."

"I'll agree to nothing of the kind," said Rainsford.

"Oh," said the general, "in that case—But why discuss that now? Three days hence we can discuss it over a bottle of Veuve Cliquot,[2] unless—"

The general sipped his wine.

Then a businesslike air animated him. "Ivan," he said to Rainsford, "will supply you with hunting clothes, food, a knife. I suggest you wear moccasins; they leave a poorer trail. I suggest too that you avoid the big swamp in the southeast corner of the island. We call it Death Swamp. There's quicksand there. One foolish fellow tried it. The deplorable part of it was that Lazarus followed him. You can imagine my feelings, Mr. Rainsford. I loved Lazarus; he was the finest hound in my pack. Well, I must beg you to excuse me now. I always take a siesta after lunch. You'll hardly have time for a nap, I fear. You'll want to start, no doubt. I shall not follow till dusk. Hunting at night is so much more exciting than by day, don't you think? Au revoir, Mr. Rainsford, au revoir."

General Zaroff, with a deep, courtly bow, strolled from the room.

From another door came Ivan. Under one arm he carried khaki hunting clothes, a haversack of food, a leather sheath containing a long-bladed hunting knife; his right hand rested on a cocked revolver thrust in the crimson sash about his waist. . . .

Rainsford had fought his way through the bush for two hours. "I must keep my nerve. I must keep my nerve," he said through tight teeth.

He had not been entirely clear-headed when the château gates snapped shut behind him. His whole idea at first was to put distance between himself and General Zaroff, and, to this end, he had plunged along, spurred on by the sharp rowels of something very like panic. Now he had got a grip on himself, had stopped, and was taking stock of himself and the situation.

He saw that straight flight was futile; inevitably it would bring him face to face with the sea. He was in a picture with a frame of water, and his operations, clearly, must take place within that frame.

"I'll give a trail to follow," muttered Rainsford, and he struck off from the rude paths he had been following into the trackless wilderness. He executed a series of intricate loops; he doubled on this trail again and again, recalling all the lore of the fox hunt, and all the dodges of the fox. Night found him leg-weary, with hands and face lashed by the branches, on a thickly wooded ridge. He knew it would be insane to blunder on through the dark, even if he had the strength. His need for rest was imperative and he thought: "I have played the fox, now I must play the cat of the fable." A big tree with a thick trunk and outspread

[2]A vintage champagne.

branches was nearby, and, taking care to leave not the slightest mark, he climbed up into the crotch, and stretching out on one of the broad limbs, after a fashion, rested. Rest brought him new confidence and almost a feeling of security. Even so zealous a hunter as General Zaroff could not trace him there, he told himself; only the devil himself could follow that complicated trail through the jungle after dark. But, perhaps, the general was a devil—

An apprehensive night crawled slowly by like a wounded snake, and sleep did not visit Rainsford, altho the silence of a dead world was on the jungle. Toward morning when a dingy gray was varnishing the sky, the cry of some startled bird focused Rainsford's attention in that direction. Something was coming through the bush, coming slowly, carefully, coming by the same winding way Rainsford had come. He flattened himself down on the limb, and through a screen of leaves almost as thick as tapestry, he watched. The thing that was approaching was a man.

It was General Zaroff. He made his way along with his eyes fixed in utmost concentration on the ground before him. He paused, almost beneath the tree, dropped to his knees and studied the ground. Rainsford's impulse was to hurl himself down like a panther, but he saw the general's right hand held something metallic—a small automatic pistol.

The hunter shook his head several times, as if he were puzzled. Then he straightened up and took from his case one of his black cigarets; its pungent incense-like smoke floated up to Rainsford's nostrils.

Rainsford held his breath. The general's eyes had left the ground and were traveling inch by inch up the tree. Rainsford froze there, every muscle tensed for a spring. But the sharp eyes of the hunter stopped before they reached the limb where Rainsford lay; a smile spread over his brown face. Very deliberately he blew a smoke ring into the air; then he turned his back on the tree and walked carelessly away, back along the trail he had come. The swish of the underbrush against his hunting boots grew fainter and fainter.

The pent-up air burst hotly from Rainsford's lungs. His first thought made him feel sick and numb. The general could follow a trail through the woods at night; he could follow an extremely difficult trail; he must have uncanny powers; only by the merest chance had the Cossack failed to see his quarry.

Rainsford's second thought was even more terrible. It sent a shudder of cold horror through his whole being. Why had the general smiled? Why had he turned back?

Rainsford did not want to believe what his reason told him was true, but the truth was as evident as the sun that had by now pushed through the morning mists. The general was playing with him! The general was saving him for another day's sport! The Cossack was the cat; he was the mouse. Then it was that Rainsford knew the full meaning of terror.

"I will not lose my nerve. I will not."

He slid down from the tree, and struck off again into the woods. His face was set and he forced the machinery of his mind to function. Three hundred yards from his hiding place he stopped where a huge dead tree leaned precariously on a smaller, living one. Throwing off his sack of food, Rainsford took his knife from its sheath and began to work with all his energy.

The job was finished at last, and he threw himself down behind a fallen log a hundred feet away. He did not have to wait long. The cat was coming again to play with the mouse.

Following the trail with the sureness of a bloodhound, came General Zaroff. Nothing escaped those searching black eyes, no crushed blade of grass, no bent twig, no mark, no matter how faint, in the moss. So intent was the Cossack on his stalking that he was upon the thing Rainsford had made before he saw it. His foot touched the protruding bough that was the trigger. Even as he touched it, the general sensed his danger and leaped back with the agility of an ape. But he was not quite quick enough; the dead tree, delicately adjusted to rest on the cut living one, crashed down and struck the general a glancing blow on the shoulder as it fell; but for his alertness, he must have been smashed beneath it. He staggered, but he did not fall; nor did he drop his revolver. He stood there, rubbing his injured shoulder, and Rainsford, with fear again gripping his heart, heard the general's mocking laugh ring through the jungle.

"Rainsford," called the general, "if you are within the sound of my voice, as I suppose you are, let me congratulate you. Not many men know how to make a Malay man-catcher. Luckily, for me, I too have hunted in Malacca. You are proving interesting, Mr. Rainsford. I am going now to have my wound dressed; it's only a slight one. But I shall be back. I shall be back."

When the general, nursing his bruised shoulder, had gone, Rainsford took up his flight again. It was a flight now, a desperate, hopeless flight, that carried him on for some hours. Dusk came, then darkness, and still he pressed on. The ground grew softer under his moccasins; the vegetation grew ranker, denser; insects bit him savagely. Then, as he stepped forward, his foot sank into the ooze. He tried to wrench it back, but the muck sucked viciously at his foot as if it were a giant leech. With a violent effort, he tore his foot loose. He knew where he was now. Death Swamp and its quicksand.

His hands were tight closed as if his nerve were something tangible that some one in the darkness was trying to tear from his grip. The softness of the earth had given him an idea. He stepped back from the quicksand a dozen feet or so, and, like some huge prehistoric beaver, he began to dig.

Rainsford had dug himself in in France when a second's delay meant death. That had been a placid pastime compared to his digging now. The pit grew deeper; when it was above his shoulders, he climbed out and from some hard saplings cut stakes and sharpened them to a fine point. These stakes he planted in the bottom of the pit with the points sticking up. With flying fingers he wove a rough carpet of weeds and branches and with it he covered the mouth of the pit. Then, wet with sweat and aching with tiredness, he crouched behind the stump of a lightning-charred tree.

He knew his pursuer was coming; he heard the padding sound of feet on the soft earth, and the night breeze brought him the perfume of the general's cigaret. It seemed to Rainsford that the general was coming with unusual swiftness; he was not feeling his way along, foot by foot. Rainsford, crouching there, could not see the general, nor could he see the pit. He lived a year in a minute. Then he felt an impulse to cry aloud with joy, for he heard the sharp crackle of the breaking branches as the cover of the pit gave way; he heard the sharp scream of pain as the pointed stakes found their mark. He leaped up from his place of concealment. Then he cowered back. Three feet from the pit a man was standing, with an electric torch in his hand.

"You've done well, Rainsford," the voice of the general called. "Your Burmese tiger pit has claimed one of my best dogs. Again you score. I think, Mr. Rainsford, I'll see what you can do against my whole pack. I'm going home for a rest now. Thank you for a most amusing evening."

At daybreak Rainsford, lying near the swamp, was awakened by a sound that made him know that he had new things to learn about fear. It was a distant sound, faint and wavering, but he knew it. It was the baying of a pack of hounds.

Rainsford knew he could do one of two things. He could stay where he was and wait. That was suicide. He could flee. That was postponing the inevitable. For a moment he stood there, thinking. An idea that held a wild chance came to him, and, tightening his belt, he headed away from the swamp.

The baying of the hounds drew nearer, then still nearer, nearer, ever nearer. On a ridge Rainsford climbed a tree. Down a watercourse, not a quarter of a mile away, he could see the bush moving. Straining his eyes, he saw the lean figure of General Zaroff; just ahead of him Rainsford made out another figure whose wide shoulders surged through the tall jungle weeds; it was the giant Ivan, and he seemed pulled forward by some unseen force; Rainsford knew that Ivan must be holding the pack in leash.

They would be on him any minute now. His mind worked frantically. He thought of a native trick he had learned in Uganda. He slid down the tree. He caught hold of a springy young sapling and to it he fastened his hunting knife, with the blade pointing down the trail; with a bit of wild grapevine he tied back the sapling. Then he ran for his life. The hounds raised their voices as they hit the fresh scent. Rainsford knew now how an animal at bay feels.

He had to stop to get his breath. The baying of the hounds stopped abruptly, and Rainsford's heart stopped too. They must have reached the knife.

He shinnied excitedly up a tree and looked back. His pursuers had stopped. But the hope that was in Rainsford's brain when he climbed died, for he saw in the shallow valley that General Zaroff was still on his feet. But Ivan was not. The knife, driven by the recoil of the springing tree, had not wholly failed.

"Nerve, nerve, nerve!" he panted, as he dashed along. A blue gap showed between the trees dead ahead. Ever nearer drew the hounds. Rainsford forced himself on toward that gap. He reached it. It was the shore of the sea. Across a cove he could see the gloomy gray stone of the château. Twenty feet below him the sea rumbled and hissed. Rainsford hesitated. He heard the hounds. Then he leaped far out into the sea. . . .

When the general and his pack reached the place by the sea, the Cossack stopped. For some minutes he stood regarding the blue-green expanse of water. He shrugged his shoulders. Then he sat down, took a drink of brandy from a silver flask, lit a perfumed cigaret, and hummed a bit from "Madame Butterfly."[3]

General Zaroff had an exceedingly good dinner in his great paneled dining hall that evening. With it he had a bottle of Pol Roger and half a bottle of Chambertin. Two slight annoyances kept him from perfect enjoyment. One was the thought that it would be difficult to replace Ivan; the other was that his quarry had escaped him; of course the American hadn't played the game—so thought the general as he tasted his after-dinner liqueur. In his library he read, to soothe himself, from the works of Marcus Aurelius.[4] At ten he went up to his bedroom. He was deliciously tired, he said to himself, as he locked himself in. There was a little moonlight, so, before turning on his light, he went to the window and looked down at the courtyard. He could see the great hounds, and he called: "Better luck another time," to them. Then he switched on the light.

A man, who had been hiding in the curtains of the bed, was standing there.

"Rainsford!" screamed the general. "How in God's name did you get here?"

"Swam," said Rainsford. "I found it quicker than walking through the jungle."

The general sucked in his breath and smiled. "I congratulate you," he said. "You have won the game."

Rainsford did not smile. "I am still a beast at bay," he said, in a low, hoarse voice. "Get ready, General Zaroff."

The general made one of his deepest bows. "I see," he said. "Splendid! One of us is to furnish a repast for the hounds. The other will sleep in this very excellent bed. On guard, Rainsford. . . ."

He had never slept in a better bed, Rainsford decided.

[3]A well-known opera.

[4]Roman philosopher who extolled reason as above life's pains and pleasures.

## FOR DISCUSSION

1. What is the story's precipitating incident? Do you find anything difficult to believe about that incident?
2. How does Rainsford's early conversation with Whitney on the yacht foreshadow what later happens to Rainsford? What purpose is served by the ideas argued in that conversation?
3. Both the receding lights of the moving yacht (just after Rainsford falls overboard) and the many lights of the palatial château (when Rainsford first comes upon the place) have a symbolic meaning or value. What are these values and how do they differ from each other?
4. A little before Rainsford makes it to the beach of Ship-Trap Island, he hears "the sound of an animal in an extremity of anguish and terror." Why does he not recognize the animal?
5. Why does the gargoyle knocker on the front door of the château creak "as if it had never before been used"?
6. Is Rainsford or General Zaroff the protagonist of the story? Which character is more thoroughly developed? Which character does the storyline follow more closely? Which character's thoughts are given?
7. What specific types of conflict does the story present? Which type dominates?
8. Physically, how do Rainsford and General Zaroff compare with each other? Does this suggest any other comparisons between the two of them?
9. Is the situation—the island, the château, the General—plausible? Why or why not?
10. What specific past incident are we told about in the story that might account for Zaroff's madness?
11. Zaroff's character seems to have two distinct sides. Describe each, pointing out details that symbolize them.
12. At what point in the story does Rainsford face a dilemma? What are his only apparent courses of action? How have we been prepared (earlier) for the course of action that he does take?
13. After following the contest between Zaroff and Rainsford closely for three days, we are told nothing about their decisive struggle. Did the outcome really surprise you? How does this affect your response to the story?
14. The final sentence of the story reads, "He had never slept in a better bed, Rainsford decided." Does this statement suggest to you that Rainsford's character has changed—because of the struggle he has undergone—or have we simply been shown more of the qualities he originally possessed?
15. What is the story's theme? Where is it stated in the story, if at all?

# By the Waters of Babylon

STEPHEN VINCENT BENÉT

The north and the west and the south are good hunting ground, but it is forbidden to go east. It is forbidden to go to any of the Dead Places except to search for metal and then he who touches the metal must be a priest or the son of a priest. Afterwards, both the man and the metal must be purified. These are the rules and the laws; they are well made. It is forbidden to cross the great river and look upon the place that was the Place of the Gods—this is most strictly forbidden. We do not even say its name though we know its name. It is there that spirits live, and demons—it is there that there are the ashes of the Great Burning. These things are forbidden—they have been forbidden since the beginning of time.

My father is a priest; I am the son of a priest. I have been in the Dead Places near us, with my father—at first, I was afraid. When my father went into the house to search for the metal, I stood by the door and my heart felt small and weak. It was a dead man's house, a spirit house. It did not have the smell of man, though there were old bones in a corner. But it is not fitting that a priest's son should show fear. I looked at the bones in the shadow and kept my voice still.

Then my father came out with the metal—a good, strong piece. He looked at me with both eyes but I had not run away. He gave me the metal to hold—I took it and did not die. So he knew that I was truly his son and would be a priest in my time. That was when I was very young—nevertheless, my brothers would not have done it, though they are good hunters. After that, they gave me the good piece of meat and the warm corner by the fire. My father watched over me—he was glad that I should be a priest. But when I boasted or wept without a reason, he punished me more strictly than my brothers. That was right.

After a time, I myself was allowed to go into the dead houses and search for metal. So I learned the ways of those houses—and if I saw bones, I was no longer afraid. The bones are light and old—sometimes they will fall into dust if you touch them. But that is a great sin.

I was taught the chants and the spells—I was taught how to stop the running of blood from a wound and many secrets. A priest must know many secrets—that was what my father said. If the hunters think we do all things by chants and spells, they may believe so—it does not hurt them. I was taught how to read in the old books and how to make the old writings—that was hard and took a long time. My knowledge made me happy—it was like a fire in my heart. Most of all, I liked to hear of the Old Days and the stories of the gods. I asked myself many questions that I could not answer, but it was good to ask them. At night, I would lie awake and listen to the wind—it seemed to me that it was the voice of the gods as they flew through the air.

We are not ignorant like the Forest People—our women spin wool on the wheel, our priests wear a white robe. We do not eat grubs from the tree, we have not forgotten the old writings, although they are hard to understand. Nevertheless, my knowledge and my lack of knowledge burned in me—I wished to know more. When I was a man at last, I came to my father and said, "It is time for me to go on my journey. Give me your leave."

He looked at me for a long time, stroking his beard, then he said at last, "Yes. It is time." That night, in the house of the priesthood, I asked for and received purification. My body hurt but my spirit was a cool stone. It was my father himself who questioned me about my dreams.

He bade me look into the smoke of the fire and see—I saw and told what I saw. It was what I have always seen—a river, and, beyond it, a great Dead Place and in it the gods walking. I have always thought about that. His eyes were stern when I told him—he was no longer my father but a priest. He said, "This is a strong dream."

"It is mine," I said, while the smoke waved and my head felt light. They were singing the Star song in the outer chamber and it was like the buzzing of bees in my head.

He asked me how the gods were dressed and I told him how they were dressed. We know how they were dressed from the book, but I saw them as if they were before me. When I had finished, he threw the sticks three times and studied them as they fell.

"This is a very strong dream," he said. "It may eat you up."

"I am not afraid," I said and looked at him with both eyes. My voice sounded thin in my ears but that was because of the smoke.

He touched me on the breast and the forehead. He gave me the bow and the three arrows.

"Take them," he said. "It is forbidden to travel east. It is forbidden to cross the river. It is forbidden to go to the Place of the Gods. All these things are forbidden."

"All these things are forbidden," I said, but it was my voice that spoke and not my spirit. He looked at me again.

"My son," he said. "Once I had young dreams. If your dreams do not eat you up, you may be a great priest. If they eat you, you are still my son. Now go on your journey."

I went fasting, as is the law. My body hurt but not my heart. When the dawn came, I was out of sight of the village. I prayed and purified myself, waiting for a sign. The sign was an eagle. It flew east.

Sometimes signs are sent by bad spirits. I waited again on the flat rock, fasting, taking no food. I was very still—I could feel the sky above me and the earth beneath. I waited till the sun was beginning to sink. Then three deer passed in the valley, going east—they did not wind me or see me. There was a white fawn with them—a very great sign.

I followed them, at a distance, waiting for what would happen. My heart was troubled about going east, yet I knew that I must go. My head hummed with my fasting—I did not even see the panther spring

upon the white fawn. But, before I knew it, the bow was in my hand.
I shouted and the panther lifted his head from the fawn. It is not easy
to kill a panther with one arrow but the arrow went through his eye
and into his brain. He died as he tried to spring—he rolled over, tearing
at the ground. Then I knew I was meant to go east—I knew that was
my journey. When the night came, I made my fire and roasted meat.

It is eight suns' journey to the east and a man passes by many Dead
Places. The Forest People are afraid of them but I am not. Once I made
my fire on the edge of a Dead Place at night and, next morning, in the
dead house, I found a good knife, little rusted. That was small to what
came afterward but it made my heart feel big. Always when I looked
for game, it was in front of my arrow, and twice I passed hunting parties
of the Forest People without their knowing. So I knew my magic was
strong and my journey clean, in spite of the law.

Toward the setting of the eighth sun, I came to the banks of the great
river. It was half-a-day's journey after I had left the god-road—we do
not use the god-roads now for they are falling apart into great blocks
of stone, and the forest is safer going. A long way off, I had seen the
water through trees but the trees were thick. At last, I came out upon
an open place at the top of a cliff. There was the great river below, like
a giant in the sun. It is very long, very wide. It could eat all the streams
we know and still be thirsty. Its name is Ou-dis-sun, the Sacred, the
Long. No man of my tribe had seen it, not even my father, the priest.
It was magic and I prayed.

Then I raised my eyes and looked south. It was there, the Place of the
Gods.

How can I tell what it was like—you do not know. It was there, in
the red light, and they were too big to be houses. It was there with the
red light upon it, mighty and ruined. I knew that in another moment
the gods would see me. I covered my eyes with my hands and crept
back into the forest.

Surely, that was enough to do, and live. Surely it was enough to
spend the night upon the cliff. The Forest People themselves do not
come near. Yet, all through the night, I knew that I should have to cross
the river and walk in the places of the gods, although the gods ate me
up. My magic did not help me at all and yet there was a fire in my
bowels, a fire in my mind. When the sun rose, I thought, "My journey
has been clean. Now I will go home from my journey." But, even as I
thought so, I knew I could not. If I went to the Place of the Gods, I
would surely die, but, if I did not go, I could never be at peace with my
spirit again. It is better to lose one's life than one's spirit, if one is a
priest and the son of a priest.

Nevertheless, as I made the raft, the tears ran out of my eyes. The
Forest People could have killed me without fight, if they had come upon
me then, but they did not come. When the raft was made, I said the
sayings for the dead and painted myself for death. My heart was cold
as a frog and my knees like water, but the burning in my mind would

not let me have peace. As I pushed the raft from the shore, I began my death song—I had the right. It was a fine song.

> "I am John, son of John," I sang. "My people are the Hill People. They
> are the men.
> I go into the Dead Places but I am not slain.
> I take the metal from the Dead Places but I am not blasted.
> I travel upon the god-roads and am not afraid. E-yah! I have killed the
> panther, I have killed the fawn!
> E-yah! I have come to the great river. No man has come there before.
> It is forbidden to go east, but I have gone, forbidden to go on the great
> river, but I am there.
> Open your hearts, you spirits, and hear my song.
>   Now I go to the Place of the Gods, I shall not return.
> My body is painted for death and my limbs weak, but my heart is big as
>   I go to the Place of the Gods!"

All the same, when I came to the Place of the Gods, I was afraid, afraid. The current of the great river is very strong—it gripped my raft with its hands. That was magic, for the river itself is wide and calm. I could feel evil spirits about me, in the bright morning; I could feel their breath on my neck as I was swept down the stream. Never have I been so much alone—I tried to think of my knowledge, but it was a squirrel's heap of winter nuts. There was no strength in my knowledge any more and I felt small and naked as a new-hatched bird—alone upon the great river, the servant of the gods.

Yet, after a while, my eyes were opened and I saw. I saw both banks of the river—I saw that once there had been god-roads across it, though now they were broken and fallen like broken vines. Very great they were, and wonderful and broken—broken in the time of the Great Burning when the fire fell out of the sky. And always the current took me nearer to the Place of the Gods, and the huge ruins rose before my eyes.

I do not know the customs of rivers—we are the People of the Hills. I tried to guide my raft with the pole but it spun around. I thought the river meant to take me past the Place of the Gods and out into the Bitter Water of the legends. I grew angry then—my heart felt strong. I said aloud, "I am a priest and the son of a priest!" The gods heard me—they showed me how to paddle with the pole on one side of the raft. The current changed itself—I drew near to the Place of the Gods.

When I was very near, my raft struck and turned over. I can swim in our lakes—I swam to the shore. There was a great spike of rusted metal sticking out into the river—I hauled myself up upon it and sat there, panting. I had saved my bow and two arrows and the knife I found in the Dead Place but that was all. My raft went whirling downstream toward the Bitter Water. I looked after it, and thought if it had trod me under, at least I would be safely dead. Nevertheless, when I had dried my bowstring and re-strung it, I walked forward to the Place of the Gods.

It felt like ground underfoot; it did not burn me. It is not true what some of the tales say, that the ground there burns forever, for I have been there. Here and there were the marks and stains of the Great Burning, on the ruins, that is true. But they were old marks and old stains. It is not true either, what some of our priests say, that it is an island covered with fogs and enchantments. It is not. It is a great Dead Place—greater than any Dead Place we know. Everywhere in it there are god-roads, though most are cracked and broken. Everywhere there are the ruins of the high towers of the gods.

How shall I tell what I saw? I went carefully, my strung bow in my hand, my skin ready for danger. There should have been the wailings of spirits and the shrieks of demons, but there were not. It was very silent and sunny where I had landed—the wind and the rain and the birds that drop seeds had done their work—the grass grew in the cracks of the broken stone. It is a fair island—no wonder the gods built there. If I had come there, a god, I also would have built.

How shall I tell what I saw? The towers are not all broken—here and there one still stands, like a great tree in a forest, and the birds nest high. But the towers themselves look blind, for the gods are gone. I saw a fish-hawk, catching fish in the river. I saw a little dance of white butterflies over a great heap of broken stones and columns. I went there and looked about me—there was a carved stone with cut-letters, broken in half. I can read letters but I could not understand these. They said UBTREAS. There was also the shattered image of a man or a god. It had been made of white stone and he wore his hair tied back like a woman's. His name was ASHING, as I read on the cracked half of a stone. I thought it wise to pray to ASHING, though I do not know that god.

How shall I tell what I saw? There was no smell of man left, on stone or metal. Nor were there many trees in that wilderness of stone. There are many pigeons, nesting and dropping in the towers—the gods must have loved them, or, perhaps, they used them for sacrifices. There are wild cats that roam the god-roads, green-eyed, unafraid of man. At night they wail like demons but they are not demons. The wild dogs are more dangerous, for they hunt in a pack, but them I did not meet till later. Everywhere there are the carved stones, carved with magical numbers or words.

I went North—I did not try to hide myself. When a god or a demon saw me, then I would die, but meanwhile I was no longer afraid. My hunger for knowledge burned in me—there was so much that I could not understand. After awhile, I knew that my belly was hungry. I could have hunted for my meat, but I did not hunt. It is known that the gods did not hunt as we do—they got their food from enchanted boxes and jars. Sometimes these are still found in the Dead Places—once, when I was a child and foolish, I opened such a jar and tasted it and found the food sweet. But my father found out and punished me for it strictly, for, often, that food is death. Now, though, I had long gone past what was forbidden, and I entered the likeliest towers, looking for the food of the gods.

I found it at last in the ruins of a great temple in the mid-city. A mighty temple it must have been, for the roof was painted like the sky at night with its stars—that much I could see, though the colors were faint and dim. It went down into great caves and tunnels—perhaps they kept their slaves there. But when I started to climb down, I heard the squeaking of rats, so I did not go—rats are unclean, and there must have been many tribes of them, from the squeaking. But near there, I found food, in the heart of a ruin, behind a door that still opened. I ate only the fruits from the jars—they had a very sweet taste. There was drink, too, in bottles of glass—the drink of the gods was strong and made my head swim. After I had eaten and drunk, I slept on the top of a stone, my bow at my side.

When I woke, the sun was low. Looking down from where I lay, I saw a dog sitting on his haunches. His tongue was hanging out of his mouth; he looked as if he were laughing. He was a big dog, with a gray-brown coat, as big as a wolf. I sprang up and shouted at him but he did not move—he just sat there as if he were laughing. I did not like that. When I reached for a stone to throw, he moved swiftly out of the way of the stone. He was not afraid of me; he looked at me as if I were meat. No doubt I could have killed him with an arrow, but I did not know if there were others. Moreover, night was falling.

I looked about me—not far away there was a great, broken god-road, leading North. The towers were high enough, but not so high, and while many of the dead-houses were wrecked, there were some that stood. I went toward this god-road, keeping to the heights of the ruins, while the dog followed. When I had reached the god-road, I saw that there were others behind him. If I had slept later, they would have come upon me asleep and torn out my throat. As it was, they were sure enough of me; they did not hurry. When I went into the dead-house, they kept watch at the entrance—doubtless they thought they would have a fine hunt. But a dog cannot open a door and I knew, from the books, that the gods did not like to live on the ground but on high.

I had just found a door I could open when the dogs decided to rush. Ha! They were surprised when I shut the door in their faces—it was a good door, of strong metal. I could hear their foolish baying beyond it but I did not stop to answer them. I was in darkness—I found stairs and climbed. There were many stairs, turning around till my head was dizzy. At the top was another door—I found the knob and opened it. I was in a long small chamber—on one side of it was a bronze door that could not be opened, for it had no handle. Perhaps there was a magic word to open it but I did not have the word. I turned to the door in the opposite side of the wall. The lock of it was broken and I opened it and went in.

Within, there was a place of great riches. The god who lived there

must have been a powerful god. The first room was a small anteroom—
I waited there for some time, telling the spirits of the place that I came
in peace and not as a robber. When it seemed to me that they had had
time to hear me, I went on. Ah, what riches! Few, even, of the windows
had been broken—it was all as it had been. The great windows that
looked over the city had not been broken at all though they were dusty
and streaked with many years. There were coverings on the floors, the
colors not greatly faded, and the chairs were soft and deep. There were
pictures upon the walls, very strange, very wonderful—I remember one
of a bunch of flowers in a jar—if you came close to it, you could see
nothing but bits of color, but if you stood away from it, the flowers
might have been picked yesterday. It made my heart feel strange to look
at this picture—and to look at the figure of a bird, in some hard clay,
on a table and see it so like our birds. Everywhere there were books
and writings, many in tongues that I could not read. The god who lived
there must have been a wise god and full of knowledge. I felt I had
right there, as I sought knowledge also.

Nevertheless, it was strange. There was a washing-place but no
water—perhaps the gods washed in air. There was a cooking-place but
no wood, and though there was a machine to cook food, there was no
place to put fire in it. Nor were there candles or lamps—there were
things that looked like lamps but they had neither oil nor wick. All these
things were magic, but I touched them and lived—the magic had gone
out of them. Let me tell one thing to show. In the washing-place, a
thing said "Hot" but it was not hot to the touch—another thing said
"Cold" but it was not cold. This must have been a strong magic but the
magic was gone. I do not understand—they had ways—I wish that I
knew.

It was close and dry and dusty in their house of the gods. I have said
the magic was gone but that is not true—it had gone from the magic
things but it had not gone from the place. I felt the spirits about me,
weighing upon me. Nor had I ever slept in a Dead Place before—and
yet, tonight, I must sleep there. When I thought of it, my tongue felt
dry in my throat, in spite of my wish for knowledge. Almost I would
have gone down again and faced the dogs, but I did not.

I had not gone through all the rooms when the darkness fell. When
it fell, I went back to the big room looking over the city and made fire.
There was a place to make fire and a box with wood in it, though I do
not think they cooked there. I wrapped myself in a floor-covering and
slept in front of the fire—I was very tired.

Now I tell what is very strong magic. I woke in the midst of the night.
When I woke, the fire had gone out and I was cold. It seemed to me
that all around me there were whisperings and voices. I closed my eyes
to shut them out. Some will say that I slept again, but I do not think
that I slept. I could feel the spirits drawing my spirit out of my body as
a fish is drawn on a line.

Why should I lie about it? I am a priest and the son of a priest. If there are spirits, as they say, in the small Dead Places near us, what spirits must there not be in that great Place of the Gods? And would not they wish to speak? After such long years? I know that I felt myself drawn as a fish is drawn on a line. I had stepped out of my body—I could see my body asleep in front of the cold fire, but it was not I. I was drawn to look out upon the city of the gods.

It should have been dark, for it was night, but it was not dark. Everywhere there were lights—lines of light—circles and blurs of light—ten thousand torches would not have been the same. The sky itself was alight—you could barely see the stars for the glow in the sky. I thought to myself "This is strong magic" and trembled. There was a roaring in my ears like the rushing of rivers. Then my eyes grew used to the light and my ears to the sound. I knew that I was seeing the city as it had been when the gods were alive.

That was a sight indeed—yes, that was a sight: I could not have seen it in the body—my body would have died. Everywhere went the gods, on foot and in chariots—there were gods beyond number and counting and their chariots blocked the streets. They had turned night to day for their pleasure—they did not sleep with the sun. The noise of their coming and going was the noise of many waters. It was magic what they could do—it was magic what they did.

I looked out of another window—the great vines of their bridges were mended and the god-roads went East and West. Restless, restless, were the gods and always in motion! They burrowed tunnels under rivers—they flew in the air. With unbelievable tools they did giant works—no part of the earth was safe from them, for, if they wished for a thing, they summoned it from the other side of the world. And always, as they labored and rested, as they feasted and made love, there was a drum in their ears—the pulse of the giant city, beating and beating like a man's heart.

Were they happy? What is happiness to the gods? They were great, they were mighty, they were wonderful and terrible. As I looked upon them and their magic, I felt like a child—but a little more, it seemed to me, and they would pull down the moon from the sky. I saw them with wisdom beyond wisdom and knowledge beyond knowledge. And yet not all they did was well done—even I could see that—and yet their wisdom could not but grow until all was peace.

Then I saw their fate come upon them and that was terrible past speech. It came upon them as they walked the streets of their city. I have been in the fights with the Forest People—I have seen men die. But this was not like that. When gods war with gods, they use weapons we do not know. It was fire falling out of the sky and a mist that poisoned. It was the time of the Great Burning and the Destruction. They ran about like ants in the streets of their city—poor gods, poor gods! Then the towers began to fall. A few escaped—yes, a few. The legends tell it. But, even after the city had become a Dead Place, for many years the poison was still in the ground. I saw it happen, I saw the last of them die. It was darkness over the broken city and I wept.

All this, I saw. I saw it as I have told it, though not in the body. When I woke in the morning, I was hungry, but I did not think first of my hunger for my heart was perplexed and confused. I knew the reason for the Dead Places but I did not see why it had happened. It seemed to me it should not have happened, with all the magic they had. I went through the house looking for an answer. There was so much in the house I could not understand—and yet I am a priest and the son of a priest. It was like being on one side of the great river, at night, with no light to show the way.

Then I saw the dead god. He was sitting in his chair, by the window, in a room I had not entered before and, for the first moment, I thought that he was alive. Then I saw the skin on the back of his hand—it was like dry leather. The room was shut, hot and dry—no doubt that had kept him as he was. At first I was afraid to approach him—then the fear left me. He was sitting looking out over the city—he was dressed in the clothes of the gods. His age was neither young nor old—I could not tell his age. But there was wisdom in his face and great sadness. You could see that he would have not run away. He had sat at his window, watching his city die—then he himself had died. But it is better to lose one's life than one's spirit—and you could see from the face that his spirit had not been lost. I knew, that, if I touched him, he would fall into dust—and yet, there was something unconquered in the face.

That is all of my story, for then I knew he was a man—I knew then that they had been men, neither gods nor demons. It is a great knowledge, hard to tell and believe. They were men—they went a dark road, but they were men. I had no fear after that—I had no fear going home, though twice I fought off the dogs and once I was hunted for two days by the Forest People. When I saw my father again, I prayed and was purified. He touched my lips and my breast, he said, "You went away a boy. You come back a man and a priest." I said, "Father, they were men! I have been in the Place of the Gods and seen it! Now slay me, if it is the law—but still I know they were men."

He looked at me out of both eyes. He said, "The law is not always the same shape—you have done what you have done. I could not have done it in my time, but you come after me. Tell!"

I told and he listened. After that, I wished to tell all the people but he showed me otherwise. He said, "Truth is a hard deer to hunt. If you eat too much truth at once, you may die of the truth. It was not idly that our fathers forbade the Dead Places." He was right—it is better the truth should come little by little. I have learned that, being a priest. Perhaps, in the old days, they ate knowledge too fast.

Nevertheless, we make a beginning. It is not for the metal alone we go to the Dead Places now—there are the books and the writings. They are hard to learn. And the magic tools are broken—but we can look at them and wonder. At least, we make a beginning. And, when I am chief priest we shall go beyond the great river. We shall go to the Place of the Gods—the place Newyork—not one man but a company. We shall look for the images of the gods and find the god ASHING and the others—the gods LICOLN and BILTMORE and MOSES. But they were men who built the city, not gods or demons. They were men. I remember the dead man's face. They were men who were here before us. We must build again.

## FOR DISCUSSION

1. From what point of view is this story told?
2. Who is the story's protagonist and central character? What is it that this character is trying to accomplish?
3. What antagonistic forces oppose the protagonist?
4. This is a story in the ancient tradition of the quest. What is a quest? What is John's quest?
5. Describe the relationship between John and his father.
6. Locate as many examples as you can of statements made by John suggesting that he believes separate parts of his body function independently of the whole. What do these statements suggest about his way of thinking?
7. John, a priest and the son of a priest, has dreams and visions. What are some of his dreams and how do they motivate him? What are John's views of a priest's position and his responsibilities in society?
8. What nuances of John's character are revealed by his attitude toward the Forest People?
9. In what ways do the Hill People differ from the Forest People? What do these differences suggest about possible symbolic values for hills and forests?
10. At one point in the story John kills a panther that has sprung upon a white fawn. Later, in his song, he says, "I have killed the panther, *I have killed the fawn.*" Many readers, viewing the panther as a symbol of the viciousness of primitivism and the fawn as a symbol of innocence and truth—even of John himself—object to John's killing the fawn. Why do you think John killed the fawn?
11. Can you read any symbolic significance into John's laborious crossing of the wide river called Ou-dis-sun? Keep in mind that he is going east rather than west; going west, toward where the sun sets, traditionally suggests decline and death.
12. Important information about the setting is withheld to the end. At what point in the story did you know the truth about the Place of the Gods? Did you learn the truth before John says he did, or at about the same time? How does this timing contribute to suspense?
13. What does John learn in his great vision in the Place of the Gods?
14. Why does the author call what had been New York City Babylon? (The reference is to the Biblical Babylon, as in Isaiah 21:9—"Babylon is fallen, is fallen; and all the graven images of her gods He hath broken unto the ground.")
15. Why do you think the author has John tell the story? What effect did this have on your response?
16. Thematically, do you think this story is basically optimistic or pessimistic? Do you know any other stories, or movies, with similar themes?

# The Lottery Ticket

ANTON CHEKHOV

Ivan Dmitritch, a middle-class man who lived with his family on an income of twelve hundred a year and was very well satisfied with his lot, sat down on the sofa after supper and began reading the newspaper.

"I forgot to look at the newspaper today," his wife said to him as she cleared the table. "Look and see whether the list of drawings is there."

"Yes, it is," said Ivan Dmitritch; "but hasn't your ticket lapsed?"

"No; I took the interest on Tuesday."

"What is the number?"

"Series 9,499, number 26."

"All right . . . we will look . . . 9,499 and 26."

Ivan Dmitritch had no faith in lottery luck, and would not, as a rule, have consented to look at the lists of winning numbers, but now, as he had nothing else to do and as the newspaper was before his eyes, he passed his finger downwards along the column of numbers. And immediately, as though in mockery of his skepticism, no further than the second line from the top, his eye was caught by the figure 9,499! Unable to believe his eyes, he hurriedly dropped the paper on his knees without looking to see the number of the ticket, and, just as though some one had given him a douche[1] of cold water, he felt an agreeable chill in the pit of his stomach; tingling and terrible and sweet!

"Masha, 9,499 is there!" he said in a hollow voice.

His wife looked at his astonished and panic-stricken face, and realized that he was not joking.

"9,499?" she asked, turning pale and dropping the folded tablecloth on the table.

"Yes, yes . . . it really is there!"

"And the number of the ticket?"

"Oh, yes! There's the number of the ticket too. But stay . . . wait! No, I say! Anyway, the number of our series is there! Anyway, you understand. . . ."

Looking at his wife, Ivan Dmitritch gave a broad, senseless smile, like a baby when a bright object is shown it. His wife smiled too; it was as pleasant to her as to him that he only mentioned the series, and did not try to find out the number of the winning ticket. To torment and tantalize oneself with hopes of possible fortune is so sweet, so thrilling!

"It is our series," said Ivan Dmitritch, after a long silence. "So there is a probability that we have won. It's only a probability, but there it is!"

"Well, now look!"

"Wait a little. We have plenty of time to be disappointed. It's on the

[1]Shower.

second line from the top, so the prize is seventy-five thousand. That's not money, but power, capital! And in a minute I shall look at the list, and there—26! Eh? I say, what if we really have won?"

The husband and wife began laughing and staring at one another in silence. The possibility of winning bewildered them; they could not have said, could not have dreamed, what they both needed that seventy-five thousand for, what they would buy, where they would go. They thought only of the figures 9,499 and 75,000 and pictured them in their imagination, while somehow they could not think of the happiness itself which was so possible.

Ivan Dmitritch, holding the paper in his hand, walked several times from corner to corner, and only when he had recovered from the first impression began dreaming a little.

"And if we have won," he said—"Why, it will be a new life, it will be a transformation! The ticket is yours, but if it were mine I should, first of all, of course spend twenty-five thousand on real property in the shape of an estate; ten thousand on immediate expenses, new furnishings . . . travelling . . . paying debts, and so on. . . . The other forty thousand I would put in the bank and get interest on it."

"Yes, an estate, that would be nice," said his wife, sitting down and dropping her hands in her lap.

"Somewhere in the Tula or Oryol provinces. . . . In the first place we shouldn't need a summer villa, and besides, it would always bring in an income."

And pictures came crowding on his imagination, each more gracious and poetical than the last. And in all these pictures he saw himself well-fed, serene, healthy, felt warm, even hot! Here, after eating a summer soup, cold as ice, he lay on his back on the burning sand close to a stream or in the garden under a lime-tree. . . . It is hot. . . . His little boy and girl are crawling about near him, digging in the sand or catching ladybirds in the grass. He dozes sweetly, thinking of nothing, and feeling all over that he need not go to the office today, tomorrow, or the day after. Or, tired of lying still, he goes to the hayfield, or to the forest for mushrooms, or watches the peasants catching fish with a net. When the sun sets he takes a towel and soap and saunters to the bathing-shed, where he undresses at his leisure, slowly rubs his bare chest with his hands, and goes into the water. And in the water, near the opaque soapy circles, little fish flit to and fro and green water-weeds nod their heads. After bathing there is tea with cream and milk rolls. . . . In the evening a walk or *vint*[2] with the neighbors.

"Yes, it would be nice to buy an estate," said his wife, also dreaming, and from her face it was evident that she was enchanted by her thoughts.

Ivan Dmitritch pictured to himself autumn with its rains, its cold evenings, and its St. Martin's summer.[3] At that season he would have

[2]A Russian card game like bridge.
[3]What Americans call Indian Summer.

to take longer walks about the garden and beside the river, so as to get thoroughly chilled, and then drink a big glass of vodka and eat a salted mushroom or a soused cucumber, and then—drink another. . . . The children would come running from the kitchen-garden, bringing a carrot and a radish smelling of fresh earth. . . . And then, he would lie stretched full length on the sofa, and in leisurely fashion turn over the pages of some illustrated magazine, or, covering his face with it and unbuttoning his waistcoat, give himself up to slumber.

The St. Martin's summer is followed by cloudy, gloomy weather. It rains day and night, the bare trees weep, the wind is damp and cold. The dogs, the horses, the fowls—all are wet, depressed, downcast. There is nowhere to walk; one can't go out for days together; one has to pace up and down the room, looking despondently at the grey window. It is dreary!

Ivan Dmitritch stopped and looked at his wife.

"I should go abroad, you know, Masha," he said.

And he began thinking how nice it would be in late autumn to go abroad somewhere to the South of France . . . to Italy . . . to India!

"I should certainly go abroad too," his wife said. "But look at the number of the ticket!"

"Wait, wait! . . ."

He walked about the room and went on thinking. It occurred to him: what if his wife really did go abroad? It is pleasant to travel alone, or in the society of light, careless women who live in the present, and not such as think and talk all the journey about nothing but their children, sigh, and tremble with dismay over every farthing. Ivan Dmitritch imagined his wife in the train with a multitude of parcels, baskets, and bags; she would be sighing over something, complaining that the train made her head ache, that she had spent so much money. . . . At the stations he would continually be having to run for boiling water, bread and butter.[4] . . . She wouldn't have dinner because of its being too dear. . . .

"She would begrudge me every farthing," he thought, with a glance at his wife. "The lottery ticket is hers, not mine! Besides, what is the use of her going abroad? What does she want there? She would shut herself up in the hotel, and not let me out of her sight . . . I know!"

And for the first time in his life his mind dwelt on the fact that his wife had grown elderly and plain, and that she was saturated through and through with the smell of cooking, while he was still young, fresh, and healthy, and might well have got married again.

"Of course, all that is silly nonsense," he thought; "but . . . why should she go abroad? What would she make of it? And yet she would go, of course. . . . I can fancy. . . . In reality it is all one to her, whether it is Naples or Klin. She would only be in my way. I should be dependent

[4]Because in those days, at the beginning of the century, there was no food service on Russian trains. The boiling water would be for making tea.

upon her. I can fancy how, like a regular woman, she will lock the money up as soon as she gets it. . . . She will look after her relations and grudge me every farthing."

Ivan Dmitritch thought of her relations. All those wretched brothers and sisters and aunts and uncles would come crawling about as soon as they heard of the winning ticket, would begin whining like beggars, and fawning upon them with oily, hypocritical smiles. Wretched, detestable people! If they were given anything, they would ask for more; while if they were refused, they would swear at them, slander them, and wish them every kind of misfortune.

Ivan Dmitritch remembered his own relations, and their faces, at which he had looked impartially in the past, struck him now as repulsive and hateful.

"They are such reptiles!" he thought.

And his wife's face, too, struck him as repulsive and hateful. Anger surged up in his heart against her, and he thought malignantly:

"She knows nothing about money, and so she is stingy. If she won it she would give me a hundred roubles, and put the rest away under lock and key."

And he looked at his wife, not with a smile now, but with hatred. She glanced at him too, and also with hatred and anger. She had her own daydreams, her own plans, her own reflections; she understood perfectly well what her husband's dreams were. She knew who would be the first to try to grab her winnings.

"It's very nice making daydreams at other people's expense!" is what her eyes expressed. "No, don't you dare!"

Her husband understood her look; hatred began stirring again in his breast, and in order to annoy his wife he glanced quickly to spite her at the fourth page on the newspaper and read out triumphantly:

"Series 9,499, number 46! Not 26!"

Hatred and hope both disappeared at once, and it began immediately to seem to Ivan Dmitritch and his wife that their rooms were dark and small and low-pitched, that the supper they had been eating was not doing them good, but lying heavy on their stomachs, that the evenings were long and wearisome. . . .

"What the devil's the meaning of it?" said Ivan Dmitritch, beginning to be ill-humored. "Wherever one steps there are bits of paper under one's feet, crumbs, husks. The rooms are never swept! One is simply forced to go out. Damnation take my soul entirely! I shall go and hang myself on the first aspen-tree!"

## FOR DISCUSSION

1. This story features what we have called an implicit or internalized plot. Contrast the significance of the few actions that actually take place with all that goes on in the minds of Ivan and Masha.

2. Why is it important to know that Ivan Dmitritch is a middle-class person? How might his reactions to the circumstances of the story differ were he either a member of the aristocracy or a penniless peasant?
3. How does the relationship between Ivan and Masha change as the story progresses? Are there any signs that there has been friction between them before the story begins?
4. What does the lottery ticket itself symbolize? How can it be viewed as an ironic symbol?
5. Do you think Ivan has an accurate view of his wife's personality? How do you think he would fare in the company of those "careless women" he dreams of? What evidence can you find in the story that Masha has also been less than enchanted with the circumstances of her life?
6. The larger setting of this story includes the horrible Russian climate. How does a whole life lived in this climate contribute to Ivan's dreams of a better life?
7. Why do you suppose Masha has continued to spend money for these lottery tickets even though Ivan has no faith in them?
8. Detail the story's precipitating incident, climax, and denouement. Is it possible that "The Lottery Ticket" has two protagonists and two antagonists?

# Night Club

KATHARINE BRUSH

Promptly at quarter of ten P.M. Mrs. Brady descended the steps of the
Elevated. She purchased from the newsdealer in the cubbyhole beneath
them a next month's magazine and a tomorrow morning's paper and,
with these tucked under one plump arm, she walked. She walked two
blocks north on Sixth Avenue; turned and went west. But not far west.
Westward half a block only, to the place where the gay green awning
marked "Club Français" paints a stripe of shade across the glimmering
sidewalk. Under this awning Mrs. Brady halted briefly, to remark to
the six-foot doorman that it looked like rain and to await his performance
of his professional duty. When the small green door yawned open, she
sighed deeply and plodded in.

The foyer was a blackness, an airless velvet blackness like the inside
of a jeweler's box. Four drum-shaped lamps of golden silk suspended
from the ceiling gave it light (a very little) and formed the jewels: gold
signets, those, or cuff-links for a giant. At the far end of the foyer there
were black stairs, faintly dusty, rippling upward toward an amber
radiance. Mrs. Brady approached and ponderously mounted the stairs,
clinging with one fist to the mangy velvet rope that railed their edge.

From the top, Miss Lena Levin observed the ascent. Miss Levin was
the checkroom girl. She had dark-at-the-roots blonde hair and slender
hips upon which, in moments of leisure, she wore her hands, like
buckles of ivory loosely attached.

This was a moment of leisure. Miss Levin waited behind her counter.
Row upon row of hooks, empty as yet, and seeming to beckon—wee
curved fingers of iron—waited behind her.

"Late," said Miss Levin, "again."

"Go wan!" said Mrs. Brady. "It's only ten to ten. *Whew!* Them *stairs!*"

She leaned heavily, sideways, against Miss Levin's counter, and,
applying one palm to the region of her heart, appeared at once to listen
and to count. "Feel!" she cried then in a pleased voice.

Miss Levin obediently felt.

"Them stairs," continued Mrs. Brady darkly, "with my bad heart,
will be the death of me. Whew! Well, dearie? What's the news?"

"You got the paper," Miss Levin languidly reminded her.

"Yeah!" agreed Mrs. Brady with sudden vehemence. "I got a paper!"
She slapped it upon the counter. "An' a lot of time I'll get to *read* my
paper, won't I now? On a Saturday night!" She moaned. "Other nights
is bad enough, dear knows—but *Saturday* nights! How I dread 'em!
Every Saturday night I say to my daughter, I say, 'Geraldine, I can't,'
I say, 'I can't go through it again, an' that's all there is to it,' I say. 'I'll
*quit!*' I say. An' I *will,* too!" added Mrs. Brady firmly, if indefinitely.

Miss Levin, in defense of Saturday nights, mumbled some vague something about tips.

"Tips!" Mrs. Brady hissed it. She almost spat it. Plainly money was nothing, nothing at all, to this lady. "I just wish," said Mrs. Brady, and glared at Miss Levin, "I just wish *you* had to spend one Saturday night, just one, in that dressing room! Bein' pushed an' stepped on and near knocked down by that gang of hussies, an' them orderin' an' bossin' you 'round like you was *black*, an' usin' your things an' then saying' they're sorry, they got no change, they'll be back. Yeah! They *never* come back!"

"There's Mr. Costello," whispered Miss Levin through lips that, like a ventriloquist's, scarcely stirred.

"An' as I was sayin'," Mrs. Brady said at once brightly, "I got to leave you. Ten to ten, time I was on the job."

She smirked at Miss Levin, nodded, and right-about-faced. There, indeed, Mr. Costello was. Mr. Billy Costello, manager, proprietor, monarch of all he surveyed. From the doorway of the big room where the little tables herded in a ring around the waxen floor, he surveyed Mrs. Brady, and in such a way that Mrs. Brady, momentarily forgetting her bad heart, walked fast, scurried faster, almost ran.

The door of her domain was set politely in an alcove, beyond silken curtains looped up at the sides. Mrs. Brady reached it breathless, shouldered it open, and groped for the electric switch. Lights sprang up, a bright white blaze, intolerable for an instant to the eyes, like sun on snow. Blinking, Mrs. Brady shut the door.

The room was a spotless, white-tiled place, half beauty shop, half dressing-room. Along one wall stood washstands, sturdy triplets in a row, with pale-green liquid soap in glass balloons afloat above them. Against the opposite wall there was a couch. A third wall backed an elongated glass-topped dressing table; and over the dressing table and over the washstands long rectangular sheets of mirror reflected lights, doors, glossy tiles, lights multiplied. . . .

Mrs. Brady moved across this glitter like a thick dark cloud in a hurry. At the dressing table she came to a halt, and upon it she laid her newspaper, her magazine, and her purse—a black purse worn gray with much clutching. She divested herself of a rusty black coat and a hat of the mushroom persuasion, and hung both up in a corner cupboard which she opened by means of one of a quite preposterous bunch of keys. From a nook in the cupboard she took down a lace-edged handkerchief with long streamers. She untied the streamers and tied them again around her chunky black alpaca waist. The handkerchief became an apron's baby cousin.

Mrs. Brady relocked the cupboard door, fumbled her key-ring over, and unlocked a capacious drawer of the dressing table. She spread a fresh towel on the plate-glass top, in the geometrical center, and upon the towel she arranged with care a procession of things fished from the drawer. Things for the hair. Things for the complexion. Things for the eyes, the lashes, the brows, the lips, and the finger nails. Things in boxes and things in jars and things in tubes and tins. Also an ash tray, matches, pins, a tiny sewing kit, a pair of scissors. Last of all, a hand-painted sign, a nudging sort of sign:

NOTICE! THESE ARTICLES, PLACED HERE FOR YOUR CONVENIENCE, ARE THE PROPERTY OF THE *MAID*.

And directly beneath the sign, propping it up against the looking-glass, a china saucer, in which Mrs. Brady now slyly laid decoy money: two quarters and two dimes, in four-leaf clover formation.

Another drawer of the dressing table yielded a bottle of bromo-seltzer, a bottle of aromatic spirits of ammonia, a tin of sodium bicarbonate, and a teaspoon. These were lined up on a shelf above the couch.

Mrs. Brady was now ready for anything. And (from the grim, thin pucker of her mouth) expecting it.

Music came to her ears. Rather, the beat of music, muffled, rhythmic, remote. *Umpa-um, umpa-um, umpa-um-umm*—Mr. "Fiddle" Baer and his band, hard at work on the first fox-trot of the night. It was teasing, foot-tapping music; but the large solemn feet of Mrs. Brady were still. She sat on the couch and opened her newspaper; and for some moments she read uninterruptedly, with special attention to the murders, the divorces, the breaches of promise, the funnies.

Then the door swung inward, admitting a blast of Mr. Fiddle Baer's best, a whiff of perfume, and a girl.

Mrs. Brady put her paper away.

The girl was *petite* and darkly beautiful; wrapped in fur and mounted on tall jeweled heels. She entered humming the rag-time song the orchestra was playing, and while she stood near the dressing table, stripping off her gloves, she continued to hum it softly to herself:

> *"Oh, I know my baby loves me,*
> *I can tell my baby loves me."*

Here the dark little girl got the left glove off, and Mrs. Brady glimpsed a platinum wedding ring.

> *"'Cause there ain't no maybe*
> *In my baby's*
> *Eyes."*

The right glove came off. The dark little girl sat down in one of the chairs that faced the dressing table. She doffed her wrap, casting it carelessly over the chair back. It had a cloth-of-gold lining, and the name of a Paris house was embroidered in curlicues on the label. Mrs. Brady hovered solicitously near.

The dark little girl, still humming, looked over the articles, "placed here for your convenience," and picked up the scissors. Having cut off a very small hangnail with the air of one peforming a perilous major operation, she seized and used the manicure buffer, and after that the eyebrow pencil. Mrs. Brady's mind, hopefully calculating the tip, jumped and jumped again like a taxi-meter.

*"Oh, I know my baby loves me—"*

The dark little girl applied powder and lipstick belonging to herself. She examined the result searchingly in the mirror and sat back, satisfied. She cast some silver *Klink! Klink!* into Mrs. Brady's saucer, and half rose. Then, remembering something, she settled down again.

The ensuing thirty seconds were spent by her in pulling off her platinum wedding ring, tying it in a corner of a lace handkerchief, and tucking the handkerchief down the bodice of her tight white velvet gown.

"There!" she said.

She swooped up her wrap and trotted toward the door, jeweled heels merrily twinkling.

*'"Cause there ain't no maybe—"*

The door fell shut.

Almost instantly it opened again, and another girl came in. A blonde, this. She was pretty in a round-eyed, doll-like way; but Mrs. Brady, regarding her, mentally grabbed the spirits of ammonia bottle. For she looked terribly ill. The round eyes were dull, the pretty silky little face was drawn. The thin hands, picking at the fastenings of a specious beaded bag, trembled and twitched.

Mrs. Brady cleared her throat. "Can I do something for you, miss?"

Evidently the blonde girl had believed herself alone in the dressing room. She started violently and glanced up, panic in her eyes. Panic, and something else. Something very like murderous hate—but for an instant only, so that Mrs. Brady, whose perceptions were never quick, missed it altogether.

"A glass of water?" suggested Mrs. Brady.

"No," said the girl, "no." She had one hand in the beaded bag now. Mrs. Brady could see it moving, causing the bag to squirm like a live thing, and the fringe to shiver. "Yes!" she cried abruptly. "A glass of water—please—you get it for me."

She dropped on to the couch. Mrs. Brady scurried to the water cooler in the corner, pressed the spigot with a determined thumb. Water trickled out thinly. Mrs. Brady pressed harder, and scowled, and thought, "Something's wrong with this thing. I mustn't forget, next time I see Mr. Costello—"

When again she faced her patient, the patient was sitting erect. She was thrusting her clenched hand back into the beaded bag again.

She took only a sip of the water, but it seemed to help her quite miraculously. Almost at once color came to her cheeks, life to her eyes. She grew young again—as young as she was. She smiled up at Mrs. Brady.

"Well!" she exclaimed. "What do you know about that!" She shook her honey-colored head. "I can't imagine what came over me."

"Are you better now?" inquired Mrs. Brady.

"Yes. Oh, yes. I'm better now. You see," said the blonde girl confidentially, "we were at the theater, my boy friend and I, and it was hot and stuffy—I guess that must have been the trouble."

She paused, and the ghost of her recent distress crossed her face. "God! I thought that last act *never* would end!" she said.

While she attended to her hair and complexion, she chattered gayly to Mrs. Brady, chattered on with scarcely a stop for breath, and laughed much. She said, among other things, that she and her "boy friend" had not known one another very long, but that she was "ga-ga" about him. "He is about me, too," she confessed. "He thinks I'm grand."

She fell silent then, and in the looking-glass her eyes were shadowed, haunted. But Mrs. Brady, from where she stood, could not see the looking-glass; and half a minute later the blonde girl laughed and began again. When she went out she seemed to dance out on little winged feet; and Mrs. Brady, sighing, thought it must be nice to be young . . . and happy like that.

The next arrivals were two. A tall, extremely smart young woman in black chiffon entered first, and held the door open for her companion; and the instant the door was shut, she said, as though it had been on the tip of her tongue for hours, "Amy, what under the sun *happened?*"

Amy, who was brown-eyed, brown-bobbed-haired, and patently annoyed about something, crossed to the dressing table and flopped into a chair before she made reply.

"Nothing," she said wearily then.

"That's nonsense!" snorted the other. "Tell me. Was it something she said? She's a tactless ass, of course. Always was."

"No, not anything she said. It was—" Amy bit her lip. "All right! I'll tell you. Before we left your apartment I just happened to notice that Tom had disappeared. So I went to look for him—I wanted to ask him if he'd remembered to tell the maid where we were going—Skippy's subject to croup, you know, and we always leave word. Well, so I went into the kitchen, thinking Tom might be there mixing cocktails—and there he was—and there *she* was!"

The full red mouth of the other young woman pursed itself slightly. Her arched brows lifted. "Well?"

Her matter-of-factness appeared to infuriate Amy. "He was *kissing* her!" she flung out.

"Well?" said the other again. She chuckled softly and patted Amy's shoulder, as if it were the shoulder of a child. "You're surely not going to let *that* spoil your whole evening? Amy *dear!* Kissing may once have been serious and significant—but it isn't nowadays. Nowadays, it's like shaking hands. It means nothing."

But Amy was not consoled. "I hate her!" she cried desperately. "Red-headed *thing!* Calling me 'darling' and 'honey,' and s-sending me handkerchiefs for C-Christmas—and then sneaking off behind closed doors and k-kissing my h-h-husband—"

At this point Amy broke down, but she recovered herself sufficiently to add with venom, "I'd like to slap her!"

"Oh, oh, oh," smiled the tall young woman. "I wouldn't do that!"

Amy wiped her eyes with what might well have been one of the Christmas handkerchiefs, and confronted her friend. "Well, what *would* you do, Vera? If you were I?"

"I'd forget it," said Vera, "and have a good time. I'd kiss somebody myself. You've no idea how much better you'd feel!"

"I don't do—" Amy began indignantly; but as the door behind her opened and a third young woman—red-headed, earringed, exquisite—lilted in, she changed her tone. "Oh, hello!" she called sweetly, beaming at the newcomer via the mirror. "We were wondering what had become of you!"

The red-headed girl, smiling easily back, dropped her cigarette on the floor and crushed it out with a silver-shod toe. "Tom and I were talking to Fiddle Baer," she explained. "He's going to play 'Clap Yo' Hands' next, because it's my favorite. Lend me a comb, will you?"

"There's a comb there," said Vera, indicating Mrs. Brady's business comb.

"But imagine using it!" murmured the red-headed girl. "Amy, darling, haven't you one?"

Amy produced a tiny comb from her rhinestone purse. "Don't forget to bring it when you come," she said, and stood up. "I'm going on out, I want to tell Tom something." She went.

The red-headed young woman and the tall black-chiffon one were alone, except for Mrs. Brady. The red-headed one beaded her incredible lashes. The tall one, the one called Vera, sat watching her. Presently she said, "Sylvia, look here." And Sylvia looked. Anybody, addressed in that tone, would have.

"There is one thing," Vera went on quietly, holding the other's eyes, "that I want understood. And that is *'Hands off!'* Do you hear me?"

"I don't known what you mean."

"You do know what I mean!"

The red-headed girl shrugged her shoulders. "Amy told you she saw us, I suppose."

"Precisely. And," went on Vera, gathering up her possessions and rising, "as I said before, you're to keep away." Her eyes blazed sudden white-hot rage. "Because, as you very well know, he belongs to *me*," she said, and departed, slamming the door.

Between eleven o'clock and one Mrs. Brady was very busy indeed. Never for more than a moment during those two hours was the dressing room empty. Often it was jammed, full to overflowing with curled cropped heads, with ivory arms and shoulders, with silk and lace and chiffon, with legs. The door flapped in and back, in and back. The mirrors caught and held—and lost—a hundred different faces. Powder veiled the dressing table with a thin white dust; cigarette stubs, scarlet at the tips, choked the ash-receiver. Dimes and quarters clattered into Mrs. Brady's saucer—and were transferred to Mrs. Brady's purse. The original seventy cents remained. That much, and no more, would Mrs. Brady gamble on the integrity of womankind.

She earned her money. She threaded needles and took stitches. She powdered the backs of necks. She supplied towels for soapy, dripping hands. She removed a speck from a teary blue eye and pounded the heel on a slipper. She curled the straggling ends of a black bob and a gray bob, pinned a velvet flower on a lithe round waist, mixed three doses of bicarbonate of soda, took charge of a shed pink-satin girdle, collected, on hands and knees, several dozen fake pearls that had wept from a broken string.

She served chorus girls and school girls, gay young matrons and gayer young mistresses, a lady who had divorced four husbands, and a lady who had poisoned one, the secret (more or less) sweetheart of a Most Distinguished Name, and the Brains of a bootleg gang. . . . She saw things. She saw a yellow check, with the ink hardly dry. She saw four tiny bruises, such as fingers might make, on an arm. She saw a girl strike another girl, not playfully. She saw a bundle of letters some man wished he had not written, safe and deep in a brocaded handbag.

About midnight the door flew open and at once was pushed shut, and a gray-eyed, lovely child stood backed against it, her palms flattened on the panels at her sides, the draperies of her white chiffon gown settling lightly to rest around her.

There were already five damsels of varying ages in the dressing room. The latest arrival marked their presence with a flick of her eyes and, standing just where she was, she called peremptorily, "Maid!"

Mrs. Brady, standing just where *she* was, said, "Yes, miss?"

"Please come here," said the girl.

Mrs. Brady, as slowly as she dared, did so.

The girl lowered her voice to a tense half-whisper. "Listen! Is there any way I can get out of here except through this door I came in?"

Mrs. Brady stared at her stupidly.

"Any window?" persisted the girl. "Or anything?"

Here they were interrupted by the exodus of two of the damsels-of-

varying-ages. Mrs. Brady opened the door for them—and in so doing
caught a glimpse of a man who waited in the hall outside, a debonair,
old-young man with a girl's furry wrap hung over his arm, and his hat
in his hand.

The door clicked. The gray-eyed girl moved out from the wall, against
which she had flattened herself—for all the world like one eluding
pursuit in a cinema.

"What about that window?" she demanded, pointing.

"That's all the farther it opens," said Mrs. Brady.

"Oh! And it's the only one—isn't it?"

"It is."

"Damn," said the girl. "Then there's *no* way out?"

"No way but the door," said Mrs. Brady testily.

The girl looked at the door. She seemed to look *through* the door, and to
despise and to fear what she saw. Then she looked at Mrs. Brady. "Well,"
she said, "then I s'pose the only thing for me to do is to stay in here."

She stayed. Minutes ticked by. Jazz crooned distantly, stopped, struck
up again. Other girls came and went. Still the gray-eyed girl sat on the
couch, with her back to the wall and her shapely legs crossed, smoking
cigarettes, one from the stub of another.

After a long while she said, "Maid!"

"Yes, miss?"

"Peek out that door, will you, and see if there's anyone standing
there."

Mrs. Brady peeked, and reported that there was. There was a gentleman with a little bit of black mustache standing there. The same gentleman, in fact, who was standing there "just after you came in."

"Oh, Lord," sighed the gray-eyed girl. "Well . . . I can't stay here all
*night*, that's one sure thing."

She slid off the couch, and went listlessly to the dressing table. There
she occupied herself for a minute or two. Suddenly, without a word,
she darted out.

Thirty seconds later Mrs. Brady was elated to find two crumpled one-
dollar bills lying in her saucer. Her joy, however, died a premature
death. For she made an almost simultaneous second discovery. A saddening one. Above all, a puzzling one.

"Now what for," marveled Mrs. Brady, "did she want to walk off
with them *scissors?*"

This at twelve twenty-five.

At twelve thirty a quartette of excited young things burst in, babbling
madly. All of them had their evening wraps with them; all talked at
once. One of them, a Dresden china girl with a heart-shaped face, was
the center of attraction. Around her the rest fluttered like monstrous
butterflies; to her they addressed their shrill exclamatory cries.

"Babe," they called her.

Mrs. Brady heard snatches: "Not in this state unless . . ." "Well, you

can in Maryland, Jimmy says." "Oh, there must be some place nearer
than . . ." "Isn't this marvelous?" "When did it happen, Babe? When
did you decide?"

"Just now," the girl with the heart-shaped face sang softly, "when
we were dancing."

The babble resumed, "But listen, Babe, what'll your mother and father
. . . ?" "Oh, never mind, let's hurry." "Shall we be warm enough with
just these thin wraps, do you think; Babe, will you be warm enough?
Sure?"

Powder flew and little pocket combs marched through bright marcels.
Flushed cheeks were painted pinker still.

"My pearls," said Babe, "are *old*. And my dress and my slippers are
*new*. *Now*, let's see—what can I *borrow?*"

A lace handkerchief, a diamond bar pin, a pair of earrings were
proffered. She chose the bar pin, and its owner unpinned it proudly,
gladly.

"I've got blue garters!" exclaimed a shrill little girl in a silver dress.

"Give me one, then," directed Babe. "I'll trade with you. . . . There!
That fixes that."

More babbling, "Hurry! Hurry up!" . . . "Listen, are you *sure* we'll
be warm enough? Because we can stop at my house, there's nobody
home." "Give me that puff, Babe, I'll powder your back." "And just
to think a week ago you'd never even met each other!" "Oh, hurry *up*,
let's get *started!*" "I'm ready." "So'm I." "Ready, Babe? You look ador-
able." "Come on, everybody."

They were gone again, and the dressing room seemed twice as still
and vacant as before.

A minute of grace, during which Mrs. Brady wiped the spilled powder
away with a damp gray rag. Then the door jumped open again. Two
evening gowns appeared and made for the dressing table in a bee line.
Slim tubular gowns they were, one green, one palest yellow. Yellow
hair went with the green gown, brown hair with the yellow. The green-
gowned, yellow-haired girl wore gardenias on her left shoulder, four
of them, and a flashing bracelet on each fragile wrist. The other girl
looked less prosperous; still, you would rather have looked at her.

Both ignored Mrs. Brady's cosmetic display as utterly as they ignored
Mrs. Brady, producing full field equipment of their own.

"Well," said the girl with gardenias, rouging energetically, "how do
you like him?"

"Oh-h—all right."

"Meaning, 'Not any,' hmm? I suspected as much!" The girl with
gardenias turned in her chair and scanned her companion's profile with
disapproval. "See here, Marilee," she drawled, "are you going to be a
damn fool *all* your life?"

"He's fat," said Marilee dreamily. "Fat, and—greasy, sort of. I mean,
greasy in his mind. Don't you know what I mean?"

"I know *one* thing," declared the other. "I know Who He Is! And if I were you, that's all I'd need to know. *Under the circumstances.*"

The last three words, stressed meaningly, affected the girl called Marilee curiously. She grew grave. Her lips and lashes dropped. For some seconds she sat frowning a little, breaking a black-sheathed lipstick in two and fitting it together again.

"She's worse," she said finally, low.

"Worse?"

Marilee nodded.

"Well," said the girl with gardenias, "there you are. It's the climate. She'll never be anything *but* worse, if she doesn't get away. Out West. Arizona or somewhere."

"I know," murmured Marilee.

The other girl open a tin of eye shadow. "Of course," she said dryly, "suit yourself. She's not *my* sister."

Marilee said nothing. Quiet she sat, breaking the lipstick, mending it, breaking it.

"Oh, well," she breathed finally, wearily, and straightened up. She propped her elbows on the plate-glass dressing table top and leaned toward the mirror, and with the lipstick she began to make her coral-pink mouth very red and gay and reckless and alluring.

Nightly at one o'clock Vane and Moreno dance for the Club Français. They dance a tango, they dance a waltz; then, by way of encore, they do a Black Bottom, and a trick of their own called the Wheel. They dance for twenty, thirty minutes. And while they dance you do not leave your table—for this is what you came to see. Vane and Moreno. The new New York thrill. The sole justification for the five-dollar couvert[1] extorted by Billy Costello.

From one until half-past, then, was Mrs. Brady's recess. She had been looking forward to it all the evening long. When it began—when the opening chords of the tango music sounded stirringly from the room outside—Mrs. Brady brightened. With a right good will she sped the parting guests.

Alone, she unlocked her cupboard and took out her magazine—the magazine she had bought three hours before. Heaving a great breath of relief and satisfaction, she lumped herself on the couch and fingered the pages.

Immediately she was absorbed, her eyes drinking up printed lines, her lips moving soundlessly.

The magazine was Mrs. Brady's favorite. Its stories were true stories, taken from life (so the editor said); and to Mrs. Brady they were alive, vivid threads in the dull, drab pattern of her night.

[1]Cover charge.

## FOR DISCUSSION

1. The immediate setting of the story is the women's dressing room at the Club Français, while the larger setting is the Roaring Twenties. How does setting contribute to the story?

2. The story includes several striking descriptive sentences and clever statements of action, such as "The foyer was a blackness, an airless velvet blackness like the inside of a jeweler's box" or "Mrs. Brady moved across this glitter like a dark cloud in a hurry." Find as many such statements as you can and discuss how they reflect the author's tone and the story's mood, and how they contribute to the dramatization of character.

3. This story includes six episodes featuring women who have come to the Club Français, but it still seems unified. What do you see as contributing to its unity?

4. Summarize each of the six dressing room episodes and discuss the personalities of the women who appear in them. Which episode do you find the most serious, the most potentially dangerous, the most reflective of the period, the most depressing, the funniest? What do all of the episodes have in common? What do they seem to suggest about human happiness?

5. How perceptive is Mrs. Brady? Does she understand what goes on around her, or does she even try to do so? What is ironic about her attitude?

6. What do you think is the story's central point or theme?

# A Passion in the Desert

HONORÉ DE BALZAC

"The whole show is dreadful," she cried, coming out of the menagerie of M. Martin. She had just been looking at that daring speculator "working with his hyena"—to speak in the style of the program.

"By what means," she continued, "can he have tamed these animals to such a point as to be certain of their affection for——."

"What seems to you a problem," said I, interrupting, "is really quite natural."

"Oh!" she cried, letting an incredulous smile wander over her lips.

"You think that beasts are wholly without passions?" I asked her. "Quite the reverse; we can communicate to them all the vices arising in our own state of civilization."

She looked at me with an air of astonishment.

"Nevertheless," I continued, "the first time I saw M. Martin, I admit, like you, I did give vent to an exclamation of surprise. I found myself next to an old soldier with the right leg amputated, who had come in with me. His face had struck me. He had one of those intrepid heads, stamped with the seal of warfare, and on which the battles of Napoleon are written. Besides, he had that frank good-humored expression which always impresses me favorably. He was without doubt one of those troopers who are surprised at nothing, who find matter for laughter in the contortions of a dying comrade, who bury or plunder him quite light-heartedly, who stand intrepidly in the way of bullets; in fact, one of those men who waste no time in deliberation, and would not hesitate to make friends with the devil himself. After looking very attentively at the proprietor of the menagerie getting out of his box, my companion pursed up his lips with an air of mockery and contempt, with that peculiar and expressive twist which superior people assume to show they are not taken in. Then when I was expatiating on the courage of M. Martin, he smiled, shook his head knowingly, and said, 'Well known.'

"How 'well known'?" I said. "If you would only explain to me the mystery I should be vastly obliged."

"After a few minutes, during which we made acquaintance, we went to dine at the first restaurateur's whose shop caught our eye. At dessert a bottle of champagne completely refreshed and brightened up the memories of this odd old soldier. He told me his story, and I said he had every reason to exclaim, " 'Well known.' "

When she got home, she teased me to that extent and made so many promises, that I consented to communicate to her the old soldier's confidences. Next day she received the following episode of an epic which one might call "The Frenchman in Egypt."

During the expedition in Upper Egypt under General Desaix,[1] a Provençal soldier fell into the hands of the Mangrabins, and was taken by these Arabs into the deserts beyond the falls of the Nile.

In order to place a sufficient distance between themselves and the French army, the Mangrabins made forced marches, and only rested during the night. They camped round a well overshadowed by palm trees under which they had previously concealed a store of provisions. Not surmising that the notion of flight would occur to their prisoner, they contented themselves with binding his hands, and after eating a few dates, and giving provender to their horses, went to sleep.

When the brave Provençal saw that his enemies were no longer watching him, he made use of his teeth to steal a scimitar, fixed the blade between his knees, and cut the cords which prevented using his hands; in a moment he was free. He at once seized a rifle and dagger, then taking the precaution to provide himself with a sack of dried dates, oats, and powder and shot, and to fasten a scimitar to his waist he leaped onto a horse, and spurred on vigorously in the direction where he thought to find the French army. So impatient was he to see a bivouac again that he pressed on the already tired courser at such speed that its flanks were lacerated with his spurs, and at last the poor animal died, leaving the Frenchman alone in the desert. After walking some time in the sand with all the courage of an escaped convict, the soldier was obliged to stop, as the day had already ended. In spite of the beauty of an oriental sky at night, he felt he had not strength enough to go on. Fortunately he had been able to find a small hill, on the summit of which a few palm trees shot up into the air; it was their verdure seen from afar which had brought hope and consolation to his heart. His fatigue was so great that he lay down upon a rock of granite, capriciously cut out like a camp-bed; there he fell asleep without taking any precaution to defend himself while he slept. He had made the sacrifice of his life. His last thought was one of regret. He repented having left the Mangrabins, whose nomad life seemed to smile on him now that he was afar from them and without help. He was awakened by the sun, whose pitiless rays fell with all their force on the granite and produced an intolerable heat—for he had had the stupidity to place himself inversely to the shadow thrown by the verdant majestic heads of the palm trees. He looked at the solitary trees and shuddered—they reminded him of the graceful shafts crowned with foliage which characterize the Saracen columns in the cathedral of Arles.[2]

But when, after counting the palm trees, he cast his eye around him, the most horrible despair was infused into his soul. Before him stretched an ocean without limit. The dark sand of the desert spread farther than sight could reach in every direction, and glittered like steel struck with

---

[1]The French general Napoleon Bonaparte led campaigns in Egypt in 1798 and 1799. Desaix, one of his chief officers, led the conquest of Upper Egypt.

[2]A city in the soldier's native Provence.

a bright light. It might have been a sea of looking-glass, or lakes melted together in a mirror. A fiery vapor carried up in streaks made a perpetual whirlwind over the quivering land. The sky was lit with an oriental splendor of insupportable purity, leaving naught for the imagination to desire. Heaven and earth were on fire.

The silence was awful in its wild and terrible majesty. Infinity, immensity, closed in upon the soul from every side. Not a cloud in the sky, not a breath in the air, not a flaw on the bosom of the sand, ever moving in diminutive waves; the horizon ended as at sea on a clear day, with one line of light, definite as the cut of a sword.

The Provençal threw his arms around the trunk of one of the palm trees, as though it were the body of a friend, and then in the shelter of the thin straight shadow that the palm cast upon the granite, he wept. Then sitting down he remained as he was, contemplating with profound sadness the implacable scene, which was all he had to look upon. He cried aloud, to measure the solitude. His voice, lost in the hollows of the hill, sounded faintly, and aroused no echo—the echo was in his own heart. The Provençal was twenty-two years old;—he loaded his carbine.

"There'll be time enough," he said to himself, laying on the ground the weapon which alone could bring him deliverance.

Looking by turns at the black expanse and the blue expanse, the soldier dreamed of France—he smelt with delight the gutters of Paris— he remembered the towns through which he had passed, the faces of his fellow-soldiers, the most minute details of his life. His southern fancy soon showed him the stones of his beloved Provence, in the play of the heat which waved over the spread sheet of the desert. Fearing the danger of this cruel mirage, he went down the opposite side of the hill to that by which he had come up the day before. The remains of a rug showed that this place of refuge had at one time been inhabited; at a short distance he saw some palm trees full of dates. Then the instinct which binds us to life awoke again in his heart. He hoped to live long enough to await the passing of some Arabs, or perhaps he might hear the sound of cannon; for at this time Bonaparte was traversing Egypt.

This thought gave him new life. The palm tree seemed to bend with the weight of the ripe fruit. He shook some of it down. When he tasted this unhoped-for manna, he felt sure that the palms had been cultivated by a former inhabitant—the savory, fresh meat of the dates was proof of the care of his predecessor. He passed suddenly from the dark despair to an almost insant joy. He went up again to the top of the hill, and spent the rest of the day in cutting down one of the sterile palm trees, which the night before had served him for shelter. A vague memory made him think of the animals of the desert; and in case they might come to drink at the spring, visible from the base of the rocks but lost farther down, he resolved to guard himself from their visits by placing a barrier at the entrance of his hermitage.

In spite of his diligence, and the strength which the fear of being devoured asleep gave him, he was unable to cut the palm in pieces, though he succeeded in cutting it down. At eventide the king of the desert fell; the sound of its fall resounded far and wide, like a sign in the solitude; the soldier shuddered as though he had heard some voice predicting woe.

But like an heir who does not long bewail a deceased parent, he tore off from this beautiful tree the tall broad green leaves which are its poetic adornment, and used them to mend the mat on which he was to sleep.

Fatigued by the heat and his work, he fell asleep under the red curtains of his wet cave.

In the middle of the night his sleep was troubled by an extraordinary noise; he sat up, and the deep silence around him allowed him to distinguish the alternative accents of a respiration whose savage energy could not belong to a human creature.

A profound terror, increased still further by the darkness, the silence, and his waking images, froze his heart within him. He almost felt his hair stand on end, when by straining his eyes to their utmost he perceived through the shadows two faint yellow lights. At first he attributed these lights to the reflection of his own pupils, but soon the vivid brilliance of the night aided him gradually to distinguish the objects around him in the cave, and he beheld a huge animal lying but two steps from him. Was it a lion, a tiger, or a crocodile?

The Provençal was not educated enough to know under what species his enemy ought to be classed; but his fright was all the greater, as his ignorance led him to imagine all terrors at once; he endured a cruel torture, noting every variation of the breathing close to him without daring to make the slightest movement. An odor, pungent like that of a fox, but more penetrating, profounder—so to speak—filled the cave, and when the Provençal became sensible of this, his terror reached its height, for he could no longer doubt the proximity of a terrible companion, whose royal dwelling served him for shelter.

Presently the reflection of the moon, descending on the horizon, lit up the den, rendering gradually visible and resplendent the spotted skin of a panther.

The lion of Egypt slept, curled up like a big dog, the peaceful possessor of a sumptuous niche at the gate of an *hôtel*;[3] its eyes opened for a moment and closed again; its face was turned toward the man. A thousand confused thoughts passed through the Frenchman's mind; first he thought of killing it with a bullet from his gun, but he saw there was not enough distance between them for him to take proper aim— the shot would miss the mark. And if it were to wake!—the thought made his limbs rigid. He listened to his own heart beating in the midst of the silence, and cursed the too violent pulsations which the flow of

[3]A great mansion.

blood brought on, fearing to disturb that sleep which allowed him time to think of some means of escape.

Twice he placed his hand on his scimitar, intending to cut off the head of the enemy; but the difficulty of cutting the stiff, short hair compelled him to abandon this daring project. To miss would be to die for certain, he thought; he preferred the chances of fair fight, and made up his mind to wait till morning; the morning did not leave him long to wait.

He could now examine the panther at ease; its muzzle was smeared with blood.

"She's had a good dinner," he thought, without troubling himself as to whether her feast might have been on human flesh. "She won't be hungry when she gets up."

It was a female. The fur on her belly and flanks was glistening white; many small marks like velvet formed beautiful bracelets round her feet; her sinuous tail was also white, ending with black rings; the overpart of her dress, yellow like unburnished gold, very lissome and soft, had the characteristic blotches in the form of rosettes, which distinguish the panther from every other feline species.

This tranquil and formidable hostess snored in an attitude as graceful as that of a cat lying on a cushion. Her blood-stained paws, nervous and well-armed, were stretched out before her face, which rested upon them, and from which radiated her straight, slender whiskers, like threads of silver.

If she had been like that in a cage, the Provençal would doubtless have admired the grace of the animal, and the vigorous contrasts of vivid color which gave her robe an imperial splendor; but just then his sight was troubled by her sinister appearance.

The presence of the panther, even asleep, could not fail to produce the effect which the magnetic eyes of the serpent are said to have on the nightingale.

For a moment the courage of the soldier began to fail before this danger, though no doubt it would have risen at the mouth of a cannon charged with shell. Nevertheless, a bold thought brought daylight to his soul and sealed up the source of the cold sweat which sprang forth on his brow. Like men driven to bay who defy death and offer their body to the smiter, so he, seeing in this merely a tragic episode, resolved to play his part with honor to the last.

"The day before yesterday the Arabs would have killed me perhaps," he said; so considering himself as good as dead already, he waited bravely, with excited curiosity, his enemy's awakening.

When the sun appeared, the panther suddenly opened her eyes; then she put out her paws with energy, as if to stretch them and get rid of cramp. At last she yawned, showing the formidable apparatus of her teeth and pointed tongue, rough as a file.

"A regular *petite maîtresse*," thought the Frenchman, seeing her roll herself about so softly and coquettishly. She licked off the blood which stained her paws and muzzle, and scratched her head with reiterated gestures full of prettiness. "All right, make a little toilet,"[4] the Frenchman said to himself, beginning to recover his gaiety with his courage; "we'll say good morning to each other presently," and he seized the small, short dagger which he had taken from the Mangrabins. At this moment the panther turned her head toward the man and looked at him fixedly without moving.

The rigidity of her metallic eyes and their insupportable luster made him shudder, especially when the animal walked toward him. But he looked at her caressingly, staring into her eyes in order to magnetize her, and let her come quite close to him; then with a movement both gentle and amorous, as though he were caressing the most beautiful of women, he passed his hand over her whole body, from the head to the tail, scratching the flexible vertebrae which divided the panther's yellow back. The animal waved her tail voluptuously, and her eyes grew gentle; and when for the third time the Frenchman accomplished this interesting flattery, she gave forth one of those purrings by which our cats express their pleasure; but this murmur issued from a throat so powerful and so deep, that it resounded through the cave like the last vibrations of an organ in a church. The man, understanding the importance of his caresses, redoubled them in such a way as to surprise and stupefy his imperious courtesan. When he felt sure of having extinguished the ferocity of his capricious companion, whose hunger had so fortunately been satisfied the day before, he got up to go out of the cave; the panther let him go out, but when he had reached the summit of the hill she sprang with the lightness of a sparrow hopping from twig to twig, and rubbed herself against his legs, putting up her back after the manner of all the race of cats. Then regarding her guest with eyes whose glare had softened a little, she gave vent to that wild cry which naturalists compare to the grating of a saw.

"She is exacting," said the Frenchman, smilingly.

He was bold enough to play with her ears; he caressed her belly and scratched her head as hard as he could.

When he saw that he was successful, he tickled her skull with the point of his dagger, watching for the right moment to kill her, but the hardness of her bones made him tremble for his success.

The sultana of the desert showed herself gracious to her slave; she lifted her head, stretched out her neck, and manifested her delight by the tranquility of her attitude. It suddenly occurred to the soldier that to kill this savage princess with one blow he must poignard her in the throat.

He raised the blade, when the panther, satisfied no doubt, laid herself gracefully at his feet, and cast up at him glances in which, in spite of their natural fierceness, was mingled confusedly a kind of good-will. The poor Provençal ate his dates, leaning against one of the palm trees,

[4]Clean and dress up for the day.

and casting his eyes alternately on the desert in quest of some liberator and on his terrible companion to watch her uncertain clemency.

The panther looked at the place where the date stones fell, and every time that he threw one down her eyes expressed an incredible mistrust.

She examined the man with an almost commercial prudence. However, this examination was favorable to him, for when he had finished his meager meal she licked his boots with her powerful rough tongue, brushing off with marvellous skill the dust gathered in the creases.

"Ah, but when she's really hungry!" thought the Frenchman. In spite of the shudder this thought caused him, the soldier began to measure curiously the proportions of the panther, certainly one of the most splendid specimens of its race. She was three feet high and four feet long without counting her tail; this powerful weapon, rounded like a cudgel, was nearly three feet long. The head, large as that of a lioness, was distinguished by a rare expression of refinement. The cold cruelty of a tiger was dominant, it was true, but there was also a vague resemblance to the face of a sensual woman. Indeed, the face of this solitary queen had something of the gaiety of a drunken Nero: she had satisfied herself with bood, and she wanted to play.

The soldier tried if he might walk up and down, and the panther left him free, contenting herself following him with her eyes, less like a faithful dog than a big Angora cat, observing everything, and every movement of her master.

When he looked around, he saw, by the spring, the remains of his horse; the panther had dragged the carcass all that way; about two-thirds of it had been devoured already. The sight reassured him.

It was easy to explain the panther's absence, and the respect she had had for him while he slept. The first piece of good luck emboldened him to tempt the future, and he conceived the wild hope of continuing on good terms with the panther during the entire day, neglecting no means of taming her, and remaining in her good graces.

He returned to her, and had the unspeakable joy of seeing her wag her tail with an almost imperceptible movement at his approach. He sat down then, without fear, by her side, and they began to play together; he took her paws and muzzle, pulled her ears, rolled her over on her back, stroked her warm, delicate flanks. She let him do whatever he liked, and when he began to stroke the hair on her feet she drew her claws in carefully.

The man, keeping the dagger in one hand, thought to plunge it into the belly of the too-confiding panther, but he was afraid that he would be immediately strangled in her last conclusive struggle; besides, he felt in his heart a sort of remorse which bid him respect a creature that had done him no harm. He seemed to have found a friend, in a boundless desert; half unconsciously he thought of his first sweetheart, whom he had nicknamed "Mignonne"[5] by way of contrast, because she was so

[5]"Darling."

atrociously jealous that all the time of their love he was in fear of the knife with which she had always threatened him.

This memory of his early days suggested to him the idea of making the young panther answer to this name, now that he began to admire with less terror her swiftness, suppleness, and softness. Toward the end of the day he had familiarized himself with his perilous position; he now almost liked the painfulness of it. At last his companion had got into the habit of looking up at him whenever he cried in a falsetto voice, "Mignonne."

At the setting of the sun Mignonne gave, several times running, a profound melancholy cry. "She's been well brought up," said the light-hearted soldier; "she says her prayers." But this mental joke only occurred to him when he noticed what a pacific attitude his companion remained in. "Come, *ma petite blonde,* I'll let you go to bed first," he said to her, counting on the activity of his own legs to run away as quickly as possible, directly she was asleep, and seek another shelter for the night.

The soldier waited with impatience the hour of his flight, and when it had arrived he walked vigorously in the direction of the Nile; but hardly had he made a quarter of a league in the sand when he heard the panther bounding after him, crying with that saw-like cry more dreadful even than the sound of her leaping.

"Ah!" he said, "then she's taken a fancy to me; she has never met any one before, and it is really quite flattering to have her first love." That instant the man fell into one of those movable quicksands so terrible to travellers and from which it is impossible to save oneself. Feeling himself caught, he gave a shriek of alarm; the panther seized him with her teeth by the collar, and, springing vigorously backward, drew him as if by magic out of the whirling sand.

"Ah, Mignonne!" cried the soldier, caressing her enthusiastically; "we're bound together for life and death—but no jokes, mind!" and he retraced his steps.

From that time the desert seemed inhabited. It contained a being to whom the man could talk, and whose ferocity was rendered gentle by him, though he could not explain to himself the reason for their strange friendship. Great as was the soldier's desire to stay upon guard, he slept.

On awakening he could not find Mignonne; he mounted the hill, and in the distance saw her springing toward him after the habit of these animals, who cannot run on account of the extreme flexibility of the vertebral column. Mignonne arrived, her jaws covered with blood; she received the wonted caress of her companion, showing with much purring how happy it made her. Her eyes, full of languor, turned still more gently than the day before toward the Provençal who talked to her as one would to a tame animal.

"Ah! Mademoiselle, you are a nice girl, aren't you? Just look at that! so we like to be made much of, don't we? Aren't you ashamed of yourself? So you have been eating some Arab or other, have you? that doesn't matter. They're animals just the same as you are; but don't you take to eating Frenchmen, or I shan't like you any longer."

She played like a dog with its master, letting herself be rolled over, knocked about, and stroked, alternately; sometimes she herself would provoke the soldier, putting up her paw with a soliciting gesture.

Some days passed in this manner. This companionship permitted the Provençal to appreciate the sublime beauty of the desert; now that he had a living thing to think about, alternations of fear and quiet, and plenty to eat, his mind became filled with contrast and his life began to be diversified.

Solitude revealed to him all her secrets, and enveloped him in her delights. He discovered in the rising and setting of the sun sights unknown to the world. He knew what it was to tremble when he heard over his head the hiss of a bird's wing, so rarely did they pass, or when he saw the clouds, changing and many-colored travellers, melt one into another. He studied in the night time the effect of the moon upon the ocean of sand, where the simoom[6] made waves swift of movement and rapid in their change. He lived the life of the Eastern day, marvelling at its wonderful pomp; then, after having revelled in the sight of a hurricane over the plain where the whirling sands made red, dry mists and death-bearing clouds, he would welcome the night with joy, for then fell the healthful freshness of the stars, and he listened to imaginary music in the skies. Then solitude taught him to unroll the treasures of dreams. He passed whole hours in remembering mere nothings, and comparing his present life with his past.

At last he grew passionately fond of the panther; for some sort of affection was a necessity.

Whether it was that his will powerfully projected had modified the character of his companion, or whether, because she found abundant food in her predatory excursions in the desert, she respected the man's life, he began to fear for it no longer, seeing her so well tamed.

He devoted the greater part of his time to sleep, but he was obliged to watch like a spider in its web that the moment of his deliverance might not escape him, if any one should pass the line marked by the horizon. He had sacrificed his shirt to make a flag with, which he hung at the top of a palm tree, whose foliage he had torn off. Taught by necessity, he found the means of keeping it spread out, by fastening it with little sticks; for the wind might not be blowing at the moment when the passing traveller was looking through the desert.

It was during the long hours, when he had abandoned hope, that he amused himself with the panther. He had come to learn the different inflections of her voice, the expressions of her eyes; he had studied the capricious patterns of all the rosettes which marked the gold of her robe. Mignonne was not even angry when he took hold of the tuft at the end

---

[6]The hot, dry wind of the desert.

of her tail to count her rings, those graceful ornaments which glittered in the sun like jewelry. It gave him pleasure to contemplate the supple, fine outlines of her form, the whiteness of her belly, the graceful pose of her head. But it was especially when she was playing that he felt most pleasure in looking at her; the agility and youthful lightness of her movements were a continual surprise to him; he wondered at the supple way in which she jumped and climbed, washed herself and arranged her fur, crouched down and prepared to spring. However rapid her spring might be, however slippery the stone she was on, she would always stop short at the word "Mignonne."

One day, in a bright mid-day sun, an enormous bird coursed through the air. The man left his panther to look at this new guest; but after waiting a moment the deserted sultana growled deeply.

"My goodness! I do believe she's jealous," he cried, seeing her eyes become hard again; "the soul of Virginie has passed into her body; that's certain."

The eagle disappeared into the air, while the soldier admired the curved contour of the panther.

But there was such youth and grace in her form! she was beautiful as a woman! the blond fur of her robe mingled well with the delicate tints of faint white which marked her flanks.

The profuse light cast down by the sun made this living gold, these russet markings, to burn in a way to give them an indefinable attraction.

The man and the panther looked at one another with a look full of meaning; the coquette quivered when she felt her friend stroke her head; her eyes flashed like lightning—then she shut them tightly.

"She has a soul," he said, looking at the stillness of this queen of the sands, golden like them, white like them, solitary and burning like them.

"Well," she said, "I have read your plea in favor of beasts; but how did two so well adapted to understand each other end?"

"Ah, well! you see, they ended as all great passions do end—by a misunderstanding. For some reason *one* suspects the other of treason; they don't come to an explanation through pride, and quarrel and part from sheer obstinacy."

"Yet sometimes at the best moments a single word or a look is enough—but anyhow go on with your story."

"It's horribly difficult, but you will understand, after what the old villain told me over his champagne.

"He said—'I don't know if I hurt her, but she turned round, as if enraged, and with sharp teeth caught hold of my leg—gently, I daresay; but I, thinking she would devour me, plunged my dagger into her throat. She rolled over, giving a cry that froze my heart; and I saw her dying, still looking at me without anger. I would have given all the world—my cross even, which I had not got then—to have brought her to life again. It was as though I had murdered a real person; and the soldiers who had seen my flag, and were come to my assistance, found me in tears.'

" 'Well sir,' he said, after a moment of silence, 'since then I have been in war in Germany, in Spain, in Russia, in France; I've certainly carried my carcass about a good deal, but never have I seen anything like the desert. Ah! yes, it is very beautiful!'

" 'What did you feel there?' I asked him.

" 'Oh! that can't be described, young man. Besides, I am not always regretting my palm trees and my panther. I should have to be very melancholy for that. In the desert, you see, there is everything, and nothing.'

" 'Yes, but explain——'

" 'Well,' he said, with an impatient gesture, 'it is God without mankind.' "

## FOR DISCUSSION

1. A story within a story is called a *frame-story*. Who has told the narrator the tale of "The Frenchman in Egypt"? What are the circumstances surrounding the narrator's retelling the story? What is the effect of the frame, as compared with the effect of telling the story directly?
2. What does the setting of the desert contribute to the story? Can you imagine the events of the story placed elsewhere? If so, would the location have to be equally extreme?
3. What is the soldier's mental state prior to his encounter with the panther?
4. What varieties of conflict are presented in the story?
5. How would you describe the relationship between the soldier and the panther?
6. What is the significance of the soldier's naming the panther *Mignonne*? Do you see any parallels between the events of the story and a brief love affair between a man and a woman?
7. What case can be made for the panther's representing femininity? Is it significant that the panther is both beautiful and dangerous?
8. Admitting that this is an unusual tale, what do you think is the point of the story? What does the last sentence mean?

# To Hell with Dying

ALICE WALKER

"To hell with dying," my father would say, "these children want Mr. Sweet!"

Mr. Sweet was a diabetic and an alcoholic and a guitar player and lived down the road from us on a neglected cotton farm. My older brothers and sisters got the most benefit from Mr. Sweet, for when they were growing up he had quite a few years ahead of him and so was capable of being called back from the brink of death any number of times—whenever the voice of my father reached him as he lay expiring. . . . "To hell with dying, man," my father would say, pushing the wife away from the bedside (in tears although she knew the death was not necessarily the last one unless Mr. Sweet really wanted it to be), "the children want Mr. Sweet!" And they did want him, for at a signal from Father they would come crowding around the bed and throw themselves on the covers and whoever was the smallest at the time would kiss him all over his wrinkled brown face and begin to tickle him so that he would laugh all down in his stomach, and his moustache which was long and sort of straggly, would shake like Spanish moss and was also that color.

Mr. Sweet had been ambitious as a boy, wanted to be a doctor or lawyer or sailor, only to find that black men fare better if they are not. Since he could be none of those things he turned to fishing as his only earnest career and playing the guitar as his only claim to doing anything extraordinarily well. His son, the only one that he and his wife, Miss Mary, had, was shiftless as the day is long and spent money as if he were trying to see the bottom of the mint, which Mr. Sweet would tell him was the clean brown palm of his hand. Miss Mary loved her "baby," however, and worked hard to get him the "li'l necessaries" of life, which turned out mostly to be women.

Mr. Sweet was a tall, thinnish man with thick kinky hair going dead white. He was dark brown, his eyes were very squinty and sort of bluish, and he chewed Brown Mule tobacco. He was constantly on the verge of being blind drunk, for he brewed his own liquor and was not in the least a stingy sort of man, and was always very melancholy and sad, though frequently when he was "feelin' good" he'd dance around the yard with us, usually keeling over just as my mother came to see what the commotion was.

Toward all of us children he was very kind, and had the grace to be shy with us, which is unusual in grown-ups. He had great respect for my mother for she never held his drunkenness against him and would let us play with him even when he was about to fall in the fireplace from drink. Although Mr. Sweet would sometimes lose complete or nearly complete control of his head and neck so that he would loll in his chair, his mind remained strangely acute and his speech not too affected. His ability to be drunk and sober at the same time made him an ideal playmate, for he was as weak as we were and we could usually best him in wrestling, all the while keeping a fairly coherent conversation going.

We never felt anything of Mr. Sweet's age when we played with him. We loved his wrinkles and would draw some on our brows to be like him, and his white hair was my special treasure and he knew it and would never come to visit us just after he had had his hair cut off at the barbershop. Once he came to our house for something, probably to see my father about fertilizer for his crops, for although he never paid the slightest attention to his crops he liked to know what things would be best to use on them if he ever did. Anyhow, he had not come with his hair since he had just had it shaved off at the barbershop. He wore a huge straw hat to keep off the sun and also to keep his head away from me. But as soon as I saw him I ran up and demanded that he take me up and kiss me, with his funny beard which smelled so strongly of tobacco. Looking forward to burying my small fingers into his woolly hair I threw away his hat only to find he had done something to his hair, that it was no longer there! I let out a squall which made my mother think that Mr. Sweet had finally dropped me in the well or something and from that day I've been wary of men in hats. However, not long after, Mr. Sweet showed up with his hair grown out and just as white and kinky and impenetrable as it ever was.

Mr. Sweet used to call me his princess, and I believed it. He made me feel pretty at five and six, and simply outrageously devastating at the blazing age of eight and a half. When he came to our house with his guitar the whole family would stop whatever they were doing to sit around him and listen to him play. He liked to play "Sweet Georgia Brown," that was what he called me sometimes, and also he liked to play "Caldonia" and all sorts of sweet, sad, wonderful songs which he sometimes made up. It was from one of these songs that I learned that he had had to marry Miss Mary when he had in fact loved somebody else (now living in Chi'-ca-go, or De-stroy, Michigan). He was not sure that Joe Lee, her "baby," was also his baby. Sometimes he would cry and that was an indication that he was about to die again. And so we would all get prepared, for we were sure to be called upon.

I was seven the first time I remember actually participating in one of Mr. Sweet's "revivals"—my parents told me I had participated before, I had been the one chosen to kiss him and tickle him long before I knew the rite of Mr. Sweet's rehabilitation. He had come to our house, it was a few years after his wife's death, and he was very sad, and also, typically, very drunk. He sat on the floor next to me and my older brother, the rest of the children were grown-up and lived elsewhere, and began to play his guitar and cry. I held his woolly head in my arms and wished I could have been old enough to have been the woman he loved so much and that I had not been lost years and years ago.

When he was leaving my mother said to us that we'd better sleep light that night for we'd probably have to go over to Mr. Sweet's before daylight. And we did. For soon after we had gone to bed one of the neighbors knocked on our door and called my father and said that Mr. Sweet was sinking fast and if he wanted to get in a word before the crossover he'd better shake a leg and get over to Mr. Sweet's house. All the neighbors knew to come to our house if something was wrong with Mr. Sweet, but they did not know how we always managed to make him well, or at least stop him from dying, when he was often so near death. As soon as we heard the cry we got up, my brother and I and my mother and father, and put on our clothes. We hurried out of the house and down the road for we were always afraid that we might someday be too late and Mr. Sweet would get tired of dallying.

When we got to the house, a very poor shack really, we found the front room full of neighbors and relatives and someone met us at the door and said that it was all very sad that old Mr. Sweet Little (for Little was his family name although we mostly ignored it) was about to kick the bucket. My parents were advised not to take my brother and me into the "death-room" seeing we were so young and all, but we were so much more accustomed to the death-room than he that we ignored him and dashed in without giving his warning a second thought. I was almost in tears, for these deaths upset me fearfully, and the thought of how much depended on me and my brother (who was such a ham most of the time) made me very nervous.

The doctor was bending over the bed and turned back to tell us for at least the tenth time in the history of my family that alas, old Mr. Sweet Little was dying and that the children had best not see the face of implacable death (I didn't know what "implacable" was, but whatever it was, Mr. Sweet was not!). My father pushed him rather abruptly out of the way saying as he always did and very loudly for he was saying it to Mr. Sweet, "To hell with dying, man, these children want Mr. Sweet!" which was my cue to throw myself upon the bed and kiss Mr. Sweet all around the whiskers and under the eyes and around the collar of his nightshirt where he smelled so strongly of all sorts of things, mostly liniment.

I was very good at bringing him around, for as soon as I saw that he was struggling to open his eyes I knew he was going to be all right and so could finish my revival sure of success. As soon as his eyes were open he would begin to smile and that way I knew that I had surely won. Once though I got a tremendous scare for he could not open his eyes and later I learned that he had had a stroke and that one side of his face was stiff and hard to get into motion. When he began to smile I could tickle him in earnest for I was sure that nothing would get in the way of his laughter, although once he began to cough so hard that he almost threw me off his stomach, but that was when I was very small, little more than a baby, and my bushy hair had gotten in his nose.

When we were sure he would listen to us we would ask him why he was in bed and when he was coming to see us again and could we play with his guitar which more than likely would be leaning against the bed. His eyes would get all misty and he would sometimes cry out loud, but we never let it embarrass us for he knew that we loved him and we sometimes cried too for no reason. My parents would leave the room to just the three of us; Mr. Sweet, by that time, would be propped up in bed with a number of pillows behind his head and with me sitting and lying on his shoulder and along his chest. Even when he had trouble breathing he would not ask me to get down. Looking into my eyes he would shake his white head and run a scratchy old finger all around my hairline, which was rather low down nearly to my eyebrows and for which some people said I looked like a baby monkey.

My brother was very generous in all this, he let me do all the re-vivaling—he had done it for years before I was born and so was glad to be able to pass it on to someone new. What he would do while I talked to Mr. Sweet was pretend to play the guitar, in fact pretend that he was a young version of Mr. Sweet, and it always made Mr. Sweet glad to think that someone wanted to be like him—of course we did not know this then, we played the thing by ear, and whatever he seemed to like, we did. We were desperately afraid that he was just going to take off one day and leave us.

It did not occur to us that we were doing anything special; we had not learned that death was final when it did come. We thought nothing of triumphing over it so many times, and in fact became a trifle con-temptuous of people who let themselves be carried away. It did not occur to us that if our own father had been dying we could not have stopped it, that Mr. Sweet was the only person over whom we had power.

When Mr. Sweet was in his eighties I was a young lady studying away in a university many miles from home. I saw him whenever I went home, but he was never on the verge of dying that I could tell and I began to feel that my anxiety for his health and psychological well-being was unnecessary. By this time he not only had a moustache but a long flowing snow-white beard which I loved and combed and braided for hours. He was still a very heavy drinker and was like an old Chinese opium-user, very peaceful, fragile, gentle, and the only jarring note about him was his old steel guitar which he still played in the old sad, sweet, downhome blues way.

On Mr. Sweet's ninetieth birthday I was finishing my doctorate in Massachusetts and had been making arrangements to go home for several weeks' rest. That morning I got a telegram telling me that Mr. Sweet was dying again and could I please drop everything and come home. Of course I could. My dissertation could wait and my teachers would understand when I explained to them when I got back. I ran to the phone, called the airport, and within four hours I was speeding along the dusty road to Mr. Sweet's.

The house was more dilapidated than when I was last there, barely a shack, but it was overgrown with yellow roses which my family had planted many years ago. The air was heavy and sweet and very peaceful. I felt strange walking through the gate and up the old rickety steps. But the strangeness left me as I caught sight of the long white beard I loved so well flowing down the thin body over the familiar quilt coverlet. Mr. Sweet!

His eyes were closed tight and his hands, crossed over his stomach, were thin and delicate, no longer rough and scratchy. I remembered how always before I had run and jumped up on him just anywhere; now I knew he would not be able to support my weight. I looked around at my parents, and was surprised to see that my father and mother also looked old and frail. My father, his own hair very gray, leaned over the quietly sleeping old man who, incidentally, smelled still of wine and tobacco, and said as he'd done so many times, "To hell with dying, man! My daughter is home to see Mr. Sweet!" My brother had not been able to come as he was in the war in Asia. I bent down and gently stroked the closed eyes and gradually they began to open. The closed, wine-stained lips twitched a little, then parted in a warm, slightly embarrassed smile. Mr. Sweet could see me and he recognized me and his eyes looked very spry and twinkly for a moment. I put my head down on the pillow next to his and we just looked at each other for a long time. Then he began to trace my peculiar hairline with a thin, smooth finger. I closed my eyes when his finger halted above my ear (he used to rejoice at the dirt in my ears when I was little), his hand stayed cupped around my cheek. When I opened my eyes, sure I had reached him in time, his were closed.

Even at twenty-four how could I believe that I had failed? that Mr. Sweet was really gone? He had never gone before. But when I looked up at my parents I saw that they were holding back tears. They had loved him dearly. He was like a piece of rare and delicate china which was always being saved from breaking and which finally fell. I looked long at the old face, the wrinkled forehead, the red lips, the hands that still reached out to me. Soon I felt my father pushing something cool into my hands. It was Mr. Sweet's guitar. He had asked them months before to give it to me, he had known that even if I came next time he would not be able to respond in the old way. He did not want me to feel that my trip had been for nothing.

The old guitar! I plucked the strings, hummed "Sweet Georgia Brown." The magic of Mr. Sweet lingered still in the cool steel box. Through the window I could catch the fragrant delicate scent of tender yellow roses. The man on the high old-fashioned bed with the quilt coverlet and the flowing white beard had been my first love.

## FOR DISCUSSION

1. This story features a single dominant character, Mr. Sweet. How would you describe the man? Is he a believable character? Why do you think so many people liked Mr. Sweet so much?
2. From what point of view is the story told? What role does the narrator play?
3. The narrator says "Mr. Sweet had been ambitious as a boy, wanted to be a doctor or lawyer or sailor, only to find that black men fare better if they are not." Within the story, what is ironic about this statement?
4. What reasons can you give for Mr. Sweet's chronic drinking, before he became a confirmed alcoholic?
5. What do you make of the incident when Mr. Sweet shaved his head, ultimately making the narrator "wary of men in hats"?
6. The narrator says, "I held his woolly head in my arms and wished I could have been old enough to have been the woman he loved so much and that I had not been lost years and years ago." What do you make of the relationship between Mr. Sweet and the narrator? Keep in mind that the narrator says she was only seven years old when she had these feelings.
7. What do you think Mr. Sweet gets from his repeated "deaths"? Do you think that the community, and especially the narrator as a little girl, really brought Mr. Sweet back from death time after time? Is Mr. Sweet a symbol of some sort to them? What does he symbolize?
8. Why would the narrator's older brother pretend to be a young Mr. Sweet?
9. When the narrator is twenty-four and a graduate student, Mr. Sweet quietly dies in her presence. What is it that she has lost?
10. Most readers, black and white, find this a very moving story. Why do you think it has such a strong emotional appeal?

# The Loudest Voice

GRACE PALEY

There is a certain place where dumb-waiters boom, doors slam, dishes crash; every window is a mother's mouth bidding the street shut up, go skate somewhere else, come home. My voice is the loudest.

There, my own mother is still as full of breathing as me and the grocer stands up to speak to her. "Mrs. Abramowitz," he says, "people should not be afraid of their children."

"Ah, Mr. Bialik," my mother replies, "if you say to her or her father 'Ssh,' they say, 'In the grave it will be quiet.' "

"From Coney Island to the cemetery," says my papa. "It's the same subway; it's the same fare."

I am right next to the pickle barrel. My pinky is making tiny whirlpools in the brine. I stop a moment to announce: "Campbell's Tomato Soup. Campbell's Vegetable Beef Soup. Campbell's S-c-otch Broth . . ."

"Be quiet," the grocer says, "the labels are coming off."

"Please, Shirley, be a little quiet," my mother begs me.

In that place the whole street groans: Be quiet! Be quiet! but steals from the happy chorus of my inside self not a tittle or a jot.

There, too, but just around the corner, is a red brick building that has been old for many years. Every morning the children stand before it in double lines which must be straight. They are not insulted. They are waiting anyway.

I am usually among them. I am, in fact, the first, since I begin with "A."

One cold morning the monitor tapped me on the shoulder. "Go to Room 409, Shirley Abramowitz," he said. I did as I was told. I went in a hurry up a down staircase to Room 409, which contained sixth-graders. I had to wait at the desk without wiggling until Mr. Hilton, their teacher, had time to speak.

After five minutes he said, "Shirley?"

"What?" I whispered.

He said, "My! My! Shirley Abramowitz! They told me you had a particularly loud, clear voice and read with lots of expression. Could that be true?"

"Oh yes," I whispered.

"In that case, don't be silly; I might very well be your teacher someday. Speak up, speak up."

"Yes," I shouted.

"More like it," he said. "Now, Shirley, can you put a ribbon in your hair or a bobby pin? It's too messy."

"Yes!" I bawled.

"Now, now, calm down." He turned to the class. "Children, not a sound. Open at page 39. Read till 52. When you finish, start again." He looked me over once more. "Now, Shirley, you know, I suppose, that Christmas is coming. We are preparing a beautiful play. Most of the parts have been given out. But I still need a child with a strong voice, lots of stamina. Do you know what stamina is? You do? Smart kid. You know, I heard you read 'The Lord is my shepherd' in Assembly yesterday. I was very impressed. Wonderful delivery. Mrs. Jordan, your teacher, speaks highly of you. Now listen to me, Shirley Abramowitz, if you want to take the part and be in the play, repeat after me, 'I swear to work harder than I ever did before.' "

I looked to heaven and said at once, "Oh, I swear." I kissed my pinky and looked at God.

"That is an actor's life, my dear," he explained. "Like a soldier's, never tardy or disobedient to his general, the director. Everything," he said "absolutely everything will depend on you."

That afternoon, all over the building, children scraped and scrubbed the turkeys and the sheaves of corn off the schoolroom windows. Goodbye Thanksgiving. The next morning a monitor brought red paper and green paper from the office. We made new shapes and hung them on the walls and glued them to the doors.

The teachers became happier and happier. Their heads were ringing like the bells of childhood. My best friend Evie was prone to evil, but she did not get a single demerit for whispering. We learned "Holy Night" without an error. "How wonderful!" said Miss Glacé, the student teacher. "To think that some of you don't even speak the language!" We learned "Deck the Halls" and "Hark! The Herald Angels." . . . They weren't ashamed and we weren't embarrassed.

Oh, but when my mother heard about it all, she said to my father: "Misha, you don't know what's going on there. Cramer is the head of the Tickets Committee."

"Who?" asked my father. "Cramer? Oh yes, an active woman."

"Active? Active has to have a reason. Listen," she said sadly, "I'm surprised to see my neighbors making tra-la-la for Christmas."

My father couldn't think of what to say to that. Then he decided: "You're in America! Clara, you wanted to come here. In Palestine the Arabs would be eating you alive. Europe you had pogroms. Argentina is full of Indians. Here you got Christmas. . . . Some joke, ha?"

"Very funny, Misha. What is becoming of you? If we came to a new country a long time ago to run away from tyrants, and instead we fall into a creeping pogrom, that our children learn a lot of lies, so what's the joke? Ach, Misha, your idealism is going away."

"So is your sense of humor."

"That I never had, but idealism you had a lot of."

"I'm the same Misha Abramovitch, I didn't change an iota. Ask anyone."

"Only ask me," says my mamma, may she rest in peace. "I got the answer."

Meanwhile the neighbors had to think of what to say too.

Marty's father said: "You know, he has a very important part, my boy."

"Mine also," said Mr. Sauerfeld.

"Not my boy!" said Mrs. Klieg. "I said to him no. The answer is no. When I say no! I mean no!"

The rabbi's wife said, "It's disgusting!" But no one listened to her. Under the narrow sky of God's great wisdom she wore a strawberry-blond wig.

Every day was noisy and full of experience. I was Right-hand Man. Mr. Hilton said: "How could I get along without you, Shirley?"

He said: "Your mother and father ought to get down on their knees every night and thank God for giving them a child like you."

He also said: "You're absolutely a pleasure to work with, my dear, dear child."

Sometimes he said: "For God's sake, what did I do with the script? Shirley! Shirley! Find it."

Then I answered quietly: "Here it is, Mr. Hilton."

Once in a while, when he was very tired, he would cry out: "Shirley, I'm just tired of screaming at those kids. Will you tell Ira Pushkov not to come in till Lester points to that star the second time?"

Then I roared: "Ira Pushkov, what's the matter with you? Dope! Mr. Hilton told you five times already, don't come in till Lester points to that star the second time."

"Ach, Clara," my father asked, "what does she do there till six o'clock she can't even put the plates on the table?"

"Christmas," said my mother coldly.

"Ho! Ho!" my father said. "Christmas. What's the harm? After all, history teaches everyone. We learn from reading this is a holiday from pagan times also, candles, lights, even Chanukah. So we learn it's not altogether Christian. So if they think it's a private holiday, they're only ignorant, not patriotic. What belongs to history, belongs to all men. You want to go back to the Middle Ages? Is it better to shave your head with a secondhand razor? Does it hurt Shirley to learn to speak up? It does not. So maybe someday she won't live between the kitchen and the shop. She's not a fool."

I thank you, Papa, for your kindness. It is true about me to this day. I am foolish but I am not a fool.

That night my father kissed me and said with great interest in my career, "Shirley, tomorrow's your big day. Congrats."

"Save it," my mother said. Then she shut all the windows in order to prevent tonsillitis.

In the morning it snowed. On the street corner a tree had been decorated for us by a kind city administration. In order to miss its chilly shadow our neighbors walked three blocks east to buy a loaf of bread. The butcher pulled down black window shades to keep the colored lights from shining on his chickens. Oh, not me. On the way to school, with both my hands I tossed it a kiss of tolerance. Poor thing, it was a stranger in Egypt.[1]

I walked straight into the auditorium past the staring children. "Go ahead, Shirley!" said the monitors. Four boys, big for their age, had already started work as propmen and stagehands.

Mr. Hilton was very nervous. He was not even happy. Whatever he started to say ended in a sideward look of sadness. He sat slumped in the middle of the first row and asked me to help Miss Glacé. I did this, although she thought my voice too resonant and said, "Show-off!"

Parents began to arrive long before we were ready. They wanted to make a good impression. From among the yards of drapes I peeked out at the audience. I saw my embarrassed mother.

Ira, Lester, and Meyer were pasted to their beards by Miss Glacé. She almost forgot to thread the star on its wire, but I reminded her. I coughed a few times to clear my throat. Miss Glacé looked around and saw that everyone was in costume and on line waiting to play his part. She whispered, "All right . . ." Then:

Jackie Sauerfeld, the prettiest boy in first grade, parted the curtains with his skinny elbow and in a high voice sang out:

> Parents dear
> We are here
> To make a Christmas play in time.
> It we give
> In narrative
> And illustrate with pantomime.

He disappeared.

My voice burst immediately from the wings to the great shock of Ira, Lester, and Meyer, who were waiting for it but were surprised all the same.

"I remember, I remember, the house where I was born . . ."

Miss Glacé yanked the curtain open and there it was, the house—an old hayloft, where Celia Kornbluh lay in the straw with Cindy Lou, her favorite doll. Ira, Lester, and Meyer moved slowly from the wings toward her, sometimes pointing to a moving star and sometimes ahead to Cindy Lou.

It was a long story and it was a sad story. I carefully pronounced all the words about my lonesome childhood, while little Eddie Braunstein wandered upstage and down with his shepherd's stick, looking for sheep. I brought up lonesomeness again, and not being understood at all except by some women everybody hated. Eddie was too small for that and Marty Groff took his place, wearing his father's prayer shawl. I announced twelve friends, and half the boys in the fourth grade

[1] A hated alien in a foreign land, like the Jews in Egyptian captivity.

gathered round Marty, who stood on an orange crate while my voice harangued. Sorrowful and loud, I declaimed about love and God and Man, but because of the terrible deceit of Abie Stock we came suddenly to a famous moment. Marty, whose remembering tongue I was, waited at the foot of the cross. He stared desperately at the audience. I groaned, "My God, my God, why hast thou forsaken me?" The soldiers who were sheiks grabbed poor Marty to pin him up to die, but he wrenched free, turned again to the audience, and spread his arms aloft to show despair and the end. I murmured at the top of my voice, "The rest is silence, but as everyone in this room, in this city—in this world—now knows, I shall have life eternal."

That night Mrs. Kornbluh visited our kitchen for a glass of tea.

"How's the virgin?" asked my father with a look of concern.

"For a man with a daughter, you got a fresh mouth, Abramovitch."

"Here," said my father kindly, "have some lemon, it'll sweeten your disposition."

They debated a little in Yiddish, then fell in a puddle of Russian and Polish. What I understood next was my father, who said, "Still and all, it was certainly a beautiful affair, you have to admit, introducing us to the beliefs of a different culture."

"Well, yes," said Mrs. Kornbluh. "The only thing . . . you know Charlie Turner—that cute boy in Celia's class—a couple others? They got very small parts or no part at all. In very bad taste, it seemed to me. After all, it's their religion."

"Ach," explained my mother, "what could Mr. Hilton do? They got very small voices; after all, why should they holler? The English language they know from the beginning by heart. They're blond like angels. You think it's so important they should get in the play? Christmas . . . the whole piece of goods . . . they own it."

I listened and listened until I couldn't listen any more. Too sleepy, I climbed out of bed and kneeled. I made a little church of my hands and said, "Hear, O Israel . . ." Then I called out in Yiddish, "Please, good night, good night. Ssh." My father said, "Ssh yourself," and slammed the kitchen door.

I was happy. I fell asleep at once. I had prayed for everybody: my talking family, cousins far away, passers-by, and all the lonesome Christians. I expected to be heard. My voice was certainly the loudest.


## FOR DISCUSSION

1. What seems to be the author's attitude toward the story and its subject?
2. Describe the personality of the story's narrator protagonist.
3. This story has almost two dozen characters. List these characters and see just how much you know about each one. Point out any striking caricatures—brief, perhaps humorous, characterizations—that you see in the story.
4. How important is the social setting to the events of the story?

5. Contrast Mrs. Abramowitz's attitude toward the Christmas play with that of Mr. Abramowitz.
6. What kind of a teacher is Mr. Hilton? How well do you think he is suited to his job? Why do you think Miss Glacé dislikes Shirley Abramowitz? Does Miss Glacé remind you of any student teachers you have ever had?
7. Why do you suppose Shirley feels like praying for "all the lonesome Christians" at the end of the story?
8. Point out a few specific remarks by the narrator that you find humorous.
9. Describe the nature of the relationship between Shirley and her father. How does it contrast with Shirley's relationship with her mother?
10. What do you see as the story's theme? Why would a loud voice be important to a young Jewish immigrant?

# The Cask of Amontillado[1]

EDGAR ALLAN POE

The thousand injuries of Fortunato I had borne as I best could, but when he ventured upon insult, I vowed revenge. You, who so well know the nature of my soul, will not suppose, however, that I gave utterance to a threat. *At length* I would be avenged; this was a point definitely settled—but the very definitiveness with which it was resolved precluded the idea of risk. I must not only punish, but punish with impunity. A wrong is unredressed when retribution overtakes its redresser. It is equally unredressed when the avenger fails to make himself felt as such to him who has done the wrong.

It must be understood that neither by word nor deed had I given Fortunato cause to doubt my good will. I continued, as was my wont, to smile in his face, and he did not perceive that my smile *now* was at the thought of his immolation.

He had a weak point—this Fortunato—although in other regards he was a man to be respected and even feared. He prided himself on his connoisseurship in wine. Few Italians have the true virtuoso spirit. For the most part their enthusiasm is adopted to suit the time and opportunity to practice imposture upon the British and Austrian *millionaires*. In painting and gemmary Fortunato, like his countrymen, was a quack, but in the matter of old wines he was sincere. In this respect I did not differ from him materially;—I was skillful in the Italian vintages myself, and bought largely whenever I could.

It was about dusk, one evening during the supreme madness of the carnival season, that I encountered my friend. He accosted me with excessive warmth, for he had been drinking much. The man wore motley. He had on a tight-fitting parti-striped dress, and his head was surmounted by the conical cap and bells. I was so pleased to see him, that I thought I should never have done wringing his hand.

I said to him—"My dear Fortunato, you are luckily met. How remarkably well you are looking to-day! But I have received a pipe[2] of what passes for Amontillado, and I have my doubts."

"How?" said he, "Amontillado? A pipe? Impossible! And in the middle of the carnival?"

"I have my doubts," I replied; "and I was silly enough to pay the full Amontillado price without consulting you in the matter. You were not to be found, and I was fearful of losing a bargain."

"Amontillado!"

"I have my doubts."

"Amontillado!"

[1]An excellent pale dry sherry from Montilla in Spain.
[2]A cask holding 126 gallons.

"And I must satisfy them."

"Amontillado!"

"As you are engaged, I am on my way to Luchesi. If any one has a critical turn, it is he. He will tell me—"

"Luchesi cannot tell Amontillado from Sherry."[3]

"And yet some fools will have it that his taste is a match for your own."

"Come, let us go."

"Whither?"

"To your vaults."

"My friend, no; I will not impose upon your good nature. I perceive you have an engagement. Luchesi—"

"I have no engagement; come."

"My friend, no. It is not the engagement, but the severe cold with which I perceive you are afflicted. The vaults are insufferably damp. They are encrusted with nitre."

"Let us go, nevertheless. The cold is merely nothing. Amontillado! You have been imposed upon; and as for Luchesi, he cannot distinguish Sherry from Amontillado."

Thus speaking, Fortunato possessed himself of my arm. Putting on a mask of black silk, and drawing a *roquelaure*[4] closely about my person, I suffered him to hurry me to my palazzo.

There were no attendants at home; they had absconded to make merry in honor of the time. I had told them that I should not return until the morning, and had given them explicit orders not to stir from the house. These orders were sufficient, I well knew, to insure their immediate disappearance, one and all, as soon as my back was turned.

I took from their sconces two flambeaux, and giving one to Fortunato, bowed him through several suites of rooms to the archway that led into the vaults. I passed down a long and winding staircase, requesting him to be cautious as he followed. We came at length to the foot of the descent, and stood together on the damp ground of the catacombs of the Montresors.

The gait of my friend was unsteady, and the bells upon his cap jingled as he strode.

"The pipe," said he.

"It it farther on," said I; "but observe the white web-work which gleams from these cavern walls."

He turned towards me, and looked into my eyes with two filmy orbs that distilled the rheum of intoxication.

"Nitre?" he asked, at length.

"Nitre," I replied. "How long have you had that cough?"

"Ugh! ugh! ugh!—ugh! ugh! ugh!—ugh! ugh! ugh!—ugh! ugh! ugh!— ugh! ugh! ugh!"

[3]That is, from common, nonvintage sherry.

[4]A short cloak.

My poor friend found it impossible to reply for many minutes.

"It is nothing," he said, at last.

"Come," I said, with decision, "we will go back; your health is precious. You are rich, respected, admired, beloved; you are happy, as once I was. You are a man to be missed. For me it is no matter. We will go back; you will be ill, and I cannot be responsible. Besides, there is Luchesi—"

"Enough," he said; "the cough is a mere nothing: it will not kill me. I shall not die of a cough."

"True—true," I replied; "and, indeed, I had no intention of alarming you unnecessarily—but you should use all proper caution. A draught of this Medoc[5] will defend us from the damps."

Here I knocked off the neck of a bottle which I drew from a long row of its fellows that lay upon the mould.

"Drink," I said, presenting him the wine.

He raised it to his lips with a leer. He paused and nodded to me familiarly, while his bells jingled.

"I drink," he said, "to the buried that repose around us."

"And I to your long life."

He again took my arm, and we proceeded.

"These vaults," he said, "are extensive."

"The Montresors," I replied, "were a great and numerous family."

"I forget your arms."

"A huge human foot d'or, in a field azure; the foot crushes a serpent rampant whose fangs are imbedded in the heel."[6]

"And the motto?"

*"Nemo me impune lacessit."*[7]

"Good!" he said.

The wine sparkled in his eyes and the bells jingled. My own fancy grew warm with the Medoc. We had passed through walls of piled bones, with casks and puncheons intermingling, into the inmost recesses of the catacombs. I paused again, and this time I made bold to seize Fortunato by an arm above the elbow.

"The nitre!" I said; "see, it increases. It hangs like moss upon the vaults. We are below the river's bed. The drops of moisture trickle among the bones. Come, we will go back ere it is too late. Your cough—"

"It is nothing," he said; "let us go on. But first, another draught of the Medoc."

I broke and reached him a flagon of De Grâve. He emptied it at a breath. His eyes flashed with a fierce light. He laughed and threw the bottle upwards with a gesticulation I did not understand.

---

[5]Red Bordeaux wine.

[6]In heraldry, *or* is gold; *azure*, blue; and *rampant*, reared up in profile.

[7]No one dares attack me with impunity.

I looked at him in surprise. He repeated the movement—a grotesque one.

"You do not comprehend?" he said.

"Not I," I replied.

"Then you are not of the brotherhood."

"How?"

"You are not of the masons."

"Yes, yes," I said, "yes, yes."

"You? Impossible! A mason?"

"A mason," I replied.

"A sign," he said.

"It is this," I answered, producing a trowel from beneath the folds of my *roquelaure*.

"You jest," he exclaimed, recoiling a few paces. "But let us proceed to the Amontillado."

"Be it so," I said, replacing the tool beneath the cloak, and again offering him my arm. He leaned upon it heavily. We continued our route in search of the Amontillado. We passed through a range of low arches, descended, passed on, and descending again, arrived at a deep crypt, in which the foulness of the air caused our flambeaux rather to glow than flame.

At the most remote end of the crypt there appeared another less spacious. Its walls had been lined with human remains piled to the vault overhead, in the fashion of the great catacombs of Paris. Three sides of this interior crypt were still ornamented in this manner. From the fourth the bones had been thrown down, and lay promiscuously upon the earth, forming at one point a mound of some size. Within the wall thus exposed by the displacing of the bones, we perceived a still interior recess, in depth about four feet, in width three, in height six or seven. It seemed to have been constructed for no especial use within itself, but formed merely the interval between two of the colossal supports of the roof of the catacombs, and was backed by one of their circumscribing walls of solid granite.

It was in vain that Fortunato, uplifting his dull torch, endeavored to pry into the depths of the recess. Its termination the feeble light did not enable us to see.

"Proceed," I said; "herein is the Amontillado. As for Luchesi—"

"He is an ignoramus," interrupted my friend, as he stepped unsteadily forward, while I followed immediately at his heels. In an instant he had reached the extremity of the niche, and finding his progress arrested by the rock, stood stupidly bewildered. A moment more and I had fettered him to the granite. In its surface were two iron staples, distant from each other about two feet, horizontally. From one of these depended a short chain, from the other a padlock. Throwing the links about his waist, it was but the work of a few seconds to secure it. He was too much astounded to resist. Withdrawing the key I stepped back from the recess.

"Pass your hand," I said, "over the wall; you cannot help feeling the nitre. Indeed it is *very* damp. Once more let me *implore* you to return. No? Then I must positively leave you. But I must first render you all the little attentions in my power."

"The Amontillado!" ejaculated my friend, not yet recovered from his astonishment.

"True," I replied; "the Amontillado."

As I said these words I busied myself among the pile of bones of which I have before spoken. Throwing them aside, I soon uncovered a quantity of building-stone and mortar. With these materials and with the aid of my trowel, I began vigorously to wall up the entrance of the niche.

I had scarcely laid the first tier of the masonry when I discovered that the intoxication of Fortunato had in a great measure worn off. The earliest indication I had of this was a low moaning cry from the depth of the recess. It was *not* the cry of a drunken man. There was then a long and obstinate silence. I laid the second tier, and the third, and the fourth; and then I heard the furious vibrations of the chain. The noise lasted for several minutes, during which, that I might hearken to it with the more satisfaction, I ceased my labors and sat down upon the bones. When at last the clanking subsided, I resumed the trowel, and finished without interruption the fifth, the sixth, and the seventh tier. The wall was now nearly upon a level with my breast. I again paused, and holding the flambeaux over the mason-work, threw a few feeble rays upon the figure within.

A succession of loud and shrill screams, bursting suddenly from the throat of the chained form, seemed to thrust me violently back. For a brief moment I hesitated—I trembled. Unsheathing my rapier, I began to grope with it about the recess; but the thought of an instant reassured me. I placed my hand upon the solid fabric of the catacombs, and felt satisfied. I reapproached the wall. I replied to the yells of him who clamored. I re-echoed—I aided—I surpassed them in volume and in strength. I did this, and the clamorer grew still.

It was now midnight, and my task was drawing to a close. I had completed the eighth, the ninth, and the tenth tier. I had finished a portion of the last and the eleventh; there remained but a single stone to be fitted and plastered in. I struggled with its weight; I placed it partially in its destined position. But now there came from out the niche a low laugh that erected the hairs upon my head. It was succeeded by a sad voice, which I had difficulty in recognizing as that of the noble Fortunato. The voice said—

"Ha! ha! ha!—he! he! he!—a very good joke indeed—an excellent jest. We will have many a rich laugh about it at the palazzo[8]—he! he! he!—over our wine—he! he! he!"

"The Amontillado!" I said.

---

[8]Italian palace.

"He! he! he!—he! he! he!—yes, the Amontillado. But is it not getting late? Will not they be awaiting us at the palazzo, the Lady Fortunato and the rest? Let us be gone."

"Yes," I said, "let us be gone."

*"For the love of God, Montresor!"*

"Yes," I said, "for the love of God!"

But to these words I hearkened in vain for a reply. I grew impatient. I called aloud;

"Fortunato!"

No answer, I called again;

"Fortunato!"

No answer still, I thrust a torch through the remaining aperture and let it fall within. There came forth in return only a jingling of the bells. My heart grew sick—on account of the dampness of the catacombs. I hastened to make an end of my labor. I forced the last stone into its position; I plastered it up. Against the new masonry I re-erected the old rampart of bones. For the half of a century no mortal has disturbed them. *In pace requiescat!*[9]

## FOR DISCUSSION

1. To what degree would you say the mood of this story is created by setting, and to what degree is it created by the author's tone? To what degree by its action?
2. What is Montresor's motive for killing Fortunato?
3. In what ways does Montresor display considerable knowledge of human psychology?
4. Point out examples of verbal irony (when Montresor speaks) and dramatic irony (when Fortunato speaks) as Montresor leads Fortunato through the catacombs.
5. What are the relative social positions of the two men? Have these positions changed in any way during the years just prior to the events of the story?
6. Of what significance is Montresor's coat of arms and his family motto?
7. Why does Montresor's heart grow sick after he finishes walling up Fortunato?
8. Keep in mind that the narrator tells this story fifty years after the event. To whom do you suppose he is speaking as he tells the tale? Why, after all these years, is he exposing his secret? Can you account for all the precise details with which the narrator remembers a murder committed so long ago?
9. Do you think Montresor was mad, either at the time of the murder or fifty years later as he confesses the deed?

[9]May he rest in peace!

# The Monkey's Paw

W. W. JACOBS

Without, the night was cold and wet, but in the small parlour of Laburnum Villa the blinds were drawn and the fire burned brightly. Father and son were at chess; the former, who possessed ideas about the game involving radical changes, putting his king into such sharp and unnecessary perils that it even provoked comment from the white-haired old lady knitting placidly by the fire.

"Hark at the wind," said Mr. White, who, having seen a fatal mistake after it was too late, was amiably desirous of preventing his son from seeing it.

"I'm listening," said the latter, grimly surveying the board as he stretched out his hand. "Check."

"I should hardly think that he'd come to-night," said his father, with his hand poised over the board.

"Mate," replied the son.

"That's the worst of living so far out," bawled Mr. White, with sudden and unlooked-for violence; "of all the beastly, slushy, out-of-the way places to live in, this is the worst. Path's a bog, and the road's a torrent. I don't know what people are thinking about. I suppose because only two houses in the road are let, they think it doesn't matter."

"Never mind, dear," said his wife soothingly; "perhaps you'll win the next one."

Mr. White looked up sharply, just in time to intercept a knowing glance between mother and son. The words died away on his lips, and he hid a guilty grin in his thin grey beard.

"There he is," said Herbert White, as the gate banged to loudly and heavy footsteps come towards the door.

The old man rose with hospitable haste, and opening the door, was heard condoling with the new arrival. The new arrival also condoled with himself, so that Mrs. White said, "Tut, tut!" and coughed gently as her husband entered the room, followed by a tall, burly man, beady of eye and rubicund of visage.

"Sergeant-Major Morris," he said, introducing him.

The sergeant-major shook hands, and taking the proffered seat by the fire, watched contentedly while his host got out whisky and tumblers and stood a small copper kettle on the fire.

At the third glass his eyes got brighter, and he began to talk, the little family circle regarding with eager interest this visitor from distant parts, as he squared his broad shoulders in the chair, and spoke of wild scenes and doughty deeds; of wars and plagues, and strange peoples.

"Twenty-one years of it," said Mr. White, nodding at his wife and son. "When he went away he was a slip of a youth in the warehouse. Now look at him."

"He don't look to have taken much harm," said Mrs. White politely.

"I'd like to go to India myself," said the old man, "just to look round a bit, you know."

"Better where you are," said the sergeant-major, shaking his head. He put down the empty glass, and sighing softly, shook it again.

"I should like to see those old temples and fakirs and jugglers," said the old man. "What was that you started telling me the other day about a monkey's paw or something, Morris?"

"Nothing," said the soldier hastily. "Leastways nothing worth hearing."

"Monkey's paw?" said Mrs. White curiously.

"Well, it's just a bit of what you might call magic, perhaps," said the sergeant-major off-handedly.

His three listeners leaned forward eagerly. The visitor absent-mindedly put his empty glass to his lips and then set it down again. His host filled it for him.

"To look at," said the sergeant-major, fumbling in his pocket, "it's just an ordinary little paw, dried to a mummy."

He took something out of his pocket and proffered it. Mrs. White drew back with a grimace, but her son, taking it, examined it curiously.

"And what is there special about it?" enquired Mr. White as he took it from his son, and having examined it, placed it upon the table.

"It had a spell put on it by an old fakir," said the sergeant-major, "a very holy man. He wanted to show that fate ruled people's lives, and that those who interfered with it did so to their sorrow. He put a spell on it so that three separate men could each have three wishes from it."

His manner was so impressive that his hearers were conscious that their light laughter jarred somewhat.

"Well, why don't you have three, sir?" said Herbert White cleverly.

The soldier regarded him in the way that middle age is wont to regard presumptuous youth. "I have," he said quietly, and his blotchy face whitened.

"And did you really have the three wishes granted?" asked Mrs. White.

"I did," said the sergeant-major, and his glass tapped against his strong teeth.

"And has anybody else wished?" persisted the old lady.

"The first man had his three wishes. Yes," was the reply; "I don't know what the first two were, but the third was for death. That's how I got the paw."

His tones were so grave that a hush fell upon the group.

"If you've had your three wishes, it's no good to you now, then, Morris," said the old man at last. "What do you keep it for?"

The soldier shook his head. "Fancy, I suppose," he said slowly. "I did have some idea of selling it, but I don't think I will. It has caused enough mischief already. Besides, people won't buy. They think it's a fairy tale, some of them; and those who do think anything of it want to try it first and pay me afterward."

"If you could have another three wishes," said the old man, eyeing him keenly, "would you have them?"

"I don't know," said the other. "I don't know."

He took the paw, and dangling it between his forefinger and thumb, suddenly threw it upon the fire. White, with a slight cry, stooped down and snatched it off.

"Better let it burn," said the soldier solemnly.

"If you don't want it, Morris," said the other, "give it to me."

"I won't," said his friend doggedly. "I threw it on the fire. If you keep it, don't blame me for what happens. Pitch it on the fire again, like a sensible man."

The other shook his head and examined his new possession closely. "How do you do it?" he enquired.

"Hold it up in your right hand and wish aloud," said the sergeant-major, "but I warn you of the consequences."

"Sounds like the *Arabian Nights*," said Mrs. White, as she rose and began to set the supper. "Don't you think you might wish for four pairs of hands for me?"

Her husband drew the talisman from his pocket, and then all three burst into laughter as the sergeant-major, with a look of alarm on his face, caught him by the arm.

"If you must wish," he said gruffly, "wish for something sensible."

Mr. White dropped it back in his pocket, and placing chairs, motioned his friend to the table. In the business of supper the talisman was partly forgotten, and afterwards the three sat listening in an enthralled fashion to a second instalment of the soldier's adventures in India.

"If the tale about the monkey's paw is not more truthful than those he has been telling us," said Herbert, as the door closed behind their guest, just in time to catch the last train, "we shan't make much out of it."

"Did you give him anything for it, father?" enquired Mrs. White, regarding her husband closely.

"A trifle," said he, colouring slightly. "He didn't want it, but I made him take it. And he pressed me again to throw it away."

"Likely," said Herbert, with pretended horror. "Why, we're going to be rich, and famous, and happy. Wish to be an emperor, father, to begin with; then you can't be henpecked."

He darted round the table, pursued by the maligned Mrs. White armed with an antimacassar.

Mr. White took the paw from his pocket and eyed it dubiously. "I don't know what to wish for, and that's a fact," he said slowly. "It seems to me I've got all I want."

"If you only cleared the house, you'd be quite happy, wouldn't you!" said Herbert, with his hand on his shoulder. "Well, wish for two hundred pounds, then; that'll just do it."

His father, smiling shamefacedly at his own credulity, held up the talisman, as his son, with a solemn face, somewhat marred by a wink at his mother, sat down at the piano and struck a few impressive chords.

"I wish for two hundred pounds," said the old man distinctly.

A fine crash from the piano greeted the words, interrupted by a shuddering cry from the old man. His wife and son ran toward him.

"It moved," he cried, with a glance of disgust at the object as it lay on the floor. "As I wished, it twisted in my hand like a snake."

"Well, I don't see the money," said his son, as he picked it up and placed it on the table, "and I bet I never shall."

"It must have been your fancy, father," said his wife, regarding him anxiously.

He shook his head. "Never mind, though; there's no harm done, but it gave me a shock all the same."

They sat down by the fire again while the two men finished their pipes. Outside, the wind was higher than ever, and the old man started nervously at the sound of a door banging upstairs. A silence unusual and depressing settled upon all three, which lasted until the old couple arose to retire for the night.

"I expect you'll find the cash tied up in a big bag in the middle of your bed," said Herbert, as he bade them good night, "and something horrible squatting up on top of the wardrobe watching you as you pocket your ill-gotten gains."

He sat alone in the darkness, gazing at the dying fire, and seeing faces in it. The last face was so horrible and so simian that he gazed at it in amazement. It got so vivid that, with a little uneasy laugh, he felt on the table for a glass containing a little water to throw over it. His hand grasped the monkey's paw, and with a little shiver he wiped his hand on his coat and went up to bed.

## II

In the brightness of the wintry sun next morning as it streamed over the breakfast table he laughed at his fears. There was an air of prosaic wholesomeness about the room which it had lacked on the previous night, and the dirty, shrivelled little paw was pitched on the side-board with a carelessness which betokened no great belief in its virtues.

"I suppose all old soldiers are the same," said Mrs. White. "The idea of our listening to such nonsense! How could wishes be granted in these days? And if they could, how could two hundred pounds hurt you, father?"

"Might drop on his head from the sky," said the frivolous Herbert.

"Morris said the things happened so naturally," said his father, "that you might if you so wished attribute it to coincidence."

"Well, don't break into the money before I come back," said Herbert as he rose from the table. "I'm afraid it'll turn you into a mean avaricious man, and we shall have to disown you."

His mother laughed, and following him to the door, watched him down the road; and returning to the breakfast table, was very merry at the expense of her husband's credulity. All of which did not prevent her from scurrying to the door at the postman's knock, nor prevent her from referring somewhat shortly to retired sergeant-majors of bibulous habits when she found that the post brought a tailor's bill.

"Herbert will have some more of his funny remarks, I expect, when he comes home," she said, as they sat at dinner.

"I dare say," said Mr. White, pouring himself out some beer; "but for all that, the thing moved in my hand; that I'll swear to."

"You thought it did," said the old lady soothingly.

"I say it did," replied the other. "There was no thought about it; I had just—What's the matter?"

His wife made no reply. She was watching the mysterious movements of a man outside, who, peering in an undecided fashion at the house, appeared to be trying to make up his mind to enter. In mental connection with the two hundred pounds, she noticed that the stranger was well dressed, and wore a silk hat of glossy newness. Three times he paused at the gate, and then walked on again. The fourth time he stood with his hand upon it, and then with sudden resolution flung it open and walked up the path. Mrs. White at the same moment placed her hands behind her, and hurriedly unfastening the strings of her apron, put that useful article of apparel beneath the cushion of her chair.

She brought the stranger, who seemed ill at ease, into the room. He gazed at her furtively, and listened in a preoccupied fashion as the old lady apologized for the appearance of the room, and her husband's coat, a garment which he usually reserved for the garden. She then waited as patiently as her sex would permit, for him to broach his business, but he was at first strangely silent.

"I—was asked to call," he said at last, and stooped and picked a piece of cotton from his trousers. "I come from 'Maw and Meggins'."

The old lady started. "Is anything the matter?" she asked breathlessly. "Has anything happened to Herbert? What is it? What is it?"

Her husband interposed. "There, there, mother," he said hastily. "Sit down, and don't jump to conclusions. You've not brought bad news, I'm sure, sir;" and he eyed the other wistfully.

"I'm sorry——" began the visitor.

"Is he hurt?" demanded the mother wildly.

The visitor bowed in assent. "Badly hurt," he said quietly, "but he is not in any pain."

"Oh, thank God!" said the old woman, clasping her hands. "Thank God for that! Thank——"

She broke off suddenly as the sinister meaning of the assurance dawned upon her, and she saw the awful confirmation of her fears in the other's averted face. She caught her breath, and turning to her slower-witted husband, laid a trembling old hand upon his. There was a long silence.

"He was caught in the machinery," said the visitor at length in a low voice.

"Caught in the machinery," repeated Mr. White, in a dazed fashion, "yes."

He sat staring blankly out at the window, and taking his wife's hand between his own, pressed it as he had been wont to do in their old courting days nearly forty years before.

"He was the only one left to us," he said, turning gently to the visitor. "It is hard."

The other coughed, and rising, walked slowly to the window. "The firm wished me to convey their sincere sympathy with you in your great loss," he said, without looking round. "I beg that you will understand I am only their servant and merely obeying orders."

There was no reply; the old woman's face was white, her eyes staring, and her breath inaudible; and on the husband's face was a look such as his friend the sergeant might have carried into his first action.

"I was to say that Maw and Meggins disclaim all responsibility," continued the other. "They admit no liability at all, but in consideration of your son's services, they wish to present you with a certain sum as compensation."

Mr. White dropped his wife's hand, and rising to his feet, gazed with a look of horror at his visitor. His dry lips shaped the words, "How much?"

"Two hundred pounds," was the answer.

Unconscious of his wife's shriek, the old man smiled faintly, put out his hands like a sightless man, and dropped, a senseless heap, to the floor.

## III

In the huge new cemetery, some two miles distant, the old people buried their dead, and came back to the house steeped in shadow and silence. It was all over so quickly that at first they could hardly realise it, and remained in a state of expectation as though of something else to happen—something else which was to lighten this load, too heavy for old hearts to bear.

But the days passed, and expectation gave place to resignation—the hopeless resignation of the old, sometimes miscalled apathy. Sometimes they hardly exchanged a word, for now they had nothing to talk about, and their days were long to weariness.

It was about a week after, that the old man, waking suddenly in the night, stretched out his hand and found himself alone. The room was in darkness, and the sound of subdued weeping came from the window. He raised himself in bed and listened.

"Come back," he said tenderly. "You will be cold."

"It is colder for my son," said the old woman, and wept afresh.

The sound of her sobs died away on his ears. The bed was warm, and his eyes heavy with sleep. He dozed fitfully, and then slept until a sudden wild cry from his wife awoke him with a start.

*"The paw!"* she cried wildly. "The monkey's paw!"

He started up in alarm. "Where? Where is it? What's the matter?"

She came stumbling across the room toward him. "I want it," she said quietly. "You've not destroyed it?"

"It's in the parlour, on the bracket," he replied, marvelling. "Why?"

She cried and laughed together, and bending over, kissed his cheek.

"I only just thought of it," she said hysterically. "Why didn't I think of it before? Why didn't *you* think of it?"

"Think of what?" he questioned.

"The other two wishes," she replied rapidly. "We've only had one."

"Was not that enough?" he demanded fiercely.

"No," she cried triumphantly; "we'll have one more. Go down and get it quickly, and wish our boy alive again."

The man sat up in bed and flung the bedclothes from his quaking limbs. "Good God, you are mad!" he cried, aghast.

"Get it," she panted; "get it quickly, and wish—Oh, my boy, my boy!"

Her husband struck a match and lit the candle. "Get back to bed," he said unsteadily. "You don't know what you are saying."

"We had the first wish granted," said the old woman feverishly; "why not the second?"

"A coincidence," stammered the old man.

"Go and get it and wish," cried his wife, quivering with excitement.

The old man turned and regarded her, and his voice shook. "He has been dead ten days, and besides he—I would not tell you else, but—I could only recognize him by his clothing. If he was too terrible for you to see then, how now?"

"Bring him back," cried the old woman, and dragged him toward the door. "Do you think I fear the child I have nursed?"

He went down in the darkness, and felt his way to the parlour, and then to the mantelpiece. The talisman was in its place, and a horrible fear that the unspoken wish might bring his mutilated son before him ere he could escape from the room seized upon him, and he caught his breath as he found that he had lost the direction of the door. His brow cold with sweat, he felt his way round the table, and groping along the wall until he found himself in the small passage with the unwholesome thing in his hand.

Even his wife's face seemed changed as he entered the room. It was white and expectant, and to his fears seemed to have an unnatural look upon it. He was afraid of her.

*"Wish!"* she cried, in a strong voice.

"It is foolish and wicked," he faltered.

*"Wish!"* repeated his wife.

He raised his hand. "I wish my son alive again."

The talisman fell to the floor, and he regarded it fearfully. Then he sank trembling into a chair as the old woman, with burning eyes, walked to the window and raised the blind.

He sat until he was chilled with the cold, glancing occasionally at the figure of the old woman peering through the window. The candle-end, which had burned below the rim of the china candle-stick, was throwing pulsating shadows on the ceiling and walls, until, with a flicker larger than the rest, it expired. The old man, with an unspeakable sense of relief at the failure of the talisman, crept back to his bed, and a minute or two afterwards the old woman came silently and apathetically beside him.

Neither spoke, but lay silently listening to the ticking of the clock. A stair creaked, and a squeaky mouse scurried noisily through the wall. The darkness was oppressive, and after lying for some time screwing up his courage, he took the box of matches, and striking one, went downstairs for a candle.

At the foot of the stairs the match went out, and he paused to strike another; and at the same moment a knock, so quiet and stealthy as to be scarcely audible, sounded on the front door.

The matches fell from his hand and spilled in the passage. He stood motionless, his breath suspended until the knock was repeated. Then he turned and fled swiftly back to his room, and closed the door behind him. A third knock sounded through the house.

"What's that?" cried the old woman, starting up.

"A rat," said the old man in shaking tones—"a rat. It passed me on the stairs."

His wife sat up in bed listening. A loud knock resounded through the house.

"It's Herbert!" she screamed. "It's Herbert!"

She ran to the door, but her husband was before her, and catching her by the arm, held her tightly.

"What are you going to do?" he whispered hoarsely.

"It's my boy; it's Herbert!" she cried, struggling mechanically. "I forgot it was two miles away. What are you holding me for? Let go. I must open the door."

"For God's sake, don't let it in," cried the old man, trembling.

"You're afraid of your own son," she cried, struggling. "Let me go. I'm coming, Herbert; I'm coming."

There was another knock, and another. The old woman with a sudden wrench broke free and ran from the room. Her husband followed to the landing, and called after her appealingly as she hurried downstairs. He heard the chain rattle back and the bottom bolt drawn slowly and stiffly from the socket. Then the old woman's voice, strained and panting.

"The bolt," she cried loudly. "Come down. I can't reach it."

But her husband was on his hands and knees groping wildly on the floor in search of the paw. If he could only find it before the thing outside got in. A perfect fusillade of knocks reverberated through the house, and he heard the scraping of a chair as his wife put it down in the passage against the door. He heard the creaking of the bolt as it came slowly back, and at the same moment he found the monkey's paw, and frantically breathed his third and last wish.

The knocking ceased suddenly, although the echoes of it were still in the house. He heard the chair drawn back, and the door opened. A cold wind rushed up the staircase, and a long loud wail of disappointment and misery from his wife gave him courage to run down to her side, and then to the gate beyond. The street lamp flickering opposite shone on a quiet and deserted road.

## FOR DISCUSSION

1. What is the story's precipitating incident? Does it occur before or after the story begins?
2. Does the story's second paragraph, in which Mr. White makes a "fatal mistake" at chess, foreshadow later events?
3. Keeping in mind the story's repeated emphasis on such things as fire, wind, cold, dampness, and darkness, what is the work's overall mood and atmosphere?
4. Describe the appearance and personality of Sergeant-Major Morris. Is he a stock character or is he plausible? Why does he tell his tale of the monkey's paw? Why does he carry the paw with him to the White household?
5. Point out significant instances of the number three in the story.
6. From various statements made by Herbert, point out any examples of dramatic irony that you can find.
7. Sergeant-Major Morris says that he has already had his three wishes. Furthermore, he says that the person who had the paw before him wished for death with his third wish. What does this suggest to you about the Sergeant-Major?
8. At the end of the first part of the story, who is it that sits before the fire and sees a horrible simian face in the dying flames? What does this suggest to you?
9. Some people read "The Monkey's Paw" as a story of the supernatural, while others view it as a clever tale of psychological horror. Can you find any concrete examples of supernatural power in the story? On the other hand, can you logically explain away all suggestions of supernaturalism? *Was* the paw magical?
10. How many possible reasons can you give for Herbert's not being outside when Mr. White ran "to the gate beyond"?

# Report

DONALD BARTHELME

Our group is against the war. But the war goes on. I was sent to
Cleveland to talk to the engineers. The engineers were meeting in
Cleveland. I was supposed to persuade them not to do what they are
going to do. I took United's 4:45 from LaGuardia arriving in Cleveland
at 6:13. Cleveland is dark blue at that hour. I went directly to the motel,
where the engineers were meeting. Hundreds of engineers attended the
Cleveland meeting. I noticed many fractures among the engineers,
bandages, traction. I noticed what appeared to be fracture of the carpal
scraphoid in six examples. I noticed numerous fractures of the humeral
shaft, of the os calcis, of the pelvic girdle. I noticed a high incidence of
clay-shoveller's fracture. I could not account for these fractures. The
engineers were making calculations, taking measurements, sketching
on the blackboard, drinking beer, throwing bread, buttonholing em-
ployers, hurling glasses into the fireplace. They were friendly.

They were friendly. They were full of love and information. The chief
engineer wore shades. Patella in Monk's traction, clamshell fracture by
the look of it. He was standing in a slum of beer bottles and microphone
cable. "Have some of this chicken à la Isambard Kingdom Brunel the
Great Ingineer," he said. "And declare who you are and what we can
do for you. What is your line, distinguished guest?"

"Software," I said. "In every sense. I am here representing a small
group of interested parties. We are interested in your thing, which seems
to be functioning. In the midst of so much dysfunction, function is
interesting. Other people's things don't seem to be working. The State
Department's thing doesn't seem to be working. The U.N.'s thing doesn't
seem to be working. The democratic left's thing doesn't seem to be
working. Buddha's thing—"

"Ask us anything about our thing, which seems to be working," the
chief engineer said. "We will open our hearts and heads to you, Software
Man, because we want to be understood and loved by the great lay
public, and have our marvels appreciated by that public, for which we
daily unsung produce tons of new marvels each more life-enhancing
than the last. Ask us anything. Do you want to know about evaporated
thin-film metallurgy? Monolithic and hybrid integrated-circuit processes?
The algebra of inequalities? Optimization theory? Complex high-speed
micro-miniature closed and open loop systems? Fixed variable mathematical cost searches? Epitaxial deposition of semi-conductor materials?
Gross interfaced space gropes? We also have specialists in the cuckoo-
flower, the doctorfish, and the dumdum bullet as these relate to aspects
of today's expanding technology, and they do in the damnedest ways."

I spoke to him then about the war. I said the same things people
always say when they speak against the war. I said that the war was

wrong. I said that large countries should not burn down small countries. I said that the government had made a series of errors. I said that these errors once small and forgivable were now immense and unforgivable. I said that the government was attempting to conceal its original errors under layers of new errors. I said that the government was sick with error, giddy with it. I said that ten thousand of our soldiers had already been killed in pursuit of the government's errors. I said that tens of thousands of the enemy's soldiers and civilians had been killed because of various errors, ours and theirs. I said that we are responsible for errors made in our name. I said that the government should not be allowed to make additional errors.

"Yes, yes," the chief engineer said, "there is doubtless much truth in what you say, but we can't possibly *lose* the war, can we? And stopping is losing, isn't it? The war regarded as a process, stopping regarded as an abort? We don't know *how* to lose a war. That skill is not among our skills. Our array smashes their array, that is what we know. That is the process. That is what is.

"But let's not have any more of this dispiriting downbeat counter-productive talk. I have a few new marvels here I'd like to discuss with you just briefly. A few new marvels that are just about ready to be gaped at by the admiring layman. Consider for instance the area of real-time online computer-controlled wish evaporation. Wish evaporation is going to be crucial in meeting the rising expectations of the world's peoples, which are as you know rising entirely too fast."

I noticed then distributed about the room a great many transverse fractures of the ulna. "The development of the pseudo-ruminant stomach for underdeveloped peoples," he went on, "is one of our interesting things you should be interested in. With the pseudo-ruminant stomach they can chew cuds, that is to say, eat grass. Blue is the most popular color worldwide and for that reason we are working with certain strains of your native Kentucky *Poa pratensis*, or bluegrass, as the staple input for the p/r stomach cycle, which would also give a shot in the arm to our balance-of-payments thing don't you know. . . ." I noticed about me then a great number of metatarsal fractures in banjo splints. "The kangaroo initiative . . . eight hundred thousand harvested last year . . . highest percentage of edible protein of any herbivore yet studied . . ."

"Have new kangaroos been planted?"

The engineer looked at me.

"I intuit your hatred and jealousy of our thing," he said. "The ineffectual always hate our thing and speak of it as anti-human, which is not at all a meaningful way to speak of our thing. Nothing mechanical is alien to me," he said (amber spots making bursts of light in his shades), "because I am human, in a sense, and if I think it up, then 'it' is human too, whatever 'it' may be. Let me tell you, Software Man, we have been damned forbearing in the matter of this little war you declare yourself to be interested in. Function is the cry, and our thing is functioning like crazy. There are things we could do that we have not done. Steps we could take that we have not taken. These steps are, regarded in a certain light, the light of our enlightened self-interest, quite justifiable steps. We could, of course, get irritated. We could, of course, *lose patience*.

"We could, of course, release thousands upon thousands of self-powered crawling-along-the-ground lengths of titanium wire eighteen inches long with a diameter of .0005 centimetres (that is to say, invisible) which, scenting an enemy, climb up his trouser leg and wrap themselves around his neck. We have developed those. They are within our capabilities. We could, of course, release in the arena of the upper air our new improved pufferfish toxin which precipitates an identity crisis. No special technical problems there. That is almost laughably easy. We could, of course, place up to two million maggots in their rice within twenty-four hours. The maggots are ready, massed in secret staging areas in Alabama. We have hypodermic darts capable of piebalding the enemy's pigmentation. We have rots, blights, and rusts capable of attacking his alphabet. Those are dandies. We have a hut-shrinking chemical which penetrates the fibres of the bamboo, causing it, the hut, to strangle its occupants. This operates only after 10 P.M., when people are sleeping. Their mathematics are at the mercy of a suppurating surd we have invented. We have a family of fishes trained to attack their fishes. We have the deadly testicle-destroying telegram. The cable-companies are coöperating. We have a green substance that, well, I'd rather not talk about. We have a secret word that, if pronounced, produces multiple fractures in all living things in an area the size of four football fields."

"That's why—"

"Yes. Some damned fool couldn't keep his mouth shut. The point is that the whole structure of enemy life is within our power to *rend, vitiate, devour,* and *crush.* But that's not the interesting thing."

"You recount these possibilities with uncommon relish."

"Yes I realize that there is too much relish here. But *you* must realize that these capabilities represent in and of themselves highly technical and complex and interesting problems and hurdles on which our boys have expended many thousands of hours of hard work and brilliance. And that the effects are often grossly exaggerated by irresponsible victims. And that the whole thing represents a fantastic series of triumphs for the multi-disciplined problem-solving team concept."

"I appreciate that."

"We *could* unleash all this technology at once. You can imagine what would happen then. But that's not the interesting thing."

"What is the interesting thing?"

"The interesting thing is that we have a *moral sense.* It is on punched cards, perhaps the most advanced and sensitive moral sense the world has ever known."

"Because it is on punched cards?"

"It considers all conisderations in endless and subtle detail," he said.

"It even quibbles. With this great new moral tool, how can we go wrong? I confidently predict that, although we *could* employ all this splendid new weaponry I've been telling you about, *we're not going to do it.*"

"We're not going to do it?"

I took United's 5:44 from Cleveland arriving at Newark at 7:19. New Jersey is bright pink at that hour. Living things move about the surface of New Jersey at that hour molesting each other only in traditional ways. I made my report to the group. I stressed the friendliness of the engineers. I said, It's all right. I said, We have a moral sense. I said, *We're not going to do it.* They didn't believe me.

## FOR DISCUSSION

1. What are the general tone and mood of the story? How does the author's selection of words and phrases contribute to tone and mood?
2. Why does the "Software Man" go to Cleveland to take issue with the engineers? What war is the narrator opposed to? To what sort of group does he belong? Is it ironic that he is opposed to the war?
3. "Do your own thing" was a catch phrase of the late 1960s and early 1970s. How does this story make fun of "doing your own thing"?
4. What do you make of the statement, "I noticed many fractures among the engineers, bandages, traction"? Is the narrator really talking about broken bones?
5. What specific segments of American society is Barthelme satirizing? Is he any harder on one group than another?
6. Compare the ending of the story with its beginning. What has changed, if anything? What are the implications for the future?
7. Barthelme's brief fictional pieces have been called bumper sticker stories. What do you think this means? Can this piece be called a bumper sticker story?
8. Consider the story's proliferation of scientific terms. Did you look any of them up? Do you think the reader must know the meaning of the terms in order to get the point of the story's satire? Would such knowledge make any other contribution to your appreciation of the story?
9. Although this story is in many ways a fantasy—that is, it presents unbelievable people in an unbelievable situation—does it still manage to deal with some real problems in modern society? What are some of these problems?
10. Do you think this is a funny story? What are the sources of its humor?

# Powerhouse

EUDORA WELTY

Powerhouse is playing!

He's here on tour from the city—"Powerhouse and His Keyboard"—
"Powerhouse and His Tasmanians"—think of the things he calls himself!
There's no one in the world like him. You can't tell what he is. "Nigger
man"?—he looks more Asiatic, monkey, Jewish, Babylonian, Peruvian,
fanatic, devil. He has pale gray eyes, heavy lids, maybe horny like a
lizard's, but big glowing eyes when they're open. He has African feet
of the greatest size, stomping, both together, on each side of the pedals.
He's not coal black—beverage colored—looks like a preacher when his
mouth is shut, but then it opens—vast and obscene. And his mouth is
going every minute: like a monkey's when it looks for something.
Improvising, coming on a light and childish melody—*smooch*—he loves
it with his mouth.

Is it possible that he could be this! When you have him there performing for you, that's what you feel. You know people on a stage—
and people of a darker race—so likely to be marvelous, frightening.

This is a white dance. Powerhouse is not a show-off like the Harlem
boys, not drunk, not crazy—he's in a trance; he's a person of joy, a
fanatic. He listens as much as he performs, a look of hideous, powerful
rapture on his face. Big arched eyebrows that never stop traveling, like
a Jew's—wandering-Jew eyebrows. When he plays he beats down piano
and seat and wears them away. He is in motion every moment—what
could be more obscene? There he is with his great head, fat stomach,
and little round piston legs, and long yellow-sectioned strong big fingers,
at rest about the size of bananas. Of course you know how he sounds—
you've heard him on records—but still you need to see him. He's going
all the time, like skating around the skating rink or rowing a boat. It
makes everybody crowd around, here in this shadowless steel-trussed
hall with the rose-like posters of Nelson Eddy and the testimonial for
the mind-reading horse in handwriting magnified five hundred times.
Then all quietly he lays his finger on a key with the promise and serenity
of a sibyl touching the book.[1]

Powerhouse is so monstrous he sends everybody into oblivion. When
any group, any performers, come to town, don't people always come
out and hover near, leaning inward about them, to learn what it is?
What is it? Listen. Remember how it was with the acrobats. Watch them
carefully, hear the least word, especially what they say to one another,
in another language—don't let them escape you; it's the only time for
hallucination, the last time. They can't stay. They'll be somewhere else
this time tomorrow.

[1] A prophetess; she can read from the book without opening it.

Powerhouse has as much as possible done by signals. Everybody, laughing as if to hide a weakness, will sooner or later hand him up a written request. Powerhouse reads each one, studying with a secret face: that is the face which looks like a mask—anybody's; there is a moment when he makes a decision. Then a light slides under his eyelids, and he says, "92!" or some combination of figures—never a name. Before a number the band is all frantic, misbehaving, pushing, like children in a schoolroom, and he is the teacher getting silence. His hands over the keys, he says sternly, "You-all ready? You-all ready to do some serious walking?"—waits—then, STAMP. Quiet. STAMP, for the second time. This is absolute. Then a set of rhythmic kicks against the floor to communicate the tempo. Then, O Lord! say the distended eyes from beyond the boundary of the trumpets, Hello and good-bye, and they are all down the first note like a waterfall.

This note marks the end of any known discipline. Powerhouse seems to abandon them all—he himself seems lost—down in the song, yelling up like somebody in a whirlpool—not guiding them—hailing them only. But he knows, really. He cries out, but he must know exactly. "Mercy! . . . What I say! . . . Yeah!" And then drifting, listening—"Where that skin beater?"—wanting drums, and starting up and pouring it out in the greatest delight and brutality. On the sweet pieces such a leer for everybody! He looks down so benevolently upon all our faces and whispers the lyrics to us. And if you could hear him at this moment on "Marie, the Dawn is Breaking"! He's going up the keyboard with a few fingers in some very derogatory triplet-routine, he gets higher and higher, and then he looks over the end of the piano, as if over a cliff. But not in a show-off way—the song makes him do it.

He loves the way they all play, too—all those next to him. The far section of the band is all studious, wearing glasses, every one—they don't count. Only those playing around Powerhouse are the real ones. He has a bass fiddler from Vicksburg, black as pitch, named Valentine, who plays with his eyes shut and talking to himself, very young: Powerhouse has to keep encouraging him. "Go on, go on, give it up, bring it on out there!" When you heard him like that on records, did you know he was really pleading?

He calls Valentine out to take a solo.

"What you going to play?" Powerhouse looks out kindly from behind the piano; he opens his mouth and shows his tongue, listening.

Valentine looks down, drawing against his instrument, and says without a lip movement, " 'Honeysuckle Rose.' "

He has a clarinet player named Little Brother, and loves to listen to anything he does. He'll smile and say, "Beautiful!" Little Brother takes a step forward when he plays and stands at the very front, with the whites of his eyes like fishes swimming. Once when he played a low note, Powerhouse muttered a dirty praise, "He went clear downstairs to get that one!"

After a long time, he holds up the number of fingers to tell the band how many choruses still to go—usually five. He keeps his directions down to signals.

It's a bad night outside. It's a white dance, and nobody dances, except a few straggling jitterbugs and two elderly couples. Everybody just stands around the band and watches Powerhouse. Sometimes they steal glances at one another, as if to say, Of course, you know how it is with *them*—Negroes—band leaders—they would play the same way, giving all they've got, for an audience of one. . . . When somebody, no matter who, gives everything, it makes people feel ashamed for him.

Late at night they play the one waltz they will ever consent to play— by request, "Pagan Love Song." Powerhouse's head rolls and sinks like a weight between his waving shoulders. He groans, and his fingers drag into the keys heavily, holding on to the notes, retrieving. It is a sad song.

"You know what happened to me?" says Powerhouse.

Valentine hums a response, dreaming at the bass.

"I got a telegram my wife is dead," says Powerhouse, with wandering fingers.

"Uh-huh?"

His mouth gathers and forms a barbarous O while his fingers walk up straight, unwillingly, three octaves.

"Gypsy? Why how come her to die, didn't you just phone her up in the night last night long distance?"

"Telegram say—here the words: Your wife is dead." He puts 4/4 over the 3/4.

"Not but four words?" This is the drummer, an unpopular boy named Scoot, a disbelieving maniac.

Powerhouse is shaking his vast cheeks. "What the hell was she trying to do? What was she up to?"

"What name has it got signed, if you got a telegram?" Scoot is spitting away with those wire brushes.

Little Brother, the clarinet player, who cannot now speak, glares and tilts back.

"Uranus Knockwood is the name signed." Powerhouse lifts his eyes open. "Ever heard of him?" A bubble shoots out on his lip like a plate on a counter.

Valentine is beating slowly on with his palm and scratching the strings with his long blue nails. He is fond of a waltz, Powerhouse interrupts him.

"I don't know him. Don't know who he is." Valentine shakes his head with the closed eyes.

"Say it again."

"Uranus Knockwood."

"That ain't Lenox Avenue."

"It ain't Broadway."

"Ain't ever seen it wrote out in any print, even for horse racing."

"Hell, that's on a star, boy, ain't it?" Crash of the cymbals.

"What the hell was she up to?" Powerhouse shudders. "Tell me, tell me, tell me." He makes triplets, and begins a new chorus. He holds three fingers up.

"You say you got a telegram." This is Valentine, patient and sleepy, beginning again.

Powerhouse is elaborate. "Yas, the time I go out, go way downstairs along a long cor-ri-dor to where they puts us: coming back along the cor-ri-dor: steps out and hands me a telegram: Your wife is dead."

"Gypsy?" The drummer like a spider over his drums.

"Aaaaaaaaa!" shouts Powerhouse, flinging out both powerful arms for three whole beats to flex his muscles, then kneading a dough of bass notes. His eyes glitter. He plays the piano like a drum sometimes— why not?

"Gypsy? Such a dancer?"

"Why you don't hear it straight from your agent? Why it ain't come from headquarters? What you been doing, getting telegrams in the *corridor*, signed nobody?"

They all laugh. End of that chorus.

"What time is it?" Powerhouse calls. "What the hell place is this? Where is my watch and chain?"

"I hang it on you," whimpers Valentine. "It still there."

There it rides on Powerhouse's great stomach, down where he can never see it.

"Sure did hear some clock striking twelve while ago. Must be *midnight*."

"It going to be intermission," Powerhouse declares, lifting up his finger with the signet ring.

He draws the chorus to an end. He pulls a big Northern hotel towel out of the deep pocket in his vast, special-cut tux pants and pushes his forehead into it.

"If she went and killed herself!" he says with a hidden face. "If she up and jumped out that window!" He gets to his feet, turning vaguely, wearing the towel on his head.

"Ha, ha!"

"Sheik, sheik!"

"She wouldn't do that." Little Brother sets down his clarinet like a precious vase, and speaks. He still looks like an East Indian queen, implacable, divine, and full of snakes. "You ain't going to expect people doing what they says over long distance."

"Come on!" roars Powerhouse. He is already at the back door, he has pulled it wide open, and with a wild, gathered-up face is smelling the terrible night.

Powerhouse, Valentine, Scoot and Little Brother step outside into the drenching rain.

"Well, they emptying buckets," says Powerhouse in a mollified voice.

On the street he holds his hands out and turns up the blanched palms like sieves.

A hundred dark, ragged, silent, delighted Negroes have come around from under the eaves of the hall, and follow wherever they go.

"Watch out Little Brother don't shrink," says Powerhouse. "You just the right size now, clarinet don't suck you in. You got a dry throat, Little Brother, you in the desert?" He reaches into the pocket and pulls out a paper of mints. "Now hold 'em in your mouth—don't chew 'em. I don't carry around nothing without limit."

"Go in that joint and have beer," says Scoot, who walks ahead.

"Beer? Beer? You know what beer is? What do they say is beer? What's beer? Where I been?"

"Down yonder where it say World Café—that do." They are in Negrotown now.

Valentine patters over and holds open a screen door warped like a sea shell, bitter in the wet, and they walk in, stained darker with the rain and leaving footprints. Inside, sheltered dry smells stand like screens around a table covered with a red-checkered cloth, in the center of which flies hang onto an obelisk-shaped ketchup bottle. The midnight walls are checkered again with admonishing "Not Responsible" signs and black-figured, smoky calendars. It is a waiting, silent, limp room. There is a burned-out-looking nickelodeon and right beside it a long-necked wall instrument labeled "Business Phone, Don't Keep Talking." Circled phone numbers are written up everywhere. There is a worn-out peacock feather hanging by a thread to an old, thin, pink, exposed light bulb, where it slowly turns around and around, whoever breathes.

A waitress watches.

"Come here, living statue, and get all this big order of beer we fixing to give."

"Never seen you before anywhere." The waitress moves and comes forward and slowly shows little gold leaves and tendrils over her teeth. She shoves up her shoulders and breasts. "How I going to know who you might be? Robbers? Coming in out of the black of night right at midnight, setting down so big at my table?"

"Boogers," says Powerhouse, his eyes opening lazily as in a cave.

The girl screams delicately with pleasure. O Lord, she likes talk and scares.

"Where you going to find enough beer to put out on this here table?"

She runs to the kitchen with bent elbows and sliding steps.

"Here's a million nickels," says Powerhouse, pulling his hand out of his pocket and sprinkling coins out, all but the last one, which he makes vanish like a magician.

Valentine and Scoot take the money over to the nickelodeon, which looks as battered as a slot machine, and read all the names of the records out loud.

"Whose 'Tuxedo Junction'?" asks Powerhouse.

"You know whose."

"Nickelodeon, I request you please to play 'Empty Bed Blues' and let Bessie Smith sing."

Silence: they hold it like a measure.

"Bring me all those nickels on back here," says Powerhouse. "Look at that! What you tell me. the name of this place?"

"White dance, week night, raining, Alligator, Mississippi, long ways from home."

"Uh-huh."

"Sent for You Yesterday and Here You Come Today" plays.

The waitress, setting the tray of beer down on a back table, comes up taut and apprehensive as a hen. "Says.in the kitchen, back there putting their eyes to little hole peeping out, that you is Mr. Powerhouse. . . . They knows from a picture they seen."

"They seeing right tonight, that is him," says Little Brother.

"You him?"

"That is him in the flesh," says Scoot.

"Does you wish to touch him?" asks Valentine. "Because he don't bite."

"You passing through?"

"Now you got everything right."

She waits like a drop, hands languishing together in front.

"Little-Bit, ain't you going to bring the beer?"

She brings it, and goes behind the cash register and smiles, turning different ways. The little fillet of gold in her mouth is gleaming.

"The Mississippi River's here," she says once.

Now all the watching Negroes press in gently and bright-eyed through the door, as many as can get in. One is a little boy in a straw sombrero which has been coated with aluminum paint all over.

Powerhouse, Valentine, Scoot and Little Brother drink beer, and their eyelids come together like curtains. The wall and the rain and the humble beautiful waitress waiting on them and the other Negroes watching enclose them.

"Listen!" whispers Powerhouse, looking into the ketchup bottle and slowly spreading his performer's hand over the damp, wrinkling cloth with the red squares. "Listen how it is. My wife gets missing me. Gypsy. She goes to the window. She looks out and.sees you know what. Street. Sign saying Hotel. People walking. Somebody looks up. Old man. She looks down, out the window. Well? . . . Sssssst! Plooey! What she do? Jump out and bust her brains all over the world."

He opens his eyes.

"That's it," agrees Valentine. "You gets a telegram."

"Sure she misses you," Little Brother adds.

"No, it's night time." How softly he tells them! "Sure. It's the night time. She say, What do I hear? Footsteps walking up the hall? That him? Footsteps go on off. It's not me. I'm in Alligator, Mississippi, she's crazy. Shaking all over. Listens till her ears and all grow out like old music-box horns but still she can't hear a thing. She says, All right! I'll jump out the window then. Got on her nightgown. I know that nightgown, and her thinking there. Says, Ho hum, all right, and jumps out the window. Is she mad at me? Is she crazy! She don't leave *nothing* behind her!"

"Ya! Ha!"

"Brains and insides everywhere, Lord, Lord."

All the watching Negroes stir in their delight, and to their higher delight he says affectionately. "Listen! Rats in here."

"That must be the way, boss."

"Only, naw, Powerhouse, that ain't true. That sound too *bad.*"

"Does? I even know who finds her," cries Powerhouse. "That no-good pussyfooted crooning creeper, that creeper that follow around after me, coming up like weeds behind me, following around after me everything I do and messing around on the trail I leave. Bets my numbers, sings my songs, gets close to my agent like a Betsybug; when I going out he just coming in. I got him now! I got my eye on him."

"Know who he is?"

"Why, it's that old Uranus Knockwood!"

"Ya! Ha!"

"Yeah, and he coming now, he going to find Gypsy. There he is, coming around that corner, and Gypsy kadoodling down, oh-oh, watch out! *Ssssst! Plooey!* See, there she is in her little old nightgown, and her insides and brains all scattered round."

A sigh fills the room.

"Hush about her brains. Hush about her insides."

"Ya! Ha! You talking about her brains and insides—old Uranus Knockwood," says Powerhouse, "look down and say Jesus! He say, Look here what I'm walking round in!"

They all burst into halloos of laughter. Powerhouse's face looks like a big hot iron stove.

"Why, he picks her up and carries her off!" he says.

"Ya! Ha!"

"Carries her *back* around the corner. . . ."

"Oh, Powerhouse!"

"You know him."

"Uranus Knockwood!"

"Yeahhh!"

"He take our wives when we gone!"

"He come in when we goes out!"

"Uh-huh!"

"He go out when we comes in!"

"Yeahhh!"

"He standing behind the door!"

"Ol Uranus Knockwood."

"You know him."

"Middle-size man."

"Wears a hat."

"That's him."

Everybody in the room moans with pleasure. The little boy in the fine silver hat opens a paper and divides out a jelly roll among his followers.

And out of the breathless ring somebody moves forward like a slave, leading a great logy Negro with bursting eyes, and says, "This here is Sugar-Stick Thompson, that dove down to the bottom of July Creek and pulled up all those drowned white people fall out of a boat. Last summer, pulled up fourteen."

"Hello," says Powerhouse, turning and looking around at them all with his great daring face until they nearly suffocate.

Sugar-Stick, their instrument, cannot speak; he can only look back at the others.

"Can't even swim. Done it by holding his breath," says the fellow with the hero.

Powerhouse looks at him seekingly.

"I his half brother," the fellow puts in.

They step back.

"Gypsy say," Powerhouse rumbles gently again, looking at *them,* " 'What is the use? I'm gonna jump out so far—so far. . . .' *Ssssst—!''*

"Don't, boss, don't do it again," says Little Brother.

"It's awful," says the waitress. "I hates that Mr. Knockwoods. All that the truth?"

"Want to see the telegram I got from him?" Powerhouse's hand goes to the vast pocket.

"Now wait, now wait, boss." They all watch him.

"It must be the real truth," says the waitress, sucking in her lower lip, her luminous eyes turning sadly, seeking the windows.

"No, babe, it ain't the truth." His eyebrows fly up, and he begins to whisper to her out of his vast oven mouth. His hand stays in his pocket. "Truth is something worse, I ain't said what, yet. It's something hasn't come to me, but I ain't saying it won't. And when it does, then want me to tell you?" He sniffs all at once, his eyes come open and turn up, almost too far. He is dreamily smiling.

"Don't, boss, don't Powerhouse!"

"Oh!" the waitress screams.

"Go on git out of here!" bellows Powerhouse, taking his hand out of his pocket and clapping after her red dress.

The ring of watchers breaks and falls away.

"*Look* at that! Intermission is up," says Powerhouse.

He folds money under a glass, and after they go out, Valentine leans back in and drops a nickel in the nickelodeon behind them, and it lights up and begins to play "The Goona Goo." The feather dangles still.

"Take a telegram!" Powerhouse shouts suddenly up into the rain over the street. "Take a answer. Now what was that name?"

They get a little tired.

"Uranus Knockwood."

"You ought to know."

"Yas? Spell it to me."

They spell it all the ways it could be spelled. It puts them in a wonderful humor.

"Here's the answer. I got it right here. 'What in the hell you talking about? Don't make any difference: I gotcha.' Name signed: Power-house."

"That going to reach him, Powerhouse?" Valentine speaks in a maternal voice.

"Yas, yas."

All hushing, following him up the dark street at a distance, like old rained-on black ghosts, the Negroes are afraid they will die laughing.

Powerhouse throws back his vast head into the steaming rain, and a look of hopeful desire seems to blow somehow like a vapor from his own dilated nostrils over his face and bring a mist to his eyes.

"Reach him and come out the other side."

"That's it, Powerhouse, that's it. You got him now."

Powerhouse lets out a long sigh.

"But ain't you going back there to call up Gypsy long distance, the way you did last night in that other place? I seen a telephone. . . . Just to see if she there at home?"

There is a measure of silence. That is one crazy drummer that's going to get his neck broken some day.

"No," growls Powerhouse. "No! How many thousand times tonight I got to say No?"

He holds up his arm in the rain.

"You sure-enough unroll your voice some night, it about reach up yonder to her," says Little Brother, dismayed.

They go on up the street, shaking the rain off and on them like birds.

Back in the dance hall, they play "San" (99). The jitterbugs start up like windmills stationed over the floor, and in their orbits—one circle, another, a long stretch and a zigzag—dance the elderly couples with old smoothness, undisturbed and stately.

When Powerhouse first came back from intermission, no doubt full of beer, they said, he got the band tuned up again in his own way. He didn't strike the piano keys for pitch—he simply opened his mouth and gave falsetto howls—in A, D and so on—they tuned by him. Then he took hold of the piano, as if he saw it for the first time in his life, and tested it for strength, hit it down in the bass, played an octave with his elbow, lifted the top, looked inside, and leaned against it with all his might. He sat down and played it for a few minutes with outrageous force and got it under his power—a bass deep and coarse as a sea net—then produced something glimmering and fragile, and smiled. And who could ever remember any of the things he says? They are just inspired remarks that roll out of his mouth like smoke.

They've requested "Somebody Loves Me," and he's already done twelve or fourteen choruses, piling them up nobody knows how, and it will be a wonder if he ever gets through. Now and then he calls and shouts, " 'Somebody loves me! Somebody loves me. I wonder who!' " His mouth gets to be nothing but a volcano. "I wonder who!"

"Maybe . . ." He uses all his right hand on a trill.

"Maybe . . ." He pulls back his spread fingers, and looks out upon the place where he is. A vast, impersonal and yet furious grimace transfigures his wet face.

". . . Maybe it's you!"

## FOR DISCUSSION

1. From what point of view is this story written?
2. The prevailing mood of the story is closely akin to the blues. What does Powerhouse have to be blue about?
3. Can you distinguish between the author's tone and the story's mood and atmosphere?
4. Why is Powerhouse such an intriguing character? How does his appeal to the white people at the dance differ from his appeal to the black people at the World Café?
5. Does the name of the World Café have any symbolic significance?
6. What is Powerhouse's marital status? Did he really have a wife named Gypsy? Did she really commit suicide by jumping out of the window?
7. At one point Powerhouse says that his story about Gypsy "ain't the truth." Then he says, "Truth is something worse, I ain't said what, yet. It's something hasn't come to me, but I ain't saying it won't." What is this greater truth that Powerhouse seems to be hinting at?
8. To what extent does Powerhouse hide his inner emotions behind a public image? How does his "white" public image differ from his "black" public image? In what specific ways is his real personality dramatized?
9. Who is Uranus Knockwood? Consider the significance of his first and last names, and what Powerhouse says about him.
10. It is almost impossible to read this story without viewing Powerhouse as a human symbol. What do you think this larger-than-life black man symbolizes?

# A Summer Tragedy

ARNA BONTEMPS

Old Jeff Patton, the black share farmer, fumbled with his bow tie. His fingers trembled and the high stiff collar pinched his throat. A fellow loses his hand for such vanities after thirty or forty years of simple life. Once a year, or maybe twice if there's a wedding among his kinfolks, he may spruce up; but generally fancy clothes do nothing but adorn the wall of the big room and feed the moths. That had been Jeff Patton's experience. He had not worn his stiff-bosomed shirt more than a dozen times in all his married life. His swallow-tailed coat lay on the bed beside him, freshly brushed and pressed, but it was as full of holes as the overalls in which he worked on weekdays. The moths had used it badly. Jeff twisted his mouth into a hideous toothless grimace as he contended with the obstinate bow. He stamped his good foot and decided to give up the struggle.

"Jennie," he called.

"What's that, Jeff?" His wife's shrunken voice came out of the adjoining room like an echo. It was hardly bigger than a whisper.

"I reckon you'll have to he'p me wid this heah bow tie, baby," he said meekly. "Dog if I can hitch it up."

Her answer was not strong enough to reach him, but presently the old woman came to the door, feeling her way with a stick. She had a wasted, dead-leaf appearance. Her body, as scrawny and gnarled as a string bean, seemed less than nothing in the ocean of frayed and faded petticoats that surrounded her. These hung an inch or two above the tops of her heavy unlaced shoes and showed little grotesque piles where the stockings had fallen down from her negligible legs.

"You oughta could do a heap mo' wid a thing like that'n me—beingst as you got yo' good sight."

"Looks like I oughta could," he admitted. "But ma fingers is gone democrat on me. I get all mixed up in the looking glass an' can't tell wicha way to twist the devilish thing."

Jennie sat on the side of the bed and old Jeff Patton got down on one knee while she tied the bow knot. It was a slow and painful ordeal for each of them in this position. Jeff's bones cracked, his knee ached, and it was only after a half dozen attempts that Jennie worked a semblance of a bow into the tie.

"I got to dress maself now," the old woman whispered. "These is ma old shoes an' stockings, and I ain't so much as unwrapped ma dress."

"Well, don't worry 'bout me no mo', baby," Jeff said. "That 'bout finishes me. All I gotta do now is slip on that old coat 'n ves' an' I'll be fixed to leave."

Jennie disappeared again through the dim passage into the shed room. Being blind was no handicap to her in that black hole. Jeff heard the cane placed against the wall beside the door and knew that his wife was on easy ground. He put on his coat, took a battered top hat from the bedpost and hobbled to the front door. He was ready to travel. As soon as Jennie could get on her Sunday shoes and her old black silk dress, they would start.

Outside the tiny log house, the day was warm and mellow with sunshine. A host of wasps were humming with busy excitement in the trunk of a dead sycamore. Gray squirrels were searching through the grass for hickory nuts and blue jays were in the trees, hopping from branch to branch. Pine woods stretched away to the left like a black sea. Among them were scattered scores of log houses like Jeff's, houses of black share farmers. Cows and pigs wandered freely among the trees. There was no danger of loss. Each farmer knew his own stock and knew his neighbor's as well as he knew his neighbor's children.

Down the slope to the right were the cultivated acres on which the colored folks worked. They extended to the river, more than two miles away, and they were today green with the unmade cotton crop. A tiny thread of a road, which passed directly in front of Jeff's place, ran through these green fields like a pencil mark.

Jeff, standing outside the door, with his absurd hat in his left hand, surveyed the wide scene tenderly. He had been forty-five years on these acres. He loved them with the unexplained affection that others have for the countries to which they belong.

The sun was hot on his head, his collar still pinched his throat, and the Sunday clothes were intolerably hot. Jeff transferred the hat to his right hand and began fanning with it. Suddenly the whisper that was Jennie's voice came out of the shed room.

"You can bring the car round front whilst you's waitin'," it said feebly. There was a tired pause; then it added, "I'll soon be fixed to go."

"A'right, baby," Jeff answered. "I'll get it in a minute."

But he didn't move. A thought struck him that made his mouth fall open. The mention of the car brought to his mind, with new intensity, the trip he and Jennie were about to take. Fear came into his eyes; excitement took his breath. Lord, Jesus!

"Jeff . . . O Jeff," the old woman's whisper called.

He awakened with a jolt. "Hunh, baby?"

"What you doin'?"

"Nuthin. Jes studyin'. I jes been turnin' things round'n round in ma mind."

"You could be gettin' the car," she said.

"Oh yes, right away, baby."

He started round to the shed, limping heavily on his bad leg. There were three frizzly chickens in the yard. All his other chickens had been killed or stolen recently. But the frizzly chickens had been saved some-how. That was fortunate indeed, for these curious creatures had a way of devouring "Poison" from the yard and in that way protecting against conjure and black luck and spells. But even the frizzly chickens seemed now to be in a stupor. Jeff thought they had some ailment; he expected all three of them to die shortly.

The shed in which the old T-model Ford stood was only a grass roof held up by four corner poles. It had been built by tremulous hands at a time when the little rattletrap car had been regarded as a peculiar treasure. And, miraculously, despite wind and downpour it still stood.

Jeff adjusted the crank and put his weight upon it. The engine came to life with a sputter and bang that rattled the old car from radiator to taillight. Jeff hopped into the seat and put his foot on the accelerator. The sputtering and banging increased. The rattling became more violent. That was good. It was good banging, good sputtering and rattling, and it meant that the aged car was still in running condition. She could be depended on for this trip.

Again Jeff's thought halted as if paralyzed. The suggestion of the trip fell into the machinery of his mind like a wrench. He felt dazed and weak. He swung the car out into the yard, made a half turn and drove around to the front door. When he took his hands off the wheel, he noticed that he was trembling violently. He cut off the motor and climbed to the ground to wait for Jennie.

A few minutes later she was at the window, her voice rattling against the pane like a broken shutter.

"I'm ready, Jeff."

He did not answer, but limped into the house and took her by the arm. He led her slowly through the big room, down the step and across the yard.

"You reckon I'd oughta lock the do'?" he asked softly.

They stopped and Jennie weighed the question. Finally she shook her head.

"Ne' mind the do'," she said. "I don't see no cause to lock up things."

"You right," Jeff agreed. "No cause to lock up."

Jeff opened the door and helped his wife into the car. A quick shudder passed over him. Jesus! Again he trembled.

"How come you shaking so?" Jennie whispered.

"I don't know," he said.

"You mus' be scairt, Jeff."

"No, baby, I ain't scairt."

He slammed the door after her and went around to crank up again. The motor started easily. Jeff wished that it had not been so responsive. He would have liked a few more minutes in which to turn things around in his head. As it was, with Jennie chiding him about being afraid, he had to keep going. He swung the car into the little pencil-mark road and started off toward the river, driving very slowly, very cautiously.

Chugging across the green countryside, the small battered Ford seemed tiny indeed. Jeff felt a familiar excitement, a thrill, as they came down the first slope to the immense levels on which the cotton was growing. He could not help reflecting that the crops were good. He knew what that meant, too; he had made forty-five of them with his own hands. It was true that he had worn out nearly a dozen mules, but that was the fault of old man Stevenson, the owner of the land. Major Stevenson had the odd notion that one mule was all a share farmer needed to work a thirty-acre plot. It was an expensive notion, the way it killed mules from overwork, but the old man held to it. Jeff thought it killed a good many share farmers as well as mules, but he had no sympathy for them. He had always been strong, and he had been taught to have no patience with weakness in men. Women or children might be tolerated if they were puny, but a weak man was a curse. Of course, his own children—

Jeff's thought halted there. He and Jennie never mentioned their dead children any more. And naturally he did not wish to dwell upon them in his mind. Before he knew it, some remark would slip out of his mouth and that would make Jennie feel blue. Perhaps she would cry. A woman like Jennie could not easily throw off the grief that comes from losing five grown children within two years. Even Jeff was still staggered by the blow. His memory had not been much good recently. He frequently talked to himself. And, although he had kept it a secret, he knew that his courage had left him. He was terrified by the least unfamiliar sound at night. He was reluctant to venture far from home in the daytime. And that habit of trembling when he felt fearful was now far beyond his control. Sometimes he became afraid and trembled without knowing what had frightened him. The feeling would just come over him like a chill.

The car rattled slowly over the dusty road. Jennie sat erect and silent, with a little absurd hat pinned to her hair. Her useless eyes seemed very large, very white in their deep sockets. Suddenly Jeff heard her voice, and he inclined his head to catch the words.

"Is we passed Delia Moore's house yet?" she asked.

"Not yet," he said.

"You must be drivin' mighty slow, Jeff."

"We might just as well take our time, baby."

There was a pause. A little puff of steam was coming out of the radiator of the car. Heat wavered above the hood. Delia Moore's house was nearly half a mile away. After a moment Jennie spoke again.

"You ain't really scairt, is you, Jeff?"

"Nah, baby, I ain't scairt."

"You know how we agreed—we gotta keep on goin'."

Jewels of perspiration appeared on Jeff's forehead. His eyes rounded, blinded, became fixed on the road.

"I don't know," he said with a shiver. "I reckon it's the only thing to do."

"Hm."

A flock of guinea fowls, pecking in the road, were scattered by the passing car. Some of them took to their wings; others hid under bushes. A blue jay, swaying on a leafy twig, was annoying a roadside squirrel.

Jeff held an even speed till he came near Delia's place. Then he slowed down noticeably.

Delia's house was really no house at all, but an abandoned store building converted into a dwelling. It sat near a crossroads, beneath a single black cedar tree. There Delia, a cattish old creature of Jennie's age, lived alone. She had been there more years than anybody could remember, and long ago had won the disfavor of such women as Jennie. For in her young days Delia had been gayer, yellower and saucier than seemed proper in those parts. Her ways with menfolks had been dark and suspicious. And the fact that she had had as many husbands as children did not help her reputation.

"Yonder's old Delia," Jeff said as they passed.

"What she doin'?"

"Jes sittin' in the do'," he said.

"She see us?"

"Hm," Jeff said. "Musta did."

That relieved Jennie. It strengthened her to know that her old enemy had seen her pass in her best clothes. That would give the old she-devil something to chew her gums and fret about, Jennie thought. Wouldn't she have a fit if she didn't find out? Old evil Delia! This would be just the thing for her. It would pay her back for being so evil. It would also pay her, Jennie thought, for the way she used to grin at Jeff—long ago when her teeth were good.

The road became smooth and red, and Jeff could tell by the smell of the air that they were nearing the river. He could see the rise where the road turned and ran along parallel to the stream. The car chugged on monotonously. After a long silent spell, Jennie leaned against Jeff and spoke.

"How many bale o' cotton you think we got standin'?" she said.

Jeff wrinkled his forehead as he calculated.

" 'Bout twenty-five, I reckon."

"How many you make las' year?"

"Twenty-eight," he said. "How come you ask that?"

"I's jes thinkin'," Jennie said quietly.

"It don't make a speck o' difference though," Jeff reflected. "If we get much or if we get little, we still gonna be in debt to old man Stevenson when he gets through counting up agin us. It's took us a long time to learn that."

Jennie was not listening to these words. She had fallen into a trance-like meditation. Her lips twitched. She chewed her gums and rubbed her gnarled hands nervously. Suddenly she leaned forward, buried her face in the nervous hands and burst into tears. She cried aloud in a dry cracked voice that suggested the rattle of fodder on dead stalks. She cried aloud like a child, for she had never learned to suppress a genuine sob. Her slight old frame shook heavily and seemed hardly able to sustain such violent grief.

"What's the matter, baby?" Jeff asked awkwardly. "Why you cryin'
like all that?"

"I's jes thinkin'," she said.

"So you the one what's scairt now, hunh?"

"I ain't scairt, Jeff. I's jes thinkin' 'bout leavin' eve'thing like this—
eve'thing we been used to. It's right sad-like."

Jeff did not answer, and presently Jennie buried her face again and
cried.

The sun was almost overhead. It beat down furiously on the dusty
wagon-path road, on the parched roadside grass and the tiny battered
car. Jeff's hands, gripping the wheel, became wet with perspiration; his
forehead sparkled. Jeff's lips parted. His mouth shaped a hideous
grimace. His face suggested the face of a man being burned. But the
torture passed and his expression softened again.

"You mustn't cry, baby," he said to his wife. "We gotta be strong.
We can't break down."

Jennie waited a few seconds, then said, "You reckon we oughta do
it, Jeff? You reckon we oughta go 'head an' do it, really?"

Jeff's voice choked; his eyes blurred. He was terrified to hear Jennie
say the thing that had been in his mind all morning. She had egged
him on when he had wanted more than anything in the world to wait,
to reconsider, to think things over a little longer. Now she was getting
cold feet. Actually there was no need of thinking the question through
again. It would only end in making the same painful decision once
more. Jeff knew that. There was no need of fooling around longer.

"We jes as well to do like we planned," he said. "They ain't nothin'
else for us now—it's the bes' thing."

Jeff thought of the handicaps, the near impossibility, of making another crop with his leg bothering him more and more each week. Then
there was always the chance that he would have another stroke, like
the one that had made him lame. Another one might kill him. The least
it could do would be to leave him helpless. Jeff gasped—Lord, Jesus!
He could not bear to think of being helpless, like a baby, on Jennie's
hands. Frail, blind Jennie.

The little pounding motor of the car worked harder and harder. The
puff of steam from the cracked radiator became larger. Jeff realized that
they were climbing a little rise. A moment later the road turned abruptly
and he looked down upon the face of the river.

"Jeff."

"Hunh?"

"Is that the water I hear?"

"Hm. Tha's it."

"Well, which way you goin' now?"

"Down this-a way," he said. "The road runs 'long 'side o' the water
a lil piece."

She waited a while calmly. Then she said, "Drive faster."

"A'right, baby," Jeff said.

The water roared in the bed of the river. It was fifty or sixty feet below the level of the road. Between the road and the water there was a long smooth slope, sharply inclined. The slope was dry, the clay hardened by prolonged summer heat. The water below, roaring in a narrow channel, was noisy and wild.

"Jeff."

"Hunh?"

"How far you goin'?"

"Jes a lil piece down the road."

"You ain't scairt, is you, Jeff?"

"Nah, baby," he said trembling. "I ain't scairt."

"Remember how we planned it, Jeff. We gotta do it like we said. Brave-like."

"Hm."

Jeff's brain darkened. Things suddenly seemed unreal, like figures in a dream. Thoughts swam in his mind foolishly, hysterically, like little blind fish in a pool within a dense cave. They rushed, crossed one another, jostled, collided, retreated and rushed again. Jeff soon became dizzy. He shuddered violently and turned to his wife.

"Jennie, I can't do it. I can't." His voice broke pitifully.

She did not appear to be listening. All the grief had gone from her face. She sat erect, her unseeing eyes wide open, strained and frightful. Her glossy black skin had become dull. She seemed as thin, as sharp and bony, as a starved bird. Now, having suffered and endured the sadness of tearing herself away from beloved things, she showed no anguish. She was absorbed with her own thoughts, and she didn't even hear Jeff's voice shouting in her ear.

Jeff said nothing more. For an instant there was light in his cavernous brain. The great chamber was, for less than a second, peopled by characters he knew and loved. They were simple, healthy creatures, and they behaved in a manner that he could understand. They had quality. But since he had already taken leave of them long ago, the remembrance did not break his heart again. Young Jeff Patton was among them, the Jeff Patton of fifty years ago who went down to New Orleans with a crowd of country boys to the Mardi Gras doings. The gay young crowd, boys with candy-striped shirts and rouged-brown girls in noisy silks, was like a picture in his head. Yet it did not make him sad. On that very trip Slim Burns had killed Joe Beasley—the crowd had been broken up. Since then Jeff Patton's world had been the Greenbriar Plantation. If there had been other Mardi Gras carnivals, he had not heard of them. Since then there had been no time; the years had fallen on him like waves. Now he was old, worn out. Another paralytic stroke (like the one he had already suffered) would put him on his back for keeps. In that condition, with a frail blind woman to look after him, he would be worse off than if he were dead.

Suddenly Jeff's hands became steady. He actually felt brave. He slowed down the motor of the car and carefully pulled off the road.

Below, the water of the stream boomed, a soft thunder in the deep channel. Jeff ran the car onto the clay slope, pointed it directly toward the stream and put his foot heavily on the accelerator. The little car leaped furiously down the steep incline toward the water. The movement was nearly as swift and direct as a fall. The two old black folks, sitting quietly side by side, showed no excitement. In another instant the car hit the water and dropped immediately out of sight.

A little later it lodged in the mud of a shallow place. One wheel of the crushed and upturned little Ford became visible above the rushing water.

## FOR DISCUSSION

1. From what point of view is this story written? Do you see anything inconsistent between the point of view and the fact that the reader does not learn until late in the story what Jeff Patton plans to do?
2. Why do you think the author spends so much time at the beginning of the story presenting ordinary details from the Pattons' daily lives? How important is setting to the story, in particular to its final emotional impact?
3. What is the point of the contrast between the dark interior of the log house and the brighter world outside?
4. What symbolic value can you assign to the frizzly chickens?
5. At what point in the story did you discover that the Pattons intended to take their own lives?
6. List as many specific details as you can that have led the Pattons to their decision.
7. Do you think that either Jeff or Jennie could have committed suicide alone?
8. What purpose do you think Delia Moore serves in the story? What do Jennie's thoughts about Delia reveal?
9. What is ironic about much of the conversation between Jeff and Jennie on the way to the river? How does the conversation contribute to your emotional response to the story?
10. In terms of both religious symbols and everyday life, why do you think the Pattons have chosen the river as the way to end their lives? Why is their choice ironic?
11. Why do you think Jeff recalls his only Mardi Gras just before driving the Model-T into the river?
12. Do you find the Pattons to be plausible characters?
13. Thematically, what do the events of the story suggest about the way old people are often treated in this country?

# The Necklace

GUY DE MAUPASSANT

She was one of those pretty and charming girls who are sometimes, as if by a mistake of destiny, born in a family of clerks. She had no dowry, no expectations, no means of being known, understood, loved, wedded by any rich and distinguished man; and she let herself be married to a little clerk at the Ministry of Public Instruction.

She dressed plainly because she could not dress well, but she was as unhappy as though she had really fallen from her proper station, since with women there is neither case nor rank; and beauty, grace, and charm act instead of family and birth. Natural fineness, instinct for what is elegant, suppleness of wit, are the sole hierarchy, and make from women of the people the equals of the very greatest ladies.

She suffered ceaselessly, feeling herself born for all the delicacies and all the luxuries. She suffered from the poverty of her dwelling, from the wretched look of the walls, from the worn-out chairs, from the ugliness of the curtains. All those things, of which another woman of her rank would never even have been conscious, tortured her and made her angry. The sight of the little Breton peasant who did her humble housework aroused in her regrets which were despairing, and distracted dreams. She thought of the silent antechambers hung with Oriental tapestry, lit by tall bronze candelabra, and of the two great footmen in knee breeches who sleep in the big armchairs, made drowsy by the heavy warmth of the hot-air stove. She thought of the long *salons*[1] fitted up with ancient silk, of the delicate furniture carrying priceless curiosities, and of the coquettish perfumed boudoirs made for talks at five o'clock with intimate friends, with men famous and sought after, whom all women envy and whose attention they all desire.

When she sat down to dinner, before the round table covered with a tablecloth three days old, opposite her husband, who uncovered the soup tureen and declared with an enchanted air, "Ah, the good *pot-au-feu!*[2] I don't know anything better than that," she thought of dainty dinners, of shining silverware, of tapestry which peopled the walls with ancient personages and with strange birds flying in the midst of a fairy forest; and she thought of delicious dishes served on marvelous plates, and of the whispered gallantries which you listen to with a sphinxlike smile, while you are eating the pink flesh of a trout or the wings of a quail.

She had no dresses, no jewels, nothing. And she loved nothing but that; she felt made for that. She would so have liked to please, to be envied, to be charming, to be sought after.

[1]Drawing rooms, used for entertaining distinguished guests.
[2]Stew.

She had a friend, a former schoolmate at the convent, who was rich, and whom she did not like to go and see any more, because she suffered so much when she came back.

But one evening, her husband returned home with a triumphant air, and holding a large envelope in his hand.

"There," said he. "Here is something for you."

She tore the paper sharply, and drew out a printed card which bore these words:

"The Minister of Public Instruction and Mme. Georges Ramponneau request the honor of M. and Mme. Loisel's company at the palace of the Ministry on Monday evening, January eighteenth."

Instead of being delighted, as her husband hoped, she threw the invitation on the table with disdain, murmuring:

"What do you want me to do with that?"

"But, my dear, I thought you would be glad. You never go out, and this is such a fine opportunity. I had awful trouble to get it. Everyone wants to go; it is very select, and they are not giving many invitations to clerks. The whole official world will be there."

She looked at him with an irritated eye, and she said, impatiently:

"And what do you want me to put on my back?"

He had not thought of that; he stammered:

"Why, the dress you go to the theater in. It looks very well, to me."

He stopped, distracted, seeing that his wife was crying. Two great tears descended slowly from the corners of her eyes toward the corners of her mouth. He stuttered:

"What's the matter? What's the matter?"

But, by violent effort, she had conquered her grief, and she replied, with a calm voice, while she wiped her wet cheeks:

"Nothing. Only I have no dress and therefore I can't go to this ball. Give your card to some colleague whose wife is better equipped than I."

He was in despair. He resumed:

"Come, let us see, Mathilde. How much would it cost, a suitable dress, which you could use on other occasions, something very simple?"

She reflected several seconds, making her calculations and wondering also what sum she could ask without drawing on herself an immediate refusal and a frightened exclamation from the economical clerk.

Finally, she replied, hesitatingly:

"I don't know exactly, but I think I could manage it with four hundred francs."

He had grown a little pale, because he was laying aside just that amount to buy a gun and treat himself to a little shooting next summer on the plain of Nanterre, with several friends who went to shoot larks down there, of a Sunday.

But he said:

"All right. I will give you four hundred francs. And try to have a pretty dress."

The day of the ball drew near, and Mme. Loisel seemed sad, uneasy, anxious. Her dress was ready, however. Her husband said to her one evening:

"What is the matter? Come, you've been so queer these last three days."

And she answered:

"It annoys me not to have a single jewel, not a single stone, nothing to put on. I shall look like distress. I should almost rather not go at all."

He resumed:

"You might wear natural flowers. It's very stylish at this time of the year. For ten francs you can get two or three magnificent roses."

She was not convinced.

"No; there's nothing more humiliating than to look poor among other women who are rich."

But her husband cried:

"How stupid you are! Go look up your friend Mme. Forestier, and ask her to lend you some jewels. You're quite thick enough with her to do that."

She uttered a cry of joy:

"It's true. I never thought of it."

The next day she went to her friend and told of her distress.

Mme. Forestier went to a wardrobe with a glass door, took out a large jewel-box, brought it back, opened it, and said to Mme. Loisel:

"Choose, my dear."

She saw first of all some bracelets, then a pearl necklace, then a Venetian cross, gold and precious stones of admirable workmanship. She tried on the ornaments before the glass, hesitated, could not make up her mind to part with them, to give them back. She kept asking:

"Haven't you any more?"

"Why, yes. Look. I don't know what you like."

All of a sudden she discovered, in a black satin box, a superb necklace of diamonds, and her heart began to beat with an immoderate desire. Her hands trembled as she took it. She fastened it around her throat, outside her high-necked dress, and remained lost in ecstasy at the sight of herself.

Then she asked, hesitating, filled with anguish:

"Can you lend me that, only that?"

"Why, yes, certainly."

She sprang upon the neck of her friend, kissed her passionately, then fled with her treasure.

The day of the ball arrived. Mme. Loisel made a great success. She was prettier than them all, elegant, gracious, smiling, and crazy with joy. All the men looked at her, asked her name, endeavored to be introduced. All the attachés of the Cabinet wanted to waltz with her. She was remarked by the minister himself.

She danced with intoxication, with passion, made drunk by pleasure, forgetting all, in the triumph of her beauty, in the glory of her success, in a sort of cloud of happiness composed of all this homage, of all this admiration, of all these awakened desires, and of that sense of complete victory which is so sweet to a woman's heart.

She went away about four o'clock in the morning. Her husband had been sleeping since midnight, in a little deserted anteroom, with three other gentlemen whose wives were having a very good time. He threw over her shoulders the wraps which he had brought, modest wraps of common life, whose poverty contrasted with the elegance of the ball dress. She felt this, and wanted to escape so as not to be remarked by the other women, who were enveloping themselves in costly furs.

Loisel held her back.

"Wait a bit. You will catch cold outside. I will go and call a cab."

But she did not listen to him, and rapidly descended the stairs. When they were in the street they did not find a carriage; and they began to look for one, shouting after the cabmen whom they saw passing by at a distance.

They went down toward the Seine, in despair, shivering with cold. At last they found on the quay one of those ancient noctambulant coupés[3] which, exactly as if they were ashamed to show their misery during the day, are never seen round Paris until after nightfall.

It took them to their door in the Rue des Martyrs, and once more, sadly, they climbed up homeward. All was ended, for her. And as to him, he reflected that he must be at the Ministry at ten o'clock.

She removed the wraps, which covered her shoulders, before the glass, so as once more to see herself in all her glory. But suddenly she uttered a cry. She had no longer the necklace around her neck!

Her husband, already half undressed, demanded:

"What is the matter with you?"

She turned madly towards him:

"I have—I have—I've lost Mme. Forestier's necklace."

He stood up, distracted.

"What!—how?—impossible!"

And they looked in the folds of her dress, in the folds of her cloak, in her pockets, everywhere. They did not find it.

He asked:

"You're sure you had it on when you left the ball?"

"Yes, I felt it in the vestibule of the palace."

"But if you had lost it in the street we should have heard it fall. It must be in the cab."

"Yes. Probably. Did you take his number?"

"No. And you, didn't you notice it?"

"No."

They looked, thunderstruck, at one another. At last Loisel put on his clothes.

[3]A small enclosed horse-drawn carriage.

"I shall go back on foot," said he, "over the whole route which we have taken to see if I can find it."

And he went out. She sat waiting on a chair in her ball dress, without strength to go to bed, overwhelmed, without fire, without a thought.

Her husband came back about seven o'clock. He had found nothing.

He went to Police Headquarters, to the newspaper offices, to offer a reward; he went to the cab companies—everywhere, in fact, whither he was urged by the least suspicion of hope.

She waited all day, in the same condition of mad fear before this terrible calamity.

Loisel returned at night with a hollow, pale face; he had discovered nothing.

"You must write to your friend," said he, "that you have broken the clasp of her necklace and that you are having it mended. That will give us time to turn round."

She wrote at his dictation.

At the end of a week they had lost all hope.

And Loisel, who had aged five years, declared:

"We must consider how to replace that ornament."

The next day they took the box which had contained it, and they went to the jeweler whose name was found within. He consulted his book.

"It was not I, madame, who sold that necklace; I must simply have furnished the case."

Then they went from jeweler to jeweler, searching for a necklace like the other, consulting their memories, sick both of them with chagrin and anguish.

They found, in a shop at the Palais Royal, a string of diamonds which seemed to them exactly like the one they looked for. It was worth forty thousand francs. They could have it for thirty-six.

So they begged the jewelers not to sell it for three days yet. And they made a bargain that he should buy it back for thirty-four thousand francs, in case they found the other one before the end of February.

Loisel possessed eighteen thousand francs which his father had left him. He would borrow the rest.

He did borrow, asking a thousand francs of one, five hundred of another, five louis[4] here, three louis there. He gave notes, took up ruinous obligations, dealt with usurers and all the race of lenders. He compromised all the rest of his life, risked his signature without even knowing if he could meet it, and, frightened by the pains yet to come, by the black misery which was about to fall upon him, by the prospect of all the physical privations and of all the moral tortures which he was to suffer, he went to get the new necklace, putting down upon the merchant's counter thirty-six thousand francs.

When Mme. Loisel took back the necklace, Mme. Forestier said to her, with a chilly manner:

[4]One louis = 20 francs.

"You should have returned it sooner; I might have needed it."

She did not open the case, as her friend had so much feared. If she had detected the substitution, what would she have thought, what would she have said? Would she not have taken Mme. Loisel for a thief?

Mme. Loisel now knew the horrible existence of the needy. She took her part, moreover, all of a sudden, with heroism. That dreadful debt must be paid. She would pay it. They dismissed their servant; they changed their lodgings; they rented a garret under the roof.

She came to know what heavy housework meant and the odious cares of the kitchen. She washed the dishes, using her rosy nails on the greasy pots and pans. She washed the dirty linen, the shirts, and the dishcloths, which she dried upon a line; she carried the slops down to the street every morning, and carried up the water, stopping for breath at every landing. And, dressed like a woman of the people, she went to the fruiterer, the grocer, the butcher, her basket on her arm, bargaining, insulted, defending her miserable money sou by sou.[5]

Each month they had to meet some notes, renew others, obtain more time.

Her husband worked in the evening making a fair copy of some tradesman's accounts, and late at night he often copied manuscript for five sous a page.

And this life lasted for ten years.

At the end of ten years, they had paid everything, everything, with the rates of usury, and the accumulations of the compound interest.

Mme. Loisel looked old now. She had become the woman of impoverished households—strong and hard and rough. With frowsy hair, skirts askew, and red hands, she talked loud while washing the floor with great swishes of water. But sometimes, when her husband was at the office, she sat down near the window, and she thought of that gay evening of long ago, of that ball where she had been so beautiful and so fêted.

What would have happened if she had not lost that necklace? Who knows? Who knows? How life is strange and changeful! How little a thing is needed for us to be lost or to be saved!

But, one Sunday, having gone to take a walk in the Champs Elysées[6] to refresh herself from the labor of the week, she suddenly perceived a woman who was leading a child. It was Mme. Forestier, still young, still beautiful, still charming.

Mme. Loisel felt moved. Was she going to speak to her? Yes, certainly. And now that she had paid, she was going to tell her all about it. Why not?

She went up.

"Good-day, Jeanne."

[5]One franc = 20 sous.
[6]Broad, fashionable boulevard in Paris.

The other, astonished to be familiarly addressed by this plain good-wife, did not recognize her at all, and stammered:

"But—madam!—I do not know—You must be mistaken."

"No. I am Mathilde Loisel."

Her friend uttered a cry.

"Oh, my poor Mathilde! How you are changed!"

"Yes, I have had days hard enough, since I have seen you, days wretched enough—and that because of you!"

"Of me! How so?"

"Do you remember that diamond necklace which you lent me to wear at the ministerial ball?"

"Yes, Well?"

"Well, I lost it."

"What do you mean? You brought it back."

"I brought you back another just like it. And for this we have been ten years paying. You can understand that it was not easy for us, us who had nothing. At last it is ended, and I am very glad."

Mme. Forestier had stopped.

"You say that you bought a necklace of diamonds to replace mine?"

"Yes. You never noticed it, then! They were very like."

And she smiled with a joy which was proud and naïve at once.

Mme. Forestier, strongly moved, took her two hands.

"Oh, my poor Mathilde! Why, my necklace was paste. It was worth at most five hundred francs!"

## FOR DISCUSSION

1. From what narrative point of view is the story told? To what extent are we allowed to know Mme. Loisel's thoughts?
2. How important are the time and social elements of setting—late nineteenth-century, French, middle-class society—to the story? Would we believe such a story were it set in Chicago in the 1950s?
3. What is Mme. Loisel's dominant character trait at the beginning of the story? How does she react to the invitation to the ball? What sort of evening does Mme. Loisel have at the ball? What does this suggest about her understanding of adult society?
4. Once Mme. is resigned to replacing the necklace, what sort of change occurs in her personality? Does the narrator present the new or the former Mme. Loisel as the more sympathetic? How? Her name, Mathilde, means "mighty battle maiden." How does it fit her character?
5. Explain the bitter irony revealed at the conclusion of the story. Is it plausible?
6. What symbolic value can you assign to each necklace?
7. Thematically, what does this story suggest about people who live in different social (economic) classes?
8. Are you bothered that the author has deliberately withheld information so as to make a surprising and ironic ending possible? Do you think this sort of thing is fair to the reader?

# De Mortuis[1]

JOHN COLLIER

Dr. Rankin was a large and rawboned man on whom the newest suit at once appeared outdated, like a suit in a photograph of twenty years ago. This was due to the squareness and flatness of his torso, which might have been put together by a manufacturer of packing cases. His face also had a wooden and a roughly constructed look; his hair was wiglike and resentful of the comb. He had those huge and clumsy hands which can be an asset to a doctor in a small upstate town where people still retain a rural relish for paradox, thinking that the more apelike the paw, the more precise it can be in the delicate business of a tonsillectomy.

This conclusion was perfectly justified in the case of Dr. Rankin. For example, on this particular fine morning, though his task was nothing more ticklish than the cementing over of a large patch on his cellar floor, he managed those large and clumsy hands with all the unflurried certainty of one who would never leave a sponge within or create an unsightly scar without.

The doctor surveyed his handiwork from all angles. He added a touch here and a touch there till he had achieved a smoothness altogether professional. He swept up a few last crumbs of soil and dropped them into the furnace. He paused before putting away the pick and shovel he had been using, and found occasion for yet another artistic sweep of his trowel, which made the new surface precisely flush with the surrounding floor. At this moment of supreme concentration the porch door upstairs slammed with the report of a minor piece of artillery, which, appropriately enough, caused Dr. Rankin to jump as if he had been shot.

The Doctor lifted a frowning face and an attentive ear. He heard two pairs of heavy feet clump across the resonant floor of the porch. He heard the house door opened and the visitors enter the hall, with which his cellar communicated by a short flight of steps. He heard whistling and then voices of Buck and Bud crying, "Doc! Hi, Doc! They're biting!"

Whether the Doctor was not inclined for fishing that day, or whether, like others of his large and heavy type, he experienced an especially sharp, unsociable reaction on being suddenly startled, or whether he was merely anxious to finish undisturbed the job in hand and proceed to more important duties, he did not respond immediately to the inviting outcry of his friends. Instead, he listened while it ran its natural course, dying down at last into a puzzled and fretful dialogue.

"I guess he's out."

"I'll write a note—say we're at the creek to come on down."

"We could tell Irene."

[1]Short for the Latin motto, *De mortuis nil nisi bonum:* Speak no ill of the dead.

"But she's not here, either. You'd think *she'd* be around."

"Ought to be, by the look of the place."

"You said it, Bud. Just look at this table. You could write your name—"

"Sh-h-h! Look!"

Evidently the last speaker had noticed that the cellar door was ajar and that a light was shining below. Next moment the door was pushed wide open and Bud and Buck looked down.

"Why, Doc! There you are!"

"Didn't you hear us yelling?"

The Doctor, not too pleased at what he had overheard, nevertheless smiled his rather wooden smile as his two friends made their way down the steps. "I thought I heard someone," he said.

"We were bawling our heads off," Buck said. "Thought nobody was home. Where's Irene?"

"Visiting," said the Doctor. "She's gone visiting."

"Hey, what goes on?" said Bud. "What are you doing? Burying one of your patients, or what?"

"Oh, there's been water seeping up through the floor," said the Doctor. "I figured it might be some spring opened up or something."

"You don't say!" said Bud, assuming instantly the high ethical standpoint of the realtor. "Gee, Doc, I sold you this property. Don't say I fixed you up with a dump where there's an underground spring."

"There was water," said the Doctor.

"Yes, but, Doc, you can look on that geological map the Kiwanis Club got up. There's not a better section of subsoil in the town."

"Looks like he sold you a pup," said Buck, grinning.

"No," said Bud, "Look. When the Doc came here he was green. You'll admit he was green. The things he didn't know!"

"He bought Ted Webber's jalopy," said Buck.

"He'd have bought the Jessop place if I'd let him," said Bud. "But I wouldn't give him a bum steer."

"Not the poor, simple city slicker from Poughkeepsie," said Buck.

"Some people would have taken him," said Bud. "Maybe some people did. Not me. I recommended this property. He and Irene moved straight in as soon as they were married. I wouldn't have put the Doc on to a dump where there'd be a spring under the foundations."

"Oh, forget it," said the Doctor, embarrassed by this conscientiousness. "I guess it was just the heavy rains."

"By gosh!" Buck said, glancing at the besmeared point of the pickaxe. "You certainly went deep enough. Right down into the clay, huh?"

"That's four feet down, the clay," Bud said.

"Eighteen inches," said the Doctor.

"Four feet," said Bud. "I can show you on the map."

"Come on. No arguments," said Buck. "How's about it, Doc? An hour or two at the creek, eh? They're biting."

"Can't do it, boys," said the Doctor. "I've got to see a patient or two."

"Aw, live and let live, Doc," Bud said. "Give 'em a chance to get better. Are you going to depopulate the whole darn town?"

The Doctor looked down, smiled, and muttered, as he always did when this particular jest was trotted out. "Sorry, boys," he said. "I can't make it."

"Well," said Bud, disappointed, "I suppose we'd better get along. How's Irene?"

"Irene?" asked the Doctor. "Never better. She's gone visiting. Albany. Got the eleven o'clock train."

"Eleven o'clock?" said Buck. "For Albany?"

"Did I say Albany?" said the Doctor. "Watertown, I meant."

"Friends in Watertown?" Buck asked.

"Mrs. Slater," said the Doctor. "Mr. and Mrs. Slater. Lived next door to 'em when she was a kid, Irene said, over on Sycamore Street."

"Slater?" said Bud. "Next door to Irene. Not in *this* town."

"Oh, yes," said the Doctor. "She was telling me all about them last night. She got a letter. Seems this Mrs. Slater looked after her when her mother was in the hospital one time."

"No," said Bud.

"That's what she told me," said the Doctor. "Of course, it was a good many years ago."

"Look, Doc," said Buck. "Bud and I were raised in this town. We've known Irene's folks all our lives. We were in and out of their house all the time. There was never anybody next door called Slater."

"Perhaps," said the Doctor, "she married again, this woman. Perhaps it was a different name."

Bud shook his head.

"What time did Irene go to the station?" Buck asked.

"Oh, about a quarter of an hour ago," said the Doctor.

"You didn't drive her?" said Buck.

"She walked," said the Doctor.

"We came down Main Street," Buck said. "We didn't meet her."

"Maybe she walked across the pasture," said the Doctor.

"That's a tough walk with a suitcase," said Buck.

"She just had a couple of things in a little bag," said the Doctor.

Bud was still shaking his head.

Buck looked at Bud, and then at the pick, at the new, damp cement on the floor. "Jesus Christ!" he said.

"Oh, God, Doc!" Bud said. "A guy like you!"

"What in the name of heaven are you two bloody fools thinking?" asked the Doctor. "What are you trying to say?"

"A spring!" said Bud. "I ought to have known right away it wasn't any spring."

The Doctor looked at his cement-work, at the pick, at the large worried faces of his two friends. His own face turned livid. "Am I crazy?" he said. "Or are you? You suggest that I've—that Irene—my wife—oh, go on! Get out! Yes, go and get the sheriff. Tell him to come here and start digging. You—get out!"

Bud and Buck looked at each other, shifted their feet, and stood still again.

"Go on," said the Doctor.

"I don't know," said Bud.

"It's not as if he didn't have the provocation," Buck said.

"God knows," Bud said.

"God knows," Buck said. "You know. I know. The whole town knows. But try telling it to a jury."

The Doctor put his hand to his head. "What's that?" he said. "What is it? Now what are you saying? What do you mean?"

"If this ain't being on the spot!" said Buck. "Doc, you can see how it is. It takes some thinking. We've been friends right from the start. Damn good friends."

"But we've got to think," said Bud. "It's serious. Provocation or not, there's a law in the land. There's such a thing as being an accomplice."

"You were talking about provocation," said the Doctor.

"You're right," said Buck. "And you're our friend. And if ever it could be called justified—"

"We've got to fix this somehow," said Bud.

"Justified?" said the Doctor.

"You were bound to get wised up sooner or later," said Buck.

"We could have told you," said Bud. "Only—what the hell?"

"We could," said Buck. "And we nearly did. Five years ago. Before ever you married her. You hadn't been here six months, but we sort of cottoned to you. Thought of giving you a hint. Spoke about it. Remember, Bud?"

Bud nodded. "Funny," he said. "I came right out in the open about that Jessop property. I wouldn't let you buy that, Doc. But getting married, that's something else again. We could have told you."

"We're that much responsible," Buck said.

"I'm fifty," said the Doctor. "I suppose it's pretty old for Irene."

"If you was Johnny Weissmuller[2] at the age of twenty-one, it wouldn't make any difference," said Buck.

"I know a lot of people think she's not exactly a perfect wife," said the Doctor. "Maybe she's not. She's young. She's full of life."

"Oh, skip it!" said Buck sharply, looking at the raw cement. "Skip it, Doc, for God's sake."

The Doctor brushed his hand across his face. "Not everybody wants the same thing," he said. "I'm a sort of dry fellow. I don't open up very easily. Irene—you'd call her gay."

"You said it," said Buck.

---

[2]Handsome Olympic champion swimmer and portrayer of Tarzan in the movies.

"She's no housekeeper," said the Doctor. "I know it. But that's not the only thing a man wants. She's enjoyed herself."

"Yeah," said Buck. "She did."

"That's what I love," said the Doctor. "Because I'm not that way myself. She's not very deep, mentally. All right. Say she's stupid. I don't care. Lazy. No system. Well, I've got plenty of system. She's enjoyed herself. It's beautiful. It's innocent. Like a child."

"Yes. If that was all," Buck said.

"But," said the Doctor, turning his eyes full on him, "You seem to know there was more."

"Everybody knows it," said Buck.

"A decent, straightforward guy comes to a place like this and marries the town floozy," Bud said bitterly. "And nobody'll tell him. Everybody just watches."

"And laughs," said Buck. "You and me, Bud, as well as the rest."

"We told her to watch her step," said Bud. "We warned her."

"Everybody warned her," said Buck. "But people get fed up. When it got to truck-drivers—"

"It was never us, Doc," said Bud, earnestly. "Not after you came along, anyway."

"The town'll be on your side," said Buck.

"That won't mean much when the case comes to trial in the county seat," said Bud.

"Oh!" cried the Doctor, suddenly. "What shall I do? What shall I do?"

"It's up to you, Bud," said Buck. "I can't turn him in."

"Take it easy, Doc," said Bud. "Calm down. Look, Buck. When we came in here the street was empty, wasn't it?"

"I guess so," said Buck. "Anyway, nobody saw us come down to the cellar."

"And we haven't been down," Bud said, addressing himself forcefully to the Doctor. "Get that, Doc? We shouted upstairs, hung around a minute or two, and cleared out. But we never came down into this cellar."

"I wish you hadn't," the Doctor said heavily.

"All you have to do is say Irene went out for a walk and never came back," said Buck. "Bud and I can swear we saw her headed out of town with a fellow in a—well, say in a Buick sedan. Everybody'll believe that, all right. We'll fix it. But later. Now we'd better scram."

"And remember, now. Stick to it. We never came down here and we haven't seen you today," said Bud. "So long!"

Buck and Bud ascended the steps, moving with a rather absurd degree of caution. "You'd better get that . . . that thing covered up," Buck said over his shoulder.

Left alone, the Doctor sat down on an empty box, holding his head with both hands. He was still sitting like this when the porch door slammed again. This time he did not start. He listened. The house door opened and closed. A voice cried, "Yoo-hoo! Yoo-hoo! I'm back."

The Doctor rose slowly to his feet. "I'm down here, Irene!" he called.

The cellar door opened. A young woman stood at the head of the steps. "Can you beat it?" she said. "I missed the damn train."

"Oh!" said the Doctor. "Did you come back across the field?"

"Yes, like a fool," she said. "I could have hitched a ride and caught the train up the line. Only I didn't think. If you'd run me over to the junction, I could still make it."

"Maybe," said the Doctor. "Did you meet anyone coming back?"

"Not a soul," she said. "Aren't you finished with that old job yet?"

"I'm afraid I'll have to take it all up again," said the Doctor. "Come down here, my dear, and I'll show you."

## FOR DISCUSSION

1. From the very beginning, what is the author's attitude toward the story and its characters? How does this contribute to the story's subsequent mood?
2. How does the initial description of Dr. Rankin help establish the man's character? Does he fit the conventional image of the capable physician?
3. Are Bud and Buck plausible characters or literary caricatures? How does their characterization serve the story?
4. What do Bud and Buck think when they see the doc's cement job and hear the story about Irene's having gone to Watertown to visit the Slaters?
5. What do we learn about Irene, the doc's wife, as a result of Bud and Buck's assumption about what the doc has been doing?
6. When Irene returns home and explains that she has missed her train, do you believe her?
7. What has the doc decided to do by the time Irene returns home? Do you think he has a chance to get away with it?
8. What devices are used to dramatize the character of Irene?
9. Explain the story's pervading irony.

# The Stone Boy

GINA BERRIAULT

Arnold drew his overalls and raveling gray sweater over his naked body. In the other narrow bed his brother Eugene went on sleeping, undisturbed by the alarm clock's rusty ring. Arnold, watching his brother sleeping, felt a peculiar dismay; he was nine, six years younger than Eugie, and in their waking hours it was he who was subordinate. To dispel emphatically his uneasy advantage over his sleeping brother, he threw himself on the hump of Eugie's body.

"Get up! Get up!" he cried.

Arnold felt his brother twist away and saw the blankets lifted in a great wing, and, all in an instant, he was lying on his back under the covers with only his face showing, like a baby, and Eugie was sprawled on top of him.

"Whassa matter with you?" asked Eugie in sleepy anger, his face hanging close.

"Get up," Arnold repeated. "You said you'd pick peas with me."

Stupidly, Eugie gazed around the room to see if morning had come into it yet. Arnold began to laugh derisively, making soft, snorting noises, and was thrown off the bed. He got up from the floor and went down the stairs, the laughter continuing, like hiccups, against his will. But when he opened the staircase door and entered the parlor, he hunched up his shoulders and was quiet because his parents slept in the bedroom downstairs.

Arnold lifted his .22-caliber rifle from the rack on the kitchen wall. It was an old lever-action that his father had given him because nobody else used it anymore. On their way down to the garden he and Eugie would go by the lake, and if there were any ducks on it he'd take a shot at them. Standing on the stool before the cupboard, he searched on the top shelf in the confusion of medicines and ointments for man and beast and found a small yellow box of .22 cartridges. Then he sat down on the stool and began to load his gun.

It was cold in the kitchen so early, but later in the day, when his mother canned the peas, the heat from the wood stove would be almost unbearable. Yesterday she had finished preserving the huckleberries that the family had picked along the mountain, and before that she had canned all the cherries his father had brought from the warehouse in Corinth. Sometimes, on these summer days, Arnold would deliberately come out from the shade where he was playing and make himself as uncomfortable as his mother was in the kitchen by standing in the sun until the sweat ran down his body.

Eugie came clomping down the stairs and into the kitchen, his head drooping with sleepiness. From his perch on the stool Arnold watched Eugie slip on his green knit cap. Eugie didn't really need a cap, he hadn't had a haircut in a long time and his brown curls grew thick and matted, close around his ears and down his neck, tapering there to a small whorl. Eugie passed his left hand through his hair before he set his cap down with his right. The very way he slipped his cap on was announcement of his status; almost everything he did was a reminder that he was eldest—first he, then Nora, then Arnold—and called attention to how tall he was, almost as tall as his father, how long his legs were, how small he was in the hips, and what a neat dip above his buttocks his thick-soled logger's boots gave him. Arnold never tired of watching Eugie offer silent praise unto himself. He wondered, as he sat enthralled, if when he got to be Eugie's age he would still be undersized and his hair still straight.

Eugie eyed the gun. "Don't you know this ain't duck season?" he asked gruffly, as if he were the sheriff.

"No, I don't know," Arnold said with a snigger.

Eugie picked up the tin washtub for the peas, unbolted the door with his free hand and kicked it open. Then, lifting the tub to his head, he went clomping down the back steps. Arnold followed, closing the door behind him.

The sky was faintly gray, almost white. The mountains behind the farm made the sun climb a long way to show itself. Several miles to the south, where the range opened up, hung an orange mist, but the valley in which the farm lay was still cold and colorless.

Eugie opened the gate to the yard and the boys passed between the barn and the row of chicken houses, their feet stirring up the carpet of brown feathers dropped by the molting chickens. They paused before going down the slope to the lake. A fluky morning wind ran among the shocks of wheat that covered the slope. It sent a shimmer northward across the lake, gently moving the rushes that formed an island in the center. Killdeer, their white markings flashing, skimmed the water, crying their shrill, sweet cry. And there at the south end of the lake were four wild ducks, swimming out from the willows into open water.

Arnold followed Eugie down the slope, stealing, as his brother did, from one shock of wheat to another. Eugie paused before climbing through the wire fence that divided the wheat field from the marshy pasture around the lake. They were screened from the ducks by the willows along the lake's edge.

"If you hit your duck, you want me to go in after it?" Eugie said.

"If you want," Arnold said.

Eugie lowered his eyelids, leaving slits of mocking blue. "You'd drown 'fore you got to it, them legs of yours are so puny," he said.

He shoved the tub under the fence and, pressing down the center wire, climbed through into the pasture.

Arnold pressed down the bottom wire, thrust a leg through and leaned forward to bring the other leg after. His rifle caught on the wire and he jerked at it. The air was rocked by the sound of the shot. Feeling foolish, he lifted his face, baring it to an expected shower of derision from his brother. But Eugie did not turn around. Instead, from his crouching position, he fell to his knees and then pitched forward onto his face. The ducks rose up crying from the lake, cleared the mountain background and beat away northward across the pale sky.

Arnold squatted beside his brother. Eugie seemed to be climbing the earth, as if the earth ran up and down, and when he found he couldn't scale it he lay still.

"Eugie?"

Then Arnold saw it, under the tendril of hair at the nape of the neck— a slow rising of bright blood. It had an obnoxious movement, like that of a parasite.

"Hey, Eugie," he said again. He was feeling the same discomfort he had felt when he had watched Eugie sleeping; his brother didn't know that he was lying face down in the pasture.

Again he said, "Hey, Eugie," an anxious nudge in his voice. But Eugie was as still as the morning around them.

Arnold set his rifle on the ground and stood up. He picked up the tub and, dragging it behind him, walked along by the willows to the garden fence and climbed through. He went down on his knees among the tangled vines. The pods were cold with the night, but his hands were strange to him, and not until some time had passed did he realize that the pods were numbing his fingers. He picked from the top of the vine first, then lifted the vine to look underneath for pods, and moved on to the next.

It was a warmth on his back, like a large hand laid firmly there, that made him raise his head. Way up the slope the gray farmhouse was struck by the sun. While his head had been bent the land had grown bright around him.

When he got up his legs were so stiff that he had to go down on his knees again to ease the pain. Then, walking sideways, he dragged the tub, half full of peas, up the slope.

The kitchen was warm now; a fire was roaring in the stove with a closed-up, rushing sound. His mother was spooning eggs from a pot of boiling water and putting them into a bowl. Her short brown hair was uncombed and fell forward across her eyes as she bent her head. Nora was lifting a frying pan full of trout from the stove, holding the handle with a dish towel. His father had just come in from bringing the cows from the north pasture to the barn, and was sitting on the stool, unbuttoning his red plaid Mackinaw.

"Did you boys fill the tub?" his mother asked.

"They ought of by now," his father said. "They went out of the house an hour ago. Eugie woke me up comin' downstairs. I heard you shootin'—did you get a duck?"

"No," Arnold said. They would want to know why Eugie wasn't coming in for breakfast, he thought. "Eugie's dead," he told them.

They stared at him. The pitch crackled in the stove.

"You kids playin' a joke?" his father asked.

"Where's Eugene?" his mother asked scoldingly. She wanted, Arnold knew, to see his eyes, and when he had glanced at her she put the bowl and spoon down on the stove and walked past him. His father stood up and went out the door after her. Nora followed them with little skipping steps, as if afraid to be left alone.

Arnold went into the barn, down along the foddering passage past the cows waiting to be milked, and climbed into the loft. After a few minutes he heard a terrifying sound coming toward the house. His parents and Nora were returning from the willows, and sounds sharp as knives were rising from his mother's breast and carrying over the sloping fields. In a short while he heard his father go down the back steps, slam the car door and drive away.

Arnold lay still as a fugitive, listening to the cows eating close by. If his parents never called him, he thought, he would stay up in the loft forever, out of the way. In the night he would sneak down for a drink of water from the faucet over the trough and for whatever food they left for him by the barn.

The rattle of his father's car as it turned down the lane recalled him to the present. He heard the voices of his Uncle Andy and Aunt Alice as they and his father went past the barn to the lake. He could feel the morning growing heavier with sun. Someone, probably Nora, had let the chickens out of their coops and they were cackling in the yard.

After a while another car turned down the road off the highway. The car drew to a stop and he heard the voices of strange men. The men also went past the barn and down to the lake. The undertakers, whom his father must have phoned from Uncle Andy's house, had arrived from Corinth. Then he heard everybody come back and heard the car turn around and leave.

"Arnold!" It was his father calling from the yard.

He climbed down the ladder and went out into the sun, picking wisps of hay from his overalls.

Corinth, nine miles away, was the county seat. Arnold sat in the front seat of the old Ford between his father, who was driving, and Uncle Andy; no one spoke. Uncle Andy was his mother's brother, and he had been fond of Eugie because Eugie had resembled him. Andy had taken Eugie hunting and had given him a knife and a lot of things, and now Andy, his eyes narrowed, sat tall and stiff beside Arnold.

Arnold's father parked the car before the courthouse. It was a two-story brick building with a lamp on each side of the bottom step. They went up the wide stone steps, Arnold and his father going first, and entered the darkly paneled hallway. The shirt-sleeved man in the sheriff's office said that the sheriff was at Carlson's Parlor examining the Curwing boy.

Andy went off to get the sheriff while Arnold and his father waited on a bench in the corridor. Arnold felt his father watching him, and he lifted his eyes with painful casualness to the announcement, on the opposite wall, of the Corinth County Annual Rodeo, and then to the clock with its loudly clucking pendulum. After he had come down from the loft his father and Uncle Andy had stood in the yard with him and asked him to tell them everything, and he had explained to them how the gun had caught on the wire. But when they had asked him why he hadn't run back to the house to tell his parents, he had had no answer—all he could say was that he had gone down into the garden to pick the peas. His father had stared at him in a pale, puzzled way, and it was then that he had felt his father and the others set their cold, turbulent silence against him. Arnold shifted on the bench, his only feeling a small one of compunction imposed by his father's eyes.

At a quarter past nine Andy and the sheriff came in. They all went into the sheriff's private office, and Arnold was sent forward to sit in the chair by the sheriff's desk; his father and Andy sat down on the bench against the wall.

The sheriff lumped down into his swivel chair and swung toward Arnold. He was an old man with white hair like wheat stubble. His restless green eyes made him seem not to be in his office but to be hurrying and bobbing around somewhere else.

"What did you say your name was?" the sheriff asked.

"Arnold," he replied, but he could not remember telling the sheriff his name before.

"Curwing?"

"Yes."

"What were you doing with a .22, Arnold?"

"It's mine," he said.

"Okay. What were you going to shoot?"

"Some ducks," he replied.

"Out of season?"

He nodded.

"That's bad," said the sheriff. "Were you and your brother good friends?"

What did he mean—good friends? Eugie was his brother. That was different from a friend, Arnold thought. A best friend was your own age, but Eugie was almost a man. Eugie had had a way of looking at him, slyly and mockingly and yet confidentially, that had summed up how they both felt about being brothers. Arnold had wanted to be with Eugie more than with anybody else but he couldn't say they had been good friends.

"Did they ever quarrel?" the sheriff asked his father.

"Not that I know," his father replied. "It seemed to me that Arnold cared a lot for Eugie."

"Did you?" the sheriff asked Arnold.

If it seemed so to his father, then it was so. Arnold nodded.

"Were you mad at him this morning?"

"No."

"How did you happen to shoot him?"

"We was crawlin' through the fence."

"Yes?"

"An' the gun got caught on the wire."

"Seems the hammer must of caught," his father put in.

"All right, that's what happened," said the sheriff. "But what I want you to tell me is this. Why didn't you go back to the house and tell your father right away? Why did you go and pick peas for an hour?"

Arnold gazed over his shoulder at his father, expecting his father to have an answer for this also. But his father's eyes, larger and even lighter blue than usual, were fixed upon him curiously. Arnold picked at a callus in his right palm. It seemed odd now that he had not run back to the house and wakened his father, but he could not remember why he had not. They were all waiting for him to answer.

"I come down to pick peas," he said.

"Didn't you think," asked the sheriff, stepping carefully from word to word, "that it was more important for you to go tell your parents what had happened?"

"The sun was gonna come up," Arnold said.

"What's that got to do with it?"

"It's better to pick peas while they're cool."

The sheriff swung away from him, laid both hands flat on his desk. "Well, all I can say is," he said across to Arnold's father and Uncle Andy, "he's either a moron or he's so reasonable that he's way ahead of us." He gave a challenging snort. "It's come to my notice that the most reasonable guys are mean ones. They don't feel nothing."

For a moment the three men sat still. Then the sheriff lifted his hand like a man taking an oath. "Take him home," he said.

Andy uncrossed his legs. "You don't want him?"

"Not now," replied the sheriff. "Maybe in a few years."

Arnold's father stood up. He held his hat against his chest. "The gun ain't his no more," he said wanly.

Arnold went first through the hallway, hearing behind him the heels of his father and Uncle Andy striking the floorboards. He went down the steps ahead of them and climbed into the back seat of the car. Andy paused as he was getting into the front seat and gazed back at Arnold, and Arnold saw that his uncle's eyes had absorbed the knowingness from the sheriff's eyes. Andy and his father and the sheriff had discovered what made him go down into the garden. It was because he was cruel, the sheriff had said, and didn't care about his brother. Arnold lowered his eyelids meekly against his uncle's stare.

The rest of the day he did his tasks around the farm, keeping apart from the family. At evening, when he saw his father stomp tiredly into the house, Arnold did not put down his hammer and leave the chicken coop he was repairing. He was afraid that they did not want him to eat supper with them. But in a few minutes another fear that they would go to the trouble of calling him and that he would be made conspicuous by his tardiness made him follow his father into the house. As he went through the kitchen he saw the jars of peas standing in rows on the workbench, a reproach to him.

No one spoke at supper, and his mother, who sat next to him, leaned her head in her hand all through the meal, curving her fingers over her eyes so as not to see him. They were finishing their small, silent supper when the visitors began to arrive, knocking hard on the back door. The men were coming from their farms now that it was growing dark and they could not work anymore.

Old Man Matthews, gray and stocky, came first, with his two sons, Orion, the elder, and Clint, who was Eugie's age. As the callers entered the parlor where the family ate, Arnold sat down in a rocking chair. Even as he had been undecided before supper whether to remain outside or take his place at the table, he now thought that he should go upstairs, and yet he stayed to avoid being conspicuous by his absence. If he stayed, he thought, as he always stayed and listened when visitors came, they would see that he was only Arnold and not the person the sheriff thought he was. He sat with his arms crossed and his hands tucked into his armpits and did not lift his eyes.

The Matthews men had hardly settled down around the table, after Arnold's mother and Nora had cleared away the dishes, when another car rattled down the road and someone else rapped on the back door. This time it was Sullivan, a spare and sandy man, so nimble of gesture and expression that Arnold had never been able to catch more than a few of his meanings. Sullivan, in dusty jeans, sat down in another rocker, shot out his skinny legs and began to talk in his fast way, recalling everything that Eugene had ever said to him. The other men interrupted to tell of occasions they remembered, and after a time Clint's young voice, hoarse like Eugene's had been, broke in to tell about the time Eugene had beat him in a wrestling match.

Out in the kitchen the voices of Orion's wife and of Mrs. Sullivan mingled with Nora's voice but not, Arnold noticed, his mother's. Then dry little Mr. Cram came, leaving large Mrs. Cram in the kitchen, and there was no chair left for Mr. Cram to sit in. No one asked Arnold to get up and he was unable to rise. He knew that the story had got around to them during the day about how he had gone and picked peas after he had shot his brother, and he knew that although they were talking only about Eugie they were thinking about him and if he got up, if he moved even his foot, they would all be alerted. Then Uncle Andy arrived and leaned his tall, lanky body against the doorjamb and there were two men standing.

Presently Arnold was aware that the talk had stopped. He knew without looking up that the men were watching him.

"Not a tear in his eye," said Andy, and Arnold knew that it was his uncle who had gestured the men to attention.

"He don't give a hoot, is that how it goes?" asked Sullivan, trippingly.

"He's a reasonable fellow," Andy explained. "That's what the sheriff said. It's us who ain't reasonable. If we'd of shot our brother, we'd of come runnin' back to the house, cryin' like a baby. Well, we'd of been unreasonable. What would of been the use of actin' like that? If your brother is shot dead, he's shot dead. What's the use of gettin' emotional about it? The thing to do is go down to the garden and pick peas. Am I right?"

The men around the room shifted their heavy, satisfying weight of unreasonableness.

Matthews' son Orion said: "If I'd of done what he done, Pa would've hung my pelt by the side of the big coyote's in the barn."

Arnold sat in the rocker until the last man had filed out. While his family was out in the kitchen bidding the callers good night and the cars were driving away down the dirt lane to the highway, he picked up one of the kerosene lamps and slipped quickly up the stairs. In his room he undressed by lamplight, although he and Eugie had always undressed in the dark, and not until he was lying in his bed did he blow out the flame. He felt nothing, not any grief. There was only the same immense silence and crawling inside of him; it was the way the house and fields felt under a merciless sun.

He awoke suddenly. He knew that his father was out in the yard, closing the doors of the chicken houses. The sound that had wakened him was the step of his father as he got up from the rocker and went down the back steps. And he knew that his mother was awake in her bed.

Throwing off the covers, he rose swiftly, went down the stairs and across the dark parlor to his parents' room. He rapped on the door.

"Mother?"

From the closed room her voice rose to him, a seeking and retreating voice. "Yes?"

"Mother?" he asked insistently. He had expected her to realize that he wanted to go down on his knees by her bed and tell her that Eugie was dead. She did not know it yet, nobody knew it, and yet she was sitting up in bed, waiting to be told, waiting for him to confirm her dread. He had expected her to tell him to come in, to allow him to dig his head into her blankets and tell her about the terror he had felt when he had knelt beside Eugie. He had come to clasp her in his arms and, in his terror, to pommel her breasts with his head. He put his hand upon the knob.

"Go back to bed, Arnold," she called sharply.

But he waited.

"Go back! Is night when you get afraid?"

At first he did not understand. Then, silently, he left the door and for a stricken moment stood by the rocker. Outside everything was still. The fences, the shocks of wheat seen through the window before him were so still it was as if they moved and breathed in the daytime and had fallen silent with the lateness of the hour. It was a silence that seemed to observe his father, a figure moving alone around the yard, his lantern casting a circle of light by his feet. In a few minutes his father would enter the dark house, the lantern still lighting his way.

Arnold was suddenly aware that he was naked. He had thrown off his blankets and come down the stairs to tell his mother how he felt about Eugie, but she had refused to listen to him and his nakedness had become unpardonable. At once he went back up the stairs, fleeing from his father's lantern.

At breakfast he kept his eyelids lowered as if to deny the humiliating night. Nora, sitting at his left, did not pass the pitcher of milk to him and he did not ask for it. He would never again, he vowed, ask them for anything, and he ate his fried eggs and potatoes only because everybody ate meals—the cattle ate, and the cats; it was customary for everybody to eat.

"Nora, you gonna keep that pitcher for yourself?" his father asked.

Nora lowered her head unsurely.

"Pass it on to Arnold," his father said.

Nora put her hands in her lap.

His father picked up the metal pitcher and set it down at Arnold's plate.

Arnold, pretending to be deaf to the discord, did not glance up, but relief rained over his shoulders at the thought that his parents recognized him again. They must have lain awake after his father had come in from the yard: had they realized together why he had come down the stairs and knocked at their door?

"Bessie's missin' this morning," his father called out to his mother, who had gone into the kitchen. "She went up the mountain last night and had her calf, most likely. Somebody's got to go up and find her 'fore the coyotes get the calf."

That had been Eugie's job, Arnold thought. Eugie would climb the cattle trails in search of a newborn calf and come down the mountain carrying the calf across his back, with the cow running behind him, mooing in alarm.

Arnold ate the few more forkfuls of his breakfast, put his hands on the edge of the table and pushed back his chair. If he went for the calf he'd be away from the farm all morning. He could switch the cow down the mountain slowly, and the calf would run along at its mother's side.

When he passed through the kitchen his mother was setting a kettle of water on the stove. "Where you going?" she asked awkwardly.

"Up to get the calf," he replied, averting his face.

"Arnold?"

At the door he paused reluctantly, his back to her, knowing that she was seeking him out, as his father was doing, and he called upon his pride to protect him from them.

"Was you knocking at my door last night?"

He looked over his shoulder at her, his eyes narrow and dry.

"What'd you want?" she asked humbly.

"I didn't want nothing," he said flatly.

Then he went out the door and down the back steps, his legs trembling from the fright his answer gave him.

## FOR DISCUSSION

1. From what point of view is the story told? Why could the author not have made Arnold a first-person narrator?
2. Arnold is the story's protagonist. What are the antagonistic forces that he struggles against? Does he have much of a chance?
3. At the beginning of the story, what is the relationship between Eugie and Arnold? How is this relationship dramatized?
4. Many readers sense that Eugie is going to be killed before they read about the accidental shooting. Is there any specific foreshadowing of this event?
5. Why did Arnold go on and pick peas after the shooting? Why can't he demonstrate any outward signs of emotion after Eugie's death? Is Arnold truly cold and emotionless? Who is it that actually proves incapable of understanding human feelings?
6. The sheriff says that he may want Arnold "in a few years." Does the story ever suggest that this may turn out to be true?
7. Arnold experiences two major emotional traumas in the story. What are they? Ultimately, which seems likely to have the greater effect on him?
8. At what point in the story does the climax occur? Describe the situation. What irony accompanies the climax?
9. The story's denouement occurs on the morning after the shooting. It involves a re-establishment of family relationships. What are these relationships likely to be? How will the relationships differ from what they were before the tragedy?
10. At the breakfast table, Nora refuses to pass Arnold the pitcher of milk. Why does she refuse to do this?
11. What evidence can you find toward the end of the story that Arnold's mother may be changing in her attitude toward her son? What seem to be her feelings?
12. By the end of the story, how has Arnold resolved to conduct himself in the future? What is ironic about his resolution?

# The Minister's Black Veil

NATHANIEL HAWTHORNE

The sexton stood in the porch of Milford meeting-house, pulling busily at the bell-rope. The old people of the village came stooping along the street. Children, with bright faces, tripped merrily beside their parents, or mimicked a graver gait, in the conscious dignity of their Sunday clothes. Spruce bachelors looked sidelong at the pretty maidens, and fancied that the Sabbath sunshine made them prettier than on week days. When the throng had mostly streamed into the porch, the sexton began to toll the bell, keeping his eye on the Reverend Mr. Hooper's door. The first glimpse of the clergyman's figure was the signal for the bell to cease its summons.

"But what has good Parson Hooper got upon his face?" cried the sexton in astonishment.

All within hearing immediately turned about, and beheld the semblance of Mr. Hooper, pacing slowly his meditative way towards the meeting-house. With one accord they started, expressing more wonder than if some strange minister were coming to dust the cushions of Mr. Hooper's pulpit.

"Are you sure it is our parson?" inquired Goodman Gray of the sexton.

"Of a certainty it is good Mr. Hooper," replied the sexton. "He was to have exchanged pulpits with Parson Shute, of Westbury; but Parson Shute sent to excuse himself yesterday, being to preach a funeral sermon."

The cause of so much amazement may appear sufficiently slight. Mr. Hooper, a gentlemanly person, of about thirty, though still a bachelor, was dressed with due clerical neatness, as if a careful wife had starched his band,[1] and brushed the weekly dust from his Sunday's garb. There was but one thing remarkable in his appearance. Swathed about his forehead, and hanging down over his face, so low as to be shaken by his breath, Mr. Hooper had on a black veil. On a nearer view it seemed to consist of two folds of crape, which entirely concealed his features, except the mouth and chin, but probably did not intercept his sight, further than to give a darkened aspect to all living and inanimate things. With this gloomy shade before him, good Mr. Hooper walked onward, at a slow and quiet pace, stooping somewhat, and looking on the ground, as is customary with abstracted men, yet nodding kindly to those of his parishioners who still waited on the meeting-house steps. But so wonder-struck were they that his greeting hardly met with a return.

"I can't really feel as if good Mr. Hooper's face was behind that piece of crape," said the sexton.

[1] Clerical collar.

"I don't like it," muttered an old woman, as she hobbled into the meeting-house. "He has changed himself into something awful, only by hiding his face."

"Our parson has gone mad!" cried Goodman[2] Gray, following him across the threshold.

A rumor of some unaccountable phenomenon had preceded Mr. Hooper into the meeting-house, and set all the congregation astir. Few could refrain from twisting their heads towards the door; many stood upright, and turned directly about; while several little boys clambered upon the seats, and came down again with a terrible racket. There was a general bustle, a rustling of the women's gowns and shuffling of the men's feet, greatly at variance with that hushed repose which should attend the entrance of the minister. But Mr. Hooper appeared not to notice the perturbation of his people. He entered with an almost noise-less step, bent his head mildly to the pews on each side, and bowed as he passed his oldest parishioner, a white-haired great-grandsire, who occupied an arm-chair in the centre of the aisle. It was strange to observe how slowly this venerable man became conscious of something singular in the appearance of his pastor. He seemed not fully to partake of the prevailing wonder, till Mr. Hooper had ascended the stairs, and showed himself in the pulpit, face to face with his congregation, except for the black veil. That mysterious emblem was never once withdrawn. It shook with his measured breath, as he gave out the psalm; it threw its obscurity between him and the holy page, as he read the Scriptures; and while he prayed, the veil lay heavily on his uplifted countenance. Did he seek to hide it from the dread Being whom he was addressing?

Such was the effect of this simple piece of crape, that more than one woman of delicate nerves was forced to leave the meeting-house. Yet perhaps the pale-faced congregation was almost as fearful a sight to the minister, as his black veil to them.

Mr. Hooper had the reputation of a good preacher but not an energetic one: he strove to win his people heavenward by mild, persuasive influences, rather than to drive them thither by the thunders of the Word. The sermon which he now delivered was marked by the same characteristics of style and manner as the general series of his pulpit oratory. But there was something, either in the sentiment of the dis-course itself, or in the imagination of the auditors, which made it greatly the most powerful effort that they had ever heard from their pastor's lips. It was tinged, rather more darkly than usual, with the gentle gloom of Mr. Hooper's temperament. The subject had reference to secret sin, and those sad mysteries which we hid from our nearest and dearest, and would fain conceal from our own consciousness, even forgetting that the Omniscient can detect them. A subtle power was breathed into his words. Each member of the congregation, the most innocent girl, and the man of hardened breast, felt as if the preacher had crept upon

[2]Honorific title for one below the rank of gentleman.

them, behind his awful veil, and discovered their hoarded iniquity of deed or thought. Many spread their clasped hands on their bosoms. There was nothing terrible in what Mr. Hooper said, at least, no violence; and yet, with every tremor of his melancholy voice, the hearers quaked. An unsought pathos came hand in hand with awe. So sensible were the audience of some unwonted attribute in their minister, that they longed for a breath of wind to blow aside the veil, almost believing that a stranger's visage would be discovered, though the form, gesture, and voice were those of Mr. Hooper.

At the close of the services, the people hurried out with indecorous confusion, eager to communicate their pent-up amazement, and conscious of lighter spirits the moment they lost sight of the black veil. Some gathered in little circles, huddled closely together, with their mouths all whispering in the centre; some went homeward alone, wrapt in silent meditation; some talked loudly, and profaned the Sabbath day with ostentatious laughter. A few shook their sagacious heads, intimating that they could penetrate the mystery; while one or two affirmed that there was no mystery at all, but only that Mr. Hooper's eyes were so weakened by the midnight lamp, as to require a shade. After a brief interval, forth came good Mr. Hooper also, in the rear of his flock. Turning his veiled face from one group to another, he paid due reverence to the hoary heads, saluted the middle aged with kind dignity as their friend and spiritual guide, greeted the young with mingled authority and love, and laid his hands on the little children's heads to bless them. Such was always his custom on the Sabbath day. Strange and bewildered looks repaid him for his courtesy. None, as on former occasions, aspired to the honor of walking by their pastor's side. Old Squire Saunders, doubtless by an accidental lapse of memory, neglected to invite Mr. Hooper to his table, where the good clergyman had been wont to bless the food, almost every Sunday since his settlement. He returned, therefore, to the parsonage, and, at the moment of closing the door, was observed to look back upon the people all of whom had their eyes fixed upon the minister. A sad smile gleamed faintly from beneath the black veil, and flickered about his mouth, glimmering as he disappeared.

"How strange," said a lady, "that a simple black veil, such as any woman might wear on her bonnet, should become such a terrible thing on Mr. Hooper's face!"

"Something must surely be amiss with Mr. Hooper's intellects," observed her husband, the physician of the village. "But the strangest part of the affair is the effect of this vagary, even on a soberminded man like myself. The black veil, though it covers only our pastor's face, throws its influence over his whole person, and makes him ghostlike from head to foot. Do you not feel it so?"

"Truly do I," replied the lady; "and I would not be alone with him for the world. I wonder he is not afraid to be alone with himself!"

"Men sometimes are so," said her husband.

The afternoon service was attended with similar circumstances. At its conclusion, the bell tolled for the funeral of a young lady. The relatives and friends were assembled in the house, and the more distant acquaintances stood about the door, speaking of the good qualities of the deceased, when their talk was interrupted by the appearance of Mr. Hooper, still covered with his black veil. It was now an appropriate emblem. The clergyman stepped into the room where the corpse was laid, and bent over the coffin, to take a last farewell of his deceased parishioner. As he stooped, the veil hung straight down from his forehead, so that, if her eyelids had not been closed forever, the dead maiden might have seen his face. Could Mr. Hooper be fearful of her glance, that he so hastily caught back the black veil? A person who watched the interview between the dead and living, scrupled not to affirm, that, at the instant when the clergyman's features were disclosed, the corpse had slightly shuddered, rustling the shroud and muslin cap, though the countenance retained the composure of death. A superstitious old woman was the only witness of this prodigy. From the coffin Mr. Hooper passed into the chamber of the mourners, and thence to the head of the staircase, to make the funeral prayer. It was a tender and heart-dissolving prayer, full of sorrow, yet so imbued with celestial hopes, that the music of a heavenly harp, swept by the fingers of the dead, seemed faintly to be heard among the saddest accents of the minister. The people trembled, though they but darkly understood him when he prayed that they, and himself, and all of mortal race, might be ready, as he trusted this young maiden had been, for the dreadful hour that should snatch the veil from their faces. The bearers went heavily forth, and the mourners followed, saddening all the street, with the dead before them, and Mr. Hooper in his black veil behind.

"Why do you look back?" said one in the procession to his partner.

"I had a fancy," replied she, "that the minister and the maiden's spirit were walking hand in hand."

"And so had I, at the same moment," said the other.

That night, the handsomest couple in Milford village were to be joined in wedlock. Though reckoned a melancholy man, Mr. Hooper had a placid cheerfulness for such occasions, which often excited a sympathetic smile where livelier merriment would have been thrown away. There was no quality of his disposition which made him more beloved than this. The company at the wedding awaited his arrival with impatience, trusting that the strange awe, which had gathered over him throughout the day, would now be dispelled. But such was not the result. When Mr. Hooper came, the first thing that their eyes rested on was the same horrible black veil, which had added deeper gloom to the funeral, and could portend nothing but evil to the wedding. Such was its immediate effect on the guests that a cloud seemed to have rolled duskily from beneath the black crape, and dimmed the light of the candles. The bridal pair stood up before the minister. But the bride's cold fingers quivered in the tremulous hand of the bridegroom, and her deathlike paleness caused a whisper that the maiden who had been buried a few hours

before was come from her grave to be married. If ever another wedding
were so dismal, it was that famous one where they tolled the wedding
knell.[3] After performing the ceremony, Mr. Hooper raised a glass of
wine to his lips, wishing happiness to the new-married couple in a
strain of mild pleasantry that ought to have brightened the features of
the guests, like a cheerful gleam from the hearth. At that instant,
catching a glimpse of his figure in the looking-glass, the black veil
involved his own spirit in the horror with which it overwhelmed all
others. His frame shuddered, his lips grew white, he spilt the untasted
wine upon the carpet, and rushed forth into the darkness. For the Earth,
too, had on her Black Veil.

The next day, the whole village of Milford talked of little else than
Parson Hooper's black veil. That, and the mystery concealed behind it,
supplied a topic for discussion between acquaintances meeting in the
street, and good women gossiping at their open windows. It was the
first item of news that the tavern-keeper told to his guests. The children
babbled of it on their way to school. One imitative little imp covered his
face with an old black handkerchief, thereby so affrighting his playmates
that the panic seized himself, and he well-nigh lost his wits by his own
waggery.

It was remarkable that of all the busybodies and impertinent people
in the parish, not one ventured to put the plain question to Mr. Hooper,
wherefore he did this thing. Hitherto, whenever there appeared the
slightest call for such interference, he had never lacked advisers, nor
shown himself adverse to be guided by their judgment. If he erred at
all, it was by so painful a degree of self-distrust, that even the mildest
censure would lead him to consider an indifferent action as a crime.
Yet, though so well acquainted with this amiable weakness, no individual among his parishioners chose to make the black veil a subject of
friendly remonstrance. There was a feeling of dread, neither plainly
confessed nor carefully concealed, which caused each to shift the responsibility upon another, till at length it was found expedient to send
a deputation of the church, in order to deal with Mr. Hooper about the
mystery, before it should grow into a scandal. Never did an embassy
so ill discharge its duties. The minister received them with friendly
courtesy, but became silent, after they were seated, leaving to his visitors
the whole burden of introducing their important business. The topic,
it might be supposed, was obvious enough. There was the black veil
swathed round Mr. Hooper's forehead, and concealing every feature
above his placid mouth, on which, at times, they could perceive the
glimmering of a melancholy smile. But that piece of crape, to their
imagination, seemed to hang down before his heart, the symbol of a
fearful secret between him and them. Were the veil but cast aside, they
might speak freely of it, but not till then. Thus they sat a considerable

[3]Refers to Hawthorne's story *The Wedding Knell,* originally published simultaneously with
this story.

time, speechless, confused, and shrinking uneasily from Mr. Hooper's eye, which they felt to be fixed upon them with an invisible glance. Finally, the deputies returned abashed to their constituents, pronouncing the matter too weighty to be handled, except by a council of the churches, if, indeed, it might not require a general synod.

But there was one person in the village unappalled by the awe with which the black veil had impressed all beside herself. When the deputies returned without an explanation, or even venturing to demand one, she, with the calm energy of her character, determined to chase away the strange cloud that appeared to be settling round Mr. Hooper, every moment more darkly than before. As his plighted wife, it should be her privilege to know what the black veil concealed. At the minister's first visit, therefore, she entered upon the subject with a direct simplicity, which made the task easier for him and her. After he had seated himself, she fixed her eyes steadfastly upon the veil, but could discern nothing of the dreadful gloom that had so overawed the multitude: it was but a double fold of crape, hanging down from his forehead to his mouth, and slightly stirring with his breath.

"No," she said aloud, and smiling, "there is nothing terrible in this piece of crape, except that it hides a face which I am always glad to look upon. Come, good sir, let the sun shine from behind the cloud. First lay aside your black veil: then tell me why you put it on."

Mr. Hooper's smile glimmered faintly.

"There is an hour to come," said he, "when all of us shall cast aside our veils. Take it not amiss, beloved friend, if I wear this piece of crape till then."

"Your words are a mystery, too," returned the young lady. "Take away the veil from them, at least."

"Elizabeth, I will," said he, "so far as my vow may suffer me. Know, then, this veil is a type and a symbol, and I am bound to wear it ever, both in light and darkness, in solitude and before the gaze of multitudes, and as with strangers, so with my familiar friends. No mortal eye will see it withdrawn. This dismal shade must separate me from the world: even you, Elizabeth, can never come behind it!"

"What grievous affliction hath befallen you," she earnestly inquired, "that you should thus darken your eyes forever?"

"If it be a sign of mourning," replied Mr. Hooper, "I, perhaps, like most other mortals, have sorrows dark enough to be typified by a black veil."

"But what if the world will not believe that it is the type of an innocent sorrow?" urged Elizabeth. "Beloved and respected as you are, there may be whispers that you hide your face under the consciousness of secret sin. For the sake of your holy office, do away this scandal!"

The color rose into her cheeks as she intimated the nature of the rumors that were already abroad in the village. But Mr. Hooper's mildness did not forsake him. He even smiled again—that same sad smile, which always appeared like a faint glimmering of light, proceeding from the obscurity beneath the veil.

"If I hide my face for sorrow, there is cause enough," he merely replied; "and if I cover it for secret sin, what mortal might not do the same?"

And with this gentle, but unconquerable obstinacy did he resist all her entreaties. At length Elizabeth sat silent. For a few moments she appeared lost in thought, considering, probably, what new methods might be tried to withdraw her lover from so dark a fantasy, which, if it had no other meaning, was perhaps a symptom of mental disease. Though of a firmer character than his own, the tears rolled down her cheeks. But, in an instant, as it were, a new feeling took the place of sorrow: her eyes were fixed insensibly on the black veil, when, like a sudden twilight in the air, its terrors fell around her. She arose, and stood trembling before him.

"And do you feel it then, at last?" said he mournfully.

She made no reply, but covered her eyes with her hand, and turned to leave the room. He rushed forward and caught her arm.

"Have patience with me, Elizabeth!" cried he, passionately. "Do not desert me, though this veil must be between us here on earth. Be mine, and hereafter there shall be no veil over my face, no darkness between our souls! It is but a mortal veil—it is not for eternity! O! you know not how lonely I am, and how frightened, to be alone behind my black veil. Do not leave me in this miserable obscurity forever!"

"Lift the veil but once, and look me in the face," said she.

"Never! It cannot be!" replied Mr. Hooper.

"Then farewell!" said Elizabeth.

She withdrew her arm from his grasp, and slowly departed, pausing at the door, to give one long shuddering gaze, that seemed almost to penetrate the mystery of the black veil. But, even amid his grief, Mr. Hooper smiled to think that only a material emblem had separated him from happiness, though the horrors, which it shadowed forth, must be drawn darkly between the fondest of lovers.

From that time no attempts were made to remove Mr. Hooper's black veil, or, by a direct appeal, to discover the secret which it was supposed to hide. By persons who claimed a superiority to popular prejudice, it was reckoned merely an eccentric whim, such as often mingles with the sober actions of men otherwise rational, and tinges them all with its own semblance of insanity. But with the multitude, good Mr. Hooper was irreparably a bugbear. He could not walk the street with any peace of mind, so conscious was he that the gentle and timid would turn aside to avoid him, and that others would make it a point of hardihood to throw themselves in his way. The impertinence of the latter class compelled him to give up his customary walk at sunset to the burial ground; for when he leaned pensively over the gate, there would always be faces behind the gravestones, peeping at his black veil. A fable went the rounds that the stare of the dead people drove him thence. It grieved him, to the very depth of his kind heart, to observe how the children fled from his approach, breaking up their merriest sports, while his melancholy figure was yet afar off. Their instinctive dread caused him to feel more strongly than aught else, that a preternatural horror was interwoven with the threads of the black crape. In truth, his own antipathy to the veil was known to be so great, that he never willingly passed before a mirror, nor stooped to drink at a still fountain, lest, in its peaceful bosom, he should be affrighted by himself. This was what gave plausibility to the whispers, that Mr. Hooper's conscience tortured him for some great crime too horrible to be entirely concealed, or otherwise than so obscurely intimated. Thus, from beneath the black veil, there rolled a cloud into the sunshine, an ambiguity of sin or sorrow, which enveloped the poor minister, so that love or sympathy could never reach him. It was said that ghost and fiend consorted with him there. With self-shudderings and outward terrors, he walked continually in its shadow, groping darkly within his own soul, or gazing through a medium that saddened the whole world. Even the lawless wind, it was believed, respected his dreadful secret, and never blew aside the veil. But still good Mr. Hooper sadly smiled at the pale visages of the worldly throng as he passed by.

Among all its bad influences, the black veil had the one desirable effect, of making its wearer a very efficient clergyman. By the aid of his mysterious emblem—for there was no other apparent cause—he became a man of awful power over souls that were in agony for sin. His converts always regarded him with a dread peculiar to themselves, affirming, though but figuratively, that, before he brought them to celestial light, they had been with him behind the black veil. Its gloom, indeed, enabled him to sympathize with all dark affections. Dying sinners cried aloud for Mr. Hooper, and would not yield their breath till he appeared; though ever, as he stooped to whisper consolation, they shuddered at the veiled face so near their own. Such were the terrors of the black veil, even when Death had bared his visage! Strangers came long distances to attend service at his church, with the mere idle purpose of gazing at his figure, because it was forbidden them to behold his face. But many were made to quake ere they departed! Once, during Governor Belcher's administration, Mr. Hooper was appointed to preach the election sermon. Covered with his black veil, he stood before the chief magistrate, the council, and the representatives, and wrought so deep an impression that the legislative measures of that year were characterized by all the gloom and piety of our earliest ancestral sway.

In this manner, Mr. Hooper spent a long life, irreproachable in outward act, yet shrouded in dismal suspicions; kind and loving, though unloved, and dimly feared; a man apart from men, shunned in their health and joy, but ever summoned to their aid in mortal anguish. As years wore on, shedding their snows above his sable veil, he acquired a name throughout the New England churches, and they called him Father Hooper. Nearly all his parishioners, who were of mature age when he was settled, had been borne away by many a funeral: he had one congregation in the church, and a more crowded one in the church-yard; and having wrought so late into the evening, and done his work so well, it was now good Father Hooper's turn to rest.

Several persons were visible by the shaded candle-light, in the death chamber of the old clergyman. Natural connections he had none. But there was the decorously grave, though unmoved physician, seeking only to mitigate the last pangs of the patient whom he could not save. There were the deacons, and other eminently pious members of his church. There, also, was the Reverend Mr. Clark, of Westbury, a young and zealous divine, who had ridden in haste to pray by the bedside of the expiring minister. There was the nurse, no hired handmaiden of death, but one whose calm affection had endured thus long in secrecy, in solitude, amid the chill of age, and would not perish, even at the dying hour. Who, but Elizabeth! And there lay the hoary head of good Father Hooper upon the death pillow, with the black veil still swathed about his brow, and reaching down over his face, so that each more difficult gasp of his faint breath caused it to stir. All through life that piece of crape had hung between him and the world: it had separated him from cheerful brotherhood and woman's love, and kept him in that saddest of all prisons, his own heart; and still it lay upon his face, as if to deepen the gloom of his darksome chamber, and shade him from the sunshine of eternity.

For some time previous, his mind had been confused, wavering doubtfully between the past and the present, and hovering forward, as it were, at intervals, into the indistinctness of the world to come. There had been feverish turns, which tossed him from side to side, and wore away what little strength he had. But in his most convulsive struggles, and in the wildest vagaries of his intellect, when no other thought retained its sober influence, he still showed an awful solicitude lest the black veil should slip aside. Even if his bewildered soul could have forgotten, there was a faithful woman at his pillow, who, with averted eyes, would have covered that aged face, which she had last beheld in the comeliness of manhood. At length the death-stricken old man lay quietly in the torpor of mental and bodily exhaustion, with an imperceptible pulse, and breath that grew fainter and fainter, except when a long, deep, and irregular inspiration seemed to prelude the flight of his spirit.

The minister of Westbury approached the bedside.

"Venerable Father Hooper," said he, "the moment of your release is at hand. Are you ready for the lifting of the veil that shuts in time from eternity?"

Father Hooper at first replied merely by a feeble motion of his head; then, apprehensive, perhaps, that his meaning might be doubtful, he exerted himself to speak.

"Yea," said he, in faint accents, "my soul hath a patient weariness until that veil be lifted."

"And is it fitting," resumed the Reverend Mr. Clark, "that a man so given to prayer, of such a blameless example, holy in deed and thought, so far as mortal judgment may pronounce; is it fitting that a father in the church should leave a shadow on his memory, that may seem to blacken a life so pure? I pray you, my venerable brother, let not this thing be! Suffer us to be gladdened by your triumphant aspect as you go to your reward. Before the veil of eternity be lifted, let me cast aside this black veil from your face!"

And thus speaking, the Reverend Mr. Clark bent forward to reveal the mystery of so many years. But, exerting a sudden energy, that made all the beholders stand aghast, Father Hooper snatched both his hands from beneath the bedclothes, and pressed them strongly on the black veil, resolute to struggle, if the minister of Westbury would contend with a dying man.

"Never!" cried the veiled clergyman. "On earth, never!"

"Dark old man!" exclaimed the affrighted minister, "with what horrible crime upon your soul are you now passing to the judgment?"

Father Hooper's breath heaved; it rattled in his throat; but, with a mighty effort, grasping forward with his hands, he caught hold of life, and held it back till he should speak. He even raised himself in bed; and there he sat, shivering with the arms of death around him, while the black veil hung down, awful at that last moment, in the gathered terrors of a lifetime. And yet the faint, sad smile, so often there, now seemed to glimmer from its obscurity, and linger on Father Hooper's lips.

"Why do you tremble at me alone?" cried he, turning his veiled face round the circle of pale spectators. "Tremble also at each other! Have men avoided me, and women shown no pity, and children screamed and fled, only for my black veil? What, but the mystery which it obscurely typifies, has made this piece of crape so awful? When the friend shows his inmost heart to his friend; the lover to his best beloved; when man does not vainly shrink from the eye of his Creator, loathsomely treasuring up the secret of his sin; then deem me a monster, for the symbol beneath which I have lived, and die! I look around me, and, lo! on every visage a Black Veil!"

While his auditors shrank from one another, in mutual affright, Father Hooper fell back upon his pillow, a veiled corpse, with a faint smile lingering on the lips. Still veiled, they laid him in his coffin, and a veiled corpse they bore him to the grave. The grass of many years has sprung up and withered on that grave, the burial stone is moss-grown, and good Mr. Hooper's face is dust; but awful is still the thought that it mouldered beneath the Black Veil!

## FOR DISCUSSION

1. This is a story dominated by a single symbol, the black veil. What is its symbolic meaning? Does that meaning change during the course of the story?

2. Do you think there is any emotional connection between the Reverend Hooper and the young lady whose funeral he conducts early in the story? Keep in mind one parishioner's remark, "I had a fancy . . . that the minister and the maiden's spirit were walking hand in hand." Or is that just gossip? Does the funeral have any other significance?

3. How do the parishioners react to the Reverend Hooper's black veil?

4. What is Elizabeth's reaction to the veil? Does she abandon the Reverend Hooper permanently?

5. What does Hooper's own attitude toward the veil appear to be?

6. Can you see any humor—or at least potential humor—suggested by any of the episodes involving the veil?

7. How do you account for the fact that in spite of the black veil the Reverend Hooper becomes a preacher of considerable renown throughout New England?

8. If the Reverend Hooper is the story's protagonist, what are the antagonistic forces that he struggles against?

9. How thoroughly detailed are the personalities of the other characters in the story? Do any of them seem like stock characters or caricatures?

10. Would you call this a traditionally plotted short story? Does it include a precipitating incident, conflict, crisis situation, climax, falling action, denouement, and so on?

11. Hawthorne himself called this story a parable. A parable is a story that illustrates a religious or moral lesson. What lesson does this story teach? Jesus Christ himself preached through parables, and at his death on the cross "the veil of the Temple was rent in twain from the top to the bottom." Does the Reverend Hooper seem at all Christlike? What parallels and differences do you find?

# Father and I

PÄR LAGERKVIST

I remember one Sunday afternoon when I was about ten years old, Daddy took my hand and we went for a walk in the woods to hear the birds sing. We waved good-bye to mother, who was staying at home to prepare supper, and so couldn't go with us. The sun was bright and warm as we set out briskly on our way. We didn't take this bird-singing too seriously, as though it was something special or unusual. We were sensible people, Daddy and I. We were used to the woods and the creatures in them, so we didn't make any fuss about it. It was just because it was Sunday afternoon and Daddy was free. We went along the railway line where other people aren't allowed to go, but Daddy belonged to the railway and had a right to. And in this way we came direct into the woods and did not need to take a roundabout way. Then the bird song and all the rest began at once. They chirped in the bushes; hedge-sparrows, thrushes, and warblers; and we heard all the noises of the little creatures as we came into the woods. The ground was thick with anemones, the birches were dressed in their new leaves, and the pines had young, green shoots. There was such a pleasant smell everywhere. The mossy ground was steaming a little, because the sun was shining upon it. Everywhere there was life and noise; bumble-bees flew out of their holes, midges circled where it was damp. The birds shot out of the bushes to catch them and then dived back again. All of a sudden a train came rushing along and we had to go down the embankment. Daddy hailed the driver with two fingers to his Sunday hat: the driver saluted and waved his hand. Everything seemed on the move. As we went on our way along the sleepers[1] which lay and oozed tar in the sunshine, there was a smell of everything, machine oil and almond blossom, tar and heather, all mixed. We took big steps from sleeper to sleeper so as not to step among the stones, which were rough to walk on, and wore your shoes out. The rails shone in the sunshine. On both sides of the line stood the telephone poles that sang as we went by them. Yes! That was a fine day! The sky was absolutely clear. There wasn't a single cloud to be seen: there just couldn't be any on a day like this, according to what Daddy said. After a while we came to a field of oats on the right side of the line, where a farmer, whom we knew, had a clearing. The oats had grown thick and even; Daddy looked at it knowingly, and I could feel that he was satisfied. I didn't understand that sort of thing much, because I was born in town. Then we came to the bridge over the brook that mostly hadn't much water in it, but now there was plenty. We took hands so that we shouldn't fall down between the sleepers. From there it wasn't far to the railway gate-keeper's little place, which was quite buried in green. There were apple trees and

[1]Railroad ties.

gooseberry bushes right close to the house. We went in there, to pay
a visit, and they offered us milk. We looked at the pigs, the hens, and
the fruit trees, which were in full blossom, and then we went on again.
We wanted to go to the river, because there it was prettier than anywhere
else. There was something special about the river, because higher up
stream it flowed past Daddy's old home. We never liked going back
before we got to it, and, as usual, this time we got there after a fair
walk. It wasn't far to the next station, but we didn't go on there. Daddy
just looked to see whether the signals were right. He thought of everything. We stopped by the river, where it flowed broad and friendly in
the sunshine, and the thick leafy trees on the banks mirrored themselves
in the calm water. It was all so fresh and bright. A breeze came from
the little lakes higher up. We climbed down the bank, went a little way
along the very edge. Daddy showed me the fishing spots. When he
was a boy he used to sit there on the stones and wait for perch all day
long. Often he didn't get a single bite, but it was a delightful way to
spend the day. Now he never had time. We played about for some time
by the side of the river, and threw in pieces of bark that the current
carried away, and we threw stones to see who could throw farthest.
We were, by nature, very merry and cheerful, Daddy and I. After a
while we felt a bit tired. We thought we had played enough, so we
started off home again.

Then it began to get dark. The woods were changed. It wasn't quite
dark yet, but almost. We made haste. Maybe mother was getting anxious,
and waiting supper. She was always afraid that something might happen, though nothing had. This had been a splendid day. Everything
had been just as it should, and we were satisfied with it all. It was
getting darker and darker, and the trees were so queer. They stood and
listened for the sound of footsteps, as though they didn't know who we
were. There was a glow-worm under one of them. It lay down there in
the dark and stared at us. I held Daddy's hand tight, but he didn't seem
to notice the strange light: he just went on. It was quite dark when we
came to the bridge over the stream. It was roaring down underneath
us as if it wanted to swallow us up, as the ground seemed to open under
us. We went along the sleepers carefully, holding hands tight so that
we shouldn't fall in. I thought Daddy would carry me over, but he
didn't say anything about it. I suppose he wanted me to be like him,
and not think anything of it. We went on. Daddy was so calm in the
darkness, walking with even steps without speaking. He was thinking
his own thoughts. I couldn't understand how he could be so calm when
everything was so ghostly. I looked round scared. It was nothing but
darkness everywhere. I hardly dared to breathe deeply, because then
the darkness comes into one, and that was dangerous, I thought. One
must die soon. I remember quite well thinking so then. The railway
embankment was very steep. It finished in black night. The telephone
posts stood up ghostlike against the sky, mumbling deep inside as
though someone were speaking, way down in the earth. The white

china hats sat there scared, cowering with fear, listening. It was all so creepy. Nothing was real, nothing was natural, all seemed a mystery. I went closer to Daddy, and whispered: "Why is it so creepy when it's dark?"

"No child, it isn't creepy," he said, and took my hand.

"Oh, yes, but it is, Daddy."

"No, you mustn't think that. We know there is a God don't we?" I felt so lonely, so abandoned. It was queer that it was only me that was frightened, and not Daddy. It was queer that we didn't feel the same about it. And it was queerer still that what he said didn't help, didn't stop me being frightened. Not even what he said about God helped. The thought of God made one feel creepy too. It was creepy to think that He was everywhere here in the darkness, down there under the trees, and in the telephone posts that mumbled so—probably that was Him everywhere. But all the same one could never see Him.

We went along silently, each of us thinking his own thoughts. My heart felt cramped as though the darkness had come in and was squeezing it.

Then, when we were in a bend, we suddenly heard a great noise behind us. We were startled out of our thoughts. Daddy pulled me down the embankment and held me tight, and a train rushed by; a black train. The lights were out in all the carriages, as it whizzed past us. What could it be? There shouldn't be any train now. We looked at it, frightened. The furnace roared in the big engine, where they shovelled in coal, and the sparks flew out into the night. It was terrible. The driver stood so pale and immovable, with such a stony look in the glare. Daddy didn't recognize him—didn't know who he was. He was just looking ahead as though he was driving straight into darkness, far into darkness, which had no end.

Startled and panting with fear I looked after the wild thing. It was swallowed up in the night. Daddy helped me up on to the line, and we hurried home. He said, "That was strange! What train was that I wonder? And I didn't know the driver either." Then he didn't say any more.

I was shaking all over. That had been for me—for my sake. I guessed what it meant. It was all the fear which would come to me, all the unknown; all that Daddy didn't know about, and couldn't save me from. That was how the world would be for me, and the strange life I should live; not like Daddy's, where everyone was known and sure. It wasn't a real world, or a real life;—it just rushed burning into the darkness which had no end.

## FOR DISCUSSION

1. From what point of view is the story written?
2. What is the author's general tone? What is the mood of the story? Does this mood change at all as the story progresses?
3. Discuss the importance of setting to the story.

4. Would you say the plot of this story is mainly overt or internalized?
5. The story has two parts, the daytime trip to the river and Father's old home and then the night trip back. What contrasts do you find between these two trips?
6. Why does the first part of the story focus on the father and the second part on the narrator as a ten-year-old child?
7. How important is dialogue to the revelation of the story?
8. Contrast the life that Father must have had both as a young boy and as an adult—"where everyone was known and sure"—with the narrator's young life and expectations of the future.
9. The point, or theme, of this story rests on a cluster of images woven together: the railway tracks, the singing birds, the clear afternoon sky, the field of oats, the apple trees and gooseberry bushes, the river, Daddy's old home, the railroad signals, the coming darkness, the glow-worm, the steep railway embankment, and the ghostlike telephone poles. What does each of these images suggest? What do they symbolize?
10. Contrast the two trains and the circumstances of their passing. What is the symbolic significance of each train?
11. Reread the last paragraph carefully. What do you think is the theme of the story?

# The Shades of Spring

D. H. LAWRENCE

## I

It was a mile nearer through the wood. Mechanically, Syson turned up
by the forge and lifted the field-gate. The blacksmith and his mate stood
still, watching the trespasser. But Syson looked too much a gentleman
to be accosted. They let him go on in silence across the small field to
the wood.

There was not the least difference between this morning and those
of the bright springs, six or eight years back. White and sandy-gold
fowls still scratched round the gate, littering the earth and the field with
feathers and scratched-up rubbish. Between the two thick holly bushes
in the wood-hedge was the hidden gap, whose fence one climbed to
get into the wood; the bars were scored just the same by the keeper's[1]
boots. He was back in the eternal.

Syson was extraordinarily glad. Like an uneasy spirit he had returned
to the country of his past, and he found it waiting for him, unaltered.
The hazel still spread glad little hands downwards, the bluebells here
were still wan and few, among the lush grass and in shade of the
bushes.

The path through the wood, on the very brow of a slope, ran winding
easily for a time. All around were twiggy oaks, just issuing their gold,
and floor spaces diapered with woodruff, with patches of dog-mercury
and tufts of hyacinth. Two fallen trees still lay across the track. Syson
jolted down a steep, rough slope, and came again upon the open land,
this time looking north as through a great window in the wood. He
stayed to gaze over the level fields of the hill-top, at the village which
strewed the bare uplands as if it had tumbled off the passing wagons
of industry, and been forsaken. There was a stiff, modern, grey little
church, and blocks and rows of red dwellings lying at random; at the
back, the twinkling headstocks of the pit,[2] and the looming pit-hill. All
was naked and out-of-doors, not a tree! It was quite unaltered.

Syson turned, satisfied, to follow the path that sheered downhill into
the wood. He was curiously elated, feeling himself back in an enduring
vision. He started. A keeper was standing a few yards in front, barring
the way.

"Where might you be going this road, sir?" asked the man. The tone
of his question had a challenging twang. Syson looked at the fellow with
an impersonal observant gaze. It was a young man of four- or five-and-
twenty, ruddy and well favoured. His dark blue eyes now stared ag-

[1]The keeper guards against trespassers and poachers.

[2]Mine or quarry. The headstocks support the pulleys used to haul excavated material out
of the pit.

gressively at the intruder. His black moustache, very thick, was cropped short over a small, rather soft mouth. In every other respect the fellow was manly and good-looking. He stood just above middle height; the strong forward thrust of his chest, and the perfect ease of his erect, self-sufficient body, gave one the feeling that he was taut with animal life, like the thick jet of a fountain balanced in itself. He stood with the butt of his gun on the ground, looking uncertainly and questioningly at Syson. The dark, restless eyes of the trespasser, examining the man and penetrating into him without heeding his office, troubled the keeper and made him flush.

"Where is Naylor? Have you got his job?" Syson asked.

"You're not from the House, are you?" inquired the keeper. It could not be, since everyone was away.

"No, I'm not from the House," the other replied. It seemed to amuse him.

"Then might I ask where you were making for?" said the keeper, nettled.

"Where I am making for?" Syson repeated. "I am going to Willey-Water Farm."

"This isn't the road."

"I think so. Down this path, past the well, and out by the white gate."

"But that's not the public road."

"I suppose not. I used to come so often, in Naylor's time, I had forgotten. Where is he, by the way?"

"Crippled with rheumatism," the keeper answered reluctantly.

"Is he?" Syson exclaimed in pain.

"And who might you be?" asked the keeper, with a new intonation.

"John Adderley Syson; I used to live in Cordy Lane."

"Used to court Hilda Millership?"

Syson's eyes opened with a pained smile. He nodded. There was an awkward silence.

"And you—who are you?" asked Syson.

"Arthur Pilbeam—Naylor's my uncle," said the other.

"You live here in Nuttall?"

"I'm lodgin' at my uncle's—at Naylor's."

"I see!"

"Did you say you was goin' down to Willey-Water?" asked the keeper.

"Yes."

There was a pause of some moments, before the keeper blurted: "I'm courtin' Hilda Millership."

The young fellow looked at the intruder with a stubborn defiance, almost pathetic. Syson opened new eyes.

"Are you?" he said, astonished. The keeper flushed dark.

"She and me are keeping company," he said.

"I didn't know!" said Syson. The other man waited uncomfortably.

"What, is the thing settled?" asked the intruder.

"How, settled?" retorted the other sulkily.

"Are you going to get married soon, and all that?"

The keeper stared in silence for some moments, impotent.

"I suppose so," he said, full of resentment.

"Ah!" Syson watched closely.

"I'm married myself," he added, after a time.

"You are?" said the other incredulously.

Syson laughed in his brilliant, unhappy way.

"This last fifteen months," he said.

The keeper gazed at him with wide, wondering eyes, apparently thinking back, and trying to make things out.

"Why, didn't you know?" asked Syson.

"No, I didn't," said the other sulkily.

There was silence for a moment.

"Ah well!" said Syson, "I will go on. I suppose I may." The keeper stood in silent opposition. The two men hesitated in the open, grassy space, set round with small sheaves of sturdy bluebells; a little open platform on the brow of the hill. Syson took a few indecisive steps forward, then stopped.

"I say, how beautiful!" he cried.

He had come in full view of the downslope. The wide path ran from his feet like a river, and it was full of bluebells, save for a green winding thread down the centre, where the keeper walked. Like a stream the path opened into azure shallows at the levels, and there were pools of bluebells, with still the green thread winding through, like a thin current of ice-water through blue lakes. And from under the twig-purple of the bushes swam the shadowed blue, as if the flowers lay in flood water over the woodland.

"Ah, isn't it lovely!" Syson exclaimed; this was his past, the country he had abandoned, and it hurt him to see it so beautiful. Wood-pigeons cooed overhead, and the air was full of the brightness of birds singing.

"If you're married, what do you keep writing to her for, and sending her poetry books and things?" asked the keeper. Syson stared at him, taken aback and humiliated. Then he began to smile.

"Well," he said, "I did not know about you . . ."

Again the keeper flushed darkly.

"But if you are married——" he charged.

"I am," answered the other cynically.

Then, looking down the blue, beautiful path, Syson felt his own humiliation. "What right *have* I to hang on to her?" he thought, bitterly self-contemptuous.

"She knows I'm married and all that," he said.

"But you keep sending her books," challenged the keeper.

Syson, silenced, looked at the other man quizzically, half pitying. Then he turned.

"Good day," he said, and was gone. Now, everything irritated him:

the two swallows, one all gold and perfume and murmur, one silver-green and bristly, reminded him that here he had taught her about pollination. What a fool he was! What god-forsaken folly it all was!

"Ah well," he said to himself; "the poor devil seems to have a grudge against me. I'll do my best for him." He grinned to himself, in a very bad temper.

## II

The farm was less than a hundred yards from the wood's edge. The wall of trees formed the fourth side to the open quadrangle. The house faced the wood. With tangled emotions, Syson noted the plum blossom falling on the profuse, coloured primroses, which he himself had brought here and set. How they had increased! There were thick tufts of scarlet, and pink, and pale purple primroses under the plum trees. He saw somebody glance at him through the kitchen window, heard men's voices.

The door opened suddenly: very womanly she had grown! He felt himself going pale.

"You?—Addy!" she exclaimed, and stood motionless.

"Who?" called the farmer's voice. Men's low voices answered. Those low voices, curious and almost jeering, roused the tormented spirit in the visitor. Smiling brilliantly at her, he waited.

"Myself—why not?" he said.

The flush burned very deep on her cheek and throat.

"We are just finishing dinner," she said.

"Then I will stay outside." He made a motion to show that he would sit on the red earthenware pipkin that stood near the door among the daffodils, and contained the drinking-water.

"Oh no, come in," she said hurriedly. He followed her. In the door-way, he glanced swiftly over the family, and bowed. Everyone was confused. The farmer, his wife, and the four sons sat at the coarsely laid dinner-table, the men with arms bare to the elbows.

"I am sorry I come at lunch-time," said Syson.

"Hello, Addy!" said the farmer, assuming the old form of address, but his tone cold. "How are you?"

And he shook hands.

"Shall you have a bit?" he invited the young visitor, but taking for granted the offer would be refused. He assumed that Syson was become too refined to eat so roughly. The young man winced at the imputation.

"Have you had any dinner?" asked the daughter.

"No," replied Syson. "It is too early. I shall be back at half-past one."

"You call it lunch, don't you?" asked the eldest son, almost ironical. He had once been an intimate friend of this young man.

"We'll give Addy something when we've finished," said the mother, an invalid, deprecating.

"No—don't trouble. I don't want to give you any trouble," said Syson.

"You could allus live on fresh air an' scenery," laughed the youngest son, a lad of nineteen.

Syson went round the buildings, and into the orchard at the back of the house, where daffodils all along the hedgerow swung like yellow, ruffled birds on their perches. He loved the place extraordinarily, the hills ranging round, with bear-skin woods covering their giant shoulders, and small red farms like brooches clasping their garments; the blue streak of water in the valley, the bareness of the home pasture, the sound of myriad-threaded bird-singing, which went mostly unheard. To his last day, he would dream of this place, when he felt the sun on his face, or saw the small handfuls of snow between the winter twigs, or smelt the coming of spring.

Hilda was very womanly. In her presence he felt constrained. She was twenty-nine, as he was, but she seemed to him much older. He felt foolish, almost unreal beside her. She was so static. As he was fingering some shed plum blossom on a low bough, she came to the back door to shake the tablecloth. Fowls raced from the stack-yard, birds rustled from the trees. Her dark hair was gathered up in a coil like a crown on her head. She was very straight, distant in her bearing. As she folded the cloth, she looked away over the hills.

Presently Syson returned indoors. She had prepared eggs and curd cheese, stewed gooseberries and cream.

"Since you will dine to-night," she said, "I have only given you a light lunch."

"It is awfully nice," he said. "You keep a real idyllic atmosphere—your belt of straw and ivy buds."

Still they hurt each other.

He was uneasy before her. Her brief, sure speech, her distant bearing, were unfamiliar to him. He admired again her grey-black eyebrows, and her lashes. Their eyes met. He saw, in the beautiful grey and black of her glance, tears and a strange light, and at the back of all, calm acceptance of herself, and triumph over him.

He felt himself shrinking. With an effort he kept up the ironic manner.

She sent him into the parlour while she washed the dishes. The long low room was refurnished from the Abbey[3] sale, with chairs upholstered in claret-coloured rep, many years old, and an oval table of polished walnut, and another piano, handsome, though still antique. In spite of the strangeness, he was pleased. Opening a high cupboard let into the thickness of the wall, he found it full of his books, his old lesson-books, and volumes of verse he had sent her, English and German. The daffodils in the white window-bottoms shone across the room, he could almost feel their rays. The old glamour caught him again. His youthful water-colours on the wall no longer made him grin; he remembered how fervently he had tried to paint for her, twelve years before.

[3]Here not a church or monastery but a nobleman's mansion.

She entered, wiping a dish, and he saw again the bright, kernel-white beauty of her arms.

"You are quite splendid here," he said, and their eyes met.

"Do you like it?" she asked. It was the old, low, husky tone of intimacy. He felt a quick change beginning in his blood. It was the old, delicious sublimation, the thinning, almost the vaporising of himself, as if his spirit were to be liberated.

"Aye," he nodded, smiling at her like a boy again. She bowed her head.

"This was the countess's chair," she said in low tones. "I found her scissors down here between the padding."

"Did you? Where are they?"

Quickly, with a lilt in her movement, she fetched her work-basket, and together they examined the long-shanked old scissors.

"What a ballad of dead ladies!"[4] he said, laughing, as he fitted his fingers into the round loops of the countess's scissors.

"I knew you could use them," she said, with certainty. He looked at his fingers, and at the scissors. She meant his fingers were fine enough for the small-looped scissors.

"That is something to be said for me," he laughed, putting the scissors aside. She turned to the window. He noticed the fine, fair down on her cheeks and her upper lip, and her soft, white neck, like the throat of a nettle flower, and her forearms, bright as newly blanched kernels. He was looking at her with new eyes, and she was a different person to him. He did not know her. But he could regard her objectively now.

"Shall we go out awhile?" she asked.

"Yes!" he answered. But the predominant emotion, that troubled the excitement and perplexity of his heart, was fear, fear of that which he saw. There was about her the same manner, the same intonation in her voice, now as then, but she was not what he had known her to be. He knew quite well what she had been for him. And gradually he was realising that she was something quite other, and always had been.

She put no covering on her head, merely took off her apron, saying: "We will go by the larches." As they passed the old orchard, she called him in to show him a blue-tit's nest in one of the apple trees, and a sycock's in the hedge. He rather wondered at her surety, at a certain hardness like arrogance hidden under her humility.

"Look at the apple buds," she said, and he then perceived myriads of little scarlet balls among the drooping boughs. Watching his face, her eyes went hard. She saw the scales were fallen from him,[5] and at last he was going to see her as she was. It was the thing she had most dreaded in the past, and most needed, for her soul's sake. Now he was

---

[4]Refers to a poetic evocation, by the French medieval poet François Villon, of the famous beauties of the past, now vanished like the snows of yesteryear.

[5]That is, from his eyes. The allusion is to the restoration of his sight to the temporarily blinded apostle St. Paul.

going to see her as she was. He would not love her, and he would know he never could have loved her. The old illusion gone, they were strangers, crude and entire. But he would give her her due—she would have her due from him.

She was brilliant as he had not known her. She showed him nests: a jenny wren's in a low bush.

"See this jinty's!" she exclaimed.

He was surprised to hear her use the local name. She reached carefully through the thorns, and put her fingers in the nest's round door.

"Five!" she said. "Tiny little things."

She showed him nests of robins, and chaffinches, and linnets, and buntings; of a wagtail beside the water.

"And if we go down, nearer the lake, I will show you a king-fisher's. . . ."

"Among the young fir trees," she said, "there's a throstle's or a blackie's on nearly every bough, every ledge. The first day, when I had seen them all, I felt as if I mustn't go in the wood. It seemed a city of birds: and in the morning, hearing them all, I thought of the noisy early markets. I was afraid to go in my own wood."

She was using the language they had both of them invented. Now it was all her own. He had done with it. She did not mind his silence, but was always dominant, letting him see her wood. As they came along a marshy path where forget-me-nots were opening in a rich blue drift: "We know all the birds, but there are many flowers we can't find out," she said. It was half an appeal to him, who had known the names of things.

She looked dreamily across to the open fields that slept in the sun.

"I have a lover as well, you know," she said, with assurance, yet dropping again almost into the intimate tone.

This woke in him the spirit to fight her.

"I think I met him. He is good-looking—also in Arcardy."[6]

Without answering, she turned into a dark path that led uphill, where the trees and undergrowth were very thick.

"They did well," she said at length, "to have various altars to various gods, in old days."

"Ah yes!" he agreed. "To whom is the new one?"

"There are no old ones," she said. "I was always looking for this."

"And whose is it?" he asked.

"I don't know," she said, looking full at him.

"I'm very glad, for your sake," he said, "that you are satisfied."

"Aye—but the man doesn't matter so much," she said. There was a pause.

"No!" he exclaimed, astonished, yet recognising her as her real self.

"It is one's self that matters," she said. "Whether one is being one's own self and serving one's own God."

---

[6]Alludes to the Latin "I, too, have lived in Arcady" (the pastoral country of myth).

There was silence, during which he pondered. The path was almost flowerless, gloomy. At the side, his heels sank into soft clay.

## III

"I," she said, very slowly, "I was married the same night as you."
He looked at her.
"Not legally, of course," she replied. "But—actually."
"To the keeper?" he said, not knowing what else to say.
She turned to him.
"You thought I could not?" she said. But the flush was deep in her cheek and throat, for all her assurance.
Still he would not say anything.
"You see"—she was making an effort to explain—"*I* had to understand also."
"And what does it amount to, this *understanding?*" he asked.
"A very great deal—does it not to you?" she replied. "One is free."
"And you are not disappointed?"
"Far from it!" Her tone was deep and sincere.
"You love him?"
"Yes, I love him."
"Good!" he said.
This silenced her for a while.
"Here, among his things, I love him," she said.
His conceit would not let him be silent.
"It needs this setting?" he asked.
"It does," she cried. "You were always making me to be not myself."
He laughed shortly.
"But is it a matter of surroundings?" he said. He had considered her all spirit.
"I am like a plant," she replied. "I can only grow in my own soil."
They came to a place where the undergrowth shrank away, leaving a bare, brown space, pillared with the brick-red and purplish trunks of pine trees. On the fringe, hung the sombre green of elder trees, with flat flowers in bud, and below were bright, unfurling pennons of fern. In the midst of the bare space stood a keeper's log hut. Pheasant-coops were lying about, some occupied by a clucking hen, some empty.
Hilda walked over the brown pine-needles to the hut, took a key from among the eaves, and opened the door. It was a bare wooden place with a carpenter's bench and form, carpenter's tools, an axe, snares, traps, some skins pegged down, everything in order. Hilda closed the door. Syson examined the weird flat coats of wild animals, that were pegged down to be cured. She turned some knotch in the side wall, and disclosed a second, small apartment.
"How romantic!" said Syson.
"Yes. He is very curious—he has some of a wild animal's cunning—

in a nice sense—and he is inventive, and thoughtful—but not beyond a certain point."

She pulled back a dark green curtain. The apartment was occupied almost entirely by a large couch of heather and bracken, on which was spread an ample rabbit-skin rug. On the floor were patchwork rugs of cat-skin, and a red calf-skin, while hanging from the wall were other furs. Hilda took down one, which she put on. It was a cloak of rabbit-skin and of white fur, with a hood, apparently of the skins of stoats. She laughed at Syson from out of this barbaric mantle, saying:

"What do you think of it?"

"Ah——! I congratulate you on your man," he replied.

"And look!" she said.

In a little jar on a shelf were some sprays, frail and white, of the first honeysuckle.

"They will scent the place at night."

He looked round curiously.

"Where does he come short, then?" he asked. She gazed at him for a few moments. Then, turning aside:

"The stars aren't the same with him," she said. "You could make them flash and quiver, and the forget-me-nots come up at me like phosphorescence. You could make things *wonderful*. I have found it out—it is true. But I have them all for myself, now."

He laughed, saying:

"After all, stars and forget-me-nots are only luxuries. You ought to make poetry."

"Aye," she assented. "But I have them all now."

Again he laughed bitterly at her.

She turned swiftly. He was leaning against the small window of the tiny, obscure room, and was watching her, who stood in the doorway, still cloaked in her mantle. His cap was removed, so she saw his face and head distinctly in the dim room. His black, straight, glossy hair was brushed clean back from his brow. His black eyes were watching her, and his face, that was clear and cream, and perfectly smooth, was flickering.

"We are very different," she said bitterly.

Again he laughed.

"I see you disapprove of me," he said.

"I disapprove of what you have become," she said.

"You think we might"—he glanced at the hut—"have been like this—you and I?"

She shook her head.

"You! No; never! You plucked a thing and looked at it till you had found out all you wanted to know about it, then you threw it away," she said.

"Did I?" he asked. "And could your way never have been my way? I suppose not."

"Why should it?" she said. "I am a separate being."

"But surely two people sometimes go the same way," he said.

"You took me away from myself," she said.

He knew he had mistaken her, had taken her for something she was not. That was his fault, not hers.

"And did you always know?" he asked.

"No—you never let me know. You bullied me. I couldn't help myself. I was glad when you left me, really."

"I know you were," he said. But his face went paler, almost deathly luminous.

"Yet," he said, "it was you who sent me the way I have gone."

"I!" she exclaimed, in pride.

"You *would* have me take the Grammar School scholarship—and you would have me foster poor little Botell's fervent attachment to me, till he couldn't live without me—and because Botell was rich and influential. You triumphed in the wine-merchant's offer to send me to Cambridge,[7] to befriend his only child. You wanted me to rise in the world. And all the time you were sending me away from you—every new success of mine put a separation between us, and more for you than for me. You never wanted to come with me: you wanted just to send me to see what it was like. I believe you even wanted me to marry a lady. You wanted to triumph over society in me."

"And I am responsible," she said, with sarcasm.

"I distinguished myself to satisfy you," he replied.

"Ah!" she cried, "you always wanted change, change, like a child."

"Very well! And I am a success, and I know it, and I do some good work. But—I thought you were different. What right have you to a man?"

"What do you want?" she cried, looking at him with wide, fearful eyes.

He looked back at her, his eyes pointed, like weapons.

"Why, nothing," he laughed shortly.

There was a rattling at the outer latch, and the keeper entered. The woman glanced round, but remained standing, fur-cloaked, in the inner doorway. Syson did not move.

The other man entered, saw, and turned away without speaking. The two also were silent.

Pilbeam attended to his skins.

"I must go," said Syson.

"Yes," she replied.

"Then I give you 'To our vast and varying fortunes.' " He lifted his hand in pledge.

" 'To our vast and varying fortunes,' " she answered gravely, and speaking in cold tones.

"Arthur!" she cried.

[7]The great English university.

The keeper pretended not to hear. Syson, watching keenly, began to smile. The woman drew herself up.

"Arthur!" she said again, with a curious upward inflection, which warned the two men that her soul was trembling on a dangerous crisis.

The keeper slowly put down his tool and came to her.

"Yes," he said.

"I wanted to introduce you," she said, trembling.

"I've met him a'ready," said the keeper.

"Have you? It is Addy, Mr. Syson, whom you know about.—This is Arthur, Mr. Pilbeam," she added, turning to Syson. The latter held out his hand to the keeper, and they shook hands in silence.

"I'm glad to have met you," said Syson. "We drop our correspondence, Hilda?"

"Why need we?" she asked.

The two men stood at a loss.

"*Is* there no need?" said Syson.

Still she was silent.

"It is as you will," she said.

They went all three together down the gloomy path.

" 'Qu'il était bleu, le ciel, et grand l'espoir,' "[8] quoted Syson, not knowing what to say.

"What do you mean?" she said. "Besides, *we* can't walk in *our* wild oats—we never sowed any."

Syson looked at her. He was startled to see his young love, his nun, his Botticelli angel,[9] so revealed. It was he who had been the fool. He and she were more separate than any two strangers could be. She only wanted to keep up a correspondence with him—and he, of course, wanted it kept up, so that he could write to her, like Dante to some Beatrice[10] who had never existed save in the man's own brain.

At the bottom of the path she left him. He went along with the keeper, towards the open, towards the gate that closed on the wood. The two men walked almost like friends. They did not broach the subject of their thoughts.

●      ●      ●      ●      ●

Instead of going straight to the high-road gate, Syson went along the woods' edge, where the brook spread out in a little bog, and under the alder trees, among the reeds, great yellow stools and bosses of marigolds shone. Threads of brown water trickled by, touched with gold from the flowers. Suddenly there was a blue flash in the air, as a kingfisher passed.

[8]"How blue the sky was, and how great was hope."

[9]The Renaissance painter Sandro Botticelli depicted women as idealistically slender and ethereal.

[10]The medieval poet Dante wrote his masterpiece, *The Divine Comedy*, under the inspiration of his idealized beloved Beatrice, and celebrated Beatrice herself in the cycle of poems, *The New Life*.

Syson was extraordinarily moved. He climbed the bank to the gorse bushes, whose sparks of blossom had not yet gathered into a flame. Lying on the dry brown turf, he discovered sprigs of tiny purple milkwort and pink spots of lousewort. What a wonderful world it was—marvellous, for ever new. He felt as if it were underground, like the fields of monotone hell, notwithstanding. Inside his breast was a pain like a wound. He remembered the poem of William Morris, where in the Chapel of Lyonesse a knight lay wounded, with the truncheon of a spear deep in his breast, lying always as dead, yet did not die, while day after day the coloured sunlight dipped from the painted window across the chancel, and passed away.[11] He knew now it never had been true, that which was between him and her, not for a moment. The truth had stood apart all the time.

Syson turned over. The air was full of the sound of larks, as if the sunshine above were condensing and falling in a shower. Amid this bright sound, voices sounded small and distinct.

"But if he's married, an' quite willing to drop it off, what has ter against it?" said the man's voice.

"I don't want to talk about it now. I want to be alone."

Syson looked through the bushes. Hilda was standing in the wood, near the gate. The man was in the field, loitering by the hedge, and playing with the bees as they settled on the white bramble flowers.

There was silence for a while, in which Syson imagined her will among the brightness of the larks. Suddenly the keeper exclaimed "Ah!" and swore. He was gripping at the sleeve of his coat, near the shoulder. Then he pulled off his jacket, threw it on the ground, and absorbedly rolled up his shirtsleeves right to the shoulder.

"Ah!" he said vindictively, as he picked out the bee and flung it away. He twisted his fine, bright arm, peering awkwardly over his shoulder.

"What is it?" asked Hilda.

"A bee—crawled up my sleeve," he answered.

"Come here to me," she said.

The keeper went to her, like a sulky boy. She took his arm in her hands.

"Here it is—and the sting left in—poor bee!"

She picked out the sting, put her mouth to his arm, and sucked away the drop of poison. As she looked at the red mark her mouth had made, and at his arm, she said, laughing:

"That is the reddest kiss you will ever have."

When Syson next looked up, at the sound of voices, he saw in the shadow the keeper with his mouth on the throat of his beloved, whose head was thrown back, and whose hair had fallen, so that one rough rope of dark brown hair hung across his bare arm.

[11]The knight's wound, like Syson's, is not physical but emotional; at the end of the poem he dies for love. Lyonesse was a legendary region in southwestern England, now submerged.

"No," the woman answered. "I am not upset because he's gone. You won't understand. . . ."

Syson could not distinguish what the man said. Hilda replied, clear and distinct:

"You know I love you. He has gone quite out of my life—don't trouble about him. . . ." He kissed her, murmuring. She laughed hollowly.

"Yes," she said, indulgent. "We will be married, we will be married. But not just yet." He spoke to her again. Syson heard nothing for a time. Then she said:

"You must go home now, dear—you will get no sleep."

Again was heard the murmur of the keeper's voice, troubled by fear and passion.

"But why should we be married at once?" she said. "What more would you have, by being married? It is most beautiful as it is."

At last he pulled on his coat and departed. She stood at the gate, not watching him, but looking over the sunny country.

When at last she had gone, Syson also departed, going back to town.

## FOR DISCUSSION

1. What is the story's precipitating incident? Why has Syson returned to the place of his youth? What does he hope to accomplish?
2. What does setting contribute to the story? How does it affect your view of the characters?
3. The stories of D. H. Lawrence often present a triangle involving a man of intellect, a man of animal feeling, and a woman possessing both qualities. Explain how this story uses such a pattern.
4. What is Syson's emotional state as he returns to the old familiar woods?
5. Discuss the initial reaction of Syson and Arthur to each other. Which man do you find more sympathetic?
6. Discuss specific ways in which Syson has allowed his emotions to be dominated by his intellect. Why does he so often express himself through literary allusions?
7. What is Hilda's first reaction to Syson when he appears outside the house? How do the members of her family regard Syson?
8. What does Hilda mean when she tells Syson that she was married the same night as he? What does this suggest about her combined intellectual-animal nature?
9. Why does Hilda take Syson to the very place—the tiny room in the hut—where she has made love with Arthur?
10. Why do you think Hilda feels that "the stars aren't the same" with Arthur as they might have been with Syson? Does Hilda still love Syson? If so, does she love Syson more than she does Arthur? Or does she love the two men equally but differently?
11. Why has Syson continued to write to Hilda even after getting married? How has Hilda contributed to the fact that she and Syson have grown apart?
12. Why does Syson disapprove of what Hilda has become? How has he misjudged Hilda's character from the first?

13. Discuss the possible symbolic significance of each of the following: Arthur's name and his gun, the woods, the path through the woods, the countess's scissors, the hut, its green curtains and rear compartment, the rabbit-fur that Hilda puts on, the honeysuckle sprays, and Arthur's bee sting. Are any or all of these sexual symbols? Are there any others?

14. At the end of the story, how is Syson like the wounded knight in the Chapel of Lyonesse?

15. What has Syson learned from his visit? What in particular is the meaning of the final scene between Hilda and Arthur? Will the two ever really marry?

16. Do you find the characters in this story plausible? Do any of them change during the course of the story, or do they remain pretty much the same?

17. The word *shades* in the title seems a little strange if you take it to mean only "shadows." Does the word have another meaning that seems relevant to the story? What is its relevance?

# The Bride Comes to Yellow Sky

STEPHEN CRANE

## I

The great Pullman was whirling onward with such dignity of motion that a glance from the window seemed simply to prove that the plains of Texas were pouring eastward. Vast flats of green grass, dull-hued spaces of mesquit and cactus, little groups of frame houses, woods of light and tender trees, all were sweeping into the east, sweeping over the horizon, a precipice.

A newly married pair had boarded this coach at San Antonio. The man's face was reddened from many days in the wind and sun, and a direct result of his new black clothes was that his brick-colored hands were constantly performing in a most conscious fashion. From time to time he looked down respectfully at his attire. He sat with a hand on each knee, like a man waiting in a barber's shop. The glances he devoted to other passengers were furtive and shy.

The bride was not pretty, nor was she very young. She wore a dress of blue cashmere, with small reservations of velvet here and there, and with steel buttons abounding. She continually twisted her head to regard her puff sleeves, very stiff, straight, and high. They embarrassed her. It was quite apparent that she had cooked, and that she expected to cook, dutifully. The blushes caused by the careless scrutiny of some passengers as she had entered the car were strange to see upon this plain, under-class countenance, which was drawn in placid, almost emotionless lines.

They were evidently very happy. "Ever been in a parlor-car before?" he asked, smiling with delight.

"No," she answered; "I never was. It's fine, ain't it?"

"Great! And then after a while we'll go forward to the diner, and get a big lay-out. Finest meal in the world. Charge a dollar."

"Oh, do they?" cried the bride. "Charge a dollar? Why, that's too much—for us—ain't it, Jack?"

"Not this trip, anyhow," he answered bravely. "We're going to go the whole thing."

Later he explained to her about the trains. "You see, it's a thousand miles from one end of Texas to the other; and this train runs right across it, and never stops but four times." He had the pride of an owner. He pointed out to her the dazzling fittings of the coach; and in truth her eyes opened wider as she contemplated the sea-green figured velvet, the shining brass, silver, and glass, the wood that gleamed as darkly brilliant as the surface of a pool of oil. At one end a bronze figure sturdily held a support for a separated chamber, and at convenient places on the ceiling were frescos in olive and silver.

To the minds of the pair, their surroundings reflected the glory of their marriage that morning in San Antonio; this was the environment of their new estate; and the man's face in particular beamed with an elation that made him appear ridiculous to the negro porter. This individual at times surveyed them from afar with an amused and superior grin. On other occasions he bullied them with skill in ways that did not make it exactly plain to them that they were being bullied. He subtly used all the manners of the most unconquerable kind of snobbery. He oppressed them; but of this oppression they had small knowledge, and they speedily forgot that infrequently a number of travellers covered them with stares of derisive enjoyment. Historically there was supposed to be something infinitely humorous in their situation.

"We are due in Yellow Sky at 3:42," he said, looking tenderly into her eyes.

"Oh, are we?" she said, as if she had not been aware of it. To evince surprise at her husband's statement was part of her wifely amiability. She took from a pocket a little silver watch; and as she held it before her, and stared at it with a frown of attention, the new husband's face shone.

"I bought it in San Anton' from a friend of mine," he told her gleefully.

"It's seventeen minutes past twelve," she said, looking up at him with a kind of shy and clumsy coquetry. A passenger, noting this play, grew excessively sardonic, and winked at himself in one of the numerous mirrors.

At last they went to the dining car. Two rows of negro waiters, in glowing white suits, surveyed their entrance with the interest, and also the equanimity, of men who had been forewarned. The pair fell to the lot of a waiter who happened to feel pleasure in steering them through their meal. He viewed them with the manner of a fatherly pilot, his countenance radiant with benevolence. The patronage, entwined with the ordinary deference, was not plain to them. And yet, as they returned to their coach, they showed in their faces a sense of escape.

To the left, miles down a long purple slope, was a little ribbon of mist where moved the keening Rio Grande. The train was approaching it at an angle, and the apex was Yellow Sky. Presently it was apparent that, as the distance from Yellow Sky grew shorter, the husband became commensurately restless. His brick-red hands were more insistent in their prominence. Occasionally he was even rather absent-minded and far-away when the bride leaned forward and addressed him.

As a matter of truth, Jack Potter was beginning to find the shadow of a deed weigh upon him a like a leaden slab. He, the town marshal of Yellow Sky, a man known, liked, and feared in his corner, a prominent person, had gone to San Antonio to meet a girl he believed he loved, and there, after the usual prayers, had actually induced her to marry him, without consulting Yellow Sky for any part of the transaction. He was now bringing his bride before an innocent and unsuspecting community.

Of course people in Yellow Sky married as it pleased them, in accordance with a general custom; but such was Potter's thought of his duty to his friends, or of their idea of his duty, or of an unspoken form which does not control men in these matters, that he felt he was heinous. He had committed an extraordinary crime. Face to face with this girl in San Antonio, and spurred by his sharp impulse, he had gone headlong over all the social hedges. At San Antonio he was like a man hidden in the dark. A knife to sever any friendly duty, any form, was easy to his hand in that remote city. But the hour of Yellow Sky—the hour of daylight—was approaching.

He knew full well that his marriage was an important thing to his town. It could only be exceeded by the burning of the new hotel. His friends could not forgive him. Frequently he had reflected on the advisability of telling them by telegraph, but a new cowardice had been upon him. He feared to do it. And now the train was hurrying him toward a scene of amazement, glee, and reproach. He glanced out of the window at the line of haze swinging slowly in toward the train.

Yellow Sky had a kind of brass band, which played painfully, to the delight of the populace. He laughed without heart as he thought of it. If the citizens could dream of his prospective arrival with his bride, they would parade the band at the station and escort them, amid cheers and laughing congratulations, to his adobe home.

He resolved that he would use all the devices of speed and plainscraft in making the journey from the station to his house. Once within that safe citadel, he could issue some sort of vocal bulletin, and then not go among the citizens until they had time to wear off a little of their enthusiasm.

The bride looked anxiously at him. "What's worrying you, Jack?"

He laughed again. "I'm not worrying, girl; I'm only thinking of Yellow Sky."

She flushed in comprehension.

A sense of mutual guilt invaded their minds and developed a finer tenderness. They looked at each other with eyes softly aglow. But Potter often laughed the same nervous laugh; the flush upon the bride's face seemed quite permanent.

The traitor to the feelings of Yellow Sky narrowly watched the speeding landscape. "We're nearly there," he said.

Presently the porter came and announced the proximity of Potter's home. He held a brush in his hand, and, with all his airy superiority gone, he brushed Potter's new clothes as the latter slowly turned this way and that way. Potter fumbled out a coin and gave it to the porter, as he had seen others do. It was a heavy and muscle-bound business, as that of a man shoeing his first horse.

The porter took their bag, and as the train began to slow they moved forward to the hooded platform of the car. Presently the two engines and their long string of coaches rushed into the station of Yellow Sky.

"They have to take water here," said Potter, from a constricted throat and in mournful cadence, as one announcing death. Before the train stopped his eye had swept the length of the platform, and he was glad and astonished to see there was none upon it but the station-agent, who, with a slightly hurried and anxious air, was walking toward the water-tanks. When the train had halted, the porter alighted first, and placed in position a little temporary step.

"Come on, girl," said Potter, hoarsely. As he helped her down they each laughed on a false note. He took the bag from the negro, and bade his wife cling to his arm. As they slunk rapidly away, his hang-dog glance perceived that they were unloading the two trunks, and also that the station-agent, far ahead near the baggage-car, had turned and was running toward him, making gestures. He laughed, and groaned as he laughed, when he noted the first effect of his marital bliss upon Yellow Sky. He gripped his wife's arm firmly to his side, and they fled. Behind them the porter stood, chuckling fatuously.

## II

The California express on the Southern Railway was due at Yellow Sky in twenty-one minutes. There were six men at the bar of the Weary Gentleman saloon. One was a drummer[1] who talked a great deal and rapidly; three were Texans who did not care to talk at that time; and two were Mexican sheep-herders, who did not talk as a general practice in the Weary Gentleman saloon. The barkeeper's dog lay on the board walk that crossed in the front of the door. His head was on his paws, and he glanced drowsily here and there with the constant vigilance of a dog that is kicked on occasion. Across the sandy street were some vivid green grass-plots, so wonderful in appearance, amid the sands that burned near them in a blazing sun, that they caused a doubt in the mind. They exactly resembled the grass mats used to represent lawns on the stage. At the cooler end of the railway station, a man without a coat sat in a tilted chair and smoked his pipe. The fresh-cut bank of the Rio Grande circled near the town, and there could be seen beyond it a great plum-colored plain of mesquit.

Save for the busy drummer and his companions in the saloon, Yellow Sky was dozing. The new-comer leaned gracefully upon the bar, and recited many tales with the confidence of a bard who has come upon a new field.

"—and at the moment that the old man fell downstairs with the bureau in his arms, the old woman was coming up with two scuttles of coal, and of course—"

The drummer's tale was interrupted by a young man who suddenly appeared in the open door. He cried: "Scratchy Wilson's drunk, and has turned loose with both hands." The two Mexicans at once set down their glasses and faded out of the rear entrance of the saloon.

[1]Traveling salesman.

The drummer, innocent and jocular, answered: "All right, old man. S'pose he has? Come in and have a drink, anyhow."

But the information had made such an obvious cleft in every skull in the room that the drummer was obliged to see its importance. All had become instantly solemn. "Say," said he, mystified, "what is this?" His three companions made the introductory gesture of eloquent speech; but the young man at the door forestalled them.

"It means, my friend," he answered, as he came into the saloon, "that for the next two hours this town won't be a health resort."

The barkeeper went to the door, and locked and barred it; reaching out of the window, he pulled in heavy wooden shutters, and barred them. Immediately a solemn, chapel-like gloom was upon the place. The drummer was looking from one to another.

"But say," he cried, "what is this, anyhow? You don't mean there is going to be a gun-fight?"

"Don't know whether there'll be a fight or not," answered one man, grimly; "but there'll be some shootin'—some good shootin'."

The young man who had warned them waved his hand. "Oh, there'll be a fight fast enough, if any one wants it. Anybody can get a fight out there in the street. There's a fight just waiting."

The drummer seemed to be swayed between the interest of a foreigner and a perception of personal danger.

"What did you say his name was?" he asked.

"Scratchy Wilson," they answered in chorus.

"And will he kill anybody? What are you going to do? Does this happen often? Does he rampage around like this once a week or so? Can he break in that door?"

"No; he can't break down that door," replied the barkeeper. "He's tried it three times. But when he comes you'd better lay down on the floor, stranger. He's dead sure to shoot at it, and a bullet may come through."

Thereafter the drummer kept a strict eye upon the door. The time had not yet been called for him to hug the floor, but, as a minor precaution, he sidled near to the wall. "Will he kill anybody?" he said again.

The men laughed low and scornfully at the question.

"He's out to shoot, and he's out for trouble. Don't see any good in experimentin' with him."

"But what do you do in a case like this? What do you do?"

A man responded: "Why, he and Jack Potter—"

"But," in chorus the other men interrupted, "Jack Potter's in San Anton'."

"Well, who is he? What's he got to do with it?"

"Oh, he's the town marshal. He goes out and fights Scratchy when he gets on one of these tears."

"Wow!" said the drummer, mopping his brow. "Nice job he's got."

The voices had toned away to mere whisperings. The drummer wished to ask further questions, which were born of an increasing anxiety and bewilderment; but when he attempted them, the men merely looked at him in irritation and motioned him to remain silent. A tense waiting hush was upon them. In the deep shadows of the room their eyes shone as they listened for sounds from the street. One man made three gestures at the barkeeper; and the latter, moving like a ghost, handed him a glass and a bottle. The man poured a full glass of whisky, and set down the bottle noiselessly. He gulped the whisky in a swallow, and turned again toward the door in immovable silence. The drummer saw that the barkeeper, without a sound, had taken a Winchester from beneath the bar. Later he saw this individual beckoning to him, so he tiptoed across the room.

"You better come with me back of the bar."

"No, thanks," said the drummer, perspiring; "I'd rather be where I can make a break for the back door."

Whereupon the man of bottles made a kindly but peremptory gesture. The drummer obeyed it, and, finding himself seated on a box with his head below the level of the bar, balm was laid upon his soul at sight of various zinc and copper fittings that bore a resemblance to armor-plate. The barkeeper took a seat comfortably upon an adjacent box.

"You see," he whispered, "this here Scratchy Wilson is a wonder with a gun—a perfect wonder; and when he goes on the wartrail, we hunt our holes—naturally. He's about the last one of the old gang that used to hang out along the river here. He's a terror when he's drunk. When he's sober he's all right—kind of simple—wouldn't hurt a fly—nicest fellow in town. But when he's drunk—whoo!"

There were periods of stillness. "I wish Jack Potter was back from San Anton'," said the barkeeper. "He shot Wilson up once—in the leg—and he would sail in and pull out the kinks in this thing."

Presently they heard from a distance the sound of a shot, followed by three wild yowls. It instantly removed a bond from the men in the darkened saloon. There was a shuffling of feet. They looked at each other. "Here he comes," they said.

## III

A man in a maroon-colored flannel shirt, which had been purchased for purposes of decoration, and made principally by some Jewish women on the East Side of New York, rounded a corner and walked into the middle of the main street of Yellow Sky. In either hand the man held a long, heavy, blue-black revolver. Often he yelled, and these cries rang through a semblance of a deserted village, shrilly flying over the roofs in a volume that seemed to have no relation to the ordinary vocal strength of a man. It was as if the surrounding stillness formed the arch of a tomb over him. These cries of ferocious challenge rang against walls of silence. And his boots had red tops with gilded imprints, of the kind beloved in winter by little sledding boys on the hillsides of New England.

The man's face flamed in a rage begot of whisky. His eyes, rolling, and yet keen for ambush, hunted the still doorways and windows. He walked with the creeping movement of the midnight cat. As it occurred to him, he roared menacing information. The long revolvers in his hands were as easy as straws; they were moved with an electric swiftness. The little fingers of each hand played sometimes in a musician's way. Plain from the low collar of the shirt, the cords of his neck straightened and sank, straightened and sank, as passion moved him. The only sounds were his terrible invitations. The calm adobes preserved their demeanor at the passing of this small thing in the middle of the street.

There was no offer of fight—no offer of fight. The man called to the sky. There were no attractions. He bellowed and fumed and swayed his revolvers here and everywhere.

The dog of the barkeeper of the Weary Gentleman saloon had not appreciated the advance of events. He yet lay dozing in front of his master's door. At sight of the dog, the man paused and raised his revolver humorously. At sight of the man, the dog sprang up and walked diagonally away, with a sullen head, and growling. The man yelled, and the dog broke into a gallop. As it was about to enter an alley, there was a loud noise, a whistling, and something spat the ground directly before it. The dog screamed, and, wheeling in terror, galloped headlong in a new direction. Again there was a noise, a whistling, and sand was kicked viciously before it. Fear-stricken, the dog turned and flurried like an animal in a pen. The man stood laughing, his weapons at his hips.

Ultimately the man was attracted by the closed door of the Weary Gentleman saloon. He went to it and, hammering with a revolver, demanded drink.

The door remaining imperturbable, he picked a bit of paper from the walk, and nailed it to the framework with a knife. He then turned his back contemptuously upon this popular resort and, walking to the opposite side of the street and spinning there on his heel quickly and lithely, fired at the bit of paper. He missed it by a half-inch. He swore at himself, and went away. Later he comfortably fusilladed the windows of his most intimate friend. The man was playing with this town; it was a toy for him.

But still there was no offer of fight. The name of Jack Potter, his ancient antagonist, entered his mind, and he concluded that it would be a glad thing if he should go to Potter's house, and by bombardment induce him to come out and fight. He moved in the direction of his desire, chanting Apache scalp-music.

When he arrived at it, Potter's house presented the same still front as had the other adobes. Taking up a strategic position, the man howled a challenge. But this house regarded him as might a great stone god. It gave no sign. After a decent wait, the man howled further challenges, mingling with them wonderful epithets.

Presently there came the spectacle of a man churning himself into deepest rage over the immobility of a house. He fumed at it as the winter wind attacks a prairie cabin in the North. To the distance there should have gone the sound of a tumult like the fighting of two hundred Mexicans. As necessity bade him, he paused for breath or to reload his revolvers.

## IV

Potter and his bride walked sheepishly and with speed. Sometimes they laughed together shamefacedly and low.

"Next corner, dear," he said finally.

They put forth the efforts of a pair walking bowed against a strong wind. Potter was about to raise a finger to point the first appearance of the new home when, as they circled the corner, they came face to face with a man in a maroon-colored shirt, who was feverishly pushing cartridges into a large revolver. Upon the instant the man dropped his revolver to the ground and, like lightning, whipped another from its holster. The second weapon was aimed at the bridegroom's chest.

There was a silence. Potter's mouth seemed to be merely a grave for his tongue. He exhibited an instinct to at once loosen his arm from the woman's grip, and he dropped the bag to the sand. As for the bride, her face had gone as yellow as old cloth. She was a slave to hideous rites, gazing at the apparitional snake.

The two men faced each other at a distance of three paces. He of the revolver smiled with a new and quiet ferocity.

"Tried to sneak up on me," he said. "Tried to sneak up on me!" His eyes grew more baleful. As Potter made a slight movement, the man thrust his revolver venomously forward. "No; don't you do it, Jack Potter. Don't you move a finger toward a gun just yet. Don't you move an eyelash. The time has come for me to settle with you, and I'm goin' to do it my own way, and loaf along with no interferin'. So if you don't want a gun bent on you, just mind what I tell you."

Potter looked at his enemy. "I ain't got a gun on me, Scratchy," he said. "Honest, I ain't." He was stiffening and steadying, but yet somewhere at the back of his mind a vision of the Pullman floated: the sea-green figured velvet, the shining brass, silver, and glass, the wood that gleamed as darkly brilliant as the surface of a pool of oil—all the glory of the marriage, the environment of the new estate. "You know I fight when it comes to fighting, Scratchy Wilson; but I ain't got a gun on me. You'll have to do all the shootin' yourself."

His enemy's face went livid. He stepped forward, and lashed his weapon to and fro before Potter's chest. "Don't tell me you ain't got no gun on you, you whelp. Don't tell me no lie like that. There ain't a man in Texas ever seen you without no gun. Don't take me for no kid." His eyes blazed with light, and his throat worked like a pump.

"I ain't takin' you for no kid," answered Potter. His heels had not moved an inch backward. "I'm takin' you for a damn fool. I tell you

I ain't got a gun, and I ain't. If you're goin' to shoot me up, you better begin now; you'll never get a chance like this again."

So much enforced reasoning had told on Wilson's rage; he was calmer. "If you ain't got a gun, why ain't you got a gun?" he sneered. "Been to Sunday-school?"

"I ain't got a gun because I've just come from San Anton' with my wife. I'm married," said Potter. "And if I'd thought there was going to be any galoots like you prowling around when I brought my wife home, I'd had a gun, and don't you forget it."

"Married!" said Scratchy, not at all comprehending.

"Yes, married. I'm married," said Potter, distinctly.

"Married?" said Scratchy. Seemingly for the first time, he saw the drooping, drowning woman at the other man's side. "No!" he said. He was like a creature allowed a glimpse of another world. He moved a pace backward, and his arm, with the revolver, dropped to his side. "Is this the lady?" he asked.

"Yes; this is the lady," answered Potter.

There was another period of silence.

"Well," said Wilson at last, slowly, "I s'pose it's all off now."

"It's all off if you say so, Scratchy. You know I didn't make the trouble." Potter lifted his valise.

"Well, I 'low it's off, Jack," said Wilson. He was looking at the ground. "Married!" He was not a student of chivalry; it was merely that in the presence of this foreign condition he was a simple child of the earlier plains. He picked up his starboard revolver, and, placing both weapons in their holsters, he went away. His feet made funnel-shaped tracks in the heavy sand.

## FOR DISCUSSION

1. What is the point of view of the story? Are there any shifts in the point of view?
2. What does setting contribute to the story?
3. What is the author's tone? Do you notice any changes in the tone in different parts of the story?
4. What symbolic meaning can you find in the train moving westward across the Texas plains? What is the reason for the elaborate descriptions of the train's interior?
5. Why does Jack Potter feel guilty—as if he has committed some crime—for having gone to San Antonio and gotten married?
6. How do the various people on the train view Jack Potter and his bride?
7. Are the men in the Weary Gentleman saloon detailed characters, or are they only briefly sketched?
8. Would you call Scratchy Wilson a stock character? What does Scratchy represent? Is he an evil person?
9. Why does the salesman in the Weary Gentleman seem so surprised by Scratchy Wilson's behavior?

10. Why is Scratchy dumbfounded when he learns that Potter has gotten married? Why is he no longer interested in a fight with Potter?
11. What symbolic meaning can you find in the story's final sentence: "His feet made funnel-shaped tracks in the sand"?
12. Thematically, what is the author suggesting about the old West by this thwarted confrontation between Scratchy Wilson, the last of the old gang, and Jack Potter, a marshal who has taken himself a bride? Can this story be read as a spoof on the traditional western shootout of popular fiction?

# The Dry Rock

IRWIN SHAW

"We're late," Helen said, as the cab stopped at a light. "We're twenty minutes late." She looked at her husband accusingly.

"All right," Fitzsimmons said. "I couldn't help it. The work was on the desk and it had to . . ."

"This is the one dinner party of the year I didn't want to be late for," Helen said. "So naturally . . ."

The cab started and was halfway across the street when the Ford sedan roared into it, twisting, with a crashing and scraping of metal, a high mournful scream of brakes, the tinkling of glass. The cab shook a little, then subsided.

The cabby, a little gray man, turned and looked back, worriedly. "Everybody is all right?" he asked nervously.

"Everybody is fine," Helen said bitterly, pulling at her cape to get it straight again after the jolting.

"No damage done," said Fitzsimmons, smiling reassuringly at the cabby, who looked very frightened.

"I am happy to hear that," the cabby said. He got out of his car and stood looking sadly at his fender, now thoroughly crumpled, and his headlight, now without a lens. The door of the Ford opened and its driver sprang out. He was a large young man with a light gray hat. He glanced hurriedly at the cab.

"Why don't you watch where the hell yer goin'?" he asked harshly.

"The light was in my favor," said the cabby. He was a small man of fifty, in a cap and a ragged coat, and he spoke with a heavy accent. "It turned green and I started across. I would like your license, Mister."

"What for?" the man in the gray hat shouted. "Yer load's all right. Get on yer way. No harm done." He started back to his car.

The cabby gently put his hand on the young man's arm. "Excuse me, friend," he said. "It is a five-dollar job, at least. I would like to see your license."

The man pulled his arm away, glared at the cabby. "Aaah," he said and swung. His fist made a loud, surprising noise against the cabby's nose. The old man sat down slowly on the running board of his cab, holding his head wearily in his hands. The young man in the gray hat stood over him, bent over, fists still clenched. "Didn't I tell yuh no harm was done?" he shouted. "Why didn't yuh lissen t' me? I got a good mind to . . ."

"Now, see here," Fitzsimmons said, opening the rear door and stepping out.

"What d'you want?" The young man turned and snarled at Fitzsimmons, his fists held higher. "Who asked for you?"

"I saw the whole thing," Fitzsimmons began, "and I don't think you . . ."

"Aaah," snarled the young man. "Dry up."

"Claude," Helen called. "Claude, keep out of this."

"Claude," the young man repeated balefully. "Dry up, Claude."

"Are you all right?" Fitzsimmons asked, bending over the cabby, who still sat reflectively on the running board, his head down, his old and swollen cap hiding his face, blood trickling down his clothes.

"I'm all right," the cabby said wearily. He stood up, looked wonderingly at the young man. "Now, my friend, you force me to make trouble. Police!" he called, loudly. *"Police!"*

"Say, lissen," the man in the gray hat shouted. "What the hell do yuh need to call the cops for? Hey, cut it out!"

*"Police!"* the old cabby shouted calmly, but with fervor deep in his voice. "Police!"

"I ought to give it to yuh good." The young man shook his fist under the cabby's nose. He jumped around nervously. "This is a small matter," he shouted, "nobody needs the cops!"

"Police!" called the cabby.

"Claude," Helen put her head out the window. "Let's get out of here and let the two gentlemen settle this any way they please."

"I apologize!" The young man held the cabby by his lapels with both large hands, shook him, to emphasize his apology. "Excuse me. I'm sorry. Stop yelling police, for God's sake!"

"I'm going to have you locked up," the cabby said. He stood there, slowly drying the blood off his shabby coat with his cap. His hair was gray, but long and full, like a musician's. He had a big head for his little shoulders, and a sad, lined, little face and he looked older than fifty, to Fitzsimmons, and very poor, neglected, badly nourished. "You have committed a crime," the cabby said, "and there is a punishment for it."

"Will yuh talk to him?" The young man turned savagely to Fitzsimmons. "Will yuh tell him I'm sorry?"

"It's entirely up to him," Fitzsimmons said.

"We're a half hour late," Helen announced bitterly. "The perfect dinner guests."

"It is not enough to be sorry," said the cab driver. *"Police . . ."*

"Say, listen, Bud," the young man said, his voice quick and confidential, "what's yer name?"

"Leopold Tarloff," the cabby said. "I have been driving a cab on the streets of New York for twenty years, and everybody thinks just because you're a cab driver they can do whatever they want to you."

"Lissen, Leopold," the young man pushed his light gray hat far back on his head. "Let's be sensible. I hit yer cab. All right. I hit you. All right."

"What's all right about it?" Tarloff asked.

"What I mean is, I admit it, I confess I did it, that's what I mean. All right." The young man grabbed Tarloff's short ragged arms as he spoke, intensely. "Why the fuss? It happens every day. Police are unnecessary. I'll tell yuh what I'll do with yuh, Leopold. Five dollars, yuh say, for the fender. All right. And for the bloody nose, another pound. What do yuh say? Everybody is satisfied. Yuh've made yerself a fiver on the transaction; these good people go to their party without no more delay."

Tarloff shook his arms free from the huge hands of the man in the gray hat. He put his head back and ran his fingers through his thick hair and spoke coldly. "I don't want to hear another word. I have never been so insulted in my whole life."

The young man stepped back, his arms wide, palms up wonderingly. "I insult him!" He turned to Fitzsimmons. "Did you hear me insult this party?" he asked.

"Claude!" Helen called. "Are we going to sit here all night?"

"A man steps up and hits me in the nose," Tarloff said. "He thinks he makes everything all right with five dollars. He is mistaken. Not with five hundred dollars."

"How much d'yuh think a clap in the puss is worth?" the young man growled. "Who d'yuh think y'are—Joe Louis?"

"Not ten thousand dollars," Tarloff said, on the surface calm, but quivering underneath. "Not for twenty thousand dollars. My dignity."

"His dignity!" the young man whispered. "For Christ's sake!"

"What do you want to do?" Fitzsimmons asked, conscious of Helen glooming in the rear seat of the cab.

"I would like to take him to the station house and make a complaint," Tarloff said. "You would have to come with me, if you'd be so kind. What is your opinion on the matter?"

"Will yuh tell him the cops are not a necessity!" the young man said hoarsely. "Will yuh tell the bastidd?"

"Claude!" called Helen.

"It's up to you," Fitzsimmons said, looking with what he hoped was an impartial, judicious expression at Tarloff, hoping he wouldn't have to waste any more time. "You do what you think you ought to do."

Tarloff smiled, showing three yellow teeth in the front of his small and childlike mouth, curved and red and surprising in the lined and weatherbeaten old hackie's face. "Thank you very much," he said. "I am glad to see you agree with me."

Fitzsimmons sighed.

"Yer drivin' me crazy!" the young man shouted at Tarloff. "Yer makin' life impossible!"

"To you," Tarloff said with dignity, "I talk from now on only in a court of law. That's my last word."

The young man stood there, breathing heavily, his fists clenching and unclenching, his pale gray hat shining in the light of a street lamp. A policeman turned the corner, walking in a leisurely and abstracted manner, his eyes on the legs of a girl across the street.

Fitzsimmons went over to him. "Officer," he said, "there's a little job for you over here." The policeman regretfully took his eyes off the girl's legs and sighed and walked slowly over to where the two cars were still nestling against each other.

"What are yuh?" the young man was asking Tarloff, when Fitzsimmons came up with the policeman. "Yuh don't act like an American citizen. What are yuh?"

"I'm a Russian," Tarloff said. "But I'm in the country twenty-five years now, I know what the rights of an individual are."

"Yeah," said the young man hopelessly. "Yeah . . ."

The Fitzsimmonses drove silently to the police station in the cab, with Tarloff driving slowly and carefully, though with hands that shook on the wheel. The policeman drove with the young man in the young man's Ford. Fitzsimmons saw the Ford stop at a cigar store and the young man jump out and go into the store, into a telephone booth.

"For three months," Helen said, as they drove, "I've been trying to get Adele Lowrie to invite us to dinner. Now we've finally managed it. Perhaps we ought to call her and invite the whole party down to night court."

"It isn't night court," Fitzsimmons said patiently. "It's a police station. And I think you might take it a little better. After all, the poor old man has no one else to speak up for him."

"Leopold Tarloff," Helen said. "It sounds impossible. Leopold Tarloff. Leopold Tarloff."

They sat in silence until Tarloff stopped the cab in front of the police station and opened the door for them. The Ford with the policeman and the young man drove up right behind them and they all went in together.

There were some people up in front of the desk lieutenant, a dejected-looking man with long mustaches and a loud, blonde woman who kept saying that the man had threatened her with a baseball bat three times that evening. Two Negroes with bloody bandages around their heads were waiting, too.

"It will take some time," said the policeman. "There are two cases ahead of you. My name is Kraus."

"Oh, my," said Helen.

"You'd better call Adele," Fitzsimmons said. "Tell her not to hold dinner for for us."

Helen held her hand out gloomily for nickels.

"I'm sorry," Tarloff said anxiously, "to interrupt your plans for the evening."

"Perfectly all right," Fitzsimmons said, trying to screen his wife's face from Tarloff by bending over to search for the nickels in his pocket.

Helen went off, disdainfully holding her long formal skirt up with her hand, as she walked down the spit- and butt-marked corridor of the police station toward a pay telephone. Fitzsimmons reflectively watched her elegant back retreat down the hallway.

"I am tired," Tarloff said. "I think I will have to sit down, if you will excuse me." He sat on the floor, looking up with a frail, apologetic smile on his red face worn by wind and rain and traffic-policemen. Fitzsimmons suddenly felt like crying, watching the old man sitting there among the spit and cigarette butts, on the floor against the wall, with his cap off and his great bush of musician's gray hair giving the lie to the tired, weathered face below it.

Four men threw open the outside doors and walked into the police station with certainty and authority. They all wore the same light-gray hats with the huge flat brims. The young man who had hit Tarloff greeted them guardedly. "I'm glad you're here, Pidgear," he said to the man who, by some subtle mixture of stance and clothing, of lift of eyebrow and droop of mouth, announced himself as leader.

They talked swiftly and quietly in a corner.

"A Russian!" Pidgear's voice rang out angrily. "There are 10,000 cab drivers in the metropolitan area, you have to pick a Russian to punch in the nose!"

"I'm excitable!" the young man yelled. "Can I help it if I'm excitable? My father was the same way; it's a family characteristic."

"Go tell that to the Russian," Pidgear said. He went over to one of the three men who had come in with him, a large man who needed a shave and whose collar was open at the throat, as though no collar could be bought large enough to go all the way around that neck. The large man nodded, went over to Tarloff, still sitting patiently against the wall.

"You speak Russian?" the man with the open collar said to Tarloff.

"Yes, sir," Tarloff said.

The large man sat down slowly beside him, gripped Tarloff's knee confidentially in his tremendous hairy hand, spoke excitedly, winningly, in Russian.

Pidgear and the young man who had hit Tarloff came over to Fitzsimmons, leaving the other two men in the gray hats, small, dark men with shining eyes, who just stood at the door and looked hotly on.

"My name is Pidgear," the man said to Fitzsimmons, who by now was impressed with the beautiful efficiency of the system that had been put into motion by the young driver of the Ford—an obviously legal mind like Pidgear, a man who spoke Russian, and two intense men with gray hats standing on call just to see justice done, and all collected in the space of fifteen minutes. "Alton Pidgear," the man said, smiling professionally at Fitzsimmons. "I represent Mr. Rusk."

"Yeah," said the young man.

"My name is Fitzsimmons."

"Frankly, Mr. Fitzsimmons," Pidgear said, "I would like to see you get Mr. Tarloff to call this whole thing off. It's an embarrassing affair for all concerned; nobody stands to gain anything by pressing it."

Helen came back and Fitzsimmons saw by the expression on her face thtt she wasn't happy. "They're at the soup by now," she said loudly to Fitzsimmons. "Adele said for us to take all the time we want, they're getting along fine."

"Mr. Rusk is willing to make a handsome offer," Pidgear said. "Five dollars for the car, five dollars for the nose . . ."

"Go out to dinner with your husband," Helen muttered, "and you wind up in a telephone booth in a police station. 'Excuse me for being late, darling, but I'm calling from the 8th precinct, this is our night for street-fighting.'"

"Sssh, Helen, please," Fitzsimmons said. He hadn't eaten since nine that morning and his stomach was growling with hunger.

"It was all a mistake," Pidgear said smoothly. "A natural mistake. Why should the man be stubborn? He is being reimbursed for everything, isn't he? I wish you would talk to him, Mr. Fitzsimmons; we don't want to keep you from your social engagements. Undoubtedly," Pidgear said, eying their evening clothes respectfully, "you and the madam were going to an important dinner party. It would be too bad to spoil an important dinner party for a little thing like this. Why, this whole affair is niggling," he said, waving his hand in front of Fitzsimmons' face. "Absolutely niggling."

Fitzsimmons looked over to where Tarloff and the other Russian were sitting on the floor. From Tarloff's face and gestures, even though he was talking in deepest Russian, Fitzsimmons could tell Tarloff was still as firm as ever. Fitzsimmons looked closely at Rusk, who was standing looking at Tarloff through narrow, baleful eyes.

"Why're you so anxious?" Fitzsimmons asked.

Rusk's eyes clouded over and his throat throbbed against his collar with rage. "I don't want to appear in court!" he yelled. "I don't want the whole goddamn business to start all over again, investigation, lawyers, fingerprints . . ."

Pidgear punched him savagely in the ribs, his fist going a short distance, but with great violence.

"Why don't you buy time on the National Broadcasting System?" Pidgear asked. "Make an address, coast to coast!"

Rusk glared murderously for a moment at Pidgear, then leaned over toward Fitzsimmons, pointing a large blunt finger at him. "Do I have to put my finger in your mouth?" he whispered hoarsely.

"What does he mean by that?" Helen asked loudly. "Put his finger in your mouth? Why should he put his finger in your mouth?"

Rusk looked at her with complete hatred, turned, too full for words, and stalked away, with Pidgear after him. The two little men in the gray hats watched the room without moving.

"Claude?" Helen began.

"Obviously," Fitzsimmons said, his voice low, "Mr. Rusk isn't anxious for anyone to look at his fingerprints. He's happier this way."

"You picked a fine night!" Helen shook her head sadly. "Why can't we just pick up and get out of here?"

Rusk, with Pidgear at his side, strode back. He stopped in front of the Fitzsimmonses. "I'm a family man," he said, trying to sound like one. "I ask yuh as a favor. Talk to the Russian."

"I had to go to Bergdorf Goodman," Helen said, too deep in her own troubles to bother with Rusk, "to get a gown to spend the evening in a police station. 'Mrs. Claude Fitzsimmons was lovely last night in blue velvet and silver fox at Officer Kraus's reception at the 8th Precinct. Other guests were the well-known Leopold Tarloff, and the Messrs. Pidgear and Rusk, in gray hats. Other guests included the Russian Ambassador and two leading Italian artillerymen, also in gray hats.' "

Pidgear laughed politely. "Your wife is a very witty woman," he said.

"Yes," said Fitzsimmons, wondering why he'd married her.

"Will yuh for Christ's sake *ask*?" Rusk demanded. "Can it hurt yuh?"

"We're willing to do our part," Pidgear said. "We even brought down a Russian to talk to him and clear up any little points in his own language. No effort is too great."

Fitzsimmons' stomach growled loudly. "Haven't eaten all day," he said, embarrassed.

"That's what happens," Pidgear said. "Naturally."

"Yeah," said Rusk.

"Perhaps I should go out and get you a malted milk," Helen suggested coldly.

Fitzsimmons went over to where Tarloff was sitting with the other Russian. The others followed him.

"Are you sure, Mr. Tarloff," Fitzsimmons said, "that you still want to prosecute?"

"Yes," Tarloff said promptly.

"Ten dollars," Rusk said. "I offer yuh ten dollars. Can a man do more?"

"Money is not the object." With his cap Tarloff patted his nose, which was still bleeding slowly and had swelled enormously, making Tarloff look lopsided and monstrous.

"What's the object?" Rusk asked.

"The object, Mr. Rusk, is principle."

"*You* talk to him," Rusk said to Fitzsimmons.

"All right," Officer Kraus said, "you can go up there now."

They all filed in in front of the lieutenant sitting high at his desk.

Tarloff told his story, the accident, the wanton punch in the nose.

"It's true," Pidgear said, "that there was an accident, that there was a slight scuffle after by mistake. But the man isn't hurt. A little swelling in the region of the nose. No more." He pointed dramatically to Tarloff.

"Physically," Tarloff said, clutching his cap, talking with difficulty because his nose was clogged, "physically that's true. I am not badly hurt. But in a mental sense . . ." He shrugged. "I have suffered an injury."

"Mr. Rusk is offering the amount of ten dollars," Pidgear said. "Also, he apologizes; he's sorry."

The lieutenant looked wearily down at Rusk. "Are you sorry?" he asked.

"I'm sorry," said Rusk, raising his right hand. "On the Bible, I swear I'm sorry."

"Mr. Tarloff," the lieutenant said, "if you wish to press charges, there are certain steps you will have to take. A deposition will have to be taken. Have you got witnesses?"

"Here," Tarloff said with a shy smile at the Fitzsimmonses.

"They will have to be present," the lieutenant said sleepily.

"Oh, God," Helen said.

"A warrant will have to be sworn out, there must be a hearing, at which the witnesses must also be present . . ."

"Oh, God," Helen said.

"Then the trial," said the lieutenant.

"Oh, God!" Helen said loudly.

"The question is, Mr. Tarloff," said the lieutenant, yawning, "are you willing to go through all that trouble?"

"The fact is," Tarloff said unhappily, "he hit me in the head without provocation. He is guilty of a crime on my person. He insulted me. He did me an injustice. The law exists for such things. One individual is not to be hit by another individual in the streets of the city without legal punishment." Tarloff was using his hands to try to get everyone, the Fitzsimmonses, the lieutenant, Pidgear, to understand. "There is a principle. The dignity of the human body. Justice. For a bad act a man suffers. It's an important thing . . ."

"I'm excitable," Rusk shouted. "If yuh want, yuh can hit me in the head."

"That is not the idea," Tarloff said.

"The man is sorry," the lieutenant said, wiping his eyes, "he is offering you the sum of ten dollars; it will be a long, hard job to bring this man to trial; it will cost a lot of the taxpayers' money; you are bothering these good people here who have other things to do. What is the sense in it, Mr. Tarloff?"

Tarloff scraped his feet slowly on the dirty floor, looked sadly, hopefully, at Fitzsimmons. Fitzsimmons looked at his wife, who was glaring at Tarloff, tapping her foot sharply again and again. Fitzsimmons looked back at Tarloff, standing there, before the high desk, small, in his ragged coat and wild gray hair, his little worn face twisted and grotesque with the swollen nose, his eyes lost and appealing. Fitzsimmons shrugged sadly. Tarloff drooped inside his old coat, shook his head wearily, shrugged, deserted once and for all before the lieutenant's desk, on the dry rock of principle.

"O.K.," he said.

"Here," Rusk brought the ten-dollar bill out with magical speed.

Tarloff pushed it away. "Get out of here," he said, without looking up.

No one talked all the way to Adele Lowrie's house. Tarloff opened the door and sat, looking straight ahead, while they got out. Helen went to the door of the house and rang. Silently, Fitzsimmons offered Tarloff the fare. Tarloff shook his head. "You have been very good," he said. "Forget it."

Fitzsimmons put the money away slowly.

"Claude!" Helen called. "The door's open."

Fitzsimmons hated his wife, suddenly, without turning to look at her. He put out his hand and Tarloff shook it wearily.

"I'm awfully sorry," Fitzsimmons said. "I wish I . . ."

Tarloff shrugged. "That's all right," he said. "I understand." His face, in the shabby light of the cab, worn and old and battered by the streets of the city, was a deep well of sorrow. "There is no time. Principle." He laughed, shrugged. "Today there is no time for anything."

He shifted gears and the taxi moved slowly off, its motor grinding noisily.

"Claude!" Helen called.

"Oh, shut up!" Fitzsimmons said as he turned and walked into Adele Lowrie's house.

## FOR DISCUSSION

1. What is the story's precipitating incident?
2. Through whose eyes are the events of the story seen? Which character is the third-person narrator submerged within?
3. Who is the protagonist of the story? What types of forces does he struggle against?
4. Does the story include a second set of characters in conflict with each other? If so, who are these other characters?
5. What do all the characters other than Tarloff and Fitzsimmons think about the key issue of the story?
6. Why is it ironic that Tarloff is of Russian descent?
7. What is Rusk's probable line of work?
8. At what point does the climax occur? What takes place during the denouement?
9. What is the "dry rock" of the title? What is the meaning of the image?
10. Why does Fitzsimmons hate his wife at the end of the story?
11. The theme of this story involves a broad comment upon our busy and impersonal society. What is that comment? Can you locate specific places in the story where various aspects of the theme are stated directly?

# The Wooing of Ariadne

HARRY MARK PETRAKIS

I knew from the beginning she must accept my love—put aside foolish female protestations. It is the distinction of the male to be the aggressor and the cloak of the female to lend grace to the pursuit. Aha! I am wise to these wiles.

I first saw Ariadne at a dance given by the Spartan brotherhood in the Legion Hall on Laramie Street. The usual assemblage of prune-faced and banana-bodied women smelling of virtuous anemia. They were an outrage to a man such as myself.

Then I saw her! A tall stately woman, perhaps in her early thirties. She had firm and slender arms bare to the shoulders and a graceful neck. Her hair was black and thick and piled in a great bun at the back of her head. That grand abundance of hair attracted me at once. This modern aberration women have of chopping their hair close to the scalp and leaving it in fantastic disarray I find revolting.

I went at once to my friend Vasili, the baker, and asked him who she was.

"Ariadne Langos," he said. "Her father is Janco Langos, the grocer."

"Is she engaged or married?"

"No." he said slyly. "They say she frightens off the young men. They say she is very spirited."

"Excellent," I said and marveled at my good fortune in finding her unpledged. "Introduce me at once."

"Marko," Vasili said with some apprehension. "Do not commit anything rash."

I pushed the little man forward. "Do not worry, little friend," I said. "I am a man suddenly possessed by a vision. I must meet her at once."

We walked together across the dance floor to where my beloved stood. The closer we came the more impressive was the majestic swell of her breasts and the fine great sweep of her thighs. She towered over the insignificant apple-core women around her. Her eyes, dark and thoughtful, seemed to be restlessly searching the room.

Be patient, my dove! Marko is coming.

"Miss Ariadne," Vasili said. "This is Mr. Marko Palamas. He desires to have the honor of your acquaintance."

She looked at me for a long and piercing moment. I imagined her gauging my mighty strength by the width of my shoulders and the circumference of my arms. I felt the tips of my mustache bristle with pleasure. Finally she nodded with the barest minimum of courtesy. I was not discouraged.

"Miss Ariadne," I said, "may I have the pleasure of this dance?"

She stared at me again with her fiery eyes. I could imagine more timid men shriveling before her fierce gaze. My heart flamed at the passion her rigid exterior concealed.

"I think not," she said.

"Don't you dance?"

Vasili gasped beside me. An old prune-face standing nearby clucked her toothless gums.

"Yes, I dance," Ariadne said coolly. "I do not wish to dance with you."

"Why?" I asked courteously.

"I do not think you heard me," she said. "I do not wish to dance with you."

Oh, the sly and lovely darling. Her subterfuge so apparent. Trying to conceal her pleasure at my interest.

"Why?" I asked again.

"I am not sure," she said. "It could be your appearance, which bears considerable resemblance to a gorilla, or your manner, which would suggest closer alliance to a pig."

"Now that you have met my family," I said engagingly, "let us dance."

"Not now," she said, and her voice rose. "Not this dance or the one after. Not tonight or tomorrow night or next month or next year. Is that clear?"

Sweet, sweet Ariadne. Ancient and eternal game of retreat and pursuit. My pulse beat more quickly.

Vasili pulled at my sleeve. He was my friend, but without the courage of a goat. I shook him off and spoke to Ariadne.

"There is a joy like fire that consumes a man's heart when he first sets eyes on his beloved," I said. "This I felt when I first saw you." My voice trembled under a mighty passion. "I swear before God from this moment that I love you."

She stared shocked out of her deep dark eyes and, beside her, old prune-face staggered as if she had been kicked. Then my beloved did something which proved indisputably that her passion was as intense as mine.

She doubled up her fist and struck me in the eye. A stout blow for a woman that brought a haze to my vision, but I shook my head and moved a step closer.

"I would not care," I said, "if you struck out both my eyes. I would cherish the memory of your beauty forever."

By this time the music had stopped, and the dancers formed a circle of idiot faces about us. I paid them no attention and ignored Vasili, who kept whining and pulling at my sleeve.

"You are crazy!" she said. "You must be mad! Remove yourself from my presence or I will tear out both your eyes and your tongue besides!"

You see! Another woman would have cried, or been frightened into silence. But my Ariadne, worthy and venerable, hurled her spirit into my teeth.

"I would like to call on your father tomorrow," I said. From the assembled dancers who watched there rose a few vagrant whispers and some rude laughter. I stared at them carefully and they hushed at once. My temper and strength of arm were well known.

Ariadne did not speak again, but in a magnificent spirit stamped from the floor. The music began, and men and women began again to dance. I permitted Vasili to pull me to a corner.

"You are insane!" he said. He wrung his withered fingers in anguish. "You assaulted her like a Turk! Her relatives will cut out your heart!"

"My intentions were honorable," I said. "I saw her and loved her and told her so." At this point I struck my fist against my chest. Poor Vasili jumped.

"But you do not court a woman that way," he said.

"*You* don't, my anemic friend," I said. "Nor do the rest of these sheep. But I court a woman that way!"

He looked to heaven and helplessly shook his head. I waved good-by and started for my hat and coat.

"Where are you going?" he asked.

"To prepare for tomorrow," I said. "In the morning I will speak to her father."

I left the hall and in the street felt the night wind cold on my flushed cheeks. My blood was inflamed. The memory of her loveliness fed fuel to the fire. For the first time I understood with a terrible clarity the driven heroes of the past performing mighty deeds in love. Paris stealing Helen in passion, and Menelaus pursuing with a great fleet.[1] In that moment if I knew the whole world would be plunged into conflict I would have followed Ariadne to Hades.

I went to my rooms above my tavern. I could not sleep. All night I tossed in restless frenzy. I touched my eye that she had struck with her spirited hand.

*Ariadne! Ariadne!* my soul cried out.

In the morning I bathed and dressed carefully. I confirmed the address of Langos, the grocer, and started to his store. It was a bright cold November morning, but I walked with spring in my step.

When I opened the door of the Langos grocery, a tiny bell rang shrilly. I stepped into the store piled with fruits and vegetables and smelling of cabbages and greens.

A stooped little old man with white bushy hair and owlish eyes came toward me. He looked as if his veins contained vegetable juice instead of blood, and if he were, in truth, the father of my beloved I marveled at how he could have produced such a paragon of women.

---

[1]This summarizes the cause of the Trojan War, the subject of Homer's great epic *The Iliad.* Menelaus was Helen's husband and king of Sparta, the warlike province of Greece from which Marko Palamas also comes. To win back Helen, Menelaus called on his allies, the other Greek kings; the war lasted more than a decade, and many heroes on both sides were killed.

"Are you Mr. Langos?"

"I am," he said and he came closer. "I am."

"I met your daughter last night," I said. "Did she mention I was going to call?"

He shook his head somberly.

"My daughter mentioned you," he said. "In thirty years I have never seen her in such a state of agitation. She was possessed."

"The effect on me was the same," I said. "We met for the first time last night, and I fell passionately in love."

"Incredible," the old man said.

"You wish to know something about me," I said. "My name is Marko Palamas. I am a Spartan emigrated to this country eleven years ago. I am forty-one years old. I have been a wrestler and a sailor and fought with the resistance movement in Greece in the war. For this service I was decorated by the king. I own a small but profitable tavern on Dart Street. I attend church regularly. I love your daughter."

As I finished he stepped back and bumped a rack of fruit. An orange rolled off to the floor. I bent and retrieved it to hand it to him and he cringed as if he thought I might bounce it off his old head.

"She is a bad-tempered girl," he said. "Stubborn, impatient and spoiled. She has been the cause of considerable concern to me. All the eligible young men have been driven away by her temper and disposition."

"Poor girl," I said. "Subjected to the courting of calves and goats."

The old man blinked his owlish eyes. The front door opened and a battleship of a woman sailed in.

"Three pounds of tomatoes, Mr. Langos," she said. "I am in a hurry. Please to give me good ones. Last week two spoiled before I had a chance to put them into Demetri's salad."

"I am very sorry," Mr. Langos said. He turned to me. "Excuse me, Mr. Poulmas."

"Palamas," I said. "Marko Palamas."

He nodded nervously. He went to wait on the battleship, and I spent a moment examining the store. Neat and small. I would not imagine he did more than hold his own. In the rear of the store there were stairs leading to what appeared to be an apartment above. My heart beat faster.

When he had bagged the tomatoes and given change, he returned to me and said, "She is also a terrible cook. She cannot fry an egg without burning it." His voice shook with woe. "She cannot make pilaf or lamb with squash." He paused. "You like pilaf and lamb with squash?"

"Certainly."

"You see?" he said in triumph. "She is useless in the kitchen. She is thirty years old, and I am resigned she will remain an old maid. In a way I am glad because I know she would drive some poor man to drink."

"Do not deride her to discourage me," I said. "You need have no fear that I will mistreat her or cause her unhappiness. When she is married to me she will cease being a problem to you." I paused. "It is true that I am not pretty by the foppish standards that prevail today. But I am a man. I wrestled Zahundos and pinned him two straight falls in Baltimore. A giant of a man. Afterward he conceded he had met his master. This from Zahundos was a mighty compliment."

"I am sure," the old man said without enthusiasm. "I am sure."

He looked toward the front door as if hoping for another customer.

"Is your daughter upstairs?"

He looked startled and tugged at his apron. "Yes," he said. "I don't know. Maybe she has gone out."

"May I speak to her? Would you kindly tell her I wish to speak with her."

"You are making a mistake," the old man said. "A terrible mistake."

"No mistake," I said firmly.

The old man shuffled toward the stairs. He climbed them slowly. At the top he paused and turned the knob of the door. He rattled it again.

"It is locked," he called down. "It has never been locked before. She has locked the door."

"Knock," I said. "Knock to let her know I am here."

"I think she knows," the old man said. "I think she knows."

He knocked gently.

"Knock harder," I suggested. "Perhaps she does not hear."

"I think she hears," the old man said. "I think she hears."

"Knock again," I said. "Shall I come up and knock for you?"

"No, no," the old man said quickly. He gave the door a sound kick. Then he groaned as if he might have hurt his foot.

"She does not answer," he said in a quavering voice. "I am very sorry she does not answer."

"The coy darling," I said and laughed. "If that is her game." I started for the front door of the store.

I went out and stood on the sidewalk before the store. Above the grocery were the front windows of their apartment. I cupped my hands about my mouth.

"Ariadne!" I shouted. "Ariadne!"

The old man came out of the door running disjointedly. He looked frantically down the street.

"Are you mad?" he asked shrilly. "You will cause a riot. The police will come. You must be mad!"

"Ariadne!" I shouted. "Beloved!"

A window slammed open, and the face of Ariadne appeared above me. Her dark hair tumbled about her ears.

"Go away!" she shrieked. "Will you go away!"

"Ariadne," I said loudly. "I have come as I promised. I have spoken to your father. I wish to call on you."

"Go away!" she shrieked. "Madman! Imbecile! Go away!"

By this time a small group of people had assembled around the store and were watching curiously. The old man stood wringing his hands and uttering what sounded like small groans.

"Ariadne," I said. "I wish to call on you. Stop this nonsense and let me in."

She pushed farther out the window and showed me her teeth.

"Be careful, beloved," I said. "You might fall."

She drew her head in quickly, and I turned then to the assembled crowd.

"A misunderstanding," I said. "Please move on."

Suddenly old Mr. Langos shrieked. A moment later something broke on the sidewalk a foot from where I stood. A vase or a plate. I looked up, and Ariadne was preparing to hurl what appeared to be a water pitcher.

"Ariadne!" I shouted. "Stop that!"

The water pitcher landed closer than the vase, and fragments of glass struck my shoes. The crowd scattered, and the old man raised his hands and wailed to heaven.

Ariadne slammed down the window.

The crowd moved in again a little closer, and somewhere among them I heard laughter. I fixed them with a cold stare and waited for some one of them to say something offensive. I would have tossed him around like sardines, but they slowly dispersed and moved on. In another moment the old man and I were alone.

I followed him into the store. He walked an awkward dance of agitation. He shut the door and peered out through the glass.

"A disgrace," he wailed. "A disgrace. The whole street will know by nightfall. A disgrace."

"A girl of heroic spirit," I said. "Will you speak to her for me? Assure her of the sincerity of my feelings. Tell her I pledge eternal love and devotion."

The old man sat down on an orange crate and weakly made his cross.

"I had hoped to see her myself," I said. "But if you promise to speak to her, I will return this evening."

"That soon?" the old man said.

"If I stayed now," I said, "it would be sooner."

"This evening," the old man said and shook his head in resignation. "This evening."

I went to my tavern for a while and set up the glasses for the evening trade. I made arrangements for Pavlakis to tend bar in my place. Afterward I sat alone in my apartment and read a little of majestic Pindar[2] to ease the agitation of my heart.

Once in the mountains of Greece when I fought with the guerillas in the last year of the great war, I suffered a wound from which it seemed

[2]Great Greek poet of the fifth century B.C., whose odes celebrate the winners in the Olympic and other Greek games and refer frequently to Greek myth.

I would die. For days high fever raged in my body. My friends brought a priest at night secretly from one of the captive villages to read the last rites. I accepted the coming of death and was grateful for many things. For the gentleness and wisdom of my old grandfather, the loyalty of my companions in war, the years I sailed between the wild ports of the seven seas, and the strength that flowed to me from the Spartan earth. For one thing only did I weep when it seemed I would leave life, that I had never set ablaze the world with a burning song of passion for one woman. Women I had known, pockets of pleasure that I tumbled for quick joy, but I had been denied mighty love for one woman. For that I wept.

In Ariadne I swore before God I had found my woman. I knew by the storm-lashed hurricane that swept within my body. A woman whose majesty was in harmony with the earth, who would be faithful and beloved to me as Penelope had been to Ulysses.[3]

That evening near seven I returned to the grocery. Deep twilight had fallen across the street, and the lights in the window of the store had been dimmed. The apples and oranges and pears had been covered with brown paper for the night.

I tried the door and found it locked. I knocked on the glass, and a moment later the old man came shuffling out of the shadows and let me in.

"Good evening, Mr. Langos."

He muttered some greeting in answer. "Ariadne is not here," he said. "She is at the church. Father Marlas wishes to speak with you."

"A fine young priest," I said. "Let us go at once."

I waited on the sidewalk while the old man locked the store. We started the short walk to the church.

"A clear and ringing night," I said. "Does it not make you feel the wonder and glory of being alive?"

The old man uttered what sounded like a groan, but a truck passed on the street at that moment and I could not be sure.

At the church we entered by a side door leading to the office of Father Marlas. I knocked on the door, and when he called to us to enter we walked in.

Young Father Marlas was sitting at his desk in his black cassock and with his black goatee trim and imposing beneath his clean-shaven cheeks. Beside the desk, in a dark blue dress sat Ariadne, looking somber and beautiful. A bald-headed, big-nosed old man with flint and fire in his eyes sat in a chair beside her.

"Good evening, Marko," Father Marlas said and smiled.

"Good evening, Father," I said.

---

[3]In Homer's other epic, *The Odyssey*, Penelope, wife of the Greek general Odysseus (or Ulysses), remained faithful to him despite the attention of many suitors during the many years it took him to make his way home from the Trojan War.

"Mr. Langos and his daughter you have met," he said and he cleared his throat. "This is Uncle Paul Langos."

"Good evening, Uncle Paul," I said. He glared at me and did not answer. I smiled warmly at Ariadne in greeting, but she was watching the priest.

"Sit down," Father Marlas said.

I sat down across from Ariadne, and old Mr. Langos took a chair beside Uncle Paul. In this way we were arrayed in battle order as if we were opposing armies.

A long silence prevailed during which Father Marlas cleared his throat several times. I observed Ariadne closely. There was grace and poise even in the way her slim-fingered hands rested in her lap. She was a dark and lovely flower, and my pulse beat more quickly at her nearness.

"Marko," Farther Marlas said finally. "Marko, I have known you well for the three years since I assumed duties in this parish. You are most regular in your devotions and very generous at the time of the Christmas and Easter offerings. Therefore, I find it hard to believe the complaint against you."

"My family are not liars!" Uncle Paul said, and he had a voice like hunks of dry cheese being grated.

"Of course not," Father Marlas said quickly. He smiled benevolently at Ariadne. "I only mean to say—"

"Tell him to stay away from my niece," Uncle Paul burst out.

"Excuse me, Uncle Paul," I said very politely. "Will you kindly keep out of what is not your business."

Uncle Paul looked shocked. "Not my business?" He looked from Ariadne to Father Marlas and then to his brother. "Not my business?"

"This matter concerns Ariadne and me," I said. "With outside interference it becomes more difficult."

"Not my business!" Uncle Paul said. He couldn't seem to get that through his head.

"Marko," Father Marlas said, and his composure was slightly shaken. "The family feels you are forcing your attention upon this girl. They are concerned."

"I understand, Father," I said. "It is natural for them to be concerned. I respect their concern. It is also natural for me to speak of love to a woman I have chosen for my wife."

"Not my business!" Uncle Paul said again, and shook his head violently.

"My daughter does not wish to become your wife," Mr. Langos said in a squeaky voice.

"That is for your daughter to say," I said courteously.

Ariadne made a sound in her throat, and we all looked at her. Her eyes were deep and cold, and she spoke slowly and carefully as if weighing each word on a scale in her father's grocery.

"I would not marry this madman if he were one of the Twelve Apostles," she said.

"See!" Mr. Langos said in triumph.

"Not my business!" Uncle Paul snarled.

"Marko," Father Marlas said. "Try to understand."

"We will call the police!" Uncle Paul raised his voice. "Put this hoodlum under a bond!"

"Please!" Father Marlas said. "Please!"

"Today he stood on the street outside the store," Mr. Langos said excitedly. "He made me a laughingstock."

"If I were a younger man," Uncle Paul growled, "I would settle this without the police. Zi-ip!" He drew a callused finger violently across his throat.

"Please," Father Marlas said.

"A disgrace!" Mr. Langos said.

"An outrage!" Uncle Paul said.

"He must leave Ariadne alone!" Mr. Langos said.

"We will call the police!" Uncle Paul said.

"Silence!" Father Marlas said loudly.

With everything suddenly quiet he turned to me. His tone softened.

"Marko," he said and he seemed to be pleading a little. "Marko, you must understand."

Suddenly a great bitterness assailed me, and anger at myself, and a terrible sadness that flowed like night through my body because I could not make them understand.

"Father," I said quietly, "I am not a fool. I am Marko Palamas and once I pinned the mighty Zahundos in Baltimore. But this battle, more important to me by far, I have lost. That which has not the grace of God is better far in silence."

I turned to leave and it would have ended there.

"Hoodlum!" Uncle Paul said. "It is time you were silent!"

I swear in that moment if he had been a younger man I would have flung him to the dome of the church. Instead I turned and spoke to them all in fire and fury.

"Listen," I said. "I feel no shame for the violence of my feelings. I am a man bred by the Spartan earth and my emotions are violent. Let those who squeak of life feel shame. Nor do I feel shame because I saw this flower and loved her. Or because I spoke at once of my love.

No one moved or made a sound.

"We live in a dark age," I said. "An age where men say one thing and mean another. A time of dwarfs afraid of life. The days are gone when mighty Pindar sang his radiant blossoms of song. When the noble passions of men set ablaze cities, and the heroic deeds of men rang like thunder to every corner of the earth."

I spoke my final words to Ariadne. "I saw you and loved you," I said gently. "I told you of my love. This is my way—the only way I know.

If this way has proved offensive to you I apologize to you alone. But understand clearly that for none of this do I feel shame."

I turned then and started to the door. I felt my heart weeping as if waves were breaking within my body.

"Marko Palamas," Ariadne said. I turned slowly. I looked at her. For the first time the warmth I was sure dwelt in her body radiated within the circles of her face. For the first time she did not look at me with her eyes like glaciers.

"Marko Palamas," she said and there was a strange moving softness in the way she spoke my name. "You may call on me tomorrow."

Uncle Paul shot out of his chair. "She is mad too!" he shouted. "He has bewitched her!"

"A disgrace!" Mr. Langos said.

"Call the police!" Uncle Paul shouted. "I'll show him if it's my business!"

"My poor daughter!" Mr. Langos wailed.

"Turk!" Uncle Paul shouted. "Robber!"

"Please!" Father Marlas said. "Please!"

I ignored them all. In that winged and zestful moment I had eyes only for my beloved, for Ariadne, blossom of my heart and black-eyed flower of my soul!

## FOR DISCUSSION

1. From what narrative point of view is the story written? Who is the narrator? Who is the protagonist and central character?
2. Some readers think that because of Marko's way of revealing his own thoughts and editorializing about himself, the story's point of view is inappropriate. Do you agree or disagree? If you agree, what other narrative point of view might have been used in order to make the character of Marko more believable? If you disagree, why?
3. What forces oppose the protagonist? Why is it necessary to oppose the protagonist with several types of antagonists?
4. What does Marko's self-image seem to be? Is it accurate?
5. In Greek mythology, Ariadne was a mortal who married Dionysos, god of wine. Do you think the author had this myth in mind in naming the daughter of Janco Langos Ariadne?
6. How does Marko view other men, especially other men who may have tried to court Ariadne?
7. Once, when Marko was close to death, only one thing made him weep. What was it? How does this help explain the ardor with which he pursues Ariadne?
8. Can you find any evidence that from the beginning of the story Ariadne wants to be pursued?
9. Why does Ariadne suddenly surrender and tell Marko, "You may call on me tomorrow"? What is ironic about how Marko finally "wins" her?
10. Might this story be considered a modern myth? Do you think the author meant it to be considered that way?

# Studs

JAMES T. FARRELL

It is raining outside; rain pouring like bullets from countless machine guns; rain spat-spattering on the wet earth and paving in endless silver crystals. Studs' grave out at Mount Olivet will be soaked and soppy, and fresh with the wet, clean odors of watered earth and flowers. And the members of Studs' family will be looking out of the windows of their apartment on the South Side, thinking of the cold, damp grave and the gloomy, muddy cemetery, and of their Studs lying at rest in peaceful acceptance of that wormy conclusion which is the common fate.

At Studs' wake last Monday evening everybody was mournful, sad that such a fine young fellow of twenty-six should go off so suddenly with double pneumonia; blown out of this world like a ripped leaf in a hurricane. They sighed and the women and girls cried, and everybody said that it was too bad. But they were consoled because he'd had the priest and had received Extreme Unction before he died, instead of going off like Sport Murphy who was killed in a saloon brawl. Poor Sport! He was a good fellow, and tough as hell. Poor Studs!

The undertaker (it was probably old man O'Reedy who used to be usher in the old parish church) laid Studs out handsomely. He was outfitted in a sombre black suit and a white silk tie. His hands were folded over his stomach, clasping a pair of black rosary beads. At his head, pressed against the satin bedding, was a spiritual bouquet, set in line with Studs' large nose. He looked handsome, and there were no lines of suffering on his planed face. But the spiritual bouquet (further assurance that his soul would arrive safely in Heaven) was a dirty trick. So was the administration of the last sacraments. For Studs will be miserable in Heaven, more miserable than he was on those Sunday nights when he would hang around the old poolroom at Fifty-eighth and the elevated station, waiting for something to happen. He will find the land of perpetual happiness and goodness dull and boresome, and he'll be resentful. There will be nothing to do in Heaven but to wait in timeless eternity. There will be no can houses,[1] speakeasies, whores (unless they are reformed) and gambling joints; and neither will there be a shortage of plasterers. He will loaf up and down gold-paved streets where there is not even the suggestion of a poolroom, thinking of Paulie Haggerty, Sport Murphy, Arnold Sheehan and Hink Weber, who are possibly in Hell together because there was no priest around to play a dirty trick on them.

I thought of these things when I stood by the coffin, waiting for Tommy Doyle, Red Kelly, Les, and Joe to finish offering a few per-

---

[1] Brothels.

functory prayers in memory of Studs. When they had showered some Hail Marys and Our Fathers on his already prayer-drenched soul, we went out into the dining room.

Years ago when I was a kid in the fifth grade in the old parish school, Studs was in the graduating class. He was one of the school leaders, a light-faced, blond kid who was able to fight like sixty and who never took any sass from Tommy Doyle, Red Kelly, or any of those fellows from the Fifty-eighth Street gang. He was quarterback on the school's football team, and liked by the girls.

My first concrete memory of him is of a rainy fall afternoon. Dick Buckford and I were fooling around in front of Helen Shires' house bumping against each other with our arms folded. We never thought of fighting but kept pushing and shoving and bumping each other. Studs, Red O'Connell, Tubby Connell, the Donoghues, and Jim Clayburn came along. Studs urged us into fighting, and I gave Dick a bloody nose. Studs congratulated me, and said that I could come along with them and play tag in Red O'Connell's basement, where there were several trick passageways.

After that day, I used to go around with Studs and his bunch. They regarded me as a sort of mascot, and they kept training me to fight other kids. But any older fellows who tried to pick on me would have a fight on their hands. Every now and then he would start boxing with me.

"Gee, you never get hurt, do you?" he would say. I would grin in answer, bearing the punishment because of the pride and the glory.

"You must be goofy. You can't be hurt."

"Well, I don't get hurt like other kids."

"You're too good for Morris and those kids. You could trim them with your eyes closed. You're good," he would say, and then he would go on training me.

I arranged for a party on one of my birthdays, and invited Studs and the fellows from his bunch. Red O'Connell, a tall, lanky, cowardly kid, went with my brother, and the two of them convinced my folks that Studs was not a fit person for me to invite. I told Studs what had happened, and he took such an insult decently. But none of the fellows he went with would accept my invitation, and most of the girls also refused. On the day of the party, with my family's permission, I again invited Studs but he never came.

I have no other concrete recollections of Studs while he was in grammar school. He went to Loyola[2] for one year, loafed about for a similar period; and then he became a plasterer for his father. He commenced going round the poolroom. The usual commonplace story resulted. What there was of the boy disappeared in slobbish dissipation. His pleasures came compressed within a hexagonal of whores, movies, pool, alky, poker, and craps. By the time I commenced going into the poolroom (my third year in high school) this process had been completed.

[2]A Catholic university in Chicago.

Studs' attitude toward me had also changed to one of contempt. I was a goofy young punk. Often he made cracks about me. Once, when I retaliated by sarcasm, he threatened to bust me, and awed by his former reputation I shut up. We said little to each other, although Studs occasionally condescended to borrow fifty or seventy-five cents from me, or to discuss Curley, the corner imbecile.

Studs' companions were more or less small-time amateur hoodlums. He had drifted away from the Donoghues and George Gogarty, who remained bourgeois young men with such interests as formal dances and shows. Perhaps Slug Mason was his closest friend; a tall, heavy-handed, good-natured, child-minded slugger, who knew the address and telephone number of almost every prostitute on the South Side. Hink Weber, who should have been in the ring and who later committed suicide in an insane asylum, Red Kelly, who was a typical wise-cracking corner habitué, Tommy Doyle, a fattening, bull-dozing, half-good-natured moron, Stan Simonsky and Joe Thomas were his other companions.

I feel sure that Studs' family, particularly his sisters, were appalled by his actions. The two sisters, one of whom I loved in an adolescently romantic and completely unsuccessful manner, were the type of middle-class girls who go in for sororities and sensibilities. One Saturday evening, when Studs got drunk earlier than usual, his older sister (who the boys always said was keen) saw him staggering around under the Fifty-eighth Street elevated station. She was with a young man in an automobile, and they stopped. Studs talked loudly to her, and finally they left. Studs reeled after the car, cursing and shaking his fists. Fellows like Johnny O'Brien (who went to the U. of C. to become a fraternity man) talked sadly of how Studs could have been more discriminating in his choice of buddies and liquor; and this, too, must have reached the ears of his two sisters.

Physical decay slowly developed. Studs, always a square-planed, broad person, began getting soft and slightly fat. He played one or two years with the corner football team. He was still an efficient quarterback, but slow. When the team finally disbanded, he gave up athletics. He fought and brawled about until one New Year's Eve he talked out of turn to Jim McGeoghan, who was a boxing champ down at Notre Dame. Jim flattened Studs' nose, and gave him a wicked black eye. Studs gave up fighting.

My associations with the corner gradually dwindled. I went to college, and became an atheist. This further convinced Studs that I wasn't right, and he occasionally remarked about my insanity. I grew up contemptuous of him and the others; and some of this feeling crept into my overt actions. I drifted into other groups and forgot the corner. Then I went to New York, and stories of legendary activities became fact on the corner. I had started a new religion, written poetry, and done countless similar monstrous things. When I returned, I did not see Studs for over a year. One evening, just before the Smith-Hoover election day,

I met him as he came out of the I.C.[3] Station at Randolph Street with Pat Carrigan and Ike Dugan. I talked to Pat and Ike, but not to Studs.

"Aren't you gonna say hello to me?" he asked in friendly fashion, and he offered me his hand.

I was curious but friendly for several minutes. We talked of Al Smith's chances in an uninformed, unintelligent fashion and I injected one joke about free love. Studs laughed at it; and then they went on.

The next I heard of him, he was dead.

When I went out into the dining room, I found all the old gang there, jabbering in the smoke-thick, crowded room. But I did not have any desire or intention of giving the world for having seen them. They were almost all fat and respectable. Cloddishly, they talked of the tragedy of his death, and then went about remembering the good old days. I sat in the corner and listened.

The scene seemed tragi-comical to me. All these fellows had been the bad boys of my boyhood, and many of them I had admired as proper models. Now they were all of the same kidney. Jackie Cooney (who once stole fifteen bottles of grape juice in one haul from under the eyes of a Greek proprietor over at Sixty-fifth and Stony Island), Monk McCarthy (who lived in a basement on his pool winnings and peanuts for over a year), Al Mumford (the good-natured, dumbly well-intentioned corner scapegoat), Pat Carrigan, the roly-poly fat boy from Saint Stanislaus high school—all as alike as so many cans of tomato soup.

Jim Nolan, now bald-headed, a public accountant, engaged to be married, and student in philosophy at Saint Vincent's evening school, was in one corner with Monk.

"Gee, Monk, remember the time we went to Plantation and I got drunk and went down the alley over-turning garbage cans?" he recalled.

"Yeh, that was some party," Monk said.

"Those were the days," Jim said.

Tubby Connell, whom I recalled as a moody, introspective kid, singled out the social Johnny O'Brien and listened to the latter talk with George Gogarty about Illinois U.

Al Mumford walked about making cracks, finally observing to me, "Jim, get a fiddle and you'll look like Paderwooski."[4]

Red Kelly sat enthroned with Les, Doyle, Simonsky, Bryan, Young Floss Campbell (waiting to be like these older fellows), talking oracularly.

"Yes, sir, it's too bad. A young fellow in the prime of life going like that. It's too bad," he said.

"Poor Studs!" Les said.

"I was out with him a week ago," Bryan said.

"He was all right then," Kelly said.

"Life is a funny thing," Doyle said.

"It's a good thing he had the priest," Kelly said.

[3]Illinois Central (Railroad).

[4]Ignace Jan Paderewski, Polish pianist and celebrity of the time.

"Yeh," Les said.

"Sa-ay, last Saturday I pushed the swellest little baby at Rosy's," Doyle said.

"Was she a blonde?" Kelly said.

"Yeh," Doyle said.

"She's cute. I jazzed her, too," Kelly said.

"Yeh, that night at Plantation was a wow," Jim Nolan said.

"We ought to pull off a drunk some night," Monk said.

"Let's," Nolan said.

"Say, Curley, are you in love?" Mumford asked Curley across the room.

"Now, Duffy," Curley said with imbecilic superiority.

"Remember the time Curley went to Burnham?" Carrigan asked.

Curley blushed.

"What happened, Curley?" Duffy asked.

"Nothing, Al," Curley said, confused.

"Go on, tell him, Curley! Tell him! Don't be bashful now! Don't be bashful! Tell him about the little broad!" Carrigan said.

"Now, Pat, you know me better than that," Curley said.

"Come on, Curley, tell me," Al said.

"Some little girl sat on Curley's knee, and he shoved her off and called her a lousy whore and left the place,"Carrigan said.

"Why, Curley, I'm ashamed of you," Al said.

Curley blushed.

"I got to get up at six every morning. But I don't mind it. This not workin' is the bunk. You ain't got any clothes or anything when you ain't got the sheets. I know. No, sir, this loafin' is all crap. You wait around all day for something to happen," Jackie Cooney said to Tommy Rourke.

"Gee, it was tough on Studs," Johnny O'Brien said to George Gogarty.

Gogarty said it was tough, too. Then they talked of some student from Illinois U. Phil Rolfe came in. Phil was professional major-domo of the wake; he was going with Studs' kid sister. Phil used to be a smart Jewboy, misplaced when he did not get into the furrier business. Now he was sorry with everybody, and thanking them for being sorry. He and Kelly talked importantly of pallbearers. Then he went out. Some fellow I didn't know started telling one of Red Kelly's brothers what time he got up to go to work. Mickey Flannagan, the corner drunk, came in and he, too, said he was working.

They kept on talking, and I thought more and more that they were a bunch of slobs. All the adventurous boy that was in them years ago had been killed. Slobs, getting fat and middle-aged, bragging of their stupid brawls, reciting the commonplaces of their days.

As I left, I saw Studs' kid sister. She was crying so pitifully that she was unable to recognize me. I didn't see how she could ever have been affectionate toward Studs. He was so outside of her understanding. I knew she never mentioned him to me the few times I took her out. But she cried pitifully.

As I left, I thought that Studs had looked handsome. He would have gotten a good break, too, if only they hadn't given him Extreme Unction. For life would have grown into fatter and fatter decay for him, just as it was starting to do with Kelly, Doyle, Cooney and McCarthy. He, too, was a slob; but he died without having to live countless slobbish years. If only they had not sent him to Heaven where there are no whores and poolrooms.

I walked home with Joe, who isn't like the others. We couldn't feel sorry over Studs. It didn't make any difference.

"Joe, he was a slob," I said.

Joe did not care to use the same language, but he did not disagree.

And now the rain keeps falling on Studs' new grave, and his family mournfully watches the leaden sky, and his old buddies are at work wishing that it was Saturday night, and that they were just getting into bed with a naked voluptuous blonde.

## FOR DISCUSSION

1. From the very beginning, what is the author's tone and the story's mood?
2. Who is the story's central character? What has been the narrator's relationship to this character?
3. The plot on the surface is a biographical narrative, like an obituary. Does it have an internalized aspect as well?
4. How does setting contribute to the story's mood and atmosphere?
5. From what narrative point of view is the story told? Who is the narrator?
6. What does the narrator think of Studs's prospects for happiness in heaven?
7. Part of the story is told largely through a series of flashbacks. Can you discover any plan or organization in the arrangement of these brief episodes?
8. What issue in the Al Smith vs. Herbert Hoover presidential election of 1928 would have been of special interest to Studs and the narrator?
9. By the time of Studs's wake, what has happened to all of the old fellows, the ones who attend the wake?
10. Describe the quality of conversation at the wake. What does it suggest about the people doing the talking?
11. How have the years separated the narrator from all of the old fellows? What is the narrator's final evaluation of the fellows? What is his final evaluation of Studs?

# The Tryst

IVAN TURGENEV

I was sitting in a birch grove in autumn, about the middle of September.
A fine drizzling rain had been descending ever since dawn, interspersed
at times with warm sunshine; the weather was inconstant. Now the sky
would be completely veiled in porous white clouds; again, all of a
sudden, it would clear up in spots for a moment, and then, from behind
the parted thunderclouds, the clear and friendly azure would show
itself, like a beautiful eye. I sat, and gazed about me, and listened. The
leaves were rustling in a barely audible manner overhead; from their
sound alone one could tell what season of the year it was. It was not
the cheerful, laughing rustle of springtime, not the soft whispering, not
the long conversation of summer, not the cold and timid stammering
of late autumn, but a barely audible, dreamy chatter. A faint breeze
swept feebly across the treetops. The interior of the grove, moist with
the rain, kept changing incessantly, according to whether the sun shone
forth, or was covered with a cloud; now it was all illuminated, as though
everything in it were suddenly smiling: the slender boles of the not too
thickly set birches suddenly assumed the tender gleam of white silk,
the small leaves which lay on the ground suddenly grew variegated and
lighted up with the golden hue of ducats, and the handsome stalks of
the tall, curly ferns, already stained with their autumnal hue, like the
colour of over-ripe grapes, seemed fairly transparent, as they intertwined
interminably and crossed one another before one's eyes; now, of a
sudden, everything round about would turn slightly blue: the brilliant
hues were extinguished for a moment, the birches stood there all white,
devoid of reflections, white as newly fallen snow, which has not yet
been touched by the sparkling rays of the winter sun; and the fine rain
began stealthily, craftily, to sprinkle and whisper through the forest.
The foliage on the trees was still almost entirely green, although it had
faded perceptibly; only here and there stood one, some young tree, all
scarlet, or all gold, and you should have seen how brilliantly it flamed
up in the sun, when the rays gliding and changing, suddenly pierced
through the thick network of the slender branches, only just washed
clean by the glittering rain. Not a single bird was to be heard; they had
all taken refuge, and fallen silent; only now and then did the jeering
little voice of the tom-tit ring out like a tiny steel bell. Before I had come
to a halt in this birch-forest I and my dog had traversed a grove of lofty
aspens. I must confess that I am not particularly fond of that tree, the
aspen, with its pale-lilac trunk, and greyish-green, metallic foliage,
which it elevates as high aloft as possible, and spreads forth to the air
in a trembling fan; I do not like the eternal rocking of its round, dirty
leaves, awkwardly fastened to their long stems. It is a fine tree only on
some summer evenings when, rising isolated amid a plot of low-growing

bushes, it stands directly in the line of the glowing rays of the setting sun, and glistens and quivers from its root to its crest, all deluged with a uniform reddish-yellow stain,—or when, on a bright, windy day, it is all noisily rippling and lisping against the blue sky, and its every leaf, caught in the current, seems to want to wrench itself free, fly off and whirl away into the distance. But, on the whole, I do not like that tree, and therefore, without halting to rest in that grove, I wended my way to the little birch-coppice, nestled down under one small tree, whose boughs began close to the ground, and, consequently, could protect me from the rain, and after having admired the surrounding view, I sank into that untroubled and benignant slumber which is known to sportsmen alone.

I cannot tell how long I slept, but when I opened my eyes,—the whole interior of the forest was filled with sunlight, and in all directions, athwart the joyously rustling foliage, the bright-blue sky seemed to be sparkling: the clouds had vanished, dispersed by the sportive breeze; the weather had cleared, and in the atmosphere was perceptible that peculiar, dry chill which, filling the heart with a sort of sensation of alterness, almost always is the harbinger of a clear evening after a stormy day. I was preparing to rise to my feet, and try my luck again, when suddenly my eyes halted on a motionless human form. I took a more attentive look; it was a young peasant maiden. She was sitting twenty paces distant from me, with her head drooping thoughtfully, and both arms lying idly on her knees; on one of them, which was half bare, lay a thick bunch of field flowers, which went slipping softly down her plaid petticoat at each breath she drew. Her clean white chemise, unbuttoned at the throat and wrists, fell in short, soft folds about her figure: two rows of large yellow pearl-beads depended from her neck upon her breasts. She was very comely. Her thick, fair hair, of a fine ash-blonde hue, fell in two carefully brushed semi-circles from beneath a narrow, red band which was pulled down almost on her very brow, as white as ivory; the rest of her face was slightly sunburned to that golden tint which only a fine skin assumes. I could not see her eyes— she did not raise them; but I did see her high, slender eyebrows, her long eyelashes; they were moist, and on one of her cheeks there glittered in the sunlight the dried trace of a tear, that had stopped short close to her lips, which had grown slightly pale. Her whole little head was extremely charming; even her rather thick and rounded nose did not spoil it. I was particularly pleased with the expression of her face: it was so simple and gentle, so sad and so full of childish surprise at its own sadness. She was evidently waiting for some one; something crackled faintly in the forest. She immediately raised her head and looked about her; in the transparent shadow her eyes flashed swiftly before me,—large, clear, timorous eyes, like those of a doe. She listened for several moments, without taking her widely opened eyes from the spot where the faint noise had resounded, sighed, gently turned away her head, bent down still lower than before, and began slowly to sort over her flowers. Her eyelids reddened, her lips moved bitterly, and a fresh tear rolled from beneath her thick eyelashes, halting and glittering radiantly on her cheek. Quite a long time passed in this manner; the poor girl did not stir,—only now and then she moved her hands about and listened, listened still. . . . Again something made a noise in the forest,—she gave a start. The noise did not cease, grew more distinct, drew nearer; at last brisk, decided footsteps made themselves audible. She drew herself up, and seemed to be frightened; her attentive glance wavered, with expectation, apparently. A man's figure flitted swiftly through the thicket. She glanced at it, suddenly flushed up, smiled joyously and happily, tried to rise to her feet, and immediately bent clear over once more, grew pale and confused,—and only raised her palpitating, almost beseeching glance to the approaching man when the latter had come to a halt by her side.

I gazed at him with interest from my ambush. I must confess that he did not produce a pleasant impression on me. From all the signs, he was the petted valet of a young, wealthy gentleman. His clothing betrayed pretensions to taste and foppish carelessness: he wore a short overcoat of bronze hue, probably the former property of his master, buttoned to the throat, a small pink neckerchief with lilac ends, and a black velvet cap, with gold galloon, pulled down to his very eyebrows. The round collar of his white shirt propped up his ears, and ruthlessly sawed his cheeks, and his starched cuffs covered the whole of his hands down to his red, crooked fingers, adorned with gold and silver rings with turquoise forget-me-nots. His fresh, rosy, bold face belonged to the category of visages which, so far as I have been able to observe, almost always irritate men and, unfortunately, very often please women. He was, obviously, trying to impart to his somewhat coarse features a scornful and bored expression; he kept incessantly screwing up his little milky-grey eyes, which were small enough without that, knitting his brows, drawing down the corners of his lips, constrainedly yawning, and with careless, although not quite skilful ease of manner he now adjusted with his hand his sandy, dashingly upturned temple-curls, now plucked at the small yellow hairs which stuck out on his thick upper lip,—in a word, he put on intolerable airs. He began to put on airs as soon as he caught sight of the young peasant girl who was waiting for him; slowly, with a swaggering stride, he approached her, stood for a moment, shrugged his shoulders, thrust both hands into the pockets of his coat, and barely vouchsafing the poor girl a fugitive and indifferent glance, he dropped down on the ground.

"Well,"—he began, continuing to gaze off somewhere to one side, dangling his foot and yawning:—"hast thou[1] been here long?"

The girl could not answer him at once.

---

[1]This form of expression translates a Russian verb form used only when talking to a lover, a child, or a social inferior.

"A long time, sir, Viktór Alexándrovitch,"[2]—she said at last, in a barely audible voice.

"Ah!" (He removed his cap, passed his hand majestically over his thick, tightly curled hair, which began almost at his very eyebrows, and after glancing around him with dignity, he carefully covered his precious head again.) "Why, I came pretty near forgetting all about it. And then, there was the rain, you know!" (He yawned again.)—"I have a lot of things to do: I can't attend to them all, and he scolds into the bargain. To-morrow we are going away. . . ."

"To-morrow?"—ejaculated the girl, and fixed a frightened glance on him.

"Yes, to-morrow. . . . Come, come, come, pray,"—he interposed hastily and with vexation, seeing that she was beginning to tremble, and had softly dropped her head:—"Pray, don't cry, Akulína. Thou knowest that I cannot endure that." (And he wrinkled up his stubby nose.)—"If thou dost, I'll go away instantly. . . . How stupid it is to whimper!"

"Well, I won't, I won't,"—hastily articulated Akulína, swallowing her tears with an effort—"So you are going away to-morrow?"—she added after a short silence:—"When will God grant me to see you again, Viktór Alexándrovitch?"

"We shall see each other again, we shall see each other again. If not next year, then later on. I think the master intends to enter the government service in Petersburg,"—he went on, uttering his words carelessly and somewhat through his nose:—"and perhaps we shall go abroad."

"You will forget me, Viktór Alexándrovitch,"—said Akulína sadly.

"No, why should I? I will not forget thee: only, thou must be sensible, don't make a fool of thyself, heed thy father. . . . And I won't forget thee—no-o-o." (And he calmly stretched himself and yawned again.)

"Do not forget me, Viktór Alexándrovitch," she continued, in a tone of entreaty. "I think that I have loved you to such a degree, it always seems as though for you, I would . . . you say, I must obey my father, Viktór Alexándrovitch. . . . But how am I to obey my father. . . ."

"But why not?" (He uttered these words as though from his stomach, as he lay on his back, with his arms under his head.)

"But what do you mean, Viktór Alexándrovitch . . . you know yourself. . . ."

She stopped short. Viktór toyed with the steel chain of his watch.

"Thou are not a stupid girl, Akulína,"—he began at last:—"therefore, don't talk nonsense. I desire thy welfare, dost understand me? Of course, thou art not stupid, not a regular peasant, so to speak; and thy mother also was not always a peasant. All the same, thou hast no education—so thou must obey when people give thee orders."

---

[2]A serious but not absolutely formal style of address in Russia.

"But I'm afraid, Viktór Alexándrovitch."

"I-i, what nonsense, my dear creature! What hast thou to be afraid of? What's that thou hast there,"—he added, moving toward her:—"flowers?"

"Yes,"—replied Akulína, dejectedly.—"I have been plucking some wild tansy,"—she went on, after a brief pause:—"'T is good for the calves. And this here is a good remedy for scrofula. See, what a wonderfully beautiful flower! I have never seen such a beautiful flower in my life. Here are forget-me-nots, and here is a violet. . . . And this, here, I got for you,"—she added, drawing from beneath the yellow tansy a small bunch of blue corn-flowers, bound together with a slender blade of grass:—"Will you take them?"

Viktór languidly put out his hand, took the flowers, smelled of them carelessly, and began to twist them about in his fingers, staring pompously upward. Akulína glanced at him. . . . In her sorrowful gaze there was a great deal of devotion, of adoring submission to him. And she was afraid of him also, and did not dare to cry, and was bidding him farewell and gloating upon him for the last time; but he lay there, sprawling out like a sultan, and tolerated her adoration with magnanimous patience and condescension. I must confess, that I gazed with indignation at his red face, whereon, athwart the feignedly-scornful indifference, there peered forth satisfied, satiated self-conceit. Akulína was so fine at that moment: her whole soul opened confidingly, passionately before him, reached out to him, fawned upon him, and he . . . he dropped the corn-flowers on the grass, pulled a round monocle in a bronze setting from the side-pocket of his paletot,[3] and began to stick it into his eye; but try as he would to hold it fast with his frowning brows, the monocle kept tumbling out and falling into his hand.

"What is that?"—inquired the amazed Akulína at last.

"A lorgnette,"—he replied pompously.

"What is it for?"

"To see better with."

"Pray let me see it."

Viktór frowned, but gave her the monocle.

"Look out, see that thou dost not break it."

"Never fear, I won't break it." (She raised it timidily to her eye.) "I can see nothing,"—she said innocently.

"Why, pucker up thine eye,"—he retorted in the tone of a displeased preceptor. (She screwed up the eye in front of which she was holding the glass.)

"Not that one, not that one, the other one!"—shouted Viktór, and without giving her a chance to repair her mistake, he snatched the lorgnette away from her.

Akulína blushed scarlet, smiled faintly, and turned away.

"Evidently, it is not suited to the like of me,"—said she.

---

[3]Overcoat.

"I should say not!"

The poor girl made no reply, and sighed deeply.

"Akh, Viktór Alexándrovitch; what shall I do without you!"—she suddenly said. Viktór wiped the lorgnette with the tail of his coat, and put it back in his pocket.

"Yes, yes,"—he said at last:—"thou wilt really find it very hard at first." (He patted her condescendingly on the shoulder; she softly removed his hand from her shoulder, and kissed it timidly.)—"Well, yes, yes, thou really art a good girl,"—he went on, with a conceited smile; "but what can one do? Judge for thyself! The master and I cannot remain here; winter will soon be here, and the country in winter—thou knowest it thyself—is simply vile. 'Tis quite another matter in Petersburg! There are simply such marvels there as thou, silly, canst not even imagine in thy dreams. Such houses, such streets, and society, culture—simply astounding! . . ." (Akulína listened to him with devouring attention, her lips slightly parted, like those of a child.)—"But what am I telling thee all this for?"—he added, turning over on the ground. "Of course, thou canst not understand!"

"Why not, Viktór Alexándrovitch? I have understood—I have understood everything."

"Did any one ever see such a girl!"

Akulína dropped her eyes.

"You did not use to talk to me formerly in that way, Viktór Alexándrovitch,"—she said, without raising her eyes.

"Formerly? . . . formerly! Just see there, now! . . . Formerly!"—he remarked, as though vexed.

Both maintained silence for a while.

"But I must be off,"—said Viktór, and began to raise himself on his elbow. . . .

"Wait a little longer,"—articulated Akulína, in a beseeching voice.

"What's the use of waiting? . . . I have already bade thee farewell, haven't I?"

"Wait,"—repeated Akulína.

Viktór stretched himself out again, and began to whistle. Still Akulína never took her eyes from him. I could perceive that she had grown somewhat agitated: her lips were twitching, her pale cheeks had taken on a faint flush. . . .

"Viktór Alexándrovitch,"—she said at last, in a broken voice:—" 't is sinful of you . . . sinful of you, Viktór Alexándrovitch: by heaven, it is!"

"What's sinful?"—he asked, knitting his brows, and he half rose and turned toward her.

" 'T is sinful, Viktór Alexándrovitch. You might at least speak a kind word to me at parting; you might at least say one little word to me, an unhappy orphan. . . ."

"But what am I to say to thee?"

"I don't know; you know that better than I do, Viktór Alexándrovitch.

Here you are going away, and not a single word. . . . How have I deserved such treatment?"

"What a queer creature thou art! What can I do?"

"You might say one little word. . . ."

"Come, thou'rt wound up to say the same thing over and over,"—he said testily, and rose to his feet.

"Don't be angry, Viktór Alexándrovitch,"—she added hurriedly, hardly able to repress her tears.

"I'm not angry, only thou art so stupid. . . . What is it thou wantest? I can't marry thee, can I? I can't, can I? Well, then, what is it thou dost want? What?" (He turned his face toward her, as though awaiting an answer, and spread his fingers far apart.)

"I want nothing . . . nothing,"—she replied, stammering, and barely venturing to stretch out to him her trembling arms:—"but yet, if you would say only one little word in farewell. . . ."

And the tears streamed down her face in a torrent.

"Well, there she goes! She's begun to cry," said Viktór coldly, pulling his cap forward over his eyes.

"I want nothing,"—she went on, sobbing, and covering her face with both hands;—"but how do I stand now with my family, what is my position? and what will happen to me, what will become of me, unhappy one? They will marry off the poor deserted one to a man she does not love. . . . Woe is me!"

"O, go on, go on,"—muttered Viktór in an undertone, shifting from foot to foot where he stood.

"And if he would say only one word, just one . . . such as: 'Akulína, I. . . .' "

Sudden sobs, which rent her breast, prevented her finishing her sentence—she fell face downward on the grass, and wept bitterly, bitterly. . . . Her whole body was convulsively agitated, the back of her neck fairly heaved. . . . Her long-suppressed woe had burst forth, at last, in a flood. Viktór stood over her, stood there a while, and shrugged his shoulders, then wheeled around, and marched off with long strides.

Several minutes elapsed. . . . She quieted down, raised her head, glanced around, and clasped her hands; she tried to run after him, but her limbs gave way under her—she fell on her knees. . . . I could not restrain myself, and rushed to her; but no sooner had she glanced at me than strength from some source made its appearance,—she rose to her feet with a faint shriek, and vanished behind the trees, leaving her flowers scattered on the ground.

I stood there for a while, picked up the bunch of corn-flowers, and emerged from the grove into the fields. The sun hung low in the palely-clear sky; its rays, too, seemed to have grown pallid, somehow, and cold: they did not beam, they disseminated an even, almost watery light. Not more than half an hour remained before night-fall, and the sunset glow was only just beginning to kindle. A gusty breeze dashed swiftly to meet me across the yellow, dried-up stubble-field; small, warped leaves rose hastily before it, and darted past, across the road, along the edge of the woods; the side of the grove, turned toward the field like a wall, was all quivering and sparkling with a drizzling glitter, distinct but not brilliant; on the reddish turf, on the blades of grass, on the straws, everywhere around, gleamed and undulated the innumerable threads of autumnal spiders' webs. I halted. . . . I felt sad: athwart the cheerful though chilly smile of fading nature, the mournful terror of not far-distant winter seemed to be creeping up. High above me, cleaving the air heavily and sharply with its wings, a cautious raven flew past, cast a sidelong glance at me, soared aloft and, floating on outstretched wings, disappeared behind the forest, croaking spasmodically; a large flock of pigeons fluttered sharply from the threshing-floor and, suddenly rising in a cloud, eagerly dispersed over the fields—a sign of autumn! Someone was driving past behind the bare hill, his empty cart rumbling loudly. . . .

I returned home; but the image of poor Akulína did not leave my mind for a long time, and her corn-flowers, long since withered, I have preserved to this day. . . .

## FOR DISCUSSION

1. From what narrative point of view is this story told? What role does the narrator play in the story?
2. How is setting specifically employed by the author to contribute to the mood and atmosphere of the story?
3. How does the narrator come to be in the birch grove and observe the events of the story?
4. The author suggests an association of one type of tree with Akulína and another with Viktór Alexándrovitch. What are the two trees? What are the narrator's feelings toward each?
5. What is ironic about the title of the story? Who are the two people in the story capable of love?
6. What do we learn about the personalities of Akulína and Alexándrovitch from the way they dress?
7. How does Akulína demonstrate her love for Alexándrovitch? How does Alexándrovitch demonstrate his rejection of Akulína?
8. How does the story's narrative point of view contribute to the reader's liking Akulína and disliking Alexándrovitch?
9. Can you see any symbolic significance in the business of the monocle, especially as it relates to the differences between Alexándrovitch's small, squinting eyes and Akulína's "large, clear, timorous eyes"? Do you see any other images with possible psychological significance?
10. Is there any evidence that the narrator is not completely reliable? What does he say, or not say, that sheds light on his credibility and his motives for telling the story?

# The Sojourner

CARSON MCCULLERS

The twilight border between sleep and waking was a Roman one this morning: splashing fountains and arched, narrow streets, the golden lavish city of blossoms and age-soft stone. Sometimes in this semi-consciousness he sojourned again in Paris, or war German rubble, or Swiss skiing and a snow hotel. Sometimes, also, in a fallow Georgia field at hunting dawn. Rome it was this morning in the yearless region of dreams.

John Ferris awoke in a room in a New York hotel. He had the feeling that something unpleasant was awaiting him—what it was, he did not know. The feeling, submerged by matinal necessities, lingered even after he had dressed and gone downstairs. It was a cloudless autumn day and the pale sunlight sliced between the pastel skyscrapers. Ferris went into the next-door drugstore and sat at the end booth next to the window glass that overlooked the sidewalk. He ordered an American breakfast with scrambled eggs and sausage.

Ferris had come from Paris to his father's funeral which had taken place the week before in his home town in Georgia. The shock of death had made him aware of youth already passed. His hair was receding and the veins in his now naked temples were pulsing and prominent and his body was spare except for an incipient belly bulge. Ferris had loved his father and the bond between them had once been extraordinarily close—but the years had somehow unraveled this filial devotion; the death, expected for a long time, had left him with an unforseen dismay. He had stayed as long as possible to be near his mother and brothers at home. His plane for Paris was to leave the next morning.

Ferris pulled out his address book to verify a number. He turned the pages with growing attentiveness. Names and addresses from New York, the capitals of Europe, a few faint ones from his home state in the South. Faded, printed names, sprawled drunken ones. Betty Wills: a random love, married now. Charlie Williams: wounded in the Hürtgen Forest, unheard of since. Grand old Williams—did he live or die? Don Walker: a B.T.O.[1] in television, getting rich. Henry Green: hit the skids after the war, in a sanitarium now, they say. Cozie Hall: he had heard that she was dead. Heedless, laughing Cozie—it was strange to think that she too, silly girl, could die. As Ferris closed the address book, he suffered a sense of hazard, transience, almost of fear.

It was then that his body jerked suddenly. He was staring out of the window when there, on the sidewalk, passing by, was his ex-wife. Elizabeth passed quite close to him, walking slowly. He could not

[1] Big-Time Operator.

understand the wild quiver of his heart, nor the following sense of recklessness and grace that lingered after she was gone.

Quickly Ferris paid his check and rushed out to the sidewalk. Elizabeth stood on the corner waiting to cross Fifth Avenue. He hurried toward her meaning to speak, but the lights changed and she crossed the street before he reached her. Ferris followed. On the other side he could easily have overtaken her, but he found himself lagging unaccountably. Her fair brown hair was plainly rolled, and as he watched her Ferris recalled that once his father had remarked that Elizabeth had a "beautiful carriage." She turned at the next corner and Ferris followed, although by now his intention to overtake her had disappeared. Ferris questioned the bodily disturbance that the sight of Elizabeth aroused in him, the dampness of his hands, the hard heartstrokes.

It was eight years since Ferris had last seen his ex-wife. He knew that long ago she had married again. And there were children. During recent years he had seldom thought of her. But at first, after the divorce, the loss had almost destroyed him. Then after the anodyne of time, he had loved again, and then again. Jeannine, she was now. Certainly his love for his ex-wife was long since past. So why the unhinged body, the shaken mind? He knew only that his clouded heart was oddly dissonant with the sunny, candid autumn day. Ferris wheeled suddenly and, walking with long strides, almost running, hurried back to the hotel.

Ferris poured himself a drink, although it was not yet eleven o'clock. He sprawled out in an armchair like a man exhausted, nursing his glass of bourbon and water. He had a full day ahead of him as he was leaving by plane the next morning for Paris. He checked over his obligations: take luggage to Air France, lunch with his boss, buy shoes and an overcoat. And something—wasn't there something else? Ferris finished his drink and opened the telephone directory.

His decision to call his ex-wife was impulsive. The number was under Bailey, the husband's name, and he called before he had much time for self-debate. He and Elizabeth had exchanged cards at Christmastime, and Ferris had sent a carving set when he received the announcement of her wedding. There was no reason *not* to call. But as he waited, listening to the ring at the other end, misgiving fretted him.

Elizabeth answered; her familiar voice was a fresh shock to him. Twice he had to repeat his name, but when he was identified, she sounded glad. He explained he was only in town for that day. They had a theater engagement, she said—but she wondered if he would come by for an early dinner. Ferris said he would be delighted.

As he went from one engagement to another, he was still bothered at odd moments by the feeling that something necessary was forgotten. Ferris bathed and changed in the late afternoon, often thinking about Jeannine: he would be with her the following night. "Jeannine," he would say, "I happened to run into my ex-wife when I was in New York. Had dinner with her. And her husband, of course. It was strange seeing her after all these years."

Elizabeth lived in the East Fifties, and as Ferris taxied uptown he glimpsed at intersections the lingering sunset, but by the time he reached his destination it was already autumn dark. The place was a building with a marquee and a doorman, and the apartment was on the seventh floor.

"Come in, Mr. Ferris."

Braced for Elizabeth or even the unimagined husband, Ferris was astonished by the freckled red-haired child; he had known of the children, but his mind had failed somehow to acknowledge them. Surprise made him step back awkwardly.

"This is our apartment," the child said politely. "Aren't you Mr. Ferris? I'm Billy. Come in."

In the living room beyond the hall, the husband provided another surprise; he too had not been acknowledged emotionally. Bailey was a lumbering red-haired man with a deliberate manner. He rose and extended a welcoming hand.

"I'm Bill Bailey. Glad to see you. Elizabeth will be in, in a minute. She's finishing dressing."

The last words struck a gliding series of vibrations, memories of the other years. Fair Elizabeth, rosy and naked before her bath. Half-dressed before the mirror of her dressing table, brushing her fine, chestnut hair. Sweet, casual intimacy, the soft-fleshed loveliness indisputably possessed. Ferris shrank from the unbidden memories and compelled himself to meet Bill Bailey's gaze.

"Billy, will you please bring that tray of drinks from the kitchen table?"

The child obeyed promptly, and when he was gone Ferris remarked conversationally, "Fine boy you have there."

"We think so."

Flat silence until the child returned with a tray of glasses and a cocktail shaker of Martinis. With the priming drinks they pumped up conversation: Russia, they spoke of, and the New York rain-making, and the apartment situation in Manhattan and Paris.

"Mr. Ferris is flying all the way across the ocean tomorrow," Bailey said to the little boy who was perched on the arm of his chair, quiet and well behaved. "I bet you would like to be a stowaway in his suitcase."

Billy pushed back his limp bangs. "I want to fly in an airplane and be a newspaperman like Mr. Ferris." He added with sudden assurance, "That's what I would like to do when I am big."

Bailey said, "I thought you wanted to be a doctor."

"I do!" said Billy. "I would like to be both. I want to be a atom-bomb scientist too."

Elizabeth came in carrying in her arms a baby girl.

"Oh, John!" she said. She settled the baby in the father's lap. "It's grand to see you. I'm awfully glad you could come."

The little girl sat demurely on Bailey's knees. She wore a pale pink crepe de Chine frock, smocked around the yoke with rose, and a matching silk hair ribbon tying back her pale soft curls. Her skin was summer tanned and her brown eyes flecked with gold and laughing. When she reached up and fingered her father's horn-rimmed glasses, he took them off and let her look through them a moment. "How's my old Candy?"

Elizabeth was very beautiful, more beautiful perhaps than he had ever realized. Her straight clean hair was shining. Her face was softer, glowing and serene. It was a madonna loveliness, dependent on the family ambiance.

"You've hardly changed at all," Elizabeth said, "but it has been a long time."

"Eight years." His hand touched his thinning hair self-consciously while further amenities were exchanged.

Ferris felt himself suddenly a spectator—an interloper among these Baileys. Why had he come? He suffered. His own life seemed so solitary, a fragile column supporting nothing amidst the wreckage of the years. He felt he could not bear much longer to stay in the family room.

He glanced at his watch. "You're going to the theater?"

"It's a shame," Elizabeth said, "but we've had this engagement for more than a month. But surely, John, you'll be staying home one of these days before long. You're not going to be an expatriate, are you?"

"Expatriate," Ferris repeated. "I don't much like the word."

"What's a better word?" she asked.

He thought for a moment. "Sojourner might do."

Ferris glanced again at his watch, and again Elizabeth apologized. "If only we had known ahead of time——"

"I just had this day in town. I came home unexpectedly. You see, Papa died last week."

"Papa Ferris is dead?"

"Yes, at Johns-Hopkins. He had been sick there nearly a year. The funeral was down home in Georgia."

"Oh, I'm so sorry, John. Papa Ferris was always one of my favorite people."

The little boy moved from behind the chair so that he could look into his mother's face. He asked, "Who is dead?"

Ferris was oblivious to apprehension; he was thinking of his father's death. He saw again the outstretched body on the quilted silk within the coffin. The corpse flesh was bizarrely rouged and the familiar hands lay massive and joined above a spread of funeral roses. The memory closed and Ferris awakened to Elizabeth's calm voice.

"Mr. Ferris' father, Billy. A really grand person. Somebody you didn't know."

"But why did you call him *Papa* Ferris?"

Bailey and Elizabeth exchanged a trapped look. It was Bailey who answered the questioning child. "A long time ago," he said, "your mother and Mr. Ferris were once married. Before you were born—a long time ago."

"Mr. Ferris?"

The little boy stared at Ferris, amazed and unbelieving. And Ferris' eyes, as he returned the gaze, were somehow unbelieving too. Was it indeed true that at one time he had called this stranger, Elizabeth, Little Butterduck during nights of love, that they had lived together, shared perhaps a thousand days and nights and—finally—endured in the misery of sudden solitude the fiber by fiber (jealousy, alcohol and money quarrels) destruction of the fabric of married love.

Bailey said to the children, "It's somebody's suppertime. Come on now."

"But Daddy! Mama and Mr. Ferris—I——"

Billy's everlasting eyes—perplexed and with a glimmer of hostility— reminded Ferris of the gaze of another child. It was the young son of Jeannine—a boy of seven with a shadowed little face and nobby knees whom Ferris avoided and usually forgot.

"Quick march!" Bailey gently turned Billy toward the door. "Say good night now, son."

"Good night, Mr. Ferris." He added resentfully, "I thought I was staying up for the cake."

"You can come in afterward for the cake," Elizabeth said. "Run along now with Daddy for your supper."

Ferris and Elizabeth were alone. The weight of the situation descended on those first moments of silence. Ferris asked permission to pour himself another drink and Elizabeth set the cocktail shaker on the table at his side. He looked at the grand piano and noticed the music on the rack.

"Do you still play as beautifully as you used to?"

"I still enjoy it."

"Please play, Elizabeth."

Elizabeth arose immediately. Her readiness to perform when asked had always been one of her amiabilities; she never hung back, apologized. Now as she approached the piano there was the added readiness of relief.

She began with a Bach prelude and fugue. The prelude was as gaily iridescent as a prism in a morning room. The first voice of the fugue, an announcement pure and solitary, was repeated intermingling with a second voice, and again repeated within an elaborated frame, the multiple music, horizontal and serene, flowed with unhurried majesty. The principal melody was woven with two other voices, embellished with countless ingenuities—now dominant, again submerged, it had the sublimity of a single thing that does not fear surrender to the whole. Toward the end, the density of the material gathered for the last enriched insistence on the dominant first motif and with a chorded final statement the fugue ended. Ferris rested his head on the chair back and closed his eyes. In the following silence a clear, high voice came from the room down the hall.

"Daddy, how *could* Mama and Mr. Ferris——" A door was closed.

The piano began again—what was this music? Unplaced, familiar, the limpid melody had lain a long while dormant in his heart. Now it spoke to him of another time, another place—it was the music Elizabeth used to play. The delicate air summoned a wilderness of memory. Ferris was lost in the riot of past longings, conflicts, ambivalent desires. Strange that the music, catalyst for this tumultuous anarchy, was so serene and clear. The singing melody was broken off by the appearance of the maid.

"Miz Bailey, dinner is out on the table now."

Even after Ferris was seated at the table between his host and hostess, the unfinished music still overcast his mood. He was a little drunk.

"*L'improvisation de la vie humaine,*" he said. "There's nothing that makes you so aware of the improvisation of human existence as a song unfinished. Or an old address book."

"Address book?" repeated Bailey. Then he stopped, noncommittal and polite.

"You're still the same old boy, Johnny," Elizabeth said with a trace of the old tenderness.

It was a Southern dinner that evening, and the dishes were his old favorites. They had fried chicken and corn pudding and rich, glazed candied sweet potatoes. During the meal Elizabeth kept alive a conversation when the silences were overlong. And it came about that Ferris was led to speak of Jeannine.

"I first knew Jeannine last autumn—about this time of the year—in Italy. She's a singer and she had an engagement in Rome. I expect we will be married soon."

The words seemed so true, inevitable, that Ferris did not at first acknowledge to himself the lie. He and Jeannine had never in that year spoken of marriage. And indeed, she was still married—to a White Russian money-changer in Paris from whom she had been separated for five years. But it was too late to correct the lie. Already Elizabeth was saying: "This really makes me glad to know. Congratulations, Johnny."

He tried to make amends with truth. "The Roman autumn is so beautiful. Balmy and blossoming." He added. "Jeannine has a little boy of six. A curious trilingual little fellow. We go to the Tuileries[2] sometimes."

A lie again. He had taken the boy once to the gardens. The sallow foreign child in shorts that bared his spindly legs had sailed his boat in the concrete pond and ridden the pony. The child had wanted to go in to the puppet show. But there was not time, for Ferris had an engagement at the Scribe Hotel. He had promised they would go to the guignol[3] another afternoon. Only once had he taken Valentin to the Tuileries.

There was a stir. The maid brought in a white-frosted cake with pink

[2]A large park in the center of Paris.
[3]Puppet show, open during the summer.

candles. The children entered in their night clothes. Ferris still did not understand.

"Happy birthday, John," Elizabeth said. "Blow out the candles."

Ferris recognized his birthday date. The candles blew out lingeringly and there was the smell of burning wax. Ferris was thirty-eight years old. The veins in his temples darkened and pulsed visibly.

"It's time you started for the theater."

Ferris thanked Elizabeth for the birthday dinner and said the appropriate good-byes. The whole family saw him to the door.

A high, thin moon shone above the jagged, dark skyscrapers. The streets were windy, cold. Ferris hurried to Third Avenue and hailed a cab. He gazed at the nocturnal city with the deliberate attentiveness of departure and perhaps farewell. He was alone. He longed for flighttime and the coming journey.

The next day he looked down on the city from the air, burnished in sunlight, toylike, precise. Then America was left behind and there was only the Atlantic and the distant European shore. The ocean was milky pale and placid beneath the clouds. Ferris dozed most of the day. Toward dark he was thinking of Elizabeth and the visit of the previous evening. He thought of Elizabeth among her family with longing, gentle envy and inexplicable regret. He sought the melody, the unfinished air, that had so moved him. The cadence, some unrelated tones, were all that remained; the melody itself evaded him. He had found instead the first voice of the fugue that Elizabeth had played—it came to him, inverted mockingly and in a minor key. Suspended above the ocean the anxieties of transcience and solitude no longer troubled him and he thought of his father's death with equanimity. During the dinner hour the plane reached the shore of France.

At midnight Ferris was in a taxi crossing Paris. It was a clouded night and mist wreathed the lights of the Place de la Concorde. The midnight bistros gleamed on the wet pavements. As always after a transocean flight the change of continents was too sudden. New York at morning, this midnight Paris. Ferris glimpsed the disorder of his life: the succession of cities, of transitory loves; and time, the sinister glissando of the years, time always.

"Vite! Vite!" he called in terror. "Dépêchez-vous."[4]

Valentin opened the door to him. The little boy wore pajamas and an outgrown red robe. His grey eyes were shadowed and, as Ferris passed into the flat, they flickered momentarily.

"J'attends Maman."[5]

Jennine was singing in a night club. She would not be home before another hour. Valentin returned to a drawing, squatting with his crayons over the paper on the floor. Ferris looked down at the drawing—it was a banjo player with notes and wavy lines inside a comic-strip balloon.

[4]"Fast! Fast! Hurry!"
[5]"I'm waiting for mama."

"We will go again to the Tuileries."

The child looked up and Ferris drew him closer to his knees. The melody, the unfinished music that Elizabeth had played, came to him suddenly. Unsought, the load of memory jettisoned—this time bringing only recognition and sudden joy.

"Monsieur Jean," the child said, "did you see him?"

Confused, Ferris thought only of another child—the freckled family-loved boy. "See who, Valentin?"

"Your dead papa in Georgia." The child added, "Was he okay?"

Ferris spoke with rapid urgency: "We will go often to the Tuileries. Ride the pony and we will go into the guignol. We will see the puppet show and never be in a hurry any more."

"Monsieur Jean," Valentin said. "The guignol is now closed."

Again, the terror the acknowledgement of wasted years and death. Valentin, responsive and confident, still nestled in his arms. His cheek touched the soft cheek and felt the brush of the delicate eyelashes. With inner desperation he pressed the child close—as though an emotion as protean as his love could dominate the pulse of time.

## FOR DISCUSSION

1. From what point of view is the story told? Within what character is the unknown narrator submerged?
2. Do you think the coincidence of John Ferris's ex-wife's walking right past him on Fifth Avenue, and on his birthday, is evidence of weak plot structure?
3. What are some of the things that have contributed to the emotional state of John Ferris as he enters his ex-wife's apartment?
4. Do you find the character of John Ferris plausible?
5. Why does Ferris prefer to call himself a sojourner rather than an expatriate?
6. What effect does little Billy's inability to understand how his mother could have ever been married to Ferris have on the protagonist?
7. Why is Elizabeth so willing to play the piano, and especially to play music from her and John's past life together?
8. What do you make of the fact that Ferris does not remember it is his birthday—and that Elizabeth does?
9. Why does Ferris tell Elizabeth lies about his personal life?
10. Thematically, what does the story suggest about people's feelings toward those they have once loved? What does it suggest about a life that excludes permanent commitments to others?

# The Boarding House

JAMES JOYCE

Mrs. Mooney was a butcher's daughter. She was a woman who was quite able to keep things to herself: a determined woman. She had married her father's foreman and opened a butcher's shop near Spring Gardens. But as soon as his father-in-law was dead Mr. Mooney began to go to the devil. He drank, plundered the till, ran headlong into debt. It was no use making him take the pledge: he was sure to break out again a few days after. By fighting his wife in the presence of customers and by buying bad meat he ruined his business. One night he went for his wife with the cleaver and she had to sleep in a neighbor's house.

After that they lived apart. She went to the priest and got a separation from him with care of the children. She would give him neither money nor food nor house-room; and so he was obliged to enlist himself as a sheriff's man.[1] He was a shabby stooped little drunkard with a white face and a white moustache and white eyebrows, pencilled above his little eyes, which were pink-veined and raw; and all day long he sat in the bailiff's room, waiting to be put on a job. Mrs. Mooney, who had taken what remained of her money out of the butcher business and set up a boarding house in Hardwicke Street, was a big imposing woman. Her house had a floating population made up of tourists from Liverpool and the Isle of Man and, occasionally, *artistes* from the music halls. Its resident population was made up of clerks from the city. She governed her house cunningly and firmly, knew when to give credit, when to be stern and when to let things pass. All the resident young men spoke of her as *The Madame*.

Mrs. Mooney's young men paid fifteen shillings a week for board and lodging (beer or stout at dinner excluded). They shared in common tastes and occupations and for this reason they were very chummy with one another. They discussed with one another the chances of favorites and outsiders. Jack Mooney, the Madam's son, who was clerk to a commission agent[2] in Fleet Street, had the reputation of being a hard case. He was fond of using soldiers' obscenities: usually he came home in the small hours. When he met his friends he had always a good one to tell them and he was always sure to be on to a good thing—that is to say, a likely horse or a likely *artiste*. He was also handy with the mits and sang comic songs. On Sunday nights there would often be a reunion in Mrs. Mooney's front drawing-room. The music-hall *artistes* would oblige; and Sheridan played waltzes and polkas and vamped accom-

---

[1] In Ireland, a sheriff is a high officer of the court; his men would summon jurors, serve summonses, and the like.

[2] One who transacts business for others on a commission basis.

paniments. Polly Mooney, the Madam's daughter would also sing. She sang:

> I'm a . . . naughty girl.
> You needn't sham:
> You know I am.

Polly was a slim girl of nineteen; she had light soft hair and a small full mouth. Her eyes, which were grey with a shade of green through them, had a habit of glancing upwards when she spoke with anyone, which made her look like a little perverse madonna. Mrs. Mooney had first sent her daughter to be a typist in a corn-factor's[3] office but, as a disreputable sheriff's man used to come every other day to the office, asking to be allowed to say a word to his daughter, she had taken her daughter home again and set her to do housework. As Polly was very lively the intention was to give her the run of the young men. Besides, young men like to feel that there is a young woman not very far away. Polly, of course, flirted with the young men but Mrs. Mooney, who was a shrewd judge, knew that the young men were only passing the time away: none of them meant business. Things went on so for a long time and Mrs. Mooney began to think of sending Polly back to type-writing when she noticed that something was going on between Polly and one of the young men. She watched the pair and kept her own counsel.

Polly knew that she was being watched, but still her mother's persistent silence could not be misunderstood. There had been no open complicity between mother and daughter, no open understanding but, though people in the house began to talk of the affair, still Mrs. Mooney did not intervene. Polly began to grow a little strange in her manner and the young man was evidently perturbed. At last, when she judged it to be the right moment, Mrs. Mooney intervened. She dealt with moral problems as a cleaver deals with meat: and in this case she had made up her mind.

It was a bright Sunday morning of early summer, promising heat, but with a fresh breeze blowing. All the windows of the boarding house were open and the lace curtains ballooned gently towards the street beneath the raised sashes. The belfry of George's Church sent out constant peals and worshippers, singly or in groups, traversed the little circus[4] before the church, revealing their purpose by their self-contained demeanor no less than by the little volumes in their gloved hands. Breakfast was over in the boarding house and the table of the breakfast-room was covered with plates on which lay yellow streaks of eggs with morsels of bacon-fat and bacon-rind. Mrs. Mooney sat in the straw arm-chair and watched the servant Mary remove the breakfast things. She

[3]A dealer in grains.

[4]Circular drive.

made Mary collect the crusts and pieces of broken bread to help make Tuesday's bread-pudding. When the table was cleared, the broken bread collected, the sugar and butter safe under lock and key, she began to reconstruct the interview which she had had the night before with Polly. Things were as she had suspected: she had been frank in her questions and Polly had been frank in her answers. Both had been somewhat awkward, of course. She had been made awkward by her not wishing to receive the news in too cavalier a fashion or to seem to have connived and Polly had been made awkward not merely because allusions of that kind always made her awkward but also because she did not wish it to be thought that in her wise innocence she had divined the intention behind her mother's tolerance.

Mrs. Mooney glanced instinctively at the little gilt clock on the mantelpiece as soon as she had become aware through her revery that the bells of George's Church had stopped ringing. It was seventeen minutes past eleven: she would have lots of time to have the matter out with Mr. Doran and then catch short twelve[5] at Marlborough Street. She was sure she would win. To begin with she had all the weight of social opinion on her side: she was an outraged mother. She had allowed him to live beneath her roof, assuming that he was a man of honor, and he had simply abused her hospitality. He was thirty-four or thirty-five years of age, so that youth could not be pleaded as his excuse; nor could ignorance be his excuse since he was a man who had seen something of the world. He had simply taken advantage of Polly's youth and inexperience: that was evident. The question was: What reparation would he make?

There must be reparation made in such cases. It is all very well for the man: he can go his ways as if nothing had happened, having had his moment of pleasure, but the girl has to bear the brunt. Some mothers would be content to patch up such an affair for a sum of money; she had known cases of it. But she would not do so. For her only one reparation could make up for the loss of her daughter's honor: marriage.

She counted all her cards again before sending Mary up to Mr. Doran's room to say that she wished to speak with him. She felt sure she would win. He was a serious young man, not rakish or loud-voiced like the others. If it had been Mr. Sheridan or Mr. Meade or Bantam Lyons her task would have been much harder. She did not think he would face publicity. All the lodgers in the house knew something of the affair; details had been invented by some. Besides, he had been employed for thirteen years in a great Catholic wine-merchant's office and publicity would mean for him, perhaps, the loss of his sit.[6] Whereas if he agreed all might be well. She knew he had a good screw[7] for one thing and she suspected he had a bit of stuff put by.

[5]Midday mass.

[6]Situation; i.e., job.

[7]Salary.

Nearly the half-hour! She stood up and surveyed herself in the pier-glass.[8] The decisive expression of her great florid face satisfied her and she thought of some mothers she knew who could not get their daughters off their hands.

Mr. Doran was very anxious indeed this Sunday morning. He had made two attempts to shave but his hand had been so unsteady that he had been obliged to desist. Three days' reddish beard fringed his jaws and every two or three minutes a mist gathered on his glasses so that he had to take them off and polish them with his pocket-handerchief. The recollection of his confession of the night before was a cause of acute pain to him; the priest had drawn out every ridiculous detail of the affair and in the end had so magnified his sin that he was almost thankful at being afforded a loophole of reparation. The harm was done. What could he do now but marry her or run away? He could not brazen it out. The affair would be sure to be talked of and his employer would be certain to hear of it. Dublin is such a small city: everyone knows everyone else's business. He felt his heart leap warmly in his throat as he heard in his excited imagination old Mr. Leonard calling out in his rasping voice: *Send Mr. Doran here, please.*

All his long years of service gone for nothing! All his industry and diligence thrown away! As a young man he had sown his wild oats, of course; he had boasted of his free-thinking and denied the existence of God to his companions in public-houses. But that was all passed and done with . . . nearly. He still bought a copy of *Reynolds's Newspaper*[9] every week but he attended to his religious duties and for nine-tenths of the year lived a regular life. He had money enough to settle down on; it was not that. But the family would look down on her. First of all there was her disreputable father and then her mother's boarding house was beginning to get a certain fame. He had a notion that he was being had. He could imagine his friends talking of the affair and laughing. She *was* a little vulgar; sometimes she said *I seen* and *If I had've known.* But what would grammar matter if he really loved her? He could not make up his mind whether to like her or despise her for what she had done. Of course, he had done it too. His instinct urged him to remain free, not to marry. Once you are married you are done for, it said.

While he was sitting helplessly on the side of the bed in shirt and trousers she tapped lightly at his door and entered. She told him all, that she had made a clean breast of it to her mother and that her mother would speak with him that morning. She cried and threw her arms round his neck, saying:

—O, Bob! Bob! What am I to do? What am I to do at all?

She would put an end to herself, she said.

He comforted her feebly, telling her not to cry, that it would be all right, never fear. He felt against his shirt the agitation of her bosom.

[8]A large mirror.

[9]A freethinkers' magazine.

It was not altogether his fault that it had happened. He remembered well, with the curious patient memory of the celibate, the first casual caresses her dress, her breath, her fingers had given him. Then late one night as he was undressing for bed she had tapped at his door, timidly. She wanted to relight her candle at his for hers had been blown out by a gust. It was her bath night. She wore a loose open combing-jacket of printed flannel. Her white instep shone in the opening of her furry slippers and the blood glowed warmly behind her perfumed skin. From her hands and wrists too as she lit and steadied her candle a faint perfume arose.

On nights when he came in very late it was she who warmed up his dinner. He scarcely knew what he was eating, feeling her beside him alone, at night, in the sleeping house. And her thoughtfulness! If the night was anyway cold or wet or windy there was sure to be a little tumbler of punch ready for him. Perhaps they could be happy together. . . .

They used to go upstairs together on tiptoe, each with a candle, and on the third landing exchange reluctant goodnights. They used to kiss. He remembered well her eyes, the touch of her hand and his delirium. . . .

But delirium passes. He echoed her phrase, applying it to himself: *What am I to do?* The instinct of the celibate warned him to hold back. But the sin was there; even his sense of honor told him that reparation must be made for such a sin.

While he was sitting with her on the side of the bed Mary came to the door and said that the missus wanted to see him in the parlor. He stood up to put on his coat and waistcoat, more helpless than ever. When he was dressed he went over to her to comfort her. It would be all right, never fear. He left her crying on the bed and moaning softly: *O my God!*

Going down the stairs his glasses became so dimmed with moisture that he had to take them off and polish them. He longed to ascend through the roof and fly away to another country where he would never hear again of his trouble, and yet a force pushed him downstairs step by step. The implacable faces of his employer and of the Madam stared upon his discomfiture. On the last flight of stairs he passed Jack Mooney who was coming up from the pantry nursing two bottles of *Bass*.[10] They saluted coldly; and the lover's eyes rested for a second or two on a thick bulldog face and a pair of thick short arms. When he reached the foot of the staircase he glanced up and saw Jack regarding him from the door of the return-room.

Suddenly he remembered the night when one of the music-hall *artistes*, a little blond Londoner, had made a rather free allusion to Polly. The reunion had been almost broken up on account of Jack's violence. Everyone tried to quiet him. The music-hall *artiste*, a little paler than

[10]An English ale.

usual, kept smiling and saying that there was no harm meant: but Jack kept shouting at him that if any fellow tried that sort of a game on with *his* sister he'd bloody well put his teeth down his throat, so he would.

Polly sat for a little time on the side of the bed, crying. Then she dried her eyes and went over to the looking-glass. She dipped the end of the towel in the water-jug and refreshed her eyes with the cool water. She looked at herself in profile and readjusted a hairpin above her ear. Then she went back to the bed again and sat at the foot. She regarded the pillows for a long time and the sight of them awakened in her mind secret amiable memories. She rested the nape of her neck against the cool iron bed-rail and fell into a revery. There was no longer any perturbation visible on her face.

She waited on patiently, almost cheerfully, without alarm, her memories gradually giving place to hopes and visions of the future. Her hopes and visions were so intricate that she no longer saw the white pillows on which her gaze was fixed or remembered that she was waiting for anything.

At last she heard her mother calling. She started to her feet and ran to the banisters.

—Polly! Polly!

—Yes, mamma?

—Come down, dear. Mr. Doran wants to speak to you.

Then she remembered what she had been waiting for.

## FOR DISCUSSION

1. From what point of view is the story written? Into which characters' minds does the unnamed narrator go?
2. What is the story's immediate setting? What is its greater or larger setting?
3. What is the author's tone?
4. Which of the story's three major characters would you call the protagonist: Mrs. Mooney, Polly Mooney, or Bob Doran?
5. Whichever character is the protagonist, what is the predominant force against which he or she struggles?
6. What are some of the things that have made Mrs. Mooney the kind of woman she is? Does she possess consistency, motivation, and plausibility?
7. Identify specific points in the story at which the narrator switches from the thoughts of one character to the thoughts of another.
8. Why did Mrs. Mooney not intervene in the affair between Polly and Bob Doran until after an intimacy had taken place?
9. Do you think Polly loves Bob Doran? What does Polly do while Bob is downstairs talking to Mrs. Mooney about the situation?
10. At what point does the story's narrative climax occur?
11. The story's denouement is foreshadowed. What is going to happen quite soon?
12. Thematically, what do the events of the story suggest about romantic love and marriage?

# You Were Perfectly Fine

DOROTHY PARKER

The pale young man eased himself carefully into the low chair, and rolled his head to the side, so that the cool chintz comforted his cheek and temple.

"Oh, dear," he said. "Oh, dear, oh, dear, oh, dear. Oh."

The clear-eyed girl, sitting light and erect on the couch, smiled brightly at him.

"Not feeling so well today?" she said.

"Oh, I'm great," he said. "Corking, I am. Know what time I got up? Four o'clock this afternoon, sharp. I kept trying to make it, and every time I took my head off the pillow, it would roll under the bed. This isn't my head I've got on now. I think this is something that used to belong to Walt Whitman. Oh, dear, oh, dear, oh, dear."

"Do you think maybe a drink would make you feel better?" she said.

"The hair of the mastiff that bit me?" he said. "Oh, no thank you. Please never speak of anything like that again. I'm through. I'm all, all through. Look at that hand; steady as a humming-bird. Tell me, was I very terrible last night?"

"Oh, goodness," she said, "everybody was feeling pretty high. You were all right."

"Yeah," he said. "I must have been dandy. Is everybody sore at me?"

"Good heavens, no," she said. "Everyone thought you were terribly funny. Of course, Jim Pierson was a little stuffy, there for a minute at dinner. But people sort of held him back in his chair, and got him calmed down. I don't think anybody at the other tables noticed it at all. Hardly anybody."

"He was going to sock me?" he said. "Oh, Lord. What did I do to him?"

"Why, you didn't do a thing," she said. "You were perfectly fine. But you know how silly Jim gets, when he thinks anybody is making too much fuss over Elinor."

"Was I making a pass at Elinor?" he said. "Did I do that?"

"Of course you didn't," she said. "You were only fooling, that's all. She thought you were awfully amusing. She was having a marvelous time. She only got a little tiny bit annoyed just once, when you poured the clam-juice down her back."

"My God," he said. "Clam-juice down that back. And every vertebra a little Cabot.[1] Dear God. What'll I ever do?"

"Oh, she'll be all right," she said. "Just send her some flowers, or something. Don't worry about it. It isn't anything."

[1] One of the leading families of Boston society.

"No, I won't worry," he said. "I haven't got a care in the world. I'm sitting pretty. Oh, dear, oh, dear. Did I do any other fascinating tricks at dinner?"

"You were fine," she said. "Don't be so foolish about it. Everybody was crazy about you. The maître d'hôtel was a little worried because you wouldn't stop singing, but he really didn't mind. All he said was, he was afraid they'd close the place again, if there was so much noise. But he didn't care a bit, himself. I think he loved seeing you have such a good time. Oh, you were just singing away, there, for about an hour. It wasn't so terribly loud, at all."

"So I sang," he said. "That must have been a treat. I sang."

"Don't you remember?" she said. "You just sang one song after another. Everybody in the place was listening. They loved it. Only you kept insisting that you wanted to sing some song about some kind of fusiliers or other, and everybody kept shushing you, and you'd keep trying to start it again. You were wonderful. We were all trying to make you stop singing for a minute, and eat something, but you wouldn't hear of it. My, you were funny."

"Didn't I eat any dinner?" he said.

"Oh, not a thing," she said. "Every time the waiter would offer you something, you'd give it right back to him, because you said that he was your long-lost brother, changed in the cradle by a gypsy band, and that anything you had was his. You had him simply roaring at you."

"I bet I did," he said. "I bet I was comical. Society's Pet, I must have been. And what happened then, after my overwhelming success with the waiter?"

"Why, nothing much," she said. "You took a sort of dislike to some old man with white hair, sitting across the room, because you didn't like his necktie and you wanted to tell him about it. But we got you out, before he got really mad."

"Oh, we got out," he said. "Did I walk?"

"Walk! Of course you did," she said. "You were absolutely all right. There was that nasty stretch of ice on the sidewalk, and you did sit down awfully hard, you poor dear. But good heavens, that might have happened to anybody."

"Oh, sure," he said. "Louisa Alcott[2] or anybody. So I fell down on the sidewalk. That would explain what's the matter with my—Yes. I see. And then what, if you don't mind?"

"Ah, now, Peter!" she said. "You can't sit there and say you don't remember what happened after that! I did think that maybe you were just a little tight at dinner—oh, you were perfectly all right, and all that, but I did know you were feeling pretty gay. But you were so serious, from the time you fell down—I never knew you to be that way. Don't you know, how you told me I had never seen your real self before? Oh,

[2]Author of books for girls, notably *Little Women*.

Peter, I just couldn't bear it, if you didn't remember that lovely long ride we took together in the taxi! Please, you do remember that, don't you? I think it would simply kill me, if you didn't."

"Oh, yes," he said. "Riding in the taxi. Oh, yes, sure. Pretty long ride, hmm?"

"Round and round and round the park," she said. "Oh, and the trees were shining so in the moonlight. And you said you never knew before that you really had a soul."

"Yes," he said. "I said that. That was me."

"You said such lovely, lovely things," she said. "And I'd never known, all this time, how you had been feeling about me, and I'd never dared to let you see how I felt about you. And then last night—oh, Peter dear, I think that taxi ride was the most important thing that ever happened to us in our lives."

"Yes," he said. "I guess it must have been."

"And we're going to be so happy," she said. "Oh, I just want to tell everybody! But I don't know—I think maybe it would be sweeter to keep it all to ourselves."

"I think it would be," he said.

"Isn't it lovely?" she said.

"Yes," he said. "Great."

"Lovely!" she said.

"Look here," he said, "do you mind if I have a drink? I mean, just medicinally, you know. I'm off the stuff for life, so help me. But I think I feel a collapse coming on."

"Oh, I think it would do you good," she said. "You poor boy, it's a shame you feel so awful. I'll go make you a whiskey and soda."

"Honestly," he said, "I don't see how you could ever want to speak to me again, after I made such a fool of myself, last night. I think I'd better go join a monastery in Tibet."

"You crazy idiot!" she said. "As if I could ever let you go away now! Stop talking like that. You were perfectly fine."

She jumped up from the couch, kissed him quickly on the forehead, and ran out of the room.

The pale young man looked after her and shook his head long and slowly, then dropped it in his damp and trembling hands.

"Oh, dear," he said. "Oh, dear, oh, dear, oh, dear."

## FOR DISCUSSION

1. From what narrative point of view is the story written?
2. Which of the two characters would you say is the story's protagonist?
3. What is the author's attitude toward the story and its characters? How do you know?
4. What is the story's precipitating incident? Did this incident occur before the story begins?

5. What is Peter's condition at the beginning of the story? Why is he unable to remember what happened at the party of the previous evening?
6. From the story's dialogue, detail as many specific incidents of the party as you can.
7. Why hasn't the woman with whom Peter is talking been put off by his behavior at the party?
8. Why does the reader learn about the events of the previous evening only gradually? How is this related to the story's narrative point of view?
9. Exactly what happened during the taxi ride?
10. Does Peter ever actually remember anything that happened the previous evening?
11. Do you think the young lady in the story is telling the truth about the events of the evening? Can you be sure?

# The Lottery

SHIRLEY JACKSON

The morning of June 27th was clear and sunny, with the fresh warmth of a full-summer day; the flowers were blossoming profusely and the grass was richly green. The people of the village began to gather in the square, between the post office and the bank, around ten o'clock; in some towns there were so many people that the lottery took two days and had to be started on June 26th, but in this village, where there were only about three hundred people, the whole lottery took less than two hours, so it could begin at ten o'clock in the morning and still be through in time to allow the villagers to get home for noon dinner.

The children assembled first, of course. School was recently over for the summer, and the feeling of liberty sat uneasily on most of them; they tended to gather together quietly for a while before they broke into boisterous play, and their talk was still of the classroom and the teacher, of books and reprimands. Bobby Martin had already stuffed his pockets full of stones, and the other boys soon followed his example, selecting the smoothest and roundest stones; Bobby and Harry Jones and Dickie Delacroix—the villagers pronounced this name "Dellacroy"—eventually made a great pile of stones in one corner of the square and guarded it against the raids of the other boys. The girls stood aside, talking among themselves, looking over their shoulders at the boys, and the very small children rolled in the dust or clung to the hands of their older brothers or sisters.

Soon the men began to gather, surveying their own children, speaking of planting and rain, tractors and taxes. They stood together, away from the pile of stones in the corner, and their jokes were quiet and they smiled rather than laughed. The women, wearing faded house dresses and sweaters, came shortly after their menfolk. They greeted one another and exchanged bits of gossip as they went to join their husbands. Soon the women, standing by their husbands, began to call to their children, and the children came reluctantly, having to be called four or five times. Bobby Martin ducked under his mother's grasping hand and ran, laughing, back to the pile of stones. His father spoke up sharply, and Bobby came quickly and took his place between his father and his oldest brother.

The lottery was conducted—as were the square dances, the teenage club, the Halloween program—by Mr. Summers, who had time and energy to devote to civic activities. He was a round-faced, jovial man and he ran the coal business, and people were sorry for him, because he had no children and his wife was a scold. When he arrived in the square, carrying the black wooden box, there was a murmur of conversation among the villagers, and he waved and called, "Little late today, folks." The postmaster, Mr. Graves, followed him, carrying a three-legged stool, and the stool was put in the center of the square and Mr. Summers set the black box down on it. The villagers kept their distance, leaving a space between themselves and the stool, and when Mr. Summers said, "Some of you fellows want to give me a hand?" there was a hesitation before two men, Mr. Martin and his oldest son, Baxter, came forward to hold the box steady on the stool while Mr. Summers stirred up the papers inside it.

The original paraphernalia for the lottery had been lost long ago, and the black box now resting on the stool had been put into use even before Old Man Warner, the oldest man in town, was born. Mr. Summers spoke frequently to the villagers about making a new box, but no one liked to upset even as much tradition as was represented by the black box. There was a story that the present box had been made with some pieces of the box that had preceded it, the one that had been constructed when the first people settled down to make a village here. Every year, after the lottery, Mr. Summers began talking again about a new box, but every year the subject was allowed to fade off without anything's being done. The black box grew shabbier each year; by now it was no longer completely black but splintered badly along one side to show the original wood color, and in some places faded or stained.

Mr. Martin and his oldest son, Baxter, held the black box securely on the stool until Mr. Summers had stirred the papers thoroughly with his hand. Because so much of the ritual had been forgotten or discarded, Mr. Summers had been successful in having slips of paper substituted for the chips of wood that had been used for generations. Chips of wood, Mr. Summers had argued, had been all very well when the village was tiny, but now that the population was more than three hundred and likely to keep on growing, it was necessary to use something that would fit more easily into the black box. The night before the lottery, Mr. Summers and Mr. Graves made up the slips of paper and put them in the box, and it was then taken to the safe of Mr. Summers's coal company and locked up until Mr. Summers was ready to take it to the square next morning. The rest of the year, the box was put away, sometimes one place, sometimes another; it had spent one year in Mr. Graves's barn and another year underfoot in the post office, and sometimes it was set on a shelf in the Martin grocery and left there.

There was a great deal of fussing to be done before Mr. Summers declared the lottery open. There were the lists to make up—of heads of families, heads of households in each family, members of each household in each family. There was the proper swearing-in of Mr. Summers by the postmaster, as the official of the lottery; at one time, some people remembered, there had been a recital of some sort, performed by the official of the lottery, a perfunctory, tuneless chant that had been rattled off duly each year; some people believed that the official of the lottery used to stand just so when he said or sang it, others believed that he was supposed to walk among the people, but years and years ago this part of the ritual had been allowed to lapse. There had been, also, a ritual salute, which the official of the lottery had had to use in addressing each person who came up to draw from the box, but this also had changed with time, until now it was felt necessary only for the official to speak to each person approaching. Mr. Summers was very good at all this; in his clean white shirt and blue jeans, with one hand resting carelessly on the black box, he seemed very proper and important as he talked interminably to Mr. Graves and the Martins.

Just as Mr. Summers finally left off talking and turned to the assembled villagers, Mrs. Hutchinson came hurriedly along the path to the square, her sweater thrown over her shoulders, and slid into place in the back of the crowd. "Clean forgot what day it was," she said to Mrs. Delacroix, who stood next to her, and they both laughed softly. "Thought my old man was out back stacking wood," Mrs. Hutchinson went on, "and then I looked out the window and the kids was gone, and then I remembered it was the twenty-seventh and came a-running." She dried her hands on her apron, and Mrs. Delacroix said, "You're in time, though. They're still talking away up there."

Mrs. Hutchinson craned her neck to see through the crowd and found her husband and children standing near the front. She tapped Mrs. Delacroix on the arm as a farewell and began to make her way through the crowd. The people separated good-humoredly to let her through; two or three people said, in voices just loud enough to be heard across the crowd, "Here comes your Missus, Hutchinson," and "Bill, she made it after all." Mrs. Hutchinson reached her husband, and Mr. Summers, who had been waiting, said cheerfully, "Thought we were going to have to get on without you, Tessie." Mrs. Hutchinson said, grinning, "Wouldn't have me leave m'dishes in the sink, now, would you, Joe?" and laughter ran through the crowd as the people stirred back into position after Mrs. Hutchinson's arrival.

"Well, now," Mr. Summers said soberly, "guess we better get started, get this over with, so's we can go back to work. Anybody ain't here?"

"Dunbar," several people said. "Dunbar, Dunbar."

Mr. Summers consulted his list. "Clyde Dunbar," he said. "That's right. He's broke his leg, hasn't he? Who's drawing for him?"

"Me, I guess," a woman said, and Mr. Summers turned to look at her. "Wife draws for her husband," Mr. Summers said. "Don't you have a grown boy to do it for you, Janey?" Although Mr. Summers and everyone else in the village knew the answer perfectly well, it was the business of the official of the lottery to ask such questions formally. Mr. Summers waited with an expression of polite interest while Mrs. Dunbar answered.

"Horace's not but sixteen yet," Mrs. Dunbar said regretfully. "Guess I gotta fill in for the old man this year."

"Right," Mr. Summers said. He made a note on the list he was holding. Then he asked, "Watson boy drawing this year?"

A tall boy in the crowd raised his hand. "Here," he said. "I'm drawing for m'mother and me." He blinked his eyes nervously and ducked his head as several voices in the crowd said things like "Good fellow, Jack," and "Glad to see your mother's got a man to do it."

"Well," Mr. Summers said, "guess that's everyone. Old Man Warner make it?"

"Here," a voice said, and Mr. Summers nodded.

A sudden hush fell on the crowd as Mr. Summers cleared his throat and looked at the list. "All ready?" he called. "Now, I'll read the names—heads of families first—and the men come up and take a paper out of the box. Keep the paper folded in your hand without looking at it until everyone has had a turn. Everything clear?"

The people had done it so many times that they only half listened to the directions; most of them were quiet, wetting their lips, not looking around. Then Mr. Summers raised one hand high and said, "Adams." A man disengaged himself from the crowd and came forward. "Hi, Steve," Mr. Summers said, and Mr. Adams said, "Hi, Joe." They grinned at one another humorlessly and nervously. Then Mr. Adams reached into the black box and took out a folded paper. He held it firmly by one corner as he turned and went hastily back to his place in the crowd, where he stood a little apart from his family, not looking down at his hand.

"Allen," Mr. Summers said. "Anderson. . . . Bentham."

"Seems like there's no time at all between lotteries any more," Mrs. Delacroix said to Mrs. Graves in the back row. "Seems like we got through with the last one only last week."

"Time sure goes fast," Mrs. Graves said.

"Clark. . . . Delacroix."

"There goes my old man," Mrs. Delacroix said. She held her breath while her husband went forward.

"Dunbar," Mr. Summers said, and Mrs. Dunbar went steadily to the box while one of the women said, "Go on, Janey," and another said, "There she goes."

"We're next," Mrs. Graves said. She watched while Mr. Graves came around from the side of the box, greeted Mr. Summers gravely, and selected a slip of paper from the box. By now, all through the crowd there were men holding the small folded papers in their large hands, turning them over and over nervously. Mrs. Dunbar and her two sons stood together, Mrs. Dunbar holding the slip of paper.

"Harburt. . . . Hutchinson."

"Get up there, Bill," Mrs. Hutchinson said, and the people near her laughed.

"Jones."

"They do say," Mr. Adams said to Old Man Warner, who stood next to him, "that over in the north village they're talking of giving up the lottery."

Old Man Warner snorted. "Pack of crazy fools," he said. "Listening to the young folks, nothing's good enough for *them*. Next thing you know, they'll be wanting to go back to living in caves, nobody work any more, live *that* way for a while. Used to be a saying about 'Lottery in June, corn be heavy soon.' First thing you know, we'd all be eating stewed chickweed and acorns. There's *always* been a lottery," he added petulantly. "Bad enough to see young Joe Summers up there joking with everybody."

"Some places have already quit lotteries," Mrs. Adams said.

"Nothing but trouble in *that*," Old Man Warner said stoutly. "Pack of young fools."

"Martin." And Bobby Martin watched his father go forward. "Overdyke. . . . Percy."

"I wish they'd hurry," Mrs. Dunbar said to her older son. "I wish they'd hurry."

"They're almost through," her son said.

"You get ready to run tell Dad," Mrs. Dunbar said.

Mr. Summers called his own name and then stepped forward precisely and selected a slip from the box. Then he called, "Warner."

"Seventy-seventh year I been in the lottery," Old Man Warner said as he went through the crowd. "Seventy-seventh time."

"Watson." The tall boy came awkwardly through the crowd. Someone said, "Don't be nervous, Jack," and Mr. Summers said, "Take your time, son."

"Zanini."

After that, there was a long pause, a breathless pause, until Mr. Summers, holding his slip of paper in the air, said, "All right, fellows." For a minute, no one moved, and then all the slips of paper were opened. Suddenly, all the women began to speak at once, saying, "Who is it?," "Who's got it?," "Is it the Dunbars?," "Is it the Watsons?" Then the voices began to say, "It's Hutchinson. It's Bill," "Bill Hutchinson's got it."

"Go tell your father," Mrs. Dunbar said to her older son.

People began to look around to see the Hutchinsons. Bill Hutchinson was standing quiet, staring down at the paper in his hand. Suddenly, Tessie Hutchinson shouted to Mr. Summers, "You didn't give him time enough to take any paper he wanted. I saw you. It wasn't fair!"

"Be a good sport, Tessie," Mrs. Delacroix called, and Mrs. Graves said, "All of us took the same chance."

"Shut up, Tessie," Bill Hutchinson said.

"Well, everyone," Mr. Summers said, "that was done pretty fast, and now we've got to be hurrying a little more to get done in time." He consulted his next list. "Bill," he said, "you draw for the Hutchinson family. You got any other households in the Hutchinsons?"

"There's Don and Eva," Mrs. Hutchinson yelled. "Make *them* take their chance!"

"Daughters draw with their husbands' families, Tessie," Mr. Summers said gently. "You know that as well as anyone else."

"It wasn't *fair*," Tessie said.

"I guess not, Joe," Bill Hutchinson said regretfully. "My daughter draws with her husband's family, that's only fair. And I've got no other family except the kids."

"Then, as far as drawing for families is concerned, it's you," Mr. Summers said in explanation, "and as far as drawing for households is concerned, that's you, too. Right?"

"Right," Bill Hutchinson said.

"How many kids, Bill?" Mr. Summers asked formally.

"Three," Bill Hutchinson said. "There's Bill, Jr., and Nancy, and little Dave. And Tessie and me."

"All right, then," Mr. Summers said. "Harry, you got their tickets back?"

Mr. Graves nodded and held up the slips of paper. "Put them in the box, then," Mr. Summers directed. "Take Bill's and put it in."

"I think we ought to start over," Mrs. Hutchinson said, as quietly as she could. "I tell you it wasn't *fair*. You didn't give him time enough to choose. *Every*body saw that."

Mr. Graves had selected the five slips and put them in the box, and he dropped all the papers but those onto the ground, where the breeze caught them and lifted them off.

"Listen, everybody," Mrs. Hutchinson was saying to the people around her.

"Ready, Bill?" Mr. Summers asked, and Bill Hutchinson, with one quick glance around at his wife and children, nodded.

"Remember," Mr. Summers said, "take the slips and keep them folded until each person has taken one. Harry, you help little Dave." Mr. Graves took the hand of the little boy, who came willingly with him up to the box. "Take a paper out of the box, Davy," Mr. Summers said. Davy put his hand into the box and laughed. "Take just *one* paper," Mr. Summers said. "Harry, you hold it for him." Mr. Graves took the child's hand and removed the folded paper from the tight fist and held it while little Dave stood next to him and looked up at him wonderingly.

"Nancy next," Mr. Summers said. Nancy was twelve, and her school friends breathed heavily as she went forward, switching her skirt, and took a slip daintily from the box. "Bill, Jr.," Mr. Summers said, and Billy, his face red and his feet overlarge, nearly knocked the box over as he got a paper out. "Tessie," Mr. Summers said. She hesitated for a minute, looking around defiantly, and then set her lips and went up to the box. She snatched a paper out and held it behind her.

"Bill," Mr. Summers said, and Bill Hutchinson reached into the box and felt around, bringing his hand out at last with the slip of paper in it.

The crowd was quiet. A girl whispered, "I hope it's not Nancy," and the sound of the whisper reached the edges of the crowd.

"It's not the way it used to be," Old Man Warner said clearly. "People ain't the way they used to be."

"All right," Mr. Summers said. "Open the papers. Harry, you open little Dave's."

Mr. Graves opened the slip of paper and there was a general sigh through the crowd as he held it up and everyone could see that it was blank. Nancy and Bill, Jr., opened theirs at the same time, and both beamed and laughed, turning around to the crowd and holding their slips of paper above their heads.

"Tessie," Mr. Summers said. There was a pause, and then Mr. Summers looked at Bill Hutchinson, and Bill unfolded his paper and showed it. It was blank.

"It's Tessie," Mr. Summers said, and his voice was hushed. "Show us her paper, Bill."

Bill Hutchinson went over to his wife and forced the slip of paper out of her hand. It had a black spot on it, the black spot Mr. Summers had made the night before with the heavy pencil in the coal-company office. Bill Hutchinson held it up, and there was a stir in the crowd.

"All right, folks," Mr. Summers said. "Let's finish quickly."

Although the villagers had forgotten the ritual and lost the original black box, they still remembered to use stones. The pile of stones the boys had made earlier was ready; there were stones on the ground with the blowing scraps of paper that had come out of the box. Mrs. Delacroix selected a stone so large she had to pick it up with both hands and turned to Mrs. Dunbar. "Come on," she said. "Hurry up."

Mrs. Dunbar had small stones in both hands, and she said, gasping for breath, "I can't run at all. You'll have to go ahead and I'll catch up with you."

The children had stones already, and someone gave little Davy Hutchinson a few pebbles.

Tessie Hutchinson was in the center of a cleared space by now, and she held her hands out desperately as the villagers moved in on her. "It isn't fair," she said. A stone hit her on the side of the head.

Old Man Warner was saying, "Come on, come on, everyone." Steve Adams was in the front of the crowd of villagers, with Mrs. Graves beside him.

"It isn't fair, it isn't right," Mrs. Hutchinson screamed, and then they were upon her.

## FOR DISCUSSION

1. From what narrative point of view is the story written?
2. What is the author's tone? What is the mood of the story?
3. Why is it "natural" that the children began to gather first on the day of the lottery? What is their role at the end of the story?
4. What is ironic about the fact that Mr. Summers conducts the lottery? Why has he been chosen to do the job?
5. This is a story with a dominant symbol. What is the symbolic object, and what about it seems particularly significant?

6. What is the official reason for holding the lottery? Are the villagers still aware of the reasons? What is suggested by the fact that the lottery is not conducted as precisely as it once was?
7. How does the ritual carried out in the story compare with the technological level at which the people of the village live?
8. Would you say the characters in the story represent stereotypes or plausible personalities?
9. What is ironic about the arguments over whether or not the lottery was fairly conducted?
10. As you read the story, at what point did you realize what was ultimately going to happen? How did you know? How early in the story did you suspect that something unusual was in the air? Is there any specific foreshadowing?
11. Do you think the people of the village are evil? Do they live evil lives? If they are not basically evil, what motivates them to commit what most people would agree is an evil act?
12. One interpretation of "The Lottery" is that it is about a scapegoat. Who is the scapegoat in the story? Why do you suppose the people of the village might need a scapegoat? Why do any people need a scapegoat? Do you find this interpretation convincing?
13. What is the theme of the story? Does it relate to any periodic rituals or practices in our own society? Does it suggest anything about the role of chance in our lives? Can you think of any other interpretations?

PART II *The Novella*

# Introduction

The novella can be tricky to define, but it is clearly distinct from either the short story or the full-length novel. The novella is a type of prose fiction of intermediate length, usually of between 12,000 and 40,000 words, perhaps thirty to a hundred pages long. It is also called by a variety of other names, such as the short novel, the novelette, or the *nouvelle*, the last being a French term meaning simply "a story."

Although many great writers have written novellas, the form has never become as popular as the modern short story or the novel. Apart from sometimes heated debate over what the form should be called, there is also the fact that it is of an inconvenient length—too long to fit into a magazine, too short to be a book. Even the Library of Congress system of classifying fictional works ignores the existence of the novella under any name. So, the novella has chronically had hard times. Nevertheless, the form has persisted, and writers still continue to write novellas.

Many readers ask whether the novella should be thought of as an expanded short story or an abbreviated novel. The answer is that it should be thought of as neither.

The novel is an entirely different type of fiction. The modern realistic novel may be viewed as a sort of fictionalized history, compared with which a novella is only an episode. The novel has room for multiple and complicated plots, a world of fully developed characters, many incidents, and great expanses of time and space.

The distinctions between the novella and the short story are less striking, but they are important. The novella's greater length makes possible a greater passage of time, more changes of scene, more incidents supporting the work's major incident, an expanded cast of characters, and much more detailed probing into the makeup of individual characters. The short story, it has often been noted, begins as near its ending as possible. The novella, on the other hand, takes the time to build more slowly toward its central incident. Still, because it is relatively short compared to the novel, the novella does not sacrifice the impact that can be gained through brevity. Most novellas can be read in a single sitting, and so readers can still enjoy the same sweep and excitement that they get from a good short story.

Indeed, much of what we have already said about the short story can also be said about the novella. The elements of plot, setting, character, tone, mood, emotion, irony, symbolism, theme, and point of view are just as important to the novella as they are to the short story. As you read the two novellas included in this section—Herman Melville's *Bartleby, the Scrivener* and Katherine Anne Porter's *Noon Wine*—pay particular attention to the more gradual changes that occur in the personalities of the major characters. Also note that these changes occur over a period of time, not in a single flash of insight, as often happens in the short story.

# Bartleby, the Scrivener

HERMAN MELVILLE

I am a rather elderly man. The nature of my avocations, for the last thirty years, has brought me into more than ordinary contact with what would seem an interesting and somewhat singular set of men, of whom, as yet, nothing, that I know of, has ever been written—I mean, the law-copyists, or scriveners, I have known very many of them, professionally and privately, and, if I pleased, could relate divers histories, at which good-natured gentlemen might smile, and sentimental souls might weep. But I waive the biographies of all other scriveners, for a few passages in the life of Bartleby, who was a scrivener, the strangest I ever saw, or heard of. While, of other law-copyists, I might write the complete life, of Bartleby nothing of that sort can be done. I believe that no materials exist, for a full and satisfactory biography of this man. It is an irreparable loss to literature. Bartleby was one of those beings of whom nothing is ascertainable, except from the original sources, and, in his case, those are very small. What my own astonished eyes saw of Bartleby, *that* is all I know of him, except, indeed, one vague report, which will appear in the sequel.

Ere introducing the scrivener, as he first appeared to me, it is fit I make some mention of myself, my *employés*, my business, my chambers, and general surroundings; because some such description is indispensable to an adequate understanding of the chief character about to be presented. Imprimis:[1] I am a man who, from his youth upwards, has been filled with a profound conviction that the easiest way of life is the best. Hence, though I belong to a profession proverbially energetic and nervous, even to turbulence, at times, yet nothing of that sort have I ever suffered to invade my peace. I am one of those unambitious lawyers who never address a jury, or in any way draw down public applause; but, in the cool tranquillity of a snug retreat, do a snug business among rich men's bonds, and mortgages, and title-deeds. All who know me, consider me an eminently *safe* man. The late John Jacob Astor, a personage little given to poetic enthusiasm, had no hesitation in pronouncing my first grand point to be prudence; my next, method. I do not speak it in vanity, but simply record the fact, that I was not unemployed in my profession by the late John Jacob Astor; a name which, I admit, I love to repeat; for it hath a rounded and orbicular sound to it, and rings like unto bullion. I will freely add, that I was not insensible to the late John Jacob Astor's good opinion.

Some time prior to the period at which this little history begins, my avocations had been largely increased. The good old office, now extinct

[1]First.

in the State of New York, of a Master in Chancery,[2] had been conferred upon me. It was not a very arduous office, but very pleasantly remunerative. I seldom lose my temper; much more seldom indulge in dangerous indignation at wrongs and outrages; but I must be permitted to be rash here and declare, that I consider the sudden and violent abrogation of the office of Master in Chancery, by the new Constitution, as a —— premature act; inasmuch as I had counted upon a life-lease of the profits, whereas I only received those of a few short years. But this is by the way.

My chambers were up stairs, at No. — Wall Street. At one end, they looked upon the white wall of the interior of a spacious sky-light shaft, penetrating the building from top to bottom.

This view might have been considered rather tame than otherwise, deficient in what landscape painters call "life." But, if so, the view from the other end of my chambers offered, at least, a contrast, if nothing more. In that direction, my windows commanded an unobstructed view of a lofty brick wall, black by age and everlasting shade; which wall required no spy-glass to bring out its lurking beauties, but, for the benefit of all near-sighted spectators, was pushed up to within ten feet of my window-panes. Owing to the great height of the surrounding buildings, and my chambers being on the second floor, the interval between this wall and mine not a little resembled a huge square cistern.

At the period just preceding the advent of Bartleby, I had two persons as copyists in my employment, and a promising lad as an office-boy. First, Turkey; second, Nippers; third, Ginger Nut. These may seem names, the like of which are not usually found in the Directory.[3] In truth, they were nicknames, mutually conferred upon each other by my three clerks, and were deemed expressive of their respective persons or characters. Turkey was a short, pursy[4] Englishman, of about my own age—that is, somewhere not far from sixty. In the morning, one might say, his face was of a fine florid hue, but after twelve o'clock, meridian—his dinner hour—it blazed like a grate full of Christmas coals; and continued blazing—but, as it were, with a gradual wane—till six o'clock, P.M., or thereabouts; after which, I saw no more of the proprietor of the face, which, gaining its meridian with the sun, seemed to set with it, to rise, culminate, and decline the following day, with the like regularity and undiminished glory. There are many singular coincidences I have known in the course of my life, not the least among which was the fact, that, exactly when Turkey displayed his fullest beams from his red and radiant countenance, just then, too, at that critical moment, began the daily period when I considered his business capacities as seriously

---

[2]The court of chancery settled matters not adequately covered by the laws, on the basis of fairness and good sense. The office of Master was abolished in 1847.

[3]The Post Office Directory.

[4]Pudgy.

disturbed for the remainder of the twenty-four hours. Not that he was absolutely idle, or averse to business then; far from it. The difficulty was, he was apt to be altogether too energetic. There was a strange, inflamed, flurried, flighty recklessness of activity about him. He would be incautious in dipping his pen into his inkstand. All his blots upon my documents were dropped there after twelve o'clock, meridian. Indeed, not only would he be reckless, and sadly given to making blots in the afternoon, but, some days, he went further, and was rather noisy. At such times, too, his face flamed with augmented blazonry, as if cannel coal had been heaped on anthracite. He made an unpleasant racket with his chair; spilled his sand-box;[5] in mending his pens, impatiently split them all to pieces, and threw them on the floor in a sudden passion; stood up, and leaned over his table, boxing his papers about in a most indecorous manner, very sad to behold in an elderly man like him. Nevertheless, as he was in many ways a most valuable person to me, and all the time before twelve o'clock, meridian, was the quickest, steadiest creature, too, accomplishing a great deal of work in a style not easily to be matched—for these reasons, I was willing to overlook his eccentricities, though, indeed, occasionally, I remonstrated with him. I did this very gently, however, because, though the civilest, nay, the blandest and most reverential of men in the morning, yet, in the afternoon, he was disposed, upon provocation, to be slightly rash with his tongue—in fact, insolent. Now, valuing his morning services as I did, and resolved not to lose them—yet, at the same time, made uncomfortable by his inflamed ways after twelve o'clock—and being a man of peace, unwilling by my admonitions to call forth unseemly retorts from him, I took upon me, one Saturday noon (he was always worse on Saturdays) to hint to him, very kindly, that, perhaps, now that he was growing old, it might be well to abridge his labors; in short, he need not come to my chambers after twelve o'clock, but, dinner over, had best go home to his lodgings, and rest himself till tea-time. But no; he insisted upon his afternoon devotions. His countenance became intolerably fervid, as he oratorically assured me—gesticulating with a long ruler at the other end of the room—that if his services in the morning were useful, how indispensable, then, in the afternoon?

"With submission, sir," said Turkey, on this occasion, "I consider myself your right-hand man. In the morning I but marshal and deploy my columns; but in the afternoon I put myself at their head, and gallantly charge the foe, thus"—and he made a violent thrust with the ruler.

"But the blots, Turkey," intimated I.

"True; but, with submission, sir, behold these hairs! I am getting old. Surely, sir, a blot or two of a warm afternoon is not to be severely urged against gray hairs. Old age—even if it blot the page—is honorable. With submission, sir, we *both* are getting old."

This appeal to my fellow-feeling was hardly to be resisted. At all

---

[5]The sand was used to speed the drying of ink.

events, I saw that go he would not. So, I made up my mind to let him stay, resolving, nevertheless, to see to it that, during the afternoon, he had to do with my less important papers.

Nippers, the second on my list, was a whiskered, sallow, and, upon the whole, rather piratical-looking young man, of about five-and-twenty. I always deemed him the victim of two evil powers—ambition and indigestion. The ambition was evinced by a certain impatience of the duties of a mere copyist, an unwarrantable usurpation of strictly professional affairs, such as the original drawing up of legal documents. The indigestion seemed betokened in an occasional nervous testiness and grinning irritability, causing the teeth to audibly grind together over mistakes committed in copying; unnecessary maledictions, hissed, rather than spoken, in the heat of business; and especially by a continual discontent with the height of the table where he worked. Though of a very ingenious mechanical turn, Nippers could never get this table to suit him. He put chips under it, blocks of various sorts, bits of pasteboard, and at last went so far as to attempt an exquisite adjustment, by final pieces of folded blotting-paper. But no invention would answer. If, for the sake of easing his back, he brought the table-lid at a sharp angle well up towards his chin, and wrote there like a man using the steep roof of a Dutch house for his desk, then he declared that it stopped the circulation in his arms. If now he lowered the table to his waistbands, and stooped over it in writing, then there was a sore aching in his back. In short, the truth of the matter was, Nippers knew not what he wanted. Or, if he wanted anything, it was to be rid of a scrivener's table altogether. Among the manifestations of his diseased ambition was a fondness he had for receiving visits from certain ambiguous-looking fellows in seedy coats, whom he called his clients. Indeed, I was aware that not only was he, at times, considerable of a ward-politician, but he occasionally did a little business at the Justices' courts, and was not unknown on the steps of the Tombs.[6] I have good reason to believe, however, that one individual who called upon him at my chambers, and who, with a grand air, he insisted was his client, was no other than a dun, and the alleged title-deed, a bill. But, with all his failings, and the annoyances he caused me, Nippers, like his compatriot Turkey, was a very useful man to me; wrote a neat, swift hand; and, when he chose, was not deficient in a gentlemanly sort of deportment. Added to this, he always dressed in a gentlemanly sort of way; and so, incidentally, reflected credit upon my chambers. Whereas, with respect to Turkey, I had much ado to keep him from being a reproach to me. His clothes were apt to look oily, and smell of eating-houses. He wore his pantaloons very loose and baggy in summer. His coats were execrable; his hat not to be handled. But while the hat was a thing of indifference to me, inasmuch as his natural civility and deference, as a dependent Englishman, always led him to doff it the moment he entered the room, yet his

---

[6]A New York prison.

coat was another matter. Concerning his coats, I reasoned with him; but with no effect. The truth was, I suppose, that a man with so small an income could not afford to sport such a lustrous face and a lustrous coat at one and the same time. As Nippers once observed, Turkey's money went chiefly for red ink. One winter day, I presented Turkey with a highly respectable-looking coat of my own—a padded gray coat, of a most comfortable warmth, and which buttoned straight up from the knee to the neck. I thought Turkey would appreciate the favor, and abate his rashness and obstreperousness of afternoons. But no; I verily believe that buttoning himself up in so downy and blanket-like a coat had a pernicious effect upon him—upon the same principle that too much oats are bad for horses. In fact, precisely as a rash, restive horse is said to feel his oats, so Turkey felt his coat. It made him insolent. He was a man whom prosperity harmed.

Though, concerning the self-indulgent habits of Turkey, I had my own private surmises, yet, touching Nippers, I was well persuaded that, whatever might be his faults in other respects, he was, at least, a temperate young man. But, indeed, nature herself seemed to have been his vintner, and, at his birth, charged him so thoroughly with an irritable, brandy-like disposition, that all subsequent potations were needless. When I consider how, amid the stillness of my chambers, Nippers would sometimes impatiently rise from his seat, and stooping over his table, spread his arms wide apart, seize the whole desk, and move it, and jerk it, with a grim, grinding motion on the floor, as if the table were a perverse voluntary agent, intent on thwarting and vexing him, I plainly perceive that, for Nippers, brandy-and-water were altogether superfluous.

It was fortunate for me that, owing to its peculiar cause—indigestion—the irritability and consequent nervousness of Nippers were mainly observable in the morning, while in the afternoon he was comparatively mild. So that, Turkey's paroxysms only coming on about twelve o'clock, I never had to do with their eccentricities at one time. Their fits relieved each other, like guards. When Nippers's was on, Turkey's was off; and vice versa. This was a good natural arrangement, under the circumstances.

Ginger Nut, the third on my list, was a lad, some twelve years old. His father was a carman,[7] ambitious of seeing his son on the bench instead of a cart, before he died. So he sent him to my office, as student at law, errand-boy, cleaner and sweeper, at the rate of one dollar a week. He had a little desk to himself, but he did not use it much. Upon inspection, the drawer exhibited a great array of the shells of various sorts of nuts. Indeed, to this quick-witted youth, the whole noble science of the law was contained in a nut-shell. Not the least among the employments of Ginger Nut, as well as one which he discharged with the most alacrity, was his duty as cake and apple purveyor for Turkey and Nippers. Copying law-papers being proverbially a dry, husky sort

[7]Teamster.

of business, my two scriveners were fain to moisten their mouths very often with Spitzenbergs,[8] to be had at the numerous stalls nigh the Custom House and Post Office. Also, they sent Ginger Nut very frequently for that peculiar cake—small, flat, round, and very spicy—after which he had been named by them. Of a cold morning, when business was but dull, Turkey would gobble up scores of these cakes, as if they were mere wafers—indeed, they sell them at the rate of six or eight for a penny—the scrape of his pen blending with the crunching of the crisp particles in his mouth. Of all the fiery afternoon blunders and flurried rashness of Turkey, was his once moistening a ginger-cake between his lips, and clapping it on to a mortgage, for a seal. I came within an ace of dismissing him then. But he mollified me by making an oriental bow, and saying—

"With submission, sir, it was generous of me to find you in[9] stationery of my own account."

Now my original business—that of a conveyancer and title hunter, and drawer-up of recondite documents of all sorts—was considerably increased by receiving the Master's office. There was now great work for scriveners. Not only must I push the clerks already with me, but I must have additional help.

In answer to my advertisement, a motionless young man one morning stood upon my office threshold, the door being open, for it was summer. I can see that figure now—pallidly neat, pitiably respectable, incurably forlorn! It was Bartleby.

After a few words touching his qualifications, I engaged him, glad to have among my corps of copyists a man of so singularly sedate an aspect, which I thought might operate beneficially upon the flighty temper of Turkey, and the fiery one of Nippers.

I should have stated before that ground-glass folding-doors divided my premises into two parts, one of which was occupied by my scriveners, the other by myself. According to my humor, I threw open these doors, or closed them. I resolved to assign Bartleby a corner by the folding-doors, but on my side of them, so as to have this quiet man within easy call, in case any trifling thing was to be done. I placed his desk close up to a small side-window in that part of the room, a window which originally had afforded a lateral view of certain grimy backyards and bricks, but which, owing to subsequent erections, commanded at present no view at all, though it gave some light. Within three feet of the panes was a wall, and the light came down from far above, between two lofty buildings, as from a very small opening in a dome. Still further to a satisfactory arrangement, I procured a high green folding screen, which might entirely isolate Bartleby from my sight, though not remove him from my voice. And thus, in a manner, privacy and society were conjoined.

[8]Apples.
[9]Supply you with.

At first Bartleby did an extraordinary quantity of writing. As if long famishing for something to copy, he seemed to gorge himself on my documents. There was no pause for digestion. He ran a day and night line, copying by sunlight and by candle-light. I should have been quite delighted with his application, had he been cheerfully industrious. But he wrote on silently, palely, mechanically.

It is, of course, an indispensable part of a scrivener's business to verify the accuracy of his copy, word by word. Where there are two or more scriveners in an office, they assist each other in this examination, one reading from the copy, the other holding the original. It is a very dull, wearisome, and lethargic affair. I can readily imagine that, to some sanguine temperaments, it would be altogether intolerable. For example, I cannot credit that the mettlesome poet, Byron, would have contentedly sat down with Bartleby to examine a law document of, say five hundred pages, closely written in a crimpy hand.

Now and then, in the haste of business, it had been my habit to assist in comparing some brief document myself, calling Turkey or Nippers for this purpose. One object I had, in placing Bartleby so handy to me behind the screen, was, to avail myself of his services on such trivial occasions. It was on the third day, I think, of his being with me, and before any necessity had arisen for having his own writing examined, that, being much hurried to complete a small affair I had in hand, I abruptly called to Bartleby. In my haste and natural expectancy of instant compliance, I sat with my head bent over the original on my desk, and my right hand sideways, and somewhat nervously extended with the copy, so that, immediately upon emerging from his retreat, Bartleby might snatch it and proceed to business without the least delay.

In this very attitude did I sit when I called to him, rapidly stating what it was I wanted him to do—namely, to examine a small paper with me. Imagine my surprise, nay, my consternation, when, without moving from his privacy, Bartleby, in a singularly mild, firm voice, replied, "I would prefer not to."

I sat awhile in perfect silence, rallying my stunned faculties. Immediately it occurred to me that my ears had deceived me, or Bartleby had entirely misunderstood my meaning. I repeated my request in the clearest tone I could assume; but in quite as clear a one came the previous reply, "I would prefer not to."

"Prefer not to," echoed I, rising in high excitement, and crossing the room with a stride. "What do you mean? Are you moon-struck? I want you to help me compare this sheet here—take it," and I thrust it towards him.

"I would prefer not to," said he.

I looked at him steadfastly. His face was leanly composed; his gray eye dimly calm. Not a wrinkle of agitation rippled him. Had there been the least uneasiness, anger, impatience or impertinence in his manner; in other words, had there been anything ordinarily human about him, doubtless I should have violently dismissed him from the premises. But as it was, I should have as soon thought of turning my pale plaster-of-paris bust of Cicero[10] out of doors. I stood gazing at him awhile, as he went on with his own writing, and then reseated myself at my desk. This is very strange, thought I. What had one best to do? But my business hurried me. I concluded to forget the matter for the present, reserving it for my future leisure. So, calling Nippers from the other room, the paper was speedily examined.

A few days after this, Bartleby concluded four lengthy documents, being quadruplicates of a week's testimony taken before me in my High Court of Chancery. It became necessary to examine them. It was an important suit, and great accuracy was imperative. Having all things arranged, I called Turkey, Nippers and Ginger Nut, from the next room, meaning to place the four copies in the hands of my four clerks, while I should read from the original. Accordingly, Turkey, Nippers, and Ginger Nut had taken their seats in a row, each with his document in his hand, when I called to Bartleby to join this interesting group.

"Bartleby! quick, I am waiting."

I heard a slow scrape of his chair legs on the uncarpeted floor, and soon he appeared standing at the entrance of his hermitage.

"What is wanted?" said he, mildly.

"The copies, the copies," said I, hurriedly. "We are going to examine them. There"—and I held towards him the fourth quadruplicate.

"I would prefer not to," he said, and gently disappeared behind the screen.

For a few moments I was turned into a pillar of salt, standing at the head of my seated column of clerks. Recovering myself, I advanced towards the screen, and demanded the reason for such extraordinary conduct.

"Why do you refuse?"

"I would prefer not to."

With any other man I should have flown outright into a dreadful passion, scorned all further words, and thrust him ignominiously from my presence. But there was something about Bartleby that not only strangely disarmed me, but in a wonderful manner, touched and disconcerted me. I began to reason with him.

"These are your own copies we are about to examine. It is labor saving to you, because one examination will answer for your four papers. It is common usage. Every copyist is bound to help examine his copy. Is it not so? Will you not speak? Answer!"

"I prefer not to," he replied in a flute-like tone. It seemed to me that, while I had been addressing him, he carefully revolved every statement that I made; fully comprehended the meaning; could not gainsay the irresistible conclusion; but, at the same time, some paramount consideration prevailed with him to reply as he did.

[10]Great Roman orator and rhetorician.

"You are decided, then, not to comply with my request—a request made according to common usage and common sense?"

He briefly gave me to understand, that on that point my judgment was sound. Yes: his decision was irreversible.

It is not seldom the case that, when a man is browbeaten in some unprecedented and violently unreasonable way, he begins to stagger in his own plainest faith. He begins, as it were, vaguely to surmise that, wonderful as it may be, all the justice and all the reason is on the other side. Accordingly, if any disinterested persons are present, he turns to them for some reinforcement for his own faltering mind.

"Turkey," said I, "what do you think of this? Am I not right?"

"With submission, sir," said Turkey, in his blandest tone, "I think that you are."

"Nippers," said I, "what do *you* think of it?"

"I think I should kick him out of the office."

(The reader of nice perceptions will here perceive that, it being morning, Turkey's answer is couched in polite and tranquil terms, but Nippers replies in ill-tempered ones. Or, to repeat a previous sentence, Nippers's ugly mood was on duty, and Turkey's off.)

"Ginger Nut," said I, willing to enlist the smallest suffrage in my behalf, "what do *you* think of it?"

"I think, sir, he's a little *luny*," replied Ginger Nut, with a grin.

"You hear what they say," said I, turning towards the screen, "come forth and do your duty."

But he vouchsafed no reply. I pondered a moment in sore perplexity. But once more business hurried me. I determined again to postpone the consideration of this dilemma to my future leisure. With a little trouble we made out to examine the papers without Bartleby, though at every page or two Turkey deferentially dropped his opinion, that this proceeding was quite out of the common; while Nippers, twitching in his chair with a dyspeptic nervousness, ground out, between his set teeth, occasional hissing maledictions against the stubborn oaf behind the scene. And for his (Nippers's) part, this was the first and the last time he would do another man's business without pay.

Meanwhile Bartleby sat in his hermitage, oblivious to everything but his own peculiar business there.

Some days passed, the scrivener being employed upon another lengthy work. His late remarkable conduct led me to regard his ways narrowly. I observed that he never went to dinner; indeed, that he never went anywhere. As yet I had never, of my personal knowledge, known him to be outside of my office. He was a perpetual sentry in the corner. At about eleven o'clock though, in the morning, I noticed that Ginger Nut would advance toward the opening in Bartleby's screen, as if silently beckoned thither by a gesture invisible to me where I sat. The boy would then leave the office, jingling a few pence, and reappear with a handful of ginger-nuts, which he delivered in the hermitage, receiving two of the cakes for his trouble.

He lives, then, on ginger-nuts, thought I; never eats a dinner, properly speaking; he must be a vegetarian, then, but no; he never eats even vegetables, he eats nothing but ginger-nuts. My mind then ran on in reveries concerning the probable effects upon the human constitution of living entirely on ginger-nuts. Ginger-nuts are so called, because they contain ginger as one of their peculiar constituents, and the final flavoring one. Now, what was ginger? A hot, spicy thing. Was Bartleby hot and spicy? Not at all. Ginger, then, had no effect upon Bartleby. Probably he preferred it should have none.

Nothing so aggravates an earnest person as a passive resistance. If the individual so resisted be of a not inhumane temper, and the resisting one perfectly harmless in his passivity, then, in the better moods of the former, he will endeavor charitably to construe to his imagination what proves impossible to be solved by his judgment. Even so, for the most part, I regarded Bartleby and his ways. Poor fellow! thought I, he means no mischief; it is plain he intends no insolence; his aspect sufficiently evinces that his eccentricities are involuntary. He is useful to me. I can get along with him. If I turn him away, the chances are he will fall in with some less indulgent employer, and then he will be rudely treated, and perhaps driven forth miserably to starve. Yes. Here I can cheaply purchase a delicious self-approval. To befriend Bartleby; to humor him in his strange wilfulness, will cost me little or nothing, while I lay up in my soul what will eventually prove a sweet morsel for my conscience. But this mood was not invariable with me. The passiveness of Bartleby sometimes irritated me. I felt strangely goaded on to encounter him in new opposition—to elicit some angry spark from him answerable to my own. But, indeed, I might as well have essayed to strike fire with my knuckles against a bit of Windsor soap. But one afternoon the evil impulse in me mastered me, and the following little scene ensued:

"Bartleby," said I, "when those papers are all copied, I will compare them with you."

"I would prefer not to."

"How? Surely you do not mean to persist in that mulish vagary?"

No answer.

I threw open the folding-doors near by, and, turning upon Turkey and Nippers, exclaimed:

"Bartleby a second time says, he won't examine his papers. What do you think of it, Turkey?"

It was afternoon, be it remembered. Turkey sat glowing like a brass boiler; his bald head steaming; his hands reeling among his blotted papers.

"Think of it?" roared Turkey. "I think I'll just step behind his screen, and black his eyes for him!"

So saying, Turkey rose to his feet and threw his arms into a pugilistic position. He was hurrying away to make good his promise, when I detained him, alarmed at the effect of incautiously rousing Turkey's combativeness after dinner.

"Sit down, Turkey," said I, "and hear what Nippers has to say. What do you think of it, Nippers? Would I not be justified in immediately dismissing Bartleby?"

"Excuse me, that is for you to decide, sir. I think his conduct quite unusual, and, indeed, unjust, as regards Turkey and myself. But it may only be a passing whim."

"Ah," exclaimed I, "you have strangely changed your mind, then— you speak very gently of him now."

"All beer," cried Turkey; "gentleness is effects of beer—Nippers and I dined together to-day. You see how gentle *I* am, sir. Shall I go and black his eyes?"

"You refer to Bartleby, I suppose. No, not to-day, Turkey," I replied; "pray, put up your fists."

I closed the doors, and again advanced towards Bartleby. I felt additional incentives tempting me to my fate. I burned to be rebelled against again. I remembered that Bartleby never left the office.

"Bartleby," said I, "Ginger Nut is away; just step around to the Post-Office, won't you?" (it was but a three minutes' walk) "and see if there is anything for me."

"I would prefer not to."

"You *will* not?"

"I *prefer* not."

I staggered to my desk, and sat there in a deep study. My blind inveteracy returned. Was there any other thing in which I could procure myself to be ignominiously repulsed by this lean, penniless wight?— my hired clerk? What added thing is there, perfectly reasonable, that he will be sure to refuse to do?

"Bartleby!"

No answer.

"Bartleby," in a louder tone.

No answer.

"Bartleby," I roared.

Like a very ghost, agreeably to the laws of magical invocation, at the third summons, he appeared at the entrance of his hermitage.

"Go to the next room, and tell Nippers to come to me."

"I prefer not to," he respectfully and slowly said, and mildly disappeared.

"Very good, Bartleby," said I, in a quiet sort of serenely-severe self-possessed tone, intimating the unalterable purpose of some terrible retribution very close at hand. At the moment I half intended something of the kind. But upon the whole, as it was drawing towards my dinner-hour, I thought it best to put on my hat and walk home for the day, suffering much from perplexity and distress of mind.

Shall I acknowledge it? The conclusion of this whole business was, that it soon became a fixed fact of my chambers, that a pale young scrivener, by the name of Bartleby, had a desk there; that he copied for me at the usual rate of four cents a folio (one hundred words); but he was permanently exempt from examining the work done by him, that duty being transferred to Turkey and Nippers, out of compliment, doubtless, to their superior acuteness; moreover, said Bartleby was never, on any account, to be dispatched on the most trivial errand of any sort; and that even if entreated to take upon him such a matter, it was generally understood that he would "prefer not to"—in other words, that he would refuse point-blank.

As days passed on, I became considerably reconciled to Bartleby. His steadiness, his freedom from all dissipation, his incessant industry (except when he chose to throw himself into a standing revery behind his screen), his great stillness, his unalterableness of demeanor under all circumstances, made him a valuable acquisition. One prime thing was this—*he was always there*—first in the morning, continually through the day, and the last at night. I had a singular confidence in his honesty. I felt my most precious papers perfectly safe in his hands. Sometimes, to be sure, I could not, for the very soul of me, avoid falling into sudden spasmodic passions with him. For it was exceeding difficult to bear in mind all the time those strange peculiarities, privileges, and unheard-of exemptions, forming the tacit stipulations on Bartleby's part under which he remained in my office. Now and then, in the eagerness of dispatching pressing business, I would inadvertently summon Bartleby, in a short, rapid tone, to put his finger, say, on the incipient tie of a bit of red tape with which I was about compressing some papers. Of course, from behind the screen the usual answer, "I prefer not to," was sure to come; and then, how could a human creature, with the common infirmities of our nature, refrain from bitterly exclaiming upon such perverseness—such unreasonableness? However, every added repulse of this sort which I received only tended to lessen the probability of my repeating the inadvertence.

Here it must be said, that, according to the custom of most legal gentlemen occupying chambers in densely-populated law buildings, there were several keys to my door. One was kept by a woman residing in the attic, which person weekly scrubbed and daily swept and dusted my apartments. Another was kept by Turkey for convenience sake. The third I sometimes carried in my own pocket. The fourth I knew not who had.

Now, one Sunday morning I happened to go to Trinity Church, to hear a celebrated preacher, and finding myself rather early on the ground I thought I would walk round to my chambers for a while. Luckily I had my key with me; but upon applying it to the lock, I found it resisted by something inserted from the inside. Quite surprised, I called out; when to my consternation a key was turned from within; and thrusting his lean visage at me, and holding the door ajar, the apparition of Bartleby appeared, in his shirt-sleeves, and otherwise in a strangely tattered deshabille, saying quietly that he was sorry, but he was deeply engaged just then, and—preferred not admitting me at present. In a brief word or two, he moreover added, that perhaps I had better walk round the block two or three times, and by that time he would probably have concluded his affairs.

Now, the utterly unsurmised appearance of Bartleby, tenanting my law-chambers of a Sunday morning, with his cadaverously gentlemanly *nonchalance*, yet withal firm and self-possessed, had such a strange effect upon me, that incontinently I slunk away from my own door, and did as desired. But not without sundry twinges of impotent rebellion against the mild effrontery of this unaccountable scrivener. Indeed, it was his wonderful mildness chiefly, which not only disarmed me, but un-manned me, as it were. For I consider that one, for the time, is a sort of unmanned when he tranquilly permits his hired clerk to dictate to him, and order him away from his own premises. Furthermore, I was full of uneasiness as to what Bartleby could possibly be doing in my office in his shirt-sleeves, and in an otherwise dismantled condition of a Sunday morning. Was anything amiss going on? Nay, that was out of the question. It was not to be thought of for a moment that Bartleby was an immoral person. But what could he be doing there?—copy-ing? Nay again, whatever might be his eccentricities, Bartleby was an eminently decorous person. He would be the last man to sit down to his desk in any state approaching to nudity. Besides, it was Sunday; and there was something about Bartleby that forbade the supposition that he would by any secular occupation violate the proprieties of the day.

Nevertheless, my mind was not pacified; and full of a restless curiosity, at last I returned to the door. Without hindrance I inserted my key, opened it, and entered. Bartleby was not to be seen. I looked round anxiously, peeped behind his screen; but it was very plain that he was gone. Upon more closely examining the place, I surmised that for an indefinite period Bartleby must have ate, dressed, and slept in my office, and that too without plate, mirror, or bed. The cushioned seat of a rickety old sofa in one corner bore the faint impress of a lean, reclining form. Rolled away under his desk, I found a blanket; under the empty grate, a blacking box and brush; on a chair, a tin basin, with soap and a ragged towel; in a newspaper a few crumbs of ginger-nuts and a morsel of cheese. Yes, thought I, it is evident enough that Bartleby has been making his home here, keeping bachelor's hall all by himself. Immediately then the thought came sweeping across me, what miserable friendlessness and loneliness are here revealed! His poverty is great; but his solitude, how horrible! Think of it. Of a Sunday, Wall Street is deserted as Petra;[11] and every night of every day it is an emptiness. This building, too, which of week-days hums with industry and life, at nightfall echoes with sheer vacancy, and all through Sunday is forlorn. And here Bartleby makes his home; sole spectator of a solitude which

[11]Ancient Middle Eastern trade center, long since in ruins.

he has seen all populous—a sort of innocent and transformed Marius brooding among the ruins of Carthage![12]

For the first time in my life a feeling of overpowering stinging melancholy seized me. Before, I had never experienced aught but a not unpleasing sadness. The bond of a common humanity now drew me irresistibly to gloom. A fraternal melancholy! For both I and Bartleby were sons of Adam. I remembered the bright silks and sparkling faces I had seen that day, in gala trim, swan-like sailing down the Mississippi of Broadway; and I contrasted them with the pallid copyist, and thought to myself, Ah, happiness courts the light, so we deem the world is gay; but misery hides aloof, so we deem that misery there is none. These sad fancyings—chimeras, doubtless, and a sick and silly brain—led on to other and more special thoughts, concerning the eccentricities of Bartleby. Presentiments of strange discoveries hovered round me. The scrivener's pale form appeared to me laid out, among uncaring strangers, in its shivering winding-sheet.

Suddenly I was attracted by Bartleby's closed desk, the key in open sight left in the lock.

I mean no mischief, seek the gratification of no heartless curiosity, thought I; besides, the desk is mine, and its contents, too, so I will make bold to look within. Everything was methodically arranged, the papers smoothly placed. The pigeon-holes were deep, and removing the files of documents, I groped into their recesses. Presently I felt something there, and dragged it out. It was an old bandanna handkerchief, heavy and knotted. I opened it, and saw it was a saving's bank.

I now recalled all the quiet mysteries which I had noted in the man. I remembered that he never spoke but to answer; that, though at intervals he had considerable time to himself, yet I had never seen him reading—no, not even a newspaper; that for long periods he would stand looking out, at his pale window behind the screen, upon the dead brick wall; I was quite sure he never visited any refectory or eating-house; while his pale face clearly indicated that he never drank beer like Turkey, or tea and coffee even, like other men; that he never went anywhere in particular that I could learn; never went out for a walk, unless, indeed, that was the case at present; that he had declined telling who he was, or whence he came, or whether he had any relatives in the world; that though so thin and pale, he never complained of ill-health. And more than all, I remembered a certain unconscious air of pallid—how shall I call it?—of pallid haughtiness, say, or rather an austere reserve about him, which had positively awed me into my tame compliance with his eccentricities, when I had feared to ask him to do the slightest incidental thing for me, even though I might know, from his long-continued motionlessness, that behind his screen he must be standing in one of those dead-wall reveries of his.

---

[12]Refers to a Roman general and political leader who, in exile, compared the change in his fortunes to the fall and destruction of the great African city-state of Carthage.

Revolving all these things, and coupling them with the recently discovered fact, that he made my office his constant abiding place and home, and not forgetful of his morbid moodiness; revolving all these things, a prudential feeling began to steal over me. My first emotions had been those of pure melancholy and sincerest pity; but just in proportion as the forlornness of Bartleby grew and grew to my imagination, did that same melancholy merge into fear, that pity into repulsion. So true it is, and so terrible, too, that up to a certain point the thought or sight of misery enlists our best affections; but, in certain special cases, beyond that point it does not. They err who would assert that invariably this is owing to the inherent selfishness of the human heart. It rather proceeds from a certain hopelessness of remedying excessive and organic ill. To a sensitive being, pity is not seldom pain. And when at last it is perceived that such pity cannot lead to effectual succor, common sense bids the soul be rid of it. What I saw that morning persuaded me that the scrivener was the victim of innate and incurable disorder. I might give alms to his body; but his body did not pain him; it was his soul that suffered, and his soul I could not reach.

I did not accomplish the purpose of going to Trinity Church that morning. Somehow, the things I had seen disqualified me for the time from church-going. I walked homeward, thinking what I would do with Bartleby. Finally, I resolved upon this—I would put certain calm questions to him the next morning, touching his history, etc., and if he declined to answer them openly and unreservedly (and I supposed he would prefer not), then to give him a twenty dollar bill over and above whatever I might owe him, and tell him his services were no longer required; but that if in any other way I could assist him, I would be happy to do so, especially if he desired to return to his native place, wherever that might be, I would willingly help to defray the expenses. Moreover, if, after reaching home, he found himself at any time in want of aid, a letter from him would be sure of a reply.

The next morning came.

"Bartleby," said I, gently calling to him behind his screen.

No reply.

"Bartleby," said I, in a still gentler tone, "come here; I am not going to ask you to do anything you would prefer not to do—I simply wish to speak to you."

Upon this he noiselessly slid into view.

"Will you tell me, Bartleby, where you were born?"

"I would prefer not to."

"Will you tell me *anything* about yourself?"

"I would prefer not to."

"But what reasonable objection can you have to speak to me? I feel friendly towards you."

He did not look at me while I spoke, but kept his glance fixed upon my bust of Cicero, which, as I then sat, was directly behind me, some six inches above my head.

"What is your answer, Bartleby?" said I, after waiting a considerable time for a reply, during which his countenance remained immovable, only there was the faintest conceivable tremor of the white attenuated mouth.

"At present I prefer to give no answer," he said, and retired into his hermitage.

It was rather weak in me I confess, but his manner, on this occasion, nettled me. Not only did there seem to lurk in it a certain calm disdain, but his perverseness seemed ungrateful, considering the undeniable good usage and indulgence he had received from me.

Again I sat ruminating what I should do. Mortified as I was at his behavior, and resolved as I had been to dismiss him when I entered my office, nevertheless I strangely felt something superstitious knocking at my heart, and forbidding me to carry out my purpose, and denouncing me for a villain if I dared to breathe one bitter word against this forlornest of mankind. At last, familiarly drawing my chair behind his screen, I sat down and said: "Bartleby, never mind, then, about revealing your history; but let me entreat you, as a friend, to comply as far as may be with the usages of this office. Say now, you will help to examine papers to-morrow or next day: in short, say now, that in a day or two you will begin to be a little reasonable:—say so, Bartleby."

"At present I would prefer not to be a little reasonable," was his mildly cadaverous reply.

Just then the folding-doors opened, and Nippers approached. He seemed suffering from an unusually bad night's rest, induced by severer indigestion than common. He overheard those final words of Bartleby.

"*Prefer not*, eh?" gritted Nippers—"I'd *prefer* him, if I were you, sir," addressing me—"I'd *prefer* him; I'd give him preferences, the stubborn mule! What is it, sir, pray, that he *prefers* not to do now?"

Bartleby moved not a limb.

"Mr. Nippers," said I, "I'd prefer that you would withdraw for the present."

Somehow, of late, I had got into the way of involuntarily using this word "prefer" upon all sorts of not exactly suitable occasions. And I trembled to think that my contact with the scrivener had already and seriously affected me in a mental way. And what further and deeper aberration might it not yet produce? This apprehension had not been without efficacy in determining me to summary measures.

As Nippers, looking very sour and sulky, was departing, Turkey blandly and deferentially approached.

"With submission sir," said he, "yesterday I was thinking about Bartleby here, and I think that if he would but prefer to take a quart of good ale every day, it would do much towards mending him, and enabling him to assist in examining his papers."

"So you have got the word, too," said I, slightly excited.

"With submission, what word, sir?" asked Turkey, respectfully crowding himself into the contracted space behind the screen, and by so doing, making me jostle the scrivener. "What word, sir?"

"I would prefer to be left alone here," said Bartleby, as if offended at being mobbed in his privacy.

"*That's* the word, Turkey," said I—"*that's it.*"

"Oh, *prefer?* oh yes—queer word. I never use it myself. But sir, as I was saying, if he would but prefer—"

"Turkey," interrupted I, "you will please withdraw."

"Oh certainly, sir, if you prefer that I should."

As he opened the folding-door to retire, Nippers at his desk caught a glimpse of me, and asked whether I would prefer to have a certain paper copied on blue paper or white. He did not in the least roguishly accent the word "prefer." It was plain that it involuntarily rolled from his tongue. I thought to myself, surely I must get rid of a demented man, who already has in some degree turned the tongues, if not the heads of myself and clerks. But I thought it prudent not to break the dismission at once.

The next day I noticed that Bartleby did nothing but stand at his window in his dead-wall revery. Upon asking him why he did not write, he said that he had decided upon doing no more writing.

"Why, how now? what next?" exclaimed I, "do no more writing?"

"No more."

"And what is the reason?"

"Do you not see the reason for yourself?" he indifferently replied.

I looked steadfastly at him, and perceived that his eyes looked dull and glazed. Instantly it occurred to me, that his unexampled diligence in copying by his dim window for the first few weeks of his stay with me might have temporarily impaired his vision.

I was touched. I said something in condolence with him. I hinted that of course he did wisely in abstaining from writing for a while; and urged him to embrace that opportunity of taking wholesome exercise in the open air. This, however, he did not do. A few days after this, my other clerks being absent, and being in a great hurry to dispatch certain letters by the mail, I thought that, having nothing else earthly to do, Bartleby would surely be less inflexible than usual, and carry these letters to the post-office. But he blankly declined. So, much to my inconvenience, I went myself.

Still added days went by. Whether Bartleby's eyes improved or not, I could not say. To all appearance, I thought they did. But when I asked him if they did, he vouchsafed no answer. At all events, he would do no copying. At last, in reply to my urgings, he informed me that he had permanently given up copying.

"What!" exclaimed I; "suppose your eyes should get entirely well—better than ever before—would you not copy then?"

"I have given up copying," he answered, and slid aside.

He remained as ever, a fixture in my chamber. Nay—if that were possible—he became still more of a fixture than before. What was to be done? He would do nothing in the office; why should he stay there? In plain fact, he had now become a millstone to me, not only useless as a necklace, but afflictive to bear. Yet I was sorry for him. I speak less than truth when I say that, on his own account, he occasioned me uneasiness. If he would but have named a single relative or friend, I would have instantly have written, and urged their taking the poor fellow away to some convenient retreat. But he seemed alone, absolutely alone in the universe. A bit of wreck in the mid-Atlantic. At length, necessities connected with my business tyrannized over all other considerations. Decently as I could, I told Bartleby that in six days' time he must unconditionally leave the office. I warned him to take measures, in the interval, for procuring some other abode. I offered to assist him in this endeavor, if he himself would but take the first step towards a removal. "And when you finally quit me, Bartleby," added I, "I shall see that you go not away entirely unprovided. Six days from this hour, remember."

At the expiration of that period, I peeped behind the screen, and lo! Bartleby was there.

I buttoned up my coat, balanced myself; advanced slowly towards him, touched his shoulder, and said, "The time has come; you must quit this place; I am sorry for you; here is money; but you must go."

"I would prefer not," he replied, with his back still towards me.

"You *must*."

He remained silent.

Now I had an unbounded confidence in this man's common honesty. He had frequently restored to me sixpences and shillings[13] carelessly dropped upon the floor, for I am apt to be very reckless in such shirt-button affairs. The proceeding, then, which followed will not be deemed extraordinary.

"Bartleby," said I, "I owe you twelve dollars on account; here are thirty-two; the odd twenty are yours—Will you take it?" and I handed the bills towards him.

But he made no motion.

"I will leave them here, then," putting them under a weight on the table. Then taking my hat and cane and going to the door, I tranquilly turned and added—"After you have removed your things from these offices, Bartleby, you will of course lock the door—since every one is now gone for the day but you—and if you please, slip your key underneath the mat, so that I may have it in the morning. I shall not see you again; so good-bye to you. If, hereafter, in your new place of abode, I can be of any service to you, do not fail to advise me by letter. Good-bye, Bartleby, and fare you well."

But he answered not a word; like the last column of some ruined temple, he remained standing mute and solitary in the middle of the otherwise deserted room.

---

[13]Small change.

As I walked home in a pensive mood, my vanity got the better of my pity. I could not but highly plume myself on my masterly management in getting rid of Bartleby. Masterly I call it, and such it must appear to any dispassionate thinker. The beauty of my procedure seemed to consist in its perfect quietness. There was no vulgar bullying, no bravado of any sort, no choleric hectoring, and striding to and fro across the apartment, jerking out vehement commands for Bartleby to bundle himself off with his beggarly traps. Nothing of the kind. Without loudly bidding Bartleby depart—as an inferior genius might have done—I *assumed* the ground that depart he must; and upon that assumption built all I had to say. The more I thought over my procedure, the more I was charmed with it. Nevertheless, next morning, upon awakening, I had my doubts—I had somehow slept off the fumes of vanity. One of the coolest and wisest hours a man has, is just after he awakes in the morning. My procedure seemed as sagacious as ever—but only in theory. How it would prove in practice—there was the rub. It was truly a beautiful thought to have assumed Bartleby's departure; but, after all, that assumption was simply my own, and none of Bartleby's. The great point was, not whether I had assumed that he would quit me, but whether he would prefer so to do. He was more a man of preferences than assumptions.

After breakfast, I walked down town, arguing the probabilities *pro* and *con.* One moment I thought it would prove a miserable failure, and Bartleby would be found all alive at my office as usual; the next moment it seemed certain that I should find his chair empty. And so I kept veering about. At the corner of Broadway and Canal Street, I saw quite an excited group of people standing in earnest conversation.

"I'll take odds he doesn't," said a voice as I passed.

"Doesn't go?—done!" said I, "put up your money."

I was instinctively putting my hand in my pocket to produce my own, when I remembered that this was an election day. The words I had overheard bore no reference to Bartleby, but to the success or non-success of some candidate for the mayoralty. In my intent frame of mind, I had, as it were, imagined that all Broadway shared in my excitement, and were debating the same question with me. I passed on, very thankful that the uproar of the street screened my momentary absent-mindedness.

As I had intended, I was earlier than usual at my office door. I stood listening for a moment. All was still. He must be gone. I tried the knob. The door was locked. Yes, my procedure had worked to a charm; he indeed must be vanished. Yet a certain melancholy mixed with this: I was almost sorry for my brilliant success. I was fumbling under the door mat for the key, which Bartleby was to have left there for me, when accidentally my knee knocked against a panel, producing a summoning sound, and in response a voice came to me from within—"Not yet; I am occupied."

It was Bartleby.

I was thunderstruck. For an instant I stood like the man who, pipe in mouth, was killed one cloudless afternoon long ago in Virginia, by summer lightning; at his own warm open window he was killed, and remained leaning out there upon the dreamy afternoon, till some one touched him, when he fell.

"Not gone!" I murmured at last. But again obeying that wondrous ascendancy which the inscrutable scrivener had over me, and from which ascendancy, for all my chafing, I could not completely escape. I slowly went down stairs and out in to the street, and while walking round the block, considered what I should next do in this unheard-of perplexity. Turn the man out by an actual thrusting I could not; to drive him away by calling him hard names would not do; calling in the police was an unpleasant idea; and yet, permit him to enjoy his cadaverous triumph over me—this, too, I could not think of. What was to be done? or, if nothing could be done, was there anything further that I could *assume* in the matter? Yes, as before I had prospectively assumed that Bartleby would depart, so now I might retrospectively assume that departed he was. In the legitimate carrying out of this assumption, I might enter my office in a great hurry, and pretending not to see Bartleby at all, walk straight against him as if he were air. Such a proceeding would in a singular degree have the appearance of a home-thrust.[14] It was hardly possible that Bartleby could withstand such an application of the doctrine of assumptions. But upon second thoughts the success of the plan seemed rather dubious. I resolved to argue the matter over with him again.

"Bartleby," said I, entering the office, with a quietly severe expression, "I am seriously displeased. I am pained, Bartleby. I had thought better of you. I had imagined you of such a gentlemanly organization, that in any delicate dilemma a slight hint would suffice—in short, an assumption. But it appears I am deceived. Why," I added, unaffectedly starting, "you have not even touched that money yet," pointing to it, just where I had left it the evening previous.

He answered nothing.

"Will you, or will you not, quit me?" I now demanded in a sudden passion, advancing close to him.

"I would prefer *not* to quit you," he replied, gently emphasizing the *not*.

"What earthly right have you to stay here? Do you pay any rent? Do you pay my taxes? Or is this property yours?"

He answered nothing.

"Are you ready to go and write now? Are your eyes recovered? Could you copy a small paper for me this morning? or help examine a few lines? or step round to the post-office? In a word, will you do anything at all, to give a coloring to your refusal to depart the premises?"

He silently retired into his hermitage.

I was now in such a state of nervous resentment that I thought it but

[14]A blow that hits the mark, as in fencing.

prudent to check myself at present from futher demonstrations. Bartleby and I were alone. I remembered the tragedy of the unfortunate Adams and the still more unfortunate Colt in the solitary office of the latter; and how poor Colt, being dreadfully incensed by Adams, and imprudently permitting himself to get wildly excited, was at unawares hurried into his fatal act—an act which certainly no man could possibly deplore more than the actor himself. Often it had occurred to me in my ponderings upon the subject that had that altercation taken place in the public street, or at a private residence, it would not have terminated as it did. It was the circumstance of being alone in a solitary office, up stairs, of a building entirely unhallowed by humanizing domestic associations—an uncarpeted office, doubtless, of a dusty, haggard sort of appearance—this it must have been, which greatly helped to enhance the irritable desperation of the hapless Colt.

But when this old Adam[15] of resentment rose in me and tempted me concerning Bartleby, I grappled him and threw him. How? Why, simply by recalling the divine injunction: "A new commandment give I unto you, that ye love one another." Yes, this it was that saved me. Aside from higher considerations, charity often operates as a vastly wise and prudent principle—a great safeguard to its possessor. Men have committed murder for jealousy's sake, and anger's sake, and hatred's sake, and selfishness' sake, and spiritual pride's sake; but no man, that ever I heard of, ever committed a diabolical murder for sweet charity's sake. Mere self-interest, then, if no better motive can be enlisted, should, especially with high-tempered men, prompt all beings to charity and philanthropy. At any rate, upon the occasion in question, I strove to drown my exasperated feelings towards the scrivener by benevolently construing his conduct. Poor fellow, poor fellow! thought I, he don't mean anything; and besides, he has seen hard times, and ought to be indulged.

I endeavored, also, immediately to occupy myself, and at the same time to comfort my despondency. I tried to fancy, that in the course of the morning, at such time as might prove agreeable to him, Bartleby, of his own free accord, would emerge from his hermitage and take up some decided line of march in the direction of the door. But no. Half-past twelve o'clock came; Turkey began to glow in the face, overturn his inkstand, and become generally obstreperous; Nippers abated down into quietude and courtesy; Ginger Nut munched his noon apple; and Bartleby remained standing at his window in one of his profoundest dead-wall reveries. Will it be credited? Ought I to acknowledge it? That afternoon I left the office without saying one further word to him.

Some days now passed, during which, at leisure intervals I looked a little into "Edwards on the Will," and "Priestley on Necessity."[16] Under

---

[15]Human inclination toward sin.

[16]Eighteenth-century theological books arguing against freedom of the will and in favor of divine predestination.

the circumstances, those books induced a salutary feeling. Gradually I slid into the persuasion that these troubles of mine, touching the scrivener, had been all predestinated from eternity, and Bartleby was billeted upon me for some mysterious purpose of an all-wise Providence, which it was not for a mere mortal like me to fathom. Yes, Bartleby, stay there behind your screen, thought I; I shall persecute you no more; you are harmless and noiseless as any of these old chairs; in short, I never feel so private as when I know you are here. At last I see it, I feel it; I penetrate to the predestinated purpose of my life. I am content. Others may have loftier parts to enact; but my mission in this world, Bartleby, is to furnish you with office-room for such period as you may see fit to remain.

I believe that this wise and blessed frame of mind would have continued with me, had it not been for the unsolicited and uncharitable remarks obtruded upon me by my professional friends who visited the rooms. But thus it often is, that the constant friction of illiberal minds wears out at last the best resolves of the more generous. Though to be sure, when I reflected upon it, it was not strange that people entering my office should be struck by the peculiar aspect of the unaccountable Bartleby, and so be tempted to throw out some sinister observations concerning him. Sometimes an attorney, having business with me, and calling at my office, and finding no one but the scrivener there, would undertake to obtain some sort of precise information from him touching my whereabouts; but without heeding his idle talk, Bartleby would remain standing immovable in the middle of the room. So after contemplating him in that position for a time, the attorney would depart, no wiser than he came.

Also, when a reference was going on, and the room full of lawyers and witnesses, and business driving fast, some deeply-occupied legal gentleman present, seeing Bartleby wholly unemployed, would request him to run round to his (the legal gentleman's) office and fetch some papers for him. Thereupon, Bartleby would tranquilly decline, and yet remain idle as before. Then the lawyer would give a great stare, and turn to me. And what could I say? At last I was made aware that all through the circle of my professional acquaintance, a whisper of wonder was running round, having reference to the strange creature I kept at my office. This worried me very much. And as the idea came upon me of his possibly turning out a long-lived man, and keep occupying my chambers, and denying my authority; and perplexing my visitors; and scandalizing my professional reputation; and casting a general gloom over the premises; keeping soul and body together to the last upon his savings (for doubtless he spent but half a dime a day), and in the end perhaps outlive me, and claim possession of my office by right of his perpetual occupancy: as all these dark anticipations crowded upon me more and more, and my friends continually intruded their relentless remarks upon the apparition in my room; a great change was wrought in me. I resolved to gather all my faculties together, and forever rid me of this intolerable incubus.

Ere revolving any complicated project, however, adapted to this end, I first simply suggested to Bartleby the propriety of his permanent departure. In a calm and serious tone, I commended the idea to his careful and mature consideration. But, having taken three days to meditate upon it, he apprised me, that his original determination remained the same; in short, that he still preferred to abide with me.

What shall I do? I now said to myself, buttoning up my coat to the last button. What shall I do? what ought I to do? what does conscience say I *should* do with this man, or, rather, ghost. Rid myself of him, I must; go, he shall. But how? You will not thrust him, the poor, pale, passive mortal—you will not thrust such a helpless creature out of your door? you will not dishonor yourself by such cruelty? No, I will not, I cannot do that. Rather would I let him live and die here, and then mason up his remains in the wall. What, then, will you do? For all your coaxing, he will not budge. Bribes he leaves under your own paper-weight on your table; in short, it is quite plain that he prefers to cling to you.

Then something severe, something unusual must be done. What! Surely you will not have him collared by a constable, and commit his innocent pallor to the common jail? And upon what ground could you procure such a thing to be done?—a vagrant, is he? What! he a vagrant, a wanderer, who refuses to budge? It is because he will *not* be a vagrant, then, that you seek to count him *as* a vagrant. That is too absurd. No visible means of support: there I have him. Wrong again: for indubitably he *does* support himself, and that is the only unanswerable proof that any man can show of his possessing the means so to do. No more, then. Since he will not quit me, I must quit him. I will change my offices; I will move elsewhere, and give him fair notice, that if I find him on my new premises I will then proceed against him as a common trespasser.

Acting accordingly, next day I thus addressed him: "I find these chambers too far from the City Hall; the air is unwholesome. In a word, I propose to remove my offices next week, and shall no longer require your services. I tell you this now, in order that you may seek another place."

He made no reply, and nothing more was said.

On the appointed day I engaged carts and men, proceeded to my chambers, and, having but little furniture, everything was removed in a few hours. Throughout, the scrivener remained standing behind the screen, which I directed to be removed the last thing. It was withdrawn; and, being folded up like a huge folio, left him the motionless occupant of a naked room. I stood in the entry watching him a moment, while something from within me upbraided me.

I re-entered, with my hand in my pocket—and—and my heart in my mouth.

"Good-bye, Bartleby; I am going—good-bye, and God some way bless you; and take that," slipping something in his hand. But it dropped upon the floor, and then—strange to say—I tore myself from him whom I had so longed to be rid of.

Established in my new quarters, for a day or two I kept the door locked, and started at every footfall in the passages. When I returned to my rooms, after any little absence, I would pause at the threshold for an instant, and attentively listen, ere applying my key. But these fears were needless. Bartleby never came nigh me.

I thought all was going well, when a perturbed-looking stranger visited me, inquiring whether I was the person who had recently occupied rooms at No. — Wall Street.

Full of forebodings, I replied that I was.

"Then, sir," said the stranger, who proved a lawyer, "you are responsible for the man you left there. He refuses to do any copying; he refuses to do anything; he says he prefers not to; and he refuses to quit the premises."

"I am very sorry, sir," said I, with assumed tranquillity, but an inward tremor, "but, really, the man you allude to is nothing to me—he is no relation or apprentice of mine, that you should hold me responsible for him."

"In mercy's name, who is he?"

"I certainly cannot inform you. I know nothing about him. Formerly I employed him as a copyist; but he has done nothing for me now for some time past."

"I shall settle him, then—good morning, sir."

Several days passed, and I heard nothing more; and, though I often felt a charitable prompting to call at the place and see poor Bartleby, yet a certain squeamishness, of I know not what, withheld me.

All is over with him, by this time, thought I, at last, when, through another week, no further intelligence reached me. But, coming to my room the day after, I found several persons waiting at my door in a high state of nervous excitement.

"That's the man—here he comes," cried the foremost one, whom I recognized as the lawyer who had previously called upon me alone.

"You must take him away, sir, at once," cried a portly person among them, advancing upon me, and whom I knew to be the landlord of No. — Wall Street. "These gentlemen, my tenants, cannot stand it any longer; Mr. B——," pointing to the lawyer, "has turned him out of his room, and he now persists in haunting the building generally, sitting upon the banisters of the stairs by day, and sleeping in the entry by night. Everybody is concerned; clients are leaving the offices; some fears are entertained of a mob; something you must do, and that without delay."

Aghast at this torrent, I fell back before it, and would fain have locked myself in my new quarters. In vain I persisted that Bartleby was nothing to me—no more than to any one else. In vain—I was the last person known to have anything to do with him, and they held me to the terrible account. Fearful, then, of being exposed in the papers (as one person present obscurely threatened), I considered the matter, and, at length, said, that if the lawyer would give me a confidential interview with the scrivener, in his (the lawyer's) own room, I would, that afternoon, strive my best to rid them of the nuisance they complained of.

Going up stairs to my old haunt, there was Bartleby silently sitting upon the banister at the landing.

"What are you doing here, Bartleby?" said I.

"Sitting upon the banister," he mildly replied.

I motioned him into the lawyer's room, who then left us.

"Bartleby," said I, "are you aware that you are the cause of great tribulation to me, by persisting in occupying the entry after being dismissed from the office?"

No answer.

"Now one of two things must take place. Either you must do something, or something must be done to you. Now what sort of business would you like to engage in? Would you like to re-engage in copying for some one?"

"No; I would prefer not to make any change."

"Would you like a clerkship in a dry-goods store?"

"There is too much confinement about that. No, I would not like a clerkship; but I am not particular."

"Too much confinement," I cried, "why, you keep yourself confined all the time!"

"I would prefer not to take a clerkship," he rejoined, as if to settle that little item at once.

"How would a bar-tender's business suit you? There is no trying of the eye-sight in that."

"I would not like it at all; though, as I said before, I am not particular."

His unwonted wordiness inspirited me. I returned to the charge.

"Well, then, would you like to travel through the country collecting bills for the merchants? That would improve your health."

"No, I would prefer to be doing something else."

"How, then, would going as a companion to Europe, to entertain some young gentleman with your conversation—how would that suit you?"

"Not at all. It does not strike me that there is anything definite about that. I like to be stationary. But I am not particular."

"Stationary you shall be, then," I cried, now losing all patience, and, for the first time in all my exasperating connection with him, fairly flying into a passion. "If you do not go away from these premises before night, I shall feel bound—indeed, I *am* bound—to—to—to quit the premises myself!" I rather absurdly concluded, knowing not with what possible threat to try to frighten his immobility into compliance. Despairing of all further efforts, I was precipitately leaving him, when a final thought occurred to me—one which had not been wholly unindulged before.

"Bartleby," said I, in the kindest tone I could assume under such exciting circumstances, "will you go home with me now—not to my office, but my dwelling—and remain there till we can conclude upon some convenient arrangement for you at our leisure? Come, let us start now, right away."

"No: at present I would prefer not to make any change at all."

I answered nothing; but, effectually dodging every one by the suddenness and rapidity of my flight, rushed from the building, ran up Wall Street towards Broadway, and, jumping into the first omnibus, was soon removed from pursuit. As soon as tranquillity returned, I distinctly perceived that I had now done all that I possibly could, both in respect to the demands of the landlord and his tenants, and with regard to my own desire and sense of duty, to benefit Bartleby, and shield him from rude persecution. I now strove to be entirely care-free and quiescent; and my conscience justified me in the attempt; though, indeed, it was not so successful as I could have wished. So fearful was I of being again hunted out by the incensed landlord and his exasperated tenants, that, surrendering my business to Nippers, for a few days, I drove about the upper part of the town and through the suburbs, in my rockaway; crossed over to Jersey City and Hoboken, and paid fugitive visits to Manhattanville and Astoria. In fact, I almost lived in my rockaway for the time.

When again I entered my office, lo, a note from the landlord lay upon the desk. I opened it with trembling hands. It informed me that the writer had sent to the police, and had Bartleby removed to the Tombs as a vagrant. Moreover, since I knew more about him than any one else, he wished me to appear at that place, and make a suitable statement of the facts. These tidings had a conflicting effect upon me. At first I was indignant; but at last, almost approved. The landlord's energetic, summary disposition, had led him to adopt a procedure which I do not think I would have decided upon myself; and yet, as a last resort, under such peculiar circumstances, it seemed the only plan.

As I afterward learned, the poor scrivener, when told that he must be conducted to the Tombs, offered not the slightest obstacle, but, in his pale, unmoving way, silently acquiesced.

Some of the compassionate and curious by-standers joined the party; and headed by one of the constables arm-in-arm with Bartleby, the silent procession filed its way through all the noise, and heat, and joy of the roaring thoroughfares at noon.

The same day I received the note, I went to the Tombs, or, to speak more properly, the Halls of Justice. Seeking the right officer, I stated the purpose of my call, and was informed that the individual I described was, indeed, within. I then assured the functionary that Bartleby was a perfectly honest man, and greatly to be compassionated, however unaccountably eccentric. I narrated all I knew, and closed by suggesting the idea of letting him remain in as indulgent confinement as possible, till something less harsh might be done—though, indeed, I hardly knew what. At all events, if nothing else could be decided upon, the alms-house must receive him. I then begged to have an interview.

Being under no disgraceful charge, and quite serene and harmless in all his ways, they had permitted him freely to wander about the prison, and, especially, in the inclosed grass-platted yards thereof. And so I found him there, standing all alone in the quietest of the yards, his face towards a high wall, while all around, from the narrow slits of the jail windows, I thought I saw peering out upon him the eyes of murderers and thieves.

"Bartleby!"

"I know you," he said, without looking round—"and I want nothing to say to you."

"It was not I that brought you here, Bartleby," said I, keenly pained at his implied suspicion. "And to you, this should not be so vile a place. Nothing reproachful attaches to you by being here. And see, it is not so sad a place as one might think. Look, there is the sky, and here is the grass."

"I know where I am," he replied, but would say nothing more, and so I left him.

As I entered the corridor again, a broad meat-like man, in an apron, accosted me, and, jerking his thumb over his shoulder, said —"Is that your friend?"

"Yes."

"Does he want to starve? If he does, let him live on the prison fare, that's all."

"Who are you?" asked I, not knowing what to make of such an unofficially speaking person in such a place.

"I am the grub-man. Such gentlemen as have friends here, hire me to provide them with something good to eat."

"Is this so?" said I, turning to the turnkey.

He said it was.

"Well, then," said I, slipping some silver into the grub-man's hands (for so they called him), "I want you to give particular attention to my friend there; let him have the best dinner you can get. And you must be as polite to him as possible."

"Introduce me, will you?" said the grub-man, looking at me with an expression which seemed to say he was all impatience for an opportunity to give a specimen of his breeding.

Thinking it would prove of benefit to the scrivener, I acquiesced; and, asking the grub-man his name, went up with him to Bartleby.

"Bartleby, this is a friend; you will find him very useful to you."

"Your sarvant, sir, your sarvant," said the grub-man, making a low salutation behind his apron. "Hope you find it pleasant here, sir; nice grounds—cool apartments—hope you'll stay with us some time—try to make it agreeable. What will you have for dinner to-day?"

"I prefer not to dine to-day," said Bartleby, turning away. "It would disagree with me; I am unused to dinners." So saying, he slowly moved to the other side of the inclosure, and took up a position fronting the dead-wall.

"How's this?" said the grub-man, addressing me with a stare of astonishment. "He's odd, ain't he?"

"I think he is a little deranged," said I, sadly.

"Deranged? deranged is it? Well, now, upon my word, I thought that friend of yourn was a gentleman forger; they are always pale and genteel-like, them forgers. I can't help pity 'em—can't help it, sir. Did you know Monroe Edwards?" he added, touchingly, and paused. Then, laying his hand piteously on my shoulder, sighed, "he died of consumption at Sing-Sing. So you weren't acquainted with Monroe?"

"No, I was never socially acquainted with any forgers. But I cannot stop longer. Look to my friend yonder. You will not lose by it. I will see you again."

Some few days after this, I again obtained admission to the Tombs, and went through the corridors in quest of Bartleby; but without finding him.

"I saw him coming from his cell not long ago," said a turnkey, "may be he's gone to loiter in the yards."

So I went in that direction.

"Are you looking for the silent man?" said another turnkey, passing me. "Yonder he lies—sleeping in the yard there. 'Tis not twenty minutes since I saw him lie down."

The yard was entirely quiet. It was not accessible to the common prisoners. The surrounding walls, of amazing thickness, kept off all sounds behind them. The Egyptian character of the masonry weighed upon me with its gloom. But a soft imprisoned turf grew under foot. The heart of the eternal pyramids, it seemed, wherein, by some strange magic, through the clefts, grass-seed, dropped by birds, had sprung.

Strangely huddled at the base of the wall, his knees drawn up, and lying on his side, his head touching the cold stones, I saw the wasted Bartleby. But nothing stirred. I paused; then went close up to him; stooped over, and saw that his dim eyes were open; otherwise he seemed profoundly sleeping. Something prompted me to touch him. I felt his hand, when a tingling shiver ran up my arm and down my spine to my feet.

The round face of the grub-man peered upon me now. "His dinner is ready. Won't he dine to-day, either? Or does he live without dining?"

"Lives without dining," said I, and closed the eyes.

"Eh!—He's asleep, ain't he?"

"With kings and counselors,"[17] murmured I.

There would seem little need for proceeding further in this history. Imagination will readily supply the meagre recital of poor Bartleby's

---

[17]That is, dead. The narrator quotes from Job 3:13–14: "Then had I been at rest, with kings and counsellors of the earth, which built desolate places for themselves."

interment. But, ere parting with the reader, let me say, that if this little narrative has sufficiently interested him, to awaken curiosity as to who Bartleby was, and what manner of life he led prior to the present narrator's making his acquaintance, I can only reply, that in such curiosity I fully share, but am wholly unable to gratify it. Yet here I hardly know whether I should divulge one little item of rumor, which came to my ear a few months after the scrivener's decease. Upon what basis it rested, I could never ascertain; and hence, how true it is I cannot now tell. But, inasmuch as this vague report has not been without a certain suggestive interest to me, however sad, it may prove the same with some others; and so I will briefly mention it. The report was this: that Bartleby had been a subordinate clerk in the Dead Letter[18] Office at Washington, from which he had been suddenly removed by a change in the administration. When I think over this rumor, hardly can I express the emotions which seize me. Dead letters! does it not sound like dead men? Conceive a man by nature and misfortune prone to a pallid hopelessness, can any business seem more fitted to heighten it than that of continually handling these dead letters, and assorting them for the flames? For by the cart-load they are annually burned. Sometimes from out the folded paper the pale clerk takes a ring—the finger it was meant for, perhaps, moulders in the grave; a bank-note sent in swiftest charity—he whom it would relieve, nor eats nor hungers any more; pardon for those who died despairing; hope for those who died un-hoping; good tidings for those who died stifled by unrelieved calamities. On errands of life, these letters speed to death.

Ah, Bartleby! Ah, humanity!

## FOR DISCUSSION

1. From what narrative point of view is *Bartleby, the Scrivener* written? Who is the narrator? Is he the protagonist or is Bartleby?
2. What is the mood of the story? Is it unchanging?
3. What is the precipitating incident?
4. How does the narrator dramatize his own personality by his writing style? Consider his tone and his vocabulary.
5. The story has an immediate setting, the lawyer's offices, and a greater setting, the Wall Street district of nineteenth-century New York. How do both contribute to the work? Are any details particularly significant?
6. How many characters in the novella are given true names? Do you attach any significance to this?
7. Is there symbolic significance in Nippers's constant attempts to adjust the height of his writing table?
8. Turkey often uses the phrase "with submission." What does this suggest about his character?

---

[18]An undeliverable letter that cannot be returned to the sender, a dead letter is held at the post office for some time, then destroyed.

9. Which character or characters develop as the tale progresses? Which do not?
10. Why do you suppose the lawyer-narrator finds it necessary to tell the story of Bartleby? After all, the lawyer admits that he is rather lazy. Is the story the narrator actually tells the same as the one he thinks he is telling? Are his observations and interpretations reliable?
11. Throughout the novella Bartleby appears to be both rebelling against something and resigned to his fate. Can you tell what Bartleby is rebelling against, or why he is resigned to the worst?
12. Why does the lawyer-narrator go to such lengths to indulge or accommodate Bartleby's eccentricities? Do his motives for doing so change?
13. What reasons can you think of for Bartleby's refusing to accept the lawyer's many offers of help and assistance?
14. In what ways does the work emphasize the passage of time?
15. Point out specific instances of humor in the story. Does Bartleby ever reveal a sense of humor?
16. Detail the specific stages of Bartleby's progressive withdrawal from the world. Why does he die?
17. How does Bartleby's eccentric behavior influence the behavior of the other characters in the story?
18. How many different ways is a wall mentioned? Does it have any symbolic meaning?
19. As you read this novella, did you find yourself sympathizing with Bartleby or with the lawyer? With neither? Why did you make this choice?
20. The lawyer seems satisfied with his final attempt to explain Bartleby's behavior. Are you? Does the dead letter office have any other significance than the one the lawyer assigns to it? What is the meaning of the last four words of the story, from the narrator's point of view and from yours?

# Noon Wine

KATHERINE ANNE PORTER

*Time:* 1896–1905
*Place:* Small South Texas Farm

The two grubby small boys with tow-colored hair who were digging among the ragweed in the front yard sat back on their heels and said, "Hello," when the tall bony man with straw-colored hair turned in at their gate. He did not pause at the gate; it had swung back, conveniently half open, long ago, and was now sunk so firmly on its broken hinges no one thought of trying to close it. He did not even glance at the small boys, much less give them good-day. He just clumped down his big square dusty shoes one after the other steadily, like a man following a plow, as if he knew the place well and knew where he was going and what he would find there. Rounding the right-hand corner of the house under the row of chinaberry trees, he walked up to the side porch where Mr. Thompson was pushing a big swing churn back and forth.

Mr. Thompson was a tough weather-beaten man with stiff black hair and a week's growth of black whiskers. He was a noisy proud man who held his neck so straight his whole face stood level with his Adam's apple, and the whiskers continued down his neck and disappeared into a black thatch under his open collar. The churn rumbled and swished like the belly of a trotting horse, and Mr. Thompson seemed somehow to be driving a horse with one hand, reining it in and urging it forward; and every now and then he turned halfway around and squirted a tremendous spit of tobacco juice out over the steps. The door stones were brown and gleaming with fresh tobacco juice. Mr. Thompson had been churning quite a while and he was tired of it. He was just fetching a mouthful of juice to squirt again when the stranger came around the corner and stopped. Mr. Thompson saw a narrow-chested man with blue eyes so pale they were almost white, looking and not looking at him from a long gaunt face, under white eyebrows. Mr. Thompson judged him to be another of these Irishmen, by his long upper lip.

"Howdy do, sir," said Mr. Thompson politely, swinging his churn.

"I need work," said the man, clearly enough but with some kind of foreign accent Mr. Thompson couldn't place. It wasn't Cajun and it wasn't Nigger and it wasn't Dutch, so it had him stumped. "You need a man here?"

Mr. Thompson gave the churn a great shove and it swung back and forth several times on its own momentum. He sat on the steps, shot his quid into the grass, and said, "Set down. Maybe we can make a deal. I been kinda lookin' round for somebody. I had two niggers but they got into a cutting scrape up the creek last week, one of 'em dead now and the other in the hoosegow at Cold Springs. Neither one of 'em worth killing, come right down to it. So it looks like I'd better get somebody. Where'd you work last?"

"North Dakota," said the man, folding himself down on the other end of the steps, but not as if he were tired. He folded up and settled down as if it would be a long time before he got up again. He never had looked at Mr. Thompson, but there wasn't anything sneaking in his eye, either. He didn't seem to be looking anywhere else. His eyes sat in his head and let things pass by them. They didn't seem to be expecting to see anything worth looking at. Mr. Thompson waited a long time for the man to say something more, but he had gone into a brown study.

"North Dakota," said Mr. Thompson, trying to remember where that was. "That's a right smart distance off, seems to me."

"I can do everything on farm," said the man; "cheap. I need work."

Mr. Thompson settled himself to get down to business. "My name's Thompson, Mr. Royal Earle Thompson," he said.

"I'm Mr. Helton," said the man, "Mr. Olaf Helton." He did not move.

"Well, now," said Mr. Thompson in his most carrying voice, "I guess we'd better talk turkey."

When Mr. Thompson expected to drive a bargain he always grew very hearty and jovial. There was nothing wrong with him except that he hated like the devil to pay wages. He said so himself. "You furnish grub and a shack," he said, "and then you got to pay 'em besides. It ain't right. Besides the wear and tear on your implements," he said, "they just let everything go to rack and ruin." So he began to laugh and shout his way through the deal.

"Now, what I want to know is, how much you fixing to gouge outa me?" he brayed, slapping his knee. After he had kept it up as long as he could, he quieted down, feeling a little sheepish, and cut himself a chew. Mr. Helton was staring out somewhere between the barn and the orchard, and seemed to be sleeping with his eyes open.

"I'm good worker," said Mr. Helton as from the tomb. "I get dollar a day."

Mr. Thompson was so shocked he forgot to start laughing again at the top his voice until it was nearly too late to do any good. "Haw, haw," he bawled. "Why, for a dollar a day I'd hire out myself. What kinda work is it where they pay you a dollar a day?"

"Wheatfields, North Dakota," said Mr. Helton, not even smiling.

Mr. Thompson stopped laughing. "Well, this ain't any wheatfield by a long shot. This more of a dairy farm," he said, feeling apologetic. "My wife, she was set on a dairy, she seemed to like working around with cows and calves, so I humored her. But it was a mistake," he said. "I got nearly everything to do, anyhow. My wife ain't very strong. She's sick today, that's a fact. She's been porely for the last few days. We plant a little feed, and a corn patch, and there's the orchard, and a few pigs and chickens, but our main hold is the cows. Now just speakin' as one man to another, there ain't any money in it. Now I can't give you no dollar a day because ackshally I don't make that much out of it. No, sir, we get along on a lot less than a dollar a day, I'd say, if we figger up everything in the long run. Now, I paid seven dollars a month to the two niggers, three-fifty each, and grub, but what I say is, one middlin'-good white man ekals a whole passel of niggers any day in the week, so I'll give you seven dollars and you eat at the table with us, and you'll be treated like a white man, as the feller says—"

"That's all right," said Mr. Helton. "I take it."

"Well, now I guess we'll call it a deal, hey?" Mr. Thompson jumped up as if he had remembered important business. "Now, you just take hold of that churn and give it a few swings, will you, while I ride to town on a coupla little errands. I ain't been able to leave the place all week. I guess you know what to do with butter after you get it, don't you?"

"I know," said Mr. Helton without turning his head. "I know butter business." He had a strange drawling voice, and even when he spoke only two words his voice waved slowly up and down and the emphasis was in the wrong place. Mr. Thompson wondered what kind of foreigner Mr. Helton could be.

"Now just where did you say you worked last?" he asked, as if he expected Mr. Helton to contradict himself.

"North Dakota," said Mr. Helton.

"Well, one place is good as another once you get used to it," said Mr. Thompson, amply. "You're a forriner, ain't you?"

"I'm a Swede," said Mr. Helton, beginning to swing the churn.

Mr. Thompson let forth a booming laugh, as if this was the best joke on somebody he'd ever heard. "Well, I'll be damned," he said at the top of his voice. "A Swede: well, now, I'm afraid you'll get pretty lonesome around here. I never seen any Swedes in this neck of the woods."

"That's all right," said Mr. Helton. He went on swinging the churn as if he had been working on the place for years.

"In fact, I might as well tell you, you're practically the first Swede I ever laid eyes on."

"That's all right," said Mr. Helton.

Mr. Thompson went into the front room where Mrs. Thompson was lying down, with the green shades drawn. She had a bowl of water by her on the table and a wet cloth over her eyes. She took the cloth off at the sound of Mr. Thompson's boots and said, "What's all the noise out there? Who is it?"

"Got a feller out there says he's a Swede, Ellie," said Mr. Thompson; "says he knows how to make butter."

"I hope it turns out to be the truth," said Mrs. Thompson. "Looks like my head never will get any better."

"Don't you worry," said Mr. Thompson. "You fret too much. Now I'm gointa ride into town and get a little order of groceries."

"Don't you linger, now, Mr. Thompson," said Mrs. Thompson.

"Don't go to the hotel." She meant the saloon; the proprietor also had rooms for rent upstairs.

"Just a coupla little toddies," said Mr. Thompson, laughing loudly, "never hurt anybody."

"I never took a dram in my life," said Mrs. Thompson, "and what's more I never will."

"I wasn't talking about the womenfolks," said Mr. Thompson.

The sound of the swinging churn rocked Mrs. Thompson first into a gentle doze, then a deep drowse from which she waked suddenly knowing that the swinging had stopped a good while ago. She sat up shading her weak eyes from the flat strips of late summer sunlight between the sill and the lowered shades. There she was, thank God, still alive, with supper to cook but no churning on hand, and her head still bewildered, but easy. Slowly she realized she had been hearing a new sound even in her sleep. Somebody was playing a tune on the harmonica, not merely shrilling up and down making a sickening noise, but really playing a pretty tune, merry and sad.

She went out through the kitchen, stepped off the porch, and stood facing the east, shading her eyes. When her vision cleared and settled, she saw a long, pale-haired man in blue jeans sitting in the doorway of the hired man's shack, tilted back in a kitchen chair, blowing away at the harmonica with his eyes shut. Mrs. Thompson's heart fluttered and sank. Heavens, he looked lazy and worthless, he did, now. First a lot of no-count fiddling darkies and then a no-count white man. It was just like Mr. Thompson to take on that kind. She did wish he would be more considerate, and take a little trouble with his business. She wanted to believe in her husband, and there were too many times when she couldn't. She wanted to believe that tomorrow, or at least the day after, life, such a battle at best, was going to be better.

She walked past the shack without glancing aside, stepping carefully, bent at the waist because of the nagging pain in her side, and went to the springhouse, trying to harden her mind to speak very plainly to that new hired man if he had not done his work.

The milk house was only another shack of weather-beaten boards nailed together hastily years before because they needed a milk house; it was meant to be temporary, and it was; already shapeless, leaning this way and that over a perpetual cool trickle of water that fell from a little grot, almost choked with pallid ferns. No one else in the whole countryside had such a spring on his land. Mr. and Mrs. Thompson felt they had a fortune in that spring, if ever they got around to doing anything with it.

Rickety wooden shelves clung at hazard in the square around the small pool where the larger pails of milk and butter stood, fresh and sweet in the cold water. One hand supporting her flat, pained side, the other shading her eyes, Mrs. Thompson leaned over and peered into the pails. The cream had been skimmed and set aside, there was a rich roll of butter, the wooden molds and shallow pans had been scrubbed

and scalded for the first time in who knows when, the barrel was full
of buttermilk ready for the pigs and the weanling calves, the hard
packed-dirt floor had been swept smooth. Mrs. Thompson straightened
up again, smiling tenderly. She had been ready to scold him, a poor
man who needed a job, who had just come there and who might not
have been expected to do things properly at first. There was nothing
she could do to make up for the injustice she had done him in her
thoughts but to tell him how she appreciated his good clean work,
finished already, in no time at all. She ventured near the door of the
shack with her careful steps; Mr. Helton opened his eyes, stopped
playing, and brought his chair down straight, but did not look at her,
or get up. She was a little frail woman with long thick brown hair in a
braid, a suffering patient mouth and diseased eyes which cried easily.
She wove her fingers into an eyeshade, thumbs on temples, and, winking
her tearful lids, said with a polite little manner, "Howdy do, sir. I'm
Miz Thompson, and I wanted to tell you I think you did real well in the
milk house. It's always been a hard place to keep."

He said, "That's all right," in a slow voice, without moving.

Mrs. Thompson waited a moment. "That's a pretty tune you're playing. Most folks don't seem to get much music out of a harmonica."

Mr. Helton sat humped over, long legs sprawling, his spine in a bow,
running his thumb over the square mouth-stops; except for his moving
hand he might have been asleep. The harmonica was a big shiny new
one, and Mrs. Thompson, her gaze wandering about, counted five
others, all good and expensive, standing in a row on the shelf beside
his cot. "He must carry them around in his jumper pocket," she thought,
and noted there was not a sign of any other possession lying about.
"I see you're mighty fond of music," she said. "We used to have an old
accordion, and Mr. Thompson could play it right smart, but the little
boys broke it up."

Mr. Helton stood up rather suddenly, the chair clattered under him,
his knees straightened though his shoulders did not, and he looked at
the floor as if he were listening carefully. "You know how little boys
are," said Mrs. Thompson. "You'd better set them harmonicas on a high
shelf or they'll be after them. They're great hands for getting into things.
I try to learn 'em, but it don't do much good."

Mr. Helton, in one wide gesture of his long arms, swept his harmonicas
up against his chest, and from there transferred them in a row to the
ledge where the roof joined to the wall. He pushed them back almost
out of sight.

"That'll do, maybe," said Mrs. Thompson. "Now I wonder," she said,
turning and closing her eyes helplessly against the stronger western
light, "I wonder what became of them little tads. I can't keep up with
them." She had a way of speaking about her children as if they were
rather troublesome nephews on a prolonged visit.

"Down by the creek," said Mr. Helton, in his hollow voice. Mrs.
Thompson, pausing confusedly, decided he had answered her question.

He stood in silent patience, not exactly waiting for her to go, perhaps, but pretty plainly not waiting for anything else. Mrs. Thompson was perfectly accustomed to all kinds of men full of all kinds of cranky ways. The point was, to find out just how Mr. Helton's crankiness was different from any other man's, and then get used to it, and let him feel at home. Her father had been cranky, her brothers and uncles had all been set in their ways and none of them alike, and every hired man she'd ever seen had quirks and crotchets of his own. Now here was Mr. Helton, who was a Swede, who wouldn't talk, and who played the harmonica besides.

"They'll be needing something to eat," said Mrs. Thompson in a vague friendly way, "pretty soon. Now I wonder what I ought to be thinking about for supper? Now what do you like to eat, Mr. Helton? We always have plenty of good butter and milk and cream, that's a blessing. Mr. Thompson says we ought to sell all of it, but I say my family comes first." Her little face went all out of shape in a pained blind smile.

"I eat anything," said Mr. Helton, his words wandering up and down.

He *can't* talk, for one thing, thought Mrs. Thompson, it's a shame to keep at him when he don't know the language good. She took a slow step away from the shack, looking back over her shoulder. "We usually have cornbread except on Sundays," she told him. "I suppose in your part of the country you don't get much good cornbread."

Not a word from Mr. Helton. She saw from her eye-corner that he had sat down again, looking at his harmonica, chair tilted. She hoped he would remember it was getting near milking time. As she moved away, he started playing again, the same tune.

Milking time came and went. Mrs. Thompson saw Mr. Helton going back and forth between the cow barn and the milk house. He swung along in an easy lope, shoulders bent, head hanging, the big buckets balancing like a pair of scales at the ends of his bony arms. Mr. Thompson rode in from town sitting straighter than usual, chin in, a towsack full of supplies swung behind the saddle. After a trip to the barn, he came into the kitchen full of good will, and gave Mrs. Thompson a hearty smack on the cheek after dusting her face off with his tough whiskers. He had been to the hotel, that was plain. "Took a look around the premises, Ellie," he shouted. "That Swede sure is grinding out the labor. But he is the closest mouthed feller I ever met up with in all my days. Looks like he's scared he'll crack his jaw if he opens his front teeth."

Mrs. Thompson was stirring up a big bowl of buttermilk cornbread. "You smell like a toper, Mr. Thompson," she said with perfect dignity. "I wish you'd get one of the little boys to bring me in an extra load of firewood. I'm thinking about baking a batch of cookies tomorrow."

Mr. Thompson, all at once smelling the liquor on his own breath, sneaked out, justly rebuked, and brought in the firewood himself. Arthur and Herbert, grubby from thatched head to toes, from skin to shirt,

came stamping in yelling for supper. "Go wash your faces and comb
your hair," said Mrs. Thompson, automatically. They retired to the
porch. Each one put his hand under the pump and wet his forelock,
combed it down with his fingers, and returned at once to the kitchen,
where all the fair prospects of life were centered. Mrs. Thompson set
an extra plate and commanded Arthur, the eldest, eight years old, to
call Mr. Helton for supper.

Arthur, without moving from the spot, bawled like a bull calf,
"Saaaaaay, Hellllllton, suuuuuupper's ready!" and added in a lower
voice, "You big Swede!"

"Listen to me," said Mrs. Thompson, "that's no way to act. Now you
go out there and ask him decent, or I'll get your daddy to give you a
good licking."

Mr. Helton loomed, long and gloomy, in the doorway. "Sit right
there," boomed Mr. Thompson, waving his arm. Mr. Helton swung his
square shoes across the kitchen in two steps, slumped onto the bench
and sat. Mr. Thompson occupied his chair at the head of the table, the
two boys scrambled into place opposite Mr. Helton, and Mrs. Thompson
sat at the end nearest the stove. Mrs. Thompson clasped her hands,
bowed her head and said aloud hastily, "Lord, for all these and Thy
other blessings we thank Thee in Jesus' name, amen," trying to finish
before Herbert's rusty little paw reached the nearest dish. Otherwise
she would be duty-bound to send him away from the table, and growing
children need their meals. Mr. Thompson and Arthur always waited,
but Herbert, aged six, was too young to take training yet.

Mr. and Mrs. Thompson tried to engage Mr. Helton in conversation,
but it was a failure. They tried first the weather, and then the crops,
and then the cows, but Mr. Helton simply did not reply. Mr. Thompson
then told something funny he had seen in town. It was about some of
the other old grangers at the hotel, friends of his, giving beer to a goat,
and the goat's subsequent behavior. Mr. Helton did not seem to hear.
Mrs. Thompson laughed dutifully, but she didn't think it was very
funny. She had heard it often before, though Mr. Thompson, each time
he told it, pretended it had happened that self-same day. It must have
happened years ago if it ever happened at all, and it had never been a
story that Mrs. Thompson thought suitable for mixed company. The
whole thing came of Mr. Thompson's weakness for a dram too much
now and then, though he voted for local option at every election. She
passed the food to Mr. Helton, who took a helping of everything, but
not much, not enough to keep him up to his full powers if he expected
to go on working the way he had started.

At last, he took a fair-sized piece of cornbread, wiped his plate up as
clean as if it had been licked by a hound dog, stuffed his mouth full,
and, still chewing, slid off the bench and started for the door.

"Good night, Mr. Helton," said Mrs. Thompson, and the other
Thompsons took it up in a scattered chorus. "Good night, Mr. Helton!"

"Good night," said Mr. Helton's wavering voice grudgingly from the darkness.

"Gude not," said Arthur, imitating Mr. Helton.

"Gude not," said Herbert, the copy-cat.

"You don't do it right," said Arthur. "Now listen to me. Guuuuuude naht," and he ran a hollow scale in a luxury of successful impersonation. Herbert almost went into a fit with joy.

"Now you *stop* that," said Mrs. Thompson. "He can't help the way he talks. You ought to be ashamed of yourselves, both of you, making fun of a poor stranger like that. How'd you like to be a stranger in a strange land?"

"I'd like it," said Arthur. "I think it would be fun."

"They're both regular heathens, Ellie," said Mr. Thompson. "Just plain ignoramuses." He turned the face of awful fatherhood upon his young. "You're both going to get sent to school next year, and that'll knock some sense into you."

"I'm going to git sent to the 'formatory when I'm old enough," piped up Herbert. "That's where I'm goin'."

"Oh, you are, are you?" asked Mr. Thompson. "Who says so?"

"The Sunday School Superintendent," said Herbert, a bright boy showing off.

"You see?" said Mr. Thompson, staring at his wife. "What did I tell you?" He became a hurricane of wrath. "Get to bed, you two," he roared until his Adam's apple shuddered. "Get now before I take the hide off you!" They got, and shortly from their attic bedroom the sounds of scuffling and snorting and giggling and growling filled the house and shook the kitchen ceiling.

Mrs. Thompson held her head and said in a small uncertain voice, "It's no use picking on them when they're so young and tender. I can't stand it."

"My goodness, Ellie," said Mr. Thompson, "we've got to raise 'em. We can't just let 'em grow up hog wild."

She went on in another tone. "That Mr. Helton seems all right, even if he can't be made to talk. Wonder how he comes to be so far from home."

"Like I said, he isn't no whamper-jaw," said Mr. Thompson, "but he sure knows how to lay out the work. I guess that's the main thing around here. Country's full of fellers trampin' round looking for work."

Mrs. Thompson was gathering up the dishes. She now gathered up Mr. Thompson's plate from under his chin. "To tell you the honest truth," she remarked, "I think it's a mighty good change to have a man round the place who knows how to work and keep his mouth shut. Means he'll keep out of our business. Not that we've got anything to hide, but it's convenient."

"That's a fact," said Mr. Thompson. "Haw, haw," he shouted suddenly. "Means you can do all the talking, huh?"

"The only thing," went on Mrs. Thompson, "is this: he don't eat hearty enough to suit me. I like to see a man set down and relish a good meal. My granma used to say it was no use putting dependence on a man who won't set down and make out his dinner. I hope it won't be that way this time."

"Tell *you* the truth, Ellie," said Mr. Thompson, picking his teeth with a fork and leaning back in the best of good humors, "I always thought your granma was a ter'ble ole fool. She'd just say the first thing that popped into her head and call it God's wisdom."

"My granma wasn't anybody's fool. Nine times out of ten she knew what she was talking about. I always say, the first thing you think is the best thing you can say."

"Well," said Mr. Thompson, going into another shout, "you're so reefined about that goat story, you just try speaking out in mixed comp'ny sometime! You just try it. S'pose you happened to be thinking about a hen and a rooster, hey? I reckon you'd shock the Babtist preacher!" He gave her a good pinch on her thin little rump. "No more meat on you than a rabbit," he said, fondly. "Now I like 'em cornfed."

Mrs. Thompson looked at him open-eyed and blushed. She could see better by lamplight. "Why, Mr. Thompson, sometimes I think you're the evilest-minded man that ever lived." She took a handful of hair on the crown of his head and gave it a good, slow pull. "That's to show you how it feels, pinching so hard when you're supposed to be playing," she said, gently.

In spite of his situation in life, Mr. Thompson had never been able to outgrow his deep conviction that running a dairy and chasing after chickens was woman's work. He was fond of saying that he could plow a furrow, cut sorghum, shuck corn, handle a team, build a corn crib, as well as any man. Buying and selling, too, were man's work. Twice a week he drove the spring wagon to market with the fresh butter, a few eggs, fruits in their proper season, sold them, pocketed the change, and spent it as seemed best, being careful not to dig into Mrs. Thompson's pin money.

But from the first the cows worried him, coming up regularly twice a day to be milked, standing there reproaching him with their smug female faces. Calves worried him, fighting the rope and strangling themselves until their eyes bulged, trying to get at the teat. Wrestling with a calf unmanned him, like having to change a baby's diaper. Milk worried him, coming bitter sometimes, drying up, turning sour. Hens worried him, cackling, clucking, hatching out when you least expected it and leading their broods into the barnyard where the horses could step on them; dying of roup and wryneck and getting plagues of chicken lice; laying eggs all over God's creation so that half of them were spoiled before a man could find them, in spite of a rack of nests Mrs. Thompson had set for them in the feed room. Hens were a blasted nuisance.

Slopping hogs was hired man's work, in Mr. Thompson's opinion.

Killing hogs was a job for the boss, but scraping them and cutting them up was for the hired man again; and again woman's proper work was dressing meat, smoking, pickling, and making lard and sausage. All his carefully limited fields of activity were related somehow to Mr. Thompson's feeling for the appearance of things, his own appearance in the sight of God and man. "It don't *look* right," was his final reason for not doing anything he did not wish to do.

It was his dignity and his reputation that he cared about, and there were only a few kinds of work manly enough for Mr. Thompson to undertake with his own hands. Mrs. Thompson, to whom so many forms of work would have been becoming, had simply gone down on him early. He saw, after a while, how short-sighted it had been of him to expect much from Mrs. Thompson; he had fallen in love with her delicate waist and lace-trimmed petticoats and big blue eyes, and, though all those charms had disappeared, she had in the meantime become Ellie to him, not at all the same person as Miss Ellen Bridges, popular Sunday School teacher in the Mountain City First Baptist Church, but his dear wife, Ellie, who was not strong. Deprived as he was, however, of the main support in life which a man might expect in marriage, he had almost without knowing it resigned himself to failure. Head erect, a prompt payer of taxes, yearly subscriber to the preacher's salary, land owner and father of a family, employer, a hearty good fellow among men, Mr. Thompson knew, without putting it into words, that he had been going steadily down hill. God amighty, it did look like somebody around the place might take a rake in hand now and then and clear up the clutter around the barn and the kitchen steps. The wagon shed was so full of broken-down machinery and ragged harness and old wagon wheels and battered milk pails and rotting lumber you could hardly drive in there any more. Not a soul on the place would raise a hand to it, and as for him, he had all he could do with his regular work. He would sometimes in the slack season sit for hours worrying about it, squirting tobacco on the ragweeds growing in a thicket against the wood pile, wondering what a fellow could do, handicapped as he was. He looked forward to the boys growing up soon; he was going to put them through the mill just as his own father had done with him when he was a boy; they were going to learn how to take hold and run the place right. He wasn't going to overdo it, but those two boys were going to earn their salt, or he'd know why. Great big lubbers sitting around whittling! Mr. Thompson sometimes grew quite enraged with them, when imagining their possible future, big lubbers sitting around whittling or thinking about fishing trips. Well, he'd put a stop to that, mighty damn quick.

As the seasons passed, and Mr. Helton took hold more and more, Mr. Thompson began to relax in his mind a little. There seemed to be nothing the fellow couldn't do, all in the day's work and as a matter of course. He got up at five o'clock in the morning, boiled his own coffee and fried his own bacon and was out in the cow lot before Mr. Thompson had even begun to yawn, stretch, groan, roar and thump around looking for his jeans. He milked the cows, kept the milk house, and churned the butter; rounded the hens up and somehow persuaded them to lay in the nests, not under the house and behind the haystacks; he fed them regularly and they hatched out until you couldn't set a foot down for them. Little by little the piles of trash around the barn and house disappeared. He carried buttermilk and corn to the hogs, and curried cockleburs out of the horses' manes. He was gentle with the calves, if a little grim with the cows and hens; judging by his conduct, Mr. Helton had never heard of the difference between man's and woman's work on a farm.

In the second year, he showed Mr. Thompson the picture of a cheese press in a mail order catalogue, and said, "This is a good thing. You buy this, I make cheese." The press was bought and Mr. Helton did make cheese, and it was sold, along with the increased butter and the crates of eggs. Sometimes Mr. Thompson felt a little contemptuous of Mr. Helton's ways. It did seem kind of picayune for a man to go around picking up half a dozen ears of corn that had fallen off the wagon on the way from the field, gathering up fallen fruit to feed to the pigs, storing up old nails and stray parts of machinery, spending good time stamping a fancy pattern on the butter before it went to market. Mr. Thompson, sitting up high on the spring-wagon seat, with the decorated butter in a five-gallon lard can wrapped in wet towsack, driving to town, chirruping to the horses and snapping the reins over their backs, sometimes thought that Mr. Helton was a pretty meeching sort of fellow; but he never gave way to these feelings, he knew a good thing when he had it. It was a fact the hogs were in better shape and sold for more money. It was a fact that Mr. Thompson stopped buying feed, Mr. Helton managed the crops so well. When beef- and hog-slaughtering time came, Mr. Helton knew how to save the scraps that Mr. Thompson had thrown away, and wasn't above scraping guts and filling them with sausages that he made by his own methods. In all, Mr. Thompson had no grounds for complaint. In the third year, he raised Mr. Helton's wages though Mr. Helton had not asked for a raise. The fourth year, when Mr. Thompson was not only out of debt but had a little cash in the bank, he raised Mr. Helton's wages again, two dollars and a half a month each time.

"The man's worth it, Ellie," said Mr. Thompson, in a glow of self-justification for his extravagance. "He's made this place pay, and I want him to know I appreciate it."

Mr. Helton's silence, the pallor of his eyebrows and hair, his long, glum jaw and eyes that refused to see anything, even the work under his hands, had grown perfectly familiar to the Thompsons. At first, Mrs. Thompson complained a little. "It's like sitting down at the table with a disembodied spirit," she said. "You'd think he'd find something to say, sooner or later."

"Let him alone," said Mr. Thompson. "When he gets ready to talk, he'll talk."

The years passed, and Mr. Helton never got ready to talk. After his work was finished for the day, he would come up from the barn or the milk house or the chicken house, swinging his lantern, his big shoes clumping like pony hoofs on the hard path. They, sitting in the kitchen in the winter, or on the back porch in summer, would hear him drag out his wooden chair, hear the creak of it tilted back, and then for a little while he would play his single tune on one or another of his harmonicas. The harmonicas were in different keys, some lower and sweeter than the others, but the same changeless tune went on, a strange tune, with sudden turns in it, night after night, and sometimes even in the afternoons when Mr. Helton sat down to catch his breath. At first the Thompsons liked it very much, and always stopped to listen. Later there came a time when they were fairly sick of it, and began to wish to each other that he would learn a new one. At last they did not hear it any more, it was as natural as the sound of the wind rising in the evenings, or the cows lowing, or their own voices.

Mrs. Thompson pondered now and then over Mr. Helton's soul. He didn't seem to be a church-goer, and worked straight through Sunday as if it were any common day of the week. "I think we ought to invite him to go to hear Dr. Martin," she told Mr. Thompson. "It isn't very Christian of us not to ask him. He's not a forward kind of man. He'd wait to be asked."

"Let him alone," said Mr. Thompson. "The way I look at it, his religion is every man's own business. Besides, he ain't got any Sunday clothes. He wouldn't want to go to church in them jeans and jumpers of his. I don't know what he does with his money. He certainly don't spend it foolishly."

Still, once the notion got into her head, Mrs. Thompson could not rest until she invited Mr. Helton to go to church with the family next Sunday. He was pitching hay into neat little piles in the field back of the orchard. Mrs. Thompson put on smoked glasses and a sunbonnet and walked all the way down there to speak to him. He stopped and leaned on his pitchfork, listening, and for a moment Mrs. Thompson was almost frightened at his face. The pale eyes seemed to glare past her, the eyebrows frowned, the long jaw hardened. "I got work," he said bluntly, and lifting his pitchfork he turned from her and began to toss the hay. Mrs. Thompson, her feelings hurt, walked back thinking that by now she should be used to Mr. Helton's ways, but it did seem like a man, even a foreigner, could be just a little polite when you gave him a Christian invitation. "He's not polite, that's the only thing I've got against him," she said to Mr. Thompson. "He just can't seem to behave like other people. You'd think he had a grudge against the world," she said. "I sometimes don't know what to make of it."

In the second year something had happened that made Mrs. Thomp-

son uneasy, the kind of thing she could not put into words, hardly into
thoughts, and if she had tried to explain to Mr. Thompson it would
have sounded worse than it was, or not bad enough. It was that kind
of queer thing that seems to be giving a warning, and yet, nearly always
nothing comes of it. It was on a hot, still spring day, and Mrs. Thompson
had been down to the garden patch to pull some new carrots and green
onions and string beans for dinner. As she worked, sunbonnet low over
her eyes, putting each kind of vegetable in a pile by itself in her basket,
she noticed how neatly Mr. Helton weeded, and how rich the soil was.
He had spread it all over with manure from the barns, and worked it
in, in the fall, and the vegetables were coming up fine and full. She
walked back under the nubbly little fig trees where the unpruned
branches leaned almost to the ground, and the thick leaves made a cool
screen. Mrs. Thompson was always looking for shade to save her eyes.
So she, looking idly about, saw through the screen a sight that struck
her as very strange. If it had been a noisy spectacle, it would have been
quite natural. It was the silence that struck her. Mr. Helton was shaking
Arthur by the shoulders, ferociously, his face most terribly fixed and
pale. Arthur's head snapped back and forth and he had not stiffened
in resistance, as he did when Mrs. Thompson tried to shake him. His
eyes were rather frightened, but surprised, too, probably more surprised
than anything else. Herbert stood by meekly, watching. Mr. Helton
dropped Arthur, and seized Herbert, and shook him with the same
methodical ferocity, the same face of hatred. Herbert's mouth crumpled
as if he would cry, but he made no sound. Mr. Helton let him go, turned
and strode into the shack, and the little boys ran, as if for their lives,
without a word. They disappeared around the corner to the front of the
house.

Mrs. Thompson took time to set her basket on the kitchen table, to
push her sunbonnet back on her head and draw it forward again, to
look in the stove and make certain the fire was going, before she followed
the boys. They were sitting huddled together under a clump of chinaberry trees in plain sight of her bedroom window, as if it were a safe
place they had discovered.

"What are you doing?" asked Mrs. Thompson.

They looked hang-dog from under their foreheads and Arthur mumbled, "Nothin'."

"Nothing *now*, you mean," said Mrs. Thompson, severely. "Well, I
have plenty for you to do. Come right in here this minute and help me
fix vegetables. This minute."

They scrambled up very eagerly and followed her close. Mrs. Thompson tried to imagine what they had been up to; she did not like the
notion of Mr. Helton taking it on himself to correct her little boys, but
she was afraid to ask them for reasons. They might tell her a lie, and
she would have to overtake them in it, and whip them. Or she would
have to pretend to believe them, and they would get in the habit of

lying. Or they might tell her the truth, and it would be something she would have to whip them for. The very thought of it gave her a headache. She supposed she might ask Mr. Helton, but it was not her place to ask. She would wait and tell Mr. Thompson, and let him get at the bottom of it. While her mind ran on, she kept the little boys hopping. "Cut those carrot tops closer, Herbert, you're just being careless. Arthur, stop breaking up the beans so little. They're little enough already. Herbert, you go get an armload of wood. Arthur, you take these onions and wash them under the pump. Herbert, as soon as you're done here, you get a broom and sweep out this kitchen. Arthur, you get a shovel and take up the ashes. Stop picking your nose, Herbert. How often must I tell you? Arthur, you go look in the top drawer of my bureau, left-hand side, and bring me the vaseline for Herbert's nose. Herbert, come here to me. . . ."

They galloped through their chores, their animal spirits rose with activity, and shortly they were out in the front yard again, engaged in a wrestling match. They sprawled and fought, scrambled, clutched, rose and fell shouting, as aimlessly, noisily, monotonously as two puppies. They imitated various animals, not a human sound from them, and their dirty faces were streaked with sweat. Mrs. Thompson, sitting at her window, watched them with baffled pride and tenderness, they were so sturdy and healthy and growing so fast; but uneasily, too, with her pained little smile and the tears rolling from her eyelids that clinched themselves against the sunlight. They were so idle and careless, as if they had no future in this world, and no immortal souls to save, and oh, what had they been up to that Mr. Helton had shaken them, with his face positively dangerous?

In the evening before supper, without a word to Mr. Thompson of the curious fear the sight had caused her she told him that Mr. Helton had shaken the little boys for some reason. He stepped out to the shack and spoke to Mr. Helton. In five minutes he was back, glaring at his young. "He says them brats been fooling with his harmonicas, Ellie, blowing in them and getting them all dirty and full of spit and they don't play good."

"Did he say all that?" asked Mrs. Thompson. "It doesn't seem possible."

"Well, that's what he meant, anyhow," said Mr. Thompson. "He didn't say it just that way. But he acted pretty worked up about it."

"That's a shame," said Mrs. Thompson, "a perfect shame. Now we've got to do something so they'll remember they mustn't go into Mr. Helton's things."

"I'll tan their hides for them," said Mr. Thompson. "I'll take a calf rope to them if they don't look out."

"Maybe you'd better leave the whipping to me," said Mrs. Thompson. "You haven't got a light enough hand for children."

"That's just what's the matter with them now," shouted Mr. Thompson, "rotten spoiled and they'll wind up in the penitentiary. You don't half whip 'em. Just little love taps. My pa used to knock me down with a stick of stove wood or anything else that came handy."

"Well, that's not saying it's right," said Mrs. Thompson. "I don't hold with that way of raising children. It makes them run away from home. I've seen too much of it."

"I'll break every bone in 'em," said Mr. Thompson, simmering down, "if they don't mind you better and stop being so bullheaded."

"Leave the table and wash your face and hands," Mrs. Thompson commanded the boys, suddenly. They slunk out and dabbled at the pump and slunk in again, trying to make themselves small. They had learned long ago that their mother always made them wash when there was trouble ahead. They looked at their plates. Mr. Thompson opened up on them.

"Well, now, what you got to say for yourselves about going into Mr. Helton's shack and ruining his harmonicas?"

The two little boys wilted, their faces drooped into the grieved hopeless lines of children's faces when they are brought to the terrible bar of blind adult justice; their eyes telegraphed each other in panic, "Now we're really going to catch a licking"; in despair, they dropped their buttered cornbread on their plates, their hands lagged on the edge of the table.

"I ought to break your ribs," said Mr. Thompson, "and I'm a good mind to do it."

"Yes, sir," whispered Arthur, faintly.

"Yes, sir," said Herbert, his lip trembling.

"Now, papa," said Mrs. Thompson in a warning tone. The children did not glance at her. They had no faith in her good will. She had betrayed them in the first place. There was no trusting her. Now she might save them and she might not. No use depending on her.

"Well, you ought to get a good thrashing. You deserve it, don't you, Arthur?"

Arthur hung his head. "Yes, sir."

"And the next time I catch either of you hanging around Mr. Helton's shack, I'm going to take the hide off *both* of you, you hear me, Herbert?"

Herbert mumbled and choked, scattering his cornbread. "Yes, sir."

"Well, now sit up and eat your supper and not another word out of you," said Mr. Thompson, beginning on his own food. The little boys perked up somewhat and started chewing, but every time they looked around they met their parents' eyes, regarding them steadily. There was no telling when they would think of something new. The boys ate warily, trying not to be seen or heard, the cornbread sticking, the buttermilk gurgling, as it went down their gullets.

"And something else, Mr. Thompson," said Mrs. Thompson after a pause. "Tell Mr. Helton he's to come straight to us when they bother him, and not to trouble shaking them himself. Tell him we'll look after that."

"They're so mean," answered Mr. Thompson, staring at them. "It's a wonder he don't kill 'em off and be done with it." But there was something in the tone that told Arthur and Herbert that nothing more worth worrying about was going to happen this time. Heaving deep sighs, they sat up, reaching for the food nearest them.

"Listen," said Mr. Thompson, suddenly. The little boys stopped eating. "Mr. Helton hasn't come for his supper. Arthur, go and tell Mr. Helton he's late for supper. Tell him nice, now."

Arthur, miserably depressed, slid out of his place and made for the door, without a word.

There were no miracles of fortune to be brought to pass on a small dairy farm. The Thompsons did not grow rich, but they kept out of the poor house, as Mr. Thompson was fond of saying, meaning he had got a little foothold in spite of Ellie's poor health, and unexpected weather, and strange declines in market prices, and his own mysterious handicaps which weighed him down. Mr. Helton was the hope and the prop of the family, and all the Thompsons became fond of him, or at any rate they ceased to regard him as in any way peculiar, and looked upon him, from a distance they did not know how to bridge, as a good man and a good friend. Mr. Helton went his way, worked, played his tune. Nine years passed. The boys grew up and learned to work. They could not remember the time when Ole Helton hadn't been there: a grouchy cuss, Brother Bones; Mr. Helton, the dairymaid; that Big Swede. If he had heard them, he might have been annoyed at some of the names they called him. But he did not hear them, and besides they meant no harm— or at least such harm as existed was all there, in the names; the boys referred to their father as the Old Man, or the Old Geezer, but not to his face. They lived through by main strength all the grimy, secret, oblique phases of growing up and got past the crisis safely if anyone does. Their parents could see they were good solid boys with hearts of gold in spite of their rough ways. Mr. Thompson was relieved to find that, without knowing how he had done it, he had succeeded in raising a set of boys who were not trifling whittlers. They were such good boys Mr. Thompson began to believe they were born that way, and that he had never spoken a harsh word to them in their lives, much less thrashed them. Herbert and Arthur never disputed his word.

Mr. Helton, his hair wet with sweat, plastered to his dripping forehead, his jumper streaked dark and light blue and clinging to his ribs, was chopping a little firewood. He chopped slowly, struck the ax into the end of the chopping log, and piled the wood up neatly. He then disappeared around the house into his shack, which shared with the wood pile a good shade from a row of mulberry trees. Mr. Thompson was lolling in a swing chair on the front porch, a place he had never liked. The chair was new, and Mrs. Thompson had wanted it on the front porch, though the side porch was the place for it, being cooler; and Mr. Thompson wanted to sit in the chair, so there he was. As soon as the new wore off of it, and Ellie's pride in it was exhausted, he would move it around to the side porch. Meantime the August heat was almost unbearable, the air so thick you could poke a hole in it. The dust was inches thick on everything, though Mr. Helton sprinkled the whole yard regularly every night. He even shot the hose upward and washed the tree tops and the roof of the house. They had laid waterpipes to the kitchen and an outside faucet. Mr. Thompson must have dozed, for he opened his eyes and shut his mouth just in time to save his face before a stranger who had driven up to the front gate. Mr. Thompson stood up, put on his hat, pulled up his jeans, and watched while the stranger tied his team, attached to a light spring wagon, to the hitching post. Mr. Thompson recognized the team and wagon. They were from a livery stable in Buda. While the stranger was opening the gate, a strong gate that Mr. Helton had built and set firmly on its hinges several years back, Mr. Thompson strolled down the path to greet him and find out what in God's world a man's business might be that would bring him out at this time of day, in all this dust and welter.

He wasn't exactly a fat man. He was more like a man who had been fat recently. His skin was baggy and his clothes were too big for him, and he somehow looked like a man who should be fat ordinarily, but who might have just got over a spell of sickness. Mr. Thompson didn't take to his looks at all, he couldn't say why.

The stranger took off his hat. He said in a loud hearty voice, "Is this Mr. Thompson, Mr. Royal Earle Thompson?"

"That's my name," said Mr. Thompson, almost quietly, he was so taken aback by the free manner of the stranger.

"My name is Hatch," said the stranger, "Mr. Homer T. Hatch, and I've come to see you about buying a horse."

"I reckon you've been misdirected," said Mr. Thompson. "I haven't got a horse for sale. Usually if I've got anything like that to sell," he said, "I tell the neighbors and tack up a little sign on the gate."

The fat man opened his mouth and roared with joy, showing rabbit teeth brown as shoeleather. Mr. Thompson saw nothing to laugh at, for once. The stranger shouted, "That's just an old joke of mine." He caught one of his hands in the other and shook hands with himself heartily. "I always say something like that when I'm calling on a stranger, because I've noticed that when a feller says he's come to buy something nobody takes him for a suspicious character. You see? Haw, haw, haw."

His joviality made Mr. Thompson nervous, because the expression in the man's eyes didn't match the sounds he was making. "Haw, haw," laughed Mr. Thompson obligingly, still not seeing the joke. "Well, that's all wasted on me because I never take any man for a suspicious character 'til he shows hisself to be one. Says or does something," he explained. "Until that happens, one man's as good as another, so far's I'm concerned."

"Well," said the stranger, suddenly very sober and sensible, "I ain't come neither to buy nor sell. Fact is, I want to see you about something that's of interest to us both. Yes, sir, I'd like to have a little talk with you, and it won't cost you a cent."

"I guess that's fair enough," said Mr. Thompson, reluctantly. "Come on around the house where there's a little shade."

They went around and seated themselves on two stumps under a chinaberry tree.

"Yes, sir, Homer T. Hatch is my name and America is my nation," said the stranger. "I reckon you must know the name? I used to have a cousin named Jameson Hatch lived up the country a ways."

"Don't think I know the name," said Mr. Thompson. "There's some Hatchers settled somewhere around Mountain City."

"Don't know the old Hatch family," cried the man in deep concern. He seemed to be pitying Mr. Thompson's ignorance. "Why, we came over from Georgia fifty years ago. Been here long yourself?"

"Just all my whole life," said Mr. Thompson, beginning to feel peevish. "And my pa and my grampap before me. Yes, sir, we've been right here all along. Anybody wants to find a Thompson knows where to look for him. My grampap immigrated in 1836."

"From Ireland, I reckon?" said the stranger.

"From Pennsylvania," said Mr. Thompson. "Now what makes you think we came from Ireland?"

The stranger opened his mouth and began to shout with merriment, and he shook hands with himself as if he hadn't met himself for a long time. "Well, what I always says is, a feller's got to come from *somewhere*, ain't he?"

While they were talking, Mr. Thompson kept glancing at the face near him. He certainly did remind Mr. Thompson of somebody, or maybe he really had seen the man himself somewhere. He couldn't just place the features. Mr. Thompson finally decided it was just that all rabbit-teethed men looked alike.

"That's right," acknowledged Mr. Thompson, rather sourly, "but what I always say is, Thompsons have been settled here for so long it don't make much difference any more *where* they come from. Now of course, this is the slack season, and we're all just laying round a little, but nevertheless we've all got our chores to do, and I don't want to hurry you, and so if you've come to see me on business maybe we'd better get down to it."

"As I said, it's not in a way, and again in a way it is," said the fat man. "Now I'm looking for a man named Helton, Mr. Olaf Eric Helton, from North Dakota, and I was told up around the country a ways that I might find him here, and I wouldn't mind having a little talk with him. No, siree, I sure wouldn't mind, if it's all the same to you."

"I never knew his middle name," said Mr. Thompson, "but Mr. Helton is right here, and been here now for going on nine years. He's a mighty steady man, and you can tell anybody I said so."

"I'm glad to hear that," said Mr. Homer T. Hatch. "I like to hear of a feller mending his ways and settling down. Now when I knew Mr.

Helton he was pretty wild, yes, sir, wild is what he was, he didn't know his own mind at all. Well, now, it's going to be a great pleasure to me to meet up with an old friend and find him all settled down and doing well by hisself."

"We've all got to be young once," said Mr. Thompson. "It's like the measles, it breaks out all over you, and you're a nuisance to yourself and everybody else, but it don't last, and it usually don't leave no ill effects." He was so pleased with this notion he forgot and broke into a guffaw. The stranger folded his arms over his stomach and went into a kind of fit, roaring until he had tears in his eyes. Mr. Thompson stopped shouting and eyed the stranger uneasily. Now he liked a good laugh as well as any man, but there ought to be a little moderation. Now this feller laughed like a perfect lunatic, that was a fact. And he wasn't laughing because he really thought things were funny, either. He was laughing for reasons of his own. Mr. Thompson fell into a moody silence, and waited until Mr. Hatch settled down a little.

Mr. Hatch got out a very dirty blue cotton bandana and wiped his eyes: "That joke just about caught me where I live," he said, almost apologetically. "Now I wish I could think up things as funny as that to say. It's a gift. It's . . ."

"If you want to speak to Mr. Helton, I'll go and round him up," said Mr. Thompson, making motions as if he might get up. "He may be in the milk house and he may be settling in his shack this time of day." It was drawing towards five o'clock. "It's right around the corner," he said.

"Oh, well, there ain't no special hurry," said Mr. Hatch. "I've been wanting to speak to him for a good long spell now and I guess a few minutes more won't make no difference. I just more wanted to locate him, like. That's all."

Mr. Thompson stopped beginning to stand up, and unbuttoned one more button of his shirt, and said, "Well, he's here, and he's this kind of man, that if he had any business with you he'd like to get it over. He don't dawdle, that's one thing you can say for him."

Mr. Hatch appeared to sulk a little at these words. He wiped his face with the bandanna and opened his mouth to speak, when round the house there came the music of Mr. Helton's harmonica. Mr. Thompson raised a finger. "There he is," said Mr. Thompson. "Now's your time."

Mr. Hatch cocked an ear towards the east side of the house and listened for a few seconds, a very strange expression on his face.

"I know that tune like I know the palm of my own hand," said Mr. Thompson, "but I never heard Mr. Helton say what it was."

"That's a kind of Scandahoovian song," said Mr. Hatch. "Where I come from they sing it a lot. In North Dakota, they sing it. It says something about starting out in the morning feeling so good you can't hardly stand it, so you drink up all your likker before noon. All the likker, y' understand, that you was saving for the noon lay-off. The words ain't much, but it's a pretty tune. It's a kind of drinking song."

He sat there drooping a little, and Mr. Thompson didn't like his expression. It was a satisfied expression, but it was more like the cat that et the canary.

"So far as I know," said Mr. Thompson, "he ain't touched a drop since he's been on the place, and that's nine years this coming September. Yes, sir, nine years, so far as I know, he ain't wetted his whistle once. And that's more than I can say for myself," he said, meekly proud.

"Yes, that's a drinking song," said Mr. Hatch. "I used to play 'Little Brown Jug' on the fiddle when I was younger than I am now," he went on, "but this Helton, he just keeps it up. He just sits and plays it by himself."

"He's been playing it off and on for nine years right here on the place," said Mr. Thompson, feeling a little proprietary.

"And he was certainly singing it as well, fifteen years before that, in North Dakota," said Mr. Hatch. "He used to sit up in a straitjacket, practically, when he was in the asylum—"

"What's that you say?" said Mr. Thompson. "What's that?"

"Shucks, I didn't mean to tell you," said Mr. Hatch, a faint leer of regret in his drooping eyelids. "Shucks, that just slipped out. Funny, now I'd made up my mind I wouldn't say a word, because it would just make a lot of excitement, and what I say is, if a man has lived harmless and quiet for nine years it don't matter if he *is* loony, does it? So long's he keeps quiet and don't do nobody harm."

"You mean they had him in a straitjacket?" asked Mr. Thompson, uneasily. "In a lunatic asylum?"

"They sure did," said Mr. Hatch. "That's right where they had him, from time to time."

"They put my Aunt Ida in one of them things in the State asylum," said Mr. Thompson. "She got vi'lent, and they put her in one of these jackets with long sleeves and tied her to an iron ring in the wall, and Aunt Ida got so wild she broke a blood vessel and when they went to look after her she was dead. I'd think one of them things was dangerous."

"Mr. Helton used to sing his drinking song when he was in a straitjacket," said Mr. Hatch. "Nothing ever bothered him, except if you tried to make him talk. That bothered him, and he'd get vi'lent, like your Aunt Ida. He'd get vi'lent and then they'd put him in the jacket and go off and leave him, and he'd lay there perfickly contented, so far's you could see, singing his song. Then one night he just disappeared. Left, you might say, just went, and nobody ever saw hide or hair of him again. And then I come along and find him here," said Mr. Hatch, "all settled down and playing the same song."

"He never acted crazy to me," said Mr. Thompson. "He always acted like a sensible man, to me. He never got married, for one thing, and he works like a horse, and I bet he's got the first cent I paid him when he landed here, and he don't drink, and he never says a word, much less swear, and he don't waste time runnin' around Saturday nights, and if he's crazy," said Mr. Thompson, "why, I think I'll go crazy myself for a change."

"Haw, ha," said Mr. Hatch, "heh, he, that's good! Ha, ha, ha, I hadn't thought of it jes like that. Yeah, that's right! Let's all go crazy and get rid of our wives and save our money, hey?" He smiled unpleasantly, showing his little rabbit teeth.

Mr. Thompson felt he was being misunderstood. He turned around and motioned toward the open window back of the honeysuckle trellis. "Let's move off down here a little," he said. "I oughta thought of that before." His visitor bothered Mr. Thompson. He had a way of taking the words out of Mr. Thompson's mouth, turning them around and mixing them up until Mr. Thompson didn't know himself what he had said. "My wife's not very strong," said Mr. Thompson. "She's been kind of invalid now goin' on fourteen years. It's mighty tough on a poor man, havin' sickness in the family. She had four operations," he said proudly, "one right after the other, but they didn't do any good. For five years handrunnin', I just turned every nickel I made over to the doctors. Upshot is, she's a mighty delicate woman."

"My old woman," said Mr. Homer T. Hatch, "had a back like a mule, yes, sir. That woman could have moved the barn with her bare hands if she'd ever took the notion. I used to say, it was a good thing she didn't know her own stren'th. She's dead now, though. That kind wear out quicker than the puny ones. I never had much use for a woman always complainin'. I'd get rid of her mighty quick, yes, sir, mighty quick. It's just as you say: a dead loss, keepin' one of 'em up."

This was not at all what Mr. Thompson had heard himself say; he had been trying to explain that a wife as expensive as his was a credit to a man. "She's a mighty reasonable woman," said Mr. Thompson, feeling baffled, "but I wouldn't answer for what she'd say or do if she found out we'd had a lunatic on the place all this time." They had moved away from the window; Mr. Thompson took Mr. Hatch the front way, because if he went the back way they would have to pass Mr. Helton's shack. For some reason he didn't want the stranger to see or talk to Mr. Helton. It was strange but that was the way Mr. Thompson felt.

Mr. Thompson sat down again, on the chopping log, offering his guest another tree stump. "Now, I mighta got upset myself at such a thing, once," said Mr. Thompson, "but now I *deefy* anything to get me lathered up." He cut himself an enormous plug of tobacco with his horn-handled pocketknife, and offered it to Mr. Hatch, who then produced his own plug and, opening a huge bowie knife with a long blade sharply whetted, cut off a large wad and put it in his mouth. They then compared plugs and both of them were astonished to see how different men's ideas of good chewing tobacco were.

"Now, for instance," said Mr. Hatch, "mine is lighter colored. That's because, for one thing, there ain't any sweetenin' in this plug. I like it dry, natural leaf, medium strong."

"A little sweetenin' don't do no harm so far as I'm concerned," said Mr. Thompson, "but it's got to be mighty little. But with me, now, I want a strong leaf, I want it heavy-cured, as the feller says. There's a man near here, named Williams, Mr. John Morgan Williams, who chews a plug—well, sir, it's black as your hat and soft as melted tar. It fairly drips with molasses, jus' plain molasses, and it chews like licorice. Now, I don't call that a good chew."

"One man's meat," said Mr. Hatch, "is another man's poison. Now, such a chew would simply gag me. I couldn't begin to put it in my mouth."

"Well," said Mr. Thompson, a tinge of apology in his voice, "I jus' barely tasted it myself, you might say. Just took a little piece in my mouth and spit it out again."

"I'm dead sure I couldn't even get that far," said Mr. Hatch. "I like a dry natural chew without any artificial flavorin' of any kind."

Mr. Thompson began to feel that Mr. Hatch was trying to make out he had the best judgment in tobacco, and was going to keep up the argument until he proved it. He began to feel seriously annoyed with the fat man. After all, who was he and where did he come from? Who was he to go around telling other people what kind of tobacco to chew?

"Artificial flavorin'," Mr. Hatch went on, doggedly, "is jes put in to cover up a cheap leaf and make a man think he's gettin' somethin' more than he *is* gettin'. Even a little sweetenin' is a sign of a cheap leaf, you can mark my words."

"I've always paid a fair price for my plug," said Mr. Thompson, stiffly. "I'm not a rich man and I don't go round settin' myself up for one, but I'll say this, when it comes to such things as tobacco, I buy the best on the market."

"Sweetenin', even a little," began Mr. Hatch, shifting his plug and squirting tobacco juice at a dry-looking little rose bush that was having a hard enough time as it was, standing all day in the blazing sun, its roots clenched in the baked earth, "is the sign of—"

"About this Mr. Helton, now," said Mr. Thompson, determinedly, "I don't see no reason to hold it against a man because he went loony once or twice in his lifetime and so I don't expect to take no steps about it. Not a step. I've got nothin' against the man, he's always treated me fair. They's things and people," he went on, "'nough to drive any man loony. The wonder to me is, more men don't wind up in straitjackets, the way things are going these days and times."

"That's right," said Mr. Hatch, promptly, entirely too promptly, as if he were turning Mr. Thompson's meaning back on him. "You took the words right out of my mouth. There ain't every man in a straitjacket that ought to be there. Ha, ha, you're right all right. You got the idea."

Mr. Thompson sat silent and chewed steadily and stared at a spot on the ground about six feet away and felt a slow muffled resentment climbing from somewhere deep down in him, climbing and spreading all through him. What was this fellow driving at? What was he trying to say? It wasn't so much his words, but his looks and his way of talking: that droopy look in the eye, that tone of voice, as if he was trying to mortify Mr. Thompson about something. Mr. Thompson didn't like it, but he couldn't get hold of it either. He wanted to turn around and shove the fellow off the stump, but it wouldn't look reasonable. Suppose something happened to the fellow when he fell off the stump, just for instance, if he fell on the ax and cut himself, and then someone should ask Mr. Thompson why he shoved him, and what could a man say? It would look mighty funny, it would sound mighty strange to say, Well him and me fell out over a plug of tobacco. He might just shove him anyway and then tell people he was a fat man not used to the heat and while he was talking he got dizzy and fell off by himself, or something like that, and it wouldn't be the truth either, because it wasn't the heat and it wasn't the tobacco. Mr. Thompson made up his mind to get the fellow off the place pretty quick, without seeming to be anxious, and watch him sharp till he was out of sight. It doesn't pay to be friendly with strangers from another part of the country. They're always up to something, or they'd stay at home where they belong.

"And they's some people," said Mr. Hatch, "would jus' as soon have a loonatic around their house as not, they can't see no difference between them and anybody else. I always say, if that's the way a man feels, don't care who he associates with, why, why, that's his business, not mine. I don't wanta have a thing to do with it. Now back home in North Dakota, we don't feel that way. I'd like to a seen anybody hiring a loonatic there, aspecially after what he done."

"I didn't understand your home was North Dakota," said Mr. Thompson. "I thought you said Georgia."

"I've got a married sister in North Dakota," said Mr. Hatch, "married a Swede, but a white man if ever I saw one. So I say *we* because we got into a little business together out that way. And it seems like home, kind of."

"What did he do?" asked Mr. Thompson, feeling very uneasy again.

"Oh, nothin' to speak of," said Mr. Hatch, jovially, "jus' went loony one day in the hayfield and shoved a pitchfork right square through his brother, when they was makin' hay. They was goin' to execute him, but they found out he had went crazy with the heat, as the feller says, and so they put him in the asylum. That's all he done. Nothin' to get lathered up about, ha, ha, ha!" he said, and taking out his sharp knife he began to slice off a chew as carefully as if he were cutting cake.

"Well," said Mr. Thompson, "I don't deny that's news. Yes, sir, news. But I still say somethin' must have drove him to it. Some men make you feel like giving 'em a good killing just by lookin' at you. His brother may a been a mean ornery cuss."

"Brother was going to get married," said Mr. Hatch; "used to go courtin' his girl nights. Borrowed Mr. Helton's harmonica to give her a serenade one evenin', and lost it. Brand new harmonica."

"He thinks a heap of his harmonicas," said Mr. Thompson. "Only money he ever spends, now and then he buys hisself a new one. Must have a dozen in that shack, all kinds and sizes."

"Brother wouldn't buy him a new one," said Mr. Hatch, "so Mr. Helton just ups, as I says, and runs his pitchfork through his brother. Now you know he musta been crazy to get all worked up over a little thing like that."

"Sounds like it," said Mr. Thompson, reluctant to agree in anything with this intrusive and disagreeable fellow. He kept thinking he couldn't remember when he had taken such a dislike to a man on first sight.

"Seems to me you'd get pretty sick of hearin' the same tune year in, year out," said Mr. Hatch.

"Well, sometimes I think it wouldn't do no harm if he learned a new one," said Mr. Thompson, "but he don't, so there's nothin' to be done about it. It's a pretty good tune, though."

"One of the Scandahoovians told me what it meant, that's how I come to know," said Mr. Hatch. "Especially that part about getting so gay you jus' go ahead and drink up all the likker you got on hand before noon. It seems like up in them Swede countries a man carries a bottle of wine around with him as a matter of course, at least that's the way I understood it. Those fellers will tell you anything, though—" He broke off and spat.

The idea of drinking any kind of liquor in this heat made Mr. Thompson dizzy. The idea of anybody feeling good on a day like this, for instance, made him tired. He felt he was really suffering from the heat. The fat man looked as if he had grown to the stump; he slumped there in his damp, dark clothes too big for him, his belly slack in his pants, his wide black felt hat pushed off his narrow forehead red with prickly heat. A bottle of good cold beer, now, would be a help, thought Mr. Thompson, remembering the four bottles sitting deep in the pool at the springhouse, and his dry tongue squirmed in his mouth. He wasn't going to offer this man anything, though, not even a drop of water. He wasn't even going to chew any more tobacco with him. He shot out his quid suddenly, and wiped his mouth on the back of his hand, and studied the head near him attentively. The man was no good, and he was there for no good, but what was he up to? Mr. Thompson made up his mind he'd give him a little more time to get his business, whatever it was, with Mr. Helton over, and then if he didn't get off the place he'd kick him off.

Mr. Hatch, as if he suspected Mr. Thompson's thoughts, turned his eyes, wicked and pig-like, on Mr. Thompson. "Fact is," he said, as if he had made up his mind about something, "I might need your help in the little matter I've got on hand, but it won't cost you any trouble. Now, this Mr. Helton here, like I tell you, he's a dangerous escaped loonatic, you might say. Now fact is, in the last twelve years or so I musta rounded up twenty-odd escaped loonatics, besides a couple of escaped convicts that I just run into by accident, like. I don't make a business of it, but if there's a reward, and there usually is a reward, of course, I get it. It amounts to a tidy little sum in the long run, but that ain't the main question. Fact is, I'm for law and order, I don't like to see lawbreakers and loonatics at large. It ain't the place for them. Now I reckon you're bound to agree with me on that, aren't you?''

Mr. Thompson said, "Well, circumstances alters cases, as the feller says. Now, what I know of Mr. Helton, he ain't dangerous, as I told you." Something serious was going to happen, Mr. Thompson could see that. He stopped thinking about it. He'd just let this fellow shoot off his head and then see what could be done about it. Without thinking he got out his knife and plug and started to cut a chew, then remembered himself and put them back in his pocket.

"The law," said Mr. Hatch, "is solidly behind me. Now this Mr. Helton, he's been one of my toughest cases. He's kept my record from being practically one hundred per cent. I knew him before he went loony, and I know the fam'ly, so I undertook to help out rounding him up. Well, sir, he was gone slick as a whistle, for all we knew the man was as good as dead long while ago. Now we never might have caught up with him, but do you know what he did? Well, sir, about two weeks ago his old mother gets a letter from him, and in that letter, what do you reckon she found? Well, it was a check on that little bank in town for eight hundred and fifty dollars, just like that; the letter wasn't nothing much, just said he was sending her a few little savings, she might need something, but there it was, name, postmark, date, everything. The old woman practically lost her mind with joy. She's getting childish, and it looked like she kinda forgot that her only living son killed his brother and went loony. Mr. Helton said he was getting along all right, and for her not to tell nobody. Well, natchally, she couldn't keep it to herself, with that check to cash and everything. So that's how I come to know." His feelings got the better of him. "You coulda knocked me down with a feather." He shook hands with himself and rocked, wagged his head, going "Heh, heh," in his throat. Mr. Thompson felt the corners of his mouth turning down. Why, the dirty low-down hound, sneaking around spying into other people's business like that. Collecting blood money, that's what it was! Let him talk!

"Yea, well, that musta been a surprise all right," he said, trying to hold his voice even. "I'd say a surprise."

"Well, siree," said Mr. Hatch, "the more I got to thinking about it, the more I just come to the conclusion that I'd better look into the matter a little, and so I talked to the old woman. She's pretty decrepit, now, half blind and all, but she was all for taking the first train out and going to see her son. I put it up to her square—how she was too feeble for the trip, and all. So, just as a favor to her, I told her for my expenses I'd come down and see Mr. Helton and bring her back all the news about him. She gave me a new shirt she made herself by hand, and a big Swedish kind of cake to bring to him, but I musta mislaid them along the road somewhere. It don't reely matter, though, he prob'ly ain't in any state of mind to appreciate 'em."

Mr. Thompson sat up and turning around on the log looked at Mr. Hatch and asked as quietly as he could, "And now what are you aiming to do? That's the question."

Mr. Hatch slouched up to his feet and shook himself. "Well, I come all prepared for a little scuffle," he said. "I got the handcuffs," he said, "but I don't want no violence if I can help it. I didn't want to say nothing around the countryside, making an uproar. I figured the two of us could overpower him." He reached into his big inside pocket and pulled them out. Handcuffs, for God's sake, thought Mr. Thompson. Coming round on a peaceable afternoon worrying a man, and making trouble, and fishing handcuffs out of his pocket on a decent family homestead, as if it was all in the day's work.

Mr. Thompson, his head buzzing, got up too. "Well," he said, roundly, "I want to tell you I think you've got a mighty sorry job on hand, you sure must be hard up for something to do, and now I want to give you a good piece of advice. You just drop the idea that you're going to come here and make trouble for Mr. Helton, and the quicker you drive that hired rig away from my front gate the better I'll be satisfied."

Mr. Hatch put one handcuff in his outside pocket, the other dangling down. He pulled his hat down over his eyes, and reminded Mr. Thompson of a sheriff, somehow. He didn't seem in the least nervous, and didn't take up Mr. Thompson's words. He said, "Now listen just a minute, it ain't reasonable to suppose that a man like yourself is going to stand in the way of getting an escaped loonatic back to the asylum where he belongs. Now I know it's enough to throw you off, coming sudden like this, but fact is I counted on your being a respectable man and helping me out to see that justice is done. Now a course, if you won't help, I'll have to look around for help somewheres else. It won't look very good to your neighbors that you was harbring an escaped loonatic who killed his own brother, and then you refused to give him up. It will look mighty funny."

Mr. Thompson knew almost before he heard the words that it would look funny. It would put him in a mighty awkward position. He said, "But I've been trying to tell you all along that the man ain't loony now. He's been perfectly harmless for nine years. He's—he's—"

Mr. Thompson couldn't think how to describe how it was with Mr. Helton. "Why, he's been like one of the family," he said, "the best standby a man ever had." Mr. Thompson tried to see his way out. It was a fact Mr. Helton might go loony again any minute, and now this fellow talking around the country would put Mr. Thompson in a fix. It was a terrible position. He couldn't think of any way out. "You're crazy," Mr. Thompson roared suddenly, "you're the crazy one around here, you're crazier then he ever was! You get off this place or I'll handcuff you and turn you over to the law. You're trespassing," shouted Mr. Thompson. "Get out of here before I knock you down!"

He took a step towards the fat man, who backed off, shrinking, "Try it, try it, go ahead!" and then something happened that Mr. Thompson tried hard afterwards to piece together in his mind, and in fact it never did come straight. He saw the fat man with his long bowie knife in his hand, he saw Mr. Helton come round the corner on the run, his long jaw dropped, his arms swinging, his eyes wild. Mr. Helton came in between them, fists doubled up, then stopped short, glaring at the fat man, his big frame seemed to collapse, he trembled like a shied horse; and then the fat man drove at him, knife in one hand, handcuffs in the other. Mr. Thompson saw it coming, he saw the blade going into Mr. Helton's stomach, he knew he had the ax out of the log in his own hands, felt his arms go up over his head and bring the ax down on Mr. Hatch's head as if he were stunning a beef.

Mrs. Thompson had been listening uneasily for some time to the voices going on, one of them strange to her, but she was too tired at first to get up and come out to see what was going on. The confused shouting that rose so suddenly brought her up to her feet and out across the front porch without her slippers, hair half-braided. Shading her eyes, she saw first Mr. Helton, running all stooped over through the orchard, running like a man with dogs after him; and Mr. Thompson supporting himself on the ax handle was leaning over shaking by the shoulder a man Mrs. Thompson had never seen, who lay doubled up with the top of his head smashed and the blood running away in a greasy-looking puddle. Mr. Thompson without taking his hand from the man's shoulder, said in a thick voice, "He killed Mr. Helton, he killed him, I saw him do it. I had to knock him out," he called loudly, "but he won't come to."

Mrs. Thompson said in a faint scream, "Why, yonder goes Mr. Helton," and she pointed. Mr. Thompson pulled himself up and looked where she pointed. Mrs. Thompson sat down slowly against the side of the house and began to slide forward on her face; she felt as if she were drowning, she couldn't rise to the top somehow, and her only thought was she was glad the boys were not there, they were out, fishing at Halifax, oh, God, she was glad the boys were not there.

Mr. and Mrs. Thompson drove up to their barn about sunset. Mr. Thompson handed the reins to his wife, got out to open the big door, and Mrs. Thompson guided old Jim in under the roof. The buggy was gray with dust and age, Mrs. Thompson's face was gray with dust and weariness, and Mr. Thompson's face, as he stood at the horse's head and began unhitching, was gray except for the dark blue of his freshly shaven jaws and chin, gray and blue and caved in, but patient, like a dead man's face.

Mrs. Thompson stepped down to the hard packed manure of the barn floor, and shook out her light flower-sprigged dress. She wore her smoked glasses, and her wide shady leghorn hat with the wreath of exhausted pink and blue forget-me-nots hid her forehead, fixed in a knot of distress.

The horse hung his head, raised a huge sigh and flexed his stiffened legs. Mr. Thompson's words came up muffled and hollow. "Poor ole Jim," he said, clearing his throat, "he looks pretty sunk in the ribs. I guess he's had a hard week." He lifted the harness up in one piece, slid it off and Jim walked out of the shafts halting a little. "Well, this is the last time," Mr. Thompson said, still talking to Jim. "Now you can get a good rest."

Mrs. Thompson closed her eyes behind her smoked glasses. The last time, and high time, and they should never have gone at all. She did not need her glasses any more, now the good darkness was coming down again, but her eyes ran full of tears steadily, though she was not crying, and she felt better with the glasses, safer, hidden away behind them. She took out her handkerchief with her hands shaking as they had been shaking ever since *that day*, and blew her nose. She said, "I see the boys have lighted the lamps. I hope they've started the stove going."

She stepped along the rough path holding her thin dress and starched petticoats around her, feeling her way between the sharp small stones, leaving the barn because she could hardly bear to be near Mr. Thompson, advancing slowly towards the house because she dreaded going there. Life was all one dread, the faces of her neighbors, of her boys, of her husband, the face of the whole world, the shape of her own house in the darkness, the very smell of the grass and the trees were horrible to her. There was no place to go, only one thing to do, bear it somehow— but how? She asked herself that question often. How was she going to keep on living now? Why had she lived at all? She wished now she had died one of those times when she had been so sick, instead of living on for this.

The boys were in the kitchen: Herbert was looking at the funny pictures from last Sunday's newspapers, the Katzenjammer Kids and Happy Hooligan. His chin was in his hands and his elbows on the table, and he was really reading and looking at the pictures, but his face was unhappy. Arthur was building the fire, adding kindling a stick at a time, watching it catch and blaze. His face was heavier and darker than Herbert's, but he was a little sullen by nature; Mrs. Thompson thought, he takes things harder, too. Arthur said, "Hello, Momma," and went on with his work. Herbert swept the papers together and moved over on the bench. They were big boys—fifteen and seventeen, and Arthur as tall as his father. Mrs. Thompson sat down beside Herbert, taking off her hat. She said, "I guess you're hungry. We were late today. We went to Log Hollow road, it's rougher than ever." Her pale mouth drooped with a sad fold on either side.

"I guess you saw the Mannings, then," said Herbert.

"Yes, and the Fergusons, and the Allbrights, and that new family McClellan."

"Anybody say anything?" asked Herbert.

"Nothing much, you know how it's been all along, some of them keeps saying, yes, they know it was a clear case and a fair trial and they say how glad they are your papa came out so well, and all that, some of 'em do, anyhow, but it looks like they don't really take sides with him. I'm about wore out," she said, the tears rolling again from under her dark glasses. "I don't know what good it does, but your papa can't seem to rest unless he's telling how it happened. I don't know."

"I don't think it does any good, not a speck," said Arthur, moving away from the stove. "It just keeps the whole question stirred up in people's minds. Everybody will go round telling what he heard, and the whole thing is going to get worse mixed up than ever. It just makes matters worse. I wish you could get Papa to stop driving round the country talking like that."

"Your papa knows best," said Mrs. Thompson. "You oughtn't to criticize him. He's got enough to put up with without that."

Arthur said nothing, his jaw stubborn. Mr. Thompson came in, his eyes hollowed out and dead-looking, his thick hands gray white and seamed from washing them clean every day before he started out to see the neighbors to tell them his side of the story. He was wearing his Sunday clothes, a thick pepper-and-salt-colored suit with a black string tie.

Mrs. Thompson stood up, her head swimming. "Now you-all get out of the kitchen, it's too hot in here and I need room. I'll get us a little bite of supper, if you'll just get out and give me some room."

They went as if they were glad to go, the boys outside, Mr. Thompson into his bedroom. She heard him groaning to himself as he took off his shoes, and heard the bed creak as he lay down. Mrs. Thompson opened the icebox and felt the sweet coldness flow out of it; she had never expected to have an icebox, much less did she hope to afford to keep it filled with ice. It still seemed like a miracle, after two or three years. There was the food, cold and clean, all ready to be warmed over. She would never have had that icebox if Mr. Helton hadn't happened along one day, just by the strangest luck; so saving, and so managing, so good, thought Mrs. Thompson, her heart swelling until she feared she would faint again, standing there with the door open and leaning her head upon it. She simply could not bear to remember Mr. Helton, with his long sad face and silent ways, who had always been so quiet and harmless, who had worked so hard and helped Mr. Thompson so much, running through the hot fields and woods, being hunted like a mad dog, everybody turning out with ropes and guns and sticks to catch and tie him. Oh, God, said Mrs. Thompson in a long dry moan, kneeling before the icebox and fumbling inside for the dishes, even if they did pile mattresses all over the jail floor and against the walls, and five men there to hold him to keep him from hurting himself any more, he was already hurt too badly, he couldn't have lived anyway. Mr. Barbee, the sheriff, told her about it. He said, well, they didn't aim to harm him but they had to catch him, he was crazy as a loon; he picked up rocks and tried to brain every man that got near him. He had two harmonicas in his jumper pocket, said the sheriff, but they fell out in the scuffle, and

Mr. Helton tried to pick 'em up again, and that's when they finally got him. "They *had* to be rough, Miz Thompson, he fought like a wildcat." Yes, thought Mrs. Thompson again with the same bitterness, of course, they had to be rough. They always have to be rough. Mr. Thompson can't argue with a man and get him off the place peaceably; no, she thought, standing up and shutting the icebox, he has to kill somebody, he has to be a murderer and ruin his boys' lives and cause Mr. Helton to be killed like a mad dog.

Her thoughts stopped with a little soundless explosion, cleared and began again. The rest of Mr. Helton's harmonicas were still in the shack, his tune ran in Mrs. Thompson's head at certain times of the day. She missed it in the evenings. It seemed so strange she had never known the name of that song, nor what it meant, until after Mr. Helton was gone. Mrs. Thompson, trembling in the knees, took a drink of water at the sink and poured the red beans into the baking dish, and began to roll the pieces of chicken in flour to fry them. There was a time, she said to herself, when I thought I had neighbors and friends, there was a time when we could hold up our heads, there was a time when my husband hadn't killed a man and I could tell the truth to anybody about anything.

Mr. Thompson, turning on his bed, figured that he had done all he could, he'd just try to let the matter rest from now on. His lawyer, Mr. Burleigh, had told him right at the beginning, "Now you keep calm and collected. You've got a fine case, even if you haven't got witnesses. Your wife must sit in court, she'll be a powerful argument with the jury. You just plead not guilty and I'll do the rest. The trial is going to be a mere formality, you haven't got a thing to worry about. You'll be clean out of this before you know it." And to make talk Mr. Burleigh had got to telling about all the men he knew around the country who for one reason or another had been forced to kill somebody, always in self-defense, and there just wasn't anything to it at all. He even told about how his own father in the old days had shot and killed a man just for setting foot inside his gate when he told him not to. "Sure, I shot the scoundrel," said Mr. Burleigh's father, "in self-defense; I *told* him I'd shoot him if he set his foot in my yard, and he did, and I did." There had been bad blood between them for years, Mr. Burleigh said, and his father had waited a long time to catch the other fellow in the wrong, and when he did he certainly made the most of his opportunity.

"But Mr. Hatch, as I told you," Mr. Thompson had said, "made a pass at Mr. Helton with his bowie knife. That's why I took a hand."

"All the better," said Mr. Burleigh. "That stranger hadn't any right coming to your house on such an errand. Why, hell," said Mr. Burleigh, "that wasn't even manslaughter you committed. So now you just hold your horses and keep your shirt on. And don't say one word without I tell you."

Wasn't even manslaughter. Mr. Thompson had to cover Mr. Hatch with a piece of wagon canvas and ride to town to tell the sheriff. It had been hard on Ellie. When they got back, the sheriff and the coroner and two deputies, they found her sitting beside the road, on a low bridge over a gulley, about half a mile from the place. He had taken her up behind his saddle and got her back to the house. He had already told the sheriff that his wife had witnessed the whole business, and now he had time, getting her to her room and in bed, to tell her what to say if they asked anything. He had left out the part about Mr. Helton being crazy all along, but it came out at the trial. By Mr. Burleigh's advice Mr. Thompson had pretended to be perfectly ignorant; Mr. Hatch hadn't said a word about that. Mr. Thompson pretended to believe that Mr. Hatch had just come looking for Mr. Helton to settle old scores, and the two members of Mr. Hatch's family who had come down to try to get Mr. Thompson convicted didn't get anywhere at all. It hadn't been much of a trial, Mr. Burleigh saw to that. He had charged a reasonable fee, and Mr. Thompson had paid him and felt grateful, but after it was over Mr. Burleigh didn't seem pleased to see him when he got to dropping into the office to talk it over, telling him things that had slipped his mind at first: trying to explain what an ornery low hound Mr. Hatch had been, anyhow. Mr. Burleigh seemed to have lost his interest; he looked sour and upset when he saw Mr. Thompson at the door. Mr. Thompson kept saying to himself that he'd got off, all right, just as Mr. Burleigh had predicted, but, but—and it was right there that Mr. Thompson's mind stuck, squirming like an angleworm on a fishhook: he had killed Mr. Hatch, and he was a murderer. That was the truth about himself that Mr. Thompson couldn't grasp, even when he said the word to himself. Why, he had not even once *thought* of killing anybody, much less Mr. Hatch, and if Mr. Helton hadn't come out so unexpectedly, hearing the row, why, then—but then, Mr. Helton had come on the run that way to help him. What he couldn't understand was what happened next. He had seen Mr. Hatch go after Mr. Helton with the knife, he had seen the point, blade up, go into Mr. Helton's stomach and slice up like you slice a hog, but when they finally caught Mr. Helton there wasn't a knife scratch on him. Mr. Thompson knew he had the ax in his own hands and felt himself lifting it, but he couldn't remember hitting Mr. Hatch. He couldn't remember it. He couldn't. He remembered only that he had been determined to stop Mr. Hatch from cutting Mr. Helton. If he was given a chance he could explain the whole matter. At the trial they hadn't let him talk. They just asked questions and he answered yes or no, and they never did get to the core of the matter. Since the trial, now, every day for a week he had washed and shaved and put on his best clothes and had taken Ellie with him to tell every neighbor he had that he never killed Mr. Hatch on purpose, and what good did it do? Nobody believed him. Even when he turned to Ellie and said, "You was there, you saw it, didn't you?" and Ellie spoke up saying, "Yes, that's the truth. Mr. Thompson was trying to save Mr. Helton's life," and he added, "If you don't believe me, you can believe my wife. She won't lie," Mr. Thompson saw something in all their faces that disheartened him, made him feel empty and tired out. They didn't believe he was not a murderer.

Even Ellie never said anything to comfort him. He hoped she would say finally, "I remember now, Mr. Thompson, I really did come round the corner in time to see everything. It's not a lie, Mr. Thompson. Don't you worry." But as they drove together in silence, with the days still hot and dry, shortening for fall, day after day, the buggy jolting in the ruts, she said nothing; they grew to dread the sight of another house, and the people in it: all houses looked alike now, and the people—old neighbors or new—had the same expression when Mr. Thompson told them why he had come and began his story. Their eyes looked as if someone had pinched the eyeball at the back; they shriveled and the light went out of them. Some of them sat with fixed tight smiles trying to be friendly. "Yes, Mr. Thompson, we know how you must feel. It must be terrible for you, Mrs. Thompson. Yes, you know, I've about come to the point where I believe in such a thing as killing in self-defense. Why, certainly, we believe you, Mr. Thompson, why shouldn't we believe you? Didn't you have a perfectly fair and above-board trial? Well, now, natchally, Mr. Thompson, we think you done right."

Mr. Thompson was satisfied they didn't think so. Sometimes the air around him was so thick with their blame he fought and pushed with his fists, and the sweat broke out all over him, he shouted his story in a dust-choked voice, he would fairly bellow at last: "My wife, here, you know her, she was there, she saw and heard it all, if you don't believe me, ask her, she won't lie!" and Mrs. Thompson, with her hands knotted together, aching, her chin trembling, would never fail to say: "Yes, that's right, that's the truth—"

The last straw had been laid on today, Mr. Thompson decided. Tom Allbright, an old beau of Ellie's, why, he had squired Ellie around a whole summer, had come out to meet them when they drove up, and standing there bareheaded had stopped them from getting out. He had looked past them with an embarrassed frown on his face, telling them his wife's sister was there with a raft of young ones, and the house was pretty full and everything upset, or he'd ask them to come in. "We've been thinking of trying to get up to your place one of these days," said Mr. Allbright, moving away trying to look busy, "we've been mighty occupied up here of late." So they had to say, "Well, we just happened to be driving this way," and go on. "The Allbrights," said Mrs. Thompson, "always was fair-weather friends." "They look out for number one, that's a fact," said Mr. Thompson. But it was cold comfort to them both.

Finally Mrs. Thompson had given up. "Let's go home," she said. "Old Jim's tired and thirsty, and we've gone far enough."

Mr. Thompson said, "Well, while we're out this way, we might as well stop at the McClellans'." They drove in, and asked a little cotton-haired boy if his mamma and papa were at home. Mr. Thompson wanted to see them. The little boy stood gazing with his mouth open, then galloped into the house shouting, "Mommer, Popper, come out hyah. That man that kilt Mr. Hatch has come ter see yer!"

The man came out in his sock feet, with one gallus up, the other broken and dangling, and said, "Light down, Mr. Thompson, and come in. The ole woman's washing, but she'll git here." Mrs. Thompson, feeling her way, stepped down and sat in a broken rocking-chair on the porch that sagged under her feet. The woman of the house, barefooted, in a calico wrapper, sat on the edge of the porch, her fat sallow face full of curiosity. Mr. Thompson began, "Well, as I reckon you happen to know, I've had some strange troubles lately, and, as the feller says, it's not the kind of troubles that happens to a man every day in the year, and there's some things I don't want no misunderstanding about in the neighbors' minds, so—" He halted and stumbled forward, and the two listening faces took on a mean look, a greedy, despising look, a look that said plain as day, "My, you must be a purty sorry feller to come round worrying about what *we* think, *we* know you wouldn't be here if you had anybody else to turn to—my, I wouldn't lower myself that much, myself." Mr. Thompson was ashamed of himself, he was suddenly in a rage, he'd like to knock their dirty skunk heads together, the low-down white trash—but he held himself down and went on to the end. "My wife will tell you," he said, and this was the hardest place, because Ellie always without moving a muscle seemed to stiffen as if somebody had threatened to hit her; "ask my wife, she won't lie."

"It's true, I saw it—"

"Well, now," said the man, drily, scratching his ribs inside his shirt, "that sholy is too bad. Well, now, I kaint see what we've got to do with all this here, however. I kaint see no good reason for us to git mixed up in these murder matters, I shore kaint. Whichever way you look at it, it ain't none of my business. However, it's mighty nice of you-all to come around and give us the straight of it, fur we've heerd some mighty queer yarns about it, mighty queer, I golly you couldn't hardly make head ner tail of it."

"Evvybody goin' round shootin' they heads off," said the woman. "Now we don't hold with killin'; the Bible says—"

"Shet yer trap," said the man, "and keep it shet 'r I'll shet it fer yer. Now it shore looks like to me—"

"We mustn't linger," said Mrs. Thompson, unclasping her hands. "We've lingered too long now. It's getting late, and we've far to go." Mr. Thompson took the hint and followed her. The man and the woman lolled against their rickety porch poles and watched them go.

Now lying on his bed, Mr. Thompson knew the end had come. Now, this minute, lying in the bed where he had slept with Ellie for eighteen years; under this roof where he had laid the shingles when he was waiting to get married; there as he was with his whiskers already sprouting since his shave that morning; with his fingers feeling his bony chin, Mr. Thompson felt he was a dead man. He was dead to his other life, he had got to the end of something without knowing why, and he had to make a fresh start, he did not know how. Something different was going to begin, he didn't know what. It was in some way not his business. He didn't feel he was going to have much to do with it. He got up, aching, hollow, and went out to the kitchen where Mrs. Thompson was just taking up the supper.

"Call the boys," said Mrs. Thompson. They had been down to the barn, and Arthur put out the lantern before hanging it on a nail near the door. Mr. Thompson didn't like their silence. They had hardly said a word about anything to him since that day. They seemed to avoid him, they ran the place together as if he wasn't there, and attended to everything without asking him for any advice. "What you boys been up to?" he asked, trying to be hearty. "Finishing your chores?"

"No, sir," said Arthur, "there ain't much to do. Just greasing some axles." Herbert said nothing. Mrs. Thompson bowed her head: "For these and all Thy blessings. . . . Amen," she whispered weakly, and the Thompsons sat there with their eyes down and their faces sorrowful, as if they were at a funeral.

Every time he shut his eyes, trying to sleep, Mr. Thompson's mind started up and began to run like a rabbit. It jumped from one thing to another, trying to pick up a trail here or there that would straighten out what had happened that day he killed Mr. Hatch. Try as he might, Mr. Thompson's mind would not go anywhere that it had not already been, he could not see anything but what he had seen once, and he knew that was not right. If he had not seen straight that first time, then everything about his killing Mr. Hatch was wrong from start to finish, and there was nothing more to be done about it, he might just as well give up. It still seemed to him that he had done, maybe not the right thing, but the only thing he could do, that day, but had he? *Did he have to kill Mr. Hatch?* He had never seen a man he hated more, the minute he laid eyes on him. He knew in his bones the fellow was there for trouble. What seemed so funny now was this: Why hadn't he just told Mr. Hatch to get out before he ever even got in?

Mrs. Thompson, her arms crossed on her breast, was lying beside him, perfectly still, but she seemed awake, somehow. "Asleep, Ellie?"

After all, he might have got rid of him peaceably, or maybe he might have had to overpower him and put those handcuffs on him and turn him over to the sheriff for disturbing the peace. The most they could have done was to lock Mr. Hatch up while he cooled off for a few days, or fine him a little something. He would try to think of things he might have said to Mr. Hatch. Why, let's see, I could just have said, Now look here, Mr. Hatch, I want to talk to you as man to man. But his brain would go empty. What could he have said or done? But if he *could* have done anything else almost except kill Mr. Hatch, then nothing would have happened to Mr. Helton. Mr. Thompson hardly ever thought of Mr. Helton. His mind just skipped over him and went on. If he stopped to think about Mr. Helton he'd never in God's world get anywhere. He tried to imagine how it might all have been, this very night even, if Mr. Helton were still safe and sound out in his shack playing his tune about feeling so good in the morning, drinking up all the wine so you'd feel even better; and Mr. Hatch safe in jail somewhere, mad as hops, maybe, but out of harm's way and ready to listen to reason and to repent of his meanness, the dirty, yellow-livered hound coming around persecuting an innocent man and ruining a whole family that never harmed him! Mr. Thompson felt the veins of his forehead start up, his fists clutched as if they seized an ax handle, the sweat broke out on him, he bounded up from the bed with a yell smothered in his throat, and Ellie started up after him, crying out, "Oh, oh, don't! Don't! Don't!" as if she were having a nightmare. He stood shaking until his bones rattled in him, crying hoarsely, "Light the lamp, light the lamp, Ellie."

Instead, Mrs. Thompson gave a shrill weak scream, almost the same scream he had heard on that day she came around the house when he was standing there with the ax in his hand. He could not see her in the dark, but she was on the bed, rolling violently. He felt for her in horror, and his groping hands found her arms, up, and her own hands pulling her hair straight out from her head, her neck strained back, and the tight screams strangling her. He shouted out for Arthur, for Herbert. "Your mother!" he bawled, his voice cracking. As he held Mrs. Thompson's arms, the boys came tumbling in, Arthur with the lamp above his head. By this light Mr. Thompson saw Mrs. Thompson's eyes, wide open, staring dreadfully at him, the tears pouring. She sat up at sight of the boys, and held out one arm towards them, the hand wagging in a crazy circle, then dropped on her back again, and suddenly went limp. Arthur set the lamp on the table and turned on Mr. Thompson. "She's scared," he said, "she's scared to death." His face was in a knot of rage, his fists were doubled up, he faced his father as if he meant to strike him. Mr. Thompson's jaw fell, he was so surprised he stepped back from the bed. Herbert went to the other side. They stood on each side of Mrs. Thompson and watched Mr. Thompson as if he were a dangerous wild beast. "What did you do to her?" shouted Arthur, in a grown man's voice. "You touch her again and I'll blow your heart out!" Herbert was pale and his cheek twitched, but he was on Arthur's side; he would do what he could to help Arthur.

Mr. Thompson had no fight left in him. His knees bent as he stood, his chest collapsed. "Why, Arthur," he said, his words crumbling and his breath coming short. "She's fainted again. Get the ammonia." Arthur did not move. Herbert brought the bottle, and handed it, shrinking, to his father.

Mr. Thompson held it under Mrs. Thompson's nose. He poured a little in the palm of his hand and rubbed it on her forehead. She gasped and opened her eyes and turned her head away from him. Herbert began a doleful hopeless sniffling. "Mamma," he kept saying, "Mamma, don't die."

"I'm all right," Mrs. Thompson said. "Now don't you worry around. Now Herbert, you mustn't do that. I'm all right." She closed her eyes. Mr. Thompson began pulling on his best pants; he put on his socks and shoes. The boys sat on each side of the bed, watching Mrs. Thompson's face. Mr. Thompson put on his shirt and coat. He said, "I reckon I'll ride over and get the doctor. Don't look like all this fainting is a good sign. Now you just keep watch until I get back." They listened, but said nothing. He said, "Don't you get any notions in your head. I never did your mother any harm in my life, on purpose." He went out, and, looking back, saw Herbert staring at him from under his brows, like a stranger. "You'll know how to look after her," said Mr. Thompson.

Mr. Thompson went through the kitchen. There he lighted the lantern, took a thin pad of scratch paper and a stub pencil from the shelf where the boys kept their schoolbooks. He swung the lantern on his arm and reached into the cupboard where he kept the guns. The shotgun was there to his hand, primed and ready, a man never knows when he may need a shotgun. He went out of the house without looking around, or looking back when he had left it, passed his barn without seeing it, and struck out to the farthest end of his fields, which ran for half a mile to the east. So many blows had been struck at Mr. Thompson and from so many directions he couldn't stop any more to find out where he was hit. He walked on, over plowed ground and over meadow, going through barbed wire fences cautiously, putting his gun through first; he could almost see in the dark, now his eyes were used to it. Finally he came to the last fence; here he sat down, back against a post, lantern at his side, and, with the pad on his knee, moistened the stub pencil and began to write:

"Before Almighty God, the great judge of all before who I am about to appear, I do hereby solemnly swear that I did not take the life of Mr. Homer T. Hatch on purpose. It was done in defense of Mr. Helton. I did not aim to hit him with the ax but only to keep him off Mr. Helton. He aimed a blow at Mr. Helton who was not looking for it. It was my belief at the time that Mr. Hatch would of taken the life of Mr. Helton if I did not interfere. I have told all this to the judge and the jury and they let me off but nobody believes it. This is the only way I can prove I am not a cold blooded murderer like everybody seems to think. If I had been in Mr. Helton's place he would have done the same for me. I still think I done the only thing there was to do. My wife—"

Mr. Thompson stopped here to think a while. He wet the pencil point with the tip of his tongue and marked out the last two words. He sat a while blacking out the words until he had made a neat oblong patch where they had been, and started again:

"It was Mr. Homer T. Hatch who came to do wrong to a harmless man. He caused all this trouble and he deserved to die but I am sorry it was me who had to kill him."

He licked the point of his pencil again, and signed his full name carefully, folded the paper and put it in his outside pocket. Taking off his right shoe and sock, he set the butt of the shotgun along the ground with the twin barrels pointed towards his head. It was very awkward. He thought about this a little, leaning his head aginst the gun mouth. He was trembling and his head was drumming until he was deaf and blind, but he lay down flat on the earth on his side, drew the barrel under his chin and fumbled for the trigger with his great toe. That way he could work it.

## FOR DISCUSSION

1. From what point of view is *Noon Wine* told? Is the narrator submerged within any one character? Do you notice any shifts?
2. What does setting contribute to the story? Remember that setting includes time, location, and the spiritual condition of all important characters.
3. What is the precipitating incident?
4. Who is the protagonist? What types of forces does the protagonist struggle against?
5. What does Mr. Thompson's early handling of the churn suggest about his ability as a farmer? What does it suggest about his disposition?
6. What purpose do you think is served by having Mr. Thompson's speech so sprinkled with clichés?
7. What do Olaf Helton's harmonicas represent—or symbolize—about the man's character? Why does he always play the same tune? What is the significance of the tune?
8. From almost the beginning of the novella, what seems to be Mrs. Thompson's knowledge of and experience with men? From their private conversations, how well would you say Mr. and Mrs. Thompson really know each other? Are they a close and affectionate husband and wife?
9. Contrast Mr. and Mrs. Thompson's styles in raising children. What do the differences suggest about the psychological stability of Mr. Thompson? Why does Mr. Thompson possess such an apparent dislike for his two sons, particularly when they are quite young? Why does he always want to smash them for minor misdeeds?
10. In what ways is the passage of time emphasized in the story? How long does Olaf work on the Thompson farm?
11. What is ironic about the way Hatch has learned the whereabouts of Olaf after so many years?
12. Detail the events of the novella's climactic scene.
13. Why does Mr. Thompson kill Hatch? Did Hatch really go for Olaf with a knife? Did Mr. Thompson think about killing Hatch before the killing occurred?
14. Can you assign any symbolic value to Mrs. Thompson's smoked glasses, or to the fact that she prefers evening and night to the bright of day?
15. Why do the people of the community want nothing to do with Mr. Thompson even after he has been legally acquitted of any wrong-doing?
16. What did Mr. Thompson lie about at the trial? Why did he lie? Why did he force Mrs. Thompson to participate in the lie?
17. What are the psychological effects of Thompson's act on himself and Mrs. Thompson? Are they foreshadowed, or did they surprise you?

18. Do you think Mr. Thompson's suicide will eventually clear his good name in the community?
19. Thematically, *Noon Wine* centers on whether Mr. Thompson's destruction results from circumstances beyond his control or from a series of bad decisions he himself has made. Which do you believe is the case?

# PART III *The Drama*

# Introduction

Like storytelling, playacting goes as far back into the history of human civilization as our written records will take us. Virtually every society has had some form of dramatic theater—that is, a stage upon which stories were acted out before an audience. Early drama developed out of local or tribal religious ceremonies, fertility rites, choral hymns of praise for fallen heroes, or the basic human impulse to act out and share in the retelling of a good story. The great tragedies and comedies of ancient Greece were first performed at the festivals of Dionysus, the god of wine and revelry, and during the middle ages well-known stories from the Old and New Testaments were dramatized and performed in churchyards. But even in the early days, dramatic theater was not a pious rite; rather, it was a popular and sometimes rowdy entertainment that soon moved away from the temples and churches to its own special places.

## Drama on the Stage

The drama is a unique type of literary art in that it is composed mainly to be acted in public, and only secondarily to be read and reflected upon in private. For example, Shakespeare seems never to have had any of his own plays published, though he did publish his poems. The great First Folio edition of Shakespeare's plays appeared years after the dramatist's death. Even today, new plays are usually performed before they are published. And in some modern dramatic forms—the movies and television, for example—the actual playscript or scenario may never be published at all. The words exist only as part of a dramatic production.

What happens to a play when it is produced in the theater, or for movies or television? What we see is a group of actors impersonating other people, within a setting and under lights. Nearly everything the actors do or say has been practiced many times in rehearsal under the guidance of a director, who has helped them understand the motivation behind each act and speech, explained the meaning of obscure parts of the play when necessary, and often told them exactly when, where, and how to move. The director has also worked with a designer or designers who chose or created the scenery, costumes, and lighting. All of these people, and the rest of the production staff as well, were hired by the producer, usually in conjunction with the director. The producer supervises the entire operation from beginning to end, and also raises the large amount of money to get a play, or a movie or television show, ready for its first audiences.

What about the playwright? If he is Sophocles or Shakespeare or Oscar Wilde, of course, he has no say in a modern production. Modern playwrights, while they are often on hand the first time a play is produced, seldom have much authority—unless the director chooses to share it. Many times the playwright will be asked to make cuts, rewrite lines or entire speeches, and sometimes even to add a new scene—all for greater theatrical effectiveness. Oscar Wilde reduced *The Importance of Being Earnest* from its original four acts to three at the request of his director, and Shakespeare's most popular plays appear to have been drastically cut when taken on tour by the acting company for which he wrote them and of which he was a member. Even today, classic plays like *Othello* are almost always cut when they are performed. This is done to spare the endurance of modern audiences and actors, and sometimes to focus the play's meaning in a particular way.

What does all this have to do with reading a play? First, it shows that unlike stories and poems, plays are written with active, creative collaboration in mind. Except at the beginnings of scenes—and often not even then—the playwright offers very little description and explanation beyond what the characters say and do, and often barely sketches in what they do. As a result, when you read a play you can be your own director and designer. You can even cast the actors as you please.

For example, Shakespeare's *Othello* contains very little descriptive information about how the characters look and dress or the settings within which they move. The first scene is announced simply as "Venice. A Street." That is not much to go on, but later in the scene Roderigo gives us a little more information, while actually speaking to Iago: "Here is her father's house." A few lines later there is a stage direction: "(Enter Brabantio, above, at a window.)" Iago shortly tells Brabantio to "Awake the snorting [i.e., snoring] citizens"—so we know that it is nighttime; toward the end of the scene Brabantio enters below, attended by servants carrying torches. But we still don't know what the house looks like, or anything about the appearance of the characters. Small wonder, then, that different productions of *Othello* may look quite different from one another. Nevertheless, Shakespeare has told us enough so that we can conjure up an image of the scene. We can even tell that the conversation between Roderigo and Iago, with which the play begins, has actually been going on for some time before the curtain rises; in the first line Roderigo cuts off some explanation from Iago with the impatient words, "Tush! Never tell me."

If, in respect to descriptive detail, plays leave much to the reader's imagination, there are other ways in which they are easier to read than stories or poems. Since there is no way during a performance for theatergoers to turn back a few pages and reread a passage, playwrights construct their plays to make such reference unnecessary. Plot and character are made very clear very quickly. And since most of the play consists of dialogue, rather than description or narration, the work tends to be less complex in terms of syntax and vocabulary than is the case in many poems and stories. Verse dramas are the one great exception to this—especially Shakespeare's, which are written in the English of some four hundred years ago. Many of the words have since changed in meaning, and many others are now rarely used at all. When these plays were new, however, they were very popular, a fact suggesting that sixteenth-century theatergoers didn't find them difficult to understand.

In general, it is fair to say that plays can be read and enjoyed purely as literary works. This is true because plays include many of the same elements found in short stories and novellas. For example, a play has a plot consisting of a series of actions, takes place within a specific period of time and within specified physical locations, and dramatizes the personalities of a group of characters interacting with one another. The playwright's tone—his or her attitude toward the work, including its subject and characters—will help produce an overall mood or atmosphere, which will in turn evoke an emotional response from the reader. Verbal irony, dramatic irony, and irony of plot are as important in a play as they are in any work of prose fiction. In many plays, symbols are used in more obvious ways than in short fiction, often appearing as images, actions, or objects that dominate key scenes. As often as not, at some point in a play a major character will articulate the work's basic thematic concerns.

# Plot

Despite an almost infinite variety of individual differences, most plays follow a similar five-part structural pattern that is very much like the structure of a short story. The first part, called the **exposition,** sets forth the dramatic situation as it exists at the beginning of the play. The exposition introduces the characters, reveals the relationships among them, details the background information needed to understand the play's basic conflicts, and moves the play forward toward its central struggle, whether that struggle be tragic, comic, social, or a combination of the three.

The second part of a play is called the **rising action** or, sometimes, the **complication.** This part consists of a sequence of events that complicates the original situation and heightens the conflicts among the major characters. As with the short story, when conflict is intensified to a level that cannot be long endured, the play reaches that part of rising action called the **crisis situation.**

The third important part of a play is the **climax,** also called the **turning point.** Often the climax will involve the protagonist's doing something that can never be undone, discovering some important truth, or making a decision or commitment that ultimately leads to success or disaster, depending on the kind of play. In some plays the climax will occur a little beyond the halfway point, but in others—especially modern plays—it may be pushed to very near the end.

The **falling action** follows the climax and concerns itself with the unwinding or unraveling of the complications set up during the rising action, and leads to the final part of the play, which may be called the **conclusion,** the **resolution,** or the **denouement.** If the play is a tragedy, the resolution may include a **catastrophe,** which usually involves the death of the hero. If the play is a comedy, the resolution will likely include a final twist that makes everything turn out happily after all. In any event, the denouement brings about a more stable situation at the end of the drama than that which existed at the beginning.

# Types of Drama

For convenience, we can place plays of all lengths into five broad categories: tragedy, comedy, melodrama, social drama, and fantasy. It must be understood, however, that many plays do not fit precisely into one particular category. For example, there are such dramatic "mixtures" as tragicomedies, melodramatic tragedies, and social fantasies. Nevertheless, a fairly precise definition of each of these five basic classifications is worth keeping in mind as you acquaint yourself with the drama.

## Tragedy

A **tragedy** is traditionally defined as a serious play written under the assumption that an absolute order of right and wrong exists in the universe and transcends individual human beings, who must obey it or pay a heavy price for disobeying it, whether or not they know about their disobedience. Among the classical Greek tragedians—Aeschylus, Sophocles, and Euripides—this order is governed by fate. Among the Elizabethans of Shakespeare's day, the order features a rigidly structured cosmos in which an individual's social or political role in life is determined by forces beyond his or her control. Both concepts, and others as well, are still alive in modern drama.

A classical tragedy typically features an individual of high position and importance who violates the cosmic order of right and wrong assumed in the play. Often this transgression is a result of **hubris,** a sort of aggressive insolence or arrogance arising from excessive pride or passion and causing the tragic hero to ignore or disregard that absolute order. From this mistake follow all of the tragic events of the drama. Even though a tragic hero may not always be guilty of hubris, he or she will possess some weakness or frailty of character that ultimately leads to his or her downfall.

Many carefully plotted tragedies include a **reversal,** which is often closely associated with the play's climax or turning point. The reversal is the point at which the hero's fortunes change from good to bad, most often as a direct result of his transgression against the play's system of values. The catastrophe at the play's end will frequently be softened by some sort of dramatic **recognition**—that is, the tragic hero achieves some insight into or understanding of the reasons for his downfall. In *Oedipus Rex* Oedipus discovers that he has killed his father and married his mother, and that he was fated to do these things. When such recognition occurs, it helps soften the impact of the misfortune.

Although classical tragedy is a serious and sometimes solemn dramatic form, the audience is seldom left in a state of depression at the conclusion of the play. As the Greek critic Aristotle pointed out, the tensions built up during the early parts of the performance are usually released as a result of an emotional response to the not-altogether deserved suffering of the tragic hero. A sort of purgation of fear and pity, resulting in an emotional cleansing, is often experienced by theatergoers as a result of having vicariously participated in what the characters in the play have endured. This is called **catharsis.** And as a result of catharsis audiences more often than not leave the performance of a tragedy with a sense of relief rather than feelings of tension or sadness.

Modern tragedies often depart from one or more of the elements of classical tragedy. For example, the central figure may be neither of high position nor arrogant. The order that he or she violates may be presented not as a universal moral order but as a local situation—perhaps an evil— in which case the play may be less a tragedy than a social drama. But the key elements—of a central character whose fortunes change for the worse and who is destroyed at the end—have remained the same.

## Comedy

The word **comedy** is derived from the Greek word *komoidia*, meaning a revel-song. Ancient Greek comedies had their origin in primitive fertility rituals, and they dramatize the joy of life triumphing over death or other obstacles that block the forces of life. Classical comedies, then, are full of high spirits and optimism. Often, in addition to provoking smiles or laughter, comedies dramatize the basic absurdities of life, especially the absurdities resulting when life is taken too seriously. Plays that take a satirical or farcical view of human nature, or that merely end happily, may all be thought of as variations of dramatic comedy.

The comic hero, in contrast with the tragic hero, is more likely to be viewed by theatergoers as "one of us." He quite often possesses various foibles, quirks, and shortcomings that we all recognize in our own personalities. While the comic hero may be knocked about by fate or accident, he tends to get tangled up in humorous situations rather than mortal ones. Furthermore, when the comic hero's fortunes change, they change from bad to good, and society—at least that part of society shown in the play—rewards him instead of casting him out as it casts out King Oedipus. Whereas theatergoers may experience a more intense emotional response to what befalls a tragic hero, they are far more likely to identify with a comic hero.

The great majority of all dramatic comedies can be placed in one of two general categories: romantic comedies and satiric comedies. **Romantic comedies** tend to take place in an idealized world of young love and stable social conditions. More often than not, the greatest complications of plot involve matching the right young man with the right young woman. **Satiric comedies,** on the other hand, are often intended to mock human behavior, and their humor may be grimly pessimistic or even bitter—anything but lighthearted. When a satiric comedy goes so far as to suggest the need for or even to advocate social reform, it has moved into the realm of dramatic theater we have called social drama.

## Melodrama

The term melodrama means, literally, "a play with music." As a specific type of dramatic theater, the melodrama became popular in the nineteenth century, just as great numbers of ordinary people—as a result of improved social and economic conditions—found themselves with free time on their hands and money to spend for entertainment. Thomas

Holcroft's *A Tale of Mystery* (1802) is believed to have been the very first English melodrama.

A **melodrama** is a play with a romantic plot that is sensationally developed to keep the audience at the highest peak of emotion from beginning to end. Almost without exception, a melodrama pits the blackest evil against the purest good, with much bombastic dialogue and exciting action thrown in to exaggerate the contrast between these two qualities. The melodramatic hero represents virtue, while the villain personifies vice. Since the whole point of such a production is to thrill the audience, little attention is paid to character motivation and plausibility. Stock characters are part of the stock in trade of melodrama. In its most blatant form, the melodrama is a play with black-caped villains, romantic young nobles who inhabit brooding castles with secret passageways, fainting maidens, breathtaking escapes, stilted moralizing, and surprise endings.

The James Bond movies, for all their cinematic polish, are contemporary melodramas. In fact, a great deal of popular entertainment, especially television drama, has much in common with melodrama. This is natural enough; there are times, many times, when we prefer simple entertainment to an intellectual challenge. And besides, perhaps down deep we are all a little corny.

## Social Drama

**Social drama** focuses upon some sociological truth, incongruity, injustice, or problem. It emerged as a distinct dramatic form in the late nineteenth century and has tended to dominate serious drama ever since. In social drama, society rather than the individual receives the main focus. While the social play, like the tragedy, may portray a heroic character experiencing some internal struggle or conflict, that conflict will most likely originate in some social dislocation that has greatly affected the character's life and personality. Likewise, this character will be "heroic" only because the struggle is intense or protracted, not because he or she possesses qualities above the average.

The social, economic, and political forces in a society, and the tensions they create, are at the heart of social plays. Such plays try to lead audiences to an understanding of these forces, often with the aim of provoking social change. Thus, the modern theater has often become a pulpit from which social dramatists preach against economic oppression, racial prejudice, excessive governmental power, sexism, and the like by showing how these forces affect the lives of dramatic characters. A social play that focuses on a single major problem in society is called a **problem play,** and a social play that tries to preach a particular political or economic doctrine is called a **propaganda play.**

# Fantasy

Plays in our final category, **fantasy,** present worlds that are intentionally unrealistic and sometimes nonsensical. Often dramatic fantasies depict events that could not happen in the real world—like people turning into rhinoceroses, or the entire black population of a small town suddenly vanishing. Ironically, though, once the unreal conditions of the play have been established, they are worked out with iron logic; and the theme of a fantasy play may be very down-to-earth.

Such a mixing of fantastic and realistic elements is typical of what has been called the Theater of the Absurd, a contemporary variety of dramatic fantasy that focuses on the ridiculous and nonsensical aspects of life in today's society. In the Theater of the Absurd actions apparently lack either motivation or purpose, many of the plays have no discernible beginning or end, and most portray a sense of meaninglessness and futility in human existence. While absurdist plays may often be very funny, or at least have their funny moments, their world view is dark and nightmarish. We laugh and shake our heads as we leave the theater, but our laughter is brittle and our heads are filled with disturbing thoughts.

Of the following plays, Sophocles' *Oedipus Rex* and William Shakespeare's *Othello* are tragedies, Anton Chekhov's *A Marriage Proposal* and Oscar Wilde's *The Importance of Being Earnest* are comedies, Thomas Holcroft's *A Tale of Mystery* is a melodrama, Susan Glaspell's *Trifles* and Arthur Miller's *A Memory of Two Mondays* are social plays, and Douglas Turner Ward's *Day of Absence* and Eugène Ionesco's *The Gap* are fantasies.

# Oedipus Rex[1]

SOPHOCLES

## Cast of Characters

| | |
|---|---|
| OEDIPUS | MESSENGER  (from Corinth) |
| A PRIEST | SHEPHERD  (of Laïos) |
| KREON | SECOND MESSENGER  (from the palace) |
| TEIRESIAS | CHORAGOS |
| IOKASTÊ | CHORUS OF THEBAN ELDERS |

THE SCENE.   *Before the palace of* OEDIPUS, *King of Thebes. A central door and two lateral doors open onto a platform which runs the length of the façade. On the platform, right and left, are altars; and three steps lead down into the orchêstra, or chorus-ground. At the beginning of the action these steps are crowded by suppliants[2] who have brought branches and chaplets of olive leaves and who sit in various attitudes of despair.* OEDIPUS *enters.*

## PROLOGUE[3]

OEDIPUS  My children, generations of the living
  In the line of Kadmos,[4] nursed at his ancient hearth:
  Why have you strewn yourselves before these altars
  In supplication, with your boughs and garlands?
  The breath of incense rises from the city                5
  With a sound of prayer and lamentation.
                                Children,
  I would not have you speak through messengers,
  And therefore I have come myself to hear you—
  I, Oedipus, who bear the famous name.
  (*To a* PRIEST) You, there, since you are eldest in the company,     10
  Speak for them all, tell me what preys upon you,
  Whether you come in dread, or crave some blessing:
  Tell me, and never doubt that I will help you
  In every way I can; I should be heartless
  Were I not moved to find you suppliant here.          15
PRIEST  Great Oedipus, O powerful king of Thebes!
  You see how all the ages of our people
  Cling to your altar steps: here are boys

---

[1] This is an English version by Dudley Fitts and Robert Fitzgerald.

[2] People entreating favors from the king.

[3] The prologue is an introduction or foreword to the action, including the exposition.

[4] (Cadmus), Son of Agenor, king of Phoenicia, and legendary founder of the city of Thebes. Here, as with most of the names throughout the play, Fitts and Fitzgerald use spellings closer to the Greek than are the usual English forms.

Who can barely stand alone, and here are priests
By weight of age, as I am a priest of God,                                    20
And young men chosen from those yet unmarried;
As for the others, all that multitude,
They wait with olive chaplets[5] in the squares,
At the two shrines of Pallas,[6] and where Apollo[7]
Speaks in the glowing embers.

                Your own eyes                                25
Must tell you: Thebes is tossed on a murdering sea
And can not lift her head from the death surge.
A rust consumes the buds and fruits of the earth;
The herds are sick; children die unborn,
And labor is vain. The god of plague and pyre                                 30
Raids like detestable lightning through the city,
And all the house of Kadmos is laid waste,
All emptied, and all darkened: Death alone
Battens upon the misery of Thebes.

You are not one of the immortal gods, we know;                                35
Yet we have come to you to make our prayer
As to the man surest in mortal ways
And wisest in the ways of God. You saved us
From the Sphinx,[8] that flinty singer, and the tribute
We paid to her so long; yet you were never                                    40
Better informed than we, nor could we teach you:
A god's touch, it seems, enabled you to help us.

Therefore, O mighty power, we turn to you:
Find us our safety, find us a remedy,
Whether by counsel of the gods or of men.                                     45
A king of wisdom tested in the past
Can act in a time of troubles, and act well.
Noblest of men, restore
Life to your city! Think how all men call you
Liberator for your boldness long ago;                                         50
Ah, when your years of kingship are remembered,
Let them not say *We rose, but later fell*—
Keep the State from going down in the storm!

---

[5] Wreaths of olive branches worn on the head, the olive symbolizing peace.

[6] A name for Athena, the goddess of wisdom. She was the patroness of Athens, where the Parthenon was her shrine.

[7] Phoebus Apollo, god of the sun, music, poetry, and prophecy. At his shrine, fortunes were told from embers.

[8] A winged monster with the head of a woman and the body of a lion. She had once terrorized Thebes, devouring all those who failed to answer her riddle: "What walks on four legs in the morning, on two at midday, and on three in the evening?" When young Oedipus answered correctly, "Man," the Sphinx killed herself, ending a plague. Subsequently, Kreon, acting as regent of Thebes after the death of Laïos, offered Oedipus not only the throne but also the hand of Iokastê, the widow of Laïos.

Once, years ago, with happy augury,
You brought us fortune; be the same again!                    55
No man questions your power to rule the land:
But rule over men, not over a dead city!
Ships are only hulls, high walls are nothing,
When no life moves in the empty passageways.

OEDIPUS  Poor children! You may be sure I know                60
All that you longed for in your coming here.
I know that you are deathly sick; and yet,
Sick as you are, not one is as sick as I.
Each of you suffers in himself alone
His anguish, not another's; but my spirit                     65
Groans for the city, for myself, for you.

I was not sleeping, you are not waking me.
No, I have been in tears for a long while
And in my restless thoughts walked many ways.
In all my search I found one remedy,                          70
And I have adopted it: I have sent Kreon,
Son of Menoikeus, brother of the queen,
To Delphi, Apollo's place of revelation,
To learn there, if he can,
What act or pledge of mine may save the city.                 75
I have counted the days, and now, this very day,
I am troubled, for he has overstayed his time.
What is he doing? He has been gone too long.
Yet whenever he comes back, I should do ill
Not to take any action the god orders.                        80

PRIEST  It is a timely promise. At this instant
They tell me Kreon is here.

OEDIPUS                        O Lord Apollo!
May his news be fair as his face is radiant!

PRIEST  Good news, I gather! he is crowned with bay,[9]
The chaplet is thick with berries.

OEDIPUS                           We shall soon know;          85
He is near enough to hear us now.

    (Enter KREON.)

                         O prince:
Brother: son of Menoikeus:
What answer do you bring us from the god?

KREON  A strong one. I can tell you, great afflictions
Will turn out well, if they are taken well.                   90

OEDIPUS  What was the oracle? These vague words
Leave me still hanging between hope and fear.

---

[9] The same as laurel, a symbol of victory or achievement.

KREON  Is it your pleasure to hear me with all these
   Gathered around us? I am prepared to speak,
   But should we not go in?
OEDIPUS               Speak to them all,         95
   It is for them I suffer, more than for myself.
KREON  Then I will tell you what I heard at Delphi.
   In plain words
   The god commands us to expel from the land of Thebes
   An old defilement we are sheltering.         100
   It is a deathly thing, beyond cure;
   We must not let it feed upon us longer.
OEDIPUS  What defilement? How shall we rid ourselves of it?
KREON  By exile or death, blood for blood. It was
   Murder that brought the plague-wind on the city.         105
OEDIPUS  Murder of whom? Surely the god has named him?
KREON  My lord: Laïos once ruled this land,
   Before you came to govern us.
OEDIPUS               I know;
   I learned of him from others; I never saw him.
KREON  He was murdered; and Apollo commands us now         110
   To take revenge upon whoever killed him.
OEDIPUS  Upon whom? Where are they? Where shall we find a clue
   To solve that crime, after so many years?
KREON  Here in this land, he said. Search reveals
   Things that escape an inattentive man.         115
OEDIPUS  Tell me: Was Laïos murdered in his house,
   Or in the fields, or in some foreign country?
KREON  He said he planned to make a pilgrimage.
   He did not come home again.
OEDIPUS             And was there no one,
   No witness, no companion, to tell what happened?         120
KREON  They were all killed but one, and he got away
   So frightened that he could remember one thing only.
OEDIPUS  What was the one thing? One may be the key
   To everything, if we resolve to use it.
KREON  He said that a band of highwaymen attacked them,         125
   Outnumbered them, and overwhelmed the king.
OEDIPUS  Strange, that a highwayman should be so daring—
   Unless some faction here bribed him to do it.
KREON  We thought of that. But after Laïos' death
   New troubles arose and we had no avenger.         130
OEDIPUS  What troubles could prevent your hunting down the killers?
KREON  The riddling Sphinx's song
   Made us deaf to all mysteries but her own.
OEDIPUS  Then once more I must bring what is dark to light.
   It is most fitting that Apollo shows,         135
   As you do, this compunction for the dead.

You shall see how I stand by you, as I should,
Avenging this country and the god as well,
And not as though it were for some distant friend,
But for my own sake, to be rid of evil.                                    140
Whoever killed King Laïos might—who knows?—
Lay violent hands even on me—and soon.
I act for the murdered king in my own interest.

Come, then, my children: leave the altar steps,
Lift up your olive boughs!
                              One of you go                                 145
And summon the people of Kadmos to gather here.
I will do all that I can; you may tell them that.        (*Exit a* PAGE.)
So, with the help of God,
We shall be saved—or else indeed we are lost.
PRIEST   Let us rise, children. It was for this we came,                   150
And now the king has promised it.
Phoibos[10] has sent us an oracle; may he descend
Himself to save us and drive out the plague.

(*Exeunt* OEDIPUS *and* KREON *into the palace by the central door. The* PRIEST *and
the* SUPPLIANTS *disperse R and L. After a short pause the* CHORUS *enters the
orchêstra.*)

## PÁRODOS[11]

*STROPHE 1*

CHORUS   What is God singing in his profound
Delphi of gold and shadow?                                                 155
What oracle for Thebes, the sunwhipped city?
Fear unjoints me, the roots of my heart tremble.
Now I remember, O Healer, your power, and wonder:
Will you send doom like a sudden cloud, or weave it
Like nightfall of the past?                                                160
Speak to me, tell me, O
Child of golden Hope, immortal Voice.

*ANTISTROPHE 1*

Let me pray to Athenê, the immortal daughter of Zeus,
And to Artemis[12] her sister
Who keeps her famous throne in the market ring,                           165

---

[10] Once again, Phoebus Apollo, the sun god. His shrine was at Delphi.

[11] The *Párodos* is a formal song (ode) delivered by the Chorus as it entered the theater,
moving down the aisles toward the dramatic or playing area. The *Strophe* is a verse song
chanted by the Chorus as it danced right to left. Then, the *Antistrophe* was sung as the
Chorus danced back left to right. Finally, the *Epode* was sung as the Chorus stood
stationary.

[12] The moon goddess and goddess of hunting. Patroness of unmarried girls and chastity.

And to Apollo, archer from distant heaven[13]—
O gods, descend! Like three streams leap against
The fires of our grief, the fires of darkness;
Be swift to bring us rest!
As in the old time from the brilliant house                    170
Of air you stepped to save us, come again!

*STROPHE 2*

Now our afflictions have no end,
Now all our stricken host lies down
And no man fights off death with his mind;
The noble plowland bears no grain,                             175
And groaning mothers can not bear—
See, how our lives like birds take wing,
Like sparks that fly when a fire soars,
To the shore of the god of evening.[14]

*ANTISTROPHE 2*

The plague burns on, it is pitiless,                           180
Though pallid children laden with death
Lie unwept in the stony ways,
And old gray women by every path
Flock to the strand about the altars
There to strike their breasts and cry                          185
Worship of Phoibos in wailing prayers:
Be kind, God's golden child!

*STROPHE 3*

There are no swords in this attack by fire,
No shields, but we are ringed with cries.
Send the besieger plunging from our homes                      190
Into the vast sea-room of the Atlantic
Or into the waves that foam eastward of Thrace—
For the day ravages what the night spares—
Destroy our enemy, lord of the thunder!
Let him be riven by lightning from heaven!                     195

*ANTISTROPHE 3*

Phoibos Apollo, stretch the sun's bowstring,
That golden cord, until it sing for us,
Flashing arrows in heaven!
                                    Artemis, Huntress,
Race with flaring lights upon our mountains!
O scarlet god, O golden-banded brow,                           200
O Theban Bacchos[15] in a storm of Maenads,

[13] Apollo was also the god of archery.

[14] The god of evening was Death.

[15] Bacchos (Dionysos) was the god of wine and revelry, hence scarlet-faced. The Maenads
were Bacchos's attendant female revelers or worshipers.

(Enter OEDIPUS, C.)

Whirl upon Death, that all the Undying hate!
Come with blinding torches, come in joy!


## SCENE I

OEDIPUS  Is this your prayer? It may be answered. Come,
    Listen to me, act as the crisis demands,                              205
    And you shall have relief from all these evils.

    Until now I was a stranger to this tale,
    As I had been a stranger to the crime.
    Could I track down the murderer without a clue?
    But now, friends,                                                    210
    As one who became a citizen after the murder,
    I make this proclamation to all Thebans:
    If any man knows by whose hand Laïos, son of Labdakos,
    Met his death, I direct that man to tell me everything,
    No matter what he fears for having so long withheld it.              215
    Let it stand as promised that no further trouble
    Will come to him, but he may leave the land in safety.

    Moreover: If anyone knows the murderer to be foreign,
    Let him not keep silent: he shall have his reward from me.
    However, if he does conceal it; if any man                          220
    Fearing for his friend or for himself disobeys this edict,
    Hear what I propose to do:

    I solemnly forbid the people of this country,
    Where power and throne are mine, ever to receive that man
    Or speak to him, no matter who he is, or let him                     225
    Join in sacrifice, lustration,[16] or in prayer.
    I decree that he be driven from every house,
    Being, as he is, corruption itself to us: the Delphic
    Voice of Apollo has pronounced this revelation.
    Thus I associate myself with the oracle                              230
    And take the side of the murdered king.

    As for the criminal, I pray to God—
    Whether it be a lurking thief, or one of a number—
    I pray that that man's life be consumed in evil and wretchedness.
    And as for me, this curse applies no less                           235
    If it should turn out that the culprit is my guest here,
    Sharing my hearth.
                You have heard the penalty.
    I lay it on you now to attend to this

[16] Purification by means of certain ceremonies.

For my sake, for Apollo's, for the sick
Sterile city that heaven has abandoned.                              240
Suppose the oracle had given you no command:
Should this defilement go uncleansed for ever?
You should have found the murderer: your king,
A noble king, had been destroyed!
                              Now I,
Having the power that he held before me,                             245
Having his bed, begetting children there
Upon his wife, as he would have, had he lived—
Their son would have been my children's brother,
If Laïos had had luck in fatherhood!
(And now his bad fortune has struck him down)—                      250
I say I take the son's part, just as though
I were his son, to press the fight for him
And see it won! I'll find the hand that brought
Death to Labdakos' and Polydoros' child,
Heir of Kadmos' and Agenor's line.[17]                              255
And as for those who fail me,
May the gods deny them the fruit of the earth,
Fruit of the womb, and may they rot utterly!
Let them be wretched as we are wretched, and worse!

For you, for loyal Thebans, and for all                             260
Who find my actions right, I pray the favor
Of justice, and of all the immortal gods.
CHORAGOS[18]  Since I am under oath, my lord, I swear
    I did not do the murder, I can not name
    The murderer. Phoibos ordained the search;                      265
    Why did he not say who the culprit was?
OEDIPUS  An honest question. But no man in the world
    Can make the gods do more than the gods will.
CHORAGOS  There is an alternative, I think—
OEDIPUS                                    Tell me.
    Any or all, you must not fail to tell me.                       270
CHORAGOS  A lord clairvoyant to the lord Apollo,
    As we all know, is the skilled Teiresias.
    One might learn much about this from him, Oedipus.
OEDIPUS  I am not wasting time:
    Kreon spoke of this, and I have sent for him—                   275
    Twice, in fact; it is strange that he is not here.
CHORAGOS  The other matter—that old report—seems useless.
OEDIPUS  What was that? I am interested in all reports.

----

[17] The royal family of Thebes, the line of succession going: Kadmos, Polydoros, Labdakos,
    and Laïos. Although he does not know it, Oedipus is next in line.

[18] The chief spokesman for the Chorus. Originally, the *Choragos* was a wealthy person
    who was also a financial patron of the play.

CHORAGOS  The king was said to have been killed by highwaymen.
OEDIPUS  I know. But we have no witnesses to that.                    280
CHORAGOS  If the killer can feel a particle of dread,
    Your curse will bring him out of hiding!
OEDIPUS                                        No.
    The man who dared that act will fear no curse.

*(Enter the blind seer* TEIRESIAS, *led by a* PAGE.)

CHORAGOS  But there is one man who may detect the criminal.
    This is Teiresias, this is the holy prophet             285
    In whom, alone of all men, truth was born.
OEDIPUS  Teiresias: seer: student of mysteries,
    Of all that's taught and all that no man tells,
    Secrets of Heaven and secrets of the earth:
    Blind though you are, you know the city lies            290
    Sick with plague; and from this plague, my lord,
    We find that you alone can guard or save us.

    Possibly you did not hear the messengers?
    Apollo, when we sent to him,
    Sent us back word that this great pestilence             295
    Would lift, but only if we established clearly
    The identity of those who murdered Laïos.
    They must be killed or exiled.
                    Can you use
    Birdflight[19] or any art of divination
    To purify yourself, and Thebes, and me                   300
    From this contagion? We are in your hands.
    There is no fairer duty
    Than that of helping others in distress.
TEIRESIAS  How dreadful knowledge of the truth can be
    When there's no help in truth! I knew this well,         305
    But did not act on it: else I should not have come.
OEDIPUS  What is troubling you? Why are your eyes so cold?
TEIRESIAS  Let me go home. Bear your own fate, and I'll
    Bear mine. It is better so: trust what I say.
OEDIPUS  What you say is ungracious and unhelpful             310
    To your native country. Do not refuse to speak.
TEIRESIAS  When it comes to speech, your own is neither temperate
    Nor opportune. I wish to be more prudent.
OEDIPUS  In God's name, we all beg you—
TEIRESIAS                                  You are all ignorant.
    No; I will never tell you what I know.                   315
    Now it is my misery; then, it would be yours.

[19] The configurations made by birds in flight were sometimes used by augurs to foretell
    the future or reveal the unknown or forgotten past.

OEDIPUS  What! You do know something, and will not tell us?
   You would betray us all and wreck the State?
TEIRESIAS  I do not intend to torture myself, or you.
   Why persist in asking? You will not persuade me.                      320
OEDIPUS  What a wicked old man you are! You'd try a stone's
   Patience! Out with it! Have you no feeling at all?
TEIRESIAS  You call me unfeeling. If you could only see
   The nature of your own feelings . . .
OEDIPUS                            Why,
   Who would not feel as I do? Who could endure                          325
   Your arrogance toward the city?
TEIRESIAS                            What does it matter?
   Whether I speak or not, it is bound to come.
OEDIPUS  Then, if "it" is bound to come, you are bound to tell me.
TEIRESIAS  No, I will not go on. Rage as you please.
OEDIPUS  Rage? Why not!
                         And I'll tell you what I think:                 330
   You planned it, you had it done, you all but
   Killed him with your own hands: if you had eyes,
   I'd say the crime was yours, and yours alone.
TEIRESIAS  So? I charge you, then,
   Abide by the proclamation you have made:                              335
   From this day forth
   Never speak again to these men or to me;
   You yourself are the pollution of this country.
OEDIPUS  You dare say that! Can you possibly think you have
   Some way of going free, after such insolence?                         340
TEIRESIAS  I have gone free. It is the truth sustains me.
OEDIPUS  Who taught you shamelessness? It was not your craft.
TEIRESIAS  You did. You made me speak. I did not want to.
OEDIPUS  Speak what? Let me hear it again more clearly.
TEIRESIAS  Was it not clear before? Are you tempting me?                 345
OEDIPUS  I did not understand it. Say it again.
TEIRESIAS  I say that you are the murderer whom you seek.
OEDIPUS  Now twice you have spat out infamy. You'll pay for it!
TEIRESIAS  Would you care for more? Do you wish to be really angry?
OEDIPUS  Say what you will. Whatever you say is worthless.                350
TEIRESIAS  I say you live in hideous shame with those
   Most dear to you. You can not see the evil.
OEDIPUS  Can you go on babbling like this for ever?
TEIRESIAS  I can, if there is power in truth.
OEDIPUS                            There is:
   But not for you, not for you,                                         355
   You sightless, witless, senseless, mad old man!
TEIRESIAS  You are the madman. There is no one here
   Who will not curse you soon, as you curse me.
OEDIPUS  You child of total night! I would not touch you;

Neither would any man who sees the sun.                                              360
TEIRESIAS  True: it is not from you my fate will come.
  That lies within Apollo's competence,
  As it is his concern.
OEDIPUS                  Tell me, who made
  These fine discoveries? Kreon? or someone else?
TEIRESIAS  Kreon is no threat. You weave your own doom.                               365
OEDIPUS  Wealth, power, craft of statesmanship!
  Kingly position, everywhere admired!
  What savage envy is stored up against these,
  If Kreon, whom I trusted, Kreon my friend,
  For this great office which the city once                                           370
  Put in my hands unsought—if for this power
  Kreon desires in secret to destroy me!

  He has bought this decrepit fortune-teller, this
  Collector of dirty pennies, this prophet fraud—
  Why, he is no more clairvoyant than I am!
                                        Tell us.                                       375
  Has your mystic mummery ever approached the truth?
  When that hellcat the Sphinx was performing here,
  What help were you to these people?
  Her magic was not for the first man who came along:
  It demanded a real exorcist. Your birds—                                            380
  What good were they? or the gods, for the matter of that?
  But I came by,
  Oedipus, the simple man, who knows nothing—
  I thought it out for myself, no birds helped me!
  And this is the man you think you can destroy,                                       385
  That you may be close to Kreon when he's king!
  Well, you and your friend Kreon, it seems to me,
  Will suffer most. If you were not an old man,
  You would have paid already for your plot.
CHORAGOS  We can not see that his words or yours                                      390
  Have been spoken except in anger, Oedipus,
  And of anger we have no need. How to accomplish
  The god's will best: that is what most concerns us.
TEIRESIAS  You are a king. But where argument's concerned
  I am your man, as much a king as you.                                               395
  I am not your servant, but Apollo's.
  I have no need of Kreon or Kreon's name.

  Listen to me. You mock my blindness, do you?
  But I say that you, with both your eyes, are blind:
  You can not see the wretchedness of your life,                                       400
  Nor in whose house you live, no, nor with whom.
  Who are your father and mother? Can you tell me?
  You do not even know the blind wrongs

That you have done them, on earth and in the world below.
But the double lash of your parents' curse will whip you                    405
Out of this land some day, with only night
Upon your precious eyes.
Your cries then—where will they not be heard?
What fastness of Kithairon[20] will not echo them?
And that bridal-descant of yours—you'll know it then,                       410
The song they sang when you came here to Thebes
And found your misguided berthing.
All this, and more, that you can not guess at now,
Will bring you to yourself among your children.

Be angry, then. Curse Kreon. Curse my words.                                415
I tell you, no man that walks upon the earth
Shall be rooted out more horribly than you.
OEDIPUS  Am I to bear this from him?—Damnation
   Take you! Out of this place! Out of my sight!
TEIRESIAS  I would not have come at all if you had not asked me.            420
OEDIPUS  Could I have told that you'd talk nonsense, that
   You'd come here to make a fool of yourself, and of me?
TEIRESIAS  A fool? Your parents thought me sane enough.
OEDIPUS  My parents again!—Wait: who were my parents?
TEIRESIAS  This day will give you a father, and break your heart.          425
OEDIPUS  Your infantile riddles! Your damned abracadabra!
TEIRESIAS  You were a great man once at solving riddles.
OEDIPUS  Mock me with that if you like; you will find it true.
TEIRESIAS  It was true enough. It brought about your ruin.
OEDIPUS  But if it saved this town?
TEIRESIAS  (to the PAGE)              Boy, give me your hand.               430
OEDIPUS  Yes, boy; lead him away.
                         —While you are here
   We can do nothing. Go; leave us in peace.
TEIRESIAS  I will go when I have said what I have to say.
   How can you hurt me? And I tell you again:
   The man you have been looking for all this time,                         435
   The damned man, the murderer of Laïos,
   That man is in Thebes. To your mind he is foreign-born,
   But it will soon be shown that he is a Theban,
   A revelation that will fail to please.
                         A blind man,
   Who has his eyes now; a penniless man, who is rich now;                  440
   And he will go tapping the strange earth with his staff.
   To the children with whom he lives now he will be
   Brother and father—the very same; to her
   Who bore him, son and husband—the very same

[20] A mountain range between Athens and Boeotia, near Thebes, where as an infant
   Oedipus was left to die.

Who came to his father's bed, wet with his father's blood.        445

Enough. Go think that over.
If later you find error in what I have said,
You may say that I have no skill in prophecy.

(*Exit* TEIRESIAS, *led by his* PAGE. OEDIPUS *goes into the palace.*)

## ODE I

*STROPHE 1*

CHORUS   The Delphic stone of prophecies[21]
Remembers ancient regicide                                        450
And a still bloody hand.
That killer's hour of flight has come.
He must be stronger than riderless
Coursers of untiring wind,
For the son of Zeus[22] armed with his father's thunder          455
Leaps in lightning after him;
And the Furies[23] hold his track, the sad Furies.

*ANTISTROPHE 1*

Holy Parnassos' peak of snow[24]
Flashes and blinds that secret man,
That all shall hunt him down:                                     460
Though he may roam the forest shade
Like a bull gone wild from pasture
To rage through glooms of stone.
Doom comes down on him; flight will not avail him;
For the world's heart calls him desolate,                         465
And the immortal voices follow, for ever follow.

*STROPHE 2*

But now a wilder thing is heard
From the old man skilled at hearing Fate in the wing-beat of a bird.
Bewildered as a blown bird, my soul hovers and can not find
Foothold in this debate, or any reason or rest of mind.          470
But no man ever brought—none can bring
Proof of strife between Thebes' royal house,

[21] Because Delphi was thought to be positioned at the earth's center, the shrine there contained a ceremonial monolith called the Earth's Navel.

[22] Apollo was the son of Zeus.

[23] The Furies were three hideous female deities whose task it was to avenge serious wrongs by driving the perpetrator mad.

[24] Parnassos, on whose southern slope was Delphi, was a mountain with two peaks, one consecrated to Apollo and the Muses—the nine daughters of Zeus and Mnemosyne—and the other to Dionysos. The "peak of snow" is the peak consecrated to Apollo.

Labdakos' line,[25] and the son of Polybos;[26]
And never until now has any man brought word
Of Laïos' dark death staining Oedipus the King.                    475

*ANTISTROPHE 2*

Divine Zeus and Apollo hold
Perfect intelligence alone of all tales ever told;
And well though this diviner[27] works, he works in his own night;
No man can judge that rough unknown or trust in second sight,
For wisdom changes hands among the wise.                          480
Shall I believe my great lord criminal
At a raging word that a blind old man let fall?
I saw him, when the carrion woman[28] faced him of old,
Prove his heroic mind. These evil words are lies.


# SCENE II

KREON  Men of Thebes:                                            485
   I am told that heavy accusations
   Have been brought against me by King Oedipus.

   I am not the kind of man to bear this tamely.

   If in these present difficulties
   He holds me accountable for any harm to him                   490
   Through anything I have said or done—why, then,
   I do not value life in this dishonor.
   It is not as though this rumor touched upon
   Some private indiscretion. The matter is grave.
   The fact is that I am being called disloyal                   495
   To the State, to my fellow citizens, to my friends.
CHORAGOS  He may have spoken in anger, not from his mind.
KREON  But did you not hear him say I was the one
   Who seduced the old prophet into lying?
CHORAGOS  The thing was said; I do not know how seriously.        500
KREON  But you were watching him! Were his eyes steady?
   Did he look like a man in his right mind?
CHORAGOS                             I do not know.
   I can not judge the behavior of great men.
   But here is the king himself.

   (*Enter* OEDIPUS.)

---

[25] The royal family of Laïos.

[26] At this point in the play both the Chorus and Oedipus think Polybos is Oedipus' father.

[27] The blind seer Teiresias.

[28] The Sphinx.

OEDIPUS                              So you dared come back.
  Why? How brazen of you to come to my house,                     505
  You murderer!
                    Do you think I do not know
  That you plotted to kill me, plotted to steal my throne?
  Tell me, in God's name: am I coward, a fool,
  That you should dream you could accomplish this?
  A fool who could not see your slippery game?                    510
  A coward, not to fight back when I saw it?
  You are the fool, Kreon, are you not? hoping
  Without support or friends to get a throne?
  Thrones may be won or bought: you could do neither.
KREON  Now listen to me. You have talked; let me talk, too.       515
  You can not judge unless you know the facts.
OEDIPUS  You speak well: there is one fact; but I find it hard
  To learn from the deadliest enemy I have.
KREON  That above all I must dispute with you.
OEDIPUS  That above all I will not hear you deny.                   520
KREON  If you think there is anything good in being stubborn
  Against all reason, then I say you are wrong.
OEDIPUS  If you think a man can sin against his own kind
  And not be punished for it, I say you are mad.
KREON  I agree. But tell me: What have I done to you?              525
OEDIPUS  You advised me to send for that wizard, did you not?
KREON  I did. I should do it again.
OEDIPUS                              Very well. Now tell me:
  How long has it been since Laïos—
KREON                              What of Laïos?
OEDIPUS  Since he vanished in that onset by the road?
KREON  It was long ago, a long time.
OEDIPUS                              And this prophet,             530
  Was he practicing here then?
KREON                              He was; and with honor, as now.
OEDIPUS  Did he speak of me at that time?
KREON                              He never did,
  At least, not when I was present.
OEDIPUS                              But . . . the enquiry?
  I suppose you held one?
KREON                              We did, but we learned nothing.
OEDIPUS  Why did the prophet not speak against me then?           535
KREON  I do not know; and I am the kind of man
  Who holds his tongue when he has no facts to go on.
OEDIPUS  There's one fact that you know, and you could tell it.
KREON  What fact is that? If I know it, you shall have it.
OEDIPUS  If he were not involved with you, he could not say       540
  That it was I who murdered Laïos.
KREON  If he says that, you are the one that knows it!—

But now it is my turn to question you.
OEDIPUS  Put your questions. I am no murderer.
KREON  First, then: You married my sister?
OEDIPUS                                    I married your sister.                 545
KREON  And you rule the kingdom equally with her?
OEDIPUS  Everything that she wants she has from me.
KREON  And I am the third, equal to both of you?
OEDIPUS  That is why I call you a bad friend.
KREON  No. Reason it out, as I have done.                                        550
  Think of this first: Would any sane man prefer
  Power, with all a king's anxieties,
  To that same power and the grace of sleep?
  Certainly not I.
  I have never longed for the king's power—only his rights.                      555
  Would any wise man differ from me in this?
  As matters stand, I have my way in everything
  With your consent, and no responsibilities.
  If I were king, I should be a slave to policy.

  How could I desire a scepter more                                             560
  Than what is now mine—untroubled influence?
  No, I have not gone mad; I need no honors,
  Except those with the perquisites I have now.
  I am welcome everywhere; every man salutes me,
  And those who want your favor seek my ear,                                    565
  Since I know how to manage what they ask.
  Should I exchange this ease for that anxiety?
  Besides, no sober mind is treasonable.
  I hate anarchy
  And never would deal with any man who likes it.                               570
  Test what I have said. Go to the priestess
  At Delphi, ask if I quoted her correctly.
  And as for this other thing: if I am found
  Guilty of treason with Teiresias,
  Then sentence me to death. You have my word                                   575
  It is a sentence I should cast my vote for—
  But not without evidence!
                          You do wrong
  When you take good men for bad, bad men for good.
  A true friend thrown aside—why, life itself
  Is not more precious!
                          In time you will know this well:                      580
  For time, and time alone, will show the just man,
  Though scoundrels are discovered in a day.
CHORAGOS  This is well said, and a prudent man would ponder it.
  Judgments too quickly formed are dangerous.
OEDIPUS  But is he not quick in his duplicity?                                   585

And shall I not be quick to parry him?
Would you have me stand still, hold my peace, and let
This man win everything, through my inaction?
KREON   And you want—what is it, then? To banish me?
OEDIPUS   No, not exile. It is your death I want,                         590
So that all the world may see what treason means.
KREON   You will persist, then? You will not believe me?
OEDIPUS   How can I believe you?
KREON                                    Then you are a fool.
OEDIPUS   To save myself?
KREON                       In justice, think of me.
OEDIPUS   You are evil incarnate.
KREON                                    But suppose that you are wrong?         595
OEDIPUS   Still I must rule.
KREON                       But not if you rule badly.
OEDIPUS   O city, city!
KREON                    It is my city, too!
CHORAGOS   Now, my lords, be still. I see the queen,
   Iokastê, coming from her palace chambers;
   And it is time she came, for the sake of you both.                  600
   This dreadful quarrel can be resolved through her.

   (Enter IOKASTÊ.)

IOKASTÊ   Poor foolish men, what wicked din is this?
   With Thebes sick to death, is it not shameful
   That you should rake some private quarrel up?
   (To OEDIPUS) Come into the house.
                                    —And you, Kreon, go now:           605
   Let us have no more of this tumult over nothing.
KREON   Nothing? No, sister: what your husband plans for me
   Is one of two great evils: exile or death.
OEDIPUS   He is right.
                    Why, woman, I have caught him squarely
   Plotting against my life.
KREON                       No! Let me die                             610
   Accurst if ever I have wished you harm!
IOKASTÊ   Ah, believe it, Oedipus!
   In the name of the gods, respect this oath of his
   For my sake, for the sake of these people here!

   STROPHE 1

CHORAGOS   Open your mind to her, my lord. Be ruled by her, I beg you!   615
OEDIPUS   What would you have me do?
CHORAGOS   Respect Kreon's word. He has never spoken like a fool,
   And now he has sworn an oath.
OEDIPUS                                    You know what you ask?
CHORAGOS                                                        I do.
OEDIPUS                                                    Speak on, then.

CHORAGOS  A friend so sworn should not be baited so,
 In blind malice, and without final proof.      620
OEDIPUS  You are aware, I hope, that what you say
 Means death for me, or exile at the least.

*STROPHE 2*

CHORAGOS  No, I swear by Helios,[29] first in Heaven!
 May I die friendless and accurst,
 The worst of deaths, if ever I meant that!     625
   It is the withering fields
    That hurt my sick heart:
  Must we bear all these ills,
    And now your bad blood as well?
OEDIPUS  Then let him go. And let me die, if I must,   630
 Or be driven by him in shame from the land of Thebes.
 It is your unhappiness, and not his talk,
 That touches me.
      As for him—
 Wherever he goes, hatred will follow him.
KREON  Ugly in yielding, as you were ugly in rage!    635
 Natures like yours chiefly torment themselves.
OEDIPUS  Can you not go? Can you not leave me?
KREON             I can.
 You do not know me; but the city knows me,
 And in its eyes I am just, if not in yours.    (*Exit* KREON.)

*ANTISTROPHE 1*

CHORAGOS  Lady Iokastê, did you not ask the King to go to his chambers? 640
IOKASTÊ  First tell me what has happened.
CHORAGOS  There was suspicion without evidence; yet it rankled
 As even false charges will.
IOKASTÊ      On both sides?
CHORAGOS        On both.
IOKASTÊ          But what was said?
CHORAGOS  Oh let it rest, let it be done with!
 Have we not suffered enough?        645
OEDIPUS  You see to what your decency has brought you:
 You have made difficulties where my heart saw none.

*ANTISTROPHE 2*

CHORAGOS  Oedipus, it is not once only I have told you—
 You must know I should count myself unwise
 To the point of madness, should I now forsake you—  650
   You, under whose hand,
    In the storm of another time,
  Our dear land sailed out free.
    But now stand fast at the helm!

---

[29] The sun god.

IOKASTÊ  In God's name, Oedipus, inform your wife as well:                    655
  Why are you so set in this hard anger?
OEDIPUS  I will tell you, for none of these men deserves
  My confidence as you do. It is Kreon's work,
  His treachery, his plotting against me.
IOKASTÊ  Go on, if you can make this clear to me.                              660
OEDIPUS  He charges me with the murder of Laïos.
IOKASTÊ  Has he some knowledge? Or does he speak from hearsay?
OEDIPUS  He would not commit himself to such a charge,
  But he has brought in that damnable soothsayer
  To tell his story.
IOKASTÊ            Set your mind at rest.                                      665
  If it is a question of soothsayers, I tell you
  That you will find no man whose craft gives knowledge
  Of the unknowable.

                    Here is my proof:

  An oracle was reported to Laïos once
  (I will not say from Phoibos himself, but from                              670
  His appointed ministers, at any rate)
  That his doom would be death at the hands of his own son—
  His son, born of his flesh and of mine!

  Now, you remember the story: Laïos was killed
  By marauding strangers where three highways meet;                          675
  But his child had not been three days in this world
  Before the king had pierced the baby's ankles
  And left him to die on a lonely mountainside.

  Thus, Apollo never caused that child
  To kill his father, and it was not Laïos' fate                             680
  To die at the hands of his son, as he had feared.
  This is what prophets and prophecies are worth!
  Have no dread of them.

                    It is God himself
  Who can show us what he wills, in his own way.
OEDIPUS  How strange a shadowy memory crossed my mind,                       685
  Just now while you were speaking; it chilled my heart.
IOKASTÊ  What do you mean? What memory do you speak of?
OEDIPUS  If I understand you, Laïos was killed
  At a place where three roads meet.
IOKASTÊ                              So it was said;
  We have no later story.
OEDIPUS                    Where did it happen?                               690
IOKASTÊ  Phokis, it is called: at a place where the Theban Way
  Divides into the roads toward Delphi and Daulia.
OEDIPUS  When?
IOKASTÊ        We had the news not long before you came
  And proved the right to your succession here.

OEDIPUS   Ah, what net has God been weaving for me?                    695
IOKASTÊ   Oedipus! Why does this trouble you?
OEDIPUS                                     Do not ask me yet.
  First, tell me how Laïos looked, and tell me
  How old he was.
IOKASTÊ                    He was tall, his hair just touched
  With white; his form was not unlike your own.
OEDIPUS   I think that I myself may be accurst                         700
  By my own ignorant edict.
IOKASTÊ                          You speak strangely.
  It makes me tremble to look at you, my king.
OEDIPUS   I am not sure that the blind man can not see.
  But I should know better if you were to tell me—
IOKASTÊ   Anything—though I dread to hear you ask it.                  705
OEDIPUS   Was the king lightly escorted, or did he ride
  With a large company, as a ruler should?
IOKASTÊ   There were five men with him in all: one was a herald.
  And a single chariot, which he was driving.
OEDIPUS   Alas, that makes it plain enough!
                        But who—                   710
  Who told you how it happened?
IOKASTÊ                                A household servant,
  The only one to escape.
OEDIPUS                      And is he still
  A servant of ours?
IOKASTÊ                   No; for when he came back at last
  And found you enthroned in the place of the dead king,
  He came to me, touched my hand with his, and begged       715
  That I would send him away to the frontier district
  Where only the shepherds go—
  As far away from the city as I could send him.
  I granted his prayer; for although the man was a slave,
  He had earned more than this favor at my hands.            720
OEDIPUS   Can he be called back quickly?
IOKASTÊ                                Easily.
  But why?
OEDIPUS      I have taken too much upon myself
  Without enquiry; therefore I wish to consult him.
IOKASTÊ   Then he shall come.
                 But am I not one also
  To whom you might confide these fears of yours?            725
OEDIPUS   That is your right; it will not be denied you,
  Now least of all; for I have reached a pitch
  Of wild foreboding. Is there anyone
  To whom I should sooner speak?

  Polybos of Corinth is my father.                            730
  My mother is a Dorian: Meropê.

I grew up chief among the men of Corinth
Until a strange thing happened—
Not worth my passion, it may be, but strange.
At a feast, a drunken man maundering in his cups                    735
Cries out that I am not my father's son!

I contained myself that night, though I felt anger
And a sinking heart. The next day I visited
My father and mother, and questioned them. They stormed,
Calling it all the slanderous rant of a fool;                       740
And this relieved me. Yet the suspicion
Remained always aching in my mind;
I knew there was talk; I could not rest;
And finally, saying nothing to my parents,
I went to the shrine at Delphi.                                     745

The god dismissed my question without reply;
He spoke of other things.
                Some were clear,

Full of wretchedness, dreadful, unbearable:
As, that I should lie with my own mother, breed
Children from whom all men would turn their eyes;                   750
And that I should be my father's murderer.

I heard all this, and fled. And from that day
Corinth to me was only in the stars
Descending in that quarter of the sky,
As I wandered farther and farther on my way                        755
To a land where I should never see the evil
Sung by the oracle. And I came to this country
Where, so you say, King Laïos was killed.

I will tell you all that happened there, my lady.

There were three highways                                          760
Coming together at a place I passed;
And there a herald came towards me, and a chariot
Drawn by horses, with a man such as you describe
Seated in it. The groom leading the horses
Forced me off the road at his lord's command;                      765
But as this charioteer lurched over towards me
I struck him in my rage. The old man saw me
And brought his double goad down upon my head
As I came abreast.
              He was paid back, and more!
Swinging my club in this right hand I knocked him                   770
Out of his car, and he rolled on the ground.
                    I killed him.

I killed them all.

Now if that stranger and Laïos were—kin,
Where is a man more miserable than I?
More hated by the gods? Citizen and alien alike          775
Must never shelter me or speak to me—
I must be shunned by all.
                          And I myself
Pronounced this malediction upon myself!

Think of it: I have touched you with these hands,
These hands that killed your husband. What defilement!          780

Am I all evil, then? It must be so,
Since I must flee from Thebes, yet never again
See my own countrymen, my own country,
For fear of joining my mother in marriage
And killing Polybos, my father.
                          Ah,          785
If I was created so, born to this fate,
Who could deny the savagery of God?

O holy majesty of heavenly powers!
May I never see that day! Never!
Rather let me vanish from the race of men          790
Than know the abomination destined me!
CHORAGOS  We too, my lord, have felt dismay at this.
    But there is hope: you have yet to hear the shepherd.
OEDIPUS  Indeed, I fear no other hope is left me.
IOKASTÊ  What do you hope from him when he comes?
OEDIPUS                                   This much:          795
    If his account of the murder tallies with yours,
    Then I am cleared.
IOKASTÊ              What was it that I said
    Of such importance?
OEDIPUS                  Why, "marauders," you said,
    Killed the king, according to this man's story.
    If he maintains that still, if there were several,          800
    Clearly the guilt is not mine: I was alone.
    But if he says one man, singlehanded, did it,
    Then the evidence all points to me.
IOKASTÊ  You may be sure that he said there were several;
    And can he call back that story now? He can not.          805
    The whole city heard it as plainly as I.
    But suppose he alters some detail of it:
    He can not ever show that Laïos' death
    Fulfilled the oracle: for Apollo said
    My child was doomed to kill him; and my child—          810
    Poor baby!—it was my child that died first.

No. From now on, where oracles are concerned,
I would not waste a second thought on any.

OEDIPUS  You may be right.

But come: let someone go
   For the shepherd at once. This matter must be settled.          815
IOKASTÊ  I will send for him.
   I would not wish to cross you in anything,
   And surely not in this.—Let us go in.          *(Exeunt into the palace.)*


## ODE II

*STROPHE 1*

CHORUS  Let me be reverent in the ways of right,
   Lowly the paths I journey on;
   Let all my words and actions keep          820
   The laws of the pure universe
   From highest Heaven handed down.
   For Heaven is their bright nurse,
   Those generations of the realms of light;          825
   Ah, never of mortal kind were they begot,
   Nor are they slaves of memory, lost in sleep:
   Their Father is greater than Time, and ages not.

*ANTISTROPHE 1*

   The tyrant is a child of Pride
   Who drinks from his great sickening cup          830
   Recklessness and vanity,
   Until from his high crest headlong
   He plummets to the dust of hope.
   That strong man is not strong.
   But let no fair ambition be denied;          835
   May God protect the wrestler for the State
   In government, in comely policy,
   Who will fear God, and on His ordinance wait.

*STROPHE 2*

   Haughtiness and the high hand of disdain
   Tempt and outrage God's holy law;          840
   And any mortal who dares hold
   No immortal Power in awe
   Will be caught up in a net of pain:
   The price for which his levity is sold.
   Let each man take due earnings, then,          845
   And keep his hands from holy things,
   And from blasphemy stand apart—
   Else the crackling blast of heaven
   Blows on his head, and on his desperate heart.
   Though fools will honor impious men,          850
   In their cities no tragic poet sings.

*ANTISTROPHE 2*

Shall we lose faith in Delphi's obscurities,
We who have heard the world's core
Discredited, and the sacred wood
Of Zeus at Elis[30] praised no more?                                    855
The deeds and the strange prophecies
Must make a pattern yet to be understood.
Zeus, if indeed you are lord of all,
Throned in light over night and day,
Mirror this in your endless mind:                                       860
Our masters call the oracle
Words on the wind, and the Delphic vision blind!
Their hearts no longer know Apollo,
And reverence for the gods has died away.


## *SCENE III*

*(Enter* IOKASTÊ.*)*

IOKASTÊ   Princes of Thebes, it has occurred to me                      865
   To visit the altars of the gods, bearing
   These branches as a suppliant, and this incense.
   Our king is not himself: his noble soul
   Is overwrought with fantasies of dread,
   Else he would consider                                               870
   The new prophecies in the light of the old.
   He will listen to any voice that speaks disaster,
   And my advice goes for nothing.

*(She approaches the altar, R.)*

                              To you, then, Apollo,
   Lycéan lord, since you are nearest, I turn in prayer.
   Receive these offerings, and grant us deliverance              875
   From defilement. Our hearts are heavy with fear
   When we see our leader distracted, as helpless sailors
   Are terrified by the confusion of their helmsman.

*(Enter* MESSENGER.*)*

MESSENGER   Friends, no doubt you can direct me:
   Where shall I find the house of Oedipus,                            880
   Or, better still, where is the king himself?
CHORAGOS   It is this very place, stranger; he is inside.
   This is his wife and mother of his children.

---

[30] Elis was the small country in which Olympia was located.

MESSENGER  I wish her happiness in a happy house,
 Blest in all the fulfillment of her marriage.                          885
IOKASTÊ  I wish as much for you: your courtesy
 Deserves a like good fortune. But now, tell me:
 Why have you come? What have you to say to us?
MESSENGER  Good news, my lady, for your house and your husband.
IOKASTÊ  What news? Who sent you here?
MESSENGER                                   I am from Corinth.             890
 The news I bring ought to mean joy for you,
 Though it may be you will find some grief in it.
IOKASTÊ  What is it? How can it touch us in both ways?
MESSENGER  The word is that the people of the Isthmus
 Intend to call Oedipus to be their king.                               895
IOKASTÊ  But old King Polybos—is he not reigning still?
MESSENGER  No. Death holds him in his sepulchre.
IOKASTÊ  What are you saying? Polybos is dead?
MESSENGER  If I am not telling the truth, may I die myself.
IOKASTÊ  (to a MAIDSERVANT)  Go in, go quickly; tell this to your master.  900

 O riddlers of God's will, where are you now!
 This was the man whom Oedipus, long ago,
 Feared so, fled so, in dread of destroying him—
 But it was another fate by which he died.

 (Enter OEDIPUS, C.)

OEDIPUS  Dearest Iokastê, why have you sent for me?                       905
IOKASTÊ  Listen to what this man says, and then tell me
 What has become of the solemn prophecies.
OEDIPUS  Who is this man? What is his news for me?
IOKASTÊ  He has come from Corinth to announce your father's death!
OEDIPUS  Is it true, stranger? Tell me in your own words.                 910
MESSENGER  I can not say it more clearly: the king is dead.
OEDIPUS  Was it by treason? Or by an attack of illness?
MESSENGER  A little thing brings old men to their rest.
OEDIPUS  It was sickness, then?
MESSENGER                         Yes, and his many years.
OEDIPUS  Ah!                                                             915
 Why should a man respect the Pythian hearth,[31] or
 Give heed to the birds that jangle above his head?
 They prophesied that I should kill Polybos,
 Kill my own father; but he is dead and buried,
 And I am here—I never touched him, never,                              920
 Unless he died of grief for my departure,
 And thus, in a sense, through me. No. Polybos
 Has packed the oracles off with him underground.
 They are empty words.

[31] The shrine at Delphi, where Apollo spoke through the oracle Pythia.

IOKASTÊ  Had I not told you so?

OEDIPUS  You had; it was my faint heart that betrayed me.  925

IOKASTÊ  From now on never think of those things again.

OEDIPUS  And yet—must I not fear my mother's bed?

IOKASTÊ  Why should anyone in this world be afraid,
Since Fate rules us and nothing can be foreseen?
A man should live only for the present day.  930

Have no more fear of sleeping with your mother:
How many men, in dreams, have lain with their mothers!
No reasonable man is troubled by such things.

OEDIPUS  That is true; only—
If only my mother were not still alive!  935
But she is alive. I can not help my dread.

IOKASTÊ  Yet this news of your father's death is wonderful.

OEDIPUS  Wonderful. But I fear the living woman.

MESSENGER  Tell me, who is this woman that you fear?

OEDIPUS  It is Meropê, man; the wife of King Polybos.  940

MESSENGER  Meropê? Why should you be afraid of her?

OEDIPUS  An oracle of the gods, a dreadful saying.

MESSENGER  Can you tell me about it or are you sworn to silence?

OEDIPUS  I can tell you, and I will.
Apollo said through his prophet that I was the man  945
Who should marry his own mother, shed his father's blood
With his own hands. And so, for all these years
I have kept clear of Corinth, and no harm has come—
Though it would have been sweet to see my parents again.

MESSENGER  And is this the fear that drove you out of Corinth?  950

OEDIPUS  Would you have me kill my father?

MESSENGER  As for that
You must be reassured by the news I gave you.

OEDIPUS  If you could reassure me, I would reward you.

MESSENGER  I had that in mind, I will confess: I thought
I could count on you when you returned to Corinth.  955

OEDIPUS  No: I will never go near my parents again

MESSENGER  Ah, son, you still do not know what you are doing—

OEDIPUS  What do you mean? In the name of God tell me!

MESSENGER  —If these are your reasons for not going home.

OEDIPUS  I tell you, I fear the oracle may come true.  960

MESSENGER  And guilt may come upon you through your parents?

OEDIPUS  That is the dread that is always in my heart.

MESSENGER  Can you not see that all your fears are groundless?

OEDIPUS  Groundless? Am I not my parents' son?

MESSENGER  Polybos was not your father.

OEDIPUS  Not my father?  965

MESSENGER  No more your father than the man speaking to you.

OEDIPUS  But you are nothing to me!

MESSENGER  Neither was he.

OEDIPUS   Then why did he call me son?

MESSENGER                              I will tell you:
  Long ago he had you from my hands, as a gift.

OEDIPUS   Then how could he love me so, if I was not his?   970

MESSENGER   He had no children, and his heart turned to you.

OEDIPUS   What of you? Did you buy me? Did you find me by chance?

MESSENGER   I came upon you in the woody vales of Kithairon.

OEDIPUS   And what were you doing there?

MESSENGER                              Tending my flocks.

OEDIPUS   A wandering shepherd?

MESSENGER                              But your savior, son, that day.   975

OEDIPUS   From what did you save me?

MESSENGER                              Your ankles should tell you that.

OEDIPUS   Ah, stranger, why do you speak of that childhood pain?

MESSENGER   I pulled the skewer that pinned your feet together.

OEDIPUS   I have had the mark as long as I can remember.

MESSENGER   That was why you were given the name you bear.[32]   980

OEDIPUS   God! Was it my father or my mother who did it?
  Tell me!

MESSENGER   I do not know. The man who gave you to me
  Can tell you better than I.

OEDIPUS   It was not you that found me, but another?

MESSENGER   It was another shepherd gave you to me.   985

OEDIPUS   Who was he? Can you tell me who he was?

MESSENGER   I think he was said to be one of Laïos' people.

OEDIPUS   You mean the Laïos who was king here years ago?

MESSENGER   Yes; King Laïos; and the man was one of his herdsmen.

OEDIPUS   Is he still alive? Can I see him?

MESSENGER                              These men here   990
  Know best about such things.

OEDIPUS                              Does anyone here
  Know this shepherd that he is talking about?
  Have you seen him in the fields, or in the town?
  If you have, tell me. It is time things were made plain.

CHORAGOS   I think the man he means is that same shepherd   995
  You have already asked to see. Iokastê perhaps
  Could tell you something.

OEDIPUS                              Do you know anything
  About him, Lady? Is he the man we have summoned?
  Is that the man this shepherd means?

IOKASTÊ                              Why think of him?
  Forget this herdsman. Forget it all.   1000
  This talk is a waste of time.

---

[32] In Greek, the name *Oedipus* means "swollen-foot." Originally, the feet of Oedipus may have been bound with the intention of keeping his ghost from moving about to fulfill the prophecy.

OEDIPUS                                    How can you say that,
  When the clues to my true birth are in my hands?
IOKASTÊ  For God's love, let us have no more questioning!
  Is your life nothing to you?
  My own is pain enough for me to bear.                                    1005
OEDIPUS  You need not worry. Suppose my mother a slave,
  And born of slaves: no baseness can touch you.
IOKASTÊ  Listen to me, I beg you: do not do this thing!
OEDIPUS  I will not listen; the truth must be made known.
IOKASTÊ  Everything that I say is for your own good!
OEDIPUS                                              My own good                 1010
  Snaps my patience, then; I want none of it.
IOKASTÊ  You are fatally wrong! May you never learn who you are!
OEDIPUS  Go, one of you, and bring the shepherd here.
  Let us leave this woman to brag of her royal name.
IOKASTÊ  Ah, miserable!                                                          1015
  That is the only word I have for you now.
  That is the only word I can ever have.            *(Exit into the palace.)*
CHORAGOS  Why has she left us, Oedipus? Why has she gone
  In such a passion of sorrow? I fear this silence:
  Something dreadful may come of it.
OEDIPUS                                          Let it come!                    1020
  However base my birth, I must know about it.
  The Queen, like a woman, is perhaps ashamed
  To think of my low origin. But I
  Am a child of Luck; I can not be dishonored.
  Luck is my mother; the passing months, my brothers,                     1025
  Have seen me rich and poor.
                    If this is so,
  How could I wish that I were someone else?
  How could I not be glad to know my birth?


## ODE III

*STROPHE*

CHORUS  If ever the coming time were known
  To my heart's pondering,                                                1030
  Kithairon, now by Heaven I see the torches
  At the festival of the next full moon,[33]
  And see the dance, and hear the choir sing
  A grace to your gentle shade:
  Mountain where Oedipus was found,                                        1035
  O mountain guard of a noble race!
  May the god who heals us[34] lend his aid,

---

[33] Almost any full moon marked the festival day for some god or other.

[34] Apollo.

And let that glory come to pass
For our king's cradling-ground.

*ANTISTROPHE*

Of the nymphs that flower beyond the years,                          1040
Who bore you, royal child,
To Pan of the hills[35] or the timberline Apollo,[36]
Cold in delight where the upland clears,
Or Hermês for whom Kyllenê's heights[37] are piled?
Or flushed as evening cloud,                                         1045
Great Dionysos, roamer of mountains,
He—was it he who found you there,
And caught you up in his own proud
Arms from the sweet god-ravisher[38]
Who laughed by the Muses' fountains?                                 1050


## SCENE IV

OEDIPUS   Sirs: though I do not know the man,
   I think I see him coming, this shepherd we want:
   He is old, like our friend here, and the men
   Bringing him seem to be servants of my house.
   But you can tell, if you have ever seen him.                      1055

*(Enter* SHEPHERD *escorted by* SERVANTS.*)*

CHORAGOS   I know him, he was Laïos' man. You can trust him.
OEDIPUS   Tell me first, you from Corinth: is this the shepherd
   We were discussing?
MESSENGER              This is the very man.
OEDIPUS *(to* SHEPHERD*)*   Come here. No, look at me. You must answer
   Everything I ask.—You belonged to Laïos?                          1060
SHEPHERD   Yes: born his slave, brought up in his house.
OEDIPUS   Tell me: what kind of work did you do for him?
SHEPHERD   I was a shepherd of his, most of my life.
OEDIPUS   Where mainly did you go for pasturage?
SHEPHERD   Sometimes Kithairon, sometimes the hills near-by.         1065
OEDIPUS   Do you remember ever seeing this man out there?
SHEPHERD   What would he be doing there? This man?
OEDIPUS   This man standing here. Have you ever seen him before?
SHEPHERD   No. At least, not to my recollection.
MESSENGER   And that is not strange, my lord. But I'll refresh       1070

---

[35] Pan, son of Hermes and Dryope, was the god of flocks and shepherds, forests and wild
life. He was the patron of shepherds and hunters.
[36] Apollo, as well, was associated with the care of flocks and herds.
[37] The mountain birthplace of Hermês, messenger of the gods.
[38] This is an allusion to the nymph who was thought to have borne Oedipus.

His memory: he must remember when we two
Spent three whole seasons together, March to September,
On Kithairon or thereabouts. He had two flocks;
I had one. Each autumn I'd drive mine home
And he would go back with his to Laïos' sheepfold.—                    1075
Is this not true, just as I have described it?
SHEPHERD  True, yes; but it was all so long ago.
MESSENGER  Well, then: do you remember, back in those days,
    That you gave me a baby boy to bring up as my own?
SHEPHERD  What if I did? What are you trying to say?                    1080
MESSENGER  King Oedipus was once that little child.
SHEPHERD  Damn you, hold your tongue!
OEDIPUS                                      No more of that!
    It is your tongue needs watching, not this man's.
SHEPHERD  My king, my master, what is it I have done wrong?
OEDIPUS  You have not answered his question about the boy.            1085
SHEPHERD  He does not know . . . He is only making trouble . . .
OEDIPUS  Come, speak plainly, or it will go hard with you.
SHEPHERD  In God's name, do not torture an old man!
OEDIPUS  Come here, one of you; bind his arms behind him.
SHEPHERD  Unhappy king! What more do you wish to learn?              1090
OEDIPUS  Did you give this man the child he speak of?
SHEPHERD                                      I did.
    And I would to God I had died that very day.
OEDIPUS  You will die now unless you speak the truth.
SHEPHERD  Yet if I speak the truth, I am worse than dead.
OEDIPUS (to ATTENDANT)  He intends to draw it out, apparently—        1095
SHEPHERD  No! I have told you already that I gave him the boy.
OEDIPUS  Where did you get him? From your house? From somewhere
    else?
SHEPHERD  Not from mine, no. A man gave him to me.
OEDIPUS  Is that man here? Whose house did he belong to?
SHEPHERD  For God's love, my king, do not ask me any more!            1100
OEDIPUS  You are a dead man if I have to ask you again.
SHEPHERD  Then . . . Then the child was from the palace of Laïos.
OEDIPUS  A slave child? or a child of his own line?
SHEPHERD  Ah, I am on the brink of dreadful speech!
OEDIPUS  And I of dreadful hearing. Yet I must hear.                   1105
SHEPHERD  If you must be told, then . . .
                                      They said it was Laïos' child;
    But it is your wife who can tell you about that.
OEDIPUS  My wife!—Did she give it to you?
SHEPHERD                                      My lord, she did.
OEDIPUS  Do you know why?
SHEPHERD                          I was told to get rid of it.
OEDIPUS  Oh heartless mother!
SHEPHERD                          But in dread of prophecies . . .     1110

OEDIPUS  Tell me.

SHEPHERD         It was said that the boy would kill his own father.

OEDIPUS  Then why did you give him over to this old man?

SHEPHERD  I pitied the baby, my king,
 And I thought that this man would take him far away
 To his own country.

                              He saved him—but for what a fate!          1115
 For if you are what this man says you are,
 No man living is more wretched than Oedipus.

OEDIPUS  Ah God!
        It was true!
                        All the prophecies!
                                 —Now,
 O Light, may I look on you for the last time!          1120
 I, Oedipus,
 Oedipus, damned in his birth, in his marriage damned,
 Damned in the blood he shed with his own hand!

                                        (He rushes into the palace.)


## ODE IV

STROPHE 1

CHORUS  Alas for the seed of men.
 What measure shall I give these generations          1125
 That breathe on the void and are void
 And exist and do not exist?
 Who bears more weight of joy
 Than mass of sunlight shifting in images,
 Or who shall make his thought stay on          1130
 That down time drifts away?
 Your splendor is all fallen.
 O naked brow of wrath and tears,
 O change of Oedipus!
 I who saw your days call no man blest—          1135
 Your great days like ghósts góne.

ANTISTROPHE 1

 That mind was a strong bow.
 Deep, how deep you drew it then, hard archer,
 At a dim fearful range,
 And brought dear glory down!          1140
 You overcame the stranger—
 The virgin with her hooking lion claws[39]—
 And though death sang, stood like a tower
 To make pale Thebes take heart.

[39] The Sphinx.

Fortress against our sorrow!   1145
True king, giver of laws,
Majestic Oedipus!
No prince in Thebes had ever such renown,
No prince won such grace of power.

*STROPHE 2*

And now of all men ever known   1150
Most pitiful is this man's story:
His fortunes are most changed, his state
Fallen to a low slave's
Ground under bitter fate.
O Oedipus, most royal one!   1155
The great door that expelled you to the light[40]
Gave at night—ah, gave night to your glory:
As to the father, to the fathering son.
All understood too late.
How could that queen whom Laïos won,   1160
The garden that he harrowed at his height,
Be silent when that act was done?

*ANTISTROPHE 2*

But all eyes fail before time's eye,
All actions come to justice there.
Though never willed, though far down the deep past,   1165
Your bed, your dred sirings,
Are brought to book at last.
Child by Laïos doomed to die,
Then doomed to lose that fortunate little death,
Would God you never took breath in this air   1170
That with my wailing lips I take to cry:
For I weep the world's outcast.
I was blind, and now I can tell why:
Asleep, for you had given ease of breath
To Thebes, while the false years went by.   1175

# ÉXODOS[41]

*(Enter, from the palace, SECOND MESSENGER.)*

SECOND MESSENGER   Elders of Thebes,[42] most honored in this land,
What horrors are yours to see and hear, what weight
Of sorrow to be endured, if, true to your birth,

---

[40] An allusion to the womb of Iokastê.
[41] The final scene of the play, containing the resolution.
[42] The Messenger is addressing the Chorus.

You venerate the line of Labdakos!
I think neither Istros nor Phasis, those great rivers, 1180
Could purify this place of all the evil
It shelters now, or soon must bring to light—
Evil not done unconsciously, but willed.

The greatest griefs are those we cause ourselves.
CHORAGOS  Surely, friend, we have grief enough already; 1185
    What new sorrow do you mean?
SECOND MESSENGER                        The queen is dead.
CHORAGOS  O miserable queen! But at whose hand!
SECOND MESSENGER                                Her own.
    The full horror of what happened you can not know,
    For you did not see it; but I, who did, will tell you
    As clearly as I can how she met her death. 1190

When she had left us,
In passionate silence, passing through the court,
She ran to her apartment in the house,
Her hair clutched by the fingers of both hands.
She closed the doors behind her; then, by that bed 1195
Where long ago the fatal son was conceived—
That son who should bring about his father's death—
We heard her call upon Laïos, dead so many years,
And heard her wail for the double fruit of her marriage,
A husband by her husband, children by her child. 1200

Exactly how she died I do not know:
For Oedipus burst out moaning and would not let us
Keep vigil to the end: it was by him
As he stormed about the room that our eyes were caught.
From one to another of us he went, begging a sword, 1205
Hunting the wife who was not his wife, the mother
Whose womb had carried his own children and himself.
I do not know: it was none of us aided him,
But surely one of the gods was in control!
For with a dreadful cry 1210
He hurled his weight, as though wrenched out of himself,
At the twin doors: the bolts gave, and he rushed in.
And there we saw her hanging, her body swaying
From the cruel cord she had noosed about her neck.
A great sob broke from him, heartbreaking to hear, 1215
As he loosed the rope and lowered her to the ground.

I would blot out from my mind what happened next!
For the king ripped from her gown the golden brooches
That were her ornament, and raised them, and plunged them down
Straight into his own eyeballs, crying, "No more, 1220
No more shall you look on the misery about me,

The horrors of my own doing! Too long you have known
The faces of those whom I should never have seen,
Too long been blind to those for whom I was searching!
From this hour, go in darkness!" And as he spoke,                    1225
He struck at his eyes—not once, but many times;
And the blood spattered his beard,
Bursting from his ruined sockets like red hail.

So from the unhappiness of two this evil has sprung,
A curse on the man and woman alike. The old                          1230
Happiness of the house of Labdakos
Was happiness enough: where is it today?
It is all wailing and ruin, disgrace, death—all
The misery of mankind that has a name—
And it is wholly and for ever theirs.                                1235

CHORAGOS  Is he in agony still? Is there no rest for him?

SECOND MESSENGER  He is calling for someone to open the doors wide
So that all the children of Kadmos may look upon
His father's murderer, his mother's—no,
I can not say it!

           And then he will leave Thebes,                  1240
Self-exiled, in order that the curse
Which he himself pronounced may depart from the house.
He is weak, and there is none to lead him,
So terrible is his suffering.

           But you will see:
Look, the doors are opening; in a moment                             1245
You will see a thing that would crush a heart of stone.

*(The central door is opened;* OEDIPUS, *blinded, is led in.)*

CHORAGOS  Dreadful indeed for men to see.
Never have my own eyes
Looked on a sight so full of fear.

Oedipus!                                                            1250
What madness came upon you, what daemon[43]
Leaped on your life with heavier
Punishment than a mortal man can bear?
No: I can not even
Look at you, poor ruined one.                                        1255
And I would speak, question, ponder,
If I were able. No.
You make me shudder.

OEDIPUS  God. God.
Is there a sorrow greater?                                           1260
Where shall I find harbor in this world?

---

[43] Daemon here means god.

My voice is hurled far on a dark wind.
What has God done to me?
CHORAGOS  Too terrible to think of, or to see.

*STROPHE 1*

OEDIPUS  O cloud of night,                                                    1265
  Never to be turned away: night coming on,
  I can not tell how: night like a shroud!
  My fair winds brought me here.
                                    O God. Again
  The pain of the spikes where I had sight,
  The flooding pain                                                           1270
  Of memory, never to be gouged out.
CHORAGOS  This is not strange.
  You suffer it all twice over, remorse in pain,
  Pain in remorse.

*ANTISTROPHE 1*

OEDIPUS  Ah dear friend                                                      1275
  Are you faithful even yet, you alone?
  Are you still standing near me, will you stay here,
  Patient, to care for the blind?
                                    The blind man!
  Yet even blind I know who it is attends me,
  By the voice's tone—                                                       1280
  Though my new darkness hide the comforter.
CHORAGOS  Oh fearful act!
  What god was it drove you to rake black
  Night across your eyes?

*STROPHE 2*

OEDIPUS  Apollo. Apollo. Dear                                                1285
  Children, the god was Apollo.
  He brought my sick, sick fate upon me.
  But the blinding hand was my own!
  How could I bear to see
  When all my sight was horror everywhere?                                   1290
CHORAGOS  Everywhere; that is true.
OEDIPUS  And now what is left?
  Images? Love? A greeting even,
  Sweet to the senses? Is there anything?
  Ah, no friends: lead me away.                                              1295
  Lead me away from Thebes.
                                    Lead the great wreck
  And hell of Oedipus, whom the gods hate.
CHORAGOS  Your misery, you are not blind to that.
  Would God you had never found it out!

*ANTISTROPHE 2*

OEDIPUS  Death take the man who unbound                    1300
  My feet on that hillside
  And delivered me from death to life! What life?
  If only I had died,
  This weight of monstrous doom
  Could not have dragged me and my darlings down.          1305
CHORAGOS  I would have wished the same.
OEDIPUS  Oh never to have come here
  With my father's blood upon me! Never
  To have been the man they call his mother's husband!
  Oh accurst! Oh child of evil,                            1310
  To have entered that wretched bed—
                          the selfsame one!
  More primal than sin itself, this fell to me.
CHORAGOS  I do not know what words to offer you.
  You were better dead than alive and blind.
OEDIPUS  Do not counsel me any more. This punishment       1315
  That I have laid upon myself is just.
  If I had eyes,
  I do not know how I could bear the sight
  Of my father, when I came to the house of Death,
  Or my mother: for I have sinned against them both        1320
  So vilely that I could not make my peace
  By strangling my own life.
                          Or do you think my children,
  Born as they were born, would be sweet to my eyes?
  Ah never, never! Nor this town with its high walls,
  Nor the holy images of the gods.
                          For I,                           1325
  Thrice miserable!—Oedipus, noblest of all the line
  Of Kadmos, have condemned myself to enjoy
  These things no more, by my own malediction
  Expelling that man whom the gods declared
  To be a defilement in the house of Laïos.                1330
  After exposing the rankness of my own guilt,
  How could I look men frankly in the eyes?
  No, I swear it,
  If I could have stifled my hearing at its source,
  I would have done it and made all this body              1335
  A tight cell of misery, blank to light and sound:
  So I should have been safe in my dark mind
  Beyond external evil.
                  Ah Kithairon!
  Why did you shelter me? When I was cast upon you,
  Why did I not die? Then I should never                   1340
  Have shown the world my execrable birth.

Ah Polybos! Corinth, city that I believed
The ancient seat of my ancestors: how fair
I seemed, your child! And all the while this evil
Was cancerous within me!

                  For I am sick           1345
In my own being, sick in my origin.

O three roads, dark ravine, woodland and way
Where three roads met: you, drinking my father's blood,
My own blood, spilled by my own hand: can you remember
The unspeakable things I did there, and the things      1350
I went on from there to do?

                O marriage, marriage!
The act that engendered me, and again the act
Performed by the son in the same bed—

                      Ah, the net
Of incest, mingling fathers, brothers, sons,
With brides, wives, mothers: the last evil        1355
That can be known by men: no tongue can say
How evil!

        No. For the love of God, conceal me
Somewhere far from Thebes; or kill me; or hurl me
Into the sea, away from men's eyes for ever.

Come, lead me. You need not fear to touch me.     1360
Of all men, I alone can bear this guilt.

(*Enter* KREON.)

CHORAGOS  Kreon is here now. As to what you ask,
  He may decide the course to take. He only
  Is left to protect the city in your place.
OEDIPUS  Alas, how can I speak to him? What right have I    1365
  To beg his courtesy whom I have deeply wronged?
KREON  I have not come to mock you, Oedipus,
  Or to reproach you, either.   (*To* ATTENDANTS)
                    —You, standing there:
  If you have lost all respect for man's dignity,
  At least respect the flame of Lord Helios:      1370
  Do not allow this pollution to show itself
  Openly here, an affront to the earth
  And Heaven's rain and the light of day. No, take him
  Into the house as quickly as you can.
  For it is proper                  1375
  That only the close kindred see his grief.
OEDIPUS  I pray you in God's name, since your courtesy
  Ignores my dark expectation, visiting
  With mercy this man of all men most execrable:
  Give me what I ask—for your good, not for mine.     1380

KREON   And what is it that you turn to me begging for?
OEDIPUS   Drive me out of this country as quickly as may be
   To a place where no human voice can ever greet me.
KREON   I should have done that before now—only,
   God's will had not been wholly revealed to me.            1385
OEDIPUS   But his command is plain: the parricide
   Must be destroyed. I am that evil man.
KREON   That is the sense of it, yes; but as things are,
   We had best discover clearly what is to be done.
OEDIPUS   You would learn more about a man like me?         1390
KREON   You are ready now to listen to the god.
OEDIPUS   I will listen. But it is to you
   That I must turn for help. I beg you, hear me.

The woman in there—
Give her whatever funeral you think proper:           1395
She is your sister.
               —But let me go, Kreon!
Let me purge my father's Thebes of the pollution
Of my living here, and go out to the wild hills,
To Kithairon, that has won such fame with me,
The tomb my mother and father appointed for me,      1400
And let me die there, as they willed I should.
And yet I know
Death will not ever come to me through sickness
Or in any natural way: I have been preserved
For some unthinkable fate. But let that be.          1405

As for my sons, you need not care for them.
They are men, they will find some way to live.
But my poor daughters, who have shared my table,
Who never before have been parted from their father—
Take care of them, Kreon; do this for me.          1410

And will you let me touch them with my hands
A last time, and let us weep together?
Be kind, my lord,
Great prince, be kind!
             Could I but touch them,
They would be mine again, as when I had my eyes.      1415

(Enter ANTIGONE and ISMENE, attended.)

Ah, God!
Is it my dearest children I hear weeping?
Has Kreon pitied me and sent my daughters?
KREON   Yes, Oedipus: I knew that they were dear to you
   In the old days, and know you must love them still.    1420
OEDIPUS   May God bless you for this—and be a friendlier
   Guardian to you than he has been to me!

Children, where are you?
Come quickly to my hands: they are your brother's—
Hands that have brought your father's once clear eyes        1425
To this way of seeing—
                    Ah dearest ones,
I had neither sight nor knowledge then, your father
By the woman who was the source of his own life!
And I weep for you—having no strength to see you—,
I weep for you when I think of the bitterness                1430
That men will visit upon you all your lives.
What homes, what festivals can you attend
Without being forced to depart again in tears?
And when you come to marriageable age,
Where is the man, my daughters, who would dare              1435
Risk the bane that lies on all my children?
Is there any evil wanting? Your father killed
His father; sowed the womb of her who bore him;
Engendered you at the fount of his own existence!
That is what they will say of you.

                              Then, whom                    1440
Can you ever marry? There are no bridegrooms for you,
And your lives must wither away in sterile dreaming.

O Kreon, son of Menoikeus!
You are the only father my daughters have,
Since we, their parents, are both of us gone for ever.      1445
They are your own blood: you will not let them
Fall into beggary and loneliness;
You will keep them from the miseries that are mine!
Take pity on them; see, they are only children,
Friendless except for you. Promise me this,                 1450
Great prince, and give me your hand in token of it.

(KREON *clasps his right hand.*)

Children:
I could say much, if you could understand me,
But as it is, I have only this prayer for you:
Live where you can, be happy as you can—                    1455
Happier, please God, than God has made your father.
KREON   Enough. You have wept enough. Now go within.
OEDIPUS   I must; but it is hard.
KREON                           Time eases all things.
OEDIPUS   You know my mind, then?
KREON                            Say what you desire.
OEDIPUS   Send me from Thebes!
KREON                           God grant that I may!        1460
OEDIPUS   But since God hates me . . .
KREON                          No, he will grant your wish.

OEDIPUS   You promise?

KREON                          I can not speak beyond my knowledge.

OEDIPUS   Then lead me in.

KREON                          Come now, and leave your children.

OEDIPUS   No! Do not take them from me!

KREON                                    Think no longer
That you are in command here, but rather think                        1465
How, when you were, you served your own destruction.

*(Exeunt into the house all but the* CHORUS; *the* CHORAGOS *chants directly to
the audience.)*

CHORAGOS   Men of Thebes: look upon Oedipus.

This is the king who solved the famous riddle
And towered up, most powerful of men.
No mortal eyes but looked on him with envy,                           1470
Yet in the end ruin swept over him.

Let every man in mankind's frailty
Consider his last day; and let none
Presume on his good fortune until he find
Life, at his death, a memory without pain.                            1475

## FOR DISCUSSION

1. What sort of a person is Oedipus presented as in the Prologue?
2. What heroic qualities does Oedipus possess? What are his character flaws?
3. Why is Oedipus so insistent about discovering the truth about the murder
   of Laïos? Does his insistence serve to make him a sympathetic character?
4. Point out specific instances of dramatic irony arising from statements made
   by Oedipus.
5. Throughout the play, what dramatic purpose is served by the Chorus?
6. At what point did you discover that Oedipus had murdered his father and
   married his mother?
7. By modern standards, guilt of any kind requires a knowledge on the part
   of the guilty person of his or her misdeeds. Assuming those standards, what
   is Oedipus actually guilty of?
8. Within the scheme of the play, is there any way that Oedipus could have
   avoided his fate? To what extent do you think Oedipus was responsible for
   his own downfall? To what extent does the play suggest that the gods—or
   fate—are unfair to man's attempts to think and act rationally?
9. Long before Oedipus knows the truth about all that he has done, he seems
   possessed by a gnawing sense of guilt. Why does he feel guilty? Does this
   seem natural to you?
10. Why does Oedipus put his eyes out? Would it not have been more "logical"
    for him to castrate himself or perhaps cut off the arm that slew Laïos? Why
    does he not commit suicide, as Iocastê did?
11. Psychoanalysis defines the *Oedipus complex* as the unconscious tendency of
    a child to be attracted to the parent of the opposite sex and hostile toward
    the parent of the same sex. Do you think this notion helps you to understand
    the play? Does Oedipus himself have an Oedipus complex?

# Othello

WILLIAM SHAKESPEARE

## Characters

DUKE OF VENICE
BRABANTIO   a Senator
SENATORS
GRATIANO   Brother to Brabantio
LODOVICO   Kinsman to Brabantio
OTHELLO   a noble Moor; in the service of the Venetian State
CASSIO   his Lieutenant
IAGO   his Ancient
RODERIGO   a Venetian Gentleman
MONTANO   Othello's predecessor in the Government of Cyprus
CLOWN   Servant to Othello
DESDEMONA   Daughter to Brabantio, and Wife to Othello
EMILIA   Wife to Iago
BIANCA   Mistress to Cassio
SAILOR, OFFICERS, GENTLEMEN, MESSENGERS, MUSICIANS, HERALDS, ATTENDANTS

*SCENE.   For the first Act, in Venice; during the rest of the Play, at a Sea-port in Cyprus*

## Act I

### SCENE 1   *Venice. A Street.*

*(Enter Roderigo and Iago.)*

RODERIGO   Tush! Never tell me; I take it much unkindly
   That thou, Iago, who hast had my purse
   As if the strings were thine, shouldst know of this.[1]
IAGO   'Sblood,[2] but you will not hear me:
   If ever I did dream of such a matter,
   Abhor me.

---

1. *I.e.*, Othello's successful courtship of Desdemona.     2. By God's blood.

RODERIGO  Thou told'st me thou didst hold him[3] in thy hate.
IAGO  Despise me if I do not. Three great ones of the city,
   In personal suit to make me his lieutenant,
   Off-capp'd[4] to him; and, by the faith of man,          10
   I know my price, I am worth no worse a place;
   But he, as loving his own pride and purposes,
   Evades them, with a bombast circumstance[5]
   Horribly stuff'd with epithets of war;
   And, in conclusion,
   Nonsuits[6] my mediators;[7] for, 'Certes,'[8] says he,
   'I have already chosen my officer.'
   And what was he?
   Forsooth, a great arithmetician,
   One Michael Cassio, A Florentine,          20
   A fellow almost damn'd in a fair wife;[9]
   That never set a squadron in the field,
   Nor the division of a battle knows
   More than a spinster; unless[10] the bookish theoric,[11]
   Wherein the toged consuls can propose
   As masterly as he: mere prattle, without practice,
   Is all his soldiership. But he, sir, had the election;
   And I—of whom his eyes had seen the proof
   At Rhodes, at Cyprus, and on other grounds
   Christian and heathen—must be be-lee'd[12] and calm'd          30
   By debitor and creditor; this counter-caster,[13]
   He, in good time, must his lieutenant be,
   And I—God bless the mark!—his Moorship's ancient.[14]
RODERIGO  By heaven, I rather would have been his hangman.
IAGO  Why, there's no remedy: 'tis the curse of the service,
   Preferment goes by letter and affection,
   Not by the old gradation,[15] where each second
   Stood heir to the first. Now, sir, be judge yourself,
   Whe'r[16] I in any just term am affin'd[17]
   To love the Moor.
RODERIGO          I would not follow him then.          40
IAGO  O! sir, content you;
   I follow him to serve my turn upon him;

---

3. *I.e.*, Othello.      4. Took off their caps.
5. Pompous wordiness, circumlocution.      6. Turns down.
7. Spokesmen.      8. In truth.      9. A much debated phrase. In the Italian source
the Captain (*i.e.*, Cassio) was married, and it may be that Shakespeare originally
intended Bianca to be Cassio's wife but later changed his mind and failed to alter the
phrase here accordingly. Or perhaps Iago simply sneers at Cassio as a notorious ladies'
man.      10. Except.      11. Theory.      12. Left without wind for my sails.
13. Bookkeeper (*cf.* "arithmetician" above).      14. Ensign (but Iago's position in the
play seems to be that of Othello's aide-de-camp).      15. Seniority.
16. Whether.      17. Obliged.

We cannot all be masters, nor all masters
Cannot be truly follow'd. You shall mark
Many a duteous and knee-crooking knave,
That, doting on his own obsequious bondage,
Wears out his time, much like his master's ass,
For nought but provender, and when he's old, cashier'd;
Whip me such honest knaves. Others there are
Who, trimm'd in forms and visages of duty,                      50
Keep yet their hearts attending on themselves,
And, throwing but shows of service on their lords,
Do well thrive by them, and when they have lin'd their coats
Do themselves homage: these fellows have some soul;
And such a one do I profess myself. For, sir,
It is as sure as you are Roderigo,
Were I the Moor, I would not be Iago:
In following him, I follow but myself;
Heaven is my judge, not I for love and duty,
But seeming so, for my peculiar end:                            60
For when my outward action doth demonstrate
The native act and figure of my heart
In compliment extern,[18] 'tis not long after
But I will wear my heart upon my sleeve
For daws to peck at: I am not what I am.
RODERIGO  What a full fortune does the thick-lips owe,[19]
    If he can carry 't thus!
IAGO                    Call up her father;
    Rouse him, make after him, poison his delight,
    Proclaim him in the streets, incense her kinsmen,
    And, though he in a fertile climate dwell,[20]             70
    Plague him with flies; though that his joy be joy,
    Yet throw such changes of vexation on 't
    As it may lose some colour.
RODERIGO  Here is her father's house; I'll call aloud.
IAGO  Do; with like timorous[21] accent and dire yell
    As when, by night and negligence, the fire
    Is spied in populous cities.
RODERIGO  What, ho! Brabantio: Signior Brabantio, ho!
IAGO  Awake! what, ho! Brabantio! thieves! thieves! thieves!
    Look to your house, your daughter, and your bags!          80
    Thieves! thieves!

    (Enter Brabantio, above, at a window.)

BRABANTIO  What is the reason of this terrible summons?
    What is the matter there?

18. External show.     19. Own.     20. I.e., is fortunate.     21. Frightening.

RODERIGO  Signior, is all your family within?

IAGO  Are your doors lock'd?

BRABANTIO                    Why? wherefore ask you this?

IAGO  'Zounds!²² sir, you're robb'd; for shame, put on your gown;
   Your heart is burst, you have lost half your soul;
   Even now, now, very now, an old black ram
   Is tupping²³ your white ewe. Arise, arise!
   Awake the snorting²⁴ citizens with the bell,                    90
   Or else the devil will make a grandsire of you.
   Arise, I say.

BRABANTIO      What! have you lost your wits?

RODERIGO  Most reverend signior, do you know my voice?

BRABANTIO  Not I, what are you?

RODERIGO  My name is Roderigo.

BRABANTIO                    The worser welcome:
   I have charg'd thee not to haunt about my doors:
   In honest plainness thou hast heard me say
   My daughter is not for thee; and now, in madness,
   Being full of supper and distempering draughts,                    100
   Upon malicious knavery dost thou come
   To start my quiet.

RODERIGO  Sir, sir, sir!

BRABANTIO            But thou must needs be sure
   My spirit and my place²⁵ have in them power
   To make this bitter to thee.

RODERIGO                    Patience, good sir.

BRABANTIO  What tell'st thou me of robbing? this is Venice;
   My house is not a grange.²⁶

RODERIGO                    Most grave Brabantio,
   In simple and pure soul I come to you.

IAGO  'Zounds! sir, you are one of those that will not serve God if the devil bid
   you. Because we come to do you service and you think we are ruffians, you'll
   have your daughter covered with a Barbary horse; you'll have your nephews
   neigh to you; you'll have coursers for cousins and gennets²⁷ for germans.²⁸

BRABANTIO  What profane wretch art thou?

IAGO  I am one, sir, that comes to tell you, your daughter and the Moor are now
   making the beast with two backs.

BRABANTIO  Thou art a villain.

IAGO                    You are—a senator.

BRABANTIO  This thou shalt answer; I know thee, Roderigo.

RODERIGO  Sir, I will answer any thing. But, I beseech you,
   If 't be your pleasure and most wise consent,—
   As partly, I find, it is,—that your fair daughter,                    120

---

22. By God's wounds.    23. Copulating.    24. Snoring.    25. Position.
26. Isolated farm house.    27. Spanish horses.    28. Blood relations.

At this odd-even[29] and dull watch o' the night,
Transported with no worse nor better guard
But with a knave of common hire, a gondolier,
To the gross clasps of a lascivious Moor,—
If this be known to you, and your allowance,[30]
We then have done you bold and saucy wrongs;
But if you know not this, my manners tell me
We have your wrong rebuke. Do not believe
That, from[31] the sense of all civility,
I thus would play and trifle with your reverence:                    130
Your daughter, if you have not given her leave,
I say again, hath made a gross revolt;
Tying her duty, beauty, wit and fortunes
In[32] an extravagant[33] and wheeling stranger
Of here and every where. Straight satisfy yourself:
If she be in her chamber or your house,
Let loose on me the justice of the state
For thus deluding you.
BRABANTIO                    Strike on the tinder, ho!
Give me a taper! call up all my people!
This accident[34] is not unlike my dream;                             140
Belief of it oppresses me already.
Light, I say! light!                              *(Exit, from above.)*
IAGO                    Farewell, for I must leave you:
It seems not meet nor wholesome to my place
To be produc'd,[35] as, if I stay, I shall,
Against the Moor; for I do know the state,
However this may gall him with some check,[36]
Cannot with safety cast him; for he's embark'd
With such loud reason to the Cyprus wars,—
Which even now stand in act,—that, for their souls,
Another of his fathom[37] they have none,                            150
To lead their business; in which regard,
Though I do hate him as I do hell-pains,
Yet, for necessity of present life,
I must show out a flag and sign of love,
Which is indeed but sign. That you shall surely find him,
Lead to the Sagittary[38] the raised search;
And there will I be with him. So, farewell.                   *(Exit.)*

*(Enter below, Brabantio, and servants with torches.)*

BRABANTIO  It is too true an evil: gone she is,
And what's to come of my despised time

---

29. Between night and morning.    30. By your approval.    31. Away
from.    32. To.    33. Expatriate.    34. Happening.    35. *I.e.*, as a
witness.    36. Restraining adversity.    37. Caliber, ability.    38. The name
of an inn (?).

Is nought but bitterness. Now, Roderigo,         160
  Where didst thou see her? O, unhappy girl!
  With the Moor, sayst thou? Who would be a father!
  How didst thou know 'twas she? O, she deceives me
  Past thought. What said she to you? Get more tapers!
  Raise all my kindred! Are they married, think you?
RODERIGO  Truly, I think they are.
BRABANTIO  O heaven! How got she out? O treason of the blood:
  Fathers, from hence trust not your daughters' minds
  By what you see them act. Are there not charms
  By which the property of youth and maidhood      170
  May be abus'd? Have you not read, Roderigo,
  Of some such thing?
RODERIGO            Yes, sir, I have indeed.
BRABANTIO  Call up my brother. O! that you had had her.
  Some one way, some another! Do you know
  Where we may apprehend her and the Moor?
RODERIGO  I think I can discover him, if you please
  To get good guard and go along with me.
BRABANTIO  Pray you, lead on. At every house I'll call;
  I may command at most. Get weapons, ho!
  And raise some special officers of night.         180
  On, good Roderigo; I'll deserve[39] your pains.        (Exeunt.)

## SCENE 2   Another street.

(Enter Othello, Iago, and Attendants, with torches.)

IAGO  Though in the trade of war I have slain men,
  Yet do I hold it very stuff o' the conscience
  To do no contriv'd murder: I lack iniquity
  Sometimes to do me service. Nine or ten times
  I had thought to have yerk'd[40] him here under the ribs.
OTHELLO  'Tis better as it is.
IAGO              Nay, but he prated,
  And spoke such scurvy and provoking terms
  Against your honour
  That, with the little godliness I have,
  I did full hard forbear him. But, I pray, sir,       10
  Are you fast married? Be assur'd of this,
  That the magnifico[41] is much belov'd,
  And hath in his effect a voice potential
  As double[42] as the duke's; he will divorce you,

39. I.e., reward.     40. Stabbed.     41. One of the grandees, or rulers, of Venice;
here, Brabantio.     42. Iago means that Brabantio's influence equals that of the
Doge's, with his double vote.

Or put upon you what restraint and grievance
The law—with all his might to enforce it on—
Will give him cable.[43]

OTHELLO               Let him do his spite:
My services which I have done the signiory[44]
Shall out-tongue his complaints. 'Tis yet to know,[45]
Which when I know that boasting is an honour           20
I shall promulgate, I fetch my life and being
From men of royal siege, and my demerits[46]
May speak unbonneted[47] to as proud a fortune
As this[48] that I have reach'd; for know, Iago,
But that I love the gentle Desdemona,
I would not my unhoused[49] free condition
Put into circumscription and confine
For the sea's worth. But, look! what lights come yond?

IAGO   Those are the raised[50] father and his friends:
You were best[51] go in.

OTHELLO               Not I; I must be found:           30
My parts, my title, and my perfect[52] soul
Shall manifest me rightly. Is it they?

IAGO   By Janus,[53] I think no.

*(Enter Cassio and certain Officers, with torches.)*

OTHELLO   The servants of the duke, and my lieutenant.
The goodness of the night upon you, friends!
What is the news?

CASSIO               The duke does greet you, general,
And he requires your haste-post-haste appearance,
Even on the instant.

OTHELLO              What is the matter, think you?

CASSIO   Something from Cyprus, as I may divine.
It is a business of some heat;[54] the galleys           40
Have sent a dozen sequent[55] messengers
This very night at one another's heels,
And many of the consuls,[56] rais'd and met,
Are at the duke's already. You have been hotly call'd for;
When, being not at your lodging to be found,
The senate hath sent about three several[57] quests
To search you out.

OTHELLO              'Tis well I am found by you.
I will but spend a word here in the house,

---

43. *I.e.*, scope.     44. The Venetian government.     45. *I.e.*, the signiory does not
as yet know.     46. Merits.     47. *I.e.*, as equals.     48. *I.e.*, that of
Desdemona's family.     49. Unconfined.     50. Aroused.     51. Had
better.     52. Untroubled by a bad conscience.     53. The two-faced Roman god
of portals and doors and (hence) of beginnings and ends.     54. Urgency.
55. Following one another.     56. *I.e.*, senators.     57. Separate.

And go with you.                                                    *(Exit.)*
CASSIO                 Ancient, what makes he here?
IAGO  Faith, he to-night hath boarded a land carrack;[58]                50
  If it prove lawful prize, he's made for ever.
CASSIO  I do not understand.
IAGO                              He's married.
CASSIO                              To who?

  *(Re-enter Othello.)*

IAGO  Marry,[59] to—Come, captain, will you go?
OTHELLO                              Have with you.
CASSIO  Here comes another troop to seek for you.
IAGO  It is Brabantio. General, be advis'd;
  He comes to bad intent.

  *(Enter Brabantio, Roderigo, and Officers, with torches and weapons.)*

OTHELLO                 Holla! stand there!
RODERIGO  Signior, it is the Moor.
BRABANTIO                 Down with him, thief!

  *(They draw on both sides.)*

IAGO  You, Roderigo! Come, sir, I am for you.[60]
OTHELLO  Keep up your bright swords, for the dew will rust them.
  Good signior, you shall more command with years                  60
  Than with your weapons.
BRABANTIO  O thou foul thief! where hast thou stow'd my daughter?
  Damn'd as thou art, thou hast enchanted her;
  For I'll refer me to all things of sense,
  If she in chains of magic were not bound,
  Whether a maid so tender, fair, and happy,
  So opposite to marriage that she shunn'd
  The wealthy curled darlings of our nation,
  Would ever have, to incur a general mock,
  Run from her guardage to the sooty bosom                         70
  Of such a thing as thou; to fear, not to delight.
  Judge me the world, if 'tis not gross in sense[61]
  That thou hast practis'd on her with foul charms,
  Abus'd her delicate youth with drugs or minerals
  That weaken motion:[62] I'll have 't disputed on;
  'Tis probable, and palpable to thinking.
  I therefore apprehend and do attach[63] thee
  For an abuser of the world, a practiser
  Of arts inhibited and out of warrant.[64]
  Lay hold upon him: if he do resist,                              80
  Subdue him at his peril.

58. Treasure ship.     59. By the Virgin Mary.     60. Let you and me fight.
61. Obvious.    62. Normal reactions.    63. Arrest.    64. Prohibited and illegal.

OTHELLO                          Hold your hands,
  Both you of my inclining,[65] and the rest:
  Were it my cue to fight, I should have known it
  Without a prompter. Where will you that I go
  To answer this your charge?
BRABANTIO                          To prison; till fit time
  Of law and course of direct session[66]
  Call thee to answer.
OTHELLO            What if I do obey?
  How may the duke be therewith satisfied,
  Whose messengers are here about my side,
  Upon some present[67] business of the state                    90
  To bring me to him?
OFFICER                     'Tis true, most worthy signior;
  The duke's in council, and your noble self,
  I am sure, is sent for.
BRABANTIO            How! the duke in council!
  In this time of the night! Bring him away.
  Mine's not an idle cause: the duke himself,
  Or any of my brothers of the state,[68]
  Cannot but feel this wrong as 'twere their own;
  For if such actions may have passage free,
  Bond-slaves and pagans shall our statesmen be.          *(Exeunt.)*


## SCENE 3   *A Council Chamber.*

*(The Duke and Senators sitting at a table. Officers attending.)*

DUKE   There is no composition[69] in these news
  That gives them credit.
FIRST SENATOR               Indeed, they are disproportion'd;
  My letters say a hundred and seven galleys.
DUKE   And mine, a hundred and forty.
SECOND SENATOR                     And mine, two hundred:
  But though they jump[70] not on a just[71] account,—
  As in these cases, where the aim[72] reports,
  'Tis oft with difference,—yet do they all confirm
  A Turkish fleet, and bearing up to Cyprus.
DUKE   Nay, it is possible enough to judgment:
  I do not so secure me in[73] the error,
  But the main article[74] I do approve[75]                    10
  In fearful sense.

---

65. Party.      66. Normal process of law.      67. Immediate, pressing.
68. Fellow senators.      69. Consistency, agreement.      70. Coincide.
71. Exact.      72. Conjecture.      73. Draw comfort from.
74. Substance.      75. Believe.

SAILOR *(within)*      What, ho! what, ho! what, ho!
OFFICER  A messenger from the galleys.

*(Enter a Sailor.)*

DUKE                                    Now, what's the business?
SAILOR  The Turkish preparation makes for Rhodes;
  So was I bid report here to the state
  By Signior Angelo.
DUKE  How say you by this change?
FIRST SENATOR                        This cannot be
  By no[76] assay[77] of reason; 'tis a pageant[78]
  To keep us in false gaze.[79] When we consider
  The importancy of Cyprus to the Turk,                           20
  And let ourselves again but understand,
  That as it more concerns the Turk than Rhodes,
  So may he with more facile question bear[80] it,
  For that it stands not in such warlike brace,[81]
  But altogether lacks the abilities
  That Rhodes is dress'd in: if we make thought of this,
  We must not think the Turk is so unskilful
  To leave that latest which concerns him first,
  Neglecting an attempt of ease and gain,
  To wake and wage a danger profitless.                           30
DUKE  Nay, in all confidence, he's not for Rhodes.
OFFICER  Here is more news.

*(Enter a Messenger.)*

MESSENGER  The Ottomites,[82] reverend and gracious,
  Steering with due course toward the isle of Rhodes,
  Have there injointed[83] them with an after fleet.[84]
FIRST SENATOR  Ay, so I thought. How many, as you guess?
MESSENGER  Of thirty sail; and now they do re-stem[85]
  Their backward course, bearing with frank appearance
  Their purposes toward Cyprus. Signior Montano,
  Your trusty and most valiant servitor,                          40
  With his free duty[86] recommends[87] you thus,
  And prays you to believe him.
DUKE  'Tis certain then, for Cyprus.
  Marcus Luccicos, is not he in town?
FIRST SENATOR  He's now in Florence.
DUKE  Write from us to him; post-post-haste dispatch.
FIRST SENATOR  Here comes Brabantio and the valiant Moor.

---

76. Any.      77. Test.      78. (Deceptive) show.      79. Looking in the wrong
direction.      80. More easily capture.      81. State of defense.
82. Turks.      83. Joined.      84. Fleet that followed after.      85. Steer
again.      86. Unqualified expressions of respect.      87. Informs.

*(Enter Brabantio, Othello, Iago, Roderigo, and Officers.)*

DUKE  Valiant Othello, we must straight employ you
  Against the general enemy Ottoman.
  *(To Brabantio)* I did not see you; welcome, gentle signior;       50
  We lack'd your counsel and your help to-night.
BRABANTIO  So did I yours. Good your Grace, pardon me;
  Neither my place nor aught I heard of business
  Hath rais'd me from my bed, nor doth the general care
  Take hold of me, for my particular grief
  Is of so flood-gate[88] and o'erbearing nature
  That it engluts and swallows other sorrows
  And it is still itself.
DUKE                 Why, what's the matter?
BRABANTIO  My daughter! O! my daughter.
DUKE
SENATORS                     Dead?
BRABANTIO                       Ay, to me;
  She is abus'd, stol'n from me, and corrupted        60
  By spells and medicines bought of mountebanks;
  For nature so preposterously to err,
  Being not deficient, blind, or lame of sense,
  Sans[89] witchcraft could not.
DUKE  Whoe'er he be that in this foul proceeding
  Hath thus beguil'd your daughter of herself
  And you of her, the bloody book of law
  You shall yourself read in the bitter letter
  After your own sense; yea, though our proper[90] son
  Stood[91] in your action.[92]
    BRABANTIO         Humbly I thank your Grace.      70
  Here is the man, this Moor; whom now, it seems,
  Your special mandate for the state affairs
  Hath hither brought.
DUKE
SENATORS         We are very sorry for it.
DUKE *(to Othello)*  What, in your own part, can you say to this?
BRABANTIO  Nothing, but this is so.
OTHELLO  Most potent, grave, and reverend signiors,
  My very noble and approv'd[93] good masters,
  That I have ta'en away this old man's daughter,
  It is most true; true, I have married her:
  The very head and front of my offending      80
  Hath this extent, no more. Rude am I in my speech,
  And little bless'd with the soft phrase of peace;
  For since these arms of mine had seven years' pith,[94]

88. Torrential.     89. Without.     90. Own.     91. Were accused.
92. Suit.     93. Tested (by past experience).     94. Strength.

Till now some nine moons wasted,[95] they have us'd
Their dearest action in the tented field;
And little of this great world can I speak,
More than pertains to feats of broil and battle;
And therefore little shall I grace my cause
In speaking for myself. Yet, by your gracious patience,
I will a round[96] unvarnish'd tale deliver                         90
Of my whole course of love; what drugs, what charms,
What conjuration, and what mighty magic,
For such proceeding I am charg'd withal,
I won his daughter.
BRABANTIO                A maiden never bold;
Of spirit so still and quiet, that her motion
Blush'd at herself;[97] and she, in spite of nature,
Of years, of country, credit, every thing,
To fall in love with what she fear'd to look on!
It is a judgment maim'd and most imperfect
That will confess[98] perfection so could err                      100
Against all rules of nature, and must be driven
To find out practices of cunning hell,
Why this should be. I therefore vouch again
That with some mixtures powerful o'er the blood,
Or with some dram conjur'd to this effect,
He wrought upon her.
DUKE                    To vouch this, is no proof,
Without more certain and more overt test
Than these thin habits[99] and poor likelihoods
Of modern[100] seeming do prefer against him.
FIRST SENATOR  But, Othello, speak:                               110
Did you by indirect and forced courses
Subdue and poison this young maid's affections;
Or came it by request and such fair question[101]
As soul to soul affordeth?
OTHELLO                    I do beseech you;
Send for the lady to the Sagittary,
And let her speak of me before her father:
If you do find me foul in her report,
The trust, the office I do hold of you,
Not only take away, but let your sentence
Even fall upon my life.
DUKE                    Fetch Desdemona hither.                   120
OTHELLO  Ancient, conduct them; you best know the place.

                    (Exeunt Iago and Attendants.)

95. Past.       96. Blunt.        97. I.e., (her modesty was such that) she blushed at her
own emotions; or: could not move without blushing.        98. Assert.        99. Weak
appearances.        100. Commonplace.        101. Conversation.

And, till she come, as truly as to heaven
I do confess the vices of my blood,
So justly to your grave ears I'll present
How I did thrive in this fair lady's love,
And she in mine.

DUKE   Say it, Othello.

OTHELLO   Her father lov'd me; oft invited me;
Still[102] question'd me the story of my life
From year to year, the battles, sieges, fortunes                    130
That I have pass'd.
I ran it through, even from my boyish days
To the very moment that he bade me tell it;
Wherein I spake of most disastrous chances,
Of moving accidents by flood and field,
Of hair-breadth 'scapes i' the imminent deadly breach,
Of being taken by the insolent foe
And sold to slavery, of my redemption thence
And portance[103] in my travel's history;
Wherein of antres[104] vast and deserts idle,[105]                   140
Rough quarries, rocks, and hills whose heads touch heaven,
It was my hint[106] to speak, such was the process;
And of the Cannibals that each other eat,
The Anthropophagi,[107] and men whose heads
Do grow beneath their shoulders. This to hear
Would Desdemona seriously incline;
But still the house-affairs would draw her thence;
Which ever as she could with haste dispatch,
She'd come again, and with a greedy ear
Devour up my discourse. Which I observing,                          150
Took once a pliant[108] hour, and found good means
To draw from her a prayer of earnest heart
That I would all my pilgrimage dilate,[109]
Whereof by parcels[110] she had something heard,
But not intentively:[111] I did consent;
And often did beguile her of her tears,
When I did speak of some distressful stroke
That my youth suffer'd. My story being done,
She gave me for my pains a world of sighs:
She swore, in faith, 'twas strange, 'twas passing[112] strange;     160
'Twas pitiful, 'twas wondrous pitiful:
She wish'd she had not heard it, yet she wish'd
That heaven had made her[113] such a man; she thank'd me,
And bade me, if I had a friend that lov'd her,

102. Always, regularly.     103. Behavior.     104. Caves.     105. Empty,
sterile.     106. Opportunity.     107. Man-eaters.     108. Suitable.
109. Relate in full.     110. Piecemeal.     111. In sequence.
112. Surpassing.     113. Direct object; not "for her."

I should but teach him how to tell my story,
And that would woo her. Upon this hint I spake.
She lov'd me for the dangers I had pass'd,
And I lov'd her that she did pity them.
This only is the witchcraft I have us'd:
Here comes the lady; let her witness it.                    170

*(Enter Desdemona, Iago, and Attendants.)*

DUKE   I think this tale would win my daughter too.
   Good Brabantio,
   Take up this mangled matter at the best;
   Men do their broken weapons rather use
   Than their bare hands.
BRABANTIO                       I pray you, hear her speak:
   If she confess that she was half the wooer,
   Destruction on my head, if my bad blame
   Light on the man! Come hither, gentle mistress:
   Do you perceive in all this noble company
   Where most you owe obedience?
DESDEMONA                        My noble father,      180
   I do perceive here a divided duty:
   To you I am bound for life and education;
   My life and education both do learn[114] me
   How to respect you; you are the lord of duty,
   I am hitherto your daughter: but here's my husband;
   And so much duty as my mother show'd
   To you, preferring you before her father,
   So much I challenge[115] that I may profess
   Due to the Moor my lord.
BRABANTIO                 God be with you! I have done.
   Please it your Grace, on to the state affairs:        190
   I had rather to adopt a child than get it.
   Come hither, Moor:
   I here do give thee that with all my heart
   Which, but thou hast[116] already, with all my heart
   I would keep from thee. For your sake,[117] jewel,
   I am glad at soul I have no other child;
   For thy escape would teach me tyranny,
   To hang clogs on them. I have done, my lord.
DUKE   Let me speak like yourself and lay a sentence,[118]
   Which as a grize[119] or step, may help these lovers     200
   Into your favour.
   When remedies are past, the griefs are ended
   By seeing the worst, which[120] late on hopes depended.

114. Teach.        115. Claim as right.    116. Didn't you have it.    117. Because
of you.        118. Provide a maxim.    119. Step.    120. The antecedent is
"griefs."

To mourn a mischief that is past and gone
Is the next way to draw new mischief on.
What cannot be preserv'd when Fortune takes,
Patience her injury a mockery makes.[121]
The robb'd that smiles steals something from the thief;
He robs himself that spends a bootless grief.

BRABANTIO  So let the Turk of Cyprus us beguile;                    210
We lose it not so long as we can smile.
He bears the sentence[122] well that nothing bears
But the free comfort which from thence he hears;
But he bears both the sentence and the sorrow
That, to pay grief, must of poor patience borrow.
These sentences, to sugar, or to gall,
Being strong on both sides, are equivocal:[123]
But words are words: I never yet did hear
That the bruis'd heart was pierced[124] through the ear.
I humbly beseech you, proceed to the affairs of state.         220

DUKE  The Turk with a most mighty preparation makes for Cyprus. Othello, the
fortitude[125] of the place is best known to you; and though we have there a
substitute of most allowed sufficiency,[126] yet opinion, a sovereign mistress of
effects, throws a more safer voice on you:[127] you must therefore be content to
slubber[128] the gloss of your new fortunes with this more stubborn[129] and
boisterous expedition.

OTHELLO  The tyrant custom, most grave senators,
Hath made the flinty and steel couch of war
My thrice-driven[130] bed of down: I do agnize[131]
A natural and prompt alacrity                                       230
I find in hardness, and do undertake
These present wars against the Ottomites.
Most humbly therefore bending to your state,[132]
I crave fit disposition[133] for my wife,
Due reference of place and exhibition,[134]
With such accommodation and besort[135]
As levels with[136] her breeding.

DUKE                              If you please,
Be 't at her father's.

BRABANTIO              I'll not have it so.

OTHELLO  Nor I.

DESDEMONA      Nor I; I would not there reside,

---

121. To suffer an irreparable loss patiently is to make light of injury (*i.e.,* to triumph
over adversity).          122. (1) Verdict, (2) Maxim.          123. Sententious comfort (like
the Duke's trite maxims) can hurt as well as soothe.          124. (1) Lanced (*i.e.,* cured),
(2) Wounded.          125. Strength.          126. Admitted competence.          127. General
opinion, which mainly determines action, thinks Cyprus safer with you in
command.          128. Besmear.          129. Rough.          130. Made as soft as
possible.          131. Recognize.          132. Submitting to your authority.
133. Disposal.          134. Provision.          135. Fitness.          136. Is proper to.

To put my father in impatient thoughts 240
By being in his eye. Most gracious duke,
To my unfolding[137] lend your gracious ear;
And let me find a charter[138] in your voice
To assist my simpleness.
DUKE  What would you, Desdemona?
DESDEMONA  That I did love the Moor to live with him,
My downright violence and storm of fortunes
May trumpet to the world; my heart's subdu'd
Even to the very quality of my lord;[139]
I saw Othello's visage in his mind, 250
And to his honours and his valiant parts
Did I my soul and fortunes consecrate.
So that, dear lords, if I be left behind,
A moth of peace, and he go to the war,
The rites[140] for which I love him are bereft me,
And I a heavy interim shall support[141]
By his dear[142] absence. Let me go with him.
OTHELLO  Let her have your voices.
Vouch with me, heaven, I therefore beg it not
To please the palate of my appetite, 260
Nor to comply with heat,—the young affects[143]
In me defunct,—and proper satisfaction,
But to be free and bounteous to her mind;
And heaven defend[144] your good souls that you think
I will your serious and great business scant
For[145] she is with me. No, when light-wing'd toys
Of feather'd Cupid seel[146] with wanton dulness
My speculative and offic'd instruments,[147]
That[148] my disports corrupt and taint my business,
Let housewives make a skillet of my helm, 270
And all indign[149] and base adversities
Make head against my estimation![150]
DUKE  Be it as you shall privately determine,
Either for her stay or going. The affair cries haste,
And speed must answer it.
FIRST SENATOR  You must away to-night.
OTHELLO                              With all my heart.
DUKE  At nine i' the morning here we'll meet again.
Othello, leave some officer behind,
And he shall our commission bring to you;

137. Explanation.      138. Permission.      139. *I.e.*, I have become a soldier, like
Othello.      140. *I.e.*, of marriage, or of war, or of both.      141. Endure.
142. Closely concerning (*i.e.*, Desdemona).      143. The passions of youth (hence,
here, *immoderate* sexual passion).      144. Forbid.      145. Because.
146. Blind (v.) by sewing up the eyelids (a term from falconry).      147. Reflective
and executive faculties and organs.      148. So that.      149. Shameful.
150. Reputation.

With such things else of quality and respect                    280
As doth import you.[151]

OTHELLO              So please your Grace, my ancient;
A man he is of honesty and trust:
To his conveyance I assign my wife,
With what else needful your good grace shall think
To be sent after me.

DUKE              Let it be so.
Good-night to every one. *(To Brabantio)* And, noble signior,
If virtue no delighted[152] beauty lack,
Your son-in-law is far more fair than black.

FIRST SENATOR  Adieu, brave Moor! use Desdemona well.

BRABANTIO  Look to her, Moor, if thou hast eyes to see:        290
She has deceiv'd her father, and may thee.

*(Exeunt Duke, Senators, Officers, &c.)*

OTHELLO  My life upon her faith! Honest Iago,
My Desdemona must I leave to thee:
I prithee, let thy wife attend on her;
And bring them after in the best advantage.[153]
Come, Desdemona; I have but an hour
Of love, of worldly matters and direction,
To spend with thee: we must obey the time.

*(Exeunt Othello and Desdemona.)*

RODERIGO  Iago!

IAGO  What sayst thou, noble heart?                            300

RODERIGO  What will I do, think'st thou?

IAGO  Why, go to bed, and sleep.

RODERIGO  I will incontinently[154] drown myself.

IAGO  Well, if thou dost, I shall never love thee after.
Why, thou silly gentleman!

RODERIGO  It is silliness to live when to live is torment; and then have we a
prescription to die when death is our physician.

IAGO  O! villanous; I have looked upon the world for four times seven years,
and since I could distinguish betwixt a benefit and an injury, I never found
man that knew how to love himself. Ere I would say, I would drown myself
for the love of a guinea-hen, I would change my humanity with a baboon.

RODERIGO  What should I do? I confess it is my shame to be so fond;[155] but it is
not in my virtue[156] to amend it.

IAGO  Virtue! a fig! 'tis in ourselves that we are thus, or thus. Our bodies are
our gardens, to the which our wills are gardeners; so that if we will plant
nettles or sow lettuce, set hyssop and weed up thyme, supply it with one
gender[157] of herbs or distract it with many, either to have it sterile with idleness

151. Concern.      152. Delightful.      153. Opportunity.
154. Forthwith.    155. Infatuated.      156. Strength.      157. Kind.

or manured with industry, why, the power and corrigible[158] authority of this lies in our wills. If the balance of our lives had not one scale of reason to poise another of sensuality, the blood and baseness of our natures would conduct us to most preposterous conclusions; but we have reason to cool our raging motions, our carnal stings, our unbitted[159] lusts, whereof I take this that you call love to be a sect or scion.[160]

RODERIGO  It cannot be.

IAGO  It is merely a lust of the blood and a permission of the will. Come, be a man. Drown thyself! drown cats and blind puppies. I have professed me thy friend, and I confess me knit to thy deserving with cables of perdurable toughness; I could never better stead thee than now. Put money in thy purse; follow these wars; defeat thy favour[161] with a usurped[162] beard; I say, put money in thy purse. It cannot be that Desdemona should long continue her love to the Moor,—put money in thy purse,—nor he his to her. It was a violent commencement in her, and thou shalt see an answerable sequestration;[163] put but money in thy purse. These Moors are changeable in their wills;—fill thy purse with money:—the food that to him now is as luscious as locusts,[164] shall be to him shortly as bitter as coloquintida.[165] She must change for youth: when she is sated with his body, she will find the error of her choice. She must have change, she must: therefore put money in thy purse. If thou wilt needs damn thyself, do it a more delicate way than drowning. Make all the money thou canst. If sanctimony and a frail vow betwixt an erring[166] barbarian and a supersubtle[167] Venetian be not too hard for my wits and all the tribe of hell, thou shalt enjoy her; therefore make money. A pox of drowning thyself! it is clean out of the way: seek thou rather to be hanged in compassing thy joy than to be drowned and go without her.

RODERIGO  Wilt thou be fast to my hopes, if I depend on the issue?[168]

IAGO  Thou art sure of me: go, make money. I have told thee often, and I retell thee again and again, I hate the Moor; my cause is hearted; thine hath no less reason. Let us be conjunctive[169] in our revenge against him; if thou canst cuckold him, thou dost thyself a pleasure, me a sport. There are many events in the womb of time which will be delivered. Traverse;[170] go: provide thy money. We will have more of this to-morrow. Adieu.

RODERIGO  Where shall we meet i' the morning?

IAGO  At my lodging.

RODERIGO  I'll be with thee betimes.

IAGO  Go to: farewell. Do you hear, Roderigo?

RODERIGO  What say you?

IAGO  No more of drowning, do you hear?

RODERIGO  I am changed. I'll sell all my land.

IAGO  Go to; farewell! put money enough in your purse.    (Exit Roderigo.)

---

158. Corrective.    159. I.e., uncontrolled.    160. Offshoot.    161. Change thy appearance (for the worse?).    162. Assumed.    163. Estrangement.
164. Sweet-tasting fruits (perhaps the carob, the edible seed-pod of an evergreen tree in the Mediterranean area).    165. Purgative derived from a bitter apple.
166. Vagabond.    167. Exceedingly refined.    168. Rely on the outcome.
169. Allied.    170. March.

Thus do I ever make my fool my purse;
For I mine own gain'd knowledge should profane,                    360
If I would time expend with such a snipe[171]
But for my sport and profit. I hate the Moor,
And it is thought abroad[172] that 'twixt my sheets
He has done my office: I know not if 't be true,
But I, for mere suspicion in that kind,
Will do as if for surety.[173] He holds me well;[174]
The better shall my purpose work on him.
Cassio's a proper[175] man; let me see now:
To get his place; and to plume up[176] my will
In double knavery; how, how? Let's see:                           370
After some time, to abuse Othello's ear
That he[177] is too familiar with his wife.
He hath a person and a smooth dispose[178]
To be suspected; framed[179] to make women false.
The Moor is of a free and open nature,
That thinks men honest that but seem to be so,
And will as tenderly be led by the nose
As asses are.
I have 't; it is engender'd: hell and night
Must bring this monstrous birth to the world's light.        (*Exit.*)  380

# Act II

### SCENE 1   *A Sea-port Town in Cyprus. An open place near the Quay.*

(*Enter Montano and two Gentlemen.*)

MONTANO  What from the cape can you discern at sea?
FIRST GENTLEMAN  Nothing at all: it is a high-wrought flood;
   I cannot 'twixt the heaven and the main[180]
   Descry a sail.
MONTANO  Methinks the wind hath spoke aloud at land;
   A fuller blast ne'er shook our battlements;
   If it hath ruffian'd so upon the sea,
   What ribs of oak, when mountains melt on them,
   Can hold the mortise?[181] what shall we hear of this?
SECOND GENTLEMAN  A segregation[182] of the Turkish fleet;        10
   For do but stand upon the foaming shore,
   The chidden billow seems to pelt the clouds;
   The wind-shak'd surge, with high and monstrous mane,

---

171. Dupe.      172. People think.      173. As if it were certain.      174. In high
regard.      175. Handsome.      176. Make ready.      177. *I.e.,* Cassio.
178. Bearing.      179. Designed, apt.      180. Ocean.      181. Hold the joints
together.      182. Scattering.

Seems to cast water on the burning bear[183]
And quench the guards of the ever-fixed pole:[184]
I never did like[185] molestation view
On the enchafed[186] flood.

MONTANO                         If that[187] the Turkish fleet
Be not enshelter'd and embay'd, they are drown'd;
It is impossible they bear it out.

*(Enter a Third Gentleman.)*

THIRD GENTLEMAN  News, lad! our wars are done.                    20
The desperate tempest hath so bang'd the Turks
That their designment halts;[188] a noble ship of Venice
Hath seen a grievous wrack and suffrance[189]
On most part of their fleet.

MONTANO  How! is this true?

THIRD GENTLEMAN                The ship is here put in,
A Veronesa;[190] Michael Cassio,
Lieutenant to the warlike Moor Othello,
Is come on shore: the Moor himself's at sea,
And is in full commission here for Cyprus.

MONTANO  I am glad on 't; 'tis a worthy governor.                  30

THIRD GENTLEMAN  But this same Cassio, though he speak of comfort
Touching the Turkish loss, yet he looks sadly
And prays the Moor be safe; for they were parted
With foul and violent tempest.

MONTANO                         Pray heaven he be;
For I have serv'd him, and the man commands
Like a full soldier. Let's to the sea-side, ho!
As well to see the vessel that's come in
As to throw out our eyes for brave Othello,
Even till we make the main and the aerial blue
An indistinct regard.[191]

THIRD GENTLEMAN       Come, let's do so;                            40
For every minute is expectancy
Of more arrivance.

*(Enter Cassio.)*

CASSIO  Thanks, you the valiant of this warlike isle,
That so approve the Moor. O! let the heavens
Give him defence against the elements,
For I have lost him on a dangerous sea.

---

183. Ursa Minor (the Little Dipper).       184. Polaris, the North Star, almost directly
above the Earth's axis, is part of the constellation of the Little Bear, or Dipper.
185. Similar.      186. Agitated.      187. If.      188. Plan is stopped.
189. Damage.       190. Probably a *type* of ship, rather than a ship from Verona—not
only because Verona is an inland city but also because of "a noble ship of Venice"
above.       191. Till our (straining) eyes can no longer distinguish sea and sky.

MONTANO   Is he well shipp'd?
CASSIO   His bark is stoutly timber'd, and his pilot
  Of very expert and approv'd allowance;[192]
  Therefore my hopes, not surfeited to death,[193]
  Stand in bold cure.[194]

  *(Within, 'A sail!—a sail!—a sail!' Enter a Messenger.)*

CASSIO   What noise?
MESSENGER   The town is empty; on the brow o' the sea
  Stand ranks of people, and they cry 'A sail!'
CASSIO   My hopes do shape him for the governor.

  *(Guns heard.)*

SECOND GENTLEMAN   They do discharge their shot of courtesy;
  Our friends at least.
CASSIO                     I pray you, sir, go forth.
  And give us truth who 'tis that is arriv'd.
SECOND GENTLEMAN   I shall.                           *(Exit.)*
MONTANO   But, good lieutenant, is your general wiv'd?
CASSIO   Most fortunately: he hath achiev'd a maid
  That paragons[195] description and wild fame;
  One that excels the quirks[196] of blazoning pens,
  And in th' essential vesture of creation[197]
  Does tire the ingener.[198]

  *(Re-enter Second Gentleman.)*

                    How now! who has put in?
SECOND GENTLEMAN   'Tis one Iago, ancient to the general.
CASSIO   He has had most favourable and happy speed:
  Tempests themselves, high seas, and howling winds,
  The gutter'd[199] rocks, and congregated sands,
  Traitors ensteep'd[200] to clog the guiltless keel,
  As having sense of beauty, do omit
  Their mortal[201] natures, letting go safely by
  The divine Desdemona.
MONTANO                     What is she?
CASSIO   She that I spake of, our great captain's captain,
  Left in the conduct of the bold Iago,
  Whose footing[202] here anticipates our thoughts
  A se'nnight's[203] speed. Great Jove, Othello guard,
  And swell his sail with thine own powerful breath,

50

60

70

192. Admitted and proven to be expert.      193. Over indulged.      194. With
good chance of being fulfilled.      195. Exceeds, surpasses.
196. Ingenuities.      197. *I.e.,* just as God made her; or: (even in) the (mere) essence
of human nature.      198. Inventor (*i.e.,* of her praises?).      199. Jagged; or:
submerged.      200. Submerged.      201. Deadly.      202. Landing.
203. Week's.

That he may bless this bay with his tall[204] ship,
Make love's quick pants in Desdemona's arms,                          80
Give renew'd fire to our extinced spirits,
And bring all Cyprus comfort!

*(Enter Desdemona, Emilia, Iago, Roderigo, and Attendants.)*

                    O! behold,
The riches of the ship is come on shore.
Ye men of Cyprus, let her have your knees.
Hail to thee, lady! and the grace of heaven,
Before, behind thee, and on every hand,
Enwheel thee round!
DESDEMONA         I thank you, valiant Cassio.
  What tidings can you tell me of my lord?
CASSIO  He is not yet arriv'd; nor know I aught
  But that he's well, and will be shortly here.                  90
DESDEMONA  O! but I fear—How lost you company?
CASSIO  The great contention of the sea and skies
  Parted our fellowship. But hark! a sail.

*(Cry within, 'A sail—a sail!' Guns heard.)*

SECOND GENTLEMAN  They give their greeting to the citadel:
  This likewise is a friend.
CASSIO           See for the news!      *(Exit Gentleman.)*
  Good ancient, you are welcome:—*(To Emilia)* welcome, mistress.
  Let it not gall your patience, good Iago,
  That I extend my manners; 'tis my breeding
  That gives me this bold show of courtesy.      *(Kissing her.)*
IAGO  Sir, would she give you so much of her lips                100
  As of her tongue she oft bestows on me,
  You'd have enough.
DESDEMONA        Alas! she has no speech.
IAGO  In faith, too much;
  I find it still when I have list[205] to sleep:
  Marry, before your ladyship, I grant,
  She puts her tongue a little in her heart,
  And chides with thinking.[206]
EMILIA  You have little cause to say so.
IAGO  Come on, come on; you are pictures[207] out of doors,
  Bells[208] in your parlours, wild cats in your kitchens,        110
  Saints in your injuries, devils being offended,
  Players[209] in your housewifery,[210] and housewives[211] in your beds.
DESDEMONA  O! fie upon thee, slanderer.
IAGO  Nay, it is true, or else I am a Turk:

204. Brave.     205. Wish.     206. *I.e.,* without words.     207. *I.e.,* made up,
"painted."     208. *I.e.,* jangly.     209. Triflers, wastrels.     210. Housekeeping.
211. (1) Hussies, (2) (unduly) frugal with their sexual favors, (3) businesslike, serious.

You rise to play and go to bed to work.

EMILIA  You shall not write my praise.

IAGO                                    No, let me not.

DESDEMONA  What wouldst thou write of me, if thou shouldst praise me?

IAGO  O gentle lady, do not put me to 't,
  For I am nothing if not critical.

DESDEMONA  Come on; assay. There's one gone to the harbour?          120

IAGO  Ay, madam.

DESDEMONA  *(aside)*  I am not merry, but I do beguile
  The thing I am by seeming otherwise.
  *(To Iago.)* Come, how wouldst thou praise me?

IAGO  I am about it; but indeed my invention
  Comes from my pate[212] as birdlime does from frize;[213]
  It plucks out brains and all: but my muse labours
  And thus she is deliver'd.
  If she be fair and wise, fairness and wit,
  The one's for use, the other useth it.                            130

DESDEMONA  Well prais'd! How if she be black and witty?

IAGO  If she be black,[214] and thereto have a wit,
  She'll find a white that shall her blackness fit.

DESDEMONA  Worse and worse.

EMILIA  How if fair and foolish?

IAGO  She never yet was foolish that was fair,
  For even her folly[215] help'd to an heir.

DESDEMONA  These are old fond[216] paradoxes to make fools laugh i' the alehouse.
  What miserable praise hast thou for her that's foul and foolish?

IAGO  There's none so foul and foolish thereunto,                   140
  But does foul pranks which fair and wise ones do.

DESDEMONA  O heavy ignorance! thou praisest the worst best. But what praise
  couldst thou bestow on a deserving woman indeed, one that, in the authority
  of her merit, did justly put on the vouch[217] of very malice itself?

IAGO  She that was ever fair and never proud,
  Had tongue at will and yet was never loud,
  Never lack'd gold and yet went never gay,
  Fled from her wish and yet said, 'Now I may,'
  She that being anger'd, her revenge being nigh,
  Bade her wrong stay and her displeasure fly,                      150
  She that in wisdom never was so frail
  To change the cod's head for the salmon's tail,[218]
  She that could think and ne'er disclose her mind,
  See suitors following and not look behind,
  She was a wight, if ever such wight were,—

DESDEMONA  To do what?

---

212. Head.      213. Coarse cloth.      214. Brunette, dark haired.      215. Here
also, wantonness.      216. Foolish.      217. Compel the approval.      218. To
make a foolish exchange (a bawdy secondary meaning is probable).

IAGO  To suckle fools and chronicle small beer.[219]

DESDEMONA  O most lame and impotent conclusion! Do not learn of him, Emilia, though he be thy husband. How say you, Cassio? Is he not a most profane and liberal[220] counsellor?                                                            160

CASSIO  He speaks home,[221] madam; you may relish him more in the soldier than in[222] the scholar.

IAGO (aside)  He takes her by the palm: ay, well said, whisper; with as little a web as this will I ensnare as great a fly as Cassio. Ay, smile upon her, do; I will gyve[223] thee in thine own courtship. You say true, 'tis so, indeed. If such tricks as these strip you out of your lieutenantry, it had been better you had not kissed your three fingers so oft, which now again you are most apt to play the sir[224] in. Very good; well kissed! an excellent courtesy! 'tis so, indeed. Yet again your fingers to your lips? would they were clyster-pipes[225] for your sake! (A trumpet heard.) The Moor! I know his trumpet.[226]

CASSIO  'Tis truly so.

DESDEMONA  Let's meet him and receive him.

CASSIO  Lo! where he comes.

(Enter Othello and Attendants.)

OTHELLO  O my fair warrior!

DESDEMONA                    My dear Othello!

OTHELLO  It gives me wonder great as my content
To see you here before me. O my soul's joy!
If after every tempest come such calms,
May the winds blow till they have waken'd death!
And let the labouring bark climb hills of seas
Olympus-high, and duck again as low                              180
As hell's from heaven! If it were now to die,
'Twere now to be most happy, for I fear
My soul hath her content so absolute
That not another comfort like to this
Succeeds in unknown fate.

DESDEMONA                    The heavens forbid
But that our loves and comforts should increase
Even as our days do grow!

OTHELLO  Amen to that, sweet powers!
I cannot speak enough of this content;
It stops me here; it is too much of joy:                         190
And this, and this, the greatest discords be        (Kissing her.)
That e'er our hearts shall make!

IAGO (aside)                    O! you are well tun'd now,
But I'll set down[227] the pegs that make this music,
As honest as I am.

219. I.e., keep petty household accounts.   220. Free-spoken, licentious.
221. To the mark, aptly.   222. As . . . as.   223. Entangle.
224. Gentleman.   225. Syringes, enema pipes.   226. I.e., Othello's distinctive trumpet call.   227. Loosen.

OTHELLO               Come, let us to the castle.
  News, friends; our wars are done, the Turks are drown'd.
  How does my old acquaintance of this isle?
  Honey, you shall be well desir'd[228] in Cyprus;
  I have found great love amongst them. O my sweet,
  I prattle out of fashion, and I dote
  In mine own comforts. I prithee, good Iago,                    200
  Go to the bay and disembark my coffers.
  Bring thou the master to the citadel;
  He is a good one, and his worthiness
  Does challenge much respect. Come, Desdemona,
  Once more well met at Cyprus.

*(Exeunt all except Iago and Roderigo.)*

IAGO  Do thou meet me presently at the harbour. Come hither. If thou be'st valiant, as they say base men being in love have then a nobility in their natures more than is native to them, list[229] me. The lieutenant to-night watches on the court of guard:[230] first, I must tell thee this, Desdemona is directly in love with him.

RODERIGO  With him! Why, 'tis not possible.

IAGO  Lay thy finger thus, and let thy soul be instructed. Mark me with what violence she first loved the Moor but for bragging and telling her fantastical lies; and will she love him still for prating? let not thy discreet heart think it. Her eye must be fed; and what delight shall she have to look on the devil? When the blood is made dull with the act of sport, there should be, again to inflame it, and to give satiety a fresh appetite, loveliness in favour, sympathy in years, manners, and beauties; all which the Moor is defective in. Now, for want of these required conveniences, her delicate tenderness will find itself abused, begin to heave the gorge,[231] disrelish and abhor the Moor; very nature will instruct her in it, and compel her to some second choice. Now, sir, this granted, as it is a most pregnant[232] and unforced position, who stands so eminently in the degree of this fortune as Cassio does? a knave very voluble, no further conscionable[233] than in putting on the mere form of civil and humane seeming, for the better compassing of his salt[234] and most hidden loose affection? why, none; why, none: a slipper[235] and subtle knave, a finder-out of occasions, that has an eye can stamp and counterfeit advantages, though true advantage never present itself; a devilish knave! Besides, the knave is handsome, young, and hath all those requisites in him that folly and green minds look after; a pestilent complete knave! and the woman hath found him already.

RODERIGO  I cannot believe that in her; she is full of most blessed condition.

IAGO  Blessed fig's end! the wine she drinks is made of grapes;[236] if she had been blessed she would never have loved the Moor; blessed pudding! Didst thou not see her paddle with the palm of his hand? didst not mark that?

228. Welcomed.    229. Listen to.    230. Guardhouse.    231. Vomit.
232. Obvious.    233. Conscientious.    234. Lecherous.
235. Slippery.    236. *I.e.,* she is only flesh and blood.

RODERIGO  Yes, that I did; but that was but courtesy.

IAGO  Lechery, by this hand! an index[237] and obscure prologue to the history of lust and foul thoughts. They met so near with their lips, that their breaths embraced together. Villanous thoughts, Roderigo! when these mutualities so marshal the way, hard at hand comes the master and main exercise, the incorporate[238] conclusion. Pish![239] But, sir, be you ruled by me: I have brought you from Venice. Watch you to-night; for the command, I'll lay 't upon you: Cassio knows you not. I'll not be far from you: do you find some occasion to anger Cassio, either by speaking too loud, or tainting[240] his discipline; or from what other course you please, which the time shall more favourably minister.

RODERIGO  Well.

IAGO  Sir, he is rash and very sudden in choler, and haply may strike at you: provoke him, that he may; for even out of that will I cause these of Cyprus to mutiny, whose qualification[241] shall come into no true taste again but by the displanting of Cassio. So shall you have a shorter journey to your desires by the means I shall then have to prefer[242] them; and the impediment most profitably removed, without the which there were no expectation of our prosperity.

RODERIGO  I will do this; if I can bring it to any opportunity.

IAGO  I warrant thee. Meet me by and by at the citadel: I must fetch his necessaries ashore. Farewell.

RODERIGO  Adieu.                                          (Exit.)

IAGO  That Cassio loves her, I do well believe it;
    That she loves him, 'tis apt,[243] and of great credit:[244]
    The Moor, howbeit that I endure him not,                   260
    Is of a constant, loving, noble nature;
    And I dare think he'll prove to Desdemona
    A most dear[245] husband. Now, I do love her too;
    Not out of absolute lust,—though peradventure[246]
    I stand accountant[247] for as great a sin,—
    But partly led to diet my revenge,
    For that I do suspect the lusty Moor
    Hath leap'd into my seat; the thought whereof
    Doth like a poisonous mineral gnaw my inwards;
    And nothing can or shall content my soul                   270
    Till I am even'd with him, wife for wife;
    Or failing so, yet that I put the Moor
    At least into a jealousy so strong
    That judgment cannot cure. Which thing to do,
    If this poor trash[248] of Venice, whom I trash[249]
    For his quick hunting, stand the putting-on,[250]
    I'll have our Michael Cassio on the hip;

---

237. Pointer.    238. Carnal.    239. Exclamation of disgust.
240. Disparaging.    241. Appeasement.    242. Advance.    243. Natural,
probable.    244. Easily believable.    245. A pun on the word in the sense of:
expensive.    246. Perchance, perhaps.    247. Accountable.    248. I.e.,
Roderigo.    249. Check, control.    250. Inciting.

Abuse him to the Moor in the rank garb,[251]
For I fear Cassio with my night-cap too,
Make the Moor thank me, love me, and reward me                    280
For making him egregiously an ass
And practising upon his peace and quiet
Even to madness. 'Tis here, but yet confus'd:
Knavery's plain face is never seen till us'd.                    *(Exit.)*


## SCENE 2   *A Street.*

*(Enter a Herald with a proclamation; people following.)*

HERALD   It is Othello's pleasure, our noble and valiant general, that, upon certain tidings now arrived, importing the mere[252] perdition of the Turkish fleet, every man put himself into triumph; some to dance, some to make bonfires, each man to what sport and revels his addiction leads him; for, besides these beneficial news, it is the celebration of his nuptial. So much was his pleasure should be proclaimed. All offices[253] are open, and there is full liberty of feasting from this present hour of five till the bell have told eleven. Heaven bless the isle of Cyprus and our noble general Othello!                    *(Exeunt.)*


## SCENE 3   *A Hall in the Castle.*

*(Enter Othello, Desdemona, Cassio, and Attendants.)*

OTHELLO   Good Michael, look you to the guard to-night:
   Let's teach ourselves that honourable stop,[254]
   Not to outsport discretion.
CASSIO   Iago hath direction what to do:
   But, notwithstanding, with my personal[255] eye
   Will I look to 't.
OTHELLO                  Iago is most honest.
   Michael, good-night; to-morrow with your earliest
   Let me have speech with you. *(To Desdemona.)* Come, my dear love,
   The purchase made, the fruits are to ensue;
   That profit's yet to come 'twixt me and you.                    10
   Good-night.

*(Exeunt Othello, Desdemona, and Attendants.)*

*(Enter Iago.)*

CASSIO   Welcome, Iago; we must to the watch.
IAGO   Not this hour, lieutenant; 'tis not yet ten o' the clock. Our general casts

---

251. Gross manner.          252. Utter.          253. Kitchens and storehouses.
254. Discipline.       255. Own.

us thus early for the love of his Desdemona, who let us not therefore blame;
he hath not yet made wanton the night with her, and she is sport for love.

CASSIO  She's a most exquisite lady.

IAGO  And, I'll warrant her, full of game.

CASSIO  Indeed, she is a most fresh and delicate creature.

IAGO  What an eye she has! methinks it sounds a parley[256] of provocation.

CASSIO  An inviting eye: and yet methinks right modest.                                    20

IAGO  And when she speaks, is it not an alarum[257] to love?

CASSIO  She is indeed perfection.

IAGO  Well, happiness to their sheets! Come, lieutenant, I have a stoup of wine,
and here without are a brace[258] of Cyprus gallants that would fain have a
measure to the health of black Othello.

CASSIO  Not to-night, good Iago: I have very poor and unhappy brains for
drinking: I could well wish courtesy would invent some other custom of
entertainment.

IAGO  O! they are our friends; but one cup: I'll drink for you.

CASSIO  I have drunk but one cup to-night, and that was craftily qualified[259] too,
and, behold, what innovation[260] it makes here: I am unfortunate in the infirmity, and dare not task my weakness with any more.

IAGO  What, man! 'tis a night of revels; the gallants desire it.

CASSIO  Where are they?

IAGO  Here at the door; I pray you, call them in.

CASSIO  I'll do 't; but it dislikes me.                                    (Exit.)

IAGO  If I can fasten but one cup upon him,
With that which he hath drunk to-night already,
He'll be as full of quarrel and offence
As my young mistress' dog. Now, my sick fool Roderigo,                    40
Whom love has turn'd almost the wrong side out,
To Desdemona hath to-night carous'd
Potations pottle-deep;[261] and he's to watch.
Three lads of Cyprus, noble swelling spirits,
That hold their honours in a wary distance,[262]
The very elements[263] of this warlike isle,
Have I to-night fluster'd with flowing cups,
And they watch too. Now, 'mongst this flock of drunkards,
Am I to put our Cassio in some action
That may offend the isle. But here they come.                    50
If consequence[264] do but approve my dream,
My boat sails freely, both with wind and stream.

(Re-enter Cassio, with him Montano, and Gentlemen. Servant following with wine.)

CASSIO  'Fore God, they have given me a rouse[265] already.

MONTANO  Good faith, a little one; not past a pint, as I am a soldier.

---

256. Conference.      257. Call-to-arms.      258. Pair.      259. Diluted.
260. Change, revolution.      261. Bottoms-up.      262. Take offense easily.
263. Types.      264. Succeeding events.      265. Drink.

IAGO  Some wine, ho!

(Sings)  And let me the canakin[266] clink, clink;
And let me the canakin clink:
A soldier's a man;
A life's but a span;
Why then let a soldier drink.   60

Some wine, boys!

CASSIO  'Fore God, an excellent song.

IAGO  I learned it in England, where indeed they are most potent in potting; your Dane, your German, and your swag-bellied[267] Hollander,—drink, ho!—are nothing to your English.

CASSIO  Is your Englishman so expert in his drinking?

IAGO  Why, he drinks you[268] with facility your Dane dead drunk; he sweats not to overthrow your Almain;[269] he gives your Hollander a vomit ere the next pottle can be filled.

CASSIO  To the health of our general!   70

MONTANO  I am for it, lieutenant; and I'll do you justice.

IAGO  O sweet England!

(Sings)  King Stephen was a worthy peer,
His breeches cost him but a crown;
He held them sixpence all too dear,
With that he call'd the tailor lown.[270]
He was a wight of high renown,
And thou art but of low degree:
'Tis pride that pulls the country down,
Then take thine auld cloak about thee.   80

Some wine, ho!

CASSIO  Why, this is a more exquisite song than the other.

IAGO  Will you hear 't again?

CASSIO  No; for I hold him to be unworthy of his place that does those things. Well, God's above all; and there be souls must be saved, and there be souls must not be saved.

IAGO  It's true, good lieutenant.

CASSIO  For mine own part,—no offence to the general, nor any man of quality,—I hope to be saved.

IAGO  And so do I too, lieutenant.   90

CASSIO  Ay; but, by your leave, not before me; the lieutenant is to be saved before the ancient. Let's have no more of this; let's to our affairs. God forgive us our sins! Gentlemen, let's look to our business. Do not think, gentlemen, I am drunk: this is my ancient; this is my right hand, and this is my left hand. I am not drunk now; I can stand well enough, and speak well enough.

ALL  Excellent well.

CASSIO  Why, very well, then; you must not think then that I am drunk.   (Exit.)

MONTANO  To the platform, masters; come, let's set the watch.

266. Small cup.   267. With a pendulous belly.   268. The "ethical" dative, i.e., you'll see that he drinks.   269. German.   270. Lout, rascal.

IAGO   You see this fellow that is gone before;                              100
  He is a soldier fit to stand by Caesar
  And give direction; and do but see his vice;
  'Tis to his virtue a just equinox,[271]
  The one as long as the other; 'tis pity of him.
  I fear the trust Othello puts him in,
  On some odd time of his infirmity,
  Will shake this island.
MONTANO                              But is he often thus?
IAGO   'Tis evermore the prologue to his sleep;
  He'll watch the horologe a double set,[272]
  If drink rock not his cradle.                                        110
MONTANO                              It were well
  The general were put in mind of it.
  Perhaps he sees it not; or his good nature
  Prizes the virtue that appears in Cassio,
  And looks not on his evils. Is not this true?

(Enter Roderigo.)

IAGO (aside to him)   How now, Roderigo!
  I pray you, after the lieutenant; go.                    (Exit Roderigo.)
MONTANO   And 'tis great pity that the noble Moor
  Should hazard such a place as his own second
  With one of an ingraft[273] infirmity;
  It were an honest action to say                                     120
  So to the Moor.
IAGO                         Not I, for this fair island:
  I do love Cassio well, and would do much
  To cure him of this evil. But hark! what noise?

(Cry within, 'Help! Help!' Re-enter Cassio, driving in Roderigo.)

CASSIO   You rogue! you rascal!
MONTANO                              What's the matter, lieutenant?
CASSIO   A knave teach me my duty!
  I'll beat the knave into a twiggen[274] bottle.
RODERIGO   Beat me!
CASSIO                         Dost thou prate, rogue?

(Striking Roderigo.)

MONTANO (staying him)   Nay, good lieutenant;
  I pray you, sir, hold your hand.
CASSIO                              Let me go, sir,
  Or I'll knock you o'er the mazzard.[275]                            130
MONTANO                              Come, come; you're drunk.

271. Equivalent.      272. Stand watch twice twelve hours.      273. Ingrained.
274. Wicker.      275. Head.

CASSIO  Drunk!

*(They fight.)*

IAGO *(aside to Roderigo)*   Away, I say! go out, and cry a mutiny.

*(Exit Roderigo.)*

Nay, good lieutenant! God's will, gentlemen!
Help, ho! Lieutenant! sir! Montano! sir!
Help, masters! Here's a goodly watch indeed!

*(Bell rings.)*

Who's that that rings the bell? Diablo, ho!
The town will rise: God's will! lieutenant, hold!
You will be sham'd for ever.

*(Re-enter Othello and Attendants.)*

OTHELLO                  What is the matter here?
MONTANO  'Zounds! I bleed still; I am hurt to the death.

*(He faints.)*

OTHELLO  Hold, for your lives!                                           140
IAGO  Hold, ho, lieutenant! Sir! Montano! gentlemen!
  Have you forgot all sense of place and duty?
  Hold! the general speaks to you; hold for shame!
OTHELLO  Why, how now, ho! from whence ariseth this?
  Are we turn'd Turks, and to ourselves do that
  Which heaven hath forbid the Ottomites?
  For Christian shame put by this barbarous brawl;
  He that stirs next to carve for his own rage
  Holds his soul light; he dies upon his motion.
  Silence that dreadful bell! it frights the isle                        150
  From her propriety. What is the matter, masters?
  Honest Iago, that look'st dead with grieving,
  Speak, who began this? On thy love, I charge thee.
IAGO  I do not know; friends all but now, even now,
  In quarter²⁷⁶ and in terms like bride and groom
  Devesting²⁷⁷ them for bed; and then, but now,—
  As if some planet had unwitted men,—
  Swords out, and tilting one at other's breast,
  In opposition bloody. I cannot speak
  Any beginning to this peevish odds,²⁷⁸                                 160
  And would in action glorious I had lost
  Those legs that brought me to a part of it!
OTHELLO  How comes it, Michael, you are thus forgot?
CASSIO  I pray you, pardon me; I cannot speak.

---

276. On duty.    277. Undressing.    278. Silly quarrel.

OTHELLO   Worthy Montano, you were wont be civil;
   The gravity and stillness of your youth
   The world hath noted, and your name is great
   In mouths of wisest censure:[279] what's the matter,
   That you unlace[280] your reputation thus
   And spend your rich opinion[281] for the name        170
   Of a night-brawler? give me answer to it.
MONTANO   Worthy Othello, I am hurt to danger;
   Your officer, Iago, can inform you,
   While I spare speech, which something now offends[282] me,
   Of all that I do know; nor know I aught
   By me that's said or done amiss this night,
   Unless self-charity be sometimes a vice,
   And to defend ourselves it be a sin
   When violence assails us.
OTHELLO             Now, by heaven,
   My blood begins my safer guides to rule,        180
   And passion, having my best judgment collied,[283]
   Assays to lead the way. If I once stir,
   Or do but lift this arm, the best of you
   Shall sink in my rebuke. Give me to know
   How this foul rout began, who set it on;
   And he that is approv'd[284] in this offence,
   Though he had twinn'd with me—both at a birth—
   Shall lose me. What! in a town of war,
   Yet wild, the people's hearts brimful of fear,
   To manage private and domestic quarrel,        190
   In night, and on the court and guard of safety!
   'Tis monstrous. Iago, who began 't?
MONTANO   If partially affin'd,[285] or leagu'd in office,
   Thou dost deliver more or less than truth,
   Thou art no soldier.
IAGO           Touch me not so near;
   I had rather[286] have this tongue cut from my mouth
   Than it should do offence to Michael Cassio;
   Yet, I persuade myself, to speak the truth
   Shall nothing wrong him. Thus it is, general.
   Montano and myself being in speech,        200
   There comes a fellow crying out for help,
   And Cassio following with determin'd sword
   To execute upon him. Sir, this gentleman
   Steps in to Cassio, and entreats his pause;
   Myself the crying fellow did pursue,
   Lest by his clamour, as it so fell out,

279. Judgment.    280. Undo.    281. High reputation.    282. Pains,
harms.    283. Clouded.    284. Proved (*i.e.*, guilty).    285. Favorably biased
(by ties of friendship, or as Cassio's fellow officer).    286. More quickly.

The town might fall in fright; he, swift of foot,
Outran my purpose, and I return'd the rather
For that I heard the clink and call of swords,
And Cassio high in oath, which till to-night          210
I ne'er might say before. When I came back,—
For this was brief,—I found them close together,
At blow and thrust, even as again they were
When you yourself did part them.
More of this matter can I not report:
But men are men; the best sometimes forget:
Though Cassio did some little wrong to him,
As men in rage strike those that wish them best,
Yet, surely Cassio, I believe, receiv'd
From him that fled some strange indignity,             220
Which patience could not pass.

OTHELLO                              I know, Iago.
Thy honesty and love doth mince[287] this matter,
Making it light to Cassio. Cassio, I love thee;
But never more be officer of mine.

*(Enter Desdemona, attended.)*

Look! if my gentle love be not rais'd up;
*(To Cassio.)* I'll make thee an example.

DESDEMONA                              What's the matter?

OTHELLO   All's well now, sweeting; come away to bed.
Sir, for your hurts, myself will be your surgeon.      230
Lead him off.                          *(Montano is led off.)*
Iago, look with care about the town,
And silence those whom this vile brawl distracted.
Come, Desdemona; 'tis the soldier's life,
To have their balmy slumbers wak'd with strife.

*(Exeunt all but Iago and Cassio.)*

IAGO   What! are you hurt, lieutenant?

CASSIO   Ay; past all surgery.

IAGO   Marry, heaven forbid!

CASSIO   Reputation, reputation, reputation! O! I have lost my reputation. I have
lost the immortal part of myself, and what remains is bestial. My reputation,
Iago, my reputation!

IAGO   As I am an honest man, I thought you had received some bodily wound;
there is more offence in that than in reputation. Reputation is an idle and
most false imposition;[288] oft got without merit, and lost without deserving:
you have lost no reputation at all, unless you repute yourself such a loser.
What! man; there are ways to recover the general again; you are but now cast
in his mood,[289] a punishment more in policy[290] than in malice; even so as one

287. Tone down.      288. Something external.      289. Dismissed because he is
angry.      290. *I.e.*, more for the sake of the example, or to show his fairness.

would beat his offenceless dog to affright an imperious lion. Sue to him again, and he is yours.

CASSIO I will rather sue to be despised than to deceive so good a commander with so slight, so drunken and so indiscreet an officer. Drunk! and speak parrot![291] and squabble, swagger, swear, and discourse fustian[292] with one's own shadow! O thou invisible spirit of wine! if thou hast no name to be known by, let us call thee devil!

IAGO What was he that you followed with your sword? What hath he done to you?

CASSIO I know not.

IAGO Is 't possible?

CASSIO I remember a mass of things, but nothing distinctly; a quarrel, but nothing wherefore. O God! that men should put an enemy in their mouths to steal away their brains; that we should, with joy, pleasance,[293] revel, and applause, transform ourselves into beasts.

IAGO Why, but you are now well enough; how came you thus recovered?

CASSIO It hath pleased the devil drunkenness to give place to the devil wrath; one unperfectness shows me another, to make me frankly despise myself.

IAGO Come, you are too severe a moraler. As the time, the place, and the condition of this country stands, I could heartily wish this had not befallen, but since it is as it is, mend it for your own good.

CASSIO I will ask him for my place again; he shall tell me I am a drunkard! Had I as many mouths as Hydra,[294] such an answer would stop them all. To be now a sensible man, by and by a fool, and presently a beast! O strange! Every inordinate cup is unblessed and the ingredient[295] is a devil.

IAGO Come, come; good wine is a good familiar creature if it be well used; exclaim no more against it. And, good lieutenant, I think you think I love you.

CASSIO I have well approved it, sir. I drunk!

IAGO You or any man living may be drunk at some time, man. I'll tell you what you shall do. Our general's wife is now the general; I may say so in this respect, for that he hath devoted and given up himself to the contemplation, mark, and denotement of her parts and graces: confess yourself freely to her; importune her; she'll help to put you in your place again. She is of so free, so kind, so apt, so blessed a disposition, that she holds it a vice in her goodness not to do more than she is requested. This broken joint between you and her husband entreat her to splinter;[296] and, my fortunes against any lay[297] worth naming, this crack of your love shall grow stronger than it was before.

CASSIO You advise me well.

IAGO I protest, in the sincerity of love and honest kindness.

CASSIO I think it freely; and betimes in the morning I will beseech the virtuous Desdemona to undertake for me. I am desperate of my fortunes if they check me here.

291. *I.e.*, without thinking. 292. *I.e.*, nonsense. 293. Pleasure. 294. Many-headed snake in Greek mythology. 295. Contents. 296. Bind up with splints. 297. Wager.

IAGO   You are in the right. Good-night, lieutenant; I must to the watch.

CASSIO   Good-night, honest Iago!                                    *(Exit.)*   290

IAGO   And what's he then that says I play the villain?
  When this advice is free I give and honest,
  Probal[298] to thinking and indeed the course
  To win the Moor again? For 'tis most easy
  The inclining Desdemona to subdue
  In any honest suit; she's fram'd as fruitful[299]
  As the free elements. And then for her
  To win the Moor, were 't to renounce his baptism,
  All seals and symbols of redeemed sin,
  His soul is so enfetter'd to her love,                          300
  That she may make, unmake, do what she list,
  Even as her appetite shall play the god
  With his weak function.[300] How am I then a villain
  To counsel Cassio to this parallel[301] course,
  Directly to his good? Divinity of hell!
  When devils will the blackest sins put on,
  They do suggest at first with heavenly shows,
  As I do now; for while this honest fool
  Plies Desdemona to repair his fortunes,
  And she for him pleads strongly to the Moor,                    310
  I'll pour this pestilence into his ear
  That she repeals[302] him for her body's lust;
  And, by how much she strives to do him good,
  She shall undo her credit with the Moor.
  So will I turn her virtue into pitch,
  And out of her own goodness make the net
  That shall enmesh them all.

*(Re-enter Roderigo.)*

How now, Roderigo!

RODERIGO   I do follow here in the chase, not like a hound that hunts, but one
that fills up the cry.[303] My money is almost spent; I have been to-night
exceedingly well cudgelled; and I think the issue will be, I shall have so much
experience for my pains; and so, with no money at all and a little more wit,
return again to Venice.

IAGO   How poor are they that have not patience!
  What wound did ever heal but by degrees?
  Thou know'st we work by wit and not by witchcraft,
  And wit depends on dilatory time.
  Does 't not go well? Cassio hath beaten thee,
  And thou by that small hurt hast cashiered Cassio.
  Though other things grow fair against the sun,
  Yet fruits that blossom first will first be ripe:                330

298. Provable.     299. Generous.     300. Faculties.     301. Purposeful.
302. *I.e.*, seeks to recall.     303. Pack (hunting term).

Content thyself awhile. By the mass, 'tis morning;
Pleasure and action make the hours seem short.
Retire thee; go where thou art billeted:
Away, I say; thou shalt know more hereafter:
Nay, get thee gone. (Exit Roderigo.) Two things are to be done,
My wife must move for Cassio to her mistress;
I'll set her on;
Myself the while to draw the Moor apart,
And bring him jump[304] when he may Cassio find
Soliciting his wife: ay, that's the way:                              340
Dull not device by coldness and delay.                    (Exit.)

# Act III

## SCENE 1   Cyprus. Before the Castle.

(Enter Cassio, and some Musicians.)

CASSIO  Masters, play here; I will content your pains;[305]
  Something that's brief; and bid 'Good-morrow, general.'       (Music.)

(Enter Clown.)

CLOWN  Why, masters, have your instruments been in Naples, that they speak
  i' the nose[306] thus?
FIRST MUSICIAN  How, sir, how?
CLOWN  Are these, I pray you, wind-instruments?
FIRST MUSICIAN  Ay, marry, are they, sir.
CLOWN  O! thereby hangs a tail.
FIRST MUSICIAN  Whereby hangs a tail, sir?
CLOWN  Marry, sir, by many a wind-instrument that I know. But, masters, here's
  money for you; and the general so likes your music, that he desires you, for
  love's sake, to make no more noise with it.
FIRST MUSICIAN  Well, sir, we will not.
CLOWN  If you have any music that may not be heard, to 't again; but, as they
  say, to hear music the general does not greatly care.
FIRST MUSICIAN  We have none such, sir.
CLOWN  Then put up your pipes in your bag, for I'll away.
  Go; vanish into air; away!                              (Exeunt Musicians.)
CASSIO  Dost thou hear, mine honest friend?
CLOWN  No, I hear not your honest friend; I hear you.                    20
CASSIO  Prithee, keep up thy quillets.[307] There's a poor piece of gold for thee. If
  the gentlewoman that attends the general's wife be stirring, tell her there's
  one Cassio entreats her a little favour of speech: wilt thou do this?
CLOWN  She is stirring, sir: if she will stir hither, I shall seem to notify unto her.

304. At the exact moment.        305. Reward your efforts.        306. Naples was
notorious for venereal disease, and syphilis was believed to affect the nose.
307. Quibbles.

CASSIO  Do, good my friend.                              *(Exit Clown.)*

*(Enter Iago.)*

In happy time, Iago.

IAGO  You have not been a-bed, then?

CASSIO  Why, no; the day had broke
Before we parted. I have made bold, Iago,
To send in to your wife; my suit to her
Is, that she will to virtuous Desdemona                                    30
Procure me some access.

IAGO                              I'll send her to you presently;
And I'll devise a mean to draw the Moor
Out of the way, that your converse and business
May be more free.

CASSIO  I humbly thank you for 't.                        *(Exit Iago.)*
                              I never knew
A Florentine more kind and honest.[308]

*(Enter Emilia.)*

EMILIA  Good-morrow, good lieutenant: I am sorry
For your displeasure,[309] but all will soon be well.
The general and his wife are talking of it,
And she speaks for you stoutly: the Moor replies                          40
The he you hurt is of great fame in Cyprus
And great affinity,[310] and that in wholesome wisdom
He might not but refuse you; but he protests he loves you,
And needs no other suitor but his likings
To take the safest occasion by the front[311]
To bring you in again.[312]

CASSIO                              Yet, I beseech you,
If you think fit, or that it may be done,
Give me advantage of some brief discourse
With Desdemona alone.

EMILIA                              Pray you, come in:
I will bestow you where you shall have time                               50
To speak your bosom[313] freely.

CASSIO                              I am much bound to you.        *(Exeunt.)*


## SCENE 2   *A Room in the Castle.*

*(Enter Othello, Iago, and Gentlemen.)*

OTHELLO  These letters give, Iago, to the pilot,

---

308. Cassio means that not even a fellow Florentine could behave to him in a friendlier
fashion than does Iago.        309. Disgrace.        310. Family connection.
311. Forelock.        312. Restore you (to Othello's favor).        313. Heart, inmost
thoughts.

And by him do my duties to the senate;
That done, I will be walking on the works;
Repair there to me.
IAGO                    Well, my good lord, I'll do 't.
OTHELLO  This fortification, gentlemen, shall we see 't?
GENTLEMEN  We'll wait upon your lordship.                    *(Exeunt.)*


## SCENE 3    *Before the Castle.*

*(Enter Desdemona, Cassio, and Emilia.)*

DESDEMONA  Be thou assur'd, good Cassio, I will do
    All my abilities in thy behalf.
EMILIA  Good madam, do: I warrant it grieves my husband,
    As if the case were his.
DESDEMONA  O! that's an honest fellow. Do not doubt, Cassio,
    But I will have my lord and you again
    As friendly as you were.
CASSIO                    Bounteous madam,
    Whatever shall become of Michael Cassio,
    He's never any thing but your true servant.
DESDEMONA  I know 't; I thank you. You do love my lord;          10
    You have known him long; and be you well assur'd
    He shall in strangeness[314] stand no further off
    Than in a politic[315] distance.
CASSIO                    Ay, but, lady,
    That policy may either last so long,
    Or feed upon such nice[316] and waterish diet,
    Or breed itself so out of circumstance,
    That, I being absent and my place supplied,
    My general will forget my love and service.
DESDEMONA  Do not doubt[317] that; before Emilia here
    I give thee warrant of thy place. Assure thee,          20
    If I do vow a friendship, I'll perform it
    To the last article; my lord shall never rest;
    I'll watch him tame,[318] and talk him out of patience;
    His bed shall seem a school, his board a shrift;[319]
    I'll intermingle every thing he does
    With Cassio's suit. Therefore be merry, Cassio;
    For thy solicitor shall rather die
    Than give thy cause away.[320]

*(Enter Othello and Iago, at a distance.)*

---

314. Aloofness.        315. *I.e.,* dictated by policy.        316. Slight, trivial.
317. Fear.        318. Outwatch him (*i.e.,* keep him awake) till he submits.
319. Confessional.        320. Abandon your cause.

EMILIA  Madam, here comes my lord.

CASSIO  Madam, I'll take my leave.                                    30

DESDEMONA  Why, stay, and hear me speak.

CASSIO  Madam, not now; I am very ill at ease,
  Unfit for mine own purposes

DESDEMONA  Well, do your discretion.                    (*Exit Cassio.*)

IAGO  Ha! I like not that.

OTHELLO                      What dost thou say?

IAGO  Nothing, my lord: or if—I know not what.

OTHELLO  Was not that Cassio parted from my wife?

IAGO  Cassio, my lord? No, sure, I cannot think it,
  That he would steal away so guilty-like,
  Seeing you coming.

OTHELLO                      I do believe 'twas he.          40

DESDEMONA  How now, my lord!
  I have been talking with a suitor here,
  A man that languishes in your displeasure.

OTHELLO  Who is 't you mean?

DESDEMONA  Why, your lieutenant, Cassio. Good my lord,
  If I have any grace or power to move you,
  His present[321] reconciliation take;
  For if he be not one that truly loves you,
  That errs in ignorance and not in cunning,
  I have no judgment in an honest face.          50
  I prithee[322] call him back.

OTHELLO                      Went he hence now?

DESDEMONA  Ay, sooth; so humbled,
  That he hath left part of his grief with me,
  To suffer with him. Good love, call him back.

OTHELLO  Not now, sweet Desdemona; some other time.

DESDEMONA  But shall 't be shortly?

OTHELLO                      The sooner, sweet, for you.

DESDEMONA  Shall 't be to-night at supper?

OTHELLO                      No, not to-night.

DESDEMONA  To-morrow dinner, then?

OTHELLO                      I shall not dine at home;
  I meet the captains at the citadel.

DESDEMONA  Why, then, to-morrow night; or Tuesday morn;      60
  Or Tuesday noon, or night; or Wednesday morn:
  I prithee name the time, but let it not
  Exceed three days: in faith, he's penitent;
  And yet his trespass, in our common reason,—
  Save that they say, the wars must make examples
  Out of their best,—is not almost[323] a fault
  To incur a private check.[324] When shall he come?

321. Immediate.    322. Pray thee.    323. Hardly.    324. (Even) a private
reprimand.

Tell me, Othello: I wonder in my soul,
What you could ask me, that I should deny,
Or stand so mammering[325] on. What! Michael Cassio,                    70
That came a wooing with you, and so many a time,
When I have spoke of you dispraisingly,
Hath ta'en your part; to have so much to do
To bring him in! Trust me, I could do much,—
OTHELLO  Prithee, no more; let him come when he will;
  I deny thee nothing.
DESDEMONA            Why, this is not a boon;
  'Tis as I should entreat you wear your gloves,
  Or feed on nourishing dishes, or keep you warm,
  Or sue to you to do a peculiar profit
  To your own person: nay, when I have a suit                    80
  Wherein I mean to touch your love indeed,
  It shall be full of poise[326] and difficult weight,
  And fearful to be granted.
OTHELLO                I will deny thee nothing:
  Whereon, I do beseech thee, grant me this,
  To leave me but a little to myself.
DESDEMONA  Shall I deny you? no: farewell, my lord.
OTHELLO  Farewell, my Desdemona: I'll come to thee straight.
DESDEMONA  Emilia, come. Be as your fancies teach you;
  Whate'er you be, I am obedient.            *(Exit, with Emilia.)*
OTHELLO  Excellent wretch![327] Perdition catch my soul,         90
  But I do love thee! and when I love thee not,
  Chaos is[328] come again.
IAGO  My noble lord,—
OTHELLO            What dost thou say, Iago?
IAGO  Did Michael Cassio, when you woo'd my lady,
  Know of your love?
OTHELLO  He did, from first to last: why dost thou ask?
IAGO  But for a satisfaction of my thought;
  No further harm.
OTHELLO          Why of thy thought, Iago?
IAGO  I did not think he had been acquainted with her.
OTHELLO  O! yes; and went between us very oft.               100
IAGO  Indeed!
OTHELLO  Indeed! ay, indeed; discern'st thou aught in that?
  Is he not honest?
IAGO          Honest, my lord?
OTHELLO                Honest! ay, honest.
IAGO  My lord, for aught I know.
OTHELLO  What dost thou think?

325. Shilly-shallying.    326. Weight.    327. Here, a term of endearment.
328. Will have.

IAGO                                  Think, my lord!

OTHELLO                                                Think, my lord!
  By heaven, he echoes me,
  As if there were some monster in his thought
  Too hideous to be shown. Thou dost mean something:
  I heard thee say but now, thou lik'dst not that,
  When Cassio left my wife; what didst not like?                    110
  And when I told thee he was of my counsel
  In my whole course of wooing, thou criedst, 'Indeed!'
  And didst contract and purse thy brow together,
  As if thou then hadst shut up in thy brain
  Some horrible conceit.[329] If thou dost love me,
  Show me thy thought.

IAGO  My lord, you know I love you.

OTHELLO                                  I think thou dost;
  And, for[330] I know thou art full of love and honesty,
  And weigh'st thy words before thou givest them breath,
  Therefore these stops[331] of thine fright me the more;          120
  For such things in a false disloyal knave
  Are tricks of custom, but in a man that's just
  They are close dilations,[332] working from the heart
  That passion cannot rule.

IAGO                          For Michael Cassio,
  I dare be sworn I think that he is honest.

OTHELLO  I think so too.

IAGO                          Men should be what they seem;
  Or those that be not, would they might seem none!

OTHELLO  Certain, men should be what they seem.

IAGO  Why then, I think Cassio's an honest man.

OTHELLO  Nay, yet there's more in this.                            130
  I pray thee, speak to me as to thy thinkings,
  As thou dost ruminate, and give thy worst of thoughts
  The worst of words.

IAGO                          Good my lord, pardon me;
  Though I am bound to every act of duty,
  I am not bound to[333] that all slaves are free to.
  Utter my thoughts? Why, say they are vile and false;
  As where's that palace whereinto foul things
  Sometimes intrude not? who has a breast so pure
  But some uncleanly apprehensions[334]
  Keep leets and law-days,[335] and in sessions sit                140
  With meditations lawful?

OTHELLO  Thou dost conspire against thy friend, Iago,

---

329. Fancy.       330. Because.       331. Interruptions, hesitations.       332. Secret
(*i.e.*, involuntary, unconscious) revelations.       333. Bound with regard to.
334. Conceptions.       335. Sittings of the local courts.

If thou but think'st him wrong'd, and mak'st his ear
A stranger to thy thoughts.
IAGO                              I do beseech you,
Though I perchance am vicious in my guess,—
As, I confess, it is my nature's plague
To spy into abuses, and oft my jealousy[336]
Shapes faults that are not,—that your wisdom yet,
From one that so imperfectly conceits,
Would take no notice, nor build yourself a trouble            150
Out of his scattering and unsure observance.
It were not for your quiet nor your good,
Nor for my manhood, honesty, or wisdom,
To let you know my thoughts.
OTHELLO                           What dost thou mean?
IAGO  Good name in man and woman, dear my lord,
Is the immediate jewel of[337] their souls:
Who steals my purse steals trash; 'tis something, nothing;
'Twas mine, 'tis his, and has been slave to thousands;
But he that filches from me my good name
Robs me of that which not enriches him,                     160
And makes me poor indeed.
OTHELLO  By heaven, I'll know thy thoughts.
IAGO  You cannot, if my heart were in your hand;
Nor shall not, whilst 'tis in my custody.
OTHELLO  Ha!
IAGO         O! beware, my lord, of jealousy;
It is the green-ey'd monster which doth mock
The meat it feeds on: that cuckold[338] lives in bliss
Who, certain of his fate, loves not his wronger;
But, O! what damned minutes tells[339] he o'er
Who dotes, yet doubts; suspects, yet soundly loves!          170
OTHELLO  O misery!
IAGO  Poor and content is rich, and rich enough,
But riches fineless[340] is as poor as winter
To him that ever fears he shall be poor.
Good heaven, the souls of all my tribe defend
From jealousy!
OTHELLO             Why, why is this?
Think'st thou I'd make a life of jealousy,
To follow still the changes of the moon
With fresh suspicions? No; to be once in doubt
Is once to be resolved. Exchange me for a goat               180
When I shall turn the business of my soul
To such exsufflicate[341] and blown[342] surmises,

336. Suspicion.     337. Jewel closest to.     338. Husband of an adulterous
woman.     339. Counts.     340. Boundless.     341. Spat out (?).
342. Fly-blown.

Matching thy inference. 'Tis not to make me jealous
To say my wife is fair, feeds well, loves company,
Is free of speech, sings, plays, and dances well;
Where virtue is, these are more virtuous:
Nor from mine own weak merits will I draw
The smallest fear, or doubt of her revolt;
For she had eyes, and chose me. No, Iago;
I'll see before I doubt; when I doubt, prove;                    190
And, on the proof, there is no more but this,
Away at once with love or jealousy!

IAGO   I am glad of it; for now I shall have reason
To show the love and duty that I bear you
With franker spirit; therefore, as I am bound,
Receive it from me; I speak not yet of proof.
Look to your wife; observe her well with Cassio;
Wear your eye thus, not jealous nor secure:
I would not have your free and noble nature
Out of self-bounty[343] be abus'd; look to 't:                  200
I know our country disposition[344] well;
In Venice they do let heaven see the pranks
They dare not show their husbands; their best conscience
Is not to leave 't undone, but keep 't unknown.

OTHELLO   Dost thou say so?

IAGO   She did deceive her father, marrying you;
And when she seem'd to shake and fear your looks,
She lov'd them most.

OTHELLO                          And so she did.

IAGO                                          Why, go to,[345] then;
She that so young could give out such a seeming,
To seel her father's eyes up close as oak,                      210
He thought 'twas witchcraft; but I am much to blame;
I humbly do beseech you of your pardon
For too much loving you.

OTHELLO                          I am bound to thee for ever.

IAGO   I see, this hath a little dash'd your spirits.

OTHELLO   Not a jot, not a jot.

IAGO                          I' faith, I fear it has.
I hope you will consider what is spoke
Comes from my love. But I do see you're mov'd;
I am to pray you not to strain my speech
To grosser issues nor to larger reach
Than to suspicion.                                              220

OTHELLO   I will not.

IAGO                          Should you do so, my lord,

343. Innate generosity.        344. *I.e.*, that of Venice.        345. Colloquialism; here,
something like "all right."

My speech should fall into such vile success
As my thoughts aim not at. Cassio's my worthy friend—
My lord, I see you're mov'd.
OTHELLO                              No, not much mov'd:
I do not think but Desdemona's honest.[346]
IAGO  Long live she so! and long live you to think so!
OTHELLO  And yet, how nature erring from itself,—
IAGO  Ay, there's the point: as, to be bold with you,
Not to affect many proposed matches
Of her own clime,[347] complexion, and degree,[348]                    230
Whereto, we see, in all things nature tends;
Foh! one may smell in such, a will most rank,
Foul disproportion, thoughts unnatural.
But pardon me; I do not in position[349]
Distinctly[350] speak of her, though I may fear
Her will, recoiling[351] to her better judgment,
May fall to match you with her country forms
And happily[352] repent.
OTHELLO                         Farewell, farewell:
If more thou dost perceive, let me know more;
Set on thy wife to observe. Leave me, Iago.                              240
IAGO  My lord, I take my leave.                          (Going.)
OTHELLO  Why did I marry? This honest creature, doubtless,
Sees and knows more, much more, than he unfolds.
IAGO (returning)  My lord, I would I might entreat your honour
To scan this thing no further; leave it to time.
Although 'tis fit that Cassio have his place,
For, sure he fills it up with great ability,
Yet, if you please to hold him off awhile,
You shall by that perceive him and his means:
Note if your lady strain his entertainment[353]                         250
With any strong or vehement importunity;
Much will be seen in that. In the mean time,
Let me be thought too busy[354] in my fears,
As worthy cause I have to fear I am,
And hold her free, I do beseech your honour.
OTHELLO  Fear not my government.
IAGO  I once more take my leave.                          (Exit.)
OTHELLO  This fellow's of exceeding honesty,
And knows all qualities, with a learned spirit,
Of human dealings; if I do prove her haggard,[355]                     260
Though that her jesses[356] were my dear heart-strings,

346. Chaste.       347. Country.       348. Social rank.       349. In definite
assertion.       350. Specifically.       351. Reverting.       352. Perhaps.
353. Urge his re-welcome (*i.e.,* to Othello's trust and favor).
354. Meddlesome.       355. Wild hawk.       356. Leather thongs by which the
hawk's legs were strapped to the trainer's wrist.

I'd whistle her off and let her down the wind,[357]
To prey at fortune. Haply, for I am black,
And have not those soft parts of conversation
That chamberers[358] have, or, for I am declin'd
Into the vale of years—yet that's not much—
She's gone, I am abus'd;[359] and my relief
Must be to loathe her. O curse of marriage!
That we can call these delicate creatures ours,
And not their appetites. I had rather be a toad,                    270
And live upon the vapour of a dungeon,
Than keep a corner in the thing I love
For others' uses. Yet, 'tis the plague of great ones;
Prerogativ'd[360] are they less than the base;
'Tis destiny unshunnable, like death:
Even then this forked plague[361] is fated to us
When we do quicken.[362]
                              Look! where she comes.
If she be false, O! then heaven mocks itself.
I'll not believe it.

*(Re-enter Desdemona and Emilia.)*

DESDEMONA          How now, my dear Othello!
   Your dinner and the generous[363] islanders                     280
   By you invited, do attend your presence.
OTHELLO  I am to blame.
DESDEMONA                     Why do you speak so faintly?
   Are you not well?
OTHELLO  I have a pain upon my forehead here.[364]
DESDEMONA  Faith, that's with watching; 'twill away again:
   Let me but bind it hard, within this hour
   It will be well.
OTHELLO          Your napkin[365] is too little:

*(She drops her handkerchief.)*

   Let it alone. Come, I'll go in with you.
DESDEMONA  I am very sorry that you are not well.

                         *(Exeunt Othello and Desdemona.)*

EMILIA  I am glad I have found this napkin;                         290
   This was her first remembrance from the Moor;
   My wayward husband hath a hundred times
   Woo'd me to steal it, but she so loves the token,

357. I'd let her go and take care of herself.          358. Courtiers; or (more specifically):
gallants, frequenters of bed chambers.          359. Deceived.          360. Privileged.
361. *I.e.*, the cuckold's proverbial horns.          362. Are conceived, come alive.
363. Noble.          364. Othello again refers to his cuckoldom.          365. Handkerchief.

For he conjur'd her she should ever keep it,
That she reserves it evermore about her
To kiss and talk to. I'll have the work ta'en out,[366]
And giv 't Iago:
What he will do with it heaven knows, not I;
I nothing but[367] to please his fantasy.[368]

*(Enter Iago.)*

IAGO   How now! what do you here alone?                           300
EMILIA   Do not you chide; I have a thing for you.
IAGO   A thing for me? It is a common thing—
EMILIA   Ha!
IAGO   To have a foolish wife.
EMILIA   O! is that all? What will you give me now
  For that same handkerchief?
IAGO                              What handkerchief?
EMILIA   What handkerchief!
  Why, that the Moor first gave to Desdemona:
  That which so often you did bid me steal.
IAGO   Hath stol'n it from her?                                    310
EMILIA   No, faith; she let it drop by negligence,
  And, to the advantage, I, being there, took 't up.
  Look, here it is.
IAGO              A good wench; give it me.
EMILIA   What will you do with 't, that you have been so earnest
  To have me filch it?
IAGO                  Why, what's that to you? *(Snatches it.)*
EMILIA   If it be not for some purpose of import
  Give 't me again; poor lady! she'll run mad
  When she shall lack it.
IAGO   Be not acknown on 't;[369] I have use for it.
  Go, leave me.                                    *(Exit Emilia.)*
  I will in Cassio's lodging lose this napkin,                     321
  And let him find it; trifles light as air
  Are to the jealous confirmations strong
  As proofs of holy writ; this may do something.
  The Moor already changes with my poison:
  Dangerous conceits are in their natures poisons,
  Which at the first are scarce found to distaste,[370]
  But with a little act upon the blood,
  Burn like the mines of sulphur. I did say so:
  Look! where he comes!

*(Enter Othello.)*

---

366. Pattern copied.     367. *I.e.,* only want.     368. Whim.     369. You know
nothing about it.     370. Scarce can be tasted.

Not poppy,[371] nor mandragora,[372]                330
Nor all the drowsy syrups[373] of the world,
Shall ever medicine thee to that sweet sleep
Which thou owedst yesterday.

OTHELLO                           Ha! ha! false to me?

IAGO  Why, how now, general! no more of that.

OTHELLO  Avaunt! be gone! thou hast set me on the rack;
I swear 'tis better to be much abus'd
Than but to know 't a little.

IAGO                           How now, my lord!

OTHELLO  What sense had I of her stol'n hours of lust?
I saw 't not, thought it not, it harm'd not me;
I slept the next night well, was free and merry;                340
I found not Cassio's kisses on her lips;
He that is robb'd, not wanting what is stol'n,
Let him not know 't, and he's not robb'd at all.

IAGO  I am sorry to hear this.

OTHELLO  I had been happy, if the general camp,[374]
Pioners[375] and all, had tasted her sweet body,
So[376] I had nothing known. O! now, for ever
Farewell the tranquil mind; farewell content!
Farewell the plumed troop and the big wars
That make ambition virtue! O, farewell!                350
Farewell the neighing steed, and the shrill trump,
The spirit-stirring drum, the ear-piercing fife,
The royal banner, and all quality,
Pride, pomp, and circumstance[377] of glorious war!
And, O you mortal engines,[378] whose rude throats
The immortal Jove's dread clamours counterfeit,
Farewell! Othello's occupation's gone!

IAGO  Is it possible, my lord?

OTHELLO  Villain, be sure thou prove my love a whore,
Be sure of it; give me the ocular proof;                360
Or, by the worth of mine eternal soul,
Thou hadst been better have been born a dog
Than answer my wak'd wrath.

IAGO                           Is 't come to this?

OTHELLO  Make me to see 't; or, at the least, so prove it,
That the probation[379] bear no hinge nor loop
To hang a doubt on; or woe upon thy life!

IAGO  My noble lord,—

OTHELLO  If thou dost slander her and torture me,
Never pray more; abandon all remorse;
On horror's head horrors accumulate;                370

371. Opium.     372. A soporific.     373. I.e., soporifics.     374. Whole
army.      375. Lowest rank of manual laborers in the army.      376. As long
as.      377. Pageantry.      378. Deadly artillery.      379. Proof.

Do deeds to make heaven weep, all earth amaz'd;
For nothing canst thou to damnation add
Greater than that.
IAGO                    O grace! O heaven forgive me!
Are you a man! have you a soul or sense?
God be wi' you; take mine office. O wretched fool!
That liv'st to make thine honesty a vice.
O monstrous world! Take note, take note, O world!
To be direct and honest is not safe.
I thank you for this profit,[380] and, from hence
I'll love no friend, sith[381] love breeds such offence.                    380
OTHELLO  Nay, stay; thou shouldst be honest.
IAGO  I should be wise; for honesty's a fool,
And loses that it works for.
OTHELLO                    By the world,
I think my wife be honest and think she is not;
I think that thou art just and think thou art not.
I'll have some proof. Her name, that was as fresh
As Dian's[382] visage, is now begrim'd and black
As mine own face. If there be cords or knives,
Poison or fire or suffocating streams,
I'll not endure it. Would I were satisfied!                    390
IAGO  I see, sir, you are eaten up with passion.
I do repent me that I put it to you.
You would be satisfied?
OTHELLO                    Would! nay, I will.
IAGO  And may; but how? how satisfied, my lord?
Would you, the supervisor,[383] grossly gape on;
Behold her tupp'd?
OTHELLO                    Death and damnation! O!
IAGO  It were a tedious[384] difficulty, I think,
To bring them to that prospect; damn them then,
If ever mortal eyes do see them bolster[385]
More[386] than their own! What then? how then?                    400
What shall I say? Where's satisfaction?
It is impossible you should see this,
Were they as prime[387] as goats, as hot as monkeys,
As salt as wolves in pride,[388] and fools as gross
As ignorance made drunk; but yet, I say,
If imputation, and strong circumstances,
Which lead directly to the door of truth,
Will give you satisfaction, you may have it.
OTHELLO  Give me a living reason she's disloyal.
IAGO  I do not like the office;                    410

380. Lesson.     381. Since.     382. Diana's, the goddess of the moon.
383. Observer.     384. Laborious.     385. Lie together.     386. Other.
387. Lustful.     388. Heat.

But, sith I am enter'd in this cause so far,
Prick'd to 't by foolish honesty and love,
I will go on. I lay with Cassio lately;
And, being troubled with a raging tooth,
I could not sleep.
There are a kind of men so loose of soul
That in their sleeps will mutter their affairs;
One of this kind is Cassio.
In sleep I heard him say, 'Sweet Desdemona,
Let us be wary, let us hide our loves!'                                   420
And then, sir, would he gripe[389] and wring my hand,
Cry, 'O, sweet creature!' and then kiss me hard,
As if he pluck'd up kisses by the roots,
That grew upon my lips; then laid his leg
Over my thigh, and sigh'd, and kiss'd; and then
Cried, 'Cursed fate, that gave thee to the Moor!'
OTHELLO   O monstrous! monstrous!
IAGO                                         Nay, this was but his dream.
OTHELLO   But this denoted a foregone conclusion:[390]
'Tis a shrewd doubt,[391] though it be but a dream.
IAGO   And this may help to thicken other proofs                          430
That do demonstrate thinly.
OTHELLO                        I'll tear her all to pieces.
IAGO   Nay, but be wise; yet we see nothing done;
She may be honest yet. Tell me but this:
Have you not sometimes seen a handkerchief
Spotted with strawberries in your wife's hand?
OTHELLO   I gave her such a one; 'twas my first gift.
IAGO   I know not that; but such a handkerchief—
I am sure it was your wife's—did I to-day
See Cassio wipe his beard with.
OTHELLO                         If it be that,—
IAGO   If it be that, or any that was hers,                               440
It speaks against her with the other proofs.
OTHELLO   O! that the slave had forty thousand lives;
One is too poor, too weak for my revenge.
Now do I see 'tis true. Look here, Iago;
All my fond love thus do I blow to heaven:
'Tis gone.
Arise, black vengeance, from the hollow hell!
Yield up, O love! thy crown and hearted throne
To tyrannous hate. Swell, bosom, with thy fraught,[392]
For 'tis of aspics'[393] tongues!
IAGO                        Yet be content.[394]                          450

389. Seize.      390. Previous consummation.      391. (1) Cursed, (2) Acute,
suspicion.      392. Burden.      393. Poisonous snakes.      394. Patient.

OTHELLO  O! blood, blood, blood!

IAGO  Patience, I say; your mind, perhaps, may change.

OTHELLO  Never, Iago. Like to the Pontic sea,[395]
  Whose icy current and compulsive course
  Ne'er feels retiring ebb, but keeps due on
  To the Propontic and the Hellespont,[396]
  Even so my bloody thoughts, with violent pace,
  Shall ne'er look back, ne'er ebb to humble love,
  Till that a capable[397] and wide revenge
  Swallow them up.                                    (Kneels)
               Now, by yond marble heaven,                    460
  In the due reverence of a sacred vow
  I here engage my words.

IAGO                    Do not rise yet.               (Kneels.)
  Witness, you ever-burning lights above!
  You elements that clip[398] us round about!
  Witness, that here Iago doth give up
  The execution of his wit, hands, heart,
  To wrong'd Othello's service! Let him command,
  And to obey shall be in me remorse,[399]
  What bloody business ever.[400]

OTHELLO                 I greet thy love,           (They rise.)
  Not with vain thanks, but with acceptance bounteous,        470
  And will upon the instant put thee to 't:
  Within these three days let me hear thee say
  That Cassio's not alive.

IAGO  My friend is dead; 'tis done at your request:
  But let her live.

OTHELLO         Damn her, lewd minx! O, damn her!
  Come, go with me apart; I will withdraw,
  To furnish me with some swift means of death
  For the fair devil. Now art thou my lieutenant.

IAGO  I am your own for ever.                          (Exeunt.)


## SCENE 4  *Before the Castle.*

*(Enter Desdemona, Emilia, and Clown.)*

DESDEMONA  Do you know, sirrah,[401] where Lieutenant Cassio lies?[402]

CLOWN  I dare not say he lies any where.

DESDEMONA  Why, man?

---

395. The Black Sea.    396. The Sea of Marmara, The Dardanelles.
397. Comprehensive.    398. Encompass.    399. Probably a corrupt line; the
meaning appears to be: "to obey shall be my solemn obligation."
400. Soever.    401. Common form of address to inferiors.    402. Lives.

CLOWN   He is a soldier; and for one to say a soldier lies, is stabbing.[403]

DESDEMONA   Go to;[404] where lodges he?

CLOWN   To tell you where he lodges is to tell you where I lie.

DESDEMONA   Can anything be made of this?

CLOWN   I know not where he lodges, and for me to devise[405] a lodging, and say he lies here or he lies there, were to lie in mine own throat.

DESDEMONA   Can you inquire him out, and be edified by report?                10

CLOWN   I will catechize the world for him; that is, make questions, and by them answer.

DESDEMONA   Seek him, bid him come hither; tell him I have moved my lord in his behalf, and hope all will be well.

CLOWN   To do this is within the compass of man's wit, and therefore I will attempt the doing it.                (Exit.)

DESDEMONA   Where should I lose that handkerchief, Emilia?

EMILIA   I know not, madam.

DESDEMONA   Believe me, I had rather have lost my purse
Full of cruzadoes;[406] and, but my noble Moor                20
Is true of mind, and made of no such baseness
As jealous creatures are, it were enough
To put him to ill thinking.

EMILIA                              Is he not jealous?

DESDEMONA   Who! he? I think the sun where he was born
Drew all such humours from him.

EMILIA                              Look! where he comes.

DESDEMONA   I will not leave him now till Cassio
Be call'd to him.

(Enter Othello.)

                              How is 't with you, my lord?

OTHELLO   Well, my good lady. (Aside) O! hardness to dissemble.
How do you, Desdemona?

DESDEMONA                      Well, my good lord.

OTHELLO   Give me your hand. This hand is moist,[407] my lady.                30

DESDEMONA   It yet has felt no age nor known no sorrow.

OTHELLO   This argues fruitfulness and liberal[408] heart;
Hot, hot, and moist; this hand of yours requires
A sequester[409] from liberty, fasting and prayer,
Much castigation, exercise devout;
For here's a young and sweating devil here,
That commonly rebels. 'Tis a good hand,
A frank one.

DESDEMONA      You may, indeed, say so;
For 'twas that hand that gave away my heart.

403. *I.e.*, is cause for stabbing.        404. Here apparently: "Come on!"
405. Invent.        406. Portuguese gold coins.        407. A supposed symptom of a
lustful nature.        408. With overtones of: too free, loose.        409. Separation.

OTHELLO   A liberal hand; the hearts of old gave hands,                    40
   But our new heraldry[410] is hands not hearts.

DESDEMONA   I cannot speak of this. Come now, your promise.

OTHELLO   What promise, chuck?[411]

DESDEMONA   I have sent to bid Cassio come speak with you.

OTHELLO   I have a salt and sorry rheum offends me.
   Lend me thy handkerchief.

DESDEMONA                    Here, my lord.

OTHELLO   That which I gave you.

DESDEMONA                         I have it not about me.

OTHELLO   Not?

DESDEMONA   No, indeed, my lord.

OTHELLO                              That is a fault.
   That handkerchief
   Did an Egyptian[412] to my mother give;                          50
   She was a charmer,[413] and could almost read
   The thoughts of people; she told her, while she kept it,
   'Twould make her amiable[414] and subdue my father
   Entirely to her love, but if she lost it
   Or made a gift of it, my father's eye
   Should hold her loathed, and his spirits should hunt
   After new fancies.[415] She dying gave it me;
   And bid me, when my fate would have me wive,
   To give it her. I did so; and take heed on 't;
   Make it a darling like your precious eye;                         60
   To lose 't or give 't away, were such perdition
   As nothing else could match.

DESDEMONA                    Is 't possible?

OTHELLO   'Tis true; there's magic in the web of it;
   A sibyl,[416] that had number'd in the world
   The sun to course two hundred compasses,
   In her prophetic fury sew'd the work;
   The worms were hallow'd that did breed the silk,
   And it was dy'd in mummy[417] which the skilful
   Conserv'd of maidens' hearts.

DESDEMONA                    Indeed! is 't true?

OTHELLO   Most veritable; therefore look to 't well.                       70

DESDEMONA   Then would to heaven that I had never seen it!

OTHELLO   Ha! wherefore?

DESDEMONA   Why do you speak so startingly and rash?

OTHELLO   Is 't lost? is 't gone? speak, is it out o' the way?

DESDEMONA   Heaven bless us!

OTHELLO   Say you?

---

410. *I.e.*, new heraldic symbolism (Othello means that the new way is not to give the
heart together with the hand).      411. Common term of endearment.
412. Gypsy.      413. Sorceress.      414. Lovable, desirable.      415. Loves.
416. Prophetess.      417. Drug (medicinal or magic) derived from embalmed bodies.

DESDEMONA   It is not lost: but what an if[418] it were?

OTHELLO   How!

DESDEMONA   I say, it is not lost.

OTHELLO                               Fetch 't, let me see 't!

DESDEMONA   Why, so I can, sir, but I will not now.                    80
   This is a trick to put me from my suit:
   Pray you let Cassio be receiv'd again.

OTHELLO   Fetch me the handkerchief; my mind misgives.

DESDEMONA   Come, come;
   You'll never meet a more sufficient[419] man.

OTHELLO   The handkerchief!

DESDEMONA                               I pray, talk[420] me of Cassio.

OTHELLO   The handkerchief!

DESDEMONA                       A man that all his time
   Hath founded his good fortunes on your love,
   Shar'd dangers with you,—

OTHELLO   The handkerchief!                                            90

DESDEMONA   In sooth, you are to blame.

OTHELLO   Away!                                            (Exit.)

EMILIA   Is not this man jealous?

DESDEMONA   I ne'er saw this before.
   Sure, there's some wonder in this handkerchief;
   I am most unhappy in the loss of it.

EMILIA   'Tis not a year or two shows us a man;
   They are all but[421] stomachs, and we all but[421] food;
   They eat us hungerly, and when they are full
   They belch us. Look you! Cassio and my husband.                100

*(Enter Iago and Cassio.)*

IAGO   There is no other way; 'tis she must do 't:
   And, lo! the happiness;[422] go and importune her.

DESDEMONA   How now, good Cassio! what's the news with you?

CASSIO   Madam, my former suit: I do beseech you
   That by your virtuous means I may again
   Exist, and be a member of his love
   Whom I with all the office[423] of my heart
   Entirely honour; I would not be delay'd.
   If my offence be of such mortal kind
   That nor my service past, nor present sorrows,              110
   Nor purpos'd merit in futurity,
   Can ransom me into his love again,
   But to know so must be my benefit;
   So shall I clothe me in a forc'd content,
   And shut myself up in some other course

---

418. If.        419. Adequate.        420. Talk to.        421. Only . . . only.
422. "What luck!"        423. Duty.

To fortune's alms.
DESDEMONA            Alas! thrice-gentle Cassio!
My advocation is not now in tune;
My lord is not my lord, nor should I know him,
Were he in favour[424] as in humour alter'd.
So help me every spirit sanctified,                              120
As I have spoken for you all my best
And stood within the blank of[425] his displeasure
For my free speech. You must awhile be patient;
What I can do I will, and more I will
Than for myself I dare: let that suffice you.
IAGO  Is my lord angry?
EMILIA                He went hence but now,
And certainly in strange unquietness.
IAGO  Can he be angry? I have seen the cannon,
When it hath blown his ranks[426] into the air,
And, like the devil, from his very arm                          130
Puff'd his own brother; and can he be angry?
Something of moment[427] then; I will go meet him;
There's matter in 't indeed, if he be angry.
DESDEMONA  I prithee, do so. (Exit Iago.) Something, sure, of state,[428]
Either from Venice, or some unhatch'd[429] practice
Made demonstrable here in Cyprus to him,
Hath puddled[430] his clear spirit; and, in such cases
Men's natures wrangle with inferior things,
Though great ones are their object. 'Tis even so;
For let our finger ache, and it indues[431]                     140
Our other healthful members even to that sense
Of pain. Nay, we must think men are not gods,
Nor of them look for such observancy[432]
As fits the bridal.[433] Beshrew me much, Emilia,
I was—unhandsome warrior as I am—
Arraigning his unkindness with[434] my soul;
But now I find I had suborn'd the witness,[435]
And he's indicted falsely.
EMILIA  Pray heaven it be state matters, as you think,
And no conception,[436] nor no jealous toy[437]                 150
Concerning you.
DESDEMONA  Alas the day! I never gave him cause.
EMILIA  But jealous souls will not be answer'd so;
They are not ever jealous for the cause,

424. Appearance.      425. As the target for.       426. I.e., his soldiers.
427. Important.     428. Public affairs.        429. Abortive or budding plot.
430. Muddied.     431. Brings, leads.     432. Attention.
433. Wedding.     434. To.      435. I.e., caused my soul to bring in wrong
charges.     436. Fancy, supposition.       437. Fancy.

But jealous for they are jealous; 'tis a monster
Begot upon itself, born on itself.
DESDEMONA  Heaven keep that monster from Othello's mind!
EMILIA  Lady, amen.
DESDEMONA  I will go seek him. Cassio, walk hereabout;
  If I do find him fit, I'll move your suit          160
  And seek to effect it to my uttermost.
CASSIO  I humbly thank your ladyship.    (Exeunt Desdemona and Emilia.)

  (Enter Bianca.)

BIANCA  Save you, friend Cassio!
CASSIO                What make you from home?
  How is it with you, my most fair Bianca?
  I' faith, sweet love, I was coming to your house.
BIANCA  And I was going to your lodging, Cassio.
  What! keep a week away? seven days and nights?
  Eight score eight hours? and lovers' absent hours,
  More tedious than the dial eight score times?
  O weary reckoning!
CASSIO           Pardon me, Bianca,        170
  I have this while with leaden thoughts been press'd;
  But I shall, in a more continuate[438] time,
  Strike off[439] this score of absence. Sweet Bianca,

  (Giving her Desdemona's handkerchief.)

  Take me this work out.
BIANCA            O Cassio! whence came this?
  This is some token from a newer friend;
  To the felt absence now I feel a cause;
  Is 't come to this? Well, well.
CASSIO           Go to, woman!
  Throw your vile guesses in the devil's teeth,
  From whence you have them. You are jealous now
  That this is from some mistress, some remembrance:  180
  No, in good troth, Bianca.
BIANCA          Why, whose is it?
CASSIO  I know not, sweet; I found it in my chamber.
  I like the work well; ere it be demanded,—[440]
  As like enough it will,—I'd have it copied;
  Take it and do 't; and leave me for this time.
BIANCA  Leave you! wherefore?
CASSIO  I do attend here on[441] the general,
  And think it no addition,[442] nor my wish,
  To have him see me woman'd.

438. Uninterrupted.    439. Cancel (I.e., make up for).    440. Asked for.
441. Wait for.    442. Advantage, credit.

BIANCA                                    Why, I pray you?
CASSIO  Not that I love you not.
BIANCA                                 But that you do not love me.                    190
  I pray you, bring me on the way a little
  And say if I shall see you soon at night.
CASSIO  'Tis but a little way that I can bring you,
  For I attend here; but I'll see you soon.
BIANCA  'Tis very good; I must be circumstanc'd.[443]          (*Exeunt.*)

# Act IV

## SCENE 1  *Cyprus. Before the Castle.*

(*Enter Othello and Iago.*)

IAGO  Will you think so?
OTHELLO                         Think so, Iago!
IAGO                                         What!
  To kiss in private?
OTHELLO              An unauthoriz'd kiss.
IAGO  Or to be naked with her friend a-bed
  An hour or more, not meaning any harm?
OTHELLO  Naked a-bed, Iago, and not mean harm?
  It is hypocrisy against the devil:[444]
  They that mean virtuously, and yet do so,
  The devil their virtue tempts, and they tempt heaven.
IAGO  If they do nothing, 'tis a venial slip;
  But if I give my wife a handkerchief,—                           10
OTHELLO  What then?
IAGO  Why, then, 'tis hers, my lord; and, being hers,
  She may, I think, bestow 't on any man.
OTHELLO  She is protectress of her honour too;
  May she give that?
IAGO  Her honour is an essence that's not seen;
  They have it very oft that have it not:[445]
  But for the handkerchief,—
OTHELLO  By heaven, I would most gladly have forgot it:—
  Thou said'st,—O! it comes o'er my memory,                    20
  As doth the raven[446] o'er the infected house,
  Boding to all,—he had my handkerchief.
IAGO  Ay, what of that?
OTHELLO                      That's not so good now.
IAGO                                          What,

443. Governed by circumstances.     444. *I.e.*, by not committing the sin which the
situation invites.     445. *I.e.*, some unchaste women are thought chaste.
446. (1) A bad omen, (2) A carrier of the plague.

If I had said I had seen him do you wrong?
Or heard him say, as knaves be such abroad,[447]
Who having, by their own importunate suit,
Or voluntary dotage[448] of some mistress,
Convinced or supplied them,[449] cannot choose
But they must blab.

OTHELLO               Hath he said any thing?
IAGO   He hath, my lord; but be you well assur'd,                        30
No more than he'll unswear.
OTHELLO                    What hath he said?
IAGO   Faith, that he did—I know not what he did.
OTHELLO   What? what?
IAGO   Lie—
OTHELLO   With her?
IAGO                With her, on her; what you will.
OTHELLO   Lie with her; lie on her! We say, lie on her, when they belie her. Lie with her! that's fulsome. Handkerchief,—confessions,—handkerchief! To confess, and be hanged for his labour. First, to be hanged, and then to confess: I tremble at it. Nature would not invest herself in such shadowing passion without some instruction.[450] It is not words that shake me thus. Pish! Noses, ears, and lips. Is it possible?—Confess!—Handkerchief!—O devil!

*(Falls in a trance.)*

IAGO   Work on,
My medicine, work! Thus credulous fools are caught;
And many worthy and chaste dames even thus,
All guiltless, meet reproach. What, ho! my lord!
My lord, I say! Othello!

*(Enter Cassio.)*

                How now, Cassio!
CASSIO   What's the matter?
IAGO   My lord is fallen into an epilepsy;[451]
This is his second fit; he had one yesterday.
CASSIO   Rub him about the temples.                                      50
                No, forbear;
The lethargy[452] must have his quiet course,
If not, he foams at mouth, and by and by
Breaks out to savage madness. Look! he stirs;
Do you withdraw yourself a little while,
He will recover straight; when he is gone,
I would on great occasion[453] speak with you.          *(Exit Cassio.)*
How is it, general? have you not hurt your head?

447. As there are some such in the world.        448. Foolish affection.
449. Overcome (their reluctance) or satisfied (their desires).        450. I would not fall
into such passion unless there were some real grounds for it.        451. Seizure,
fit.        452. Coma.        453. Important matter.

OTHELLO   Dost thou mock me?[454]

IAGO                           I mock you! no, by heaven.
   Would you would bear your fortune like a man!

OTHELLO   A horned man's a monster and a beast.                    60

IAGO   There's many a beast then, in a populous city,
   And many a civil[455] monster.

OTHELLO   Did he confess it?

IAGO                           Good sir, be a man;
   Think every bearded fellow that's but yok'd
   May draw[456] with you; there's millions now alive
   That nightly lie in those unproper[457] beds
   Which they dare swear peculiar;[458] your case is better.
   O! 'tis the spite of hell, the fiend's arch-mock,
   To lip[459] a wanton in a secure[460] couch,
   And to suppose her chaste. No, let me know;                     70
   And knowing what I am, I know what she shall be.

OTHELLO   O! thou art wise; 'tis certain.

IAGO                           Stand you awhile apart;
   Confine yourself but in a patient list.[461]
   Whilst you were here o'erwhelmed with your grief,—
   A passion most unsuiting such a man,—
   Cassio came hither; I shifted him away,
   And laid good 'scuse upon your ecstasy;[462]
   Bade him anon return and here speak with me;
   The which he promis'd. Do but encave yourself,
   And mark the fleers, the gibes, and notable scorns,             80
   That dwell in every region of his face;
   For I will make him tell the tale anew,
   Where, how, how oft, how long ago, and when
   He hath, and is again to cope[463] your wife:
   I say, but mark his gesture. Marry, patience;
   Or I shall say you are all in all in spleen,[464]
   And nothing of a man.

OTHELLO                     Dost thou hear, Iago?
   I will be found most cunning in my patience;
   But—dost thou hear?—most bloody.

IAGO                           That's not amiss:
   But yet keep time[465] in all. Will you withdraw?     (Othello goes apart.)   90
   Now will I question Cassio of Bianca,
   A housewife[466] that by selling her desires
   Buys herself bread and clothes; it is a creature

---

454. Another allusion to the cuckold's horns.     455. Citizen.     456. I.e., pull the
burden of cuckoldom.     457. Not exclusively their own.     458. Exclusively their
own.     459. Kiss.     460. I.e., without suspicion of having a rival.
461. Bounds of patience.     462. Derangement, trance.     463. Close with.
464. Completely overcome by passion.     465. Maintain control.     466. Hussy.

That dotes on Cassio; as 'tis the strumpet's plague
To beguile many and be beguil'd by one.
He, when he hears of her, cannot refrain
From the excess of laughter. Here he comes:

*(Re-enter Cassio.)*

As he shall smile, Othello shall go mad;
And his unbookish[467] jealousy must construe
Poor Cassio's smiles, gestures, and light behaviour                    100
Quite in the wrong. How do you now, lieutenant?
CASSIO  The worser that you give me the addition[468]
Whose want[469] even kills me.
IAGO  Ply Desdemona well, and you are sure on 't.
(*Speaking lower*) Now, if this suit lay in Bianca's power,
How quickly should you speed!
CASSIO                              Alas! poor caitiff![470]
OTHELLO  Look! how he laughs already!
IAGO  I never knew woman love man so.
CASSIO  Alas! poor rogue, I think, i' faith, she loves me.
OTHELLO  Now he denies it faintly, and laughs it out.                   110
IAGO  Do you hear, Cassio?
OTHELLO                      Now he importunes him
To tell it o'er: go to; well said, well said.
IAGO  She gives it out that you shall marry her;
Do you intend it?
CASSIO  Ha, ha, ha!
OTHELLO  Do you triumph, Roman?[471] do you triumph?
CASSIO  I marry her! what? a customer?[472] I prithee, bear some charity to my
wit;[473] do not think it so unwholesome. Ha, ha, ha!
OTHELLO  So, so, so, so. They laugh that win.[474]
IAGO  Faith, the cry goes that you shall marry her.                     120
CASSIO  Prithee, say true.
IAGO  I am a very villain else.
OTHELLO  Have you scored me?[475] Well.
CASSIO  This is the monkey's own giving out: she is persuaded I will marry her,
out of her own love and flattery, not out of my promise.
OTHELLO  Iago beckons me;[476] now he begins the story.
CASSIO  She was here even now; she haunts me in every place. I was the other
day talking on the sea-bank with certain Venetians, and thither comes this
bauble,[477] and, by this hand, she falls me thus about my neck;—
OTHELLO  Crying, 'O dear Cassio!' as it were; his gesture imports it.    130

---

467. Unpracticed, naive.      468. Title.      469. The want of which.
470. Wretch.      471. *I.e.*, one who triumphs (?).      472. Courtesan,
prostitute.      473. Give me credit for some sense.      474. "He who laughs last
laughs longest"(?).      475. Wounded, defaced (?); or: settled my account (?).
476. Signals.      477. Plaything.

CASSIO  So hangs and lolls and weeps upon me; so hales[478] and pulls me; ha, ha, ha!

OTHELLO  Now he tells how she plucked him to my chamber. O! I see that nose of yours, but not the dog I shall throw it to.

CASSIO  Well, I must leave her company.

IAGO  Before me![479] look, where she comes.

CASSIO  'Tis such another fitchew![480] marry, a perfumed one.

*(Enter Bianca.)*

What do you mean by this haunting of me?

BIANCA  Let the devil and his dam haunt you! What did you mean by that same handkerchief you gave me even now? I was a fine fool to take it. I must take out the work! A likely piece of work, that you should find it in your chamber, and not know who left it there! This is some minx's token, and I must take out the work! There, give it your hobby-horse;[481] wheresoever you had it I'll take out no work on 't.

CASSIO  How now, my sweet Bianca! how now, how now!

OTHELLO  By heaven, that should be[482] my handkerchief!

BIANCA  An you'll come to supper to-night, you may; an you will not, come when you are next prepared[483] for. *(Exit.)*

IAGO  After her, after her.

CASSIO  Faith, I must; she'll rail in the street else.                                    150

IAGO  Will you sup there?

CASSIO  Faith, I intend so.

IAGO  Well, I may chance to see you, for I would very fain[484] speak with you.

CASSIO  Prithee come; will you?

IAGO  Go to; say no more. *(Exit Cassio.)*

OTHELLO *(advancing)*  How shall I murder him, Iago?

IAGO  Did you perceive how he laughed at his vice?

OTHELLO  O! Iago!

IAGO  And did you see the handkerchief?

OTHELLO  Was that mine?                                                                  160

IAGO  Yours, by this hand; and to see how he prizes the foolish woman your wife! she gave it him, and he hath given it his whore.

OTHELLO  I would have him nine years a-killing. A fine woman! a fair woman! a sweet woman!

IAGO  Nay, you must forget that.

OTHELLO  Ay, let her rot, and perish, and be damned to-night; for she shall not live. No, my heart is turned to stone; I strike it, and it hurts my hand. O! the world hath not a sweeter creature; she might lie by an emperor's side and command him tasks.

IAGO  Nay, that's not your way.[485]                                                   170

---

478. Hauls.        479. An exclamation of surprise.        480. Polecat, noted both for its strong smell and for its lechery.        481. Harlot.        482. *I.e.*, I think that is.
483. Expected (Bianca means that if he does not come that night, she will never want to see him again).        484. Gladly.        485. Proper course.

OTHELLO  Hang her! I do but say what she is. So delicate with her needle! An admirable musician! O, she will sing the savageness out of a bear. Of so high and plenteous wit and invention!

IAGO  She's the worse for all this.

OTHELLO  O! a thousand, a thousand times. And then, of so gentle a condition![486]

IAGO  Ay, too gentle.[487]

OTHELLO  Nay, that's certain;—but yet the pity of it, Iago!
O! Iago, the pity of it, Iago!

IAGO  If you are so fond over her iniquity, give her patent to offend; for, if it touch not you, it comes near nobody.

OTHELLO  I will chop her into messes.[488] Cuckold me!

IAGO  O! 'tis foul in her.

OTHELLO  With mine officer!

IAGO  That's fouler.

OTHELLO  Get me some poison, Iago; this night: I'll not expostulate with her, lest her body and beauty unprovide my mind again.[489] This night, Iago.

IAGO  Do it not with poison, strangle her in her bed, even the bed she hath contaminated.

OTHELLO  Good, good; the justice of it pleases; very good.                    190

IAGO  And for Cassio, let me be his undertaker;[490] you shall hear more by midnight.

OTHELLO  Excellent good. *(A trumpet within.)* What trumpet is that same?

IAGO  Something from Venice, sure. 'Tis Lodovico,
Come from the duke; and see, your wife is with him.

*(Enter Lodovico, Desdemona, and Attendants.)*

LODOVICO  God save you, worthy general!

OTHELLO                                        With all my heart, sir.

LODOVICO  The duke and senators of Venice greet you.

*(Gives him a packet.)*

OTHELLO  I kiss the instrument of their pleasures.

*(Opens the packet, and reads.)*

DESDEMONA  And what's the news, good cousin Lodovico?

IAGO  I am very glad to see you, signior;                    200
Welcome to Cyprus.

LODOVICO  I thank you. How does Lieutenant Cassio?

IAGO  Lives, sir.

DESDEMONA  Cousin, there's fall'n between him and my lord
An unkind[491] breach; but you shall make all well.

OTHELLO  Are you sure of that?

DESDEMONA  My lord?

486. So much the high-born lady.    487. *I.e.*, yielding.    488. Bits.
489. Unsettle my intention.    490. Dispatcher.    491. Unnatural.

OTHELLO (*reads*) 'This fail you not to do, as you will'—
LODOVICO  He did not call; he's busy in the paper.
   Is there division⁴⁹² twixt my lord and Cassio?           210
DESDEMONA  A most unhappy one; I would do much
   To atone⁴⁹³ them, for the love I bear to Cassio.
OTHELLO  Fire and brimstone!
DESDEMONA          My lord?
OTHELLO               Are you wise?
DESDEMONA  What! is he angry?
LODOVICO             May be the letter mov'd him;
   For, as I think, they do command him home,
   Deputing Cassio in his government.
DESDEMONA  Trust me, I am glad on 't.
OTHELLO            Indeed!
DESDEMONA             My lord?
OTHELLO  I am glad to see you mad.
DESDEMONA          Why, sweet Othello?
OTHELLO  Devil!                 (*Strikes her.*)
DESDEMONA  I have not deserved this.
LODOVICO  My lord, this would not be believ'd in Venice,     220
   Though I should swear I saw 't; 'tis very much;
   Make her amends, she weeps.
OTHELLO           O devil, devil!
   If that the earth could teem with women's tears,
   Each drop she falls⁴⁹⁴ would prove a crocodile.⁴⁹⁵
   Out of my sight!
DESDEMONA      I will not stay to offend you.        (*Going.*)
LODOVICO  Truly, an obedient lady;
   I do beseech your lordship, call her back.
OTHELLO  Mistress!
DESDEMONA      My lord?
OTHELLO           What would you with her, sir?
LODOVICO  Why, I, my lord?
OTHELLO  Ay; you did wish that I would make her turn:     230
   Sir, she can turn, and turn, and yet go on,
   And turn again; and she can weep, sir, weep;
   And she's obedient, as you say, obedient,
   Very obedient. Proceed you in your tears.
   Concerning this, sir,—O well-painted passion!—
   I am commanded home. Get you away;
   I'll send for you anon. Sir, I obey the mandate,
   And will return to Venice. Hence! avaunt!⁴⁹⁶   (*Exit Desdemona.*)
   Cassio shall have my place. And, sir, to-night,
   I do entreat that we may sup together;           240

---

492. Estrangement.     493. Reconcile.     494. Lets fall.     495. The crocodile's
tears were supposed to be hypocritical.     496. Begone!

You are welcome, sir, to Cyprus. Goats and monkeys!        *(Exit.)*

LODOVICO  Is this the noble Moor whom our full senate
  Call all-in-all sufficient? is this the noble nature
  Whom passion could not shake? whose solid virtue
  The shot of accident nor dart of chance
  Could neither graze nor pierce?

IAGO                          He is much chang'd.

LODOVICO  Are his wits safe? is he not light of brain?

IAGO  He's that he is; I may not breathe my censure.
  What he might be, if, what he might, he is not,
  I would to heaven he were!⁴⁹⁷                            250

LODOVICO                  What! strike his wife!

IAGO  Faith, that was not so well; yet would I knew
  That stroke would prove the worst!

LODOVICO                          Is it his use?
  Or did the letters work upon his blood,
  And new-create this fault?

IAGO                      Alas, alas!
  It is not honesty in me to speak
  What I have seen and known. You shall observe him,
  And his own courses⁴⁹⁸ will denote him so
  That I may save my speech. Do but go after
  And mark how he continues.

LODOVICO  I am sorry that I am deceiv'd in him.        *(Exeunt.)*  260


## SCENE 2    *A Room in the Castle.*

*(Enter Othello and Emilia.)*

OTHELLO  You have seen nothing, then?

EMILIA  Nor ever heard, nor ever did suspect.

OTHELLO  Yes, you have seen Cassio and her together.

EMILIA  But then I saw no harm, and then I heard
  Each syllable that breath made up between them.

OTHELLO  What! did they never whisper?

EMILIA                          Never, my lord.

OTHELLO  Nor send you out o' the way?

EMILIA  Never.

OTHELLO  To fetch her fan, her gloves, her mask, nor nothing?⁴⁹⁹

EMILIA  Never, my lord.                                  10

OTHELLO  That's strange.

EMILIA  I durst, my lord, to wager she is honest,
  Lay down my soul at stake: if you think other,
  Remove your thought; it doth abuse your bosom.

497. Another of Iago's gnomic speeches; perhaps approximately: "If now he is not
himself, I wish he would be what he could be!"    498. Actions.    499. Anything.

If any wretch have put this in your head,
Let heaven requite it with the serpent's curse!
For, if she be not honest, chaste, and true,
There's no man happy; the purest of their wives
Is foul as slander.

OTHELLO                Bid her come hither; go.            *(Exit Emilia.)*
  She says enough; yet she's a simple[500] bawd            20
  That cannot say as much. This is a subtle whore,
  A closet lock and key of villanous secrets;
  And yet she'll kneel and pray; I have seen her do 't.

*(Re-enter Emilia with Desdemona.)*

DESDEMONA   My lord, what is your will?
OTHELLO                        Pray, chuck, come hither.
DESDEMONA   What is your pleasure?
OTHELLO                    Let me see your eyes;
  Look in my face.
DESDEMONA           What horrible fancy's this?
OTHELLO *(to Emilia)*   Some of your function,[501] mistress;
  Leave procreants alone and shut the door;
  Cough or cry 'hem' if any body come;
  Your mystery,[502] your mystery; nay, dispatch.          *(Exit Emilia.)*
DESDEMONA   Upon my knees, what doth your speech import?    31
  I understand a fury in your words.
  But not the words.
OTHELLO   Why, what art thou?
DESDEMONA                        Your wife, my lord; your true
  and loyal wife.
OTHELLO         Come, swear it, damn thyself;
  Lest, being like one of heaven, the devils themselves
  Should fear to seize thee; therefore be double-damn'd;
  Swear thou art honest.
DESDEMONA               Heaven doth truly know it.
OTHELLO   Heaven truly knows that thou art false as hell.
DESDEMONA   To whom, my lord? with whom? how am I false?    40
OTHELLO   Ah! Desdemona; away, away, away!
DESDEMONA   Alas, the heavy day!—Why do you weep?
  Am I the motive of these tears, my lord?
  If haply you my father do suspect
  An instrument of this your calling back,
  Lay not your blame on me; if you have lost him,
  Why, I have lost him too.
OTHELLO                Had it pleas'd heaven
  To try me with affliction, had he rain'd
  All kinds of sores and shames on my bare head,

500. Simpleminded.      501. To your duty, business.      502. Trade.

Steep'd me in poverty to the very lips,                                   50
Given to captivity me and my utmost hopes,
I should have found in some part of my soul
A drop of patience; but, alas! to make me
The fixed figure for the time of scorn[503]
To point his slow and moving finger at;
Yet could I bear that too; well, very well:
But there, where I have garner'd[504] up my heart,
Where either I must live or bear no life,
The fountain from the which my current runs
Or else dries up; to be discarded thence!                                 60
Or keep it as a cistern for foul toads
To knot and gender in![505] Turn thy complexion there,[506]
Patience, thou young and rose-lipp'd cherubin;
Ay, there, look grim as hell!

DESDEMONA  I hope my noble lord esteems me honest.

OTHELLO  O! ay; as summer flies in the shambles,[507]
That quicken even with blowing. O thou weed!
Who art so lovely fair and smell'st so sweet
That the sense aches at thee, would thou hadst ne'er been born.

DESDEMONA  Alas! what ignorant sin have I committed?                      70

OTHELLO  Was this fair paper, this most goodly book,
Made to write 'whore' upon? What committed!
Committed! O thou public commoner![508]
I should make very forges of my cheeks,
That would to cinders burn up modesty,
Did I but speak thy deeds. What committed!
Heaven stops the nose at it and the moon winks,[509]
The bawdy wind that kisses all it meets
Is hush'd within the hollow mine of earth,
And will not hear it. What committed!                                     80
Impudent strumpet!

DESDEMONA            By heaven, you do me wrong.

OTHELLO  Are not you a strumpet?

DESDEMONA                    No  as I am a Christian.
If to preserve this vessel for my lord
From any other foul unlawful touch
Be not to be a strumpet, I am none.

OTHELLO  What! not a whore?

DESDEMONA                    No, as I shall be sav'd.

OTHELLO  Is it possible?

DESDEMONA  O! heaven forgive us.

OTHELLO                  I cry you mercy,[510] then;

503. *I.e.*, the scornful world.      504. Stored.      505. Bunch up and
procreate.      506. *I.e.*, change your color to suit the "cistern for foul toads."
507. Slaughterhouse.      508. Harlot.      509. Closes her eyes.      510. Beg your
pardon.

I took you for that cunning whore of Venice
That married with Othello. You, mistress,                          90
That have the office opposite to Saint Peter,
And keep the gate of hell!

*(Re-enter Emilia.)*

                              You, you, ay, you!
We have done our course; there's money for your pains.
I pray you, turn the key and keep our counsel.                    *(Exit.)*
EMILIA  Alas! what does this gentleman conceive?[511]
  How do you, madam? how do you, my good lady?
DESDEMONA  Faith, half asleep.
EMILIA  Good madam, what's the matter with my lord?
DESDEMONA  With who?
EMILIA  Why, with my lord, madam.                             100
DESDEMONA  Who is thy lord?
EMILIA                     He that is yours, sweet lady.
DESDEMONA  I have none; do not talk to me, Emilia;
  I cannot weep, nor answer have I none,
  But what should go by water.[512] Prithee, to-night
  Lay on my bed my wedding sheets: remember:
  And call thy husband hither.
EMILIA                Here is a change indeed!                   *(Exit.)*
DESDEMONA  'Tis meet I should be us'd so, very meet.
  How have I been behav'd, that he might stick
  The small'st opinion on my least misuse?[513]

*(Re-enter Emilia, with Iago.)*

IAGO  What is your pleasure, madam? How is it with you?      110
DESDEMONA  I cannot tell. Those that do teach young babes
  Do it with gentle means and easy tasks;
  He might have chid me so; for, in good faith,
  I am a child to chiding.
IAGO                What's the matter, lady?
EMILIA  Alas, Iago, my lord hath so bewhor'd her,
  Thrown such despite[514] and heavy terms upon her,
  As true hearts cannot bear.
DESDEMONA  Am I that name, Iago?
IAGO                 What name, fair lady?
DESDEMONA  Such as she says my lord did say I was.
EMILIA  He call'd her whore; a beggar in his drink                120
  Could not have laid such terms upon his callat.[515]
IAGO  Why did he so?
DESDEMONA  I do not know; I am sure I am none such.

---

511. Imagine.     512. Be conveyed by means of tears.     513. The least suspicion
on my slightest misconduct.     514. Abuse.     515. Slut.

IAGO  Do not weep, do not weep. Alas the day!

EMILIA  Has she forsook so many noble matches,
　Her father and her country and her friends,
　To be call'd whore? would it not make one weep?

DESDEMONA  It is my wretched fortune.

IAGO　　　　　　　　　　　　Beshrew[516] him for it!
　How comes this trick upon him?

DESDEMONA　　　　　　　　Nay, heaven doth know.

EMILIA  I will be hang'd, if some eternal villain,　　　　　　　130
　Some busy and insinuating rogue,
　Some cogging[517] cozening slave, to get some office,
　Have not devis'd this slander; I'll be hang'd else.

IAGO  Fie! there is no such man; it is impossible.

DESDEMONA  If any such there be, heaven pardon him!

EMILIA  A halter pardon him, and hell gnaw his bones!
　Why should he call her whore? who keeps her company?
　What place? what time? what form? what likelihood?
　The Moor's abus'd by some most villanous knave,
　Some base notorious knave, some scurvy fellow.　　　　　　140
　O heaven! that such companions[518] thou'dst unfold,
　And put in every honest hand a whip
　To lash the rascals naked through the world,
　Even from the east to the west!

IAGO　　　　　　　　　　　Speak within door.

EMILIA  O! fie upon them. Some such squire he was
　That turn'd your wit the seamy side without,[519]
　And made you to suspect me with the Moor.

IAGO  You are a fool; go to.

DESDEMONA　　　　　　　　O good Iago,
　What shall I do to win my lord again?
　Good friend, go to him; for, by this light of heaven,　　　　150
　I know not how I lost him. Here I kneel:
　If e'er my will did trespass 'gainst his love,
　Either in discourse of thought or actual deed,
　Or that mine eyes, mine ears, or any sense,
　Delighted them[520] in any other form;
　Or that I do not yet,[521] and ever did,
　And ever will, though he do shake me off
　To beggarly divorcement, love him dearly,
　Comfort forswear me! Unkindness may do much;
　And his unkindness may defeat[522] my life,　　　　　　　　160
　But never taint my love. I cannot say 'whore':
　It does abhor me now I speak the word;
　To do the act that might the addition earn

516. Curse.　　517. Cheating.　　518. Fellows (derogatory).
519. Outward.　　520. Found delight.　　521. Still.　　522. Destroy.

Not the world's mass of vanity could make me.
IAGO  I pray you be content, 'tis but his humour;
  The business of the state does him offence,
  And he does chide with you.
DESDEMONA               If 'twere no other,—
IAGO  'Tis but so, I warrant.                *(Trumpets.)*
  Hark! how these instruments summon to supper;
  The messengers of Venice stay the meat:          170
  Go in, and weep not; all things shall be well.

                    *(Exeunt Desdemona and Emilia.)*

*(Enter Roderigo.)*

  How now, Roderigo!
RODERIGO  I do not find that thou dealest justly with me.
IAGO  What in the contrary?[523]
RODERIGO  Every day thou daffest me[524] with some device, Iago; and rather, as
  it seems to me now, keepest from me all conveniency,[525] than suppliest me
  with the least advantage of hope. I will indeed no longer endure it, nor am
  I yet persuaded to put up[526] in peace what already I have foolishly suffered.
IAGO  Will you hear me, Roderigo?          180
RODERIGO  Faith, I have heard too much, for your words and performances are
  no kin together.
IAGO  You charge me most unjustly.
RODERIGO  With nought but truth. I have wasted myself out of my means. The
  jewels you have had from me to deliver to Desdemona would half have
  corrupted a votarist;[527] you have told me she has received them, and returned
  me expectations and comforts of sudden respect[528] and acquaintance, but I
  find none.
IAGO  Well; go to; very well.
RODERIGO  Very well! go to! I cannot go to, man; nor 'tis not very well: by this
  hand, I say, it is very scurvy, and begin to find myself fobbed[529] in it.
IAGO  Very well.
RODERIGO  I tell you 'tis not very well. I will make myself known to Desdemona;
  if she will return me my jewels, I will give over my suit and repent my
  unlawful solicitation; if not, assure yourself I will seek satisfaction of you.
IAGO  You have said now.[530]
RODERIGO  Ay, and said nothing, but what I protest intendment of doing.
IAGO  Why, now I see there's mettle in thee, and even from this instant do build
  on thee a better opinion than ever before. Give me thy hand, Roderigo; thou
  hast taken against me a most just exception; but yet, I protest, I have dealt
  most directly in thy affair.
RODERIGO  It hath not appeared.

---

523. I.e., what reason do you have for saying that?    524. You put me off.
525. Favorable circumstances.    526. Put up with.    527. Nun.
528. Immediate consideration.    529. Cheated.    530. I.e., "I suppose you're
through?" (?); or: "Now you're talking" (?).

IAGO  I grant indeed it hath not appeared, and your suspicion is not without wit and judgment. But, Roderigo, if thou hast that in thee indeed, which I have greater reason to believe now than ever, I mean purpose, courage, and valour, this night show it: if thou the next night following enjoy not Desdemona, take me from this world with treachery and devise engines for[531] my life.

RODERIGO  Well, what is it? is it within reason and compass?

IAGO  Sir, there is especial commission come from Venice to depute Cassio in Othello's place.                                                      210

RODERIGO  Is that true? why, then Othello and Desdemona return again to Venice.

IAGO  O, no! he goes into Mauritania, and takes away with him the fair Desdemona, unless his abode be lingered here by some accident; wherein none can be so determinate[532] as the removing of Cassio.

RODERIGO  How do you mean, removing of him?

IAGO  Why, by making him uncapable of Othello's place; knocking out his brains.

RODERIGO  And that you would have me do?

IAGO  Ay; if you dare do yourself a profit and a right. He sups to-night with a harlotry,[533] and thither will I go to him; he knows not yet of his honourable fortune. If you will watch his going thence,—which I will fashion to fall out between twelve and one,—you may take him at your pleasure; I will be near to second your attempt, and he shall fall between us. Come, stand not amazed at it, but go along with me; I will show you such a necessity in his death that you shall think yourself bound to put it on him. It is now high supper-time, and the night grows to waste; about it.

RODERIGO  I will hear further reason for this.

IAGO  And you shall be satisfied.                                    (Exeunt.)


## SCENE 3   *Another Room in the Castle.*

*(Enter Othello, Lodovico, Desdemona, Emilia, and Attendants.)*

LODOVICO  I do beseech you, sir, trouble yourself no further.

OTHELLO  O! pardon me; 'twill do me good to walk.

LODOVICO  Madam, good-night; I humbly thank your ladyship.

DESDEMONA  Your honour is most welcome.

OTHELLO                                          Will you walk, sir?
   O! Desdemona,—

DESDEMONA  My lord?

OTHELLO  Get you to bed on the instant; I will be returned forthwith; dismiss your attendant there; look it be done.

DESDEMONA  I will, my lord.      *(Exeunt Othello, Lodovico, and Attendants.)*

EMILIA  How goes it now? He looks gentler than he did.                   10

531. Devices against.      532. Effective.      533. Harlot.

DESDEMONA  He says he will return incontinent;[534]
  He hath commanded me to go to bed,
  And bade me to dismiss you.
EMILIA                         Dismiss me!
DESDEMONA  It was his bidding; therefore, good Emilia,
  Give me my nightly wearing, and adieu:
  We must not now displease him.
EMILIA  I would you had never seen him.
DESDEMONA  So would not I; my love doth so approve him,
  That even his stubbornness,[535] his checks[536] and frowns,—
  Prithee, unpin me,—have grace and favour in them.          20
EMILIA  I have laid those sheets you bade me on the bed.
DESDEMONA  All's one.[537] Good faith! how foolish are our minds!
  If I do die before thee, prithee, shroud me
  In one of those same sheets.
EMILIA              Come, come, you talk.
DESDEMONA  My mother had a maid call'd Barbara;
  She was in love, and he she lov'd prov'd mad[538]
  And did forsake her; she had a song of 'willow';
  An old thing 'twas, but it express'd her fortune,
  And she died singing it; that song to-night
  Will not go from my mind; I have much to do          30
  But to go hang my head all at one side,
  And sing it like poor Barbara. Prithee, dispatch.
EMILIA  Shall I go fetch your night-gown?
DESDEMONA                    No, unpin me here.
  This Lodovico is a proper man.
EMILIA  A very handsome man.
DESDEMONA  He speaks well.
EMILIA  I know a lady in Venice would have walked barefoot to Palestine for a
  touch of his nether lip.
DESDEMONA *(sings)*

    The poor soul sat sighing by a sycamore tree,
      Sing all a green willow;          40
    Her hand on her bosom, her head on her knee,
      Sing willow, willow, willow:
    The fresh streams ran by her, and murmur'd her moans;
      Sing willow, willow, willow:
    Her salt tears fell from her, and soften'd the stones;—

  Lay by these:—

      Sing willow, willow, willow:

  Prithee, hie thee;[539] he'll come anon.—

---

534. At once.    535. Roughness.    536. Rebukes.    537. *I.e.,* it doesn't
matter.    538. Wild.    539. Hurry.

Sing all a green willow must be my garland.

Let nobody blame him, his scorn I approve,— 50

Nay, that's not next. Hark! who is it that knocks?

EMILIA  It is the wind.

DESDEMONA

I call'd my love false love; but what said he then?

Sing willow, willow, willow:

If I court moe[540] women, you'll couch with moe men.

So, get thee gone; good-night. Mine eyes do itch;

Doth that bode weeping?

EMILIA                    'Tis neither here nor there.

DESDEMONA  I have heard it said so. O! these men, these men!

Dost thou in conscience think, tell me, Emilia,

That there be women do abuse their husbands 60

In such gross kind?

EMILIA                There be some such, no question.

DESDEMONA  Wouldst thou do such a deed for all the world?

EMILIA  Why, would not you?

DESDEMONA                No, by this heavenly light!

EMILIA  Nor I neither by this heavenly light;

I might do 't as well i' the dark.

DESDEMONA  Wouldst thou do such a deed for all the world?

EMILIA  The world is a huge thing; 'tis a great price

For a small vice.

DESDEMONA        In troth, I think thou wouldst not.

EMILIA  In troth, I think I should, and undo 't when I had done. Marry, I would
not do such a thing for a joint-ring,[541] nor measures of lawn,[542] nor for gowns,
petticoats, nor caps, nor any petty exhibition;[543] but for the whole world, who
would not make her husband a cuckold to make him a monarch? I should
venture purgatory for 't.

DESDEMONA  Beshrew me, if I would do such a wrong

For the whole world.

EMILIA  Why, the wrong is but a wrong i' the world; and having the world for
your labour, 'tis a wrong in your own world, and you might quickly make it
right.

DESDEMONA  I do not think there is any such woman.

EMILIA  Yes, a dozen; and as many to the vantage,[544] as 80

Would store[545] the world they played for.

But I do think it is their husbands' faults

If wives do fall. Say that they slack their duties,

And pour our treasures into foreign laps,

Or else break out in peevish jealousies,

Throwing restraint upon us; or say they strike us,

540. More.     541. Ring made in separable halves.     542. Fine linen.
543. Offer, gift.     544. Over and above.     545. Populate.

Or scant[546] our former having[547] in despite;
  Why, we have galls,[548] and though we have some grace,
  Yet have we some revenge. Let husbands know
  Their wives have sense like them; they see and smell,                          90
  And have their palates both for sweet and sour,
  As husbands have. What is it that they do
  When they change us for others? Is it sport?[549]
  I think it is; and doth affection breed it?
  I think it doth; is 't frailty that thus errs?
  It is so too; and have not we affections,
  Desires for sport, and frailty, as men have?
  Then, let them use us well; else let them know,
  The ills we do, their ills instruct us so.
DESDEMONA   Good-night, good-night; heaven me such usage[550] send,          100
  Not to pick bad from bad, but by bad mend!                    (Exeunt.)

# Act V

## SCENE 1   Cyprus. A Street.

(Enter Iago and Roderigo.)

IAGO   Here, stand behind this bulk;[551] straight will he come:
  Wear thy good rapier bare, and put it home.
  Quick, quick; fear nothing; I'll be at thy elbow.
  It makes us, or it mars us; think on that,
  And fix most firm thy resolution.
RODERIGO   Be near at hand; I may miscarry in 't.
IAGO   Here, at thy hand: be bold, and take thy stand.              (Retires.)
RODERIGO   I have no great devotion to the deed;
  And yet he has given me satisfying reasons:
  'Tis but a man gone: forth, my sword; he dies.                               10
IAGO   I have rubb'd this young quat[552] almost to the sense,[553]
  And he grows angry. Now, whether he kill Cassio,
  Or Cassio him, or each do kill the other,
  Every way makes my gain: live Roderigo,
  He calls me to a restitution large
  Of gold and jewels that I bobb'd[554] from him,
  As gifts to Desdemona;
  It must not be: if Cassio do remain,
  He hath a daily beauty in his life
  That makes me ugly: and, besides, the Moor                                   20

546. Reduce.     547. Allowance.     548. Spirits, temper.     549. Lust, sexual
enjoyment.     550. Habits (?), treatment (?).     551. Jutting part of a wall.
552. Pimple.     553. To the quick.     554. Swindled.

May unfold me to him; there stand I in much peril.
No, he must die. But so;[555] I hear him coming.

*(Enter Cassio.)*

RODERIGO   I know his gait; 'tis he. Villain, thou diest!

*(Makes a pass at Cassio.)*

CASSIO   That thrust had been mine enemy indeed
But that my coat is better than thou know'st;
I will make proof of thine.

*(Draws, and wounds Roderigo.)*

RODERIGO                    O! I am slain.

*(Iago from behind wounds Cassio in the leg, and exit.)*

CASSIO   I am maim'd for ever. Help, ho! murder! murder!          *(Falls.)*

*(Enter Othello, at a distance.)*

OTHELLO   The voice of Cassio: Iago keeps his word.
RODERIGO   Oh! villain that I am!
OTHELLO                              It is e'en so.
CASSIO   O, help, ho! light! a surgeon!                                          30
OTHELLO   'Tis he: O brave Iago, honest and just!
That hast such noble sense of thy friend's wrong;
Thou teachest me. Minion,[556] your dear lies dead,
And your unblest fate hies; strumpet, I come!
Forth of my heart those charms, thine eyes, are blotted;
Thy bed lust-stain'd shall with lust's blood be spotted.          *(Exit.)*

*(Enter Lodovico and Gratiano, at a distance.)*

CASSIO   What ho! no watch? no passage?[557] murder! murder!
GRATIANO   'Tis some mischance; the cry is very direful.
CASSIO   O, help!
LODOVICO   Hark!                                                                  40
RODERIGO   O wretched villain!
LODOVICO   Two or three groans: it is a heavy[558] night;
These may be counterfeits; let's think 't unsafe
To come in to the cry[559] without more help.
RODERIGO   Nobody come? then shall I bleed to death.
LODOVICO   Hark!

*(Re-enter Iago, with a light.)*

GRATIANO   Here's one comes in his shirt, with light and weapons.
IAGO   Who's there? whose noise is this that cries on murder?

555. *I.e.,* that's the only way.      556. (Cassio's) darling, *i.e.,* Desdemona.
557. Passer-by.        558. Dark.      559. Where the cry comes from.

LODOVICO  We do not know.

IAGO                    Did not you hear a cry?

CASSIO  Here, here! for heaven's sake, help me.

IAGO                              What's the matter?                    50

GRATIANO  This is Othello's ancient, as I take it.

LODOVICO  The same indeed; a very valiant fellow.

IAGO  What are you here that cry so grievously?

CASSIO  Iago? O! I am spoil'd, undone by villains!
  Give me some help.

IAGO  O me, lieutenant! what villains have done this?

CASSIO  I think that one of them is hereabout,
  And cannot make away.

IAGO                    O treacherous villains!
  (To Lodovico and Gratiano.) What are you there? come in, and give some help.

RODERIGO  O! help me here.                              60

CASSIO  That's one of them.

IAGO                    O murderous slave! O villain!

  (Stabs Roderigo.)

RODERIGO  O damn'd Iago! O inhuman dog!

IAGO  Kill men i' the dark! Where be these bloody thieves?
  How silent is this town! Ho! murder! murder!
  What may you be? are you of good or evil?

LODOVICO  As you shall prove us, praise us.

IAGO  Signior Lodovico?

LODOVICO  He, sir.

IAGO  I cry you mercy. Here's Cassio hurt by villains.

GRATIANO  Cassio!                                      70

IAGO  How is it, brother?

CASSIO  My leg is cut in two.

IAGO                    Marry, heaven forbid.
  Light, gentlemen; I'll bind it with my shirt.

  (Enter Bianca.)

BIANCA  What is the matter, ho? who is 't that cried?

IAGO  Who is 't that cried!

BIANCA  O my dear Cassio! my sweet Cassio!
  O Cassio, Cassio, Cassio!

IAGO  O notable strumpet! Cassio, may you suspect
  Who they should be that have thus mangled you?

CASSIO  No.                                           80

GRATIANO  I am sorry to find you thus; I have been to seek you.

IAGO  Lend me a garter. So. O! for a chair,
  To bear him easily hence!

BIANCA  Alas; he faints! O Cassio, Cassio, Cassio!

IAGO  Gentlemen all, I do suspect this trash[560]

560. I.e., Bianca.

To be a party in this injury.
Patience awhile, good Cassio. Come, come.
Lend me a light. Know we this face, or no?
Alas! my friend and my dear countryman,
Roderigo? no: yes, sure, O heaven! Roderigo.          90
GRATIANO  What! of Venice?
IAGO  Even he, sir: did you know him?
GRATIANO                              Know him! ay.
IAGO  Signior Gratiano? I cry you gentle pardon;
  These bloody accidents must excuse my manners,
  That so neglected you.
GRATIANO                I am glad to see you.
IAGO  How do you, Cassio? O! a chair, a chair!
GRATIANO  Roderigo!

    (A chair brought in.)

IAGO  He, he, 'tis he,—O! that's well said; the chair:
  Some good men bear him carefully from hence;
  I'll fetch the general's surgeon. (To Bianca.) For you, mistress,     100
  Save you your labour. He that lies slain here, Cassio,
  Was my dear friend. What malice was between you?
CASSIO  None in the world; nor do I know that man.
IAGO (to Bianca)  What! look you pale? O! bear him out o' the air—

    (Cassio and Roderigo are borne off.)

  Stay you, good gentlemen. Look you pale, mistress?—
  Do you perceive the gastness[561] of her eye?
  Nay, if you stare, we shall hear more anon.
  Behold her well; I pray you, look upon her.
  Do you see, gentlemen? nay, guiltiness will speak
  Though tongues were out of use.          110

    (Enter Emilia.)

EMILIA  'Las! what 's the matter? what 's the matter, husband?
IAGO  Cassio hath here been set on in the dark
  By Roderigo and fellows that are 'scaped:
  He 's almost slain, and Roderigo dead.
EMILIA  Alas! good gentleman; alas! good Cassio!
IAGO  This is the fruit of whoring. Prithee, Emilia,
  Go know of Cassio where he supp'd to-night.
    (To Bianca.) What! do you shake at that?
BIANCA  He supp'd at my house; but I therefore shake not.
IAGO  O! did he so? I charge you, go with me.          120
EMILIA  Fie, fie, upon thee, strumpet!
BIANCA  I am no strumpet, but of life as honest
  As you that thus abuse me.

561. Terror.

EMILIA                As I! foh! fie upon thee!

IAGO  Kind gentlemen, let's go see poor Cassio dress'd.[562]
   Come, mistress, you must tell's another tale.
   Emilia, run you to the citadel,
   And tell my lord and lady what hath happ'd.
   Will you go on afore? *(Aside.)* This is the night
   That either makes me or fordoes[563] me quite.                    *(Exeunt.)*


SCENE 2   *A Bedchamber in the Castle. Desdemona in bed asleep.*
          *A light burning.*

*(Enter Othello.)*

OTHELLO  It is the cause,[564] it is the cause, my soul;
   Let me not name it to you, you chaste stars!
   It is the cause. Yet I'll not shed her blood,
   Nor scar that whiter skin of hers than snow,
   And smooth as monumental alabaster.
   Yet she must die, else she'll betray more men.
   Put out the light, and then put out the light:
   If I quench thee, thou flaming minister,[565]
   I can again thy former light restore,
   Should I repent me; but once put out thy light,                  10
   Thou cunning'st[566] pattern of excelling nature,
   I know not where is that Promethean[567] heat
   That can thy light relume.[568] When I have pluck'd the rose,
   I cannot give it vital growth again,
   It needs must wither: I'll smell it on the tree. *(Kisses her.)*
   O balmy breath, that dost almost persuade
   Justice to break her sword! One more, one more.
   Be thus when thou art dead, and I will kill thee,
   And love thee after. One more, and this the last:
   So sweet was ne'er so fatal. I must weep,                        20
   But they are cruel tears; this sorrow's heavenly,
   It strikes where it doth love. She wakes.
DESDEMONA  Who 's there? Othello?
OTHELLO                        Ay, Desdemona.
DESDEMONA  Will you come to bed, my lord?
OTHELLO  Have you pray'd to-night, Desdemona?
DESDEMONA                                 Ay, my lord.
OTHELLO  If you bethink yourself of any crime

---

562. Bandaged.        563. Ruins.        564. *I.e.,* Desdemona's unchastity (Othello
means that the severity of the punishment is required by the nature of her sin).
565. *I.e.,* the candle.        566. Most intricately wrought.        567. In Greek
mythology the demi-god Prometheus stole fire from the gods and gave it to man.
568. Relight.

Unreconcil'd as yet to heaven and grace,
  Solicit for it straight.

DESDEMONA  Alas! my lord, what may you mean by that?

OTHELLO  Well, do it, and be brief; I will walk by:[569]        30
  I would not kill thy unprepared spirit;
  No; heaven forfend![570] I would not kill thy soul.

DESDEMONA  Talk you of killing?

OTHELLO                          Ay, I do.

DESDEMONA                                Then heaven
  Have mercy on me!

OTHELLO                Amen! with all my heart.

DESDEMONA  If you say so, I hope you will not kill me.

OTHELLO  Hum!

DESDEMONA  And yet I fear you; for you are fatal then
  When your eyes roll so. Why I should fear I know not,
  Since guiltiness I know not; but yet I feel I fear.

OTHELLO  Think on thy sins.

DESDEMONA                    They are loves I bear to you.       40

OTHELLO  Ay, and for that thou diest.

DESDEMONA  That death's unnatural that kills for loving.
  Alas! why gnaw you so your nether lip?
  Some bloody passion shakes your very frame;
  These are portents,[571] but yet, I hope, I hope
  They do not point on me.

OTHELLO                      Peace, and be still!

DESDEMONA  I will so. What's the matter?

OTHELLO  That handkerchief which I so lov'd and gave thee
  Thou gav'st to Cassio.

DESDEMONA                No, by my life and soul!
  Send for the man and ask him.

OTHELLO                          Sweet soul, take heed,         50
  Take heed of perjury; thou 'rt on thy death-bed.

DESDEMONA  Ay, but not yet to die.

OTHELLO                             Yes, presently;[572]
  Therefore confess thee freely of thy sin;
  For to deny each article with oath
  Cannot remove nor choke the strong conception[573]
  That I do groan withal. Thou art to die.

DESDEMONA  Then Lord have mercy on me!

OTHELLO                                  I say, amen.

DESDEMONA  And have you mercy too! I never did
  Offend you in my life; never lov'd Cassio
  But with such general warranty[574] of heaven                 60
  As I might love; I never gave him token.

569. Nearby.     570. Forbid.     571. Omens.     572. At once.
573. Belief.     574. Permission.

OTHELLO   By heaven, I saw my handkerchief in 's hand.
O perjur'd woman! thou dost stone[575] my heart,
And mak'st me call what I intend to do
A murder, which I thought a sacrifice:
I saw the handkerchief.
DESDEMONA                    He found it then;
I never gave it him. Send for him hither;
Let him confess a truth.
OTHELLO                       He hath confessed.
DESDEMONA   What, my lord?
OTHELLO   That he hath us'd thee.
DESDEMONA                       How? Unlawfully?
OTHELLO                                      Ay.                              70
DESDEMONA   He will not say so.
OTHELLO                         No; his mouth is stopp'd:
Honest Iago hath ta'en order for 't.[576]
DESDEMONA   O! my fear interprets. What! is he dead?
OTHELLO   Had all his hairs been lives, my great revenge
Had stomach[577] for them all.
DESDEMONA   Alas! he is betray'd and I undone.
OTHELLO   Out, strumpet! Weep'st thou for him to my face?
DESDEMONA   O! banish me, my lord, but kill me not!
OTHELLO   Down, strumpet!
DESDEMONA   Kill me to-morrow; let me live to-night!          80
OTHELLO   Nay, if you strive,—
DESDEMONA   But half an hour!
OTHELLO                         Being done, there is no pause.
DESDEMONA   But while I say one prayer!
OTHELLO                            It is too late.   (He smothers her.)
EMILIA (within)   My lord, my lord! what, ho! my lord, my lord!
OTHELLO   What noise is this? Not dead? not yet quite dead?
I that am cruel am yet merciful;
I would not have thee linger in thy pain.
So, so.
EMILIA (within)   What, ho! my lord, my lord!
OTHELLO                                      Who's there?
EMILIA (within)   O! good my lord, I would speak a word with you!     90
OTHELLO   Yes; 'tis Emilia: by and by.[578] She's dead.
'Tis like[579] she comes to speak of Cassio's death;
The noise was high. Ha! no more moving?
Still as the grave. Shall she come in? Were 't good?[580]
I think she stirs again: no. What's best to do?
If she come in she'll sure speak to my wife:
My wife! my wife! what wife? I have no wife;

575. Turn to stone.     576. Taken steps.     577. Appetite.     578. I.e., "just a
moment."     579. Likely.     580. Would that be wise?

O, insupportable! O heavy hour!
Methinks it should be now a huge eclipse
Of sun and moon, and that the affrighted globe                                    100
Should yawn[581] at alteration.

EMILIA *(within)*                    I do beseech you
That I may speak with you, O! good my lord.

OTHELLO   I had forgot thee: O! come in, Emilia:
Soft, by and by: let me the curtains draw.
Where art thou?                                    *(Unlocks the door.)*

*(Enter Emilia.)*

                    What's the matter with thee now?

EMILIA   O! my good lord, yonder's foul murder done.

OTHELLO   What! now?

EMILIA   But now, my lord.

OTHELLO   It is the very error[582] of the moon;
She comes more near the earth than she was wont,                                    110
And makes men mad.

EMILIA   Cassio, my lord, has kill'd a young Venetian
Call'd Roderigo.

OTHELLO                    Roderigo kill'd!
And Cassio kill'd?

EMILIA                    No, Cassio is not kill'd.

OTHELLO   Not Cassio kill'd! then murder's out of tune,
And sweet revenge grows harsh.

DESDEMONA   O! falsely, falsely murder'd.

EMILIA                                    Alas! what cry is that?

OTHELLO   That! what?

EMILIA   Out, and alas! that was my lady's voice:
Help! Help, ho! help! O lady, speak again!                                    120
Sweet Desdemona! O! sweet mistress, speak.

DESDEMONA   A guiltless death I die.

EMILIA   O! who hath done this deed?

DESDEMONA   Nobody; I myself; farewell:
Commend me to my kind lord. O! farewell!                                    *(Dies.)*

OTHELLO   Why, how should she be murder'd?

EMILIA                                    Alas! who knows?

OTHELLO   You heard her say herself it was not I.

EMILIA   She said so; I must needs report the truth.

OTHELLO   She's like a liar gone to burning hell;
'Twas I that kill'd her.

EMILIA                    O! the more angel she,                                    130
And you the blacker devil.

OTHELLO   She turn'd to folly, and she was a whore.

EMILIA   Thou dost belie her, and thou art a devil.

581. Open up (as in an earthquake).     582. Straying.

OTHELLO   She was false as water.

EMILIA                               Thou art rash as fire to say
That she was false! O! she was heavenly true.

OTHELLO   Cassio did tup her; ask thy husband else.
O! I were damn'd beneath all depth in hell
But that I did proceed[583] upon just grounds
To this extremity. Thy husband knew it all.

EMILIA   My husband!                                                      140

OTHELLO   Thy husband.

EMILIA   That she was false to wedlock?

OTHELLO   Ay, with Cassio. Nay, had she been true,
If heaven would make me such another world
Of one entire and perfect chrysolite,[584]
I'd not have sold her for it.

EMILIA   My husband!

OTHELLO                        Ay, 'twas he that told me first:
An honest man he is, and hates the slime
That sticks on filthy deeds.

EMILIA                        My husband!

OTHELLO   What needs this iterance,[585] woman? I say thy husband.        150

EMILIA   O mistress! villany hath made mocks with love.
My husband say that she was false!

OTHELLO                              He, woman;
I say, thy husband: dost understand the word?
My friend, thy husband, honest, honest Iago.

EMILIA   If he say so, may his pernicious soul
Rot half a grain a day! he lies to the heart:
She was too fond of her most filthy bargain.[586]

OTHELLO   Ha!

EMILIA   Do thy worst:
This deed of thine is no more worthy heaven                              160
Than thou wast worthy her.

OTHELLO                        Peace! you were best.[587]

EMILIA   Thou hast not half the power to do me harm
As I have to be hurt. O gull! O dolt!
As ignorant as dirt! thou hast done a deed,—
I care not for thy sword; I'll make thee known,
Though I lost twenty lives. Help! help, ho! help!
The Moor has kill'd my mistress! murder! murder!

(Enter Montano, Gratiano, Iago, and others.)

MONTANO   What is the matter? How now, general!

EMILIA   O! are you come, Iago? you have done well,
That men must lay their murders on your neck.                            170

583. Had I not proceeded.    584. Topaz.    585. Repetition.    586. I.e.,
Othello.    587. You'd better be quiet.

GRATIANO   What is the matter?

EMILIA   Disprove this villain if thou be'st a man:
He says thou told'st him that his wife was false.
I know thou didst not, thou'rt not such a villain.
Speak, for my heart is full.

IAGO   I told him what I thought, and told no more
Than what he found himself was apt and true.

EMILIA   But did you ever tell him she was false?

IAGO   I did.

EMILIA   You told a lie, an odious damned lie;                    180
Upon my soul, a lie, a wicked lie;
She false with Cassio! Did you say with Cassio?

IAGO   With Cassio, mistress. Go to, charm[588] your tongue.

EMILIA   I will not charm my tongue; I am bound to speak.
My mistress here lies murder'd in her bed.

ALL   O heavens forfend!

EMILIA   And your reports have set the murder on.

OTHELLO   Nay, stare not, masters; it is true, indeed.

GRATIANO   'Tis a strange truth.

MONTANO   O monstrous act!

EMILIA                           Villany! villany! villany!         190
I think upon 't, I think, I smell 't; O villany!
I thought so then;[589] I'll kill myself for grief.
O! villany, villany!

IAGO   What! are you mad? I charge you, get you home.

EMILIA   Good gentlemen, let me have leave to speak:
'Tis proper I obey him, but not now.
Perchance, Iago, I will ne'er go home.

OTHELLO   O! O! O!                                    (Falls on the bed.)

EMILIA                       Nay, lay thee down and roar,
For thou hast kill'd the sweetest innocent
That e'er did lift up eye.

OTHELLO                       O! she was foul.              (Rises.)
I scarce did know you, uncle. There lies your niece,        201
Whose breath, indeed, these hands have newly stopp'd:
I know this act shows terrible and grim.

GRATIANO   Poor Desdemona! I am glad thy father's dead.
Thy match was mortal to him, and pure grief
Shore[590] his old thread in twain: did he live now,
This sight would make him do a desperate turn,
Yea, curse his better angel from his side,
And fall to reprobation.[591]

---

588. *I.e.*, into silence.        589. *Cf.* "I will be hang'd, if some eternal villain,/Some
busy and insinuating rogue,/Some cogging cozening slave, to get some office,/Have not
devis'd this slander; . . ." (IV, ii, 130 ff.). Emilia means, not that she guessed Iago's
guilt, but that she rightly guessed the slanderer's motive.        590. Cut.
591. Damnation.

OTHELLO  'Tis pitiful; but yet Iago knows                          210
  That she with Cassio hath the act of shame
  A thousand times committed; Cassio confess'd it:
  And she did gratify[592] his amorous works
  With that recognizance and pledge of love
  Which I first gave her. I saw it in his hand:
  It was a handkerchief, an antique token
  My father gave my mother.
EMILIA  O heaven! O heavenly powers!
IAGO                          Come, hold your peace.
EMILIA  'Twill out, 'twill out; I hold my peace, sir? no;
  No, I will speak as liberal as the north;[593]            220
  Let heaven and men and devils, let them all,
  All, all, cry shame against me, yet I'll speak.
IAGO  Be wise, and get you home.
EMILIA                          I will not.

  *(Iago threatens to stab Emilia.)*

GRATIANO                          Fie!
  Your sword upon a woman!
EMILIA  O thou dull Moor! that handkerchief thou speak'st of
  I found by fortune and did give my husband;
  For often, with a solemn earnestness,
  More than, indeed, belong'd to such a trifle,
  He begg'd of me to steal it.
IAGO                          Villainous whore!
EMILIA  She give it Cassio! no, alas! I found it,            230
  And I did give 't my husband.
IAGO                          Filth, thou liest!
EMILIA  By heaven, I do not, I do not, gentlemen.
  O murderous coxcomb![594] what should such a fool
  Do with so good a wife?
OTHELLO                          Are there no stones[595] in heaven
  But what serve for the thunder? Precious villain!

  *(He runs at Iago. Iago stabs Emilia.)*

GRATIANO  The woman falls; sure, he has kill'd his wife.    *(Exit Iago.)*
EMILIA  Ay, ay; O! lay me by my mistress' side.
GRATIANO  He's gone; but his wife's kill'd.
MONTANO  'Tis a notorious[596] villain. Take you this weapon,
  Which I have here recover'd from the Moor.                240
  Come, guard the door without; let him not pass,
  But kill him rather. I'll after that same villain,
  For 'tis a damned slave.            *(Exeunt Montano and Gratiano.)*

592. Reward.  593. *I.e.,* the north wind (?), the supposedly free-spoken people of
north England (?).  594. Idiot.  595. *I.e.,* thunderbolts (to strike Iago
down).  596. Notable.

OTHELLO                    I am not valiant neither,
   But every puny whipster⁵⁹⁷ gets my sword.
   But why should honour outlive honesty?
   Let it go all.
EMILIA          What did thy song bode, lady?
   Hark, canst thou hear me? I will play the swan,
   And die in music:—
   *(Sings.)*          Willow, willow, willow.
   Moor, she was chaste; she lov'd thee, cruel Moor;
   So come my soul to bliss as I speak true;                    250
   So speaking as I think, I die, I die.          *(Dies.)*
OTHELLO  I have another weapon in this chamber;
   It is a sword of Spain, the ice-brook's temper.⁵⁹⁸
   O! here it is. Uncle, I must come forth.
GRATIANO *(within)*  If thou attempt it, it will cost thee dear:
   Thou hast no weapon, and perforce must suffer.
OTHELLO  Look in upon me then, and speak with me,
   Or, naked⁵⁹⁹ as I am, I will assault thee.

   *(Re-enter Gratiano.)*

GRATIANO  What is the matter?
OTHELLO                    Behold! I have a weapon;
   A better never did itself sustain                    260
   Upon a soldier's thigh: I have seen the day,
   That with this little arm, and this good sword,
   I have made my way through more impediments
   Than twenty times your stop: but, O vain boast!
   Who can control his fate? 'tis not so now.
   Be not afraid, though you do see me weapon'd;
   Here is my journey's end, here is my butt,⁶⁰⁰
   And very sea-mark of my utmost sail.⁶⁰¹
   Do you go back dismay'd? 'tis a lost fear;
   Man but a rush⁶⁰² against Othello's breast,                    270
   And he retires. Where should Othello go?
   Now how dost thou look now? O ill-starr'd wench!
   Pale as thy smock! when we shall meet at compt,⁶⁰³
   This look of thine will hurl my soul from heaven,
   And fiends will snatch at it. Cold, cold, my girl!
   Even like thy chastity.
   O! cursed, cursed slave. Whip me, ye devils,
   From the possession of this heavenly sight!
   Blow me about in winds! roast me in sulphur!

---

597. *I.e.*, a small boy whipping a top.      598. Tempered in icy water (or the reference may be to Innsbruck, famed for the quality of its steel, but this hardly fits "a sword of Spain").      599. Unarmed.      600. Goal, end, limit.
601. Destination of my farthest journey.      602. Wield but a reed.      603. On the day of judgment.

Wash me in steep-down gulfs of liquid fire!                                    280
O Desdemona! Desdemona! dead!
Oh! Oh! Oh!

*(Enter Lodovico, Montano, Cassio carried in a chair, and Officers with Iago,
prisoner.)*

LODOVICO   Where is this rash and most unfortunate man?
OTHELLO   That's he that was Othello; here I am.
LODOVICO   Where is that viper? bring the villain forth.
OTHELLO   I look down towards his feet;[604] but that's a fable.
  If that thou be'st a devil, I cannot kill thee.            *(Wounds Iago.)*
LODOVICO   Wrench his sword from him.            *(Othello is disarmed.)*
IAGO                                           I bleed, sir; but not kill'd.
OTHELLO   I am not sorry neither; I'd have thee live;
  For, in my sense,[605] 'tis happiness to die.                            290
LODOVICO   O thou Othello! that wert once so good,
  Fall'n in the practice[606] of a damned slave,[607]
  What shall be said to thee?
OTHELLO                        Why, any thing:
  An honourable murderer, if you will;
  For nought did I in hate, but all in honour.
LODOVICO   This wretch hath part confess'd his villany:
  Did you and he consent in Cassio's death?
OTHELLO   Ay.
CASSIO   Dear general, I never gave you cause.
OTHELLO   I do believe it, and I ask your pardon.                            300
  Will you, I pray, demand that demi-devil
  Why he hath thus ensnar'd my soul and body?
IAGO   Demand me nothing: what you know, you know:
  From this time forth I never will speak word.
LODOVICO   What! not to pray?
GRATIANO                          Torments will ope[608] your lips.
OTHELLO   Well, thou dost best.
LODOVICO   Sir, you shall understand what hath befall'n,
  Which, as I think, you know not. Here is a letter
  Found in the pocket of the slain Roderigo,
  And here another; the one of them imports                            310
  The death of Cassio to be undertook
  By Roderigo.
OTHELLO   O villain!
CASSIO                  Most heathenish and most gross!
LODOVICO   Now here's another discontented paper,
  Found in his pocket too; and this, it seems,
  Roderigo meant to have sent this damned villain,

---

604. *I.e.,* for the Devil's cloven hoof.    605. The way I feel.    606. Plot,
machination.    607. *I.e.,* Iago.    608. Open.

But that, belike,[609] Iago in the interim[610]
　Came in and satisfied him.
OTHELLO　　　　　　　　O the pernicious caitiff!
　How came you, Cassio, by that handkerchief
　That was my wife's?
CASSIO　　　　　　　I found it in my chamber;　　　　　　320
　And he himself confess'd but even now
　That there he dropp'd it for a special purpose
　Which wrought to his desire.
OTHELLO　　　　　　　　O fool! fool! fool!
CASSIO　There is besides in Roderigo's letter
　How he upbraids Iago that he made him
　Brave me upon the watch; whereon it came
　That I was cast:[611] and even but now he spake,
　After long seeming dead, Iago hurt him,
　Iago set him on.
LODOVICO　You must forsake this room and go with us;　　330
　Your power and your command is taken off,
　And Cassio rules in Cyprus. For this slave,
　If there be any cunning cruelty
　That can torment him much and hold him long,
　It shall be his. You shall close prisoner rest,
　Till that the nature of your fault be known
　To the Venetian state. Come, bring him away.
OTHELLO　Soft you; a word or two before you go.
　I have done the state some service, and they know 't;
　No more of that. I pray you, in your letters,　　　　340
　When you shall these unlucky deeds relate,
　Speak of me as I am; nothing extenuate,
　Nor set down aught[612] in malice: then, must you speak
　Of one that lov'd not wisely but too well;
　Of one not easily jealous, but, being wrought,
　Perplex'd[613] in the extreme; of one whose hand
　Like the base Indian,[614] threw a pearl away
　Richer than all his tribe; of one whose subdu'd[615] eyes
　Albeit unused to the melting mood,
　Drop tears as fast as the Arabian trees　　　　　　350
　Their med'cinable gum. Set you down this;
　And say besides, that in Aleppo once,
　Where a malignant and a turban'd Turk
　Beat a Venetian and traduc'd the state,
　I took by the throat the circumcised dog,
　And smote him, thus.　　　　　　　　　　(Stabs himself.)

609. Most likely.　　　610. In the meantime.　　　611. Dismissed.
612. Anything.　　　613. Distracted.　　　614. The Folio reads "ludean." Both
readings denote the foolish infidel who fails to appreciate the treasure he
possesses.　　　615. Overcome (by grief).

LODOVICO   O bloody period![616]
GRATIANO                    All that's spoke is marr'd.
OTHELLO   I kiss'd thee ere I killed thee; no way but this,

*(Falling upon Desdemona.)*

Killing myself to die upon a kiss.                              *(Dies.)*
CASSIO   This did I fear, but thought he had no weapon;        360
    For he was great of heart.
LODOVICO *(to Iago)*           O Spartan dog!
    More fell[617] than anguish, hunger, or the sea.
    Look on the tragic loading of this bed;
    This is thy work; the object poisons sight;
    Let it be hid. Gratiano, keep the house,
    And seize upon the fortunes of the Moor,
    For they succeed on you. To you, lord governor,
    Remains the censure of this hellish villain,
    The time, the place, the torture; O! enforce it.
    Myself will straight aboard, and to the state            370
    This heavy act with heavy heart relate.                  *(Exeunt.)*


## FOR DISCUSSION

1. At the very beginning of the play, does Iago have substantial reason to be angry with Othello? Do you think Iago's subsequent villainies are in proportion to what has been done to him?
2. What do you make of Iago's fondness for likening men to animals? Find some specific examples. What does this habit suggest about Iago's character?
3. For what reasons is Brabantio so outraged that his daughter, Desdemona, would marry Othello? Is there any racial enmity involved? By what devices does Brabantio think Othello was able to win Desdemona?
4. How, in fact, did Othello win Desdemona's love? Why did she fall in love with him? In turn, why did he love her?
5. Near the end of Act I, Brabantio says to Othello of Desdemona, "Look to her, Moor, if thou hast eyes to see:/She has deceiv'd her father, and may thee." What dramatic device is here being employed? Does Desdemona, in fact, ever deceive Othello? Does Othello remember the charge later on, or is he reminded of it by someone else?
6. From early in the play, why is Othello so disposed to trust Iago, to believe anything Iago says?
7. By what devices does Iago enlist Roderigo in his plot against Othello? Why does Roderigo allow Iago to use him in this way?
8. Why is Cassio an appropriate man for Iago to use to make Othello jealous? What circumstances combine to make Othello dismiss Cassio as his Lieutenant?
9. Trace the steps by which Iago manages to rouse Othello's suspicions of Desdemona's fidelity. Why does Othello seem so willing to suspect Des-

616. Ending.      617. Terrible.

demona of unfaithfulness? What does this willingness suggest about his character?

10. *Othello* is a good example of a play featuring an important symbol that dominates a major dramatic scene and continues to influence later scenes. What is the symbolic object? What does it symbolize? Why is it so important to the entire play?

11. At the beginning of Act IV, Othello falls into a trance. Does the play give you reasons to find such behavior plausible? After all, Othello is presented as noble and heroic.

12. Why does Othello not believe Emilia when she tells him that Desdemona is true to him?

13. Who is the first person to suspect Iago's treachery? What provokes this suspicion? How is Iago at last found out?

14. Near the end of Act IV, Emilia says, "Who would not make her husband a cuckold to make him a monarch"? What does this mean? What does the statement suggest about the station of womanhood?

15. What finally provokes Othello to murder Desdemona? What is the grim irony in this?

16. Why is it beyond Othello's power to forgive Desdemona, had she indeed been guilty as he believes?

17. What dramatic purpose is served when Iago kills Emilia?

18. Does Othello deserve to die? Does the fact that he kills himself in any way mitigate what he has done?

19. Who would you say is the more clever person, Othello or Iago? What does your answer suggest about the nature of nobility and villainy?

20. Historically, *Othello* has been one of the most popular tragedies in English literature. Do you see Othello as a tragic hero? In what ways is he heroic?

21. Several key elements of *Othello*—the black man in a white society, the role of women as daughters and wives, the motivations of evil—are also major issues today. How did this affect your reading of the play? Are its characters and attitudes still relevant, or not?

# A Marriage Proposal

ANTON CHEKHOV

## Cast of Characters

STEPAN STEPANOVITCH TSCHUBUKOV   a country farmer
NATALIA STEPANOVNA   his daughter (aged 25)
IVAN VASSILIYITCH LOMOV   Tschubukov's neighbor

SCENE.  *The reception room in* TSCHUBUKOV's *home.* TSCHUBUKOV *discovered as the curtain rises. Enter* LOMOV, *wearing a dress-suit.*

TSCHUB  *(going toward him and greeting him)*  Who is this I see? My dear fellow! Ivan Vassiliyitch! I'm so glad to see you! *(Shakes hands.)* But this is a surprise! How are you?

LOMOV  Thank you! And how are you?

TSCHUB  Oh, so-so, my friend. Please sit down. It isn't right to forget one's neighbor. But tell me, why all this ceremony? Dress clothes, white gloves and all? Are you on your way to some engagement, my good fellow?

LOMOV  No, I have no engagement except with you, Stepan Stepanovitch. .

TSCHUB  But why in evening clothes, my friend? This isn't New Year's!

LOMOV  You see, it's simply this, that—*(composing himself)* I have come to you, Stepan Stepanovitch, to trouble you with a request. It is not the first time I have had the honor of turning to you for assistance, and you have always, that is—I beg your pardon, I am a bit excited! I'll take a drink of water first, dear Stepan Stepanovitch. *(He drinks.)*

TSCHUB  *(aside)*  He's come to borrow money! I won't give him any! *(to LOMOV)*  What is it, then, dear Lomov?

LOMOV  You see—dear—Stepanovitch, pardon me, Stepan—Stepan—dear-vitch—I mean—I am terribly nervous, as you will be so good as to see—! What I mean to say—you are the only one who can help me, though I don't deserve it, and—and I have no right whatever to make this request of you.

TSCHUB  Oh, don't beat about the bush, my dear fellow. Tell me!

LOMOV  Immediately—in a moment. Here it is, then: I have come to ask for the hand of your daughter, Natalia Stepanovna.

TSCHUB  *(joyfully)*  Angel! Ivan Vassiliyitch! Say that once again! I didn't quite hear it!

LOMOV  I have the honor to beg—

TSCHUB  *(interrupting)*  My dear, dear man! I am so happy that everything is so—everything! *(Embraces and kisses him.)* I have wanted this to happen for so long. It has been my dearest wish! *(He represses a tear.)* And I have always loved you, my dear fellow, as my own son! May God give you His blessings and His grace and—I always wanted it to happen. But why am I standing here like a blockhead? I am completely dumbfounded with pleasure, completely dumbfounded. My whole being—! I'll call Natalia—

LOMOV  Dear Stepan Stepanovitch, what do you think? May I hope for Natalia Stepanovna's acceptance?

TSCHUB   Really! A fine boy like you—and you think she won't accept on the minute? Lovesick as a cat and all that—! *(He goes out, right.)*

LOMOV   I'm cold. My whole body is trembling as though I was going to take my examination! But the chief thing is to settle matters! If a person meditates too much, or hesitates, or talks about it, waits for an ideal or for true love, he never gets it. Brrr! It's cold! Natalia is an excellent housekeeper, not at all bad-looking, well educated—what more could I ask? I'm so excited my ears are roaring! *(He drinks water.)* And not to marry, that won't do! In the first place, I'm thirty-five—a critical age, you might say. In the second place, I must live a well-regulated life. I have a weak heart, continual palpitation, and I am very sensitive and always getting excited. My lips begin to tremble and the pulse in my right temple throbs terribly. But the worst of all is sleep! I hardly lie down and begin to doze before something in my left side begins to pull and tug, and something begins to hammer in my left shoulder—and in my head, too! I jump up like a madman, walk about a little, lie down again, but the moment I fall asleep I have a terrible cramp in the side. And so it is all night long! *(Enter NATALIA STEPANOVNA.)*

NATALIA   Ah! It's you. Papa said to go in: there was a dealer in there who'd come to buy something. Good afternoon, Ivan Vassiliyitch.

LOMOV   Good day, my dear Natalia Stepanovna.

NATALIA   You must pardon me for wearing my apron and this old dress: we are working to-day. Why haven't you come to see us oftener? You've not been here for so long! Sit down. *(They sit down.)* Won't you have something to eat?

LOMOV   Thank you, I have just had lunch.

NATALIA   Smoke, do, there are the matches. To-day it is beautiful and only yesterday it rained so hard that the workmen couldn't do a stroke of work. How many bricks have you cut? Think of it! I was so anxious that I had the whole field mowed, and now I'm sorry I did it, because I'm afraid the hay will rot. It would have been better if I had waited. But what on earth is this? You are in evening clothes! The latest cut! Are you on your way to a ball? And you seem to be looking better, too—really. Why are you dressed up so gorgeously?

LOMOV *(excited)*   You see, my dear Natalia Stepanovna—it's simply this: I have decided to ask you to listen to me—of course it will be a surprise, and indeed you'll be angry, but I—*(aside)* How fearfully cold it is!

NATALIA   What is it? *(A pause.)* Well?

LOMOV   I'll try to be brief. My dear Natalia Stepanovna, as you know, for many years, since my childhood, I have had the honor to know your family. My poor aunt and her husband, from whom, as you know, I inherited the estate, always had the greatest respect for your father and your poor mother. The Lomovs and the Tschubukovs have been for decades on the friendliest, indeed the closest, terms with each other, and furthermore my property, as you know, adjoins your own. If you will be so good as to remember, my meadows touch your birch woods.

NATALIA   Pardon the interruption. You said "my meadows"—but are they yours?

LOMOV   Yes, they belong to me.

NATALIA   What nonsense! The meadows belong to us—not to you!

LOMOV   No, to me! Now, my dear Natalia Stepanovna!

NATALIA  Well, that is certainly news to me. How do they belong to you?

LOMOV  How? I am speaking of the meadows lying between your birch woods and my brick-earth.

NATALIA  Yes, exactly. They belong to us.

LOMOV  No, you are mistaken, my dear Natalia Stepanovna, they belong to me.

NATALIA  Try to remember exactly, Ivan Vassiliyitch. Is it so long ago that you inherited them?

LOMOV  Long ago! As far back as I can remember they have always belonged to us.

NATALIA  But that isn't true! You'll pardon my saying so.

LOMOV  It is all a matter of record, my dear Natalia Stepanovna. It is true that at one time the title to the meadows was disputed, but now everyone knows they belong to me. There is no room for discussion. Be so good as to listen: my aunt's grandmother put these meadows, free from all costs, into the hands of your father's grandfather's peasants for a certain time while they were making bricks for my grandmother. These people used the meadows free of cost for about forty years, living there as they would on their own property. Later, however, when—

NATALIA  There's not a word of truth in that! My grandfather, and my great-grandfather, too, knew that their estate reached back to the swamp, so that the meadows belong to us. What further discussion can there be? I can't understand it. It is really most annoying.

LOMOV  I'll show you the papers, Natalia Stepanovna.

NATALIA  No, either you are joking, or trying to lead me into a discussion. That's not at all nice! We have owned this property for nearly three hundred years, and now all at once we hear that it doesn't belong to us. Ivan Vassiliyitch, you will pardon me, but I really can't believe my ears. So far as I am concerned, the meadows are worth very little. In all they don't contain more than five acres and they are worth only a few hundred roubles, say three hundred, but the injustice of the thing is what affects me. Say what you will, I can't bear injustice.

LOMOV  Only listen until I have finished, please! The peasants of your respected father's grandfather, as I have already had the honor to tell you, baked bricks for my grandmother. My aunt's grandmother wished to do them a favor—

NATALIA  Grandfather! Grandmother! Aunt! I know nothing about them. All I know is that the meadows belong to us, and that ends the matter.

LOMOV  No, they belong to me!

NATALIA  And if you keep on explaining it for two days, and put on five suits of evening clothes, the meadows are still ours, ours, ours! I don't want to take your property, but I refuse to give up what belongs to us!

LOMOV  Natalia Stepanovna, I don't need the meadows, I am only concerned with the principle. If you are agreeable, I beg of you, accept them as a gift from me!

NATALIA  But I can give them to you, because they belong to me! That is very peculiar, Ivan Vassiliyitch! Until now we have considered you as a good neighbor and a good friend; only last year we lent you our threshing machine so that we couldn't thresh until November, and now you treat us like thieves! You offer to give me my own land. Excuse me, but neighbors don't treat each other that way. In my opinion, it's a very low trick—to speak frankly—

LOMOV   According to you I'm a usurper, then, am I? My dear lady, I have never appropriated other people's property, and I shall permit no one to accuse me of such a thing! (*He goes quickly to the bottle and drinks water.*) The meadows are mine!

NATALIA   That's not the truth! They are mine!

LOMOV   Mine!

NATALIA   Eh? I'll prove it to you! This afternoon I'll send my reapers into the meadows.

LOMOV   W—h—a—t?

NATALIA   My reapers will be there to-day!

LOMOV   And I'll chase them off!

NATALIA   If you dare!

LOMOV   The meadows are mine, you understand? Mine!

NATALIA   Really, you needn't scream so! If you want to scream and snort and rage you may do it at home, but here please keep yourself within the limits of common decency.

LOMOV   My dear lady, if it weren't that I were suffering from palpitation of the heart and hammering of the arteries in my temples, I would deal with you very differently! (*in a loud voice*) The meadows belong to me!

NATALIA   Us!

LOMOV   Me!

(*Enter* TSCHUBUKOV, *right.*)

TSCHUB   What's going on here? What is he yelling about?

NATALIA   Papa, please tell this gentleman to whom the meadows belong, to us or to him?

TSCHUB (*to* LOMOV)   My dear fellow, the meadows are ours.

LOMOV   But, merciful heavens, Stepan Stepanovitch, how do you make that out? You at least might be reasonable. My aunt's grandmother gave the use of the meadows free of cost to your grandfather's peasants; the peasants lived on the land for forty years and used it as their own, but later when—

TSCHUB   Permit me, my dear friend. You forget that your grandmother's peasants never paid, because there had been a lawsuit over the meadows, and everyone knows that the meadows belong to us. You haven't looked at the map.

LOMOV   I'll prove to you that they belong to me!

TSCHUB   Don't try to prove it, my dear fellow.

LOMOV.   I will!

TSCHUB   My good fellow, what are you shrieking about? You can't prove anything by yelling, you know. I don't ask for anything that belongs to you, nor do I intend to give up anything of my own. Why should I? If it has gone so far, my dear man, that you really intend to claim the meadows, I'd rather give them to the peasants than you, and I certainly shall!

LOMOV   I can't believe it! By what right can you give away property that doesn't belong to you?

TSCHUB   Really, you must allow me to decide what I am to do with my own land! I'm not accustomed, young man, to have people address me in that tone of voice. I, young man, am twice your age, and I beg you to address me respectfully.

LOMOV No! No! You think I'm a fool! You're making fun of me! You call my property yours and then expect me to stand quietly by and talk to you like a human being. That isn't the way a good neighbor behaves, Stepan Stepanovitch! You are no neighbor, you're no better than a landgrabber. That's what you are!

TSCHUB Wh—at? What did he say?

NATALIA Papa, send the reapers into the meadows this minute!

TSCHUB (to LOMOV) What was that you said, sir?

NATALIA The meadows belong to us and I won't give them up! I won't give them up! I won't give them up!

LOMOV We'll see about that! I'll prove in court that they belong to me.

TSCHUB In court! You may sue in court, sir, if you like! Oh, I know you, you are only waiting to find an excuse to go to law! You're an intriguer, that's what you are! Your whole family were always looking for quarrels. The whole lot!

LOMOV Kindly refrain from insulting my family. The entire race of Lomov has always been honorable! And never has one been brought to trial for embezzlement, as your dear uncle was!

TSCHUB And the whole Lomov family were insane!

NATALIA Every one of them!

TSCHUB Your grandmother was a dipsomaniac, and the younger aunt, Nastasia Michailovna, ran off with an architect.

LOMOV And your mother limped. (He puts his hand over his heart.) Oh, my side pains! My temples are bursting! Lord in Heaven! Water!

TSCHUB And your dear father was a gambler—and a glutton!

NATALIA And your aunt was a gossip like few others!

LOMOV And you are an intriguer. Oh, my heart! And it's an open secret that you cheated at the elections—my eyes are blurred! Where is my hat?

NATALIA Oh, how low! Liar! Disgusting thing!

LOMOV Where's the hat—? My heart! Where shall I go? Where is the door—? Oh—it seems—as though I were dying! I can't—my legs won't hold me—(Goes to the door.)

TSCHUB (following him) May you never darken my door again!

NATALIA Bring your suit to court! We'll see! (LOMOV staggers out, center.)

TSCHUB (angrily) The devil!

NATALIA Such a good-for-nothing! And then they talk about being good neighbors!

TSCHUB Loafer! Scarecrow! Monster!

NATALIA A swindler like that takes over a piece of property that doesn't belong to him and then dares to argue about it!

TSCHUB And to think that this fool dares to make a proposal of marriage!

NATALIA What? A proposal of marriage?

TSCHUB Why, yes! He came here to make you a proposal of marriage.

NATALIA Why didn't you tell me that before?

TSCHUB That's why he had on his evening clothes! The poor fool!

NATALIA   Proposal for me? Oh! *(Falls into an armchair and groans.)* Bring him back! Bring him back!

TSCHUB   Bring whom back?

NATALIA   Faster, faster, I'm sinking! Bring him back! *(She becomes hysterical.)*

TSCHUB   What is it? What's wrong with you? *(his hands to his head)* I'm cursed with bad luck! I'll shoot myself! I'll hang myself!

NATALIA   I'm dying! Bring him back!

TSCHUB   Bah! In a minute! Don't bawl! *(He rushes out, center.)*

NATALIA   *(groaning)*   What have they done to me? Bring him back! Bring him back!

TSCHUB   *(comes running in)*   He's coming at once! The devil take him! Ugh! Talk to him yourself, I can't.

NATALIA   *(groaning)*   Bring him back!

TSCHUB   He's coming, I tell you! "Oh, Lord! What a task it is to be the father of a grown daughter!" I'll cut my throat! I really will cut my throat! We've argued with the fellow, insulted him, and now we've thrown him out!—and you did it all, you!

NATALIA   No, you! You haven't any manners, you are brutal! If it weren't for you, he wouldn't have gone!

TSCHUB   Oh, yes, I'm to blame! If I shoot or hang myself, remember *you'll* be to blame. You forced me to it! You! *(LOMOV appears in the doorway.)* There, talk to him yourself! *(He goes out.)*

LOMOV   Terrible palpitation!— My leg is lamed! My side hurts me——

NATALIA   Pardon us, we were angry, Ivan Vassiliyitch. I remember now—the meadows really belong to you.

LOMOV   My heart is beating terribly! My meadows—my eyelids tremble—*(They sit down.)* We were wrong. It was only the principle of the thing—the property isn't worth much to me, but the principle is worth a great deal.

NATALIA   Exactly, the principle! Let us talk about something else.

LOMOV   Because I have proofs that my aunt's grandmother had, with the peasants of your good father——

NATALIA   Enough, enough. *(aside)* I don't know how to begin. *(to LOMOV)* Are you going hunting soon?

LOMOV   Yes, heath-cock shooting, respected Natalia Stepanovna. I expect to begin after the harvest. Oh, did you hear? My dog, Ugadi, you know him—limps!

NATALIA   What a shame! How did that happen?

LOMOV   I don't know. Perhaps it's a dislocation, or maybe he was bitten by some other dog. *(He sighs.)* The best dog I ever had—to say nothing of his price! I paid Mironov a hundred and twenty-five roubles for him.

NATALIA   That was too much to pay, Ivan Vassiliyitch.

LOMOV   In my opinion it was very cheap. A wonderful dog!

NATALIA   Papa paid eighty-five roubles for his Otkatai, and Otkatai is much better than your Ugadi.

LOMOV   Really? Otkatai is better than Ugadi? What an idea! *(He laughs.)* Otkatai better than Ugadi!

NATALIA   Of course he is better. It is true Otkatai is still young; he isn't full-grown yet, but in the pack or on the leash with two or three, there is no better than he, even——

LOMOV  I really beg your pardon, Natalia Stepanovna, but you quite overlooked the fact that he has a short lower jaw, and a dog with a short lower jaw can't snap.

NATALIA  Short lower jaw? That's the first time I ever heard that!

LOMOV  I assure you, his lower jaw is shorter than the upper.

NATALIA  Have you measured it?

LOMOV  I have measured it. He is good at running, though.

NATALIA  In the first place, our Otkatai is pure-bred, a full-blooded son of Sapragavas and Stameskis, and as for your mongrel, nobody could ever figure out his pedigree; he's old and ugly, and as skinny as an old hag.

LOMOV  Old, certainly! I wouldn't take five of your Otkatais for him! Ugadi is a dog and Otkatai is—it is laughable to argue about it! Dogs like your Otkatai can be found by the dozens at any dog dealer's, a whole pound-full!

NATALIA  Ivan Vassiliyitch, you are very contrary to-day. First our meadows belong to you and then Ugadi is better than Otkatai. I don't like it when a person doesn't say what he really thinks. You know perfectly well that Otkatai is a hundred times better than your silly Ugadi. What makes you keep on saying he isn't?

LOMOV  I can see, Natalia Stepanovna, that you consider me either a blindman or a fool. But at least you may as well admit that Otkatai has a short lower jaw!

NATALIA  It isn't so!

LOMOV  Yes, a short lower jaw!

NATALIA  (loudly)  It's not so!

LOMOV  What makes you scream, my dear lady?

NATALIA  What makes you talk such nonsense? It's disgusting! It is high time that Ugadi was shot, and yet you compare him with Otkatai!

LOMOV  Pardon me, but I can't carry on this argument any longer. I have palpitation of the heart!

NATALIA  I have always noticed that the hunters who do the most talking know the least about hunting.

LOMOV  My dear lady, I beg of you to be still. My heart is bursting! (He shouts.) Be still!

NATALIA  I won't be still until you admit that Otkatai is better! (Enter TSCHUBUKOV.)

TSCHUB  Well, has it begun again?

NATALIA  Papa, say frankly, on your honor, which dog is better: Otkatai or Ugadi?

LOMOV  Stepan Stepanovitch, I beg of you, just answer this: has your dog a short lower jaw or not? Yes or no?

TSCHUB  And what if he has? Is it of such importance? There is no better dog in the whole country.

LOMOV  My Ugadi is better. Tell the truth, now!

TSCHUB  Don't get so excited, my dear fellow! Permit me. Your Ugadi certainly has his good points. He is from a good breed, has a good stride, strong haunches, and so forth. But the dog, if you really want to know it, has two faults; he is old and he has a short lower jaw.

LOMOV   Pardon me, I have palpitation of the heart!—Let us keep to facts—just remember in Maruskins's meadows, my Ugadi kept ear to ear with the Count Rasvachai and your dog.

TSCHUB   He was behind, because the Count struck him with his whip.

LOMOV   Quite right. All the other dogs were on the fox's scent, but Otkatai found it necessary to bite a sheep.

TSCHUB   That isn't so!—I am sensitive about that and beg you to stop this argument. He struck him because everybody looks on a strange dog of good blood with envy. Even you, sir, aren't free from the sin. No sooner do you find a dog better than Ugadi than you begin to—this, that—his, mine—and so forth! I remember distinctly.

LOMOV   I remember something, too!

TSCHUB (mimicking him)   I remember something, too! What do you remember?

LOMOV   Palpitation! My leg is lame—I can't——

NATALIA   Palpitation! What kind of hunter are you? You ought to stay in the kitchen by the stove and wrestle with the potato peelings, and not go fox-hunting! Palpitation!

TSCHUB   And what kind of hunter are you? A man with your diseases ought to stay at home and not jolt around in the saddle. If you were a hunter—! But you only ride round in order to find out about other people's dogs, and make trouble for everyone. I am sensitive! Let's drop the subject. Besides, you're no hunter.

LOMOV   You only ride around to flatter the Count!—My heart! You intriguer! Swindler!

TSCHUB   And what of it? (shouting) Be still!

LOMOV   Intriguer!

TSCHUB   Baby! Puppy! Walking drug-store!

LOMOV   Old rat! Jesuit! Oh, I know you!

TSCHUB   Be still! Or I'll shoot you—with my worst gun, like a partridge! Fool! Loafer!

LOMOV   Everyone knows that—oh, my heart!—that your poor late wife beat you. My leg—my temples—Heavens—I'm dying—I——

TSCHUB   And your housekeeper wears the trousers in your house!

LOMOV   Here—here—there—there—my heart has burst! My shoulder is torn apart. Where is my shoulder? I'm dying! (He falls into a chair.) The doctor! (Faints.)

TSCHUB   Baby! Half-baked clam! Fool!

NATALIA   Nice sort of hunter you are! You can't even sit on a horse. (to TSCHUB) Papa, what's the matter with him? (She screams.) Ivan Vassiliyitch! He is dead!

LOMOV   I'm ill! I can't breathe! Air!

NATALIA   He is dead! (She shakes LOMOV in the chair.) Ivan Vassiliyitch! What have we done! He is dead! (She sinks into a chair.) The doctor—doctor! (She goes into hysterics.)

TSCHUB   Ahh! What is it? What's the matter with you?

NATALIA (groaning)   He's dead!—Dead!

TSCHUB   Who is dead? Who? (looking at LOMOV) Yes, he is dead! Good God!

Water! The doctor! *(holding the glass to* LOMOV's *lips)* Drink! No, he won't drink! He's dead! What a terrible situation! Why didn't I shoot myself? Why have I never cut my throat? What am I waiting for now? Only give me a knife! Give me a pistol! *(LOMOV moves.)* He's coming to! Drink some water—there!

LOMOV  Sparks! Mists! Where am I?

TSCHUB  Get married! Quick, and then go to the devil! She's willing! *(He joins the hands of* LOMOV *and* NATALIA.*)* She's agreed! Only leave me in peace!

LOMOV  Wh—what? *(getting up)* Whom?

TSCHUB  She's willing! Well? Kiss each other and—the devil take you both!

NATALIA  *(groans)*  He lives! Yes, yes, I'm willing!

TSCHUB  Kiss each other!

LOMOV  Eh? Whom? *(*NATALIA *and* LOMOV *kiss.)* Very nice—! Pardon me, but what is this for? Oh, yes, I understand! My heart—sparks—I am happy, Natalia Stepanovna. *(He kisses her hand.)* My leg is lame!

NATALIA  I'm happy too!

TSCHUB  Ahh! A load off my shoulders! Ahh!

NATALIA  And now at least you'll admit that Ugadi is worse than Otkatai!

LOMOV  Better!

NATALIA  Worse!

TSCHUB  Now the domestic joys have begun.—Champagne!

LOMOV  Better!

NATALIA  Worse, worse, worse!

TSCHUB  *(trying to drown them out)*  Champagne, champagne!

*Curtain*


## FOR DISCUSSION

1. Who is the play's comic hero?
2. At the very beginning, what is it that Tschubukov fears has occasioned Lomov's visit? Why has Lomov really come to visit Tschubukov?
3. When Tschubukov learns the true reason for Lomov's visit, what change comes over Tschubukov? Exactly why does this change occur?
4. What part of the play would you label as the exposition? What do we learn during the exposition? Is Tschubukov's discovery of the truth about Lomov's visit a part of the exposition?
5. Does Natalia's age affect Tschubukov's reaction to the reason for Lomov's visit?
6. What kind of a person is Lomov? In what specific ways is he not heroic?
7. Why is it ironic that Natalia gets into an argument with Lomov? What particular type of irony is at work during this part of the play?
8. At what point does the climax of the play occur?
9. The high point in the humor of this little comedy is, of course, the repeated exclamation, "Bring him back!" Why is this so funny? What does it suggest about Natalia's priorities in life?
10. Summarize all of the events that occur during the play's falling action. Specifically, how is the resolution handled?
11. What are some of the things that the play suggests about human nature in general?

# The Importance of Being Earnest

OSCAR WILDE

## Characters

JOHN WORTHING, J.P.
ALGERNON MONCRIEFF
REV. CANON CHASUBLE, D.D.
MERRIMAN  butler
LANE  manservant
LADY BRACKNELL
HON. GWENDOLEN FAIRFAX
CECILY CARDEW
MISS PRISM  governess

*THE SCENES OF THE PLAY*

**Act I**  *Algernon Moncrieff's Flat in Half-Moon Street, W.*
**Act II**  *The Garden at the Manor House, Woolton.*
**Act III**  *Drawing-Room of the Manor House, Woolton.*

**Time**—The Present.
**Place**—London.

# Act I

*SCENE  Morning-room in* ALGERNON'S *flat in Half-Moon Street. The room is luxuriously and artistically furnished. The sound of a piano is heard in the adjoining room.*

*(*LANE *is arranging afternoon tea on the table, and after the music has ceased,* ALGERNON *enters.)*

ALGERNON  Did you hear what I was playing, Lane?
LANE  I didn't think it polite to listen, sir.
ALGERNON  I'm sorry for that, for your sake. I don't play accurately—any one can play accurately—but I play with wonderful expression. As far as the piano is concerned, sentiment is my forte. I keep science for Life.
LANE  Yes, sir.
ALGERNON  And, speaking of the science of Life, have you got the cucumber sandwiches cut for Lady Bracknell?
LANE  Yes, sir. *(Hands them on a salver.)*
ALGERNON *(Inspects them, takes two, and sits down on the sofa.)*  Oh! . . . by the way, Lane, I see from your book[1] that on Thursday night, when Lord Shoreman

---

[1] The catalog of Algernon's wine cellar. Lane's duty is to keep it up to date.

and Mr. Worthing were dining with me, eight bottles of champagne are entered as having been consumed.

LANE  Yes, sir; eight bottles and a pint.

ALGERNON  Why is it that at a bachelor's establishment the servants invariably drink the champagne? I ask merely for information.

LANE  I attribute it to the superior quality of the wine, sir. I have often observed that in married households the champagne is rarely of a first-rate brand.

ALGERNON  Good Heavens! Is marriage so demoralizing as that?

LANE  I believe it *is* a very pleasant state, sir. I have had very little experience of it myself up to the present. I have only been married once. That was in consequence of a misunderstanding between myself and a young woman.

ALGERNON *(languidly)*  I don't know that I am much interested in your family life, Lane.

LANE  No, sir; it is not a very interesting subject. I never think of it myself.

ALGERNON  Very natural, I am sure. That will do, Lane, thank you.

LANE  Thank you, sir.  (LANE *goes out.*)

ALGERNON  Lane's views on marriage seem somewhat lax. Really, if the lower orders don't set us a good example, what on earth is the use of them? They seem, as a class, to have absolutely no sense of moral responsibility.

*Enter* LANE.

LANE  Mr. Ernest Worthing.

*Enter* JACK. LANE *goes out.*

ALGERNON  How are you, my dear Ernest? What brings you up to town?

JACK  Oh, pleasure, pleasure! What else should bring one anywhere? Eating as usual, I see, Algy!

ALGERNON *(stiffly)*  I believe it is customary in good society to take some slight refreshment at five o'clock. Where have you been since last Thursday?

JACK *(sitting down on the sofa)*  In the country.

ALGERNON  What on earth do you do there?

JACK *(pulling off his gloves)*  When one is in town one amuses oneself. When one is in the country one amuses other people. It is excessively boring.

ALGERNON  And who are the people you amuse?

JACK *(airily)*  Oh, neighbors, neighbors.

ALGERNON  Got nice neighbors in your part of Shropshire?

JACK  Perfectly horrid! Never speak to one of them.

ALGERNON  How immensely you must amuse them! *(Goes over and takes sandwich.)* By the way, Shropshire is your county, is it not?

JACK  Eh? Shropshire? Yes, of course.[2] Hallo! Why all these cups? Why cucumber sandwiches? Why such reckless extravagance in one so young? Who is coming to tea?

ALGERNON  Oh! merely Aunt Augusta and Gwendolen.

JACK  How perfectly delightful!

[2] It later turns out that Jack really lives in Hertfordshire, which is over 100 miles nearer—just north of London, in fact.

ALGERNON  Yes, that is all very well; but I am afraid Aunt Augusta won't quite approve of your being here.

JACK  May I ask why?

ALGERNON  My dear fellow, the way you flirt with Gwendolen is perfectly disgraceful. It is almost as bad as the way Gwendolen flirts with you.

JACK  I am in love with Gwendolen. I have come up to town expressly to propose to her.

ALGERNON  I thought you had come up for pleasure? . . . I call that business.

JACK  How utterly unromantic you are!

ALGERNON  I really don't see anything romantic in proposing. It is very romantic to be in love. But there is nothing romantic about a definite proposal. Why, one may be accepted. One usually is, I believe. Then the excitement is all over. The very essence of romance is uncertainty. If ever I get married, I'll certainly try to forget the fact.

JACK  I have no doubt about that, dear Algy. The Divorce Court was specially invented for people whose memories are so curiously constituted.

ALGERNON  Oh! there is no use speculating on that subject. Divorces are made in Heaven— (JACK *puts out his hand to take a sandwich.* ALGERNON *at once interferes.*) Please don't touch the cucumber sandwiches. They are ordered specially for Aunt Augusta. (*Takes one and eats it.*)

JACK  Well, you have been eating them all the time.

ALGERNON  That is quite a different matter. She is my aunt. (*Takes plate from below.*) Have some bread and butter. The bread and butter is for Gwendolen. Gwendolen is devoted to bread and butter.

JACK (*advancing to table and helping himself*)  And very good bread and butter it is, too.

ALGERNON  Well, my dear fellow, you need not eat as if you were going to eat it all. You behave as if you were married to her already. You are not married to her already, and I don't think you ever will be.

JACK  Why on earth do you say that?

ALGERNON  Well, in the first place girls never marry the men they flirt with. Girls don't think it right.

JACK  Oh, that is nonsense!

ALGERNON  It isn't. It is a great truth. It accounts for the extraordinary number of bachelors that one sees all over the place. In the second place, I don't give my consent.

JACK  Your consent!

ALGERNON  My dear fellow, Gwendolen is my first cousin. And before I allow you to marry her, you will have to clear up the whole question of Cecily. (*Rings bell.*)

JACK  Cecily! What on earth do you mean? What do you mean, Algy, by Cecily? I don't know any one of the name of Cecily.

*Enter* LANE.

ALGERNON  Bring me that cigarette case Mr. Worthing left in the smoking-room the last time he dined here.

LANE  Yes, sir. (LANE *goes out.*)

JACK  Do you mean to say you have had my cigarette case all this time? I wish to goodness you had let me know. I have been writing frantic letters to Scotland Yard about it. I was very nearly offering a large reward.

ALGERNON  Well, I wish you would offer one. I happen to be more than usually hard up.

JACK  There is no good offering a large reward now that the thing is found.

*Enter* LANE *with the cigarette case on a salver.* ALGERNON *takes it at once.* LANE *goes out.*

ALGERNON  I think that is rather mean of you, Ernest, I must say. *(Opens case and examines it.)* However, it makes no matter, for, now that I look at the inscription, I find that the thing isn't yours after all.

JACK  Of course it's mine. *(Moving to him.)* You have seen me with it a hundred times, and you have no right whatsoever to read what is written inside. It is a very ungentlemanly thing to read a private cigarette case.

ALGERNON  Oh! it is absurd to have a hard-and-fast rule about what one should read and what one shouldn't. More than half of modern culture depends on what one shouldn't read.

JACK  I am quite aware of the fact, and I don't propose to discuss modern culture. It isn't the sort of thing one should talk of in private. I simply want my cigarette case back.

ALGERNON  Yes; but this isn't your cigarette case. This cigarette case is a present from some one of the name of Cecily, and you said you didn't know any one of that name.

JACK  Well, if you want to know, Cecily happens to be my aunt.

ALGERNON  Your aunt!

JACK  Yes. Charming old lady she is, too. Lives at Tunbridge Wells. Just give it back to me, Algy.

ALGERNON  *(retreating to back of sofa)*  But why does she call herself little Cecily if she is your aunt and lives at Tunbridge Wells? *(Reading.)* "From little Cecily with her fondest love."

JACK  *(moving to sofa and kneeling upon it)*  My dear fellow, what on earth is there in that? Some aunts are tall, some aunts are not tall. That is a matter that surely an aunt may be allowed to decide for herself. You seem to think that every aunt should be exactly like your aunt! That is absurd! For Heaven's sake give me back my cigarette case. *(Follows* ALGERNON *round the room.)*

ALGERNON  Yes. But why does your aunt call you her uncle? "From little Cecily, with her fondest love to her dear Uncle Jack." There is no objection, I admit, to an aunt being a small aunt, but why an aunt, no matter what her size may be, should call her own nephew her uncle, I can't quite make out. Besides, your name isn't Jack at all; it is Ernest.

JACK  It isn't Ernest; it's Jack.

ALGERNON  You have always told me it was Ernest. I have introduced you to every one as Ernest. You answer to the name of Ernest. You look as if your name was Ernest. You are the most earnest looking person I ever saw in my life. It is perfectly absurd your saying that your name isn't Ernest. It's on your cards. Here is one of them. *(taking it from case)* "Mr. Ernest Worthing, B 4,

The Albany." I'll keep this as a proof your name is Ernest if ever you attempt to deny it to me, or to Gwendolen, or to any one else. *(Puts the card in his pocket.)*

JACK    Well, my name is Ernest in town and Jack in the country, and the cigarette case was given to me in the country.

ALGERNON    Yes, but that does not account for the fact that your small Aunt Cecily, who lives at Tunbridge Wells, calls you her dear uncle. Come, old boy, you had much better have the thing out at once.

JACK    My dear Algy, you talk exactly as if you were a dentist. It is very vulgar to talk like a dentist when one isn't a dentist. It produces a false impression.

ALGERNON    Well, that is exactly what dentists always do. Now, go on! Tell me the whole thing. I may mention that I have always suspected you of being a confirmed and secret Bunburyist; and I am quite sure of it now.

JACK    Bunburyist? What on earth do you mean by a Bunburyist?

ALGERNON    I'll reveal to you the meaning of that incomparable expression as soon as you are kind enough to inform me why you are Ernest in town and Jack in the country.

JACK    Well, produce my cigarette case first.

ALGERNON    Here it is. *(Hands cigarette case.)* Now produce your explanation, and pray make it improbable. *(Sits on sofa.)*

JACK    My dear fellow, there is nothing improbable about my explanation at all. In fact it's perfectly ordinary. Old Mr. Thomas Cardew, who adopted me when I was a little boy, made me in his will guardian to his grand-daughter, Miss Cecily Cardew. Cecily, who addressed me as her uncle from motives of respect that you could not possibly appreciate, lives at my place in the country under the charge of her admirable governess, Miss Prism.

ALGERNON    Where is that place in the country, by the way?

JACK    That is nothing to you, dear boy. You are not going to be invited. . . . . I may tell you candidly that the place is not in Shropshire.

ALGERNON    I suspected that, my dear fellow! I have Bunburyed all over Shropshire on two separate occasions. Now, go on. Why are you Ernest in town and Jack in the country?

JACK    My dear Algy, I don't know whether you will be able to understand my real motives. You are hardly serious enough. When one is placed in the position of guardian, one has to adopt a very high moral tone on all subjects. It's one's duty to do so. And as a high moral tone can hardly be said to conduce very much to either one's health or one's happiness, in order to get up to town I have always pretended to have a younger brother of the name Ernest, who lives in the Albany, and gets into the most dreadful scrapes. That, my dear Algy, is the whole truth pure and simple.

ALGERNON    The truth is rarely pure and never simple. Modern life would be very tedious if it were either, and modern literature a complete impossibility!

JACK    That wouldn't be at all a bad thing.

ALGERNON    Literary criticism is not your forte, my dear follow. Don't try it. You should leave that to people who haven't been at a University. They do it so well in the daily papers. What you really are is a Bunburyist. I was quite right in saying you were a Bunburyist. You are one of the most advanced Bunburyists I know.

JACK   What on earth do you mean?

ALGERNON   You have invented a very useful younger brother called Ernest, in order that you may be able to come up to town as often as you like. I have invented an invaluable permanent invalid called Bunbury, in order that I may be able to go down into the country whenever I choose. Bunbury is perfectly invaluable. If it wasn't for Bunbury's extraordinary bad health, for instance, I wouldn't be able to dine with you at Willis's to-night, for I have been really engaged to Aunt Augusta[3] for more than a week.

JACK   I haven't asked you to dine with me anywhere to-night.

ALGERNON:   I know. You are absolutely careless about sending out invitations. It is very foolish of you. Nothing annoys people so much as not receiving invitations.

JACK   You had much better dine with your Aunt Augusta.

ALGERNON   I haven't the smallest intention of doing anything of the kind. To begin with, I dined there on Monday, and once a week is quite enough to dine with one's own relatives. In the second place, whenever I do dine there I am always treated as a member of the family, and sent down with[4] either no woman at all, or two. In the third place, I know perfectly well whom she will place me next to, to-night. She will place me next Mary Farquhar, who always flirts with her own husband across the dinner-table. That is not very pleasant. Indeed, it is not even decent . . . and that sort of thing is enormously on the increase. The amount of women in London who flirt with their own husbands is perfectly scandalous. It looks so bad. It is simply washing one's clean linen in public. Besides, now that I know you to be a confirmed Bunburyist I naturally want to talk to you about Bunburying. I want to tell you the rules.

JACK   I'm not a Bunburyist at all. If Gwendolen accepts me, I am going to kill my brother, indeed I think I'll kill him in any case. Cecily is a little too much interested in him. It is rather a bore. So I am going to get rid of Ernest. And I strongly advise you to do the same with Mr. —— with your invalid friend who has the absurd name.

ALGERNON   Nothing will induce me to part with Bunbury, and if you ever get married, which seems to me extremely problematic, you will be very glad to know Bunbury. A man who married without knowing Bunbury has a very tedious time of it.

JACK   That is nonsense. If I marry a charming girl like Gwendolen, and she is the only girl I ever saw in my life that I would marry, I certainly won't want to know Bunbury.

ALGERNON   Then your wife will. You don't seem to realize, that in married life three is company and two is none.

---

[3] That is, engaged to be a guest at her dinner party.

[4] Required to escort.

JACK (*sententiously*)   That, my dear young friend, is the theory that the corrupt French Drama has been propounding for the last fifty years.

ALGERNON   Yes; and that the happy English home has proved in half the time.

JACK   For heaven's sake, don't try to be cynical. It's perfectly easy to be cynical.

ALGERNON   My dear fellow, it isn't easy to be anything now-a-days. There's such a lot of beastly competition about. (*The sound of an electric bell is heard.*) Ah! that must be Aunt Augusta. Only relatives, or creditors, ever ring in that Wagnerian manner.[5] Now, if I get her out of the way for ten minutes, so that you have an opportunity for proposing to Gwendolen, may I dine with you to-night at Willis's?

JACK   I suppose so, if you want to.

ALGERNON   Yes, but you must be serious about it. I hate people who are not serious about meals. It is so shallow of them.

*Enter* LANE.

LANE   Lady Bracknell and Miss Fairfax. (ALGERNON *goes forward to meet them. Enter* LADY BRACKNELL *and* GWENDOLEN.)

LADY BRACKNELL   Good afternoon, dear Algernon, I hope you are behaving very well.

ALGERNON   I'm feeling very well, Aunt Augusta.

LADY BRACKNELL   That's not quite the same thing. In fact the two things rarely go together. (*Sees* JACK *and bows to him with icy coldness.*)

ALGERNON (*to* GWENDOLEN)   Dear me, you are smart![6]

GWENDOLEN   I am always smart! Aren't I, Mr. Worthing?

JACK   You're quite perfect, Miss Fairfax.

GWENDOLEN   Oh! I hope I am not that. It would leave no room for developments, and I intend to develop in *many directions*. (GWENDOLEN *and* JACK *sit down together in the corner.*)

LADY BRACKNELL   I'm sorry if we are a little late, Algernon, but I was obliged to call on dear Lady Harbury. I hadn't been there since her poor husband's death. I never saw a woman so altered; she looks quite twenty years younger. And now I'll have a cup of tea, and one of those nice cucumber sandwiches you promised me.

ALGERNON   Certainly, Aunt Augusta. (*Goes over to tea-table.*)

LADY BRACKNELL   Won't you come and sit here, Gwendolen?

GWENDOLEN   Thanks, mamma, I'm quite comfortable where I am.

ALGERNON (*picking up empty plate in horror*)   Good heavens! Lane! Why are there no cucumber sandwiches? I ordered them specially.

LANE (*gravely*)   There were no cucumbers in the market this morning, sir. I went down twice.

ALGERNON   No cucumbers!

LANE   No, sir. Not even for ready money.[7]

ALGERNON   That will do, Lane, thank you.

---

[5] That is, loudly and for very long, as in Wagner's operas.
[6] Stylishly dressed.
[7] As opposed to credit.

LANE  Thank you, sir. *(Goes out.)*

ALGERNON  I am greatly distressed, Aunt Augusta, about there being no cucumbers, not even for ready money.

LADY BRACKNELL  It really makes no matter, Algernon. I had some crumpets with Lady Harbury, who seems to me to be living entirely for pleasure now.

ALGERNON  I hear her hair has turned quite gold from grief.

LADY BRACKNELL  It certainly has changed its color. From what cause I, of course, cannot say. (ALGERNON *crosses and hands tea.)* Thank you. I've quite a treat for you to-night, Algernon. I am going to send you down with Mary Farquhar. She is such a nice woman, and so attentive to her husband. It's delightful to watch them.

ALGERNON  I am afraid, Aunt Augusta, I shall have to give up the pleasure of dining with you to-night after all.

LADY BRACKNELL  *(frowning)*  I hope not, Algernon. It would put my table completely out. Your uncle would have to dine upstairs. Fortunately he is accustomed to that.

ALGERNON  It is a great bore, and, I need hardly say, a terrible disappointment to me, but the fact is I have just had a telegram to say that my poor friend Bunbury is very ill again. *(Exchanges glances with* JACK.*)* They seem to think I should be with him.

LADY BRACKNELL  It is very strange. This Mr. Bunbury seems to suffer from curiously bad health.

ALGERNON  Yes; poor Bunbury is a dreadful invalid.

LADY BRACKNELL  Well, I must say, Algernon, that I think it is high time that Mr. Bunbury made up his mind whether he was going to live or to die. This shilly-shallying with the question is absurd. Nor do I in any way approve of the modern sympathy with invalids. I consider it morbid. Illness of any kind is hardly a thing to be encouraged in others. Health is the primary duty of life. I am always telling that to your poor uncle, but he never seems to take much notice . . . as far as any improvement in his ailments goes. I should be much obliged if you would ask Mr. Bunbury, from me, to be kind enough not to have a relapse on Saturday, for I rely on you to arrange my music for me. It is my last reception and one wants something that will encourage conversation, particularly at the end of the season[8] when every one has practically said whatever they had to say, which, in most cases, was probably not much.

ALGERNON  I'll speak to Bunbury, Aunt Augusta, if he is still conscious, and I think I can promise you he'll be all right by Saturday. You see, if one plays good music, people don't listen, and if one plays bad music people don't talk. But I'll run over the program I've drawn out, if you will kindly come into the next room for a moment.

LADY BRACKNELL  Thank you, Algernon. It is very thoughtful of you. *(rising, and following* ALGERNON*)* I'm sure the program will be delightful, after a few expurgations. French songs I cannot possibly allow. People always seem to think that they are improper, and either look shocked, which is vulgar, or

---

[8] The three-month English social season ends in July.

laugh, which is worse. But German sounds a thoroughly respectable language, and indeed, I believe is so. Gwendolen, you will accompany me.

GWENDOLEN  Certainly, mamma. (LADY BRACKNELL *and* ALGERNON *go into the music-room;* GWENDOLEN *remains behind.*)

JACK  Charming day it has been, Miss Fairfax.

GWENDOLEN  Pray don't talk to me about the weather, Mr. Worthing. Whenever people talk to me about the weather, I always feel quite certain that they mean something else. And that makes me so nervous.

JACK  I do mean something else.

GWENDOLEN  I thought so. In fact, I am never wrong.

JACK  And I would like to be allowed to take advantage of Lady Bracknell's temporary absence . . .

GWENDOLEN  I would certainly advise you to do so. Mamma has a way of coming back suddenly into a room that I have often had to speak to her about.

JACK  (*nervously*)  Miss Fairfax, ever since I met you I have admired you more than any girl . . . I have ever met since . . . I met you.

GWENDOLEN  Yes, I am quite aware of the fact. And I often wish that in public, at any rate, you had been more demonstrative. For me you have always had an irresistible fascination. Even before I met you I was far from indifferent to you. (JACK *looks at her in amazement.*) We live, as I hope you know, Mr. Worthing, in an age of ideals. The fact is constantly mentioned in the more expensive monthly magazines, and has reached the provincial pulpits I am told: and my ideal has always been to love some one of the name of Ernest. There is something in that name that inspires absolute confidence. The moment Algernon first mentioned to me that he had a friend called Ernest, I knew I was destined to love you.

JACK  You really love me, Gwendolen?

GWENDOLEN  Passionately!

JACK  Darling! You don't know how happy you've made me.

GWENDOLEN  My own Ernest!

JACK  But you don't really mean to say that you couldn't love me if my name wasn't Ernest?

GWENDOLEN  But your name is Ernest.

JACK  Yes, I know it is. But supposing it was something else? Do you mean to say you couldn't love me then?

GWENDOLEN  (*glibly*)  Ah! that is clearly a metaphysical speculation, and like most metaphysical speculations has very little reference at all to the actual facts of real life, as we know them.

JACK  Personally, darling, to speak quite candidly, I don't much care about the name of Ernest . . . I don't think that name suits me at all.

GWENDOLEN  It suits you perfectly. It is a divine name. It has a music of its own. It produces vibrations.

JACK  Well, really, Gwendolen, I must say that I think there are lots of other much nicer names. I think, Jack, for instance, a charming name.

GWENDOLEN  Jack? . . . No, there is very little music in the name Jack, if any at all, indeed. It does not thrill. It produces absolutely no vibrations. . . . I have known several Jacks, and they all, without exception, were more than usually plain. Besides, Jack is a notorious domesticity for John! And I pity any woman who is married to a man called John. She would probably never be allowed to know the entrancing pleasure of a single moment's solitude. The only really safe name is Ernest.

JACK  Gwendolen, I must get christened at once—I mean we must get married at once. There is no time to be lost.

GWENDOLEN  Married, Mr. Worthing?

JACK  *(astounded)*  Well . . . surely. You know that I love you, and you led me to believe, Miss Fairfax, that you were not absolutely indifferent to me.

GWENDOLEN  I adore you. But you haven't proposed to me yet. Nothing has been said at all about marriage. The subject has not even been touched on.

JACK  Well . . . may I propose to you now?

GWENDOLEN  I think it would be an admirable opportunity. And to spare you any possible disappointment, Mr. Worthing, I think it only fair to tell you quite frankly beforehand that I am fully determined to accept you.

JACK  Gwendolen!

GWENDOLEN  Yes, Mr. Worthing, what have you got to say to me?

JACK  You know what I have got to say to you.

GWENDOLEN  Yes, but you don't say it.

JACK  Gwendolen, will you marry me? *(Goes on his knees.)*

GWENDOLEN  Of course I will, darling. How long you have been about it! I am afraid you have had very little experience in how to propose.

JACK  My own one, I have never loved any one in the world but you.

GWENDOLEN  Yes, but men often propose for practice. I know my brother Gerald does. All my girl-friends tell me so. What wonderfully blue eyes you have, Ernest! They are quite, quite blue. I hope you will always look at me just like that, especially when there are other people present.

*Enter* LADY BRACKNELL.

LADY BRACKNELL  Mr. Worthing! Rise, sir, from this semi-recumbent posture. It is most indecorous.

GWENDOLEN  Mamma! *(He tries to rise; she restrains him.)* I must beg you to retire. This is no place for you. Besides, Mr. Worthing has not quite finished yet.

LADY BRACKNELL  Finished what, may I ask?

GWENDOLEN  I am engaged to Mr. Worthing, mamma. *(They rise together.)*

LADY BRACKNELL  Pardon me, you are not engaged to any one. When you do become engaged to some one, I, or your father, should his health permit him, will inform you of the fact. An engagement should come on a young girl as a surprise, pleasant or unpleasant, as the case may be. It is hardly a matter that she could be allowed to arrange for herself. . . . And now I have a few questions to put to you, Mr. Worthing. While I am making these inquiries, you, Gwendolen, will wait for me below in the carriage.

GWENDOLEN  *(reproachfully)*  Mamma!

LADY BRACKNELL  In the carriage, Gwendolen! (GWENDOLEN *goes to the door. She and* JACK *blow kisses to each other behind* LADY BRACKNELL'S *back.* LADY BRACKNELL *looks vaguely about as if she could not understand what the noise was. Finally turns round.)* Gwendolen, the carriage!

GWENDOLEN   Yes, mamma. (*Goes out, looking back at* JACK.)

LADY BRACKNELL (*sitting down*)   You can take a seat, Mr. Worthing. (*Looks in her pocket for note-book and pencil.*)

JACK   Thank you, Lady Bracknell, I prefer standing.

LADY BRACKNELL (*pencil and note-book in hand*)   I feel bound to tell you that you are not down on my list of eligible young men, although I have the same list as the dear Duchess of Bolton has. We work together, in fact. However, I am quite ready to enter your name, should your answers be what a really affectionate mother requires. Do you smoke?

JACK   Well, yes, I must admit I smoke.

LADY BRACKNELL   I am glad to hear it. A man should always have an occupation of some kind. There are far too many idle men in London as it is. How old are you?

JACK   Twenty-nine.

LADY BRACKNELL   A very good age to be married at. I have always been of opinion that a man who desires to get married should know either everything or nothing. Which do you know?

JACK (*after some hesitation*)   I know nothing, Lady Bracknell.

LADY BRACKNELL   I am pleased to hear it. I do not approve of anything that tampers with natural ignorance. Ignorance is like a delicate exotic fruit; touch it and the bloom is gone. The whole theory of modern education is radically unsound. Fortunately in England, at any rate, education produces no effect whatsoever. If it did, it would prove a serious danger to the upper classes, and probably lead to acts of violence in Grosvenor Square.[9] What is your income?

JACK   Between seven and eight thousand a year.

LADY BRACKNELL (*Makes a note in her book.*)   In land, or in investments?

JACK   In investments, chiefly.

LADY BRACKNELL   That is satisfactory. What between the duties expected of one during one's life-time, and the duties[10] exacted from one after one's death, land has ceased to be either a profit or a pleasure. It gives one position, and prevents one from keeping it up. That's all that can be said about land.

JACK   I have a country house with some land, of course, attached to it, about fifteen hundred acres, I believe; but I don't depend on that for my real income. In fact, as far as I can make out, the poachers are the only people who make anything out of it.

LADY BRACKNELL   A country house! How many bedrooms? Well, that point can be cleared up afterwards. You have a town house, I hope? A girl with a simple, unspoiled nature, like Gwendolen, could hardly be expected to reside in the country.

JACK   Well, I own a house in Belgrave Square, but it is let by the year to Lady Bloxham. Of course, I can get it back whenever I like, at six months's notice.

LADY BRACKNELL   Lady Bloxham? I don't know her.

---

[9] A particularly elegant residential area in London.

[10] Taxes.

JACK  Oh, she goes about very little. She is a lady considerably advanced in years.

LADY BRACKNELL  Ah, now-a-days that is no guarantee of respectability of character. What number in Belgrave Square?

JACK  149.

LADY BRACKNELL (*shaking her head*)  The unfashionable side. I thought there was something. However, that could easily be altered.

JACK  Do you mean the fashion, or the side?

LADY BRACKNELL (*sternly*)  Both, if necessary, I presume. What are your politics?

JACK  Well, I am afraid I really have none. I am a Liberal Unionist.

LADY BRACKNELL  Oh, they count as Tories.[11] They dine with us. Or come in the evening, at any rate. Now to minor matters. Are your parents living?

JACK  I have lost both my parents.

LADY BRACKNELL  Both? . . . That seems like carelessness. Who was your father? He was evidently a man of some wealth. Was he born in what the Radical papers call the purple of commerce, or did he rise from the ranks of the aristocracy?

JACK  I am afraid I really don't know. The fact is, Lady Bracknell, I said I had lost my parents. It would be nearer the truth to say that my parents seem to have lost me . . . I don't actually know who I am by birth. I was . . . well, I was found.

LADY BRACKNELL  Found!

JACK  The late Mr. Thomas Cardew, an old gentleman of a very charitable and kindly disposition, found me, and gave me the name of Worthing, because he happened to have a first-class ticket for Worthing in his pocket at the time. Worthing is a place in Sussex. It is a seaside resort.

LADY BRACKNELL  Where did the charitable gentleman who had a first-class ticket for this seaside resort find you?

JACK (*gravely*)  In a hand-bag.

LADY BRACKNELL  A hand-bag?

JACK (*very seriously*)  Yes, Lady Bracknell. I was in a hand-bag—a somewhat large, black leather hand-bag, with handles to it—an ordinary hand-bag in fact.

LADY BRACKNELL  In what locality did this Mr. James, or Thomas, Cardew come across this ordinary hand-bag?

JACK  In the cloak-room[12] at Victoria Station. It was given to him in mistake for his own.

LADY BRACKNELL  The cloak-room at Victoria Station?

JACK  Yes. The Brighton line.

LADY BRACKNELL  The line is immaterial. Mr. Worthing, I confess I feel somewhat bewildered by what you have just told me. To be born, or at any rate bred, in a hand-bag, whether it had handles or not, seems to me to display a

---

[11] Conservatives. The Liberal Unionists were a splinter group of the opposition party, the Liberals, and joined the Conservatives only in supporting the continued union of Ireland and Great Britain.

[12] Checkroom.

contempt for the ordinary decencies of family life that remind one of the worst excesses of the French Revolution. And I presume you know what that unfortunate movement led to? As for the particular locality in which the hand-bag was found, a cloak-room at a railway station might serve to conceal a social indiscretion—has probably, indeed, been used for that purpose before now—but it could hardly be regarded as an assured basis for a recognized position in good society.

JACK   May I ask you then what you would advise me to do? I need hardly say I would do anything in the world to ensure Gwendolen's happiness.

LADY BRACKNELL   I would strongly advise you, Mr. Worthing, to try and acquire some relations as soon as possible, and to make a definite effort to produce at any rate one parent, of either sex, before the season is quite over.

JACK   Well, I don't see how I could possibly manage to do that. I can produce the hand-bag at any moment. It is in my dressing-room at home. I really think that should satisfy you, Lady Bracknell.

LADY BRACKNELL   Me, sir! What has it to do with me? You can hardly imagine that I and Lord Bracknell would dream of allowing our only daughter—a girl brought up with the utmost care—to marry into a cloak-room, and form an alliance with a parcel? Good morning, Mr. Worthing! (LADY BRACKNELL *sweeps out in majestic indignation.*)

JACK   Good morning! (ALGERNON, *from the other room, strikes up the Wedding March.* JACK *looks perfectly furious, and goes to the door.*) For goodness' sake don't play that ghastly tune, Algy! How idiotic you are! (*The music stops, and* ALGERNON *enters cheerily.*)

ALGERNON   Didn't it go off all right, old boy? You don't mean to say Gwendolen refused you? I know it is a way she has. She is always refusing people. I think it is most ill-natured of her.

JACK   Oh, Gwendolen is as right as a trivet.[13] As far as she is concerned, we are engaged. Her mother is perfectly unbearable. Never met such a Gorgon[14] . . . I don't really know what a Gorgon is like, but I am quite sure that Lady Bracknell is one. In any case, she is a monster, without being a myth, which is rather unfair. . . . I beg your pardon, Algy, I suppose I shouldn't talk about your own aunt in that way before you.

ALGERNON   My dear boy, I love hearing my relations abused. It is the only thing that makes me put up with them at all. Relations are simply a tedious pack of people, who haven't got the remotest knowledge of how to live, nor the smallest instinct about when to die.

JACK   Oh, that is nonsense!

ALGERNON   It isn't!

JACK   Well, I won't argue about the matter. You always want to argue about things.

ALGERNON   That is exactly what things were originally made for.

JACK   Upon my word, if I thought that, I'd shoot myself . . . (*a pause*) You don't think there is any chance of Gwendolen becoming like her mother in about a hundred and fifty years, do you, Algy?

[13] Roughly, steady as a tripod; just fine.
[14] Mythical creature whose stare turned mortals to stone.

ALGERNON   All women become like their mothers. That is their tragedy. No man does. That's his.

JACK   Is that clever?

ALGERNON   It is perfectly phrased! and quite as true as any observation in civilized life should be.

JACK   I am sick to death of cleverness. Everybody is clever now-a-days. You can't go anywhere without meeting clever people. The thing has become an absolute public nuisance. I wish to goodness we had a few fools left.

ALGERNON   We have.

JACK   I should extremely like to meet them. What do they talk about?

ALGERNON   The fools? Oh! about the clever people, of course.

JACK   What fools!

ALGERNON   By the way, did you tell Gwendolen the truth about your being Ernest in town, and Jack in the country?

JACK   (in a very patronizing manner)   My dear fellow, the truth isn't quite the sort of thing one tells to a nice, sweet, refined girl. What extraordinary ideas you have about the way to behave to a woman!

ALGERNON   The only way to behave to a woman is to make love to her, if she is pretty, and to some one else if she is plain.

JACK   Oh, that is nonsense.

ALGERNON   What about your brother? What about the profligate Ernest?

JACK   Oh, before the end of the week I shall have got rid of him. I'll say he died in Paris of apoplexy. Lots of people die of apoplexy, quite suddenly, don't they?

ALGERNON   Yes, but it's hereditary, my dear fellow. It's a sort of thing that runs in families. You had much better say a severe chill.

JACK   You are sure a severe chill isn't hereditary, or anything of that kind?

ALGERNON   Of course it isn't!

JACK   Very well, then. My poor brother Ernest is carried off suddenly in Paris, by a severe chill. That gets rid of him.

ALGERNON   But I thought you said that . . . Miss Cardew was a little too much interested in your poor brother Ernest? Won't she feel his loss a good deal?

JACK   Oh, that is all right. Cecily is not a silly, romantic girl, I am glad to say. She has got a capital appetite, goes for long walks, and pays no attention at all to her lessons.

ALGERNON   I would rather like to see Cecily.

JACK   I will take very good care you never do. She is excessively pretty, and she is only just eighteen.

ALGERNON   Have you told Gwendolen yet that you have an excessively pretty ward who is only just eighteen?

JACK   Oh, one doesn't blurt these things out to people. Cecily and Gwendolen are perfectly certain to be extremely great friends. I'll bet you anything you like that half an hour after they have met, they will be calling each other sister.

ALGERNON   Women only do that when they have called each other a lot of other things first. Now, my dear boy, if we want to get a good table at Willis's, we really must go and dress. Do you know it is nearly seven?

JACK   (irritably)   Oh! it always is nearly seven.

ALGERNON  Well, I'm hungry.

JACK  I never knew you when you weren't. . . .

ALGERNON  What shall we do after dinner? Go to a theater?

JACK  Oh, no! I loathe listening.

ALGERNON  Well, let us go to the Club?

JACK  Oh, no! I hate talking.

ALGERNON  Well, we might trot round to the Empire[15] at ten?

JACK  Oh, no! I can't bear looking at things. It is so silly.

ALGERNON  Well, what shall we do?

JACK  Nothing!

ALGERNON  It is awfully hard work doing nothing. However, I don't mind hard work where there is no definite object of any kind.

*Enter* LANE.

LANE  Miss Fairfax.

*Enter* GWENDOLEN. LANE *goes out.*

ALGERNON  Gwendolen, upon my word!

GWENDOLEN  Algy, kindly turn your back. I have something very particular to say to Mr. Worthing.

ALGERNON  Really, Gwendolen, I don't think I can allow this at all.

GWENDOLEN  Algy, you always adopt a strictly immoral attitude towards life. You are not quite old enough to do that. (ALGERNON *retires to the fireplace.*)

JACK  My own darling!

GWENDOLEN  Ernest, we may never be married. From the expression on mamma's face I fear we never shall. Few parents now-a-days pay any regard to what their children say to them. The old-fashioned respect for the young is fast dying out. Whatever influence I ever had over mamma, I lost at the age of three. But although she may prevent us from becoming man and wife, and I may marry some one else, and marry often, nothing that she can possibly do can alter my eternal devotion to you.

JACK  Dear Gwendolen.

GWENDOLEN  The story of your romantic origin, as related to me by mamma, with unpleasing comments, has naturally stirred the deeper fibers of my nature. Your Christian name has an irresistible fascination. The simplicity of your character makes you exquisitely incomprehensible to me. Your town address at the Albany I have. What is your address in the country?

JACK  The Manor House, Woolton, Hertfordshire. (ALGERNON, *who has been carefully listening, smiles to himself, and writes the address on his shirt-cuff. Then picks up the Railway Guide.*)

GWENDOLEN  There is a good postal service, I suppose? It may be necessary to do something desperate. That, of course, will require serious consideration. I will communicate with you daily.

JACK  My own one!

[15] A famous music hall, where one could find popular and sometimes rowdy entertainment—the opposite of one's private club, whose atmosphere would be hushed and civilized.

GWENDOLEN  How long do you remain in town?

JACK  Till Monday.

GWENDOLEN  Good! Algy, you may turn round now.

ALGERNON  Thanks, I've turned round already.

GWENDOLEN  You may also ring the bell.

JACK  You will let me see you to your carriage, my own darling?

GWENDOLEN  Certainly.

JACK (to LANE, *who now enters*)    I will see Miss Fairfax out.

LANE  Yes, sir. (JACK *and* GWENDOLEN *go off.* LANE *presents several letters on a salver to* ALGERNON. *It is to be surmised that they are bills, as* ALGERNON, *after looking at the envelopes, tears them up.*)

ALGERNON  A glass of sherry, Lane.

LANE  Yes, sir.

ALGERNON  To-morrow, Lane, I'm going Bunburying.

LANE  Yes, sir.

ALGERNON  I shall probably not be back till Monday. You can put up my dress clothes, my smoking jacket, and all the Bunbury suits . . .

LANE  Yes, sir. (*Handing sherry.*)

ALGERNON  I hope to-morrow will be a fine day, Lane.

LANE  It never is, sir.

ALGERNON  Lane, you're a perfect pessimist.

LANE  I do my best to give satisfaction, sir.

*Enter* JACK. LANE *goes off.*

JACK  There's a sensible, intelligent girl! the only girl I ever cared for in my life. (ALGERNON *is laughing immoderately.*) What on earth are you so amused at?

ALGERNON  Oh, I'm a little anxious about poor Bunbury, that's all.

JACK  If you don't take care, your friend Bunbury will get you into a serious scrape some day.

ALGERNON  I love scrapes. They are the only things that are never serious.

JACK  Oh, that's nonsense, Algy. You never talk anything but nonsense.

ALGERNON  Nobody ever does. (JACK *looks indignantly at him, and leaves the room.* ALGERNON *lights a cigarette, reads his shirt-cuff and smiles.*)

*Curtain*

# Act II

*SCENE   Garden at the Manor House. A flight of gray stone steps leads up to the house. The garden, an old-fashioned one, full of roses. Time of year, July. Basket chairs, and a table covered with books, are set under a large yew tree.*

(MISS PRISM *discovered seated at the table.* CECILY *is at the back watering flowers.*)

MISS PRISM (*calling*)  Cecily, Cecily! Surely such a utilitarian occupation as the watering of flowers is rather Moulton's duty than yours? Especially at a moment when intellectual pleasures await you. Your German grammar is on the table. Pray open it at page fifteen. We will repeat yesterday's lesson.

CECILY (*coming over very slowly*)   But I don't like German. It isn't at all a becoming language. I know perfectly well that I look quite plain after my German lesson.

MISS PRISM   Child, you know how anxious your guardian is that you should improve yourself in every way. He laid particular stress on your German, as he was leaving for town yesterday. Indeed, he always lays stress on your German when he is leaving for town.

CECILY   Dear Uncle Jack is so very serious! Sometimes he is so serious that I think he cannot be quite well.

MISS PRISM (*drawing herself up*)   Your guardian enjoys the best of health, and his gravity of demeanor is especially to be commended in one so comparatively young as he is. I know no one who has a higher sense of duty and responsibility.

CECiLY   I suppose that is why he often looks a little bored when we three are together.

MISS PRISM   Cecily! I am surprised at you. Mr. Worthing has many troubles in his life. Idle merriment and triviality would be out of place in his conversation. You must remember his constant anxiety about that unfortunate young man, his brother.

CECILY   I wish Uncle Jack would allow that unfortunate young man, his brother, to come down here sometimes. We might have a good influence over him, Miss Prism. I am sure you certainly would. You know German, and geology, and things of that kind influence a man very much. (CECILY *begins to write in her diary.*)

MISS PRISM (*shaking her head*)   I do not think that even I could produce any effect on a character that, according to his own brother's admission, is irretrievably weak and vacillating. Indeed, I am not sure that I would desire to reclaim him. I am not in favor of this modern mania for turning bad people into good people at a moment's notice. As a man sows so let him reap. You must put away your diary, Cecily. I really don't see why you should keep a diary at all.

CECILY   I keep a diary in order to enter the wonderful secrets of my life. If I didn't write them down I should probably forget all about them.

MISS PRISM   Memory, my dear Cecily, is the diary that we all carry about with us.

CECILY   Yes, but it usually chronicles the things that have never happened, and couldn't possibly have happened. I believe that Memory is responsible for nearly all the three-volume novels that Mudie[16] sends us.

MISS PRISM   Do not speak slightingly of the three-volume novel, Cecily. I wrote one myself in earlier days.

CECILY   Did you really, Miss Prism? How wonderfully clever you are! I hope it did not end happily? I don't like novels that end happily. They depress me so much.

MISS PRISM   The good ended happily, and the bad unhappily. That is what Fiction means.

---

[16] Mudie's circulating library. The three-volume novels were sentimental and improbable romances popular at the time.

CECILY  I suppose so. But it seems very unfair. And was your novel ever published?

MISS PRISM  Alas! no. The manuscript unfortunately was abandoned. I use the word in the sense of lost or mislaid. To your work, child, these speculations are profitless.

CECILY (*smiling*)  But I see dear Dr. Chasuble coming up through the garden.

MISS PRISM (*rising and advancing*)  Dr. Chasuble! This is indeed a pleasure.

*Enter* CANON CHASUBLE.

CHASUBLE  And how are we this morning? Miss Prism, you are, I trust, well?

CECILY  Miss Prism has just been complaining of a slight headache. I think it would do her so much good to have a short stroll with you in the park, Dr. Chasuble.

MISS PRISM  Cecily, I have not mentioned anything about a headache.

CECILY  No, dear Miss Prism, I know that, but I felt instinctively that you had a headache. Indeed I was thinking about that, and not about my German lesson, when the Rector came in.

CHASUBLE  I hope, Cecily, you are not inattentive.

CECILY  Oh, I am afraid I am.

CHASUBLE  That is strange. Were I fortunate enough to be Miss Prism's pupil, I would hang upon her lips. (MISS PRISM *glares.*) I spoke metaphorically.—My metaphor was drawn from bees. Ahem! Mr. Worthing, I suppose, has not returned from town yet?

MISS PRISM  We do not expect him till Monday afternoon.

CHASUBLE  Ah, yes, he usually likes to spend his Sunday in London. He is not one of those whose sole aim is enjoyment, as, by all accounts, that unfortunate young man, his brother, seems to be. But I must not disturb Egeria and her pupil any longer.

MISS PRISM  Egeria? My name is Laetitia, Doctor.

CHASUBLE (*bowing*)  A classical allusion merely, drawn from the Pagan authors.[17] I shall see you both no doubt at Evensong.

MISS PRISM  I think, dear Doctor, I will have a stroll with you. I find I have a headache after all, and a walk might do it good.

CHASUBLE  With pleasure, Miss Prism, with pleasure. We might go as far as the schools and back.

MISS PRISM  That would be delightful. Cecily, you will read your Political Economy in my absence. The chapter on the Fall of the Rupee[18] you may omit. It is somewhat too sensational. Even these metallic problems have their melo-dramatic side. (*Goes down the garden with* DR. CHASUBLE.)

CECILY (*Picks up books and throws them back on table.*)  Horrid Political Economy! Horrid Geography! Horrid, horrid German!

*Enter* MERRIMAN *with a card on a salver.*

---

[17] That is, the ancient Romans. Egeria was a nymph said by King Numa Pompilius to have been his mistress and to have advised him concerning legislation and the forms of worship.

[18] The currency of India; "political economy" is the subject now called economics.

MERRIMAN   Mr. Ernest Worthing has just driven over from the station. He has brought his luggage with him.

CECILY *(Takes the card and reads it.)*   "Mr. Ernest Worthing, B 4, The Albany, W." Uncle Jack's brother! Did you tell him Mr. Worthing was in town?

MERRIMAN   Yes, Miss. He seemed very much disappointed. I mentioned that you and Miss Prism were in the garden. He said he was anxious to speak to you privately for a moment.

CECILY   Ask Mr. Ernest Worthing to come here. I suppose you had better talk to the housekeeper about a room for him.

MERRIMAN   Yes, Miss. (MERRIMAN *goes off.*)

CECILY   I have never met any really wicked person before. I feel rather frightened. I am so afraid he will look just like every one else.

*Enter* ALGERNON, *very gay and debonair.*

He does!

ALGERNON *(raising his hat)*   You are my little cousin Cecily, I'm sure.

CECILY   You are under some strange mistake. I am not little. In fact, I am more than usually tall for my age. (ALGERNON *is rather taken aback.*) But I am your cousin Cecily. You, I see from your card, are Uncle Jack's brother, my cousin Ernest, my wicked cousin Ernest.

ALGERNON   Oh! I am not really wicked at all, cousin Cecily. You mustn't think that I am wicked.

CECILY   If you are not, then you have certainly been deceiving us all in a very inexcusable manner. I hope you have not been leading a double life, pretending to be wicked and being really good all the time. That would be hypocrisy.

ALGERNON *(Looks at her in amazement.)*   Oh! of course I have been rather reckless.

CECILY   I am glad to hear it.

ALGERNON   In fact, now you mention the subject, I have been very bad in my own small way.

CECILY   I don't think you should be so proud of that, though I am sure it must have been very pleasant.

ALGERNON   It is much pleasanter being here with you.

CECILY   I can't understand how you are here at all. Uncle Jack won't be back till Monday afternoon.

ALGERNON   That is a great disappointment. I am obliged to go up by the first train on Monday morning. I have a business appointment that I am anxious . . . to miss.

CECILY   Couldn't you miss it anywhere but in London?

ALGERNON   No; the appointment is in London.

CECILY   Well, I know, of course, how important it is not to keep a business engagement, if one wants to retain any sense of the beauty of life, but still I think you had better wait till Uncle Jack arrives. I know he wants to speak to you about your emigrating.

ALGERNON   About my what?

CECILY   Your emigrating. He has gone up to buy your outfit.

ALGERNON   I certainly wouldn't let Jack buy my outfit. He has no taste in neckties at all.

CECILY  I don't think you will require neckties. Uncle Jack is sending you to Australia.

ALGERNON  Australia! I'd sooner die.

CECILY  Well, he said at dinner on Wednesday night, that you would have to choose between this world, the next world, and Australia.

ALGERNON  Oh, well! The accounts I have received of Australia and the next world are not particularly encouraging. This world is good enough for me, cousin Cecily.

CECILY  Yes, but are you good enough for it?

ALGERNON  I'm afraid I'm not that. That is why I want you to reform me. You might make that your mission, if you don't mind, cousin Cecily.

CECILY  I'm afraid I've not time, this afternoon.

ALGERNON  Well, would you mind my reforming myself this afternoon?

CECILY  That is rather Quixotic of you. But I think you should try.

ALGERNON  I will. I feel better already.

CECILY  You are looking a little worse.

ALGERNON  That is because I am hungry.

CECILY  How thoughtless of me. I should have remembered that when one is going to lead an entirely new life, one requires regular and wholesome meals. Won't you come in?

ALGERNON  Thank you. Might I have a button-hole first? I never have any appetite unless I have a button-hole first.

CECILY  A Maréchal Niel?[19] (Picks up scissors.)

ALGERNON  No, I'd sooner have a pink rose.

CECILY  Why? (Cuts a flower.)

ALGERNON  Because you are like a pink rose, cousin Cecily.

CECILY  I don't think it can be right for you to talk to me like that. Miss Prism never says such things to me.

ALGERNON  Then Miss Prism is a short-sighted old lady. (CECILY puts the rose in his button-hole.) You are the prettiest girl I ever saw.

CECILY  Miss Prism says that all good looks are a snare.

ALGERNON  They are a snare that every sensible man would like to be caught in.

CECILY  Oh! I don't think I would care to catch a sensible man. I shouldn't know what to talk to him about.

(They pass into the house. MISS PRISM and DR. CHASUBLE return.)

MISS PRISM  You are too much alone, dear Dr. Chasuble. You should get married. A misanthrope I can understand—a womanthrope, never!

CHASUBLE  (with a scholar's shudder)  Believe me, I do not deserve so neologistic a phrase. The precept as well as the practice of the Primitive Church was distinctly against matrimony.

MISS PRISM  (sententiously)  That is obviously the reason why the Primitive Church has not lasted up to the present day. And you do not seem to realize, dear Doctor, that by persistently remaining single, a man converts himself into a

---

[19] A yellow rose, to be pinned to Algernon's lapel.

permanent public temptation. Men should be careful; this very celibacy leads weaker vessels astray.

CHASUBLE  But is a man not equally attractive when married?

MISS PRISM  No married man is ever attractive except to his wife.

CHASUBLE  And often, I've been told, not even to her.

MISS PRISM  That depends on the intellectual sympathies of the woman. Maturity can always be depended on. Ripeness can be trusted. Young women are green. (DR. CHASUBLE *starts.*) I spoke horticulturally. My metaphor was drawn from fruits. But where is Cecily?

CHASUBLE  Perhaps she followed us to the schools.

*Enter* JACK *slowly from the back of the garden. He is dressed in the deepest mourning, with crape hatband and black gloves.*

MISS PRISM  Mr. Worthing!

CHASUBLE  Mr. Worthing?

MISS PRISM  This is indeed a surprise. We did not look for you till Monday afternoon.

JACK  (*Shakes* MISS PRISM'S *hand in a tragic manner.*)  I have returned sooner than I expected. Dr. Chasuble, I hope you are well?

CHASUBLE  Dear Mr. Worthing, I trust this garb of woe does not betoken some terrible calamity?

JACK  My brother.

MISS PRISM  More shameful debts and extravagance?

CHASUBLE  Still leading his life of pleasure?

JACK  (*shaking his head*)  Dead!

CHASUBLE  Your brother Ernest dead?

JACK  Quite dead.

MISS PRISM  What a lesson for him! I trust he will profit by it.

CHASUBLE  Mr. Worthing, I offer you my sincere condolence. You have at least the consolation of knowing that you were always the most generous and forgiving of brothers.

JACK  Poor Ernest! He had many faults, but it is a sad, sad blow.

CHASUBLE  Very sad indeed. Were you with him at the end?

JACK  No. He died abroad; in Paris, in fact. I had a telegram last night from the manager of the Grand Hotel.

CHASUBLE  Was the cause of death mentioned?

JACK  A severe chill, it seems.

MISS PRISM  As a man sows, so shall he reap.

CHASUBLE  (*raising his hand*)  Charity, dear Miss Prism, charity! None of us are perfect. I myself am peculiarly susceptible to draughts. Will the interment take place here?

JACK  No. He seems to have expressed a desire to be buried in Paris.

CHASUBLE  In Paris! (*Shakes his head.*) I fear that hardly points to any very serious state of mind at the last. You would no doubt wish me to make some slight allusion to this tragic domestic affliction next Sunday. (JACK *presses his hand convulsively.*) My sermon on the meaning of the manna in the wilderness can be adapted to almost any occasion, joyful, or, as in the present case, distressing. (*All sigh.*) I have preached it at harvest celebrations, christenings, confirmations, on days of humiliation and festal days. The last time I delivered it was in the Cathedral, as a charity sermon on behalf of the Society for the Prevention of Discontentment among the Upper Orders. The Bishop, who was present, was much struck by some of the analogies I drew.

JACK  Ah, that reminds me, you mentioned christenings I think, Dr. Chasuble? I suppose you know how to christen all right? (DR. CHASUBLE *looks astounded.*) I mean, of course, you are continually christening, aren't you?

MISS PRISM  It is, I regret to say, one of the Rector's most constant duties in this parish. I have often spoken to the poorer classes on the subject. But they don't seem to know what thrift is.

CHASUBLE  But is there any particular infant in whom you are interested, Mr. Worthing? Your brother was, I believe, unmarried, was he not?

JACK  Oh, yes.

MISS PRISM  (*bitterly*)  People who live entirely for pleasure usually are.

JACK  But it is not for any child, dear Doctor. I am very fond of children. No! the fact is, I would like to be christened myself, this afternoon, if you have nothing better to do.

CHASUBLE  But surely, Mr. Worthing, you have been christened already?

JACK  I don't remember anything about it.

CHASUBLE  But have you any grave doubts on the subject?

JACK  I certainly intend to have. Of course, I don't know if the thing would bother you in any way, or if you think I am a little too old now.

CHASUBLE  Not at all. The sprinkling, and, indeed, the immersion of adults is a perfectly canonical practice.

JACK  Immersion!

CHASUBLE  You need have no apprehensions. Sprinkling is all that is necessary, or indeed I think advisable. Our weather is so changeable. At what hour would you wish the ceremony performed?

JACK  Oh, I might trot around about five if that would suit you.

CHASUBLE  Perfectly, perfectly! In fact I have two similar ceremonies to perform at that time. A case of twins that occurred recently in one of the outlying cottages on your own estate. Poor Jenkins the carter, a most hardworking man.

JACK  Oh! I don't see much fun in being christened along with other babies. It would be childish. Would half-past five do?

CHASUBLE  Admirably! Admirably! (*Takes out watch.*) And now, dear Mr. Worthing, I will not intrude any longer into a house of sorrow. I would merely beg you not to be too much bowed down by grief. What seem to us bitter trials at the moment are often blessings in disguise.

MISS PRISM  This seems to me a blessing of an extremely obvious kind.

*Enter* CECILY *from the house.*

CECILY  Uncle Jack! Oh, I am pleased to see you back. But what horrid clothes you have on! Do go and change them.

MISS PRISM   Cecily!

CHASUBLE   My child! my child! (CECILY *goes towards* JACK; *he kisses her brow in a melancholy manner.*)

CECILY   What is the matter, Uncle Jack? Do look happy! You look as if you had a toothache and I have such a surprise for you. Who do you think is in the dining-room? Your brother!

JACK   Who?

CECILY   Your brother Ernest. He arrived about half an hour ago.

JACK   What nonsense! I haven't got a brother.

CECILY   Oh, don't say that. However badly he may have behaved to you in the past he is still your brother. You couldn't be so heartless as to disown him. I'll tell him to come out. And you will shake hands with him, won't you, Uncle Jack? (*Runs back into the house.*)

CHASUBLE   These are very joyful tidings.

MISS PRISM   After we had all been resigned to his loss, his sudden return seems to me peculiarly distressing.

JACK   My brother is in the dining-room? I don't know what it all means. I think it is perfectly absurd.

*Enter* ALGERNON *and* CECILY *hand in hand. They come slowly up to* JACK.

JACK   Good heavens! (*Motions* ALGERNON *away.*)

ALGERNON   Brother John, I have come down from town to tell you that I am very sorry for all the trouble I have given you, and that I intend to lead a better life in the future. (JACK *glares at him and does not take his hand.*)

CECILY   Uncle Jack, you are not going to refuse your own brother's hand?

JACK   Nothing will induce me to take his hand. I think his coming down here disgraceful. He knows perfectly well why.

CECILY   Uncle Jack, do be nice. There is some good in every one. Ernest has just been telling me about his poor invalid friend, Mr. Bunbury, whom he goes to visit so often. And surely there must be much good in one who is kind to an invalid, and leaves the pleasures of London to sit by a bed of pain.

JACK   Oh, he has been talking about Bunbury, has he?

CECILY   Yes, he has told me all about poor Mr. Bunbury, and his terrible state of health.

JACK   Bunbury! Well, I won't have him talk to you about Bunbury or about anything else. It is enough to drive one perfectly frantic.

ALGERNON   Of course I admit that the faults were all on my side. But I must say that I think that Brother John's coldness to me is peculiarly painful. I expected a more enthusiastic welcome, especially considering it is the first time I have come here.

CECILY   Uncle Jack, if you don't shake hands with Ernest I will never forgive you.

JACK   Never forgive me?

CECILY   Never, never, never!

JACK   Well, this is the last time I shall ever do it. (*Shakes hands with* ALGERNON *and glares.*)

CHASUBLE  It's pleasant, is it not, to see so perfect a reconciliation? I think we might leave the two brothers together.

MISS PRISM  Cecily, you will come with us.

CECILY  Certainly, Miss Prism. My little task of reconciliation is over.

CHASUBLE  You have done a beautiful action to-day, dear child.

MISS PRISM  We must not be premature in our judgments.

CECILY  I feel very happy. *(They all go off.)*

JACK  You young scoundrel, Algy, you must get out of this place as soon as possible. I don't allow any Bunburying here.

*Enter* MERRIMAN.

MERRIMAN  I have put Mr. Ernest's things in the room next to yours, sir. I suppose that is all right?

JACK  What?

MERRIMAN  Mr. Ernest's luggage, sir. I have unpacked it and put it in the room next to your own.

JACK  His luggage?

MERRIMAN  Yes, sir. Three portmanteaus, a dressing-case, two hat-boxes, and a large luncheon-basket.

ALGERNON  I am afraid I can't stay more than a week this time.

JACK  Merriman, order the dog-cart[20] at once. Mr. Ernest has been suddenly called back to town.

MERRIMAN  Yes, sir. *(Goes back into the house.)*

ALGERNON  What a fearful liar you are, Jack. I have not been called back to town at all.

JACK  Yes, you have.

ALGERNON  I haven't heard any one call me.

JACK  Your duty as a gentleman calls you back.

ALGERNON  My duty as a gentleman has never interfered with my pleasures in the smallest degree.

JACK  I can quite understand that.

ALGERNON  Well, Cecily is a darling.

JACK  You are not to talk of Miss Cardew like that. I don't like it.

ALGERNON  Well, I don't like your clothes. You look perfectly ridiculous in them. Why on earth don't you go up and change? It is perfectly childish to be in deep mourning for a man who is actually staying for a whole week with you in your house as a guest. I call it grotesque.

JACK  You are certainly not staying with me for a whole week as a guest or anything else. You have got to leave . . . by the four-five train.

ALGERNON  I certainly won't leave you so long as you are in mourning. It would be most unfriendly. If I were in mourning you would stay with me, I suppose. I should think it very unkind if you didn't.

JACK  Well, will you go if I change my clothes?

ALGERNON  Yes, if you are not too long. I never saw anybody take so long to dress, and with such little result.

---

20 A horse-drawn cart, originally to carry hunters and their dogs.

JACK  Well, at any rate, that is better than being always over-dressed as you are.

ALGERNON  If I am occasionally a little over-dressed, I make up for it by being always immensely over-educated.

JACK  Your vanity is ridiculous, your conduct an outrage, and your presence in my garden utterly absurd. However, you have got to catch the four-five, and I hope you will have a pleasant journey back to town. This Bunburying, as you call it, has not been a great success for you. *(Goes into the house.)*

ALGERNON  I think it has been a great success. I'm in love with Cecily, and that is everything. *(Enter* CECILY *at the back of the garden. She picks up the can and begins to water the flowers.)* But I must see her before I go, and make arrangements for another Bunbury. Ah, there she is.

CECILY  Oh, I merely came back to water the roses. I thought you were with Uncle Jack.

ALGERNON  He's gone to order the dog-cart for me.

CECILY  Oh, is he going to take you for a nice drive?

ALGERNON  He's going to send me away.

CECILY  Then have we got to part?

ALGERNON  I am afraid so. It's a very painful parting.

CECILY  It is always painful to part from people whom one has known for a very brief space of time. The absence of old friends one can endure with equanimity. But even a momentary separation from any one to whom one has just been introduced is almost unbearable.

ALGERNON  Thank you.

*Enter* MERRIMAN.

MERRIMAN  The dog-cart is at the door, sir. *(*ALGERNON *looks appealingly at* CECILY.*)*

CECILY  It can wait, Merriman . . . for . . . five minutes.

MERRIMAN  Yes, miss.

*(Exit* MERRIMAN.*)*

ALGERNON  I hope, Cecily, I shall not offend you if I state quite frankly and openly that you seem to me to be in every way the visible personification of absolute perfection.

CECILY  I think your frankness does you great credit, Ernest. If you will allow me I will copy your remarks into my diary. *(Goes over to table and begins writing in diary.)*

ALGERNON  Do you really keep a diary? I'd give anything to look at it. May I?

CECILY  Oh, no. *(Puts her hand over it.)* You see it is simply a very young girl's record of her own thoughts and impressions, and consequently meant for publication. When it appears in volume form I hope you will order a copy. But pray, Ernest, don't stop. I delight in taking down from dictation. I have reached "absolute perfection." You can go on. I am quite ready for more.

ALGERNON  *(somewhat taken aback)*  Ahem! Ahem!

CECILY  Oh, don't cough, Ernest. When one is dictating one should speak fluently and not cough. Besides, I don't know how to spell a cough. *(Writes as* ALGERNON *speaks.)*

ALGERNON  *(speaking very rapidly)*  Cecily, ever since I first looked upon your wonderful and incomparable beauty, I have dared to love you wildly, passionately, devotedly, hopelessly.

CECILY  I don't think that you should tell me that you love me wildly, passionately, devotedly, hopelessly. Hopelessly doesn't seem to make much sense, does it?

ALGERNON  Cecily!

*Enter* MERRIMAN.

MERRIMAN  The dog-cart is waiting, sir.

ALGERNON  Tell it to come round next week, at the same hour.

MERRIMAN  (*Looks at* CECILY, *who makes no sign.*)  Yes, sir.

(MERRIMAN *retires.*)

CECILY  Uncle Jack would be very much annoyed if he knew you were staying on till next week, at the same hour.

ALGERNON  Oh, I don't care about Jack. I don't care for anybody in the whole world but you. I love you, Cecily. You will marry me, won't you?

CECILY  You silly you! Of course. Why, we have been engaged for the last three months.

ALGERNON  For the last three months?

CECILY  Yes, it will be exactly three months on Thursday.

ALGERNON  But how did we become engaged?

CECILY  Well, ever since dear Uncle Jack first confessed to us that he had a younger brother who was very wicked and bad, you of course have formed the chief topic of conversation between myself and Miss Prism. And of course a man who is much talked about is always very attractive. One feels there must be something in him after all. I daresay it was foolish of me, but I fell in love with you, Ernest.

ALGERNON  Darling! And when was the engagement actually settled?

CECILY  On the 14th of February last. Worn out by your entire ignorance of my existence, I determined to end the matter one way or the other, and after a long struggle with myself I accepted you under this dear old tree here. The next day I bought this little ring in your name, and this is the little bangle with the true lovers' knot I promised you always to wear.

ALGERNON  Did I give you this? It's very pretty, isn't it?

CECILY  Yes, you've wonderfully good taste, Ernest. It's the excuse I've always given for your leading such a bad life. And this is the box in which I keep all your dear letters. (*Kneels at table, opens box, and produces letters tied up with blue ribbon.*)

ALGERNON  My letters! But my own sweet Cecily, I have never written you any letters.

CECILY  You need hardly remind me of that, Ernest. I remember only too well that I was forced to write your letters for you. I wrote always three times a week, and sometimes oftener.

ALGERNON  Oh, do let me read them, Cecily?

CECILY  Oh, I couldn't possibly. They would make you far too conceited. (*Replaces box.*) The three you wrote me after I had broken off the engagement are so beautiful, and so badly spelled, that even now I can hardly read them without crying a little.

ALGERNON  But was our engagement ever broken off?

CECILY  Of course it was. On the 22nd of last March. You can see the entry if you like. *(Shows diary.)* "To-day I broke off my engagement with Ernest. I feel it is better to do so. The weather still continues charming."

ALGERNON  But why on earth did you break it off? What had I done? I had done nothing at all. Cecily, I am very much hurt indeed to hear you broke it off. Particularly when the weather was so charming.

CECILY  It would hardly have been a really serious engagement if it hadn't been broken off at least once. But I forgave you before the week was out.

ALGERNON  *(crossing to her, and kneeling)*  What a perfect angel you are, Cecily.

CECILY  You dear romantic boy. *(He kisses her, she puts her fingers through his hair.)* I hope your hair curls naturally, does it?

ALGERNON  Yes, darling, with a little help from others.

CECILY  I am so glad.

ALGERNON  You'll never break off our engagement again, Cecily?

CECILY  I don't think I could break it off now that I have actually met you. Besides, of course, there is the question of your name.

ALGERNON  Yes, of course. *(nervously)*

CECILY  You must not laugh at me, darling, but it had always been a girlish dream of mine to love some one whose name was Ernest. (ALGERNON *rises,* CECILY *also.)* There is something in that name that seems to inspire absolute confidence. I pity any poor married woman whose husband is not called Ernest.

ALGERNON  But, my dear child, do you mean to say you could not love me if I had some other name?

CECILY  But what name?

ALGERNON  Oh, any name you like—Algernon, for instance. . . .

CECILY  But I don't like the name of Algernon.

ALGERNON  Well, my own dear, sweet, loving little darling, I really can't see why you should object to the name of Algernon. It is not at all a bad name. In fact, it is rather an aristocratic name. Half of the chaps who get into the Bankruptcy Court are called Algernon. But seriously, Cecily . . . *(moving to her)* . . . if my name was Algy, couldn't you love me?

CECILY  *(rising)*  I might respect you, Ernest, I might admire your character, but I fear that I should not be able to give you my undivided attention.

ALGERNON  Ahem! Cecily! *(picking up hat)* Your Rector here is, I suppose, thoroughly experienced in the practice of all the rites and ceremonials of the church?

CECILY  Oh, yes. Dr. Chasuble is a most learned man. He has never written a single book, so you can imagine how much he knows.

ALGERNON  I must see him at once on a most important christening—I mean on most important business.

CECILY  Oh!

ALGERNON  I sha'n't be away more than half an hour.

CECILY  Considering that we have been engaged since February the 14th, and that I only met you to-day for the first time, I think it is rather hard that you should leave me for so long a period as half an hour. Couldn't you make it twenty minutes?

ALGERNON  I'll be back in no time. (Kisses her and rushes down the garden.)

CECILY  What an impetuous boy he is. I like his hair so much. I must enter his proposal in my dairy.

Enter MERRIMAN.

MERRIMAN  A Miss Fairfax has just called to see Mr. Worthing. On very important business, Miss Fairfax states.

CECILY  Isn't Mr. Worthing in his library?

MERRIMAN  Mr. Worthing went over in the direction of the Rectory some time ago.

CECILY  Pray ask the lady to come out here; Mr. Worthing is sure to be back soon. And you can bring tea.

MERRIMAN  Yes, miss. (Goes out.)

CECILY  Miss Fairfax! I suppose one of the many good elderly women who are associated with Uncle Jack in some of his philanthropic work in London. I don't quite like women who are interested in philanthropic work. I think it is so forward of them.

Enter MERRIMAN.

MERRIMAN  Miss Fairfax.

Enter GWENDOLEN.

(Exit MERRIMAN)

CECILY (advancing to meet her)  Pray let me introduce myself to you. My name is Cecily Cardew.

GWENDOLEN  Cecily Cardew? (moving to her and shaking hands) What a very sweet name! Something tells me that we are going to be great friends. I like you already more than I can say. My first impressions of people are never wrong.

CECILY  How nice of you to like me so much after we have known each other such a comparatively short time. Pray sit down.

GWENDOLEN (still standing up)  I may call you Cecily, may I not?

CECILY  With pleasure!

GWENDOLEN  And you will always call me Gwendolen, won't you?

CECILY  If you wish.

GWENDOLEN  Then that is all quite settled, it it not?

CECILY  I hope so. (A pause. They both sit down together.)

GWENDOLEN  Perhaps this might be a favorable opportunity for my mentioning who I am. My father is Lord Bracknell. You have never heard of papa, I suppose?

CECILY  I don't think so.

GWENDOLEN  Outside the family circle, papa, I am glad to say, is entirely unknown. I think that is quite as it should be. The home seems to me to be the proper sphere for the man. And certainly once a man begins to neglect his domestic duties he becomes painfully effeminate, does he not? And I don't like that. It makes men so very attractive. Cecily, mamma, whose views on education are remarkably strict, has brought me up to be extremely short-sighted; it is part of her system; so do you mind my looking at you through my glasses?

CECILY   Oh, not at all, Gwendolen. I am very fond of being looked at.

GWENDOLEN   (after examining CECILY carefully through a lorgnette)   You are here on a short visit, I suppose.

CECILY   Oh, no, I live here.

GWENDOLEN   (severely)   Really? Your mother, no doubt, or some female relative of advanced years, resides here also?

CECILY   Oh, no. I have no mother, nor, in fact, any relations.

GWENDOLEN   Indeed?

CECILY   My dear guardian, with the assistance of Miss Prism, has the arduous task of looking after me.

GWENDOLEN   Your guardian?

CECILY   Yes, I am Mr. Worthing's ward.

GWENDOLEN   Oh! It is strange he never mentioned to me that he had a ward. How secretive of him! He grows more interesting hourly. I am not sure, however, that the news inspires me with feelings of unmixed delight. (rising and going to her) I am very fond of you, Cecily; I have liked you ever since I met you. But I am bound to state that now that I know that you are Mr. Worthing's ward, I cannot help expressing a wish you were—well, just a little older than you seem to be—and not quite so very alluring in appearance. In fact, if I may speak candidly—

CECILY   Pray do! I think that whenever one has anything unpleasant to say, one should always be quite candid.

GWENDOLEN   Well, to speak with perfect candor, Cecily, I wish that you were fully forty-two, and more than usually plain for your age. Ernest has a strong upright nature. He is the very soul of truth and honor. Disloyalty would be as impossible to him as deception. But even men of the noblest possible moral character are extremely susceptible to the influence of the physical charms of others. Modern, no less than Ancient History, supplies us with many most painful examples of what I refer to. If it were not so, indeed, History would be quite unreadable.

CECILY   I beg your pardon, Gwendolen, did you say Ernest?

GWENDOLEN   Yes.

CECILY   Oh, but it is not Mr. Ernest Worthing who is my guardian. It is his brother—his elder brother.

GWENDOLEN   (sitting down again)   Ernest never mentioned to me that he had a brother.

CECILY   I am sorry to say they have not been on good terms for a long time.

GWENDOLEN   Ah! that accounts for it. And now that I think of it I have never heard any man mention his brother. The subject seems distasteful to most men. Cecily, you have lifted a load from my mind. I was growing almost anxious. It would have been terrible if any cloud had come across a friendship like ours, would it not? Of course you are quite, quite sure that it is not Mr. Ernest Worthing who is your guardian?

CECILY  Quite sure. *(a pause)* In fact, I am going to be his.

GWENDOLEN  *(enquiringly)*  I beg your pardon?

CECILY  *(rather shy and confidingly)*  Dearest Gwendolen, there is no reason why I should make a secret of it to you. Our little county newspaper is sure to chronicle the fact next week. Mr. Ernest Worthing and I are engaged to be married.

GWENDOLEN  *(quite politely, rising)*  My darling Cecily, I think there must be some slight error. Mr. Ernest Worthing is engaged to me. The announcement will appear in the *Morning Post* on Saturday at the latest.

CECILY  *(very politely, rising)*  I am afraid you must be under some misconception. Ernest proposed to me exactly ten minutes ago. *(Shows diary.)*

GWENDOLEN  *(Examines diary through her lorgnette carefully.)*  It is certainly very curious, for he asked me to be his wife yesterday afternoon at 5:30. If you would care to verify the incident, pray do so. *(Produces diary of her own.)* I never travel without my diary. One should always have something sensational to read in the train. I am so sorry, dear Cecily, if it is any disappointment to you, but I'm afraid *I* have the prior claim.

CECILY  It would distress me more than I can tell you, dear Gwendolen, if it caused you any mental or physical anguish, but I feel bound to point out that since Ernest proposed to you he clearly has changed his mind.

GWENDOLEN  *(meditatively)*  If the poor fellow has been entrapped into any foolish promise I shall consider it my duty to rescue him at once, and with a firm hand.

CECILY  *(thoughtfully and sadly)*  Whatever unfortunate entanglement my dear boy may have got into, I will never reproach him with it after we are married.

GWENDOLEN  Do you allude to me, Miss Cardew, as an entanglement? You are presumptuous. On an occasion of this kind it becomes more than a moral duty to speak one's mind. It becomes a pleasure.

CECILY  Do you suggest, Miss Fairfax, that I entrapped Ernest into an engagement? How dare you? This is no time for wearing the shallow mask of manners. When I see a spade I call it a spade.

GWENDOLEN *(satirically)*  I am glad to say that I have never seen a spade. It is obvious that our social spheres have been widely different.

*Enter* MERRIMAN, *followed by the footman. He carries a salver, tablecloth, and plate-stand.* CECILY *is about to retort. The presence of the servants exercises a restraining influence, under which both girls chafe.*

MERRIMAN  Shall I lay tea here as usual, miss?

CECILY *(sternly, in a calm voice)*  Yes, as usual. *(*MERRIMAN *begins to clear and lay cloth. A long pause.* CECILY *and* GWENDOLEN *glare at each other.)*

GWENDOLEN  Are there many interesting walks in the vicinity, Miss Cardew?

CECILY  Oh, yes, a great many. From the top of one of the hills quite close one can see five counties.

GWENDOLEN  Five counties! I don't think I should like that. I hate crowds.

CECILY *(sweetly)*  I suppose that is why you live in town? *(*GWENDOLEN *bites her lip, and beats her foot nervously with her parasol.)*

GWENDOLEN *(looking round)*  Quite a well-kept garden this is, Miss Cardew.

CECILY  So glad you like it, Miss Fairfax.

GWENDOLEN  I had no idea there were any flowers in the country.

CECILY  Oh, flowers are as common here, Miss Fairfax, as people are in London.

GWENDOLEN  Personally I cannot understand how anybody manages to exist in the country, if anybody who is anybody does. The country always bores me to death.

CECILY  Ah! This is what the newspapers call agricultural depression, is it not? I believe the aristocracy are suffering very much from it just at present. It is almost an epidemic amongst them, I have been told. May I offer you some tea, Miss Fairfax?

GWENDOLEN  *(with elaborate politeness)*  Thank you. *(Aside.)* Detestable girl! But I require tea!

CECILY  *(sweetly)*  Sugar?

GWENDOLEN  *(superciliously)*  No, thank you. Sugar is not fashionable any more. *(CECILY looks angrily at her, takes up the tongs and puts four lumps of sugar into the cup.)*

CECILY  *(severely)*  Cake or bread and butter?

GWENDOLEN  *(in a bored manner)*  Bread and butter, please. Cake is rarely seen at the best houses now-a-days.

CECILY  *(Cuts a very large slice of cake, and puts it on the tray.)*  Hand that to Miss Fairfax. *(MERRIMAN does so, and goes out with footman. GWENDOLEN drinks the tea and makes a grimace. Puts down cup at once, reaches out her hand to the bread and butter, looks at it, and finds it is cake. Rises in indignation.)*

GWENDOLEN  You have filled my tea with lumps of sugar, and though I asked most distinctly for bread and butter, you have given me cake. I am known for the gentleness of my disposition, and the extraordinary sweetness of my nature, but I warn you, Miss Cardew, you may go too far.

CECILY  *(rising)*  To save my poor, innocent, trusting boy from the machinations of any other girl there are no lengths to which I would not go.

GWENDOLEN  From the moment I saw you I distrusted you. I felt that you were false and deceitful. I am never deceived in such matters. My first impressions of people are invariably right.

CECILY  It seems to me, Miss Fairfax, that I am trespassing on your valuable time. No doubt you have many other calls of a similar character to make in the neighborhood.

*Enter JACK.*

GWENDOLEN  *(catching sight of him)*  Ernest! My own Ernest!

JACK  Gwendolen! Darling! *(Offers to kiss her.)*

GWENDOLEN  *(drawing back)*  A moment! May I ask if you are engaged to be married to this young lady? *(Points to CECILY.)*

JACK  *(laughing)*  To dear little Cecily! Of course not! What could have put such an idea into your pretty little head?

GWENDOLEN  Thank you. You may. *(Offers her cheek.)*

CECILY  *(very sweetly)*  I knew there must be some misunderstanding, Miss Fairfax. The gentleman whose arm is at present around your waist is my dear guardian, Mr. John Worthing.

GWENDOLEN  I beg your pardon?

CECILY  This is Uncle Jack.

GWENDOLEN *(receding)*  Jack! Oh!

*Enter* ALGERNON.

CECILY  Here is Ernest.

ALGERNON *(Goes straight over to* CECILY *without noticing any one else.)*  My own love! *(Offers to kiss her.)*

CECILY *(drawing back)*  A moment, Ernest! May I ask you—are you engaged to be married to this young lady?

ALGERNON *(looking round)*  To what young lady? Good heavens! Gwendolen!

CECILY  Yes, to good heavens, Gwendolen, I mean to Gwendolen.

ALGERNON *(laughing)*  Of course not! What could have put such an idea into your pretty little head?

CECILY  Thank you. *(presenting her cheek to be kissed)* You may. *(*ALGERNON *kisses her.)*

GWENDOLEN  I felt there was some slight error, Miss Cardew. The gentleman who is now embracing you is my cousin, Mr. Algernon Moncrieff.

CECILY *(breaking away from* ALGERNON*)*  Algernon Moncrieff! Oh! *(The two girls move towards each other and put their arms round each other's waists as if for protection.)*

CECILY  Are you called Algernon?

ALGERNON  I cannot deny it.

CECILY  Oh!

GWENDOLEN  Is your name really John?

JACK *(standing rather proudly)*  I could deny it if I liked. I could deny anything if I liked. But my name certainly is John. It has been John for years.

CECILY *(to* GWENDOLEN*)*  A gross deception has been practiced on both of us.

GWENDOLEN  My poor wounded Cecily!

CECILY  My sweet, wronged Gwendolen!

GWENDOLEN *(slowly and seriously)*  You will call me sister, will you not? *(They embrace.* JACK *and* ALGERNON *groan and walk up and down.)*

CECILY *(rather brightly)*  There is just one question I would like to be allowed to ask my guardian.

GWENDOLEN  An admirable idea! Mr. Worthing, there is just one question I would like to be permitted to put to you. Where is your brother Ernest? We are both engaged to be married to your brother Ernest, so it is a matter of some importance to us to know where your brother Ernest is at present.

JACK *(slowly and hesitatingly)*  Gwendolen—Cecily—it is very painful for me to be forced to speak the truth. It is the first time in my life that I have ever been reduced to such a painful position, and I am really quite inexperienced in doing anything of the kind. However I will tell you quite frankly that I have no brother Ernest. I have no brother at all. I never had a brother in my life, and I certainly have not the smallest intention of ever having one in the future.

CECILY *(surprised)*  No brother at all?

JACK *(cheerily)*  None!

GWENDOLEN *(severely)*  Had you never a brother of any kind?

JACK (*pleasantly*)   Never. Not even of any kind.

GWENDOLEN   I am afraid it is quite clear, Cecily, that neither of us is engaged to be married to any one.

CECILY   It is not a very pleasant position for a young girl suddenly to find herself in. Is it?

GWENDOLEN   Let us go into the house. They will hardly venture to come after us there.

CECILY   No, men are so cowardly, aren't they? (*They retire into the house with scornful looks.*)

JACK   This ghastly state of things is what you call Bunburying, I suppose?

ALGERNON   Yes, and a perfectly wonderful Bunbury it is. The most wonderful Bunbury I have ever had in my life.

JACK   Well, you've no right whatsoever to Bunbury here.

ALGERNON   That is absurd. One has a right to Bunbury anywhere one chooses. Every serious Bunburyist knows that.

JACK   Serious Bunburyist! Good heavens!

ALGERNON   Well, one must be serious about something, if one wants to have any amusement in life. I happen to be serious about Bunburying. What on earth you are serious about I haven't got the remotest idea. About everything, I should fancy. You have such an absolutely trivial nature.

JACK   Well, the only small satisfaction I have in the whole of this wretched business is that your friend Bunbury is quite exploded. You won't be able to run down to the country quite so often as you used to do, dear Algy. And a very good thing, too.

ALGERNON   Your brother is a little off color, isn't he, dear Jack? You won't be able to disappear to London quite so frequently as your wicked custom was. And not a bad thing, either.

JACK   As for your conduct towards Miss Cardew, I must say that your taking in a sweet, simple, innocent girl like that is quite inexcusable. To say nothing of the fact that she is my ward.

ALGERNON   I can see no possible defense at all for your deceiving a brilliant, clever, thoroughly experienced young lady like Miss Fairfax. To say nothing of the fact that she is my cousin.

JACK   I wanted to be engaged to Gwendolen, that is all. I love her.

ALGERNON   Well, I simply wanted to be engaged to Cecily. I adore her.

JACK   There is certainly no chance of your marrying Miss Cardew.

ALGERNON   I don't think there is much likelihood, Jack, of you and Miss Fairfax being united.

JACK   Well, that is no business of yours.

ALGERNON   If it was my business, I wouldn't talk about it. (*Begins to eat muffins.*) It is very vulgar to talk about one's business. Only people like stock-brokers do that, and then merely at dinner parties.

JACK   How you can sit there, calmly eating muffins, when we are in this horrible trouble, I can't make out. You seem to me to be perfectly heartless.

ALGERNON   Well, I can't eat muffins in an agitated manner. The butter would probably get on my cuffs. One should always eat muffins quite calmly. It is the only way to eat them.

JACK  I say it's perfectly heartless your eating muffins at all, under the circumstances.

ALGERNON  When I am in trouble, eating is the only thing that consoles me. Indeed, when I am in really great trouble, as any one who knows me intimately will tell you, I refuse everything except food and drink. At the present moment I am eating muffins because I am unhappy. Besides, I am particularly fond of muffins. *(rising)*

JACK *(rising)*  Well, that is no reason why you should eat them all in that greedy way. *(Takes muffins from* ALGERNON.*)*

ALGERNON *(offering tea-cake)*  I wish you would have tea-cake instead. I don't like tea-cake.

JACK  Good heavens! I suppose a man may eat his own muffins in his own garden.

ALGERNON  But you have just said it was perfectly heartless to eat muffins.

JACK  I said it was perfectly heartless of you, under the circumstances. That is a very different thing.

ALGERNON  That may be. But the muffins are the same. *(He seizes the muffin-dish from* JACK.*)*

JACK  Algy, I wish to goodness you would go.

ALGERNON  You can't possibly ask me to go without having some dinner. It's absurd. I never go without my dinner. No one ever does, except vegetarians and people like that. Besides I have just made arrangements with Dr. Chasuble to be christened at a quarter to six under the name of Ernest.

JACK  My dear fellow, the sooner you give up that nonsense the better. I made arrangements this morning with Dr. Chasuble to be christened myself at 5:30, and I naturally will take the name of Ernest. Gwendolen would wish it. We can't both be christened Ernest. It's absurd. Besides, I have a perfect right to be christened if I like. There is no evidence at all that I ever have been christened by anybody. I should think it extremely probable I never was, and so does Dr. Chasuble. It is entirely different in your case. You have been christened already.

ALGERNON  Yes, but I have not been christened for years.

JACK  Yes, but you have been christened. That is the important thing.

ALGERNON  Quite so. So I know my constitution can stand it. If you are not quite sure about your ever having been christened, I must say I think it rather dangerous your venturing on it now. It might make you very unwell. You can hardly have forgotten that some one very closely connected with you was very nearly carried off this week in Paris by a severe chill.

JACK  Yes, but you said yourself that a severe chill was not hereditary.

ALGERNON  It usedn't to be, I know—but I daresay it is now. Science is always making wonderful improvements in things.

JACK *(picking up the muffin-dish)*  Oh, that is nonsense; you are always talking nonsense.

ALGERNON  Jack, you are at the muffins again! I wish you wouldn't. There are only two left. *(Takes them.)* I told you I was particularly fond of muffins.

JACK  But I hate tea-cake.

ALGERNON   Why on earth then do you allow tea-cake to be served up for your guests? What ideas you have of hospitality!

JACK   Algernon! I have already told you to go. I don't want you here. Why don't you go?

ALGERNON   I haven't quite finished my tea yet, and there is still one muffin left. (JACK *groans, and sinks into a chair.* ALGERNON *still continues eating.*)

*Curtain*

# Act III

*SCENE   Morning-room at the Manor House.* GWENDOLEN *and* CECILY *are at the window, looking out into the garden.*

GWENDOLEN   The fact that they did not follow us at once into the house, as any one else would have done, seems to me to show that they have some sense of shame left.

CECILY   They have been eating muffins. That looks like repentance.

GWENDOLEN *(after a pause)*   They don't seem to notice us at all. Couldn't you cough?

GWENDOLEN   They're looking at us. What effrontery!

CECILY   They're approaching. That's very forward of them.

GWENDOLEN   Let us preserve a dignified silence.

CECILY   Certainly. It's the only thing to do now.

*Enter* JACK, *followed by* ALGERNON. *They whistle some dreadful popular air from a British opera.*

GWENDOLEN   This dignified silence seems to produce an unpleasant effect.

CECILY   A most distasteful one.

GWENDOLEN   But we will not be the first to speak.

CECILY   Certainly not.

GWENDOLEN   Mr. Worthing, I have something very particular to ask you. Much depends on your reply.

CECILY   Gwendolen, your common sense is invaluable. Mr. Moncrieff, kindly answer me the following question. Why did you pretend to be my guardian's brother?

ALGERNON   In order that I might have an opportunity of meeting you.

CECILY *(to* GWENDOLEN*)*   That certainly seems a satisfactory explanation, does it not?

GWENDOLEN   Yes, dear, if you can believe him.

CECILY   I don't. But that does not affect the wonderful beauty of his answer.

GWENDOLEN   True. In matters of grave importance, style, not sincerity, is the vital thing. Mr. Worthing, what explanation can you offer to me for pretending to have a brother? Was it in order that you might have an opportunity of coming up to town to see me as often as possible?

JACK   Can you doubt it, Miss Fairfax?

GWENDOLEN   I have the gravest doubts upon the subject. But I intend to crush them. This is not the moment for German skepticism.[21] (*Moving to* CECILY.) Their explanations appear to be quite satisfactory, especially Mr. Worthing's. That seems to me to have the stamp of truth upon it.

CECILY  I am more than content with what Mr. Moncrieff said. His voice alone inspires one with absolute credulity.

GWENDOLEN  Then you think we should forgive them?

CECILY  Yes. I mean no.

GWENDOLEN  True! I had forgotten. There are principles at stake that one cannot surrender. Which of us should tell them? The task is not a pleasant one.

CECILY  Could we not both speak at the same time?

GWENDOLEN  An excellent idea! I nearly always speak at the same time as other people. Will you take the time from me?

CECILY  Certainly. (GWENDOLEN *beats time with up-lifted finger.*)

GWENDOLEN and CECILY (*speaking together*)  Your Christian names are still an insuperable barrier. That is all!

JACK and ALGERNON (*speaking together*)  Our Christian names! Is that all? But we are going to be christened this afternoon.

GWENDOLEN (*to* JACK)  For my sake you are prepared to do this terrible thing?

JACK  I am.

CECILY (*to* ALGERNON)  To please me you are ready to face this fearful ordeal?

ALGERNON  I am!

GWENDOLEN  How absurd to talk of the equality of the sexes! Where questions of self-sacrifice are concerned, men are infinitely beyond us.

JACK  We are. (*Clasps hands with* ALGERNON.)

CECILY  They have moments of physical courage of which we women know absolutely nothing.

GWENDOLEN (*to* JACK)  Darling!

ALGERNON (*to* CECILY)  Darling! (*They fall into each other's arms.*)

*Enter* MERRIMAN. *When he enters he coughs loudly, seeing the situation.*

MERRIMAN  Ahem! Ahem! Lady Bracknell!

JACK  Good heavens!

*Enter* LADY BRACKNELL. *The couples separate in alarm. Exit* MERRIMAN.

LADY BRACKNELL  Gwendolen! What does this mean?

GWENDOLEN  Merely that I am engaged to be married to Mr. Worthing, Mamma.

LADY BRACKNELL  Come here. Sit down. Sit down immediately. Hesitation of any kind is a sign of mental decay in the young, of physical weakness in the old. (*Turns to* JACK.) Apprised, sir, of my daughter's sudden flight by her trusty maid, whose confidence I purchased by means of a small coin, I followed her at once by a luggage train. Her unhappy father is, I am glad to say, under the impression that she is attending a more than usually lengthy lecture by the University Extension Scheme on the Influence of a Permanent Income on Thought. I do not propose to undeceive him. Indeed I have never undeceived him on any question. I would consider it wrong. But of course you will clearly

[21] The particular German skeptics referred to here are nineteenth-century biblical scholars.

understand that all communication between yourself and my daughter must cease immediately from this moment. On this point, as indeed on all points, I am firm.

JACK   I am engaged to be married to Gwendolen, Lady Bracknell!

LADY BRACKNELL   You are nothing of the kind, sir. And now, as regards Algernon! . . . Algernon!

ALGERNON   Yes, Aunt Augusta.

LADY BRACKNELL   May I ask if it is in this house that your invalid friend Mr. Bunbury resides?

ALGERNON (*stammering*)   Oh, no! Bunbury doesn't live here. Bunbury is somewhere else at present. In fact, Bunbury is dead.

LADY BRACKNELL   Dead! When did Mr. Bunbury die? His death must have been extremely sudden.

ALGERNON (*airily*)   Oh, I killed Bunbury this afternoon. I mean poor Bunbury died this afternoon.

LADY BRACKNELL   What did he die of?

ALGERNON   Bunbury? Oh, he was quite exploded.

LADY BRACKNELL   Exploded! Was he the victim of a revolutionary outrage? I was not aware that Mr. Bunbury was interested in social legislation. If so, he is well punished for his morbidity.

ALGERNON   My dear Aunt Augusta, I mean he was found out! The doctors found out that Bunbury could not live, that is what I mean—so Bunbury died.

LADY BRACKNELL   He seems to have had great confidence in the opinion of his physicians. I am glad, however, that he made up his mind at the last to some definite course of action, and acted under proper medical advice. And now that we have finally got rid of this Mr. Bunbury, may I ask, Mr. Worthing, who is that young person whose hand my nephew Algernon is now holding in what seems to me a peculiarly unnecessary manner?

JACK   That lady is Miss Cecily Cardew, my ward. (LADY BRACKNELL *bows coldly to* CECILY.)

ALGERNON   I am engaged to be married to Cecily, Aunt Augusta.

LADY BRACKNELL   I beg your pardon?

CECILY   Mr. Moncrieff and I are engaged to be married, Lady Bracknell.

LADY BRACKNELL (*with a shiver, crossing to the sofa and sitting down*)   I do not know whether there is anything peculiarly exciting in the air of this particular part of Hertfordshire, but the number of engagements that go on seems to me considerably above the proper average that statistics have laid down for our guidance. I think some preliminary enquiry on my part would not be out of place. Mr. Worthing, is Miss Cardew at all connected with any of the larger railway stations in London? I merely desire information. Until yesterday I had no idea that there were any families or persons whose origin was a Terminus. (JACK *looks perfectly furious, but restrains himself.*)

JACK (*in a clear, cold voice*)   Miss Cardew is the granddaughter of the late Mr. Thomas Cardew of 149, Belgrave Square, S.W.; Gervase Park, Dorking, Surrey; and the Sporran, Fifeshire, N.B.[22]

---

[22] North Britain; that is, Scotland. S.W. stands for South West (London). Surrey is the county just south of London.

LADY BRACKNELL   That sounds not unsatisfactory. Three addresses always inspire confidence, even in tradesmen. But what proof have I of their authenticity?

JACK   I have carefully preserved the Court Guide[23] of the period. They are open to your inspection, Lady Bracknell.

LADY BRACKNELL *(grimly)*   I have known strange errors in that publication.

JACK   Miss Cardew's family solicitors are Messrs. Markby, Markby, and Markby.

LADY BRACKNELL   Markby, Markby, and Markby? A firm of the very highest position in their profession. Indeed I am told that one of the Mr. Markbys is occasionally to be seen at dinner parties. So far I am satisfied.

JACK *(very irritably)*   How extremely kind of you, Lady Bracknell! I have also in my possession, you will be pleased to hear, certificates of Miss Cardew's birth, baptism, whooping cough, registration, vaccination, confirmation, and the measles; both the German and the English variety.

LADY BRACKNELL   Ah! A life crowded with incident, I see; though perhaps somewhat too exciting for a young girl. I am not myself in favor of premature experiences. *(Rises, looks at her watch.)* Gwendolen! the time approaches for our departure. We have not a moment to lose. As a matter of form, Mr. Worthing, I had better ask you if Miss Cardew has any little fortune?

JACK   Oh, about a hundred and thirty thousand pounds in the Funds.[24] That is all. Good-by, Lady Bracknell. So pleased to have seen you.

LADY BRACKNELL *(sitting down again)*   A moment, Mr. Worthing. A hundred and thirty thousand pounds! And in the Funds! Miss Cardew seems to me a most attractive young lady, now that I look at her. Few girls of the present day have any really solid qualities, any of the qualities that last, and improve with time. We live, I regret to say, in an age of surfaces. *(To* CECILY.*)* Come over here, dear. *(*CECILY *goes across.)* Pretty child! your dress is sadly simple, and your hair seems almost as Nature might have left it. But we can soon alter all that. A thoroughly experienced French maid produces a really marvelous result in a very brief space of time. I remember recommending one to young Lady Lancing, and after three months her own husband did not know her.

JACK *(aside)*   And after six months nobody knew her.

LADY BRACKNELL *(Glares at* JACK *for a few moments. Then bends, with a practiced smile, to* CECILY.*)*   Kindly turn round, sweet child. *(*CECILY *turns completely round.)* No, the side view is what I want. *(*CECILY *presents her profile.)* Yes, quite as I expected. There are distinct social possibilities in your profile. The two weak points in our age are its want of principle and its want of profile. The chin a little higher, dear. Style largely depends on the way the chin is worn. They are worn very high, just at present. Algernon!

ALGERNON   Yes, Aunt Augusta!

LADY BRACKNELL   There are distinct social possibilities in Miss Cardew's profile.

ALGERNON   Cecily is the sweetest, dearest, prettiest girl in the whole world. And I don't care twopence about social possibilities.

LADY BRACKNELL   Never speak disrespectfully of society, Algernon. Only people who can't get into it do that. *(to* CECILY*)* Dear child, of course you know that Algernon has nothing but his debts to depend upon. But I do not approve

---

[23] A list of those who have been received at court; in effect, a social register.

[24] Government bonds.

of mercenary marriages. When I married Lord Bracknell I had no fortune of any kind. But I never dreamed for a moment of allowing that to stand in my way. Well, I suppose I must give my consent.

ALGERNON  Thank you, Aunt Augusta.

LADY BRACKNELL  Cecily, you may kiss me!

CECILY (*Kisses her.*)  Thank you, Lady Bracknell.

LADY BRACKNELL  You may also address me as Aunt Augusta for the future.

CECILY  Thank you, Aunt Augusta.

LADY BRACKNELL  The marriage, I think, had better take place quite soon.

ALGERNON  Thank you, Aunt Augusta.

CECILY  Thank you, Aunt Augusta.

LADY BRACKNELL  To speak frankly, I am not in favor of long engagements. They give people the opportunity of finding out each other's character before marriage, which I think is never advisable.

JACK  I beg your pardon for interrupting you, Lady Bracknell, but this engagement is quite out of the question. I am Miss Cardew's guardian, and she cannot marry without my consent until she comes of age. That consent I absolutely decline to give.

LADY BRACKNELL  Upon what grounds, may I ask? Algernon is an extremely, I may almost say an ostentatiously, eligible young man. He has nothing, but he looks everything. What more can one desire?

JACK  It pains me very much to have to speak frankly to you, Lady Bracknell, about your nephew, but the fact is that I do not approve at all of his moral character. I suspect him of being untruthful. (ALGERNON *and* CECILY *look at him in indignant amazement.*)

LADY BRACKNELL  Untruthful! My nephew Algernon? Impossible! He is an Oxonian.[25]

JACK  I fear there can be no possible doubt about the matter. This afternoon, during my temporary absence in London on an important question of romance, he obtained admission to my house by means of the false pretense of being my brother. Under an assumed name he drank, I've just been informed by my butler, an entire pint bottle of my Perrier-Jouet, Brut, '89;[26] a wine I was specially reserving for myself. Continuing his disgraceful deception, he succeeded in the course of the afternoon in alienating the affections of my only ward. He subsequently stayed to tea, and devoured every single muffin. And what makes his conduct all the more heartless is, that he was perfectly well aware from the first that I have no brother, that I never had a brother, and that I don't intend to have a brother, not even of any kind. I distinctly told him so myself yesterday afternoon.

LADY BRACKNELL  Ahem! Mr. Worthing, after careful consideration I have decided entirely to overlook my nephew's conduct to you.

JACK  That is very generous of you, Lady Bracknell. My own decision, however, is unalterable. I decline to give my consent.

[25] A graduate of Oxford University.

[26] A particularly excellent champagne.

LADY BRACKNELL *(to* CECILY*)*   Come here, sweet child. *(*CECILY *goes over.)* How old are you, dear?

CECILY   Well, I am really only eighteen, but I always admit to twenty when I go to evening parties.

LADY BRACKNELL   You are perfectly right in making some slight alteration. Indeed, no woman should ever be quite accurate about her age. It looks so calculating. . . . *(in meditative manner)* Eighteen, but admitting to twenty at evening parties. Well, it will not be very long before you are of age and free from the restraints of tutelage. So I don't think your guardian's consent is, after all, a matter of any importance.

JACK   Pray excuse me, Lady Bracknell, for interrupting you again, but it is only fair to tell you that according to the terms of her grandfather's will Miss Cardew does not come legally of age till she is thirty-five.

LADY BRACKNELL   That does not seem to me to be a grave objection. Thirty-five is a very attractive age. London society is full of women of the very highest birth who have, of their own free choice, remained thirty-five for years. Lady Dumbleton is an instance in point. To my own knowledge she has been thirty-five ever since she arrived at the age of forty, which was many years ago now. I see no reason why our dear Cecily should not be even still more attractive at the age you mention than she is at present. There will be a large accumulation of property.

CECILY   Algy, could you wait for me till I was thirty-five?

ALGERNON   Of course I could, Cecily. You know I could.

CECILY   Yes, I felt it instinctively, but I couldn't wait all that time. I hate waiting even five minutes for anybody. It always makes me rather cross. I am not punctual myself, I know, but I do like punctuality in others, and waiting, even to be married, is quite out of the question.

ALGERNON   Then what is to be done, Cecily?

CECILY   I don't know, Mr. Moncrieff.

LADY BRACKNELL   My dear Mr. Worthing, as Miss Cardew states positively that she cannot wait till she is thirty-five—a remark which I am bound to say seems to me to show a somewhat impatient nature—I would beg of you to reconsider your decision.

JACK   But, my dear Lady Bracknell, the matter is entirely in your own hands. The moment you consent to my marriage with Gwendolen, I will most gladly allow your nephew to form an alliance with my ward.

LADY BRACKNELL   *(rising and drawing herself up)*   You must be quite aware that what you propose is out of the question.

JACK   Then a passionate celibacy is all that any of us can look forward to.

LADY BRACKNELL   That is not the destiny I propose for Gwendolen. Algernon, of course, can choose for himself. *(Pulls out her watch.)* Come, dear *(*GWENDOLEN *rises),* we have already missed, five, if not six, trains. To miss any more might expose us to comment on the platform.

*Enter* DR. CHASUBLE.

CHASUBLE   Everything is quite ready for the christenings.

LADY BRACKNELL   The christenings, sir! Is not that somewhat premature?

CHASUBLE *(looking rather puzzled, and pointing to* JACK *and* ALGERNON*)*   Both these gentlemen have expressed a desire for immediate baptism.

LADY BRACKNELL   At their age? The idea is grotesque and irreligious! Algernon, I forbid you to be baptized. I will not hear of such excesses. Lord Bracknell would be highly displeased if he learned that that was the way in which you wasted your time and money.

CHASUBLE   Am I to understand then that there are to be no christenings at all this afternoon?

JACK   I don't think that, as things are now, it would be of much practical value to either of us, Dr. Chasuble.

CHASUBLE   I am grieved to hear such sentiments from you, Mr. Worthing. They savor of the heretical views of the Anabaptists,[27] views that I have completely refuted in four of my unpublished sermons. However, as your present mood seems to be one peculiarly secular, I will return to the church at once. Indeed, I have just been informed by the pew-opener[28] that for the last hour and a half Miss Prism has been waiting for me in the vestry.

LADY BRACKNELL *(starting)*   Miss Prism! Did I hear you mention a Miss Prism?

CHASUBLE   Yes, Lady Bracknell. I am on my way to join her.

LADY BRACKNELL   Pray allow me to detain you for a moment. This matter may prove to be one of vital importance to Lord Bracknell and myself. Is this Miss Prism a female of repellent aspect, remotely connected with education?

CHASUBLE *(somewhat indignantly)*   She is the most cultivated of ladies, and the very picture of respectability.

LADY BRACKNELL   It is obviously the same person. May I ask what position she holds in your household?

CHASUBLE *(severely)*   I am a celibate, madam.

JACK *(interposing)*   Miss Prism, Lady Bracknell, has been for the last three years Miss Cardew's esteemed governess and valued companion.

LADY BRACKNELL   In spite of what I hear of her, I must see her at once. Let her be sent for.

CHASUBLE *(looking off)*   She approaches; she is nigh.

*Enter* MISS PRISM *hurriedly.*

MISS PRISM   I was told you expected me in the vestry, dear Canon. I have been waiting for you there for an hour and three-quarters. *(Catches sight of* LADY BRACKNELL, *who has fixed her with a stony glare.* MISS PRISM *grows pale and quails. She looks anxiously round as if desirous to escape.)*

LADY BRACKNELL *(in a severe, judicial voice)*   Prism! *(*MISS PRISM *bows her head in shame.)* Come here, Prism! *(*MISS PRISM *approaches in a humble manner.)* Prism! Where is that baby? *(General consternation. The Canon starts back in horror.* ALGERNON *and* JACK *pretend to be anxious to shield* CECILY *and* GWENDOLEN *from hearing the details of a terrible public scandal.)* Twenty-eight years ago, Prism, you left Lord Bracknell's house, Number 104, Upper Grosvenor Street, in

[27] A seventeenth century Protestant sect which held that baptism was useless unless the person baptized was a believer.

[28] One who ushers worshipers to their pews and opens the pew door for them.

charge of a perambulator that contained a baby, of the male sex. You never returned. A few weeks later, through the elaborate investigations of the Metropolitan police, the perambulator was discovered at midnight, standing by itself in a remote corner of Bayswater.[29] It contained the manuscript of a three-volume novel of more than usually revolting sentimentality. (MISS PRISM *starts in involuntary indignation.*) But the baby was not there! (*Every one looks at* MISS PRISM.) Prism, where is that baby? (*a pause*)

MISS PRISM   Lady Bracknell, I admit with shame that I do not know. I only wish I did. The plain facts of the case are these. On the morning of the day you mention, a day that is forever branded on my memory, I prepared as usual to take the baby out in its perambulator. I had also with me a somewhat old but capacious hand-bag in which I had intended to place the manuscript of a work of fiction that I had written during my few unoccupied hours. In a moment of mental abstraction, for which I never can forgive myself, I deposited the manuscript in the bassinet, and placed the baby in the hand-bag.

JACK (*who has been listening attentively*)   But where did you deposit the hand-bag?

MISS PRISM   Do not ask me, Mr. Worthing.

JACK   Miss Prism, this is a matter of no small importance to me. I insist on knowing where you deposited the hand-bag that contained that infant.

MISS PRISM   I left it in the cloak-room of one of the larger railway stations in London.

JACK   What railway station?

MISS PRISM (*quite crushed*)   Victoria. The Brighton line. (*Sinks into a chair.*)

JACK   I must retire to my room for a moment. Gwendolen, wait here for me.

GWENDOLEN   If you are not too long, I will wait here for you all my life.

(*Exit* JACK *in great excitement.*)

CHASUBLE   What do you think this means, Lady Bracknell?

LADY BRACKNELL   I dare not even suspect, Dr. Chasuble. I need hardly tell you that in families of high position strange coincidences are not supposed to occur. They are hardly considered the thing. (*Noises heard overhead as if some one was throwing trunks about. Everybody looks up.*)

CECILY   Uncle Jack seems strangely agitated.

CHASUBLE   Your guardian has a very emotional nature.

LADY BRACKNELL   This noise is extremely unpleasant. It sounds as if he was having an argument. I dislike arguments of any kind. They are always vulgar, and often convincing.

CHASUBLE (*looking up*)   It has stopped now. (*The noise is redoubled.*)

LADY BRACKNELL   I wish he would arrive at some conclusion.

GWENDOLEN   This suspense is terrible. I hope it will last.

*Enter* JACK *with a hand-bag of black leather in his hand.*

JACK (*rushing over to* MISS PRISM)   Is this the hand-bag, Miss Prism? Examine it carefully before you speak. The happiness of more than one life depends on your answer.

[29] An unfashionable residential district in west London.

MISS PRISM (*calmly*)  It seems to be mine. Yes, here is the injury it received through the upsetting of a Gower Street omnibus in younger and happier days. Here is the stain on the lining caused by the explosion of a temperance beverage, an incident that occurred at Leamington. And here, on the lock, are my initials. I had forgotten that in an extravagant mood I had had them placed there. The bag is undoubtedly mine. I am delighted to have it so unexpectedly restored to me. It has been a great inconvenience being without it all these years.

JACK (*in a pathetic voice*)  Miss Prism, more is restored to you than this hand-bag. I was the baby you placed in it.

MISS PRISM (*amazed*)  You?

JACK (*embracing her*)  Yes . . . mother!

MISS PRISM (*recoiling in indignant astonishment*)  Mr. Worthing! I am unmarried!

JACK  Unmarried! I do not deny that is a serious blow. But after all, who has the right to cast a stone against one who has suffered? Cannot repentance wipe out an act of folly? Why should there be one law for men and another for women? Mother, I forgive you. (*Tries to embrace her again.*)

MISS PRISM (*still more indignant*)  Mr. Worthing, there is some error. (*Pointing to* LADY BRACKNELL.) There is the lady who can tell you who you really are.

JACK (*after a pause*)  Lady Bracknell, I hate to seem inquisitive, but would you kindly inform me who I am?

LADY BRACKNELL  I am afraid that the news I have to give you will not altogether please you. You are the son of my poor sister, Mrs. Moncrieff, and consequently Algernon's elder brother.

JACK  Algy's elder brother! Then I have a brother after all. I knew I had a brother! I always said I had a brother! Cecily,—how could you have ever doubted that I had a brother? (*Seizes hold of* ALGERNON.) Dr. Chasuble, my unfortunate brother. Miss Prism, my unfortunate brother. Gwendolen, my unfortunate brother. Algy, you young scoundrel, you will have to treat me with more respect in the future. You have never behaved to me like a brother in all your life.

ALGERNON  Well, not till to-day, old boy, I admit. I did my best, however, though I was out of practice. (*Shakes hands.*)

GWENDOLEN (*to* JACK)  My own! But what own are you? What is your Christian name, now that you have become some one else?

JACK  Good heavens! . . . I had quite forgotten that point. Your decision on the subject of my name is irrevocable, I suppose?

GWENDOLEN  I never change, except in my affections.

CECILY  What a noble nature you have, Gwendolen!

JACK  Then the question had better be cleared up at once. Aunt Augusta, a moment. At the time when Miss Prism left me in the hand-bag, had I been christened already?

LADY BRACKNELL  Every luxury that money could buy, including christening, had been lavished on you by your fond and doting parents.

JACK  Then I was christened! That is settled. Now, what name was I given? Let me know the worst.

LADY BRACKNELL  Being the eldest son you were naturally christened after your father.

JACK (*irritably*)   Yes, but what was my father's Christian name?

LADY BRACKNELL (*meditatively*)   I cannot at the present moment recall what the General's Christian name was. But I have no doubt he had one. He was eccentric, I admit. But only in later years. And that was the result of the Indian climate, and marriage, and indigestion, and other things of that kind.

JACK   Algy! Can't you recollect what our father's Christian name was?

ALGERNON   My dear boy, we were never even on speaking terms. He died before I was a year old.

JACK   His name would appear in the Army Lists of the period, I suppose, Aunt Augusta?

LADY BRACKNELL   The General was essentially a man of peace, except in his domestic life. But I have no doubt his name would appear in any military directory.

JACK   The Army Lists of the last forty years are here. These delightful records should have been my constant study. (*Rushes to bookcase and tears the books out.*) M. Generals . . . Mallam, Maxbohm, Magley, what ghastly names they have—Markby, Migsby, Mobbs, Moncrieff! Lieutenant 1840, Captain, Lieutenant-Colonel, Colonel, General 1869, Christian names, Ernest John. (*Puts book very quietly down and speaks quite calmly.*) I always told you, Gwendolen, my name was Ernest, didn't I? Well, it is Ernest after all. I mean it naturally is Ernest.

LADY BRACKNELL   Yes, I remember that the General was called Ernest. I knew I had some particular reason for disliking the name.

GWENDOLEN   Ernest! My own Ernest! I felt from the first that you could have no other name!

JACK   Gwendolen, it is a terrible thing for a man to find out suddenly that all his life he has been speaking nothing but the truth. Can you forgive me?

GWENDOLEN   I can. For I feel that you are sure to change.

JACK   My own one!

CHASUBLE (*to* MISS PRISM)   Laetitia! (*Embraces her.*)

MISS PRISM (*enthusiastically*)   Frederick! At last!

ALGERNON   Cecily! (*Embraces her.*) At last!

JACK   Gwendolen! (*Embraces her.*) At last!

LADY BRACKNELL   My nephew, you seem to be displaying signs of triviality.

JACK   On the contrary, Aunt Augusta, I've now realized for the first time in my life the vital Importance of Being Earnest.

*Tableau*

*Curtain*

## FOR DISCUSSION

1. This play comes under the heading of a comedy of manners—that is, a comedy that mocks or satirizes the conventions, behavior, or manners of a segment of a particular society. What society is Wilde satirizing? What specific segment of this society is he exposing?

2. What seems to be the author's tone? Is he angry or bitter? Does he have a particular ax to grind? What is his attitude toward the major characters in the play?
3. Do the characters in the play represent types or plausible personalities?
4. Early in the play Algernon says, "As far as the piano is concerned, sentiment is my forte." How is this statement a pun? Can you point out other clever puns in the play?
5. Why does Jack Worthing use the name Ernest when he comes to London? Why, in fact, does he live in the country at all since he likes so much to come to London? What does this situation suggest to you about the moral standards of Victorian society?
6. What is "Bunburying"? How does the term come up in the play? Where do you think Algernon got this idea of Bunburying? Why do you think he chose the name Bunbury?
7. Jack frequently tells Algernon that Algernon is talking nonsense. Which of the two, in fact, talks the greatest nonsense?
8. Who has the more romantic view of life generally, Jack or Algernon? Which is the older of the two men?
9. Algernon says of Lady Harbury, whose husband has died, "I hear her hair has turned quite gold from grief." What does this mean?
10. Why does Gwendolen desire Jack to show his interest and affection for her in public?
11. Oscar Wilde was a master of the *epigram*, a brief and witty observation ending with a twist. For example, at one point Algernon says to Jack Worthing, "All women become like their mothers. That is their tragedy. No man does. That is his." Point out a few additional examples of epigrams.
12. What are Lady Bracknell's ideas about the procedure by which a young lady becomes engaged and married? Why does she object to Jack Worthing's proposal to Gwendolen? What does she suggest to Jack that he might do to overcome her objections?
13. Why does Lady Bracknell want to know how many bedrooms Jack's country house has?
14. Exactly how did Jack come by his last name—Worthing?
15. What is Jack Worthing's country address? How does Algernon learn it?
16. Why does Cecily prefer her diary to her studies? What does she write in her diary? What does her scribbling suggest about her character?
17. What is the relationship between Canon Chasuble and Miss Prism?
18. Canon Chasuble makes an allusion to "Egeria and her pupil." Is the allusion appropriate to the relationship between Miss Prism and Gwendolen or is it more appropriate to some other relationship in the play? What does this allusion suggest about the Canon's reading habits?
19. With Canon Chasuble in mind, what would you say is Wilde's view of the church's role in the social and spiritual lives of the main characters?
20. The "argument" scene between Gwendolen and Cecily is one of the play's most famous. Which of the two women would you say "wins" the scene?
21. At what specific point does the climax or turning point of the play occur? Detail the events of the climactic scene.
22. All of Act III may be viewed as the play's resolution or denouement. What important "twists" make it possible for everything to turn out happily?
23. Thematically, does the play really preach the importance of being earnest? If not, what does it preach?

# A Tale of Mystery

THOMAS HOLCROFT

## Cast of Characters

| | |
|---|---|
| BONAMO | PIERO |
| ROMALDI | EXEMPT |
| FRANCISCO | SELINA |
| STEPHANO | FIAMETTA |
| MONTANO | GARDENERS, PEASANTS, MUSICIANS, DANCERS, ARCHERS |
| MICHELLI | |
| MALVOGLIO | |

## Act I

*A hall in the house of Bonamo, with two side doors, and folding doors in the back scene: a table, pen, ink, and paper, chairs, etc. Music to express discontent and alarm. Enter Selina and Fiametta.*

SELINA  You seem hurried, Fiametta.

FIAMETTA  Hurried, truly! Yes, yes, and you'll be hurried too.

SELINA  I?

FIAMETTA  Fine news!

SELINA  Of what kind?

FIAMETTA  A very bad kind. The Count Romaldi—

SELINA *(alarmed)*  What of him?

FIAMETTA  Is coming.

SELINA  When?

FIAMETTA  This evening.

SELINA  Heavens! What can he want?

FIAMETTA  Want? He wants mischief. We all know he wants you to marry his son, because you're a rich heiress.

SELINA  Surely, my uncle will never consent?

FIAMETTA  Your uncle and all Savoy fear him.

BONAMO *(calling without)*  Fiametta!

FIAMETTA  I am here, sir.

BONAMO  But I want you here.

FIAMETTA  Lord, sir, I am busy.

SELINA  Go, run to my uncle.

FIAMETTA  It's a shame that he should not think of marrying you to his own son, when he knows how dearly you love each other.

SELINA  It is the excellence of my dear uncle's heart, that disdains the appearance of self-interest.

FIAMETTA  So, rather than be blamed himself, he'll make you and I and everybody miserable! But I'll talk to him.

BONAMO *(without)*   Fiametta, I say!

FIAMETTA   Coming! *(going)* He shall hear of it. I'm in the proper cue. He knows I'm right, and I'll not spare him.                              *Exit, talking.*

*Hunting music. Enter Stephano, with his fowling-piece, net, and game.*

SELINA   Why are you so late, Stephano? I had a thousand alarms.

STEPHANO   Forgive me, dear Selina. The pursuit of game led me too far among the mountains.

SELINA   Do you know—?

STEPHANO   What?

SELINA   I almost dread to tell you. Count Romaldi is coming.

STEPHANO   Romaldi!

SELINA   I shudder, when I recollect the selfishness of his views, and the violence of his character.

STEPHANO   Add, the wickedness of his heart.

*Music, to express chattering contention. Enter Bonamo and Fiametta.*

FIAMETTA   I tell you again, sir, it is uncharitable, it is cruel, it is hard-hearted in you to give any such orders.

BONAMO   And I tell you they shall be obeyed. Have not I a right to do as I please in my own house?

FIAMETTA   No, sir, you have no right to do wrong anywhere.

STEPHANO   What is the dispute, sir?

FIAMETTA   He has ordered me to turn the poor Francisco out of doors, because, forsooth, the house is not large enough to hold this Count Romaldi.

SELINA   Think, my dear uncle, how grateful and kind is his heart.

STEPHANO   And that he is a man of misfortune.

BONAMO   Folly and misfortune are twins: nobody can tell one from the other. He has got footing here, and you seem all determined he shall keep it.

SELINA   I own I am interested in his favor. His manners are so mild!

STEPHANO   His eye so expressive!

SELINA   His behaviour so proper!

FIAMETTA   I'll be bound he is of genteel parentage!

BONAMO   Who told you so?

FIAMETTA   Not he, himself, for certain, because, poor creature, he is dumb. But only observe his sorrowful looks. What it is I don't know, but there is something on his mind so—

BONAMO   You are a fool!

FIAMETTA   Fool or not, I have served you faithfully these three-and-twenty years; so you may turn me out of doors at last, if you please.

BONAMO   I?

FIAMETTA   Yes; for if you turn Francisco out, I'll never enter them again.

BONAMO   You certainly know more concerning this man?

FIAMETTA   Since it must be told, I do.

BONAMO   Then speak.

FIAMETTA   It is quite a tragedy!

BONAMO   Indeed! Let us hear.

FIAMETTA  It is now seven or eight years ago, when, you having sent me to Chamberry, I was coming home. It was almost dark; everything was still; I was winding along the dale, and the rocks were all as it were turning black. Of a sudden, I heard cries! A man was murdering! I shook from head to foot! Presently the cries died away; and I beheld two bloody men, with their daggers in their hands, stealing off under the crags at the foot of the mill. I stood like a stone, for I was frightened out of my wits! So I thought I heard groans; and, *afeared* as I was, I had the sense to think they must come from the poor murdered creature. So I listened, and followed my ears, and presently I saw this very man—

SELINA  Francisco?

FIAMETTA  Weltering in his blood! To be sure I screamed and called loud enough; for what could I do by myself? So presently my cries *was* heard; and honest Michelli, the miller, with his man, came running.

BONAMO  I now remember the tale. The poor man recovered, and everybody praised Michelli.

FIAMETTA  So they ought; he is an honest good soul! What then, sir, can you suppose I thought, when about a week ago, I again saw Francisco's *apparition* standing before me, making signs that he was famished with hunger and thirst? I knew him at once and he soon bethought himself of me. If you had *seen* his clasped hands, and his thankful looks, and his dumb notes, and his signs of joy at having found me!—While I have a morsel, he shall never want. I'll hire him a cottage; I'll wait upon him; I'll work for him; so turn him out of doors, if you have the heart.

STEPHANO  Fiametta, you wrong my father.

BONAMO  I'll hear his story from himself.

FIAMETTA  He can't speak.

BONAMO  But he can write.

FIAMETTA  I'll warrant him. I'm sure he's a gentleman.

BONAMO  Bring him here: if he prove himself an honest man, I am his friend.

FIAMETTA  I know that, or you should be no master of mine.          *Exit.*

STEPHANO  His kind attentions to Selina are singular.

SELINA  Every morning I find him waiting for me with fresh gathered flowers, which he offers with such modest yet affectionate looks!

*Fiametta returns with Francisco, the latter poor in appearance, but clean, with a reserved, placid, and dignified air.*

BONAMO  Come near, friend. You understand his gestures, Fiametta; so stay where you are.

FIAMETTA  I intend it.

BONAMO  *(to himself)* He has a manly form! a benevolent eye! *(aloud)* Sit down, sir. Leave us, my children. *(Francisco suddenly rises, as Stephano and Selina offer to go, brings them back, and intreats they may remain.)* Since he desires it, stay.— There is pen, ink, and paper: when you cannot give answer by signs, write, but be strict to the truth. *(Francisco, with dignity, points to heaven and his heart.)* Who are you? *(Francisco writes; and Stephano, standing behind him, takes up the paper and reads the answers.)*

FRANCISCO  "A noble Roman!"

BONAMO  Your family?—

FRANCISCO  (*Gives a sudden sign of Forbear! and writes.*)   "Must not be known."

BONAMO  Why?

FRANCISCO  "It is disgraced."

BONAMO  By you? (*Francisco gesticulates.*)

FIAMETTA   (*interpreting*) No, no, no!

BONAMO  Who made you dumb?

FRANCISCO  "The Algerines."[1]

BONAMO  How came you in their power?

FRANCISCO  "By treachery."

BONAMO  Do you know the traitors? (*Francisco gesticulates.*)

FIAMETTA (*eagerly*)   He does! he does!

BONAMO  Who are they?

FRANCISCO  "The same who stabbed me among the rocks." (*a general expression of horror*)

BONAMO  Name them.

FRANCISCO  (*Gesticulates violently, denoting painful recollection; then writes.*) "Never!"

BONAMO  Are they known by me?

FIAMETTA (*interpreting*)   They are! They are!

BONAMO  Are they rich?

FRANCISCO  "Rich and powerful."

BONAMO  Astonishing! Your refusal to name them gives strange suspicions. I must know more; tell me all, or quit my house.

*Music to express pain and disorder. Enter Piero.*

PIERO  Count Romaldi, sir. (*Francisco starts up, struck with alarm.*)

STEPHANO  So soon!

BONAMO  Show him up.

PIERO  He's here.

*Similar music. Romaldi suddenly enters, as Francisco is attempting to pass the door: they start back at the sight of each other. Romaldi recovers himself; and Francisco, in an agony of mind, leaves the room.*

BONAMO  What is all this!—Where is he gone?—Call him back, Fiametta.

*Exeunt Fiametta and Stephano, both regarding Romaldi with dislike.*

ROMALDI (*with forced ease*)   At length, my good friend, I am here. I have long promised myself the pleasure of seeing you. Your hand. How hearty you look! And your lovely niece! Her father's picture!

BONAMO  Rather her mother's.

ROMALDI  My son will adore her. In two days I expect him here. I have serious business to communicate.

---

[1] Pirates.

SELINA *(to her uncle)*  Permit me to retire, sir.

BONAMO *(tenderly)*  Go, my child; go.

SELINA *(aside)*  Grant, oh merciful Heaven, I may not fall a sacrifice to avarice.                                                                          *Exit.*

BONAMO  And now your pleasure, Count?

ROMALDI  Nay, I imagine, you can guess my errand. You know my friendship for my son, who, let me tell you, is your great admirer. The care you have bestowed upon your niece, her education, mind and manners, and the faithful guardian you have been, both of her wealth and person, well deserve praise.

BONAMO  If I have done my duty, I am greatly fortunate.

ROMALDI  She is a lovely young lady, and you are not ignorant of my son's passion; to which your duty towards your niece must make you a friend. I therefore come, with open frankness, to propose their union.

BONAMO  And I, with equal candor, must tell you, I can give no answer.

ROMALDI *(haughtily affecting surprise)*  No answer?

BONAMO  Your rank and wealth make the proposal flattering; but there is a question still more serious.

ROMALDI *(in the same tone)*  What can that be?

BONAMO  One which my niece only can resolve.

ROMALDI  Inexperience like hers should have no opinion.

BONAMO  How, my lord? Drag the bride, by force, to that solemn altar, where, in the face of Heaven, she is to declare her choice is free?

ROMALDI  Mere ceremonies!

BONAMO  Ceremonies! Bethink yourself; lest marriage become a farce, libertinism a thing to laugh at, and adultery itself a finable offence!

ROMALDI  Ay, ay; you are a moralist, a conscientious man. Your son is reported to have designs on Selina.

BONAMO  My lord!

ROMALDI  No anger: I speak as a friend. Her fortune is tempting; but you disdain to be influenced. The wealth and rank of our family—

BONAMO  Surpass mine. True; still my niece, I say, must be consulted.

ROMALDI  Indeed! *(sternly)* Then my alliance, it seems, is refused?

BONAMO  By no means: I have neither the right to refuse nor to accept. If Selina—

*Re-enter Selina with a letter.*

SELINA *(presenting it to Bonamo)*  From the unfortunate Francisco.

ROMALDI  What, that strange fellow I met as I came in?

SELINA *(aside)*  He knows his name!

ROMALDI  I forgot to ask you how he got admittance here?

SELINA *(with marked displeasure)*  I should hope, my lord, there would always be some charitable door open to the unfortunate!

ROMALDI *(with courteous resentment)*  I address your uncle, lovely lady.

BONAMO  When you came in, he was relating his adventures, which have been strange.

ROMALDI *(retaining himself)*  And are you, my friend, simple enough to believe such tales?

SELINA  What tales, my lord?

BONAMO   The proofs are convincing! The mutilations he has suffered; the wounds he received, not a league from hence; the—

ROMALDI *(alarmed)*   Did he name—?

BONAMO   Who? The monsters that gave them?—No; but they are not unknown to him.

ROMALDI   That—that is fortunate.

BONAMO   I was amazed to learn—

SELINA   That they are rich and powerful. But I forget: the story can have no interest for you.

ROMALDI *(eagerly)*   You mistake: I—*(recollecting himself)* my feelings are as keen as yours.

BONAMO   But what has he written? *(Offers to open the letter.)*

ROMALDI   If you will take my advice, you will not read. Doubtless he has more complaints, more tales, more favors to request. Be kind and hospitable; but do not be a dupe.

BONAMO   Of which, I own, there is danger.

ROMALDI *(seizing the letter, which Bonamo carelessly holds)*   Then let me guard you against it.

SELINA *(After continually watching and suspecting Romaldi, snatches the letter back; while he, remarking her suspicions, is confused.)*   This letter, my lord, was given in charge to me; I promised to bring an answer, and I respectfully intreat my uncle will read it.

BONAMO   Well, well. *(Reads.)* "Friend of humanity, should I remain, the peace of your family might be disturbed. I therefore go; but earnestly intreat you will neither think me capable of falsehood nor ingratitude.—Wherever I am, my wishes and my heart will be here.—Farewell." He shall not go.

ROMALDI   Why not? He owns the peace of your family may be disturbed.

BONAMO   Fly, Selina; tell him I require, I request, him to sleep here to-night, that I may speak with him to-morrow.

ROMALDI *(aside)*   That must not be.

SELINA   Thanks, my dear uncle! you have made me happy.          *Exit in haste.*

*Confused music. Enter Piero.*

BONAMO   What now, Piero?

PIERO   Signor Montano is below.

ROMALDI *(alarmed and aside)*   Montano!

BONAMO   I'm very glad of it, for I wanted his advice. *(to Romaldi)* The best of men!

PIERO   Please to come up, sir.

ROMALDI   With your permission, I will retire.

*Enter Montano. Music plays alarmingly, but piano when he enters and while he stays.*

MONTANO   I beg pardon, good sir, but—

*Music loud and discordant at the moment the eye of Montano catches the figure of Romaldi; at which Montano starts with terror and indignation. He then assumes the eye and attitude of menace, which Romaldi returns. The music ceases.*

Can it be possible!

ROMALDI *(returning his threatening looks)*  Sir!

MONTANO  You here!

ROMALDI  Not having the honor of your acquaintance, I know not why my presence should please or displease you.

MONTANO *(after a look of stern contempt at Romaldi, and addressing Bonamo)*  Good night, my friend; I will see you to-morrow.

*Exit suddenly. Hurrying music, but half piano.*

BONAMO *(calling)*  Nay, but signor! Signor Montano! Are the people all mad? Fiametta!

FIAMETTA *(without)*  Sir!

BONAMO  Run, overtake him; and say I must speak with him. *(Music ceases.)* Excuse me for going. *(to Romaldi)*

ROMALDI  Why in such haste? I have heard of this Montano: a credulous person, a relator of strange stories.

BONAMO  Signor Montano credulous! There is not in all Savoy a man of sounder understanding. Good night, my lord; I will send your servant: that door leads to your bedroom. Call for whatever you want; the house is at your command.

*Exit with looks of suspicion. Music of doubt and terror.*

ROMALDI  What am I to think? How act?—The arm of Providence seems raised to strike!—Am I become a coward? Shall I betray, rather than defend myself? I am not yet an idiot.

*Threatening music. Enter the Count's servant, Malvoglio, who observes his master. Music ceases.*

MALVOGLIO  Your lordship seems disturbed.

ROMALDI  Francisco is here.

MALVOGLIO  I saw him.

ROMALDI  And did not your blood freeze?

MALVOGLIO  I was sorry.

ROMALDI  For what?

MALVOGLIO  That my dagger had missed its aim.

ROMALDI  We are in his power.

MALVOGLIO  He is in ours.

ROMALDI  What are your thoughts?

MALVOGLIO  What are yours, my lord?

ROMALDI  Guess them.

MALVOGLIO  Executioners!

ROMALDI  Infamy!

MALVOGLIO  Racks!

ROMALDI  Maledictions!

MALVOGLIO  From all which a blow may yet deliver us.

*Selina, entering and hiding behind the door, opposite to the chamber of Romaldi, overhears them.*

ROMALDI  'Tis a damning crime!

MALVOGLIO  Were it the first.

ROMALDI  Where is he to sleep?

MALVOGLIO  There! *(pointing to the chamber opposite to Romaldi's)*

SELINA *(behind the door)*  They mean Francisco!

ROMALDI  Obstinate fool! Since he will stay—

MALVOGLIO  He must die.

SELINA  The monsters!

ROMALDI  I heard a noise.

MALVOGLIO *(looking towards the folding doors)*  He's coming.

ROMALDI  Let us retire and concert—

MALVOGLIO  Then, at midnight—

ROMALDI  When he sleeps—

MALVOGLIO  He'll wake no more!

*Exeunt to the chamber of the Count.*

*The stage dark: soft music, but expressing first pain and alarm, then the successive feelings of the scene. Fiametta enters, with Francisco and a lamp, which she places on the table. She regards him with compassion, points to his bedroom, then curtsies with kindness and respect, and retires; he returning her kindness. He seats himself as if to write, rises, takes the lamp, looks round with apprehension, goes to the chamber-door of Romaldi, starts away with horror, recovers himself, again places the lamp on the table, and sits down to write. The door of Romaldi opens; Malvoglio half appears, watching Francisco; but, as he turns, again retires. Enter Selina, who gently pulls the sleeve of Francisco: he starts, but seeing her, his countenance expands with pleasure. Music pauses on a half close.*

SELINA *(in a low voice)*  Dare not to sleep! I will be on the watch! Your life is in danger!                                              *Exit. Music continues tremendous.*

*Francisco, greatly agitated, draws a pair of pistols, lays them on the table, and seats himself to consider if he should write more. Romaldi and Malvoglio appear. Music suddenly stops.*

ROMALDI *(to Malvoglio)*  Watch that entrance. *(to Francisco)* Wretched fool! Why are you here?

*Music: terror, confusion, menace, command. Francisco starts up, seizes his pistols, points them towards Romaldi and Malvoglio, and commands the former, by signs, to read the paper that lies on the table. Music ceases.*

ROMALDI *(Reads.)*  "Repent; leave the house. Oblige me not to betray you. Force me not on self-defence." Fool! Do you pretend to command? *(Throws him a purse.)* We are two. Take that, and fly. *(Music. Francisco, after a look of compassionate appeal, spurns it from him, and commands them to go. After which, sudden pause of music.—aside to Malvoglio)* I know him; he will not fire.

*Music. They draw their daggers; he at first avoids them; at length they each seize him by the arm, and are in the attitude of threatening to strike, when the shrieks of Selina, joining the music, which likewise shrieks, suddenly brings Bonamo, Stephano, and Servants, through the folding doors.*

SELINA  Uncle! Stephano! Murder!

*Romaldi and Malvoglio, at hearing the noise behind, quit Francisco, and feign to be standing on self-defence.—Music ceases.*

BONAMO  What mean these cries? What strange proceedings are here?

SELINA  They are horrible.

BONAMO  Why, my lord, are these daggers drawn against a man under my protection?

ROMALDI  Self-defence is a duty. Is not his pistol levelled at my breast?

BONAMO *(to Francisco)*  Can it be? *(Francisco inclines his head.)* Do you thus repay hospitality?

SELINA  Sir, you are deceived: his life was threatened.

ROMALDI *(sternly)*  Madam—

SELINA  I fear you not! I watched, I overheard you!

BONAMO  Is this true?

ROMALDI  No.

SELINA  By the purity of heaven, yes! Behind that door, I heard the whole; Francisco must quit the house, or be murdered.

ROMALDI *(to Bonamo sternly)*  I expect, sir, my word will not be doubted.

BONAMO  My lord, there is one thing of which I cannot doubt: the moment you appeared, terror was spread through my house. Men's minds are troubled at the sight of you: they seem all to avoid you. Good seldom accompanies mystery; I therefore now decidedly reply to your proposal, that my niece cannot be the wife of your son; and must further add, you oblige me to decline the honor of your present visit.

ROMALDI *(with threatening haughtiness)*  Speak the truth, old man, and own you are glad to find a pretext to colour refusal, and gratify ambition. Selina and Stephano; you want her wealth, and mean in that way to make it secure. But beware! Dare to pursue your project, and tremble at the consequences! To-morrow, before ten o'clock, send your written consent; or dread what shall be done.

*Exeunt Romaldi and Malvoglio: appropriate music.*

BONAMO  Dangerous and haughty man! But his threats are vain; my doubts are removed; Selina shall not be the victim of mean precaution, and cowardly fears. I know your wishes, children. Let us retire. *(To his Servants)* Make preparations for rejoicing: early to-morrow, Stephano and Selina shall be affianced. *(music of sudden joy, while they kneel)*

STEPHANO  My kind father!

SELINA  Dearest, best of guardians! *(Music pauses.)*

BONAMO  Francisco shall partake the common happiness.

FIAMETTA *(as they are all retiring)*  Dear, dear! I shan't sleep to-night.

*Exeunt: Bonamo expressing friendship to all, which all return, Francisco with joy equal to that of the lovers. Sweet and cheerful music, gradually dying away.*

*End of the First Act.*

# Act II

## SCENE 1

*A beautiful garden and pleasure grounds, with garlands, festoons, love devices[2] and every preparation for a marriage festival. Joyful music. First and Second Gardeners, Piero and his Companions, all busy.*

PIERO   Come, come; bestir yourselves! The company will soon be here.

FIRST GARDENER   Well; let them come: all is ready.

PIERO   It has a nice look, by my fackins!

FIRST GARDENER   I believe it has! thanks to me.

PIERO   Thanks to *you?*

SECOND GARDENER   And me.

PIERO   And *you?* Here's impudence! I say it is thanks to me.

FIRST and SECOND GARDENERS   You, indeed!

PIERO   Why, surely, you'll not have the face to pretend to deny my incapacity?

FIRST GARDENER   Yours?

SECOND GARDENER   Yours?

PIERO   Mine! mine!

*Enter Stephano.*

STEPHANO   What is the matter, my honest friends?

FIRST GARDENER   Why, here's Mr. Piero pretends to dispute his claim to all that has been done.

SECOND GARDENER   Yes; and says everything is owing to his incapacity.

FIRST GARDENER   Now I maintain the incapacity was all my own. *(To Stephano)* Saving and excepting yours, sir.

SECOND GARDENER   And mine.

FIRST GARDENER   Seeing you gave the first orders.

PIERO   But *wasn't* they given to me, sir? Didn't you say to me, Piero, says you—

STEPHANO   *(interrupting)* Ay, ay; each man has done his part: all is excellent, and I thank you kindly. Are the villagers invited?

PIERO   Invited! They no sooner heard of the wedding than they were half out of their wits! There will be such dancing and sporting! Then the music! Little Nanine, with her hurdy-gurdy; her brother, with the tabor and pipe; the blind fiddler, the lame piper, I and my jew's harp! such a band!

STEPHANO   Bravo! Order everything for the best.

PIERO   But who is to order? Please to tell me that, sir?

STEPHANO   Why, you.

PIERO   There! *(to his companions)* Mind! I am to order! Mark that!

STEPHANO   You shall be major-domo for the day.

PIERO   You hear. I am to be—do—drum-major for the day!

STEPHANO   Selina is coming. To your posts.

[2] Emblems.

*Music. They hurry each to his garland, and conceal themselves by the trees and bushes. Enter Bonamo, Selina, and Fiametta. Music ceases.*

BONAMO *(looking round)*   Vastly well, upon my word!

SELINA *(tenderly)*   I fear, Stephano, you have slept but little?

BONAMO *(gaily)*   Sleep indeed! He had something better to think of. Come, come; we'll breakfast here in the bower. Order it, Fiametta.

FIAMETTA   Directly, sir. *(She goes, and returns with the Servants; aiding them to arrange the breakfast table.)*

BONAMO   How reviving to age is the happiness of the young! And yet—*(Sighs.)*—thou hast long been an orphan, Selina; it has more than doubled thy fortune, which was great at my brother's sudden death. Would thou hadst less wealth, or I more!

SELINA   And why, my dear uncle?

BONAMO   Evil tongues—this Romaldi—

STEPHANO   Forget him.

SELINA   Would that were possible! his menace—before ten o'clock—oh! that the hour were over!

BONAMO   Come, come; we'll not disturb our hearts with fears. To breakfast, and then to the notary. I forgot Francisco; why is he not here?

SELINA   Shall I bring him?

BONAMO   Do you go, Fiametta.

FIAMETTA   Most willingly.

BONAMO   Come, sit down. *(They seat themselves. Sweet music. Piero peeps from behind a shrub. Stephano gives a gentle clap with his hands, and the Peasants all rise from their hiding-places, and suspend their garlands in a picturesque group, over Bonamo, Selina, and Stephano. Music ceases.)*

PIERO   What say you to that, now?

BONAMO   Charming! charming!

PIERO   I hope I am not made a major for nothing.

BONAMO *(to Francisco, who enters with Fiametta)*   Come, sir, please to take your seat.

PIERO *(to Stephano)*   Shall the sports begin? *(Stephano gives an affirmative sign.)* Here! dancers! pipers! strummers! thrummers! to your places. This bench is for the band of music—mount.

*Here the dancing, which should be of the gay, comic, and grotesque kind; with droll attitudes, gesticulations, and bounds, in imitation of the mountaineers, the goats they keep, etc., that is, the humorous dancing of the Italian peasants. In the midst of the rejoicing the clock strikes; the dancing suddenly ceases; the changing music inspires alarm and dismay. Enter Malvoglio. He stops in the middle of the stage; the company start up; Francisco, Stephano, Selina, and Bonamo, all with more or less terror. The Peasants, alarmed and watching: the whole, during a short pause, forming a picture. Malvoglio then presents a letter to Bonamo, with a malignant assurance, and turns away, gratified by the consternation he has occasioned: with which audacious air and feeling, he retires. While Bonamo opens the letter and reads with great agitation, the music expresses confusion and pain of thought; then ceases.*

BONAMO  Oh, shame! dishonor! treachery!

STEPHANO  My father!—

SELINA  My uncle!

FIAMETTA  What treachery? *(Francisco is in an attitude of despair.)*

BONAMO  No more of love or marriage! no more of sports, rejoicing, and mirth.

STEPHANO  Good Heavens!

SELINA  My guardian! my friend! my uncle!

BONAMO *(repelling her)*  I am not your uncle.

SELINA  Sir!

STEPHANO  Not?

BONAMO  She is the child of crime! of adultery. *(a general stupefaction: the despair of Francisco at its height)*

STEPHANO  'Tis malice, my father.

BONAMO  Read.

STEPHANO  The calumny of Romaldi!

BONAMO *(seriously)*  Read.

STEPHANO *(Reads.)*  "Selina is not your brother's daughter. To prove I speak nothing but the truth, I send you the certificate of her baptism."

BONAMO  'Tis here—authenticated. Once more read.

STEPHANO *(Reads.)*  "May the 11th, 1584, at ten o'clock this evening was baptized Selina Bianchi, the daughter of Francisco Bianchi." *(Francisco utters a cry, and falls on the seat.)*

SELINA  Is it possible! my father! *(Francisco opens his arms, and Selina falls on his neck)*

STEPHANO  Amazement!

BONAMO  Sinful man! Not satisfied with having dishonored my brother, after claiming my pity, would you aid in making me contract a most shameful alliance? Begone! you and the offspring of your guilt.

STEPHANO  Selina is innocent. *(Francisco confirms it.)*

BONAMO  Her father is—a wretch! Once more, begone. *(Francisco during this dialogue had held his daughter in his arms; he now rises with a sense of injury and is leading her away.)* Hold, miserable man. *(to himself)* Houseless—penniless—without bread—without asylum—must she perish because her father has been wicked? *(to Francisco)* Take this purse, conceal your shame, and, when 'tis empty, let me know your hiding place. *(Francisco expresses gratitude, but rejects the purse.)*

SELINA *(with affection)*  Spare your benefits, sir, till you think we deserve them.

BONAMO  Poor Selina!

STEPHANO *(eagerly)*  What say you, sir?

BONAMO  Nothing—let them begone.

SELINA  Stephano! farewell.

STEPHANO  She shall not go! or—I will follow.

BONAMO  And forsake your father! ungrateful boy! *(to Francisco)* Begone, I say. Let me never see you more. *(to the Peasants)* Confine that frantic youth.

*Violent distracted music. Stephano endeavours to force his way to Selina. Fiametta passionately embraces her; and by gesture reproaches Bonamo, who persists, yet is tormented by doubt. Stephano escapes, and suddenly hurries Selina forward, to detain her; after violent efforts, they are again forced asunder; and, as they are retiring on opposite sides, with struggles and passion, the Scene closes.*

## SCENE 2

*The house of Bonamo. Bonamo; Stephano, brought on by the Peasants, who then leave the room.*

BONAMO  Disobedient, senseless boy!

STEPHANO  *(Exhausted)*  Selina! give me back Selina, or take my life!

BONAMO  Forbear these complaints.

STEPHANO  She is the woman I love.

BONAMO  Dare you—

STEPHANO  None but she shall be my wife.

BONAMO  Your wife!

STEPHANO  To the world's end I'll follow her!

BONAMO  And quit your father? Now, when age and infirmity bend him to the grave?

STEPHANO  We will return to claim your blessing.

BONAMO  Stephano! I have loved you like a father; beware of my malediction.

STEPHANO  When a father's malediction is unjust, Heaven is deaf.

*Enter Fiametta, retaining her anger.*

FIAMETTA  Very well! It's all very right! But you will see how it will end!

BONAMO  *(to Stephano)*  I no longer wonder Count Romaldi should advise me to drive such a wretch from my house.

FIAMETTA  Count Romaldi is himself a wretch.

BONAMO  Fiametta!—

FIAMETTA  *(overcome by her passion)*  I say it again: a vile wicked wretch! and has written—

BONAMO  *(imperiously)*  The truth. The certificate is incontestable.

FIAMETTA  I would not for all the world be guilty of your sins.

BONAMO  Woman!

FIAMETTA  I don't care for you. I loved you this morning; I would have lost my life for you, but you are grown wicked.

BONAMO  Will you be silent?

FIAMETTA  Is it not wickedness to turn a sweet innocent helpless young creature out of doors, one who has behaved with such tenderness, and leave her at last to starve? Oh, it is abominable!

BONAMO  Once more, hold your tongue.

FIAMETTA  I won't! I can't! Poor Stephano! And do you think he'll forbear to love her? If he did, I should hate him! But he'll make his escape. You may hold him to-day, but he'll be gone to-morrow. He'll overtake and find his dear forlorn Selina; and they will marry, and live in poverty: but they will work, and eat their morsel with a good conscience; while you will turn from your dainties with an aching heart!

BONAMO   For the last time, I warn you—

FIAMETTA   I know the worst: I have worked for you all the prime of my youth; and now you'll serve me as you have served the innocent wretched Selina; you'll turn me out of doors. Do it! But I'll not go till I've said out my say: so I tell you again, you are a hard-hearted uncle, an unfeeling father, and an unjust master! Everybody will shun you! You will dwindle out a life of misery, and nobody will pity you, because you don't deserve pity. So now I'll go, as soon as you please.

*Enter Signor Montano, hastily. Fiametta and Stephano eagerly attentive.*

MONTANO   What is it I have just heard, my friend? Have you driven away your niece?

BONAMO   She is not my niece.

MONTANO   'Tis true.

FIAMETTA   How?

MONTANO   But where did you learn that?

BONAMO   From these papers.

MONTANO   Who sent them?

BONAMO   Count Romaldi.

MONTANO   Count Romaldi is—a villain.

FIAMETTA   There! There!

STEPHANO   You hear, Sir!

FIAMETTA   I hope I shall be believed another time.

BONAMO *(greatly interested)*   Silence, woman!—By a man like you such an accusation cannot be made without sufficient proofs.

MONTANO   You shall have them. Be attentive.

FIAMETTA   I won't breathe! A word shan't escape my lips. *(They press round Montano.)*

MONTANO   Eight years ago, before I had the honor to know you, returning one evening after visiting my friends, I was leisurely ascending the rock of Arpennaz.

FIAMETTA   So, so! The rock of Arpennaz! You hear! But I'll not say a word.

MONTANO   Two men, wild in their looks and smeared with blood, passed hastily by me, with every appearance of guilt impressed upon their contenances.

FIAMETTA   The very same! Eight years ago! The rock of Arpennaz! The—

BONAMO   Silence!

FIAMETTA   I'll not say a word. Tell all, sir, I am dumb.

MONTANO   They had not gone a hundred paces before he, who appeared the master, staggered and fell. I hastened to him: he bled much, and I and his servant supported him to my house. They said they had been attacked by banditti, yet their torn clothes, a deep bite, which the master had on the back of his hand, and other hurts appearing to be given by an unarmed man, made me doubt. Their embarrassment increased suspicion, which was confirmed next day by Michelli, the honest miller of Arpennaz, who, the evening before, near the spot from which I saw these men ascend, had succoured a poor wretch, dreadfully cut and mangled.

FIAMETTA  It's all true! 'Twas I! I myself! My cries made Michelli come! Eight years—

BONAMO  Again?

FIAMETTA  I've done.

MONTANO  I no longer doubted I had entertained men of blood, and hastened to deliver them up to justice; but, when I returned, they had flown, having left a purse, and this letter.

BONAMO *(having seen it)*  'Tis the hand of Romaldi.

MONTANO  Imagine my surprise and indignation, yesterday evening, when I here once more beheld the assassin! I could not disguise my emotion; and I left you with such abruptness to give immediate information. The archers are now in pursuit: I have no doubt they will soon secure him, as they already have secured his accomplice.

STEPHANO  Malvoglio?

MONTANO  Yes, who has confessed—

STEPHANO  What?

MONTANO  That the real name of this pretended Romaldi is Bianchi.

BONAMO  Just heaven! Francisco's brother!

MONTANO  Whose wife this wicked brother loved. Privately married, and she pregnant, Francisco put her under the protection of his friend here in Savoy.

STEPHANO  My uncle! His sudden death occasioned the mystery.

MONTANO  But the false Romaldi decoyed Francisco into the power of the Algerines, seized his estates, and, finding he had escaped, attempted to assassinate him.

FIAMETTA  Now are you convinced! He would not 'peach his brother of abomination! *(raising her clasped hands)* I told you Francisco was an angel! but, for all you knew me so well, I'm not to be believed.

BONAMO  You are not to be silenced.

FIAMETTA  No; I'm not. Francisco is an angel, Selina is an angel, Stephano is an angel: they shall be married, and all make one family, of which, if you repent, you shall be received into the bosom.

BONAMO *(slowly, earnestly)*  Pray, good woman, hold your tongue.

FIAMETTA  Repent, then! Repent! *(Here the distant thunder is heard, and the rising storm perceived.)*

BONAMO *(to Montano and Stephano)*  I do repent!

FIAMETTA *(affectionately)*  Then I forgive you. *(Sobs.)* I won't turn away. You're my master again. *(Kisses his hand and wipes her eyes.)*

BONAMO  But where shall we find Selina, and—?

FIAMETTA  Oh, I know where!

STEPHANO *(eagerly)*  Do you?

FIAMETTA  Why, could you think that—*(her heart full)* Follow me! Only follow me.

*Exeunt hastily. Thunder heard, while the Scene changes. Music.*

## SCENE 3

*The wild mountainous country called the Nant of Arpennaz; with pines and mossy rocks. A rude wooden bridge on a small height thrown from rock to rock; a rugged mill stream a little in the background; the miller's house on the right; a steep ascent by a narrow path to the bridge; a stone or bank to sit on, on the right-hand side. The increasing storm of lightning, thunder, hail, and rain, becomes terrible. Suitable music. Enter Romaldi from the rocks, disguised like a peasant, with terror, pursued, as it were, by heaven and earth.*

ROMALDI   Whither fly? Where shield me from pursuit, and death, and ignominy? My hour is come! The fiends that tempted me now tear me. *(dreadful thunder)* The heavens shoot their fires at me! Save! Spare! Oh spare me. *(Falls on the bank.)*

*Music, hail, etc. continue; after a pause, he raises his head. More fearful claps of thunder are heard, and he again falls on his face. The storm gradually abates. Pause in the music. A very distant voice is heard:* Holloa! *Music continues. He half rises, starts, and runs from side to side, looking and listening. Music ceases. Voice again:* Holloa!

ROMALDI   They are after me! Some one points me out! No den, no cave, can hide me! *(Looks the way he came.)* I cannot return that way, I cannot. It is the place of blood! A robbed and wretched brother! 'Tis his blood, by which I am covered! Ay! There! There have I been driven for shelter! Under those very rocks! Oh, that they would open! Cover me, earth! Cover my crimes! Cover my shame!

*Falls motionless again. Music of painful remorse; then changes to the cheerful pastorale, etc. Michelli is seen coming toward the bridge, which he crosses, stopping to look round and speak; then speaks as he descends by the rugged narrow path, and then in the front of the stage.*

MICHELLI *(on the bridge)*   'Tis a fearful storm! One's very heart shrinks! It makes a poor mortal think of his sins—and his danger.

ROMALDI *(after listening)*   Danger! What?—Is it me? *(listening)*

MICHELLI *(descending)*   Every thunder clap seems to flash vengeance in his face!

ROMALDI   I am known; or must be!—Shall I yield; or shall I—*(Points his pistol at Michelli, then shrinks.)* More murder!

MICHELLI *(in the front of the stage)*   At such terrible times, a clear conscience is better than kingdoms of gold mines.

ROMALDI *(in hesitation whether he shall or shall not murder)*   How to act?

MICHELLI *(perceiving Romaldi, who conceals his pistol)*   Now, friend!

ROMALDI   Now, miller!

MICHELLI *(observing his agitation)*   You look—

ROMALDI   How do I look? *(fearing, and still undetermined)*

MICHELLI   I—What have you there?

ROMALDI   Where?

MICHELLI  Under your coat.

ROMALDI  *(leaving the pistol in his inside pocket, and showing his hands)*  Nothing.

MICHELLI  Something is the matter with you.

ROMALDI  *(sudden emotion to shoot: restrained)*  I am tired.

MICHELLI  Come in, then, and rest yourself.

ROMALDI  Thank you! *(moved)* Thank you!

MICHELLI  Whence do you come?

ROMALDI  From—the neighbourhood of Geneva.

MICHELLI  *(as if with meaning)*  Did you pass through Sallancha?

ROMALDI  *(alarmed)*  Sallancha? Why do you ask?

MICHELLI  You have heard of what has happened?

ROMALDI  Where?

MICHELLI  There! At Sallancha! One Count Romaldi—

ROMALDI  What of him?

MICHELLI  *(observing)*  Do you know him?

ROMALDI  I—How should a poor—?

MICHELLI  Justice is at his heels. He has escaped: but he'll be taken. The executioner will have him.

ROMALDI  *(Shudders.)*  Ay?

MICHELLI  As sure as you are here.

ROMALDI  *(aside)*  All men hate me! Why should I spare him?

MICHELLI  I saved the good Francisco.

ROMALDI  *(gazing steadfastly at him)*  You! Was it you?

MICHELLI  I.

ROMALDI  Then—live.

MICHELLI  Live?

ROMALDI  To be rewarded.

MICHELLI  I'd have done the same for you.

ROMALDI  Live—live!

MICHELLI  I will, my friend, as long as I can; and when I die, I'll die with an honest heart.

ROMALDI  Miserable wretch!

MICHELLI  Who?

ROMALDI  That Count Romaldi.

MICHELLI  Why ay! Unless he is a devil, he is miserable indeed. *(music, quick march)* He'll be taken; for, look, yonder are the archers. *(They cross the bridge.)*

ROMALDI  *(fearing Michelli knows him)*  What then? Where is Romaldi?

MICHELLI  How should I know?

ROMALDI  *(aside)*  Does he dissemble? They are here! I am lost! *(Retires. Music. The Archers come forward.)*

MICHELLI  Good day, worthy Sirs.

EXEMPT  Honest miller, good day. We are in search of Count Romaldi, whom we are to take, dead or alive. Do you know his person?

MICHELLI  No.

ROMALDI  *(aside, and out of sight of the Archers)*  Thanks, merciful heaven!

EXEMPT  *(Reads.)*  "Five feet eight" *(The description must be that of the actor's voice, size and person: to which add:)* "with a large scar on the back of the right hand."

ROMALDI *(thrusting his hand in his bosom)* 'Twill betray me!

EXEMPT 'Twas a bite! The wretch Malvoglio has deposed that good Francisco is the brother of the vile Romaldi.

MICHELLI How!

EXEMPT And that Francisco, tho' robbed, betrayed and mutilated, has endured every misery, and lived in continual dread of steel or poison, rather than bring this monster to the scaffold.

MICHELLI But he'll come there at last!

EXEMPT We are told, he is among these mountains.

MICHELLI Oh, could I catch him by the collar!

EXEMPT Should you meet him, beware: he's not unarmed.

MICHELLI There is no passing for him or you by this valley after the storm; the mountain torrents are falling. You must go back.

EXEMPT Many thanks. We must lose no time.

MICHELLI Success to you.

*Archers re-ascend the hill. Music. Quick march, as when they entered.*

ROMALDI Death! Infamy! Is there no escaping?

MICHELLI The day declines, and you look—

ROMALDI How?

MICHELLI Um—I wish you looked better. Come in; pass the evening here: recover your strength and spirits.

ROMALDI *(with great emotion, forgetting and holding out his hand)* You are a worthy man.

MICHELLI I wish to be. *(feeling Romaldi's hand after shaking)* Zounds! What? Hey?

ROMALDI *(concealing his confusion)* A scar—

MICHELLI On the back of the right hand!

ROMALDI I have served. A hussar with his sabre gave the cut.

MICHELLI *(after considering)* Humph! It may be.

ROMALDI It is.

MICHELLI At least it *may* be; and the innocent—

ROMALDI Ay! Might suffer for the guilty.

MICHELLI *(after looking at him)* Rather than that—I will run all risks. I am alone; my family is at the fair, and cannot be home tonight. But you are a stranger; you want protection—

ROMALDI *(with great emotion)* I do, indeed!

MICHELLI You shall have it. Come. Never shall my door be shut against the houseless wretch.              *Exeunt to the house.*

*Music expressing dejection. Francisco and Selina approaching the bridge, he points to the Miller's house. Cheerful music; she testifies joy, and admiration of the Miller. They descend, he carefully guiding and aiding her. The Miller, supposed to hear a noise, comes to inquire, sees Francisco, and they run into each other's arms.*

MICHELLI Welcome! A thousand times welcome!

SELINA Ten thousand thanks to the saviour of my father!

MICHELLI Your father, sweet lady?

SELINA Oh yes! discovered to me by his mortal enemy.

MICHELLI  The monster Romaldi!

SELINA (*dejectedly*)  Alas!

MICHELLI  For your father's sake, for your own sake, welcome both.

ROMALDI (*half from the door*)  I heard my name!

MICHELLI (*leading them to the door, just as Romaldi advances a step*)  Come. I have a stranger—

SELINA (*Seeing Romaldi, shrieks.*)  Ah! (*Francisco falls back and covers his eyes, with agony.*)

MICHELLI  How now? (*Romaldi retires.*)

SELINA  'Tis he!

*Music of hurry, terror, etc. Francisco, putting his hand towards her mouth, enjoins her silence with great eagerness. Michelli, by making the sign of biting his right hand, asks Francisco if it be Romaldi. Francisco turns away without answering. Michelli denotes his conviction it is Romaldi, and hastily ascends to cross the bridge in search of the Archers; Francisco intreats him back in vain. Romaldi, in terror, enters from the house presenting his pistol. Francisco opens his breast for him to shoot if he pleases. Selina falls between them. The whole scene passes in a mysterious and rapid manner. Music suddenly stops.*

ROMALDI  No! Too much of your blood is upon my head! Be justly revenged: take mine!

*Music continues as Romaldi offers the pistol; which Francisco throws to a distance, and intreats him to fly by the valley.—Romaldi signifies the impossibility, and runs distractedly from side to side: then after Francisco and Selina's intreaties, ascends to cross the bridge. Met at the edge of the hill by an Archer, he is driven back; they struggle on the bridge. The Archer's sword taken by Romaldi; who, again attempting flight, is again met by several Archers. Romaldi maintains a retreating fight. Fiametta, Bonamo, Stephano, Montano, and Peasants follow the Archers. Francisco and Selina, in the greatest agitation, several times throw themselves between the assailants and Romaldi. When the combatants have descended the hill, Romaldi's foot slips, he falls, and Francisco intervenes to guard his body. By this time all the principal characters are near the front. The Archers appear prepared to shoot, and strike with their sabres; when the intreaties and efforts of Francisco and Selina are renewed. The Archers forbear for a moment; and Francisco shields his brother. The music ceases.*

SELINA  Oh, forbear. Let my father's virtues plead for my uncle's errors!

BONAMO  We will all intreat for mercy; since of mercy we all have need: for his sake, and for our own, may it be freely granted!

*The Curtain falls to slow and solemn music.*

*The End*

## FOR DISCUSSION

1. How does the setting contribute to the general melodramatic mood of the play? For what purpose is music used in the play?

2. Who is the play's evil villain? What characterizes him as such?
3. What is the basic problem that precipitates the events of the play?
4. Why will Francisco not reveal who has maimed him?
5. Explain how Fiametta may be viewed both as a comic character and as the conscience of Bonamo.
6. What is ironic about the timing of Count Romaldi's first entrance?
7. Why will Bonamo not give Selina's hand in marriage to Count Romaldi's son? How does this establish Bonamo as a good person?
8. What does Selina overhear during the night of Count Romaldi's visit?
9. Why does Bonamo order Count Romaldi out of the house?
10. What preparations are being made at the beginning of Act II? What is the mood of the play at this point?
11. What are Bonamo's views on adultery? How does he react to the mysterious letter?
12. What is the true relationship between Francisco and Selina? How does the knowledge of this relationship change Bonamo's attitude?
13. How does Romaldi meet his end? Does he repent his evildoing?
14. Why do the good people of the play forgive Romaldi his treacheries at the end?

# Trifles

## SUSAN GLASPELL

### Cast of Characters

COUNTY ATTORNEY
SHERIFF
HALE
MRS. HALE
MRS. PETERS   (the Sheriff's wife)

*SCENE.   The kitchen in the now abandoned farmhouse of* JOHN WRIGHT, *a gloomy kitchen, and left without having been put in order—the walls covered with a faded wall paper.* D.R. *is a door leading to the parlor. On the* R. *wall above this door is a built-in kitchen cupboard with shelves in the upper portion and drawers below. In the rear wall at* R., *up two steps is a door opening onto stairs leading to the second floor. In the rear wall at* L. *is a door to the shed and from there to the outside. Between these two doors is an old-fashioned black iron stove. Running along the* L. *wall from the shed door is an old iron sink and sink shelf, in which is set a hand pump. Downstage of the sink is an uncurtained window. Near the window is an old wooden rocker. Center stage is an unpainted wooden kitchen table with straight chairs on either side. There is a small chair* D.R. *Unwashed pans under the sink, a loaf of bread outside the breadbox, a dish towel on the table—other signs of incompleted work. At the rear the shed door opens and the* SHERIFF *comes in followed by the* COUNTY ATTORNEY *and* HALE. *The* SHERIFF *and* HALE *are men in middle life, the* COUNTY ATTORNEY *is a young man; all are much bundled up and go at once to the stove. They are followed by the two women—the* SHERIFF'S *wife,* MRS. PETERS, *first; she is a slight wiry woman, a thin nervous face.* MRS. HALE *is larger and would ordinarily be called more comfortable looking, but she is disturbed now and looks fearfully about as she enters. The women have come in slowly, and stand close together near the door.*

COUNTY ATTORNEY *(at stove rubbing his hands)*   This feels good. Come up to the fire, ladies.
MRS. PETERS *(after taking a step forward)*   I'm not—cold.
SHERIFF *(unbuttoning his overcoat and stepping away from the stove to right of table as if to mark the beginning of official business)*   Now, Mr. Hale, before we move things about, you explain to Mr. Henderson just what you saw when you came here yesterday morning.
COUNTY ATTORNEY *(crossing down to left of the table)*   By the way, has anything been moved? Are things just as you left them yesterday?
SHERIFF *(looking about)*   It's just the same. When it dropped below zero last night I thought I'd better send Frank out this morning to make a fire for us—*(sits right of center table)* no use getting pneumonia with a big case on, but I told him not to touch anything except the stove—and you know Frank.
COUNTY ATTORNEY   Somebody should have been left here yesterday.

SHERIFF  Oh—yesterday. When I had to send Frank to Morris Center for that man who went crazy—I want you to know I had my hands full yesterday. I knew you could get back from Omaha by today and as long as I went over everything here myself—

COUNTY ATTORNEY  Well, Mr. Hale, tell just what happened when you came here yesterday morning.

HALE *(crossing down to above table)*  Harry and I had started to town with a load of potatoes. We came along the road from my place and as I got here I said, "I'm going to see if I can't get John Wright to go in with me on a party telephone." I spoke to Wright about it once before and he put me off, saying folks talked too much anyway, and all he asked was peace and quiet—I guess you know about how much he talked himself; but I thought maybe if I went to the house and talked about it before his wife, though I said to Harry that I didn't know as what his wife wanted made much differece to John—

COUNTY ATTORNEY  Let's talk about that later, Mr. Hale. I do want to talk about that, but tell now just what happened when you got to the house.

HALE  I didn't hear or see anything; I knocked at the door, and still it was all quiet inside. I knew they must be up, it was past eight o'clock. So I knocked again, and I thought I heard somebody say, "Come in." I wasn't sure, I'm not sure yet, but I opened the door—this door *(indicating the door by which the two women are still standing)* and there in that rocker—*(pointing to it)* sat Mrs. Wright. *(They all look at the rocker* D.L.*)*

COUNTY ATTORNEY  What—was she doing?

HALE  She was rockin' back and forth. She had her apron in her hand and was kind of—pleating it.

COUNTY ATTORNEY  And how did she—look?

HALE  Well, she looked queer.

COUNTY ATTORNEY  How do you mean—queer?

HALE  Well, as if she didn't know what she was going to do next. And kind of done up.

COUNTY ATTORNEY  *(takes out notebook and pencil and sits left of center table)*  How did she seem to feel about your coming?

HALE  Why, I don't think she minded—one way or other. She didn't pay much attention. I said, "How do, Mrs. Wright, it's cold, ain't it?" And she said, "Is it?"—and went on kind of pleating at her apron. Well, I was surprised; she didn't ask me to come up to the stove, or to set down, but just sat there, not even looking at me, so I said, "I want to see John." And then she—laughed. I guess you would call it a laugh. I thought of Harry and the team outside, so I said a little sharp: "Can't I see John?" "No," she says, kind o' dull like. "Ain't he home?" says I. "Yes," says she, "he's home." "Then why can't I see him?" I asked her, out of patience. " 'Cause he's dead," says she. *"Dead?"* says I. She just nodded her head, not getting a bit excited, but rockin' back and forth. "Why—where is he?" says I, not knowing what to say. She just pointed upstairs—like that. *(himself pointing to the room above)* I started for the stairs, with the idea of going up there. I walked from there to here—then I says, "Why, what did he die of?" "He died of a rope round his neck," says she, and just went on pleatin' at her apron. Well, I went out and called

Harry. I thought I might—need help. We went upstairs and there he was lyin'—

COUNTY ATTORNEY  I think I'd rather have you go into that upstairs, where you can point it all out. Just go on now with the rest of the story.

HALE  Well, my first thought was to get that rope off. It looked . . . *(stops, his face twitches)* . . . but Harry, he went up to him, and he said, "No, he's dead all right, and we'd better not touch anything." So we went back downstairs. She was still sitting that same way. "Has anybody been notified?" I asked. "No," says she, unconcerned. "Who did this, Mrs. Wright?" said Harry. He said it business-like—and she stopped pleatin' of her apron. "I don't know," she says. "You don't *know*?" says Harry. "No," says she. "Weren't you sleepin' in the bed with him?" says Harry. "Yes," says she, "but I was on the inside." "Somebody slipped a rope round his neck and strangled him and you didn't wake up?" says Harry. "I didn't wake up," she said after him. We must 'a' looked as if we didn't see how that could be, for after a minute she said, "I sleep sound." Harry was going to ask her more questions but I said maybe we ought to let her tell her story first to the coroner, or the sheriff, so Harry went fast as he could to Rivers' place, where there's a telephone.

COUNTY ATTORNEY  And what did Mrs. Wright do when she knew that you had gone for the coroner?

HALE  She moved from the rocker to that chair over there *(pointing to a small chair in the D.R. corner)* and just sat there with her hands held together and looking down. I got a feeling that I ought to make some conversation, so I said I had come in to see if John wanted to put in a telephone, and at that she started to laugh, and then she stopped and looked at me—scared. *(The COUNTY ATTORNEY, who has had his notebook out, makes a note.)* I dunno, maybe it wasn't scared. I wouldn't like to say it was. Soon Harry got back, and then Dr. Lloyd came, and you, Mr. Peters, and so I guess that's all I know that you don't.

COUNTY ATTORNEY  *(rising and looking around)*  I guess we'll go upstairs first—and then out to the barn and around there. *(to the SHERIFF)* You're convinced that there was nothing important here—nothing that would point to any motive?

SHERIFF  Nothing here but kitchen things. *(The COUNTY ATTORNEY, after again looking around the kitchen, opens the door of a cupboard closet in R. wall. He brings a small chair from R.—gets up on it and looks on a shelf. Pulls his hand away, sticky.)*

COUNTY ATTORNEY  Here's a nice mess. *(The women draw nearer U.C.)*

MRS. PETERS *(to the other woman)*  Oh, her fruit; it did freeze. *(to the LAWYER)* She worried about that when it turned so cold. She said the fire'd go out and her jars would break.

SHERIFF *(rises)*  Well, can you beat the woman! Held for murder and worryin' about her preserves.

COUNTY ATTORNEY *(getting down from chair)*  I guess before we're through she may have something more serious than preserves to worry about. *(Crosses down R.C.)*

HALE  Well, women are used to worrying over trifles. *(The two women move a little closer together.)*

COUNTY ATTORNEY *(with the gallantry of a young politician)*  And yet, for all their worries, what would we do without the ladies? *(The women do not unbend. He goes below the center table to the sink, takes a dipperful of water from the pail and pouring it into a basin, washes his hands. While he is doing this the* SHERIFF *and* HALE *cross to cupboard, which they inspect. The* COUNTY ATTORNEY *starts to wipe his hands on the roller towel, turns it for a cleaner place.)* Dirty towels! *(Kicks his foot against the pans under the sink.)* Not much of a housekeeper, would you say, ladies?

MRS. HALE *(stiffly)* There's a great deal of work to be done on a farm.

COUNTY ATTORNEY  To be sure. And yet *(with a little bow to her)* I know there are some Dickson County farmhouses which do not have such roller towels. *(He gives it a pull to expose its full length again.)*

MRS. HALE  Those towels get dirty awful quick. Men's hands aren't always as clean as they might be.

COUNTY ATTORNEY  Ah, loyal to your sex, I see. But you and Mrs. Wright were neighbors. I suppose you were friends, too.

MRS. HALE *(shaking her head)*  I've not seen much of her of late years. I've not been in this house—it's more than a year.

COUNTY ATTORNEY *(crossing to women* U. C.*)*  And why was that? You didn't like her?

MRS. HALE  I like her all well enough. Farmers' wives have their hands full, Mr. Henderson. And then——

COUNTY ATTORNEY  Yes——?

MRS. HALE *(looking about)*  It never seemed a very cheerful place.

COUNTY ATTORNEY  No—it's not cheerful. I shouldn't say she had the home-making instinct.

MRS. HALE  Well, I don't know as Wright had, either.

COUNTY ATTORNEY  You mean that they didn't get on very well?

MRS. HALE  No, I don't mean anything. But I don't think a place'd be any cheerfuller for John Wright's being in it.

COUNTY ATTORNEY  I'd like to talk more of that a little later. I want to get the lay of things upstairs now. *(He goes past the women to* U. R. *where steps lead to a stair door.)*

SHERIFF  I suppose anything Mrs. Peters does'll be all right. She was to take in some clothes for her, you know, and a few little things. We left in such a hurry yesterday.

COUNTY ATTORNEY  Yes, but I would like to see what you take, Mrs. Peters, and keep an eye out for anything that might be of use to us.

MRS. PETERS  Yes, Mr. Henderson. *(The men leave by* U. R. *door to stairs. The women listen to the men's steps on the stairs, then look about the kitchen.)*

MRS. HALE *(crossing* L. *to sink)*  I'd hate to have men coming into my kitchen, snooping around and criticizing. *(She arranges the pans under sink which the* LAWYER *had shoved out of place.)*

MRS. PETERS  Of course it's no more than their duty. *(Crosses to cupboard* U. R.*)*

MRS. HALE  Duty's all right, but I guess that deputy sheriff that came out to make the fire might have got a little of this on. *(Gives the roller towel a pull.)* Wish I'd thought of that sooner. Seems mean to talk about her for not having things slicked up when she had to come away in such a hurry. *(Crosses* R. *to* MRS. PETERS *at cupboard.)*

MRS. PETERS *(who has been looking through cupboard, lifts one end of a towel that covers a pan)*  She had bread set. *(Stands still.)*

MRS. HALE (*eyes fixed on a loaf of bread beside the breadbox, which is on a low shelf of the cupboard*)  She was going to put this in there. (*Picks up loaf, then abruptly drops it. In a manner of returning to familiar things.*) It's a shame about her fruit. I wonder if it's all gone. (*Gets up on the chair and looks.*) I think there's some here that's all right, Mrs. Peters. Yes—here; (*holding it toward the window*) this is cherries, too. (*Looking again.*) I declare I believe that's the only one. (*Gets down, jar in her hand. Goes to the sink and wipes it off on the outside.*) She'll feel awful bad after all her hard work in the hot weather. I remember the afternoon I put up my cherries last summer. (*She puts the jar on the big kitchen table, center of the room. With a sigh, is about to sit down in the rocking chair. Before she is seated realizes what chair it is; with a slow look at it, steps back. The chair which she has touched rocks back and forth.* MRS. PETERS *moves to center table and they both watch the chair rock for a moment or two.*)

MRS. PETERS (*shaking off the mood which the empty rocking chair has evoked. Now in a businesslike manner she speaks.*)  Well, I must get those things from the front room closet. (*She goes to the door at the* R., *but, after looking into the other room, steps back.*) You coming with me, Mrs. Hale? You could help me carry them. (*They go in the other room; reappear,* MRS. PETERS *carrying a dress, petticoat and skirt,* MRS. HALE *following with a pair of shoes.*) My, it's cold in there. (*She puts the clothes on the big table, and hurries to the stove.*)

MRS. HALE (*right of center table examining the skirt*)  Wright was close. I think maybe that's why she kept so much to herself. She didn't even belong to the Ladies' Aid. I suppose she felt she couldn't do her part, and then you don't enjoy things when you feel shabby. I heard she used to wear pretty clothes and be lively, when she was Minnie Foster, one of the town girls singing in the choir. But that—oh, that was thirty years ago. This all you was to take in?

MRS. PETERS  She said she wanted an apron. Funny thing to want, for there isn't much to get you dirty in jail, goodness knows. But I suppose just to make her feel more natural. (*Crosses to cupboard.*) She said they was in the top drawer in this cupboard. Yes, here. And then her little shawl that always hung behind the door. (*Opens stair door and looks.*) Yes, here it is. (*Quickly shuts door leading upstairs.*)

MRS. HALE (*abruptly moving toward her*)  Mrs. Peters?

MRS. PETERS  Yes, Mrs. Hale? (*At* U. R. *door.*)

MRS. HALE  Do you think she did it?

MRS. PETERS (*in a frightened voice*)  Oh, I don't know.

MRS. HALE  Well, I don't think she did. Asking for an apron and her little shawl. Worrying about her fruit.

MRS. PETERS (*Starts to speak, glances up, where footsteps are heard in the room above. in a low voice*)  Mr. Peters says it looks bad for her. Mr. Henderson is awful sarcastic in a speech and he'll make fun of her sayin' she didn't wake up.

MRS. HALE  Well, I guess John Wright didn't wake when they was slipping that rope under his neck.

MRS. PETERS (*crossing slowly to table and placing shawl and apron on table with other clothing*)  No, it's strange. It must have been done awful crafty and still. They say it was such a—funny way to kill a man, rigging it all up like that.

MRS. HALE (*crossing to left of* MRS. PETERS *at table*)  That's just what Mr. Hale said. There was a gun in the house. He says that's what he can't understand.

MRS. PETERS.   Mr. Henderson said coming out that what was needed for the case was a motive; something to show anger, or—sudden feeling.

MRS. HALE (*who is standing by the table*)   Well, I don't see any signs of anger around here. (*She puts her hand on the dish towel which lies on the table, stands looking down at table, one-half of which is clean, the other half messy.*) It's wiped to here. (*Makes a move as if to finish work, then turns and looks at loaf of bread outside the breadbox. Drops towel. in that voice of coming back to familiar things*) Wonder how they are finding things upstairs. (*crossing below table to* D. R.) I hope she had it a little more red-up up there. You know, it seems kind of *sneaking*. Locking her up in town and then coming out here and trying to get her own house to turn against her!

MRS. PETERS   But, Mrs. Hale, the law is the law.

MRS. HALE   I s'pose 'tis. (*unbuttoning her coat*) Better loosen up your things, Mrs. Peters. You won't feel them when you go out. (MRS. PETERS *takes off her fur tippet, goes to hang it on chair back left of table, stands looking at the work basket on floor near* D. L. *window.*)

MRS. PETERS   She was piecing a quilt. (*She brings the large sewing basket to the center table and they look at the bright pieces,* MRS. HALE *above the table and* MRS. PETERS *left of it.*)

MRS. HALE   It's a log cabin pattern. Pretty, isn't it? I wonder if she was goin' to quilt it or just knot it? (*Footsteps have been heard coming down the stairs. The* SHERIFF *enters followed by* HALE *and the* COUNTY ATTORNEY.)

SHERIFF   They wonder if she was going to quilt it or just knot it! (*The men laugh; the women look abashed.*)

COUNTY ATTORNEY (*rubbing his hands over the stove*)   Frank's fire didn't do much up there, did it? Well, let's go out to the barn and get that cleared up. (*The men go outside by* U. L. *door.*)

MRS. HALE (*resentfully*)   I don't know as there's anything so strange, our takin' up our time with little things while we're waiting for them to get the evidence. (*She sits in chair right of table smoothing out a block with decision.*) I don't see as it's anything to laugh about.

MRS. PETERS (*apologetically*)   Of course they've got awful important things on their minds. (*Pulls up a chair and joins* MRS. HALE *at the left of the table.*)

MRS. HALE (*examining another block*)   Mrs. Peters, look at this one. Here, this is the one she was working on, and look at the sewing! All the rest of it has been so nice and even. And look at this! It's all over the place! Why, it looks as if she didn't know what she was about! (*After she has said this they look at each other, then start to glance back at the door. After an instant* MRS. HALE *has pulled at a knot and ripped the sewing.*)

MRS. PETERS   Oh, what are you doing, Mrs. Hale?

MRS. HALE (*mildly*)   Just pulling out a stitch or two that's not sewed very good. (*threading a needle*) Bad sewing always made me fidgety.

MRS. PETERS (*with a glance at door, nervously*)   I don't think we ought to touch things.

MRS. HALE   I'll just finish up this end. (*suddenly stopping and leaning forward*) Mrs. Peters?

MRS. PETERS   Yes, Mrs. Hale?

MRS. HALE   What do you suppose she was so nervous about?

MRS. PETERS   Oh—I don't know. I don't know as she was nervous. I sometimes sew awful queer when I'm just tired. (MRS. HALE *starts to say something, looks at* MRS. PETERS, *then goes on sewing.*) Well, I must get these things wrapped up. They may be through sooner than we think. (*putting apron and other things together*) I wonder where I can find a piece of paper, and string. (*Rises.*)

MRS. HALE   In that cupboard, maybe.

MRS. PETERS   (*crosses* R. *looking in cupboard*)   Why, here's a birdcage. (*Holds it up.*) Did she have a bird, Mrs. Hale?

MRS. HALE   Why, I don't know whether she did or not—I've not been here for so long. There was a man around last year selling canaries cheap, but I don't know as she took one; maybe she did. She used to sing real pretty herself.

MRS. PETERS   (*glancing around*)   Seems funny to think of a bird here. But she must have had one, or why would she have a cage? I wonder what happened to it?

MRS. HALE   I s'pose maybe the cat got it.

MRS. PETERS   No, she didn't have a cat. She's got that feeling some people have about cats—being afraid of them. My cat got in her room and she was real upset and asked me to take it out.

MRS. HALE   My sister Bessie was like that. Queer, ain't it?

MRS. PETERS   (*examining the cage*)   Why, look at this door. It's broke. One hinge is pulled apart. (*Takes a step down to* MRS. HALE's *right.*)

MRS. HALE   (*looking too*)   Looks as if someone must have been rough with it.

MRS. PETERS   Why, yes. (*She brings the cage forward and puts it on the table.*)

MRS. HALE   (*glancing toward* U. L. *door*)   I wish if they're going to find any evidence they'd be about it. I don't like this place.

MRS. PETERS   But I'm awful glad you came with me, Mrs. Hale. It would be lonesome for me sitting here alone.

MRS. HALE   It would, wouldn't it? (*Dropping her sewing.*) But I tell you what I do wish, Mrs. Peters. I wish I had come over sometimes when *she* was here. I—(*looking around the room*)—wish I had.

MRS. PETERS   But of course you were awful busy, Mrs. Hale—your house and your children.

MRS. HALE   (*rises and crosses* L.)   I could've come. I stayed away because it weren't cheerful—and that's why I ought to have come. I—(*looking out* L. *window*) I've never liked this place. Maybe because it's down in a hollow and you don't see the road. I dunno what it is, but it's a lonesome place and always was. I wish I had come over to see Minnie Foster sometimes. I can see now— (*Shakes her head.*)

MRS. PETERS   (*left of table and above it*)   Well, you mustn't reproach yourself, Mrs. Hale. Somehow we just don't see how it is with other folks until—something turns up.

MRS. HALE   Not having children makes less work—but it makes a quiet house, and Wright out to work all day, and no company when he did come in. (*turning from window*) Did you know John Wright, Mrs. Peters?

MRS. PETERS   Not to know him; I've seen him in town. They say he was a good man.

MRS. HALE   Yes—good; he didn't drink, and kept his word as well as most, I guess, and paid his debts. But he was a hard man, Mrs. Peters. Just to pass the time of day with him—(*Shivers.*) Like a raw wind that gets to the bone.

*(Pauses, her eye falling on the cage.)* I should think she would 'a' wanted a bird. But what do you suppose went with it?

MRS. PETERS   I don't know, unless it got sick and died. *(She reaches over and swings the broken door; swings it again. Both women watch it.)*

MRS. HALE   You weren't raised round here, were you? (MRS. PETERS *shakes her head.)* You didn't know—her?

MRS. PETERS   Not till they brought her yesterday.

MRS. HALE   She—come to think of it, she was kind of like a bird herself—real sweet and pretty, but kind of timid and—fluttery. How—she—did—change. *(Silence; then as if struck by a happy thought and relieved to get back to everyday things. Crosses R. above* MRS. PETERS *to cupboard, replaces small chair used to stand on to its original place* D. R.*)* Tell you what, Mrs. Peters, why don't you take the quilt in with you? It might take up her mind.

MRS. PETERS   Why, I think that's a real nice idea, Mrs. Hale. There couldn't possibly be any objection to it, could there? Now, just what would I take? I wonder if her patches are in here—and her things. *(They look in the sewing basket.)*

MRS. HALE *(Crosses to right of table.)*   Here's some red. I expect this has got sewing things in it. *(Brings out a fancy box.)* What a pretty box. Looks like something somebody would give you. Maybe her scissors are in here. *(Opens box. Suddenly puts her hand to her nose.)* Why—— (MRS. PETERS *bends nearer, then turns her face away.)* There's something wrapped up in this piece of silk.

MRS. PETERS   Why, this isn't her scissors.

MRS. HALE *(lifting the silk)*   Oh, Mrs. Peters—it's—— (MRS. PETERS *bends closer.)*

MRS. PETERS   It's the bird.

MRS. HALE   But, Mrs. Peters—look at it! Its neck! Look at its neck! It's all—other side *to.*

MRS. PETERS   Somebody—wrung—its—neck. *(Their eyes meet. A look of growing comprehension, of horror. Steps are heard outside.* MRS. HALE *slips box under quilt pieces, and sinks into her chair. Enter* SHERIFF *and* COUNTY ATTORNEY. MRS. PETERS *steps* D. L. *and stands looking out of window.)*

COUNTY ATTORNEY *(as one turning from serious things to little pleasantries)*   Well, ladies, have you decided whether she was going to quilt it or knot it? *(Crosses to* C. *above table.)*

MRS. PETERS   We think she was going to—knot it. (SHERIFF *crosses to right of stove, lifts stove lid and glances at fire, then stands warming hands at stove.)*

COUNTY ATTORNEY   Well, that's interesting, I'm sure. *(seeing the birdcage)* Has the bird flown?

MRS. HALE *(putting more quilt pieces over the box)*   We think the—cat got it.

COUNTY ATTORNEY *(preoccupied)*   Is there a cat? (MRS. HALE *glances in a quick covert way at* MRS. PETERS.*)*

MRS. PETERS *(turning from window takes a step in)*   Well, not *now.* They're superstitious, you know. They leave.

COUNTY ATTORNEY *(to* SHERIFF PETERS, *continuing an interrupted conversation)*   No sign at all of anyone having come from the outside. Their own rope. Now let's go up again and go over it piece by piece. *(They start upstairs.)* It would have to have been someone who knew just the—— (MRS. PETERS *sits down left of table. The two women sit there not looking at one another, but as if peering into something and at the same time holding back. When they talk now it is in the manner of feeling their way over ground, as if afraid of what they are saying, but as if they cannot help saying it.)*

MRS. HALE *(hesitatively and in hushed voice)*  She liked the bird. She was going to bury it in that pretty box.

MRS. PETERS *(in a whisper)*  When I was a girl—my kitten—there was a boy took a hatchet, and before my eyes—and before I could get there—— *(Covers her face an instant.)* If they hadn't held me back I would have—*(catches herself, looks upstairs where steps are heard, falters weakly)*—hurt him.

MRS. HALE *(with a slow look around her)*  I wonder how it would seem never to have had any children around. *(pause)* No, Wright wouldn't like the bird—a thing that sang. She used to sing. He killed that, too.

MRS. PETERS *(moving uneasily)*  We don't know who killed the bird.

MRS. HALE  I knew John Wright.

MRS. PETERS  It was an awful thing was done in this house that night, Mrs. Hale. Killing a man while he slept, slipping a rope around his neck that choked the life out of him.

MRS. HALE  His neck. Choked the life out of him. *(Her hand goes out and rests on the birdcage.)*

MRS. PETERS *(with rising voice)*  We don't know who killed him. We don't know.

MRS. HALE *(her own feeling not interrupted)*  If there'd been years and years of nothing, then a bird to sing to you, it would be awful—still, after the bird was still.

MRS. PETERS *(something within her speaking)*  I know what stillness is. When we homesteaded in Dakota, and my first baby died—after he was two years old, and me with no other then——

MRS. HALE *(moving)*  How soon do you suppose they'll be through looking for the evidence?

MRS. PETERS  I know what stillness is. *(pulling herself back)* The law has got to punish crime, Mrs. Hale.

MRS. HALE *(not as if answering that)*  I wish you'd seen Minnie Foster when she wore a white dress with blue ribbons and stood up there in the choir and sang. *(a look around the room)* Oh, I wish I'd come over here once in a while! That was a crime! That was a crime! Who's going to punish that?

MRS. PETERS *(looking upstairs)*  We mustn't—take on.

MRS. HALE  I might have known she needed help! I know how things can be— for women. I tell you, it's queer, Mrs. Peters. We live close together and we live far apart. We all go through the same things—it's all just a different kind of the same thing. *(Brushes her eyes, noticing the jar of fruit, reaches out for it.)* If I was you I wouldn't tell her her fruit was gone. Tell her it *ain't*. Tell her it's all right. Take this in to prove it to her. She—she may never know whether it was broke or not.

MRS. PETERS *(Takes the jar, looks about for something to wrap it in; takes petticoat from the clothes brought from the other room, very nervously begins winding this around the jar.)* *(in a false voice)*  My, it's a good thing the men couldn't hear us.

Wouldn't they just laugh! Getting all stirred up over a little thing like a—dead
canary. As if that could have anything to do with—with—wouldn't they *laugh!*
*(The men are heard coming downstairs.)*

MRS. HALE *(under her breath)*   Maybe they would—maybe they wouldn't.

COUNTY ATTORNEY   No, Peters, it's all perfectly clear except a reason for doing
it. But you know juries when it comes to women. If there was some definite
thing. *(Crosses slowly to above table.* SHERIFF *crosses* D. R. MRS. HALE *and* MRS.
PETERS *remain seated at either side of table.)* Something to show—something to
make a story about—a thing that would connect up with this strange way of
doing it—— *(The women's eyes meet for an instant. Enter* HALE *from outer door.)*

HALE *(remaining* U. L. *by door)*   Well, I've got the team around. Pretty cold out
there.

COUNTY ATTORNEY   I'm going to stay awhile by myself. *(to the* SHERIFF*)* You can
send Frank out for me, can't you? I want to go over everything. I'm not
satisfied that we can't do better.

SHERIFF   Do you want to see what Mrs. Peters is going to take in? *(The* LAWYER
*picks up the apron; laughs.)*

COUNTY ATTORNEY   Oh, I guess they're not very dangerous things the ladies
have picked out. *(Moves a few things about, disturbing the quilt pieces which cover
the box. Steps back.)* No, Mrs. Peters doesn't need supervising. For that matter
a sheriff's wife is married to the law. Ever think of it that way, Mrs. Peters?

MRS. PETERS   Not—just that way.

SHERIFF *(chuckling)*   Married to the law. *(Moves to* D. R. *door to the other room.)* I
just want you to come in here a minute, George. We ought to take a look at
these windows.

COUNTY ATTORNEY *(scoffingly)*   Oh, windows!

SHERIFF   We'll be right out, Mr. Hale. *(*HALE *goes outside. The* SHERIFF *follows the*
COUNTY ATTORNEY *into the other room. Then* MRS. HALE *rises, hands tight together,
looking intensely at* MRS. PETERS, *whose eyes make a slow turn, finally meeting* MRS.
HALE*'s. A moment* MRS. HALE *holds her, then her own eyes point the way to where
the box is concealed. Suddenly* MRS. PETERS *throws back quilt pieces and tries to put
the box in the bag she is carrying. It is too big. She opens box, starts to take bird out,
cannot touch it, goes to pieces, stands there helpless. Sound of a knob turning in the
other room.* MRS. HALE *snatches the box and puts it in the pocket of her big coat. Enter*
COUNTY ATTORNEY *and* SHERIFF, *who remains* D. R.*)*

COUNTY ATTORNEY *(crosses to* U. L. *door facetiously)*   Well, Henry, at least we found
out that she was not going to quilt it. She was going to—what is it you call
it, ladies?

MRS. HALE *(standing* C. *below table facing front, her hand against her pocket)*   We call
it—knot it, Mr. Henderson.

*Curtain*

## FOR DISCUSSION

1. How does the setting, including stage properties, contribute to the general mood of the play?
2. What has happened to precipitate the events of the play?
3. What was Mrs. Wright's condition when Mr. Hale found her in the rocker?
4. Describe the personality of Mr. Henderson, the County Attorney.
5. Compare the personalities of Mrs. Hale and Mrs. Peters. Which woman do you find more perceptive?
6. What symbolic value can you assign to Mrs. Wright's frozen fruit? What does the play's constant emphasis on coldness suggest?
7. What is the point of whether Mrs. Wright was going to quilt or knot the quilt she had been working on? Why does Mrs. Hale pull out the stitches in the quilt that were "not sewed very good"?
8. Why does Mrs. Hale suddenly wish that she had come to visit Mrs. Wright from time to time? Why had she not visited her very often before?
9. What kind of a girl had Mrs. Wright been when she was the young Minnie Foster? What kind of a man had Mr. Wright been?
10. What is the climax of the play?
11. What is ironic about who finds the evidence of how the murder took place?
12. Do Mrs. Peters and Mrs. Hale know that they are concealing evidence? Do they know that they have discovered the motive for the murder?
13. In a paragraph or two, detail the probable events of the murder.
14. *Trifles* is a social play, and it deals with a very serious human problem. What is that problem? What is the play's central problem?

# A Memory of Two Mondays

ARTHUR MILLER

## Cast of Characters

| | |
|---|---|
| BERT | LARRY |
| RAYMOND | FRANK |
| AGNES | JERRY |
| PATRICIA | WILLIAM |
| GUS | TOM |
| JIM | MECHANIC |
| KENNETH | MISTER EAGLE |

*The shipping room of a large auto-parts warehouse. This is but the back of a large loft in an industrial section of New York. The front of the loft, where we cannot see, is filled with office machinery, records, the telephone switchboard, and the counter where customers may come who do not order by letter or phone.*

*The two basic structures are the long packing table which curves upstage at the left, and the factory-type windows which reach from floor to ceiling and are encrusted with the hard dirt of years. These windows are the background and seem to surround the entire stage.*

*At the back, near the center, is a door to the toilet; on it are hooks for clothing. The back wall is bare but for a large spindle on which orders are impaled every morning and taken off and filled by the workers all day long. At center there is an ancient desk and chair. Downstage right is a small bench. Boxes, a roll of packing paper on the table, and general untidiness. This place is rarely swept.*

*The right and left walls are composed of corridor openings, a louverlike effect, leading out into the alleys which are lined with bins reaching to the ceiling. Downstage center there is a large cast-iron floor scale with weights and balance exposed.*

*The nature of the work is simple. The men take orders off the hook, go out into the bin-lined alleys, fill the orders, bring the merchandise back to the table, where Kenneth packs and addresses everything. The desk is used by Gus and/or Tom Kelly to figure postage or express rates on, to eat on, to lean on, or to hide things in. It is just home base, generally.*

*A warning: The place must seem dirty and unmanageably chaotic, but since it is seen in this play with two separate visions it is also romantic. It is a little world, a home to which, unbelievably perhaps, these people like to come every Monday morning, despite what they say.*

*It is a hot Monday morning in summer, just before nine.*

*The stage is empty for a moment; then Bert enters. He is eighteen. His trousers are worn at the knees but not unrespectable; he has rolled-up sleeves and is tieless. He carries a thick book, a large lunch in a brown paper bag, and a* New York Times. *He stores the lunch behind the packing table, clears a place on the table, sits and opens the paper, reads.*

*Enter Raymond Ryan, the manager. He wears a tie, white shirt, pressed pants, carries a clean towel, a tabloid, and in the other hand a sheaf of orders.*

*Raymond is forty, weighed down by responsibilities, afraid to be kind, quite able to be tough. He walks with the suggestion of a stoop.*

*He goes directly to a large hook set in the back wall and impales the orders. Bert sees him but, getting no greeting, returns to his paper. Preoccupied, Raymond walks past Bert toward the toilet, then halts in thought, turns back to Bert.*

RAYMOND  Tommy Kelly get in yet?

BERT  I haven't seen him, but I just got here myself. *(Raymond nods slightly, worried.)* He'll probably make it all right.

RAYMOND  What are you doing in so early?

BERT  I wanted to get a seat on the subway for once. Boy, it's nice to walk around in the streets before the crowds get out . . .

RAYMOND *(He has never paid much attention to Bert, is now curious, has time for it.)*  How do you get time to read that paper?

BERT  Well, I've got an hour and ten minutes on the subway. I don't read it all, though. Just reading about Hitler.

RAYMOND  Who's that?

BERT  He took over the German government last week.[1]

RAYMOND *(nodding, uninterested)*  Listen, I want you to sweep up that excelsior laying around the freight elevator.

BERT  Okay. I had a lot of orders on Saturday, so I didn't get to it.

RAYMOND *(self-consciously; thus almost in mockery)*  I hear you're going to go to college. Is that true?

BERT *(embarrassed)*  Oh, I don't know, Mr. Ryan. They may not even let me in, I got such bad marks in high school.

RAYMOND  *You* did?

BERT  Oh, yeah. I just played ball and fooled around, that's all. I think I wasn't listening, y'know?

RAYMOND  How much it going to cost you?

BERT  I guess about four, five hundred for the first year. So I'll be here a long time—if I ever do go. You ever go to college?

RAYMOND *(shaking his head negatively)*  My kid brother went to pharmacy, though. What are you going to take up?

BERT  I really don't know. You look through that catalogue—boy, you feel like taking it all, you know?

RAYMOND  This the same book you been reading?

BERT  Well, it's pretty long, and I fall asleep right after supper.

RAYMOND *(turning the book up)*  "War and Peace"?

BERT  Yeah, he's supposed to be a great writer.

RAYMOND  How long it take you to read a book like this?

BERT  Oh, probably about three, four months, I guess. It's hard on the subway, with all those Russian names.

RAYMOND *(putting the book down)*  What do you get out of a book like that?

BERT  Well, it's—it's literature.

---

[1] The play is set at the end of March 1933, shortly after the German government granted Hitler dictatorial powers, and one month into the "hundred days" during which Franklin D. Roosevelt's New Deal programs were made law.

RAYMOND *(nodding, mystified)*   Be sure to open those three crates of axles that came in Saturday, will you? *(He starts to go toward the toilet.)*

BERT   I'll get to it this morning.

RAYMOND   And let me know when you decide to leave. I'll have to get somebody—

BERT   Oh, that'll be another year. Don't worry about it. I've got to save it all up first. I'm probably just dreaming anyway.

RAYMOND   How much do you save?

BERT   About eleven or twelve a week.

RAYMOND   Out of fifteen?

BERT   Well, I don't buy much. And my mother gives me my lunch.

RAYMOND   Well, sweep up around the elevator, will you?

*Raymond starts for the toilet as Agnes enters. She is a spinster in her late forties, always on the verge of laughter.*

AGNES   Morning, Ray!

RAYMOND   Morning, Agnes. *(He exits into the toilet.)*

AGNES *(to Bert)*   Bet you wish you could go swimming, heh?

BERT   Boy, I wouldn't mind. It's starting to boil already.

AGNES   You ought to meet my nephew sometime, Bert. He's a wonderful swimmer. Really, you'd like him. He's very serious.

BERT   How old is he now?

AGNES   He's only thirteen, but he reads the *New York Times* too.

BERT   Yeah?

AGNES *(noticing the book)*   You still reading that book?

BERT *(embarrassed)*   Well I only get time on the subway, Agnes—

AGNES   Don't let any of them kid you, Bert. You go ahead. You read the *New York Times* and all that. What happened today?

BERT   Hitler took over the German government.

AGNES   Oh, yes; my nephew knows about him. He loves civics. Last week one night he made a regular speech to all of us in the living room, and I realized that everything Roosevelt has done is absolutely illegal. Did you know that? Even my brother-in-law had to admit it, and he's a Democrat.

*Enter Patricia on her way to the toilet. She is twenty-three, blankly pretty, dressed just a little too tightly. She is not quite sure who she is yet.*

PATRICIA   Morning!

AGNES   Morning, Patricia! Where did you get that pin?

PATRICIA   It was given. *(She glances at Bert, who blushes.)*

AGNES   Oh, Patricia! Which one is he?

PATRICIA   Oh, somebody. *(She starts past for the toilet; Bert utters a warning "Ugh," and she remains.)*

AGNES *(She tends to laugh constantly, softly.)*   Did you go to the dance Saturday night?

PATRICIA *(fixing her clothing)*   Well, they're always ending up with six guys in the hospital at that dance, and like that, so we went bowling.

AGNES   Did he give you that pin?

PATRICIA   No, I had a date after him.

AGNES (*laughing, titillated*)   Pat!

PATRICIA   Well, I forgot all about him. So when I got home he was still sitting in front of the house in his car. I thought he was going to murder me. But isn't it an unusual pin? (*to Bert, who has moved off*) What are you always running away for?

BERT (*embarrassed*)   I was just getting ready to work, that's all.

*Enter Gus. He is sixty-eight, a barrel-bellied man, totally bald, with a long, fierce, gray mustache that droops on the right side. He wears a bowler, and his pants are a little too short. He has a ready-made clip-on tie. He wears winter underwear all summer long, changes once a week. There is something neat and dusty about him—a rolling gait, bandy legs, a belly hard as a rock and full of beer. He speaks with a gruff Slavic accent.*

PATRICIA   Oh, God, here's King Kong. (*She goes out up one of the corridors.*)

GUS (*calling after her halfheartedly—he is not completely sober, not bright yet*)   You let me get my hands on you I give you King Kong!

AGNES (*laughing*)   Oh, Gus, don't say those things!

GUS (*going for her*)   Aggie, you make me crazy for you!

AGNES (*laughing and running from him toward the toilet door*)   Gus!

GUS   Agnes, let's go Atlantic City! (*Agnes starts to open the toilet door. Raymond emerges from it.*)

AGNES (*surprised by Raymond*)   Oh!

RAYMOND (*with plaintive anger*)   Gus! Why don't you cut it out, heh?

GUS   Oh, I'm sick and tired, Raymond.

*Agnes goes into the toilet.*

RAYMOND   How about getting all the orders shipped out by tonight, heh, Gus—for once?

GUS   What I did? I did something?

RAYMOND   Where's Jim?

GUS   How do I know where's Jim? Jim is my brother?

*Jim enters, stiff. He is in his mid-seventies, wears bent eyeglasses; has a full head of hair; pads about with careful tread.*

JIM (*dimly*)   Morning, Raymond. (*He walks as though he will fall forward. All watch as Jim aims his jacket for a hook, then, with a sudden motion, makes it. But he never really sways.*)

GUS   Attaboy, Jim! (*to Raymond*) What you criticize Jim? Look at that!

JIM (*turning to Raymond with an apologetic smile*)   Morning, Raymond. Hot day today. (*He goes to the spike and takes orders off it.*)

RAYMOND   Now look, Gus. Mr. Eagle is probably going to come today, so let's have everything going good, huh?

GUS   You can take Mr. Eagle and you shove him!

*Agnes enters from the toilet.*

RAYMOND   What's the matter with you? I don't want that language around here any more. I'm not kidding, either. It's getting worse and worse, and we've got orders left over every night. Let's get straightened out here, will you? It's the same circus every Monday morning. *(He goes out.)*

AGNES  How's Lilly? Feeling better?

GUS  She's all the time sick, Agnes. I think she gonna die.

AGNES  Oh, don't say that. Pray to God, Gus.

GUS *(routinely)*  Aggie, come with me Atlantic City. *(He starts taking off his shirt.)*

AGNES *(going from him)*  Oh, how you smell!

GUS *(loudly)*  I stink, Aggie!

AGNES *(closing her ears, laughing)*  Oh, Gus, you're so terrible! *(She rushes out.)*

GUS *(laughs loudly, tauntingly, and turns to Bert)*  What are you doin'? It's nine o'clock.

BERT  Oh. *(He gets off the bench.)* I've got five to. Is your wife really sick? *(He gets an order from the hook.)*

GUS  You don't see Jim wait till nine o'clock! *(He goes to Jim, who is looking through the orders, and puts an arm around him.)* Goddam Raymond. You hear what he says to me?

JIM  Ssh, Gus, it's all right. Maybe better call Lilly.

GUS *(grasping Jim's arm)*  Wanna beer?

JIM *(trying to disengage himself)*  No, Gus, let's behave ourselves. Come on.

GUS *(looking around)*  Oh, boy. Oh goddam boy. Monday morning. Ach.

JIM *(to Bert, as he starts out)*  Did you unpack those axles yet?

GUS *(taking the order out of Jim's hand)*  What are you doing with axles? Man your age! *(He gives Bert Jim's order.)* Bert! Here! You let him pick up heavy stuff I show you something! Go!

BERT  I always take Jim's heavy orders, Gus. *(He goes out with the orders.)*

GUS  Nice girls, heh, Jim?

JIM  Oh, darn nice. Darn nice girls, Gus.

GUS  I keep my promise, hah, Jim?

JIM  You did, Gus. I enjoyed myself. But maybe you ought to call up your wife. She might be wonderin' about you. You been missin' since Saturday, Gus.

GUS *(asking for a reminder)*  Where we was yesterday?

JIM  That's when we went to Staten Island, I think. On the ferry? Remember? With the girls? I think we was on a ferry. So it must've been to Staten Island. You better call her.

GUS  Ach— She don't hear nothing, Jim.

JIM  But if the phone rings, Gus, she'll know you're all right.

GUS  All right, I ring the phone. *(He goes and dials. Jim leaves with his orders.)*

*Patricia enters.*

PATRICIA  Morning, Kong!

GUS  Shatap. *(She goes into the toilet as Gus listens on the phone. Then he roars:)* Hallo! *Hallo! Lilly! Gus! Gus!* How you feel? *Gus!* Working! Ya! Ya! *Gus!* Oh, shatap! *(He hangs up the phone angrily, confused. Jim enters with a few small boxes, which he sets in a pile on the table.)*

JIM  You call her?

GUS  Oh, Jim, she don't hear nothing. *(He goes idly to the toilet, opens the door. Patricia screams within, and Gus stands there in the open doorway, screaming with her in parody, then lets the door shut.)*

*Jim starts out, examining his order, a pencil in his hand, as Kenneth enters, lunch in hand. Kenneth is twenty-six, a strapping, fair-skinned man, with thinning hair, delicately shy, very strong. He has only recently come to the country.*

JIM   Morning, Kenneth.

KENNETH   And how are you this fine exemplary morning, James?

JIM   Oh, comin' along. Goin' to be hot today. *(He goes out.)*

*Kenneth hangs up his jacket and stores his lunch. Gus is standing in thought, picking his ear with a pencil.*

KENNETH   Havin' yourself a thought this morning, Gus? *(Gus just looks at him, then goes back to his thought and his excavation.)* Gus, don't you think something could be done about the dust constantly fallin' through the air of this place? Don't you imagine a thing or two could be done about that?

GUS   Because it's dusty, that's why. *(He goes to the desk, sits.)*

KENNETH   That's what I was sayin'—its dusty. Tommy Kelly get in?

GUS   No.

KENNETH   Oh, poor Tommy Kelly. *(Bert enters.)* Good morning to you, Bert. Have you finished your book yet?

BERT *(setting two heavy axles on the bench)*   Not yet, Kenneth.

KENNETH *(his jacket in his hand)*   Well, don't lose heart. *(He orates:)*

> "Courage, brother! do not stumble
> Though thy path be dark as night;
> There's a star to guide the humble;
> Trust in God, and do the Right."

By Norman Macleod.[2]

BERT *(with wonder, respect)*   How'd you learn all that poetry?

KENNETH *(hanging up his jacket)*   Why, in Ireland, Bert; there's all kinds of useless occupations in Ireland. "When lilacs last in the dooryard bloomed . . ."

GUS *(from the desk)*   What the hell you doin'? *(Bert goes to order hook.)*

KENNETH   Why, it's the poetry hour, Gus, don't you know that? This is the hour all men rise to thank God for the blue of the sky, the roundness of the everlasting globe, and the cheerful cleanliness of the subway system. And here we have some axles. Oh, Bert, I never thought I would end me life wrappin' brown paper around strange axles. *(He wraps.)* And what's the latest in the *New York Times* this morning?

BERT *(looking through orders on the hook)*   Hitler took over the German government.

KENNETH   Oh, did he! Strange, isn't it, about the Germans? A great people they are for mustaches. You take Bismarck, now, or you take Frederick the Great, or even take Gus over here—

GUS   I'm no Heinie.

KENNETH   Why, I always thought you were, Gus. What are you, then?

GUS   American.

KENNETH   I know that, but what *are* you?

GUS   I fought in submarine.

---

[2] Nineteenth-century Scottish clergyman and poet. Kenneth next quotes from Walt Whitman.

KENNETH   Did you, now? An American submarine?

GUS   What the hell kind of submarine I fight in, Hungarian? (*He turns back to his desk.*)

KENNETH   Well, don't take offense, Gus. There's all kinds of submarines, y'know. (*Bert starts out, examining his order.*) How's this to be wrapped, Bert? Express?

BERT   I think that goes parcel post. It's for Skaneateles.

GUS (*erupting at his desk*)   Axles parcel post? You crazy? You know how much gonna cost axles parcel post?

BERT   That's right. I guess it goes express.

GUS   And you gonna go college? Barber college you gonna go!

BERT   Well, I forgot it was axles, Gus.

GUS (*muttering over his desk*)   Stupid.

KENNETH   I've never been to Skaneateles. Where would that be?

BERT   It's a little town upstate. It's supposed to be pretty there.

KENNETH   That a sweet thought? Sendin' these two grimy axles out into the green countryside? I spent yesterday in the park. What did you do, Bert? Go swimmin' again, I suppose?

GUS (*turning*)   You gonna talk all day?

BERT   We're working. (*He goes out. Kenneth wraps.*)

KENNETH   You're rubbin' that poor kid pretty hard, Gus; he's got other things on his mind than parcel post and—

GUS   What the hell I care what he got on his mind? Axles he gonna send parcel post! (*He returns to his work on the desk.*)

KENNETH (*wraps, then*)   Can you feel the heat rising in this building! If only some of it could be saved for the winter. (*Pause. He is wrapping.*) The fiery furnace. Nebuchadnezzar was the architect. (*Pause.*) What do you suppose would happen, Gus, if a man took it into his head to wash these windows? They'd snatch him off to the nuthouse, heh? (*Pause.*) I wonder if he's only kiddin'— Bert. About goin' to college someday.

GUS (*not turning from his desk*)   Barber college he gonna go.

KENNETH (*he works, thinking*)   He must have a wealthy family. Still and all, he don't spend much. I suppose he's just got some strong idea in his mind. That's the thing, y'know. I often conceive them myself, but I'm all the time losin' them, though. It's the holdin' on—that's what does it. You can almost see it in him, y'know? He's holdin' on to somethin'. (*He shakes his head in wonder, then sings:*)

> Oh, the heat of the summer,
> The cool of the fall.
> The lady went swimming
> With nothing at all.

Ah, that's a filthy song, isn't it! (*Pause. He wraps.*) Gus, you suppose Mr. Roosevelt'll be makin' it any better than it is? (*He sings:*)

> The minstrel boy to the war has gone,
> In the ranks of death . . .

*Patricia enters from the toilet.*

PATRICIA   Was that an Irish song?

KENNETH (*shyly*)   All Irish here and none of yiz knows an Irish song.

PATRICIA　You have a terrific voice, Kenneth.

GUS *(to Patricia)*　Why don't you make date with him?

KENNETH *(stamping his foot)*　Oh, that's a nasty thing to say in front of a girl, Gus!

*Gus rises.*

PATRICIA *(backing away from Gus)*　Now don't start with me, kid, because—

*Gus lunges for her. She turns to run, and he squeezes her buttocks mercilessly as she runs out and almost collides with Larry, who is entering. Larry is thirty-nine, a troubled but phlegmatic man, good-looking. He is carrying a container of coffee and a lighted cigarette. On the collision he spills a little coffee.*

LARRY *(with a slight humor)*　Hey! Take it easy.

PATRICIA *(quite suddenly all concerned for Larry, to Gus)*　Look what you did, you big horse!

*Larry sets the coffee on the table.*

LARRY　Jesus, Gus.

GUS　Tell her stop makin' all the men crazy! *(He returns to his desk.)*

PATRICIA　I'm sorry, Larry. *(She is alone, in effect, with Larry. Both of them wipe the spot on his shirt.)* Did you buy it?

LARRY *(embarrassed but courageous, as though inwardly flaunting his own fears)*　Yeah, I got it yesterday.

PATRICIA　Gee, I'd love to see it. You ever going to bring it to work?

LARRY *(Now he meets her eyes.)*　I might. On a Saturday, maybe.

PATRICIA　'Cause I love those Auburns, y'know?

LARRY　Yeah, they got nice valves. Maybe I'll drive you home some night. For the ride.

PATRICIA *(The news stuns her.)*　Oh, boy! Well—I'll see ya. *(She goes.)*

GUS　You crazy? Buy Auburn?

LARRY *(with depth—a profound conclusion)*　I like the valves, Gus.

GUS　Yeah, but when you gonna go sell it who gonna buy an Auburn?

LARRY　Didn't you ever get to where you don't care about that? I *always* liked those valves, and I decided, that's all.

GUS　Yeah, but when you gonna go sell it—

LARRY　I don't care.

GUS　You don't care!

LARRY　I'm sick of dreaming about things. They've got the most beautifully laid-out valves in the country on that car, and I want it, that's all.

*Kenneth is weighing a package on the scales.*

GUS　Yeah, but when you gonna go sell it—

LARRY　I just don't care, Gus. Can't you understand that? *(He stares away, inhaling his cigarette.)*

KENNETH *(stooped over, sliding the scale weights)*　There's a remarkable circumstance, Larry. Raymond's got twins, and now you with the triplets. And both in the same corporation. We ought to send that to the *Daily News* or something. I think they give you a dollar for an item like that.

*Bert enters, puts goods on the table.*

BERT   Gee, I'm getting hungry. Want a sandwich, Kenneth? *(He reaches behind the packing table for his lunch bag.)*

KENNETH   Thank you, Bert. I might take one later.

GUS *(turning from the desk to Bert)*   Lunch you gonna eat nine o'clock?

BERT   I got up too early this morning. You want some?

KENNETH   He's only a growing boy, Gus—and by the way, if you care to bend down, Gus *(indicating under the scale platform)* there's more mice than ever under here.

GUS *(without turning)*   Leave them mice alone.

KENNETH   Well, you're always complainin' the number of crayons I'm using, and I'm only tellin' you they're the ones is eatin' them up. *(He turns to Larry.)* It's a feast of crayons goin' on here every night, Larry.

*Enter Jim with goods, padding along.*

JIM   Goin' to be hot today, Gus.

GUS   Take easy, what you running for? *(Jim stops to light his cigar butt.)*

KENNETH *(reading off the scale weights)*   Eighty-one pounds, Gus. For Skaneateles, in the green countryside of upper New York State.

GUS   What? What you want?

KENNETH   I want the express order—eighty-one pounds to Skaneateles, New York.

GUS   Then why don't you say that, goddam Irishman? You talk so much. When you gonna stop talkin'? *(He proceeds to make out the slip.)*

KENNETH   Oh, when I'm rich, Gus, I'll have very little more to say. *(Gus is busy making out the slip; Kenneth turns to Larry.)* No sign yet of Tommy Kelly in the place, Larry.

LARRY   What'd you, cut a hole in your shoe?

KENNETH   A breath of air for me little toe. I only paid a quarter for them, y'know; feller was sellin' them in Bryant Park. Slightly used, but they're a fine pair of shoes, you can see that.

LARRY   They look small for you.

KENNETH   They are at that. But you can't complain for a quarter, I guess.

GUS   Here.

*Gus hands Kenneth an express slip, which Kenneth now proceeds to attach to the package on the table. Meanwhile Jim has been leafing through the orders on the hook and is now leaving with two in his hand.*

KENNETH   How do you keep up your strength, Jim? I'm always exhausted. You never stop movin', do ya? *(Jim just shakes his head with a "Heh, heh.")* I bet it's because you never got married, eh?

JIM   No, I guess I done everything there is but that.

LARRY   How come you never did get married, Jim?

JIM   Well, I was out West so long, you know, Larry. Out West. *(He starts to go again.)*

KENNETH   Oh, don't they get married much out there?

JIM   Well, the cavalry was amongst the Indians most of the time.

BERT   How old are you now, Jim? No kidding.

KENNETH   I'll bet he's a hundred.

JIM   Me? No. I ain't no hunderd. I ain't near a hunderd. You don't have to be a hunderd to've fought the Indians. They was more Indians was fought than they tells in the schoolbooks, y'know. They was a hell of a lot of fightin' up to McKinley and all in there. I ain't no hunderd. *(He starts out.)*

KENNETH   Well, how old would you say you are, Jim?

JIM   Oh, I'm seventy-four, seventy-five, seventy-six—around in there. But I ain't no hunderd. *(He exits, and Kenneth sneezes.)*

BERT   *(He has put his lunch bag away and is about to leave.)*   Boy, I was hungry!

KENNETH   *(irritated)*   Larry, don't you suppose a word might be passed to Mr. Eagle about the dust? It's rainin' dust from the ceiling!

*Bert goes out.*

GUS   What the hell Mr. Eagle gonna do about the dust?

KENNETH   Why, he's supposed to be a brilliant man, isn't he? Dartmouth College graduate and all? I've been five and a half months in this country, and I never sneezed so much in my entire life before. My nose is all—

*Enter Frank, the truckdriver, an impassive, burly man in his thirties.*

FRANK   Anything for the West Bronx?

KENNETH   Nothin' yet, Frank. I've only started, though.

*Jim enters with little boxes, which he adds to the pile on the bench.*

FRANK   You got anything for West Bronx, Jim? I've got the truck on the elevator.

GUS   What's the hurry?

FRANK   I got the truck on the elevator.

GUS   Well, take it off the elevator! You got one little box of bearings for the West Bronx. You can't go West Bronx with one little box.

FRANK   Well, I gotta go.

GUS   You got a little pussy in the West Bronx.

FRANK   Yeah, I gotta make it before lunch.

JIM   *(riffling through his orders)*   I think I got something for the East Bronx.

FRANK   No, West Bronx.

JIM   *(removing one order from his batch)*   How about Brooklyn?

FRANK   What part? *(He takes Jim's order, reads the address, looks up, thinking.)*

JIM   Didn't you have a girl around Williamsburg?

FRANK   I'll have to make a call. I'll be right back.

GUS   You gonna deliver only where you got a woman?

FRANK   No, Gus, I go any place you tell me. But as long as I'm goin' someplace I might as well—you know. *(He starts out.)*

GUS   You some truckdriver.

FRANK   You said it, Gus. *(He goes out.)*

GUS   Why don't you go with him sometime, Kenneth? Get yourself nice piece ding-a-ling—

KENNETH   Oh, don't be nasty now, Gus. You're only tryin' to be nasty to taunt me.

*Raymond enters.*

RAYMOND  Didn't Tommy Kelly get here?

GUS  Don't worry for Tommy. Tommy going to be all right.

LARRY  Can I see you a minute, Ray? *(He moves with Raymond over to the left.)*

RAYMOND  Eagle's coming today, and if he sees him drunk again I don't know what I'm going to do.

LARRY  Ray, I'd like you to ask Eagle something for me.

RAYMOND  What?

LARRY  I've got to have more money.

RAYMOND  You and me both, boy.

LARRY  No, I can't make it any more. Ray. I mean it. The car put me a hundred and thirty bucks in the hole. If one of the kids get sick I'll be strapped.

RAYMOND  Well, what'd you buy the car for?

LARRY  I'm almost forty, Ray. What am I going to be careful for?

RAYMOND  See, the problem is, Larry, if you go up, I'm only making thirty-eight myself, and I'm the manager, so it's two raises—

LARRY  Ray, I hate to make it tough for you, but my wife is driving me nuts. Now—

*Enter Jerry Maxwell and Willy Hogan, both twenty-three. Jerry has a black eye; both are slick dressers.*

JERRY AND WILLY  Morning. Morning, Gus.

RAYMOND  Aren't you late, fellas?

JERRY *(glancing at his gold wristwatch)*  I've got one minute to nine, Mr. Ryan.

WILLY  That's Hudson Tubes[3] time, Mr. Ryan.

GUS  The stopwatch twins.

RAYMOND *(to Jerry)*  You got a black eye?

JERRY  Yeah, we went to a dance in Jersey City last night.

WILLY  Ran into a wise guy in Jersey City, Mr. Ryan.

JERRY *(with his taunting grin; he is very happy with himself)*  Tried to take his girl away from us.

RAYMOND  Well, get on the ball. Mr. Eagle's—

*Enter Tom Kelly. Gus rises from the desk. Bert enters, stands still. Raymond and Larry stand watching. Kenneth stops wrapping. Tom is stiff; he moves in a dream to the chair Gus has left and sits rigidly. He is a slight, graying clerk in his late forties.*

GUS *(to Raymond)*  Go 'way, go 'head.

*Raymond comes up and around the desk to face Tom, who sits there, staring ahead, immobile, his hands in his lap.*

RAYMOND  Tommy.

*Jerry and Willy titter.*

GUS *(to them)*  Shatap, goddam bums!

JERRY  Hey, don't call me—

---

[3] That is, according to the clocks in the Hudson Tubes, subways connecting New York City and New Jersey.

GUS  Shatap, goddamit I break you goddam head! (*He has an axle in his hand, and Raymond and Larry are pulling his arm down. Jim enters and goes directly to him. All are crying, "Gus! Cut it out! Put it down!"*)

JERRY  What'd we do? What'd I say?

GUS  Watch out! Just watch out you make fun of this man! I break you head, both of you! (*Silence. He goes to Tom, who has not moved since arriving.*) Tommy. Tommy, you hear Gus? Tommy? (*Tom is transfixed.*)

RAYMOND  Mr. Eagle is coming today, Tommy.

GUS (*to all*)  Go 'head, go to work, go to work! (*They all move; Jerry and Willy go out.*)

RAYMOND  Can you hear me, Tom? Mr. Eagle is coming to look things over today, Tom.

JIM  Little shot of whisky might bring him to.

GUS  Bert! (*He reaches into his pocket.*) Here, go downstairs bring a shot. Tell him for Tommy. (*He sees what is in his hand.*) I only got ten cents.

RAYMOND  Here. (*He reaches into his pocket as Jim, Kenneth, and Larry all reach into their own pockets.*)

BERT (*taking a coin from Raymond*)  Okay, I'll be right up. (*He hurries out.*)

RAYMOND  Well, this is it, Gus. I gave him his final warning.

GUS (*He is worried.*)  All right, go 'way, go 'way.

*Agnes enters.*

AGNES  Is he—?

RAYMOND  You heard me, Agnes. I told him on Saturday, didn't I? (*He starts past her.*)

AGNES  But Ray, look how nice and clean he came in today. His hair is all combed, and he's much neater.

RAYMOND  I did my best, Agnes. (*He goes out.*)

GUS (*staring into Tommy's dead eyes*)  Ach. He don't see nothin', Agnes.

AGNES (*looking into Tommy's face*)  And he's supposed to be saving for his daughter's confirmation dress! Oh, Tommy. I'd better cool his face. (*She goes into the toilet.*)

KENNETH (*to Larry*)  Ah, you can't blame the poor feller; sixteen years of his life in this place.

LARRY  You said it.

KENNETH  There's a good deal of monotony connected with the life, isn't it?

LARRY  You ain't kiddin'.

KENNETH  Oh, there must be a terrible lot of Monday mornings in sixteen years. And no philosophical idea at all, y'know, to pass the time?

GUS (*to Kenneth*)  When you gonna shut up?

*Agnes comes from the toilet with a wet cloth. They watch as she washes Tom's face.*

KENNETH  Larry, you suppose we could get these windows washed sometime? I've often thought if we could see a bit of the sky now and again it would help matters now and again.

LARRY  They've never been washed since I've been here.

KENNETH  I'd do it myself if I thought they wouldn't all be laughin' at me for a greenhorn. (*He looks out through the open window, which only opens out a few*) *inches.)* With all this glass we might observe the clouds and the various signs of approaching storms. And there might even be a bird now and again.

AGNES  Look at that—he doesn't even move. And he's been trying so hard! Nobody gives him credit, but he does try hard. *(to Larry)* See how nice and clean he comes in now?

*Jim enters, carrying parts.*

JIM  Did you try blowing in his ear?

GUS  Blow in his ear?

JIM  Yeah, the Indians used to do that. Here, wait a minute. *(He comes over, takes a deep breath, and blows into Tom's ear. A faint smile begins to appear on Tom's face, but, as Jim runs out of breath, it fades.)*

KENNETH  Well, I guess he's not an Indian.

JIM  That's the truth, y'know. Out West, whenever there'd be a drunken Indian, they used to blow in his ear.

*Enter Bert, carefully carrying a shotglass of whisky.*

GUS  Here, gimme that. *(He takes it.)*

BERT  *(licking his fingers)*  Boy, that stuff is strong.

GUS  Tommy? *(He holds the glass in front of Tom's nose.)* Whisky. *(Tom doesn't move.)* Mr. Eagle is coming today, Tommy.

JIM  Leave it on the desk. He might wake up to it.

BERT  How's he manage to make it here, I wonder.

AGNES  Oh, he's awake. Somewhere inside, y'know. He just can't show it, somehow. It's not really like being drunk, even.

KENNETH  Well, it's pretty close, though, Agnes.

*Agnes resumes wetting Tom's brow.*

LARRY  Is that a fact, Jim, about blowing in a guy's ear?

JIM  Oh, sure. Indians always done that. *(He goes to the order hook, leafs through.)*

KENNETH  What did yiz all have against the Indians?

JIM  The Indians? Oh, we don't have nothin' against the Indians. Just law and order, that's all. Talk about heat, though. It was so hot out there we—

*Jim exits with an order as Frank enters.*

FRANK  All right, I'll go to Brooklyn.

GUS  Where you running? I got nothing packed yet.

*Enter Jerry, who puts goods on the table.*

FRANK  Well, you beefed that I want to go Bronx, so I'm tellin' you now I'll go to Brooklyn.

GUS  You all fixed up in Brooklyn?

FRANK  Yeah, I just made a call.

AGNES  *(laughing)*  Oh, you're all so terrible! *(She goes out.)*

JERRY  How you doin', Kenny? You gittin' any?

KENNETH  Is that all two fine young fellas like you is got on your minds?

JERRY  Yeah, that's all. What's on your mind?

*Frank is loading himself with packages.*

GUS *(of Tommy)*   What am I gonna do with him, Larry? The old man's comin'.

LARRY   Tell you the truth, Gus, I'm sick and tired of worrying about him, y'know? Let him take care of himself.

*Gus goes to Larry, concerned, and they speak quietly.*

GUS   What's the matter with you these days?

LARRY   Two years I'm asking for a lousy five-dollar raise. Meantime my brother's into me for fifty bucks for his wife's special shoes; my sister's got me for sixty-five to have her kid's teeth fixed. So I buy a car, and they're all on my back—how'd I dare buy a car! Whose money is it? Y'know, Gus? I mean—

GUS   Yeah, but an Auburn, Larry—

LARRY *(getting hot)*   I happen to like the valves! What's so unusual about that?

*Enter Willy and Jerry with goods.*

WILLY *(to Jerry)*   Here! Ask Frank. *(to Frank)* Who played shortstop for Pittsburgh in nineteen-twenty-four?

FRANK   Pittsburgh? Honus Wagner, wasn't it?

WILLY *(to Jerry)*   What I tell ya?

JERRY   How could it be Honus Wagner? Honus Wagner—

*Raymond enters with a mechanic, and Willy and Jerry exit, arguing. Frank goes out with his packages. Gus returns to his desk.*

RAYMOND   Larry, you want to help this man? He's got a part here.

*Larry simply turns, silent, with a hurt and angry look. The mechanic goes to him, holds out the part; but Larry does not take it, merely inspects it, for it is greasy, as is the man.*

RAYMOND *(going to the desk, where Gus is now seated at work beside Tom Kelly)*   Did he move at all, Gus?

GUS   He's feeling much better, I can see. Go, go 'way, Raymond. *(Raymond worriedly stands there.)*

LARRY *(to mechanic)*   Where you from?

MECHANIC   I'm mechanic over General Truck.

LARRY   What's that off?

MECHANIC *(as Bert stops to watch, and Kenneth stops packing to observe)*   That's the thing—I don't know. It's a very old coal truck, see, and I thought it was a Mack, because it says Mack on the radiator, see? But I went over to Mack, and they says there's no part like that on any Mack in their whole history, see?

LARRY   Is there any name on the engine?

MECHANIC   I'm tellin' you; on the engine it says American-LaFrance—must be a replacement engine.

LARRY   That's not off a LaFrance.

MECHANIC   I know! I went over to American-LaFrance, but they says they never seen nothin' like that in their whole life since the year one.

*Raymond joins them.*

LARRY   What is it, off the manifold?

MECHANIC   Well, it ain't exactly off the manifold. It like sticks out, see, except it don't stick out, it's like stuck in there—I mean it's like in a little hole there on top of the head, except it ain't exactly a hole, it's a thing that comes up in like a bump, see, and then it goes down. Two days I'm walkin' the streets with this, my boss is goin' crazy.

LARRY   Well, go and find out what it is, and if we got it we'll sell it to you.

RAYMOND   Don't you have any idea, Larry?

LARRY   I might, Ray, but I'm not getting paid for being an encyclopedia. There's ten thousand obsolete parts upstairs—it was never my job to keep all that in my head. If the old man wants that service, let him pay somebody to do it.

RAYMOND   Ah, Larry, the guy's here with the part.

LARRY   The guy is always here with the part, Ray. Let him hire somebody to take an inventory up there and see what it costs him.

RAYMOND   *(taking the part off the table)*   Well, I'll see what I can find up there.

LARRY   You won't find it, Ray. Put it down. *(Raymond does, and Larry, blinking with hurt, turns to the mechanic.)* What is that truck, about nineteen-twenty-two?

MECHANIC   That truck? *(He shifts onto his right foot in thought.)*

LARRY   Nineteen-twenty?

MECHANIC   *(in a higher voice, shifting to the left foot)*   That truck?

LARRY   Well, it's at least nineteen-twenty, isn't it?

MECHANIC   Oh, it's at least. I brung over a couple a friend of mines, and one of them is an old man and he says when he was a boy already that truck was an old truck, and he's an old, old man, that guy. *(Larry takes the part now and sets on the packing bench. Now even Gus gets up to watch as he stares at the part. There is a hush. Raymond goes out. Larry turns the part a little and stares at it again. Now he sips his coffee.)* I understand this company's got a lot of old parts from the olden days, heh?

LARRY   We may have one left, if it's what I think it is, but you'll have to pay for it.

MECHANIC   Oh, I know; that's why my boss says try all the other places first, because he says youse guys charge. But looks to me like we're stuck.

LARRY   Bert. *(He stares in thought.)* Get the key to the third floor from Miss Molloy. Go up there, and when you open the door you'll see those Model-T mufflers stacked up.

BERT   Okay.

LARRY   You ever been up there?

BERT   No, but I always wanted to go.

LARRY   Well, go past the mufflers and you'll see a lot of bins going up to the ceiling. They're full of Marmon valves and ignition stuff.

BERT   Yeah?

LARRY   Go past them, and you'll come to a little corridor, see?

BERT   Yeah?

LARRY   At the end of the corridor is a pile of crates—I think there's some Maxwell differentials in there.

BERT   Yeah?

LARRY Climb over the crates, but don't keep goin', see. Stand on top of the crates and turn right. Then bend down, and there's a bin—No, I tell you, get off the crates, and you can reach behind them, but to the right, and reach into that bin. There's a lot of Locomobile headnuts in there, but way back—you gotta stick your hand way in, see, and you'll find one of these.

BERT Geez, Larry, how do you remember all that?

*Agnes rushes in.*

AGNES Eagle's here! Eagle's here!

LARRY *(to the mechanic)* Go out front and wait at the counter, will ya? *(The mechanic nods and leaves. Larry indicates the glass on the desk.)* Better put that whisky away, Gus.

GUS *(alarmed now)* What should we do with him?

*Larry goes to Tom, peeved, and speaks in his ear.*

LARRY Tommy, Tommy!

AGNES Larry, why don't you put him up on the third floor? He got a dozen warnings already. Eagle's disgusted—

GUS Maybe he's sick. I never seen him like this.

*Jim enters with goods.*

JIM Eagle's here.

LARRY Let's try to walk him around. Come on.

*Gus looks for a place to hide the whisky, then drinks it.*

GUS All right, Tommy, come on, get up. *(They hoist him up to his feet, then let him go. He starts to sag; they catch him.)* I don't think he feel so good.

LARRY Come on, walk him. *(to Agnes)* Watch out for Eagle. *(She stands looking off and praying silently.)* Let's go, Tom. *(They try to walk Tom, but he doesn't lift his feet.)*

AGNES *(trembling, watching Tommy)* He's so kindhearted, y'see? That's his whole trouble—he's too kindhearted.

LARRY *(angering, but restrained, shaking Tom)* For God's sake, Tom, come on! Eagle's here! *(He shakes Tom more violently.)* Come on! What the hell is the matter with you, you want to lose your job? Goddamit, you a baby or something?

AGNES Sssh!

*They all turn to the left. In the distance is heard the clacking of heel taps on a concrete floor.*

GUS Put him down, Larry! *(They seat Tom before the desk. Agnes swipes back his mussed hair. Gus sets his right hand on top of an invoice on the desk.)* Here, put him like he's writing. Where's my pencil? Who's got pencil? *(Larry, Kenneth, Agnes search themselves for a pencil.)*

KENNETH Here's a crayon.

GUS Goddam, who take my pencil! Bert! Where's that Bert! He always take my pencil!

*Bert enters, carrying a heavy axle.*

BERT    Hey, Eagle's here!

GUS    Goddam you, why you take my pencil?

BERT    I haven't got your pencil. This is mine.

*Gus grabs the pencil out of Bert's shirt pocket and sticks it upright into Tom's hand. They have set him up to look as if he is writing. They step away. Tom starts sagging toward one side.*

AGNES *(in a loud whisper)*    Here he comes!

*She goes to the order spike and pretends she is examining it. Larry meanwhile rushes to Tom, sets him upright, then walks away, pretending to busy himself. But Tom starts falling off the chair again, and Bert rushes and props him up.*

*The sound of the heel taps is on us now, and Bert starts talking to Tom, meantime supporting him with one hand on his shoulder.*

BERT *(overloudly)*    Tommy, the reason I ask, see, is because on Friday I filled an order for the same amount of coils for Scranton, see, and it just seems they wouldn't be ordering the same exact amount again.

*During his speech Eagle has entered—a good-looking man in his late forties, wearing palm beach trousers, a shirt and tie, sleeves neatly folded up, a new towel over one arm. He walks across the shipping room, not exactly looking at anyone, but clearly observing everything. He goes into the toilet, past Agnes who turns.*

AGNES    Good morning, Mr. Eagle.

EAGLE *(nodding)*    Morning. *(He goes into the toilet.)*

KENNETH *(indicating the toilet)*    Keep it up, keep it up now!

BERT *(loudly)*    Ah—another thing that's bothering me, Tommy, is those rear-end gears for Riverhead. I can't find any invoice for Riverhead. I can't find any invoice for gears to Riverhead. *(He is getting desperate, looks to the others, but they only urge him on.)* So what happened to the invoice? That's the thing we're all wondering about, Tommy. What happened to that invoice? You see, Tom? That invoice—it was blue, I remember, blue with a little red around the edges—

KENNETH *(loudly)*    That's right there, Bert, it was a blue invoice—and it had numbers on it—

*Suddenly Tom stands, swaying a little, blinking. There is a moment's silence.*

TOM    No, no, Glen Wright was shortstop for Pittsburgh, not Honus Wagner.

*Eagle emerges from the toilet. Bert goes to the order spike.*

LARRY    Morning, sir. *(He goes out.)*

TOM *(half bewildered, shifting from foot to foot)*    Who was talking about Pittsburgh? *(He turns about and almost collides with Eagle.)* Morning, Mr. Eagle.

EAGLE *(As he passes Tom he lets his look linger on his face.)*    Morning, Kelly.

*Eagle crosses the shipping room and goes out. Agnes, Kenneth, and Gus wait an instant. Jim enters, sees Tom is up.*

JIM    Attaboy, Tommy, knew you'd make it.

TOM    Glen Wright was shortstop. Who asked about that?

GUS *(nodding sternly his approbation to Bert)* Very good, Bert, you done good.

BERT *(wiping his forehead)* Boy!

TOM Who was talking about Pittsburgh? *(Agnes is heard weeping. They turn.)* Agnes? *(He goes to her.)* What's the matter, Ag?

AGNES Oh, Tommy, why do you do that?

PATRICIA *(calling from offstage left)* Aggie? Your switchboard's ringing.

AGNES Oh, Tommy! *(Weeping, she hurries out.)*

TOM *(to the others)* What happened? What is she cryin' for?

GUS *(indicating the desk)* Why don't you go to work, Tommy? You got lotta parcel post this morning.

*Tom always has a defensive smile. He shifts from foot to foot as he talks, as though he were always standing on a hot stove. He turns to the desk, sees Kenneth. He wants to normalize everything.*

TOM Kenny! I didn't even see ya!

KENNETH Morning, Tommy. Good to see you up and about.

TOM *(with a put-on brogue)* Jasus, me bye, y'r hair is fallin' like the dew of the evenin.'

KENNETH *(self-consciously wiping his hair)* Oh, Tommy, now—

TOM Kenny, bye, y'r gittin' an awful long face to wash!

KENNETH *(gently cuffing him)* Oh, now, stop that talk!

TOM *(backing toward his desk)* Why, ya donkey, ya. I bet they had to back you off the boat!

KENNETH *(with mock anger)* Oh, don't you be callin' me a donkey now!

*Enter Raymond.*

RAYMOND Tom? *(He is very earnest, even deadly.)*

TOM *(instantly perceiving his own guilt)* Oh, mornin', Ray, how's the twins? *(He gasps little chuckles as he sits at his desk, feeling about for a pencil.)*

*Raymond goes up close to the desk and leans over, as the others watch—pretending not to.*

RAYMOND *(quietly)* Eagle wants to see you.

TOM *(with foreboding, looking up into Raymond's face)* Eagle? I got a lot of parcel post this morning, Ray. *(He automatically presses down his hair.)*

RAYMOND He's in his office waiting for you now, Tom.

TOM Oh, sure. It's just that there's a lot of parcel post on Monday. . . . *(He feels for his tie as he rises, and walks out. Raymond starts out after him, but Gus intercedes.)*

GUS *(going up to Raymond)* What Eagle wants?

RAYMOND I warned him, Gus, I warned him a dozen times.

GUS He's no gonna fire him.

RAYMOND Look, it's all over, Gus, so there's nothing—

GUS He gonna fire Tommy?

RAYMOND Now don't raise your voice.

GUS Sixteen year Tommy work here! He got daughter gonna be in church confirmation!

RAYMOND Now listen, I been nursing him along for—

GUS Then you fire me! You fire Tommy, you fire me!

RAYMOND Gus!

*With a stride Gus goes to the hook, takes his shirt down, thrusts himself into it.*

GUS    Goddam son-of-a-bitch.

RAYMOND    Now don't be crazy, Gus.

GUS    I show who crazy! Tommy Kelly he gonna fire! *(He grabs his bowler off the hook. Enter Agnes, agitated.)*

AGNES    Gus! Go to the phone!

GUS    *(not noticing her, and with bowler on, to Raymond)*    Come on, he gonna fire me now, son-of-a-bitch! *(He starts out, shirttails flying, and Agnes stops him.)*

AGNES    *(indicating the phone)*    Gus, your neighbor's—

GUS    *(trying to disengage himself)*    No, he gonna fire me now. He fire Tommy Kelly, he fire me!

AGNES    Lilly, Gus! Your neighbor wants to talk to you. Go, go to the phone.

*Gus halts, looks at Agnes.*

GUS    What, Lilly?

AGNES    Something's happened. Go, go to the phone.

GUS    Lilly? *(Perplexed, he goes to the phone.)* Hallo. Yeah, Gus. Ha? *(He listens, stunned. His hand, of itself, goes to his hatbrim as though to doff the hat, but it stays there. Jim enters, comes to a halt, sensing the attention, and watches Gus.)* When? When it happen? *(He listens, and then mumbles)* Ya. Thank you. I come home right away. *(He hangs up. Jim comes forward to him questioningly. To Jim, perplexed)* My Lilly. Die.

JIM    Oh? Hm!

*Larry enters. Gus dumbly turns to him.*

GUS    *(to Larry)*    Die. My Lilly.

LARRY    Oh, that's tough, Gus.

RAYMOND    You better go home. *(Pause.)* Go ahead, Gus. Go home.

*Gus stands blinking. Raymond takes his jacket from the hook and helps him on with it. Agnes starts to push his shirttails into his pants.*

GUS    We shouldn't've go to Staten Island, Jim. Maybe she don't feel good yesterday. Ts, I was in Staten Island, maybe she was sick. *(Tommy Kelly enters, goes directly to his desk, sits, his back to the others. Pause. To Tom)* He fire you, Tommy?

TOM    *(holding tears back)*    No, Gus, I'm all right.

GUS    *(going up next to him)*    Give you another chance?

TOM    *(He is speaking with his head lowered.)*    Yeah. It's all right, Gus, I'm goin' to be all right from now on.

GUS    Sure. Be a man, Tommy. Don't be no drunken bum. Be a man. You hear? Don't let nobody walk on top you. Be man.

TOM    I'm gonna be all right, Gus.

GUS    *(nodding)*    One more time you come in drunk I gonna show you something. *(Agnes sobs. He turns to her.)* What for you cry all the time? *(He goes past her and out. Agnes then goes. A silence.)*

RAYMOND    *(breaking the silence)*    What do you say, fellas, let's get going, heh? *(He claps his hands and walks out as all move about their work. Soon all are gone but*

*Tommy Kelly, slumped at his desk; Kenneth, wrapping; and Bert, picking an order from the hook. Now Kenneth faces Bert suddenly.)*

KENNETH *(he has taken his feeling from the departing Gus, and turns now to Bert)*    Bert? How would you feel about washing these windows—you and I—once and for all? Let a little of God's light in the place?

BERT *(excitedly, happily)*    Would you?

KENNETH    Well, I would if you would.

BERT    Okay, come on! Let's do a little every day; couple of months it'll all be clean! Gee! Look at the sun!

KENNETH    Hey, look down there!

See the old man sitting in a chair?

And roses all over the fence!

Oh, that's a lovely back yard!

*A rag in hand, Bert mounts the table; they make one slow swipe of the window before them and instantly all the windows around the stage burst into the yellow light of summer that floods into the room.*

BERT    Boy, they've got a tree!

And all those cats!

KENNETH    It'll be nice to watch the seasons pass.

That pretty up there now, a real summer sky

And a little white cloud goin' over?

I can just see autumn comin' in

And the leaves falling on the gray days.

You've got to have a sky to look at!

*Gradually, as they speak, all light hardens to that of winter, finally.*

BERT *(turning to Kenneth)*    Kenny, were you ever fired from a job?

KENNETH    Oh, sure; two-three times.

BERT    Did you feel bad?

KENNETH    The first time, maybe. But you have to get used to that, Bert. I'll bet you never went hungry in your life, did you?

BERT    No, I never did. Did you?

KENNETH    Oh, many and many a time. You get used to that too, though.

BERT *(turning and looking out)*    That tree is turning red.

KENNETH    It must be spectacular out in the country now.

BERT    How does the cold get through these walls? Feel it, it's almost a wind!

KENNETH    Don't cats walk daintly in the snow!

BERT    Gee, you'd never know it was the same place—

How clean it is when it's white!

Gus doesn't say much any more, y'know?

KENNETH    Well, he's showin' his age. Gus is old.

When do you buy your ticket for the train?

BERT    I did. I've got it.

KENNETH    Oh, then you're off soon!

You'll confound all the professors, I'll bet!

*(He sings softly.)*

"The minstrel boy to the war has gone . . ."

*Bert moves a few feet away; thus he is alone. Kenneth remains at the window, looking out, polishing, and singing softly.*

BERT  There's something so terrible here!
   There always was, and I don't know what.
   Gus, and Agnes, and Tommy and Larry, Jim and Patricia—
   Why does it make me so sad to see them every morning?
   It's like the subway;
   Every day I see the same people getting on
   And the same people getting off,
   And all that happens is that they get older. God!
   Sometimes it scares me; like all of us in the world
   Were riding back and forth across a great big room,
   From wall to wall and back again,
   And no end ever! Just no end!
   *(He turns to Kenneth, but not quite looking at him, and with a deeper anxiety.)*
   Didn't you ever want to be anything, Kenneth?
KENNETH  I've never been able to keep my mind on it, Bert. . . .
   I shouldn't've cut a hole in me shoe.
   Now the snow's slushin' in, and me feet's all wet.
BERT  If you studied, Kenneth, if you put your mind to something great, I know
   you'd be able to learn anything, because you're clever, you're much smarter
   than I am!
KENNETH  You've got something steady in your mind, Bert;
   Something far away and steady.
   I never could hold my mind on a far-away thing . . .
   *(His tone changes as though he were addressing a group of men; his manner is rougher,
   angrier, less careful of proprieties.)*
   She's not giving me the heat I'm entitled to.
   Eleven dollars a week room and board,
   And all she puts in the bag is a lousy pork sandwich,
   The same every day and no surprises.
   Is that right? Is that right now?
   How's a man to live.
   Freezing all day in this palace of dust
   And night comes with one window and a bed
   And the streets full of strangers
   And not one of them's read a book through,
   Or seen a poem from beginning to end
   Or knows a song worth singing.
   Oh, this is an ice-cold city, Mother,
   And Roosevelt's not makin' it warmer, somehow.
   *(He sits on the table, holding his head.)*
   And here's another grand Monday!
   *(They are gradually appearing in natural light now, but it is a cold wintry light which
   has gradually supplanted the hot light of summer. Bert goes to the hook for a sweater.)*
   Jesus, me head'll murder me. I never had the headache till this year.
BERT  *(delicately)*  You're not taking up drinking, are you?

KENNETH *(he doesn't reply. Suddenly, as though to retrieve something slipping by, he gets to his feet, and roars out)*
"The Ship of State," by Walt Whitman!
"O Captain! my Captain! our fearful trip is done!
The ship has weathered every wrack,
The prize we sought is won . . ."
Now what in the world comes after that?

BERT  I don't know that poem.

KENNETH  Dammit all! I don't remember the bloody poems any more the way I did! It's the drinkin' does it, I think. I've got to stop the drinkin'!

BERT  Well, why do you drink, Kenny, if it makes you feel—

KENNETH  Good God, Bert, you can't always be doin' what you're better off to do! There's all kinds of unexpected turns, y'know, and things not workin' out the way they ought! What in hell *is* the next stanza of that poem? "The prize we sought is won . . ." God, I'd never believe I could forget that poem! I'm thinkin', Bert, y'know—maybe I ought to go into the Civil Service. The only trouble is there's no jobs open except for the guard in the insane asylum. And that'd be a nervous place to work, I think.

BERT  It might be interesting, though.

KENNETH  I suppose it might. They tell me it's only the more intelligent people goes mad, y'know. But it's sixteen hundred a year, Bert, and I've a feelin' I'd never dare leave it, y'know? And I'm not ready for me last job yet, I think. I don't want nothin' to be the last, yet. Still and all . . .

*Raymond enters, going to toilet. He wears a blue button-up sweater.*

RAYMOND  Morning, boys. *(He impales a batch of orders on the desk.)*

KENNETH  *(in a routine way)*  Morning, Mr. Ryan. Have a nice New Year's, did you?

RAYMOND  Good enough. *(to Bert, seeing the book on the table)* Still reading that book?

BERT  Oh, I'm almost finished now. *(Raymond nods, continues on. Bert jumps off the table.)* Mr. Ryan? Can I see you a minute? *(He goes to Raymond.)* I wondered if you hired anybody yet, to take my place.

RAYMOND  *(pleasantly surprised)*  Why? Don't you have enough money to go?

BERT  No, I'm going. I just thought maybe I could help you break in the new boy. I won't be leaving till after lunch tomorrow.

RAYMOND  *(with resentment, even an edge of sarcasm)*  We'll break him in all right. Why don't you just get on to your own work? There's a lot of excelsior laying around the freight elevator.

*Raymond turns and goes into the toilet. For an instant Bert is left staring after him. Then he turns to Kenneth, perplexed.*

BERT  Is he sore at me?

KENNETH  *(deprecatingly)*  Ah, why would he be sore at you? *(He starts busying himself at the table, avoiding Bert's eyes. Bert moves toward him, halts.)*

BERT  I hope you're not, are you?

KENNETH  *(with an evasive air)*  Me? Ha! Why, Bert, you've got the heartfelt good wishes of everybody in the place for your goin'-away! *(But he turns away to busy himself at the table—and on his line Larry has entered with a container of coffee and a cigarette.)*

BERT  Morning, Larry. *(He goes to the hook, takes an order.)*

LARRY *(leaning against the table)*  Jesus, it'd be just about perfect in here for penguins. *(Bert passes him.)* You actually leaving tomorrow?

BERT *(eagerly)*  I guess so, yeah.

LARRY *(with a certain embarrassed envy)*  Got all the dough, heh?

BERT  Well, for the first year anyway. *(He grins in embarrassment.)* You mind if I thank you?

LARRY  What for?

BERT  I don't know—just for teaching me everything. I'd have been fired the first month without you, Larry.

LARRY *(with some wonder, respect)*  Got all your dough, heh?

BERT  Well, that's all I've been doing is saving.

*Enter Tom Kelly. He is bright, clean, sober.*

TOM  Morning!

KENNETH *(with an empty kind of heartiness)*  Why, here comes Tommy Kelly!

TOM *(passing to hang up his coat and hat)*  Ah, y're gettin' an awful long face to wash, Kenny, me bye.

KENNETH  Oh, cut it out with me face, Tommy. I'm as sick of it as you are.

TOM  Go on, ya donkey ya, they backed you off the boat.

KENNETH  Why, I'll tear you limb from limb, Tom Kelly! *(He mocks a fury, and Tom laughs as he is swung about. And then, with a quick hug and a laugh:)* Oh, Tommy, you're the first man I ever heard of done it. How'd you do it, Tom?

TOM  Will power, Kenny. *(He walks to his desk, sits.)* Just made up my mind, that's all.

KENNETH  Y'know the whole world is talking about you, Tom—the way you mixed all the drinks at the Christmas party and never weakened? Y'know, when I heard it was you going to mix the drinks I was prepared to light a candle for you.

TOM  I just wanted to see if I could do it, that's all. When I done that—mixin' the drinks for three hours, and givin' them away—I realized I made it. You don't look so hot to me, you know that?

KENNETH *(with a sigh)*  Oh, I'm all right. It's the sight of Monday, that's all, is got me down.

TOM  You better get yourself a little will power, Kenny. I think you're gettin' a fine taste for the hard stuff.

KENNETH  Ah, no, I'll never be a drunk, Tommy.

TOM  You're a drunk now.

KENNETH  Oh, don't say that, please!

TOM  I'm tellin' you, I can see it comin' on you.

KENNETH *(deeply disturbed)*  You can't either. Don't say that, Tommy!

*Agnes enters.*

AGNES  Morning! *(She wears sheets of brown paper for leggins.)*

KENNETH  Winter's surely here when Agnes is wearin' her leggins.

AGNES  *(with her laughter)*  Don't they look awful? But that draft under the switchboard is enough to kill ya.

LARRY  This place is just right for penguins.

AGNES  Haven't you got a heavier sweater, Bert? I'm surprised at your mother.

BERT  Oh, it's warm; she knitted it.

KENNETH  Bert's got the idea. Get yourself an education.

TOM  College guys are sellin' ties all over Macy's. Accountancy, Bert, that's my advice to you. You don't even have to go to college for it either.

BERT  Yeah, but I don't want to be an accountant.

TOM  *(with a superior grin)*  You don't want to be an accountant?

LARRY  What's so hot about an accountant?

TOM  Well, try runnin' a business without one. That's what you should've done, Larry. If you'd a took accountancy, you'd a—

LARRY  You know, Tommy, I'm beginning to like you better drunk? *(Tommy laughs, beyond criticism.)* I mean it. Before, we only had to pick you up all the time; now you got opinions about everything.

TOM  Well, if I happen to know something, why shouldn't I say—

*Enter Raymond from the toilet.*

RAYMOND  What do you say we get on the ball early today, fellas? Eagle's coming today. Bert, how about gettin' those carburetor crates open, will ya?

BERT  I was just going to do that.

*Bert and Raymond are starting out, and Agnes is moving to go, when Gus and Jim enter. Both of them are on the verge of staggering. Gus has a bright new suit and checked overcoat, a new bowler, and new shoes. He is carrying upright a pair of Ford fenders, still in their brown paper wrappings—they stand about seven feet in height. Jim aids him in carefully resting the fenders against the wall.*

*Kenneth, Agnes, and Larry watch in silence.*

*Patricia enters and watches. She is wearing leggins.*

*Willy and Jerry enter in overcoats, all jazzed up.*

WILLY  Morning!

JERRY  Morn—*(Both break off and slowly remove their coats as they note the scene and the mood. Gus, now that the fenders are safely stacked, turns.)*

GUS  *(dimly)*  Who's got a hanger?

KENNETH  Hanger? You mean a coat-hanger, Gus?

GUS  Coat-hanger.

JERRY  Here! Here's mine! *(He gives a wire hanger to Gus. Gus is aided by Jim in removing his overcoat, and they both hang it on the hanger, then on a hook. Both give it a brush or two, and Gus goes to his chair, sits. He raises his eyes to them all.)*

GUS  So what everybody is looking at?

*Bert, Willy, Jerry go to work, gradually going out with orders. Jim also takes orders off the hook, and the pattern of going-and-coming emerges. Patricia goes to the toilet. Tom Kelly works at the desk.*

LARRY *(half-kidding, but in a careful tone)*   What are you all dressed up about?

*Gus simply glowers in his fumes and thoughts. Raymond goes over to Jim.*

RAYMOND   What's he all dressed up for?

JIM   Oh, don't talk to me about him, Ray, I'm sick and tired of him. Spent all Saturday buyin' new clothes to go to the cemetery; then all the way the hell over to Long Island City to get these damned fenders for that old wreck of a Ford he's got. Never got to the cemetery, never got the fenders on—and we been walkin' around all weekend carryin' them damn things.

RAYMOND   Eagle'll be here this morning. See if you can get him upstairs. I don't want him to see him crocked again.

JIM   I'd just let him sit there, Ray, if I was you. I ain't goin' to touch him. You know what he went and done? Took all his insurance money outa the bank Saturday. Walkin' around with all that cash in his pocket—I tell ya, I ain't been to sleep since Friday night. 'Cause you can't let him loose with all that money and so low in his mind, y'know . . .

GUS   Irishman! *(All turn to him. He takes a wad out of his pocket, peels one bill off.)* Here. Buy new pair shoes.

KENNETH   Ah, thank you, no, Gus, I couldn't take that.

RAYMOND   Gus, Eagle's coming this morning; why don't you—

GUS *(stuffing a bill into Kenneth's pocket)*   Go buy pair shoes.

RAYMOND   Gus, he's going to be here right away; why don't you—

GUS   I don't give one goddam for Eagle! Why he don't make one more toilet?

RAYMOND   What?

*Bert enters with goods.*

GUS   Toilet! That's right? Have one toilet for so many people? That's very bad, Raymond. That's no nice. *(offering Bert a bill)* Here, boy, go—buy book, buy candy.

*Larry goes to Gus before he gives the bill, puts an arm around him, and walks away from the group.*

LARRY   Come on, Gussy, let me take you upstairs.

GUS   I don't care Eagle sees me, I got my money now, goddam. Oh, Larry, Larry, twenty-two year I workin' here.

LARRY   Why don't you give me the money, Gus? I'll put in the bank for you.

GUS   What for I put in bank? I'm sixty-eight years old, Larry. I got no children, nothing. What for I put in bank? *(Suddenly, reminded, he turns back to Raymond, pointing at the floor scale.)* Why them goddam mice nobody does nothing?

RAYMOND *(alarmed by Gus's incipient anger)*   Gus, I want you to go upstairs!

*Patricia enters from toilet.*

GUS *(at the scale)*   Twenty-two years them goddam mice! That's very bad, Raymond, so much mice! *(He starts rocking the scale.)* Look at them goddam mice! *(Patricia screams as mice come running out from under the scale. A mêlée of shouts begins, everyone dodging mice or swinging brooms and boxes at them. Raymond is pulling Gus away from the scale, yelling at him to stop it. Agnes rushes in and, seeing the mice, screams and rushes out. Jerry and Willy rush in and join in chasing the mice, laughing. Patricia, wearing leggins, is helped onto the packing table by Larry, and Gus shouts up at her.)* Come with me Atlantic City, Patricia! *(He pulls out the wad.)* Five thousand dollars I got for my wife!

PATRICIA   You rotten thing, you! You dirty rotten thing, Gus!

GUS   I make you happy, Patricia! I make you—*(Suddenly his hand goes to his head; he is dizzy. Larry goes to him, takes one look.)*

LARRY   Come, come on. *(He walks Gus into the toilet.)*

PATRICIA *(out of the momentary silence)*   Oh, that louse! Did you see what he did, that louse? *(She gets down off the table, and, glancing angrily toward the toilet, she goes out.)*

RAYMOND   All right, fellas, what do you say, heh? Let's get going.

*Work proceeds—the going and coming.*

TOM *(as Raymond passes him)*   I tried talking to him a couple of times, Ray, but he's got no will power! There's nothing you can do if there's no will power, y'know?

RAYMOND   Brother! It's a circus around here. Every Monday morning! I never saw anything like . . .

*He is gone. Kenneth is packing. Tom works at his desk. Jim comes and, leaving goods on the packing table, goes to the toilet, peeks in, and then goes out, studying an order. Bert enters with goods.*

KENNETH   There's one thing you have to say for the Civil Service; it seals the fate and locks the door. A man needn't wonder what he'll do with his life any more.

*Jerry enters with goods.*

BERT *(glancing at the toilet door)*   Gee, I never would've thought Gus liked his wife, would you?

*Tom, studying a letter, goes out.*

JERRY *(looking up and out the window)*   Jesus!

BERT *(not attending to Jerry)*   I thought he always hated his wife—

JERRY   Jesus, boy!

KENNETH *(to Jerry)*   What're you doin'? What's—?

JERRY   Look at the girls up in there. One, two, three, four windows—full a girls, look at them! Them two is naked!

*Willy enters with goods.*

KENNETH   Oh, my God!

WILLY *(rushing to the windows)*   Where? Where?

KENNETH   Well, what're you gawkin' at them for!

*Gus and Larry enter from the toilet.*

JERRY   There's another one down there! Look at her on the bed! What a beast!

WILLY *(overjoyed)*   It's a cathouse! Gus! A whole cathouse moved in!

*Willy and Jerry embrace and dance around wildly; Gus stands with Larry, staring out, as does Bert.*

KENNETH   Aren't you ashamed of yourself!!

*Tom enters with his letter.*

TOM   Hey, fellas, Eagle's here.

JERRY *(pointing out)*   There's a new cathouse, Tommy! *(Tom goes and looks out the windows.)*

KENNETH   Oh, that's a terrible thing to be lookin' at, Tommy! *(Agnes enters; Kenneth instantly goes to her to get her out.)* Oh, Agnes, you'd best not be comin' back here any more now—

AGNES   What? What's the matter?

*Jerry has opened a window, and he and Willy whistle sharply through their fingers. Agnes looks out.*

KENNETH   Don't, Agnes, don't look at that!

AGNES   Well, for heaven's sake! What are all those women doing there?

GUS   That's whorehouse, Aggie.

KENNETH   Gus, for God's sake! *(He walks away in pain.)*

AGNES   What are they sitting on the beds like that for?

TOM   The sun is pretty warm this morning—probably trying to get a little tan.

AGNES   Oh, my heavens. Oh, Bert, it's good you're leaving! *(She turns to them.)* You're not all going, are you? *(Gus starts to laugh, then Tom, then Jerry and Willy, then Larry, and she is unstrung and laughing herself, but shocked.)* Oh, my heavens! *(She is gone, as Jim enters with goods.)*

KENNETH   All right, now, clear off, all of you. I can't be workin' with a lot of sex maniacs blockin' off me table!

GUS   Look, Jim! *(Jim looks out.)*

JIM   Oh, nice.

JERRY   How about it, fellas? Let's all go lunchtime! What do you say, Kenny? I'll pay for you!

*Gus goes to the desk, drags the chair over to the window.*

KENNETH   I'd sooner roll meself around in the horse manure of the gutter!

JERRY   I betcha you wouldn't even know what to do!

KENNETH *(bristling, fists shut)*   I'll show you what I do! I'll show you right now!

*Enter Raymond, furious.*

RAYMOND   What the hell is this? What's going on here?

GUS *(sitting in his chair, facing the windows)*   Whorehouse. *(Raymond looks out the windows.)*

KENNETH   You'd better pass a word to Mr. Eagle about this, Raymond, or the corporation's done for. Poor Agnes, she's all mortified, y'know.

RAYMOND   Oh, my God! *(To all:)* All right, break it up, come on, break it up, Eagle's here. *(Willy, Jerry, Bert, and Jim disperse, leaving with orders. Tommy returns to the desk.)* What're you going to do, Gus? You going to sit there? *(Gus doesn't answer; sits staring out thoughtfully.)* What's going on with you? Gus! Eagle's here! All right, cook in your own juice. Sit there. *(He glances out the windows.)* Brother, I needed this now! *(He goes out angrily.)*

LARRY  Give me the money, Gus, come on. I'll hold it for you.

GUS *(an enormous sadness is on him)*  Go 'way.

*Enter Patricia. She glances at Larry and Gus, then looks out the windows.*

KENNETH *(wrapping)*  Ah, Patricia, don't look out there. It's disgraceful.

TOM  It's only a lot of naked women.

KENNETH  Oh, Tommy, now! In front of a girl!

PATRICIA *(to Kenneth)*  What's the matter? Didn't you ever see that before? *(She sees Gus sitting there.)* Look at Kong, will ya? *(She laughs.)* Rememberin' the old days, heh, Kong?

*Larry is walking toward an exit at left.*

GUS  Oh, shatap!

PATRICIA *(catching up with Larry at the edge of the stage, quietly)*  What's Ray sayin' about you sellin' the Auburn?

LARRY  Yeah, I'm kinda fed up with it. It's out of my class anyway.

PATRICIA  That's too bad. I was just gettin' to enjoy it.

LARRY *(very doubtfully)*  Yeah?

PATRICIA  What're you mad at me for?

LARRY  Why should I be mad?

PATRICIA  You're married, what're you—?

LARRY  Let me worry about that, will you?

PATRICIA  Well, I gotta worry about it too, don't I?

LARRY  Since when do you worry about anything, Pat?

PATRICIA  Well, what did you expect me to do? How did I know you were serious?

*Gus goes to his coat, searches in a pocket.*

LARRY  What did you think I was telling you all the time?

PATRICIA  Yeah, but Larry, anybody could say those kinda things.

LARRY  I know, Pat. But I never did. *(With a cool, hurt smile.)* You know, kid, you better start believing people when they tell you something. Or else you're liable to end up in there. *(He points out the windows.)*

PATRICIA *(with quiet fury)*  You take that back! *(He walks away; she goes after him.)* You're going to take that back, Larry!

*Eagle enters, nods to Larry and Patricia.*

EAGLE  Morning.

PATRICIA *(with a mercurial change to sunny charm)*  Good morning, Mr. Eagle!

*Larry is gone, and she exits. Eagle crosses, noticing Gus, who is standing beside his coat, drinking out of a pint whisky bottle.*

EAGLE  Morning, Gus.

GUS *(lowering the bottle)*  Good morning. *(Eagle exits into the toilet.)*

TOM *(to Gus)*  You gone nuts?

*Gus returns, holding the bottle, to his chair, where he sits, looking out the window. He is growing sodden and mean. Bert enters with goods.*

KENNETH *(sotto voce)*    Eagle's in there, and look at him. He'll get the back of it now for sure.

TOM *(going to Gus)*    Gimme the bottle, Gus!

GUS    I goin' go someplace, Tommy. I goin' go cemetery. I wasn't one time in cemetery. I go see my Lilly. My Lilly die, I was in Staten Island. All alone she was in the house. Ts! *(Jerry enters with goods, sees him, and laughs.)*

BERT    Gus, why don't you give Tommy the bottle?

GUS    Twenty-two years I work here.

KENNETH *(to Jerry, who is staring out the window)*    Will you quit hangin' around me table, please?

JERRY    Can't I look out the window?

*Willy enters with goods.*

WILLY    How's all the little pussies?

KENNETH    Now cut that out! *(They laugh at him.)*

TOM *(sotto voce)*    Eagle's in there!

KENNETH    Is that all yiz know of the world—filthy women and dirty jokes and the ignorance drippin' off your faces? *(Eagle enters from the toilet.)* There's got to be somethin' done about this, Mr. Eagle. It's an awful humiliation for the women here. *(He points, and Eagle looks.)* I mean to say, it's a terrible disorganizing sight starin' a man in the face eight hours a day, sir.

EAGLE    Shouldn't have washed the windows, I guess. *(He glances down at Gus and his bottle and walks out.)*

KENNETH    Shouldn't have washed the windows, he says! *(They are laughing; Gus is tipping the bottle up. Jim enters with goods.)*

JERRY    What a donkey that guy is!

*Kenneth lunges for Jerry and grabs him by the tie, one fist ready.*

KENNETH    I'll donkey you! *(Jerry starts a swing at him, and Bert and Tom rush to separate them as Raymond enters.)*

RAYMOND    Hey! Hey!

JERRY *(as they part)*    All right, donkey, I'll see you later.

KENNETH    You'll see me later, all right—with one eye closed!

RAYMOND    Cut it out! *(Kenneth, muttering, returns to work at his table. Jerry rips an order off the hook and goes out. Willy takes an order. Bert goes out with an order. Raymond has been looking down at Gus, who is sitting with the bottle.)* You going to work, Gus? Or you going to do that? *(Gus gets up and goes to his coat, takes it off the hanger.)* What're you doing?

GUS    Come on, Jim, we go someplace. Here—put on you coat.

RAYMOND    Where you going? It's half-past nine in the morning.

*Enter Agnes.*

AGNES    What's all the noise here? *(She breaks off, seeing Gus dressing.)*

GUS    That's when I wanna go—half-past nine. *(He hands Jim his coat.)* Here. Put on. Cold outside.

JIM *(quietly)*    Maybe I better go ʼvith him, Ray. He's got all his money in—

*Bert enters with goods.*

RAYMOND *(reasonably, deeply concerned)*   Gus, now look; where you gonna go now? Why don't you lie down upstairs?

GUS *(swaying, to Bert)*   Twenty-two years I was here.

BERT   I know, Gus.

*Larry enters, watches.*

GUS   I was here before you was born I was here.

BERT   I know.

GUS   Them mice was here before you was born. *(Bert nods uncomfortably, full of sadness.)* When Mr. Eagle was in high school I was already here. When there was Winton Six I was here. When was Minerva car I was here. When was Stanley Steamer I was here, and Stearns Knight, and Marmon was good car; I was here all them times. I was here first day Raymond come; he was young boy; work hard be manager. When Agnes still think she was gonna get married I was here. When was Locomobile, and Model K Ford and Model N Ford— all them different Fords, and Franklin was good car, Jordan car, Reo car, Pierce Arrow, Cleveland car—all them was good cars. All them times I was here.

BERT   I know.

GUS   You don't know nothing. Come on, Jim. *(He goes and gets a fender. Jim gets the other.)* Button up you coat, cold outside. Tommy? Take care everything good.

*He walks out with Jim behind him, each carrying a fender upright. Raymond turns and goes out, then Larry. Agnes goes into the toilet. The lights lower as this movement takes place, until Bert is alone in light, still staring at the point where Gus left.*

BERT   I don't understand;
    I don't know anything:
    How is it me that gets out?
    I don't know half the poems Kenneth does,
    Or a quarter of what Larry knows about an engine.

    I don't understand how they come every morning,
    Every morning and every morning,
    And no end in sight.
    That's the thing—there's no end!
    Oh, there ought to be a statue in the park—
    "To All the Ones That Stay."
    One to Larry, to Agnes, Tom Kelly, Gus . . .

    Gee, it's peculiar to leave a place—forever!
    Still, I always hated coming here;
    The same dried-up jokes, the dust;
    Especially in spring, walking in from the sunshine,
    Or any Monday morning in the hot days.

*In the darkness men appear and gather around the packing table, eating lunch out of bags; we see them as ghostly figures, silent.*

God, it's so peculiar to leave a place!
I know I'll remember them as long as I live,
As long as I live they'll never die,
And still I know that in a month or two
They'll forget my name, and mix me up
With another boy who worked here once,
And went. Gee, it's a mystery!

*As full light rises Bert moves into the group, begins eating from a bag.*

JERRY *(looking out the window)*   You know what's a funny thing? It's a funny thing
   how you get used to that.
WILLY   Tommy, what would you say Cobb's average was for lifetime?
TOM   Cobb? Lifetime? *(He thinks. Pause. Kenneth sings.)*
KENNETH   "The minstrel boy to the war has gone—

*Patricia enters, crossing to toilet.*

In the ranks of death you will find him."
PATRICIA   Is that an Irish song?
KENNETH   All Irish here, and none of yiz knows an Irish song!

*She laughs, exits into the toilet.*

TOM   I'd say three-eighty lifetime for Ty Cobb. *(to Larry)* You're foolish sellin'
   that car with all the work you put in it.
LARRY   Well, it was one of those crazy ideas. Funny how you get an idea, and
   then suddenly you wake up and you look at it and it's like—dead or something.
   I can't afford a car.

*Agnes enters, going toward the toilet.*

AGNES   I think it's even colder today than yesterday.

*Raymond enters.*

RAYMOND   It's five after one, fellas; what do you say?

*They begin to get up as Jim enters in his overcoat and hat.*

KENNETH   Well! The old soldier returns!
RAYMOND   Where's Gus, Jim?

*Agnes has opened the toilet door as Patricia emerges.*

AGNES   Oh! You scared me. I didn't know you were in there!
JIM *(removing his coat)*   He died, Ray.
RAYMOND   What?

*The news halts everyone—but one by one—in midair, as it were.*

LARRY   He what?
AGNES   What'd you say?
JIM   Gus died.
KENNETH   Gus died!
BERT   Gus?

AGNES *(going to Jim)*   Oh, good heavens. When? What happened?

LARRY   What'd you have an accident?

JIM   No, we—we went home and got the fenders on all right, and he wanted to go over and start at the bottom, and go right up Third Avenue and hit the bars on both sides. And we got up to about Fourteenth Street, in around there, and we kinda lost track of the car someplace. I have to go back there tonight, see if I can find—

AGNES   Well, what happened?

JIM   Well, these girls got in the cab, y'know, and we seen a lot of places and all that—we was to some real high-class places, forty cents for a cup of coffee[4] and all that; and then he put me in another cab, and we rode around a while; and then he got another cab to follow us. Case one of our cabs got a flat, see? He just didn't want to be held up for a minute, Gus didn't.

LARRY   Where were you going?

JIM   Oh, just all over. And we stopped for a light, y'know, and I thought I'd go up and see how he was gettin' along, y'know, and I open his cab door, and— the girl was fast asleep, see—and he—was dead. Right there in the seat. It was just gettin' to be morning.

AGNES   Oh, poor Gus!

JIM   I tell ya, Agnes, he didn't look too good to me since she died, the old lady. I never knowed it. He—liked that woman.

RAYMOND   Where's his money?

JIM   Oh *(with a wasting wave of the hand)* it's gone, Ray. We was stoppin' off every couple minutes so he call long distance. I didn't even know it, he had a brother someplace in California. Called him half a dozen times. And there was somebody he was talkin' to in Texas someplace, somebody that was in the Navy with him. He was tryin' to call all the guys that was in the submarine with him, and he was callin' all over hell and gone—and givin' big tips, and he bought a new suit, and give the cab driver a wristwatch and all like that. I think he got himself too sweated. Y'know it got pretty cold last night, and he was all sweated up. I kept tellin' him, I says, "Gus," I says, "you're gettin' yourself all sweated, y'know, and it's a cold night," I says; and all he kept sayin' to me all night he says, "Jim," he says, "I'm gonna do it right, Jim." That's all he says practically all night. "I'm gonna do it right," he says. "I'm gonna do it right." *(Pause. Jim shakes his head.)* Oh, when I open that door I knowed it right away. I takes one look at him and I knowed it. *(There is a moment of silence, and Agnes turns and goes into the toilet.)* Oh, poor Agnes, I bet she's gonna cry now.

*Jim goes to the order hook, takes an order off, and, putting a cigar into his mouth, he goes out, studying the order. Raymond crosses and goes out; then Patricia goes. Willy and Jerry exit in different directions with orders in their hands; Kenneth begins wrapping. Tom goes to his desk and sits, clasps his hands, and for a moment he prays.*

*Bert goes and gets his jacket. He slowly puts it on.*

*Enter Frank, the truckdriver.*

[4] The more usual price was less than five cents.

FRANK  Anything for West Bronx, Tommy?

TOM  There's some stuff for Sullivan's there.

FRANK  Okay. *(He pokes through the packages, picks some.)*

KENNETH  Gus died.

FRANK  No kiddin'!

KENNETH  Ya, last night.

FRANK  What do you know. Hm. *(He goes on picking packages out.)* Is this all for West Bronx, Tom?

TOM  I guess so for now.

FRANK  *(to Kenneth)*  Died.

KENNETH  Yes, Jim was with him. Last night.

FRANK  Jesus. *(Pause. He stares, shakes his head.)* I'll take Brooklyn when I get back, Tommy. *(He goes out, loaded with packages. Bert is buttoning his overcoat. Agnes comes out of the toilet.)*

BERT  Agnes?

AGNES  *(seeing the coat on, the book in his hand)*  Oh, you're leaving, Bert!

BERT  Yeah.

AGNES  Well. You're leaving.

BERT  *(expectantly)*  Yeah.

*Patricia enters.*

PATRICIA  Agnes? Your switchboard's ringing.

*Jerry enters with goods.*

AGNES  Okay! *(Patricia goes out.)* Well, good luck. I hope you pass everything.

BERT  Thanks, Aggie. *(She walks across and out, wiping a hair across her forehead. Willy enters with goods as Jerry goes out. Jim enters with goods.)*

*(Bert seems about to say good-by to each of them, but they are engrossed and he doesn't quite want to start a scene with them; but now Jim is putting his goods on the table, so Bert goes over to him.)* I'm leaving, Jim, so—uh—

JIM  Oh, leavin'? Heh! Well, that's—

TOM  *(from his place at the desk, offering an order to Jim)*  Jim? See if these transmissions came in yet, will ya? This guy's been ordering them all month.

JIM  Sure, Tom.

*Jim goes out past Bert, studying his order. Bert glances at Kenneth, who is busy wrapping. He goes to Tom, who is working at the desk.*

BERT  Well, so long, Tommy.

TOM  *(turning)*  Oh, you goin', heh?

BERT  Yeah, I'm leavin' right now.

TOM  Well, keep up the will power, y'know. That's what does it.

BERT  Yeah, I—uh—I wanted to—

*Raymond enters.*

RAYMOND  *(handing Tom an order)*  Tommy, make this a special, will you? The guy's truck broke down in Peekskill. Send it out special today.

TOM  Right.

*Raymond turns to go out, sees Bert, who seems to expect some moment from him.*

RAYMOND  Oh! 'By, Bert.

BERT  So long, Raymond, I—(*Raymond is already on his way, and he is gone. Jim enters with goods. Bert goes over to Kenneth and touches his back. Kenneth turns to him. Jim goes out as Willy enters with goods—Jerry too, and this work goes on without halt.*) Well, good-by, Kenny.

KENNETH  (*He is embarrassed as he turns to Bert.*)   Well, it's our last look, I suppose, isn't it?

BERT  No, I'll come back sometime. I'll visit you.

KENNETH  Oh, not likely; it'll all be out of mind as soon as you turn the corner. I'll probably not be here anyway.

BERT  You made up your mind for Civil Service?

KENNETH  Well, you've got to keep movin', and—I'll move there, I guess. I done a shockin' thing last night, Bert; I knocked over a bar.

BERT  Knocked it over?

KENNETH  It's disgraceful, what I done. I'm standin' there, havin' a decent conversation, that's all, and before I know it I start rockin' the damned thing, and it toppled over and broke every glass in the place, and the beer spoutin' out of the pipes all over the floor. They took all me money; I'll be six weeks payin' them back. I'm for the Civil Service, I think; I'll get back to regular there, I think.

BERT  Well—good luck, Kenny. (*blushing*) I hope you'll remember the poems again.

KENNETH  (*as though they were unimportant*)   No, they're gone, Bert. There's too much to do in this country for that kinda stuff.

*Willy enters with goods.*

TOM  Hey, Willy, get this right away; it's a special for Peekskill.

WILLY  Okay.

*Willy takes the order and goes, and when Bert turns back to Kenneth he is wrapping again. So Bert moves away from the table. Jerry enters, leaves; and Jim enters, drops goods on the table, and leaves. Larry enters with a container of coffee, goes to the order hook, and checks through the orders. Bert goes to him.*

BERT  I'm goin', Larry.

LARRY  (*over his shoulder*)  Take it easy, kid.

*Patricia enters and crosses past Bert, looking out through the windows. Tom gets up and bumbles through a pile of goods on the table, checking against an order in his hand. It is as though Bert wished it could stop for a moment, and as each person enters he looks expectantly, but nothing much happens. And so he gradually moves—almost is moved—toward an exit, and with his book in his hand he leaves.*

*Now Kenneth turns and looks about, sees Bert is gone. He resumes his work and softly sings.*

KENNETH  "The minstrel boy to the war has gone!" Tommy, I'll be needin' more crayon before the day is out.

TOM  (*without turning from the desk*)  I'll get some for you.

**568   The Drama**

KENNETH (*looking at a crayon, peeling it down to a nub*)   Oh, the damn mice. But
they've got to live, too, I suppose. (*He marks a package and softly sings:*)
> ". . . in the ranks of death you will find him.
> His father's sword he has girded on,
> And his wild harp slung behind him."

*The Curtain Falls*

## FOR DISCUSSION

1. How does the setting contribute to the play's overall mood and atmosphere? How important is the larger setting of the Great Depression?
2. Why does Bert's dream of going to college seem like such an impossible dream to most of the characters in the play?
3. Who is Mr. Eagle? Can you see any symbolic significance in his name?
4. Mr. Ryan says that the warehouse is "the same circus every Monday morning." This suggests that the place may be different during the other days of the week. Why might Mondays be different from other days?
5. Why are Jim and Gus unclear about what they did the day before the play begins? What is it that several of the characters seek in drinking so much?
6. Why does Patricia call Gus "Kong"? Does this tell us more about Gus or about Patricia?
7. What is Gus's relationship with his wife? How is this relationship revealed in greater detail as the play moves along?
8. Point out early examples of Kenneth's witty sarcasm. Why do you suppose his conversation is so filled with such remarks? Is he a bitter person?
9. What symbolic value can you assign to the warehouse's dirty windows or to the dust falling from the ceiling?
10. Why does Larry buy the Auburn? Was it a sensible purchase? What does the car symbolize for him?
11. What is Tommy Kelly's condition when he finally shows up for work? Why are the others so sympathetic toward him?
12. What do we learn about Larry as a result of his amazing memory of exactly where the old truck part was stored? How does his memory help explain his heightened sense of frustration?
13. Of all the characters in the play, which exhibits the greatest tendency to look after the others?
14. At what point in the play does the climax occur? What is ironic about which character is most affected by the climax?
15. What is suggested by the window-washing episode? Why does Kenneth so much want to clean the windows? What is ironic about what is later seen through the clean windows? Who is most unprepared to deal with what is seen?
16. Twice during the play, scenes depicting life at the warehouse are divided by interludes in verse. What is the function of those interludes? Whose "vision" (to use Miller's term) do they present? What does this suggest about that character's role in the play?

17. Why does Mr. Ryan become short-tempered with Bert as the time for Bert to leave to go to college approaches?
18. What kind of a person does Tommy Kelly become once he has stopped drinking? What do the other characters think of the sober Tommy Kelly?
19. What qualities does Bert possess that make possible his escape from the warehouse? If he is not smarter or more talented than the others, what makes him different?
20. What did Gus die of? Was he ready to die? Did he in fact "do it right"?

# Day of Absence

DOUGLAS TURNER WARD

## Characters

| | |
|---|---|
| CLEM | INDUSTRIALIST |
| LUKE | BUSINESSMAN |
| JOHN | CLUBWOMAN |
| MARY | COURIER |
| FIRST OPERATOR | ANNOUNCER |
| SECOND OPERATOR | CLAN |
| THIRD OPERATOR | AIDE |
| SUPERVISOR | PIOUS |
| JACKSON | DOLL WOMAN |
| MAYOR | BRUSH MAN |
| FIRST CITIZEN | MOP MAN |
| SECOND CITIZEN | RASTUS |
| THIRD CITIZEN | |

*The time is now. Play opens in unnamed Southern town of medium population on a somnolent cracker morning—meaning no matter the early temperature, it's gonna get hot. The hamlet is just beginning to rouse itself from the sleepy lassitude of night.*

## NOTES ON PRODUCTION

No scenery is necessary—only actors shifting in and out on an almost bare stage and freezing into immobility as focuses change or blackouts occur.

Play is conceived for performance by a Negro cast, a reverse minstrel show done in white-face. Logically, it might also be performed by whites—at their own risk. If any producer is faced with choosing between opposite hues, author strongly suggests: "Go 'long wit' the blacks—besides all else, they need the work more."

If acted by the latter, race members are urged to go for broke, yet cautioned not to ham it up too broadly. In fact—it just might be more effective if they aspire for serious tragedy. Only qualification needed for Caucasian casting is that the company fit a uniform pattern—insipid white; also played in white-face.

Before any horrifying discrimination doubts arise, I hasten to add that a bonafide white actor should be cast as the Announcer in all productions, likewise a Negro thespian in pure native black as Rastus. This will truly subvert any charge that the production is unintegrated.

All props, except essential items (chairs, brooms, rags, mops, debris), should be imaginary (phones, switchboard, mikes, eating utensils, food, etc.). Actors should indicate their presence through mime.

The cast of characters develops as the play progresses. In the interest of economical casting, actors should double or triple in roles wherever possible.

## PRODUCTION CONCEPT

This is a red-white-and-blue play—meaning the entire production should be designed around the basic color scheme of our patriotic trinity. *Lighting* should illustrate, highlight and detail time, action and mood. Opening scenes stage-lit with white rays of morning, transforming to panic reds of afternoon, flowing into ominous blues of evening. *Costuming* should be orchestrated around the same color scheme. In addition, subsidiary usage of grays, khakis, yellows, pinks, and combinated patterns of stars-and-bars should be employed. Some actors (Announcer and Rastus excepted, of course) might wear white shoes or sneakers, and some women characters clothed in knee-length frocks might wear white stockings. Blonde wigs, both for males and females, can be used in selected instances. *Makeup* should have uniform consistency, with individual touches thrown in to enhance personal identity.

## SAMPLE MODELS OF MAKEUP AND COSTUMING

Mary: Kewpie-doll face, ruby-red lips painted to valentine-pursing, moon-shaped rouge circles implanted on each cheek, blond wig of fat-flowing ringlets, dazzling ankle-length snow-white nightie.

Mayor: Seersucker white ensemble, ten-gallon hat, red string-tie and blue belt.

Clem: Khaki pants, bareheaded and blond.

Luke: Blue work-jeans, straw-hatted.

Club Woman: Yellow dress patterned with symbols of Dixie, gray hat.

Clan: A veritable, riotous advertisement of red-white-and-blue combinations with stars-and-bars tossed in.

Pious: White ministerial garb with *black* cleric's collar topping his snow-white shirt.

Operators: All in red with different color wigs.

All other characters should be carefully defined through costuming which typifies their identity.

SCENE    *Street.*
TIME    *Early morning.*

CLEM (*Sitting under a sign suspended by invisible wires and bold-printed with the lettering: "STORE."*) 'Morning, Luke. . . .

LUKE (*Sitting a few paces away under an identical sign.*) 'Morning, Clem. . . .

CLEM  Go'n' be a hot day.

LUKE  Looks that way. . . .

CLEM  Might rain though. . . .

LUKE  Might.

CLEM  Hope it does. . . .

LUKE  Me, too. . . .

CLEM  Farmers could use a little wet spell for a change. . . . How's the Missis?

LUKE   Same.

CLEM   'N' the kids?

LUKE   Them, too. . . . How's yourns?

CLEM   Fine, thank you. . . . *(They both lapse into drowsy silence waving lethargically from time to time at imaginary passersby.)* Hi, Joe. . . .

LUKE   Joe. . . .

CLEM   . . . How'd it go yesterday, Luke?

LUKE   Fair.

CLEM   Same wit' me. . . . Business don't seem to git no better or no worse. Guess we in a rut, Luke, don't it 'pear that way to you?—Morning, ma'am.

LUKE   Morning. . . .

CLEM   Tried display, sales, advertisement, stamps—everything, yet merchandising stumbles 'round in the same old groove. . . . But—that's better than plunging downwards, I reckon.

LUKE   Guess it is.

CLEM   Morning, Bret. How's the family?·. . . That's good.

LUKE   Bret—

CLEM   Morning, Sue.

LUKE   How do, Sue.

CLEM   *(Staring after her.)*   . . . Fine hunk of woman.

LUKE   Sure is.

CLEM   Wonder if it's any good?

LUKE   Bet it is.

CLEM   Sure like to find out!

LUKE   So would I.

CLEM   You ever try?

LUKE   Never did. . . .

CLEM   Morning, Gus. . . .

LUKE   Howdy, Gus.

CLEM   Fine, thank you. *(They lapse into silence again.* CLEM *rouses himself slowly, begins to look around quizzically.)*   Luke . . . ?

LUKE   Huh?

CLEM   Do you . . . er, er—feel anything—funny . . . ?

LUKE   Like what?

CLEM   Like . . . er—something—strange?

LUKE   I dunno . . . haven't thought about it.

CLEM   I mean . . . like something's wrong—outta place, unusual?

LUKE   I don't know. . . . What you got in mind?

CLEM   Nothing . . . just that—just that—like somp'ums outta kilter. I got a funny feeling somp'ums not up to snuff. Can't figger out what it is . . .

LUKE   Maybe it's in your haid?

CLEM   No, not like that. . . . Like somp'ums happened—or happening—gone haywire, loony.

LUKE   Well, don't worry 'bout it, it'll pass.

CLEM   Guess you right. *(Attempts return to somnolence but doesn't succeed.)* . . . I'm sorry, Luke, but you sure you don't feel nothing peculiar . . . ?

LUKE   *(Slightly irked.)*   Toss it out your mind, Clem! We got a long day ahead of us. If something's wrong, you'll know 'bout it in due time. No use worrying about it 'till it comes and if it's coming, it will. Now, relax!

CLEM  All right, you right. . . . Hi, Margie. . . .

LUKE  Marge.

CLEM *(Unable to control himself.)*  Luke, I don't give a damn what you say. Somp'ums topsy-turvy, I just know it!

LUKE *(Increasingly irritated.)*  Now look here, Clem—it's a bright day, it looks like it's go'n' git hotter. You say the wife and kids are fine and the business is no better or no worse? Well, what else could be wrong? . . . If somp'ums go'n' happen, it's go'n' happen anyway and there ain't a damn fool thing you kin do to stop it! So you ain't helping me, yourself or nobody else by thinking 'bout it. It's not go'n' be no better or no worse when it gits here. It'll come to you when it gits ready to come and it's go'n' be the same whether you worry about it or not. So stop letting it upset you!

*(LUKE settles back in his chair. CLEM does likewise. LUKE shuts his eyes. After a few moments, they reopen. He forces them shut again. They reopen in greater curiosity. Finally, he rises slowly to an upright position in the chair, looks around frowningly. Turns slowly to CLEM.)*  . . . Clem? . . . You know something? . . . Somp'um is peculiar . . .

CLEM *(Vindicated.)*  I knew it, Luke! I just knew it! Ever since we been sitting here, I been having that feeling!

*(Scene is blacked out abruptly. Lights rise on another section of the stage where a young couple lie in bed under an invisible-wire-suspension-sign lettered: "HOME." Loud insistent sounds of baby yells are heard. JOHN, the husband, turns over trying to ignore the cries, MARY, the wife, is undisturbed. JOHN's efforts are futile, the cries continue until they cannot be denied. He bolts upright, jumps out of bed and disappears off-stage. Returns quickly and tries to rouse MARY.)*

JOHN  Mary . . . *(Nudges her, pushes her, yells into her ear, but she fails to respond.)* Mary, get up . . . Get up!

MARY  Ummm . . . *(Shrugs away, still sleeping.)*

JOHN  GET UP!

MARY  UMMMMMMMMMM!

JOHN  Don't you hear the baby bawling! . . . NOW GET UP!

MARY *(Mumbling drowsily.)*  . . . What baby . . . whose baby . . . ?

JOHN  Yours!

MARY  Mine? That's ridiculous. . . . what'd you say . . . ? Somebody's baby bawling? . . . How could that be so? *(Hearing screams.)* Who's crying? Somebody's crying! . . . What's crying? . . . WHERE'S LULA?!

JOHN  I don't know. You better get up.

MARY  That's outrageous! . . . What time is it?

JOHN  Late 'nuff! Now rise up!

MARY  You must be joking. . . . I'm sure I still have four or five hours sleep in store—even more after that head-splittin' blow-out last night . . . *(Tumbles back under covers.)*

JOHN  Nobody told you to gulp those last six bourbons—

MARY  Don't tell me how many bourbons to swallow, not after you guzzled the whole stinking bar! . . . Get up? . . . You must be cracked. . . . Where's Lula? She must be here, she always is . . .

JOHN  Well, she ain't here yet, so get up and muzzle that brat before she does drive me cuckoo!

MARY  (*Springing upright, finally realizing gravity of situation.*)   Whaddaya mean Lula's not here? She's always here, she must be here. . . . Where else kin she be? She supposed to be. . . . She just can't *not* be here—CALL HER!

(*Blackout as* JOHN *rushes offstage. Scene shifts to a trio of Telephone Operators perched on stools before imaginary switchboards. Chaos and bedlam are taking place to the sound of buzzes. Production Note: Effect of following dialogue should simulate rising pandemonium.*)

FIRST OPERATOR  The line is busy—
SECOND OPERATOR  Line is busy—
THIRD OPERATOR  Is busy—
FIRST OPERATOR  Doing best we can—
SECOND OPERATOR  Having difficulty—
THIRD OPERATOR  Soon as possible—
FIRST OPERATOR  Just one moment—
SECOND OPERATOR  Would you hold on—
THIRD OPERATOR  Awful sorry, madam—
FIRST OPERATOR  Would you hold on, please—
SECOND OPERATOR  Just a second, please—
THIRD OPERATOR  Please hold on, please—
FIRST OPERATOR  The line is busy—
SECOND OPERATOR  The line is busy—
THIRD OPERATOR  The line is busy—
FIRST OPERATOR  Doing best we can—
SECOND OPERATOR  Hold on please—
THIRD OPERATOR  Can't make connections—
FIRST OPERATOR  Unable to put it in—
SECOND OPERATOR  Won't plug through—
THIRD OPERATOR  Sorry madam—
FIRST OPERATOR  If you'd wait a moment—
SECOND OPERATOR  Doing best we can—
THIRD OPERATOR  Sorry—
FIRST OPERATOR  One moment—
SECOND OPERATOR  Just a second—
THIRD OPERATOR  Hold on—
FIRST OPERATOR  Yes—
SECOND OPERATOR  STOP IT!—
THIRD OPERATOR  HOW DO I KNOW—
FIRST OPERATOR  YOU ANOTHER ONE!
SECOND OPERATOR  HOLD ON DAMMIT!
THIRD OPERATOR  UP YOURS, TOO!
FIRST OPERATOR  THE LINE IS BUSY—

SECOND OPERATOR   THE LINE IS BUSY—

THIRD OPERATOR   THE LINE IS BUSY—

(*The switchboard clamors a cacophony of buzzes as* OPERATORS *plug connections with the frenzy of a Chaplin movie. Their replies degenerate into a babble of gibberish. At the height of frenzy, the* SUPERVISOR *appears.*)

SUPERVISOR   WHAT'S THE SNARL-UP???!!!

FIRST OPERATOR   Everybody calling at the same time, ma'am!

SECOND OPERATOR   Board can't handle it!

THIRD OPERATOR   Like everybody in big New York City is trying to squeeze a call through to li'l' ole us!

SUPERVISOR   God! . . . Somp'um terrible musta happened! . . . Buzz the emergency frequency hookup to the Mayor's office and find out what the hell's going on!

(*Scene blacks out quickly to* CLEM *and* LUKE.)

CLEM   (*Something slowly dawning on him.*)   Luke . . .?

LUKE   Yes, Clem?

CLEM   (*Eyes roving around in puzzlement.*)   Luke . . .?

LUKE   (*Irked.*)   I said what, Clem!

CLEM   Luke . . .? Where—where is—the—the—?

LUKE   THE WHAT?!

CLEM   Nigras . . .?

LUKE   ?????What . . .?

CLEM   Nigras. . . . Where is the Nigras, where is they, Luke . . .? ALL THE NIGRAS! . . . I don't see no Nigras . . .?!

LUKE   Whatcha mean . . .?

CLEM   (*Agitatedly.*)   Luke, there ain't a darky in sight. . . . And if you remember, we ain't spied a nappy hair all morning. . . . The Nigras, Luke! We ain't laid eyes on nary a coon this whole morning!!!

LUKE   You must be crazy or something, Clem!

CLEM   Think about it, Luke, we been sitting here for an hour or more—try and recollect if you remember seeing jist *one* go by?!!!

LUKE   (*Confused.*)   . . . I don't recall . . . But . . . but there musta been some. . . . The heat musta got you, Clem! How in hell could that be so?!!!

CLEM   (*Triumphantly.*)   Just think, Luke! . . . Look around ya. . . . Now, every morning mosta people walkin' 'long this street is colored. They's strolling by going to work, they's waiting for the buses, they's sweeping sidewalks, cleaning stores, starting to shine shoes and wetting the mops—right?! . . . Well, look around you, Luke—where is they? (*Luke paces up and down, checking.*) I told you, Luke, they ain't nowheres to be seen.

LUKE   ???? . . . This . . . this . . . some kind of holiday for 'em—or something?

CLEM   I don't know, Luke . . . but . . . but what I do know is they ain't here 'n' we haven't seen a solitary one. . . . It's scaryfying. Luke . . .!

LUKE   Well . . . maybe they's jist standing 'n' walking and shining on other streets.—Let's go look!

(*Scene blacks out to* JOHN *and* MARY. *Baby cries are as insistent as ever.*)

MARY *(At end of patience.)*   SMOTHER IT!

JOHN *(Beyond his.)*   That's a hell of a thing to say 'bout your own child! You should know what to do to hush her up!

MARY   Why don't you try?!

JOHN   You had her!

MARY   You shared in borning her?!

JOHN   Possibly not!

MARY   Why, you lousy—!

JOHN   What good is a mother who can't shut up her own daughter?!

MARY   I told you she yells louder every time I try to lay hands on her.—Where's Lula? Didn't you call her?!

JOHN   I told you I can't get the call through!

MARY   Try ag'in—

JOHN   It's no use! I tried numerous times and can't even git through to the switchboard. You've got to quiet her down yourself. *(Firmly.)* Now, go in there and clam her up 'fore I lose my patience!

*(MARY exits. Soon, we hear the yells increase. She rushes back in.)*

MARY   She won't let me touch her, just screams louder!

JOHN   Probably wet 'n' soppy!

MARY   Yes! Stinks something awful! Phooooey! I can't stand that filth and odor!

JOHN   That's why she's screaming! Needs her didee changed.—Go change it!

MARY   How you 'spect me to when I don't know how?! Suppose I faint?!

JOHN   Well let her blast away. I'm getting outta here.

MARY   You can't leave me here like this!

JOHN   Just watch me! . . . See this nice split-level cottage, peachy furniture, multi-colored teevee, hi-fi set 'n' the rest? . . . Well, how you think I scraped 'em together while you curled up on your fat li'l' fanny? . . . By gitting outta here—not only *on time* . . . but EARLIER!—Beating a frantic crew of nice young executives to the punch—gitting there fustest with the mostest brown-nosing you ever saw! Now if I goof one day—just ONE DAY!—You reckon I'd stay ahead? NO! . . . There'd be a wolf-pack trampling over my prostrate body, racing to replace my smiling face against the boss' left rump! . . . NO, MAM! I'm zooming outta here on time, just as I always have and what's more—you go'n' fix me some breakfast, I'M HUNGRY!

MARY   But—

JOHN   No buts about it!

*(Flash blackout as he gags on a mouthful of coffee.)*

What you trying to do, STRANGLE ME!!! *(Jumps up and starts putting on jacket.)*

MARY *(Sarcastically.)*   What did you expect?

JOHN *(In biting fury.)*   That you could possibly boil a pot of water, toast a few slices of bread and fry a coupler eggs! . . . It was a mistaken assumption!

MARY   So they aren't as good as Lula's!

JOHN   That is an overstatement. Your efforts don't result in anything that could possibly be digested by man, mammal, or insect! . . . When I married you, I thought I was fairly acquainted with your faults and weaknesses—I chalked 'em up to human imperfection. . . . But now I know I was being extremely generous, over-optimistic and phenomenally deluded!—You have no idea how useless you really are!

MARY Then why'd you marry me?!

JOHN Decoration!

MARY You shoulda married Lula!

JOHN I might've if it wasn't 'gainst the segregation law! . . . But for the sake of my home, my child and my sanity, I will even take a chance in sacrificing my slippery grip on the status pole and drive by her shanty to find out whether she or someone like her kin come over here and prevent some ultimate disaster.

*(Storms toward door, stopping abruptly at exit.)*

Are you sure you kin make it to the bathroom wit'out Lula backing you up?!!!

*(Blackout. Scene shifts to Mayor's office where a cluttered desk stands center amid papered debris.)*

MAYOR *(Striding determinedly toward desk, stopping midways, bellowing.)* WOODFENCE! . . . WOODFENCE! . . . WOODFENCE! *(Receiving no reply, completes distance to desk.)* JACKSON! . . . JACKSON!

JACKSON *(Entering worriedly.)* Yes sir . . .?

MAYOR Where's Vice-Mayor Woodfence, that no-good brother-in-law of mine?!

JACKSON Hasn't come in yet, sir.

MAYOR HASN'T COME IN?!!! . . . Damn bastard! Knows we have a crucial conference. Soon as he staggers through that door, tell him to shoot in here! *(Angrily focusing on his disorderly desk and littered surroundings.)* And git Mandy here to straighten up this mess—Rufus too! You know he shoulda been waiting to knock dust off my shoes soon as I step in. Get 'em in here! . . . What's the matter wit' them lazy Nigras? . . . Already had to dress myself because of JC, fix my own coffee without MayBelle, drive myself to work 'counta Bubba, feel my old Hag's tits after Sapphi—NEVER MIND!—Git 'em in here—QUICK!

JACKSON *(Meekly.)* They aren't . . . they aren't here, sir . . .

MAYOR Whaddaya mean they aren't here? Find out where they at. We got important business, man! You can't run a town wit' laxity like this. Can't allow things to git snafued jist because a bunch of lazy Nigras been out gitting drunk and living it up all night! Discipline, man, discipline!

JACKSON That's what I'm trying to tell you, sir . . . they didn't come in, can't be found . . . none of 'em.

MAYOR Ridiculous, boy! Scare 'em up and tell 'em scoot here in a hurry befo' I git mad and fire the whole goddamn lot of 'em!

JACKSON But we can't find 'em, sir.

MAYOR Hogwash! Can't nobody in this office do anything right?! Do I hafta handle every piddling little matter myself?! Git me their numbers, I'll have 'em here befo' you kin shout to—

*(Three men burst into room in various states of undress.)*

ONE Henry—they vanished!

TWO  Disappeared into thin air!

THREE  Gone wit'out a trace!

TWO  Not a one on the street!

THREE  In the house!

ONE  On the job!

MAYOR  Wait a minute!! . . . Hold your water! Calm down—!

ONE  But they've gone, Henry—GONE! All of 'em!

MAYOR  What the hell you talking 'bout? Who's gone—?

ONE  The Nigras, Henry! They gone!

MAYOR  Gone? . . . Gone where?

TWO  That's what we trying to tell ya—they just disappeared! The Nigras have disappeared, swallowed up, vanished! All of 'em! Every last one!

MAYOR  Have everybody 'round here gone batty? . . . That's impossible, how could the Nigras vanish?

THREE  Beats me, but it's happened!

MAYOR  You mean a whole town of Nigras just evaporate like this—poof!— Overnight?

ONE  Right!

MAYOR  Y'all must be drunk! Why, half this town is colored. How could they just sneak out!

TWO  Don't ask me, but there ain't one in sight!

MAYOR  Simmer down 'n' put it to me easy-like.

ONE  Well . . . I first suspected somp'um smelly when Sarah Jo didn't show up this morning and I couldn't reach her—

TWO  Dorothy Jane didn't 'rive at my house—

THREE  Georgia Mae wasn't at mine neither—and SHE sleeps in!

ONE  When I reached the office, I realized I hadn't seen nary one Nigra all morning! Nobody else had either—wait a minute—Henry, have you?!

MAYOR  ???Now that you mention it . . . no, I haven't . . .

ONE  They gone, Henry. . . . Not a one on the street, not a one in our homes, not a single, last living one to be found nowheres in town. What we gon' do?!

MAYOR  (Thinking.)  Keep heads on your shoulders 'n' put clothes on your back. . . . They can't be far. . . . Must be 'round somewheres. . . . Probably playing hide 'n' seek, that's it! . . . JACKSON!

JACKSON  Yessir?

MAYOR  Immediately mobilize our Citizens Emergency Distress Committee!— Order a fleet of sound trucks to patrol streets urging the population to remain calm—situation's not as bad as it looks—everything's under control! Then have another squadron of squawk buggies drive slowly through all Nigra alleys, ordering them to come out wherever they are. If that don't git 'em organize a vigilante search-squad to flush 'em outta hiding! But most important of all, track down that lazy goldbricker, Woodfence, and tell him to git on top of the situation! By God, we'll find 'em even if we hafta dig 'em outta the ground!

*(Blackout. Scene shifts back to JOHN and MARY a few hours later. A funereal solemnity pervades their mood. JOHN stands behind MARY who sits, in a scene duplicating the famous "American Gothic" painting.)*

JOHN  . . . Walked up to the shack, knocked on door, didn't git no answer. Hollered "LULA? LULA . . .?—Not a thing. Went 'round the side, peeped in window—nobody stirred. Next door—nobody there. Crossed other side of street and banged on five or six other doors—not a colored person could be found! Not a man, neither women or child—not even a little black dog could be seen, smelt or heard for blocks around. . . . They've gone, Mary.

MARY  What does it all mean, John?

JOHN  I don't know, Mary . . .

MARY  I always had Lula, John. She never missed a day at my side. . . . That's why I couldn't accept your wedding proposal until I was sure you'd welcome me and her together as a package. How am I gonna git through the day? My baby don't know *me*, I ain't acquainted wit' *it*. I've never lifted cover off pot, swung a mop or broom, dunked a dish or even pushed a dustrag. I'm lost wit'out Lula, I need her, John, I need her. (*Begins to weep softly.* JOHN *pats her consolingly.*)

JOHN  Courage, honey. . . . Everybody in town is facing the same dilemma. We mustn't crack up . . .

(*Blackout. Scene shifts back to* MAYOR's *office later in day. Atmosphere and tone resembles a wartime headquarters at the front.* MAYOR *is poring over huge map.*)

INDUSTRIALIST  Half the day is gone already, Henry. On behalf of the factory owners of this town, you've got to bail us out! Seventy-five percent of all production is paralyzed. With the Nigra absent, men are waiting for machines to be cleaned, floors to be swept, crates lifted, equipment delivered and bathrooms to be deodorized. Why, restrooms and toilets are so filthy until they not only cannot be sat in, but it's virtually impossible to get within hailing distance because of the stench!

MAYOR  Keep your shirt on, Jeb—

BUSINESSMAN  Business is even in worse condition, Henry. The volume of goods moving 'cross counters has slowed down to a trickle—almost negligible. Customers are not only not purchasing—but the absence of handymen, porters, sweepers, stock-movers, deliverers and miscellaneous dirty-work doers is disrupting the smooth harmony of marketing!

CLUB WOMAN  Food poisoning, severe indigestitis, chronic diarrhea, advanced diaper chafings and a plethora of unsanitary household disasters dangerous to life, limb and property! . . . As a representative of the Federation of Ladies' Clubs, I must sadly report that unless the trend is reversed, a complete breakdown in family unity is imminent. . . . Just as homosexuality and debauchery signalled the fall of Greece and Rome, the downgrading of Southern Bellesdom might very well prophesy the collapse of our indigenous institutions. . . . Remember—it has always been pure, delicate, lily-white images of Dixie femininity which provided backbone, inspiration and ideology for our male warriors in their defense against the on-rushing black horde. If our gallant men are drained of this worship and idolatry—God knows! The cause won't be worth a Confederate Nickel!

MAYOR  Stop this panicky defeatism, y'all hear me! All machinery at my disposal is being utilized. I assure you wit' great confidence the damage will soon repair itself.—Cheerful progress reporters are expected any moment now.—Wait! See, here's Jackson. . . . Well, Jackson?

JACKSON *(Entering.)*   As of now, sir, all efforts are fruitless. Neither hide nor hair of them has been located. We have not unearthed a single one in our shack-to-shack search. Not a single one has heeded our appeal. Scoured every crick and cranny inside their hovels, turning furniture upside down and inside out, breaking down walls and tearing through ceilings. We made determined efforts to discover where 'bouts of our faithful uncle Toms and informers—but even they have vanished without a trace. . . . Searching squads are on the verge of panic and hysteria, sir, wit' hotheads among 'em campaigning for scorched earth policies. Nigras on a whole lack cellars, but there's rising sentiment favoring burning to find out whether they're underground—DUG IN!

MAYOR   Absolutely counter such foolhardy suggestions! Suppose they are tombed in? We'd only accelerate the gravity of the situation using incendiary tactics! Besides, when they're rounded up where will we put 'em if we've already burned up their shacks—IN OUR OWN BEDROOMS?!!!

JACKSON   I agree, sir, but the mood of the crowd is becoming irrational. In anger and frustration, they's forgetting their original purpose was to FIND the Nigras!

MAYOR   At all costs! Stamp out all burning proposals! Must prevent extremist notions from gaining ascendancy. Git wit' it. . . . Wait—'n' for Jehovah's sake, find out where the hell is that trifling slacker, WOODFENCE!

COURIER *(Rushing in.)*   Mr. Mayor! Mr. Mayor! . . . We've found some! We've found some!

MAYOR *(Excitedly.)*   Where?!

COURIER   In the—in the— *(Can't catch breath.)*

MAYOR *(Impatiently.)*   Where, man? Where?!!!

COURIER   In the colored wing of the city hospital!

MAYOR   The hos—? The hospital! I shoulda known! How could those helpless, crippled, cut and shot Nigras disappear from a hospital! Shoulda thought of that! . . . Tell me more, man!

COURIER   I—I didn't wait, sir. . . . I—I ran in to report soon as I heard—

MAYOR   WELL GIT BACK ON THE PHONE, YOU IDIOT, DON'T YOU KNOW WHAT THIS MEANS!

COURIER   Yes, sir. *(Races out.)*

MAYOR   Now we gitting somewhere! . . . Gentlemen, if one sole Nigra is among us, we're well on the road to rehabilitation! Those Nigras in the hospital must know somp'um 'bout the others where'bouts. . . . Scat back to your colleagues, boost up their morale and inform 'em that things will zip back to normal in a jiffy! *(They start to file out, then pause to observe the* COURIER *reentering dazedly.)* Well . . . ? Well, man . . . ? WHAT'S THE MATTER WIT' YOU, NINNY, TELL ME WHAT ELSE WAS SAID?!

COURIER   They all . . . they all . . . they all in a—in a—a coma, sir . . .

MAYOR   They all in a what . . . ?

COURIER   In a coma, sir . . .

MAYOR   Talk sense, man! . . . Whaddaya mean, they all in a coma?

COURIER   Doctor says every last one of the Nigras are jist laying in bed . . . STILL . . . not moving . . . neither live or dead . . . laying up there in a coma . . . every last one of 'em . . .

MAYOR   (Sputters, then grabs phone.)   Get me Confederate Memorial. . . . Put me through to the Staff Chief. . . . YES, this is the Mayor. . . . Sam? . . . What's this I hear? . . . But how could they be in a coma, Sam? . . . You don't know! Well, what the hell you think the city's paying you for! . . . You've got 'nuff damn hacks and quacks there to find out! . . . How could it be somp'um unknown? You mean Nigras know somp'um 'bout drugs your damn butchers don't? . . . Well, what the crap good are they! . . . All right, all right, I'll be calm. . . . Now, tell me. . . . Uh huh, uh huh. . . . Well, can't you give 'em some injections or somp'um . . . ?—You did . . . uh huh . . . DID YOU TRY A LI'L' ROUGH TREATMENT?—that too, huh. . . . All right, Sam, keep trying. . . . (Puts phone down delicately, continuing absently.) Can't wake 'em up. Just lay there. Them that's sick won't git no sicker, them that's half-well won't git no better, babies that's due won't be born and them that's come won't show no life. Nigras wit' cuts won't bleed and them which need blood won't be transfused. . . . He say dying Nigras is even refusing to pass away! (Is silently perplexed for a moment, then suddenly breaks into action.) JACKSON?! . . . Call up the police—THE JAIL! Find out what's going on there! Them Nigras are captives! If there's one place we got darkies under control, it's there! Them sonsabitches too onery to act right either for colored or white!

(JACKSON exits. The COURIER follows.)

Keep your fingers crossed, citizens, them Nigras in jail are the most important Nigras we got!

(All hands are raised conspicuously aloft, fingers prominently ex-ed. Seconds tick by. Soon JACKSON returns crestfallen.)

JACKSON   Sheriff Bull says they don't know whether they still on premises or not. When they went to rouse Nigra jailbirds this morning, cell-block doors refused to swing open. Tried everything—even exploded dynamite charges— but it just wouldn't budge. . . . Then they hoisted guards up to peep through barred windows, but couldn't see good 'nuff to tell whether Nigras was inside or not. Finally, gitting desperate, they power-hosed the cells wit' water but had to cease 'cause Sheriff Bull said he didn't wanta jeopardize drowning the Nigras since it might spoil his chance of shipping a record load of cotton pickers to the State Penitentiary for cotton-snatching jubilee. . . . Anyway— they ain't heard a Nigra-squeak all day.

MAYOR   ???That so . . . ? WHAT 'BOUT TRAINS 'N' BUSSES PASSING THROUGH? There must be some dinges riding through?

JACKSON   We checked . . . not a one on board.

MAYOR   Did you hear whether any other towns lost their Nigras?

JACKSON   Things are status-quo everywhere else.

MAYOR   (Angrily.)   Then what the hell they picking on us for!

COURIER *(Rushing in.)*   MR. MAYOR! Your sister jist called—HYSTERICAL! She says Vice-Mayor Woodfence went to bed wit her last night, but when she woke up this morning he was gone! Been missing all day!

MAYOR   ???Could Nigras be holding brother-in-law Woodfence hostage?

COURIER   No, sir. Besides him—investigations reveal that dozens of more prominent citizens—two City Council members, the chairman of the Junior Chamber of Commerce, our City College All-Southern half-back, the chairlady of the Daughters of the Confederate Rebellion, Miss Cotton-Sack Festival of the Year and numerous other miscellaneous nobodies—are all absent wit'out leave. Dangerous evidence points to the conclusion that they have been infiltrating!

MAYOR   Infiltrating???

COURIER   Passing all along!

MAYOR   ???PASSING ALL ALONG???

COURIER   Secret Nigras all the while!

MAYOR   NAW! (CLUB WOMAN *keels over in faint.* JACKSON, BUSINESSMAN *and* INDUSTRIALIST *begin to eye each other suspiciously.)*

COURIER   Yessir!

MAYOR   PASSING???

COURIER   Yessir!

MAYOR   SECRET NIG—!???

COURIER   Yessir!

MAYOR *(Momentarily stunned to silence.)*   The dirty mongrelizers! . . . Gentlemen, this is a grave predicament indeed. . . . It pains me to surrender priority to our states' right credo, but it is my solemn task and frightening duty to inform you that we have no other recourse but to seek outside help for deliverance.

*(Blackout. Lights re-rise on Huntley-Brinkley-Murrow-Sevareid-Cronkite-Reasoner-type* ANNOUNCER *grasping a hand-held microphone [imaginary] a few hours later. He is vigorously, excitedly mouthing his commentary, but no sound escapes his lips. . . . During this dumb, wordless section of his broadcast, a bedraggled assortment of figures marching with picket signs occupy his attention. On their picket signs are inscribed various appeals and slogans. "CINDY LOU UNFAIR TO BABY JOE" . . . "CAP'N SAM MISS BIG BOY" . . . "RETURN LI'L' BLUE TO MARSE JIM" . . . "INFORMATION REQUESTED 'BOUT MAMMY GAIL" . . . "BOSS NATHAN PROTEST TO FAST LEROY." Trailing behind the marchers, forcibly isolated, is a woman dressed in widow-black holding a placard which reads: "WHY DIDN'T YOU TELL US—YOUR DEFILED WIFE AND TWO ABSENT MONGRELS.")*

ANNOUNCER *(Who has been silently mouthing his delivery during the picketing procession, is suddenly heard as if caught in the midst of commentary.)*   . . . Factories standing idle from the loss of non-essential workers. Stores shuttered from the absconding of uncrucial personnel. Uncollected garbage threatening pestilence and pollution. . . . Also, each second somewheres in this former utopia below the Mason and Dixon, dozens of decrepit old men and women usually tended by faithful nurses and servants are popping off like flies—abandoned by sons, daughters and grandchildren whose refusal to provide their doddering relatives with bedpans and other soothing necessities result in their hasty, nasty, messy corpus delicties. . . . But most critically affected of all by this complete drought of Afro-American resources are policemen and other public safety guardians denied their daily quota of Negro arrests. One officer known affectionately as "TWO-A-DAY-PETE" because of his unblemished record of TWO Negro headwhippings per day has already been carted off to the County Insane Asylum—straight-jacketed, screaming and biting, unable to withstand the shock of having his spotless slate sullied by interruption. . . . It is feared that similar attacks are soon expected among municipal judges prevented for the first time in years of distinguished bench-sitting from sentencing one single Negro to a hoose-gow or pokey. . . . Ladies and gentlemen, as you trudge in from the joys and headaches of workday chores and dusk begins to descend on this sleepy Southern hamlet, we REPEAT—today—before early morning dew had dried upon magnolia blossoms, your comrade citizens of this lovely Dixie village awoke to the realization that some—pardon me! Not some—but ALL OF THEIR NEGROES were missing. . . . Absent, vamoosed, departed, at bay, fugitive, away, gone and so-far unretrieved. . . . In order to dispel your incredulity, gauge the temper of your suffering compatriots and just possibly prepare you for the likelihood of an equally nightmarish eventuality, we have gathered a cross-section of this city's most distinguished leaders for exclusive interviews. . . . First, Mr. Council Clan, grand-dragoon of this area's most active civic organizations and staunch bell-wether of the political opposition. . . . Mr. Clan, how do you ACCOUNT for this incredible disappearance?

CLAN    A PLOT, plain and simple, that's what it is, as plain as the corns on your feet!

ANNOUNCER    Whom would you consider responsible?

CLAN    I could go on all night.

ANNOUNCER    Cite a few?

CLAN    Too numerous.

ANNOUNCER    Just one?

CLAN    Name names when time comes.

ANNOUNCER    Could you be referring to native Negroes?

CLAN    Ever try quarantining lepers from their spots?

ANNOUNCER    Their organizations?

CLAN    Could you slice a nose off a mouth and still keep a face?

ANNOUNCER    Commies?

CLAN    Would you lop off a titty from a chest and still have a breast?

ANNOUNCER    Your city government?

CLAN    Now you talkin'!

ANNOUNCER    State administration?

CLAN    Warming up!

ANNOUNCER    Federal?

CLAN    Kin a blind man see?!

ANNOUNCER    The Court?

CLAN    Is a pig clean?!

ANNOUNCER    Clergy?

CLAN  Do a polecat stink?!

ANNOUNCER  Well, Mr. Clan, with this massive complicity, how do you think the plot could've been prevented from succeeding?

CLAN  If I'da been in office, it never woulda happened.

ANNOUNCER  Then you're laying major blame at the doorstep of the present administration?

CLAN  Damn tooting!

ANNOUNCER  But from your oft-expressed views, Mr. Clan, shouldn't you and your followers be delighted at the turn of events? After all—isn't it one of the main policies of your society to *drive* Negroes away? *Drive* 'em back where they came from?

CLAN  DRIVVVE, BOY! DRIIIIVVVE! That's right! . . . When we say so and not befo'. Ain't supposed to do nothing 'til we tell 'em. Got to stay put until we exercise our God-given right to tell 'em when to git!

ANNOUNCER  But why argue if they've merely jumped the gun? Why not rejoice at this premature purging of undesirables?

CLAN  The time ain't ripe yet, boy. . . . The time ain't ripe yet.

ANNOUNCER  Thank you for being so informative, Mr. Clan—Mrs. Aide? Mrs. Aide? Over here, Mrs. Aide. . . . Ladies and gentlemen, this city's Social Welfare Commissioner, Mrs. Handy Anna Aide. . . . Mrs. Aide, with all your Negroes AWOL, haven't developments alleviated the staggering demands made upon your Welfare Department? Reduction of relief requests, elimination of case loads, removal of chronic welfare dependents, et cetera?

AIDE  Quite the contrary. Disruption of our pilot projects among Nigras saddles our white community with extreme hardship. . . . You see, historically, our agencies have always been foremost contributors to the Nigra Git-A-Job movement. We pioneered in enforcing social welfare theories which oppose coddling the fakers. We strenuously believe in helping Nigras help themselves by particiating in meaningful labor. "Relief is Out, Work is In," is our motto. We place them as maids, cooks, butlers, and breast-feeders, cesspool-diggers, wash-basin maintainers, shoe-shine boys, and so on—mostly on a volunteer self-work basis.

ANNOUNCER  Hired at prevailing salaried rates, of course?

AIDE  God forbid! Money is unimportant. Would only make 'em worse. Our main goal is to improve their ethical behavior. "Rehabilitation Through Positive Participation" is another motto of ours. All unwed mothers, loose-living malingering fathers, bastard children and shiftless grandparents are kept occupied through constructive muscle-therapy. This provides the Nigra with less opportunity to indulge his pleasure-loving amoral inclinations.

ANNOUNCER  They volunteer to participate in these pilot projects?

AIDE  Heavens no! They're notorious shirkers. When I said the program is voluntary, I meant white citizens in overwhelming majorities do the volunteering. Placing their homes, offices, appliances and persons at our disposal for use in "Operation Uplift." . . . We would never dare place such a decision in the hands of the Nigra. It would never get off the ground! . . . No, they have no choice in the matter. "Work or Starve" is the slogan we use to stimulate Nigra awareness of what's good for survival.

ANNOUNCER  Thank you, Mrs. Aide, and good luck. . . . Rev? . . . Rev? . . . Ladies and gentlemen, this city's foremost spiritual guidance counselor, Reverend Reb Pious. . . . How does it look to you, Reb Pious?

PIOUS  (*Continuing to gaze skyward.*)  It's in *His* hands, son, it's in *His* hands.

ANNOUNCER  How would you assess the disappearance, from a moral standpoint?

PIOUS  An immoral act, son, morally wrong and ethically indefensible. A perversion of Christian principles to be condemned from every pulpit of this nation.

ANNOUNCER  Can you account for its occurrence after the many decades of the Church's missionary activity among them?

PIOUS  It's basically a reversion of the Nigra to his deep-rooted primitivism. . . . Now, at last, you can understand the difficulties of the Church in attempting to anchor God's kingdom among ungratefuls. It's a constant, unrelenting, no-holds-barred struggle against Satan to wrestle away souls locked in his possession for countless centuries! Despite all our aid, guidance, solace and protection, Old BeezleBub still retains tenacious grips upon the Nigras, childish loyalty—comparable to the lure of bright flames to an infant.

ANNOUNCER  But actual physical departure, Reb Pious? How do you explain that?

PIOUS  Voodoo, my son, voodoo. . . . With Satan's assist, they have probably employed some heathen magic which we cultivated, sophisticated Christians know absolutely nothing about. However, before long we are confident about counteracting this evil witch-doctory and triumphing in our Holy Savior's name. At this perilous juncture, true believers of all denominations are participating in joint, 'round-the-clock observances, offering prayers for our Master's swiftest intercession. I'm optimistic about the outcome of his intervention. . . . Which prompts me—if I may, sir—to offer these words of counsel to our delinquent Nigras. . . . I say to you without rancor or vengeance, quoting a phrase of one of your greatest prophets, Booker T. Washington: "Return your buckets to where they lay and all will be forgiven."

ANNOUNCER  A very inspirational appeal, Reb Pious. I'm certain they will find the tug of its magnetic sincerity irresistible. Thank you, Reb Pious. . . . All in all—as you have witnessed, ladies and gentlemen—this town symbolizes the face of disaster. Suffering as severe a prostration as any city wrecked, ravaged, and devastated by the holocaust of war. A vital, lively, throbbing organism brought to a screeching halt by the strange enigma of the missing Negroes. . . . We take you now to offices of the one man into whose hands has been thrust the final responsibility of rescuing this shuddering metropolis from the precipice of destruction. . . . We give you the honorable Mayor, Henry R. E. Lee. . . . Hello, Mayor Lee.

MAYOR  (*Jovially.*)  Hello, Jack.

ANNOUNCER  Mayor Lee, we have just concluded interviews with some of your city's leading spokesmen. If I may say so, they don't sound too encouraging about the situation.

MAYOR  Nonsense, Jack! The situation's well-in-hand as it could be under the circumstances. Couldn't be better in hand. Underneath every dark cloud, Jack, there's always a ray of sunlight, ha, ha, ha.

ANNOUNCER  Have you discovered one, sir?

MAYOR  Well, Jack, I'll tell you. . . . Of course we've been faced wit' a little crisis, but look at it like this—we've faced 'em befo': Sherman marched through Georgia—ONCE! Lincoln freed the slaves—MOMENTARILY! Carpetbaggers even put Nigras in the Governor's mansion, state legislature, Congress and the Senate of the United States. But what happened?—Old Dixie bounced right on back up. . . . At this moment the Supreme Court's trying to put Nigras in our schools and the Nigra has got it in his haid to put hisself everywhere. . . . But what you 'spect go'n' happen?—Ole Dixie will kangaroo back even higher. Southern courage, fortitude, chivalry and superiority always wins out. . . . SHUCKS! We'll have us some Nigras befo' daylight is gone!

ANNOUNCER  Mr. Mayor, I hate to introduce this note, but in an earlier interview, one of your chief opponents, Mr. Clan, hinted at your own complicity in the affair—

MAYOR  A LOT OF POPPYCOCK! Clan is politicking! I've beaten him four times outta four and I'll beat him four more times outta four! This is no time for partisan politics! What we need now is level-headedness and across-the-board unity. This typical, rash, mealy-mouth, shooting-off-at-the-lip of Clan and his ilk proves their insincerity and voters will remember that in the next election! Won't you, voters?! *(Has risen to the height of his campaign oratory.)*

ANNOUNCER  Mr. Mayor! . . . Mr. Mayor! . . . Please—

MAYOR  . . . I tell you, I promise you—

ANNOUNCER  PLEASE, MR. MAYOR!

MAYOR  Huh? . . . Oh—yes, carry on.

ANNOUNCER  Mr. Mayor, your cheerfulness and infectious good spirits lead me to conclude that startling new developments warrant fresh-found optimism. What concrete, declassified information do you have to support your claim that Negroes will reappear before nightfall?

MAYOR  Because we are presently awaiting the pay-off of a masterful five-point supra-recovery program which can't help but reap us a bonanza of Nigras 'fore sundown! . . . First: Exhaustive efforts to pinpoint the where'bouts of our own missing darkies continue to zero in on the bullseye. . . . Second: The President of the United States, following an emergency cabinet meeting, has designated us the prime disaster area of the century—National Guard is already on the way. . . . Third: In an unusual, but bold maneuver, we have appealed to the NAACP 'n' all other Nigra conspirators to help us git to the bottom of the vanishing act. . . . Fourth: We have exercised our nonreciprocal option and requested that all fraternal southern states express their solidarity by lending us some of their Nigras temporarily on credit. . . . Fifth and foremost: We have already gotten consent of the Governor to round up all the stray, excess and incorrigible Nigras to be shipped to us under escort of the State Militia. . . . That's why we've stifled pessimism and are brimming wit' confidence that this full-scale concerted mobilization will ring down a jackpot of jigaboos 'fore light vanishes from sky!—

ANNOUNCER  Congratulations! What happens if it fails?

MAYOR  Don't even think THAT! Absolutely no reason to suspect it will. . . .*(Peers over shoulder, then whispers confidentially while placing hand over mouth by* AN-

NOUNCER's *imaginary mike.*) . . . But speculating on the dark side of your question—if we don't turn up some by nightfall, it may be all over. The harm has already been done. You see the South has always been glued together by the uninterrupted presence of its darkies. No telling how unstuck we might git if things keep on like they have.—Wait a minute, it musta paid off already! Mission accomplished 'cause here's Jackson head a time wit' the word. . . . Well, Jackson, what's new?

JACKSON  Situation on the home front remains static, sir—can't uncover scent or shadow. The NAACP and all other Nigra front groups 'n' plotters deny any knowledge or connection wit' the missing Nigras. Maintained this even after appearing befo' a Senate Emergency Investigating Committee which subpoenaed 'em to Washington post haste and threw 'em in jail for contempt. A handful of Nigras who agreed to make spectacular appeals for ours to come back to us have themselves mysteriously disappeared. But, worst news of all, sir, is our sister cities and counties, inside and outside the state, have changed their minds, fallen back on their promises and refused to lend us any Nigras, claiming they don't have 'nuff for themselves.

MAYOR  What 'bout Nigras promised by the Governor?!

JACKSON  Jailbirds and vagrants escorted here from chain-gangs and other reservations either revolted and escaped enroute or else vanished mysteriously on approaching our city limits. . . . Deterioration rapidly escalates, sir. Estimates predict we kin hold out only one more hour before being overtaken by anarchistic turmoil. . . . Some citizens seeking haven elsewheres have already fled, but on last report were being forcibly turned back by armed sentinels in other cities who wanted no parts of 'em—claiming they carried a jinx.

MAYOR  That bad, huh?

JACKSON  Worse, sir . . . we've received at least five reports of plots on your life.

MAYOR  What?!—We've gotta act quickly then!

JACKSON  Run out of ideas, sir.

MAYOR  Think harder, boy!

JACKSON  Don't have much time, sir. One measly hour, then all hell go'n' break loose.

MAYOR  Gotta think of something drastic, Jackson!

JACKSON  I'm dry, sir.

MAYOR  Jackson! Is there any planes outta here in the next hour?

JACKSON  All transportation's been knocked out, sir.

MAYOR  I thought so!

JACKSON  What were you contemplating, sir?

MAYOR  Don't ask me what I was contemplating! I'm still boss 'round here! Don't forgit it!

JACKSON  Sorry, sir.

MAYOR  . . . Hold the wire! . . . Wait a minute . . . ! Waaaaait a minute— GODAMNIT! All this time crapping 'round, diddling and fotsing wit' puny li'l' solutions—all the while neglecting our ace in the hole, our trump card! Most potent weapon for digging Nigras outta the woodpile!!! All the while right befo' our eyes! . . . Ass! Why didn't you remind me?!!!

JACKSON   What is it, sir?

MAYOR   . . . ME—THAT'S WHAT! ME! A personal appeal from ME! *Directly to them!* . . . Although we wouldn't let 'em march to the polls and express their affection for me through the ballot box, we've always known I'm held highest in their esteem. A direct address from their beloved Mayor! . . . If they's anywheres close within the sound of my voice, they'll shape up! Or let us know by a sign they's ready to!

JACKSON   You sure *that'll* turn the trick, sir?

MAYOR   As sure as my ancestors befo' me who knew that when they puckered their lips to whistle, ole Sambo was gonna come a-lickety-splitting to answer the call! . . . That same chips-down blood courses through these Confederate gray veins of Henry R. E. Lee!!!

ANNOUNCER   I'm delighted to offer our network's facilities for such a crucial public interest address, sir. We'll arrange immediately for your appearance on an international hookup, placing you in the widest proximity to contact them wherever they may be.

MAYOR   Thank you, I'm very grateful. . . . Jackson, re-grease the machinery and set wheels in motion. Inform townspeople what's being done. Tell 'em we're all in this together. The next hour is countdown. I demand absolute cooperation, city-wide silence and inactivity. I don't want the Nigras frightened if they's nearby. This is the most important hour in town's history. Tell 'em if one single Nigra shows up during hour of decision, victory is within sight. I'm gonna git 'em that one—maybe all! Hurry and crack to it!

(ANNOUNCER *rushes out, followed by* JACKSON. *Blackout. Scene re-opens, with* MAYOR *seated, eyes front, spotlight illuminating him in semidarkness. Shadowy figures stand in the background, prepared to answer phones or aid in any other manner.* MAYOR *waits patiently until "GO!" signal is given. Then begins, his voice combining elements of confidence, tremolo and gravity.*)

Good evening. . . . Despite the fact that millions of you wonderful people throughout the nation are viewing and listening to this momentous broadcast—and I thank you for your concern and sympathy in this hour of our peril—I primarily want to concentrate my attention and address these remarks solely for the benefit of our departed Nigra friends who may be listening somewhere in our far-flung land to the sound of my voice. . . . If you are—it is with heart-felt emotion and fond memories of our happy association that I ask—"Where are you . . . ?" Your absence has left a void in the bosom of every single man, woman and child of our great city. I tell you—you don't know what it means for us to wake up in the morning and discover that your cheerful, grinning, happy-go-lucky faces are missing! . . . From the depths of my heart, I can only meekly, humbly suggest what it means to me personally. . . . You see—the one face I will never be able to erase from my memory is the face—not of my Ma, not of Pa, neither wife or child—but the image of the first woman I came to love so well when just a wee lad—the vision of the first human I laid clear sight on at childbirth—the profile—better yet, the full face of my dear old . . . Jemimah—God rest her soul. . . . Yes! My dear ole mammy, wit' her round ebony moonbeam gleaming down upon me in the crib, teeth shining, blood-red bandana standing starched, peaked and proud, gazing down upon me affectionately as she crooned me a Southern lullaby. . . . OH! It's a memorable picture I will eternally cherish in permanent treasure chambers of my heart, now and forever always. . . . Well, if this radiant image can remain so infinitely vivid to me all these many years after her unfortunate demise in the Po' folks home—THINK of the misery the rest of us must be suffering after being *freshly* denied your soothing presence?! We need ya. If you kin hear me, just contact this station 'n' I will welcome you back personally. Let me just tell you that since you eloped, nothing has been the same. How could it? You're part of us, you belong to us. Just give us a sign and we'll be contented that all is well. . . . Now if you've skipped away on a little fun-fest, we understand, ha, ha. We know you like a good time and we don't begrudge it to ya. Hell—er, er, we like a good time ourselves—who doesn't? . . . In fact, think of all the good times we've had together, huh? We've had some real fun, you and us, yesiree! . . . Nobody knows better than you and I what fun we've had together. You singing us those old Southern coon songs and dancing those Nigra jigs and us clapping, prodding 'n' spurring you on! Lots of fun, huh?! . . . OH BOY! The times we've had together. . . . If you've snucked away for a bit of fun by yourself, we'll go 'long wit' ya—long as you let us know where you at so we won't be worried about you. . . . We'll go 'long wit' you long as you don't take the joke too far. I'll admit a joke is a joke and you've played a LULU! . . . I'm warning you, we can't stand much more horsing 'round from you! Business is business 'n' fun is fun! You've had your fun so now let's get down to business! Come on back, YOU HEAR ME!!! . . . . If you been hoodwinked by agents of some foreign government, I've been authorized by the President of these United States to inform you that this liberty-loving Republic is prepared to rescue you from their clutches. Don't pay no 'tention to their sireen songs and atheistic promises! You better off under our control and you know it! . . . If you been bamboozled by rabble-rousing nonsense of your own so-called leaders, we prepared to offer same protection. Just call us up! Just give us a sign! . . . Come on, give us a sign . . . give us a sign—even a teeny-weeny one . . . ??!! (*Glances around checking on possible communications. A bevy of headshakes indicate no success.* MAYOR *returns to address with desperate fervor.*) Now look—you don't know what you doing! If you persist in this disobedience, you know all too well the consequences! We'll track you to the end of the earth, beyond the galaxy, across the stars! We'll capture you and chastise you with all the vengeance we command! 'N' you know only too well how stern we kin be when double-crossed! The city, the state and the entire nation will crucify you for this unpardonable defiance! (*Checks again.*) No call . . . ? No sign . . . ? Time is running out! Deadline slipping past! They gotta respond! They gotta! (*Resuming.*) Listen to me! I'm begging y'all, you gotta come back . . . ! LOOK, GEORGE! (*Waves dirty rag aloft.*) I brought the rag you wax the car wit'. . . . Don't this bring back memories, George, of all the days you spent shining that automobile to shimmering perfection . . . ? And you, Rufus?! . . . . Here's the shoe polisher and the brush! . . . 'Member, Rufus? . . . Remember the happy mornings you spent popping this rag and whisking this brush so furiously 'till it created music that was sympho-nee to the ear . . . ? And you—MANDY? . . . Here's the waste-basket you didn't dump this morning. I saved it just for you! . . . LOOK, all y'all out there . . . ?

*(Signals and a three-person procession parades one after the other before the imaginary camera.)*

DOLL WOMAN *(Brandishing a crying baby [doll] as she strolls past and exits.)*  She's been crying ever since you left, Caldonia . . .

MOP MAN *(Flashing mop.)*  It's been waiting in the same corner, Buster . . .

BRUSH MAN *(Flagging toilet brush in one hand and toilet plunger in other.)*  It's been dry ever since you left, Washington . . .

MAYOR *(Jumping in on the heels of the last exit.)*  Don't these things mean anything to y'all? By God! Are your memories so short?! Is there nothing sacred to ya? . . . Please come back, for my sake, please! All of you—even you questionable ones! I promise no harm will be done to you! Revenge is disallowed! We'll forgive everything! Just come on back and I'll git down on my knees— *(Immediately drops to knees.)* I'll be kneeling in the middle of Dixie Avenue to kiss the first shoe of the first on 'a you to show up. . . . *I'll smooch any other spot you request.* . . . Erase this nightmare 'n' we'll concede any demand you make, just come on back—please???!! . . . PLEEEEEEEZE?!!!

VOICE *(Shouting.)*  TIME!!!

MAYOR *(Remaining on knees, frozen in a pose of supplication. After a brief, deadly silence, he whispers almost inaudibly.)*  They wouldn't answer . . . they wouldn't answer . . .

*(Blackout as bedlam erupts offstage. Total blackness holds during a sufficient interval where offstage sound-effects create the illusion of complete pandemonium, followed by a diminution which trails off into an expressionistic simulation of a city coming to a stricken standstill: industrial machinery clanks to halt, traffic blares to silence, etc. . . . The stage remains dark and silent for a long moment, then lights re-arise on the ANNOUNCER.)*

ANNOUNCER  A pitiful sight, ladies and gentlemen. Soon after his unsuccessful appeal Mayor Lee suffered a vicious pummeling from the mob and barely escaped with his life. National Guardsmen and State Militia were impotent in quelling the fury of a town venting its frustration in an orgy of destruction— a frenzy of rioting, looting and all other aberrations of a town gone berserk. . . . Then—suddenly—as if a magic wand had been waved, madness evaporated and something more frightening replaced it: Submission. . . . Even whimperings ceased. The city: exhausted, benumbed.—Slowly its occupants slinked off into shadows, and by midnight, the town was occupied exclusively by zombies. The fight and life had been drained out. . . . Pooped. . . . Hope ebbed away as completely as the beloved, absent Negroes. . . . As our crew packed gear and crept away silently, we treaded softly—as if we were stealing away from a mausoleum. . . . The Face Of A Defeated City.

*(Blackout. Lights rise slowly at the sound of rooster-crowing, signalling the approach of a new day, the next morning. Scene is same as opening of play.* CLEM *and* LUKE *are huddled over dazedly, trancelike. They remain so for a long count. Finally, a figure drifts on stage, shuffling slowly.)*

LUKE *(Gazing in silent fascination at the approaching figure.)* . . . Clem . . . ? Do you see what I see or am I dreaming . . . ?

CLEM  It's a . . . a Nigra, ain't it, Luke . . . ?

LUKE  Sure looks like one, Clem—but we better make sure—eyes could be playing tricks on us. . . . Does he still look like one to you, Clem?

CLEM  He still does, Luke—but I'm scared to believe—

LUKE  . . . Why . . . ? It looks like Rastus, Clem!

CLEM  Sure does, Luke . . . but we better not jump to no hasty conclusion . . .

LUKE *(In timid softness.)*   That you, Rastus . . . ?

RASTUS *(Stepin Fetchit, Willie Best, Nicodemus, B. McQueen and all the rest rolled into one.)*   Why . . . howdy . . . Mr. Luke . . . Mr. Clem . . .

CLEM  It is him, Luke! It is him!

LUKE  Rastus?

RASTUS  Yas . . . sah?

LUKE  Where was you yesterday?

RASTUS *(Very, very puzzled.)*  Yes . . . ter . . . day? . . . Yester . . . day . . . ? Why . . . right . . . here . . . Mr. Luke . . .

LUKE  No you warn't, Rastus, don't lie to me! Where was you yestiddy?

RASTUS  Why . . . I'm sure I was . . . Mr. Luke . . . Remember . . . I made . . . that . . . delivery for you . . .

LUKE  That was MONDAY, Rastus, yestiddy was TUESDAY.

RASTUS  Tues . . . day . . . ? You don't say. . . . Well . . . well . . . well . . .

LUKE  Where was you 'n' all the other Nigras yesterday, Rastus?

RASTUS  I . . . thought . . . yestiddy . . . was Monday, Mr. Luke—I coulda swore it . . . ! . . . See how . . . things . . . kin git all mixed up? . . . I coulda swore it . . .

LUKE  TODAY is WEDNESDAY, Rastus. Where was you TUESDAY?

RASTUS  Tuesday . . . huh? That's somp'um . . . I . . . don't . . . remember . . . missing . . . a day . . . Mr. Luke . . . but I guess you right . . .

LUKE  Then where was you!!!???

RASTUS  Don't rightly know, Mr. Luke. I didn't know I had skipped a day—But that jist goes to show you how time kin fly, don't it, Mr. Luke. . . . Uuh, uuh, uuh . . . *(He starts shuffling off, scratching head, a flicker of a smile playing across his lips.* CLEM *and* LUKE *gaze dumbfoundedly as he disappears.)*

LUKE *(Eyes sweeping around in all directions.)*   Well. . . . There's the others, Clem. . . . Back jist like they useta be. . . . Everything's same as always . . .

CLEM  ??? . . . . . . . . . . . . Is it . . . Luke . . . ! *(Slow fade.)*

*Curtain*

## FOR DISCUSSION

1. How does the author's tone in the "Notes on Production" and "Production Concept" sections establish the mood for the entire play? Is it possible to imagine the play done in a style of "serious tragedy"? Why do you think the author made the suggestion?
2. How do Clem's feelings of uneasiness in the opening scene foreshadow later events?
3. Why is it such a catastrophe for all of the "Nigras" in this small community to disappear? What roles have the blacks played in this society?
4. What is suggested by the fact that the few "Nigras" left in town—those in the hospital—are all in a coma?
5. Why have several prominent white citizens disappeared along with all of the "Nigras"? What is suggested about these vanished whites?
6. Why is Council Clan so upset by the disappearance of the "Nigras," since it is his supposed goal to clear the society of all Negroes? What type of irony is involved in this situation?
7. How do Aide and Pious exemplify white people with standard prejudices against blacks?
8. Why does the Mayor allow himself to include threats in his plea for the Negroes to return?
9. In the closing scene, is Rastus as innocent as he seems to be?
10. At the end of the play, is everything indeed going to be the "same as always"?
11. Although this play is a fantasy, it contains some strong social commentary. What are some of the social points that it makes?
12. Point out specific ways in which the play stereotypes both whites and blacks. Is the stereotyping an advantage or a disadvantage in this play?
13. *Day of Absence* was first produced—off Broadway—in 1965. Do you think theatergoers in the 1980s would see it any differently from theatergoers in the mid-1960s?

# The Gap

EUGÈNE IONESCO

Translated by Rosette Lamont

## List of Characters

THE FRIEND
THE ACADEMICIAN
THE ACADEMICIAN'S WIFE
THE MAID

**Set.** *A rich bourgeois living room with artistic pretensions. One or two sofas, a number of armchairs, among which, a green, Régence style¹ one, right in the middle of the room. The walls are covered with framed diplomas. One can make out, written in heavy script at the top of a particularly large one, "Doctor Honoris causa."² This is followed by an almost illegible Latin inscription. Another equally impressive diploma states: "Doctorat honoris causa," again followed by a long, illegible text. There is an abundance of smaller diplomas, each of which bears a clearly written "doctorate."*
    *A door to the right of the audience.*
    *As the curtain rises, one can see* THE ACADEMICIAN'S WIFE *dressed in a rather crumpled robe. She has obviously just gotten out of bed, and has not had time to dress.* THE FRIEND *faces her. He is well dressed: hat, umbrella in hand, stiff collar, black jacket and striped trousers, shiny black shoes.*


THE WIFE  Dear friend, tell me all.

THE FRIEND  I don't know what to say.

THE WIFE  I know.

THE FRIEND  I heard the news last night. I did not want to call you. At the same time I couldn't wait any longer. Please forgive me for coming so early with such terrible news.

THE WIFE  He didn't make it! How terrible! We were still hoping. . . .

THE FRIEND  It's hard, I know. He still had a chance. Not much of one. We had to expect it.

THE WIFE  I didn't expect it. He was always so successful. He could always manage somehow, at the last moment.

THE FRIEND  In that state of exhaustion. You shouldn't have let him!

THE WIFE  What can we do, what can we do! . . . How awful!

THE FRIEND  Come on, dear friend, be brave. That's life.

THE WIFE  I feel faint: I'm going to faint. *(She falls in one of the armchairs.)*

THE FRIEND  *(holding her, gently slapping her cheeks and hands)* I shouldn't have blurted it out like that. I'm sorry.

¹ Of the late seventeenth and early eighteenth centuries; particularly elegant.
² An honorary doctorate.

THE WIFE   No, you were right to do so. I had to find out somehow or other.

THE FRIEND   I should have prepared you, carefully.

THE WIFE   I've got to be strong. I can't help thinking of him, the wretched man. I hope they won't put it in the papers. Can we count on the journalists' discretion?

THE FRIEND   Close your door. Don't answer the telephone. It will still get around. You could go to the country. In a couple of months, when you are better, you'll come back, you'll go on with your life. People forget such things.

THE WIFE   People won't forget so fast. That's all they were waiting for. Some friends will feel sorry, but the others, the others. . . . (THE ACADEMICIAN *comes in, fully dressed: uniform, chest covered with decorations, his sword on his side.*)

THE ACADEMICIAN   Up so early, my dear? (*to* THE FRIEND) You've come early too. What's happening? Do you have the final results?

THE WIFE   What a disgrace!

THE FRIEND   You mustn't crush him like this, dear friend. (*to* THE ACADEMICIAN) You have failed.

THE ACADEMICIAN   Are you quite sure?

THE FRIEND   You should never have tried to pass the baccalaureate examination.

THE ACADEMICIAN   They failed me. The rats! How dare they do this to me!

THE FRIEND   The marks were posted late in the evening.

THE ACADEMICIAN   Perhaps it was difficult to make them out in the dark. How could you read them?

THE FRIEND   They had set up spotlights.

THE ACADEMICIAN   They're doing everything to ruin me.

THE FRIEND   I passed by in the morning; the marks were still up.

THE ACADEMICIAN   You could have bribed the concierge[3] into pulling them down.

THE FRIEND   That's exactly what I did. Unfortunately the police were there. Your name heads the list of those who failed. Everyone's standing in line to get a look. There's an awful crush.

THE ACADEMICIAN   Who's there? The parents of the candidates?

THE FRIEND   Not only they.

THE WIFE   All your rivals, all your colleagues must be there. All those you attacked in the press for ignorance: your undergraduates, your graduate students, all those you failed when you were chairman of the board of examiners.

THE ACADEMICIAN   I am discredited! But I won't let them. There must be some mistake.

THE FRIEND   I saw the examiners. I spoke with them. They gave me your marks. Zero in mathematics.

THE ACADEMICIAN   I had no scientific training.

THE FRIEND   Zero in Greek, zero in Latin.

THE WIFE   (*to her husband*)   You, a humanist, the spokesman for humanism, the author of that famous treatise "The Defense of Poesy and Humanism."

THE ACADEMICIAN   I beg your pardon, but my book concerns itself with twentieth

---

[3] Janitor.

century humanism. *(to* THE FRIEND*)* What about composition? What grade did
I get in composition?

THE FRIEND  Nine hundred. You have nine hundred points.

THE ACADEMICIAN  That's perfect. My average must be all the way up.

THE FRIEND  Unfortunately not. They're marking on the basis of two thousand.
The passing grade is one thousand.

THE ACADEMICIAN  They must have changed the regulations.

THE WIFE  They didn't change them just for you. You have a frightful persecution
complex.

THE ACADEMICIAN  I tell you they changed them.

THE FRIEND  They went back to the old ones, back to the time of Napoleon.[4]

THE ACADEMICIAN  Utterly outmoded. Besides, when did they make those
changes? It isn't legal. I'm chairman of the Baccalaureate Commission of the
Ministry of Public Education. They didn't consult me, and they cannot make
any changes without my approval. I'm going to expose them. I'm going to
bring government charges against them.

THE WIFE  Darling, you don't know what you're doing. You're in your dotage.
Don't you recall handing in your resignation just before taking the examination
so that no one could doubt the complete objectivity of the board of examiners?

THE ACADEMICIAN  I'll take it back.

THE WIFE  You should never have taken that test. I warned you. After all, it's
not as if you needed it. But you have to collect all the honors, don't you?
You're never satisfied. What did you need this diploma for? Now all is lost.
You have your Doctorate, your Master's, your high school diploma, your
elementary school certificate, and even the first part of the baccalaureate.[5]

THE ACADEMICIAN  There was a gap.

THE WIFE  No one suspected it.

THE ACADEMICIAN  But *I* knew it. Others might have found out. I went to the
office of the Registrar and asked for a transcript of my record. They said to
me: "Certainly Professor, Mr. President, Your Excellency. . . ." Then they
looked up my file, and the Chief Registrar came back looking embarrassed,
most embarrassed indeed. He said: "There's something peculiar, very peculiar.
You have your Master's, certainly, but it's no longer valid." I asked him why,
of course. He answered: "There's a gap behind your Master's. I don't know
how it happened. You must have registered and been accepted at the University without having passed the second part of the baccalaureate examination."

THE FRIEND  And then?

THE WIFE  Your Master's degree is no longer valid?

THE ACADEMICIAN  No, not quite. It's suspended. "The duplicate you are asking
for will be delivered to you upon completion of the baccalaureate. Of course

---

[4] The early nineteenth century.

[5] A very difficult exam in two parts—oral and written—taken in France at about the age
of eighteen to qualify for higher education. The exam is mainly general and philosophical
in nature.

you will pass the examination with no trouble." That's what I was told, so you see now that I had to take it.

THE FRIEND  Your husband, dear friend, wanted to fill the gap. He's a conscientious person.

THE WIFE  It's clear you don't know him as I do. That's not it at all. He wants fame, honors. He never had enough. What does one diploma more or less matter? No one notices them anyway, but he sneaks in at night, on tiptoe, into the living room, just to look at them, and count them.

THE ACADEMICIAN  What else can I do when I have insomnia?

THE FRIEND  The questions asked at the baccalaureate are usually known in advance. You were admirably situated to get this particular information. You could also have sent in a replacement to take the test for you. One of your students, perhaps. Or if you wanted to take the test without people realizing that you already knew the questions, you could have sent your maid to the black market, where one can buy them.

THE ACADEMICIAN  I don't understand how I could have failed in my composition. I filled three sheets of paper, I treated the subject fully, taking into account the historical background. I interpreted the situation accurately . . . at least plausibly. I didn't deserve a bad grade.

THE FRIEND  Do you recall the subject?

THE ACADEMICIAN  Hum . . . let's see. . . .

THE FRIEND  He doesn't even remember what he discussed.

THE ACADEMICIAN  I do . . . wait . . . hum.

THE FRIEND  The subject to be treated was the following: "Discuss the influence of Renaissance painters on novelists of the Third Republic."[6] I have here a photostatic copy of your examination paper. Here is what you wrote.

THE ACADEMICIAN  (*grabbing the photostat reading*)  "The trial of Benjamin: After Benjamin was tried and acquitted, the assessors holding a different opinion from that of the President murdered him, and condemned Benjamin to the suspension of his civic rights, imposing on him a fine of nine hundred francs. . . ."

THE FRIEND  That's where the nine hundred points come from.

THE ACADEMICIAN  "Benjamin appealed his case . . . Benjamin appealed his case. . . ." I can't make out the rest. I've always had bad handwriting. I ought to have taken a typewriter along with me.

THE WIFE  Horrible handwriting, scribbling and crossing out; ink spots didn't help you much.

THE ACADEMICIAN  (*goes on with his reading after having retrieved the text his wife had pulled out of his hand*)  "Benjamin appealed his case. Flanked by policemen dressed in zouave uniforms . . . in zouave uniforms. . . ." It's getting dark. I can't see the rest. . . . I don't have my glasses.

THE WIFE  What you've written has nothing to do with the subject.

THE FRIEND  Your wife's quite right, friend. It has nothing to do with the subject

THE ACADEMICIAN  Yes, it has. Indirectly.

THE FRIEND  Not even indirectly.

[6] That is, of the period 1870–1940.

THE ACADEMICIAN  Perhaps I chose the second question.

THE FRIEND  There was only one.

THE ACADEMICIAN  Even if there was only that one, I treated another quite adequately. I went to the end of the story. I stressed the important points, explaining the motivations of the characters, highlighting their behavior. I explained the mystery, making it plain and clear. There was even a conclusion at the end. I can't make out the rest. (to THE FRIEND) Can you read it?

THE FRIEND  It's illegible. I don't have my glasses either.

THE WIFE (taking the text)  It's illegible and I have excellent eyes. You pretended to write. Mere scribbling.

THE ACADEMICIAN  That's not true. I've even provided a conclusion. It's clearly marked here in heavy print: "Conclusion or sanction . . . Conclusion or sanction. . . ." They can't get away with it. I'll have this examination rendered null and void.

THE WIFE  Since you treated the wrong subject, and treated it badly, setting down only titles, and writing nothing in between, the mark you received is justified. You'd lose your case.

THE FRIEND  You'd most certainly lose. Drop it. Take a vacation.

THE ACADEMICIAN  You're always on the side of the Others.

THE WIFE  After all, these professors know what they're doing. They haven't been granted their rank for nothing. They passed examinations, received serious training. They know the rules of composition.

THE ACADEMICIAN  Who was on the board of examiners?

THE FRIEND  For Mathematics, a movie star. For Greek, one of the Beatles. For Latin, the champion of the automobile race, and many others.

THE ACADEMICIAN  But these people aren't any more qualified than I am. And for composition?

THE FRIEND  A woman, a secretary in the editorial division of the review Yesterday, the Day Before Yesterday, and Today.

THE ACADEMICIAN  Now I know. This wretch gave me a poor grade out of spite because I never joined her political party. It's an act of vengeance. But I have ways and means of rendering the examination null and void. I'm going to call the President.

THE WIFE  Don't. You'll make yourself look even more ridiculous. (to THE FRIEND) Please try to restrain him. He listens to you more than to me. (THE FRIEND shrugs his shoulders, unable to cope with the situation. THE WIFE turns to her husband, who has just lifted the receiver off the hook.) Don't call!

THE ACADEMICIAN (on the telephone)  Hello, John? It is I . . . What? . . . What did you say? . . . But, listen, my dear friend . . . but, listen to me . . . Hello! Hello! (Puts down the receiver.)

THE FRIEND  What did he say?

THE ACADEMICIAN  He said . . . He said . . . , "I don't want to talk to you. My mummy won't let me make friends with boys at the bottom of the class." Then he hung up on me.

THE WIFE  You should have expected it. All is lost. How could you do this to me? How could you do this to me?

THE ACADEMICIAN  Think of it! I lectured at the Sorbonne, at Oxford, at American universities. Ten thousand theses have been written on my work; hundreds of critics have analyzed it. I hold an *honoris causa* doctorate from Amsterdam as well as a secret university Chair with the Duchy of Luxembourg. I received the Nobel Prize three times. The King of Sweden himself was amazed by my erudition. A doctorate *honoris causa, honoris causa . . .* and I failed the baccalaureate examination!

THE WIFE  Everyone will laugh at us!

THE ACADEMICIAN *takes off his sword and breaks it on his knee.*

THE FRIEND (*picking up the two pieces*)  I wish to preserve these in memory of our ancient glory.

THE ACADEMICIAN *meanwhile in a fit of rage is tearing down his decorations, throwing them on the floor, and stepping on them.*

THE WIFE (*trying to salvage the remains*)  Don't do this! Don't! That's all we've got left.

*Curtain*


## FOR DISCUSSION

1. What do you make of the fact that until the Academician makes his entrance the two women seem to be talking about someone's death?
2. Why are none of the characters in the play given proper names?
3. Why was the Academician so distressed by the gap in his education? Why did he take the baccalaureate (undergraduate) examination?
4. What is ironic about the Academician's being the author of a famous book on twentieth-century humanism?
5. Why did the Academician fail the examination?
6. How is it possible for a person whose book has engendered "ten thousand theses" to be unable to write a coherent paragraph?
7. Although *The Gap* is a clear example of a modern dramatic fantasy, the play nonetheless has a serious purpose. What do you think that purpose is? What is the play's theme?

PART IV *Poetry*

# Introduction

Not only is poetry the oldest of all the types of literature, but it is also the first that most people encounter in life. When we are children, our parents sing lullabies and recite nursery rhymes to us long before telling us stories. As we grow up, we often hear verse on radio and television— in the form of popular songs and commercials. And few of us manage to escape the feeble verses produced by the makers of greeting cards. Good poetry, however, is more than nursery rhymes, popular songs, and greeting card verse; even though these things may have given us a certain amount of enjoyment, many students discover a much greater enjoyment in learning about more serious poetry.

Since poetry calls so much attention to its own form and structure, you will find poetic form one suitable starting place for learning to appreciate poetry. In several respects poetry has much in common with music. Poetry's words are often chosen for sound as much as meaning, and they are arranged into lines that are much like musical phrases, with the rhythms and sounds of the words blended to produce a musical or lyric effect. Also like music, poetry benefits from being heard as well as read. Indeed, many great poems have been set to music.

Another possible starting point for learning about poetry is with a consideration of poetry's distinctive way of communicating—the kinds of things a poem might say that an essay, a story, or a nonpoetic play would not, and poetry's distinctive way of saying them. Earlier we discussed imagery in the context of the short story, where it enhances the narrative flow of the story. In poetry, however, an image or symbol may be what an entire poem is about.

Finally, one can also begin a study of poetry by noting what elements a poem shares with other kinds of literature. For example, just as every short story has a narrator with a point of view, every poem has a persona—a person or voice that speaks the poem. Just as every work of fiction or drama has its distinctive tone, which expresses the author's attitude toward the work and its audience, so does every poem. Irony— both verbal irony and irony of situation—is often employed in poetry as it is in fiction and drama. A poem can tell a story, argue a position, make a joke, create a character, sketch a picture, or do whatever the poet has the craft to make it do. Plays, and even autobiographies and works of philosophy, have been written in verse.

Our discussion will take roughly the following order: poetic form, poetic meaning, and the elements that poetry has in common with other kinds of literature. Unlike the other introductions in the book, this one will include many complete poems and parts of poems, besides referring to others collected together as an anthology for further reading. Finally, we have provided a series of questions that you can ask about any poem, rather than separate questions about each selection.

## Foot and Meter

Until this century, most verse was written in regular rhythms—what are called **meters.** All writing and speech have rhythm, but the rhythm of metrical verse is more strikingly accented and more repetitive than the rhythms of ordinary speech and prose. As in music, the rhythms of poetry are marked off into recurring patterns of strong and weak sounds. These patterns, which are the individual units of rhythm in a line of verse, are called **feet.**

A poetic foot consists, usually, of two or three syllables, with at least one of them receiving a strong stress; and a line of metrical poetry consists, rhythmically, of several feet—usually four, five, or six, but occasionally as many as eight or as few as one. The feet repeat the poem's basic rhythmic pattern, or stay very close to it. And all the lines of the poem are metrically related to one another, either repeating the same rhythmic pattern or varying from it in ways that remain harmonious.

The two most important types of metrical feet containing two syllables are the iambic foot and the trochaic foot. The **iambic foot** consists of an unstressed syllable followed by a strongly accented syllable (ta-DUM, marked ◡ ／ ). It may be thought of as the "skipping" foot. Such words as *alive, believe, delight,* and *return* are iambic. The **trochaic foot,** on the other hand, consists of a strongly stressed syllable followed by an unaccented syllable (DUM-ta, marked / ˘ ). It may be thought of as the "marching" foot. Such words as *anger, badly, loosen,* and *whisper* are trochaic.

The following two excerpts illustrate iambic and trochaic feet:

Whose woods | these are | I think | I know.

His house | is in | the vill | age, though;

He will | not see | me stopp | ing here

To watch | his woods | fill up | with snow.

> (Robert Frost, from "Stopping by
> Woods on a Snowy Evening")

At the | door on | summer | evenings

Sat the | little | Hia | watha;

Heard the | whispering | of the | pine trees,

Heard the | lapping | of the | water,

Sounds of | music, | words of | wonder . . .

> (Henry Wadsworth Longfellow,
> from "Firefly Song")

Marking off the rhythm of a line into feet, and into strong and weak stresses, is called **scansion** (SKAN-shun). Scansion can be both subtle and inexact, and it can therefore be tricky, especially if the exercise is new to you. For example, if you read the lines by Frost aloud several times, you may be able to "feel" that forcing the entire stanza into an unvarying iambic pattern violates the usual rhythms of the words and leaves little room for rhythmic emphasis. A more experienced scansion of the stanza might read as follows:

Whose woods | these are | I think | I know.

His house | is in | the vill | age, though;

He will | not see | me stopp | ing here

To watch | his woods | fill up | with snow.

The first two feet in the first line are not iambic; each consists of a pair of strongly accented syllables. Such a foot is called a **spondee**. And in the third and fourth lines, an iambic foot has been turned around to form a trochee. Such variations keep the rhythm alive and the reader alert, just as syncopations do in music.

The two most important feet containing three syllables are the anapestic foot and the dactylic foot. The **anapestic foot** consists of two unaccented syllables followed by a strongly stressed syllable (ta-ta-DUM, marked ⌣ ⌣ / ). The anapest may be thought of as the "galloping" foot. Here is an excerpt featuring the anapestic foot:

```
   ⌣    /       ⌣  ⌣   /    ⌣  ⌣ /    ⌣  ⌣   /
And there | lay the ri | der distort | ed and pale,

   ⌣   ⌣   /    ⌣   ⌣   /     ⌣  ⌣   /    ⌣  ⌣   /
With the dew | on his brow, | and the rust | on his mail;

   ⌣  ⌣   /       ⌣  ⌣  /   ⌣   ⌣   /     ⌣ ⌣ /
And the tents | were all si | lent, the bann | ers alone,

 ⌣   /     ⌣  ⌣ /    ⌣   ⌣   /     ⌣  ⌣   /
The lan | ces unlif | ted, the trum | pet unblown.
```

(George Gordon, Lord Byron, from
"The Destruction of Sennacherib")

The **dactylic foot** consists of a strongly stressed syllable followed by two unaccented syllables (DUM-ta-ta, marked / ⌣ ⌣ ). The dactyl may be thought of as the "waltzing" foot. The following excerpt is mainly dactylic:

```
  /   ⌣   ⌣      /    ⌣  ⌣
Cannon to | right of them,

  /   ⌣  ⌣    /   ⌣   ⌣
Cannon to | left of them,

  /   ⌣  ⌣     /   ⌣   ⌣
Cannon in | front of them

    /   ⌣   ⌣      /   ⌣
  Volleyed and | thundered;

  /    ⌣   ⌣     /   ⌣   ⌣
Stormed at with | shot and shell,

  /  ⌣  ⌣     /   ⌣   ⌣
Boldly they | rode and well,

 / ⌣  ⌣    /   ⌣  ⌣
Into the | jaws of Death,

 / ⌣  ⌣      /    ⌣ ⌣
Into the | mouth of Hell,

   /   ⌣  ⌣    /   ⌣
  Rode the six | hundred.
```

(Alfred, Lord Tennyson, from "The
Charge of the Light Brigade")

Many times poems blend two or more types of feet. The following poem presents a nice blending of iambic and anapestic feet, with anapests dominating just a little. Also notice that line three consists of two feet marked ⌣ / ⌣ . Line seven ends with the same foot. This is a less frequently used three-syllable foot called an **amphibrach** (ta-DUM-ta).

## Do You Fear the Wind?

Do you fear | the force | of the wind,

The slash | of the rain?

Go face them | and fight them,

Be sav | age again.

Go hun | gry and cold | like the wolf,                5

Go wade | like the crane:

The palms | of your hands | will thicken,

The skin | of your cheek | will tan,

You'll grow ragg | ed and wear | y and swar | thy,

But you'll walk | like a man!                10

Hamlin Garland

The next excerpt includes mostly trochees and dactyls, but the rhythm is such that a few lines end with iambs.

Mowers, | weary | and brown, | and blithe,

What is | the word | methinks | ye know,

Endless | over- | word that | the Scythe

Sings to the | blades of | the grass | below?

Scythes that | swing in the | grass and | clover,

Something, | still, they | say as | they pass;

What is the | word that, | over and | over,

Sings the | Scythe to the | flowers | and grass?

(Andrew Lang, from "Scythe Song")

The **amphimacer,** an additional kind of three-syllable foot used for variation, consists of a stressed syllable, followed by a weak syllable, followed by another stressed syllable (DUM-ta-DUM; / ◡ / ). Here is a rare poem written almost entirely in amphimacers:

# The Oak

Live thy Life,

Young and old,

Like yon oak,

Bright in spring,

Living gold;                                                                                    5

Summer-rich

Then; and then

Autumn-changed,

Soberer-hued

Gold again.                                                                                    10

All his leaves

Fallen at length,

Look, he stands,

Trunk and bough,

Naked strength.                                                                              15

Alfred, Lord Tennyson

In the examples so far, you may have noticed that each line is divided into one or more feet, and you probably also noticed that the number of feet per line forms a pattern within the poem. All of the lines may have the same number of feet, or the number may vary from line to line in a regular way. The number of feet in a poetic line is called the **quantity** of its meter. Here are some useful terms for naming the various metrical quantities:

| | |
|---|---|
| **monometer** | one foot |
| **dimeter** | two feet |
| **trimeter** | three feet |
| **tetrameter** | four feet |
| **pentameter** | five feet |
| **hexameter** | six feet |
| **heptameter** | seven feet |
| **octameter** | eight feet |

To name a poem's meter, you combine the term for its prevailing foot and the term for the number of feet that appear in each line. For example:

The Cur | few tolls | the knell | of par | ting day,

The low | ing herd | wind slow | ly o'er | the lea,

The plow | man home | ward plods | his wear | y way,

And leaves | the world | to dark | ness and | to me.

> (Thomas Gray, from "Elegy
> Written in a Country Churchyard")

The feet are iambic, and there are five feet in each line. The meter, therefore, is **iambic pentameter**—for centuries the most often used meter in English poetry.

## Rhyme and Other Devices of Sound

Rhythm, the pattern of weak and strong stresses, is only one aspect of the sound of poetry. Another centers on the sounds of vowels and consonants. In everyday speech, we tend to take the sounds of the words we use for granted, not paying much attention to the music they might make. But poets use the materials of language the way a sculptor might use a rock or a block of wood, to transform the shapeless into the well-formed, the meaningless into the meaningful. And so it follows that they pay close attention to the sounds of words, and turn them to special and prominent use.

The most obvious use of sound in poetry is **rhyme.** In fact, many people think of rhyme as the one essential element of poetry—even though neither the earliest poetry nor much new poetry rhymes at all. For two words to form a perfect rhyme three specific things must happen. First, the two words must have the same vowel sound in their last stressed syllables. Second, the consonant sounds preceding that vowel sound must be different. Third, all sounds following that vowel sound must be the same. Thus, all of the following words—*ways, gaze, praise, neighs, repays,* and *mayonnaise*—are perfect rhymes for one another. And *position, suspicion,* and *recognition* all rhyme as well.

Rhyming words in which the last stressed syllable is also the last syllable, like *gaze* and *repays,* may form **single rhymes;** those with two consecutive rhyming syllables, like *position* and *recognition,* form **double rhymes.** (An old usage, which now seems quaint and perhaps wrong-headed, has it that single rhymes are "masculine" because they end with a strong stress, and double rhymes are "feminine" because they end with a weak stress. But the more neutral terms are just as good.) As you will see, single rhymes are far more common than any other kind, but double rhymes have their uses, for example in lines written in trochaic rhythm. Sometimes you may even come across a **triple rhyme,** as in *call to me* and *all to me,* when the rhythm is dactylic.

Look for the rhymes in this old English song:

# Sleighing Song

On Christmas night the moon sheds its light
   And the road is white below;
Make merry today! The horse knows the way;
   So hey! for the sleigh and the snow!

We skim o'er the ground with never a sound;
   We bound like a hounded doe;
When the skies are gray we cannot delay,
   So hey! for the sleigh and the snow!

Anonymous

The second, fourth, sixth, and eighth lines rhyme: *below, snow, doe,* and again *snow.* Since the poem is in iambic rhythm, and each line ends with a strong stress, these are all single rhymes. And since they all come at the ends of lines, they are known as **end-rhymes.** But perhaps you noticed that there are many other rhymes in this poem:

On Christmas *night* the moon sheds its *light*
   And the road is *white* below . . .

These are called **internal rhymes.** Most of them fall within a line; and *light*, though it ends a line, cannot be an end-rhyme because no other line in the poem ends with a rhyme-word for *light*.

What are rhymes for? Most obviously, they emphasize a sound by repeating it, and so draw attention to the words containing those sounds. What is less obvious is that the arrangement of rhymes, particularly end-rhymes, gives many poems their structure. We will discuss this aspect of rhyming later.

But poets are not limited to rhyme in their uses of word sounds. They may choose to repeat a particular vowel or consonant, or a particular kind of vowel or consonant, to create subtle effects. For example, the poet may repeat the same vowel sound in words that do not rhyme, a quality called **assonance:**

> When I was a child,
>    My dreams were my flying times;
> And daily my waking hours
>    Awaited those flights in wilder climes.

Here, the sound of *I* is repeated in ten syllables, only two of which (*times* and *climes*) are rhymes; and, less obviously, *daily* and *waking* and *Awaited* are in assonance with one another.

A specific kind of assonance occurs at the ends of lines and is called a **near rhyme** or a **false rhyme.** It meets all of the requirements for a perfect rhyme except that the sounds following the rhyming vowel are not the same. In this old ballad stanza, *split* and *ship* are in assonance, as are *storm* and *morn:*

> The anchor broke, the topmast split,
>    'Twas such a deadly storm;
> The waves came over the broken ship
>    Till all her sides were torn.

> (Anonymous, from "Sir Patrick Spens")

False rhyme is fairly common in popular verse and song, but rare in serious poetry, because it suggests that the poet tried but failed to find perfect rhymes.

**Alliteration,** the repetition of a consonant sound, usually occurs at the beginning of stressed syllables. For example:

> To sit in solemn silence in a dull, dark dock,
> In a pestilential prison, with a lifelong lock,
> Awaiting the sensation of a short, sharp shock,
> From a cheap and chippy chopper on a big black block!

> (W. S. Gilbert, from *The Mikado*)

Here the alliteration comes on so strong and fast that it is funny—as it was meant to be. But alliteration can also contribute to serious poetry:

> By the bivouac's fitful flame,
> A procession winding around me, solemn and sweet and slow—but first
>   I note
> The tents of the sleeping army, the fields' and woods' dim outline,
> The darkness lit by spots of kindled fire, the silence,
> Like a phantom far or near an occasional figure moving . . .
>
> (Walt Whitman, from "By the<br>Bivouac's Fitful Flame")

**Consonance**, another form of near rhyme, involves the pairing of words in which the final consonants of the stressed syllables agree but the preceding vowel sounds differ. Sometimes, however, the consonants preceding the differing vowel sounds will also agree. The following example presents both varieties of consonance.

## Arms and the Boy

Let the boy try along this bayonet-blade
How cold steel is, and keen with hunger for blood;
Blue with all malice, like a madman's flash;
And thinly drawn with famishing for flesh.

Lend him to stroke these blind, blunt bullet-heads                5
Which long to nuzzle in the heart of lads,
Or give him cartridges of fine zinc teeth,
Sharp with the sharpness of grief and death.

For his teeth seem for laughing round an apple.
There lurk no claws behind his fingers supple;                   10
And God will grow no talons at his heels,
Nor antlers through the thickness of his curls.

Wilfred Owen

All of these devices for managing sound within a poem are more or less arbitrary, as they do not attempt to imitate the sounds of the world outside the poem. But language does sometimes attempt this kind of imitation, called **onomatopoeia** (*ahn*-uh-*mat*-uh-PEE-uh), in words like *hiss, bang, honk, whirr,* and *quack*; and so does poetry:

> Hear the sledges with the bells—
>   Silver bells!

What a world of merriment their melody foretells!
How they tinkle, tinkle, tinkle,
In the icy air of night!
While the stars that oversprinkle
All the heavens seem to twinkle
With a crystalline delight;
Keeping time, time, time,
In a sort of Runic rhyme,
To the tintinnabulation that so musically wells
From the bells, bells, bells, bells,
Bells, bells, bells—
From the jingling and the tinkling of the bells.

(Edgar Allan Poe, from "The Bells")

The bell imitations in this poem come mainly from the use of onomatopoetic words (*tinkle, tintinnabulation, jingling*) or rhymes on them—even *time* and *rhyme* suggest the missing, onomatopoetic *chime*. But the effect is so obvious and insistent that it soon becomes tiresome—perhaps even a bit silly. More subtle is the following:

. . . but every sound is sweet;
Myriads of rivulets hurrying through the lawn,
The moan of doves in immemorial elms,
And murmuring of innumerable bees.

(Alfred, Lord Tennyson, from *The Princess*)

The *m*'s and *b*'s in the last line suggest, quietly, just the sound that the words describe. And in the following poem, the *s*'s in the first stanza and the repeated use of the word *hush* in the second suggest the sound made by the scythes as they mow the grass, and they help to create an eerie, chilling mood

## Scythe Song

Mowers, weary and brown, and blithe,
  What is the word methinks ye know,
Endless over-word that the Scythe
  Sings to the blades of the grass below?
Scythes that swing in the grass and clover,
  Something, still, they say as they pass;
What is the word that, over and over,
  Sings the Scythe to the flowers and grass?

5

*Hush, ah hush,* the Scythes are saying,
  *Hush, and heed not, and fall asleep;*                           10
*Hush,* they say to the grasses swaying,
  *Hush,* they sing to the clover deep!
*Hush*—'tis the lullaby Time is singing—
  *Hush, and heed not, for all things pass,*
*Hush, ah hush!* and the Scythes are swinging                      15
  Over the clover, over the grass!

Andrew Lang

## Verse Forms

There are many different patterns of rhyme, called **rhyme-schemes.**
The most simple is the **couplet,** in which two successive lines rhyme
with each other. For example:

## On the Collar of a Dog

I am his Highness' dog at Kew;[1]
Pray tell me, sir, whose dog are you?

Alexander Pope

Alexander Pope was a master of the couplet, and wrote not only epigrams
but long philosophical poems in that rhyme-scheme. Here is a selection
from such a poem:

   Know then thyself, presume not God to scan;
   The proper study of mankind is Man.
   Placed on this isthmus of a middle state,
   A being darkly wise, and rudely great:
   With too much knowledge for the skeptic side,
   With too much weakness for the stoic's pride,
   He hangs between; in doubt to act, or rest,
   In doubt to deem himself a god, or beast;
   In doubt his mind or body to prefer,
   Born but to die, and reasoning but to err;
   Alike in ignorance, his reason such,
   Whether he thinks too little, or too much:
   Chaos of thought and passion, all confused;
   Still by himself abused, or disabused;
   Created half to rise, and half to fall;

---

[1] Kew Palace, London, then the residence of King George III.

Great lord of all things, yet a prey to all;
Sole judge of truth, in endless error hurled:
The glory, jest, and riddle of the world!

(Alexander Pope, from *An Essay on Man*)

These couplets are in iambic pentameter, and are called **heroic couplets.** When heroic couplets are strung together, as here, the result is called **heroic verse.** When a couplet includes a complete grammatical unit and can stand alone as an independent idea or statement, it is a **closed couplet,** as in the first two lines above. Couplets make us read a poem in pairs of lines, and are ideal both for formally balanced rhetoric and for epigrams and even jokes.

Long poems written in couplets may be divided into smaller sections of irregular length according to the sense of the poem. These sections, logically enough, are called **verse paragraphs,** and serve about the same function as prose paragraphs do. But more often a poem will be divided into groups of lines called **stanzas,** usually alike in meter and rhyme-scheme, like the verses of a song. Here is an example:

## Loveliest of Trees, the Cherry Now

Loveliest of trees, the cherry now
Is hung with bloom along the bough,
And stands about the woodland ride
Wearing white for Eastertide.

Now, of my threescore years and ten,    5
Twenty will not come again,
And take from seventy springs a score,
It only leaves me fifty more.

And since to look at things in bloom
Fifty springs are little room,    10
About the woodlands I will go
To see the cherry hung with snow.

        A. E. Housman

The poem is written in couplets, but it is also in three four-line stanzas called **quatrains,** two couplets each. (Add to this information the fact that the poem is in iambic tetrameter, and you have a brief but accurate description of its form.) Like a verse paragraph, each stanza corresponds to a different thought, but each also matches the length, rhyme-scheme, and meter of the others. The form is not very complicated, and the thought is not very profound, but they are perfectly matched, and that is the first requirement for a fine poem.

Of course, poets do not always write in couplets or quatrains. But let's stay with the quatrain a little longer to see what else can be done with it.

> All in a hot and copper sky,
> The bloody Sun, at noon,
> Right up above the mast did stand,
> No bigger than the Moon.

> (Samuel Taylor Coleridge, from "The Rime of the Ancient Mariner")

> Sound, sound the clarion, fill the fife!
>   To all the sensual world proclaim,
> One crowded hour of glorious life
>   Is worth an age without a name.

> (Sir Walter Scott, from "One Crowded Hour")

> Ring out the old, ring in the new,
>   Ring, happy bells, across the snow:
>   The year is going, let him go;
> Ring out the false, ring in the true.

> (Alfred, Lord Tennyson, from *In Memoriam A. H. H.*)

As you read the Coleridge, you probably wondered when and how it would rhyme. None of the first three lines forms a rhyme, and it was not until literally the last word of all that you could be sure there would even *be* a rhyme. This is a very different sort of effect from that of a couplet, even though each rhyme-scheme is based on a single pair of rhymes. The difference is in scale, in the distance you must read and the time you must wait until you learn where and what the rhyme will be. Scott's four lines rhyme alternately, so that the suspense of not knowing how the stanza will rhyme is resolved partly in line 3 and partly in line 4. It is mainly the last two lines that count: the first two merely set up the rhyme-scheme, and announce that an important statement is to follow. Finally, Tennyson rhymes his first and fourth lines, with a couplet in between.

There is a standard shorthand that you can use to label the rhymes in a poem and refer to them in discussion. You begin by labeling the sound with which the first line ends *a*. If the second line ends with a different sound, you label that sound *b*. If the third line ends with yet another sound, you label that *c*, and so on; each new sound gets a new letter. Then, when a line repeats the sound of the ending of the first line, you have another *a*. When another line repeats the sound of the ending of the second line, you have another *b*. So, the rhyme-scheme of the Coleridge stanza is *abcb*, the Scott *abab*, and the Tennyson *abba*. The following five-line stanza, called a **quintet**, has a rhyme-scheme of *abbba*. Notice that all of the *b* rhymes are double rhymes.

> Underneath the growing grass,
>   Underneath the living flowers,
>   Deeper than the sound of showers:
>   There we shall not count the hours
> By the shadows as they pass.

> (Christina Rossetti, from
>                     "The Bourne")

The next poem is in four six-line stanzas, or **sestets,** each with a rhyme-scheme of *ababcc*.

## I Wandered Lonely as a Cloud

I wandered lonely as a cloud
That floats on high o'er vales and hills,
When all at once I saw a crowd,
A host, of golden daffodils;
Beside the lake, beneath the trees,     5
Fluttering and dancing in the breeze.

Continuous as the stars that shine
And twinkle in the milky way,
They stretched in never-ending line
Along the margin of a bay:     10
Ten thousand saw I at a glance,
Tossing their heads in sprightly dance.

The waves beside them danced; but they
Outdid the sparkling waves in glee;
A poet could not but be gay     15
In such a jocund company;
I gazed—and gazed—but little thought
What wealth the show to me had brought:

For oft, when on my couch I lie
In vacant or in pensive mood,                                          20
They flash upon that inward eye
Which is the bliss of solitude;
And then my heart with pleasure fills,
And dances with the daffodils.

William Wordsworth

The **tercet**—sometimes called a **triplet**—is a stanza of three lines all rhyming together. Usually, but not always, the lines contain the same number of feet. Observe the following little poem, which is made up of two tercets.

## Upon Julia's Clothes

Whenas in silks my Julia goes,
Then, then, methinks, how sweetly flows
That liquefaction of her clothes.

Next, when I cast mine eyes, and see
That brave[1] vibration, each way free,                                5
O, how that glittering taketh me!

Robert Herrick

When tercets are strung together in such a way that the middle line of one stanza forms a rhyme with the first and third lines of the following stanza, the stanza form of **terza rima** is created. Observe the following excerpt:

O wild West Wind, thou breath of Autumn's being,
Thou, from whose unseen presence the leaves dead
Are driven, like ghosts from an enchanter fleeing,

Yellow, and black and pale, and hectic red,
Pestilence-stricken multitudes: O thou,
Who chariotest to their dark wintry bed

The winged seeds, where they lie cold and low,
Each like a corpse within its grave, until
Thine azure sister of the Spring shall blow . . .

(Percy Bysshe Shelley, from
"Ode to the West Wind")

[1]Glorious.

A quatrain that has four feet in the first and third lines and three feet in the second and fourth lines, with a rhyme-scheme of *abcb*, is called a **ballad stanza**. The quatrain by Coleridge was in the ballad stanza form. So is this example:

# John Barleycorn

## A Ballad

There were three Kings into the east
  Three Kings both great and high,
And they hae sworn a solemn oath
  John Barleycorn should die.

They took a plow and plowed him down,       5
  Put clods upon his head,
And they hae sworn a solemn oath
  John Barleycorn was dead.

But the cheerfu' Spring came kindly on,
  And show'rs began to fall;       10
John Barleycorn got up again,
  And sore surprised them all.

The sultry suns of Summer came,
  And he grew thick and strong,
His head weel armed wi' pointed spears,       15
  That no one should him wrong.

The sober Autumn entered mild,
  When he grew wan and pale;
His bending joints and drooping head
  Showed he began to fail.       20

His color sickened more and more,
  He faded into age;
And then his enemies began
  To show their deadly rage.

They've ta'en a weapon, long and sharp,       25
  And cut him by the knee;
Then tied him fast upon a cart,
  Like a rogue for forgerie.

They laid him down upon his back,
  And cudgelled him full sore;       30

They hung him up before the storm,
  And turned him o'er and o'er.

They filléd up a darksome pit
  With water to the brim,
They heavéd in John Barleycorn,          35
  There let him sink or swim.

They laid him out upon the floor,
  To work him further woe,
And still, as signs of life appeared,
  They tossed him to and fro.          40

They wasted, o'er a scorching flame,
  The marrow of his bones;
But a miller used him worst of all,
  For he crushed him between two stones.

And they hae ta'en his very heart's blood,          45
  And drank it round and round;
And still the more and more they drank,
  Their joy did more abound.

John Barleycorn was a hero bold,
  Of noble enterprise,          50
For if you do but taste his blood,
  'Twill make your courage rise;

'Twill make a man forget his woe;
  'Twill heighten all his joy:
'Twill make the widow's heart to sing,          55
  Tho' the tear were in her eye.

Then let us toast John Barleycorn,
  Each man a glass in hand;
And may his great posterity
  Ne'er fail in old Scotland.          60

## Robert Burns

We have already seen one example of the **quintet,** or five-line stanza. Many other rhyme-schemes are possible with the quintet, and the length of the lines may vary as well. However, the most frequently used rhyme-schemes are *ababa, abaab,* and *ababb.* Here is an example of *ababa:*

  I would that you were all to me,
    You that are just so much, no more,

Nor yours, nor mine, nor slave nor free!
　Where does the fault lie? What the core
O' the wound, since wound must be?

　　　　　(Robert Browning, from "Two in
　　　　　　　the Campagna")


The six-line stanza is called a **sestet**. As with the quintet, the sestet may have a variety of rhyme-schemes. We have already seen an example with a rhyme-scheme of *ababcc* in William Wordsworth's poem "I Wandered Lonely as a Cloud." The following example has a rhyme-scheme of *ababab*.


## She Walks in Beauty

### 1

She walks in beauty, like the night
Of cloudless climes and starry skies;
And all that's best of dark and bright
Meet in her aspect and her eyes:
Thus mellowed to that tender light                          5
Which heaven to gaudy day denies.

### 2

One shade the more, one ray the less,
Had half impaired the nameless grace
Which waves in every raven tress,
Or softly lightens o'er her face;                          10
Where thoughts serenely sweet express
How pure, how dear their dwelling place.

### 3

And on that cheek, and o'er that brow,
So soft, so calm, yet eloquent,
The smiles that win, the tints that glow,                  15
But tell of days in goodness spent,
A mind at peace with all below,
A heart whose love is innocent!

#### George Gordon, Lord Byron


The seven-line stanza is called a **septet**. In English poetry the dominant type of septet is composed of iambic pentameter lines with a rhyme-scheme of *ababbcc* and called *rhyme royal*. Here is an example:

Of Heaven or Hell I have no power to sing,
I cannot ease the burden of your fears,
Or make quick-coming death a little thing,
Or bring again the pleasure of past years,
Nor for my words shall ye forget your tears,
Or hope again for aught that I can say,
The idle singer of an empty day.

But rather, when, aweary of your mirth,
From full hearts still unsatisfied ye sigh,
And, feeling kindly unto all the earth,
Grudge every minute as it passes by,
Made the more mindful that the sweet days die—
Remember me a little then, I pray,
The idle singer of an empty day.

The heavy trouble, the bewildering care
That weighs us down who live and earn our bread,
These idle verses have no power to bear;
So let me sing of names rememberéd,
Because they, living not, can ne'er be dead,
Or long time take their memory quite away
From us poor singers of an empty day.

Dreamer of dreams, born out of my due time,
Why should I strive to set the crooked straight?
Let it suffice me that my murmuring rhyme
Beats with light wing against the ivory gate,
Telling a tale not too importunate
To those who in the sleepy region stay,
Lulled by the singer of an empty day.

(William Morris, from "The Earthly
Paradise")

The eight-line stanza is called an **octet**. Of course, with a stanza of this length, many rhyme-schemes are possible. For example:

# The Solitary Reaper

Behold her, single in the field,
Yon solitary Highland Lass!
Reaping and singing by herself;
Stop here, or gently pass!
Alone she cuts and binds the grain,
And sings a melancholy strain;

5

O listen! for the Vale profound
Is overflowing with the sound.

No Nightingale did ever chaunt
More welcome notes to weary bands          10
Of travelers in some shady haunt,
Among Arabian sands;
A voice so thrilling ne'er was heard
In springtime from the Cuckoo bird,
Breaking the silence of the seas          15
Among the farthest Hebrides.

Will no one tell me what she sings?—
Perhaps the plaintive numbers flow
For old, unhappy, far-off things,
And battles long ago;                      20
Or is it some more humble lay,
Familiar matter of today?
Some natural sorrow, loss, or pain,
That has been, and may be again?

Whate'er the theme, the Maiden sang        25
As if her song could have no ending;
I saw her singing at her work,
And o'er the sickle bending—
I listened, motionless and still;
And, as I mounted up the hill,            30
The music in my heart I bore,
Long after it was heard no more.

William Wordsworth

An octet comprised of iambic pentameter lines and rhyming *abababcc* is called **ottava rima.** Here is an example of ottava rima:

# Sailing to Byzantium

## 1

That is no country for old men. The young
In one another's arms, birds in the trees
—Those dying generations—at their song,
The salmon-falls, the mackerel-crowded seas,
Fish, flesh, or fowl, commend all summer long          5
Whatever is begotten, born, and dies.

Caught in that sensual music all neglect
Monuments of unageing intellect.

### 2

An aged man is but a paltry thing,
A tattered coat upon a stick, unless                                          10
Soul clap its hands and sing, and louder sing
For every tatter in its mortal dress,
Nor is there singing school but studying
Monuments of its own magnificence;
And therefore I have sailed the seas and come                                 15
To the holy city of Byzantium.

### 3

O sages standing in God's holy fire
As in the gold mosaic of a wall,
Come from the holy fire, perne in a gyre,[1]
And be the singing-masters of my soul.                                        20
Consume my heart away; sick with desire
And fastened to a dying animal
It knows not what it is; and gather me
Into the artifice of eternity.

### 4

Once out of nature I shall never take                                         25
My bodily form from any natural thing,
But such a form as Grecian goldsmiths make
Of hammered gold and gold enameling[2]
To keep a drowsy Emperor awake;
Or set upon a golden bough to sing                                            30
To lords and ladies of Byzantium
Of what is past, or passing, or to come.

#### William Butler Yeats

The stanza forms we have shown you, from couplet to octet, are all highly versatile, lending themselves to use by many poets writing about many different subjects. But poets sometimes also invent stanza forms to be used in a particular poem and never again. The younger contemporaries of Shakespeare were especially fond of devising new and individual stanza forms. Here are two examples:

[1]Spin in a spiral.
[2]According to Yeats, "A tree made of gold and silver, and artificial birds that sang."

## Easter Wings

Lord, who createdst man in wealth and store,[1]
   Though foolishly he lost the same,
      Decaying  more  and  more
        Till  he  became
          Most  poor:               5
          With   thee
        O  let  me  rise
    As    larks,    harmoniously,
   And  sing  this  day  thy  victories:
Then  shall  the  fall  further  the  flight  in  me.    10

My   tender  age  in   sorrow   did   begin;
   And still with sicknesses and shame
      Thou  didst  so  punish  sin,
        That  I  became
          Most  thin.               15
          With   thee
        Let me combine,
   And feel this day thy victory;
   For,  if  I  imp[2]  my  wing  on  thine,
Affliction  shall  advance  the  flight  in  me.    20

George Herbert

## To Daffodils

Fair daffodils, we weep to see
  You haste away so soon:
As yet the early-rising sun
  Has not attained his noon.
    Stay, stay,             5
  Until the hasting day
    Has run
  But to the evensong;
And having prayed together, we
  Will go with you along.        10

[1]Abundance.
[2]Graft.

We have short time to stay as you;
  We have as short a spring;
As quick a growth to meet decay,
  As you or anything.
    We die,                                                    15
  As your hours do, and dry
    Away
Like to the summer's rain;
Or as the pearls of morning's dew,
  Ne'er to be found again.                                     20

Robert Herrick

"Easter Wings" is a **shaped poem** whose appearance on the page suggests its subject or meaning. Turn this page sideways and you will see the wings of the poem's title.

Some poems are made of more than one kind of stanza. In the long poem from which the following excerpt is taken, each stanza has its own unique form, as intricately organized as the stanza of Herrick's "To Daffodils" but, once used, never repeated. Here are the first two stanzas:

I

There was a time when meadow, grove, and stream,
The earth, and every common sight,
    To me did seem
    Appareled in celestial light,
The glory and the freshness of a dream.                        5
It is not now as it hath been of yore—
    Turn whereso'er I may,
      By night or day,
The things which I have seen I now can see no more.

II

    The Rainbow comes and goes,                                10
    And lovely is the Rose,
    The Moon doth with delight
Look round her when the heavens are bare,
    Waters on a starry night
    Are beautiful and fair;                                    15
  The sunshine is a glorious birth;
  But yet I know, where'er I go,
That there hath passed away a glory from the earth.

(William Wordsworth, from "Ode:
Intimations of Immortality from
Recollections of Early Childhood")

## The Sonnet

Just as there are traditional forms for stanzas, there are traditional forms for whole poems. The most-used and best-known such form is the sonnet. A **sonnet** is a poem of fourteen lines, almost always in iambic pentameter, following one of several specific rhyme-schemes. Each kind of sonnet is best suited to a particular kind of poetic thought, and each has been popular among poets and readers from the Renaissance through the twentieth century.

The earliest form of the sonnet dates back to thirteenth-century Italy, and was perfected in the fourteenth century by the Italian poet Petrarch; it has therefore been named for him as the **Petrarchan sonnet.** Though continuous, it consists of two distinct parts. The first eight lines, called an **octave** (not an octet, which is an eight-line stanza), always follow the rhyme-scheme *abbaabba*. The last six lines, called the **sestet** (like the six-line stanza), has a somewhat more flexible rhyme-scheme. The usual scheme is *cdecde, cdccdc, cdedce,* or the like. However, no Petrarchan sonnet may contain more than five rhymes.

The form of the Petrarchan sonnet is mirrored in its thought. The octave usually states an idea or a problem. When the sonnet turns from the octave to the sestet, it also turns from idea to resolution, from question to answer, from problem to solution. Here are two examples:

## On His Blindness

When I consider how my light is spent
   Ere half my days, in this dark world and wide,
   And that one talent which is death to hide,
   Lodged with me useless, though my soul more bent
To serve therewith my Maker, and present           5
   My true account, lest he returning chide;
   "Doth God exact day-labor, light denied?"
   I fondly[1] ask; but Patience, to prevent[2]
That murmur, soon replies, "God doth not need
   Either man's work or his own gifts; who best       10
   Bear his mild yoke, they serve him best. His state
Is kingly. Thousands at his bidding speed
   And post o'er land and ocean without rest:
   They also serve who only stand and wait."

John Milton

[1]Foolishly.

[2]Forestall.

# Composed upon Westminster Bridge, September 3, 1802

Earth has not anything to show more fair:
Dull would he be of soul who could pass by
A sight so touching in its majesty;
This City now doth, like a garment, wear
The beauty of the morning; silent, bare,                              5
Ships, towers, domes, theaters, and temples lie
Open unto the fields, and to the sky;
All bright and glittering in the smokeless air.
Never did sun more beautifully steep
In his first splendor, valley, rock, or hill;                         10
Ne'er saw I, never felt, a calm so deep!
The river glideth at his own sweet will:
Dear God! the very houses seem asleep;
And all that mighty heart is lying still!

William Wordsworth

The sonnet was introduced into England in the fifteenth century, and soon became enormously popular there; Shakespeare alone wrote 154 sonnets. The form in which he wrote, however, was very different from Petrarch's, and has in fact become known as the **Shakespearean sonnet.** It consists of three quatrains and a couplet, all independently rhymed: *abab cdcd efef gg.* In this kind of sonnet, the turn of thought often occurs in the final couplet. Here are two examples:

# That Time of Year Thou Mayst in Me Behold

That time of year thou mayst in me behold
When yellow leaves, or none, or few, do hang
Upon those boughs which shake against the cold,
Bare ruined choirs, where late the sweet birds sang.
In me thou see'st the twilight of such day                           5
As after sunset fadeth in the West;
Which by and by black night doth take away,
Death's second self that seals up all in rest.
In me thou see'st the glowing of such fire
That on the ashes of his youth doth lie,                              10
As the deathbed whereon it must expire,
Consumed with that which it was nourished by.
  This thou perceiv'st, which makes thy love more strong,
  To love that well which thou must leave ere long.

William Shakespeare

# When I Have Fears That I May Cease to Be

When I have fears that I may cease to be
Before my pen has glean'd my teeming brain,
Before high-piléd books, in charact'ry,
Hold like rich garners the full-ripen'd grain;
When I behold, upon the night's starr'd face,                              5
Huge cloudy symbols of a high romance,
And think that I may never live to trace
Their shadows, with the magic hand of chance;
And when I feel, fair creature of an hour,
That I shall never look upon thee more,                                    10
Never have relish in the fairy power
Of unreflecting love;—then on the shore
Of the wide world I stand alone, and think
Till love and fame to nothingness do sink.

John Keats

The **irregular sonnet** encompasses all of the many other rhyme-schemes which fall within fourteen lines and are "sonnet-like"—that is, use octaves, sestets, or quatrains, or couplets, and are written in iambic pentameter. Here is an irregular sonnet that starts with a Petrarchan octave and ends like a Shakespearean sonnet with a quatrain and a couplet. The rhyme-scheme is *abba abba cdcd ee.*

# No More, My Dear, No More These Counsels Try

No more, my dear, no more these counsels try!
O give my passions leave to run their race;
Let Fortune lay on me her worst disgrace;
Let folk o'ercharged with brain against me cry;
Let clouds bedim my face, break in mine eye;                              5
Let me no steps but of lost labor trace;
Let all the earth in scorn recount my case;
But do not will me from my love to fly.
I do not envy Aristotle's wit,
Nor do aspire to Caesar's bleeding fame,                                  10
Nor ought do care, though some above me sit,
Nor hope, nor wish another course to frame,
But that which once may win thy cruel heart:
Thou art my wit, and thou my virtue art.

(Sir Philip Sidney, from
*Astrophel and Stella*)

The next irregular sonnet at first appears to have a rhyme-scheme of *ababacdcedefef*, but in fact line 4 ends in consonance with line 2, and line 9 ends in consonance with lines 11 and 13.

## Ozymandias

I met a traveler from an antique land
Who said: Two vast and trunkless legs of stone
Stand in the desert . . . Near them, on the sand,
Half sunk, a shattered visage lies, whose frown,
And wrinkled lip, and sneer of cold command,                                5
Tell that its sculptor well those passions read
Which yet survive, stamped on these lifeless things,
The hand that mocked them and the heart that fed.
And on the pedestal these words appear:
"My name is Ozymandias, king of kings;                                       10
Look on my works, ye Mighty, and despair!"
Nothing beside remains. Round the decay
Of that colossal wreck, boundless and bare,
The lone and level sands stretch far away.

> Percy Bysshe Shelley

Another irregular sonnet is divided after the eighth line by a space, but as you read it you will see that it is no conventional Petrarchan sonnet.

## if i have made,my lady,intricate

if i have made,my lady,intricate
imperfect various things chiefly which wrong
your eyes(frailer than most deep dreams are frail)
songs less firm than your body's whitest song
upon my mind—if i have failed to snare                                       5
the glance too shy—if through my singing slips
the very skilful strangeness of your smile
the keen primeval silence of your hair

—let the world say"his most wise music stole
nothing from death"—
                              you only will create                           10
(who are so perfectly alive)my shame:
lady through whose profound and fragile lips
the sweet small clumsy feet of April came

into the ragged meadow of my soul.

> E. E. Cummings

The poem itself is one of the "intricate/imperfect various things" Cummings has made for his lady: imperfect, perhaps, because of the off-rhyme of *frail* and *smile* (though Cummings could obviously have made a perfect rhyme had he wished to), and intricate in many ways, including the spacing of the lines—dividing the tenth line into halves—and the rhyme-scheme, which is *abcbdecd fageg f*.

## Blank Verse

**Blank verse** consists of unrhymed lines in iambic pentameter. Historically, the form has often been used in verse plays like Shakespeare's *Othello* as well as in poems. The following passage of blank verse is from another Shakespeare play, *Macbeth*.

>    . . . We fail?
> But screw your courage to the sticking place
> And we'll not fail. When Duncan is asleep
> (Whereto the rather shall his day's hard journey
> Soundly invite him), his two chamberlains
> Will I with wine and wassail so convince[1]
> That memory, the warder of the brain,
> Shall be a fume, and the receipt[2] of reason
> A limbeck[3] only. When in swinish sleep
> Their drenchéd natures lie as in a death,
> What cannot you and I perform upon
> Th' unguarded Duncan? what not put upon
> His spongy officers, who shall bear the guilt
> Of our great quell?[4]

5

10

(William Shakespeare, from *Macbeth*)

The next excerpt is an example of non-dramatic blank verse; it does not come from a play but from a poem. You might note that the initial foot in several of the lines is reversed, becoming a trochee rather than an iamb.

> Deep in the shady sadness of a vale
> Far sunken from the healthy breath of morn,
> Far from the fiery noon, and eve's one star,

[1]Overwhelm.
[2]Receptacle.
[3]A still.
[4]Killing.

Sat gray-hair'd Saturn,[1] quiet as a stone,
Still as the silence round about his lair;
Forest on forest hung about his head
Like cloud on cloud. No stir of air was there,
Not so much life as on a summer's day
Robs not one light seed from the feather'd grass,
But where the dead leaf fell, there did it rest.

(John Keats, from "Hyperion")

# Free Verse

Free verse is poetry that conforms to no strict metrical structure. Most often, free verse poets attempt to duplicate the rhythms of everyday speech, but also to lend them the musicality associated with conventional poetry. Free verse is not nearly as old as metrical poetry: the epics of Homer, for example, written in dactylic hexameter, are nearly three thousand years old, but free verse as a conscious poetic statement dates only to the late nineteenth century, when French poets such as Arthur Rimbaud began to experiment with it. Many modern scholars, however, consider parts of the King James Bible, translated during the sixteenth and early seventeenth centuries, to be free verse.

Still, there are people who insist that free verse is not really poetry, that it is only a pretentious kind of prose. Robert Frost once compared writing free verse with playing tennis with the net down. Of course, free verse may look like poetry on the page, but it cannot be relied on to rhyme or scan. Couldn't a sly author (you may ask) simply take a piece of prose, cut it up into lines, and fool us into accepting it as poetry? Let's see.

The morning of June 27th was clear and sunny,
with the fresh warmth
of a full-summer day;
the flowers were blossoming profusely
and
    the grass was richly green.

The people of the village
began to gather in the square,
between the post office and the bank,
around ten o'clock;
in some towns there were so many people that the lottery took two days
    and had to be started on June 26th,
but in this village,

[1]One of the oldest of the Roman gods.

where there were only about three hundred people,
the whole lottery took less than two hours,
so that it could begin

    at ten o'clock in the morning
and still
  be through in time
    to allow the villagers

to get home for noon dinner.

The first sentence, divided into six lines, is almost like real poetry. Read aloud, it has a strong if irregular rhythm, and the sentence does one of the things poetry does well: it presents a strong sensory image vividly and economically. But by halfway through the second sentence one can hear that verse is not the natural form for this writing. The author is bent on getting important information across, and by the fifth "line" we can no longer believe that she is choosing each word not only for what it means but also for how it sounds.

  The passage is, in fact, the opening of Shirley Jackson's short story "The Lottery," which you may have read. If you have, you already know that it is an exceptionally carefully and skillfully written story, and we are not suggesting that it isn't. To expect prose to work as poetry is like expecting a marathon runner to excel in the sprints. But free verse *can* reasonably be expected to work as poetry, and in fact it does. Let's look at an example, marked to show its rhythm:

## A Noiseless Patient Spider

˘ / ˘ / ˘ / ˘
A noiseless patient spider

˘ / / ˘˘/˘ / ˘ /˘˘ / ˘˘/˘
I mark'd where on a little promontory it stood isolated

/ / ˘˘ / ˘ /˘ / ˘ / ˘
Mark'd how to explore the vacant vast surrounding,

˘ / / /˘ ˘ /˘˘ /˘˘ / ˘˘/
It launch'd forth filament, filament, filament, out of itself,

/˘˘/ ˘ ˘ /˘/˘˘ / ˘ ˘
Ever unreeling them, ever tirelessly speeding them.

  ˘ / ˘ ˘ / ˘ ˘ /
And you O my soul where you stand,

˘ /˘ ˘ / ˘ / ˘˘/ ˘ ˘ /
Surrounded, detached, in measureless oceans of space,

/ ˘˘ / ˘ /˘˘ / ˘ / ˘˘ / ˘˘ / ˘
Ceaselessly musing, venturing, throwing, seeking the spheres to connect them,

5

  ᴗ ᴗ   /    ᴗ ᴗ   /  ᴗ  /   ᴗ ᴗ   / ᴗ /  ᴗ   /

Till the bridge you will need be form'd, till the ductile anchor hold,

  ᴗ ᴗ   / ᴗ ᴗ   /  ᴗ  /  /  /   ᴗ  ᴗ ᴗ   /

Till the gossamer thread you fling catch somewhere, O my soul.        10

Walt Whitman

Though the lines are irregular in length, they fall into a strong musical rhythm that often sounds like anapests and dactyls. Highly organized, symmetrical rhythmic phrases like these are called **cadences**. Early examples of the skillful arrangement of free verse cadences may be seen even in this sixteenth-century English translation of an Old Testament psalm:

## Psalm 23

The Lord is my shepherd; I shall not want.  
He maketh me to lie down in green pastures:  
He leadeth me beside the still waters.  
He restoreth my soul:  
He leadeth me in the paths of righteousness for his name's sake.     5  
Yea, though I walk through the valley of the shadow of death,  
I will fear no evil: for thou art with me;  
Thy rod and thy staff they comfort me.  
Thou preparest a table before me in the presence of mine enemies:  
Thou anointest my head with oil; my cup runneth over.     10  
Surely goodness and mercy shall follow me all the days of my life:  
And I will dwell in the house of the Lord forever.

Since Whitman, many poets have written in long, rhythmic lines that echo Whitman's cadences. For example:

## Signpost

Civilized, crying how to be human again: this will tell you how.  
Turn outward, love things, not men, turn right away from humanity,  
Let that doll lie. Consider if you like how the lilies grow,  
Lean on the silent rock until you feel its divinity  
Make your veins cold, a look at the silent stars, let your eyes     5  
Climb the great ladder out of the pit of yourself and man.  
Things are so beautiful, your love will follow your eyes;  
Things are the God, you will love God, and not in vain,  
For what we love, we grow to it, we share its nature. At length  
You will look back along the stars' rays and see that even     10  
The poor doll humanity has a place under heaven.

Its qualities repair their mosaic around you, the chips of strength
And sickness; but now you are free, even to become human,
But born of the rock and the air, not of a woman.

Robinson Jeffers

When reading a poem in free verse closely, or planning to read it aloud, you should mark its strong and weak stresses to make yourself aware of how regular or irregular the rhythm may be. However, it is pointless to divide each line into feet, since the foot is a unit of meter and has nothing to do with nonmetrical verse.

All of the free verse poems above look quite different from metrical poems. But some others adopt conventions from metrical verse. The following poem, for example, is divided into groups of three lines that look like stanzas. The usual term for such groups of lines in free verse is **strophes** (STROH-fees).

## Waking from Sleep

Inside the veins there are navies setting forth,
Tiny explosions at the water lines,
And seagulls weaving in the wind of the salty blood.

It is the morning. The country has slept the whole winter.
Window seats were covered with fur skins, the yard was full     5
Of stiff dogs, and hands that clumsily held heavy books.

Now we wake, and rise from bed, and eat breakfast!—
Shouts rise from the harbor of the blood,
Mist, and masts rising, the knock of wooden tackle in the sunlight.

Now we sing, and do tiny dances on the kitchen floor.     10
Our whole body is like a harbor at dawn;
We know that our master has left us for the day.

Robert Bly

And the following excerpt from a free verse poem is rhymed in an *abbcca* pattern:

But though I have wept and fasted, wept and prayed,
Though I have seen my head (grown slightly bald) brought in upon a
    platter,
I am no prophet—and here's no great matter;

I have seen the moment of my greatness flicker,
And I have seen the eternal Footman hold my coat, and snicker,
And in short, I was afraid.

(T. S. Eliot, from "The Love Song
of J. Alfred Prufrock")

Some free verse poems look very odd on the page. Here is an example:

## Portrait

Buffalo Bill    's
defunct
            who used to
            ride a watersmooth-silver
                                                stallion                                5
and break onetwothreefourfive pigeonsjustlikethat
                                                Jesus

he was a handsome man
                        and what i want to know is
how do you like your blueeyed boy                                          10
Mister Death

E. E. Cummings

Cummings was also a painter, and he gave more than usual care to the appearance of his poems, using a typewriter for his final draft. (Yes, the space before the apostrophe in *Bill*    's is correct; it is not a printer's error.) But Cummings also meant poems like this to sound the way they look, with a pause at the end of each line, and with "onetwothreefourfive" rattled off like five quick shots from Buffalo Bill's revolver.

In reading free verse, then, you should pay just as much attention to the way the poem sounds—its rhythms and occasional rhymes, the sounds of its words—as you do in reading metrical verse. After all, the poet was just as careful in composing those sounds for you.

## Imagery and Figurative Language

**Imagery** involves the use of language to represent objects, sensations, or emotions, and can be thought of as the conversion of nonverbal things into words. We show elsewhere how writers of short stories create literary images, and poets do much the same. For example:

The sea is calm tonight,
The tide is full, the moon lies fair
Upon the straits;—on the French coast the light
Gleams and is gone; the cliffs of England stand,
Glimmering and vast, out in the tranquil bay.
Come to the window, sweet is the night-air!
Only, from the long line of spray
Where the sea meets the moon-blanched land,
Listen! you hear the grating roar
Of pebbles which the waves draw back, and fling,
At their return, up the high strand,
Begin, and cease, and then again begin,
With tremulous cadence slow . . .

(Matthew Arnold, from "Dover Beach")

Using sights and sounds, the poem builds up an expansive and detailed image of the English coast at Dover. But poets do not very often write extended descriptions such as this one. Poems tend to be much shorter and therefore more concentrated than other forms of writing—this description is only one line shorter than a complete sonnet—and so, usually, are poetic images. Also, many poets prefer to create images indirectly, through various kinds of comparisons that we call **figurative language.**

Figurative language does not belong only in poetry; all of us use it in everyday speech, often without even thinking about it. When someone speaks of "taking the bull by the horns," we know he does not mean that he will wrestle steers in a rodeo, merely that he will stop delaying and do an unpleasant or frightening task. A football coach will call a defensive maneuver a *blitz* without realizing that he is comparing it with Hitler's *Blitzkrieg* (literally, "lightning war"), the German army's sudden and rapid conquests to the east and west during World War II. For that matter, the word *Blitzkrieg* itself compares a military strategy with a bolt of lightning. These figures of speech do not really describe the actions they refer to, but rather make those actions seem more vivid and dramatic, and also tell us what the speaker's attitude is. The same is true of the two comparisons in the opening stanza of this poem:

# A Red, Red Rose

O My Luve's like a red, red rose,
  That's newly sprung in June;
O My Luve's like the melodie
  That's sweetly played in tune.

As fair art thou, my bonnie lass,                                    5
   So deep in luve am I;
And I will luve thee still, my dear,
   Till a' the seas gang dry.

Till a' the seas gang dry, my dear,
   And the rocks melt wi' the sun:                                  10
And I will luve thee still, my dear,
   While the sands o' life shall run.

And fare thee weel, my only luve,
   And fare thee weel awhile!
And I will come again, my luve,                                     15
   Though it were ten thousand mile.

Robert Burns

   The two comparisons are examples of a figure of speech called a simile.
A **simile** makes a direct comparison by using the words *like* or *as*. The
poet's love is like a rose in only a limited way; Burns does not want us
to think her prickly, or rooted in the earth, or even bright red. Nor does
he say she is like any particular tune. His love, the rose, and the sweetly
played melody have in common only that all three are softly beautiful—
"fair."
   A **metaphor** is a figure of speech that implies a comparison between
two things or situations by saying that one is the other. Since neither
*like* nor *as* is actually used, the comparison must be made in the mind
of the reader. In a full metaphor, a linking verb like *is, are, was, were,*
and *am* will always be present. The following brief poem begins with
a pair of full metaphors:

## Poet to His Love

An old silver church in a forest
Is my love for you.
The trees around it
Are words that I have stolen from your heart.
An old silver bell, the last smile you gave,                        5
Hangs at the top of my church.
It rings only when you come through the forest
And stand beside it.
And then it has no need for ringing,
For your voice takes its place.                                     10

Maxwell Bodenheim

A variation on the full metaphor is the submerged metaphor. A **submerged metaphor** occurs when the metaphorical image does not include a linking verb. "My winged heart," "a sea of troubles," "the ragged truth," and "frozen thought" are all examples of submerged metaphors. The following quatrain—which is taken from a Shakespeare sonnet we have already looked at—employs several submerged metaphors, the first making an implied comparison between a man's life and a single year, and the second suggesting a comparison between tree limbs and that part of a church or cathedral called the choir, leading to a further comparison between the singers in the choir and singing birds.

> That time of year thou mayst in me behold
> When yellow leaves, or none, or few, do hang
> Upon those boughs which shake against the cold,
> Bare ruined choirs where late the sweet birds sang.

> (William Shakespeare, from "That Time
> of Year Thou Mayst in Me Behold")

If you take this quatrain as a whole, you will also find that it is an extended metaphor comparing a person's later years and late autumn, and comparing coldness with death. Advancing age is in fact what the poem is about.

**Personification** is a particular kind of submerged metaphor that assigns human qualities or feelings to animals, plants, objects, or abstractions. In the last six lines of the following sonnet love, passion, faith, and innocence are all personified.

## Since There's No Help, Come Let Us Kiss and Part

Since there's no help, come let us kiss and part;
Nay, I have done, you get no more of me,
And I am glad, yea glad with all my heart
That thus so cleanly I myself can free.
Shake hands for ever, cancel all our vows,          5
And when we meet at any time again,
Be it not seen in either of our brows
That we one jot of former love retain.
Now at the last gasp of love's latest breath,
When, his pulse failing, passion speechless lies,          10
When faith is kneeling by his bed of death,
And innocence is closing up his eyes;
Now if thou wouldst, when all have given him over,
From death to life thou mightst him yet recover.

Michael Drayton

When personification is carried to the point that an inanimate object is actually spoken to as if it could hear and understand, we have what is called a poetic **apostrophe**. Notice how in the following poem a tree is both personified and spoken to.

## Tree at My Window

Tree at my window, window tree,
My sash is lowered when night comes on;
But let there never be curtain drawn
Between you and me.

Vague dream-head lifted out of the ground,                    5
And thing next most diffuse to cloud,
Not all your light tongues talking aloud
Could be profound.

But, tree, I have seen you taken and tossed,
And if you have seen me when I slept,                         10
You have seen me when I was taken and swept
And all but lost.

That day she put our heads together,
Fate had her imagination about her,
Your head so much concerned with outer,                       15
Mine with inner, weather.

> Robert Frost

A **metonymy**, pronounced (muh-TAHN-uh-mee), is another form of metaphor in which the name of some object or idea is substituted for the name of something closely related to it. For example, in the statement "I earn my living by the sweat of my brow," the expression "sweat of my brow" replaces "hard labor," *sweat* being an item having a close relationship to *labor*. In the following stanza, "blood," "state," "armor," "scepter and crown," "dust," and "scythe and spade" are each used in place of another word or expression with which it has some close relationship. Each of these substitutions forms a metonymy.

The glories of our blood and state
Are shadows, not substantial things;
There is no armor against fate;

Death lays his icy hand on kings.
  Scepter and crown
  Must tumble down
And in the dust be equal made
With the poor crooked scythe and spade.

(James Shirley, from "The Glories
of Our Blood and State")

The **synecdoche** (si-NEK-duh-kee) is a figure of speech—sometimes thought to be a kind of metonymy—in which a typical or important part is used to signify the whole, or the whole is used to signify the part. For example, in the statement "Man cannot live by bread alone," the word *bread* stands in place of all food, and so the part represents the whole. In the following stanza, the word *hand* stands for the sovereign ruler to whom the hand belonged, and all the forces that the ruler commanded.

The hand that signed the paper felled a city;
Five sovereign fingers taxed the breath,
Doubled the globe of dead and halved a country;
These five kings did a king to death.

(Dylan Thomas, from "The Hand
That Signed the Paper")

In all these kinds of imagery, in similes and the various forms of metaphor, it is almost always clear which part of the comparison is "real," and which is included only to make the comparison. Few readers would suppose that Maxwell Bodenheim's "Poet to His Love" is about churches or forests; it is about love, specifically the love between the speaker of the poem and a woman mentioned in it. For convenience's sake, we can call the subject of the comparison the **primary term,** and the objects with which it is compared—the trees, the forests—the **secondary terms.**

But there is another kind of imagery in which the primary term is never stated, and it is up to readers to supply the primary term from their understanding of the poem. This figure of speech is called a **symbol.** Here is an example:

## The Sick Rose

O Rose, thou art sick.
The invisible worm
That flies in the night
In the howling storm

Has found out thy bed                                                    5
Of crimson joy,
And his dark secret love
Does thy life destroy.

William Blake

What kind of worm is invisible, flies through howling storms at night, and kills roses? There is no such animal today, nor was there in Blake's time nearly two centuries ago, so Blake must have invented it as a symbol for something else, something terrifying and deadly. And if the worm is a symbol, so is the rose; real roses are killed by real worms but not by invisible ones. The rose stands for something alive, beautiful, and capable of sensuality in its "bed of crimson joy"—the phrase suggests more than a mere flowerbed. If you feel that "dark, secret love" is the key to the poem's meaning, you might conclude that the rose stands for something that such a love would destroy—sexual innocence, perhaps—and that the worm, then, represents a kind of irresistible, dark passion that could overpower such innocence.

But this is not the only possible interpretation of the poem's symbolism. The worm's supernatural qualities—it is invisible and can fly—and its identification with storms and the night are among the qualities often assigned to Satan. And Satan once took on the shape of a kind of worm—a serpent—when he appeared to Eve in the garden of Eden. If the worm is Satan, then, what kind of life does it destroy? The life of a soul, its chance for redemption and eternal life after death. So the rose would represent the human soul, its "bed of crimson joy" would represent our weakness for sensual corruption, and "his dark secret love" might be Satan's kind of dark secret love, a love incompatible with the love of God.

There are other possible interpretations as well, all different in detail but all sharing the theme of something beautiful but vulnerable that is dying from some kind of corruption. Which interpretation would the poet accept, and which would he consider wrong? We can never know for sure because Blake does not say. All we can be sure of is that his poem is not about garden pests!

## Persona, Tone, and Irony

A poem is something that should be heard as well as seen. Even if you do not read it aloud, you should try to hear it as you read, to imagine a voice speaking the poem to you. But whose voice is it that you hear? The easy—and wrong—answer is that it's the poet's voice. The **speaker** of a poem, who is technically known as the **persona,** is as much an invention as is the poem's form. For example:

## Love Equals Swift and Slow

Love equals swift and slow,
    And high and low,
Racer and lame,
    The hunter and his game.

Henry David Thoreau

There is nothing in the poem to suggest that this thought is not Thoreau's own, that he is inventing anyone other than himself as the poem's speaker. But the voice we hear speaks in rhymed couplets; and people, including Thoreau, do not normally speak that way in their everyday lives. So even in this poem, the persona is the poet's invention, a Thoreau who speaks in verse.

This may seem like splitting hairs, and indeed many experienced poetry teachers and critics would refer to the speaker in "Love Equals Swift and Slow" as "the poet" or "Thoreau." But it is best to be careful, and to use the terms "speaker" and "persona" instead, to avoid being confused. For example, here are four lines from a poem by A. E. Housman:

Now, of my threescore years and ten,
Twenty will not come again,
And take from seventy springs a score,
It only leaves me fifty more.

(A. E. Housman, from "Loveliest<br>of Trees, the Cherry Now")

The speaker is, in effect, saying that of his seventy-year life expectancy he has used up twenty—that he is twenty years old. If you concluded from this that Housman was twenty when he wrote the poem, you would be wrong, because he was actually in his late thirties. A scholar of Latin literature at University College, London, he invented for this and many of his other poems the persona of a young man living in the country. Of course, most readers of Housman's poems know nothing about the poet's life, and Housman did not expect them to. But without direct biographical evidence, it is very risky to assume that the poet is speaking directly in the poem, and not through an invented character.

Sometimes a poet will invent a persona so distinctive and well-characterized that it is like a character in a play. The speaker of the following poem is an envious, bad-tempered, and evil-minded monk muttering to himself about an inoffensive friar named Lawrence.

# Soliloquy of the Spanish Cloister

## 1

Gr-r-r—there go, my heart's abhorrence!
    Water your damned flower-pots, do!
If hate killed men, Brother Lawrence,
    God's blood, would not mine kill you!
What? your myrtle-bush wants trimming?                    5
    Oh, that rose has prior claims—
Needs its leaden vase filled brimming?
    Hell dry you up with its flames!

## 2

At the meal we sit together:
    *Salve tibi!*[1] I must hear                          10
Wise talk of the kind of weather,
    Sort of season, time of year:
*Not a plenteous cork-crop: scarcely*
    *Dare we hope oak-galls, I doubt:*
*What's the Latin name for "parsley"?*                    15
    What's the Greek name for Swine's Snout?

## 3

Whew! We'll have our platter burnished,
    Laid with care on our own shelf!
With a fire-new spoon we're furnished,
    And a goblet for ourself,                             20
Rinsed like something sacrificial
    Ere 'tis fit to touch our chaps—
Marked with L for our initial!
    (He-he! There his lily snaps!)

## 4

*Saint*, forsooth! While brown Dolores                   25
    Squats outside the Convent bank
With Sanchicha, telling stories,
    Steeping tresses in the tank,
Blue-black, lustrous, thick like horsehairs,
    —Can't I see his dead eye glow,                       30
Bright as 'twere a Barbary corsair's?[2]
    (That is, if he'd let it show!)

[1]Hail to thee!
[2]A north African pirate.

### 5

When he finishes refection,
   Knife and fork he never lays
Cross-wise, to my recollection,                35
   As do I, in Jesu's praise.
I the Trinity illustrate,
   Drinking watered orange-pulp—
In three sips the Arian[3] frustrate;
   While he drains his at one gulp.         40

### 6

Oh, those melons? If he's able
   We're to have a feast! so nice!
One goes to the Abbot's table,
   All of us get each a slice.
How go on your flowers? None double?      45
   Not one fruit-sort can you spy?
Strange! And I, too, at such trouble,
   Keep them close-nipped on the sly!

### 7

There's a great text in Galatians,
   Once you trip on it, entails          50
Twenty-nine distinct damnations,
   One sure, if another fails:
If I trip him just a-dying,
   Sure of heaven as sure can be,
Spin him around and send him flying      55
   Off to hell, a Manichee?[4]

### 8

Or, my scrofulous French novel
   On grey paper with blunt type!
Simply glance at it, you grovel
   Hand and foot in Belial's[5] gripe:      60
If I double down its pages
   At the woeful sixteenth print,
When he gathers his greengages,
   Ope a sieve and slip it in't?

---

[3] A heresy that denied the doctrine of the Trinity.

[4] Manicheanism is another heresy based on the belief that the world is split between forces of good and evil.

[5] The devil's.

**9**

Or, there's Satan! one might venture                                           65
  Pledge one's soul to him, yet leave
Such a flaw in the indenture
  As he'd miss till, past retrieve,
Blasted lay that rose-acacia
  We're so proud of! *Hy, Zy, Hine* . . .                                      70
'St, there's vespers! *Plena gratiâ*
  *Ave, Virgo!*⁶ Gr-r-r—you swine!

## Robert Browning

Browning's poem also has a very strong **tone,** showing the poet's attitude toward the work and toward its audience. The speaker's foul temper and foul mouth are so exaggerated that they become comical: Browning is laughing at his persona, and wants us to do so too. The tone is not only humorous but also satiric, as Browning is making fun not just of a certain kind of person but of all religious hypocrisy.

The poem also makes much use of **irony,** both verbal irony and irony of situation. In the sixth stanza, the speaker pretends to believe that he is trying to help Brother Lawrence by secretly clipping off the buds before they blossom or produce fruit, but we know from the rest of the poem that the words are ironic, that he is doing the damage on purpose. And the whole poem is ironic in its situation: a monk in a cloister, supposedly dedicated to the service of God and of the good, is actually more evil-minded and corrupt than many nonbelievers outside the monastery.

## Some Questions to Ask about a Poem

When you read a poem closely, you must keep in mind that every word, every sound, may be important to its meaning. Here are some questions whose answers will help you to focus on any poem's form and meaning.

### POETIC FORM:

1. Mark the strong and weak stresses of the poem. Is the rhythm metrical, or is the poem in free verse?
2. Look at the ends of the lines. Is the poem rhymed? Are the words at the ends of lines in consonance or assonance? What is the rhyme-scheme, if any? Can you name the stanza form? How does rhyme contribute to the meaning of the poem?

---

⁶"Hail, Virgin, full of grace"—a prayer to the Virgin Mary.

3. If the poem is metrical, divide the lines into feet, keeping in mind the various kinds of metrical feet discussed in this book. What is the most frequent foot? Do all of the lines have the same number of feet? Can you name the meter?
4. If the poem is in free verse, is the verse still written in cadences—that is, long lines with a strong, consistent rhythm? If the rhythm is not regular, what other qualities and features does it have?
5. Whether the poem is in meter or in free verse, what types of variations (in the feet, or in the rhythm) can you see? Do these variations occur regularly in more than one line, or do they occur irregularly? Can you make any connection between these variations and the total impression the poet is trying to create?
6. Does the poem make use of alliteration, consonance, assonance, or onomatopoeia?

## IMAGERY

7. What specific images does the poem create? Are these images literal or figurative? Can you name the poem's figures of speech by type?
8. What do the poem's similes and metaphors, if there are any, tell you about the poet's attitude towards the things being compared? Do these figures of speech merely make the poem more vivid, or do they add a dimension to its meaning?
9. If the poem is partly or wholly symbolic, what meaning would you assign to its symbols? Are several meanings possible? Which do you find the most convincing, and why?

## PERSONA, TONE, and IRONY

10. Who is the persona or speaker in the poem? Are there more than one? Can you point out any specific differences between the persona and the poet? Is the speaker addressing the reader, or someone else in the poem, or himself?
11. What is the poet's tone? What seems to be the poet's attitude toward the subject and situation of the poem? How does this attitude affect your own response to the poem?
12. Are any specific parts or elements of the poem ironic? Point out any instances of verbal irony or irony of situation. What is ironic about each?

## GENERAL

13. Go through the poem line by line, looking up any words which are not familiar to you or which do not seem to fit the context (in case there are other meanings unknown to you). Are there any words which seem to have been chosen mainly for their rhythm, or because they rhyme or otherwise fit the sound scheme of the poem? Are there any that you find particularly striking and effective?

14. Depending on the poem's length, write a prose paraphrase or summary. Which parts of the poem were easiest to restate in your own words, and which parts were hardest? What did you have to leave out?

15. How would you describe the poem's primary intention? Does the poem sing a cheerful song, tell a story, celebrate or satirize people or events, argue a philosophical or political issue, tell of love or passion, create a character, lament a death, or do anything else? Does the way the poem carries out its intention seem fitting, or unusual, or both?

16. Did you like the poem? What particularly did you like or dislike about it? Did it tell you anything you did not already know? How did the poem's structure and poetic devices contribute to your liking or disliking the work?

# Poems

## Western Wind

ANONYMOUS

Western wind, when will thou blow,
   The small rain down can rain?
Christ, if my love were in my arms
   And I in my bed again!

## A Lyke-Wake Dirge

ANONYMOUS

This ae° night, this ae night,                           *one*
   Every night and all,
Fire and sleet and candle-light,
   And Christ receive thy saul.°                   *soul*

When thou from hence away are past,
   Every night and all,
To Whinny-muir° thou comest at last:       *thorny-moor*
   And Christ receive thy saul.

If ever thou gavest hosen and shoon,°    *socks and shoes*
   Every night and all,                             10
Sit thee down and put them on:
   And Christ receive thy saul.

If hosen and shoon thou ne'er gavest nane,
   Every night and all,
The whins shall prick thee to bare bane:
   And Christ receive thy saul.

From Whinny-muir when thou mayst pass,
   Every night and all,
To Brig° o' Dread thou comest at last:       *Bridge*
   And Christ receive thy saul.                  20

From Brig o' Dread when thou mayst pass,
   Every night and all,
To purgatory fire thou comest at last:
   And Christ receive thy saul.

If ever thou gavest meat or drink,
   Every night and all,
The fire shall never make thee shrink:
   And Christ receive thy saul.

If meat or drink thou ne'er gavest nane,
   Every night and all,                                     30
The fire will burn thee to the bare bane:
   And Christ receive thy saul.

This ae night, this ae night,
   Every night and all,
Fire and sleet and candle-light,
   And Christ receive thy saul.


# Jolly Good Ale and Old

ANONYMOUS

   Back and side go bare, go bare,
     Both foot and hand go cold;
   But, belly, God send thee good ale enough,
     Whether it be new or old.

I cannot eat but little meat,
   My stomach is not good;
But sure I think that I can drink
   With him that wears a hood.°                 *a friar*
Though I go bare, take ye no care,
   I am nothing a-cold;                         10
I stuff my skin so full within
   Of jolly good ale and old.

   Back and side go bare, go bare,
     Both foot and hand go cold;
   But, belly, God send thee good ale enough,
     Whether it be new or old.

I love no roast but a nut-brown toast,
   And a crab° laid in the fire;              *crab apple*

A little bread shall do me stead,
  Much bread I not desire.                                               20
No frost nor snow, no wind, I trow,
  Can hurt me if it would,
I am so wrapped and throughly lapped
  Of jolly good ale and old.

      Back and side go bare, go bare,
        Both foot and hand go cold;
      But, belly, God send thee good ale enough,
        Whether it be new or old.

And Tib, my wife, that as her life
  Loveth well good ale to seek,                                          30
Full oft drinks she till ye may see
  The tears run down her cheek.
Then doth she troll° to me the bowl,                                     *pass*
  Even as a maltworm° should,                                           *drinker*
And saith, "Sweetheart, I took my part
  Of this jolly good ale and old."

      Back and side go bare, go bare,
        Both foot and hand go cold;
      But, belly, God send thee good ale enough,
        Whether it be new or old.                                        40

Now let them drink till they nod and wink,
  Even as good fellows should do;
They shall not miss to have the bliss
  Good ale doth bring men to.
And all poor souls that have scoured bowls
  Or have them lustily trolled—
God save the lives of them and their wives,
  Whether they be young or old.

      Back and side go bare, go bare,
        Both foot and hand go cold;
      But, belly, God send thee good ale enough,                        50
        Whether it be new or old.


# When I Was Fair and Young

QUEEN ELIZABETH I


When I was fair and young, and favor gracéd me,
Of many was I sought, their mistress for to be;

But I did scorn them all, and answered them therefore,
  "Go, go, go seek some otherwhere!
    Importune me no more!"

How many weeping eyes I made to pine with woe,
How many sighing hearts, I have no skill to show;
Yet I the prouder grew, and answered them therefore,
  "Go, go, go seek some otherwhere!
    Importune me no more!"        10

Then spake fair Venus' son,[1] that proud victorious boy,
And said, "Fine dame, since that you be so coy,
I will so pluck your plumes that you shall say no more,
  'Go, go, go seek some otherwhere!
    Importune me no more!' "

When he had spake these words, such change grew in my breast
That neither night nor day since that, I could take any rest.
Then lo! I did repent that I had said before,
  "Go, go, go seek some otherwhere!
    Importune me no more!"        20


# The Passionate Shepherd to His Love

CHRISTOPHER MARLOWE

Come live with me, and be my love,
And we will all the pleasures prove
That valleys, groves, hills and fields,
Woods, or steepy mountains yields.

And we will sit upon the rocks,
Seeing the shepherds feed their flocks,
By shallow rivers, to whose falls
Melodious birds sing madrigals.

And I will make thee beds of roses
And a thousand fragrant posies,        10
A cap of flowers, and a kirtle
Embroidered all with leaves of myrtle;

A gown made of the finest wool
Which from our pretty lambs we pull,

[1] Cupid, god of love and sexual desire.

Fair-linéd slippers for the cold,
With buckles of the purest gold;

A belt of straw and ivy buds,
With coral clasps and amber studs:
And if these pleasures may thee move,
Come live with me, and be my love.                    20

The shepherd swains shall dance and sing,
For thy delight each May morning:
If these delights thy mind may move,
Then live with me, and be my love.


## The Nymph's Reply to the Shepherd

SIR WALTER RALEGH

If all the world and love were young,
And truth in every shepherd's tongue,
These pretty pleasures might me move
To live with thee and be thy love.

Time drives the flocks from field to fold
When rivers rage, and rocks grow cold;
And Philomel° becometh dumb;                          *the nightingale*
The rest complain of cares to come.

The flowers do fade, and wanton fields
To wayward winter reckoning yields;                   10
A honey tongue, a heart of gall,
Is fancy's spring, but sorrow's fall.

Thy gowns, thy shoes, thy beds of roses,
Thy cap, thy kirtle, and thy posies
Soon break, soon wither, soon forgotten—
In folly ripe, in reason rotten.

Thy belt of straw and ivy buds,
Thy coral clasps and amber studs,
All these in me no means can move
To come to thee and be thy love.                      20

But could youth last and love still breed,
Had joys no date° nor age no need,                    *ending date*
Then these delights my mind might move
To live with thee and be thy love.

# All the World's a Stage[1]

WILLIAM SHAKESPEARE

All the world's a stage,

And all the men and women merely players:
They have their exits and their entrances,
And one man in his time plays many parts,
His acts being seven ages. At first the infant,
Mewling and puking in the nurse's arms.
Then the whining schoolboy, with his satchel
And shining morning face, creeping like snail
Unwillingly to school. And then the lover,
Sighing like furnace, with a woeful ballad           10
Made to his mistress' eyebrow. Then a soldier,
Full of strange oaths and bearded like the pard,°        *leopard*
Jealous in honor, sudden and quick in quarrel,
Seeking the bubble reputation
Even in the cannon's mouth. And then the justice,
In fair round belly with good capon lined,
With eyes severe and beard of formal cut,
Full of wise saws and modern instances;°        *examples*
And so he plays his part. The sixth age shifts
Into the lean and slipper'd pantaloon,[2]        20
With spectacles on nose and pouch on side,
His youthful hose, well saved, a world too wide
For his shrunk shank; and his big manly voice,
Turning again toward childish treble, pipes
And whistles in his° sound. Last scene of all,        *its*
That ends this strange eventful history,
Is second childishness and mere oblivion,
Sans° teeth, sans eyes, sans taste, sans everything.        *without*

# When I Do Count the Clock That Tells the Time

WILLIAM SHAKESPEARE

When I do count the clock that tells the time,
And see the brave day sunk in hideous night;
When I behold the violet past prime,
And sable curls all silver'd o'er with white;

[1] From the play *As You Like It*, Act II, Scene vii, 139–166.

[2] Old man of Italian comedy, rich and retired, traditionally with a young daughter or wife who makes a fool of him.

When lofty trees I see barren of leaves,
Which erst° from heat did canopy the herd,                          *once*
And summer's green all girded up in sheaves,
Borne on the bier with white and bristly beard,
Then of thy beauty do I question make,
That thou among the wastes of time must go,                          10
Since sweets and beauties do themselves forsake
And die as fast as they see others grow;
And nothing 'gainst Time's scythe can make defence
Save breed,° to brave him when he takes thee hence.                  *children*

## Shall I Compare Thee to a Summer's Day?

WILLIAM SHAKESPEARE

Shall I compare thee to a summer's day?
Thou art more lovely and more temperate:
Rough winds do shake the darling buds of May,
And summer's lease hath all too short a date:
Sometimes too hot the eye of heaven shines,
And often is his gold complexion dimmed;
And every fair from fair sometime declines,
By chance or nature's changing course untrimmed;¹
But thy eternal summer shall not fade,
Nor lose possession of that fair thou ow'st;°                        *ownest*
Nor shall Death brag thou wander'st in his shade,
When in eternal lines to time thou grow'st:
So long as men can breathe, or eyes can see,
So long lives this, and this gives life to thee.

## When, in Disgrace with Fortune and Men's Eyes

WILLIAM SHAKESPEARE

When, in disgrace with fortune and men's eyes,
I all alone beweep my outcast state,
And trouble deaf heaven with my bootless° cries,                     *useless*
And look upon myself, and curse my fate,
Wishing me like to one more rich in hope,
Featured like him, like him with friends possessed,
Desiring this man's art and that man's scope,
With what I most enjoy contented least;

¹ Divested of beauty, as with a fading flower.

Yet in these thoughts myself almost despising,
Haply I think on thee, and then my state,                                    10
Like to the lark at break of day arising
From sullen earth, sings hymns at heaven's gate;
For thy sweet love rememb'red such wealth brings
That then I scorn to change my state with kings.


# My Mistress' Eyes Are Nothing Like the Sun

WILLIAM SHAKESPEARE

My mistress' eyes are nothing like the sun;
Coral is far more red than her lips' red;
If snow be white, why then her breasts are dun;
If hairs be wires, black wires grow on her head.
I have seen roses damasked,° red and white,                          *pink*
But no such roses see I in her cheeks;
And in some perfumes is there more delight
Than in the breath that from my mistress reeks.
I love to hear her speak, yet well I know
That music hath a far more pleasing sound;                              10
I grant I never saw a goddess go;
My mistress, when she walks, treads on the ground.
And yet, by heaven, I think my love as rare
As any she belied with false compare.


# Song (Go and Catch a Falling Star)

JOHN DONNE

Go and catch a falling star,
    Get with child a mandrake root,[1]
Tell me where all past years are,
    Or who cleft the devil's foot,
Teach me to hear mermaids singing,
    Or to keep off envy's stinging,
        And find
        What wind
Serves to advance an honest mind.

If thou be'st born to strange sights,                                        10
    Things invisible to see,

[1] The root of the mandrake plant is forked, roughly resembling the human body.

Ride ten thousand days and nights,
    Till age snow white hairs on thee,
Thou, when thou return'st, wilt tell me
    All strange wonders that befell thee,
        And swear
        Nowhere
Lives a woman true, and fair.

If thou find'st one, let me know;
    Such a pilgrimage were sweet.                                    20
Yet do not; I would not go,
    Though at next door we might meet.
Though she were true when you met her,
    And last till you write your letter,
        Yet she
        Will be
False, ere I come, to two or three.


# The Sun Rising

JOHN DONNE

    Busy old fool, unruly sun,
        Why dost thou thus
Through windows and through curtains call on us?
Must to thy motions lovers' seasons run?
        Saucy pedantic wretch, go chide
        Late schoolboys and sour prentices,
    Go tell court huntsmen that the king will ride,
    Call country ants to harvest offices;°                       *duties*
Love, all alike, no season knows, nor clime,
Nor hours, days, months, which are the rags of time.             10

    Thy beams, so reverend and strong
        Why shouldst thou think?
I could eclipse and cloud them with a wink,
But that I would not lose her sight so long;
        If her eyes have not blinded thine,
        Look, and tomorrow late tell me
    Whether both the Indias[1] of spice and mine°                  *gold*
    Be where thou left'st them, or lie here with me.
Ask for those kings whom thou saw'st yesterday,
And thou shalt hear, All here in one bed lay.                    20

---

[1] India and the West Indies.

> She's all states, and all princes I;
>> Nothing else is.
> Princes do but play us; compared to this,
> All honor's mimic, all wealth alchemy.
>> Thou, sun, art half as happy as we,
>> In that the world's contracted thus;
>> Thine age asks ease, and since thy duties be
>> To warm the world, that's done in warming us.
> Shine here to us, and thou art everywhere;
> This bed thy center is, these walls thy sphere.                    30

# The Bait

JOHN DONNE

Come live with me, and be my love,
And we will some new pleasures prove,
Of golden sands, and crystal brooks,
With silken lines, and silver hooks.

There will the river whispering run,
Warmed by thy eyes more than the sun.
And there th' enamor'd fish will stay,
Begging themselves they may betray.

When thou wilt swim in that live bath,
Each fish, which every channel hath,                    10
Will amorously to thee swim,
Gladder to catch thee, than thou him.

If thou, to be so seen, be'st loth,
By sun or moon, thou dark'nest both;
And if myself have leave to see,
I need not their light, having thee.

Let others freeze with angling reeds,
And cut their legs with shells and weeds,
Or treacherously poor fish beset
With strangling snare, or windowy net.                    20

Let coarse bold hands from slimy nest
The bedded fish in banks out-wrest,
Or curious traitors, sleave-silk° flies,                    *silk thread*
Bewitch poor fishes' wand'ring eyes.

For thee, thou need'st no such deceit,
For thou thyself art thine own bait;
That fish that is not catched thereby,
Alas, is wiser far than I.

# At the Round Earth's Imagined Corners, Blow

JOHN DONNE

At the round earth's imagined corners, blow
Your trumpets, Angels, and arise, arise
From death, you numberless infinities
Of souls, and to your scattered bodies go,
All whom the flood did, and fire shall o'erthrow,
All whom war, dearth, age, agues, tyrannies,
Despair, law, chance, hath slain, and you whose eyes
Shall behold God, and never taste death's woe.
But let them sleep, Lord, and me mourn a space;
For if, above all these, my sins abound,                    10
'Tis late to ask abundance of Thy grace
When we are there. Here on this lowly ground,
Teach me how to repent; for that's as good
As if Thou hadst sealed my pardon with Thy blood.

# Death, Be Not Proud

JOHN DONNE

Death, be not proud, though some have callèd thee
Mighty and dreadful, for thou art not so;
For those whom thou think'st thou dost overthrow
Die not, poor Death, nor yet canst thou kill me.
From rest and sleep, which but thy pictures be,
Much pleasure, then from thee much more must flow,
And soonest our best men with thee do go,
Rest of their bones and souls' delivery.
Thou art slave to fate, chance, kings, and desperate men,
And dost with poison, war, and sickness dwell,          10
And poppy° or charms can make us sleep as well          *opium*
And better than thy stroke; why swell'st thou then?
One short sleep past, we wake eternally,
And Death shall be no more; Death, thou shalt die.

# Delight in Disorder

ROBERT HERRICK

A sweet disorder in the dress
Kindles in clothes a wantonness.
A lawn about the shoulders thrown
Into a fine distractiön;
An erring lace, which here and there
Enthralls the crimson stomacher;
A cuff neglectful, and thereby
Ribbons to flow confusedly;
A winning wave (deserving note)
In the tempestuous petticoat;                                    10
A careless shoestring, in whose tie
I see a wild civility;
Do more bewitch me than when art
Is too precise in every part.

# To the Virgins, to Make Much of Time

ROBERT HERRICK

Gather ye rosebuds while ye may:
   Old Time is still a-flying,
And this same flower that smiles today
   Tomorrow will be dying.

The glorious lamp of heaven, the sun,
   The higher he's a-getting,
The sooner will his race be run,
   And nearer he's to setting.

That age is best which is the first,
   When youth and blood are warmer;                             10
But, being spent, the worse, and worst
   Times still succeed the former.

Then be not coy, but use your time,
   And while ye may, go marry:
For having lost but once your prime,
   You may forever tarry.

## To His Coy Mistress

ANDREW MARVELL

Had we but world enough, and time,
This coyness, lady, were no crime.
We would sit down, and think which way
To walk, and pass our long love's day.
Thou by the Indian Ganges' side
Shouldst rubies find; I by the tide
Of Humber[1] would complain. I would
Love you ten years before the flood,
And you should, if you please, refuse
Till the conversion of the Jews.[2]                                                    10
My vegetable love should grow
Vaster than empires and more slow;
An hundred years should go to praise
Thine eyes, and on thy forehead gaze;
Two hundred to adore each breast,
But thirty thousand to the rest;
An age at least to every part,
And the last age should show your heart.
For, lady, you deserve this state,°                          *dignified ceremony*
Nor would I love at lower rate.                                                        20
    But at my back I always hear
Time's wingéd chariot hurrying near;
And yonder all before us lie
Deserts of vast eternity.
Thy beauty shall no more be found;
Nor, in thy marble vault, shall sound
My echoing song; then worms shall try
That long-preserved virginity,
And your quaint honor turn to dust,
And into ashes all my lust:                                                            30
The grave's a fine and private place,
But none, I think, do there embrace.
    Now therefore, while the youthful hue
Sits on thy skin like morning glow,
And while thy willing soul transpires°                          *breathes out*
At every pore with instant fires,
Now let us sport us while we may,
And now, like amorous birds of prey,
Rather at once our time devour

[1] A muddy English river.

[2] According to tradition, the Jews would not be converted to Christianity until the end of
  recorded history.

Than languish in his slow-chapped° power.                    *slow-jawed*
Let us roll all our strength and all
Our sweetness up into one ball,
And tear our pleasures with rough strife
Thorough the iron gates of life:
Thus, though we cannot make our sun
Stand still, yet we will make him run.


# Ode on Solitude

ALEXANDER POPE

Happy the man whose wish and care
   A few paternal acres bound,
Content to breathe his native air,
      In his own ground.

Whose herds with milk, whose fields with bread,
   Whose flocks supply him with attire,
Whose trees in summer yield him shade,
      In winter fire.

Blest, who can unconcern'dly find
   Hours, days, and years slide soft away,                    10
In health of body, peace of mind,
      Quiet by day,

Sound sleep by night; study and ease,
   Together mixed; sweet recreation;
And Innocence, which most does please
      With meditation.

Thus let me live, unseen, unknown;
   Thus unlamented let me die,
Steal from the world, and not a stone
      Tell where I lie.                                        20


# The Lamb

WILLIAM BLAKE

   Little Lamb, who made thee?
   Dost thou know who made thee?
Gave thee life and bid thee feed,
By the stream and o'er the mead;

Gave thee clothing of delight,
Softest clothing, wooly, bright;
Gave thee such a tender voice,
Making all the vales rejoice?
   Little Lamb, who made thee?
   Dost thou know who made thee?          10

   Little Lamb, I'll tell thee,
   Little Lamb, I'll tell thee!
He is calléd by thy name,
For he calls himself a Lamb:
He is meek and he is mild,
He became a little child:
I a child and thou a lamb,
We are calléd by his name.
   Little Lamb, God bless thee.
   Little Lamb, God bless thee.          20

# The Tiger

WILLIAM BLAKE

Tiger! Tiger! burning bright
In the forests of the night,
What immortal hand or eye
Could frame thy fearful symmetry?

In what distant deeps or skies
Burnt the fire of thine eyes?
On what wings dare he aspire?
What the hand dare seize the fire?

And what shoulder, and what art,
Could twist the sinews of thy heart?
And when thy heart began to beat,          10
What dread hand? and what dread feet?

What the hammer? what the chain?
In what furnace was thy brain?
What the anvil? what dread grasp
Dare its deadly terrors clasp?

When the stars threw down their spears,
And watered heaven with their tears,
Did he smile his work to see?
Did he who made the Lamb make thee?       20

Tiger! Tiger! burning bright
In the forests of the night,
What immortal hand or eye
Dare frame thy fearful symmetry?


# The Garden of Love

WILLIAM BLAKE

I went to the Garden of Love,
And saw what I never had seen:
A Chapel was built in the midst,
Where I used to play on the green.

And the gates of this Chapel were shut,
And "Thou shalt not" writ over the door;
So I turned to the Garden of Love,
That so many sweet flowers bore,

And I saw it was filled with graves,
And tomb-stones where flowers should be:                    10
And Priests in black gowns were walking their rounds,
And binding with briars my joys and desires.


# London

WILLIAM BLAKE

I wander through each chartered° street                    *legally defined*
Near where the chartered Thames does flow,
And mark in every face I meet
Marks of weakness, marks of woe.

In every cry of every man,
In every infant's cry of fear,
In every voice, in every ban,
The mind-forged manacles I hear.

How the chimney-sweeper's cry
Every black'ning church appalls;                          10
And the hapless soldier's sigh
Runs in blood down palace walls.

But most through midnight streets I hear
How the youthful harlot's curse
Blasts the newborn infant's tear,
And blights with plagues the marriage hearse.


# Lines

## Composed a Few Miles above Tintern Abbey on Revisiting the Banks of the Wye during a Tour, July 13, 1798[1]

WILLIAM WORDSWORTH

Five years have passed; five summers, with the length
Of five long winters! and again I hear
These waters, rolling from their mountain-springs
With a soft inland murmur. Once again
Do I behold these steep and lofty cliffs,
That on a wild secluded scene impress
Thoughts of more deep seclusion; and connect
The landscape with the quiet of the sky.
The day is come when I again repose
Here, under this dark sycamore, and view                          10
These plots of cottage ground, these orchard tufts,
Which at this season, with their unripe fruits,
Are clad in one green hue, and lose themselves
'Mid groves and copses. Once again I see
These hedgerows, hardly hedgerows, little lines
Of sportive wood run wild; these pastoral farms,
Green to the very door; and wreaths of smoke
Sent up, in silence, from among the trees!
With some uncertain notice, as might seem
Of vagrant dwellers in the houseless woods,                       20
Or of some Hermit's cave, where by his fire
The Hermit sits alone.

                    These beauteous forms,
Through a long absence, have not been to me
As is a landscape to a blind man's eye;
But oft, in lonely rooms, and 'mid the din
Of towns and cities, I have owed to them,
In hours of weariness, sensations sweet,

---

[1] Wordsworth had previously visited the ruined medieval abbey five years earlier. That scenic site is in southeast Wales.

Felt in the blood, and felt along the heart;
And passing even into my purer mind,
With tranquil restoration—feelings too                          30
Of unremembered pleasure; such, perhaps,
As have no slight or trivial influence
On that best portion of a good man's life,
His little, nameless, unremembered acts
Of kindness and of love. Nor less, I trust,
To them I may have owed another gift,
Of aspect more sublime; that blessed mood,
In which the burthen of the mystery,
In which the heavy and the weary weight
Of all this unintelligible world,                               40
Is lightened—that serene and blessed mood,
In which the affections gently lead us on—
Until, the breath of this corporeal frame
And even the motion of our human blood
Almost suspended, we are laid asleep
In body, and become a living soul;
While with an eye made quiet by the power
Of harmony, and the deep power of joy,
We see into the life of things.

                     If this
Be but a vain belief, yet, oh! how oft—                         50
In darkness and amid the many shapes
Of joyless daylight; when the fretful stir
Unprofitable, and the fever of the world,
Have hung upon the beatings of my heart—
How oft, in spirit, have I turned to thee,
O sylvan Wye! thou wanderer through the woods,
How often has my spirit turned to thee!

   And now, with gleams of half-extinguished thought,
With many recognitions dim and faint,
And somewhat of a sad perplexity,                               60
The picture of the mind revives again;
While here I stand, not only with the sense
Of present pleasure, but with pleasing thoughts
That in this moment there is life and food
For future years. And so I dare to hope,
Though changed, no doubt, from what I was when first
I came among these hills; when like a roe
I bounded o'er the mountains, by the sides
Of the deep rivers, and the lonely streams,
Wherever nature led—more like a man                             70
Flying from something that he dreads than one

Who sought the thing he loved. For nature then
(The coarser pleasures of my boyish days,
And their glad animal movements all gone by)
To me was all in all.—I cannot paint
What then I was. The sounding cataract
Haunted me like a passion; the tall rock,
The mountain, and the deep and gloomy wood,
Their colors and their forms, were then to me
An appetite; a feeling and a love, 80
That had no need of a remoter charm,
By thought supplied, nor any interest
Unborrowed from the eye.—That time is past,
And all its aching joys are now no more,
And all its dizzy raptures. Not for this
Faint° I, nor mourn nor murmur; other gifts *become discouraged*
Have followed; for such loss, I would believe,
Abundant recompense. For I have learned
To look on nature, not as in the hour
Of thoughtless youth; but hearing oftentimes 90
The still, sad music of humanity,
Nor harsh nor grating, though of ample power
To chasten and subdue. And I have felt
A presence that disturbs me with the joy
Of elevated thoughts; a sense sublime
Of something far more deeply interfused,
Whose dwelling is the light of setting suns,
And the round ocean and the living air,
And the blue sky, and in the mind of man:
A motion and a spirit, that impels 100
All thinking things, all objects of all thought,
And rolls through all things. Therefore am I still
A lover of the meadows and the woods,
And mountains; and of all that we behold
From this green earth; of all the mighty world
Of eye, and ear—both what they half create,
And what perceive; well pleased to recognize
In nature and the language of the sense
The anchor of my purest thoughts, the nurse,
The guide, the guardian of my heart, and soul 110
Of all my moral being.

          Nor perchance,
If I were not thus taught, should I the more
Suffer my genial spirits² to decay:
For thou art with me here upon the banks

² Vital energy.

Of this fair river; thou my dearest Friend,
My dear, dear Friend;[3] and in thy voice I catch
The language of my former heart, and read
My former pleasures in the shooting lights
Of thy wild eyes. Oh! yet a little while
May I behold in thee what I was once,                           120
My dear, dear Sister! and this prayer I make,
Knowing that Nature never did betray
The heart that loved her; 'tis her privilege,
Through all the years of this our life, to lead
From joy to joy: for she can so inform
The mind that is within us, so impress
With quietness and beauty, and so feed
With lofty thoughts, that neither evil tongues,
Rash judgments, nor the sneers of selfish men,
Nor greetings where no kindness is, nor all            130
The dreary intercourse of daily life,
Shall e'er prevail against us, or disturb
Our cheerful faith, that all which we behold
Is full of blessings. Therefore let the moon
Shine on thee in thy solitary walk;
And let the misty mountain winds be free
To blow against thee: and, in after years,
When these wild ecstasies shall be matured
Into a sober pleasure; when thy mind
Shall be a mansion for all lovely forms,               140
Thy memory be as a dwelling place
For all sweet sounds and harmonies; oh! then,
If solitude, or fear, or pain, or grief
Should be thy portion, with what healing thoughts
Of tender joy wilt thou remember me,
And these my exhortations! Nor, perchance—
If I should be where I no more can hear
Thy voice, nor catch from thy wild eyes these gleams
Of past existence—wilt thou then forget
That on the banks of this delightful stream            150
We stood together; and that I, so long
A worshiper of Nature, hither came
Unwearied in that service; rather say
With warmer love—oh! with far deeper zeal
Of holier love. Nor wilt thou then forget,
That after many wanderings, many years
Of absence, these steep woods and lofty cliffs,
And this green pastoral landscape, were to me
More dear, both for themselves and for thy sake!

[3] Wordsworth's sister Dorothy.

# Lochinvar

SIR WALTER SCOTT

Oh, young Lochinvar is come out of the west:
Through all the wide border his steed was the best;
And save his good broadsword he weapons had none;
He rode all unarmed and he rode all alone.
So faithful in love, and so dauntless in war,
There never was knight like young Lochinvar!

He stayed not for brake, and he stopped not for stone;
He swam the Esk River where ford there was none:
But ere he alighted at Netherby gate,
The bride had consented, the gallant came late;                    10
For a laggard in love, and a dastard in war,
Was to wed the fair Ellen of brave Lochinvar.

So boldly he entered the Netherby Hall,
Among bride'smen, and kinsmen, and brothers, and all:
Then spoke the bride's father, his hand on his sword
(For the poor craven bridegroom said never a word),
"O come ye in peace here, or come ye in war,
Or to dance at our bridal, young Lord Lochinvar?"—

"I long wooed your daughter, my suit you denied;—
Love swells like the Solway, but ebbs like its tide!              20
And now am I come, with this lost love of mine,
To lead but one measure,° drink one cup of wine:          *dance*
There are maidens in Scotland more lovely by far,
That would gladly be bride to the young Lochinvar."

The bride kissed the goblet; the knight took it up,
He quaffed off the wine, and he threw down the cup.
She looked down to blush, and she looked up to sigh,
With a smile on her lips, and a tear in her eye.
He took her soft hand, ere her mother could bar,—
"Now tread me a measure!" said young Lochinvar.                  30

So stately his form, and so lovely her face,
That never a hall such a galliard did grace:
While her mother did fret, and her father did fume,
And the bridegroom stood dangling his bonnet and plume;
And the bride-maidens whispered, " 'T were better by far
To have matched our fair cousin with young Lochinvar."

One touch to her hand, and one word in her ear,
When they reached the hall door, and the charger stood near;
So light to the croup the fair lady he swung.
So light to the saddle before her he sprung!                                    40
"She is won! we are gone, over bank, bush, and scaur:°                           rock
They'll have fleet steeds that follow," quoth young Lochinvar.

There was mounting 'mong Graemes of the Netherby clan:
Forsters, Fenwicks, and Musgraves, they rode and they ran;
There was racing and chasing on Canobie Lee,
But the lost bride of Netherby ne'er did they see.
So daring in love, and so dauntless in war,
Have ye e'er hear of gallant like young Lochinvar?


# How the Waters Come Down at Lodore

ROBERT SOUTHEY

"How does the Water
Come down at Lodore?"
    From its sources which well
        In the tarn on the fell;°                                               mountain
            From its fountains,
            In the mountains,
        Its rills and its gills, —

Through moss and through brake
    It runs and it creeps
    For awhile, till it sleeps                                                  10
        In its own little lake.
    And thence at departing,
    Awakening and starting,
    It runs through the reeds,
        And away it proceeds
    Through meadow and glade,
        In sun and in shade,
And through the wood-shelter,
    Among crags in its flurry,
            Helter-skelter,                                                     20
            Hurry-skurry.
        Here it comes sparkling,
    And there it lies darkling;
    Now smoking and frothing
        Its tumult and wrath in,
            Till, in this rapid race

On which it is bent,
It reaches the place
Of its steep descent.
The cataract strong                                    30
Then plunges along,
Striking and raging,
As if a war waging
Its caverns and rocks among;
Rising and leaping,
Sinking and creeping,
Swelling and sweeping,
Showering and springing,
Flying and flinging,
Writhing and wringing,                                 40
Eddying and whisking,
Spouting and frisking,
Turning and twisting,
Around and around
With endless rebound!
Smiting and fighting,
A sight to delight in;
Confounding, astounding,
Dizzying and deafening the ear with its sound.

Dividing and gliding and sliding,                      50
And falling and brawling and sprawling,
And driving and riving and striving,
And sprinkling and twinkling and wrinkling,
And sounding and bounding and rounding,
And bubbling and troubling and doubling,
And grumbling and rumbling and tumbling,
And clattering and battering and shattering:

Retreating and beating and meeting and sheeting,
Delaying and straying and playing and spraying,
Advancing and prancing and glancing and dancing,      60
Recoiling, turmoiling, toiling and boiling,
And gleaming and steaming and streaming and beaming,
And rushing and flushing and brushing and gushing,
And flapping and rapping and clapping and slapping,
And curling and whirling and purling and twirling,
And thumping and plumping and bumping and jumping,
And dashing and flashing and splashing and clashing:
And so never ending, but always descending,
Sounds and motions for ever and ever are blending,
All at once and all o'er, with a mighty uproar;        70
And this way the water comes down at Lodore.

# So We'll Go No More a-Roving

GEORGE GORDON, LORD BYRON

So we'll go no more a-roving
 So late into the night,
Though the heart be still as loving,
 And the moon be still as bright.

For the sword outwears its sheath,
 And the soul wears out the breast,
And the heart must pause to breathe,
 And Love itself have rest.

Though the night was made for loving,
 And the day returns too soon,          10
Yet we'll go no more a-roving
 By the light of the moon.

# Stanzas

### When a Man Hath No Freedom to Fight for at Home

GEORGE GORDON, LORD BYRON

When a man hath no freedom to fight for at home,
 Let him combat for that of his neighbors;
Let him think of the glories of Greece and of Rome,
 And get knocked on his head for his labors.

To do good to mankind is the chivalrous plan,
 And is always as nobly requited;
Then battle for freedom wherever you can,
 And, if not shot or hanged, you'll get knighted.

# A Song: "Men of England"

PERCY BYSSHE SHELLEY

Men of England, wherefore plough
For the lords who lay ye low?
Wherefore weave with toil and care
The rich robes your tyrants wear?

Wherefore feed and clothe and save
From the cradle to the grave
Those ungrateful drones who would
Drain your sweat—nay, drink your blood?

Wherefore, Bees of England, forge
Many a weapon, chain, and scourge,                              10
That these stingless drones may spoil
The forced produce of your toil?

Have ye leisure, comfort, calm,
Shelter, food, love's gentle balm?
Or what is it ye buy so dear
With your pain and with your fear?

The seed ye sow, another reaps;
The wealth ye find, another keeps;
The robes ye weave, another wears;
The arms ye forge, another bears.                              20

Sow seed—but let no tyrant reap:
Find wealth—let no imposter heap:
Weave robes—let not the idle wear:
Forge arms—in your defence to bear.

Shrink to your cellars, holes, and cells—
In halls ye deck, another dwells.
Why shake the chains ye wrought? Ye see
The steel ye tempered glance on ye.

With plough and spade and hoe and loom
Trace your grave and build your tomb                            30
And weave your winding-sheet—till fair
England be your sepulchre.


# Mutability

PERCY BYSSHE SHELLEY


The flower that smiles today
    Tomorrow dies;
All that we wish to stay
    Tempts and then flies.
What is this world's delight?
Lightning that mocks the night,
  Brief even as bright.

Virtue, how frail it is!
    Friendship how rare!
Love, how it sells poor bliss                                                      10
    For proud despair!
But we, though soon they fall,
Survive their joy, and all
    Which ours we call.

Whilst skies are blue and bright,
    Whilst flowers are gay,
Whilst eyes that change ere night
    Make glad the day,
Whilst yet the calm hours creep,
Dream thou—and from thy sleep                                           20
    Then wake to weep.

# Lines:

## When the Lamp Is Shattered

PERCY BYSSHE SHELLEY

    When the lamp is shattered
The light in the dust lies dead—
    When the cloud is scattered
The rainbow's glory is shed.
    When the lute is broken,
Sweet tones are remembered not;
    When the lips have spoken,
Loved accents are soon forgot.

    As music and splendor
Survive not the lamp and the lute,                               10
    The heart's echoes render
No song when the spirit is mute—
    No song but sad dirges,
Like the wind through a ruined cell,
    Or the mournful surges
That ring the dead seaman's knell.

    When hearts have once mingled
Love first leaves the well-built nest;
    The weak one is singled
To endure what it once possessed.                                20
    O Love! who bewailest

The frailty of all things here,
   Why choose you the frailest
For your cradle, your home, and your bier?

   Its passions will rock thee
As the storms rock the ravens on high;
   Bright reason will mock thee,
Like the sun from a wintry sky.
   From thy nest every rafter
Will rot, and thine eagle home                                    30
   Leave thee naked to laughter,
When leaves fall and cold winds come.


## To a Waterfowl

WILLIAM CULLEN BRYANT

   Whither, 'midst falling dew,
While glow the heavens with the last steps of day,
Far, through their rosy depths, dost thou pursue
   Thy solitary way?

   Vainly the fowler's° eye                                      *hunter of birds*
Might mark thy distant flight to do thee wrong,
As, darkly seen against the crimson sky,
   Thy figure floats along.

   Seek'st thou the plashy brink
Of weedy lake, or marge of river wide,                           10
Or where the rocking billows rise and sink
   On the chaféd ocean-side?

   There is a Power whose care
Teaches thy way along that pathless coast—
The desert and illimitable air—
   Lone wandering, but not lost.

   All day thy wings have fanned,
At that far height, the cold, thin atmosphere,
Yet stoop not, weary, to the welcome land,
   Though the dark night is near.                                20

   And soon that toil shall end;
Soon shalt thou find a summer home, and rest,

And scream among thy fellows; reeds shall bend,
    Soon, o'er thy sheltered nest.

Thou'rt gone, the abyss of heaven
Hath swallowed up thy form; yet, on my heart
Deeply hath sunk the lesson thou hast given,
    And shall not soon depart.

    He who, from zone to zone,
Guides through the boundless sky thy certain flight,          30
In the long way that I must trace alone,
    Will lead my steps aright.

# To the Fringed Gentian

WILLIAM CULLEN BRYANT

Thou blossom bright with autumn dew,
And colored with the heaven's own blue,
That openest when the quiet light
Succeeds the keen and frosty night—

Thou comest not when violets lean
O'er wandering brooks and springs unseen,
Or columbines, in purple dressed,
Nod o'er the ground-bird's hidden nest.

Thou waitest late and com'st alone,
When woods are bare and birds are flown,          10
And frosts and shortening days portend
The aged year is near his end.

Then doth thy sweet and quiet eye
Look through its fringes to the sky,
Blue—blue—as if that sky let fall
A flower from its cerulean wall.

I would that thus, when I shall see
The hour of death draw near to me,
Hope, blossoming within my heart,
May look to heaven as I depart.          20

# La Belle Dame sans Merci[1]

JOHN KEATS

O what can ail thee, knight at arms,
   Alone and palely loitering?
The sedge has withered from the lake,
   And no birds sing.

O what can ail thee, knight at arms,
   So haggard and so woebegone?
The squirrel's granary is full,
   And the harvest's done.

I see a lily on thy brow
   With anguish moist and fever dew,                    10
And on thy cheeks a fading rose
   Fast withereth too.

I met a lady in the meads,
   Full beautiful, a faery's child:
Her hair was long, her foot was light,
   And her eyes were wild.

I made a garland for her head,
   And bracelets too, and fragrant zone;°         *belt*
She looked at me as° she did love,              *as if*
   And made sweet moan.                         20

I set her on my pacing steed,
   And nothing else saw all day long;
For sidelong would she bend and sing
   A faery's song.

She found me roots of relish sweet,
   And honey wild, and manna dew,
And sure in language strange she said,
   "I love thee true!"

She took me to her elfin grot,
   And there she wept and sighed full sore;°        *greatly*
And there I shut her wild, wild eyes
   With kisses four.

And there she lullèd me asleep,
   And there I dreamed—Ah! woe betide!

[1] The Beautiful Lady without Pity.

The latest° dream I ever dreamed                                    *last*
    On the cold hill side.

I saw pale kings, and princes too,
    Pale warriors, death-pale were they all;
They cried—"La Belle Dame Sans Merci
    Hath thee in thrall!"                                          40

I saw their starved lips in the gloam,°                            *twilight*
    With horrid warning gapéd wide,
And I awoke and found me here,
    On the cold hill's side.

And this is why I sojourn here,
    Alone and palely loitering,
Though the sedge is withered from the lake,
    And no birds sing.


# Sonnet to Sleep

JOHN KEATS

O soft embalmer of the still midnight,
    Shutting, with careful fingers and benign,
Our gloom-pleased eyes, embowered from the light,
    Enshaded in forgetfulness divine;
O soothest° Sleep! if so it please thee, close,                   *truest*
    In midst of this thine hymn, my willing eyes,
Or wait the amen, ere thy poppy throws
    Around my bed its lulling charities;
    Then save me, or the passéd day will shine
Upon my pillow, breeding many woes;                               10
    Save me from curious conscience, that still lords
Its strength for darkness, burrowing like a mole;
    Turn the key deftly in the oiléd wards,
And seal the hushéd casket of my soul.


# Ode on a Grecian Urn

JOHN KEATS

## 1

Thou still unravished bride of quietness,
    Thou foster child of silence and slow time,
Sylvan historian, who canst thus express

A flowery tale more sweetly than our rhyme:
What leaf-fringed legend haunts about thy shape
   Of deities or mortals, or of both,
     In Tempe or the dales of Arcady?[1]
   What men or gods are these? What maidens loath?
What mad pursuit? What struggle to escape?
     What pipes and timbrels? What wild ecstasy?     10

### 2

Heard melodies are sweet, but those unheard
   Are sweeter; therefore, ye soft pipes, play on;
Not to the sensual ear, but, more endeared,
   Pipe to the spirit ditties of no tone:
Fair youth, beneath the trees, thou canst not leave
   Thy song, nor ever can those trees be bare;
     Bold lover, never, never canst thou kiss,
Though winning near the goal—yet, do not grieve;
     She cannot fade, though thou hast not thy bliss,
   Forever wilt thou love, and she be fair!     20

### 3

Ah, happy, happy boughs! that cannot shed
   Your leaves, nor ever bid the Spring adieu;
And, happy melodist, unweariéd,
   Forever piping songs forever new;
More happy love! more happy, happy love!
   Forever warm and still to be enjoyed,
     Forever panting, and forever young;
All breathing human passion far above,
   That leaves a heart high-sorrowful and cloyed,
     A burning forehead, and a parching tongue.     30

### 4

Who are these coming to the sacrifice?
   To what green altar, O mysterious priest,
Lead'st thou that heifer lowing at the skies,
   And all her silken flanks with garlands dressed?
What little town by river or sea shore,
   Or mountain-built with peaceful citadel,
     Is emptied of this folk, this pious morn?
And, little town, thy streets forevermore
   Will silent be; and not a soul to tell
     Why thou art desolate, can e'er return.     40

---

[1] Idealized Grecian landscapes, respectively a valley and a mountainous region.

## 5

O Attic° shape! Fair attitude! with brede°            *Grecian/woven pattern*
  Of marble men and maidens overwrought,
With forest branches and the trodden weed;
  Thou, silent form, dost tease us out of thought
As doth eternity: Cold Pastoral!
   When old age shall this generation waste,
    Thou shalt remain, in midst of other woe
   Than ours, a friend to man, to whom thou say'st,
"Beauty is truth, truth beauty,"—that is all
    Ye know on earth, and all ye need to know.        50

# To Autumn

JOHN KEATS

Season of mists and mellow fruitfulness,
   Close bosom-friend of the maturing sun;
Conspiring with him how to load and bless
   With fruit the vines that round the thatch-eaves run;
To bend with apples the mossed cottage-trees,
   And fill all fruit with ripeness to the core;
    To swell the gourd, and plump the hazel shells
   With a sweet kernel; to set budding more,
And still more, later flowers for the bees,
Until they think warm days will never cease,        10
    For Summer has o'er-brimmed their clammy cells.

Who hath not seen thee oft amid thy store?
   Sometimes whoever seeks abroad may find
Thee sitting careless on a granary floor,
   Thy hair soft-lifted by the winnowing wind;
Or on a half-reaped furrow sound asleep,
    Drowsed with the fume of poppies, while thy hook°       *scythe*
     Spares the next swath and all its twinéd flowers:
And sometimes like a gleaner thou dost keep
   Steady thy laden head across a brook;        20
   Or by a cider-press, with patient look,
    Thou watchest the last oozings hours by hours.

Where are the songs of Spring? Ay, where are they?
   Think not of them, thou hast thy music too—
While barréd clouds bloom the soft-dying day,
   And touch the stubble-plains with rosy hue;

Then in a wailful choir the small gnats mourn
   Among the river sallows, borne aloft
     Or sinking as the light wind lives or dies;
And full-grown lambs loud bleat from hilly bourn;          30
   Hedge crickets sing; and now with treble soft
   The redbreast whistles from a garden-croft;
     And gathering swallows twitter in the skies.

# Concord Hymn

## Sung at the Completion of the Battle Monument, July 4, 1837

RALPH WALDO EMERSON

By the rude bridge that arched the flood,
   Their flag to April's breeze unfurled,
Here once the embattled farmers stood
   And fired the shot heard round the world.

The foe long since in silence slept;
   Alike the conqueror silent sleeps;
And Time the ruined bridge has swept
   Down the dark stream which seaward creeps.

On this green bank, by this soft stream,
   We set today a votive stone;          10
That memory may their deed redeem,
   When, like our sires, our sons are gone.

Spirit, that made those heroes dare
   To die, and leave their children free,
Bid Time and Nature gently spare
   The shaft we raise to them and thee.

# Brahma[1]

RALPH WALDO EMERSON

If the red slayer think he slays,
   Or if the slain think he is slain,

---

[1] The highest god in Hindu mythology. The poem is based on the great Hindu mystical poem, the Bhagavad Gita, which teaches that only those who put off all desires and egotism may escape the cycle of rebirth and join the Universal Soul.

They know not well the subtle ways
   I keep, and pass, and turn again.

Far or forgot to me is near;
   Shadow and sunlight are the same;
The vanished gods to me appear;
   And one to me are shame and fame.

They reckon ill who leave me out;
   When me they fly, I am the wings;          10
I am the doubter and the doubt,
   And I the hymn the Brahmin sings.

The strong gods pine for my abode,
   And pine in vain the sacred Seven;
But thou, meek lover of the good!
   Find me, and turn thy back on heaven.


# Forbearance

RALPH WALDO EMERSON

Hast thou named all the birds without a gun?
Loved the wood-rose, and left it on its stalk?
At rich men's tables eaten bread and pulse?
Unarmed, faced danger with a heart of trust?
And loved so well a high behavior,
In man or maid, that thou from speech refrained,
Nobility more nobly to repay?—
O, be my friend, and teach me to be thine!


# How Do I Love Thee? Let Me Count the Ways

ELIZABETH BARRETT BROWNING

How do I love thee? Let me count the ways.
I love thee to the depth and breadth and height
My soul can reach, when feeling out of sight
For the ends of Being and ideal Grace.
I love thee to the level of every day's
Most quiet need, by sun and candle light.
I love thee freely, as men strive for right;
I love thee purely, as they turn from praise.

I love thee with the passion put to use
In my old griefs, and with my childhood's faith.          10
I love thee with a love I seemed to lose
With my lost saints—I love thee with the breath,
Smiles, tears, of all my life!—and, if God choose,
I shall but love thee better after death.

## If Thou Must Love Me, Let It Be for Nought

ELIZABETH BARRETT BROWNING

If thou must love me, let it be for nought
Except for love's sake only. Do not say,
"I love her for her smile—her look—her way
Of speaking gently,—for a trick of thought
That falls in well with mine, and certes brought
A sense of pleasant ease on such a day"—
For these things in themselves, Belovéd, may
Be changed, or change for thee,—and love, so wrought,
May be unwrought so. Neither love me for
Thine own dear pity's wiping my cheeks dry,—          10
A creature might forget to weep, who bore
Thy comfort long, and lose thy love thereby!
But love me for love's sake, that evermore
Thou mayest love on, through love's eternity.

## Go from Me. Yet I Feel That I Shall Stand

ELIZABETH BARRETT BROWNING

Go from me. Yet I feel that I shall stand
Henceforward in thy shadow. Nevermore
Alone upon the threshold of my door
Of individual life, I shall command
The uses of my soul, nor lift my hand
Serenely in the sunshine as before,
Without the sense of that which I forbore, . . .
Thy touch upon the palm. The widest land
Doom takes to part us, leaves thy heart in mine
With pulses that beat double. What I do          10
And what I dream include thee, as the wine
Must taste of its own grapes. And when I sue
God for myself, he hears that name of thine,
And sees within my eyes the tears of two.

# The Eagle

ALFRED, LORD TENNYSON

He clasps the crag with crooked hands;
Close to the sun in lonely lands,
Ringed with the azure world, he stands.

The wrinkled sea beneath him crawls;
He watches from his mountain walls,
And like a thunderbolt he falls.

# The Splendor Falls

ALFRED, LORD TENNYSON

The splendor falls on castle walls
    And snowy summits old in story:
The long light shakes across the lakes,
    And the wild cataract leaps in glory.
Blow, bugle, blow, set the wild echoes flying,
Blow, bugle; answer, echoes, dying, dying, dying.

O hark, O hear! how thin and clear,
    And thinner, clearer, farther going!
O sweet and far from cliff and scar
    The horns of Elfland faintly blowing!
Blow, let us hear the purple glens replying:
Blow, bugle; answer, echoes, dying, dying, dying.

O love, they die in yon rich sky,
    They faint on hill or field or river:
Our echoes roll from soul to soul,
    And grow for ever and for ever.
Blow, bugle, blow, set the wild echoes flying,
And answer, echoes, answer, dying, dying, dying.

# Tears, Idle Tears

ALFRED, LORD TENNYSON

Tears, idle tears, I know not what they mean,
Tears from the depth of some divine despair
Rise in the heart, and gather to the eyes,
In looking on the happy autumn-fields,
And thinking of the days that are no more.

Fresh as the first beam glittering on a sail,
That brings our friends up from the underworld,
Sad as the last which reddens over one
That sinks with all we love below the verge;
So sad, so fresh, the days that are no more.          10

Ah, sad and strange as in dark summer dawns
The earliest pipe of half-awakened birds
To dying ears, when unto dying eyes
The casement slowly grows a glimmering square;
So sad, so strange, the days that are no more.

Dear as remembered kisses after death,
And sweet as those by hopeless fancy feigned
On lips that are for others; deep as love,
Deep as first love, and wild with all regret;
O Death in Life, the days that are no more!          20

## Dark House, by Which Once More I Stand

ALFRED, LORD TENNYSON

Dark house, by which once more I stand
  Here in the long unlovely street,
  Doors, where my heart was used to beat
So quickly, waiting for a hand,

A hand that can be clasped no more—
  Behold me, for I cannot sleep,
  And like a guilty thing I creep
At earliest morning to the door.

He is not here; but far away
  The noise of life begins again,          10
  And ghastly through the drizzling rain
On the bald street breaks the blank day.

## Ring Out, Wild Bells

ALFRED, LORD TENNYSON

Ring out, wild bells, to the wild sky,
  The flying cloud, the frosty light:
  The year is dying in the night;
Ring out, wild bells, and let him die.

Ring out the old, ring in the new,
  Ring, happy bells, across the snow:
  The year is going, let him go;
Ring out the false, ring in the true.

Ring out the grief that saps the mind,
  For those that here we see no more;            10
  Ring out the feud of rich and poor,
Ring in redress to all mankind.

Ring out a slowly dying cause,
  And ancient forms of party strife;
  Ring in the nobler modes of life,
With sweeter manners, purer laws.

Ring out the want, the care, the sin,
  The faithless coldness of the times;
  Ring out, ring out my mournful rhymes,
But ring the fuller minstrel in.            20

Ring out false pride in place and blood,
  The civic slander and the spite:
  Ring in the love of truth and right,
Ring in the common love of good.

Ring out old shapes of foul disease;
  Ring out the narrowing lust of gold;
  Ring out the thousand wars of old,
Ring in the thousand years of peace.

Ring in the valiant man and free,
  The larger heart, the kindlier hand;           30
  Ring out the darkness of the land,
Ring in the Christ that is to be.

# My Last Duchess

ROBERT BROWNING

### Ferrara[1]

That's my last duchess painted on the wall,
Looking as if she were alive. I call

---

[1] Italian city, seat of the Duke who speaks the poem.

That piece a wonder, now: Frà Pandolf's[2] hands
Worked busily a day, and there she stands.
Will't please you sit and look at her? I said
"Frà Pandolf" by design, for never read
Strangers like you that pictured countenance,
The depth and passion of its earnest glance,
But to myself they turned (since none puts by
The curtain I have drawn for you, but I)                              10
And seemed as they would ask me, if they durst,
How such a glance came there; so, not the first
Are you to turn and ask thus. Sir, 'twas not
Her husband's presence only, called that spot
Of joy into the Duchess' cheek: perhaps
Frà Pandolf chanced to say "Her mantle laps
Over my lady's wrist too much," or "Paint
Must never hope to reproduce the faint
Half-flush that dies along her throat": such stuff
Was courtesy, she thought, and cause enough                           20
For calling up that spot of joy. She had
A heart—how shall I say?—too soon made glad,
Too easily impressed; she liked whate'er
She looked on, and her looks went everywhere.
Sir, 'twas all one! My favor at her breast,
The dropping of the daylight in the West,
The bough of cherries some officious fool
Broke in the orchard for her, the white mule
She rode with round the terrace—all and each
Would draw from her alike the approving speech,                       30
Or blush, at least. She thanked men—good! but thanked
Somehow—I know not how—as if she ranked
My gift of a nine-hundred-years-old name
With anybody's gift. Who'd stoop to blame
This sort of trifling? Even had you skill
In speech—which I have not—to make your will
Quite clear to such an one, and say, "Just this
Or that in you disgusts me; here you miss,
Or there exceed the mark"—and if she let
Herself be lessoned so, nor plainly set                               40
Her wits to yours, forsooth, and made excuse,
—E'en then would be some stooping; and I choose
Never to stoop. Oh sir, she smiled, no doubt,
Whene'er I passed her; but who passed without
Much the same smile? This grew; I gave commands;
Then all smiles stopped together. There she stands

---

[2] Or Brother Pandolf, a fictitious Italian Renaissance painter who, like the real painter Frà
Angelico, was also a member of a religious order.

As if alive. Will 't please you rise? We'll meet
The company below, then. I repeat,
The Count your master's known munificence
Is ample warrant that no just pretense                               50
Of mine for dowry will be disallowed;
Though his fair daughter's self, as I avowed
At starting, is my object. Nay, we'll go
Together down, sir. Notice Neptune,[3] though,
Taming a sea-horse, thought a rarity,
Which Claus of Innsbruck cast in bronze for me!


# Meeting at Night

ROBERT BROWNING

The grey sea and the long black land;
And the yellow half-moon large and low;
And the startled little waves that leap
In fiery ringlets from their sleep,
As I gain the cove with pushing prow,
And quench its speed i' the slushy sand.

Then a mile of warm sea-scented beach;
Three fields to cross till a farm appears;
A tap at the pane, the quick sharp scratch
And blue spurt of a lighted match,                                   10
And a voice less loud, through its joys and fears,
Than the two hearts beating each to each!


# Parting at Morning

ROBERT BROWNING

Round the cape of a sudden came the sea,
And the sun looked over the mountain's rim:
And straight was a path of gold for him,
And the need of a world of men for me.

[3] Roman god of the sea.

# Two in the Campagna¹

ROBERT BROWNING

I wonder do you feel today
   As I have felt since, hand in hand,
We sat down on the grass, to stray
   In spirit better through the land,
This morn of Rome and May?

For me, I touched a thought, I know,
   Has tantalized me many times,
(Like turns of thread the spiders throw
   Mocking across our path) for rhymes
To catch at and let go.                                          10

Help me to hold it! First it left
   The yellowing fennel, run to seed
There, branching from the brickwork's cleft,
   Some old tomb's ruin; yonder weed
Took up the floating weft,

Where one small orange cup amassed
   Five beetles—blind and green they grope
Among the honey-meal; and last,
   Everywhere on the grassy slope
I traced it. Hold it fast!                                       20

The champaign° with its endless fleece                  *plain*
   Of feathery grasses everywhere!
Silence and passion, joy and peace,
   An everlasting wash of air—
Rome's ghost since her decease.

Such life here, through such lengths of hours,
   Such miracles performed in play,
Such primal naked forms of flowers,
   Such letting nature have her way
While heaven looks from its towers!                              30

How say you? Let us, O my dove,
   Let us be unashamed of soul,
As earth lies bare to heaven above!
   How is it under our control
To love or not to love?

¹ The grassy, rolling plain around Rome.

I would that you were all to me,
   You that are just so much, no more,
Nor yours, nor mine, nor slave nor free!
   Where does the fault lie? What the core
O' the wound, since wound must be?          40

I would I could adopt your will,
   See with your eyes, and set my heart
Beating by yours, and drink my fill
   At your soul's springs—your part, my part
In life, for good and ill.

No. I yearn upward, touch you close,
   Then stand away. I kiss your cheek,
Catch your soul's warmth—I pluck the rose
   And love it more than tongue can speak—
Then the good minute goes.          50

Already how am I so far
   Out of that minute? Must I go
Still like the thistle-ball, no bar,
   Onward, whenever light winds blow,
Fixed by no friendly star?

Just when I seemed about to learn!
   Where is the thread now? Off again!
The old trick! Only I discern
   Infinite passion and the pain
Of finite hearts that yearn.          60

# Remembrance

EMILY BRONTË

Cold in the earth—and the deep snow piled above thee,
Far, far removed, cold in the dreary grave!
Have I forgot, my only Love, to love thee,
Severed at last by Time's all-severing wave?

Now, when alone, do my thoughts no longer hover
Over the mountains, on that northern shore,
Resting their wings where heath and fern leaves cover
Thy noble heart forever, ever more?

Cold in the earth—and fifteen wild Decembers,
From those brown hills, have melted into spring; 10
Faithful, indeed, is the spirit that remembers
After such years of change and suffering!

Sweet Love of youth, forgive, if I forget thee,
While the world's tide is bearing me along;
Other desires and other hopes beset me,
Hopes which obscure, but cannot do thee wrong!

No later light has lightened up my heaven,
No second morn has ever shone for me;
All my life's bliss from thy dear life was given,
All my life's bliss is in the grave with thee. 20

But, when the days of golden dreams had perished,
And even Despair was powerless to destroy,
Then did I learn how existence could be cherished,
Strengthened, and fed without the aid of joy.

Then did I check the tears of useless passion—
Weaned my young soul from yearning after thine;
Sternly denied its burning wish to hasten
Down to that tomb already more than mine.

And, even yet, I dare not let it languish,
Dare not indulge in memory's rapturous pain; 30
Once drinking deep of the divinest anguish,
How could I seek the empty world again?


# No Coward Soul Is Mine

EMILY BRONTË

No coward soul is mine,
No trembler in the world's storm-troubled sphere:
  I see Heaven's glories shine,
And Faith shines equal, arming me from Fear.

  O God within my breast,
Almighty, ever-present Deity!
  Life, that in me hast rest
As I, undying Life, have power in Thee!

Vain are the thousand creeds
That move men's hearts: unutterably vain;                                    10
   Worthless as withered weeds,
Or idlest froth amid the boundless main,

   To waken doubt in one
Holding so fast by Thy infinity,
   So surely anchored on
The steadfast rock of Immortality.

   With wide-embracing love
Thy Spirit animates eternal years,
   Pervades and broods above,
Changes, sustains, dissolves, creates, and rears.                            20

   Though earth and moon were gone,
And suns and universes ceased to be,
   And Thou wert left alone,
Every existence would exist in Thee.

   There is not room for Death,
Nor atom that his might could render void:
   Since Thou art Being and Breath
And what Thou art may never be destroyed.

# There Was a Child Went Forth

WALT WHITMAN

There was a child went forth every day,
And the first object he looked upon, that object he became,
And that object became part of him for the day or a certain part of the day,
Or for many years or stretching cycles of years.

The early lilacs became part of this child,
And grass and white and red morning-glories, and white and red clover, and
   the song of the phoebe-bird,
And the Third-month° lambs and the sow's pink-faint litter, and the          *March*
   mare's foal and the cow's calf,
And the noisy brood of the barnyard or by the mire of the pond-side,
And the fish suspending themselves so curiously below there, and the
   beautiful curious liquid,
And the water-plants with their graceful flat heads, all became part of him.  10

The field-sprouts of Fourth-month and Fifth-month became part of him,
Winter-grain sprouts and those of the light-yellow corn, and the esculent
  roots of the garden,
And the apple-trees covered with blossoms and the fruit afterward, and
  wood-berries, and the commonest weeds by the road,
And the old drunkard staggering home from the outhouse of the tavern
  whence he had lately risen,
And the schoolmistress that passed on her way to the school,
And the friendly boys that passed, and the quarrelsome boys,
And the tidy and fresh-cheeked girls, and the barefoot negro boy and girl,
And all the changes of city and country wherever he went.

His own parents, he that had fathered him and she that had conceived him
  in her womb and birthed him,
They gave this child more of themselves than that,                          20
They gave him afterward every day, they became part of him.

The mother at home quietly placing the dishes on the supper-table,
The mother with mild words, clean her cap and gown, a wholesome odor
  falling off her person and clothes as she walks by,
The father, strong, self-sufficient, manly, mean, angered, unjust,
The blow, the quick loud word, the tight bargain, the crafty lure,
The family usages, the language, the company, the furniture, the yearning
  and swelling heart,
Affection that will not be gainsaid, the sense of what is real, the thought if
  after all it should prove unreal,
The doubts of day-time and the doubts of night-time, the curious whether
  and how,
Whether that which appears so is so, or is it all flashes and specks?
Men and women crowding fast in the streets, if they are not flashes and
  specks what are they?                                                     30
The streets themselves and the façades of houses, and goods in the windows,
Vehicles, teams, the heavy-planked wharves, the huge crossing at the ferries,
The village on the highland seen from afar at sunset, the river between,
Shadows, aureola and mist, the light falling on roofs and gables of white or
  brown two miles off,
The schooner near by sleepily dropping down the tide, the little boat slack-
  towed astern,
The hurrying tumbling waves, quick-broken crests, slapping,
The strata of colored clouds, the long bar of maroon-tint away solitary by
  itself, the spread of purity it lies motionless in,
The horizon's edge, the flying sea-crow, the fragrance of salt marsh and shore
  mud,
These became part of that child who went forth every day, and who now
  goes, and will always go forth every day.

# When Lilacs Last in the Dooryard Bloomed

WALT WHITMAN

### 1

When lilacs last in the dooryard bloomed,
And the great star[1] early drooped in the western sky in the night,
I mourned, and yet shall mourn with ever-returning spring.

Ever-returning spring, trinity sure to me you bring,
Lilac blooming perennial and drooping star in the west,
And thought of him I love.[2]

### 2

O powerful western fallen star!
O shades of night—O moody, tearful night!
O great star disappeared—O the black murk that hides the star!
O cruel hands that hold me powerless—O helpless soul of me!                10
O harsh surrounding cloud that will not free my soul.

### 3

In the dooryard fronting an old farm-house near the white-washed palings,
Stands the lilac-bush tall-growing with heart-shaped leaves of rich green,
With many a pointed blossom rising delicate, with the perfume strong I love,
With every leaf a miracle—and from this bush in the dooryard,
With delicate-colored blossoms and heart-shaped leaves of rich green,
A sprig with its flower I break.

### 4

In the swamp in secluded recesses,
A shy and hidden bird is warbling a song.
Solitary the thrush,                                                      20
The hermit withdrawn to himself, avoiding the settlements,
Sings by himself a song.

Song of the bleeding throat,
Death's outlet song of life (for well, dear brother, I know,
If thou wast not granted to sing thou would'st surely die).

### 5

Over the breast of the spring, the land, amid cities,
Amid lanes and through old woods, where lately the violets peeped from the
    ground, spotting the grey debris,

[1] The planet Venus.
[2] Abraham Lincoln; the poem was written shortly after his assassination.

Amid the grass in the fields each side of the lanes, passing the endless grass,
Passing the yellow-speared wheat, every grain from its shroud in the dark-
   brown fields uprisen,
Passing the apple-tree blows° of white and pink in the orchards,         *blossoms*
Carrying a corpse to where it shall rest in the grave,                        31
Night and day journeys a coffin.

### 6

Coffin that passes through lanes and streets,
Through day and night with the great cloud darkening the land,
With the pomp of the inlooped flags with the cities draped in black,
With the show of the States themselves as of crepe-veiled women standing,
With processions long and winding and the flambeaus° of the night,     *torches*
With the countless torches lit, with the silent sea of faces and the unbared
   heads,
With the waiting depot, the arriving coffin, and the somber faces,
With dirges through the night, with the thousand voices rising strong and
   solemn,
                                                                              40
With all the mournful voices of the dirges poured around the coffin,
The dim-lit churches and the shuddering organs—where amid these you
   journey,
With the tolling tolling bells' perpetual clang,
Here, coffin that slowly passes,
I give you my sprig of lilac.

### 7

(Nor for you, for one alone,
Blossoms and branches green to coffins all I bring,
For fresh as the morning, thus would I chant a song for you O sane and
   sacred death.

All over bouquets of roses,
O death, I cover you over with roses and early lilies,                         50
But mostly and now the lilac that blooms the first,
Copious I break, I break the sprigs from the bushes,
With loaded arms I come, pouring for you,
For you and the coffins all of you O death.)

### 8

O western orb sailing the heaven,
Now I know what you must have meant as a month since I walked,
As I walked in silence the transparent shadowy night,
As I saw you had something to tell as you bent to me night after night,
As you drooped from the sky low down as if to my side (while the other
   stars all looked on),
As we wandered together the solemn night (for something I know not what
   kept me from sleep),                                                         60

As the night advanced, and I saw on the rim of the west how full you were
    of woe,
As I stood on the rising ground in the breeze in the cool transparent night,
As I watched where you passed and was lost in the netherward black of the
    night,
As my soul in its trouble dissatisfied sank, as where you, sad orb,
Concluded, dropped in the night, and was gone.

### 9

Sing on there in the swamp,
O singer bashful and tender, I hear your notes, I hear your call,
I hear, I come presently, I understand you,
But a moment I linger, for the lustrous star has detained me,
The star, my departing comrade, holds and detains me.      70

### 10

O how shall I warble myself for the dead one there I loved?
And how shall I deck my song for the large sweet soul that has gone?
And what shall my perfume be for the grave of him I love?

Sea-winds blown from east and west,
Blown from the Eastern sea and blown from the Western sea, till there on the
    prairies meeting,
These and with these and the breath of my chant,
I'll perfume the grave of him I love.

### 11

O what shall I hang on the chamber walls?
And what shall the pictures be that I hang on the walls,
To adorn the burial-house of him I love?      80

Pictures of growing spring and farms and homes,
With the Fourth-month° eve at sundown, and the gray smoke lucid and   *April*
    bright,
With floods of the yellow gold of the gorgeous, indolent, sinking sun,
    burning, expanding the air,
With the fresh sweet herbage under foot, and the pale green leaves of the
    trees prolific,
In the distance the flowing glaze, the breast of the river, with a wind-dapple
    here and there,
With ranging hills on the banks, with many a line against the sky, and
    shadows,
And the city at hand with dwellings so dense, and stacks of chimneys,
And all the scenes of life and the workshops, and the workmen homeward
    returning.

## 12

Lo, body and soul—this land,
My own Manhattan with spires, and the sparkling and hurrying tides, and
    the ships,         90
The varied and ample land, the South and the North in the light, Ohio's
    shores and flashing Missouri,
And ever the far-spreading prairies covered with grass and corn.

Lo, the most excellent sun so calm and haughty,
The violet and purple morn with just-felt breezes,
The gentle soft-born measureless light,
The miracle spreading, bathing all, the fulfilled noon,
The coming eve delicious, the welcome night and the stars,
Over my cities shining all, enveloping man and land.

## 13

Sing on, sing on you gray-brown bird,
Sing from the swamps, the recesses, pour your chant from the bushes,    100
Limitless out of the dusk, out of the cedars and pines.

Sing on dearest brother, warble your reedy song,
Loud human song, with voice of uttermost woe.

O liquid and free and tender!
O wild and loose to my soul—O wondrous singer!
You only I hear—yet the star holds me (but will soon depart),
Yet the lilac with mastering odor holds me.

## 14

Now while I sat in the day and looked forth,
In the close of the day with its light and the fields of spring, and the farmers
    preparing their crops,
In the large unconscious scenery of my land with its lakes and forests,    110
In the heavenly aerial beauty (after the perturbed winds and the storms),
Under the arching heavens of the afternoon swift passing, and the voices of
    children and women,
The many-moving sea-tides, and I saw the ships how they sailed,
And the summer approaching with richness, and the fields all busy with
    labor,
And the infinite separate houses, how they all went on, each with its meals
    and minutia of daily usages,
And the streets how their throbbings throbbed, and the cities pent—lo, then
    and there,
Falling upon them all and among them all, enveloping me with the rest,
Appeared the cloud, appeared the long black trail,
And I knew death, its thought, and the sacred knowledge of death.

Then with the knowledge of death as walking one side of me,                    120
And the thought of death close-walking the other side of me,
And I in the middle as with companions, and as holding the hands of
   companions,
I fled forth to the hiding receiving night that talks not,
Down to the shores of the water, the path by the swamp in the dimness,
To the solemn shadowy cedars and ghostly pines so still.

And the singer so shy to the rest received me,
The gray-brown bird I know received us comrades three,
And he sang the carol of death, and a verse for him I love.

From deep secluded recesses,
From the fragrant cedars and the ghostly pines so still,                       130
Came the carol of the bird.

And the charm of the carol rapt me,
As I held as if by their hands my comrades in the night,
And the voice of my spirit tallied the song of the bird.

*Come lovely and soothing death,*
*Undulate round the world, serenely arriving, arriving,*
*In the day, in the night, to all, to each,*
*Sooner or later delicate death.*

*Praised be the fathomless universe,*
*For life and joy, and for objects and knowledge curious,*                     140
*And for love, sweet love—but praise! praise! praise!*
*For the sure-enwinding arms of cool-enfolding death.*

*Dark mother always gliding near with soft feet,*
*Have none chanted for thee a chant of fullest welcome?*
*Then I chant it for thee, I glorify thee above all,*
*I bring thee a song that when thou must indeed come, come unfalteringly.*

*Approach strong deliveress,*
*When it is so, when thou hast taken them, I joyously sing the dead,*
*Lost in the loving floating ocean of thee,*
*Laved in the flood of thy bliss, O death.*                                    150

*From me to thee glad serenades,*
*Dances for thee I propose saluting thee, adornments and feastings for thee,*
*And the sights of the open landscape and the high-spread sky are fitting,*
*And life and the fields, and the huge and thoughtful night.*

*The night in silence under many a star,*
*The ocean shore and the husky whispering wave whose voice I know,*

*And the soul turning to thee, O vast and well-veiled death,*
*And the body gratefully nestling close to thee.*

*Over the tree-tops I float thee a song,*
*Over the rising and sinking waves, over the myriad fields and the prairies*
  *wide,*                                                                    160
*Over the dense-packed cities all and the teeming wharves and ways,*
*I float this carol with joy, with joy to thee, O death.*

### 15

To the tally of my soul,
Loud and strong kept up the gray-brown bird,
With pure deliberate notes spreading, filling the night.

Loud in the pines and cedars dim,
Clear in the freshness moist and the swamp-perfume,
And I with my comrades there in the night.

While my sight that was bound in my eyes unclosed,
As to long panoramas of visions.                                            170

And I saw askant° the armies,                                        *sideways*
I saw as in noiseless dreams hundreds of battle-flags,
Borne through the smoke of the battles and pierced with missiles I saw them,
And carried hither and yon through the smoke, and torn and bloody,
And at last but a few shreds left on the staffs (and all in silence),
And the staffs all splintered and broken.

I saw battle-corpses, myriads of them,
And the white skeletons of young men, I saw them,
I saw the debris and debris of all the slain soldiers of the war,
But I saw they were not as was thought,                                      180
They themselves were fully at rest, they suffered not,
The living remained and suffered, the mother suffered,
And the wife and the child and the musing comrade suffered,
And the armies that remained suffered.

### 16

Passing the visions, passing the night,
Passing, unloosing the hold of my comrades' hands,
Passing the song of the hermit bird and the tallying song of my soul,
Victorious song, death's outlet song, yet varying, ever-altering song,
As low and wailing, yet clear the notes, rising and falling, flooding the night,
Sadly sinking and fainting, as warning and warning, and yet again bursting
  with joy,                                                                  190
Covering the earth and filling the spread of the heaven,
As that powerful psalm in the night I heard from recesses,

Passing, I leave thee lilac with heart-shaped leaves,
I leave thee there in the dooryard, blooming, returning with spring.

I cease from my song for thee,
From my gaze on thee in the west, fronting the west, communing with thee,
O comrade lustrous with silver face in the night.

Yet each to keep and all, retrievements out of the night,
The song, the wondrous chant of the gray-brown bird,
And the tallying chant, the echo aroused in my soul,                    200
With the lustrous and drooping star with the countenance full of woe,
With the holders holding my hand nearing the call of the bird,
Comrades mine and I in the midst, and their memory ever to keep, for the
    dead I loved so well,
For the sweetest, wisest soul of all my days and lands—and this for his dear
    sake,
Lilac and star and bird twined with the chant of my soul,
There in the fragrant pines and the cedars dusk and dim.


# Dover Beach

MATTHEW ARNOLD

The sea is calm tonight.
The tide is full, the moon lies fair
Upon the straits; on the French coast the light
Gleams and is gone; the cliffs of England stand,
Glimmering and vast, out in the tranquil bay.
Come to the window, sweet is the night air!
Only, from the long line of spray
Where the sea meets the moon-blanched land,
Listen! you hear the grating roar
Of pebbles which the waves draw back, and fling,                    10
At their return, up the high strand,
Begin, and cease, and then again begin,
With tremulous cadence slow, and bring
The eternal note of sadness in.

Sophocles long ago
Heard it on the Aegean,[1] and it brought
Into his mind the turbid ebb and flow

---

[1] The great sea to the east of Greece. The reference is to Sophocles's tragedy *Antigone*, in
   which the poet likens the blows of fate that destroy the family of Oedipus to the shock
   of a great sea striking the headland.

Of human misery; we
Find also in the sound a thought,
Hearing it by this distant northern sea.                    20

The Sea of Faith
Was once, too, at the full, and round earth's shore
Lay like the folds of a bright girdle furled.
But now I only hear
Its melancholy, long, withdrawing roar,
Retreating, to the breath
Of the night wind, down the vast edges drear
And naked shingles of the world.

Ah, love, let us be true
To one another! for the world, which seems               30
To lie before us like a land of dreams,
So various, so beautiful, so new,
Hath really neither joy, nor love, nor light,
Nor certitude, nor peace, nor help for pain;
And we are here as on a darkling plain
Swept with confused alarms of struggle and flight,
Where ignorant armies clash by night.

# Growing Old

MATTHEW ARNOLD

What is it to grow old?
Is it to lose the glory of the form,
The luster of the eye?
Is it for beauty to forego her wreath?
—Yes, but not this alone.

Is it to feel our strength—
Not our bloom only, but our strength—decay?
Is it to feel each limb
Grow stiffer, every function less exact,
Each nerve more loosely strung?                          10

Yes, this, and more; but not
Ah, 'tis not what in youth we dreamed 'twould be!
'Tis not to have our life
Mellowed and softened as with sunset glow,
A golden day's decline.

'Tis not to see the world
As from a height, with rapt prophetic eyes,
And heart profoundly stirred;
And weep, and feel the fullness of the past,
The years that are no more.                                        20

It is to spend long days
And not once feel that we were ever young;
It is to add, immured
In the hot prison of the present, month
To month with weary pain.

It is to suffer this,
And feel but half, and feebly, what we feel.
Deep in our hidden heart
Festers the dull remembrance of a change,
But no emotion—none.                                              30

It is—last stage of all—
When we are frozen up within, and quite
The phantom of ourselves,
To hear the world applaud the hollow ghost
Which blamed the living man.

# The Soul Selects Her Own Society

EMILY DICKINSON

The Soul selects her own Society—
Then—shuts the Door—
To her divine Majority—
Present no more—

Unmoved—she notes the Chariots—pausing—
At her low Gate—
Unmoved—an Emperor be kneeling
Upon her Mat—

I've known her—from an ample nation—
Choose One—                                                        10
Then—close the Valves of her attention—
Like Stone—

## There's Been a Death, in the Opposite House

EMILY DICKINSON

There's been a Death, in the Opposite House,
As lately as Today—
I know it, by the numb look
Such Houses have—alway—

The Neighbors rustle in and out—
The Doctor—drives away—
A Window opens like a Pod—
Abrupt—mechanically—

Somebody flings a Mattress out—
The Children hurry by—                                              10
They wonder if it died—on that—
I used to—when a Boy—

The Minister—goes stiffly in—
As if the House were His—
And He owned all the Mourners—now—
And little Boys—besides—

And then the Milliner—and the Man
Of the Appalling Trade—
To take the measure of the House—

There'll be that Dark Parade—                                      20

Of Tassels—and of Coaches—soon—
It's easy as a Sign—
The Intuition of the News—
In just a Country Town—


## Because I Could Not Stop for Death

EMILY DICKINSON

Because I could not stop for Death—
He kindly stopped for me—
The Carriage held but just Ourselves—
And Immortality.

We slowly drove—He knew no haste
And I had put away

My labor and my leisure too,
For His Civility—

We passed the School, where Children strove
At Recess—in the Ring—
We passed the Fields of Gazing Grain—
We passed the Setting Sun—

Or rather—He passed Us—
The Dews drew quivering and chill—
For only Gossamer, my Gown—
My Tippet—only Tulle—

We paused before a House that seemed
A Swelling of the Ground—
The Roof was scarcely visible—
The Cornice—in the Ground—

Since then—'tis Centuries—and yet
Feels shorter than the Day
I first surmised the Horses' Heads
Were toward Eternity—

# A Narrow Fellow in the Grass

EMILY DICKINSON

A narrow Fellow in the Grass
Occasionally rides—
You may have met Him—did you not
His notice sudden is—

The Grass divides as with a Comb—
A spotted shaft is seen—
And then it closes at your feet
And opens further on—

He likes a Boggy Acre
A Floor too cool for Corn—
Yet when a Boy, and Barefoot—
I more than once at Noon

Have passed, I thought, a Whip lash
Unbraiding in the Sun
When stooping to secure it
It wrinkled, and was gone—

Several of Nature's People
I know, and they know me—
I feel for them a transport
Of cordiality—                                         20

But never met this Fellow
Attended, or alone
Without a tighter breathing
And Zero at the Bone—


# Uphill

CHRISTINA ROSSETTI

Does the road wind uphill all the way?
   Yes, to the very end.
Will the day's journey take the whole long day?
   From morn to night, my friend.

But is there for the night a resting-place?
   A roof for when the slow dark hours begin.
May not the darkness hide it from my face?
   You cannot miss that inn.

Shall I meet other wayfarers at night?
   Those who have gone before.                          10
Then must I knock, or call when just in sight?
   They will not keep you standing at that door.

Shall I find comfort, travel-sore and weak?
   Of labor you shall find the sum.
Will there be beds for me and all who seek?
   Yea, beds for all who come.


# Sleeping at Last

CHRISTINA ROSSETTI

Sleeping at last, the trouble and tumult over,
   Sleeping at last, the struggle and horror past,
Cold and white, out of sight of friend and of lover,
      Sleeping at last.

No more a tired heart downcast or overcast,
No more pangs that wring or shifting fears that hover,
    Sleeping at last in a dreamless sleep locked fast.

Fast asleep. Singing birds in their leafy cover
    Cannot wake her, nor shake her the gusty blast.
Under the purple thyme and the purple clover                    10
            Sleeping at last.


# To an Athlete Dying Young

A. E. HOUSMAN

The time you won your town the race
We chaired you through the market-place;
Man and boy stood cheering by,
And home we brought you shoulder-high.

Today, the road all runners come,
Shoulder-high we bring you home,
And set you at your threshold down,
Townsman of a stiller town.

Smart lad, to slip betimes away
From fields where glory does not stay,                          10
And early though the laurel grows
It withers quicker than the rose.

Eyes the shady night has shut
Cannot see the record cut,
And silence sounds no worse than cheers
After earth has stopped the ears:

Now you will not swell the rout
Of lads that wore their honors out,
Runners whom renown outran
And the name died before the man.                               20

So set, before its echoes fade,
The fleet foot on the sill of shade,
And hold to the low lintel up
The still-defended challenge-cup.

And round that early-laureled head
Will flock to gaze the strengthless dead,
And find unwithered on its curls
The garland briefer than a girl's.

# Terence, This Is Stupid Stuff

A. E. HOUSMAN

"Terence, this is stupid stuff:
You eat your victuals fast enough;
There can't be much amiss, 'tis clear,
To see the rate you drink your beer.
But oh, good Lord, the verse you make,
It gives a chap the belly-ache.
The cow, the old cow, she is dead;
It sleeps well, the horned head:
We poor lads, 'tis our turn now
To hear such tunes as killed the cow.          10
Pretty friendship 'tis to rhyme
Your friends to death before their time
Moping melancholy mad:
Come, pipe a tune to dance to, lad."

Why, if 'tis dancing you would be,
There's brisker pipes than poetry.
Say, for what were hop-yards meant,
Or why was Burton built on Trent?[1]
Oh, many a peer of England brews
Livelier liquor than the Muse,          20
And malt does more than Milton can
To justify God's ways to man.[2]
Ale, man, ale's the stuff to drink
For fellows whom it hurts to think:
Look into the pewter pot
To see the world as the world's not.
And faith, 'tis pleasant till 'tis past:
The mischief is that 'twill not last.
Oh, I have been to Ludlow fair
And left my necktie God knows where,          30
And carried halfway home, or near,
Pints and quarts of Ludlow beer:
Then the world seemed none so bad,
And I myself a sterling lad;
And down in lovely muck I've lain,
Happy till I woke again.

[1] The English city of Burton, on the river Trent, was famous for its breweries.

[2] John Milton's intent, stated at the outset of his epic poem *Paradise Lost*, was through the loss of Eden and the redemption by Christ to "justify the ways of God to men."

Then I saw the morning sky:
Heigho, the tale was all a lie;
The world, it was the old world yet,
I was I, my things were wet,                                    40
And nothing now remained to do
But begin the game anew.

   Therefore, since the world has still
Much good, but much less good than ill,
And while the sun and moon endure
Luck's a chance, but trouble's sure,
I'd face it as a wise man would,
And train for ill and not for good.
'Tis true, the stuff I bring for sale
Is not so brisk a brew as ale:                                 50
Out of a stem that scored the hand
I wrung it in a weary land.
But take it: if the smack is sour,
The better for the embittered hour;
It should do good to heart and head
When your soul is in my soul's stead;
And I will friend you, if I may,
In the dark and cloudy day.

   There was a king³ reigned in the East:
There, when kings will sit to feast,                           60
They get their fill before they think
With poisoned meat and poisoned drink.
He gathered all that springs to birth
From the many-venomed earth;
First a little, thence to more,
He sampled all her killing store;
And easy, smiling, seasoned sound,
Sat the king when healths went round.
They put arsenic in his meat
And stared aghast to watch him eat;                            70
They poured strychnine in his cup
And shook to see him drink it up:
They shook, they stared as white's their shirt:
Them it was their poison hurt.
—I tell the tale that I heard told.
Mithridates, he died old.

³ Mithridates, king of ancient Pontus.

# The Lake Isle of Innisfree

WILLIAM BUTLER YEATS

I will arise and go now, and go to Innisfree,
And a small cabin build there, of clay and wattles made:
Nine bean-rows will I have there, a hive for the honeybee,
And live alone in the bee-loud glade.

And I shall have some peace there, for peace comes dropping slow,
Dropping from the veils of the morning to where the cricket sings;
There midnight's all a glimmer, and noon a purple glow,
And evening full of the linnet's wings.

I will arise and go now, for always night and day
I hear lake water lapping with low sounds by the shore;                    10
While I stand on the roadway, or on the pavements grey,
I hear it in the deep heart's core.

# The Wild Swans at Coole

WILLIAM BUTLER YEATS

The trees are in their autumn beauty,
The woodland paths are dry,
Under the October twilight the water
Mirrors a still sky;
Upon the brimming water among the stones
Are nine-and-fifty swans.

The nineteenth autumn has come upon me
Since I first made my count;
I saw, before I had well finished,
All suddenly mount                                                          10
And scatter wheeling in great broken rings
Upon their clamorous wings.

I have looked upon those brilliant creatures,
And now my heart is sore.
All's changed since I, hearing at twilight,
The first time on this shore,
The bell-beat of their wings above my head,
Trod with a lighter tread.

Unwearied still, lover by lover,
They paddle in the cold                                                     20

Companionable streams or climb the air;
Their hearts have not grown old;
Passion or conquest, wander where they will,
Attend upon them still.

But now they drift on the still water,
Mysterious, beautiful;
Among what rushes will they build,
By what lake's edge or pool
Delight men's eyes when I awake some day
To find they have flown away?                                    30

# The Scholars

WILLIAM BUTLER YEATS

Bald heads forgetful of their sins,
Old, learned, respectable bald heads
Edit and annotate the lines
That young men, tossing on their beds,
Rhymed out in love's despair
To flatter beauty's ignorant ear.

All shuffle there; all cough in ink;
All wear the carpet with their shoes;
All think what other people think;
All know the man their neighbor knows.                          10
Lord, what would they say
Did their Catullus[1] walk that way?

# The Second Coming

WILLIAM BUTLER YEATS

Turning and turning in the widening gyre°                        *spiral*
The falcon cannot hear the falconer;
Things fall apart; the center cannot hold;
Mere anarchy is loosed upon the world,
The blood-dimmed tide is loosed, and everywhere
The ceremony of innocence is drowned;
The best lack all conviction, while the worst
Are full of passionate intensity.

[1] Roman poet, author of passionate love poems and of satires against Julius Caesar.

Surely some revelation is at hand;
Surely the Second Coming is at hand.                                    10
The Second Coming! Hardly are those words out
When a vast image out of *Spiritus Mundi* [1]
Troubles my sight: somewhere in sands of the desert
A shape with lion body and the head of a man,
A gaze blank and pitiless as the sun,
Is moving its slow thighs, while all about it
Reel shadows of the indignant desert birds.
The darkness drops again; but now I know
That twenty centuries of stony sleep
Were vexed to nightmare by a rocking cradle,                            20
And what rough beast, its hour come round at last,
Slouches towards Bethlehem to be born?

# Richard Cory

EDWIN ARLINGTON ROBINSON

Whenever Richard Cory went down town,
We people on the pavement looked at him:
He was a gentleman from sole to crown,
Clean favored, and imperially slim.

And he was always quietly arrayed,
And he was always human when he talked;
But still he fluttered pulses when he said,
"Good-morning," and he glittered when he walked.

And he was rich—yes, richer than a king—
And admirably schooled in every grace:                                  10
In fine,° we thought that he was everything                    *in conclusion*
To make us wish that we were in his place.

So on we worked, and waited for the light,
And went without the meat, and cursed the bread;
And Richard Cory, one calm summer night,
Went home and put a bullet through his head.

---

[1] Soul of the World, a collective unconscious with which Yeats believed all human souls
  are connected.

# Miniver Cheevy

EDWIN ARLINGTON ROBINSON

Miniver Cheevy, child of scorn,
  Grew lean while he assailed the seasons;
He wept that he was ever born,
  And he had reasons.

Miniver loved the days of old
  When swords were bright and steeds were prancing;
The vision of a warrior bold
  Would set him dancing.

Miniver sighed for what was not,
  And dreamed, and rested from his labors;                    10
He dreamed of Thebes and Camelot,
  And Priam's neighbors.[1]

Miniver mourned the ripe renown
  That made so many a name so fragrant;
He mourned Romance, now on the town,
  And Art, a vagrant.

Miniver loved the Medici,[2]
  Albeit he had never seen one;
He would have sinned incessantly
  Could he have been one.                                     20

Miniver cursed the commonplace
  And eyed a khaki suit with loathing;
He missed the medieval grace
  Of iron clothing.

Miniver scorned the gold he sought,
  But sore annoyed was he without it;
Miniver thought, and thought, and thought,
  And thought about it.

---

[1] Refers to the sites of legendary heroic tragedies: Thebes is where Oedipus was king, Camelot was the court of King Arthur, and Priam was king of Troy and his "neighbors" were such heroes as Hector and Aeneas who fought the Greeks in the Trojan War.
[2] Powerful family of Renaissance Florence, whose members were successful merchants, art patrons, and leaders.

Miniver Cheevy, born too late,
   Scratched his head and kept on thinking;          30
Miniver coughed, and called it fate,
   And kept on drinking.


# Mr. Flood's Party

EDWIN ARLINGTON ROBINSON

Old Eben Flood, climbing alone one night
Over the hill between the town below
And the forsaken upland hermitage
That held as much as he should ever know
On earth again of home, paused warily.
The road was his with not a native near;
And Eben, having leisure, said aloud,
For no man else in Tilbury Town to hear:

"Well, Mr. Flood, we have the harvest moon
Again, and we may not have many more;          10
The bird is on the wing, the poet says,[1]
And you and I have said it here before.
Drink to the bird." He raised up to the light
The jug that he had gone so far to fill,
And answered huskily: "Well, Mr. Flood,
Since you propose it, I believe I will."

Alone, as if enduring to the end
A valiant armor of scarred hopes outworn,
He stood there in the middle of the road
Like Roland's ghost winding a silent horn.[2]          20
Below him, in the town among the trees,
Where friends of other days had honored him,
A phantom salutation of the dead
Rang thinly till old Eben's eyes were dim.

Then, as a mother lays her sleeping child
Down tenderly, fearing it may awake,

---

[1] The ancient Persian poet Omar Khayyam, in the *Rubaiyat* (translated by Edward FitzGerald): "The Bird of Time has but a little way/To flutter and the Bird is on the Wing." The poet therefore urges his hearers to drink and celebrate the moment.

[2] The medieval knight Roland, leading the rear guard of his uncle Charlemagne's army, would not sound his horn to summon help until his forces were defeated by the enemy and he himself lay dying.

He set the jug down slowly at his feet
With trembling care, knowing that most things break;
And only when assured that on firm earth
It stood, as the uncertain lives of men                                    30
Assuredly did not, he paced away,
And with his hand extended paused again:

"Well, Mr. Flood, we have not met like this
In a long time; and many a change has come
To both of us, I fear, since last it was
We had a drop together. Welcome home!"
Convivially returning with himself,
Again he raised the jug up to the light;
And with an acquiescent quaver said:
"Well, Mr. Flood, if you insist, I might.                                   40

"Only a very little, Mr. Flood—
For auld lang syne. No more, sir; that will do."
So, for the time, apparently it did,
And Eben evidently thought so too;
For soon amid the silver loneliness
Of night he lifted up his voice and sang,
Secure, with only two moons listening,
Until the whole harmonious landscape rang—

"For auld lang syne." The weary throat gave out,
The last word wavered, and the song was done.                              50
He raised again the jug regretfully
And shook his head, and was again alone.
There was not much that was ahead of him,
And there was nothing in the town below—
Where strangers would have shut the many doors
That many friends had opened long ago.


# O Black and Unknown Bards

JAMES WELDON JOHNSON

O black and unknown bards of long ago,
How came your lips to touch the sacred fire?
How, in your darkness, did you come to know
The power and beauty of the minstrel's lyre?
Who first from midst his bonds lifted his eyes?
Who first from out the still watch, lone and long,

Feeling the ancient faith of prophets rise
Within his dark-kept soul, burst into song?

Heart of what slave poured out such melody
As "Steal away to Jesus"? On its strains                          10
His spirit must have nightly floated free,
Though still about his hands he felt his chains.
Who heard great "Jordan roll"? Whose starward eye
Saw chariot "swing low"? And who was he
That breathed that comforting, melodic sigh,
"Nobody knows de trouble I see"?

What merely living clod, what captive thing,
Could up toward God through all its darkness grope,
And find within its deadened heart to sing
These songs of sorrow, love and faith, and hope?                  20
How did it catch that subtle undertone,
That note in music heard not with the ears?
How sound the elusive reed so seldom blown,
Which stirs the soul or melts the heart to tears.

Not that great German master in his dream
Of harmonies that thundered amongst the stars
At the creation, ever heard a theme
Nobler than "Go down, Moses." Mark its bars
How like a mighty trumpet-call they stir
The blood. Such are the notes that men have sung                  30
Going to valorous deeds; such tones there were
That helped make history when Time was young.

There is a wide, wide wonder in it all,
That from degraded rest and servile toil
The fiery spirit of the seer should call
These simple children of the sun and soil.
O black slave singers, gone, forgot, unfamed,
You—you alone, of all the long, long line
Of those who've sung untaught, unknown, unnamed,
Have stretched out upward, seeking the divine.                    40

You sang not deeds of heroes or of kings;
No chant of bloody war, no exulting paean
Of arms-won triumphs; but your humble strings
You touched in chord with music empyrean.
You sang far better than you knew; the songs
That for your listeners' hungry hearts sufficed
Still live,—but more than this to you belongs:
You sang a race from wood and stone to Christ.

# The Road Not Taken

ROBERT FROST

Two roads diverged in a yellow wood,
And sorry I could not travel both
And be one traveler, long I stood
And looked down one as far as I could
To where it bent in the undergrowth;

Then took the other, as just as fair,
And having perhaps the better claim,
Because it was grassy and wanted wear;
Though as for that the passing there
Had worn them really about the same,                        10

And both that morning equally lay
In leaves no step had trodden black.
Oh, I kept the first for another day!
Yet knowing how way leads on to way,
I doubted if I should ever come back.

I shall be telling this with a sigh
Somewhere ages and ages hence:
Two roads diverged in a wood, and I—
I took the one less traveled by,
And that has made all the difference.                        20


# Stopping by Woods on a Snowy Evening

ROBERT FROST

Whose woods these are I think I know.
His house is in the village, though;
He will not see me stopping here
To watch his woods fill up with snow.

My little horse must think it queer
To stop without a farmhouse near
Between the woods and frozen lake
The darkest evening of the year.

He gives his harness bells a shake
To ask if there is some mistake.                        10

The only other sound's the sweep
Of easy wind and downy flake.

The woods are lovely, dark, and deep,
But I have promises to keep,
And miles to go before I sleep,
And miles to go before I sleep.


# Mending Wall

ROBERT FROST

Something there is that doesn't love a wall,
That sends the frozen-ground-swell under it
And spills the upper boulders in the sun,
And makes gaps even two can pass abreast.
The work of hunters is another thing:
I have come after them and made repair
Where they have left not one stone on a stone,
But they would have the rabbit out of hiding,
To please the yelping dogs. The gaps I mean,
No one has seen them made or heard them made,          10
But at spring mending-time we find them there.
I let my neighbor know beyond the hill;
And on a day we meet to walk the line
And set the wall between us once again.
We keep the wall between us as we go.
To each the boulders that have fallen to each.
And some are loaves and some so nearly balls
We have to use a spell to make them balance:
"Stay where you are until our backs are turned!"
We wear our fingers rough with handling them.          20
Oh, just another kind of outdoor game,
One on a side. It comes to little more:
There where it is we do not need the wall:
He is all pine and I am apple orchard.
My apple trees will never get across
And eat the cones under his pines, I tell him.
He only says, "Good fences make good neighbors."
Spring is the mischief in me, and I wonder
If I could put a notion in his head:
"*Why* do they make good neighbors? Isn't it          30
Where there are cows? But here there are no cows.
Before I built a wall I'd ask to know
What I was walling in or walling out,

And to whom I was like to give offense.
Something there is that doesn't love a wall,
That wants it down." I could say "Elves" to him,
But it's not elves exactly, and I'd rather
He said it for himself. I see him there,
Bringing a stone grasped firmly by the top
In each hand, like an old-stone savage armed.                    40
He moves in darkness as it seems to me,
Not of woods only and the shade of trees.
He will not go behind his father's saying,
And he likes having thought of it so well
He says again, "Good fences make good neighbors."

# The Wood-Pile

ROBERT FROST

Out walking in the frozen swamp one gray day,
I paused and said, "I will turn back from here.
No, I will go on farther—and we shall see."
The hard snow held me, save where now and then
One foot went through. The view was all in lines
Straight up and down of tall slim trees
Too much alike to mark or name a place by
So as to say for certain I was here
Or somewhere else: I was just far from home.
A small bird flew before me. He was careful                      10
To put a tree between us when he lighted,
And say no word to tell me who he was
Who was so foolish as to think what *he* thought.
He thought that I was after him for a feather—
The white one in his tail; like one who takes
Everything said as personal to himself.
One flight out sideways would have undeceived him.
And then there was a pile of wood for which
I forgot him and let his little fear
Carry him off the way I might have gone,                         20
Without so much as wishing him good-night.
He went behind it to make his last stand.
It was a cord of maple, cut and split
And piled—and measured, four by four by eight.
And not another like it could I see.
No runner tracks in this year's snow looped near it.
And it was older sure than this year's cutting,
Or even last year's or the year's before.

The wood was gray and the bark warping off it
And the pile somewhat sunken. Clematis 30
Had wound strings round and round it like a bundle.
What held it, though, on one side was a tree
Still growing, and on one a stake and prop,
These latter about to fall. I thought that only
Someone who lived in turning to fresh tasks
Could so forget his handiwork on which
He spent himself, the labor of his ax,
And leave it there far from a useful fireplace
To warm the frozen swamp as best it could
With the slow smokeless burning of decay. 40

# Anecdote of the Jar

WALLACE STEVENS

I placed a jar in Tennessee,
And round it was, upon a hill.
It made the slovenly wilderness
Surround that hill.

The wilderness rose up to it,
And sprawled around, no longer wild.
The jar was round upon the ground
And tall and of a port in air.

It took dominion everywhere.
The jar was gray and bare. 10
It did not give of bird or bush,
Like nothing else in Tennessee.

# A Postcard from the Volcano

WALLACE STEVENS

Children picking up our bones
Will never know that these were once
As quick as foxes on the hill;

And that in autumn, when the grapes
Made sharp air sharper by their smell
These had a being, breathing frost;

And least will guess that with our bones
We left much more, left what still is
The look of things, left what we felt

At what we saw. The spring clouds blow                10
Above the shuttered mansion-house,
Beyond our gate and the windy sky

Cries out a literate despair.
We knew for long the mansion's look
And what we said of it became

A part of what it is . . . Children,
Still weaving budded aureoles,
Will speak our speech and never know,

Will say of the mansion that it seems
As if he that lived there left behind                20
A spirit storming in blank walls,

A dirty house in a gutted world,
A tatter of shadows peaked to white,
Smeared with the gold of the opulent sun.


# A Glass of Beer

JAMES STEPHENS

The lanky hank of a she in the inn over there
Nearly killed me for asking the loan of a glass of beer;
May the devil grip the whey-faced slut by the hair,
And beat bad manners out of her skin for a year.

That parboiled ape, with the toughest jaw you will see
On virtue's path, and a voice that would rasp the dead,
Came roaring and raging the minute she looked at me,
And threw me out of the house on the back of my head!

If I asked her master he'd give me a cask a day;
But she, with the beer at hand, not a gill would arrange!      10
May she marry a ghost and bear him a kitten, and may
The High King of Glory permit her to get the mange.

# Queen-Anne's-Lace

WILLIAM CARLOS WILLIAMS

Her body is not so white as
anemone petals nor so smooth—nor
so remote a thing. It is a field
of the wild carrot taking
the field by force; the grass
does not raise above it.
Here is no question of whiteness,
white as can be, with a purple mole
at the center of each flower.
Each flower is a hand's span                              10
of her whiteness. Wherever
his hand has lain there is
a tiny purple blemish. Each part
is a blossom under his touch
to which the fibers of her being
stem one by one, each to its end,
until the whole field is a
white desire, empty, a single stem,
a cluster, flower by flower,
a pious wish to whiteness gone over—                     20
or nothing.

# The Red Wheelbarrow

WILLIAM CARLOS WILLIAMS

so much depends
upon

a red wheel
barrow

glazed with rain
water

beside the white
chickens.

# This Is Just to Say

WILLIAM CARLOS WILLIAMS

I have eaten
the plums
that were in
the icebox

and which
you were probably
saving
for breakfast

Forgive me
they were delicious                                                    10
so sweet
and so cold

# The Dance

WILLIAM CARLOS WILLIAMS

In Breughel's great picture, The Kermess,°                    *outdoor fair*
the dancers go round, they go round and
around, the squeal and the blare and the
tweedle of bagpipes, a bugle and fiddles
tipping their bellies (round as the thick-
sided glasses whose wash they impound)
their hips and their bellies off balance
to turn them. Kicking and rolling about
the Fair Grounds, swinging their butts, those
shanks must be sound to bear up under such          10
rollicking measures, prance as they dance
in Breughel's great picture, The Kermess.

# Piano

D. H. LAWRENCE

Softly, in the dusk, a woman is singing to me;
Taking me back down the vista of years, till I see

A child sitting under the piano, in the boom of the tingling strings
And pressing the small, poised feet of a mother who smiles as she sings.

In spite of myself, the insidious mastery of song
Betrays me back, till the heart of me weeps to belong
To the old Sunday evenings at home, with winter outside
And hymns in the cosy parlor, the tinkling piano our guide.

So now it is vain for the singer to burst into clamor
With the great black piano appassionato. The glamor                    10
Of childish days is upon me, my manhood is cast
Down in the flood of remembrance, I weep like a child for the past.


# Snake

D. H. LAWRENCE

A snake came to my water-trough
On a hot, hot day, and I in pajamas for the heat,
To drink there.

In the deep, strange-scented shade of the great dark carob-tree
I came down the steps with my pitcher
And must wait, must stand and wait, for there he was at the trough before
   me.

He reached down from a fissure in the earth-wall in the gloom
And trailed his yellow-brown slackness soft-bellied down, over the edge of
   the stone trough
And rested his throat upon the stone bottom,
And where the water had dripped from the tap, in a small clearness,        10
He sipped with his straight mouth,
Softly drank through his straight gums, into his slack long body,
Silently.

Someone was before me at my water-trough,
And I, like a second comer, waiting.

He lifted his head from his drinking, as cattle do,
And looked at me vaguely, as drinking cattle do,
And flickered his two-forked tongue from his lips, and mused a moment,
And stooped and drank a little more,

Being earth-brown, earth-golden from the burning bowels of the earth          20
On the day of Sicilian July, with Etna[1] smoking.

The voice of my education said to me
He must be killed,
For in Sicily the black, black snakes are innocent, the gold are venomous.

And voices in me said, If you were a man
You would take a stick and break him now, and finish him off.

But must I confess how I liked him,
How glad I was he had come like a guest in quiet, to drink at my water-
    trough
And depart peaceful, pacified, and thankless,
Into the burning bowels of this earth?          30

Was it cowardice, that I dared not kill him?
Was it perversity, that I longed to talk to him?
Was it humility, to feel so honored?
I felt so honored.

And yet those voices:
*If you were not afraid, you would kill him!*

And truly I was afraid, I was most afraid,
But even so, honored still more
That he should seek my hospitality
From out the dark door of the secret earth.          40

He drank enough
And lifted his head, dreamily, as one who has drunken,
And flickered his tongue like a forked night on the air, so black;
Seeming to lick his lips,
And looked around like a god, unseeing, into the air,
And slowly turned his head,
And slowly, very slowly, as if thrice adream,
Proceeded to draw his slow length curving round
And climb again the broken bank of my wall-face.

And as he put his head into that dreadful hole,          50
And as he slowly drew up, snake-easing his shoulders, and entered farther,
A sort of horror, a sort of protest against his withdrawing into that horrid
    black hole,
Deliberately going into the blackness, and slowly drawing himself after,
Overcame me now his back was turned.

[1] The great Sicilian volcano.

I looked round, I put down my pitcher,
I picked up a clumsy log
And threw it at the water-trough with a clatter.

I think it did not hit him,
But suddenly that part of him that was left behind convulsed in undignified
    haste,
Writhed like lightning, and was gone                                        60
Into the black hole, the earth-lipped fissure in the wall-front,
At which, in the intense still noon, I stared with fascination.

And immediately I regretted it.
I thought how paltry, how vulgar, what a mean act!
I despised myself and the voices of my accursed human education.

And I thought of the albatross,[1]
And I wished he would come back, my snake.

For he seemed to me again like a king,
Like a king in exile, uncrowned in the underworld,
Now due to be crowned again.                                               70

And so, I missed my chance with one of the lords
Of life.
And I have something to expiate;
A pettiness.


# Bavarian Gentians

D. H. LAWRENCE

Not every man has gentians in his house
in Soft September, at slow, sad Michaelmas.

Bavarian gentians, big and dark, only dark
darkening the day-time, torch-like with the smoking blueness of Pluto's[2]
    gloom,

[1] In Samuel Taylor Coleridge's poem *The Rime of the Ancient Mariner*, the mariner wantonly shoots an albatross, bringing a curse on his ship and its crew.

[2] Ancient god of the underworld, also called Dis, who in Greek myth abducted Persephone, daughter of the crop goddess Demeter. Persephone is permitted to rejoin her mother for six months of the year, and during those months the land is fertile; but the autumn and winter must be spent with her husband in the underworld, and during those months Demeter mourns and the earth is barren.

ribbed and torch-like, with their blaze of darkness spread blue
down flattening into points, flattened under the sweep of white day
torch-flower of the blue-smoking darkness, Pluto's dark-blue daze,
black lamps from the halls of Dis, burning dark blue,
giving off darkness, blue darkness, as Demeter's pale lamps give off light,
lead me then, lead the way.                                          10

Reach me a gentian, give me a torch!
let me guide myself with the blue, forked torch of this flower
down the darker and darker stairs, where blue is darkened on blueness
even where Persephone goes, just now, from the frosted September
to the sightless realm where darkness is awake upon the dark
and Persephone herself is but a voice
of a darkness invisible enfolded in the deeper dark
of the arms Plutonic, and pierced with the passion of dense gloom,
among the splendor of torches of darkness, shedding darkness on the lost
    bride and her groom.


# Heat

## H. D. (HILDA DOOLITTLE)

O wind, rend open the heat,
cut apart the heat,
rend it to tatters.

Fruit cannot drop
through this thick air—
fruit cannot fall into heat
that presses up and blunts
the points of pears
and rounds the grapes.

Cut the heat—                                                       10
plough through it,
turning it on either side
of your path.


# The Horses

EDWIN MUIR

Barely a twelvemonth after
The seven days war that put the world to sleep,

Late in the evening the strange horses came.
By then we had made our covenant with silence,
But in the first few days it was so still
We listened to our breathing and were afraid.
On the second day
The radios failed; we turned the knobs; no answer.
On the third day a warship passed us, heading north,
Dead bodies piled on the deck. On the sixth day          10
A plane plunged over us into the sea. Thereafter
Nothing. The radios dumb;
And still they stand in corners of our kitchens,
And stand, perhaps, turned on, in a million rooms
All over the world. But now if they should speak,
If on a sudden they should speak again,
If on the stroke of noon a voice should speak,
We would not listen, we would not let it bring
That old bad world that swallowed its children quick°      *alive*
At one great gulp. We would not have it again.          20
Sometimes we think of the nations lying asleep,
Curled blindly in impenetrable sorrow,
And then the thought confounds us with its strangeness.
The tractors lie about our fields; at evening
They look like dank sea-monsters crouched and waiting.
We leave them where they are and let them rust:
"They'll moulder away and be like other loam."
We make our oxen drag our rusty plows,
Long laid aside. We have gone back
Far past our fathers' land.
                And then, that evening          30
Late in the summer the strange horses came.
We heard a distant tapping on the road,
A deepening drumming; it stopped, went on again
And at the corner changed to hollow thunder.
We saw the heads
Like a wild wave charging and were afraid.
We had sold our horses in our fathers' time
To buy new tractors. Now they were strange to us
As fabulous steeds set on an ancient shield
Or illustrations in a book of knights.          40
We did not dare go near them. Yet they waited,
Stubborn and shy, as if they had been sent
By an old command to find our whereabouts
And that long-lost archaic companionship.
In the first moment we had never a thought
That they were creatures to be owned and used.
Among them were some half-a-dozen colts
Dropped in some wilderness of the broken world,

Yet new as if they had come from their own Eden.
Since then they have pulled our plows and borne our loads,                    50
But that free servitude still can pierce our hearts.
Our life is changed; their coming our beginning.


# Poetry

MARIANNE MOORE

I, too, dislike it: there are things that are important beyond all this fiddle.
     Reading it, however, with a perfect contempt for it, one discovers in
     it after all, a place for the genuine.
          Hands that can grasp, eyes
          that can dilate, hair that can rise
               if it must, these things are important not because a

high-sounding interpretation can be put upon them but because they are
     useful. When they become so derivative as to become unintelligible,
     the same thing may be said for all of us, that we
          do not admire what                                               10
          we cannot understand: the bat
               holding on upside down or in quest of something to

eat, elephants pushing, a wild horse taking a roll, a tireless wolf under
     a tree, the immovable critic twitching his skin like a horse that feels a flea,
     the base-
     ball fan, the statistician—
          nor is it valid
               to discriminate against "business documents and

school-books"; all these phenomena are important. One must make a
          distinction
     however: when dragged into prominence by half poets, the result is not
          poetry,
     nor till the poets among us can be                                    20
          "literalists of
          the imagination"—above
               insolence and triviality and can present

for inspection, "imaginary gardens with real toads in them," shall we have
     it. In the meantime, if you demand on the one hand,
     the raw material of poetry in
          all its rawness and
          that which is on the other hand
               genuine, you are interested in poetry.

# The Love Song of J. Alfred Prufrock

T. S. ELIOT

> *S'io credessi che mia risposta fosse*
> *a persona che mai tornasse al mondo,*
> *questa fiamma staria senza più scosse.*
> *Ma per ciò che giammai di questo fondo*
> *non tornò vivo alcun, s'i'odo il vero,*
> *senza tema d'infamia ti rispondo.*[1]

Let us go then, you and I,
When the evening is spread out against the sky
Like a patient etherized upon a table;
Let us go, through certain half-deserted streets,
The muttering retreats
Of restless nights in one-night cheap hotels
And sawdust restaurants with oyster-shells:
Streets that follow like a tedious argument
Of insidious intent
To lead you to an overwhelming question . . .      10
Oh, do not ask, "What is it?"
Let us go and make our visit.

In the room the women come and go
Talking of Michelangelo.

The yellow fog that rubs its back upon the window-panes,
The yellow smoke that rubs its muzzle on the window-panes,
Licked its tongue into the corners of the evening,
Lingered upon the pools that stand in drains,
Let fall upon its back the soot that falls from chimneys,
Slipped by the terrace, made a sudden leap,      20
And seeing that it was a soft October night,
Curled once about the house, and fell asleep.

And indeed there will be time
For the yellow smoke that slides along the street
Rubbing its back upon the window-panes;
There will be time, there will be time
To prepare a face to meet the faces that you meet;

---

[1] During Dante's voyage through Hell (*Inferno*, XXVII 61–66), he finds himself among souls that speak through flickering flames, and asks one of them who it is. The reply: "If I thought that I were speaking to someone / who someday might return to see the world, / most certainly this flame would cease to flicker; / but since no one, if I have heard the truth, / ever returns alive from this deep pit, / with no fear of dishonor I answer you . . ."

There will be time to murder and create,
And time for all the works and days of hands
That lift and drop a question on your plate;                                      30
Time for you and time for me,
And time yet for a hundred indecisions,
And for a hundred visions and revisions,
Before the taking of a toast and tea.

In the room the women come and go
Talking of Michelangelo.
And indeed there will be time
To wonder, "Do I dare?" and, "Do I dare?"
Time to turn back and descend the stair,
With a bald spot in the middle of my hair—                                       40
(They will say: "How his hair is growing thin!")
My morning coat, my collar mounting firmly to the chin,
My necktie rich and modest, but asserted by a simple pin—
(They will say: "But how his arms and legs are thin!")
Do I dare
Disturb the universe?
In a minute there is time
For decisions and revisions which a minute will reverse.

For I have known them all already, known them all—
Have known the evenings, mornings, afternoons,                                   50
I have measured out my life with coffee spoons;
I know the voices dying with a dying fall
Beneath the music from a farther room.
    So how should I presume?

And I have known the eyes already, known them all—
The eyes that fix you in a formulated phrase,
And when I am formulated, sprawling on a pin,
When I am pinned and wriggling on the wall,
Then how should I begin
To spit out all the butt-ends of my days and ways?                              60
    And how should I presume?

And I have known the arms already, known them all—
Arms that are braceleted and white and bare
(But in the lamplight, downed with light brown hair!)
Is it perfume from a dress
That makes me so digress?
Arms that lie along a table, or wrap about a shawl.
    And should I then presume?
    And how should I begin?

                    .   .   .   .   .

Shall I say, I have gone at dusk through narrow streets                    70
And watched the smoke that rises from the pipes
Of lonely men in shirt-sleeves, leaning out of windows? . . .

I should have been a pair of ragged claws
Scuttling across the floors of silent seas.

　　　　　　·　·　·　·　·

And the afternoon, the evening, sleeps so peacefully!
Smoothed by long fingers,
Asleep . . . tired . . . or it malingers,
Stretched on the floor, here beside you and me.
Should I, after tea and cakes and ices,
Have the strength to force the moment to its crisis?                    80
But though I have wept and fasted, wept and prayed,
Though I have seen my head (grown slightly bald) brought in upon a platter,
I am no prophet[1]—and here's no great matter;
I have seen the moment of my greatness flicker,
And I have seen the eternal Footman hold my coat, and snicker,
And in short, I was afraid.

And would it have been worth it, after all,
After the cups, the marmalade, the tea,
Among the porcelain, among some talk of you and me,
Would it have been worth while,                    90
To have bitten off the matter with a smile,
To have squeezed the universe into a ball
To roll it towards some overwhelming question,
To say: "I am Lazarus, come from the dead,
Come back to tell you all, I shall tell you all"—
If one, settling a pillow by her head,
　　Should say: "That is not what I meant at all.
　　That is not it, at all."

And would it have been worth it, after all,
Would it have been worth while,                    100
After the sunsets and the dooryards and the sprinkled streets,
After the novels, after the teacups, after the skirts that trail along the floor—
And this, and so much more?—
It is impossible to say just what I mean!
But as if a magic lantern threw the nerves in patterns on a screen:
Would it have been worth while
If one, settling a pillow or throwing off a shawl,
And turning toward the window, should say:

[1] Unlike St. John the Baptist, who prophesied the coming of Christ, was beheaded at the princess Salome's request, and whose head was presented to her on a plate.

"That is not it at all,
That is not what I meant, at all."                                    110

    •   •   •   •   •

No! I am not Prince Hamlet, nor was meant to be;
Am an attendant lord, one that will do
To swell a progress,° start a scene or two,                   *royal journey*
Advise the prince; no doubt, an easy tool,
Deferential, glad to be of use,
Politic, cautious, and meticulous;
Full of high sentence,° but a bit obtuse;                      *moralizing*
At times, indeed, almost ridiculous—
Almost, at times, the Fool.

I grow old . . . I grow old . . .                                     120
I shall wear the bottoms of my trousers rolled.

Shall I part my hair behind? Do I dare to eat a peach?
I shall wear white flannel trousers, and walk upon the beach.
I have heard the mermaids singing, each to each.

I do not think that they will sing to me.

I have seen them riding seaward on the waves
Combing the white hair of the waves blown back
When the wind blows the water white and black.

We have lingered in the chambers of the sea
By sea-girls wreathed with seaweed red and brown              130
Till human voices wake us, and we drown.

# The Hollow Men

T. S. ELIOT

> *Mistah Kurtz—he dead.*
> *A penny for the Old Guy*[1]

### 1

We are the hollow men
We are the stuffed men
Leaning together

---

[1] Kurtz is the mysterious, corrupt European of Joseph Conrad's novella, *The Heart of Darkness;* he is described as a "hollow sham," "avid of . . . all the appearances of success and power." The Old Guy is Guy Fawkes, or rather the straw-stuffed effigy of him which children burn on the anniversary of his attempt to blow up the Houses of Parliament.

Headpiece filled with straw. Alas!
Our dried voices, when
We whisper together
Are quiet and meaningless
As wind in dry grass
Or rats' feet over broken glass
In our dry cellar                                                                                                   10


    Shape without form, shade without color,
Paralyzed force, gesture without motion;


    Those who have crossed
With direct eyes, to death's other Kingdom
Remember us—if at all—not as lost
Violent souls, but only
As the hollow men
The stuffed men.


## 2

Eyes I dare not meet in dreams
In death's dream kingdom                                                                            20
These do not appear:
There, the eyes are
Sunlight on a broken column
There, is a tree swinging
And voices are
In the wind's singing
More distant and more solemn
Than a fading star.


    Let me be no nearer
In death's dream kingdom                                                                            30
Let me also wear
Such deliberate disguises
Rat's coat, crowskin, crossed staves
In a field
Behaving as the wind behaves
No nearer—


    Not that final meeting
In the twilight kingdom

### 3

This is the dead land
This is cactus land                                                40
Here the stone images
Are raised, here they receive
The supplication of a dead man's hand
Under the twinkle of a fading star.
  Is it like this
In death's other kingdom
Waking alone
At the hour when we are
Trembling with tenderness
Lips that would kiss                                              50
Form prayers to broken stone.

### 4

The eyes are not here
There are no eyes here
In this valley of dying stars
In this hollow valley
This broken jaw of our lost kingdoms

  In this last of meeting places
We grope together
And avoid speech
Gathered on this beach of the tumid river                        60

  Sightless, unless
The eyes reappear
As the perpetual star
Multifoliate rose
Of death's twilight kingdom
The hope only
Of empty men.

### 5

*Here we go round the prickly pear*
*Prickly pear prickly pear*
*Here we go round the prickly pear*                              70
*At five o'clock in the morning.*

Between the idea
And the reality
Between the motion

And the act
Falls the Shadow
               *For Thine is the Kingdom*


Between the conception
And the creation
Between the emotion                                                    80
And the response
Falls the Shadow
                    *Life is very long*


  Between the desire
And the spasm
Between the potency
And the existence
Between the essence
And the descent
Falls the Shadow                                                      90
          *For Thine is the Kingdom*


  For Thine is
Life is
For Thine is the


  *This is the way the world ends*
*This is the way the world ends*
*This is the way the world ends*
*Not with a bang but a whimper.*


# Macavity: The Mystery Cat

## T. S. ELIOT


Macavity's a Mystery Cat: he's called the Hidden Paw—
For he's the master criminal who can defy the Law.
He's the bafflement of Scotland Yard, the Flying Squad's[1] despair:
For when they reach the scene of crime—*Macavity's not there!*

---

[1] Elite detective unit of Scotland Yard, called in to deal with the most puzzling or important crimes.

Macavity, Macavity, there's no one like Macavity,
He's broken every human law, he breaks the law of gravity.
His powers of levitation would make a fakir stare,
And when you reach the scene of crime—*Macavity's not there!*
You may seek him in the basement, you may look up in the air—
But I tell you once and once again, *Macavity's not there!*          10

Macavity's a ginger cat, he's very tall and thin;
You would know him if you saw him, for his eyes are sunken in.
His brow is deeply lined with thought, his head is highly domed;
His coat is dusty from neglect, his whiskers are uncombed.
He sways his head from side to side, with movements like a snake;
And when you think he's half asleep, he's always wide awake.

Macavity, Macavity, there's no one like Macavity,
For he's a fiend in feline shape, a monster of depravity.
You may meet him in a by-street, you may see him in the square—
But when a crime's discovered, then *Macavity's not there!*          20

He's outwardly respectable. (They say he cheats at cards.)
And his footprints are not found in any file of Scotland Yard's.
And when the larder's looted, or the jewel-case is rifled,
Or when the milk is missing, or another Peke's been stifled,
Or the greenhouse glass is broken, and the trellis past repair—
Ay, there's the wonder of the thing! *Macavity's not there!*

And when the Foreign Office find a Treaty's gone astray,
Or the Admiralty lose some plans and drawings by the way,
There may be a scrap of paper in the hall or on the stair—
But it's useless to investigate—*Macavity's not there!*          30
And when the loss has been disclosed, the Secret Service say:
"It *must* have been Macavity!"—but he's a mile away.
You'll be sure to find him resting, or a-licking of his thumbs,
Or engaged in doing complicated long division sums.

Macavity, Macavity, there's no one like Macavity,
There never was a Cat of such deceitfulness and suavity.
He always has an alibi, and one or two to spare:
At whatever time the deed took place—MACAVITY WASN'T THERE!

And they say that all the Cats whose wicked deeds are widely known
(I might mention Mungojerrie, I might mention Griddlebone)          40

Are nothing more than agents for the Cat who all the time
Just controls their operations: the Napoleon of Crime!

## Euclid alone has looked on Beauty bare

EDNA ST. VINCENT MILLAY

Euclid[1] alone has looked on Beauty bare.
Let all who prate of Beauty hold their peace,
And lay them prone upon the earth and cease
To ponder on themselves, the while they stare
At nothing, intricately drawn nowhere                                    5
In shapes of shifting lineage; let geese
Gabble and hiss, but heroes seek release
From dusty bondage into luminous air.
O blinding hour, O holy, terrible day,

When first the shaft into his vision shone                              10
Of light anatomized! Euclid alone
Has looked on Beauty bare. Fortunate they
Who, though once only and then but far away,
Have heard her massive sandal set on stone.

## The End of the World

ARCHIBALD MacLEISH

Quite unexpectedly as Vasserot
The armless ambidextrian was lighting
A match between his great and second toe
And Ralph the lion was engaged in biting
The neck of Madame Sossman while the drum
Pointed, and Teeny was about to cough
In waltz-time swinging Jocko by the thumb—
Quite unexpectedly the top blew off:

And there, there overhead, there, there, hung over
Those thousands of white faces, those dazed eyes,                      10
There in the starless dark the poise, the hover,

---

[1] The great geometer of ancient Greece.

There with vast wings across the canceled skies,
There in the sudden blackness the black pall
Of nothing, nothing, nothing—nothing at all.


# O sweet spontaneous

E. E. CUMMINGS

O sweet spontaneous
earth how often have
the
doting

     fingers of
prurient philosophers pinched
and
poked

thee
,has the naughty thumb                                    10
of science prodded
thy

     beauty        how
often have religions taken
thee upon their scraggy knees
squeezing and

buffeting thee that thou mightest conceive
gods
    (but
true                                                      20

to the incomparable
couch of death thy
rhythmic
lover

    thou answerest


them only with

      spring)

## next to of course god america i

E. E. CUMMINGS

"next to of course god america i
love you land of the pilgrims' and so forth oh
say can you see by the dawn's early my
country 'tis of centuries come and go
and are no more what of it we should worry
in every language even deafanddumb
thy sons acclaim your glorious name by gorry
by jingo by gee by gosh by gum
why talk of beauty what could be more beaut-
iful than these heroic happy dead                                    10
who rushed like lions to the roaring slaughter
they did not stop to think they died instead
then shall the voice of liberty be mute?"

He spoke. And drank rapidly a glass of water

## The Cool Web

ROBERT GRAVES

Children are dumb to say how hot the day is,
How hot the scent is of the summer rose,
How dreadful the black wastes of evening sky,
How dreadful the tall soldiers drumming by.

But we have speech, to chill the angry day,
And speech, to dull the rose's cruel scent.
We spell away the overhanging night,
We spell away the soldiers and the fright.

There's a cool web of language winds us in,
Retreat from too much joy or too much fear:            10
We grow sea-green at last and coldly die
In brininess and volubility.

But if we let our tongues lose self-possession,
Throwing off language and its watery clasp
Before our death, instead of when death comes,

Facing the wide glare of the children's day,
Facing the rose, the dark sky and the drums,
We shall go mad no doubt and die that way.

## Dream Variation

LANGSTON HUGHES

To fling my arms wide
In some place of the sun,
To whirl and to dance
Till the white day is done.
Then rest at cool evening
Beneath a tall tree
While night comes on gently,
     Dark like me—
That is my dream!

To fling my arms wide                               10
In the face of the sun,
Dance! Whirl! Whirl!
Till the quick day is done.
Rest at pale evening . . .
A tall, slim tree . . .
Night coming tenderly
     Black like me.

## The Weary Blues

LANGSTON HUGHES

Droning a drowsy syncopated tune,
Rocking back and forth to a mellow croon,
     I heard a Negro play.
Down on Lenox Avenue the other night
By the pale dull pallor of an old gas light
     He did a lazy sway. . . .
     He did a lazy sway. . . .
To the tune o' those Weary Blues.
With his ebony hands on each ivory key
He made that poor piano moan with melody.      10
     O Blues!
Swaying to and fro on his rickety stool

He played that sad raggy tune like a musical fool.
    Sweet Blues!
Coming from a black man's soul.
    O Blues!
In a deep song voice with a melancholy tone
I heard that Negro sing, that old piano moan—
    "Ain't got nobody in all this world,
    Ain't got nobody but ma self.                    20
    I's gwine to quit ma frownin'
    And put ma troubles on the shelf."
Thump, thump, thump, went his foot on the floor.
He played a few chords then he sang some more—
    "I got the Weary Blues
    And I can't be satisfied.
    Got the Weary Blues
    And can't be satisfied—
    I ain't happy no mo'
    And I wish that I had died."                 30
And far into the night he crooned that tune.

    The stars went out and so did the moon.
    The singer stopped playing and went to bed
    While the Weary Blues echoed through his head.
    He slept like a rock or a man that's dead.

# I, Too

LANGSTON HUGHES

I, too, sing America.

I am the darker brother.
They send me to eat in the kitchen
When company comes,
But I laugh,
And eat well,
And grow strong.

Tomorrow,
I'll be at the table
When company comes.                           10
Nobody'll dare
Say to me,
"Eat in the kitchen,"
Then.

Besides,
They'll see how beautiful I am
And be ashamed—

I, too, am America.


# Dream Deferred

LANGSTON HUGHES

What happens to a dream deferred?

    Does it dry up
    like a raisin in the sun?
    Or fester like a sore—
    And then run?
    Does it stink like rotten meat?
    Or crust and sugar over—
    like a syrupy sweet?

    Maybe it just sags
    like a heavy load.                    10

    *Or does it explode?*


# Souvenir de Monsieur Poop

STEVIE SMITH

I am the self-appointed guardian of English literature,
I believe tremendously in the significance of age;
I believe that a writer is wise at 50,
Ten years wiser at 60, at 70 a sage.
I believe that juniors are lively, to be encouraged with discretion and snubbed,
I believe also that they are bouncing, communistic, ill mannered and, of course,
    young.
But I never define what I mean by youth
Because the word undefined is more useful for general purposes of abuse.
I believe that literature is a school where only those who apply themselves
    diligently to their tasks acquire merit.
And only they after the passage of a good many years (see above).          10
But then I am an old fogey.

I always write more in sorrow than in anger.
I am, after all, devoted to Shakespeare, Milton,
And, coming to our own times,
Of course
Housman.
I have never been known to say a word against the established classics,
I am in fact devoted to the established classics.
In the service of literature I believe absolutely in the principle of division;
I divide into age groups and also into schools.                                    20
This is in keeping with my scholastic mind, and enables me to trounce
Not only youth
(Which might be thought intellectually frivolous by pedants) but also periodical
    tendencies,
To ventilate, in a word, my own political and moral philosophy.
(When I say that I am an old fogey, I am, of course, joking.)
English literature, as I see it, requires to be defended
By a person of integrity and essential good humor
Against the forces of fanaticism, idiosyncrasy and anarchy.
I perfectly apprehend the perilous nature of my convictions
And I am prepared to go to the stake                                              30
For Shakespeare, Milton,
And, coming to our own times,
Of course
Housman.
I cannot say more than that, can I?
And I do not deem it advisable, in the interests of the editor to whom I am
    spatially contracted,
To say less.


# Song

CECIL DAY LEWIS

Come, live with me and be my love,
And we will all the pleasures prove
Of peace and plenty, bed and board,
That chance employment may afford.

I'll handle dainties on the docks
And thou shalt read of summer frocks:
At evening by the sour canals
We'll hope to hear some madrigals.

Care on the maiden brow shall put
A wreath of wrinkles, and thy foot                    10
Be shod with pain: not silken dress
But toil shall tire thy loveliness.

Hunger shall make thy modest zone°             *waist*
And cheat fond death of all but bone—
If these delights thy mind may move,
Then live with me and be my love.

# As I Walked Out One Evening

W. H. AUDEN

As I walked out one evening,
  Walking down Bristol Street,
The crowds upon the pavement
  Were fields of harvest wheat.

And down by the brimming river
  I heard a lover sing
Under an arch of the railway:
  "Love has no ending.

"I'll love you, dear, I'll love you
  Till China and Africa meet,                    10
And the river jumps over the mountain
  And the salmon sing in the street,

"I'll love you till the ocean
  Is folded and hung up to dry
And the seven stars go squawking
  Like geese about the sky.

"The years shall run like rabbits,
  For in my arms I hold
The Flower of the Ages,
  And the first love of the world."           20

But all the clocks in the city
  Began to whirr and chime:

"O let not Time deceive you,
You cannot conquer Time.

"In the burrows of the Nightmare
Where Justice naked is,
Time watches from the shadow
And coughs when you would kiss.

"In headaches and in worry
Vaguely life leaks away,
And Time will have his fancy
Tomorrow or today.

"Into many a green valley
Drifts the appalling snow;
Time breaks the threaded dances
And the diver's brilliant bow.

"O plunge your hands in water,
Plunge them in up to the wrist;
Stare, stare in the basin
And wonder what you've missed.

"The glacier knocks in the cupboard,
The desert sighs in the bed,
And the crack in the teacup opens
A lane to the land of the dead.

"Where the beggars raffle the banknotes
And the Giant is enchanting to Jack,
And the Lily-white Boy is a Roarer,°                              *noisy bully*
And Jill goes down on her back.

"O look, look in the mirror,
O look in your distress;
Life remains a blessing
Although you cannot bless.

"O stand, stand at the window
As the tears scald and start;
You shall love your crooked neighbor
With your crooked heart."

It was late, late in the evening,
The lovers they were gone;
The clocks had ceased their chiming,
And the deep river ran on.

30

40

50

60

# O What Is That Sound

W. H. AUDEN

O what is that sound which so thrills the ear
  Down in the valley drumming, drumming?
Only the scarlet soldiers, dear,
  The soldiers coming.

O what is that light I see flashing so clear
  Over the distance brightly, brightly?
Only the sun on their weapons, dear,
  As they step lightly.

O what are they doing with all that gear,
  What are they doing this morning, this morning?      10
Only their usual maneuvers, dear,
  Or perhaps a warning.

O why have they left the road down there,
  Why are they suddenly wheeling, wheeling?
Perhaps a change in their orders, dear.
  Why are you kneeling?

O haven't they stopped for the doctor's care,
  Haven't they reined their horses, their horses?
Why, they are none of them wounded, dear,
  None of these forces.      20

O is it the parson they want, with white hair,
  Is it the parson, is it, is it?
No, they are passing his gateway, dear,
  Without a visit.

O it must be the farmer who lives so near.
  It must be the farmer so cunning, so cunning?
They have passed the farmyard already, dear,
  And now they are running.

O where are you going? Stay with me here!
  Were the vows you swore deceiving, deceiving?      30
No, I promised to love you, dear,
  But I must be leaving.

O it's broken the lock and splintered the door,
  O it's the gate where they're turning, turning;
Their boots are heavy on the floor
  And their eyes are burning.

## My Papa's Waltz

THEODORE ROETHKE

The whiskey on your breath
Could make a small boy dizzy;
But I hung on like death:
Such waltzing was not easy.

We romped until the pans
Slid from the kitchen shelf;
My mother's countenance
Could not unfrown itself.

The hand that held my wrist
Was battered on one knuckle;                          10
At every step you missed
My right ear scraped a buckle.

You beat time on my head
With a palm caked hard by dirt,
Then waltzed me off to bed
Still clinging to your shirt.

## Dolor

THEODORE ROETHKE

I have known the inexorable sadness of pencils,
Neat in their boxes, dolor of pad and paper-weight,
All the misery of manilla folders and mucilage,
Desolation in immaculate public places,
Lonely reception room, lavatory, switchboard,
The unalterable pathos of basin and pitcher,
Ritual of multigraph, paper-clip, comma,
Endless duplication of lives and objects.
And I have seen dust from the walls of institutions,
Finer than flour, alive, more dangerous than silica,          10
Sift, almost invisible, through long afternoons of tedium,
Dropping a fine film on nails and delicate eyebrows,
Glazing the pale hair, the duplicate gray standard faces.

# The Waking

THEODORE ROETHKE

I wake to sleep, and take my waking slow.
I feel my fate in what I cannot fear.
I learn by going where I have to go.

We think by feeling. What is there to know?
I hear my being dance from ear to ear.
I wake to sleep, and take my waking slow.

Of those so close beside me, which are you?
God bless the Ground! I shall walk softly there,
And learn by going where I have to go.

Light takes the Tree; but who can tell us how?                    10
The lowly worm climbs up a winding stair;
I wake to sleep, and take my waking slow.

Great Nature has another thing to do
To you and me; so take the lively air,
And, lovely, learn by going where to go.

This shaking keeps me steady. I should know.
What falls away is always. And is near.
I wake to sleep, and take my waking slow.
I learn by going where I have to go.


# I Knew a Woman

THEODORE ROETHKE

I knew a woman, lovely in her bones,
When small birds sighed, she would sigh back at them;
Ah, when she moved, she moved more ways than one:
The shapes a bright container can contain!
Of her choice virtues only gods should speak,
Or English poets who grew up on Greek
(I'd have them sing in chorus, cheek to cheek).

How well her wishes went! She stroked my chin,
She taught me Turn, and Counter-turn, and Stand;[1]
She taught me Touch, that undulant white skin;        10
I nibbled meekly from her proffered hand;
She was the sickle; I, poor I, the rake,
Coming behind her for her pretty sake
(But what prodigious mowing we did make).

Love likes a gander, and adores a goose:
Her full lips pursed, the errant note to seize;
She played it quick, she played it light and loose;
My eyes, they dazzled at her flowing knees;
Her several parts could keep a pure repose,
Or one hip quiver with a mobile nose        20
(She moved in circles, and those circles moved).

Let seed be grass, and grass turn into hay:
I'm martyr to a motion not my own;
What's freedom for? To know eternity.
I swear she cast a shadow white as stone.
But who would count eternity in days?
These old bones live to learn her wanton ways:
(I measure time by how a body sways).

## Reason

JOSEPHINE MILES

Said, Pull her up a bit will you, Mac, I want to unload there.
Said, Pull her up my rear end, first come first serve.
Said, Give her the gun, Bud, he needs a taste of his own bumper.
Then the usher came out and got into the act:

Said, Pull her up, pull her up a bit, we need this space, sir.
Said, For God's sake, is this still a free country or what?
You go back and take care of Gary Cooper's horse
And leave me to handle my own car.

Saw them unloading the lame old lady,
Ducked out under the wheel and gave her an elbow,    10
Said, All you needed to do was just explain;
*Reason, Reason* is my middle name.

[1] Terms for the three parts of the regular ode, whose first two stanzas are similar in form and the third different.

# Those Winter Sundays

ROBERT HAYDEN

Sundays too my father got up early
and put his clothes on in the blueblack cold,
then with cracked hands that ached
from labor in the weekday weather made
banked fires blaze. No one ever thanked him.

I'd wake and hear the cold splintering, breaking.
When the rooms were warm, he'd call,
and slowly I would rise and dress,
fearing the chronic angers of that house,

Speaking indifferently to him,                          10
who had driven out the cold
and polished my good shoes as well.
What did I know, what did I know
of love's austere and lonely offices?

# The Performers

ROBERT HAYDEN

Easily, almost matter-of-factly they step,
two minor Wallendas,[1] with pail and squeegee along
the wintry ledge, hook their harness to the wall
and leaning back into a seven-story angle of space
begin washing the office windows. I
am up there too until straps break
and iron paper apple of iron I fall
through plateglass wind onto stalagmites below.

But am safely at my desk again by the time
the hairline walkers, high-edge                          10
balancers end their center-ring routine
and crawl inside. A rough day, I remark,
for such a risky business. Many thanks.
Thank *you*, sir, one of the men replies.

[1] A famous family of circus tightrope-walkers.

# The Heavy Bear Who Goes with Me

DELMORE SCHWARTZ

"the withness of the body"

The heavy bear who goes with me,
A manifold honey to smear his face,
Clumsy and lumbering here and there,
The central ton of every place,
The hungry beating brutish one
In love with candy, anger, and sleep,
Crazy factotum, dishevelling all,
Climbs the building, kicks the football,
Boxes his brother in the hate-ridden city.

Breathing at my side, the heavy animal,                   10
That heavy bear who sleeps with me,
Howls in his sleep for a world of sugar,
A sweetness intimate as the water's clasp,
Howls in his sleep because the tight-rope
Trembles and shows the darkness beneath.
—The strutting show-off is terrified,
Dressed in his dress-suit, bulging his pants,
Trembles to think that his quivering meat
Must finally wince to nothing at all.

That inescapable animal walks with me,                    20
Has followed me since the black womb held,
Moves where I move, distorting my gesture,
A caricature, a swollen shadow,
A stupid clown of the spirit's motive,
Perplexes and affronts with his own darkness,
The secret life of belly and bone,
Opaque, too near, my private, yet unknown,
Stretches to embrace the very dear
With whom I would walk without him near,
Touches her grossly, although a word                      30
Would bare my heart and make me clear,
Stumbles, flounders, and strives to be fed
Dragging me with him in his mouthing care,
Amid the hundred million of his kind,
The scrimmage of appetite everywhere.

# Naming of Parts

HENRY REED

Today we have naming of parts. Yesterday,
We had daily cleaning. And tomorrow morning,
We shall have what to do after firing. But today,
Today we have naming of parts. Japonica
Glistens like coral in all of the neighboring gardens,
    And today we have naming of parts.


This is the lower sling swivel. And this
Is the upper sling swivel, whose use you will see,
When you are given your slings. And this is the piling swivel,
Which in your case you have not got. The branches          10
Hold in the gardens their silent, eloquent gestures,
    Which in our case we have not got.


This is the safety-catch, which is always released
With an easy flick of the thumb. And please do not let me
See anyone using his finger. You can do it quite easy
If you have any strength in your thumb. The blossoms
Are fragile and motionless, never letting anyone see
    Any of them using their finger.


And this you can see is the bolt. The purpose of this
Is to open the breech, as you see. We can slide it         20
Rapidly backwards and forwards: we call this
Easing the spring. And rapidly backwards and forwards
The early bees are assaulting and fumbling the flowers:
    They call it easing the Spring.


They call it easing the Spring: it is perfectly easy
If you have any strength in your thumb: like the bolt,
And the breech, and the cocking-piece, and the point of balance,
Which in our case we have not got; and the almond-blossom
Silent in all of the gardens and the bees going backwards and forwards,
    For today we have naming of parts.        30

# The Force That through the Green Fuse Drives the Flower

DYLAN THOMAS

The force that through the green fuse drives the flower
Drives my green age; that blasts the roots of trees
Is my destroyer.
And I am dumb to tell the crooked rose
My youth is bent by the same wintry fever.

The force that drives the water through the rocks
Drives my red blood; that dries the mouthing streams
Turns mine to wax.
And I am dumb to mouth unto my veins
How at the mountain spring the same mouth sucks.                    10

The hand that whirls the water in the pool
Stirs the quicksand; that ropes the blowing wind
Hauls my shroud sail.
And I am dumb to tell the hanging man
How of my clay is made the hangman's lime.[1]

The lips to time leech to the fountain head;
Love drips and gathers, but the fallen blood
Shall calm her sores.
And I am dumb to tell a weather's wind
How time has ticked a heaven round the stars.                    20

And I am dumb to tell the lover's tomb
How at my sheet goes the same crooked worm.

# In My Craft or Sullen Art

DYLAN THOMAS

In my craft or sullen art
Exercised in the still night
When only the moon rages
And the lovers lie abed
With all their griefs in their arms,
I labor by singing light

[1] Formerly used in burying executed prisoners in England to destroy the body rapidly.

Not for ambition or bread
Or the strut and trade of charms
On the ivory stages
But for the common wages                                    10
Of their most secret heart.

Not for the proud man apart
From the raging moon I write
On these spindrift pages
Nor for the towering dead
With their nightingales and psalms
But for the lovers, their arms
Round the griefs of the ages,
Who pay no praise or wages
Nor heed my craft or art.                                    20

# Do Not Go Gentle into That Good Night

DYLAN THOMAS

Do not go gentle into that good night,
Old age should burn and rave at close of day;
Rage, rage against the dying of the light.

Though wise men at their end know dark is right,
Because their words had forked no lightning they
Do not go gentle into that good night.

Good men, the last wave by, crying how bright
Their frail deeds might have danced in a green bay,
Rage, rage against the dying of the light.

Wild men who caught and sang the sun in flight,          10
And learn, too late, they grieved it on its way,
Do not go gentle into that good night.

Grave men, near death, who see with blinding sight
Blind eyes could blaze like meteors and be gay,
Rage, rage against the dying of the light.

And you, my father, there on the sad height,
Curse, bless, me now with your fierce tears, I pray.
Do not go gentle into that good night.
Rage, rage against the dying of the light.

# A Song in the Front Yard

GWENDOLYN BROOKS

I've stayed in the front yard all my life.
I want a peek at the back
Where it's rough and untended and hungry weed grows.
A girl gets sick of a rose.

I want to go in the back yard now
And maybe down the alley,
To where the charity children play.
I want a good time today.

They do some wonderful things.
They have some wonderful fun.                                    10
My mother sneers, but I say it's fine
How they don't have to go in at quarter to nine.
My mother, she tells me that Johnnie Mae
Will grow up to be a bad woman.
That George'll be taken to Jail soon or late
(On account of last winter he sold our back gate).

But I say it's fine. Honest, I do.
And I'd like to be a bad woman, too,
And wear the brave stockings of night-black lace
And strut down the streets with paint on my face.        20

# We Real Cool

**The Pool Players.**
**Seven at the Golden Shovel.**

GWENDOLYN BROOKS

We real cool. We
Left school. We

Lurk late. We
Strike straight. We

Sing sin. We
Thin gin. We

Jazz June. We
Die soon.

# New Year's Eve

ROBERT LOWELL

By miracle, I left the party half
an hour behind you, reached home five hours drunker,
imagining I would live a million years,
a million quarts drunker than the gods of Jutland—
live through another life and two more wives.
Life is too short to silver over this tarnish.
The gods, employed to haunt and punish husbands,
have no hand for trigger-fine distinctions,
their myopia makes all error mortal. . . .
My Darling, prickly hedgehog of the hearth,                    10
chocolates, cherries, hairshirt, pinks and glass—
when we joined in the sublime blindness of courtship,
loving lost all its vice with half its virtue.
Cards will never be dealt to us fairly again.

# Dog

LAWRENCE FERLINGHETTI

The dog trots freely in the street
and sees reality
and the things he sees
are bigger than himself
and the things he sees
are his reality
Drunks in doorways
Moons on trees
The dog trots freely thru the street
and the things he sees                                          10
are smaller than himself
Fish on newsprint
Ants in holes
Chickens in Chinatown windows
their heads a block away
The dog trots freely in the street
and the things he smells
smell something like himself
The dog trots freely in the street
past puddles and babies                                         20
cats and cigars
poolrooms and policemen

He doesn't hate cops
He merely has no use for them
and he goes past them
and past the dead cows hung up whole
in front of the San Francisco Meat Market
He would rather eat a tender cow
than a tough policeman
though either might do                                          30
And he goes past the Romeo Ravioli Factory
and past Coit's Tower
and past Congressman Doyle
He's afraid of Coit's Tower
but he's not afraid of Congressman Doyle
although what he hears is very discouraging
very depressing
very absurd
to a sad young dog like himself
to a serious dog like himself                                   40
But he has his own free world to live in
His own fleas to eat
He will not be muzzled
Congressman Doyle is just another
fire hydrant
to him
The dog trots freely in the street
and has his own dog's life to live
and to think about
and to reflect upon                                             50
touching and tasting and testing everything
investigating everything
without benefit of perjury
a real realist
with a real tale to tell
and a real tail to tell it with
a real live
          barking
                    democratic dog
engaged in real                                                 60
                    free enterprise
with something to say
                    about ontology
something to say
          about reality
                    and how to see it
                              and how to hear it
with his head cocked sideways
          at streetcorners

as if he is just about to have                                            70
                    his picture taken
                                for Victor Records
            listening for
                        His Master's Voice
        and looking
                    like a living questionmark
                                into the
                            great gramaphone
                        of puzzling existence
        with its wondrous hollow horn
                which always seems                                80
            just about to spout forth
                            some Victorious answer
                            to everything


# The May Day Dancing

HOWARD NEMEROV

The kindergarten children first come forth
In couples dressed as little brides and grooms.
By dancing in, by dancing round and out,
They braid the Maypole with a double thread;
Keep time, keep faith, is what the music says.

The corporal piano now leads out
Successively the older boys and girls,
Grade after grade, all for the dancing paired,
All dressed in the fashion of forgotten folk;
Those nymphs and shepherds, maybe, never were.                   10

And all the parents standing in a ring,
With cameras some, and some with only eyes,
Attend to the dancing's measurable rule
Bemused, or hypnotized, so that they see
Not seven classes of children, but only one,

One class of children seven times again
That ever enters on the dancing floor
One year advanced in their compliant skill
To patterns ever with more varied styles
Clothing the naked order of the bass.                            20

Some here relate the May with wanton rites,
Some with the Haymarket Riots,[1] some with nothing
Beyond the present scene and circumstance
Which by the camera's thin incisive blade
They hope to take a frozen section through,

Keeping their child with one foot on the ground
And one foot off, and with a solemn face
Or one bewildered between grin and tears,
As many times repeating time and faith
He follows the compulsions of the dance                30

Around the brilliant morning with the sun,
The dance that leads him out to bring him home,
The May Day dance that tramples down the grass
And raises dust, that braids a double thread
Around the pole, in the great room of the sun.


# Toads

PHILIP LARKIN

What should I let the toad *work*
    Squat on my life?
Can't I use my wit as a pitchfork
    And drive the brute off?

Six days of the week it soils
    With its sickening poison—
Just for paying a few bills!
    That's out of proportion.

Lots of folk live on their wits:
    Lecturers, lispers,                                    10
Losels,° loblolly-men,° louts—                    loafers/louts
    They don't end as paupers;

Lots of folk live up lanes
    With fires in a bucket,
Eat windfalls and tinned sardines—
    They seem to like it.

---

[1] In Chicago in 1886; an anarchists' meeting in Haymarket Square was being broken up
by the police when a bomb went off, killing seven policemen.

Their nippers have got bare feet,
   Their unspeakable wives
Are skinny as whippets—and yet
   No one actually *starves*.                                                    20

Ah, were I courageous enough
   To shout *Stuff your pension!*
But I know, all too well, that's the stuff
   That dreams are made on:

For something sufficiently toad-like
   Squats in me, too;
Its hunkers are heavy as hard luck,
   And cold as snow,

And will never allow me to blarney
   My way to getting                                                            30
The fame and the girl and the money
   All at one sitting.

I don't say, one bodies the other
   One's spiritual truth;
But I do say it's hard to lose either,
   When you have both.


# Buckdancer's Choice

JAMES DICKEY

So I would hear out those lungs,
The air split into nine levels,
Some gift of tongues of the whistler

In the invalid's bed: my mother,
Warbling all day to herself
The thousand variations of one song;

It is called Buckdancer's Choice.
For years, they have all been dying
Out, the classic buck-and-wing° men                          *a tapdance*

Of traveling minstrel shows;                                            10
With them also an old woman
Was dying of breathless angina,

Yet still found breath enough
To whistle up in my head
A sight like a one-man band,

Freed black, with cymbals at heel,
An ex-slave who thrivingly danced
To the ring of his own clashing light

Through the thousand variations of one song
All day to my mother's prone music,                              20
The invalid's warbler's note,

While I crept close to the wall
Sock-footed, to hear the sounds alter,
Her tongue like a mockingbird's break

Through stratum after stratum of a tone
Proclaiming what choices there are
For the last dancers of their kind,

For ill women and for all slaves
Of death, and children enchanted at walls
With a brass-beating glow underfoot,                             30

Not dancing but nearly risen
Through barnlike, theatrelike houses
On the wings of the buck and wing.


# The Dover Bitch[1]

## A Criticism of Life

ANTHONY HECHT

So there stood Matthew Arnold and this girl
With the cliffs of England crumbling away behind them,
And he said to her, "Try to be true to me,
And I'll do the same for you, for things are bad
All over, etc., etc."
Well now, I knew this girl. It's true she had read
Sophocles in a fairly good translation
And caught that bitter allusion to the sea,
But all the time he was talking she had in mind

[1] Compare Matthew Arnold, "Dover Beach."

The notion of what his whiskers would feel like                    10
On the back of her neck. She told me later on
That after a while she got to looking out
At the lights across the channel, and really felt sad,
Thinking of all the wine and enormous beds
And blandishments in French and the perfumes.
And then she got really angry. To have been brought
All the way down from London, and then be addressed
As a sort of mournful cosmic last resort
Is really tough on a girl, and she was pretty.
Anyway, she watched him pace the room                              20
And finger his watch-chain and seem to sweat a bit,
And then she said one or two unprintable things.
But you mustn't judge her by that. What I mean to say is,
She's really all right. I still see her once in a while
And she always treats me right. We have a drink
And I give her a good time, and perhaps it's a year
Before I see her again, but there she is,
Running to fat, but dependable as they come.
And sometimes I bring her a bottle of *Nuit d'Amour.*

# In Mind

DENISE LEVERTOV

There's in my mind a woman
of innocence, unadorned but

fair-featured, and smelling of
apples or grass. She wears

a utopian smock or shift, her hair
is light brown and smooth, and she

is kind and very clean without
ostentation—
                        but she has
no imagination.                                                    10
                        And there's a
turbulent moon-ridden girl

or old woman, or both,
dressed in opals and rags, feathers

and torn taffeta,
who knows strange songs—

but she is not kind.


## The Great Society[1]

ROBERT BLY

Dentists continue to water their lawns even in the rain;
Hands developed with terrible labor by apes
Hang from the sleeves of evangelists;
There are murdered kings in the light-bulbs outside movie theaters;
The coffins of the poor are hibernating in piles of new tires.

The janitor sits troubled by the boiler,
And the hotel keeper shuffles the cards of insanity.
The President dreams of invading Cuba.
Bushes are growing over the outdoor grills,
Vines over the yachts and the leather seats.                                    10

The city broods over ash cans and darkening mortar.
On the far shore, at Coney Island, dark children
Play on the chilling beach: a sprig of black seaweed,
Shells, a skyful of birds,
While the mayor sits with his head in his hands.


## A Supermarket in California

ALLEN GINSBERG

   What thoughts I have of you tonight, Walt Whitman, for I walked down the
sidestreets under the trees with a headache self-conscious looking at the full
moon.
   In my hungry fatigue, and shopping for images, I went into the neon fruit
supermarket, dreaming of your enumerations!

[1] Lyndon B. Johnson's campaign theme in the Presidential election of 1964.

What peaches and what penumbras! Whole families shopping at night! Aisles full of husbands! Wives in the avocados, babies in the tomatoes!—and you, Garcia Lorca,[1] what were you doing down by the watermelons?

I saw you, Walt Whitman, childless, lonely old grubber, poking among the meats in the refrigerator and eyeing the grocery boys.

I heard you asking questions of each: Who killed the pork chops? What price bananas? Are you my Angel?

I wandered in and out of the brilliant stacks of cans following you, and followed in my imagination by the store detective.

We strode down the open corridors together in our solitary fancy tasting artichokes, possessing every frozen delicacy, and never passing the cashier.

Where are we going, Walt Whitman? The doors close in an hour. Which way does your beard point tonight?

(I touch your book and dream of our odyssey in the supermarket and feel absurd.)

Will we walk all night through solitary streets? The trees add shade to shade, lights out in the houses, we'll both be lonely.

Will we stroll dreaming of the lost America of love past blue automobiles in driveways, home to our silent cottage?

Ah, dear father, graybeard, lonely old courage-teacher, what America did you have when Charon[2] quit poling his ferry and you got out on a smoking bank and stood watching the boat disappear on the black waters of Lethe?

# The Correspondence School Instructor Says Goodbye to His Poetry Students

GALWAY KINNELL

Goodbye, lady in Bangor, who sent me
snapshots of yourself, after definitely hinting
you were beautiful; goodbye,
Miami Beach urologist, who enclosed plain
brown envelopes for the return of your *very*
"Clinical Sonnets"; goodbye, manufacturer
of brassieres on the Coast, whose eclogues
give the fullest treatment in literature yet
to the sagging breast motif; goodbye, you in San Quentin,
who wrote, "Being German my hero is Hitler,"                    10

[1] Modern Spanish poet, assassinated in 1936 at the beginning of the Spanish Civil War.
[2] Mythical ferryman who rows the souls of the dead across Lethe, the black river of forgetfulness, to the underworld.

instead of "Sincerely yours," at the end of long,
neat-scripted letters demolishing
the pre-Raphaelites:[1]

I swear to you, it was just my way
of cheering myself up, as I licked
the stamped, self-addressed envelopes,
the game I had
of trying to guess which one of you, this time,
had poisoned his glue. I did care.
I did read each poem entire.                                                    20
I did say what I thought was the truth
in the mildest words I knew. And now,
in this poem, or chopped prose, not any better,
I realize, than those troubled lines
I kept sending back to you,
I have to say I am relieved it is over:
at the end I could feel only pity
for that urge toward more life
your poems kept smothering in words, the smell
of which, days later, would tingle                                             30
in your nostrils as new, God-given impulses
to write.

Goodbye,
you who are, for me, the postmarks again
of shattered towns—Xenia, Burnt Cabins, Hornell—
their loneliness
given away in poems, only their solitude kept.

## Their Week

W. S. MERWIN

The loneliness of Sundays grows
tall there as the light
and from it they weave
bells of different sizes
to hang in empty cupboards and in doorways
and from branches
like blossoms like fruit
and in barns

[1] Mid-nineteenth-century English poets and artists who sought to limit their work to
idealized, uplifting subjects.

and in each room like lamps
like the light                                                          10

they believe it was on a Sunday
that the animals were divided
so that the flood could happen
and on a Sunday that we were severed
from the animals
with a wound that never heals
but is still the gate where the nameless
cries out

they believe that everything
that is divided                                                         20
was divided on a Sunday
and they weave the bells
whose echoes
are all the days in the week

# Unknown Girl in the Maternity Ward

ANNE SEXTON

Child, the current of your breath is six days long.
You lie, a small knuckle on my white bed;
lie, fisted like a snail, so small and strong
at my breast. Your lips are animals; you are fed
with love. At first hunger is not wrong.
The nurses nod their caps; you are shepherded
down starch halls with the other unnested throng
in wheeling baskets. You tip like a cup; your head
moving to my touch. You sense the way we belong.
But this is an institution bed.                                         10
You will not know me very long.

The doctors are enamel. They want to know
the facts. They guess about the man who left me,
some pendulum soul, going the way men go
and leave you full of child. But our case history
stays blank. All I did was let you grow.
Now we are here for all the ward to see.
They thought I was strange, although
I never spoke a word. I burst empty
of you, letting you learn how the air is so.                            20

The doctors chart the riddle they ask of me
and I turn my head away. I do not know.

Yours is the only face I recognize.
Bone at my bone, you drink my answers in.
Six times a day I prize
your need, the animals of your lips, your skin
growing warm and plump. I see your eyes
lifting their tents. They are blue stones, they begin
to outgrow their moss. You blink in surprise
and I wonder what you can see, my funny kin,                    30
as you trouble my silence. I am a shelter of lies
Should I learn to speak again, or hopeless in
such sanity will I touch some face I recognize?

Down the hall the baskets start back. My arms
fit you like a sleeve, they hold
catkins of your willows, the wild bee farms
of your nerves, each muscle and fold
of your first days. Your old man's face disarms
the nurses. But the doctors return to scold
me. I speak. It is you my silence harms.                       40
I should have known; I should have told
them something to write down. My voice alarms
my throat. "Name of father—none." I hold
you and name you bastard in my arms.

And now that's that. There is nothing more
that I can say or lose.
Others have traded life before
and could not speak. I tighten to refuse
your owling eyes, my fragile visitor.
I touch your cheeks, like flowers. You bruise                  50
against me. We unlearn. I am a shore
rocking you off. You break from me. I choose
your only way, my small inheritor
and hand you off, trembling the selves we lose.
Go child, who is my sin and nothing more.


## Thomas Beemer Ashburton

HERBERT L. CARSON

I call to witness Thomas Beemer Ashburton
age 11

dead before age 12
of an enflamed appendix

he simply died, you see
of an enflamed appendix
at age 11, before age 12
although he had no such idea

nor had I such an idea
that last afternoon when we idly stoned                    10
the back windows of p.s. 27
then walked over to the park

down by where the wissahickon
was flowed into by the sewage outlet
where we peered into the yellow stream
browned by floating filth

then went our ways as the day waned
to homes, and hearths, and mothers
he age 11, not yet 12
to die of an enflamed appendix                             20

simply died, that's really it
wasn't there when roll was read
wasn't there when the thunderous voice
warned he knew who stoned the windows

wasn't there when I wandered to the wissahickon
far down from the big sewage outlet
threw a stone to ripple the gloss of its littered waters
destroy the dull gloss of the crystal stream

wasn't there as I stood above the wissahickon
that damned old, good old creek                            30
a swell place to swim in summer
skate in winter

wasn't there when I wondered
just what does really happen
when one is not yet age 12, just 11
and dies of an enflamed appendix

I call to witness Thomas Beemer Ashburton
dead of an enflamed appendix
to give expert testimony that I
was once age 11, not yet 12                                40

# London Is Full of Chickens on Electric Spits

PETER PORTER

London is full of chickens on electric spits,
 Cooking in windows where the public pass.
This, say the chickens, is their Auschwitz,
 And all poultry eaters are psychopaths.


# I Dream I'm the Death of Orpheus[1]

ADRIENNE RICH

I am walking rapidly through striations of light and dark thrown under an
 arcade.

I am a woman in the prime of life, with certain powers
and those powers severely limited
by authorities whose faces I rarely see.
I am a woman in the prime of life
driving her dead poet in a black Rolls-Royce
through a landscape of twilight and thorns.
A woman with a certain mission
which if obeyed to the letter will leave her intact.
A woman with the nerves of a panther
a woman with contacts among Hell's Angels[2]
a woman feeling the fullness of her powers
at the precise moment when she must not use them
a woman sworn to lucidity
who sees through the mayhem, the smoky fires
of these underground streets
her dead poet learning to walk backward against the wind
on the wrong side of the mirror

10

[1] Refers to the mysterious woman in Jean Cocteau's film, *Orphée*, who symbolizes the death of the musician Orpheus and leads him through a mirror into an underworld of ruined buildings, nearly deserted streets, and high winds.

[2] In the film, the woman who is the Death of Orpheus is often escorted, and sometimes represented, by motorcyclists in black leather.

# Both Sheep Are Gone

JOYE S. GIROUX

To kill is to be
killed,
     for no two are
separate—
        the bond of humanhood
binds
     each to each
            and
     all to all,
        forever.                                                          10
When madness overruns
civility,
     each bullet smashing
bone and brain,
        each
blade-rent gash disgorging crimson pain
on torn and shuddering flesh,
two are robbed
        of fruitful years
           forfeited.                                          20
Lost and slain,
        both sheep are gone
who once seemed safe
within the fold,
        and uneasy
is the slumber
of the flock.

# In Laughter

TED HUGHES

Cars collide and erupt luggage and babies
In laughter
The steamer upends and goes under saluting like a stuntman
In laughter
The nosediving aircraft concludes with a boom
In laughter
People's arms and legs fly off and fly on again
In laughter
The haggard mask on the bed rediscovers its pang

In laughter, in laughter                                        10
The meteorite crashes
With extraordinarily ill-luck on the pram

The ears and eyes are bundled up
Are folded up in the hair,
Wrapped in the carpet, the wallpaper, tied with the lampflex
Only the teeth work on
And the heart, dancing on in its open cave
Helpless on the strings of laughter

While the tears are nickel-plated and come through doors with a bang

And the wails stun with fear                                    20
And the bones
Jump from the torment flesh has to stay for

Stagger some distance and fall in full view

Still laughter scampers around on centipede boots
Still it runs all over on caterpillar tread
And rolls back onto the mattress, legs in the air
But it's only human

And finally it's had enough—enough!
And slowly sits up, exhausted,
And slowly starts to fasten buttons,                            30
With long pauses,

Like somebody the police have come for.


# The Snow on Saddle Mountain[1]

GARY SNYDER

The only thing that can be relied on
is the snow on Kurakake Mountain.
fields and woods
thawing, freezing, and thawing,
totally untrustworthy.
it's true, a great fuzzy windstorm
like yeast up there today, still
the only faint source of hope
is the snow on Kurakake mountain.

[1] A rendering of a poem by the modern Japanese poet Miyazawa Kenji.

# Lady Lazarus

SYLVIA PLATH

I have done it again.
One year in every ten
I manage it——

A sort of walking miracle, my skin
Bright as a Nazi lampshade,
My right foot

A paperweight,
My face a featureless, fine
Jew linen.

Peel off the napkin                                            10
O my enemy.
Do I terrify?——

The nose, the eye pits, the full set of teeth?
The sour breath
Will vanish in a day.

Soon, soon the flesh
The grave cave ate will be
At home on me

And I a smiling woman.
I am only thirty.                                              20
And like the cat I have nine times to die.

This is Number Three.
What a trash
To annihilate each decade.

What a million filaments.
The peanut-crunching crowd
Shoves in to see

Them unwrap me hand and foot——
The big strip tease.
Gentleman, ladies,                                             30

These are my hands,
My knees.
I may be skin and bone,

Nevertheless, I am the same, identical woman.
The first time it happened I was ten.
It was an accident.

The second time I meant
To last it out and not come back at all.
I rocked shut

As a seashell.                                                    40
They had to call and call
And pick the worms off me like sticky pearls.

Dying
Is an art, like everything else.
I do it exceptionally well.

I do it so it feels like hell.
I do it so it feels real.
I guess you could say I've a call.

It's easy enough to do it in a cell.
It's easy enough to do it and stay put.                          50
It's the theatrical

Comeback in broad day
To the same place, the same face, the same brute
Amused shout:

"A miracle!"
That knocks me out.
There is a charge

For the eyeing of my scars, there is a charge
For the hearing of my heart——
It really goes.                                                  60

And there is a charge, a very large charge,
For a word or a touch
Or a bit of blood

Or a piece of my hair or my clothes.
So, so, Herr Doktor.
So, Herr Enemy.

I am your opus,
I am your valuable,
The pure gold baby

That melts to a shriek.
I turn and burn.
Do not think I underestimate your great concern.                    70

Ash, ash—
You poke and stir.
Flesh, bone, there is nothing there——

A cake of soap,
A wedding ring,
A gold filling.

Herr God, Herr Lucifer,
Beware                                                             80
Beware.

Out of the ash
I rise with my red hair
And I eat men like air.


# Preface to a Twenty Volume Suicide Note

AMIRI BARAKA

       (FOR KELLIE JONES, BORN 16 MAY 1959)

Lately, I've become accustomed to the way
The ground opens up and envelopes me
Each time I go out to walk the dog.
Or the broad edged silly music the wind
Makes when I run for a bus . . .

Things have come to that.

And now, each night I count the stars,
And each night I get the same number.
And when they will not come to be counted,
I count the holes they leave.                                      10

Nobody sings anymore.

And then last night, I tiptoed up
To my daughter's room and heard her

Talking to someone, and when I opened
The door, there was no one there . . .
Only she on her knees, peeking into

Her own clasped hands.


# Steely Silence

DIANE WAKOSKI

If a man calls himself a poet
(and many do)
he is expected to charm you
with his speech.
Yet the time for speaking
is best
a formal time
and speech best
when prepared / for a purpose.
Dinner time is for eating                                            10
and afternoon for reading.
Night for sleep and love.
Most talk is simple communication
          "Pass the butter."
          "How do you get to the post office?"
          "What is your name?"
Yet talk is often created
where none need be.

Forgive me.
I have no light conversation.                                        20
Forgive me,
I have no literary or witty remarks.
My nature is dark
I am heavy to walk with
and silent in the company of friends.
I am limited to the subjects
most people don't care to discuss.
My tongue is my weapon.
I only use it
in moments of danger.                                               30
Forgive me then, for my silence.

It is a sign of trust.

# Ego Tripping

NIKKI GIOVANNI

*(there may be a reason why)*

I was born in the congo
I walked to the fertile crescent and built
    the sphinx
I designed a pyramid so tough that a star
      that only glows every one hundred years falls
      into the center giving divine perfect light
I am bad

I sat on the throne
    drinking nectar with allah
I got hot and sent an ice age to europe             10
    to cool my thirst
My oldest daughter is nefertiti[1]
    the tears from my birth pains
    created the nile
I am a beautiful woman

I gazed on the forest and burned
    out the sahara desert
    with a packet of goat's meat
    and a change of clothes
I crossed it in two hours                20
I am a gazelle so swift
    so swift you can't catch me

    For a birthday present when he was three
I gave my son hannibal an elephant
    He gave me rome for mother's day[2]
My strength flows ever on

My son noah built new/ark[3] and
I stood proudly at the helm
    as we sailed on a soft summer day

[1] Beautiful queen of Egypt, ca. fourteenth century B.C.

[2] General from the ancient North African nation of Carthage; campaigned in Italy successfully in the third century B.C., using elephants as transport to cross the Alps, but never actually conquered Rome.

[3] Also a special pronunciation of Newark (N.J.), which when this poem was written had just passed from Italian to Black political dominance.

I turned myself into myself and was                          30
    jesus
      men intone my loving name
      All praises All praises
I am the one who would save

I sowed diamonds in my back yard
My bowels deliver uranium
      the filings from my fingernails are
      semi-precious jewels
      On a trip north
I caught a cold and blew                                     40
My nose giving oil to the arab world
I am so hip even my errors are correct
I sailed west to reach east and had to round off
      the earth as I went
      The hair from my head thinned and gold was laid
      across three continents

I am so perfect so divine so ethereal so surreal
I cannot be comprehended
   except by my permission

I mean . . . I . . . can fly                                 50
    like a bird in the sky . . .


# A Blade of Grass

BRIAN PATTEN

You ask for a poem.
I offer you a blade of grass.
You say it is not good enough.
You ask for a poem.

I say this blade of grass will do.
It has dressed itself in frost,
It is more immediate
Than any image of my making.

You say it is not a poem,
It is a blade of grass and grass                             10
Is not quite good enough.
I offer you a blade of grass.

You are indignant.
You say it is too easy to offer grass.
It is absurd.
Anyone can offer a blade of grass.

You ask for a poem.
And so I write you a tragedy about
How a blade of grass
Becomes more and more difficult to offer,                    20

And about how as you grow older
A blade of grass
Becomes more difficult to accept.


# Another Afterword on Hurricane Jackson

CARL JUDSON LAUNIUS

When Hurricane left the fight game for good,
he took the dog-eared wages of his trade
and laid down cash for a shoeshine box,
and worked the walks by Grand Central Station.

He got a reputation for fast hands,                          5
and a thorough knowledge of the combinations:
Black polish for shoes which were black;
Brown polish for shoes which were brown;
Neutral polish for a classy finish.

When the last Long Island club car                          10
rumbled away to martinis and the *Times*,
Hurricane sometimes threw a vague look
northward toward Madison Square,
where he saw through cock-eyes a jab-and-hook
connect in the grey sky, and dreams                         15
flurried in the dancing lights
of crosstown buses, counting out the nights.

# Writing

PART V **Short**

# Papers

# About

# Literature

# Introduction

Students just learning to read literature closely are sometimes worried when asked to write papers using their new knowledge. Even short papers about literature are a kind of literary criticism, and literary criticism seems to require a great deal of sophistication, special knowledge, and originality. If you are not going to make a career in the study or teaching of literature—and the odds are that you have other plans—you may feel as unsure of yourself attacking such an assignment as a weekend tennis hacker going up against a seasoned professional.

What you should realize is that the purpose of writing papers about literature in an introductory course is not to produce original contributions to literary scholarship. The exercise is intended to help you understand more fully what a particular story, play, or poem means, and how it achieves its effects. And this kind of understanding is really all that most authors hope for in the first place. Few writers write for a special, scholarly audience. In fact, many writers, like most readers, have been unable to give themselves to literature full-time. The poet William Carlos Williams was a doctor with a busy general practice, and his contemporary Wallace Stevens worked for an insurance company. They, like most writers, ask only to be read with intelligent appreciation and understanding by people like you.

Nevertheless, you may still wonder why it is necessary to write about literature. Isn't it enough to arrive at an understanding in one's own mind, or to offer ideas in discussions with other readers? No one would question that these activities can be productive, but the process of writing offers you something more: the opportunity to organize and record your ideas so that you can look at them and test them more closely. Often when you think about something, your mind seems to work in disjointed flashes of understanding, leaving you the difficulty of putting all your insights together in a coherent form. And while discussion does get ideas out of your head and into the air, you can all too easily get sidetracked or forget important details. Putting your thoughts down on paper somehow helps to reveal any fuzzy or incomplete ideas, and often you will discover new things you want to say about a work as a result of the writing process itself. Finally, when you have to write in complete sentences and structured paragraphs, and to order your thoughts into some logical or persuasive sequence for someone else to read, you naturally think more carefully; you examine both your subject and the way you have dealt with it.

As you approach the task of writing on a literary topic, you should know that there are certain things you need not do. First, don't adopt any special, lofty, or high-sounding tone or style. Academese isn't necessary. In fact, by trying to impress your readers you will only bore them. Likewise, don't try to create a literary work of your own. It is easy to fall into the trap of imitating the author you are writing about. Straightforward expository prose, with clear and precise sentences arranged in a logical sequence, will do the job. The sentences should have subjects and verbs, and the paragraphs should have clear topic sentences sensibly developed by a sufficient number of specific details. Your readers will appreciate your clarity as well as your honesty. Finally, don't equate writing good papers with writing long papers. Few of the papers we suggest in the following sections need be longer than five or six paragraphs, and a good many can be completed in a single paragraph. Your goal should be to begin with a limited topic—one that can be fully treated in a relatively brief space—and then say what you have to say with crispness and precision.

## Writing About Short Stories, Novellas, and Plays

Most papers that you are likely to write about a short story, novella, or play in an introduction-to-literature course will in some way treat one or more of the essential elements first discussed in the introduction to the short story section and further dealt with in both the novella and drama sections. As you will recall, these elements include plot; setting; character; tone, mood, and emotion; irony; imagery and symbolism; theme; and point of view. Plot is a good place to begin thinking about how to write a paper on a literary topic.

PLOT

Probably the most basic paper you can write is a plot summary. To prepare a decent plot summary, you must first read the story or play very carefully, perhaps two or three times, and take notes. Afterwards, as you are organizing the paper, you will probably have to consult the work again from time to time for specific information. Although some stories and full-length plays are too long and complex to be treated on a single page, the plots of many stories and one-act plays can be summarized adequately in a few paragraphs.

Actually, there are two fundamental types of plot summaries: the one that recounts what happened, and nothing more; and the one that makes some observation or judgment at the beginning and then substantiates the judgment by presenting specifically chosen details of the plot. This second type is sometimes called a plot analysis. Analysis is a type of exposition that separates a topic or subject into component parts and then shows, for the purpose of an overall understanding, how each part relates to the whole. You can analyze almost anything about a literary work—plot, setting, character, symbolism, theme, irony—by breaking the topic down into manageable parts and then dealing with those parts one by one.

To see how the two types of plot summaries differ, consider this pair of opening sentences for two summaries of Richard Connell's story "The Most Dangerous Game." If you are doing a summary that only recounts the plot, your first sentence should be something like the following:

> As the story opens, Sanger Rainsford, a famous hunter and author, and his old friend Whitney are standing on the deck of a yacht discussing a mysterious island—Ship-Trap Island—as the boat passes near the place on a "moonless Caribbean night."

The remainder of this summary will simply tell what happens in the story. (Many students, however, will want to end such a paper with a concluding judgment of their own.) On the other hand, for a plot summary that offers a little analysis, your opening sentence might read something like this:

"The Most Dangerous Game" is elaborately plotted for a short story, and the piece is carefully structured to generate great suspense for the reader.

The remainder of this summary would detail pertinent events of the plot to show how the story does generate great suspense for the reader.

The opening sentence for the second type of summary is sometimes called a thesis statement. This is another name for a main-idea sentence—that is, a sentence telling what the paper will focus upon or try to prove.

Since "The Most Dangerous Game" is obviously too long to be summarized in a single paragraph, sensible paragraph divisions become important. We would suggest a separate paragraph for each of the following plot sections: the opening episode, while Rainsford is still on the yacht; the period between the time Rainsford falls into the water and first meets General Zaroff; the interval at the chateau before the hunt; all four hunting episodes; and the conclusion, wherein the hunted becomes the hunter. Thus, five paragraphs can accommodate the plot summary.

When you write a plot summary of either type, include as much important specific information as you can; and *be accurate*. When characters have names, use those names, rather than the characters' social roles or positions—"Ivan" rather than "the servant." Be sure to check dates (days) and time spans as well as locations. Nothing is more irritating to the reader who knows the story than a plot summary in which the wrong character is stoned to death in the wrong place or at the wrong time. Your plot summary should include enough connective words and phrases to indicate the passage of time—for example, "after a short time," "at the same time," "in the meantime," "later on," "meanwhile," "shortly thereafter," and "subsequently."

The following sentences are for you to use as opening sentences or thesis statements for plot summaries of some of the stories, novellas, and plays in the text. You may, however, wish to devise your own opening statements for either straight summaries or plot analyses of these works.

1. "By the Waters of Babylon" is an eerie story of humankind's starting over again after a nuclear holocaust.

2. Most of what takes place in "The Lottery Ticket" occurs in the minds of Ivan Dmitritch and his wife, Masha.

3. W. W. Jacobs's "The Monkey's Paw" begins, innocently enough, with a chess game between Mr. White and Herbert, his son.

4. The events of "A Summer Tragedy" take place within a brief period of time on a single afternoon.

5. "The Stone Boy" tells the story of how a young boy is forever alienated from other people as a result of the behavior of unperceptive adults, especially his mother, following a family calamity.

6. "The Shades of Spring" relates some unexpected revelations to a man who has been clinging to romantic illusions about the sweetheart of his youth.

7. "The Wooing of Ariadne" presents a robust story of romantic victory through surrender.

8. In Melville's *Bartleby, the Scrivener*, Bartleby stops working gradually, not all at once.

9. *Oedipus Rex* provides an almost perfect example of what can be called a "discovery" plot.

10. In Shakespeare's *Othello*, Othello goes from love to jealousy to murder with unbelievable speed.

11. The events presented in Susan Glaspell's play *Trifles* could occur in real life in about the same span of time required to dramatize them on the stage.

12. *Day of Absence* cleverly employs a fantastic dramatic situation to deal with a deadly serious social situation in real life.

Not all papers that deal with plot need be plot summaries. In fact, as you will recall from earlier introductions, there are many plot elements that may be worth considering in a paper. Following are some of these elements:

| | |
|---|---|
| protagonist | multiple struggle |
| antagonist | crisis situation |
| conflict | climax |
| precipitating incident | dilemma |
| foreshadowing | flashbacks |
| balancing of forces | denouement |

Writing a short paper that considers one of these items need not be any more difficult than doing a plot summary. First, however, you have to make up your mind whether your paper is simply going to point out the presence of some element in the work, or whether you are going to analyze that element. For example, consider the following first sentences for two papers dealing with antagonists in Stephen Vincent Benét's "By the Waters of Babylon":

1. John, the young priest of the Hill People, encounters a variety of antagonists on his journey to the Place of the Gods.

2. It is principally through John's reactions to encounters with a variety of antagonists that the young priest's character is revealed.

The first sentence sets up a situation wherein the remainder of the paper can simply describe the antagonists that John encounters. This statement is much like the opening sentence in a plot summary that only recounts the important events of plot. The second sentence, however, is really a thesis statement for a paper that would go on to analyze the antagonists in the story, breaking the topic down into separate considerations of each encounter with an antagonist, and pointing out how each encounter serves to reveal some important quality in John's character.

The key to writing the paper that would follow either of these opening sentences is, first, an awareness of what the opening sentence promises you will do and, second, the careful presentation of concrete details from the story to fulfill that promise. The arrangement of these details should follow a logical sequence, and the logic of the sequence should be obvious to your reader. Nothing should be included in the paper that does not directly contribute to substantiating your opening sentence.

Following are a few opening sentences, some of them thesis statements, which you can use in papers treating these elements of plot as they occur in some of this book's stories, novellas, and plays·

1. The protagonist in "The Most Dangerous Game" is Sanger Rainsford, not General Zaroff.

2. Because the story involves a double plot, there are actually two protagonists in Irwin Shaw's "The Dry Rock."

3. In Donald Barthelme's "Report," the Software Man hasn't a chance against the engineers.

4. Marko's antagonists in "The Wooing of Ariadne" include almost the entire Greek community.

5. Iago proves himself a formidable antagonist in William Shakespeare's *Othello.*

6. The conflict between Ivan Dmitritch and his wife in "The Lottery Ticket" has been going on for a long time.

7. The struggle in *Oedipus Rex* is uneven because a mortal is pitted against fate.

8. The central conflict in Thomas Holcroft's melodrama *A Tale of Mystery* is between good and evil.

9. The precipitating incident in *Bartleby, the Scrivener* actually takes place before the story begins.

10. Ironic foreshadowing is an especially important element of "The Monkey's Paw."

11. In "The Shades of Spring," balancing of forces renders both Syson and Arthur Pilbeam equally vulnerable to Hilda's independence.

12. In "The Stone Boy," little Arnold faces a multiple struggle as he tries to deal with his own internal trauma following the accidental shooting of Eugie and the brutal response of the adults around him.

13. The police station scene in "The Dry Rock" is an elaborately staged crisis situation.

14. The climax in "The Stone Boy" does not occur when Arnold shoots Eugie.

15. The climax in Guy de Maupassant's story "The Necklace" does not occur when Mme. Loisel discovers that the borrowed necklace has been lost.

16. The funniest moment of Anton Chekhov's one-act play *A Marriage Proposal* occurs precisely at the climax of the work.

17. In James Joyce's "The Boarding House," Bob Doran faces a dilemma as he awaits his Sunday meeting with Mrs. Mooney as a result of his affair with Polly.

18. In "The Most Dangerous Game," Sanger Rainsford actually faces a series of dilemmas.

19. In *Noon Wine,* Mr. Thompson faces a dilemma of sorts when he realizes what Homer T. Hatch intends to do to Olaf Helton.

20. As Dorothy Parker's story "You Were Perfectly Fine" ends, Peter faces a dilemma that he is unlikely ever to sort out for himself.

21. James T. Farrell's "Studs" includes several important flashbacks.

22. The flashbacks in "The Wooing of Ariadne" are detailed by the narrator himself.

23. The denouement in "The Shades of Spring" involves Syson over-hearing a conversation between Arthur Pilbeam and Hilda.

24. The denouement of "The Dry Rock" reveals the conclusion of the story's second plot.

25. In the denouement of Shakespeare's *Othello,* all of the leading characters meet their ends.


## SETTING

When writing about setting, you should keep in mind the three basic ways writers use it: to provide a scenic backdrop, to help establish mood and atmosphere, and to represent symbolically the thoughts and emotions of characters. You should understand that none of these uses is necessarily exclusive of the others. Quite often, your paper on setting will also need to say a thing or two about tone and mood, because authors so often use setting as a device for creating emotional as well as physical atmosphere.

A work's physical setting may be divided into two parts—the immediate setting and the greater setting. For example, the immediate setting of Katharine Brush's "Night Club" is the women's dressing room in the Club Français, and the greater setting is the 1920s in the United States. Similarly, the immediate setting of Arthur Miller's *A Memory of Two Mondays* is a Manhattan warehouse for automobile parts, and the greater setting is the Great Depression of the 1930s. The relation between a work's immediate and greater settings and its emotional atmosphere can be very intricate.

As you begin your paper on setting, be sure that your opening sentence tells the reader whether you intend to cover the entire setting of a work or simply to focus on certain important details. And again, be sure an analysis of setting begins with a thesis statement. Following are a few suggested opening sentences for papers that focus on setting:

1. In "The Most Dangerous Game," the setting of Ship-Trap Island provides a perfect arena for the confrontation between Sanger Rainsford and General Zaroff.

2. The weather is an important part of setting in "The Monkey's Paw."

3. Nightfall is an important element of setting in Pär Lagerkvist's "Father and I."

4. The last years of the old West provide the greater setting for Stephen Crane's "The Bride Comes to Yellow Sky."

5. "The Wooing of Ariadne" is largely a work about an ethnic neighborhood.

6. In "The Tryst," various items of setting are identified with either Akulína or Alexándrovitch, the two characters in conflict with each other.

7. In "The Boarding House," the attitudes and actions of Mrs. Mooney, Bob Doran, and Polly are essentially the result of the social and religious climate of Dublin at the time the story takes place.

8. The legal-financial district of nineteenth-century New York provides the greater setting for Melville's *Bartleby, the Scrivener*.

9. The grimness of life on a Texas farm at the turn of the century is central to an understanding of Katherine Anne Porter's *Noon Wine*.

10. Douglas Turner Ward's *A Day of Absence* could hardly have been set anywhere but in a small town in the American South.

## CHARACTER

Most papers that treat character will in some way focus on one or more of the three most important qualities of good characterization: consistency, motivation, and plausibility. Such papers usually try to show whether major characters do or do not possess these qualities. Other types of character papers analyze the personality of an important character or examine the relationships among characters or groups of characters.

To begin a character analysis, you should try to answer such questions as the following:

What, if anything, does the author say directly about the character's personality? How does the character behave? What sort of thoughts go through his or her mind?

What is the character's background? What does the character look like? What sort of surroundings does the character live in? What generally is his or her life style?

How does the character regard the other people in the story or play? What do these other people think of him or her? Are their opinions accurate?

What changes, if any, does the character undergo during the course of the story or play? Why do these changes occur? Is there any apparent reason for the sequence of these changes?

Having satisfied yourself with answers to such questions as these, you should then write a general statement about the character you are analyzing. This statement will serve as your thesis statement and indicate the approach your paper will take. For example, if you were doing a character analysis of Tarloff, the taxi driver in "The Dry Rock," your thesis statement might read as follows:

> Although Tarloff is clearly victimized by Rusk at the beginning of the story, the cabby's rigid desire for recrimination suggests that the man takes both life and himself a little too seriously.

Then, the remainder of your paper should carefully present—in a logical sequence—a series of specific incidents, statements, actions, or other details from the story to substantiate your opening evaluation of Tarloff's character.

Some of the following suggested opening sentences are intended for papers of character analysis, some for papers that examine relationships between characters, and some for papers that simply recount the revelation of character in a story or play:

1. In "The Most Dangerous Game," General Zaroff is a little too singly motivated to be considered a plausible character.

2. Scattered throughout "The Most Dangerous Game" are many hints that Sanger Rainsford and General Zaroff are not such dissimilar individuals after all.

3. Mrs. Brady, the central character in Katharine Brush's "Night Club," is a very unperceptive person.

4. In Shakespeare's *Othello*, Iago is always ready to explain his motivation, but his reasons are never quite plausible.

5. In "The Necklace," Mme. Loisel undergoes a transformation of her character after the borrowed necklace is lost.

6. Dr. Rankin, the central character in John Collier's "De Mortuis," seems to have been consistently gullible all of his life.

7. In "The Stone Boy," the relationship between Arnold and Eugie before the shooting was entirely normal and psychologically healthy.

8. In "The Shades of Spring," there is a mixture of love and hate in the relationship between Syson and Hilda.

9. In "The Bride Comes to Yellow Sky," Stephen Crane manages to make the reader sympathize with a stock character.

10. From the very beginning of "The Wooing of Ariadne," there is evidence that Ariadne, despite her abrasive behavior, really wants to be courted.

11. Viktór Alexándrovitch, the repugnant valet in "The Tryst," has made himself into a caricature of his master.

12. In *Bartleby, the Scrivener*, Bartleby's strange behavior may have been motivated, in part at least, by the conditions of his employment.

13. Oedipus seems to be one of those persons whom fate has chosen to destroy.

14. Although Othello is called "noble," and has noble qualities, there is much in his character that is base.

15. Emilia, the wife of Iago, shows a few sparks of feminist consciousness.

16. Lomov, the neurotic suitor in *A Marriage Proposal*, is an outstanding example of a minor comic hero.

17. The fact that Natalia is willing to consider Lomov's marriage proposal says much about her view of a woman's place in society.

18. The characters in *The Importance of Being Earnest* are humorous presentations of types rather than plausible people.

19. What separates Bert from the other characters in *A Memory of Two Mondays* is mainly that he wishes to control his own life.

20. The characters in *The Gap* are intended to be absurd caricatures.

## TONE, MOOD, AND EMOTION

When writing a paper about tone, mood, or emotion, keep in mind that tone generally encompasses the author's attitude toward the work, mood refers to the predominating atmosphere of the work itself, and emotion may include both the emotions experienced by the characters and those experienced by readers or theatergoers. Once again, be sure that your opening sentence tells the reader whether you are going to present an analysis, or whether you intend only to point out the presence in the work of some element of tone, mood, or emotion. Here are a few suggested opening sentences, some of which are thesis statements for analytical papers:

1. The humorous tone in which "The Loudest Voice" is narrated is so dominant that the story's serious subject is easy to overlook.

2. The tone of John Collier's "De Mortuis" is so flippant that the reader almost laughs as Dr. Rankin prepares to murder his wife.

3. The narrator's tone in "The Tryst" changes each time the focus shifts from Akulína to Alexándrovitch.

4. The psalm-like sentence structure used by Stephen Vincent Benét in "By the Waters of Babylon" greatly contributes to the story's strange mood.

5. The emotional atmosphere of Richard Connell's "The Most Dangerous Game" becomes increasingly intense as Rainsford's chances for survival appear to worsen.

6. The setting of Arthur Miller's *A Memory of Two Mondays* contributes greatly to the play's mood.

7. Montresor's emotional state in "The Cask of Amontillado" is cleverly reflected in the description of the catacombs.

8. In Alice Walker's "To Hell with Dying," the narrator's emotional attachment to Mr. Sweet at times becomes almost sexual.

9. Arna Bontemps's "A Summer Tragedy" is a good example of a story that provokes greater emotional intensity in the reader than is demonstrated by either of the work's two major characters.

10. In "The Stone Boy," Arnold's inability to express his own emotions after accidentally shooting his brother contributes to the reader's emotional response to the story.

11. The emotional extravagance of Thomas Holcroft's melodrama *A Tale of Mystery* makes modern readers laugh rather than believe in the characters' emotions.

12. The fact that Mr. and Mrs. White never actually see the mutilated body of Herbert outside their door actually increases the reader's emotional response to W. W. Jacobs's "The Monkey's Paw."

## IRONY

For a paper on irony, you should distinguish among the types of irony used in the work you are considering. Three important types are verbal irony, dramatic irony, and irony of plot. Virtually any element of a story or play can be used ironically, so long as there is a clear discrepancy between appearance and reality. For example, it is ironic that in "The Most Dangerous Game" Sanger Rainsford, one of the world's most skillful big game hunters, becomes one of the world's most skillful hunted creatures. Similarly, in "The Wooing of Ariadne" it is ironic that Marko wins Ariadne just when he gives up his pursuit and admits he has failed. And in *Othello* it is ironic that the handkerchief Othello has given Desdemona as a token of his love for her becomes the crucial, though false, evidence that she has been unfaithful to him.

A paper on irony is always analytical because it must discuss the important relation between appearance and reality. Your paper should begin by clearly stating what the irony is that you plan to talk about. (Students are sometimes tempted to let their readers discover the irony as the paper moves along. This technique might be appropriate if you were writing a story or a play, but it is not suitable in a critical paper.) After stating what the irony is, tell how it is ironic: explain the contrast between apparent truth and real truth. Finally, if you choose, explain the effect of the irony on the whole work.

Following are a few suggested opening sentences for papers focusing on one or another type of irony:

1. It is ironic that John, the young priest of the Hill People in "By the Waters of Babylon," discovers that the "gods" were only men.

2. In "The Lottery Ticket," it is grimly ironic that an apparent chance for comfortable financial security results in Ivan and Masha realizing that they dislike each other.

3. As a result of Mrs. Brady's lack of perception, "Night Club" includes several incidents of dramatic irony.

4. The supreme irony in "The Monkey's Paw" is that Mr. White gets his wish for 200 pounds, but at the expense of his son's life.

5. The beauty of the day on which Jeff and Jennie Patton commit suicide in "A Summer Tragedy" may be taken as an example of irony of setting.

6. Without the irony that the lost necklace was made of paste, Maupassant's "The Necklace" would be a story of little interest.

7. In *Trifles* there is an overriding irony resulting from who discovers the truth about the murder of Mr. Wright.

8. In *A Memory of Two Mondays*, the cleaning of the warehouse windows results in certain ironic discoveries about the neighborhood.

## SYMBOLISM

When approaching a paper on symbolism, you should remember that in fiction and drama virtually all symbols arise from literal images. In fact, we can define a literary symbol as a literal image placed in a story or play to suggest some meaning beyond its ordinary function. Almost any image, then, may take on symbolic value—the image of a person, an object, some action being performed or a statement being repeated, or a natural scene being described. More often than not writers use symbols to reinforce the major points of the work or to inform the reader or theatergoer about the motivations of the central characters.

You should begin your paper on symbolism with a thesis statement naming the object, person, situation, or action that you maintain has a symbolic value. Then you should explain what you think the symbolic value is and how the symbol expresses or affects the meaning of the work. Following are a few suggested opening sentences for symbol papers:

1. General Zaroff, the villain in "The Most Dangerous Game," is surrounded by a cluster of contradictory symbols.

2. The pieces of metal collected by John, the young priest of the Hill People in "By the Waters of Babylon," take on a symbolic religious value.

3. In Anton Chekhov's story "The Lottery Ticket," the ticket itself becomes a pervasive symbol.

4. In "A Passion in the Desert," Honoré de Balzac presents the panther as a symbol of feminine sexuality.

5. The symbolic meaning of the veil in "The Minister's Black Veil" seems to change as the story moves along.

6. The mysterious roaring train that passes in the night is an important symbol in Pär Lagerkvist's story "Father and I."

7. In "The Shades of Spring," D. H. Lawrence employs a cluster of Freudian symbols in the scene in the hut.

8. In "The Tryst," Ivan Turgenev uses various natural objects to symbolize the characters of Akulína and Viktór Alexándrovitch.

9. The final sentence of "The Bride Comes to Yellow Sky" contains a symbolic image important to an understanding of the whole story.

10. In "The Lottery," the black box is an ominous symbol hinting at what ultimately takes place in the story.

11. Various walls have important symbolic meaning in Bartleby, the Scrivener.

12. The dead bird is a central symbol in Trifles.

## THEME

Because theme arises from all of the elements of a story or play working together, it is sometimes easy for a paper on theme to get out of hand. For this reason, we suggest that you begin with a thematic statement—one or more sentences that present what you believe the theme to be. (Later, of course, you may find that in assembling supporting details you have changed your mind about the work's theme, and need to revise your statement.) To formulate your thematic statement, start by searching the story or play to see whether any of the characters offers remarks that seem to have thematic significance. For example, in Irwin Shaw's "The Dry Rock," Leopold Tarloff makes several statements that directly relate to what the story is all about. One such group of statements goes as follows:

He [Rusk] hit me in the head without provocation. He is guilty of a crime on my person. He insulted me. He did me an injustice. The law exists for such things. One individual is not to be hit by another individual in the street of the city without legal punishment. . . . There is a principle. The dignity of the human body. Justice. For a bad act a man suffers.

Later on, as Tarloff comes to realize that even in America society is imperfect, he says to Fitzsimmons: "There is no time. Principle. . . . Today there is no time for anything." From such statements, you can state the theme in your own words.

When the author provides no directly thematic comments, the theme must be deduced by an examination of the whole pattern of events of the work. However, since different works feature one element more than another—there is more action in "The Most Dangerous Game" than in "Studs," and better character dramatization in "The Dry Rock" than in "Report"—you cannot always weigh each element equally in determining theme. You should also keep in mind that short stories and plays often have more than one theme, and each of these may be worth considering separately.

Since thematic papers will always be analytical, all of the following suggested opening sentences are thesis statements:

1. Thematically, Katharine Brush's "Night Club" explores several varieties of desperation.

2. The need of immigrants to America to make themselves heard in their new homeland is an important theme in Grace Paley's "The Loudest Voice."

3. Our cold mistreatment of the elderly is a major thematic concern of Arna Bontemps's "A Summer Tragedy."

4. The damaging effects that the actions of unperceptive adults can have on a desperate child is the dominant theme of Gina Berriault's "The Stone Boy."

5. The initiation of youth into the real world is the central theme in Pär Lagerkvist's story "Father and I."

6. One of the themes of D. H. Lawrence's "The Shades of Spring" involves a young man's learning that some women do not wish to be viewed as fragile objects.

7. The overriding theme of "The Bride Comes to Yellow Sky" is the passing of the old West.

8. The fundamental human need to make permanent commitments to others is an important thematic consideration in Carson McCullers's "The Sojourner."

9. The danger of blind adherence to tradition is the central theme of Shirley Jackson's story "The Lottery."

10. One of the major themes of Herman Melville's novella *Bartleby, the Scrivener* is the growing intellectual alienation of the worker in nineteenth-century American society.

11. Thematically, *Oedipus* suggests that no mortal can escape his fate.

12. On a thematic level, *Othello* reveals the vulnerability of an outsider, however powerful and successful, in an alien society.

13. Thematically, *The Importance of Being Earnest* actually argues that one should never be over-earnest.


POINT OF VIEW

Point of view we have defined as the physical vantage point from which the events of a short story or novella are told. Papers treating this element can therefore deal only with fiction, not with drama. Any short paper on point of view should begin by establishing, and perhaps explaining, the point of view the author has employed. An analytical paper should then go on to discuss how this point of view contributes to the total structure or impact of the work.

Remember, we have divided all possible narrative points of view into two broad types: first-person and third-person. Then we said that there are three important varieties of each. For first-person we gave first-person central character, first-person secondary character, and first-person observer. For third-person we included third-person limited, third-person omniscient, and third-person dramatic. (To review the qualities and uses of each of these points of view, look back at the introduction to Part One.)

Following are a few suggested opening sentences for papers that focus on point of view in a specific story:

1. Since the point of view employed in "By the Waters of Babylon" eliminates the possibility of John being killed, the story's suspense rests on what John learns on his journey to the Place of the Gods.

2. The third-person point of view employed in "The Lottery Ticket" is limited, but in an unusual way.

3. "A Passion in the Desert" actually employs two different points of view, one for the section called "The Frenchman in Egypt," and another for the rest of the story.

4. Only once in "The Monkey's Paw" does the point of view shift to give the reader a peek into the mind of Herbert, but this single shift is very important to an understanding of the meaning of the entire story.

5. The point of view in "A Summer Tragedy" is inconsistent with the withholding of important narrative information until near the end of the story.

6. Point of view is employed in "The Stone Boy" to reveal Arnold's emotional state.

7. The point of view employed in "The Tryst" stretches credibility because of the narrator-observer's unlikely physical nearness to Akulína and Alexándrovitch.

8. Three specific characters are involved in the narrative omniscience of James Joyce's "The Boarding House."

9. If "The Lottery" were told from any but the dramatic point of view, the suspense of the whole story would fall apart.

10. The fact that the lawyer-narrator so dominates everything in *Bartleby, the Scrivener* argues that the story is really about the narrator, not about Bartleby.

# Writing About Poems

Writing a short paper about a poem is not quite the same kind of exercise as writing about a short story, novella, or play. In the first place, since most poems you read will be shorter than the shortest work of fiction or drama, you will probably write about a poem in greater detail. Secondly, the kinds of things you write about will often—though not always—be quite different. For example, you might decide to write a whole paper on the rhythm of a poem, and how that rhythm relates to the poem's meaning. Or you might examine a poem's rhyme scheme or stanza form. Since some plays, including Shakespeare's *Othello*, are written in verse, it is possible that you might be writing one of these kinds of papers about a play. But in general, stories and plays do not require so close a look at the effects of the sounds of words as do poems.

Nevertheless, writing about poetry is not completely different from writing about fiction or drama. There are still the same two basic approaches: the paper that simply recounts what happens or points out the presence of one or more elements, and the analytical paper that explains how those happenings or elements affect meaning. Although poems do tend to be short, they are so full of special features of sound and meaning that you will often have to limit your paper to one or two specific aspects of the poem rather than try to deal with the whole piece. And there are several kinds of papers that are very much like papers you might write about stories or plays.

THE PARAPHRASE

The paraphrase is a paper that restates in prose, and in your own words, what the poem says. As you know, the language of poetry is different from the language of everyday talk. It is more condensed, sometimes because it uses words more economically and other times because it leaves out words that would be needed in ordinary prose. Also, a poem is often filled with figurative images and carefully crafted rhythms and rhymes that force a close, careful reading. Consequently, the paraphrase is a natural type of paper for you to want to write about a poem. Just as you might write a plot summary to be sure you have the facts of a short story well in mind, you write a paraphrase to be sure you have grasped the most overt meaning of a poem.

Read Edwin Arlington Robinson's "Richard Cory," and then read the following paraphrase:

> Whenever Richard Cory came into town, we ordinary townspeople couldn't help looking at him with admiration. From head to toe, he was our ideal of a perfect gentleman. He was handsome and slim, and he always dressed in quiet good taste. Although there was not the slightest hint of haughtiness or condescension in his voice when he talked to people, the very way that he said good morning could excite a person. The man even seemed to sparkle as he moved among us.
>
> Richard Cory was also rich, very rich, and he knew every rule of good manners and proper behavior. To most of us local people, he seemed to have everything that a person could want. Few of us would have refused to change places with him. But that's the way things are, we figured, and went on living our ordinary lives, working hard and doing without the things we didn't have. Then, to our complete amazement, Richard Cory went home one summer night and committed suicide by shooting himself in the head.

As you can see, a paraphrase is not an analysis. It does not attempt to explain or fit together the information it reports, nor does it need a thesis statement. Neither is a paraphrase a summary: it is a restatement of the poem, line by line and almost word by word, and it is at least as long as the poem—often longer. And you will soon see that a paraphrase paper sets you up to write other kinds of papers about the same poem.

There are two further important requirements for writing a paraphrase. The first is that you try to assume the "voice" and overall tone of the poem. This means that you must be clear in your mind who the speaker— or persona—is. If necessary, you should identify him or her directly. (The first sentence of the "Richard Cory" paraphrase says "we ordinary townspeople," identifying the speaker as one of the townspeople.) The paraphrase thus maintains the poem's tone, which is at the same time ironic and conversational, with a note of wonder at Richard Cory's aura and amazement at what Cory finally does. The second requirement is that you be sure to paraphrase each word that is unfamiliar to you or used in an unusual way, either by including a brief definition in the paper itself or by using a synonym that you are more comfortable with.

Here are some poems for you to try your hand at paraphrasing:

1. Queen Elizabeth I, "When I Was Fair and Young."

2. Robert Browning, "My Last Duchess."

3. Emily Dickinson, "Because I Could Not Stop for Death."

4. William Butler Yeats, "The Second Coming."

5. Edwin Arlington Robinson, "Miniver Cheevy."

6. Robert Frost, "The Road Not Taken."

7. Marianne Moore, "Poetry."

8. Robert Graves, "The Cool Web."

9. Langston Hughes, "I, Too."

10. Diane Wakoski, "Steely Silence."

## IMAGERY AND FIGURATIVE LANGUAGE

Another important type of paper to write about a poem discusses its imagery. This is essentially an analytical paper because it draws conclusions about the meaning of the poem and explains the meaning of its images.

Read Robert Hayden's poem "Those Winter Sundays" and then the following short analytical paper:

> Robert Hayden's poem "Those Winter Sundays" points out how insensitive young people can be to the love a parent offers them. The poem begins with the speaker—who is not distinguished from the poet—recalling how his father, even on Sundays after a hard week's work, got up before everyone else in the house to build a fire and drive away the cold. And no one ever bothered to thank him. The speaker, as a youth, used to lie in bed as the house warmed up. Then he would reluctantly rise and dress in comfort, treating his father with indifference. Even though the father had polished the boy's good shoes, the boy acknowledged nothing. After all, his family always seemed angry, and he was afraid of their anger. But now, older and more perceptive, the poet thinks back to those cold winter Sundays and asks himself what he then knew about the kind of love that shows itself through service rather than talk and embraces. The answer is, of course, that he knew nothing.

So far, this paper is a paraphrase of the poem, with an opening sentence that states the poem's main theme. But now the paper turns to the poem's images:

> The word "cold" is used twice in a figurative way. First, it is a metonym for morning in "the blueblack cold" (line 2), and then it is a metonym for the house, and particularly for its water pipes that make cracking noises as they warm up (line 6). These instances of metonomy alert the reader to the possibility that "cold" might represent a still larger concept. The word "offices" (line 14) is a submerged metaphor, comparing the father's loving services to his son with the kind of religious rites known as offices.

Throughout the poem coldness and warmth are both literal and symbolic. Coldness suggests not only frigid temperatures but also the absence of love; and in this poem it may more specifically symbolize the speaker's failure, as a boy, to recognize or acknowledge love. The warmth of the furnace corresponds with the father's love and perhaps—since the poem ends with a general statement—all such silent demonstrations of love.

An analysis of this kind may seem terribly sophisticated and impressive when you first read it, but actually such a paper is not so difficult to put together—the writing is more difficult than the thinking. First, read the poem through several times. Then write a paraphrase by working your way through the poem and picking up each specific detail as you go. Next, having the meaning of the poem firmly in mind, write an opening sentence—a thesis statement—that states the theme of the poem or otherwise sums it up, and place that sentence at the beginning of your paraphrase. You will then have something like the first paragraph of this sample paper. Next, reread the poem, looking for those words or phrases that are likely to be figures of speech. For example, since cold has no color and makes no noise, the expressions "blueblack cold" and "the cold splintering, breaking" must be figurative. You need to determine what "cold" means. (It turns out that the first two meanings of cold combine to mean "the house early on a winter morning," and that in a larger sense "cold" symbolizes the emotional atmosphere of the house of "chronic angers.") Then look at the poem again for other details that might have symbolic value. Just as coldness symbolizes indifference, warmth is a well-known symbol for love and affection. So, these traditional associations fit the poem and increase its depth.

To write a short paper analyzing a poem's imagery, you may begin with one of the paraphrases you have already written, supply it with a thesis sentence, and then add on your analysis of the poem's images. Or you may begin with another poem, write a paraphrase, and then analyze the poem's images. Following are some thesis sentences for papers about poems suited to this type of analysis:

1. William Shakespeare's sonnet "That Time of Year Thou Mayst in Me Behold" laments the coming of old age. (The first four lines are analyzed in the discussion of the sonnet in the introduction to Part IV.)

2. "The Sun Rising," by John Donne, celebrates love and exalts two lovers by insulting the sun.

3. William Blake's "The Tiger" goes beyond description to offer a powerful symbol.

4. The whole of Christina Rossetti's poem "Uphill" is a symbolic statement about life.

5. "Heat," by the poet H. D., presents striking and powerful images of wind and heat.

6. E. E. Cummings, in "O sweet spontaneous," praises the earth while satirizing people who try to reduce it to abstract concepts.

7. "The Heavy Bear Who Goes with Me," by Delmore Schwartz, complains that the spirit can never escape the flesh.

8. The speaker in Gwendolyn Brooks's poem "A Song in the Front Yard" wants to experience a side of life that she has never seen.

9. "Toads," by Philip Larkin, is a gripe about being ordinary.

10. The two women in Denise Levertov's "In Mind" have personalities that fit together like pieces of a puzzle.

## POETIC FORM

A short paper about a poem's structure will discuss rhythm, rhyme-scheme, and stanza form—if rhyme-scheme and stanza form are present—and other uses of the sounds of words. To prepare to write such a paper, then, you will have to do more than read and reread the poem. You will have to mark it up in various ways. If you have the time, copy the poem down, leaving plenty of space between the lines. Be sure to check your copy carefully against the original to make sure you have made no mistakes.

First, mark the poem's rhythm. Each strong stress, you remember, should be marked /, and each weak stress ᴗ. If you see that the poem is written in meter, mark the lines off into feet, following the rules of scansion discussed in the introduction to Part IV. Identify and name the meter, and mark all deviations from it. If the poem is written in free verse, do not try to mark it into feet; rather, look to see whether it contains many repetitions of a basic rhythm.

Next, look at the poem's line endings to see whether they rhyme. If they do, mark off the rhyme-scheme by labeling each end-rhyme a, b, c, and so on, as we have shown. Determine whether the rhyme-scheme is constant throughout the poem, or whether it changes at any point. Look at the poem's basic divisions, if there are any. Does each stanza repeat the same rhyme-scheme? Does each stanza express a complete thought and include complete grammatical units? Finally, is the rhyme-scheme of the stanzas, or of the poem as a whole, traditional?

Finally, look for effects of sound other than rhyme—assonance, consonance, alliteration, internal rhyme, onomatopoeia. Mark any frequently repeated sounds, or sounds repeated prominently within a line, and take special note of any that are used extensively throughout the poem, or that seem particularly striking or effective.

In a paper that only describes a poem's form you do not have to organize your findings into conclusions about the way all of the structural elements relate to one another, or how they relate to the meaning of the poem. You simply report what you have found. Read Robert Frost's

"Stopping by Woods on a Snowy Evening" and then read the following short paper detailing the poem's form:

> "Stopping by Woods on a Snowy Evening" is a highly structured and regular metrical poem. The stanza form is the quatrain, and there are four quatrains bound together by an interlocking rhyme-scheme. The first stanza has a rhyme-scheme of *aaba*, the second stanza is *bbcb*, and the third is *ccdc*, while the fourth is *dddd*—the last two lines being exactly the same word for word. All of the end-rhymes are of one syllable, and the poem's meter is an almost unvaried iambic tetrameter. The first two feet of line 1 are spondees, and there is a trochee in the first foot of line 3 and another in the third foot of line 4; but these are the only variations.
>
> Repetition of sound is frequent in the poem. In the first stanza, the words *his* and *is* in line 2 rhyme, and in the next line there is a triple internal rhyme among the words *He, see,* and *me.* The word *fill* in line 4 rhymes with the word *will* in line 3. The sound of *i* in *fill* is heard many times in the poem—in the first stanza for example it appears in *think, His, is, in, village, will, his* again, and *with*—forming an extended pattern of assonance. The same is true with the *ee* sound, which is featured not only in the end-rhymes of stanzas 2 and 3 but also in such words as *these, see, Between, evening, He, easy, downy, lovely,* and *before* throughout the poem.
>
> Alliterations are scattered throughout the poem. In the first stanza the *h* sound occurs in every line, beginning with the stanza's first word—*Whose*—and it recurs through to the end of the poem. In the fourth line, *watch, woods,* and *with* form a *w* alliteration, and the sound also recurs in lines 6 (*without*), 7 (*Between* and *woods*), 11 (*sweep*), 12 (*wind*), and 13 (*woods* again).

A short analytical paper about the form of "Stopping by Woods on a Snowy Evening" would use much of this same information, but would use it to support thesis statements about the poem's overall formal effect and the relation of details to the poem's meaning. Some of the information, however, might be left out. For example, while it is true that *will* in line 3 is a full rhyme with *fill* in line 4, the first receives a weak stress and the second a strong stress; consequently you might not even notice the rhyme when listening to the poem being read aloud. So, an analytical paper might not even mention the point. Following is an example of an analytical paper about the poem's form:

> "Stopping by Woods on a Snowy Evening" is a highly structured metrical poem, but it does not draw attention to its form and in fact strikes a listener as surprisingly informal. The iambic tetrameter is almost unvaried after the first stanza—where there are two spondees at the very beginning, and trochees at the beginning of line 3 and in the third foot of line 4—and yet this regular rhythm does not result in a singsong effect. Perhaps this is because so many of the words are of one syllable—or occasionally two— so that the contrast between weak and strong stress is not great.
>
> The stanza form is the quatrain, and the rhyme-scheme is *aaba, bbcb, ccdc,* and *dddd.* Although this interlocking rhyme-scheme looks very rigid on paper, when the poem is read aloud, the third line of the first stanza,

for example, does not sound like a forecast of how the next stanza will rhyme; rather, it has the effect of an unrhymed line in its own stanza, breaking up a series of rhymes, and it actually seems to make the rhyme-scheme less rigid. In the last stanza, Frost solves the problem of what to do about the third line by simply repeating it in the last line. This repetition—along with the fact that for the first time in the poem all four lines of a stanza rhyme—gives the end of the poem a strong sense of finality.

Frost also makes subtle use of assonance and alliteration throughout the poem. The sound of *ee* appears not only in the rhymes of more than half the lines but also in ten other words within lines, and the sound of *i* (as in *wind*) occurs in assonance twice as often as *ee*. The sound of *w* occurs more than ten times, including an obvious alliteration on *watch* and *woods* in line 4, and the *h* sound occurs just as often. The most frequent consonant sound, however, is *s*, which, unlike the *w* and *h*, is also repeated several times in the last stanza. These repetitions of sound have a quiet but consistent effect on the sound of the poem as a whole, and may even suggest the "sweep / Of easy wind and downy flake."

All of the following metrical poems are appropriate for short papers about their structure:

1. Christopher Marlowe, "Come Live with Me and Be My Love."
2. William Shakespeare, "When in Disgrace with Fortune and Men's Eyes."
3. John Donne, "Go and Catch a Falling Star."
4. William Blake, "The Garden of Love."
5. Robert Southey, "How the Waters Come Down at Lodore."
6. Ralph Waldo Emerson, "Forbearance."
7. Alfred, Lord Tennyson, "The Splendor Falls."
8. Emily Dickinson, "Because I Could Not Stop for Death."
9. James Weldon Johnson, "O Black and Unknown Bards."
10. D. H. Lawrence, "Piano."
11. T. S. Eliot, "Macavity: The Mystery Cat."
12. Archibald MacLeish, "The End of the World."
13. W. H. Auden, "O What Is That Sound."
14. Dylan Thomas, "The Force That Through the Green Fuse Drives the Flower."

A short paper about the form of a free verse poem will be different in some ways from what you would write about a metrical poem. But the process you go through in preparing to write the paper is much the same, and such devices as assonance, consonance, alliteration, onomatopoeia, and even rhyme have their place in free verse. Read "Both

Sheep Are Gone" by Joye S. Giroux, scanned here to show its surprisingly regular and familiar rhythm. Then read the formal analysis of the poem.

## Both Sheep Are Gone

˘   /   ˘  ˘  /
To kill is to be

/
killed,

˘   /   /  ˘
for no two are

/ ˘ ˘
separate—

˘    /    ˘   /   ˘   /
the bond of humanhood

/
binds

/   ˘  /
each to each

˘
and

/ ˘ /
all to all,

˘ / ˘
forever.

˘    /    ˘    /  ˘ /
When madness overruns

˘ /˘/
civility,

/    /˘   /   ˘
each bullet smashing

/   ˘   /
bone and brain,

/
each

/   /   /   ˘  /  ˘  /  ˘   /
blade-rent gash disgorging crimson pain

˘  /   ˘   /   ˘˘  /
on torn and shuddering flesh,

/   ˘  /
two are robbed

˘  /  ˘   /
of fruitful years

/ ˘ ˘
forfeited.

/   ˘  /
Lost and slain,

                    /    /   ∪  /
                both sheep are gone

/    /    /    /
who once seemed safe

   ∪  /  ∪  /
within the fold,

           ∪  ∪  /  ∪
        and uneasy

/  ∪  /  ∪
is the slumber

∪  ∪  /
of the flock.

## Joye S. Giroux

"Both Sheep Are Gone," by Joye S. Giroux, at first appears to be written in the freest of free verse. Although it is not divided into regular strophes, it makes use of many different indentations, so that a new line might begin almost anywhere on the page. The effect of this is to make us read the poem very slowly and carefully, and to set off key words like "killed," "separate," "binds," and "civility" into lines of their own, giving each special emphasis. Yet the division of lines goes along with the punctuation, as each comma comes at the end of a line, and so does each period that ends one of the three long sentences that make up the poem. And parallel expressions like "each to each" and "all to all" (lines 7 and 9) are lined up with each other. So, the division into lines seems designed not just to make the poem look unique, but to affect how it is read aloud.

The cadence, too, is controlled. In fact, it is surprisingly regular, often falling into sequences of iambs interrupted by spondees—though the line endings often cut across the flow of the rhythm. There is a concentration of strong stresses at the point where the poem makes its final thematic statement—"both sheep are gone/who once seemed safe"—and after twenty-one lines of mainly iambic rhythm this passage has a strong impact.

The poem makes frequent use of the repetition of words and of alliteration. Such repetitions as "kill" and "killed" (lines 1 and 2), "each to each" (line 7) and "all to all" (line 8), and the consonance (as well as the related meanings) of "bond" and "bind" (lines 5 and 6) reinforce the opening statement that "no two are/separate"—even if one is the killer and the other the victim. Alliteration reinforces the connection between words describing violence, as in "bullet" and "bone" and "brain" (lines 10 and 11) and "gash" and "disgorging" (line 13), or the results of violence, as in "fruitful years/forfeited" (lines 19 and 20). There is even one use of end-rhyme, between "brain" (line 14) and "pain" (line 16), again at the point of greatest violence in the poem; and the rhyme is picked up again in line 21 with "slain."

The comments in the first two paragraphs of this analysis have little in common with those on Frost's "Stopping by Woods on a Snowy Evening." The reason is that Frost's poem, though original, structurally has much in common with thousands of other poems written in the same meter and stanza form, so that the writer of the paper had only to find the right names for the poem's basic techniques and point out Frost's variations. In free verse this is not the case; there are few special names for free verse structure. We have explained only two—*cadence* and *strophe*.

The latter does not apply to the Giroux poem, because it is not divided into strophes. The second paragraph of the paper notes that the short and choppy lines of the poem "cut across the flow of the rhythm" to form unusual but controlled cadences. The paper's last paragraph, on the other hand, had a good deal in common with the last paragraph on Frost, because free verse often uses the sounds of words in the same ways that metrical verse uses them.

In analyzing free verse, then, you too are free—free to analyze the poem in its own terms, without having to recognize forms or remember the names of meters and rhyme-schemes. You need only remember that poets who write free verse are no less careful and skillful than metrical poets, and that every word, every sound—even every space on the page—is used for a reason. Your paper should try to find and explain the reason.

The following free verse poems are all appropriate for short papers about their structure:

1. Walt Whitman, "There Was a Child Went Forth."

2. Matthew Arnold, "Dover Beach."

3. H. D., "Heat."

4. Marianne Moore, "Poetry."

5. T. S. Eliot, "The Hollow Men."

6. Langston Hughes, "I, Too."

7. Henry Reed, "Naming of Parts."

8. James Dickey, "Buckdancer's Choice."

9. Denise Levertov, "In Mind."

10. Allen Ginsberg, "A Supermarket in California."

11. Sylvia Plath, "Lady Lazarus."

12. Nikki Giovanni, "Ego Tripping."

## Writing Comparison and Contrast Papers

A logical extension of a paper that deals with a single story, play, or poem is a paper that deals with some element in a pair of works. Most often such papers involve comparison and contrast. Comparison and contrast papers reflect our natural inclination to notice similarities and differences between plots, settings, characters, themes, rhyme schemes, stanza forms, and other elements of stories, plays, and poems that have interested us.

Suppose you want to compare the possible symbolic values of rain in James T. Farrell's "Studs" and Ivan Turgenev's "The Tryst." A sensible procedure would be to begin with a thesis statement that tells your reader whether you intend to concentrate on similarities or differences. Then use a couple of paragraphs to present the important circumstances of rain, first in one story and then in the other, including its symbolic value in each story. Then use another paragraph to explain the similarities or differences that you want to feature.

When you set out to write a comparison and contrast paper, it is usually not a good idea to try to compare and contrast two entire works. The paper will run far too long, even for a pair of short stories or average length poems. However, you need not confine yourself to discussing only the elements of fiction or the form and structure of poems. To the contrary, you may write about almost any similarities and differences that you have noticed in a pair of works. You may even compare and contrast unlike types of works, say, the handling of a particular theme or the presentation of similar symbols in a poem and a short story. You can expect the differences to exceed the similarities in almost all cases.

Following are a few suggested opening sentences to help get you started on a comparison and contrast paper:

1. The level of suspense is much greater in Richard Connell's "The Most Dangerous Game" than in Stephen Vincent Benét's "By the Waters of Babylon."

2. A permanent intimate relationship with a woman seems as difficult for John Adderley Syson in D. H. Lawrence's "The Shades of Spring" as it is for John Ferris in Carson McCullers's "The Sojourner."

3. Although both Ivan and Masha Dmitritch in Anton Chekhov's "The Lottery Ticket" and Jeff and Jennie Patton in Arna Bontemps's "A Summer Tragedy" are married couples, the two couples illustrate vastly different relationships.

4. Some knowledge of the situation of blacks in America is important for a full reading of both Arna Bontemps's "A Summer Tragedy" and Eudora Welty's "Powerhouse."

5. The humor in Grace Paley's "The Loudest Voice" is of a completely different kind from the humor in Donald Barthelme's "Report."

6. There is an ocean of difference between the way Marko courts Ariadne in Harry Mark Petrakis's "The Wooing of Ariadne" and the way Bob Doran "wins" Polly in James Joyce's "The Boarding House."

7. Although the eccentricities of the Reverend Hooper in Nathaniel Hawthorne's "The Minister's Black Veil" and those of Bartleby in Herman Melville's *Bartleby, the Scrivener* baffle and confuse the people around them in similar ways, the motivation for each man's behavior is quite different.

8. Even though there are obvious differences between the screaming night train in Pär Lagerkvist's "Father and I" and the great Pullman in which Jack Potter and his bride travel in Stephen Crane's "The Bride Comes to Yellow Sky," there are also some symbolic similarities.

9. Although both Dorothy Parker's "You Were Perfectly Fine" and Shirley Jackson's "The Lottery" are told from the dramatic point of view, there is a great difference in tone and mood between the two stories.

10. Depressing working conditions characterize both Arthur Miller's play *A Memory of Two Mondays* and Herman Melville's novella *Bartleby, the Scrivener*.

11. The major characters in Thomas Holcroft's melodrama *A Tale of Mystery* are far less plausible than those in Susan Glaspell's *Trifles*.

12. Emily Dickinson's poems "A Death in the Opposite House" and "Because I Could Not Stop for Death" have similar subjects but are otherwise very different.

13. Allen Ginsberg's "A Supermarket in California" not only invokes Walt Whitman but resembles Whitman's poems in rhythm and form.

14. Theodore Roethke's "The Waking" and Dylan Thomas's "Do Not Go Gentle into That Good Night" are examples of an unusual poetic form. (Note: The form is called a villanelle.)

15. Though their themes and poetic forms are different, Shelley's "Ozymandias" and Yeats's "The Second Coming" have several other elements in common.

16. Wallace Stevens's "Anecdote of the Jar" and Robert Frost's "The Wood-Pile" offer contrasting poetic views of the relation between wild nature and the products of humankind.

17. William Wordsworth's "I Wandered Lonely as a Cloud" and Robert Herrick's "To Daffodils" are both poems about daffodils, but each poet assigns to the flower a different symbolic value.

18. Both William Cullen Bryant's "To the Fringed Gentian" and D. H. Lawrence's "Bavarian Gentians" are poems about the same kind of flower, but each poet assigns to the gentian a different symbolic value.

19. Many love poems share the theme that the pleasures of love are reserved for the young, and should be enjoyed without delay. (Note: This theme is known by the Latin motto *carpe diem*, "seize the day." Two *carpe diem* poems are Herrick, "To the Virgins, to Make Much of Time," and Marvell, "To His Coy Mistress.")

20. Three poems in this anthology echo a fourth—Marlowe's shepherd's "Come live with me and by my love"—but each of the four poems presents a very different idea of the good life. (Note: The four poems are Marlowe's "The Passionate Shepherd to His Love," the earliest written, Ralegh's "The Nymph's Reply to the Shepherd," written in response, Donne's "The Bait," which was written third and deliberately recalls the earlier poems, and Day Lewis's contemporary "Song.")

21. The aftermath of nuclear war is the setting for Stephen Vincent Benét's story "By the Waters of Babylon" and Edwin Muir's "The Horses," and the works have other elements in common as well.

22. A black musician is the central figure in Eudora Welty's story "Powerhouse" and Langston Hughes's poem "The Weary Blues," but each work takes a very different view of the black experience.

## Acknowledgments (continued from page iv)

GWENDOLYN BROOKS: "A Song in the Front Yard" from *The World of Gwendolyn Brooks* by Gwendolyn Brooks. Copyright 1945 by Gwendolyn Brooks Blakely. "We Real Cool" ("We Real Cool. The Pool Players. Seven at the Golden Shovel") from *The World of Gwendolyn Brooks* by Gwendolyn Brooks. Copyright © 1959 by Gwendolyn Brooks. Reprinted by permission of Harper & Row, Publishers, Inc.

KATHARINE BRUSH: "Night Club." Reprinted by permission of Harold Ober Associates, Inc. Copyright © 1927 by Katharine Brush. Renewed.

HERBERT L. CARSON: "Thomas Beemer Ashburton." Originally appeared in *Kansas Quarterly*. Reprinted by permission of the author.

ANTON CHEKHOV: "The Lottery Ticket." Reprinted with permission of Macmillan Publishing Co., Inc., David Garnett, and Chatto & Windus Ltd., Publishers, from *The Wife and Other Stories* by Anton Chekhov, translated from the Russian by Constance Garnett. Copyright 1918 by Macmillan Publishing Co., Inc., renewed 1946 by Constance Garnett. *A Marriage Proposal* by Anton Chekhov; English version by Hilmar Baukhage and Barrett H. Clark. Copyright, 1914, by Barrett H. Clark. Copyright 1942 (In Renewal) by Barrett H. Clark. Reprinted by permission of Samuel French, Inc. *Caution:* Professionals and amateurs are hereby warned that *A Marriage Proposal*, being fully protected under the copyright laws of the United States of America, the British Empire, including the Dominion of Canada, and all other countries of the Copyright Union, is subject to a royalty. All rights, including professional, amateur, motion pictures, recitation, public reading, radio and television broadcasting and the rights of translation in foreign languages are strictly reserved. Amateurs may give stage production of this play without the payment of royalty. For all other rights contact Samuel French, Inc., at 25 West 45th St., New York, N.Y. 10036, or 7623 Sunset Blvd., Hollywood, Calif., or if in Canada to Samuel French (Canada) Ltd., at 80 Richmond Street East, Toronto M5C 1P1, Canada. Copies of this play, in individual paper covered acting editions, are available from Samuel French, Inc., 25 W. 45th St., New York, N.Y. 10036 or 7623 Sunset Blvd., Hollywood, Calif. 90046 or in Canada from Samuel French, (Canada) Ltd., 80 Richmond Street East, Toronto M5C 1P1, Canada.

JOHN COLLIER: "De Mortuis." Copyright © 1942 by John Collier, © renewed 1969 by John Collier. Reprinted by permission of the Harold Matson Company, Inc.

RICHARD CONNELL: "The Most Dangerous Game" by Richard Connell. Copyright, 1924 by Richard Connell. Copyright renewed, 1952 by Louise Fox Connell. Reprinted by permission of Brandt & Brandt Literary Agents, Inc.

E. E. CUMMINGS: "Portrait" ("Buffalo Bill 's") and "O sweet spontaneous" are reprinted from *Tulips & Chimneys* by E. E. Cummings, with permission of Liveright Publishing Corporation. Copyright 1923, 1925 and renewed 1951, 1953 by E. E. Cummings. Copyright © 1973, 1976 by Nancy T. Andrews. Copyright © 1973, 1976 by George James Firmage. "next to of course god america i" and "if i have made,my lady,intricate" are reprinted from *ViVa* by E. E. Cummings, with permission of Liveright Publishing Corporation. Copyright 1926 by Horace Liveright. Copyright renewed 1953 by E. E. Cummings.

H. D. (HILDA DOOLITTLE): "Heat." Hilda Doolittle, *Selected Poems of H. D.* Copyright © 1957 by Norman Holmes Pearson. Reprinted by permission of New Directions.

JAMES DICKEY: "Buckdancer's Choice." Copyright © 1965 by James Dickey. Reprinted from *Buckdancer's Choice* by permission of Wesleyan University Press. "Buckdancer's Choice" first appeared in *The New Yorker*.

EMILY DICKINSON: "The Soul Selects Her Own Society," "A Death in the Opposite House," "Because I Could Not Stop for Death" and "A Narrow Fellow in the Grass." Reprinted by permission of the publishers and the Trustees of Amherst College from *The Poems of Emily Dickinson*, edited by Thomas H. Johnson, Cambridge, Mass.: The Belknap Press of Harvard University Press, Copyright 1951, © 1955, 1979 by the President and Fellows of Harvard College.

T. S. ELIOT: "The Love Song of J. Alfred Prufrock" and "The Hollow Men." From *Collected Poems 1909-1962* by T. S. Eliot, copyright, 1936, by Harcourt Brace Jovanovich, Inc.; copyright © 1963, 1964 by T. S. Eliot. Reprinted by permission of the publisher and Faber and Faber Ltd. "Macavity: the Mystery Cat." From *Old Possum's Book of Practical Cats*, copyright, 1939, by T. S. Eliot; copyright, 1967, by Esme Valerie Eliot. Reprinted by permission of Harcourt Brace Jovanovich, Inc. and Faber and Faber Ltd.

JAMES T. FARRELL: "Studs." Reprinted from *The Short Stories of James T. Farrell* by James T. Farrell by permission of the publisher, Vanguard Press, Inc. Copyright 1937; Copyright © renewed 1964 by James T. Farrell.

LAWRENCE FERLINGHETTI: "Dog." Lawrence Ferlinghetti, *A Coney Island of the Mind.* Copright © 1958 by Lawrence Ferlinghetti. Reprinted by permission of New Directions.

ROBERT FROST: "Tree at My Window," "Stopping by Woods on a Snowy Evening," "The Road Not Taken," "Mending Wall" and "The Wood-Pile." From *The Poetry of Robert Frost* edited by Edward Connery Lathem. Copright 1916, 1923, 1928, 1930, 1939, © 1969 by Holt, Rinehart and Winston. Copyright 1944, 1951, © 1956, 1958 by Robert Frost. Copyright © 1967 by Lesley Frost Ballantine. Reprinted by permission of Holt, Rinehart and Winston, Publishers.

ALLEN GINSBERG: "A Supermarket in California." Copyright © 1956, 1959 by Allen Ginsberg. Reprinted by permission of City Lights Books.

NIKKI GIOVANNI: "Ego Tripping." From *Re: Creation* by Nikki Giovanni, "Ego Tripping," copyright 1970. Reprinted with permission from Broadside/Crummell Press, Detroit, Michigan.

JOYE S. GIROUX: "Both Sheep Are Gone." Reprinted by permission of the author.

SUSAN GLASPELL: *Trifles.* Reprinted by permission of Dodd, Mead & Company, Inc. from *Plays* by Susan Glaspell. Copyright 1920 by Dodd, Mead & Company. Copyright renewed 1948 by Susan Glaspell.

ROBERT GRAVES: "The Cool Web." Reprinted by permission of the author and A. P. Watt Ltd., literary agents.

ROBERT HAYDEN: "Those Winter Sundays" and "The Performers" are reprinted from *Angle of Ascent,* New and Selected Poems, by Robert Hayden, with the permission of Liveright Publishing Corporation. Copyright © 1975, 1972, 1970, 1966 by Robert Hayden.

ANTHONY HECHT: "The Dover Bitch" from *The Hard Hours* by Anthony Hecht. Copyright © 1960 by Anthony Hecht. Reprinted by permission of Atheneum Publishers.

A. E. HOUSMAN: "To an Athlete Dying Young," "Terence, This Is Stupid Stuff" and "Loveliest of Trees, the Cherry Now." From "A Shropshire Lad"—Authorised Edition—from *The Collected Poems of A. E. Housman.* Copyright 1939, 1940, © 1965 by Holt, Rinehart and Winston. Copyright © 1967, 1968 by Robert E. Symons. Reprinted by permission of Holt, Rinehart and Winston, Publishers, The Society of Authors as the literary representative of the Estate of A. E. Housman, and Jonathan Cape Ltd., publishers of A. E. Housman's *Collected Poems.*

LANGSTON HUGHES: "Dream Variations," "The Weary Blues" and "I, Too (Sing America)." Copyright 1926 by Alfred A. Knopf, Inc. and renewed 1954 by Langston Hughes. Reprinted from *Selected Poems of Langston Hughes,* by Langston Hughes, by permission of Alfred A. Knopf, Inc. "Harlem" ("Dream Deferred"). Copyright 1951 by Langston Hughes. Reprinted from *The Panther and the Lash,* by Langston Hughes, by permission of Alfred A. Knopf, Inc.

TED HUGHES: "In Laughter" from *Crow* by Ted Hughes. Copyright © 1971 by Ted Hughes. Reprinted by permission of Harper & Row, Publishers, Inc. and Faber and Faber Ltd.

EUGÈNE IONESCO: *The Gap,* Rosette Lamont (translation). Reprinted from *The Massachusetts Review,* 1969, Vol. X, No. 1, © 1969 The Massachusetts Review, Inc.

SHIRLEY JACKSON: "The Lottery" from *The Lottery* by Shirley Jackson. Copyright 1948, 1949 by Shirley Jackson. Copyright renewed © 1976, 1977 by Laurence Hyman, Barry Hyman, Mrs. Sarah Webster, and Mrs. Joanne Schnurer. "The Lottery" originally appeared in *The New Yorker.* Reprinted by permission of Farrar, Straus and Giroux, Inc.

ROBINSON JEFFERS: "Signpost." Copyright 1935 and renewed 1963 by Donnan Jeffers and Garth Jeffers. Reprinted from *The Selected Poetry of Robinson Jeffers,* by Robinson Jeffers, by permission of Random House, Inc.

JAMES WELDON JOHNSON: "O Black and Unknown Bards" from *Saint Peter Relates An Incident* by James Weldon Johnson. Reprinted by permission of Viking Penguin Inc.

JAMES JOYCE: "The Boarding House" from *Dubliners* by James Joyce. Copyright © 1967 by the Estate of James Joyce. Reprinted by permission of Viking Penguin Inc.

GALWAY KINNELL: "The Correspondence School Instructor Says Goodbye to His Poetry Students." From *Body Rags* by Galway Kinnell, published by Houghton Mifflin Company. Copyright © by Galway Kinnell. Reprinted by permission.

PÄR LAGERKVIST: "Father and I." From *The Marriage Feast and Other Stories.* Copyright © Pär Lagerkvist; first published by Albert Bonniers Forlag and reprinted with their permission, and the permission of the Author's Literary Estate and Chatto & Windus Ltd.

PHILIP LARKIN: "Toads" by Philip Larkin is from *The Less Deceived*, copyright © 1955, 1972 by The Marvell Press, and appears by permission of the Marvell Press.

CARL JUDSON LAUNIUS: "Another Afterword on Hurricane Jackson," from *Neutral-Tinted Haps*, by Carl Judson Launius. Reprinted by permission of the author.

D. H. LAWRENCE: "The Shades of Spring" from *The Complete Short Stories of D. H. Lawrence*, vol. I. Copyright 1922 by Thomas Seltzer, Inc. Copyright renewed 1950 by Frieda Lawrence. "Piano," "Snake" and "Bavarian Gentians" from *The Complete Poems of D. H. Lawrence.* Copyright © 1964, 1971 by Angelo Ravagli and C. M. Weekley, Executors of the Estate of Frieda Lawrence Ravagli. Reprinted by permission of Viking Penguin Inc.

DENISE LEVERTOV: "In Mind." Denise Levertov, *O Taste and See.* Copyright © 1963 by Denise Levertov Goodman. "In Mind" was first published in *Poetry.* Reprinted by permission of New Directions.

CECIL DAY LEWIS: "Song" ('Come, live with me and be my love') from "Two Songs" from *Selected Poems* (1967) by C. Day Lewis. Copyright 1935 by C. Day Lewis. Reprinted by permission of Harper & Row, Publishers, Inc. From *Collected Poems 1954* by C. Day Lewis. Reprinted by permission of the Executors of the Estate of C. Day Lewis, and Jonathan Cape Ltd. and the Hogarth Press, publishers.

ROBERT LOWELL: "New Year's Eve" from *For Lizzie and Harriett* by Robert Lowell. Copyright © 1967, 1968, 1969, 1970, 1973 by Robert Lowell. Reprinted by permission of Farrar, Straus and Giroux, Inc.

ARCHIBALD MacLEISH: "The End of the World." From *New and Collected Poems 1917–1976* by Archibald MacLeish, published by Houghton Mifflin Company. Copyright © 1976 by Archibald MacLeish. Reprinted by permission.

GUY de MAUPASSANT: "The Necklace." Anonymous translation. Reprinted from *Studies in the Short Story*, 4th edition, edited by Virgil Scott and David Madden. Courtesy of Holt, Rinehart and Winston, Publishers.

CARSON McCULLERS: "The Sojourner." From *Collected Short Stories & The Novel, The Ballad of the Sad Cafe* by Carson McCullers, published by Houghton Mifflin Company. Copyright 1955 by Carson McCullers. Reprinted by permission.

W. S. MERWIN: "Their Week." From *Writings to An Unfinished Accompaniment* by W. S. Merwin. Copyright © 1970 by W. S. Merwin. Reprinted by permission of Atheneum Publishers.

JOSEPHINE MILES: "Reason." From *Poems 1930–1960* by Josephine Miles. Copyright © 1960 by Indiana University Press. Reprinted by permission of the publisher.

EDNA ST. VINCENT MILLAY: "Euclid alone has looked on Beauty bare." From *Collected Poems*, Harper & Row. Copyright 1923, 1951 by Edna St. Vincent Millay and Norma Millay Ellis. Reprinted by permission of Norma Millay (Ellis), Literary Executor.

ARTHUR MILLER: *A Memory of Two Mondays* from *A View From the Bridge: Two One-Act Plays* by Arthur Miller. Copyright 1955, 1957 by Arthur Miller. Reprinted by permission of Viking Penguin, Inc. *Caution: A Memory of Two Mondays* in its printed form is designed for the reading public only. All dramatic rights in it are fully protected by copyrights and no private performance—professional or amateur—and no public readings for profit may be given without the written permission of the author and the payment of royalty. Anyone disregarding the author's rights renders himself liable to prosecution. Communications should be addressed to the author's representative, International Creative Management, 40 West 57 Street, New York, N. Y. 10019.

MARIANNE MOORE: "Poetry." Reprinted with permission of Macmillan Publishing Co., Inc. from *Collected Poems* by Marianne Moore. Copyright 1935 by Marianne Moore, renewed 1963 by Marianne Moore and T. S. Eliot.

EDWIN MUIR: "The Horses." From *Collected Poems* by Edwin Muir. Copyright © 1960 by Willa Muir. Reprinted by permission of Oxford University Press, Inc. and Faber and Faber Ltd.

HOWARD NEMEROV: "The May Day Dancing." From *The Collected Poems of Howard Nemerov*. The University of Chicago Press, 1977. Reprinted by permission of the author.

WILFRED OWEN: "Arms and the Boy." From *Collected Poems of Wilfred Owen*. Edited by C. Day Lewis. Copyright © Chatto & Windus, Ltd., 1946, 1963. Reprinted by permission of New Directions, The Owen Estate and Chatto & Windus Ltd.

GRACE PALEY: "The Loudest Voice" from *Little Disturbances of Man* by Grace Paley. Copyright © 1959 by Grace Paley. Reprinted by permission of Viking Penguin Inc.

DOROTHY PARKER: "You Were Perfectly Fine" from *The Portable Dorothy Parker*. Copyright 1929 by Dorothy Parker. Copyright renewed © 1957 by Dorothy Parker. "You Were Perfectly Fine" appeared originally in *The New Yorker*. Reprinted by permission of Viking Penguin Inc.

BRIAN PATTEN: "A Blade of Grass." From *Vanishing Trick* by Brian Patten, published by George Allen & Unwin (Publishers) Ltd. Reprinted by permission.

HARRY MARK PETRAKIS: "The Wooing of Ariadne," from *A Petrakis Reader*, by Harry Mark Petrakis. Reprinted by permission of the author.

SYLVIA PLATH: "Lady Lazarus" from *Ariel* by Sylvia Plath. Copyright © 1963 by Ted Hughes. Reprinted by permission of Harper & Row, Publishers, Inc. Copyright © 1965 by Ted Hughes. Reprinted by permission of Faber and Faber Ltd. and Olwyn Hughes, literary agent.

KATHERINE ANNE PORTER: "Noon Wine." Copyright 1936, 1964 by Katherine Anne Porter. Reprinted from her volume *Pale Horse, Pale Rider* by permission of Harcourt Brace Jovanovich, Inc.

PETER PORTER: "London Is Full of Chickens on Electric Spits." Part 7 of "Annotations of Auschwitz" (poem). Reprinted by permission of the author.

HENRY REED: "Naming of Parts." From *A Map of Verona* by Henry Reed. Reprinted by permission of the author and Jonathan Cape Ltd., publishers.

OTTO REINERT: Footnotes to *Othello* by William Shakespeare. From *Drama: An Introductory Anthology*, Alternate Edition, by Otto Reinert. Copyright © 1961, 1974 by Little, Brown and Company (Inc.). Reprinted by permission.

ADRIENNE RICH: "I Dream I'm the Death of Orpheus" is reprinted from *The Will to Change*, Poems 1968–1970, by Adrienne Rich, with permission of W. W. Norton & Company, Inc. Copyright © 1971 by W. W. Norton & Company, Inc.

EDWIN ARLINGTON ROBINSON: "Miniver Cheevy." From *The Town Down the River* by Edwin Arlington Robinson. Copyright 1907, Charles Scribner's Sons; renewal copyright 1935. Reprinted by permission of the publisher. "Richard Cory." From *The Children of the Night* by Edwin Arlington Robinson. Copyright 1897 by Charles Scribner's Sons. Reprinted by permission of the publisher. "Mr. Flood's Party." Reprinted with permission of Macmillan Publishing Co., Inc. from *Collected Poems* by Edwin Arlington Robinson. Copyright 1921 by Edwin Arlington Robinson, renewed 1949 by Ruth Nivison.

THEODORE ROETHKE: "My Papa's Waltz," copyright 1942 by Hearst Magazines, Inc.; "Dolor," copyright 1943 by Modern Poetry Association; "The Waking," copyright 1953 by Theodore Roethke; and "I Knew a Woman," copyright 1954 by Theodore Roethke from the book *The Collected Poems of Theodore Roethke*. Reprinted by permission of Doubleday & Company, Inc.

DELMORE SCHWARTZ: "The Heavy Bear Who Goes With Me." Delmore Schwartz, *Selected Poems: Summer Knowledge*. Copyright 1938 by New Directions. Reprinted by permission of New Directions.

ANNE SEXTON: "Unknown Girl in the Maternity Ward." From *To Bedlam and Part Way Back* by Anne Sexton, published by Houghton Mifflin Company. Copyright © 1960 by Anne Sexton. Reprinted by permission.

IRWIN SHAW: "The Dry Rock," from *Mixed Company: Collected Short Stories of Irwin Shaw*. Copyright by Irwin Shaw. Reprinted by permission of Irwin Shaw.

STEVIE SMITH: "Souvenir de Monsieur Poop." From *Collected Poems* by Stevie Smith. Copyright © 1976 by James MacGibbon. Reprinted by permission of Oxford University Press, Inc.

GARY SNYDER: "The Snow on Saddle Mountain." Translations of Mujanawa Kenji. Gary Snyder, *The Back Country*. Copyright © 1957, 1968 by Gary Snyder. Reprinted by permission of New Directions.

SOPHOCLES: *Oedipus Rex. The Oedipus Rex of Sophocles:* An English Version by Dudley Fitts and Robert Fitzgerald, copyright 1949 by Harcourt Brace Jovanovich, Inc.; copyright 1977 by Cornelia Fitts and Robert Fitzgerald. Reprinted by permission of the publisher. *Caution:* All rights, including professional, amateur, motion picture, recitation, lecturing, performance, public reading, radio broadcasting, and television are strictly reserved. Inquiries on all rights should be addressed to Harcourt Brace Jovanovich, Inc., 757 Third Ave., New York 10017.

JAMES STEPHENS: "A Glass of Beer." From *Collected Poems* by James Stephens. Copyright 1918 by Macmillan Publishing Co., Inc., renewed 1946 by James Stephens. Reprinted with permission of Macmillan Publishing Co., Inc., Macmillan, London and Basingstoke and Mrs. Iris Wise.

WALLACE STEVENS: "Anecdote of the Jar" and "A Postcard from the Volcano." Copyright 1936 by Wallace Stevens and renewed 1964 by Holly Stevens. Reprinted from *The Collected Poems of Wallace Stevens*, by Wallace Stevens, by permission of Alfred A. Knopf, Inc.

DYLAN THOMAS: "The Force That Through the Green Fuse Drives the Flower," "In My Craft or Sullen Art" and "Do Not Go Gentle into That Good Night." *The Poems* of Dylan Thomas. Copyright 1939, 1946 by New Directions Publishing Corporation. Reprinted by permission of New Directions. From *Collected Poems* by Dylan Thomas. Reprinted by permission of J. M. Dent, Publishers, the Trustees for the copyright of the late Dylan Thomas, and David Higham Associates Limited.

DIANE WAKOSKI: "Steely Silence." Copyright © 1970 by Diane Wakoski and published in *The Magellanic Clouds*, published by Black Sparrow Press. Reprinted by permission.

ALICE WALKER: "To Hell With Dying." Copyright © 1967 by Alice Walker. Reprinted from her volume *In Love and Trouble* by permission of Harcourt Brace Jovanovich, Inc.

DOUGLAS TURNER WARD: *Day of Absence.* © Copyright, 1966, by Douglas Turner Ward. Reprinted by permission of the author and of Dramatists Play Service, Inc. *Caution: Day of Absence*, being duly copyrighted, is subject to a royalty. The amateur acting rights in the play are controlled exclusively by the Dramatists Play Service, Inc., 440 Park Avenue South, New York, N. Y. 10016. No amateur production of the play may be given without obtaining in advance the written permission of the Dramatists Play Service, Inc., and paying the requisite fee.

EUDORA WELTY: "Powerhouse." Copyright 1941, 1969 by Eudora Welty. Reprinted from her volume *A Curtain of Green and Other Stories* by permission of Harcourt Brace Jovanovich, Inc.

WILLIAM CARLOS WILLIAMS: "Queen–Anne's–Lace," "The Red Wheelbarrow" and "This Is Just to Say." *Collected Earlier Poems* of William Carlos Williams. Copyright 1938 by New Directions Publishing Corporation. "The Dance." William Carlos Williams, *Pictures From Brueghel*. Copyright © 1962 by William Carlos Williams. Reprinted by permission of New Directions.

WILLIAM BUTLER YEATS: "Sailing to Byzantium." Copyright 1928 by Macmillan Publishing Co., Inc., renewed 1956 by Georgie Yeats. "The Lake Isle of Innisfree." Copyright 1906 by Macmillan Publishing Co., Inc. renewed 1934 by W. B. Yeats. "The Wild Swans at Coole" and "The Scholars." Copyright 1919 by Macmillan Publishing Co., Inc., renewed 1947 by Bertha Georgie Yeats. "The Second Coming." Copyright 1924 by Macmillan Publishing Co., Inc., renewed 1952 by Bertha Georgie Yeats. All reprinted from *Collected Poems* by William Butler Yeats with permission of Macmillan Publishing Co., Inc., M. B. Yeats, Anne Yeats, Macmillan London Limited, and A. P. Watt Ltd.

# Index of Literary Terms

# Index of Authors, Titles, and First Lines

Authors' names are in **bold** type, titles are in *italics*, and first lines of poems appear in roman (standard) type.

# CONFIDENT KIDS®

## Guides for Growing a Healthy Family

To my dear friend Joyce Poley,
who remained my friend
through the times
when I *didn't* know how
to communicate very well!

**Books in the
"Guides for Growing a Healthy Family" Series**

*I Always, Always Have Choices*
*All My Feelings Are Okay*
*Let's Talk, Let's Listen Too*

**Future books planned on these topics:**

*Handling Significant Changes*
*Characteristics of a Healthy Family*
*Self-Esteem*

# Let's Talk, Let's Listen Too

## LINDA KONDRACKI

Fleming H. Revell
A Division of Baker Book House Co
Grand Rapids, Michigan 49516

*Scripture identified* ICB *is from the*
International Children's Bible, New Century Version,
*copyright © 1986 by Sweet Publishing, Fort Worth, Texas.*
*Used by permission.*

*Scripture identified* NIV *is from the* New International Version,
*copyright 1973, 1978, 1984 by International Bible Society.*
*Used by permission of Zondervan Publishing House.*

The quote by Virginia Satir in the introduction
is from *The New Peoplemaking*, Science and Behavior Books,
Mountain View, California, 1988.

*Art direction and series design by Joy Chu*
*Production layout by Ellen Flaster*
*Illustrations by Cat Bowman Smith*
*Initial caps and logo on* Read-Along Pages *by Rita Lascaro*

Kondracki, Linda.
Let's talk, let's listen too / Linda Kondracki.
p. cm. — (Guides for growing a healthy family)
ISBN 0-8007-1697-3
1. Interpersonal communication.
2. Child rearing. 3. Family. 4. Interpersonal communication—Religious aspects—
Christianity.
5. Child rearing—Religious aspects—Christianity.
6. Family—Religious life. I. Title. II. Series: Kondracki, Linda. Guides for growing a
healthy family.
BF637.C45K62 1993
646.7'8—dc20 93-21685

*Copyright © 1993 by The Recovery Partnership*
*Published by Fleming H. Revell, a division of Baker Book House Company,*
*Box 6287, Grand Rapids, Michigan 49516-6287*
*Printed in the United States of America*

"Confident Kids" is a registered trademark.

# CONTENTS

# About the "Guides for Growing a Healthy Family" Series

The "Guides for Growing a Healthy Family" series is a collection of innovative programs written especially for parents of elementary-age children (although—with a little ingenuity—they can be adapted to include preschoolers and teenaged members of a family). Each book combines stories, discussion topics, and group activities that serve as a practical resource for teaching all family members a set of skills they need to have productive and emotionally healthy lives. For example, the first book introduced a guide for making wise choices; this one focuses on identifying feelings and expressing them in healthy ways. Future topics to be considered are family communication skills, characteristics of a healthy family, handling significant changes (grief), and self-esteem.

However, there is no particular order to the series. Parents are invited to start with any one book of their choice and proceed through the series in whatever sequence seems to best suit their family situation.

# Goals
# of the Series

**THE FAMILY GUIDES HAVE THREE PURPOSES AND ARE DESIGNED TO BE:**

1. **A "next step" resource to parents in recovery.** Many parents are still struggling with destructive behavior patterns they learned in childhood. Recovery groups, "inner child" workshops, and individual or family therapy sessions are helping millions of adults replace those patterns with new and healthier ways of living. Nevertheless, parents in such support programs often discover that their individual recovery journeys are not adequately preparing them to parent their own children. It is our natural instinct to repeat the patterns we saw in our family of origin, yet many people in recovery typically grew up in dysfunctional homes where the models of parenting were, at best, inadequate. Most recovery agendas do not directly address how parents can translate what they are learning about themselves into the skills needed to raise emotionally healthy children. The family guides can help parents in recovery take this next step.

2. **A tool parents can use to teach healthy living skills to their children.** Good parenting is mainly about teaching children sound values and behavior patterns that reflect their responsibility to themselves and others. Even parents who are quite clear on the values may be confused about what the related skills are, and how to go about teaching those skills in

the midst of the hectic, often fragmented family life so common in many modern American homes. The books in this series identify the key skills needed to grow a healthy family life and provide an easy-to-use, hands-on tool to enable all members to learn these important skills together.

3. **A means to build family connectedness.** A common problem for families today is a loss of a sense of solidarity. Here again, busy schedules and a variety of social and economic factors make it increasingly difficult for families to create and maintain strong bonds of togetherness. The family guides help in this area by suggesting both occasions and agendas for meaningful times of family interaction. By spending quality time together, your family will not only be learning new skills but also building lifelong relationships.

## Format of the Family Guides

All the chapters, or units, in the family guides contain three sections, each of which approaches a particular aspect of a life skill from a different angle.

1. **"Getting Ready"—Parents' Pages**
   This introductory section is for your own growth, and it should be thoroughly worked through before getting the family involved. You cannot teach a skill to your children until you are on the way to mastering it yourself or at the very least understand why it is important. These pages

invite you to examine your own attitudes and behavior patterns and prepare you to personalize the material so as to meet the unique needs of your own family. Included here are *teaching pages* (the main point of the chapter, written at an adult level); *reflection questions* that relate the principle to your own experiences; and a *biblical truth* that will connect you to God and His Word.

2. **"Talking Together"—Read-Along Pages**

The middle section translates the main idea of the chapter into language your children can understand. Reading these pages together and talking through the questions will communicate valuable information on life skills in a relaxed family setting. Included here are *teaching pages* (written at a child's level); a *short activity* that invites group discussion and participation; a *story* and related questions; and a *summary statement* that clearly states a principle and relates it to God's Word.

3. **"Growing Together"—Family Activities**

This final section is perhaps the most important one of all. Doing one or more of the suggested activities not only reinforces the skills building but will also provide occasions for bonding as a family. Included here are a *biblical teaching* that connects the skill to God's Word by memorizing a Bible verse and/or sharing a short Bible study; *conversation starters* (a time for open communication); and *family night activities* through which everyone can enjoy a fun time together and learn valuable skills at the same time. There are instructions for a variety of things to do, including crafts, plays, family outings, and more.

# How to
# Use the Guides

Getting maximum benefit from the family guides will require planning and work on your part. Once you have chosen a book in this series, here is a suggested way to proceed:

1. **Familiarize yourself with the "Stages of Skill Development" (see Appendix A).** Always remember that learning new skills takes time and feels uncomfortable at first!

2. **Study the material in each chapter before presenting it to your family.** This means not only working through the Parents' Pages, but reading the other two sections as well. For example, understanding the Read-Along Pages and relating them to your own situation at home will prepare you for possible answers to the discussion questions.

3. **Work through the book systematically, preferably by dealing with one chapter each week.** Difficult as it may be to arrange, try to set aside a weekly time slot for family interaction, whether in the early evening or during the weekend. Mark it on the calendar and be sure all family members understand the importance of being there.

4. **Make advance preparations by gathering any items needed for family activities.** It will spoil everyone's fun if there is a last-minute search for supplies.

5. **Have fun together!** Perhaps the greatest benefit of using these guides comes when you can all learn to relax and enjoy just being together. As a parent, having realistic expectations increases the possibility that this will happen more and more frequently, as will your insistence on everyone's following the "Rules for Family Interaction" outlined in Appendix B.

Because the discussions and activities will not always happen as smoothly as they sound in this book, visible moments of growth may seem slow in appearing. In fact, there will be times when you think your kids are not learning a thing. But, even then, you will not be wasting your time, because you are accomplishing a great deal just by being together.

# INTRODUCTION

I see communication as a huge umbrella that covers and affects all that goes on between human beings. Once a human being has arrived on this earth, *communication is the largest single factor determining what kinds of relationships she or he makes with others and what happens to each in the world.* How we manage survival, how we develop intimacy, how productive we are, how we make sense, how we connect with our own divinity—all depend largely on our communication skills.

Virginia Satir

*T*first read these words from Virginia Satir in my college days, and I remember thinking at the time that I thought them to be an over-statement of the importance of communication skills. But over the years as I have struggled to survive, develop intimacy, be productive, make sense of the world, and connect with God—and have seen others do the same—I have come to see this quote as an accurate portrayal of reality. I now believe there is a direct relationship between the extent of our communication skills and how successfully we make our way through life.

Sounds simple, doesn't it? But there is nothing simple about communicating well. Remember the children's party game called "Gossip" or "Telephone"? One person in a circle thinks of a phrase and whispers it into the ear of the person sitting next to him or her. That person then whispers it into the ear of the next person, and so on around the room. Then the last person says the phrase aloud—to everyone's amusement. Why? Because the message always comes out as something totally different from what was said originally. As it passed through all those ears and mouths, it got distorted by people passing on what they *thought* they heard the person before them say. As a child, I loved to play that game. As an adult, I've seen it to be powerfully like the reality of our day-to-day communication. And it is not always amusing.

This book is based on the belief that clear communication is *not* something any of us automatically knows how to do, but rather is a skill we must work hard at learning to do well. In the pages that follow, you will have the opportunity to explore six skills, or "communication building blocks" as I have chosen to call them, that your family can use to improve the quality of their everyday communication. But before we get into the specifics, we need to define a few terms that will be used throughout the book:

▶ **Communication** is any means we use to make connections with another person. The purpose of communication is to get what is in my head and heart into your head and heart *in such a way that you will understand and feel exactly what I am meaning to say to you.*

▶ **The Sender** refers to the person who is saying something to someone else—the one who is sending a message to another person.

▶ **The Receiver** is the person who is receiving the message and trying to understand what the sender is intending to say.

▶ **A Communication Transaction** happens any time someone sends a message and someone else receives it. We can think of it as the basic unit of communication. It may take many such transactions between a sender and a receiver to achieve clear communication on a particular topic.

The key to understanding clear communication lies in the phrase from the first definition above: "in such a way that you will understand and feel exactly what I am meaning to say to you." Our natural tendency when sending a message is to assume that the other person knows exactly what we mean and are feeling. After all, since we are intending to communicate when we say or do something, we are sure we made ourselves perfectly clear. On the other hand, when we receive a message, we assume we have received it in exactly the way it was intended. Like the children's game, however, what was said and how it was heard are often two very different things. The result is communication that is incomplete and confusing—which in turn causes relationships that are incomplete and confusing. But we never seem to understand what's wrong!

In the chapters of this book we will explore six building blocks to clear communication. Using them can help you and your family close the gap of understanding between the messages you send to each other and the way they are received. As you begin your journey, it is my prayer that the experience of learning healthy communication skills will enrich the quality of life in your family. In the weeks ahead, I hope you and your children will relax and have a good time together as you experience new levels of communicating with one another.

COMMUNICATION
BUILDING
BLOCK #1

# Say What You're Feeling

# GETTING READY

## And How Do You *Feel* about That?*

Six-year-old Jeremy sat at the dinner table with his parents, staring quietly at his food. "How did school go today?" asked his mother.

"Fine," he replied, staring at his mashed potatoes.

"Did you have to go to time-out today?" Mom asked.

"No."

"Did you get a yellow light?" In Jeremy's classroom a yellow light was a warning; a red light resulted in a time-out.

"Yes." Jeremy squirmed uncomfortably.

"Really? What was the yellow light for?" his dad asked.

"Nothing. I don't want to talk about it. Okay?"

"Well, we'd like to know. It's okay that you got a yellow light, but we're interested in why you got one."

Jeremy looked up from his plate with a strange look in his eyes.

"We're not mad at you, son. Do you feel scared to tell us?"

Jeremy looked at his parents and exploded, "Look, I'm having a bad day and I don't want to talk about it. Can we just forget about the yellow light, *please?*"

Surprised by his outburst, Jeremy's parents began staring at their plates—and quickly changed the subject.

*Parents are urged to read "How to Use the Guides," Appendix A, and Appendix B for helpful directions to receive maximum benefit from this series.

The starting point for learning good communication is to realize that all communication happens at two levels. First, there is the factual data that we report to one another—the who-what-when-where-how details of the events of our lives—as we tell another person what happened or is happening to us. The second level contains the whole range of feelings stirred up within us as a result of those events. Reporting the facts is the level of communication that is usually the easiest for us. It is relatively nonthreatening to talk about who, what, when, where, and how. But facts mean little or nothing without the feelings that are attached to them. This is where communication begins to be complex, because now we must pay attention not only to what is being said, but the *feelings* involved as well.

The heart of good communication is to understand that how a conversation goes—what we say and the way we say it—depends on how we feel about the event and the persons we are talking to. After an opening remark, how much we continue to say depends on how we feel about their response. Likewise, how we react to another person's words depends on how we feel about that individual and/or what is being shared. Communication either opens up or shuts down according to how we respond at the feeling level.

Many of us, however, are uncomfortable with communicating and responding to feelings. As Jeremy did, we often choose to shut down communication rather than deal with the feelings involved. We do that by using this common barrier to good communication:

### Communication Barrier #1
### Denying, or Refusing to Talk About, What I Am Feeling

There is no faster way to shut down communication than to deny the feelings involved. Consider these responses:

**Denying my own feelings:**

> "It's no big deal."
> "Nothing's going on. I'm fine."
> "So what if I'm angry? Just get off my case. Okay?"

**Denying someone else's feelings:**

> "Stop that crying!"
> "So what's the big deal anyway?"
> "Don't be ridiculous."

Where does a conversation go after statements like these? It will either break off completely, as it did in Jeremy's family, or become defensive and uncomfortable. To keep communication open, we can use this simple skill:

**Communication Building Block #1**
**Report the Facts *and* How You Feel About Them**

Although this is a simple skill to learn, it is not always easy to do. It can help to follow this little formula:

*Fact . . . "and I feel . . ."*

Whenever you make a factual statement, be sure to add a phrase that fulfills the "and I feel" part of the formula.

**Statement of fact**

> "I got a D in English this term."
> "My grandmother is coming to live with us."

Now notice the significant change in meaning when the feeling level is reported along with the fact:

"I got a D in English this term—*and I feel really disappointed with myself.*"

"I got a D in English this term—*and I'm thrilled! I've already failed this class twice!*"

"My grandmother's coming to live with us—*and I'm so excited! She's so fun to have around.*"

"My grandmother's coming to live with us—*and I feel really angry.* She's taking my room and I have to move in with my little brother!"

Notice, too, how reporting our feelings leads us to share more information (why we feel the way we do), with the result that we are led into deeper levels of communication. It may take a little practice, but learning to use the *Fact* . . . "*and I feel* . . . " formula will help you reach others on both the fact and feeling level of communication.

Fortunately, there is more to Jeremy's story. At bedtime that night, his mom created an opportunity to return to the subject of the yellow light: "I know you don't want to talk about this, but I really want to know why you got the yellow light today. Will you please tell me what happened?"

"It was no big deal, Mom, and it wasn't even my fault! Terry keeps talking to me in class and I get in trouble for it! He started it, but Miss Baker yelled at me in front of the class and gave me a yellow light."

"That must have been hard. How did you feel when she did that?"

"Really stupid and like everyone in the class was looking at me."

"I'm sure it was an embarrassing moment. Do you need me to talk to Miss Baker about moving you away from Terry?"

"He doesn't even sit next to me! But it'll be okay, Mom. I'll just ignore him next time."

Through this exchange, this mom was able to help her son communicate clearly about what happened *and* express how he felt about it. The result? Jeremy was able to release his feeling of embarrassment and discover a new way to handle it in the future.

## *F o r    R e f l e c t i o n*

1. As you were growing up, how open were family members about reporting their feelings?
   - ☐ We were uncomfortable expressing feelings.
   - ☐ We received lots of "don't feel that way" messages.
   - ☐ We were supposed to know what others were feeling without them having to say it.
   - ☐ We often had open conversations about what we were feeling.
   - ☐ Other: _____

2. Place an X on the line below, indicating your present comfort level with reporting your feelings to others.

   ├────┼────┼────┼────┼────┼────┼────┤

   I never talk about                          My feelings gush
   what I'm feeling.                            out all the time.

3. In what situations, and with which people, do you feel most comfortable reporting your feelings? _____
   _____

   What criteria are necessary for you to feel comfortable enough to tell others what you are feeling? _____
   _____

4. Observe your children for a few days. Then mark an X on the continuum in #2 for each of them. How is their ability to report their feelings like or unlike yours? _____

_____

## Building On God's Word

Perhaps the greatest communication barrier of all is an inability to express our feelings openly and honestly to God. Many of us were raised to believe that we cannot tell God that we feel angry or resentful or frightened. The Bible, however, is full of examples of people who poured out their deepest feelings to God and discovered that He not only accepted their feelings, but took the time to provide them with whatever they needed most. Read the Scriptures below, taking note of the feelings being expressed to God and His response to each one:

1 Kings 19:1–9 _____

Psalms 88 & 89:1 _____

Jonah 4 _____

Luke 22:39–46 _____

Take a moment right now to communicate your deepest feelings to God, and look for Him to meet you during your time of prayer.

# S ay What You're Feeling

Do you know any hermits? A hermit is someone who chooses to live all by himself, away from
people so he'll never have to talk to anyone.
Hermits never get into fights or have to share or
get yelled at. But most of us would never choose
to be a hermit. In fact, the best part of living is

having friends and family members we can talk to and share with and learn from. How we talk to and listen to others is called *communication*, and that's what this book is about. Communication is probably the most important thing we do. In fact, how well we get along in life depends on how well we can communicate.

Sounds easy, doesn't it? But it's really not. Communicating with others is hard work, and many times we don't do it very well—even grown-ups get into trouble because they don't know the right way to communicate. But there are things we can all learn to help us communicate better, and learning them now, while you are growing up, is a great idea. So, in this book we are going to talk about things that keep us from communicating well—we'll call those **communication traps**—and other things that help us communicate well—we'll call those **communication helpers.** Now let's get started!

The biggest part of communication is telling something to another person. There are two kinds of things we can tell:

▶ Things that have happened or are happening to us. It is telling others about what's going on *outside* of us, like saying "I hit a home run in the game yesterday," or "We had a substitute teacher today."

▶ Things that we are feeling, or telling others what is happening *inside* of us, like saying, "My parents had a big fight and I'm scared they're going to get a divorce."

Telling someone what happened on the outside of us is usually easy. Telling someone what is happening on the inside, however, is much harder. Especially when our inside feelings are uncomfortable, we may try to pretend we aren't feeling them by not talking about them. That's our first communication trap:

**Communication Trap #1**
**Ignoring My Feelings**

Here's an example of kids who are ignoring their feelings:

Brian: "I was the first one down in the spelling bee. It's no big deal."

Laura: "Julie invited all her friends to her slumber party except me. So what? They probably won't have much fun anyway."

Brian and Laura are really feeling hurt inside. But they are making a big mistake by believing that if they don't talk about their feelings, the feelings will go away. However, just the opposite is true. Telling our feelings to someone else is the only way they will go away! It's better to use this communication helper:

**Communication Helper #1**
**Say How I'm Feeling**

You can learn to do this by using an easy formula:

**Say what happened *and* how I feel about it.**

Brian can use this formula to say how he really feels: "I was the first one down in the spelling bee, and I feel really dumb. I'll bet everyone thinks I am dumb!"

Help Laura say what she really feels: "Julie invited all her friends to her slumber party except me, and I feel _____

_____

Can you think of something that happened to you recently? Use the formula to tell about it:

What happened: _____

How you felt: _____

Look at these two cartoons about a problem in the life of a boy named Joseph. Can you find the communication trap? How about the communication helper?

# Grandma's Coming to Live with Us

17 ▶

## Remember...

**You can tell others what you are thinking *and* feeling.**

And remember, too, that the one person you can *always* tell what you are thinking and feeling is God. He loves to have you talk with Him.

**The Lord is close to everyone who prays to him, to all who truly pray to him.**
***Psalm 145:18 ICB***

# Growing Together

## BUILDING ON GOD'S WORD

**Dear God, I Feel . . .** Involve your family in making posters to help them focus on expressing their feelings to God. Give everyone paper and crayons, markers, or paints to create a prayer poster. Begin by writing the phrase, "Dear God, I feel . . ." across the top of each paper, and then dividing it into four sections. Next read Psalm 145:18 together. Explain that telling God what we are feeling is one of the most important ways we have of praying to Him openly and honestly. Then have all family members think of feelings they had during that day or the past week that they would like to express to God. They are to write a different "feelings" word in each section and briefly describe what happened, using words or pictures (young children may need help). When completed, talk together about each poster. (*Caution:* Be careful to respond with statements that validate, rather than deny or ignore, the feelings being expressed.)

End this time with a family prayer circle, thanking God for accepting and wanting to hear all our feelings.

## CONVERSATION STARTERS

The best way to learn about communication is to communicate, but that may be easier said than done at first. If your family is not used to sharing their thoughts and feelings with one another, it

19 ▶

# Growing Together

may feel awkward and uncomfortable the first few times. It won't take long for your family to begin enjoying the opportunity of sharing their thoughts and feelings with each other. You can use mealtimes, just before bedtime, and/or riding in the car to play the communication games listed throughout this book. Begin with the following "sharing" activity.

Write the numbers 1 through 3 on slips of paper, writing one number on each slip. Repeat numbers as necessary so that there is at least one slip for each family member. Fold the slips and place them in a basket or hat. Have family members take turns drawing a slip from the container and reading their number. They will then answer the corresponding question from the list below. Remind everyone to report both facts and feelings in his or her answer.

1. The hardest thing I ever had to do was . . .
2. If I could wish on a real wishing star, I'd wish for . . .
3. I can hardly wait until . . .

## FAMILY NIGHT ACTIVITIES

1. **Practice Reporting Feelings.** You can make a game out of learning the formula of "Fact . . . 'and I feel.'" The repetition of the game will make remembering to add the feeling statement easier in real life. To play, one family member begins by making a statement of fact. Then go around the family circle, taking turns adding "and I feel" statements that could be true in that situation.

# Growing Together

Be creative and keep going until you run out of ideas. Then let another person start a new round by telling a new fact. Example:

*Fact*

> Our class went on a field trip today . . .

*"I Feel" Statements*

> . . . and I feel happy because it was lots of fun.
>
> . . . and I feel glad it's over.
>
> . . . and I felt bored because I've been there a zillion times.

2. **"Feelings" Alphabet Race.** Handling the feeling level of communication is much easier when we have an acquaintance with a wide spectrum of feelings words. This game can help family members broaden their "feelings" vocabulary. The object is to work through the alphabet, making a list of feelings words for each letter. To play, divide into two teams, giving each team a sheet of paper and a pencil. Set a timer for five minutes (a little longer for younger children) and then go to it! At the end of the time, compare lists, scoring one point for each word on a list *that the other team does not have.*

COMMUNICATION

BUILDING

BLOCK #2

# Make
# Yourself
# Perfectly
# Clear

# GETTING READY

## You Figure
## It Out!

When I was growing up, I remember playing a game we called Skid Talking. Skid Talking was a way of mixing words together that left you scratching your head and saying, "What???" Or feeling like someone had just scrambled your brain. For example:

> "If my grandmother were alive today, she'd roll over
> in her grave."
> "Isn't it neat the way the water comes right up to
> the shore like that?"
> "It's so dark out tonight that you can't see your face
> in front of you."

As a game, it was fun to think up statements that qualified as Skid Talking. But Skid Talking as a form of communication is very confusing. As the sender of messages to others, our job is to make those messages as clear and understandable as possible. Many of us, however, have learned to use unclear statements and manipulative behavior in our person-to-person communications. Instead of sending straight, clear messages, we use a kind of cryptic code system to get others to do what we want or give us what we need. The basis for these unhealthy communication patterns lies in two assumptions:

1. Since *I* know what I am trying to say, I naturally assume that what I communicated was quite understandable.
2. I assume that I must use manipulative behavior to get my needs met, particularly if I have been conditioned to believe it is wrong to ask for what I need.

These assumptions hook us into the next communication problem:

**Communication Barrier #2**
**Sending Unclear Messages**

Unclear messages take a variety of forms:

**Blaming Messages**
"If you ever came to dinner on time, maybe we all could enjoy a hot meal."
"If you cared at all about how exhausting *my* day has been, you'd have the table set by now!"

**Guilt or Shame Messages**
"If you had not come along, I would have my degree by now."
"What's the matter with you? Your dirty clothes are all over the house. Can't you ever do anything right?"

**Guesswork Messages**
"What does a person have to do to get a clean shirt around here?"
"If that garage doesn't get cleaned out, you'll be sorry."

**Silence/Withdrawal/Pouting**
By these actions, I send a clear message that something is wrong. It is your job to notice and pry out of me what it is.

If you don't, I pout more until you ask, and then, of course, you will have to persist through several rounds of "nothing's wrong" before I finally tell you what is really going on.

## Acting Sick or Needy

Complaining about stomach pains, headaches, or loneliness (all the time) and acting as if I'm always on the brink of falling apart are some of the ways I can get others to give me the time and attention I need.

These forms of communication engage us in a type of fantasy. We send the messages with the hope/wish that another person will know what we mean and give us what we need. We may even believe that if others really loved us, they would automatically know what we want and need without our having to say anything at all. The end result, however, is disappointment and anger when they don't respond the way we fantasized they would. Unfortunately, we blame *them* for their lack of love rather than realizing *we* have sent an unclear message that they honestly did not understand.

It is much better to use the next communication skill:

**Communication Building Block #2**
**Send Straight, Clear Messages**

We send straight, clear messages by saying exactly what we mean and asking directly for what we need. Keeping in mind a few simple guidelines makes this possible:

▸ **Use "I" statements.** Blaming messages usually begin with "you." Using "I" instead of "you" shifts the focus from blaming another person to owning our own feelings and taking responsibility for our own actions.

- ▶ **Focus on behavior rather than personhood.** Guilt or shame messages are powerful because they communicate that the other person is somehow bad or stupid for acting the way he or she did. By focusing on the behavior alone, we address the problem without attacking the person.
- ▶ **Ask for what you need.** As children, many of us received negative messages about our needs. If our legitimate needs were ignored or criticized, we learned to either pretend we didn't have any needs or we resorted to unclear statements and manipulative behavior to try to get our needs met. Rather than pouting, acting sick or needy, slamming doors, or sighing deeply, we can give straight, clear messages about what we need from others.

Notice the difference in meaning *and* feeling tone when we use these guidelines to change the unclear messages from above into straight, clear communication:

"Dinner is at six. I need you to come to the table the first time I call."

"My day was exhausting and I'm beat! Will you please help me with dinner by setting the table? Thanks!"

"I'm thinking about going back to school to work on my degree. We need to talk about what that will mean for all of us."

"Your dirty clothes belong in the laundry basket, not on the bathroom floor. Please pick them up now."

"I need a clean shirt tomorrow and I'm all out."

"I can't stand that messy garage anymore! It's first on the

agenda for Saturday. Please don't plan to do anything else until we're done."

Children can learn early to ask for what they need instead of acting sick or needy to get our attention. My favorite illustration of this comes from a kindergarten teacher who once asked me what she could do about a student who constantly complained about feeling sick. I asked the teacher how she usually responded to the child. "Well," she replied, "I usually try to talk her out of it, give her a big hug, and send her back to her seat." I suggested that perhaps the girl was really looking for the hug, and that the next time she complained of feeling sick, the teacher could give her permission to ask for the hug without having to act sick to get it. The next week the teacher reported, "She asks me for a hug every day now, but no longer complains about being sick!"

To summarize, we can send straight clear statements to others by following this formula:

**Report the Facts**
**+ Say What You Are Feeling**
**+ Ask for What You Need**
**= A Clear Communication Transaction**

A wise father-in-law illustrates this formula. Graciously allowing his daughter's husband, Joe, to use his lawn mower any time he wanted to, he asked only one thing in return—that it be returned promptly. Joe was often forgetful and the mower would sit in his garage for days. Finally, his father-in-law initiated a confrontation.

"Joe," he began, "I don't mind your borrowing the lawn mower. However, I feel frustrated when I go to mow the lawn on Saturday and the mower's not there. You're welcome to use it any time you want, but I need you to return it before Saturday morning."

By simply stating the facts, reporting how he was feeling, and asking for what he needed, this father-in-law gave a straight, clear message without resorting to blaming, manipulation, or hidden messages. The result? Joe didn't have to be reminded again, and their relationship was strengthened.

## *F o r   R e f l e c t i o n*

1. Which kind(s) of messages did you receive (or are still receiving) most often from your parents?
   - ☐ Blaming: Everything was always somehow my fault.
   - ☐ Guesswork: I was never quite sure what was expected of me.
   - ☐ Guilt- or shame-producing: No matter what I did, it was never right or good enough.
   - ☐ Manipulative behavior: Silence, withdrawal, pouting, acting sick or needy.
   - ☐ Most of the time communication was straight and clear, and I knew what was expected of me.

2. What communication pattern do you use most frequently now? _____

   _____

   _____

   If you are unsure, keep a written record of your communication transactions this week, noting the number of times you use the following:

| Unclear Statements | Manipulative Behavior | Straight, Clear Statements |
|---|---|---|
| _____ | _____ | _____ |
| _____ | _____ | _____ |
| _____ | _____ | _____ |
| _____ | _____ | _____ |
| _____ | _____ | _____ |
| _____ | _____ | _____ |
| _____ | _____ | _____ |

3. What insights did you gain from the above exercise? (*Examples:* I use manipulative behavior with my spouse but not with my kids; I can communicate fairly well *except when* anger is involved; etc.) _____

_____

_____

4. Which is hardest for you?
   ☐ Saying what I mean in straight, clear messages.
   ☐ Asking for what I need.

## Building On God's Word

God invites us to ask Him for what we need. He also gives us the assurance that He is the one person we can trust to know what we need better than we do ourselves. That trust allows us to approach Him openly, knowing that He will respond to us out of love, providing for us as a loving parent. Jesus said:

> Which of you, if his son asks for bread, will give him a stone? Or if he asks for a fish, will give him a snake? If you, then, though you are evil, know how to give good gifts to your children, how much more will your Father in heaven give good gifts to those who ask him!
> *Matthew 7:9–11 NIV*

Record your immediate impressions of these verses below:

_____

_____

_____

Talk with God right now, and use straight, clear messages to boldly ask God for what you need!

**TALKING · TOGETHER**

*ake Yourself*
*Perfectly*
*Clear*

Do you know anyone who is a Skid Talker? A Skid Talker is anyone who says things in ways that make you feel like your brain is all scrambled up. Skid Talkers say things like:
"If Susie calls, tell her she's not home."

31 ▶

"I'm so upset that I'm happy."

"That dog's tail is wagging his whole head."

Skid Talkers are fun, because they make us laugh. But they're also hard to understand, and most of the time we don't know exactly what they mean. That's okay as a game, but it's not very funny when we are trying to tell someone something and they laugh at us or look all confused because they didn't understand what we were trying to say. We might even get mad at them because they didn't understand us. After all, *we* know what we meant, so we think something must be wrong with the other person for not understanding us! That's another communication trap:

### Communication Trap #2
### Blaming the Other Person for Not
### Understanding What We Are Saying

We can't blame others if we haven't sent them a straight, clear message. Whining, pouting, laying a guilt trip on Mom or Dad, acting sick, or not saying anything at all does not let others know what we want or need. For instance, let's say your mom puts a tuna sandwich in your lunch bag every day for a whole month, and you're pretty sick of it. In fact, you feel like you can't ever face another tuna sandwich again in your whole life! How are you going to get your mom to stop? You could try:

> **Skid Talking:** "I think tunas are becoming extinct, and we better protect them."
>
> **Blaming:** "You never make me anything good for lunch!"
>
> **Guilt Trip:** "How come you never give me a good lunch like all the other kids?"
>
> **Pouting, Whining, or The Silent Treatment:** "If you don't give me something else in my lunch tomorrow, I'll never speak to you again!" Then you stomp out of the room and refuse to talk the rest of the night. Or, you may simply throw your tuna sandwich away each day and hope your mom will give you something else one of these days.

The problem with all these ways is that none of them helps your mom know what you really want. It's much better to use this communication helper:

33 ▶

## Communication Helper #2
## Say Exactly What You Mean

When we need to get a message across, we have to say exactly what we want or need—Skid Talking won't get the job done. You can do this by using the formula we learned in the last chapter and adding one more part to it:

**Say what happened + How you feel about it + What you need**

Let's see how this works:

> **Say what happened:** "Mom, I'm tired of tuna sandwiches."
>
> **+ How you feel about it:** "I've had them so many times I hate them now."
>
> **+ What you need:** "I need a break from tuna for a while. Can I have bologna instead?"

It's hard for others to know what we really want when we say things that are not really true, or we act in ways that we hope will get their attention.

For instance, if you are feeling hurt or left out, you might not say anything at all but sit in the corner and pout. What you are thinking inside, however, is, "I wish someone would come and talk to me or play with me." As long as you are only thinking it inside, no one will know what you are feeling or what you need. It's much better to use the formula to give a straight, clear message like this:

> **Say what happened:** "You and Julie are playing my favorite game."
> **+ How you feel about it:** "I feel left out."
> **+ What you need:** "Can I play, too?"

Here's one for you to try:
> Stacey: *"You cheat! I hate you and I never want to play with you again!"*
> Jonathan: *"Okay with me! I'll take my game and go home."*

Using the formula, help Stacey and Jonathan communicate better:

Stacey: _____

Jonathan: _____

(Possible answers: Stacey: "You cheated on that move and I feel angry. I need you to do it over again." Jonathan: "You weren't supposed to see that. Okay, I'll do it over.")

Here's a story about a girl who learned to give a straight, clear message.

# The New Baby

## Remember...

**You can say exactly what you mean
and ask clearly for what you need.**

Remember, too, that you can *always* tell God

what you need. He loves to care for us and give us what we need:

Give all your worries to him, because he cares for you. *1 Peter 5:7 ICB*

# Growing Together

## BUILDING ON GOD'S WORD

**Family Prayer Boxes.** Prayer boxes can be a tangible way for your children to learn to ask God for what they need. Decorate two small boxes, labeling one "Requests" and the other "Answers." Several times a week, gather your family together for a prayer time, using the boxes as a focal point. Encourage family members to talk about what they most need from God at that time. Write out each request on a slip of paper and place it in the "Requests" box. The next time you get together, begin by opening that box and talking about each request inside. Then talk about what God has done or is doing about that need. When a request has been answered, write the answer on the slip and place it in the "Answers" box. In the future, you can open the "Answers" box and review the slips as a way to celebrate what God is doing in your family's lives.

## CONVERSATION STARTERS

Plan a whole week of conversation starters by copying the questions listed below on slips of paper, rolling them up like scrolls, and tying them with ribbons. Put them in a container and place them on your dinner table. Each day for a week, pick a different family member to choose one scroll, open it, and answer the question. Then let all the other family members answer it, too.

# Growing Together

1. The person I most want to be like is . . .
2. The hardest thing about being a kid [or parent] is . . .
3. This summer [or next summer] I want to . . .
4. *Tell everyone at the table one thing you like about him or her.*
5. My favorite relative is . . . [*tell why, too*]
6. *Make up two questions of your own.*

## FAMILY NIGHT ACTIVITIES

1. **Play "Feelings" Charades.** Try making yourself perfectly clear without using words. Write the following feelings words on individual slips of paper and place them in a basket or other container. To play, family members take turns choosing a slip from the container and acting out the feeling for the rest of the family. When the feeling has been correctly guessed, ask family members to tell about a time they have experienced that feeling (or something they think might cause them to feel it). Then talk about what they might need in that situation and how they might go about getting that need met. *Example:* "I would feel angry if my best friend told my secret to someone else. First I would tell Mom that I was feeling angry, then I would need to tell my friend that I was angry and ask her to apologize."

   | | | |
   |---|---|---|
   | Angry | Ashamed | Frightened |
   | Sad | Excited | Proud |
   | Jealous | Lonely | Worried |

## Growing Together

2. **Skid Talking.** Each of the statements below is an example of Skid Talking (making an unclear or twisted statement). Talk together about each one. What makes it confusing? What do you think the statement means? How could you say it differently so it would be a straight, clear message?

"We miss you almost as much as if you were here."
"This ice cream is so cold it sets my teeth on fire!"
"I never liked you and I always will."
"If we had some ham we could have some ham and eggs, if we had some eggs."

Write some Skid Talking statements of your own: _____
_____
_____

Make a commitment to help each other eliminate unclear or twisted messages from your family's communication by calling a Skid Talking alert. When a family member says something confusing, others can call out "Skid Talking!" and think together of a clearer way to say whatever that person is trying to say.

End your time with some "twisted" snacks, like pretzels or cinnamon rolls. You can also make "unclear" punch by having each family member choose one drink and then mixing them all together—for instance, orange juice, grape Kool Aid, and root beer would definitely be an "unclear" punch!

COMMUNICATION
BUILDING
BLOCK #3

# Check
# for
# Meaning

# GETTING READY

## I Know Just What You Mean...I Think

*D*rew was having a great time playing "Cowboys and Indians" with all his favorite stuffed animals. Deep into it, he never heard his mom enter the den.

"What did you say?" she yelled at him. "Don't you ever let me hear you say *that* again!"

"What do you mean? I didn't say anything!" Drew was so into his play, he had not realized he'd said a swear word. He was legitimately confused.

"Don't give me that," Mom counteracted. "You know perfectly well what you said. Clean up here and go to your room!"

This mother and son got caught in a common communication problem. Drew had no idea why Mom was yelling at him—the meaning of "don't you ever say *that* again" was unclear. On the other hand, Mom assumed he knew "perfectly well" what he had said and was manipulating her by pretending not to know. The result was a missing of meaning on both parts and therefore an unpleasant experience.

In the last chapter, we looked at our job as the *sender* of messages to be sure we send straight, clear messages to others. Here we will look at how, as the *receiver* of messages, it is our job to be sure we have accurately picked up the meaning of what another person is trying to communicate to us. Just as it is natural for us as the sender of a message to assume that another person knows what we were trying to say, so, too, as the receiver of a message is it natural for us to assume we have accurately understood what the other person intended to say. That leads us to the next problem in communicating with others:

**Communication Barrier #3**
**Assuming We Understand What**
**Another Person Is Saying to Us**

Consider what happens to a message between the time the sender sends it and the receiver receives it:

1. You send a message to me.
2. On its way to me it passes through many filters affecting the way I receive it. Some of the filters are:

   My reaction to the tone of voice you used
   The words you used may mean something different to me
      than they do to you
   My interpretation of your nonverbal actions
   My emotional state, based on things that happened to me
      that day
   My feelings about you and/or what you are saying
   Whether or not this is a good time for me to listen

3. I receive the message, but probably not exactly as you sent it.

As the receiver, I must be aware of all the things that could change the meaning of what you intended to say. When I'm *not* aware of this, I will assume that the message I received is exactly the same as the one you sent. And if I'm not exactly sure what you meant, I will make up the meaning on my own rather than ask you to clarify it for me.

This is a particularly powerful dynamic for those of us who grew up in homes with some level of dysfunction. If we grew up with alcoholism or a messy divorce, or with physical, sexual, or emotional abuse, we also experienced communication that was unclear and incomplete. That meant we were left on our own to make sense out of what was happening in our homes and the conflicting verbal messages we received from our parents. Because we were children, we distorted the meaning of what was happening in some way—almost always in a way that placed us at fault. Unfortunately, that pattern of making incorrect assumptions, or making up the meaning of events and words in our lives, stays with us even as adults.

It is possible to change all that by using this skill:

**Communication Building Block #3**
**Check to Be Sure You Accurately Understand**
**What a Message Means**

We can quickly understand the importance of this skill by thinking about the many different meanings that are possible in a communication transaction. For instance, consider the meaning of each of the following:

- **"What are you doing tonight?"** can mean, "Do you already have plans?" or, "I have plans for tonight and I want you to watch the kids," or, "I'd really like to spend time with you and I hope you're free."
- **"My boss hates me!"** can mean, "My boss yelled at me today and I felt hurt," or, "My work is not up to speed and I got confronted about it today," or, "My boss has a real personality problem!"
- **Silence/withdrawal** can mean, "Please leave me alone," or, "Please notice and ask me what's wrong."

We can only know what the sender really means by his or her words or actions when we "check for meaning." We do this by asking simple questions, such as:

> "Do you mean. . . ?"
> "What do you mean by. . . ?"
> "Is there something you're not telling me?"
> "What do you need from me right now?"
> "You seem upset. Are you angry with me?"

And so on. It may take several attempts at "checking it out" before we arrive at the proper meaning. But taking the time to check for meaning has unlimited benefits, such as:

It eliminates misunderstandings.
It lets others know we care about them enough to want to understand what they are saying to us.
It builds trust and intimacy as we learn to understand each other.
It leads us into deeper levels of communication.

At the speed we move through life today, it's easy to miss—or misinterpret—the meaning of the messages we receive each day. Checking for meaning helps us slow down long enough to avoid painful misunderstandings *and* build trusting relationships with those we love.

## For Reflection

1. What experiences or messages can you remember from your childhood that left you confused about what they meant?
   ☐ Chemical abuse in the home
   ☐ Parents divorced
   ☐ Physical, sexual, verbal, or emotional abuse
   ☐ Other: _____
   ☐ Other: _____

2. Describe a time when you assumed you knew what someone's words or behavior meant, and you were wrong. What consequences resulted? _____
   _____
   _____

**3.** In the above situation, what could you have done that would have enabled you to understand the meaning of the words or behavior? How would that have changed the consequences?

_____

_____

Spend a few days observing your family life. What cryptic codes (words and behaviors that carry a meaning different from the obvious one) are a part of your family's communication patterns? For instance:

Does your child's silence mean:
☐ "Leave me alone."
☐ "Please notice I'm hurting and I want to talk."

Does the response "fine" mean:
☐ "I'm angry and I want you to know it."
☐ "I give up."

Describe some of your family's words and behaviors that need to be checked for meaning: _____

_____

## Building On God's Word

Perhaps one of the most difficult relationships of all to understand is God's relationship to us. Jesus came to make God understandable to us. Both His words and actions communicated the meaning of who God is and our relationship to Him.

Read the following verses and briefly describe what Jesus is communicating about our relationship to God.

Matthew 6:25–34; 10:29–30 _____

Luke 15:1–7 _____

Luke 15:11–32 _____

John 14:25–27 _____

Reading through the Gospels is the best way to "check for meaning" about who God is. As you read, ask God to make Himself clear to you through the words and events of Jesus' life.

## Check It Out!

Do you like riddles? A riddle is fun because it's tricky. You have to think hard about what it means, and it could mean more than one thing. You've probably heard this riddle:

*Question:* What's black and white and *red* all over?

*Answer:* A newspaper! It's "read" all over.

But maybe you thought of another way to solve the riddle:

> *Question:* What's black and white and *red* all over?
>
> *Answer:* An embarrassed zebra! (He's "red" all over.)

Although a newspaper and a zebra are very different, either of them could be the right answer to this riddle. It all depends on which of the two sound-alike words—"red" or "read"— was meant when you heard the question. So, the way you solve the riddle depends on understanding what the speaker intended.

Sound confusing? Well, that's what we want to talk about now. In the last chapter you learned about giving clear messages to others so they will know what you are trying to say to them: *Say what you mean and ask for what you need.* But what about when someone else is telling you something and you are the listener instead of the talker? Riddles might be fun when we can't figure out what they mean, but talking to other people is *not* fun when we don't understand what they are saying to us. As listeners, we can easily get in trouble with the next communication trap:

### Communication Trap #3
### Thinking We Understand What Another Person's Words or Actions Mean When We Really Don't

This is very easy to do, and it happens when:

▶ We are confused, but don't take the time to say we don't understand.
▶ We don't stop to think that another person's words or actions can mean more than one thing (like solving a riddle).
▶ We don't listen carefully.

For example, let's say your best friend says to you, "I hate you and I never want to see you again!" Is it true that she hates you and that you'll never be able to talk to her again? Probably not. So what could her words really mean?

▶ You did something that upset her.
▶ She misunderstood what you really said or did.

▶ She's having a bad day.
▶ Other: _____

Here's another example. Suppose your mom comes to the door of your room and says, "This room is a disaster area!" Now what could that mean?

▶ Your room is messy.
▶ Your taste in interior decorating is really weird.
▶ Mom wants you to clean up your room.
▶ Other: _____

Suppose you decide Mom means your room is messy. You could still be really confused—especially if you just finished cleaning it up and you think it looks great! You might be wondering, "What's wrong with my room?" or, "Did she just make a comment or does she expect me to clean it up again?"

Before you decide you've lost your best friend forever, or you spend a whole afternoon cleaning your room again, you can use the next communication helper:

## Communication Helper #3
## Find Out What the Other Person Really Means

We do this with one easy step—ask! Use the same questions that detectives and reporters use to get more information:

**Who:** "Who are you talking to?"

**What:** "What do you mean?" or, "What do you want me to do?"

**When:** "When do I have to do it?"

**Where:** "Where is it, exactly?"

**Why:** "Why did you say [or do] that?"

**How:** "How should I do this?"

So, if your mom says, "Your room is a disaster area," you could check out what she means by asking:

▶ "What about my room makes you say that?" (*Why* did you say that?)
▶ "Do you mean you want me to clean it up better?" (*What* do you want me to do?)
▶ "Do I have to clean it now or can it wait until Saturday?" (*When* should I do it?)

By listening to Mom's answers, you'll get the information you need. Now try it out. What questions might you ask in the following situation to check for meaning?

Your mom and dad had a big fight at dinnertime. Every time they have a fight you feel frightened that they might get a divorce. At bedtime your dad comes in to say good-night, and it's just you and him. You ask:

1. _____
2. _____

(Possible answers: "Are you and Mom mad at each other?" or, "Are you thinking about getting a divorce?" or, "Did *I* do anything to make you mad?")

If you didn't ask questions, you might just assume that your parents are going to get a divorce and you would go on feeling scared every time they had a fight. By asking, you will most likely get the information you need to know exactly what is going on, and you won't have to wonder or make up things in your mind any longer.

Checking for meaning can save us lots of time and trouble and worry. Here's a story about a boy and his mom who both learned it's best to stop and check it out!

# Taking out the Garbage

INSTANT REPLAY

# Remember...

You don't have to be confused.
You can "check out" what others
are saying to you.

And you never have to be confused about whether or not God loves you. Jesus came to show you just how much God loves you and to invite you to love Him. Here is a clear message that Jesus gave us about God's love:

For God loved the world so much that he gave his only Son. God gave his Son so that whoever believes in him may not be lost, but have eternal life.
*John 3:16* ICB

# Growing Together

## BUILDING ON GOD'S WORD

Make a Parable Box. The imagery of Jesus' story of the lost sheep is a powerful means for communicating to children (and adults!) the meaning of who God is. Young children, especially, will enjoy using a parable box to retell this story of God's tender love and care for them.

You will need the following materials for each parable box:

A shoe box
A 12"x18" piece of felt or fabric for the story mat
A round-headed clothespin
A small piece of Play-Doh or clay
Scraps of fabric, felt, and yarn
Cotton balls
A pipe cleaner, preferably brown
Sixteen popsicle sticks
White glue
A picture of Jesus as the Good Shepherd [optional]

Read Matthew 18:2–5, 10–14. Then talk about how important children are to God. Jesus told the adults they would have to become *like children* if they wanted to know God. And He told the parable of the lost sheep to illustrate the fact that God cares deeply for even one little child that is hurt or lost—and that's still true today. The parable box will help you remember God's love for you.

Begin by gluing four popsicle sticks together to form a square sheepfold. Use the rest of the sticks to build it higher. Then make the shepherd by anchoring the clothespin in the Play-Doh or clay

# Growing Together

so it will stand up. Use scraps of fabric and yarn to make clothes for the shepherd, and a small piece of the pipe cleaner to make his arms. Take the rest of the pipe cleaner and wad it up to look like a thorn bush.

To tell the story, place the sheepfold on one end of the story mat, and the thorn bush on the other end. Fill the sheepfold with cotton balls (the sheep) and stand the shepherd nearby. Then place one cotton ball in the thorn bush. Now you are ready to tell the story. Let children embellish the story as they wish. When they are through, place all items in the shoe box to store until next time.

## CONVERSATION STARTERS

There is tremendous value in having a child listen to what life was like for his or her parents when they were young. Even if your family is a blended family or an adoptive family, the following questions can provide occasions for good sharing. Let your children choose which question(s) they would like to ask you.

1. Who was the best teacher you had in school? The meanest?
2. What did you do for fun when you were growing up?
3. What did you do that you got in trouble for?
4. What was your favorite story about Grandma and Grandpa?
5. Are there any family secrets you haven't told us about yet?
6. *Kids' choice—let them ask you a question of their own.*

# Growing Together

## FAMILY NIGHT ACTIVITIES

1. **Play the Gossip Game.** This game is an excellent example of how messages get twisted as they pass from senders to receivers. Since the game is more effective when there are about ten players, this would be a great night to ask extended family or family friends to join you. To play, sit in a straight line or a circle. One person thinks of a phrase and whispers it into the ear of the person sitting next to him or her. That person then whispers it into the ear of the next person, and so on around the group. The last person says the phrase aloud. Then compare it with the phrase as it was originally stated. To emphasize the role of checking for meaning, play two rounds of the game, changing the rounds as follows:

*Round #1: Assuming the Meaning.* In this version, the receivers may *not* ask the senders to repeat the phrase. They must pass on to the next person exactly what they heard (or thought they heard). The end result will be lots of twisted communication.

*Round #2: Checking for Meaning.* Now change the game so that the receivers can ask to have the phrase repeated until they feel fairly certain they have received the proper message. At the end of the round, compare how much closer to the real message you were able to come when you stopped to check for meaning.

Here are a few phrases to get you started:

1. Sing a song of sixpence [or sevenpence, or eightpence!].

# Growing Together

2. The early bird catches the worm, which is okay if you like worms.

3. Hickory, dickory dock. Something's running up the clock!

**2. Practice "Checking for Meaning."** The best way to learn about the various ways we can miscommunicate is to practice identifying all the shades of meaning in various messages. You can make a game of it around the table or in the car. Start with one of

# Growing Together

the statements below and give all family members a turn to say what it could mean. When you have thought of all possibilities, move on to the next one. After you have the idea, use statements common to your family.

"I'm bored."
"I'm full."
"My teacher hates me!"
"We never get to see any good movies!"
"I don't want to go to Aunt Susie's house."

# COMMUNICATION BUILDING BLOCK #4

# Listen Well!

# GETTING READY

## I *Am* Listening!

F ive-year-old Marissa was frustrated that her mother continued to fix dinner while she was trying to tell her about her morning in kindergarten. Finally, she pulled a stool over to the counter where Mom was chopping celery, took her mom's head in her little hands, and turned her face toward her until they were nose to nose. "Mom," Marissa said in her most serious tone, "will you please *listen* to me?"

At five, Marissa had learned to give a straight, clear message about one of her biggest needs—the need to be listened to. She also had a pretty good grasp of what it means to be listened to. The first requirement was to know that she had her mom's full attention, which she was determined to get in any way she could!

Good listening means much more than simply being in the same room with someone who is talking. In fact, the quality of our communication with others is in direct proportion to our ability to listen well. Good listening opens up communication and poor listening shuts it down. Our listening skills can be evaluated by one criterion: Am I able to set aside my own needs so I can pay attention to the needs of the person I am listening to?

Poor listeners are subject to the next communication barrier:

## Communication Barrier #4
### Ignoring the Needs of the Other Person

Good listening focuses on the needs of the other person. It is always easier, however, to remain focused on our own needs. Remaining self-focused on our own needs results in one or more of these behaviors:

▶ **Not taking time to listen:** "Not now, dear, I'm busy. We'll talk later, okay?"

▶ **Withholding attention:** "I *am* listening. I can read the paper and listen to you at the same time."

▶ **Reacting too quickly to content:** "What do you mean you got into a fight at school today? How many times have I told you never to fight?"

▶ **Giving advice or lectures where none are needed or wanted:** "You shouldn't talk to your best friend that way. Good friends are hard to find, and if you treat them that way you'll lose them. I think you should get on the phone right now and apologize."

▶ **Invalidating the other's feelings or experience:** "You shouldn't feel angry with your husband just because he stays out late. After all, boys will be boys!"

Notice how all these responses keep the focus of the communication transaction on ourselves, such as our need to do what we want to do, our need to control our children's behavior, and our need to deny feelings or experiences that make us uncomfortable. If we want to truly listen well, we must set aside our own needs and use this communication building block:

### Communication Building Block #4
### Give Full Attention to the Needs of the Other Person

We all need to have people in our lives who will truly listen to us. As parents, one of the greatest gifts we can give our children is the kind of listening that centers on *their* needs rather than our own. We do that by:

▶ **Taking time to listen:** "That's a pretty important question. Let's sit down and talk about it."

▶ **Giving full attention:** "Wait a minute. I can't listen to you and watch TV, too. I'll turn off the set so we can talk."

▶ **Listening for meaning, rather than reacting to content:** "You got into a fight at school today? Must have been something serious to get you that mad. Tell me all about it."

▶ **Withholding advice and lectures:** "Having a fight with your best friend can be pretty painful."

▶ **Validating the other's feelings or experience:** "I'm not surprised you're feeling angry. I'd be angry, too, if my husband went out with the boys *every* night and left me home alone with the kids."

Because being a good listener takes a tremendous amount of time and energy, we can't always be available to listen well to those who want us to listen to them, at the exact moment they want our attention. This is particularly true for parents in today's stress-filled society. The key is to find your own way to create times for heart-to-heart listening to your child's concerns. Recently, I heard a panel of parents talking about the different ways they had found to listen to their kids with undivided attention. One mother said she learned to sit on the floor with her daughter when she really wanted to talk. "There's nothing to do on the floor except listen," she said. Another parent reported that her son would only start talking when they were alone in the car.

"I guess he figured it was the only place I wasn't trying to do something else while he talked. I can't tell you how many times we took the long way home or I drove around the block a dozen times, knowing that as soon as the car stopped, our conversation would be over!" Another couple told about their routine of taking their two daughters out for dinner every other Wednesday, with each parent taking one girl to a different restaurant for one-on-one time. "One night over dinner with our older girl," the mother told us, "she told me about a very hurtful event that had taken place two days before. I realized that I had been 'listening' to her for two days, yet she had never felt free to tell me what was really going on in her life until we were sitting quietly together over dinner."

There is tremendous power in being listened to. We all need safe, nonjudgmental places to tell our stories. As a parent, if you want your children to come to you when they need to share their hearts, start learning now the skills of listening well.

*F o r    R e f l e c t i o n*

1. How well were you listened to as a child?
   - ☐ No one ever had time to listen to me. I talked mostly to a pet or my stuffed animals.
   - ☐ Conversations always resulted in criticism and lectures on what I did wrong.
   - ☐ My family listened well, and I grew up believing that what I have to say is valuable and worthwhile.
   - ☐ My family didn't listen well, but I found others who listened to me.
   - ☐ Other: _____

2. Think of a time you were profoundly helped by someone who really listened to you. What did he or she do that made you feel heard? _____

_____

_____

3. Who in your life listens to you now? _____

_____

4. How well do you listen to others in your life? Rate yourself for each member of your family by using the scale below:

1 = I never seem to have time to listen well.

2 = I listen, but am quick to be critical and give unnecessary advice.

3 = I work hard at taking the time to listen well. We have regular times of significant sharing.

___ My spouse
___ Child #1
___ Child #2
___ Child #3
___ Other: _____
___ Other: _____

# Building On God's Word

One of the most remarkable aspects of our relationship to God is that He never tires of listening to us. An equally remarkable fact, however, is that we can also listen to God speak to us, offering us guidance and instruction. As we work to learn the skills of listening to others, it is equally important for us to learn the skills of listening to God's voice within our hearts.

Read 1 Kings 19:3–13. What do you learn about listening to God from this episode in the life of Elijah? _____
_____
_____

What are the earthquakes, fires, and strong winds in your life that are keeping you from hearing the "still, small voice" of God? Set those things aside today, and find the time to focus your full attention on Him as you invite Him to speak to you in the quietness of your heart.

TALKING · TOGETHER

re You Listening to Me?

What if you could learn to do something that would make living in your family a lot easier, help you make lots of friends, and do better in school? Would you want to learn that thing? Well, there is something that will help you do all those things—it's being a good listener! That sounds easy, doesn't it? But there's a difference between just listening and being a *good* listener. In fact, listening well is hard work, and many people never learn how to do it. Instead, they get caught in this trap:

### Communication Trap #4
### Not Paying Attention When Someone Is Talking to You

Have you ever been frustrated when you've tried to tell something to your mom or dad, but they were doing something else at the same time? Or have you ever felt hurt inside because you told your best friend your deepest, darkest secret—and your friend just said, "That's nice," or, "That's too bad," and walked away? Those are examples of people who are not being good listeners—they are not really paying attention to the person who is talking to them. When that happens, the person who is talking doesn't feel like he or she is being listened to at all, and that causes lots of communication problems.

To be a good listener, use this communication helper:

### Communication Helper #4
### Concentrate on What Another Person Is Saying to You

What does it mean to concentrate on what someone is saying to you? It means you have to do these three things:

1. **Give the other person your full attention.** As much as you may think you can be a good listener and keep playing Nintendo, or stare out the window, or interrupt with something you want to say—you can't. The first rule of being a good listener is to stop what you are doing, look at the other person, and think only about what he or she is saying to you.

2. **Ask questions.** Sometimes when we are listening, we don't understand and our mind wanders. When that happens, good listeners ask questions, like these:

"Gosh, Jason, what do you mean you're going to Texas? Are you going for a visit or are you moving away?"
"I'm sorry, Mrs. Smith, but could you repeat that? Are we supposed to write out all the math problems, or just write down the answers?"

**3.** **Try to understand what the other person is feeling.** Good listening is much more than hearing someone else's words. Good listening means we also try to feel what the other person is feeling. For instance, suppose your mom says to you, "I have asked you three times to clean your room, and you've just ignored me! You can't play outside today until it's done. Go and do it *now!*" How will you respond? You could say to yourself, "Wow! Is she grouchy or what?" or, "There she goes again, yelling at me! Why is Mom always yelling at me?" But if you want to try to understand what the other person is feeling, ask yourself this question instead: "How do *I* feel when I ask Mom to do something for me three times and she doesn't do it?" You probably feel frustrated and angry when you ask people to do something for you and they don't do it—and so does your mom when you ignore her!

As you can see, listening is hard work. Let's see if you can find the kids in the following examples who are being good listeners. For each one, check whether he or she is being a "good listener" or "poor listener":

**1.** She is a

☐ good listener    ☐ poor listener

**2.** He is a

☐ good listener    ☐ poor listener

**3.** He is a

☐ good listener  ☐ poor listener

**4.** He is a

☐ good listener  ☐ poor listener

Answers: 1. poor listener; 2. good listener; 3. poor listener; 4. good listener

Now here's a story about a father who learned to be a good listener.

# The School Fight

## Remember...

**You can be a good listener by concentrating on what others are saying to you.**

Remember, too, that learning to listen to God is as important as learning to listen to people. God's voice will guide you through your life when you trust Him. Here's a promise from the Bible:

Trust the Lord with all your heart. Don't depend on your own understanding. Remember the Lord in everything you do. And he will give you success.

***Proverbs 3:5–6*** *ICB*

# Growing Together

## BUILDING ON GOD'S WORD

**Learning to Listen to God.** Listening to God can be a difficult concept for kids to grasp. This activity will help your children experience "listening" on more than one level.

Read Proverbs 3:5–6 together. Then talk about how part of trusting the Lord and remembering Him in everything we do is learning to listen to His voice as He directs us in the way we should go. That can be hard, unless we understand that there is more than one way to listen.

Divide your family into pairs and blindfold one person in each pair. The people who are *not* blindfolded must now guide their partners through the house (or yard, or both, depending on your situation) by using only their voice. After five minutes, switch roles and continue for another five minutes. Then gather everyone back together again and start over, this time instructing the guides to lead their partners through the house using only touch (no words). When everyone has had a chance to be both blindfolded and a guide, discuss the following questions:

1. What did it feel like to have to walk through the house in total darkness?
2. How did you feel about having to depend on someone else to get you through the house safely?
3. Did not being able to see change the way you listened in any way?
4. What was it like to be led by touch only—no sight or sound?

# Growing Together

As you trusted your guide and your senses, you were led safely through the house in a way you usually do not go. Listening to God and trusting Him is like that. Even though we can't see Him or hear Him in the way we can see and hear people around us, that doesn't mean we cannot communicate with Him. It simply means we must listen in ways we do not normally use. When we do, we are led safely through our lives by trusting our Guide— even in those times when we don't understand exactly what's happening to us.

End with a time of prayer, asking God to help each of you learn to listen and follow His leading in new ways.

## CONVERSATION STARTERS

Much of our conversation consists of things we say to each other without even thinking. The following activity will help your family identify the words you say to each other day after day that are pleasant to hear, and those that are unpleasant or hurtful.

Give out paper and pencils. (*Note:* If you have young children in your family, this activity can be done verbally.) Ask everyone to make a list of the words they *most* like to hear from other members of the family. Examples might be: "You did a great job!" or, "Let's go get a pizza." After everyone has made a list, read them to each other. How many phrases showed up on more than one list?

# Growing Together

Now ask everyone to make a list of the words they *least* like to hear from each other. Examples might be: "You dummy!" or, "What did you do *now?*" When everyone is done, compare the lists again. Talk together about possible ways to eliminate at least some of these unpleasant words from your family's day-to-day communication.

## FAMILY NIGHT ACTIVITIES

1. **"Getting To Know You" Game.** One of the results of listening well is that we get to know each other better. This game provides an opportunity for family members to get "better acquainted" by listening to each other's answers to certain questions.

Begin by reading the first question on the list below and have everyone write down his or her answer *secretly* (you may want to pair up children who cannot write with another family member). Choose one family member to be "it." Everyone else takes a turn guessing how "it" answered the question. After everyone has guessed, "it" reveals what he or she wrote, and why. Be sure all family members "listen well" to the answer; you may be surprised at how much you will learn about each other that you did not know! Everyone who guessed correctly scores one point, and another person is chosen to be "it." When everyone has had a chance to be "it" on the first question, start a new round using the second question, and so on. The questions are:

# Growing Together

1. What is your favorite dessert?
2. Name one place in the world you would really like to visit.
3. What is your favorite holiday?
4. Name one thing that makes you afraid.
5. What is your favorite family activity?
6. Name a person you want to be like.
7. *Write a few questions that fit your family.*

2. **Take Time Out to Listen Well.** Listening well does not happen automatically. Establishing a regular listening time with each of your children (one-on-one) will increase your ability to listen well. Follow these steps:

▶ *Find a regular place and time that works for you and your child.* Each child is different. Times to try are bedtime, after school, on a weekly "date," or any other time your child seems inclined to talk. Let your child know that you are committed to setting aside everything else and really listening to him or her during these special times.

▶ *Begin with nonthreatening conversation starters.* Start with conversation about their activities, moving on to simple questions like, "What was the best thing that happened today?" "What was the worst thing?" With older children, ask their opinion about subjects of general concern. "I read that kids your age are confronted with drugs all the time. Is that true at your school?"

## Growing Together

▶ ***Set aside the "critical parent" role.*** Critical parents hear only what their children are doing wrong and are quick to deliver a lecture or scolding to straighten them out. Instead, frame your responses to show that you want to understand their feelings and hear *all* of what they have to say. Try responding only with questions that invite them to say more. For example, "I'm sorry you had such a bad day in school today. What else happened?"

▶ ***Keep at it!*** Don't expect a child to share his or her deepest, darkest feelings every time you are together. If conversation does not come easily, try reading a book or playing a game together. The point is to establish a regular time for you to be with each other. Children have to trust that you will stay with them and listen to little things before they will share big things.

# COMMUNICATION BUILDING BLOCK #5

# Skills for Fighting Fair

# G E T T I N G   R E A D Y

## Fighting Is
## Just So *Emotional!*

"The problem with fighting," a mother shared in our parents' group one night, "is that it's just so *emotional!* It would be so much easier if everyone just stayed calm and acted rationally instead of flying off the handle."

Fighting, however, is seldom a rational action. In fact, when our anger or some other powerful emotion is triggered, it is not our reason that guides us but the reaction patterns we learned when we were growing up. Since fighting is not a pleasant experience, we tend to spend more time avoiding it than learning how to do it well.

As hard as it may be to believe, fighting is actually a necessary part of building intimacy and trust in our relationships. Like it or not, we *will* irritate and offend each other in the course of living from day to day. Those experiences must be dealt with in order for our communication to be connected and clear. When we hold things inside in an effort to protect our relationships, we are actually building up resentments that don't go away and will eventually come out in a destructive way. The bottom line is that if we want to keep our relationships healthy, we must learn to fight well.

Since fighting happens at an emotionally charged moment, the potential for getting hooked into the next communication barrier is very real:

**Communication Barrier #5**
**Using Destructive Behaviors When Fighting**

Our first inclination in a conflict or threatening situation is to protect ourselves. The way many of us have learned to do that is by using actions that are unhealthy or destructive. For example:

▶ **The Ostrich** avoids the conflict altogether by walking away, stuffing the feelings inside, or sending children to their rooms before the conflict is resolved.
▶ **Mr. (or Ms.) Tough Guy** responds to every conflict with physical violence, such as hitting another person or destroying property.
▶ **The Verbal Swordsman** handles conflict with name-calling and cutting remarks, using the tongue as a double-edged sword to defeat opponents and leave them bleeding emotionally.
▶ **The Revengeful Gravedigger** continuously brings up old, unrelated hurts and wounds that have nothing to do with the present conflict and should have been resolved and buried long ago.

If we respond with destructive behaviors such as these, fighting understandably becomes something we want to avoid at all costs. It also becomes counterproductive. Instead of building intimacy and deepening our relationships, it tears them apart.

Although fighting is always stressful and difficult, we can use it to further our relationships when we use this communication skill:

## Communication Building Block #5
## Remember to Use Healthy Communication
## in Conflict Situations

Of course, in the heat of the moment the last thing we are thinking about is how well we are communicating. But as we grow in our ability to use good communication skills (as discussed throughout this book), they become easier and more natural to use at all times—even in conflict situations.

Notice how using the following skills can turn a potentially destructive conflict into an occasion for deepening intimacy and trust:

▶ **Focus on feelings, not personhood.** (Refer to chapter 2.) In conflict situations our first impulse is to attack the other person by using "you" statements in a way that blames and/or shames: "You make me so mad!" or, "You jerk! Why can't you ever do anything right?" By taking responsibility for our own feelings, we can defuse much of the unpleasantness of a conflict. "I feel angry" is much less volatile than either of the above statements.

▶ **"Check it out."** (Refer to chapter 3.) Often our conflicts result from a misunderstanding. When we find ourselves in an escalating conflict, we can take time to check for meaning before reacting: "I need to ask you a question. What did you mean when you said _____?"

▶ **Listen well.** (Refer to chapter 4.) When we are fighting, we are usually not listening—we're too busy defending our position or letting our feelings take their course. Using good listening skills can help us see the conflict from the other person's point of view and keep us from saying something we'll regret later.

▶ **Focus on present issues.** Our fights need to be centered on only one conflict at a time—the present one! You can say something like: "If you need to talk about the way I yelled at your mother last summer, we can do that another time. Right now we're talking about Jamie's behavior in school."

▶ **Come to resolution.** Healthy fights come to resolution, even if that means simply agreeing to disagree. Sometimes we can resolve the conflict at the time of the fight, and other times it may take a while. There may be the need for a cooling-down period, or it may take some time for both parties to see the issue from each other's perspective. Even if it is an hour or several days later, we can still come to resolution by bringing up the issue again at a less emotionally charged moment. By doing so, we are completing the communication transaction and bringing closure: "Billy, remember the fight we had last Saturday? I didn't handle myself very well, and I'm sorry. Can we talk about it again?"

▶ **Allow for reconciliation.** Sometimes it's hard to know when a fight is over, or to make the first move toward reconnecting emotionally. As hard as it may be, it is important that when the fight is over, we have a way to open our arms to each other again. Dolores Curran, in her book *Traits of a Healthy Family*, records how several families dealt with this issue:

"Everyone comes out of their room," responded every single member of one family. Three members of another family said, "Mom says, 'Anybody want a Pepsi?'" My favorite, though, was the little five-year-old who scratched his head and furrowed his forehead in deep thought after I asked him how he knew the family fight was over. Finally, he said, "Well . . . Daddy gives a great big yawn and says, 'Well . . .'"

The great big yawn and the "Well" say a lot more than a stretch to this family. They say it's time to end the fighting and to pull together again as a family. (Dolores Curran, *Traits of a Healthy Family*, Ballantine Books, page 60)

The old adage that making up is the best part of fighting has more truth than we may realize. When we "kiss and make up," our relationship will be stronger, the intimacy between us deeper, and the communication between us clearer—provided that we have used the communication skills listed above to fight in healthy ways.

## For Reflection

1. How were conflicts handled in your family of origin?
   - ☐ They were never allowed. Kids were sent to their rooms whenever a conflict started.
   - ☐ We fought often, but we never brought anything to resolution.
   - ☐ Our fights always were clouded by unresolved past conflicts.
   - ☐ Parents were always right; kids were always wrong.
   - ☐ I grew up with healthy models of how to handle conflict.
   - ☐ Other: _____

2. How do *you* handle conflict today?
   - ☐ I shut down and do not allow myself to feel angry.
   - ☐ I blow up and rant and rave about anything and everything.
   - ☐ I lash out and hurt others with my anger.

☐  I work things out in ways that further my relationships with others instead of hurting them.

☐  Other: _____

3. How was reconciliation achieved in your family of origin?

☐  It wasn't—we are still carrying grudges against each other to this day.

☐  This is how we "kissed and made up" in our family:

_____

_____

_____

4. Answer questions 1 and 3 as they apply to your present family. What similarities/differences are there? _____

_____

What insights do you gain about how you handle conflict in your present family? (e.g., "I blow up at my kids in the same way my dad blew up in our family.") _____

_____

_____

## Building On God's Word

*True or false?*—God's Word teaches us that being angry is wrong.

Many of us have grown up believing the answer to that question is *true*, and therefore that fighting is an offense to God.

This is usually based on a misunderstanding of these verses:

> In your anger, do not sin: Do not let the sun go down
> while you are still angry, and do not give the devil a
> foothold. *Ephesians 4:26–27* NIV

At first glance, these verses may seem to say that we should not be angry. A closer look, however, reveals that the problem with anger is not *having* it, but what we *do* with it once we have it.

How does the phrase "In your anger, do not sin" relate to the communication barrier described in this chapter? _____

_____

_____

How are the skills for healthy fighting reinforced by the second part of these verses? _____

_____

_____

TALKING · TOGETHER

## *ules for Fighting Fair*

Do you like fighting? Probably not. It's not fun to get our feelings hurt—or our bodies! Maybe you know someone who fights all the time. He or she is probably not very well liked in school or a very happy person.

But like many unpleasant things in life, fighting is something we can't avoid. We'll *always* get into conflicts in our families and with our friends. That's why it's important to know that there are two ways to handle fighting— ways that *hurt* us and ways that *help* us. Fighting hurts us when we use this communication stopper:

### Communication Trap #5
### Hurting Others on Purpose When We Fight

Someone almost always gets hurt in a fight. But the things we do and say when we fight make a big difference as to who gets hurt and how badly. Do you ever do these things when you fight?

Hitting or punching
Breaking someone else's things
Saying hurtful things, like name-calling
Telling lies about the person you're mad at

In a fight, it's natural to want to hurt the person we're angry with. But when we do, we are really hurting ourselves by saying or doing things we really don't mean and making it hard for others to want to be our friends. There is a way to fight that can help you get your anger and hurt feelings out *without* being hurtful to the other person. Use this communication helper:

### Communication Helper #5
### Remember to Use Communication Helpers Even When You Fight

In the other chapters of this book, you've learned new ways to communicate with others that help you get along better and avoid fights. But you probably forget all of them when you get angry and get into a fight! Using those same helpers when you get mad, however, can make your fights less hurtful and even make your friendships and family relationships better.

Rather than reacting in the hurtful ways listed above, try using these the next time you fight:

▶ **Own your own feelings.** Remember to talk about what you are feeling, rather than attacking the other person.

▶ **Check it out.** Be sure to "check for meaning" by asking questions before you blow up.

▶ **Listen well.** By trying to see what happened from the other person's point of view, you might not feel mad anymore.

Here's a new one to add:

▶ **Work it out.** Rather than running away and staying mad forever, you can find a way to end the fight and be friends again. Staying mad only hurts you and the other person more.

Let's see how using communication helpers can make a difference in these fights:

*Fight #1:* As Michael ran out the door to play with his friends, Mom shouted, "I have to go to the market. Take your little brother with you and let him play, too." Michael was really mad, and wanted to react by ignoring and being mean to his brother. Instead, he *chose to see it from his brother's point of view*, and to treat him like he would want to be treated. "It's not his fault Mom made him come," he thought. "I guess I can find something for him to do that he'll like, and then he won't get in the way of our game."

*Fight #2:* Lana's best friend, Jennifer, came up to her on the playground and yelled at her, "How could you tell everyone in school that I like Jason? It was a secret and I hate you for telling! I don't ever want to talk to you again!" Since Jennifer had never said it was a secret, Lana didn't feel she had done anything wrong. Now she wants to get even with Jennifer by making fun of her to everyone in school. How could each of these communication helpers give her a better way to handle the conflict?

Check it out: _____

Listen well: _____

Work it out: _____

(Possible answers: "Check it out" —Find out what really happened to upset her friend so much. Was she the one responsible? "Listen well"—By thinking about how hurt *she* would be if she thought someone had told her secret. "Work it out" —Go to her friend and talk it over.)

# I Didn't Do It!

# Remember...

## You can fight without hurting yourself or others.

Here's a verse from the Bible to remember when you fight:

> When you are angry, do not sin. And do not go on being angry all day. Do not give the devil a way to defeat you.
> *Ephesians 4:26–27 ICB*

# Growing Together

## BUILDING ON GOD'S WORD

**Family Bible Study on Ephesians 4:26–27.** Before you begin, prepare two pieces of poster board by writing "Unhealthy Ways to Fight" across the top of one, and "Healthy Ways to Fight" across the top of the other. You will also need markers or crayons and (possibly) old magazines and newspapers, as suggested below.

Begin by reading Ephesians 4:26–27 aloud. Talk about the meaning of these verses as they apply to fighting. Notice that the point is not that it is wrong to be angry, but that we are *not to sin* when we are angry. Ask all family members to make a statement about what they think it means "to sin" when we are angry. Then, on the first poster board, depict these ideas by drawing scenes from their own experiences, or pasting pictures/articles cut from old magazines and newspapers. The idea here is to focus on the destructive side of anger and fighting.

Now ask family members to respond to this question: "Since the verses in Ephesians make it clear that God knows we will be angry at times, what are some ways to express our anger that are both healthy and pleasing to God?" To facilitate discussion, on the second poster board, draw each of the following symbols (if you are not an artist, you can find pictures of these items ahead of time and paste them on the board as you talk about them). Share ideas of how each item can be used to express anger in a healthy (non-sinful) way:

# Growing Together

▸ **Shoes.** (I can walk away instead of fist-fighting, or I can cool down by running around the block.)

▸ **Pillow.** (I can punch a pillow instead of punching someone else.)

▸ **Stationery and Pens.** _____

▸ **Drawing Paper and Markers.** _____

▸ **Telephone.** _____

▸ **Others?** _____

Now take a closer look at the two poster boards. Which one feels safer? Which is the better way to handle conflict? End with a prayer time, asking God to help each family member handle fights in healthy ways.

# Growing Together

## CONVERSATION STARTERS

Spend time as a family discussing the following statements:

1. The things that make me angry are . . .
2. When I'm angry, I usually . . .
3. I know a family fight is over when . . .
4. The next time I'm in a fight, I'll try to . . .

## FAMILY NIGHT ACTIVITIES

1. **"If Our House Were on Fire" Game.** Playing this game together is not only fun, it might give you some practice in handling family conflict! Give everyone paper and pencil and then set the scene as follows:

*It's the middle of the night and we are all sleeping, when suddenly the smoke alarm goes off. We get up and realize there is a fire in our house and we have to get out. As we go, each of us will have time to grab five things to take out with us. What five things will you take?*

Now give everyone time to secretly write down the five things they would want to save (children who can't write can draw pictures or answer verbally). Explain that these items should be chosen on the basis of importance to the person, not on the basis of whether or not he or she could actually take them out. *Example:* "I've been so exhausted lately. I would take my bed so at least I could get a good night's sleep!" When everyone is done, share your lists with each other, telling what was listed and why. Then read the following:

*As we are gathering our things, we become aware that the*

# Growing Together

*house is burning faster than we realized, and we will have time to take only five things for the whole family! We have just a moment or two to decide which things we will take out with us.*

Your task now is to combine everyone's lists into one list by deciding *as a family* which five items you will take out. The goal is to come to a consensus, which means that everyone in the family must agree that the five items selected are the most important to rescue. (It's not enough to simply "give in." Everyone must be convinced that the choices made are the best ones.) Be aware that as you all share your opinions and try to convince others to see your point of view, you are setting up a potential conflict situation. Remind everyone to use all the rules of good communication as you listen to one another and make your choices.

When you have reached consensus on the five items, work together to narrow the list to three, and finally to the one item all of you agree is the most important item to your family. Talk about why that item has special meaning for your family.

Before finishing the game, be sure to remind children that in case of a real fire, they would leave the house immediately and not spend time gathering things to take out. This could also be a time to remind your kids about other rules of safety around your home.

**2. Practice the Skills of Good Communication.** The best way to learn to use good communication skills when you are fighting is to practice those skills when you're *not* fighting! Look back over the activities in the first four chapters of this book and pick out one or two that deal with what seems hardest for your family to remember in conflict situations. Do those activities again now, remembering that the more you practice the skills, the easier it will be to use them in conflict situations.

105 ▶

# COMMUNICATION BUILDING BLOCK #6

# Say It without Words Too

# GETTING READY

## Actions *Do* Speak Louder Than Words!

Words are only one of the many ways we communicate with others. In fact, most of the other ways we communicate are *more* powerful than our words. I remember watching an episode of a TV sitcom a number of years ago, in which two dear friends were saying good-bye before one of them moved away. In a tender embrace, one friend said, "In all the years we've been together, have I ever told you that I loved you?" Without a moment's hesitation, the other replied, "Every moment we were together." I've never forgotten that interchange. To me, it said clearly that communication is about more than what we *say* to each other—it's about how we *act* with each other.

In those times when the people in our lives don't seem to be receiving the messages we are trying to send them, the problem often lies in this immutable law of communication: When *what we do* does not match *what we say*, it is our actions that others believe—not our words. That leads us to our final communication barrier:

**Communication Barrier #6**
**Acting in Ways That Are Contradictory to Our Words**

There are a number of aspects to this barrier:

▶ **When our nonverbal communication does not match our words.** Examples of this are: Saying "I love you" without eye contact, expression in the voice, or touch; saying "I'm *not* angry" with clenched teeth and fists; saying "I'm listening" from behind a newspaper or while staring at the TV or computer screen.

▶ **When we don't make time for another person.** Missing our children's activities, or never taking one-on-one time with family members and friends communicates: "You don't matter enough for me to spend my time with you." That message will negate anything we may try to say to the contrary.

▶ **When we don't act in ways that take the needs of the other person into consideration.** Continuing to do things that we know bother or hurt someone else, or never surprising loved ones with an act of love, is another way we say, "You don't matter."

If we want to be sure our messages are received in the way we really mean them, we can learn this communication skill:

**Communication Building Block #6**
**Making Sure Our Actions Communicate the Same Message As Our Words**

Although this principle holds true in any level of communication, it is particularly important in families when the message we want to send is: "I love you and you matter to me." We can do that by offering these three gifts:

▶ **The gift of our nonverbal warmth and affection.**

Everyone needs to hear the words "I love you." But we also need other signs that those words are true. A warm hug or time to cuddle, getting on the same level with a child, putting down the newspaper and maintaining eye contact, using voice tones that are warm and tender—these are all powerful means of communicating "I love you—and I really mean it!"

▶ **The gift of our time.** We have no greater commodity to invest in life than our time. How we choose to invest our time paints a clear picture of what we value and cherish. This is particularly true in our high-paced society, where there are so many demands on our time. When we spend time with another—particularly when we *make time* by setting aside something else we wanted to do—we are sending a powerful message that says, "You matter to me more than the other things I could be doing right now. I'm here with you because I *choose* to be." No amount of words can communicate that message better than simply taking time to be together.

▶ **The gift of acts of love.** Part of the work—and fun—of loving someone is discovering the little things that make that person happy and doing them unexpectedly, or recognizing the little things that irritate the person and remembering not to do them. For instance, you may discover that your son hates to make his bed, or your wife loves fresh flowers, or your husband is really bugged when you leave the dresser drawers open, or that your family really enjoys a spontaneous trip to the beach. Acting on this information from time to time is another powerful form of communicating "I love you, and I'm thinking about you."

Sometimes we miss the power of giving acts of love to others by not understanding the difference between what we might choose to *offer* as an act of love, and what the other person wants to *receive*. The question we must answer is, "What does the other person need from me to feel loved?" Oftentimes the answer to that question is something we would not want for ourselves. Or we may have personal reasons for holding back the gift. A powerful example of this came in one of our support groups when a young mother shared how she was struggling with her relationship with her own mother. "Mom was never there for me as a child," she recalled, "but when I became an adult, she suddenly wanted to be friends. At first, I just couldn't do it. Then one day I realized that I didn't *want* to do it. I was really withholding my friendship from my mom as a way to get revenge. I can see now that by punishing her, I am really punishing myself, but since I've never really connected with her, I don't know how to be any different."

At that point, the group helped her become unstuck by asking her to answer this question: "What does your mom need from you in order to feel you love her?" The young mom thought for only a few minutes and then replied, "All she wants is for me to talk to her and let her in on the events of my life. I guess that's not too much to ask." In later weeks, she reported to the group that, as hard as it was at first, she was now enjoying giving her mother the gift of telling her the details of her life. "I don't know that Mom and I will ever be close friends," she added, "and sometimes I don't really feel like telling her about what's going on with me. But I do love my mother, and this is the best thing I can do to *show* her that I do."

Using this Communication Building Block—making our actions match our words—does not come automatically. It demands that we pay close attention to others in our lives, ask questions, and expend energy on them when we might rather be spending it on ourselves. But, without question, it is our nonverbal expressions, the time spent together, and our acts of kindness that carry the message of our words, particularly the words "I love you."

*F   o   r        R   e   f   l   e   c   t   i   o   n*

1. In your family of origin, how did your parents show love to each other? _____
   _____
   _____

   To you? _____
   _____

   Which memories from your family of origin are clearest to you?
   ☐ Showing love to one another.
   ☐ Anger and conflict.
   ☐ It's a blank; we hardly ever showed any strong emotions in our home.

2. In what ways do you show love to family and friends today?
   _____

   In which area do you need the most improvement?
   ☐ Offering gifts of nonverbal warmth and affection.
   ☐ Offering gifts of my time.
   ☐ Offering gifts of acts of love.

3. What would each member of your family perceive as the greatest expression of love you could give?

Spouse _____

Child #1 _____

Child #2 _____

Child #3 _____

Parent(s) _____

Other _____

# Building On God's Word

Sometimes the hardest time to give love to others is when we are upset with them for doing something wrong. Many of us learned to give love as a reward for being good, believing that to love others when they act inappropriately is condoning their "bad" behavior. God, however, shows us a different model for giving love:

> This is how God showed his love among us: He sent his one and only Son into the world that we might live through him. This is love: not that we loved God, but that he loved us and sent his Son as an atoning sacrifice for our sins. Dear friends, since God so loved us, we also ought to love one another.
> *1 John 4:9–11 NIV*

By receiving God's gift of love instead of the deserved payment for our actions, we are empowered to turn around and love others in the same way God loves us. Likewise, when we offer our gifts of love to others unconditionally, they are empowered to turn around and act in loving ways themselves. In short, human beings learn to be loving by being loved.

Mark two Xs on the line below, one indicating the extent to which you are able to accept God's free gift of love to you, and the other the extent to which you are able to extend unconditional love to others. Do you see a correlation between the two marks?

├──────┼──────┼──────┼──────┼──────┼──────┤

Love is given as a free gift          Love must be earned

Spend time in prayer, talking to God about your ability—or inability—to give and receive empowering, unconditional love.

## Say It without Words Too

Have you ever heard expressions like these?
What do you think they mean?

*Say it with flowers.*
*Actions speak louder than words.*
*One picture is worth 1,000 words.*

So far in this book, we've talked about how to communicate with others by using words. But there are many ways to get a message across to another person without actually saying anything. For instance, what message do you think each of these kids is sending to the other person?

There were no words in these pictures, yet you probably didn't have any trouble figuring out what messages were being sent. In the first picture, we know the boy is angry by looking at his face and hands—we call that "body language." In the second one, the boy is communicating his love for his mother by giving her a gift, and

Mom is obviously very happy that he did.

The point to remember is that what we *do* communicates as much as what we *say*. In fact, what we *do* communicates *more* than what we say. That leads us to our last communication trap:

### Communication Trap #6
### Acting in Ways That Don't Match Our Words

It's very important to understand this trap, because when our actions don't match our words, it is always our *actions* the other person will believe. Let's see how this works by looking at the same two pictures again, adding words this time.

In the first picture, the boy's words are saying that he is not angry. Do you believe him? In the second, Mom's words are saying that her son should not have given her flowers. Do you think that's what she really means?

It can be very confusing when a person's actions and words don't match. For instance, have you ever had someone make a promise to do something with you, and then call at the last minute and cancel because he or she found something better to do instead? It's hard to know if people like that really care about us—do we believe their words or their actions?

If we want to be good communicators, we must use this last communication helper:

**Communication Helper #6
Making Sure Our Actions Carry the Same
Message As Our Words**

There are two things we need to pay attention to in order to do this.

▶ **Body Language.** Our bodies communicate what we are really feeling. No matter what we say—or even if we don't say anything—people can tell just by looking at us that what we are saying is not what we really mean.

▶ **Actions.** We can always find lots of things to do to tell others we are thinking about them and care about them. What do each of these actions communicate?

Doing a good job on homework and turning it in on time

Doing chores without being told

Choosing *not* to tease a younger brother or sister

Keeping a promise you made, even if it's hard

Making and sending a card to someone who lives far away

You can probably think of many more ways to use actions to send messages to other people in your life. Taking the time to do things we know will make another person happy is a powerful way to say "I love you!"

Using body language and actions to communicate can be fun, too. Looking at people when they talk to you, surprising someone with a little gift, hugging a friend—those are all fun ways to show what you're feeling. Just remember, when your words and actions *don't* match, it's how you act that people will believe.

Here are some more examples of this important communication helper.

# Actions Speak Louder Than Words

Can you pick out the kids who are making their words and actions match?

## Remember...

**Your actions *do* speak louder than your words!**

Remember, too, that God teaches us to use actions to treat others in loving ways. Here's a Bible verse to remember:

**This is love: not that we loved God, but that he loved us and sent his Son as an atoning sacrifice for our sins. Dear friends, since God so loved us, we also ought to love one another.**
***1 John 4:10–11*** NIV

# Growing Together

## BUILDING ON GOD'S WORD

**Memorize Bible Verses.** Memorizing key verses of Scripture gives family members the truths of God's Word in a form that will always be available to them. You can make it a fun family project by playing Bible memory games. Around the dinner table, in the car, or at bedtime are good times to learn one or more of the key verses from this book. For example:

*Verse #1:* The Lord is close to everyone who prays to him, to all who truly pray to him (Psalm 145:18 ICB).

*Verse #2:* Give all your worries to him, because he cares for you (1 Peter 5:7 ICB).

*Verse #3:* When you are angry, do not sin. And do not go on being angry all day. Do not give the devil a way to defeat you (Ephesians 4:26–27 ICB).

*Verse #4:* This is love: not that we loved God, but that he loved us and sent his Son as an atoning sacrifice for our sins. Dear friends, since God so loved us, we also ought to love one another (1 John 4:10–11 NIV).

**Bible Memory Games.** *Family Circle.* One person in the family starts by saying the first word of a verse everyone has been learning. The next person must say the second word, and so on around the circle. If someone misses, the next person must start over with the first word. Continue until the whole verse, including the reference, can be said around the circle quickly and easily.

# Growing Together

*Verse Race.* Make several duplicate sets of verse cards for a verse the family has memorized—cut 3" x 5" cards in half and print one word of the verse on each card, putting the reference on a separate card. Mix the cards up and give a set to each person (or teams of two). Then race to see who can put the verse in order the quickest. Repeat for other verses you have worked on together.

## CONVERSATION STARTERS

The Sunday comics can be a great starting place for conversations about communication. Try reading them together this week, looking for examples of the Communication Barriers (Traps) and Communication Building Blocks (Helpers) presented in this book. Talk about how the cartoon characters could change unhealthy communication transactions into healthy ones by using the new skills you are learning.

## FAMILY NIGHT ACTIVITIES

**1. Secret Pals.** Being a secret pal is a great way to learn about doing acts of kindness for others. This project can be done in a single family setting (if there are more than three members in your family), or you can ask neighboring families or extended

# Growing Together

family members to participate with you. Begin with an orientation party, during which you will do the following:

▸ *Explain the rules.* Designate a specific length of time for this project—one week if all participants live under the same roof; two or more weeks if the secret pals live in separate houses. Then decide how many things everyone will do for his or her secret pal (i.e., one thing per day, two per week, etc.).

▸ *Give examples of things to do for a secret pal.* Ask everyone present to tell the others what kinds of things they would like done for them. For example: make my bed, leave cards or notes where I can find them, hide candy bars or other small gifts in unexpected places, give me coupons I can cash in later ("Good for one load of laundry" or "Good for one night of doing dishes" or "Good for one ice cream cone," etc.). Encourage everyone to suggest as many ideas as possible.

▸ *Distribute the secret pal assignments*—secretly, of course. You might make this more fun by scratching the names in squares of chocolate, so all the participants can keep their pal truly "secret" by eating their assigned name!

When the designated time for the project is over, have a special party to reveal the identity of the secret pals. Share about the different things the secret pals did for each other, and give a small prize to anyone who managed to keep his or her identity a secret for the whole time. End by enjoying heart-shaped cookies and ice cream sundaes together.

# Growing Together

**2. Family Acts of Love to Others.** Teach your children to have a heart of love for others by involving the whole family in activities that are gifts of love to people outside your home. Some ideas are:

Visit a nursing or retirement home and bring small gifts to the residents.

Host a neighborhood block party to allow neighbors to get better acquainted.

Spend a day doing chores around the house and yard of an elderly family friend or neighbor, or at your church.

Take care of a young couple's or single parent's children for a weekend so the parent(s) can get some needed time away.

Start a clothing or food drive for community shelters.

You can probably think of many other things to do. Just be prepared for the results! Your family is likely to receive a huge quantity of love in return for the time and effort it took to give these acts of love to others.

**1** Say What You're Feeling

**2** Make Yourself Perfectly Clear

**3** Check for Meaning

**4** Listen Well!

**5** Skills for Fighting Fair

**6** Say It without Words, Too

Learning to use these six Communication Building Blocks to enhance your family's communication can be both an exciting and a difficult experience. Here are the key points to remember:

- Be sure to tell others what you are *feeling* as well as what you are thinking.
- Give others a straight, clear message by using this formula: **Report the facts + Say what you are feeling + Ask for what you need.**
- "Check it out" to be sure you accurately understand what a message means before reacting to it.
- Listen well by setting aside your own needs and focusing on the needs of the other person.
- Remember that fighting can be good for your relationships *if* you use all the skills of good communication to fight fair.
- Your actions *do* speak louder than your words!

## And above all else . . .

. . . remember that communicating with God is the most important communication of all!

> The Lord is close to everyone who prays to him, to all who truly pray to him. *Psalm 145:18 ICB*

# APPENDIX A

## STAGES OF SKILL DEVELOPMENT

The key point to remember as you start using any of the family guides in this series is this:

**Learning new skills takes time and feels uncomfortable at first!**

Remember when you were first learning to ride a bicycle or play a musical instrument or hit a baseball? It took time to perfect the skills you needed to accomplish those tasks, and much of that time was spent in boring practice sessions. You probably went through periods of discouragement and thought you would never improve. But persistence and practice eventually paid off, especially if the learning process was a group experience that took place in a friendly environment where everyone's efforts were treated with respect. It helped even more if you were guided by someone who had already mastered the skill and encouraged your every sign of progress.

Developing healthy life skills in a family setting is like that. Learning to live together in new ways will take time and commitment and patience on the part of every family member. Both you and your children will sometimes feel awkward and uncomfortable, as if things will never change for the better.

There are no shortcuts to making healthy life skills a reality in your home, but knowing what to expect can keep you going. Skills development normally occurs in five stages, as the following acrostic illustrates:

**S** = Seeing the Need
**K** = Keeping On
**I** = Increasing Confidence
**L** = Letting Go
**L** = Living It

**S** **Stage 1: Seeing the Need.** All change begins here. It is only when we are motivated by the need for change that we will go through the hard work of learning a new skill.

**K** **Stage 2: Keeping On.** This is the stage of greatest discouragement and the point at which many people give up. As you start practicing a new skill, it is natural to feel awkward, so you may want to revert to behavior patterns that are familiar and comfortable. At this point, you will need lots of encouragement and the determination to keep going.

**I** **Stage 3: Increasing Confidence.** Over time, you will begin to see changes, and the ability to use the new skill will take root. Learning to recognize and celebrate small steps of growth will build your confidence and keep you going.

**L** **Stage 4: Letting Go.** As your skill level improves, more and more you will find yourself letting go of past behavior patterns and replacing them with the new and healthier ones.

**L** **Stage 5: Living It.** In this last stage, the new skill has become so integrated into your life that it becomes almost automatic. When you find yourself using it easily, you realize that the hard work of the earlier stages has paid off!

# RULES FOR FAMILY INTERACTION

It must be kept in mind that the family guides are only a tool to help you create times of learning and connectedness in your family. That cannot happen unless the books are used in an atmosphere of openness and safety for all family members. You can make your "growing together" conversations and your Family Night activities times of heart-to-heart sharing and fun for everyone by setting and consistently maintaining the following rules:

▶ **Family Rule #1: Every member will actively participate in all discussions and Family Nights.** This lets everyone know that he or she is an important part of the family. Parents are expected to participate with their children, not sit on the sidelines and watch the action!

▶ **Family Rule #2: All members will show respect for one another's feelings.** Modeling how to identify and talk about feelings is the best way to help your kids open up to you. Although you will need to use some discretion, letting your children know that you, too, feel a wide spectrum of feelings teaches them to acknowledge their own feelings and honor the feelings of others. If mutual respect is shown when discussing feelings, it encourages family members to feel safe enough to share openly. This rule means that no put-downs, name calling, hitting, or other destructive behaviors are allowed during family sharing times!

▶ **Family Rule #3: Everyone will speak only for themselves.** In many families, one member often acts as the spokesperson for everyone else. This can be a child or a parent, but the result is the same: The other family members are not encouraged or even permitted to express their own feelings or opinions. You will need to carefully monitor your sharing times to be sure all family members feel free to openly share what they are thinking and feeling.

*Special Note for Parents: Listen well!* When asked what they most want from adults, children invariably report that they want to be listened to. Many parents unknowingly close off communication with their children by talking too much. Giving your children full attention and affirming what they are telling you will work wonders in building relationships with them.

▶ **Family Rule #4: No unsolicited advice will be given.** A continuation of Rule #3, this rule is particularly important for parents whose communication style with their children tends to be one of lecturing or telling them what they should or should not do. Many parents see this as their primary role and do not realize that their well-intended instructions often close off communication with their children. In your sharing times, encourage all family members to replace such confrontational statements as *"you* should" or "If *you* would only" with "I" messages.

Of course, there will be times when your children do need guidance from you. If you sense that a child needs help, try giving permission to ask for it. "Would you like some help in thinking that through?" or "I'd be glad to help if you need help with that" is much more affirming to a child than "do it *my* way" messages. One word of caution: You must respect your child's right to say no to your offer of help. Hard as it may be to do, hold your advice until your child is ready to hear it.

▶ **Family Rule #5: It's okay to "pass."** It is important to let all members know they can be active participants and still have times when they do not feel ready to share their deepest thoughts and feelings. Sometimes opening up may feel painful or threatening, and at those times family members need to have the freedom to pass. An environment is not "friendly" or safe if people fear being pressured to talk about things they are not yet ready to share openly.

▶ **Family Rule #6: It's okay to laugh and have fun together.** In today's high-stress world, many families have lost the ability to simply enjoy being with each other. Give your family permission to use the suggested activities as occasions to laugh, play, and make a mess together. You will find that much significant sharing and relationship building happens when family members are relaxed and enjoying one another's company.

There may be other family rules you would like to include for your family. Just remember that the purpose of each rule is to assure an environment that is safe, growth producing, and enjoyable for everyone!

If you would like more information about starting a Confident Kids® Support Group program in your congregation or community, please write:

# C O N F I D E N T   K I D S®

% Christian Recovery International
P.O. Box 11095
Whittier, CA 90603